Island Moods
and
Reflections

ISLAND MOODS

AND

REFLECTIONS

An anthology of verse
of the
British Isles

Peter B. Jones
Publisher and Managing Editor

Steve Sydenham
Consultant

Editors
Vanessa Sydenham
Catherine Jones

*with love
to Ben
from
Dodie*

ISBN 0-9699334-1-X

Published by
Poetry Institute of the British Isles Ltd.
5 Athol Street
Douglas, Isle of Man
IM1 1LD

Typesetting by Calico Communications

Printed in England
by Bath Press Ltd., Avon

INTRODUCTION

This fine anthology of verse is a result of our Winter 1994/95 British Isles Poetry Contest, in which we received thousands of entries. The contest was open to all poets without regard to sex, age or experience. We have selected only the best of these entries for publication. As will be evident from the following pages, we received numerous fine poems, many of which are outstanding.

We congratulate all our poets, whether new or already established, whose poems have been published within these pages. Many are talented undiscovered poets whose work appears in a poetry anthology for the first time.

Inevitably, this volume contains many poems that reflect the changing trends in our society.

In recent years, there has been a good deal of theorizing about poetry as an art form. These theories are often interesting and perhaps ingenious, but so far as they have influenced the writers of poetry, they are of little importance.

The editors and selection committee of this collection have approached the task with open minds. They have not allowed themselves to be influenced by any theory of what a poem should be, except that which requires that the poem should be interesting and within the bounds of poetry. The wide variety of poems chosen are designed to appeal to the general reader and to the student as well, and to give pleasure to all who enjoy poetry for its own sake.

Our final selection of prize winners was not an easy task. We consider all poems published within this volume to be of a high standard and representing the best of today's British poetry.

ACKNOWLEDGEMENTS

The publisher and editors are grateful for the efforts of the following individuals
in making this anthology possible:

Deborah Palmer, Des Armishaw, Arlene Beck, Keith Daniel,
Madeleine Jones, Miranda Jones, Nicola Sydenham and Lis Muise

Illustration: M.B. Foster

Let me here,
Content and grateful, wait the appointed time,
And ripen for the skies; the hour will come
When all these splendours bursting on my sight
Shall stand unveil'd, and to my ravishe'd sense
Unlock the glories of the world unknown.

ANNA LETITIA BARBAULD
(A Summer Evening's Meditation)

Grand Prize Winner

Muriel Altham, Lancs.

Second Prize Winners

Doreen Pinder, Clwyd
Angela Douse, Essex
David Tomkinson, Notts.

Alan Tilmouth, Corn.
Paul Clark, Corn.

Third Prize Winners

Audrey Rigby, Cumb.
Ernest Netherwood, Yorks.
Richard Styles, Cambs.
Leah A. Goddard, Gwent.
Diana Momber, Corn.

Linda De Winter, Surrey
Roger Gibson, Derbs.
John T. Norwood, W. Mids.
A.F.J. Wakeford, Kent
P. McGowan, W. Mids.

Fourth Prize Winners

Norman Acaster, Kent
Alan Titley, Norf.
Patricia Campbell-Lyons, Surrey
Denis Cheason, Cambs.
John Rumming, Avon.
Greta Hopper, Norf.
Mandy Parker, Ches.
M.E. Fitness, Lancs.
Winifred V. Stubbs, Yorks.
Alison Thomson, Fife
Moreen Place, Man.
Christine Molloy, Cumb.
Joyce Bushby, Kent

Kenneth W. White, Middx.
W.G. Ralph, Norf.
Beryl Drummond, Dorset
George Crosby, Avon.
Kevin G. Jones, Avon.
Edna Wight, Cambs.
Kathy King, Essex.
Shona White, Kent
Vernon E. Taylor, Yorks.
D. Bailey, Ches.
J. Bunn, Norf.
Bill Underwood, Wilts.

BEST POEM 10 and under, Danielle Fitzsimons, Cumb.
BEST POEM 10 to 15 years, Scott Nixon, Cleve.

Congratulations also to our Awards of Excellence winners

Grand Prize Winner

Old Lancashire Bath Night

Friday night were bath night, in our house when I were small,
We used to have an old tin bath, that hung on backyard wall.
An' when the tea were over, an' we'd cleared away each cup,
The lads would bring the old bath in, an' mam would fill it up.
Wi' pans she boiled on gas stove, 'cos we'd no hot water then,
It seemed to take for ages to fill it to the brim.
But when at last the bath were full, the lads 'ad come off worst
'Cos they'd have to sit in parlour, while the girls 'ad their bath first.
An' there in front of fire, wi' mam there to attend,
Two girls got in together, one at either end.
Then mam set to wi' loofah, an' scrubbed till we were sore,
While we just squirmed an' wriggled, sloppin' water on to floor,
Then dried an' in were nighty, hot cocoa we would have,
An' we'd have to go in parlour, an' change places wi' the lads.
An' we'd sit an' hear 'em squealin', but if they got too bad,
Mam clipped 'em round the earhole, an' threatened 'em wi' Dad.
Then when at last mam finished, an' we stood there shining pink
Mam set to an' emptied all the water down the sink,
An' we'd all sit round the fireside, till one by one we'd yawn
An' mam would say, "Right, off to bed, you'll not get up in morn."
Then we toddled off up wooden stairs, wi' candle in were hand
An' before me mam could say goodnight, we'd be in noddy land.

Muriel Altham

Second Prize Winners

The Pebble Band

One moment still, then out of reach,
Travelling stones on a moving beach,
Hitching a lift on the evening tide,
Jostling with others on top, below, beside
In the rush and tumble down the sand.
A maze of shapes this Pebble Band
Of water glazed colours of differing hue,
A motley lot, this salt laden crew.

Serpentine nuggets and granite fines,
Black grey rounds with rail white lines,
Rough smooth sticks of sanding stone,
Hard chips of flint by salt sea hone;
Playing percussion on each others' backs
In a crescendo of roaring butted sacks
With crashing waves of Double bassed rollers,
All for the love of two salt sprayed strollers.

Alan Tilmouth

The Telephone Call

When the phone rang the other night I knew it was for me,
That took no great deduction as I live alone you see.
Well I picked it up and said 'Hello' the way you always do,
And this female voice said, 'Sandra, how lovely to hear you.

It's been absolutely ages, so I thought I'd give a call
To bring you up to date with latest news about us all.'
I tried to interrupt but she went on at such a pace,
'Did you hear about Amelia? Such a scandal and disgrace.

I've told her father often he was never strict enough,
So he's turned her out without a bean and now she's sleeping rough.
And my dear, what of poor Stephen? Such a pity, what a shame,
But after all, he really only had himself to blame.

Do you see Joanne often? She was more your friend than mine,
In fact we've hardly spoken since that quite dreadful time
When she turned up wearing purple on Roberto's opening night,
And the press boys overheard me tell her that she looked a fright.'

'Excuse me,' I began, but she went on without a pause,
'John and Sal are splitting up, which is no surprise of course,
He always had a roving eye where ladies were concerned,
And heaven knows I've warned him that he'd get his fingers burned.

Well Sandra darling, no more now, I'll really have to fly,
So much to do, it's six o'clock, I'll have to say goodbye.'
The phone went dead, and she was gone, which really was a pity,
She never gave me chance to tell her that my name was Kitty.

Doreen Pinder

Ode To Autumn

Best loved of all the seasons, now proud Autumn shows her worth.
The sizzling heat of Summer past. The richness of the earth
In radiant beauty, heaven sent, to bless all of Mankind,
And with her wealth embracing us, true glories now we find.
While Bacchus lies upon his couch, his goblet filled once more,
The fields have offered up their grain, a precious golden store.
The morning mists bring mystery to every hedge and tree,
Where spider's webs like jewels hang, and when the sun breaks free
The orange, red, and golden leaves set every tree ablaze,
The beauty of the country-side revealed within its haze.
And hymns of praise are sung in Church amid the scent of flowers,
With vegetables, and harvest bread, arrangements taking hours.
Perfection linked with gratitude to God who is divine.
Who sends this cornucopia, blessed is this food and wine.
Now is the time when hedgehogs gorge before their winter sleep,
And creatures hoard their food away, and gardeners dig deep
Awaiting frosts, to sweeten up the fertile dark brown soil,
And take life easy for a while, after their months of toil.
The Autumn shows and Festivals have all now taken place,
The logs are stacked, and larders filled, the country-side's dear face
Provides its harvest for all birds when Winter days are here,
Oh glorious mellow Autumn — Hail the crowning of the year.

Angela Douse

Thoughts At St. Enedoc
(remembering Sir John Betjeman)

We drove with him on motorways
Then wandered down a lane
To sun drenched cliffs of Cornwall
Or Putney in the rain.
He shared his childhood memories
Of trains and teddy bears —
To sounds of bells he had us run
Up flights of college stairs.

He wrote about the Undergound
Of Hammersmith and Slough
Word pictures to transport us
From Edward's reign to now.
Suburban scenes he underlined
Where rows of breeze block boxes
Had gobbled into countryside
Leaving Harrow for the foxes.

If you pass by the tamarisk
Then through the old lych gate
Look on the modest marker
Not knight nor Laureate —
Although he left to millions
More than the written page
He is remembered just as 'John' —
A poet of his age.

Paul Clark

Sleepless Nights

It's three o'clock in the morning
And I think that our Tom is awake
It's worse than the four minute warning
Oh why won't he give me a break?
Does he know that the night is for sleeping?
Can't he see the dark rings round my eyes?
Is it some special secret he's keeping
As to why it's at night that he cries?
It isn't the fact that he's tired
Cos if he's put into our bed
He won't settle down there either
He's wanting to climb on my head.
I tell him, "Look Thomas, it's night-time,
I'm not in the mood to play,
I have to get up in the morning
While you, Tom, can sleep through the day!"

The morning arrives all too quickly
and finds me tired and stressed.
My face in the mirror looks sickly
and it's time to get up and get dressed.
Then coming back into the bedroom
I suddenly feel I could weep
I stand there as numb as a zombie
And you, Tom, are laid there asleep.

David Tomkinson

Third Prize Winners

Birdsong

Between dazzling links of neon chain the old songbird weaves her way,
To find a roost, she's searched in vain, now night succumbs to day.
Large flocks of downy fledgling chicks strut by without a glance,
Her eyes gaze on in hollow fix, her visage in a trance.
Not long ago they swarmed in throngs to wonder and to swoon,
They loved her beauty and her songs, enchanted by her tune.
Oh throstle voice which swelled the air and lifted hearts with gladness,
Where has it gone, the chords are bare, the song now croaks of sadness.
The wings which spanned the billboard's ink and hoisted her to fame,
Are drooping now she seems to sink on legs and feet so lame.
Her well preened plumes and fantailed dress, once the envy of the town,
Are ousted by a ruffled mess, her coat now faded brown.
She ambles on with weary gait, then stops to beg a crust,
But before the crumbs have met their fate she falls down in the dust.
The stage is set, the lights now shine for her final curtain call,
Her descant notes rise so divine, immortal in her soul.

Audrey Rigby

"WAR"

I crouch in the shell-wrecked cottage and watch the smoking plain,
Where the leafless trees of April bow to metal rain,
I think of the blessed Springtime at home in field and wood,
And the joyous meadow voices where I had often stood.

I dream of the little children who smiled so sweetly there,
And their lovely upturned faces, so young, so clear, so fair.
Then back to the reeking cannon and back to the plain of death,
Where the ghastly struggling armies defy the dragon's breath.

I ponder the burning madness, of men who made this war,
Of the men who sat in Council and steeped the world in gore.
Oh where was the cool clear reason that made so loathsome fray?
In a fight for fancied freedom which none can have a day.

I start as I see them coming to climb our scar faced hill,
As they thrust their bayonets forward intent to wound and kill.
My fingers grip my machine-gun, I know what I shall do,
Yet I cannot hate the soldier who fights for freedom too.

Whose loves are as sweet as mine are, whose home he holds as dear,
Are we mad? or only children who fight through wretched fear?
I hear my machine-gun firing, I see the young men fall,
As they fling their arms up wildly and clutch the smoking pall.

I mow down the children's children whose seed was sown in vain,
I have slain the sons of women who raised them up in pain,
And this was the soldiers' duty to slay or to be slain,
And the proud and noble Nations have gone to war again.

Richard Styles

The Conservationist

I saw him on a roadside, "Are you a tramp" I said.
He took some time to think it through,
    then shook his tousled head.
"I do not like neat pigeon holes but if you must persist,
just put me on the record as a conservationist.

The need for conservation is constantly impressed
to use resources wisely will serve the whole world best.
I do my bit to help the cause, recycle others clothes,
I have no car to foul the air, that anybody knows.

Some wash or shower every day; obsessive I would think.
I take the waters every day but boiled to make a drink.
To bathe of course is needful, say once or twice a year,
more would be quite excessive and wasteful too I fear.

My life-style does no damage to the environment.
Consumer goods are not for me, no power, no gas, no rent.
Well ventilated lodgings, a doorway or a bridge,
and for at least six months a year I do not need a fridge.

The ozone layer is safe with me, a friend of all the earth.
That sums up my philosophy for what you think it's worth.
Yes, I think 'conservationist' is what describes me well
Yet people stand up wind of me for reasons hard to tell."

J.T. Norwood

Morning

I hear the sound of music
That's carried on the breeze
Smell the sweet-sweet scent of Primroses
That grow among the trees
I hear the ringing of the Blue-Bells
As they nod their pretty heads
and I see the little Doormouse
As he scurries home to bed
The silver moon has long since gone
A new day has begun
I see the shimmering Spider's Webs
As they catch the morning sun
The wise old Owl sits all alone
On his branch high in the tree
And a brilliant coloured Butterfly
Performs a dance for me
The sun shines down and a Blackbird sings
And light reflects on gossamer wings
As a Dragonfly flits slowly by
Warmed by the sun in a cloudless sky
I wish that everyone could see
All the beautiful things that are shown to me.

A.F.J. Wakeford

Sun After Rain At The Railway Station

Pigeons blow-dried by the westerly wind
fluff out lucent feathers,
which trap iridescence in rainbow hues
about their necks like collared gems.

The sun gilds wet pavements with sudden prisms
and flashes unexpected sapphire from a raven's wing.
Even the sparrows turn tawny, honeyed by the light.

The railway lines between the platforms
are quicksilver bright; mercurial serpents.
A broken bottle gleams emerald,
another amber
and bottle caps too are silvered.

The light lies like a lambent benison, mantling
the new spun earth and each leaf blade
and each pearled cob's web
becomes precious within its caress.

Linda de Winter

Growth Cycles

In autumn storm the trees shed leaves that disappear whirlwinding down
To when, frost fractured into dust, worm-turned to soil that feeds the flow
Of leachings permeating buds of green, that signal start of spring.
Until the night when lightning strikes, or drought destroys ascending sap
Or alien virus ferments harm, then crashing down the noble bole
Returns to ground and starts to rot, and soften as decay abounds
With fungal mould and mushroom cap, and goodness flows back to the soil
Small seeds to succour into sprigs, that flex against the autumn storm

My father was a gentle man, who served in two world wars, and lived
A noble life, tree like and sound. Advancing others was his call
Taught skills and crafts for his career, and then struck down, ashen, infirm
Immobile, muted, yet the eyes, still bright, that told of bygone love
Of life, and times of joy, now ended by the blight as slow torment
Coursed through his body's branches, to the core, then smothered out the light
His teachings caused the buds to grow in others minds, and make them free
I am that sprig that, raised by him, have flexed to storms, matured to tree

Roger Gibson

Sensible Eating

The standard English breakfast please with bacon, eggs and toast;
and butter, tea and marmalade, I like the chunky most.

The Boffins said NO!

Bacon's made from pork meat, preserved by adding salt.
Salt gives you blood pressure and may cause your heart to halt.
Eggs have Salmonella, the bugs which make you quell;
White bread has no roughage and is finely ground as well.
Marmalade's half sugar the stuff you should avoid;
Tea contains much caffeine, the dreaded alkaloid.

For dinner, I'll have T-bone steak with onions and mushrooms fried;
and cheese laced roast potatoes and a salad on the side.
For sweet I'll have Peach Melba with lots of creamy sauce;
and coffee, cheese and biscuits and chocolate mints of course.

The Boffins said NO!

If you insist on T-bone steak, it's rather rich for starters;
the animal rights societies will have your gust for garters.
Cheese laced roast potatoes are foods you cannot hate;
You may find your clothes won't fit you when you're on that special date.
Coffee, cheese and biscuits with chocolate mints, oh dear!
You'll get more fat and calories than you'll need in half a year.

Now all this set me thinking, just where have I gone wrong?
The good advice from Boffins, I have ignored all along.
Calories and cholesterol I've eaten without fears;
So how come with forbidden food, I've lived for ninety years?

Ernest Netherwood

Winged Victory

Once round your feet the warm tide washed; sweet air
Fanned your cold marble, blown from shores of flowers;
Your wings spread open to the sun and showers,
You, at the dawn of time, supremely fair.

Over the azure waves, through rainbowed spray,
Far on a great ship's prow, below the white
High, dazzling clouds, you sailed till lost in light;
One with the splendour of a southern day.

Now you are broken; through cold winter night
No star shines on you, nor will the sun's beam
In summer touch you. Only in a dream
We see you as you were in the sunlight.

And yet your wings are spread; your robes flow free,
Lifted by unfelt winds; while like a tide
The crowds pass by. You, still triumphant, glide,
Beauty undimmed, into eternity.

Diana Momber

Pitfalls

Wales is the land of rugby and song
There used to be coal mines, but now they have gone.
Our valleys once echoed with beautiful singing
As miners trekked home, the coal dust still clinging.

The good Lord created our valley to cherish
To hold in esteem and never to perish.
Now old men reflect on much happier times
When they carved out a living from work in the mines.

But memories now are all that remain
The pits now have gone like the snow after rain.
Coal mining prospered, with Wales at the hub.
Now old men reminisce as they chat in the pub.

How busy our valley when I was a kid
Now tower blocks stand where those coal mines once did.
With the pits' sad demise a heritage died
And stout-hearted men sat down and cried.

With their lifeblood now gone, resistance is low
They linger on corners with nowhere to go.
"Get on yer bike and go look for work".
They're told by the rich, with an arrogant smirk.

With time on their hands they search round for kicks
And some turn to drugs and steal for a 'fix'.
Their livelihood gone, just life on the dole.
Oh! Where are the pits gone, our valley of coal?

Leah Amelia Goddard

King of the Road for a Minute

I watched an old man cross the road
His limbs were stiff with age;
His white hair ruffled by the breeze;
He was like an ancient sage.

With faltering steps he made his way
To the centre of the street,
Then waved his stick at traffic till
They halted with a screech.

He stood there for a 'minute',
Enjoying his little fling —
'Cause the traffic had obeyed him
And he felt just like a king ...

No longer was he set aside
By others in their prime,
Just because he's lived too long
If that was his only crime.

But today he'd left his calling card
On the busy world at large —
Out there in the middle of the road
He'd felt he was in charge.

Then slowly as he ambled on
And crossed to the other side —
With twinkling eyes, he bowed to all
With that age-old gentle pride ...

P. McGowan

A Special Place

It isn't a National Monument, it's not a Stately Home,
It doesn't have lots of towers or a folly or a dome.
They don't keep lions or peacocks or exotica like that -
But, lots of other birds are about and occasionally next door's cat.
There isn't a ghost or a haunting by someone who's lost his head;
Just a frightening noise in the chimney which you hear when you've gone to bed.
There's a definite lack of a river or water for quiet contemplating,
But the drains overflow every time that it rains and they flood 'til the storm starts abating.
The garden is quite far from pretty. Just some grass and a little old shed
And a couple of pots of pansies which are known as the front flower bed.
No stables or cars with chauffeurs whose expenses 'quite get one down.'
Their stately coach is the bus twice a week, back and forth to the nearby small town.
They don't stage an annual social event - to dress up for all to see
But they do have the odd little party; tea and buns and admission is free.
There's no plaque to remind the Public who has lived there in days gone before
Just a prettily painted china disc which says that it's number four.
T'was originally called 'prestigious' then was altered to 'Tudor Style'
'Though lately the point in its favour is 'from the shops it's under a mile!'
No objects d'art, no portraits in oil, no scenes brushed in colour and water
But it's Heaven on Earth and a house full of love. I should know; I'm their only grand daughter.

Audrey A. Adams

Season Of Love

Spring is here, the sky is blue, birds sing as if
they knew that I love you.
I'll be yours and you'll be mine.
I'll love you until end of time, true love means
planning a life for two, true love means being together.
I know I'll make you happy, my darling I need
you here with me, it hurts when you're not here.
Take my passion and let it happen.
I wonder if you'll still love me tomorrow.

Waheeda Abbas

Down In Black And White

White scratched on the Blackness
So black poured over white
The Dover stone,
Scratched you sadness,
Here? I pour out my own.

Whiteness taints the black,
Blackness breaks the white,
An empty void,
swallows the light.

Stephanie Acton

Moonlit Scene

The phosphorescent breakers gently cream
Against the beach, steeply sloping
The leafy-fingered palm are groping
Skyward, where heaven's jewels gleam.
Moonlight frosts the land
Silhouetting sharply, shapes and trees
While, from the sea, a cooling breeze
Gently shifts the soft sand
Still warmed by the tropical heat
Of the glaring noon-day sun.
For men, days work is done
And distantly, hand-drums beat,
As with muffled steps I stray
My thought go soaring — far away.

Norman Acaster

Astral Projection

The day was cold and all was still
When I stood on that windy hill
And waited.
The Question mark Inside my head
Was, am I alive or am I dead?
Or sedated.
A fine gossamer of silver thread
Floated high above my head,
My spirit looking down on me
Waited very patiently,
I heard the church bells start to ring
The congregation began to sing
I urged my spirit to jump back In,
So — elated.

Vera Veronica Adams

Forever An Ache

I could see the Firth of Forth from my bedroom window,
  For me a familiar scene,
The moon peeped out from behind a cloud,
  Lit up the sea, t'was an artist's dream,
I saw ancient Ravenscraig Castle,
  Massive, gaunt and bare,
My heart was sore, was I doing right?
  I asked the Lord in prayer.

I was flying to a new land,
  Leaving behind the folks that I loved so,
To find a new life for myself,
  On the morrow it was time to go,
Would I ever return to my homeland?
  Would my own folks still be there?
With a heart benumbed with sorrow,
  I continued to stand and stare.

Thirty years have come and gone,
  Since I left old Scotia's shore.
Hand work provided dividends,
  I have had my share and more,
I came home to visit Kirkcaldy,
  To find things changed, unfamiliar, all new,
Now I know I will live the rest of my life,
  With a heart divided in two.

Mary Adamson

The Pig On The Wall

In deepest Bucks, three score years ago,
In a place renowned called Drayton Parslow
There's the tale of the pig, that sat on a wall
Whilst the brass band passed by, I do recall.

First Percy Pig drinks a quart of ale
Served in a gold dish; — no, not a pail —
By the local landlord. No charge he makes,
We all watch in awe, as Percy Pig partakes.

Fortified and full, out of the door he does trot,
Watched by his many friends — a motley lot.
All keen and eager to not miss the sight
Of our beloved pig, in almost full flight.

For he scrambles up to the top of the wall
And sits proud and straight, nearly six feet tall.
And if by magic and in the nick of time
The brass band comes marching in perfect line.

Percy Pig, agog, grins from ear to ear.
He waves to his friends he holds so dear
The band plays loud and passes by
And our friend Mr. Pig, gleefully winks his eye!

Right down the ages, so brave and bold,
Our friend Percy Pig is a sight to behold
He sits on this wall, with not a care,
I know it happens, for I'm always there!

Kathleen Aldridge

Suicide

As she sat in her room
With her window ajar,
All she had left,
Was the pain and the scar.

The hurt of her life,
When she was wounded by love,
But now it has ended,
And she's safe up above.

She knew he'd never love her,
She knew he'd never care,
The child's pain has ended,
And now she's loved up there.

Gemma Adnitt

Middle Age

You're not really ninety; it's all a mistake,
Although the back hurts and all your bones ache.
The veins all are throbbing, you think they'll explode
You are sure you are nearing the end of the road.
It's your birthday today and you think you're in Heaven
You suddenly realise you are just fifty-seven.
The children are coming, who you really adore,
But oh, the relief when they head for the door.
The hormone replacement's not working too well
I must put up my feet for I'm feeling like hell.
I will have a nap — the fifth today
Will this ever go away
The consolation, so I'm told,
It only lasts until you're old.

Mrs. M. Ailles

Over The Top

The cool wind ices the sweat on his skin,
As he watches the grey mist-veil clear.
Peering past the dirt wall with fear-brightened eyes,
While his heartbeat sound swift in his ears.
"One minute!" they shout from the depths of the line,
And each second is marked by a beat.
He knows at a glance that it's not only he,
Who feels more than mud clogging his feet.
Knees slack as the whistle blast rends the cold air,
With a rush the push forwards begun.
Hands slow to react, it's his turn for the ladder,
Then "Walking pace, boys! Don't run!"
Weighted by pack and watery bowelled,
He's over, scraping the top rung.
Youth's features stunned into bloodied surprise,
At the solitary crack of a gun.

G. Adkin

Suffolk

Oh to walk down
Suffolk's country lanes
My thoughts turn,
Back to happy bygone days.

Of happy visits to loving grandparents,
No longer there,
Of walks in the woods,
And romps in the harvest field,
And to watch the men bring in their yield.

Now in my later years
And to be back again in my beloved Suffolk
With walks to the River Deben and about.
Now I find life has turned full circle,
To live here,
And to have my little grandchildren come and visit us,
And together we enjoy our trips to the sea near here.

So I feel God has been good, in His grace,
To let me enjoy this lovely place.

Mrs. G. Adams

On The Streets

People are homeless.
Living in cardboard boxes
Begging
Coughing
Crying
Searching in bins
In need.
Drinking
Pick pockets
Washing in gutters
Living in shop doorways.
Why? Why?
Redundancies, divorce, no hope.
They are sad, cold, hungry —
They haven't got any money
For a bag of chips, a cup of tea,
A biscuit.
These people can't help it
They need help.
Help them
Please.

Simon Adcock (Age 10)

The Spider's Web

It wis spun by a big black spider frae a corner in the room,
It made a lacey pattern as it twirl't it roon an' roon,
It didna tak' it very lang tae spin a fit or twa,
For the next time that I lookit it wis half wye doon the wa',
It hung aboot there for a while, syne it startit climmin' doon,
On a threed o' shiney gossamer it swung aboot the room.

It spun a length tae tak' it richt doon tae the skirtin' boord,
An' there's ay thing that it proved tae me, a spider's nae a coord,
For it dangle't on that silky threed till it landed on it's feet,
An' efter fixin' doon the ein' it startit tae retreat,
It made a bee-line for the licht an' gaed roon an' roon the shade,
Till ye cwidna see the licht bulb for the cobweb that it made.

Fin the spider finish't spinnin' it crawl't doon inside the licht,
It haul't upon the hin'maist threed an' pul't it in real ticht,
It hidna lang tae wait till it heard a buzzin' soun'
It peepit oot an' sa' a flea gan tearin' roon the room,
It cam' buzzin' roon aboot the licht, the spider lowered it's heid,
An' patiently it waited there, pretendin' tae be deid.

The flea it took a closer look, that's fin it met it's fate,
It's wing got tangle't in the web, the spider didna wait
It ran oot on the ticht rope, jist like a circus clown,
The flea jist shook it's heid, on it's face there wis a frown,
It kint it cwidna get awa, it hid fairly met it's doom,
An' a' because a spider made a cobweb in the room.

Hazel L.R. Addison

A Night Of Noise

Outside the wind is howling.
The sound of rustling leaves
People shivering.
I close my curtains,
Get undressed,
Put on my warm pyjamas
And curl up in my bed.

I lie silently for a while;
I hear some strange noises.

The sound of sirens;
Cats climbing in bins —
Calling their friends.
The sound of floor boards creaking,
Central heating pipes bumping and banging —
Like a prowler surveying the house.
The hisses of steam,
Released from the factory boiler house.
Clang! The dustbin lid falls over,
Milk bottles topple.

The sound of heavy breathing,
A creaking bed,
Then snoring.

The night is silent.

Robert Adcock (Age 12)

Bluebells

Sapphire flowers on emerald leaves,
What precious jewels are these,
Bluebells

Growing strong, wild and free,
A carpet of blue for all to see,
Bluebells

Bells of blue that gently ring
To cast out Winter, and celebrate Spring
Bluebells

Mrs. C. Allen

The Rain

The wet thick grey trousers of the rain man,
Drips on to the soggy ground,
And the soaking navy blue shirt,
The water suddenly slithers down his sleeves,
And his sweat appears to be rain drops,
And the cloudy headed man
Does not care any more.

Andrew Aitcheson

Foreboding

As I approach the bed each morn
In mood akin to dread
To gaze at her recumbent form
Alive or maybe dead.

I lift the cover from her face
To seek assurance there
That life remains within that form
Which once was young and fair.

And when she makes responsive stir
Relief comes flooding o'er.
Another day seems now assured
Before the crisis hour.

What remains of life for me
Is tinged with no remorse,
But filled with wistful memory,
And the failing of life's force.

Robert M. Aitken

Untitled

Life and love dealt such cruel blows,
you gave me compassion and faith.

I had no love for myself,
you gave me love for mankind.

Events crushed and pained,
you made me embrace life with both hands.

The darkness closed around,
you kept me fighting the battle.

My will was on bloodied knees,
you lifted my head up toward the light

My shoulders were bent with burden,
you gave me release and ease.

I asked you why,
you said you loved me.

Russell Aiton

The Spires of Oxford

How proudly they rise and gaze at the sky,
Midst towers and turrets and clouds passing by,
A stately St. Mary's all history aglow,
Silently gazes on life down below
Where footsteps and people go scurrying by,
Not stopping to wonder if treasure be nigh.

Great Christ Church and Magdalen with buttress and bell,
Bring monarch and bishop and scholar to dwell,
An architect's dream presenting a view
Which time in its wisdom sent man to pursue,
No diamond is needed nor any such stone,
The bright spires of Oxford shine forth on their own.

Ruth D. Alderman

The Hunters Causing Extinction

Through the dark deserted woods I tread,
The hunter hunting — the only thing I dread,
Running free and fast, moving through the trees
Leaving a trail for the hunter to tease
I enjoy freedom now, for one day I will pay
I hope and pray, for that day to stay away

The day I come across the hunter I fear
An arrow from his bow will pierce my tear
The day my hide will be strung out to dry
The day I kiss my world good-bye.

Marc Adams

The Blackbird

Here I sit on the highest tree,
Watching the world go by,
The month is May, it's been a lovely day,
I've been able to just fly and fly.

At moments like this when I'm resting,
I think of the winter that's past.
I had to fight hard for survival,
At times I thought "will I last."

But thanks to my friends the humans
I found my food morning and night,
On a table they left bread and water,
I was grateful for each last bite.

So now it's my turn to reward them,
To sit here and sing my refrain,
To say thanks for the chance of survival,
Maybe next year they will do it again.

Mrs. C. A'Len

Protect the Innocent

Hey Mum and Dad what's going on
Where have all your offspring gone
Growing up in this world of fear
You know you really should be near.

Do you know where your children play
What evil force is there today
Enticing your siblings to a life of hell
Will you be there when they want to tell.

Protect your children as they grow
Innocent precious wherever they go
Your fledglings come first in every way
Treat with kindness or they'll go astray.

Keep your family close love them dear
They will survive another year
These little ones have hearts of gold
Let your love for them unfold..

Christine Allison

Just You And I

A wooded glade where bluebells grow,
The birds nest happily above,
We're young, and all the world is ours,
Just you and I.

Flowers grow wild between the grass,
The leaves are full upon the trees,
As hand in hand we walk along,
Face to the sun and summer breeze,
Just you and I.

All is golden in the lane,
The autumn leaves turn russet brown,
They crush to dust beneath our feet,
We watch the golden sun go down,
Just you and I.

The snow lies deep upon the ground,
The wintry sky looks cold and chill,
The trees wrapped round with cloaks of snow,
And all is white and still.
Before the fire we needs must stay,
My love, today.

Muriel Allen

Pastoral Dream

In a field of cornflowers blue
I sat amidst its azure hue
Nature spread its soothing hand
Across the fields and rolling land.

The tall pines stirred with waking birds
Whose soft sweet voices then I heard
The darkened woods from black of night
Awoke with silver shafts of light.

I passed the hedgerows full with flowers
That opened in the sun's first hours
Velvet wallflowers, wild dog rose
Such scents to give a sweet repose.

Spiders flew on gossamer threads
On dew-strewn grass amongst the reds
Of poppies delicate and fair
A wondrous sight beyond compare.

And in the valley quietly stirred
The soft-breathed warmth of gentle herd
Their rich and satin milk to give
Their young who need its good, to live.

Catherine Allen

Remission

Bright cherry breast nipples —
Dimpled in the coming dawn
Languishing on the satin quilt of her desires
Waiting for her lover on that bright light morn
Touching her skin — the eruption of desires to explore
A Phoenix rising from the ashes

Heliotrope heavy lidded eyes — spins the pencil line
across the dent of her eyeball —
Pumps Rouge Absolute on her swollen waiting lips

Daisy petals on the floor, one, two, three
He loved me once — Didn't he?

Carol Ayres

Don't Laugh At Me

Don't laugh at the boys with their funny ways
Don't stand and stare with your eyes agaze
Or snigger at the way they walk
Or be two-faced at the way they talk.
Can you not see their own love twisted
By man's own hand he has assisted?
They are caught up between their souls
And cannot find their true love roles.
Please don't smirk or make them cry
Because they love from a gentleman's eye.
We're all born innocent, gay and free
So please, please don't laugh at me.

Paul Atherton

Animal Experiments

Animal testing is it good, or bad?
A lot of people think it's sad,
That animals suffer for our needs
And we live our lives at ease.

Do we realise the pain they go through
Or is it just we don't really want to?
Animals placed in little cages
Unaware of the dangers.

But as the time starts ticking by
Another little animal has to die
But at the end of the day we have to say
Who has the right to take a life away?

Sharon Anderson

Thoughts On An Expected Grandchild

My knitting needles click away,
Fine wool locks firmly into place,
And so your shawl grows day by day,
A warm and cosy nest of lace.

As yet you are unseen, unknown,
Busy in your wondrous cavern,
Where with love your seed was sown
To grow, in its abundant tavern.

One day in this shawl you'll sleep,
Dear love, of me a tiny part,
Another precious jewel to keep
And treasure, set inside my heart.

Mary Allen

Pater Noster

I have travelled far and wide
Have seen many a tide
There have been several dawns
Before many's a yawn
Much happiness
But also much sadness
I have followed other paths
Heard many loud laughs
Throughout all my life
There has been trouble and strife
Never has by thirst been quenched
Nor my mind been drenched
With anyone as wonderful as you Lord
Nothing compares to a love
Such as yours, God.

Dawn P. Allison

Her Mind

Her mind was like a deep dark house,
where nothing lived not even a mouse.
Old animal bones lay on the ground,
memories scattered, shall never be found.
Shrieks and screams all flew round her brain
banging her head to drive her insane.
Dark and dingy, dusty and small,
thoughts flowing through the cracks in the wall.
Worries hovering through the air,
each single thought entered the lair,
until they slowly fell in the pit,
endlessly falling to the ground they'd soon hit,
to be forgotten for eternity,
to stay there forever for no one to see...

Rebecca Leigh Allen

Two's Enough

As I close their bedroom doors, memories stir of days gone past —
Full of mischief, always wanting. Would my patience ever last?
Bikes and Go-cart in the driveway, doll's pram in the hall.
Carpets strewn with toys and marbles, trainset, books, a ball ...
Bathroom battles: "Clean you teeth and wash your dirty face."
(Where's the daughter I once hoped for, dressed in frills and lace?)
Gerbils, hamsters, cats and budgies, rabbits and a pup.
(Always nagging! ...) "It's your pet, now go and clean it up!"
Muddy shoes and rugby shorts, P.E. vests and skirts,
Washing line full each day with jumpers, jeans and shirts.
Teenage years then came along, with diets and P.M.T.
Fashion talk and rugby songs, ... Discos, ... friends for tea.
Soon the bathroom was in vogue, a never-ending queue.
"Whatever do they do in there? Quick, we need the loo"
Transformations now took place (He actually changed his clothes!)
She swapped her jeans for blouse and skirt and sandals with peep-toes.
And so, as things are meant to be, each met their future spouse.
They both left home all starry-eyed, so keen to set up house —
My job is done, I've brought them up and sent them on their way
Now is the time for me to rest and savour every day.
But as I gaze around my home, so quiet and so still,
I thank the Lord for those precious years ...
    (... and my Doctor for The Pill!)

Rosemary Atherton

The Family Circle

The family gathering around the Christmas tree
Creates feelings of thankfulness to be
Part of the seasons rejoicing at yuletide
The past year such a rough and tumble ride

Christmas is a time of heartfelt reflection
Reminiscent of loved ones with deep affection
Viewing the cards of Nativity scenes
Brings thoughts of family and all it means

Forming part of the hub in the wheel of life
Journeying through happiness, peace and strife
Protecting childhood and hurts of young love
Throughout life's storms, our guide from above

Til love's troth is promised on bended knee
Yet each have roots from a differing tree
Alas there's sadness as the funeral bell tolls
At the loss of a loved one to the land of souls

But oh, the joyous celebration of the new arrival
Assuring kith and kin's undoubted survival
A blessing of love arrives on the family scene
Symbol of the future, a gift of life supreme

As the wheel of life turns throughout the year
Christmas festivities bring new hope and cheer
Vibrantly the hub revolves for all in mind
Given freely to the world's family of mankind

V. T. Allsop

A Wish For You

I hope that you have seen the way
To find some happiness each day
In simple things, that lift us far
Above the hurt, the wounding scar.

I hope, each day, that peace you'll find
With quiet and contented mind
That gazes with appreciation
On the Almighty's great creation.

I hope that you will seek and see
The beauty in a graceful tree
With petal blossoms drifting down
To make, for earth, a perfumed gown.

I hope sometimes you've time to stand,
See doggy footprints in wet sand
And join him in his bounding glee
A-racing down to meet the sea.

I hope when Winter's world we share,
When trimming's shed and all is bare,
When snow lies thick on blackened boughs
And ice-cold wind bemoans and soughs,
That you'll see beauty in the scene,
Knowing it's just an in-between,
That days will soon be lighter, warmer
With Spring that's just around the corner.

Margery Harrington Allan

Winter Comin' On

A futtret slinkit ben the dyke faur leaves were furlin doon
The cauldrife nichts had brawed his coat tae fite fae fechie broon
The wastlin' win', forebodin' snaw gaart larricks creak an' groan
The Autumn days wir knypin' by an' Winter comin' on.

The futtret coored ahin' a stane an' hearkned tae the win'
He snuffed the air an' kent that snaw wid seen be blawin' blin'
A thraw moose reeshlt throu' the leaves an' aiblens wid been gone
But the futtret's need gaed double speed for Winter's comin' on.

A craggie raxt his spin'le trams an primpit up the ditch
Faur strippit roddins hung their heids like geets withoot a stitch
An' hoodie craws stravaiged the Straths the stibbled rapes amon'
Tae gether grubs fae plytered dubs for Winter's comin' on.

Syne frosty days that nip oor taes wi' win' that's snell an' keen
Gaars man an' moose tak' tae the hoose an' oolets scraich abeen
Fan driftin' snaw in corries blaw an' straiks the hills beyon'
An' hummle doddies hap oor knieves, the Winter's ferly on.

Robert Adam

Memories

Cometh the night,
A chill wind that blows,
When all yearnings crumble
To dust, as grains of sand
Fly scattered in the wind.
Of happiness that lasted such a short time,
Once stood majestic like a castle in the air,
Solid bastions around a stable calm,
Festooned with aspirations, yet
Darkened with a lingering doubt,
Circling as smoke round embers of a fire.
Dying, and calling the wind for breath
To kindle anew.

Cometh the night,
Mystic songs upon the morning breeze,
Carry salutations of another day,
Sweet as the dew an incense coat,
Warms the rustic calm.
Clinging like spider's silken weave
Beneath the dusty beam of darkened shed,
Memories of leafy days, haystacks, fields,
Filtering again through dusty corners of the mind.
Polish them well, replace them with care,
To draw yet again, whenever the need,
From the peaceful portals which surround
The library of your mind.

David Ambler

Our Children

It really would appear to me that the days of cosseting,
Your children number one, two, or three
In this the year '95, our children must be kept alive,
No putting on of reins when toddling,
And when school starts they go on trodding,
The green cross code is taught at school,
The lollypop man he too has rules,
And not forgetting strangers to talk to them is out,
Accept no sweets and take no lifts,
And if they bother you then kick, scream and shout,
To have your Mammy take your hand,
And leave you up to school,
Now that's just not done any more
It is your unwritten rule,
So children dear your childhood's gone
Grown up before your time,
You do your stuff and show your tough
No cotton wool for you, a rugby ball to
Tackle it seems that's what you'll do,
But there's more to life than
Rugby, computers and TV,
If you don't learn at school
You won't get a job you see,
And how will you do for your boys
Numbered One, Two or Three.

N. Armstrong

Resurrection

I see the snowdrops are through again, once more
Thrusting green spears into the pale January sunshine
And I feel again, as I have felt so many times before;
A joy that brings sadness to my eyes and spills the tears
As if some wished for hope, so long since lost
Might with the snowdrops come again'
The hope, nay indeed, the trust
That no matter how dark and final
The Winter seems,
There will always be a Spring.

Thomas Anibal

The Gift of Life

The greatest gift I ever had
A little lass and a little lad
My daughter gave them to me
Her husband helped her too
Our darling Danielle
And our Jon who's gorgeous too
I talk about them all the time
They give me so much pleasure
But I suppose that's just because
They are my greatest treasure
When I am down and feeling low
I think of them and up I go
I've never wanted money
Or clothes or dress or style
I have what I only want
The sunshine of their smile.

Margaret Atkinson

A Prayer for the Living

Say a prayer for the living and hope it is heard,
In these troubled times it's a pitiful world,
The storm is upon us as the sun sets again,
But still there is suffering and still there is pain.

Say a prayer for the living, for they are the ones,
Who must pick up the pieces and life must go on,
Help them to survive through these difficult years,
Let the memories of happiness soak up the tears.

Say a prayer for the living and show them you care,
Help them to see that you're always there.
Look into their darkness and let your light shine,
Help them to heal in the passing of time.

Say a prayer for the living, for the meek and the mild,
For the poor and the lonely and the 'to be born' child,
Say a prayer for the land and the air that we breathe,
A prayer of healing, for hope and for peace.

Paul Andrews

Daffodil

Daffodil, Daffodil, so yellow and bright
What gives you your beauty, the sun and the light,
Daffodil, Daffodil, great beauty I see
While man is cutting and killing trees
How long must it take for them to realise
They can't own the land, sea or skies
No money or wealth can buy one of these
But they still close their eyes and kill with ease,
Daffodil, Daffodil, forgive them and me
No more will you dance, nor sway in the breeze.

Philip Allsworth

Bedtime

My little boy with tired eyes said
'Mummy, is it time for bed?'
And then he had a little look
For his bedtime story book.

Up the wooden stairs we go
His little head sways to and fro
Through the door and into bed
Where he lays down his sleepy head.

He then gave me a little kiss
The story he wants not to miss
But not a sound - not a peep
My little boy lay fast asleep.

Mrs. K. Amendola

Travelling Companion

I fish out
The toiletries and shaver
From my travelling companion,
Not really noticing
The sellotape that tries
To stick the lining.

Exploring for underpants
Beneath waves of towels,
Not really noticing
The worn and battered pattern.

But the handle's strong and sturdy
And the lid will always close,
And lock.

And I wonder, how many stations,
Hallways, hotels, and bus stops
You've seen,
When my Great Aunt knew you
In Castle Eden, Hartlepool.

Chris Antcliff

Birth

As dawn breaks the sun shimmers and dances its way
Across the bay
Bringing to life all in its way and slowly
Awakening to the sounds of morning
A cry, a tear, at last he's here
Feelings of hope, of joy, of fear
Smiles abound all around
While voices chatter in muffled sound
Emotions rise and fall like a tide lapping a
Harbour wall
Unknown sounds echo wall to wall and fade into
The eternal hall
Misty murky waters await for the dawn of that
New date
For thoughts of distant memories come back to
Haunt the new of age
As minutes tick the hours away each of us accept
The way

Maxwell Anderson

Depression

I look in the mirror, and all that I see,
Is someone, or something, they say that is me.
I feel very small, just cold and still,
My mind is a void, empty of will.
I don't care the colour - my dress or my coat,
I feel so light headed, with a tightness of throat.
I'm told the sun's shining,
        and it should make me feel good.
And to 'pull myself together',
If only I could.
People are laughing,
But I have no part,
Just an ache in my shoulders and a heavy heart.
I'll walk to the window,
Then back to my chair.
I'm made to eat food, but I really don't care.
There's very little difference from night or day.
January, February, March or May.
I have this idea, going round in my head.
That life is so pointless -
- I wish I were dead. -

Jean Ashford

Odyssey

The day was hot and sunny, we went down to the beach.
A father threw a frisbee, it landed out of reach.
A coach disgorged some children on a trip round France.
One lay down to have a nap while she had the chance.
A little one made castles with a bucket and a spade.
Some were playing football, others had a wade.
A mum sat gently knocking sand out of a shoe.
Then a chill crept over us and grew and grew and grew.
Looking from this happy scene
I raised my eyes and turned my gaze
To the sea, there was a haze
And a continuous thundering boom
Which echoed and echoed and echoed
Through the growing gloom,
Within the veil, a silhouette,
Ship-shape, perhaps a corvette?
Bearing pilgrims from the past.
An ensign flying at half-mast.
Drops of rain, like teardrops fell, helter skelter
From the beach they run for shelter,
Just before the chime of noon,
1994, the date ... the 6th of June.

Judith M. Appleby

Thorg The Warrior

Today I'm a great warrior,
And fighting to defend the land,
My sword stands by my side,
My life at your command,

And he who dares to take lives,
Of the innocent and the forgotten,
Shall pay the price — oh so high,
And their lives will be trodden.

For I am here for them to face,
For I am here to put their lives in place,
And with my sword, a mighty blow,
There shall be peace wherever you go.

And round the world it shall be known,
No rich, no poor, no hunger alone,
And let the colours of life shine through,
And let this world be happy too.

So now you've heard the warrior speak,
Take heed, my friend, my word I keep,
So here I'll stand and watch over you,
And keep the land so safe — and the children too.

Karen Anthony

Misnomer

What is this thing we call fresh air?
It's really a 'something' we all share.
In and out, polluted by all
It's the ultimate political ball.
It can't be defined, it can't be refined,
Without it all is paralysed.
Thank God it can't be nationalised.

Verna Avill

Why

Why? I ask continually.
Why? But no one answers.
There is no one left to answer —
No one here but me.
They all left as the sun burned up
And the moon became a redhot and boiling,
Steaming ball.
And only I stayed:
One person from amongst them all.

In my time of need you did not forsake me,
You held me and fed me and
Rested my head.
Mother Earth I belong to you,
Owe my last breath to you,
But still I'm asking why.

Polly Atkin

The Changing Age

"It's good for you" they used to say,
To walk instead of ride.
"It's good for you" to graft and slave,
It gives a man some pride.
"It's good for you when day is done
To share your family's chatter,
And not to fume and fret and crave
For things that do not matter."

What have now but noise and speed?
No time to look around us.
With bingo halls to foster greed,
And vandals, muggers, scroungers.
Have we improved? Are we content?
Or do we hanker after
The friendly pavement gossip,
The homeliness and laughter?

Mrs. J. Armitage

Reflections

The water's edge so calm and clear
ripples gently showing only truth,
Nature once bountiful and pure yet so
greatly abused struggles endlessly to survive.
Ignorance shapes our way of life
casting no true reflections only shadows,
The water's edge so calm and clear
ripples gently showing only truth.

Margaret Ashworth

Lost Love

When time stands still,
And you've time to think
You'll wonder why, it all went wrong,
and what you miss, will give great pain,
The answer is near and always with you,
Shed the load, accept the truth,
Then come on home, it's I you love.

As time passes and waters run,
The yearn and longing will return,
You might shout out in rebuke,
No, no, no, go away,
But forever we will remain,
Two parted lovers on the same plain.

Never will you find,
What you are looking for,
In something hollow, that is lost,
For it, itself, lost its way,
In life, ———— so very long ago.

D. Atkinson

My Poppy Day

A poem you want, a poem you'll get
What it's about - I don't know yet
Sitting alone by my non-ringing phone
I've time in plenty to complete my entry.

Growing old and put out to grass
All you can think of is the years gone past.
Specs on your nose, a plug in your ear.
No wonder there's no one around to hear
Of you aches and pains, swollen knees
Varicose veins and talk with a wheeze.

Don't get me wrong, my poem has a quirk
I'm thankful to all that died at Dunkirk
They had no chance, don't you see
To have a large loving family like me.

Sue Arnold

A Ladies Night Out

Two pounds in my pocket a bottle in my bag
It was the highlight of the week, my night at the local rag
We ran like the wind to the bus stop to catch the 9.03
Dashed to the club to get in before ten which meant we got in for free
Around 12 o'clock the place came alive, the fella's arrive you see
They came in all shapes and sizes with egos as big as can be
So many John Travoltas and Romeos all in one place
I didn't know there were so many in the whole of the human race
They came with the usual patter, wonna dance luv or wonna drink,
Me dance with a slobbering drunk, he must be mad I think
I look around at all the blokes not many worth a glance
Then suddenly one will catch my eye that might be worth one dance
In for the kill, I have a drink then give the bloke the eye
I've done I've hooked him, we have the last dance
Then I tell him goodnight and goodbye
We grab our coats and dash outside to join the taxi queue
And discuss what we're wearing next week, what else has a girl got to do
They called it grab a grannies, I didn't care it was fun anyway
But they sure would be grabbing a grannie if I was to go there today

Jean Atherton

Quietly Grazing

Thunder rolled
    across the plain,
A thousand hooves
    or prairie rain.

Ponies prancing
    neighing fright
Motionless beings
    arrows bright.

Suddenly;
    before their eyes
Creatures of
    each shape, and size.

Quietly grazing
    without fear
Until the Bull
    felt sharp the spear.

As the dawn
    came softly round
A hundred carcasses
    lay aground.

Young Indian braves
    with hearts elated,
Manhood prove,
    hunger sated.

Mrs. E.A. Ambler

Still of the Swamp

It's sticky sweet hot
transparent vapours rise and burst
your throat is dried to a knot

the Gator blinks his probing eyes
the curved six inch head
his disguise for the submerged six feet

dappled jades and greys
the Cormorant takes to the frozen haze
suspended for a second

etched to the sea sky blue
like a hook in an eye
intruder to the above void of floating land

the perfect 'm' swipe of the wings
a letter curved so proud when young
look - birds flying in my sky

turtles bask on dazzled hot rocks
Spanish Moss teases the darker shadows
wading around the Cypress Knees

framed to a peaceful lull with floating hyacinths
tranquil beauty inhaled in a fraction of the beating sun
tranced into a false security by the unmoving Gator

until you tread to the depths
now you can see him move.

Joanna Ashwell

The Car Boot Sale

One day when I was walking around the countryside,
I'd just approached a village green when a notice I espied.
CAR BOOT SALE TODAY it said in letters large and black.
"Car Boot Sale?" I asked myself, "Now who'd have thought of that?"

Who can be buying all these boots and what sort can they be,
How many people wear them, that's what puzzled me.
There's fishermen who wear their boots for wading in the water,
And many people wear fur boots as Winter days grown shorter.

There's Army boots that soldiers wear for bashing up the squares,
And airmen's thick warm flying boots for him who really dares.
There's football boots for scoring goals and polished ones for riding,
Farm boots for walking through the mire or Wellies when it's raining.

The vendors were early to open their cars
And set out goods fit for a Queen.
They seemed to sell everything under the sun,
But there wasn't a boot to be seen!

Pauline Anderson

I'm Biased Against Bowl

The shelf in the corner is beginning to sag,
From the weight of his trophies my husband will brag,
Testimony to his love of sport, a love I'd willingly abort.
That shelf and its contents I would gladly abolish
'Cause I'm the one with the spit and the polish.

Golf takes care of two days in the week
For the rest a sport he endeavoured to seek,
Despite my rage and plaintive howls
He casually declared, he'd decided on bowls,
Thumb and finger, bias and end,
This game I cannot comprehend.

Now, we've had the fishing, football and cricket
But now he's batting on a sticky wicket,
My patience it is wearing thin
As I contrive to keep him in,
He roams the greens and the golf courses
While I am left to my own resources.

The weeds in the garden are doing fine
The paint on the windows is in decline,
The lawns are growing decidely fast
Oh! How long will this game last?
I'll be hopeful when the icy wind howls
Goodness! Did someone mention 'indoor' bowls?

Edna Auty

The Estonia Is No More

The mass of heads at the port,
Had no idea, had no thought,
Of the trauma that lay ahead,
Of the grief, of the dread.

The night was harsh, windy and cold,
But the passengers drove into the hold,
The Baltic Sea that night was rough,
But never the less the ship cast off.

Off it went into the ocean,
The Estonia rode it with a graceful motion,
But, alas the journey didn't last long,
Someone had done something vitally wrong.

The cargo doors weren't tightly closed,
The water level in the hold just rose,
Until it seeped up through the floors,
Oh why didn't someone close the doors?

People shouted, people yelled,
People prayed and people held
Their breath as they sank into the sea,
And the sea their graveyard proved to be.

Nine hundred plus did die that night,
To the world this was a fright,
But that was the price for pure carelessness,
That is something we must confess.

Alastair Brian Atkinson

The Orphanage - Romania

Sow and reap!
The News flashes on
M.P.'s parliament, a bomb;
And then the picture zooming in
On children — children silent, ill, thin.
No-one to care or love or play
They sit and wait their lives away,
Or rock and rock, then bang their heads
helpless prisoners in their beds!
Too hurt to weep.
"It is not right" the 'experts' say "To take these children far away"
"National Culture is the need. We will clothe, we will feed"
Sow and reap?
But who will LOVE and comfort them? Who will guide and teach?
Who will agonise and pray as every childhood stage is reached?
Who will show what family means when they explode as violent teens?
Thinking just of 'No. 1'; becoming leaders by the gun. Shoot or be shot!
Fighting in vain, just to attain — normal humanity!
Remember then
We have sown.
We will surely reap.
Sow and reap.

Fiona Arnold

Golden Boy

I look at him.
An angel's face;
The hair alight
With a golden flame;
His eyes a wide
forget-me-not blue,
He looks at me.
I smile.
No answering there.
He looks away
his gaze is not for me.
The mind is where? ...
I wish I knew
how to kindle the spark
that brings release
to the soul in the dark ...
My golden boy.

Lorna Alexander

Yesterday

A friend called yesterday,
A friend we used to meet on sunlit shores
Of golden sand, and blue secluded bays,
And sweet warm days.
We smiled and talked, and as our glances met
Behind the warmth and pleasure of our meeting
A deeper well of happiness was stirred,
Remembering the joys we all had shared —
The children clambering on the sea-wet rocks,
The bright wet towels and assorted socks;
Laughter and frolic in the tumbling waves,
The sheer delight of boats and pools and caves;
A singing kettle on a wobbly stove
Beside the tiny harbour that we love;
Our evening strolls along the quiet quay,
Watching the lighted boats slip out to sea;
The storing up of all we'd seen and heard,
Too dear to lose.
We need no pile of photos, garish views,
No written story or recorded news
Can tell the joy that lies behind our eyes,
Remembering the living, loving days
We spent — as though they were but yesterday.

E. Bailey

Victory

I still hear thee now,
Oh battle cry,
Because of thee I slowly die,
And as I look on blood red soil,
My body crushed from battle's toil,
And as I wait for my life to end,
I hear thy whisper in the wind.

So now I hang from rusted barbs,
The dead lay around me for a hundred yards,
Their flesh torn and bloody,
No spirits remain here,
Only the sounds of death,
And the smell of fear.

With dying eyes,
Limbs crushed and muddy,
Oh gallant youth your lives ended bloody,
No life in your bodies,
Not even to cry,
All you now do is stare up to the sky,
And as I toil with my final breath,
The angels are singing,
As they herald my death.

John Ansty

Our Daily Talk

I spend my life with a gentleman.
He has riches beyond compare.
His Father made the universe,
the sky and earth and air.

We talk about all sorts of things.
He listens and says not a word.
For he answers me in different ways,
like the song of a little bird.

Or the cobweb clinging on for life,
as the heavy dew weighs it down.
The sun brings out the diamonds
Gold, silver, yellow and brown.

The whisper of a gentle breeze
as it comes and goes nowhere.
The fragile little butterfly
that doesn't have a care.

Or the boldness of the sunset
at the end of a beautiful day;
And tomorrow we will go on talking
in the same wonderful way.

Cassarndra Bailey

Nostalgic Fire

As you get older you'll find that it's true
The past seems to take on a rosier hue
Like sitting at home with fire burning bright
And curtains drawn close to keep out the night.

Watching the flames as they leapt in coal fires
It was easy to talk of your hopes and desires.
The family around to encourage or tease
The image conveyed must everyone please.

But if you dig deeper you'll doubtless recall
That few winter evenings were like that at all.
Granted you sat by the fire, but alack
You'd be moaning like hell at the draught on your back.

And then you'll remember days by the score
When for reasons unknown the fire wouldn't draw.
And when the wind blew you'd be cast into gloom
As soot laden smoke billowed into the room.

But even remembering the work and the grime
The joy of a fire doesn't lessen with time.
So for comfort and cheer coal fires I espouse
As long as they're in someone else's house.

Barbara G. Baker

The Country Road

How well I love the road I take,
To visit, my darling daughter.
I know it well, when blossoms break,
That Springtime garb, has brought her.
The bird songs echo from the trees,
Refreshing is the air I breathe.

How well I love the road I take,
To visit my darling daughter.
When summer sun did overtake,
How willingly I sought her.
Noisy tractors made their din,
Harvest then, being gathered in.

How well I love the road I take,
To visit my darling daughter.
I thrilled at Autumn's golden fate.
The changing scene had taught her.
The leaves, now falling all around,
Carpeting my walk, across the ground.

How well I love the road I take,
To visit my darling daughter.
Though winter's grip makes me shake,
And my stride begins to falter.
The welcome lights of North Lodge glow,
Eases my battle, against the snow.

G.F. Allen

Myriad

"Are you afraid?", said the old man, a twinkle in
his dark, cool eyes
Without whisper of sound, the floor dipped
away and walls of delicate thunder opened
up to my innocent eyes

"Don't shout, for you'll wake the Master,
Just follow me ..." and after
a twist of ancient wrist, the sky
curled up and huddled shy in the
palm of his hand

"What do you see?", he asked as his coat became
mountains of shifting breeze.
"Why, me of course," I replied
and suddenly realised
that I was ... part of the illusion

I could scream off the edge
of the world and yet
only find me
sitting there waiting patiently

"Sometimes to keep something
you first have to let it go ..."
The old man smiled and
silence drowned the noise of
my breath as Time itself
grew old and laughed, all ... part of the illusion.

Adam Bailey

Patchwork Quilt

In my coat of many colours I lie, washed and clean - smelling sweet scent
As I rest, soft and resplendent, thoughts pass by
    of kind hands which stitched my silk and satin
    of gentle hands like mist of Matin
    of soft hands which stroke my wrinkles smooth
    over my body to caress and soothe.

In my coat of many colours I lie, stilled and calm - aging but gay
As I rest, alone every day, thoughts pass by
    of kind hands which tend my worn tattered seams
    of gentle hands with warmth of sunbeams
    of soft hands which ease my satin tears
    my body drenched in love throughout the years.

In my coat of many colours I lie, patched and neat - with blended shades
As I rest, and my beauty fades, thoughts pass by
    of kind hands which sometimes mend and patch me
    of gentle hands I feel but cannot see
    of soft hands which nightly fold with care
    and yet of all these things I am aware.

In my coat of many colours I lie, bathed and snug in warm sunlight
As I rest, in quiet respite, thoughts pass by
    of kind hands which made me with silken thread
    of gentle hands making me to spread
    of soft hands creating without guilt
    yet I am but a humble Patchwork Quilt!

Sonya Brahms

Realization

She comes, silently seductive,
sensuous as Salome,
the temptress.

Slithering with soundless ease,
her beauty iridescent
amongst the trees
of forbidden fruit,
she coils,
shimmering in the sunlight,
and with supercilious smile
beguiles the unsuspecting Eve.

She has all time to tantalize.
Her eyes mesmerize Eve's
true and spotless spouse,
who stands transfixed.

Suspended, resplendent,
with hypnotizing stare
she waits her moment.

Then with specious calm
she breaks her silence,
and the insidious hiss
of her soft breath
becomes the kiss of death
to Innocence.

Marguerita Bailey

What is a Christian?

What is a Christian? Let me see.
I'm sure that's someone just like me.
I think of others in a mess
And sympathize with their distress.
And when the paper is unfurled,
I read of troubles in the world—
Famine, illness, deprivation—
It seems in almost every nation.
Then someone passes and rattles a tin;
I dutifully put some pennies in
And walk on by and think, 'That's it,
At least I've tried to do my bit.'
When everything's fine, it's easy to be
An upstanding Christian — just like me!
I go to church and there I pray.
But do we really listen to the words we say?
'Forgive us our trespasses, as we forgive them
That trespass against us'—now that's a gem!
To come home and find out your home's been ransacked,
Ornaments broken that you've lovingly stacked.
TV is missing, video too.
Who could have done it? I haven't a clue.
I only know, for as long as I live,
It's really not easy to say, 'I forgive'.

Wally Bailey

Full Circle

I started life in a farmhouse
Where the amenities were poor;
No hot water or inside loo,
With a latch on the bedroom door.

No holidays then, but enough to eat
And fields in which to play.
Across the fields to the village school
And we always went — every day.

I moved from the country to live in a town
And ended up by the sea;
From there to a town and now I have come
Right back where I used to be.

It's sheltered accommodation now
In the village I used to know.
I've come full circle and settled at last
With memories of long ago.

It's nice to be back where I began
With amenities all laid on.
I've a cord to pull if I'm ever in need,
And I don't sigh for the days that are gone.

Dulcie Bailey

Our Dad

I wonder why Dad, who's full of fun
And so friendly with everyone,
Always gets in such a stew,
When he has a job to do.
Mother asks him to fix a shelf,
But does he do it all by himself?
Oh no' Tommy must stand by at the ready,
I must hold the ladder steady,
Mother's there to help him too,
The screwdriver is held by brother Hugh.
And when the work is all complete,
Dad's well pleased and things it's neat,
He's quite forgotten our help, I'm afraid,
And talks about the shelf he made.

J. Bailey

November Day

I looked out on a cold November day
with mist o'er field and mire,
I turned around, looked at the grate
and thought, I'll light a fire.

I looked out on a cold November day
dark and wet o'er leaf and lea,
I turned around, looked at the pot
and thought, I'll make some tea.

I looked out on a cold November day
the weather it was dire,
I turned around and sipped my tea
and sat before the fire.

Susan M. Bacon

Alone With The Ocean

My awakening call is the seagulls cry
soaring amongst my dawning thoughts,
another morning to peruse my way
along this seaweed straddled shore.

It is a bitter morn today
on this fine Atlantic stretch,
my walk is brutally brisk
no lingering with the wind,
only visions in my mind
of a warming kitchen stove.

An old fisherman, I am,
cornered in a past
of gathered ghosts colliding
in a dense seaward fog,
the cut of mesh, grasp of rope,
haul of nets be done,
only sun emblazoned hands
now shaking with the cold.

I am alone with the ocean
the borrower of my youth,
as white horses dance before
the horizon's perfect line,
rising with the swell
to jig and reel my way.

Tomorrow I will rest with the lapping of the wave
no more to awake to the seagulls morning call,
she will cushion my fall, as I descend
with my final breath of cold salt air.

Mark Baine

Different Inside

She's somehow different, sometimes strange
Doesn't fit in, in the normal range;
Listens to conversations, but doesn't really hear
About everyday things in this everyday sphere.
She's not of this world, she doesn't exist
So why must all around her persist
With trying to make here normal and sane
When it's much more fun on a higher plane.

The flowers have a language all of their own,
She understands every whisper, giggle and moan.
For men are so blind, they miss such a lot
Buy it, sell it, scheme and plot.
Hark, the daisy's got something to say,
And the bluebells whisper come and play.
The rabbits dance til the sun goes down
In each and every busy town.

But no-one sees and no-one will care,
For twilight vision is extremely rare.
Don't they know that the sun can sing
And elves make their home on a nightingales wing?
She plays the squirrels with their dainty cards,
At dawn the badgers play charades
She lives a whole lifetime in every day
In her very own misunderstood way.

Heather Baker

If Love Were ...

If love were an ocean, how deep would it be?
How many ships would sail on that sea?
If love were a flower, would it be a rose?
Fragrant and dewy, until a thorn grows.
If love were a colour, would it be white?
Pure, and faithful, until out of sight.
If love were a movie, would the ending be bad?
All tearful and tragic and terribly sad.
If love were a season, would it be spring?
Full of hope for what the future will bring.
If love is any of these things to you,
Then you will understand what love can put you through,
The moments of pleasure, the moments of doubt,
It makes you happy, it makes you shout,
Love to each one is different, yet the same,
For we each know the joy, and also the pain.

Jayne E. Bailey

Eastbourne

Eastbourne is a beautiful place.
  With sun that shines upon its face.
Walk through the streets
  with style and ease
And you will find there's
  lots of trees.
The shops are bright
  the streets are clean,
Flowers are everywhere to be seen.
  Theatres and shows in certain places
And lots of visitors with sun tanned faces.
  Eating fruits and lovely ices
And probably food with lots of spices.
  Children in the sea, inviting,
And grown ups are a-letter writing.
  When the sun goes down at night
There's plenty to see with great delight.
  This town of ours is not forlorn,
But bears a great name,
  Eastbourne.

E.J. Baker

The Lost One

Once cold and early January morn
my darling baby son was born.
From my body this tiny new life
sent to meet our world of strife.

Then spirits gave a new life inside.
But deep within your nest you cried
so God saw fit to take you away,
and there you remain forever and a day.

Through my window I see the tree
that we planted, in your memory.
Through this living thing you have life,
but oh! my heart, that knife, that knife.

The blessed again a December son
who helped to heal with all his fun.
They grew and grew so fair and strong
and independence would not be long.

Two so precious and so very alive
contrast to the mystery who did not survive.
My mind has visions of unknown face
that went to God without a trace.

I did not know you, a stranger you'll be
as you look down from the clouds, so free.
I love you though, and will always mourn,
for my child who remains unborn.

Kay Baker

Poetic Therapy

Milton, Tennyson and Keats,
Renowned for lettering feats,
Byron, Shelley, Ferguson
Illustrious poets, every one.

But what of us, the common heard,
Oblivious to poetic word.
Condemned to ignorance of rhyme,
All consumed by passing time.

What do we know of lover's love,
Of birds or flowers or skies above.
No time to see, or hear, or feel,
Pursuing wealth with fervent zeal.

But should we pause and close our eyes,
And think of childhood lullabies,
Of a red, red rose or daffodil,
Our panting, heaving breast would still.

Our days are plagued by strain and stress,
Of keeping pace with style and dress.
Our nights are filled with sighs and moans,
Concerned by thoughts of Mr. Jones.

O lucky man, whose leisure time,
Is spent in solitude sublime,
With Wordsworth, Scott or Robert Burns
Ah, only then, sanity returns.

Thomas Balfour

Tempus Fugit

When I was young, a month at school, seemed more like a year.
And every year beyond my teens, time stepped up a gear.
By the time I got to middle age, I started looking for the brake,
But time will wait for no man, whatever steps we take.

Soon I reached retirement age, and time kept speeding on,
I recalled those fleeting years, and wondered where they'd gone.
Though time's flown past, and youth is gone,
Inside my head, those years live on.

The warp of time and weft of life, have woven in my mind,
A tapestry more graphic, than in Bayeux you'll find.
Every stitch a point in time, in colours of every shade,
Reflecting both successes, and mistakes I've made.

The band of gold and silver threads, recurring frequently,
Are memories of happy times, that loved ones shared with me.
The wartime years left patches, of sombre blue and grey,
Though bleached by time and mellowed, they will never fade away.

Ray Baker

Thoughts of a Blind Person

They come from every direction,
But mainly from behind,
I dearly wish they wouldn't,
Especially when you're blind.

They're talking all together,
My patience wearing thin,
They talk to someone else about me
And treat me like I'm dim.

When I'm on the pavement,
I'm lifted from either side,
Please don't take me across the road
I don't want the other side.

And when I board the buses,
I really do despair,
People shove me down the bus
And push me into a chair.

I sometimes try to socialize,
But no-one seems to care,
I can hear a load of voices
And imagine that they stare.

If I could only have one wish,
I know what it would be,
I'd love to get my eyesight back
And be treated normally.

Elaine Barlow

Old Age

I have a birthday coming up
It really should be fun
I'm all of sixty-nine you see
But I feel more like ninety-one

I woke up this morning
To see the sun shining through
But my gout toe was playing up
So I'm feeling rather blue

I got up to make a cuppa
Pleased, the day has begun
But the postman left a stack of bills
And I've an ache in my gum

I sat to read the paper
With a cushion to support
The boil upon my left cheek
It feels worse than I thought

I've got a friend coming to see me
To tidy up the place
Arthritis in my hands and feet
Makes life for me a disgrace

Well it's no use sitting here moaning
I've got a lot to do
With Bingo coming up tonight
I have to clean me shoes

Bev Balkwill

Deceitful Lies

The love we felt between us is shattered on the ground,
A million little pieces represent the joy I'd found.
The hours we passed together sitting, having fun,
Those days of laughter and happiness have now all surely gone.
I know you didn't love her, it was just a little fling.
But where is the comfort in the words, "I'm sorry" or the flowers that you bring?
I can never again kiss you or tell you it's all right,
Your pathetic words don't move me, I won't cry for you in the night.
You can go to her now and not feel guilty, take your clothes and possessions too,
You're a fool and both deserve each other, but can she love you like I do?
Because really I can't forget you, your voice and gentle caress,
The warmth that radiated around you, some of the best times I'll ever get.
But now that it's all over, promise me one thing please.
When you're arguing and screaming at each other don't come back to me.
My heart can't stand to be broken, too many tears have fallen from my eyes.
No don't ever come near me you and your deceitful lies.

Victoria Barber

Haunted House

Open the door to the house
Nothing was stirring not even a louse
There was damp, stale blood on the walls,
And even in spook house, there's ears on the walls.
Tiptoe across to the aid out table, and gave a scream
Yuck! What's this blood and bone cream —
I don't think I'll try it with my banana supreme.

Go the then next room now, it was only my first.
What do I see, Morticia and worse.
Then thinking I'm not scared of spiders
Well something hairy, like a tarantula went down.

I started to scream. Then I got my arm in my pullover
Threw it out and did a runner.
I ran down the stairs and as I did,
I ran through some monsters eating baby hamsters.
They started to run after me
So I threw some garlic in a cup of tea.
I clapped my hands and counted to four
Soon as I knew it I was out of the door.

I was in such an awful state
That when I reach the garden gate
Around I turned and before my eyes,
The ghost house was really a steak 'n kidney pie!

Amy Balkwill

The Infinite Moment

If time allows, how much joy and anguish
Must correlate in equal passion through the senses
Equal? — the pain is a flood tide
Blotting out all pinnacles of hope,
There is no *present* joy, no hope.

If time allows, the retrospective mind
Will grope and still discover the joy the flood tide left;
The flotsam in the still clear pools,
The overshadowed heart has need of these.

If time allows, the memory of all
The joys — that remain obscured until the tortured brain
Finds them, as jewels in a cave,
When the daylight is lessening — will
Lengthen their chain of brilliance.

But oh, if time allows, let once more that
Ecstasy pervade with startling wonder all the earth
Heavens and seas in one great joy.
The one colossal *Now*, I am. I live.

If time allows, just one moment caught
From life, to hover in eternity and to feel
A present and ultimate rapture
A pearl in the core of sweetness
For then is time defeated.

Pam Banks

Regards, I'm Blue

Postcard from a sunny place. Happy words from smiling face.
Wish you were here, glad I'm not there, washed away worry, cast away care.
Pictures of a foreign port - market, lido, new resort.
Hotel's arrowed, so's the bar. Note the distance, not too far.
On the back two funny stamps. Local heroes, twenty franks.
Postmarked island, dot on map. Fishing village now tourist trap.
Should be home before the card. Writing in this heat is hard.
Done the boat trip, seen the sights. Found the Disco, had two fights.
Studied brochure on the flight "cuisine charming, varied, light."
Eat at sign "We've got fresh laid ... eggs, chips like mother made."
Bottled water costs a lot, stick to lager when I'm hot.
Top up suntan on the beach. Wink at girls, each one a peach.
Got no space to write much more, Sorry if my spelling's poor.
Found a new girl, don't tell Dad. He'll tell Barbara, she'll get mad.
Sell my jacket, helmet, bike. Sell the blue suit I don't like.

That bitch is kissing someone new. Signing off, Regards, I'm blue.

D. Bailey

An Ode to the Countryside

Entrepreneurs in business
Are few and far between
Especially when they sacrifice
The issues which are 'green'

The trees are spreading life you see,
And oxygen around, and orchards in the countryside are
Rarely to be found ...

The beauty of their presence enrich our daily life,
Forget about the struggle, the trouble and the strife.

Up will go the building block —
That's hideous and grey,
Really mate, I never dreamt I'd ever see the day,
When timber, bricks, and blocks of breeze ...
Would take the place of all our trees.

It's punishment for you my son,
And it will be a pleasure,
To give you such a thrashing
For axing trees we treasure,

But then you'll make a million, or
Hopefully it's two ...
Oh, forget about the orchard ...
I'll run away with you.

Pauline Barnes

The Rock

Come let us sit upon yon rock.
I have a tale to tell
Of folks who lived amongst the hills,
Folks I knew so well.
See yonder croft way o'er there.
T'is where my granny once did stay.
Long hours she'd sit at spinning Jenny
Aged eyes looking o'er the bay.
There's Tod the ferryman and his dog,
As lonely a sight there'll ever be.
He talks to no-one but himself,
Since that last day he came from sea.
And young Fiona, grown up now,
She's getting wed I hear;
To John Mcdougal, Mary's lad,
When he comes home from sea next year.
But come wee Jamie, lets away,
There's things that must be done.
We'll come again another time,
When all the snow has gone.
Was fine to sit upon yon rock,
And dwell on memories not long gone,
To tell of tales remembered.
Of my hills, my folks, my home.

J.F. Barnard

On First Hearing Beethoven's 'Appassionata Sonata'

When, with the assurance of perfected art
A master's hands his master's soul reveal,
Drawing aside the curtains that conceal
The joy and suffering of a passionate heart,
Then, on the flood of music borne apart,
The tide of our humanity we feel
Sweep us toward the vision now made real
And hopefully towards the truth we start.

But as the last notes die, flows in despair,
And all our new born faith does ebb away.
How in our vain presumption can we dare
To lift our candles in the sun's bright day?
Yet when clouds hide the stars, a glowworm's light
Can cheer a traveller in the darkest night.

F.M. Barnes

Only Yesterday

If I could see your face again
Hear you speak to me,
My heart would be free of pain
And loneliness would flee.

If I could see those dear eyes
Hold you again to my breast,
For you gave me paradise
Now you are there at rest.

Was it only yesterday we said good-bye
Was it only yesterday you left my heart to die

In my dreams you come to me
You quieten all my fears,
Comes the dawn and reality
And my bitter tears

How can one erase a loving face
How can a heart be re-born
Lord give me grace to find a place
Until the hurt has gone

Was it only yesterday we said good-bye
Was it only yesterday you left my heart to die?

Rose W. Barnett

The Passing Of The Elms

Oh trees I knew you fifty years ago,
Our children played beneath your leafy shade.
Unbroken then, a tall majestic row,
But sadly, passing time, great gaps has made.

In windy March atop your swaying heights,
Were twiggy nests with cawing rooks around.
And oft on rough and stormy nights,
Your leaves and twigs lay scattered on the ground.

The rooks have left the park these many years,
Did they have presage of your coming fate?
For menace deadly to your kind, appeared,
And spread across our land at fearsome rate.

A fungus blight, it seems no man can stay,
Which dams the rising sap - trees' very blood.
Starved of its flow, it wilts, then comes the day,
With shrivelled leaves it stands, insentient wood.

In copse and field, in town where traffic roars,
Stand stricken giants, early in decay,
A tiny beetle, carrier of doom spores,
Infects their bark and signs their life away.

A few more years may bring extinction near,
Familiar native, famed in verse and lore,
Oh stately elms of Clifton Park, I fear,
A spring will come when you will bud no more.

W.L. Barringer

To A Very Special Someone

Someone to hold me when times got tough,
Someone to reassure me when enough was enough,
Someone just to be there when I wasn't able to talk,
Someone to guide me on those little crucial walks

Someone to encourage me each step of the way,
Someone who knew just what I was trying to say,
Someone always there to wipe away my tears,
Someone ready to allay those worst fears

Someone to be by my side when I couldn't cope alone,
Someone who never thought it necessary to moan,
Someone whose patience never ever ran out,
Someone who showed me what loving's about

Someone who for one year gave up everything for me,
Someone who taught me to look forward and see,
Someone who proved tears are rain that makes love grow,
Someone who's loved much more than he'll ever know

Someone who nursed me back to good health again
Someone, who through this, ignored all of his own pain,
Someone to whom I feel I simply owe my life,
To that very special someone
From his ever grateful wife.

Susan Barrow

Evolution

The world has phases of a kind,
I can but think what it brings to mind.
The Earth revolves around the Sun,
Its endless job is never done.
The Sun revolves around the Moon,
The time is coming very soon
When light leaves darkness and everything fades
And the Moon becomes new again with varying shades
One day things will change
And light will shine through
When light leaves darkness
A passage anew.

Elaine C. Barter

Sir Winston Churchill

This grand, famous Englishman we are proud to own.
His courage and determination to the world was shown.

A spirit unconquered, undefeated all through
He inspired, and gave strength to fight anew.

We can all read his works, enjoy his art.
Remember his quotations, and know in our heart
He was true British, a fighter all through
With a strength and power to win and stand anew.
Nobody can ever take his place, no one ever will.
There can only be one "Sir Winston Churchill".

Trudy Barratt-Brown

Old Coach Road

Snow covered fields lay all around,
Millions of glistening diamonds
I have just found.

A coloured flower starts to bloom
As birds of the air begin to sing,
These true miracles of Spring.

The comforting warmth of a summer breeze,
Sunshine glaring through the branches of a tree,
Then, early nights of Autumn with its rustic,
Swirling, falling leaves,
And the One who loves us most in life,
Created for us all of these.

Anthony Bates

Homeless

I walk the streets
I beg for food
It's not my scene
It's very rude
There's not a lot
For me to do
I have to wash
In a public loo
I have no house
I have no friends
I have no job
I have no spends
I find a doorway
In which to lie
This is the place
Where I will die.

Andrew Barnes

Back To School

I return,
Through corridors, pristine and white,
Through corridors, lined with mirrors of confusion,
My memory.

I live again, days of carefree relaxation,
The summer wave of growing adolescence,
It passes through me.
Expression denied, none needed here.
Time folds, and I am lost,
Only to be found deep in the water of the past.

And there,
Celebrate unknowing, undying love for life,
Exultant in simplicity.
At last I return.

Paul Barrass

The Journey Of The Tweed

A trickle high up in the hill
Meandering down so quiet and still
Getting wider, see how it grows,
Gently on its way it flows
Under bridges through valleys by trees
You might even see fishermen up to their knees
Hoping to catch something worthwhile.
And on it goes mile after mile
It flows through towns both large and small
Throughout the seasons it will rise and fall
And after is passes each turn and bend
This part of the journey has come to an end
This river so beautiful, peaceful and free
Arrives at Berwick and joins the sea.

Wilma Barrett

Earth

How beautiful is earth, the lights and shadows of her myriad hills,
Her rushing gleaming streams that race below the scurrying clouds on high,
the beauty of her vale and meadow.

A chime of bells to falling waters tuned.
How beautiful the wind, that creates her silence into sound
and blows on all the petalled flowers,
that sit beneath a hiding place, from rain and snow.
How beautiful is earth, that yields her silent sun
that glows with an exhilarating light.
The unchanged wind, with a wail, that rushes freely among the stars.

Earth is old in breezy laughter, and youthful mirth,
Earth is beautiful, by the birds that stir and sing in every bush,
by the valleys warm and green, by the waves that move aloud
by the copses elms between.

How beautiful is earth, her starry sights look down and sing symphonious,
How beautiful is earth.

Phyllis Barton

What's Happening In The World

People say "Hello"
Then they wave good-bye,
Living their life
Before they die.

Sometimes it's a cruel world
But we try to put it right,
Whether it be violence or famine
We still fail to see the light.

Ignorant people
Walk down the street
Past homeless looking for shelter
And food to eat.

People faced with illness
Go on living day by day,
While others take drugs or suicide
And throw their life away.

Unemployment all around
When is it all going to end,
Surely there will be a time
When the healing will start to mend.

Amanda Barry

Red Pool

Come all you brave and fearless men
Come listen now to me:
For you went hunting hares today
At Pett Pools by the sea.

The scent was strong, the blood was up,
The hounds were running free;
The hunt was on and sport was good
At Pett Pools by the sea.

And did you kill a hare today?
And was it fun to see
The hare that died there in the pool
At Pett Pools by the sea?

And did you shout and blow your horn
And strut about with glee
When hounds had torn warm flesh apart
At Pett Pools by the sea?

And were there others sad as I
That by the pool did see
The reddening of the waters edge
At Pett Pools by the sea?

When time shall come for earthly score
To be tallied against thee
There's one more dead in pool of red
At Pett Pools by the sea.

Cliff Barwood

A Cry from the Heart

I want to live, so why should I die?
To say I'll not mind would be a lie;
I see their eyes following me round,
Wond'ring how long 'fore I'm 'neath the ground.

But life to me holds pleasures great
And many more, at a later date
Will come, of that I know
If only I don't have to go.

But no! I'll not die yet
I'll will myself the strength to kneel
And pray to God who'll not forget
To listen to my humble cry.

I know that He'll not let me die,
If in his wondrous works I'll trust.
Tho' if it be that I must go,
'twill be because He wills it so.

Mrs. D.M. Bass

The Railway Station

What a bustle and a clatter
Rushing bodies, hurrying feet.
Farewell kissing, children's chatter,
Tatty workers, town elite.

So it was I stood and watched them
Wondr'ing how it all began.
Everybody moving somewhere,
Hands that waved and feet that ran.

Was it progress? So they tell us.
Grim set faces hurrying on.
Not a minute spare to wonder
Where had most of their lives gone?

Slow the pace and slow the chatter,
Stop to look around and stare.
Just take in the things that matter,
All this pressure leaves life bare!

Jean Barton

A View From A Window

There, seeped in sodden grass it stands
With crippled ashen brown forked hands,
Its feeble fingers wave at me
The naked fruitless apple tree.

And to the right a rose bush leans
On a mossy fence that mars the scene,
A blushing bloom tosses her dew dotted head
And proudly towers over her limp leafy bed.

A little further down there clings
Some bruised and battered sallow leaves,
That flutter like lethargic wings
Yet doomed to die ... their destiny.

And what dominates this stilly scene?
Not the proud red rose or leafy green,
But the begging boughs reaching out to me
From the naked fruitless apple tree.

Maeve Batten

Hard Sad Times

In these sad days of our ever green land
Trees being axed by mankind and his hand,
Crops are burned, people they starve
Empty bellies food by the halve.

A young wee child waits for its rice
While we eat our meal not thinking twice,
The earth is dug to make a hole
For that wee child who was holding his bowl
We must act fast, we must prevent
The slaughter of these innocent.

We must work together, never let go
Even tho' worlds apart let them know
They will not be forgotten, we won't walk by
Why should we let the innocent children die
We'll call out for help from our God above
Please give us the strength, the power and love
To do what we can for those people in need
Give them our help, our all in a good deed.

Mrs. M. Batchelor

Evolution

God first made a man.
That is how human life began.
He then made him a wife.
But not for life.

That is how nature works:
life is a mixture of quirks.
It was not at that time a quest
to fill the treasure chest.

They were content with the simple things —
the joys and the sorrows that marriage brings.
Two people cannot always agree,
otherwise they would not be free.

Adam and Eve had two sons, Cain and Abel,
and all four sat at the primitive table
to eat their dinner.
And one of the sons was a sinner.

One brother
murdered the other.
Cain was his name
and today many are doing the same.

Throughout the ages
history books are full of pages
of murder and greed.
Cain set the seed.

Joseph Bell

Alone

No one ever told him how to run his life.
No one ever told him how to choose a wife.
It never seemed important,
But now the end is near,
The old man by the fire,
Dries a lonely tear.

Friends would come,
If he were young.
But as he's very old,
No one calls. No one cares,
That he could die of cold.
Memories are all he has,
Of the life that he has had.
Thinking back, it wasn't good,
Life was often sad.
But now he doesn't seem to mind.
Death is at the door,
Waiting to take him to the place,
Where sorrow is no more.

"Did you hear?
Old Smith is dead.
They say he died last year."
"If only we had cared for him
When he was living here."

Frank Beattie

Goodbye

You lived your life with courage, love and dignity
To your friends, you were steadfastly true
And those whose lives you touched, but briefly
Were proud to say they knew you.

We'll always remember the times that we shared
The tears, the laughter, nothing were you spared
And, with all your troubles, it was for others you cared
So we thank you, Michelle, for the times that we shared.

Despair and humour went hand in hand
We prayed so hard to understand,
And I speak for many when I say:
A light's gone out in our lives today.

It's always hard to say goodbye
Perhaps, we shouldn't try
You strived for peace and tranquility,
God bless, Michelle, sleep peacefully.

V.F. Beadle

A Lost Soul

A knock comes upon the door,
Who is it they are looking for?
Is it me? I hope not, that's for sure,
To hide away from man and his demands
I seek loneliness, not friends wanting reassurance
Or a chat of this and that.
A new relationship with all the risks involved,
No not for me.
I don't long to see into the future or the past,
Just this moment, with all its glory, to last
From now until forever.
I am not wise or clever, just a simple soul
With no goal, or purpose in my life
To wander aimlessly through the passing years,
Avoiding strife.
No more heartache, I've had enough
To last from now until the end of time.
The peak of ecstasy to me is just a heady wine.
No more, no more emotions exposed for all to see
The hurt that lies deep within the heart of me.

Richard Beard

Identity Crisis

Hey you there, look at me.
I'm having a breakdown,
    can't you see?
Inside this outer shell, there's
    someone going mad.
I'm not just Sally's husband, or
    John and Susan's dad.
I used to be a person, I used to
    be I think.
My identity's like water, and its
    flowing down the sink.
Please, someone put the plug in,
    and save what's left of me,
If you knew me, won't you tell me,
    who did I used to be?

Rhona Bayliss

The Atom

Day is born
In a crimson flame,
Not to adorn
A window shorn
With mushroom shape
It came
The bang, the shame
That made the world lame
People's shadows
All life gone
No sweet life
No sweet song
Men talk of how and where and when
But Hiroshima came and went.
And also Nagasaki too was spent
And Kashuma could have gone the same
Only beauty saved its name
Still men talk and say
Yea or nay.

Leslie William Beadles

Know Yourself

Passing down a darkened street
Who do you think I chanced to meet
It was a man with long, white hair
A balding head of that I'm sure
He had one leg as long as the other
Two black eyes that crossed together.
A nose that drooped to meet his chin
His shoes were patched and wearing thin
He wore a coat that reached the floor
His gloves had holes, his fingers sore.
I stopped to talk to him a while
We had a laugh, a chat, a smile.
I wondered who that old man was
I wondered why and what the cause
That made him look so old and frail
And lean upon the cold, dark rail
That ran along that darkened street
Where we did only by chance meet.
Next time I will look out for him
Although my eyes are getting dim.
Reflections in the lighted shops
Made me start with quite a shock
It was only me left standing there
With balding head and long white hair. Ah!

Mary Bertram

The Gypsy Girl

She danced like the wind, the gypsy girl
Arms outstretched skirts a-whirl.
Jet black hair, dark brown eyes,
She swayed with the wind as it swirled to the skies.
The fire it glowed, the stars shone bright
The dance continued throughout the night.
While fiddlers played, the gypsies sang
A song so sweet, the echoes rang.
Freedom and life her steps outlined
The wonder; the joy and pain.
No bonds or chains her soul entwined
Free as the air, the sun and the rain.
She twisted and turned, did not tire
Till the dawn lit the sky above
Lifted her head, her soul afire,
Mother Nature she worshipped with love.

Lilly Baynard

Autumn Colours And Fruits

Radiant colours red and gold,
Autumnal days slowly unfold,
Pale sun filters through turning leaves,
As they fall and dance in the breeze.

Ripening fruit on trailing briar,
Rich harvest of berries for all who desire,
Hawthorn berry, rose-hip red,
Creatures of field and air will be fed.

Virginia Creeper in her crimson gown,
Covering dull walls in country towns.
Making her last glorious show
Before the strong winds and falling snow.

Nature's great gifts are bountiful and free,
Praise and thank God for all we see.
Many colours, many shades,
Before the start of wintry days.

Irene Beckwith

Hindsight

The train at six thirty gave start to the day
But with daily pressures what cost for delay
To travel home with briefcase and sweat
Perhaps look back with somewhat regret
Take the attitudes of people around
But always keep your feet on the ground
Take a drink help the despair
But then a soft voice from above says, "Take care"
The Moat is dark and always there

And now I walk the garden each morning tea in hand
And reminisce of dropping a promising stand
I have been tempted to return to the brim
But again the voice from above says, "The Moat's
Still there and you can't swim"

Many people look into a mirror
But never see the reflection

Edward Beck

The Tree

Oh woe is me! Oh woe is me
They've cut down that lovely tree
For so many years, there it stood
In a built up street, not in a wood.

My soul cries out oh why, oh why
As majestically it reached the sky
Did you destroy so lovely a thing
Its beauty made my heart sing.

A copper beech so proud, so tall,
It stood, its boughs shading all
A thing of splendour by nature made
To go on living from age to age.

But progress reared its ugly head
Chop it down, remove it, dead,
We need to build more houses there
Did they really thing no one would care?

How Mother Nature cried that day
So let us make a pledge and say
No more trees die, for progress' sake
Give to the environment, don't take, take, take.

Norah M. Bennett

Old Folk's Home

Once I was beautiful dear, like you
Now I have hairs upon my chin,
Liver spots and wrinkled skin.
That scarf you admire hides a neck that sags,
Eyes are dim, beneath them bags.
Thinning hair that's turning white — it's not right!
It's not wrong?
Yes, I know I'm lucky to have lived so long.
But dear, I hate this growing old.
No more the sight of handsome knight,
Only our diminishing fold.
Staring ahead, staring ahead.
What do they see? They've never said.
I've asked them, dear, they just look blank,
Chairs in rows, rank on rank,
Within them all those figures stiff,
Ancient limbs they cannot shift,
Gazing at infinity until the staff come in with tea.
No, of course life's not all misery,
I have a friend who's older than me,
Who takes no note of ageing face,
Nor criticises a slower pace.
In human terms, he's a hundred plus,
The cat Matron bought to live with us!

Sheila Bell

Lost Heritage

I knew a vale which held a stream
where fat brown trout did glide
along the banks
wild flowers grew and small bird's nests did hide

days seemed hot much longer then
the nights a cool respite
the only sound a night bird's call
passing in swift flight

all was still beneath the moon
till dawn's first hazy light
came slowly glinting through the trees
to make the whole vale bright

but now alas this lovely vale
where happy childhood spent
is lost beneath the bricks and glass
        of new development.

M.D. Bennett

Gypsy Lee

I was lost in time and space
Looking for my true identity
Roaming from place to place
It must be the gypsy in me.
I can almost smell the camp fires
Where the people gather around
It is something that my heart desires
A part of me which must be found.

They came from Tipperary
And travelled far and wide
Speaking Shelte and Romany
It's something that fills me with pride.
Wanderers living off the land
Free to go where they please
To me it's a life that is so good
A life that is full of ease.

Jennifer Bell

The Call of Cymru
(The Call of Wales)

Land of poets, land of song,
        I hear your soft whisper, how long? how long?
Ere the prodigal shall return
        to Llewellwyn's land and adjourn,
amidst the hills and valleys fair
        of childhood dreams that knew no care.

I recall long days of hazy sun,
        voices rich with lilting tongue,
where time stood still, earth and I one,
        as lovers when their passion done.
Oh! As surely as this love shall burn
        to the Land of My Fathers a son will return.

Frank Beer

To My Grandson Nicholas

I know a boy who is only ten
But a fine man he will make like his father Ben.
If he works very hard, I am sure
That Nicholas will never be poor.
But harder still he must work at his books
To get to the top needs more than good looks.
Truth, courage and wisdom are just three seeds
You must sew on your heart for your future needs
So Nicholas, take this advice from me
Of one who loves you and hopes to see
What a fine man you'll grow up to be.

In this great big world of today
Things will not always go your way.
But I know when put to the test
You'll always try to do your best
So when in doubt, don't be blue
All good fortune will come to you.
For an honest man has no fear
And joy will come to you, my dear.
So go ahead and prosper
All these things will come to pass
If you stay just Nicholas.

N. Bennett

Heartfall

Heartfall's named after the lovely pools
Which are sometimes hot and sometimes cool
I would enjoy the tunes of the singing leaves
Which blow around in the summer breeze.
Heartfall, heartfall I wish I was there
I wish I was laying in the sweet, sweet air.
Heartfall has a strawberry scent,
But bad smells we try to prevent.
In this world it has a golden sea,
If only I could find the key.

Danny Benn (Age 10)

Lovers' Madness

I sometimes lie awake at night just thinking of you dear,
And long to hold you in mly arms till morning doth appear.
The nights are long without you,
The days are just the same,
When you're away from me dear
My heart is filled with pain.
You may think that I am crazy.
Perhaps I really am.
But even though we're miles apart
My heart's yours to command.
My love for you will never die
As long as I shall live.
'Tis only a lovers' madness
Such as lovers give.

Kathleen Benton

Nightfall

Mist is rising over meadows
Where the languid river dreams;
In the last sad rays of daylight
Leaden water palely gleams.

The pallid setting sun, like moonlight,
Barely pierces through the cloud;
Wisps of vapour, drifting upward,
Close around it like a shroud.

Trees are shadows, growing fainter,
Etched against the fading light.
Mist and darkness swamp the landscape;
Pasture lands sink into night.

Allan W. Berry

Fidelity

Silently the cortege wound
Through the sacred burial-ground,
Past the columns of the dead
Forward, to the earthen bed
Where now the parted friend would lie
Till dusk dropped on eternity.

Reverently the following stood,
Cloaked in holy solitude.

Solemnly, the act, the prayer,
Tears of sorrow and despair,
Lingered some, then all were gone,
All the mourners - All but one,
Whimpering, - it remained.

T.W. Berwick

Even' Song

I sit on a bench wooden and cold
Waiting for the bells to cease ringing
The organ erupts and the sheep of the fold
Stagger to their feet and start singing
Down the aisle shuffling past half empty pews
Chants the vicar and choir in white smocks
So what's that I spy 'neath cassock? not shoes!
But a pair of very holy grey socks!

Lance Beeke

At The Beer Festival

The white marquee welcomes the crowd,
Bodies enter and pay the price for a dream,
With thirsty eyes they search for a champion nectar,
Studying a programme for the sweetest prize,
Amber lava is poured, with not a drop to waste,
It presses boldly against the rim,
Tantalising and teasing; a blatant invitation to be sampled,
They weave, carefully dodging the same rhythmic mass.
Until a retreat of their own they find in which to remain oblivious,
Lost in their own enjoyment with their lover in a glass.

Yani Birt

Silver Wedding

The love that I once felt for him
Has faded and grown rather dim.
The stomach-churning feelings felt
Have long since gone and left.

Instead there is a deeper love
That grows and comes from up above.
I know him well, and he does me,
Something special now have we.

There is a comfort in the love we have,
The things we share, our memories, our life.
But new love is fleeting, it doesn't last
The deep love of years does, it has a past.

Mrs. M. Barber

Penfriend

My pen and I have travelled
through this imagination that is mine
sorting out my many feelings
writing them down line after line.

We have written of my heaven
we have written of my hell
travelled through the heartaches
returned to all being well.

We have hurt in hidden feelings
hidden deep within my pride
over troubled times and torment
I have watched as my pen cried.

Yet we have laughed away the morning
smiled deep into the night
my pen and I have travelled
through the dark into the light.

If at times I may be lonely
I am unlike other men
for I have a special friend
when I have with me my pen.

Dennis Best

Old-Fashioned Christmas 'Pud'

Today's the day we make the 'pud'
Stirring in all sorts really good.
Sticky, sweety, gooey things,
Lucky charms and silver rings,
Eggs tossed in with gay abandon
We rush to stir and wish at random.
Stoning raisins with sticky, wet fingers
How the memory fondly lingers.
Skinning almonds in a hot water bowl
Who cares whether it rains or snows
And when Mother was not looking,
Into our mouths one went a 'poppin'
Crunching sugar from the candied peel
And we knew this stuff was real.
Suet and nuts chopped, Oh! What a racket,
Now we buy it in a packet!
Here comes Mum, in goes the stout,
All us kids give such a shout.
The flaming 'pud', Oh! What a delight,
The cat and dog took off in fright.
Came Christmas Day — the 'pud' was a hit
Funny, Dad always got the three-penny bit.

Mollie Betchley

Heart of 'Mine'

I shed no tears, nor feel the pain
When men and machines tear at my brain.
High speed drills drive through my veins,
The blast that follows sears my face.

Along the face the shearer drives,
Rotating picks gouge out my sides.
No body or soul do I possess
Yet, I have the miners respect.

A fall of stone like thunder roars,
Down the 'gate' past the doors.
No life or limb was lost today,
Yet part of me was taken away.

No clump of boots or idle chatter,
Lights go dim, whatever's the matter?
Silence reigns, I'm left in the dark.
My friends the mice, will not depart!

Soon they'll seal my downward shaft.
Buried alive, a thing of the past.
The pillars of coal will unite and band,
While men and machine let them stand.

Thomas William Best

Aging

I didn't think, I never thought
When I was young and in my prime
That there would ever come a time
To bend my back, or a knee
Would be quite beyond me

I didn't think, I never thought
As I rushed round, here and there
Doing all without a care,
That it would ever be a strain
Or that I would be in pain

I didn't think, I never thought
But then you don't when all is well
You have not time to sit and dwell
On what could be and what could not
Until finally, well ... that's your lot

I didn't think, I never thought
And I don't wish that I had
It would only have made me sad
Life is for living as you see fit
It's yours, enjoy it — but please don't waste it.

Mrs. M. Barker

If Only

Why is the world so bleak and grey,
Drugs and violence, where e'er we look.
No time to stop, no time to stare,
No time to love, no time to care.
A man alone, who walks the streets,
No bed, no roof, just damp and cold,
No hope of a future, he just exists,
To grow lonely and old.

How did he come to be this way,
Has life led him a dance.
I wonder, would he do the same again,
If life gave him a chance.
Such sadness in a human face,
Makes one's heart so sad.
Does he look back in regret,
For the life he might have had?

Evelyn Bishop

Then Only Are You Old

Then only are you old,
When you see no loveliness in life
When you see not
Corn swaying in the courtyards
Of the sun,
Not trees giving to birds
Their endless charities.
But granaries and wealth
From nature newly won
Then only are you old
And ceased from living
When crouched
In the chill, dark room of self
Blind and cold
You count your gains
And not your giving

Norman Bentley

The Climb

As we climbed slowly up the slopes,
We felt the ice forming on the ropes,
This we knew was the testing time,
As this was our highest climb.
We felt the tingling on our ears,
And watery eyes as if like tears,
But on we went, our aim the top,
Scrambling on this frozen rock,
On we went hour after hour,
Climbing up this frozen tower.
Then as night began to fall,
We set up camp and in we crawled.
This would be our worst night,
But we must wait until morning light,
Then as dawn began to break,
We gathered gear and pulled up stakes.
This we knew must be the day,
To reach the summit come what may.
Although the snow still drifted down,
We struggled on and made good ground.
Then all at once within my reach,
I could see we had made the peak.
This must be our finest hour,
'Success' we had beaten the freezing tower.

Kenneth Billingsley

Christmas Glow

Mum shouldn't have built up the fire
For we told her that Santa was nigh.
She pushed on the logs and plenty of coal,
And retired to bed with a sigh.
When Santa got stuck in the chimney,
His coat and his beard, they were black!
With smoke in his eyes, he was shocked and surprised
And he'd burnt a large hole in his sack!
Poor Santa, we heard him a wailing
And so to the rescue we flew.
We all grabbed the ladder, and climbed on the roof
And we pulled poor old Santa back through.
Well, Santa was ever so grateful
As he stood like a sweep on the grass
But mum she played hell, when he rang the doorbell
And showed her the burn on his 'ass'.
We gave him a mince pie and some sherry.
We stitched up his toy sack as well.
Old Santa was happy, he gave us a wink,
And wished us a fond farewell.
It's nearly Christmas Eve again,
We've reminded our mam before bed.
She wrote on a note, stuck it on to the glass
Saying, "Please use the back door instead."

Mrs. S.M. Birkett

Question Mark

She hid behind a question mark
In an effort to forestall
What really was inside her
And keep it from them all.
A comma was her friend at times
As a prevaricating display
Helped to hold back feelings
Holding truth and honesty at bay.
The psychological make up
Made her character water-tight
Until someone appeared to query
Realising seeing was not sight.
The mind became companion
Not needing to explain
Hiding behind, fooling everyone
Who thought she was insane.
But she wasn't really was she?
The question mark held the clue
As she looked across the table
Declaring, "I'm not me, I'm you."

Irene Billington

Dandelion Clock
(In Memory of Clare)

Deep in the meadow green
She grew where the earth smelled warm and sweet.
Her petals, saffron gold, sang joy
And radiance was this youth.
To please the season she shed her dress
And laid bare her simple beauty,
A perfect gossamer globe, a moon to illumine the night.
And when the sun bloomed whole
A Summer breath whispered her name
And wafted her ripe flower
To float as a fan of airy parasols upon the ether.
Her fine slim pedestal,
Still rooted in the earth,
Looked bare between the daisies and willowy grass.
Yet, far above them all,
Her life awoke to a new world
And she flew with the freedom of gods.

Elizabeth Bickerstaffe

Yesterday's Gold

I felt an intruder as I wandered today
Though an old fashioned house on auction day.
So many items all privately kept
For a great many years and then suddenly laid
For the world to see, and a price to be paid.

I walked in peace round that moated farm
Stock yards to keep the cattle from harm
Aisled barn standing against the sky.
With copper and brass and oak galore
The family treasure's upon the barn floor.

A kitchen range with fire aglow
With kneading trough to make the dough.
Oil filled lamps and wooden chairs
A settle tall to keep out draughts
In a family room where children laughed.

Embroidered samplers no longer made
Old fashioned clothes so neatly laid
In drawers and wardrobes came to light.
To give a view into the past
Where bygone items were made to last.

As one by one each lot was sold
The auctioneer a story told
Reminding us and friends alike
To remember all these things we see
For this is how it used to be.

Mary Bisset

Death Of A Mill

The mill finally died last night
There was no last minute reprieve
Nor any dignity in death
Its red brick body, battered and bludgeoned into submission

I saw a hundred windowed eyes plucked out
Its noble head
That towering chimney stack laid low
And tumble in the dust

The sacred engine
That once proud beating heart
That measured, pulsating, driving force
Broken, ripped out, stilled forever

King cotton is dying
Its knights of the cloth are falling one by one
No more carding, nor more spinning, no more weaving here
Redundancy, that economic curse, has woven its deadly spell

The cloth capped streets are deserted now
Yet sometimes in the early morn, when we are still abed
I hear the sound of clog clad feet
Still echoing on the grey and cobbled millside street

Again, as through the mists of time,
I see the old faces, the muffled figures
some long since dead
Drift by in ghostly groups

George A. Mackay Bird

The Choice is Ours

In a world full of anger, torment and rage
We all have our small parts, actors on a stage
Some play it badly, others quite well,
They compare with the difference 'tween heaven and hell.

Each one has their moment to be good or bad!
And all have a chance at being happy or sad.
Envious some are, jealous a lot
Emotions run cold or extremely hot.

But one thing's for sure as the days they go by
Each moment in time somebody will die
We cant' all be lucky and live a long life,
In this world full of anger, torment and strife.

So we must count our blessings for each precious day
As towards our destiny we toil upon our hard way.
Grasp hold of the good and cast off the bad
Be always joyful, not down-hearted and sad.

Look to the future, remember fondly the past
And if you're lucky, life a long time will last.

John S. Black

Intolerance

Forcing the engine to speak
you unearth a cry of rebellion
unheard of since primitive times.

You wait until darkness when meat
is on the table and saliva fills the mouth
like gravy for a tender tongue.

The screaming is pitted with lulls of peace
made uneasy by the tap-tap-tap
of your tools, an anthem for a lost nation.

The beast's roar comes through a ribcage
purged of air, under a trembling breast
glistening with spit from the circling night.

What sounds like death throes breaks free
into the clearing with a clash of metal
and a spilling of light from its leathery heart.

You retreat inside where the tortured strains
will paint the cave walls of your sleep
in colours drained from healthy cheeks.

Iain Black

Mother

We always say we understand
When the Mother we love speaks of pain
But then we think 'Oh why go on. Must I hear it all again'.
Understand we never will
Too anxious are we our dreams to fulfil
In short it is just thoughtlessness
But she knows or she will guess
We haven't the time to tolerate
Our elders when they're not feeling great
and how often is that, as age creeps on
Their pain becomes permanent and they're not so strong
Yet still we are deaf when they complain
And rush off to live our lives again ...

There she sits in her sadness and pain all alone
She prays for her children but they rarely phone
They know she's unhappy, but they don't show they care
And rarely consider her plight and despair
Is it simply that they do not understand?
Are they really too busy with things they have planned?
I'm beginning to think, if the truth was told,
They themselves are frightened of growing old
And visiting Mother can make one see
That one day, maybe, that could be me
Sitting in sadness and pain all alone
By then we will know, but it's too late to phone
Or visit the Mother we all loved and shared
But we didn't take time to show her we cared.

Dee Blything

The Hurricane

The Hurricane arrived one Autumn night,
left many places in an awful plight,
destroying many things that stood in its path,
left death and destruction in its aftermath.

Trees torn by their roots out of the ground,
roofs sent crashing with an horrendous sound,
lorry overturns, skids along on its side,
river banks crumbled from the force of the tide.

Fences crash down, bins hurtle across the lawn,
the storm roared on, flattening the corn,
boats ripped from their anchors and blown out to sea,
bus is crushed under a fallen tree.

Rotary lines spinning crazily around,
toys blown away, never to be found,
gates try to resist, to no avail,
soon blown away by the strength of the gale.

Power lines fall with a flash and a spark,
leaving towns and villages in the dark,
glass is shattered as windows are blown in,
chimneys crash down to an almighty din.

Schools were closed, workers were late,
everywhere around was in such a state,
the wind subsided during the morning,
Hurricane left as it arrived, with no warning.

J. Bocking

Shell Shock

I didn't know what it was, rasping,
A movement, unrelated to the surround.
Curious and apprehensive I approached
The bag by the sink, still again.

Carelessly handled, some inverted,
Backs clashing, pincers twitching,
The crabs lay, dry and downcast -
Lives sold at three for a pound.

Swinging all the way, like in
The child's plastic pail, saline,
Colliding in the turbulence now,
Cracked and finished forever.

Sharon Bishop

The Lifeboatmen

In the quiet of the night there's a sound of running feet
As our gallant lifeboatmen are rushing down the street.
They've no fear for themselves or the danger ahead,
Spare a thought for these men, while we're safe in bed.
They and their families are disturbed from sleep
For there is someone in peril on the deep.
The waves may be high and stormy winds blow,
Nothing daunts them when the skipper says, 'Go!'
Their skill is renowned, and bravery too
Whatever the trials, they'll see the job through.
Thank you, God, for the men so brave
Who risk their lives for those they save.

Mrs. J. Boast

My Mum

Mum you are everything
A son could ever need
You are my friend you are my Mum
You are the best indeed

Mum you have been everything
You need to know how much
You need to know how much I care
I love you very much

You taught me to see right from wrong
You taught me to see right
You taught me to see everything
You brought me up just right

Thanks Mum

S. Bick

The Awakening

Calm is the day; a softness in the air
Overwhelms the spirit. Can Spring be here?
Rain and sleet that made the rivers rise seem far away,
Nullified and forgotten on this, this glorious day.
Wait, don't pass, just bend to see
A primrose bud, the first of many who, in all their glory,
Lie like stars upon the bank. The tired Winter,
Once severe, now
Longingly sleeps. Yes! Spring is here.

Mrs. K.L. Booker

George

I can still see George,
unobtrusive back of homeknit jersey
steadily weeding our smalltown garden borders,
mowing the twice-a-week lawns
or pruning the roses.
Plots that did not employ him
shabby as poor relations.
Now the general beginning to look uncared for.

Annuals he planted last spring
were finished by autumn;
nobody tidied the borders and grass grew longer.
But in today's March wind
freshly open daffs blow golden trumpets
for George on the other side.

Joan Bidwell

Old Age

What is it like being old,
Will we be lonesome — will we be cold.
Will we be happy and full of joy,
Because we are the grandparents of a baby boy.

Will we have enough money,
Just to buy a jar of honey.
Will we have a pension,
To buy everything we mention.

We should treat old people today,
As we shall want to be treated someday.
We shouldn't lock them away in a home,
We should just leave them alone,
And give them the freedom they rightfully own.

Claire Bloor (Age 13)

Oh To See Ourselves

There she goes down the street
With sensible shoes on her feet,
Her grey hair blown wispy by the wind,
If I were she, I'd get it trimmed.

Thick stockings to defy the cold,
A plastic mac that's getting old.
To her chest her bag she hugs
In case that man comes and mugs.

She turns to see the bus is coming
Now she's breathless from her running,
The brolly's stuck and won't collapse,
Her fingers in its ribs she traps:
Fumbling for the fare she drops the lot
Her cheeks by now are burning hot.

I vow as I stare through the pane
At the middle-aged woman in the rain,
That I shall never look like that
I'll wear high heels and a posh fur hat.
Now as she boards a number three
I suddenly realise that she is me.

H.M. Bishop

Now Is The Time

Your wounds have healed through time and rest,
Your knights are rested, too.
It's time to wake and lead the quest
Much work there is to do.

It's time to leave you crystal cave
And face the world again.
Good men need you to help them save
Their land from evil men.

Come Arthur now, and help us rid
Our country of the curse
Of politicians who would bid
To Quislings be, or worse.

Our country they would give away
To foreign lands and powers.
Traitors they are they should pay
By death, or chained in towers.

King Arthur, come and cleanse your land
Of traitors, rogues and knaves.
With you to lead this honest band
Again we'd rule the waves.

Raymond Black

Man Is Born Free But Everywhere He Is In Chains

Every second a baby is born into the world,
His tiny fingers and toes uncurl,
He takes a breath and starts to scream.
The harmless creature is helpless.
He's shoved in a cot with bars all around.
The baby can't get out, the world out of bounds.
He grows up trapped in buildings
Schools, houses, rooms with doors.
His life is already written for him.
"Go to school"
"You need your education"
The next step is university,
Then a house, a wife, children and a mortgage!
Work at nine everyday.
The man would love to break free but he can't,
He's still in his cot. He can only scream,
But no one can save him.
He goes quietly to his grave.
He is a name on a stone free to do what he wants;
Or is his mind never free from the life he's led
The lies he's told
Under the ground he tosses and turns
Screaming behind the bars of his cot
He can never get out.

Sarah Blake

Westminster

Hell is a ship to replace a white cross;
Uniform rows, in haste filled by their dross
That are lost and alone so they call for some more
That will take all our homes and will keep us all poor.

Hell is unsavoury, bearded and foul;
That will sell off our past to earn one swift buck now,
And a frown on the faceless men; Quangos galore,
Factoids sell us short; they will keep us all poor.

Hell is a black house with gold on its shield;
Selfishly grabbing all money we yield,
And a field sliced in two for a road so that more
Arrive taking our jobs and still keeping us poor.

Hell is not distant, we live it today;
In the land of the free for their fee we must pay,
Disproportionate bills; stealing from us by law,
Taxes abused just to keep us all poor.

QUATRAIN KERNOW

For a rigid regime, crushing all for its profit,
Pleas fall on deaf ears and requests will not stop it,
Polluting our towns, moorland, rivers and sea;
May Westminster be dealt with as it dealt with me.

Matthew Blewett

The Sea

The sea is a hungry hunter
A lone wolf snatching its prey
The sea is a steely, shimmering sword blade
Menacing, ruthless, fiercesome, grey.

The sea is a friend of the children
Rippling, twinkling, tickling their toes
Intriguing, exciting, cold yet inviting
With hidden secrets that nobody knows.

The sea is the land of the swarthy swashbuckler
Of pirates bold, adventurous bands,
Plundering, thundering, delighting in fighting
In search of new territories, unexplored lands.

The sea is a lover's tender touch
A gentle caress upon the sand
Young, silk-smooth skin, old wrinkled fold,
The strokings of an ageless, rhythmic hand.

Anonymous

On The Swings

So lazily we sour towards the sun
And dropping down again above the grass
We cannot hear the sighs of anyone
Nor count our precious hours that slowly pass.

There is no past, no present, and the day
Is frozen still as youthful spirits rise,
Blind as the world upends, and our dismay
Is only real when opening our eyes.

We see about the swings the silent trees
Listening to other children's shouts than ours,
And coming softly on the evening breeze
The menace of the dark and savage powers.

That make us shiver with unknowing dread
For we have glimpsed beyond the joyful swings
And seen our happy days, now lost and dead,
And seen the sadness that our growing brings.

Robert Blake

The Storm

Darkness veiled the valley of the river Teign
As we settled down in our holiday caravan again
At the end of a beautiful day in May
To rest, to sleep, to awake to enjoy a new day.

When suddenly, silently the room was alight
We had no idea what was before us that night
In the distance the grumbling, rumbling, rolling noise of thunder
As we lay in our bed full of intrepid wonder.

With a bump and a bang the black cloud burst overhead
For a moment I thought that we'd both been shot dead
As the raging rain hit the roof, it came down in a rush
Laying all tense, thinking I won't make a fuss.

Again the night sky lit up with a fiery fierce flash
Long licking fingers of lightening, another crash
Angry the air, orangey-red streaks in the sky
Slinking, snarling. Will it never pass by!

Like arms the branches of a tree overhead flapped in a rage
Inside the caravan we felt like we were trapped in a cage
Hour after hour the rumbling, racing storm continued to rattle
Clapping, cracking, crashing like an angry battle.

Horrendous hurricane, she caused such havoc and stress
Roofs ripped off, thatches on fire. Oh! What a mess
Near dawn the storm moved calmly and quietly away
And we got up to enjoy the rest of our Devon holiday.

Barbara Ann Board

If ... If ... If

If everyone were equal,
And each and everyone
Had equal share, fair and square,
Would our troubles all be gone
If we never knew the feelings
Of sorrow strife and pain,
How could we find peace of mind
And learn to smile again

If we never lost, how could we win
And can someone tell me why
After tears still comes the laughter
After rain a sun-filled sky.
If all the hopes and dreams we had
Came true beyond compare,
How would we replace them
With no hopes or dreams to share.

"If" may be a little word
But can mean a lot,
If we all learn to be thankful
For all that we have got.
So if we use this little word
With care and thought so wise
The "If's" that once were obstacles
Can be a blessing in disguise.

Mrs. R. Blower

Danny

My darling, darling son,
Where are you little one?
I'm standing in your bedroom and know that you have gone.
The wish I've made today would be my only one,
To see your lovely face, and kiss again my darling, darling son.
I love you little one.

I miss your sunshine smile, upon your happy face,
We faced some storms together, and talked of brighter days,
And throughout your lifelong illness,
Just with your winning ways,
You gave me strength and courage, to face the bitter days.

'Everyday is different', that's what I tell myself,
But then there's your empty bedroom, and games still on the shelf,
I'd love to see you one more time, and tell you 'help yourself',
To see you smiling, laughing, means more to me than wealth.
My darling, darling Danny, if only you'd had good health.

Susan Bowes

To My Wife
(After 21 Years Of Marriage)

One day two openers went in to bat,
Of course, there is nothing unusual in that;
But these two batted for twenty-one years,
And shared together their hopes and their fears,
Determined they are to add to their score,
And remain at the crease for many years more.

What do I see before me today?
Thousands of pieces adorning a tray,
Slowly but surely they take on new life
Deftly arranged by my patient wife;
Although some pieces fall on the floor,
Soon she will finish another jigsaw.

Books with her form a kind of addiction,
With Cookson and Heyer and other such fiction,
Tom Sawyer is followed by Huckleberry Finn,
In 'Wind In The Willows', Badger would win,
If you feel about nothing we make 'Much Ado'
There's Tigger and Piglet and Winnie The Pooh.

When partners have been at the wicket so long,
From each to the other reaction is strong,
No need for appeals or shouts of 'Howzat'
But after each over just stop for a chat,
Then pat down the pitch, and take up the guard,
Let everyone see what's on the score card.

Donald Bolton

Farewell to Scilly

As I sail from these Isles and all that I love,
I ask the good Lord in Heaven above
How could they do this dire thing to me?
And send me away across the sea.

No more will I see the daffodils bloom,
Or the sea in a storm with its great waves and spume,
The small country lanes with elm trees so tall
And even the fortress, they call Harry's Wall.

The hot summer sunshine, the cool gentle rain.
The sunset o'er Samson, will I see them again?
The churchyard near Old Town where my dear husband lies
The thoughts bring again the tears to my eyes.

The future is bleak, I'm alone and afraid
How can they live with decisions they made?
The cruel heartless system that made me depart
Can't someone, somewhere, hear the cry from my heart?

No shout of farewell drifts across the blue bay,
No welcome voice calls .. 'We want you to stay'
Only the seagulls cry out their good-bye
As free as the wind, they soar in the sky.

In the years yet to come, I'll think of the Isles
Where my life was a haven of laughter and smiles,
In my misery now, I'll work for and strive
To return to my love ... for that ... I'll survive.

Mrs. C.H. Boone

Good and Bad

I close my eyes, what do I find
I have shut out everything unkind
I tried to search inside my heart
And take the pieces all apart.

There is some good beside the bad
I keep the good and I feel glad
My eyes I open once again
The things that's good they still remain.

The bad things I put them to test
And then I try to do my best
And then when I have understood
Without the bad there is no good.

Mrs. M.A. Bonnar

My Dentist

My dentist is a man so rare,
I feel at ease sitting in his chair,
He puts the needle in my gum,
And asks me to wait until it's numb,
Then he asks me to open wide,
And then he proceeds to go inside,
He pulls my teeth with great ease,
Puts in a swab and tells me to squeeze,
He's got my false teeth ready now,
He fixes them in and I say "Wow",
Home I go as pleased as punch,
Pity I cannot eat my lunch,
But I can a week later.

Margaret Blomfield

Daydreamer

I have full flight of fantasy
in hours of nightlong day
I dream unreal in total hold
with past regrets that fast unfold

Must I move to clear reality
Guard the minds frail stability
Time spent is to labour lost
Computer man will count the cost

Yet a thing so precious has no price
even urgent needs will not suffice
to change this silent way sublime
The mind works best when out of line

Hubert Bond

Waves in My Heart

If only to live by the sea
I would write such poetry
Captivated and drawn am I
by the sea breeze I sigh.

Oh, to be near when calmed or feared
The ecstasy I feel within the vast depth
Could take no place but here in my soul
To arise in waves when my heart is cold.

As this world continues to spin
And I am feeling so closed in
I dream of the sea so free and wild
Until this fierce anxiety in me
Subsides to the calm compassionate form
Surly synchronism would rhyme
With the strange events of time.

Offer me wealth with its priceless gifts
But the sea for me is the treasure I hold
With its peaceful chanting, I am sleeping
With its forceful anger, I am weeping
May it surge forever powerful and bold
Never cease to flow.
When our land has grown old.

Carole Anne Boone

Sweet Life, Sweet Death

Good-bye my sweet love, good-bye
these are my last words of life
for the time is drawing closer for me to die
Oh it was so nice, so sweet
for you were my life, and now death I must greet

This lonely, lonely desolate path
has led me through a sweet life
and now will lead me to a sweet death
where the cold darkness
is a warm welcoming embrace

You gave me laughter, gave me tears
gave me strength and gave me fears
though not of this release
of a sweet life and a sweet death
and this final release
when my love, you, will take away my breath

Good-bye my sweet love, good-bye
this will be my final chapter
as time now, draws me nearer to die
and into that realm of the hereafter
oh sweet life, oh sweet death
make it easy, for now is my final breath.

John Bosco

To God

In the iron studs of an old door
And in the keys of a computer
You are there.
In the intangibility of the blue sky,
And in the dominance of a skyscraper
You are there.
In the completed beauty of unsullied nature
And in the squalor of man's clutter
You are there.
So why is inside me so far away?

Susan Bromilow Smith

The Wonder of Winter

The days grow short,
And the nights draw in,
As the Winter air,
Begins to thin,
All the Summer flowers have gone,
And all the trees are bare,
Yet when I look around me,
I feel a Magic in the air.
It's waiting for Jack Frost to come,
And transform the garden into a silvery scene,
To put icicles on the trees,
Where the Summer leaves have been.
Or am I waiting for the snowflakes,
To come floating down,
To make a snow white carpet,
And so transform the Town?

Enid Bourbonneux

Mary Raboni

The little time between the dusk and daylight;
The black outline of a woman,
Walks bowed to the bouldered tomb,
And as she stands in bowed and deepest sorrow,
I see Mary's rainbow mantle 'gainst the daybreak.
A man in white robes appears before her,
And as the dusk turns slowly into dawning,
He says in gentlest tones the name of Mary
And she looks up and loving weeps Raboni.

G. A. Burgess

Partners

Someone was expected
The door was open wide,
Who could it be? The one I loved
Was no longer by my side.

Outside, the sun was shining
The garden full of flowers,
The lawns had been cut
We'd enjoyed the garden for hours.

Inside, two arms were empty
The house felt cold and bare,
No pipe, no slippers
Just your empty chair.

My heart was broken in two
When God came and got you.
I thought about you today,
Just to see you, nightly I pray.

Please keep him safe above
And tell him I miss his love.
I will leave my door open wide
He'll need no key to come inside.

Carol Bowen

Kinswomen

Sisters, aunties, cousins and mothers,
Nieces, daughters and grandmothers.

These are the womenfolk of our family,
Most of the time we get on famously,
And it has always been that way,
Right up and to the present day.

Clothes were once always passed down,
Those party frocks all did the round,
Moth ball smelling coats and trousers,
Became peg rugs in their houses.

As guarded secrets recipes were kept,
And if you couldn't make them, you wept.
That awful, awful rich fruit cake,
Today it's a Marks and Spencers bake.

Aunties rowed over grannies bits,
Cousins driven to their end wits
Sisters that are as thick as thieves.
Mothers and daughters that like to please.

We are frilly and feminine when we want our way,
At the same time strong enough to save the day.
It's the womenfolk keep a family together,
And we'll do just that forever and ever.

Joan D. Bond

Hedgehog

The hedgehog thinks he's free from harm
When rolled up in a ball.
But when the traffic starts to move
He isn't safe at all.
I wish he'd learn to run away
Instead of standing still.
And not become a target
For speeding cars to kill.
We see him here, we see him there,
We see him round, we see him square.
Poor little hedgehog, pancake flat
Poor little hedgehog, fancy that.

S.H.J. Boulton

Giving

If you think that no one loves you
And that life's not worth a toss
If you are sick of taking orders
And often wish you were 'the boss'
Then you've got to change your life-style
And take a look at how you are living
If you've always been a 'taker'
Then you really must start *giving*
If you give the hand of friendship
Then you'll never walk alone
And give all you meet a cheerful smile
(It's better than a frown!)

Mrs. R. Butler

Positive Mental Attitude

Be positive, say yes
Be certain, look bright.
Assertive and right - be positive.
Never say no - I can't.
But ye must - I will - I can.
Be positive, I'm right.
A good thought, a right thought.
I can, I will, I shall, I am.
Assertive, positive, correct and right
I shall overcome and will.

Brendan Boylan

Untie The Knots

I don't have to invite you into my mind
You are already there.
I just let my barriers down and
You creep inside.
The complex patterns of my thoughts
Are a tangled web,
Some are knotted, some are stuck together
Yet you unravel them.
You untie the knots and break free the strands
So they lie side by side
In some kind of order.
I do not feel you creep away.

Mary Brennan

Ode To The Brontes

Oh rugged hills, oh heather gay
How may feet have passed your way,
Since Charlotte, Emily and Anne
Made history from their life's short span.
Could they but know that through the years
Their prose, though often wet with tears,
Would travel down the sands of time,
To inspire men from many climes.
Could they but stand and gaze in awe
As men step out from every shore
To view their home, to tread the moors
Which thrilled them through their literature
Could they but see the pen and quill,
Their loves still living on the hill,
Would they not count it little cost
That men find joy where tears were lost.

Gladys Bradley

Washday 1945

Fires made — now kettle's on
A cup of tea will follow
The bucket's heavy filled with water
Oh dear! Out goes the kitchen boiler
Water hot-into the tubs
Posser — Dolly and lots of rubs
The scrubbing board works very well
Now the mangle — who can tell?
What time the whites will ring the bell
Pegging out — fresh air at last
And now the floor needs look its best
By now it's five and time to tea
Washday once a week 'enough for me'.

Enid Bowden

My Bike

I hae a bike,
All bony polished too,
An if ye gee it ony damege
I'll be shoore tae damege you.

So a wik an a half later, aye
Georgie comes up tae me,
Sye that's a bony bike yev got,
Wid ye mind gee in it tae me?

I'll buy it for a quid,
And al hae wee it much, much fun,
I'll come aroon tae visit ye
Fan a me choors are done.

But this bike's for a lassie —
It's a shinie pink ye see
So dinna bother gee in me a quid cause
Yer nae gettin ony bike frae me.

So jist awa' an leave me
Ask for a bike fae yer ma,
But a will tak the quid
Tae buy me sweeties, ta!

Lee Anne Booth (Age 12)

Rubber Ducky

Oh, Rubber Ducky, the secrets you must have,
as you sit there at the end of the bath,
and though you have been there for quite a while,
you say nothing, but on your face is a smile.

You know who it was, you seen their face,
as they squeezed on the sink all the toothpaste,
you see all, but they don't notice you,
as they stick all their junk down the loo!
And who was the culprit, who left in a rush,
or did they just not bother to flush!

Yes duck, you've seen it all, the shy and the vain,
and you have suffered all the smell and the strain!
You watch them all as they dally and dither,
or as they squeeze their plooks on the mirror!

And all in the bath you see from your place on the taps,
it's a wonder that you don't start to laugh!
Why not tell us your secrets of the things you have seen,
the dirty, the filthy, the funny and the clean?

Now tell it all duck, why don't you confide?
Perhaps you too have something to hide!

Eddie Boyd

Peace

How fortunate they are, the Astronauts,
Who view the Earth from far away in Space,
Who see, in true perspective from above,
The unique beauty of her lovely face.

How came she into being is not sure,
We guess and theorize, but do not know —
Did God, or Chance create this little sphere
On which alone all natural Life may grow?

If we would save it, and indeed Mankind,
We must have Peace that now can be enjoyed,
(There will be Peace, a dreadful barren Peace —
The aftermath — if it should be destroyed!)

If only we could ALL go into Space
And see our Planet steady on her course
We might be shamed, and vow to alter ours,
Ere we succumb to sorrow and remorse!

The common soul yearns earnestly for Peace —
Oh, 'Powers that be' heed now the still small voice
Of that Goodwill which pleads for Humankind —
Make PEACE not Arms, while still you have the choice!

Nancy Bowyer-Smith

Summer 16

Where are my khaki clad warriors
Why can I not hear them sing
Which way did they go, did you see them
Could I wait til the last ones come in

How did it all go so badly
We really believed at the time
I told young Chapman and Dormer
Take courage, take heart, you'll be fine

I must write to their wives and mothers
No summer should know of such things
Kind words so trite, yet so hurtful
"Missed by his company" and things

We'll build a fine tribute to all
With bands and clergy for praise
The young shall learn it was folly
The old will mellow with age.

Where are my khaki clad warriors
Why do they not heed my call
Which way did they go, did you see them
Could I wait for them here by the wall

Ray Bradshaw

The Wedding

We've a wedding in spring, isn't it great,
May 20th that's the date.
There's heaps to be done before the big day,
I'm sure my hair is turning grey.
The bride's father, he's grousing about his top hat,
We're fed up with hearing "I'm not wearing that".
The guests have been counted, there's far too many,
Whoops we've forgotten great Aunt Jenny.
Dear cousin Marg has promised to bake,
A traditional three tier wedding cake.
The church is booked, the hotel too,
Things must be perfect for that special "I do".
Invites printed, hymns chosen with care,
Bridesmaid's aged three, one dark and one fair.
The bride's beautiful dress, it fits like a glove,
We pray the sun shines on this day filled with love.
As she walks down the aisle, I'll stand there with pride,
Yes, you've guessed, I'm mum of the bride.

Diane M. Bradshaw

Strangers

The old man's hair was sparse and grey,
Face wrinkled, worn with care;
The young boy's head had curls as fair
As his face.

The old one, the young one, glanced once to unite,
Upon the perfect moment within sight,
The old man's thoughts flew far away,
Back to his childhood days;

"We played together, you and I
In the loft, amid the hay".

I remember the last time
Our slings did sail
Over the dairy, to hit the milking pail;
To sit down for days was poor aspect,
Showing not ourselves till the sun was set;

Only once was the look that passed,
Tow strangers no more, are we, this day.

V.M. Brackstone

It Comes To Us All

Languishing upon his bed
The wise old man looked up and said
My life is coming to an end
But Oh, my dear, I don't intend
To end my life full of despair
Because I know there is something there on the other side.
To be born or die is just the same
In doing both there may be pain
One is joy the other sorrow
Neither caring for the morrow,
The coming in and going out
Are intermingled there's no doubt
When we are born into this place
We know nothing of the human race
Or what we are sent here to achieve
Upon this earth before we leave.
When we pass on we are no wiser
But cling to life we human misers
Loath to breath our last on earth
And leave this land that gave us birth,
But have no fear it comes to all
Whether we be rich or poor
And through that doorway we must pass
Like Alice through the looking glass.

Rosemary Bray

The Lift

I was standing on the ground floor
A sad and lonely wife
When this friend of mine got close to me
And soon became my life.
He took me on this lift to love
I knew I never should
But the lift kept going higher
Than I ever thought it would.
It went soaring up into the clouds
Right to the very top
I didn't know that very soon
That lift was going to drop.
It fell right to the basement
My body, it was shattered
I couldn't see, it was so dark
Not that it really mattered.
But I've pieced myself together
I must get to the ground floor
I'll struggle up the dismal stairs
And open up the door.
I've very nearly made it
Though there's still a little pain
But I know that I will never, ever
Ride that lift again.

M. Bramley

Parental Guidance

"If I beat you hard enough
You'll be like me, smart and tough
That's my way of loving you."
A love I wished I never knew.

Taught that pain was quite the norm
Whenever Father's moods would storm
Unaware his ways were wrong
Until our own kids came along.

I recognised their hopes and fears,
Their questioning eyes, the sudden tears.
My own, of course, and curse the cost
As I recall my childhood lost.

Emotions scarred by discipline keen
Without their guidance, what might I have been?
How proud they'd be, if only they knew
Their handiwork wrecked manhood too.

Roger Bourne

The Gentle Giant

Shimmering in the sunlight
The ocean's waters sparkle
Blue, green and rippling silver
The summer's spray

Therapeutic waves calm and soothe
As do the sounds of the sea
Back and forth, in and out, it's never ending
The gentle giant

The air is fresh
The smell, salty
Seagulls are crying above
Awaiting the catch of the day

Shimmering in the sunlight
The ocean's waters sparkle
But now the summers' gone
And all that's left is the memory

Linda Lee Booth

Twilight

Wing of night on the river
Hovers with darkness of thought
Dark and light on the water
And the lengthening shadow of trees
Dark hints into dark essence blending.

Reflecting shadows, dark and light
Blurring, merging indistinct
In rare fluid moment of becoming
Certain and uncertain fuse.
Accidents and essence equal in oneness
Combine in strange revelation.

Dark and light and flowing
Into oneness.
In and out of focus
Fleeting, fragmenting into harmony.

Images, dissolving outer self of things
Flash inspiring inner life, secret, hidden
As lovers coital oneness coincides, separates
Taking, imparting, self forming into unself
Reshaping lonely into self.

Dark and light
Washing in the sky of rising moon
Pieces of light, crescent,
Refluent on darkness of water.

Michael J. Breen

That Last Smile

I sat beside the bed and watched my wife
I knew the end was very near
The pulse was weak she was so calm
Somehow she did not fear.

I grasped her tiny hand in mine
She looked at me and oh, she smiled
And then with a fleeting breath
She passed into what we call Death.

There was golden silence
The tears came to my eyes
But somehow I was given strength
And realised my wife was at peace.

The suffering which she bore so well
Has left its marks on me
No grumbling or complaining
It was another Calvary.

I am lonely now, I miss my wife
But I believe she is watching me
I have memories and sometimes dreams
Which bring her close to me.

And so today I struggle on
Life's not what it used to be
But I thank the Lord for His great love
And that smile which means so much to me.

J.H. Bridgeman

St. Ives, Cornwall

Soft sea and harbour fall below the granite hills
With passages in sunlight down below.
Pot geraniums stand on whitewashed steps of stone
And all that narrow world I feel I know.

I know 'The Sloop' below the roofs, the glistening tiles of grey.
The feeling that you're there; the edge of time.
The pottery shops with shapes of clay beguile the passers-by,
And all that place I feel is really mine.

I feel that time has little place in corners hiding cats.
The shadows from the clouds on harbour walls.
Large Hepworths stand by garden walls of stone;
A white bird soars above the masts and caws.

Michael Bolan

Old Age

The wrinkled skin, a memory now into decline,
Eyes are failing, a shaking hand, that cannot sign,
Breathe now laboured, when taking a step,
People cannot understand, when you forget,
You want to listen, but its hard to hear,
This is old age, but you have no fear,
Through all the years, you have stood life's test,
Now all you want, is one long last rest,
To go to bed, and close your eyes,
And leave this world, with no good-byes,
To those left behind, who used to care,
You leave memories, for them to share.

Peter Brewer

Spare A Thought

Spare a thought this Christmas-time,
As we eat our food, and drink our wine,
For the homeless with nowhere to go,
Trudging around in the deep snow.
The cold winds blow, never still,
Through to their bones they feel the chill,
The soup kitchen's their only salvation,
As they queue with anticipation.
At night we lay snug in our beds,
While on the pavement, they lay their heads.
So spare a thought this Christmas Day,
For the homeless, we should pray.

Barbara J. Brittain

The Gift of Summer

Welcome summer, halcyon days and azure skies,
Scented flowers and gentle breeze,
Multi-coloured butterflies,
Sweet honey seek, bumble bees.

On leafy bough the blackbirds sing,
And homey bees their nectar seed,
And swallows swoop on velvet wing,
Whilst purple violets shyly peek.

Forgotten are bleak winter's days,
As nature in oblivion,
Soaks up the summer sun's warm rays,
And once bare trees their green cloaks don.

And in the evening's heady balm,
When crimson sun sinks in the west,
And all around is peace and calm,
Then nature takes her well earned rest.

Betty Bramma

Sea Girl

O that new day! That new day of blue
Up sparkling and bright on shingle spread
In the first breaking sun, and the wind -
The wind, not shivery, playing the hair
With its cool and tingling hands; that so
Seldom morning when the distant shouts
Were single shafts across the sea's bow.
Then your eyes, yes, always were your eyes
Merry, lips were nimble; the sun's flare
Held in curls about your bending head
With the swish of waves across your voice,
With the tided sands of yesterday
Smoothed in grace beneath your body's curve -
Girl of oceans! Child of elements!
With the broken jewels of the surf,
Sky and sun, drawn to the point of You,
You arising, matched with their glory.

Rory Brierley

A Drowning Scot

The sun rises to a headache reality.
A hare and a dog begin to chase the world,
To a grey slope down and an arduous alleyway up,
To a sweated atmosphere with smells of home forgotten.

The gold tipped ivory cane is pulled
To a bubbling trophy gold of his travels to an ivory head,
At the drop of a loyal hat handed over by a tired conscience,
Sliced by thirst clean off to a sunshine smile.

"And only five past eleven."

The evening staggers in with smells of a lady, beautifully fresh,
Smelt by a covetous eye tongue-tied by memories;
An ex-wife, Beattie, kindling a log with fire
Now quenched by saturated nights of many moons.

The doors toasted locked to old times repeated.
An escape becomes a routine for acceptance in a glass,
To become absolute with the flowers of the highland, meadows and streets
Of a constructed world alone for one pair of drowned eyes.

"Oh! how elegant does this vintage taste!"

Lloyd Brazier

"Is It True?"

There is no plan; no reason, for our living:
There is no pleasure, no reward, in giving.
There is no satisfaction, in a job sincerely done.
There is no warmth, well-being, basking in the sun.
There is no wonder, no miracle, in spring:
There is no balance, 'twixt Man and living thing.
There is no refreshment, in gentle April showers:
There is no future, in this tired world of ours.
There is no benefit, in developing the mind:
There is no love, in Man, for all Mankind.
There is no life, when the soul has left the shell:
There is no Heaven haven, there also is no Hell.
There is no being, for us beyond the grave:
There is no Tomorrow, no need to treasures save.
There is no tenderness, no selflessness, in love:
There is no prospect, in vast galaxies above.
There is no fulfillment, no joy, at baby's birth:
There is no humour, our lives are void of mirth.

If this be really true, then suicide I understand:
If this be really true, then speed the lethal hand.
If this be really true, then I, for one, take fright:
If this be really true, why did great authors write?
If this be really true, then all the poets lied:
If this be really true, then in vain have millions died.

Michael Trewern Bree

This Old House

When we first settled there it looked forlorn
The walls a mess, the paint all worn.
Windows tiny, the sun couldn't shine
The garden overgrown, the weeds entwined.
It had been neglected, no one cared
All little tasks had not been shared.
We all worked hard with a cheerful grin
To make it shine like a brand new pin.
It took us an age, there was a lot to do,
The jobs a plenty, the hours so few.
We made it our home and had some fun
The happy times with our daughter and son
And Tammy the dog, what a treasure she be
Plus Peter the pussy, a ginger she
Peter the second, a poor stray cat
Paul and George, two mice, very fat.
So many friends who dropped in for tea
These memories belong to me.
But what bad luck for our abode
The council required it to widen the road.
So we packed our bags and said good-bye
We tried to be brave, but had a good cry.
Our loving home which we had made so sound
Was eventually bulldozed to the ground.

Mrs. D. Brettell

My Disaster Days

When I woke up and reached for my 'specs' by my bed
And tried to put them on — I dropped them instead,
Bent down to pick them up — oh! my back's gone again!
Then kicked my bare foot 'gainst bedroom door — oh, the pain!

No more disasters till I'd brewed my morning 'cuppa',
Then, when I'd toasted my bread — I dropped the butter,
Knelt down to wipe it up off the kitchen floor
And when I stood up, banged my head on the door!

What a start to the day, I thought, as at last
I ate my breakfast, but, by then the die was cast
'Cause when I went to get my milk in from outside
I kicked a bottle, scattering glass far and wide.

I cleaned up the mess, tried to straighten my poor back,
Then went to get the newspaper off the door mat
But it was stuck in the letter-box, half in - half out,
When I pulled if free 'twas ruined beyond doubt.

After that lot, I thought, nothing else can go wrong
So I cheered myself up by singing a song,
The cat took one look at me, jumped off the chair
Fled out, through the cat-door, into the fresh air.

That's it, I thought, that's enough for today
And then I remembered what the "Good Book" says,
"Everyday is the day that the Lord has made
Rejoice and glad in it, now and always."

Kathleen Briers

The Parted Veil

A poet's soul is strong and bold,
Ever youthful, never old,
A poet's soul is strong and free
Ever seeking eternity.
Through time, the flesh is mortified
But the soul refreshed is fortified
To journey on.
To reach that star in a velvet sky,
Pass the moon in the blackest night,
And ride on the side of the westward wind
To the heavenly realms of light,
And there to pluck the purple bow,
And silken arrows from the cosmos' glow
Guiding the soul to onward go
Through the blue, blue, veil of heaven.

Rosemary Branson

A Walk At Dawn

As I walked along a country lane
The light seeped through, it ceased to rain,
All was silent, 'cept for me
Whistling tunes, merrily.
Suddenly I heard on high
A skylark singing, a pee-wit cry,
Cows in the meadow began to moo
Lambs cried for mother, they often do.
The farmer's dog added his gruff voice
Birds sang songs of their own choice.
A joyous feeling did abound
A touch of heaven all around
And, as I walked this country lane
I promised God I'd be back again.

Edward Bramley

Paradise Cottage

One lovely day in the midst of June,
When all the world seemed to be in tune,
A large oaken gate confronted me,
Behind which I was invited to see.

Some winding lanes and a farm ahead,
With bluebells and ferns where pedestrians tread,
Some beautiful woods adorned with flowers,
What an ideal way to spend the hours.

Still stolling along with great expectation,
There was in my view a delightful plantation,
Inhabited by hares, rabbits and pheasants,
Holidays here would make lovely presents.

A lovely little cottage with a welcome all its own,
To waken in the early hours and see the break of dawn,
And hear the songbirds, apparently without a care,
For me it is a dream far, far beyond compare.

Margaret Alice Brierley

The Road

Long, long miles that steal away our neighbourly love,
twist around still painful corners,
stranded in nowhere lands.
Long, long yards fall through painted visions,
these landscaped glories
trust and travel with the journey's end
no more than a horizon's breech away.

Hopefully carving through peaks and dales
of considered leniency.
Expecting no more than to arrive in good condition.
Disappointing to reveal the fear that fizzles
on in anticipation of beyond,
they flank the pathways.

We forgive our ancestral ignorance,
but bless the wayfarer's challenge
as they record progress for posterity.

Eric Brown

Seeds of Life

Inside each adult, the baby still lies,
Attached to the soul with invisible ties,
Still learning and yearning, for his needs to be fed
With loving and caring, for this child's not dead.

His body grew, but his unmet needs
Lie there waiting like dormant seeds,
Able to flourish with tender care,
Into precious blooms with talents rare.

He could be special, this child inside,
By the love he could spread both far and wide,
Each of us have him though he may lie deep
So please don't damn him to eternal sleep.

Rouse and love him, allow him space,
To show the world his innocent face,
If the baby in each of us recognised the other,
Peace would reign on the earth, our Mother.

Each child inside, has no Creed or Colour,
Doesn't discriminate 'twixt one or the other,
All are born equal, though blessings are varied.
Let him out, let him grow! Don't let him stay buried.

Brenda Brookes

Healing Light

O diamond bright, white ray supreme
Help me to bring about my dream,
To help those who are in pain
That they may be well again.
For those who are sick in body and mind
Help me to help all of mankind.
O Spirit of the universe
Let man see the light and feel thy worth.
If man could see the inner light
I feel sure it would help them to do what is right,
For we get out of life what we put in
And we should try more to be free from sin.
May I do absent healing for the sick far away
And those nearer home that I see every day.
Please shine bright on our family
And free from suffering let them be.
My husband Fred, he's the right one for me
We will be together through eternity.
Let us all live happily on this plane for a while
Then one day we will see my Mother's sweet smile,
She'll be waiting to greet us with her tender love
Just like all who have gone to the plane up above.
Only when we have done all that is right
One day we will see God's own eternal light.

Marilyn Brierley

Icarus

On leaden legs,
I run deep,
And fast, faster
Through trees
Bathed in autumn light.
From shocked eyes,
I cry out,
And blind, blinded -
Despair
My dying sight.
Here at summer's death.
I witness,
A small, smaller
Passing -
Falling from a height.

Kevin Briffett

Our Loved Ones

Our family and our loved ones
Live far across the sea
But I always feel their presence
Here inside of me,
I see them come with laughter
These moments I do prize
I seem them go with sorrow,
Tears running from my eyes.
I see them come with pale skin
To feel our sun's warm rays
To see our native animals
And feel our scorching days,
But now my relatives have gone
Back far across the sea
But ever more these memories
Shall here remain with me

Benjamin Breeds (Age 12)

Ageing

Three score years and ten we're told
Are what our years should be
From babies, youth and middle age
To Ageing gracefully.

We get around, but not too fast
To keep the home fires burning
Us O.A.P.'s were built to last
And help we're often spurning.

On 'Pension day' with strength renewed
We go to fill our coffers
Then armed with all our rightful dues
We shop around for 'Offers'

We Bingo, Disco, Dance and Sing
For fun were not found wanting
With prices cheaper in the Spring
We're haring off to 'Pontins'

At times when feeling low or ill
We say "I've lost me clout"
Says doctor as he gives a pill
There's a lot of it about.

At close of day, we hit the hay
At times that we can choose
And with a sigh we say 'Oh My'
A good lie-in and snooze.

Ivy Brown

On Visiting The Somme

Like you and I they came
Along these self-same tree-lined roads,
Now smooth with asphalt to where corn meets sky,
But wearily they trod through dust and mud,
To that place where they had to die.

The sun beats down from a cloudless sky
As all around the yellow corn stands high,
I wonder what they must have felt,
As to the front they went
Seventy years ago on another bright, clear summer's day.

What thoughts went through their minds
As there they lay,
Waiting for the coming of the dawning day.
Thoughts of home and loved ones dear,
As the appointed hour drew nearer.

Suddenly the barrage stops,
Now's the time to go 'over the top',
And bravely, in ordered line they made their way,
But far too many were to fall that day.

But rest my fellow countrymen,
Rest, you battle's been won,
Time cannot weary you now,
As you sleep beneath the corn, blue sky and sun.

Michael M. Brockett

Time Marches On

This day and Age
Is sometimes fraught with danger
One never knows what to say or do
Right or wrong who holds the clue.

Our policemen are courageous men
Without them we lose a friend
They drive a car, walk the beat
Help people to find a seat.

Knowing they are about the streets
You feel safe no need to retreat
In your home or out for a walk
Enjoying the scenery in the park

So walk with pride
The sun still shines
Safe and secure
With peace of mind.

Mrs. M. I. Brooks

Susie

Oh little cat with wild green eyes
Sometimes seen to eat the flies
Soft warm fur, but I must pause
Not to forget the hidden claws
Like the rose which smells so sweet
It hides a thorn which one can meet
You cuddle up into a ball
Always on your feet you fall
Ever watchful even in rest
One eye open for the pests
Who might pass by and flick your ear
A scratch from you, will, I fear
Send them off in great haste
Wishing they had never faced
Up to this ball of fluff
Turning out to be quite tough
Go to sleep my little Sue
And dream about what pleases you.

Doreen Brooks

Ethiopia

The days are not within their power,
Famine rules at every hour,
Saddened eyes from saddened faces stare
At their inheritance; starvation and despair

Whose children's eyes are empty eyes
That blankly stare at empty skies,
One final look to heaven above
To blame, or thank, for life's short love.

They turn to us with outstretched hand
No word is said; we understand.
From birth to death with nothing e're possessed
These starving lives will soon find peace and rest.

Don't banish from your heart their plight,
By fortune's stroke, we there, be might;
Help dry their tears, by what we do alone,
Our greatest gift, to give, and conscience to atone.

God's laws are just and justly plead
That those who have shall share with those who need.
Erase those names which on a cross they carve,
For God said in His book, 'Let no man starve'.

R. Brockett

Light Refreshment

After weeks and weeks of rain
it's good to get out and about again.
To feel the sun upon my face
enveloped in its warm embrace.

A drive into the countryside
hubby takes me for the ride
and the chance to be together,
not always in the best of weather.

The hills and dales our spirits renew.
Greens and greys of varied hue
we notice on our journey past,
free from the noisome town at last.

We park up over Burnsall bridge,
enjoy hot flasks and sandwiches.
Put on our boots and haversacks
to wander over country tracks.

Thankful for the motorcar
which transports us near or far
every time we feel the need
to leave the town for moor and field.

Ruth B. Brook

Losing It

Today I lost my tooth.
I waggle and worry and work at it, till the single strand snaps
And my tongue slithers into a warm jelly hole.
A matchbox coffin holds my decay just to the side of the pillow.
Then the fairy can slip in a sixpence and carry my childhood
To where Santa Claus and the Bogey Man,
Walk together over a ball-pool shingle of yellow and browns.

Carolyn Brookes

Independent

I'm all grown up now, mother, I don't need you anymore
I've just got time to shout good-bye as I walk out the door
You've lived your life around me, now go out and see the world
Please face the fact that I'm no longer your sweet little girl
I can't come down to see you, I expect you're feeling fine
And I will try to phone, if I can only find the time
Where were you last night mother? when I needed you
I feel under the weather and Johnny's got the flu
The baby won't stop crying, the house is such a mess
I know that you will sort it out for that's what you do best
You can go home now mother, everything is fine
And although I'm really busy, I will phone if I have time.

Sylvia Brotherdale

What Is It?

Like sweet royal icing, all smooth, white and soft,
And the last piece of pudding; not cold and not hot.

Oh my heart overflows with the visions I see,
When I get this feeling that happens to me.

Not the sun's warm red glow, at the end of the day,
Nor the sight of a kitten, when it goes out to play.

What I feel has no measure, it is priceless but free,
But all of those things can't compare much for me.

There is one thing in millions, that can drive away pain,
That brings joy into heartache, strength restored once again.

It can change angry temper to calm and serene,
Bring sharing and goodness from bad and the mean.

A touch of some magic, a wonderful sight,
To be given so eagerly both day and night.

All the bad times and struggles seem all the worth while,
What is it? Just simply WHEN MY CHILDREN SMILE.

Caren Tania Brown

The Trugmaker

The old Sussex trugmaker
Sits by himself.
Gnarled old hands
Busy at work
Moulding and shaping
The pieces of wood.
Here is a craftsman
Plying his trade
With an air of contentment
And a deep sense of pride.
No noisy shop floors
With clanging machines
To mass reproduce
Some impersonal things.
No shouting and swearing
And ruled by the clock.
But alone in the quiet
And busy all day
Creating the trugs
Each so lovingly made.

Rosalie Bungard

Teddy

He lies in the corner,
all tattered and torn.
His ears fallen off
and his fur is all worn.
His eye's hanging out
of his sweet little head.
Yet once he was favourite
and slept in my bed.

I look at that teddy
all lost and forlorn
(cast aside in the attic)
brought when I was born.
It's funny how sometimes
I felt like this toy,
alone and neglected,
unloved, cast off boy.

But now that I'm older
with a child of my own.
I'm getting you down
to give you a home.
I'll mend you and clean you,
you'll sleep in his cot.
Watch over my angel,
he means such a lot.

Sue Browning

Why Me? Why Not?

Why is their life so much better than mine?
Why is their life so incredibly fine?
Why are they richer than me?
Why can their spending be so free?
Why do they look so slim?
Why are their figures so trim?
Why are they gourmets without guilt?
Why do I end up fat, and they, well-built?
Why are their eyes so bright and clear?
Why are mine a watery leer?
Why is my hair as straight as a die?
Why does theirs curl and dutifully lie?
Why is their brain so sharp, so quick?
Whilst mine so depressingly thick?
Why does their voice impressively thrill?
Why is mine stridently shrill?
Why are they sparkling and witty?
Why am I such an object of pity?
Why is their movement of such style and grace?
Why am I clumsy, prone to fall flat on my face?
Why are they never sick or unwell?
Why is my body a living hell?
Why am I the victim of some plot?
Why me? I ask ... but then again, why not?

D.W. Brown

Seasons Of Life

Autumn is with us once again
The leaves are turning brown
The winds whip them up in frenzy
And dash them back to the ground
The evenings are darkening in
Everything is slowing down
The season of mellow fruitfulness
Is with us all around

We draw the curtains and snuggle in the warmth
To keep the winter chills at bay
A good brisk walk does us good, and helps along the way
The seasons come the seasons go
And we must go with them
Our lives are so conditioned, we have to go along
Each season has its goodness, some can bring you pain
One thing is certain, we cannot relive them again.

We enjoy the sun, the sea, the sand
The flowers, the birds, the trees
And pleasures that joy can bring to every living being
We should be grateful for what we have
And thankful for what is to come
And live in love and harmony with everyone
And give our love and praise to God for giving this to us
And giving life and a chance for everyone.

Miss D.M. Brown

Shadow Birth

"An existential crisis" she called it once,
in a blaze of hair and porcelain skin,
(we envied her then - that edge of brilliance)
smoking, curled against the sofa. "Suicide" ...
"Determinism" ... "The stoics chose it" ...
She told us, as words played on 'til dawn.
Embryonic, timed for birth beneath the surface,
a shadow stirred, recoiled, We saw success
rise to noon. The night eclipsed. She got her
'First' in sunlight, shadowless July and heat and
raised a good-bye toast: "Disaster or Success!"
(Or just the middle road?) She chose the former.

Four years on she called it depression.
Shuffling the wards, full blown and dull;
pasted, pill ridden, (Imipramine, Prosac or even
Melleril - "I'll be on them for life" she told us)
as shadows stalked, matured and we chatted,
saw the words sucked in again, the gulf of
carrot hair and said good-bye. (She got her
'First' in shadowless July.) We walked the
darkening road to town and trained it home and
smoked, through open windows, into October rain.

Helen Rosemary Brown

Junkyard Demon

Somewhere in time
a man searches through a rubbish tip
like a child who has lost his favourite toy.

One hundred yards away
a shrouded figure stand alone
on a rusting mountain of cars.
Day and night he guards their souls from Satan.

Fifty yards away
a small schoolgirl scrambles over a dish-washing machine
to clutch a crust of mouldy bread.
Eating means surviving
is today's lesson.

Two hundred yards away
images flicker across the screen of a broken TV set.
Curious, a mouse sits entranced
as the actors mouth silent words and the picture
fades and jumps across the screen.

And besides all this and above it all
a gentle snickering can be heard.

Bob Brown

That Man ...

That man
That dark man
That black man
Standing in the night
Standing in the light
That light
Coming from above.
The gold lining
A flash of silver
Then it's gone.
The gold lining
Gone
The light
Gone
That man
Gone
That man.

Robin Brown

Knitting For Rwanda

Each stitch in this small garment,
Will contribute toward the struggling population
Of yet another despotic area of Africa,
Deep in the throes of political genocide.

As you knit, remember the pattern thus:
k1. - pestilence
k1. - plague
k1. - famine
k1. - lack of water
k1. - untimely birth
k1. - untimely death
k1. - k1. - k1. - k1. - k.1. - k1. - k1. - k1. - k1. - k1.
Repeat until finished ...
Then start again.
Remember ...
Humanity never learns ...
Your talent will be needed for
E-ter-Knit-y ...

Marion Brown

R.I.P.

The aim of mankind
Is to leave something behind
That will make life worth living
In future.

The tide is turning.
Sense is lapping
A littered shore,
Gently smoothing
The jagged bones
of
War.

Elisabeth Brown

The Walking Stick

Quick, short steps
Supported with brass
ferrule tapping,
Also used for pointing
at places used to be.
A story to tell of each
remembered.
An old man now
his sons mature.
Time is short,
and much to tell
while tapping, tapping, tapping
on the brass ferrule.

Reg Browne

Creation

The earth was once a barren land
'Til God stretched forth his mighty hand
And in an instant all was green
It was a sight none yet had seen

He made the rivers and the seas
And fish to swim and stately trees
He called forth birds to sail the skies
And listened to their joyful cries

He made the beasts both great and small
He made the raging waterfall
And then as part of His great plan
He took some dust and formed man

Then so he wouldn't be alone
From Adam's side he took a bone
He fashioned His greatest work of art
And Adam loved her with all his heart

Their happiness did not last long
For the serpent taught them to do wrong
Now for their sin there was no pardon
And they were banished from the garden

So that is how mankind began
Now we must do the best we can
For they fell victim to temptation
And left us all without salvation.

J.S. Brown

Imitation

The house reflected on the lake,
Is just as real
Just as opaque
Yet upside down and in the air,
Without a way of getting there.

Suspended in the shiny blue,
Water's facade mocking you
Throw in a pebble to call it's bluff
The image ripples away in a huff
Soon to return to the seen of the crime,
Insisting it's been there all the time.

Yet unaware of what's spoiling the show,
Are reeds which seem from the chimney to grow
But raising one's eyes with relief to the bricks,
It's only nature playing tricks.

Imitation fades on reflection
However still the day,
It never finds perfection.

Katharine Clare Brown

E.T.

Engines thumping
Turbo's pumping
Belching forth its flames of life
thrusting, ever thrusting
Man into the dark unknown
Searching
Ever searching
For the being called E.T.

Past the moon
Beyond the dark side of the sun
The craft goes onward
Noiseless in the silent void
Through the seas of time beginning
Searching
Ever searching
For the being called E.T.

Yet if we find him
And with welcome hand he greets us
Will we be shaking hands
With **GOD**.

David Brownley

Values

The hammer fell, the auctioneer cried, "sold"
A mumur filled the room, then faded out,
and was this picture worth it's weight in gold?
Of this, the wealthy buyer had no doubt.
It made me wonder, were I as rich as he,
what picture I'd commission, just for me.

A landscape or, perhaps, a local scene.
A portrait of myself? No, I think that
a group of dancers on the village green,
would be more suitable for my small flat.
And so I asked my daughter what she thought.
What, if she'd had the money, she'd have bought.

"I like the smell of roses," she replied,
"The cool breeze on a summer day.
The cry of seagulls on a rising tide.
The sound of children, going out to play.
No matter what the cost, how high the fee,
no artist ever, could paint these for me."

And with these words came understanding clear.
A new and different viewpoint had I found.
Cruel poverty I'll never need to fear,
while I have nature's beauty all around.
The longed for riches are already there.
A gift, like life, for everyone to share.

Roger Brougham

My Granny

When I was just a wee lassie, sitting on my grannies knee,
Listening to the stories, she would tell to me.
She would gaze into the fire, watching the dancing flames,
And speak of far away places, with lovely exotic names.

She would tell me of the forest in Germany,
Castles in France, bull fights in Spain,
And I would want to hear them again and again.
I loved to hear of people, in these foreign lands,
Their glowing eyes and sparkling teeth,
And the colour of their hands.

For Gran said God made people,
All of a different hue,
but they had hearts as white, as me or you.
I used to feel sad when she told me of the poverty,
Where little children begged for food,
And missionaries crossed the sea,
To give aid as best they could.

Looking back now that I am grown up,
I realize the lessons Granny taught me,
Not to judge people by their race or creed,
To have pity on those who have less,
For as Granny used to say,
You can only do your best.

Vera Brown

Child's Talk

How can it be
said the child to the tree
that you stand there as naked as life.
Well, it's plain to see
there are no leaves on me
said the lifeless tree in reply.

But you look so old
and feel so cold
as you stand there so still, proud and tall.
Well, the answer is easy
it's been rather breezy
which has caused all of my leaves to fall.

The child looked glum
and her fingers lay numb
as she tried to search for the reason.
She looked all around
at the foliage on the ground
when it dawned, it must be the season.

Neil Brunton

The Wembley Exhibition

The grown-ups were excited too
We were heading for the station
By this time you may have guessed
To the Wembley Exhibition

We dressed in our very best
Fashions of the twenties age
My mother's cloche hat of beige
Framed her pretty oval face.

Apart from senior ladies preference
But in contrast to tied and laced
Most of ladies coats and dresses
Were devoid of any waist

Father was very smart in a suit of navy blue
Cricket medals bright and shiny
On his watch chain new

There was magic in the air that day
Laughing crowds, large hats, some with feathers
I'd never seen all those guards before

So splendid they were
With "Bearskins" for all weathers
It's hard to recall the journey home
After enjoying such a treat
When you're very little, you have a knack
Of falling fast asleep.

Ella Buckley

Disability, Now

Give me a shoulder to cry on,
For things are too much for me -
Just for a while may I tell you
My dread of what may come to be.

Give me a cushion to kneel on,
While I unload my grief and my fear,
Give me the comfort of knowing
At bedrock, you'll always be near.

Give me a faith that is steady,
A measure of strength to endure,
Give me more courage to face life,
And a love all-embracing, mature.

Elizabeth Brown

Untitled

I cradled the dead sea bird in my hands
The feathers like a wet suit moulded
The thin body. Sightless eyes oil blinded
The once swift wings black clogged and folded.

Oil slick they call it but 'tis creeping death
That floats an evil veil upon the sea
Silent insidious, wrapping with soft embrace
That held you fast and would not let you free.

There high above stretched out the limitless sky
Where once you flew with light and lifting wings
Its beauty mocking. Sunshine, freedom, life
They were for you the last remembered things.

Mrs. Bull

Yorkshire

The sun was like a ball of fire
Raining down for man's desire,
Valleys so green looking across the hill
To gladden my heart and give me a thrill,
O the Yorkshire dales are in my mind
One wondrous creation to be given mankind.
Two hundred miles from west to east
To walk in hot summers is really a feast
Where young lambs in the April breeze
Frolic and flick, as quick as a sneeze,
In winter the snow lays thick on the ground,
And the air so silent, as there's no one around,
Jack Frost comes daily as the farmer knows well
For his buckets and troughs are frozen to hell,
But to Yorkshire each year I know I must go
For its beauty to see even in snow.

Stuart Peter Bull

And In The End

Alone with our thoughts
And alone with our dreams,
Not everything
Is quite what it seems.

Emotions colour our every moment,
Bring pain to the quietest mood,
The mind fills with questions
And memories brood.

Evening closes in,
Followed by lonely night,
With never ending wonderings
Of all the things that might.

Of course we know there will be a day
When time will ease the pain,
But in our hearts we dread that feeling
Of here it comes again.

Margaret Burgess

Time on a Park Bench

An old man sitting on a bench
In the park, thinking of when
He was a young man.

A young man, sitting on a bench
In the park, thinking of when he
Was a boy on this bench.

A boy sitting on a bench
In the park remembering when
He was a child.

A baby boy, was sitting
On his mother's knee.
On that bench.

A young mother, hoping
Her first born, would be a boy.
As she sat there on that bench.

An old man sitting on a bench
In the park looking at his
watch ...

Edward Burke

Men in the House

My father died this year;
Within this silent house
Much evidence of being here remains,
His empty chair, the coat I can't throw out
The morning tray, no longer laid
Having no drugs to claim.

And all is changed; the bed removed,
The place where he was dressed
For other men now reign
Who make unheedless mess,
Rampage through every room
Knocking the windows out
Using their drills
To track, to whine, to bore
They leave for me the splintered glass
The rubble and the dust,
Their teabags on the floor.

But each day ends, for end must come
To endless push and shove
And then, a kind of chivalry appears
The hand upon the door,
The head put round,
"Now don't forget,
Shut all the windows love."

Iris Bull

Winter's Blast

Winter's icy blast is gripping
People on the pavement slipping
Their bodies bent against the snow
As they battle to and fro.

The sky is heavily overcast
Snowflakes falling thick and fast,
The cold north wind bites at the nose
Numbing fingers and the toes.

The snow continues through the night
And in the early morning light,
A new and silent world revealed
Ugly contours now concealed.

Winter has cast her mantle wide
Snow covers town and countryside,
A thick white blanket dazzles the eye
As the sun shines down from a clear blue sky.

Snow upon ice over river and stream
Whilst overhead the seagulls scream,
A farmer searching for lost cattle
Against the elements — a constant battle.

Winter has beauty, but can be grim
For when the snow melts, so the floods begin,
Man and beast are put to the test
Only the fittest surviving the rest.

Mrs. J. Bunn

70

What Does That Mean?

The White Queen said,
"It's a poor sort of memory
that only works backwards."
I know what she means,
it's not only the words,
but the spaces in between.

Imagine a today,
where no tomorrows are there,
to get in the way,
and there is nothing,
left of yesterday.

One hand clapping
trees falling without
a sound,
a child's mind
free and unbound.

With hope that only works forward,
and memory that only works backwards.
How ever will we learn?
What does that mean?
It's none of your concern.

Michael Burley

The Flying Fool

I am a 'gull on the ocean
A dot, almost nothing to
The beautiful, blue expanse,
Like a lone star in an ebony sky, only
I do not shine out so bright,
I am winged, I could fly free,
But for love! Love for the sea
Has lured me down;
Her waves of beauty have me besotted
And, intrigued by the depths of her soul
I sit, floating wayward, yet
Happily resigned, for freedom in not my need,
But the deep, Oh 'tis my every need!
And here looms the danger - My wings
Shall seize by love and leave me
Powerless, to her every whim -
My weakness! She must not see, nor ever know, but
No! Sensibility kneels before need,
I become obvious, helpless, vulnerable, oh
My God! My ocean, my essence, my love
I plead. Keep this wisdom hush'd,
Shield my shaken sanity, for this bird,
This flying fool's fate, is in your hands.

J. Burke

A Christmas Wish

If I had a wish to give this merry time
It would be for the whole wide world.
A wish of love, happiness for the lonely, sick
Mum and dad for the children who have not got one.
A loving family for you, that's what I would give,
Feel the warmth, love that a family could give.
So you could join in all the fun and laughter
Unwrap presents large and small,
For the lonely who think of merry Christmas' past
Someone to love, and laugh, share this happy time.
Hospitals would close your doors, home the sick would go
To share the fun with family and friends
War torn countries peace over all
Shake hands with each other this merry time.
Even families who have drifted apart,
Open your eyes, open your hearts
This may turn out a glorious time
The church bells will be ringing out loud and clear
For snow to fall, a white Christmas to bring
A glorious carol for all to sing.

Evelyn Burkitt

What Dreams?

What dreams now for Rwanda's child
Born into a time of nightmares,
As neighbours grew into murderers and pangas
Were used to harvest a human crop
And a dread-filled silence was gathered in;
But now even the dead are allowed no rest
As the annual rains come and drum upon the ground
Shaking loose the bodies from their earthy shroud,
Moving without will they can only blankly stare
Into a future they can only shape but darkly,
Where the seeds of hate and fear, well-nourished
By their blood will strongly flourish, and hope
Becomes a stranger amongst the displaced throng,
And the survivors, inheritors of a silent land
Still sleep uneasily with their pangas near to hand,
As those who killed and were in turn forced to flee
Now plot and dream of an end to their desperate exile.

George B. Burns

My Lovely Granny Yates

My Granny did not have a lot, she had a very hard life.
My Granny had no husband although she was a wife.
Five children she had to bring up alone and she did it very well,
She never said she was unhappy, with Gran you could not tell.
She wore a little black straw hat straight upon her head,
And her long black umbrella helped Granny's weary tread.
Her eyes were a lovely brown, her hair a snowy white,
And when I looked into her gentle face, Granny's smile was sheer delight.
She gave me a slice of home made cake, and a drink of her sweet tea,
I loved to go Granny's house, for she meant the world to me.
Yes, I shall always love my Granny, till the end of my own life,
For Granny was a lady, war widow, mother and wife.

Mrs. N. Burton

Duet For Father And Son

How much do you love me daddy?
How can I tell that you care?
    By the way that I hold and hug you
    And ruffle your spiky hair.
How deep is your love for me daddy
How can I know it is there?
    It's as deep as the deepest ocean,
    It's a love we shall always share.
How high is your love my daddy?
    As high as the heavens above,
    When you were born, God smiled
    And gave *us* unending love.

    How much do *I love you* my daddy
    How much will I always care
    By the way I hug and hold you
    Bend down, so I can ruffle your hair.

D.M. Burge

Florence

Other poets and writers have had reams to write about you
But you did not show such a face to me
Why did you seem so dirty, old and sad
As though you could not be bothered to make the effort any more
Like your cathedral, ornate and showy from a distance
Inside your core was bare, your finery just so much glamour
That seems so wonderful, until you look too close
I could not wait to escape your bustle and noise
Go back to my Tuscan hills that enveloped me in peace.

Melanie M. Burgess

Comfortable

Getting up in the morning
I pull on my old shirt,
My warmest socks
And you.

My eyes half shut
I spread brown toast with butter,
Heather honey
And you.

Walking down the drive
My handbag's full of Kleenex,
My Parker pen
And you.

At lunchtime, hot soup
And steaming windows
And streaming rain
And you.

In the gentle dusk
Newspaper in the porch,
Cat under my feet
And you.

I close my eyes
To falling, drifting dreams
Of leaves, and stars, and clouds, and silk
And you.

Penny Burton

Anniversaries

Today's an anniversary, and so was yesterday;
So, too, will be tomorrow, whate'er may be the day.
Mondays, Tuesdays, Wednesdays, Thursdays, Fridays too can be
As with Saturdays and Sundays, full of joy for you and me,
Birthdays are anniversaries, and so are wedding days,
We remember them, by numbers; oft seen in rosy haze.
One thing they have in common, as months pass into years,
As the numbers become bigger, each one left soon disappears.
Hopes of anniversaries weaken, while the numbers pile up high,
The precious gift of happy thoughts, can passing time defy.

Anniversaries are personal, of family, faith — or national;
And we, important times in life, can mark in ways traditional.
To celebrate, we eat and drink; make music, play and dance;
On national anniversaries, we can see fine horses prance,
A celebration can be both expansive and spectacular,
But — two can celebrate a day that is, for them, particular;
It does not need a gift or card to bring another pleasure,
A tune, smile, touched hands, memory shared;
warm words that each will treasure.
But each date can be special; each unique in every year;
For which all those who live and thrive
should be of right good cheer.

Constance M. Burrows

The Stalk

As I went to the kitchen to turn on the light
I jumped, I had a terrible fright.
For there on the worktop I saw something black
Not daring to move much I turned my back
I turned around slowly looked through squinted eyes
To where the black thing on my worktop lies
But it was still there looking big and bold
I felt my blood starting to run cold
So I went a bit nearer to have another look
I've got to get in there, I've got something to cook
So bravely I blew it with one mighty blow
But it never moved, it just didn't go
So out came the jam jar to trap it at last
Down it came, I had it trapped and fast.
I moved the jar from side to side
The ugly black thing was having a ride.
So I picked up the jar, thinking it might run off
But it never moved, I'd had enough.
So on went my glasses to inspect it some more
I pushed the jar - it fell onto the floor
I stood there in terror, not able to scream
Is it a nightmare or is it a dream?
The black thing didn't move, it didn't walk
Would you believe it, it was a tomato stalk.

Mrs. J.E. Burrows

On Our Own

Youth perceptions and the law enforcement
They lay the blame on us
I lay the blame on ignorance of our elders
And recession.
Attention is not my virtue
It is boredom and the lust for fun.

Give us occupations and watch crime
Disappear from the streets.
I am lonely — that's all I'm qualified to be.
No education because of my parents
A broken home marks my revenge.
Show them — do your best to defy them
Crime is a strong return.

The Police, the Council, let's stop discrimination
Consuming peer pressure like an angel does wings
But what do they have to offer
For taking in the rain when I'm feeling dry?
Someone has to draw blood first
Will it go on forever, or just tonight?
I am an impressionable child in a turbulent world.
Every nerve is on the edge
And breathing is becoming no fun.

Mark Burnside

Insignificance

As sinking hours
Pass slowly by
As sky turns black
I wonder why.
As sunshine rays
Glint oceans green
I silently think
What does it mean?
As gentle breeze
Slips through the air
On quiet reflection
Do I care?
As heavens burn
Will it be
Does it matter
You and me?

Lorraine Buse

Life

Here I sit alone but warm,
Outside it pours, the sky's so grey,
The trees so bare, the light so frail.

The snow will come,
And then will go,
Let's all be happy,
Like years ago.

Share our thoughts,
And let's be glad,
No love's been bought,
Life isn't bad.

Now I'm not so all alone,
My friend, my family,
Have all come home.

Nancy Burns

Heroica

The Sands of Time run out and having run
Are stilled, nor all Man's wit since Time begun
Shall sift the Sands to cancel out a grain,
Nor all Man's wisdom weft an Age that's spun.

To Thee, to Me, what are Ten Thousand Years,
What is a Day, if shackled by our fears
We choose regret, the Scourge of Yesterdays,
Than find ourselves with Love that Truth reveres?

Dreaming ere Dark Nocturn's pale eye came,
The Spirit moved me from veiled Morpheus' wame
Awake, my son, and seek the tavern where
The Cup of Life will drain thee of thy shame.

But we are Mortals weak, there is no Cup,
The tavern is mirage, we dare not sup.
Life's Liquor, stuff of Dreams, we dare not taste,
Love's thirst unsate, lest Gorgon tongues rear up.

There is no comfort in the way or wit
When Freedom dies, when self-doubt conquers it
A thousand deaths a thousand times prefer
Than die but once, in Spirit, who submit.

Take courage from the sin of mortal fate.
This Earth was made proud, fallen Man's estate.
If Fate must cast its Cross, but bear it well,
Your Destiny is not Earth's Cross to expiate.

H.G. Burnside

Night

As we lay in our beds at night
Our hopes and fears take winged flight
Hope in us eternal springs
To spur us on to better things

We think of loves long gone and past
Of friendships gone of those that last
We think of things that might have been
We heave a sigh — Ah well, to dream

The night it silently creeps by
We lie awake till dawn is nigh
The rain beats on your window pane
Your tears they fall but all in vain

Your heart beats fast you think you're dying
But you're not, you're only crying
Not another day to face
With this so unkind human race
I'll go to sleep and think no more
Just what tomorrow has in store

You look in to your soul at night
And ponder on your many plights
And can you give your soul away
A'h wait a minute — it is day

Mary Buttle

74

Cry

They watch us both together
Walking hand-in-hand
Dust of gold beneath our feet
No longer in the sand

The gentle ocean breeze
Murmurs my name to you
As above the seagulls circle
A most fantastic view

They watch me walk alone now
My head is held so low
The sand is merely sand
Where did the gold dust go

The gentle ocean breeze
Now hums a sad, sad song
As I climb the jagged black, wet rock
Our lovely kingdom gone

And so I watch them hover
So lonely in the sky
A love has gone forever
That's why the seagulls cry

Brenda Butler

Running On Empty

We are trains running
Endlessly running

Not slowly smoky.
Charging down the turbo track.

We are motors turning
Endlessly turning

Not cranked hard to start.
Speeding down the motorway.

We are trains running
We are motors turning
Not stopping to think
Not thinking to care
Not caring to stop
Or take a turn back.

We are trains and
We are motors and
We are running.
On empty.

Martin Royston Bush

The Wading Party

A line of seabirds huddle on the shingle
Buffeted by strong winds and salt spray,
Anxiously awaiting the turn of the tide
On this bleak and cold winter's day.

Small waves break on the shoreline
As the tide begins to recede,
And large herring gulls preen their plumage
Before descending to the water's edge to feed.

A flock of oyster catchers wheel and turn
Above the lonely windswept strand
To settle in the shallow pools
Their long beaks probing in the sand.

Close to the foaming edge of the sea
Where the east wind is biting and keen
Scurrying to and fro in the shallows
A group of shy turnstones are seen.

As the pale sun disappears from view
The birds begin to fly up from the shore
To sit in feathered ranks on the shingle
As the tide returns once more.

Joyce Bushby

Moment of Revelation

Yesterday I caught my son unawares
Cuddling his month-old baby in his arms.
His arrogant Viking face was so transformed
By love that I was astonished.
His eyes so shining with love,
His smile so transformed with tenderness
That I thought his bright red hair
Served as a saint's halo.

Then he saw me, standing in the open doorway
And the light went out abruptly. No saint now.
"Like to hold her?" he asked gruffly
His eyes narrowed defensively ...

But for a moment I had seen
What no camera could ever capture,
Nor any artist ever put on canvas.
And I knew that picture
Would flicker on my mind's eye
For a long time yet
And that I should be glad of it.

J.B. Bywood

Questions

I remember the time, and it wasn't long ago
When there was hardly any crime, strangers nodded 'n said 'Hello'
And old ladies didn't cuss when they got on a bus
and couldn't find a seat
an' yesterday's kids ... Lord help us, tried to assist us ... not belt us
Should we pray? What's that you say?
We can't expect the same respect
From the kids of today?
In my day, young girls when they reached their teens
Wore effeminate clothes then ... not boots and men's jeans
Then came the mini-skirt ... God help me ... was there ever anything more sexy?
Gave birth to the Beatles ... the Stones, an' could make a blind man see
No wonder today young boys are confused
Can't tell if they're being loved ... or being abused
After dark not many wander from behind closed door
Except for policemen and slit-skirted whores
It was good in my day, how come we lost the fight?
'Course, maybe it was never meant for us to get it right?
My only hope now is, before I die
that my last words are not
WHO ... WHAT ... WHERE and WHY?

D.V. Canale

Poetic Licence

We have poetic licence to illuminate our dreams.
An invention so created to illustrate our schemes.
Words of rhyme for usage of ways to express,
Of laughter, of laments, of tales of the very best.

Words that where mediocre now have frills and lace.
Expressions full of meanings are now given full grace.
Delicate, beautiful as butterflies on the wing.
Matched evenly with chords makes music for voices to sing.

There language has a tongue of there very own.
Like roses in buds to full grown blooms.
A labyrinth, a maze, just for us to explore.
Who could ask for even a fraction more.

A passion for our enthusiasm to create.
Expressing mental pictures for up to relate.
A story ever ready for us to unfold.
A creation to cultivate until a story is told ...

Jean Best

Making Love

Their energies are spent in separate worlds
On cares which lack encroachment; coming back
Together, stranger to the other's home.
But, sometimes, they can push these cares aside
And rediscover feelings both had lost.

Between them then, no word is passed; no thought
Has been communicated consciously,
And yet, in synchrony, they step across
That aching space dividing them and what
She feels for him from what he feels for her.

Desire gives way to mutual, lusting zeal
Whose powerful interacting force makes keen
Their scent and every tactile sense, while sight's
Surroundings faint and voice, in muted gasps,
Expresses shock at lack of usefulness.

Then when the cadent afterglow has set,
She wanders round the paradox wherein
An act, whose quintessential quality
Is sensual, their souls did touch; and yet
His separateness of mind remains intact.

Dominic Clarke

The Kitten

Snow is my little kitten,
With one black patch upon one eye,
She is as soft as a wooly mitten,
But like a pirate, she is sly,
She snuggles up to me for treats,
Then in a flash! She darts away
To pursue an unseen prey.
A moment late I take a peep,
And she has fallen fast asleep.

Magdalene Chadwick

Grandma's Smile

Seraphic smile, serene beneath
White hair, blue eyes and glowing cheeks.
"I was a devon dumpling", she said.
Safe in her carbolic embrace
That spoke of healing
When I misbehaved or wet the bed
That smile was absolution.
"Bless him", she said.

No dumpling now,
As she lies huddled in a geriatric bed,
The room suffused with essence of incontinence.
The eyes unseeing now,
The cheeks more parchment than peach,
And last sad relic of that smile
A glass with a set of teeth.

John Callow

The Waterfall

Waterfall waterfall wild and free
Tumbling down to the mighty sea
The rocks below turn your waters to foam
Like a weary wanderer seeking his home

Ever restless never still
Flowing along by the old windmill
The mighty sea with her arms held wide
A warm embrace for her restless child

Flow on, flow on thou waterfall
Through the darkest night till the seabirds call
Till the midday sun o'er your waters gleam
Thou lovely restless artist's dream

Rosaleen Caffrey

Remember?

The tan has gone,
Faded like the memories
Of the golden sands,
Children running on the beach,
Laughing, crying, looking for treats.
Crabs and shells to watch and play
Daily worries far away.
"What's that Boss. Where have we been?"
"O.K. I will attend to my machine!"

Alan Joseph Calvert

Autumn

When Mother Nature shakes her head,
The leaves fall gently down,
Like a cloak of crimson velvet,
Clinging to the ground.

Her face of untouched beauty,
Is magical to see,
Like a stainglass window,
Cascading through the trees.

With sunlight in her hair,
Of tints gold, and brown,
Her feet, rustling gently,
On leaves, fallen down.

The amber season begins to show,
Mother Nature takes her rest,
Of all the seasons that I know,
Autumn is the best.

June Cameron

Moment in Time

Quietly, in the pause 'twixt dark and day,
When dusk softens outlines and thought,
Words come tumbling softly
Stirring from the heart where caught.

So too, you in your deep sorrow
Come seeking the peace you need.
Struggling with confused emotions
On which bewilderment and sadness feed.

And across the darkening room
I scarced breathed, the mood to hold;
And wondered, had I reached to touch you
... Would I have breached an unspoken code.

Alice J. Campbell

Autumn

The wind is blowing all around
Leaves are falling on the ground
Autumn is the time of year
Pretty soon Jack Frost will be here.

Bonfire Night and Hallowe'en
Plenty of children to be seen
Kids on corners with guys in prams
Penny for the Guy I hear them cry.

Before Christmas arrives there's one more thing.
Remembrance Sunday
It's no fun day
A time for remembering the soldiers who were lost.
So wear your red poppy and don't count the cost.

Mrs. A. Carroll

Autumn

Now flowers are bowing out
Centre stage is taken by trees
And on the cue of autumn
Dance their lovely strip tease.

Beautiful leafy costumes
Begin floating to the ground
In colours of palest yellow
Through all shades red to brown.

The sun in charge of lighting
Swathes the trees in gold
While tossing their leafy garments
So enchantingly wanton and bold.

And now the grand finale
Trees appear naked and stark
But no, they wear body stockings
Of opaque but beautiful bark.

Amelia Canning

Escape

She's leaving tomorrow, finally
He's full of sorrow — pity
He should have said sorry ages ago
Did he say sorry ... no.
Her dignity left on a runaway train,
But another arrived with a cargo of pain — for her to collect.

She could never forget,
He cheated and lied, her poor soul it cried.
Tormented and scarred, with the thorns of his roses.
Each Saturday night his guilt in full flight
Resulted in vases of roses,
Not velvety red, but withered and dead.
In her eyes anyway, they would be in a day.

She's had enough, suffered it tough
The alarms sounded in her head —
Depart now instead
Crying over the roses — fragrances extinct.
A tear falls on a petal
As this survivor blinks,
Looks around one last time — her fallen heart begins to climb.
Up from the depths of despair,
Slowly into the fragrant air
A slammed door — a new life
No more nicks from Despair's swift knife.

Lorraine Carey

From An Open Window

From an open window,
In my own front room,
I gaze out on a garden
Of flowers all in bloom..

I see majestic roses,
In shades of white and red;
And I see pink carnations,
That grow in the flower bed.

I see the lush green grass,
As I look across the lawn,
And see dainty water lilies
Gently float on garden pond.

I hear the wild birds singing,
In the branches of the trees,
I see beautiful butterflies,
And hear humming of the bees.

I see the clear blue sky,
And the sun shines bright above,
Yes from an open window,
I see all these things I love.
Yes from an open window,
I see all these things I love.

Anthony Vincent Carlin

Loss

I sit, silent as the silver moon,
Wrapped in my own caress; please come soon!
I close my eyes and visualize a place of equanimity,
A place where to you I am not an anonymity.
When the sun's warmth sinks out of sight,
Our profound love burns on bright.

A stranded shell, neglected by the sea,
Sings its son to you and me.
We dance, in harmony,
As the seaweed strangles our feet;
This summer downpour, oh what a treat!
The warm scented rain (sweet on my lips) makes my eyes glisten.
Your spiced cologne enhanced by the rain. I listen.
I hear the heaving weaves, and the sound, which I was later to discover,
Was the beautiful sound of simply being your lover.

I open my eyes. The reality is just too much to bear,
Melancholy pervades my dreams, haunted by memories of despair.
A rose your only token of love, mine an eternal pain,
Of a love that's so profane.

Anxiety, confusion, anticipation and grief
My friends, my work — no happiness, no relief.
A heart that's shattered, and trapped and bound. A heart to mend,
As the city dawn breaks, my nightmare begins, and never will it cease to end.

Beth Cartwright

Untitled

I've grown old and my steps are slow,
Now I'm pushed to and fro,
"Go here dear, sit down there,
Wait until I've time to spare."

Yet had you seen me years ago,
With my dark brown hair all aglow,
The spring in my step the envy of all,
How proud I was, how I stood tall.

Please, don't look at me that way
As if I'd always been like today
It's not so, I was young like you
Living and working the whole day through.

.So think before you turn your head
At this frail old body in the hospital bed
Please hold my hand and tell me you care
Understand, it's so hard to bear.

Stay a while dear and just be near
And take away this loneliness fear
Then when I go to the place unknown
I'll know I shall not have been on my own.

Lilian Chandler

Consequences Of A Small Indiscretion

Nothing could calm what she suffered form,
Finding no words that meant anything,
Deprived sensuality from an unfaithful man,
A desire for contact and understanding,
Her mind sour with disgust,
Infuriated out of all proportion,
The glower, the non-communication, the two,
Singling out criticisms and injustice,
Each inclined to despise the other,
Committed to passionate love, yet hatred,
A tremor of pure agony,
An extremity of feeling,
Sparking at each other in screaming protest,
Her words cutting but brutally true,
Waves of violence fed a reckless vengeance,
His wicked shame was primitive,
Never had she felt so afraid,
Non perception of her true feelings,
Arrogantly determined, a tear on his cheek,
The conviction went out of his eyes,
He gave her a long slow look,
Then silence — "just like old times",
The tension relieved by an engulfing sigh,
What now? Forgiveness? Trust? A relationship?

Sarah J. Carter

God's Garden

Bluebell, buttercup, daisy and foxglove,
Just a few of the flowers I love,
Tulip, daffodil, rose and anemone
Their beauty and colour, in my memory,
Round petals, big petals, tight little buds
Frilly and frothy, like soapy suds,
All shapes and sizes, big and small
They are just perfect, one and all.

Oh, what a pleasure it would be
To sit, now and forever under a tree,
Looking around at the wonderful spread
Of God's miraculous flower bed.

Fluffy white blossoms like winter snow
Flying off to where, we do not know,
Dancing and wheeling, and soaring away
In the blue sky of a hot summer day,
Bright green grass and leaves on a tree,
All so innocent, pure and free,
Bulrushes and reeds in a sparkling stream
Caught in a warm, dazzling sunbeam.

Oh what a pleasure it would be
To sit, now and forever under a tree,
Looking around at the wonderful spread
Of God's miraculous flower bed.

Laura Carlisle

The Bright Side

"Unlucky in love, lucky in cards"
That's what the professionals say.
Up to this point I haven't played cards,
But I'll now take it up straight away.
I could pull all four aces
Straight out of the pack,
Be dealt a high straight,
Ace, ten, king, queen, jack.
I'd laugh in pontoon,
Twenty-one would be mine,
Say 'snap' straight away
At the appropriate time.
The casinos would ban me,
I'd break all their banks.
I'd give cash away,
And receive tons of thanks.
But I hope I'd start losing
Because that would mean
That love's luck was changing:
Someone new on the scene.

Tim Caroe

Thoughts

In my memory things locked away
Playing the piano all the day
In my system many things not said
All on my own tears not shed

I feel affection even rejection
In floods of my mind many thoughts I find
Dreams I once had failing to be
Thoughts and shadows of things that were me

I look out the window at things that I see
I take notice of things that surround me
The seas all around drowned in sorrow
But I seek happiness for the days tomorrow

Happiness and love I have found
Instead of clouds I see sunshine around
Thoughts that I've had always been spare
All that I see are people that care
At breaking point of glory I see
But still in my mind I see only me.

Jane Carpenter

The Mirror

Time passes slowly, and I feel the cold,
My bones are sore for I'm getting old.
I look in the mirror and what do I see,
This funny old woman looking at me.

But also in the mirror a picture I see,
Of a laughing young girl, that once was me.
I see fair hair with a brilliant shine
And lovely white teeth, that were all mine.

I see a slim figure and cheeks like silk.
A girl full of vigour, with a lively wit.
I see bright eyes that are filled with hope,
And trust in the future, ready to cope.

I can see all this clearly, though my eyes are dim
I did my best, determined to win.
All life's little battles, the ups and the downs,
And to meet each day without any frowns.

As I gaze in the mirror, the picture has gone,
And I'm back in the present, feeling forlorn.
But just for a second, as life's been fair
And I'm glad there's a little of that girl still there.

Kathleen Carney

Winter Sleeping Woodland

Sombre leafless boughs outlined skeleton shaping
Open viewed skyward, spaces, winter's gaze reveal
Recuperating silent woodland, midst varied weather, defences seal
Silent sentinels, woodland trees, ground surround fallen leaves draping
Remnants of summer past, greenery coat shed, underfoot carpet feel
Contrast be provided, green holly trees, fir trees, woodland bareness breaking
Plants mostly sleeping, grasses intervene, ferns spacing reveal
Some woodland life present, birds, insects, rabbits scuttering
Winter's slumber drags on, pale sunshine, snow or ice, rain darkness sunrise
Seeming times pass every slowly, dimly viewed awakening greet
Slowly daylight grows stronger, birds seem lively, Springtime sense
Wondering anticipation may beguile, impatience expecting return foliage green
Depending nature's variance unfold whether kind or otherwise
All of sleeping woodland, eventual display green foliage, beauty sheen

F.J. Carradus

"Meridian"

A necklace of stars
lights up the night sky,
Jewels of perfection
on black velvet lie.

Pale shafts of moonlight
oblique silver strands,
probing the darkness
that covers the land.

The fox, he is rampant
yellow green eyes,
searching for victims
mids't unearthly cries.

The hoot of the owl,
the screech of wild cat
competing with reynard
and radar of bat.

Mysterious nightfall,
a pattern in time,
dreamtime of mortals
somnolent, sublime.

Patricia Campbell-Lyons

The Old Town of Warsaw

During the occupation Poles put up a gallant fight
doing everything they could to thwart the German might.
They often crawled through sewers to escape the German guns,
urged on by their desire to defeat the brutal huns.
During those heroic battles, guns and tanks roared out,
and when those fights were over, there was devastation all about.
The bombing and the shelling had razed the Old Town to the ground
so ancient plans and drawings were searched for, and were found.
The old Town was to be rebuilt in the same old-fashioned way,
and work was started on it without too much delay.
Many Polish people gave up their leisure days
working on the project without any thought of pay.
The old, the young, and in-betweens, worked solidly side-by-side
creating a "memorial" to all the Poles who'd died.
It took many hard and weary years to rebuild it all anew,
now it's seen by all the world that dreams really do come true.
For out of death and devastation from all those dreadful fights
has emerged from total darkness a wondrous moving sight.
Now every day many people come to roam through cobbled streets
and look around with awe and joy at this amazing feat.
They realize that this Old Town is the symbol of a nation
Who, despite all odds, they rose again through total dedication.
From high upon his column Kin Zygmunt lovingly looks down
for once again he's very proud of his beautiful Old Town.

Mrs. J.E.H. Caxton

Under The Glow

Movement in shadows
I stare, in the glow
Of the sodium lamp
Into a time long ago
Here in this street
Where love was first shown
Are memories of people
Are memories in stone
Here on this pavement
With my heart in my head
Echoes of time
Resurrecting the dead.

So here I step
Into a time, long ago
Chasing the shadows
In the sodium glow
Here are my memories
In the amber of night
Ghosts of the past
Living in life
Here on this pavement
Under the glow
I haunt the steps
Of a child's life, long ago.

Mrs. D.C.S. Childs

The Drowning Woman

Her eyes are heavy from unshed tears, the recollection of those lonely years,
The memories that taunted her into dying, no more brooding, no more crying.

Her breath, a white flame on the cold night air
She lingered on the edge; would she dare?
To die in peace, as life's unfair.
Her bated breath; the smell of death
She hesitated; her life waited.

She jumped in with all her might
Her lungs filled with water; she tried to fight
She tried to shout, she tried to scream
It was all just like a horrible dream.

Then tiredness began to overcome her
No more panic left inside her
No more pain, no more shame
No-one else left to blame.

She finally lost her grip on life
No more trouble, no more strife
As the last bubbles of air escaped from those blood red lips
All you could see were her fingertips.

As the black veil of death descended upon her
And took her pitiful life away from her
No thought of God, no questions why
Nothing to live for, just the will to die.

No more hatred, no more sorrow, no more life, no more horror
Free of emotion, free of pain, no-one will hurt her ever again.

Scott Causer

Holidays

Happy families, donkey rides,
deck chairs, blue skies.
Ice creams, and golden sands,
the big green sea rolling by.
Cherry coke, sunny days,
and lovers holding hands.
Hotels, restaurants,
the nightclub scene.
Takeaways, taxis,
and savoury cuisine.
Big macs, and sailing ships,
shellfish stalls, novelty shops.
Postcards, and fish 'n' chips,
the amusement arcades,
children's rides.
Water slides,
crisps, candy bars, and lemonade.

A. Chapman

Untitled

She paints her pristine canvas
With a sure and practised ease
Each dab of paint and stroke of brush
So swift the eye deceives
Her colours used are not the ones
We would expect to see
Although the image looks like flowers
In those hues how can it be
She seldom sees her finished work
In its resplendent glory
Its finished off by someone else
But that's another story
She paints all day on bits of clay
Then sends them off to bake
They then, like butterflies, emerge
Exquisite cups and plates.

John Candler

Your Love's Immanence

In every summer, monsoon, winter and spring,
Your words in my ears always ring.
You taught me to fill life with thought and deed,
And helped me emerge victorious in every feat.
To struggle when life's adverse currents hold,
To smile at fate with courage bold.
To make my dreams their truths unfold,
To better my life these things you told.
To be successful in every feat in life,
You taught me how to strive and survive.
With your loving care and affection,
You helped my struggling self achieve perfection.
God's gift of life is simply great,
Which you made me always appreciate.
I poured my mind's harvest; its chaff and grain,
You sifted them., kept what's worth and blew away the remains.
Then as you walked out of my world,
The world around me twirled.
No matter how hard I try — I can't bring you back — can I?
You bid me forever good-bye and all I could do was sigh and cry!
I may forget all those I'll meet and have ever met,
But never you, for with you — I've wept.
With remembrance and affection ever thine —
I shall forever follow the footsteps you left behind on the sands of time.

Anita Chakravarty

Mercian Man

Imagine if you'd walked two hundred years ago,
Across the heaths of mercia that now you'd find it so,
For flinty-eyed steel masters and greedy mining men,
All flocked to make their fortunes then slipped away again,
They didn't want to live here amongst the filth they'd made,
They left men here to toil and sweat for the pittance they were paid,
Thousands of Irish peasants were brought to navigate,
The miles and miles of water ways to take the goods away
The belching smoke and feted air ensured a short lived span,
Victoria closed her curtains, shutting out the mercian man,
But other women not so nesh, took stand beside their men
They hammered brads and linked the chain and painted porcelain,
A land earned dignity descended upon the mercian man,
His crystal graced the tables of the highest in the land,
His chains held ships at anchor on every foreign shore,
His children gained the university and left the factory floor
Now as he sits in penthouse suite and breathes contented sighs
Just gently, faintly, on the wind does he here the curlews cries.

Pamela Cerrato

Wondering

What would you do,
If I wrote you a song,
That had no title or theme,
What would you do,
If I showed you a butterfly,
No other eyes had seen,
What would you do,
If I took you a walk,
Where no other feet had been,
What would you do,
If I told you a word,
No other could say or mean,
Because I'd like to write a song,
But there is no music there,
I'd like to catch a butterfly,
But the best are slightly rare,
I'd like to take you walking,
Can't think of anywhere,
I' like to create a beautiful word,
That says how much I care.

Kate-anna Clark-Smith (Age 14)

Perchance

Perchance there'll be another spring for me
    To laze and gaze 'neath the greenwood tree,
To hear the lark as he takes to wing
    His ode of joy on the return of spring.

Could this dark earth new birth release somehow
    Would blossoms sway from the hedgerow bough
Ah' - as the year unfolds will days seem to linger
    Will blackbird and thrush in greenwood sing stronger,
And nightowl's cry twhit - twhoo-O-O longer,
    When bright eyed redbreast - as always his will
Returns each dawn to the casement sill,
    And sunshine in splendour embraces fair earth
When this is so 'tis then I'll know -
    There was another spring for me.

Mrs. S. Carter

You Are A Good Boy

Close the door and run into the dark
The streets shining in the pavement's wetted face
The raindrops on my lashes look like stars
Flash Gordon's on a mission to base and then to Mars.
Just thumb the latch that's almost out of reach.
The bell rings, lovely smells a warm and friendly place.
"Come in lad, what's the want this late?"
"Sugar, Mrs. M., could you put it on the slate?"
"Aye and ere's a sweet, now see you run, don't stop."
Sugar under coat to keep it dry and go!
Count the lampposts, mind the dog, Hello Mrs. B.
Down the entry, across the yard and back inside for tea.
"You are a good boy, sit down, I've made jam tarts,
Wireless is on, I've made some tea,
Your programme's 'bout to start."

Michelle Carlton

Yesteryear

Over the threshold - stand there a moment,
See all the things I remember so well.
Memorabilia, cherished reminders,
Memories poignant, with stories to tell.

Flames upwards flickering, yellow and orange,
Exciting the shadows that dance on the wall.
Stories at bedtime of castles and kingdoms,
Fairy princesses. How well I recall.

Grandfather clock in its place by the doorway,
Solid, reliable, comforting sight.
Sounds of its ticking and hourly chiming
Quelled childish fears in the dead of the night.

Cat on the hearth rug, placidly purring,
Just like the one sat on grandmother's knee.
She'd smile as she knitted and told of her childhood,
Days of enchantment, happy and free.

Grandfather's chair by the side of the ingle.
Long gone the evenings when once he sat there.
Sometimes I think that I see the chair rocking
And smell his tobacco smoke still in the air.

Gone are those halcyon days of my childhood,
Gone, too, the old folk of yesterday's time.
Cherish my memories, fanciful dreamings,
Now that I'm long past the days of my prime.

Tony Channon

My Mother

Who fed me from her gentle breast,
    Then lay me gently down to rest,
    And on my cheek sweet kisses pressed?
    My mother

Who was it watched my infant head,
    Whilst sleeping on my cradle bed
    Did tears of sweet affection shed?
    Dear mother.

When pain and sickness made me cry
    Who gazed upon my heavy eye
    And wept for fear that I should die?
    Sweet mother.

Who was it taught my lips to pray
    And love God's Holy Book each day
    And walked in wisdom's pleasant way?
    Good mother.

So when I see thee hang thy head,
    T'will be my turn to watch thy bed
    And tears of sweet affection shed
    My mother.

When thou art feeble, old and grey,
    My healthy arm shall be thy stay
    And I shall soothe thy pain away
    My mother.

R.J. Chapman

The River Trent

I appear a placid river but alas that is not so
I'm a fast flowing lady not caring where I go.
I worry little when I flood, o'er hamlet field or lane.
Through countless years I've changed my course and altered yet again.

I'm a river of importance as through the land I flow
With many hidden dangers tho' those I do not show.
Many folk have tried to take me even tried to check my force
Their lives I've taken, for I'm strong and never show remorse.

I started life in Staffordshire as just a little rill,
I meandered on through Derbyshire just growing wider still.
I then arrive in Nottingham, this is a city grand,
Where Robin Hood once plundered and in Sherwood took his stand
There's a beautiful embankment here where people stroll at leisure
And watch the oarsmen in their boats now past with utmost pleasure
I flow beneath that famous bridge away past Colwick Park,
And into fairest Lincolnshire by daylight and by dark
I wander on through villages bearing barges without number
But then alas my life is o'er for I have reached the Humber.

Vera Coleman

Merry Christmas

It is a right war, a courageous war and a just war,
Arjun, why do you lament
    for those people who are trivial
       and pawns in God's plan.
Truth is often a curious planet
    Whose sublimity takes sometimes
       curious falsehood
Never, never be afraid to defend justice.

Whether it is Jesus or
    Ramakrishna or Muhammad
It is the same truth in different religion.

All dykes have one tendency
    to flow into rivulets
All rivulets have one direction —
    to submerge into sea
All seas know where to characteristically finish
    — but to become one ocean
It is one, always one, one only
    and nothing but one,
    in God's plan of life.

Monoj K. Chaudhuri

A Hope for Ireland

From Rathlin's lone isle to deep Bantry Bay,
From fine Dublin City — west to Galway,
This island, this Ireland so green and so fair,
But look very closely — What else see you there?

Dark ages of famine, torture and greed,
Evil for evil so fully repaid.
Bombs at the ready, set to explode,
Then in a second, more blood on the road.

Fire, turning fine buildings into a shell
Making a city into a hell.
So much to forgive — so much to forget,
The killing and maiming go on — but yet —

Not forever shall evil hold sway,
Peace edges nearer — so we all pray.
My hopes for you Ireland, in this coming year,
An end to the hatred, sadness and fear.

Accept that men differently worship their Lord,
Cast a new ploughshare from every sword.
Then Ireland, from terror at last will be free
As sure as the Shannon flows down to the sea.

Denis Cheason

Down By The Beach

The place is Old Laxey, it's humble and quaint
Little white wash cottages and plenty of paint.
With Shore Road, and Tent Road, and Pig Street why yes?
The pretty little gardens all looking their best.
Some with rockeries, made with stones form the shore,
And others with roses hanging over the door.
Friendly Manx people their neighbours adorning,
With a smile, and a welcome, and a cheerful, "Good Morning"
And the harbour so lovely, to some it may seem
A thing of the past and visitors dream.
Fishing boats, pleasure craft, some big, some small,
Anchored in the harbour, or moored by the wall.
With the Cairn in its glory, a rich golden brown,
Its bright purple heather in profusion abounds.
Or out by the breakwater the tide comes in swishing,
A spot where the lads spend many hours fishing.
Visitors love it, they come back for more
It's a nice sandy beach 'neath a stony old shore.
A wonderful picture of children at play,
And tall yachts with sails skimming over the bay.
There's a nice little Cafe, if you're wanting eats,
Pop and ice cream, and all kinds of sweets.
So for somewhere to go by bus, car or taxi,
There's no better place than that beach down at Laxey.

J.R.M. Clague

A Poem Of Love

I love you for your thoughtfulness,
Your kindliness and care,
And it's because my love for you
My life with you I'll share.
You mean so very much to me
I need you more each day,
In times of sadness
You appear
And drive dull cares away.
Oh! How I'm waiting for that day,
That precious happy day
When at the altar
My hand you'll hold
Slip on my finger
A band of gold
Then my life
Will be sublime
And I will know
You're really mine
Forever.

Mrs. V.G.M. Chapman

The Living Heart Of Nature

Dawn, the heart of nature begins to show, mystic majestic a
show second to none, nature's jewels in various colours there
to see, for flowers of red don't bleed and of this man should
take heed.

The living heart of nature does not beat for war, peace is
felt in a garden with charm for God in his wisdom created a
garden called Eden hoping it's beauty and tranquility would
linger for all species to see, a place where all living things
could be free.

However happiness is such a transient thing, like the tide that
is ebbing and flowing, the fates spinning webs to snare the
unwary and that is why in 1995 we have a planet so scary.

God controls the elements, gives the seasons with reasons for
man to observe, nature's soul draped with colour, monuments in
the ages that live and die but nothing can match nature how hard
it does try.

God wants to see his Earth ruled by love, no hating, no baiting,
no fighting, no killings, for young and old to appreciate his
creation a wonderful gift to all nations.

So let the living heart beat with hope, let species under threat
not be neglected, the dream of warmer pleasures to come can be
achieved with respect for what was given and to see it slowly
being put under threat, a lot on Earth with no regrets.

Fred Spencer Chesworth

Unspoken Words

If only I could speak to you
To release my stifled thought
And reaffirm my love for you
That to express I now cannot.

No more my usual interjections,
Nor more my points of view.
I now must sit in quite reflection
And sadly smile on cue.

To late to murmur gentle words
That in the past were spoken.
The situation seems absurd —
My voice has truly broken.

I listen to your conversation
While my aching heart just pounds;
Are you aware of my frustration?
Can you hear my silent sound?

Be patient with me when I'm low,
Be there when I most need you,
Hold me closely then to show
Your love will guide me through.

If all of you can give support
And never let it wane,
I'll understand it will purport
That my living's not in vain.

Barbara M. Cherrie

The Beautiful Countryside

I stood on a hill and looked around at the wonderful, wonderful view,
Fields of corn waving in the breeze, creating a golden hue.
Bright red poppies amongst the gold, a different green to every tree,
And there on the skyline a glowing red sunset in all its majesty.
Then hovering, hovering in the air, a kestrel caught my eye.
All of a sudden he swept down to earth giving a strange, unusual cry.
Around my feet wild flowers abound, yellow, white and blue,
Daisies, tares and buttercups, and even scabious too.
Mother Nature caught me in her spell, and I stood as if in a dream.
Transfixed by the wonders of this earth revealed in this rural scene.
This is my home, here I abide and give thanks to God for the beautiful countryside.

Joy Chinnery

Dark Side

Moonlight masking mysteries,
Murders, mayhem and tragedies.
Lurking under its misty air,
Feel the lull of its despair.
Skyline beams stretch afar,
Clothing for a naked star.
Whispering willows crackle in the dim,
Disguised as dreamers deep within.
Sleepy light trickles down,
Demolishing darkness, the evil clown.

Kathleen Clarke

Ten Seconds
(On visiting the National Gallery)

Enough yes, yes, we've seen this one:
Focus, click, flash, move on

Where now? We've only time for some:
Focus, click, flash, move on

Wish they'd group the famous ones:
Focus, click, flash, move on

A postcard set and now we're done:
Focus, click, flash, move on

Emma C. Clarke

Innocent Love

The love of a child is a precious thing,
To our lives such joy they bring.
Two innocent eyes shining bright,
Two little arms to squeeze you tight.
A sticky face for you to kiss,
Could anyone want more that this.
A trusting look so free of guile,
A little imp who makes you smile.
As you sit with your child upon your knee,
Remember the best things in life are free.
The only thing for which they yearn
Is that you love them in return.

June Clark

Untitled

The gardens green and
Slender beauty.
A stately order all around,
Bring to me a wholesome wonder.
A luscious spring is here again
Living bouquet of great wonder.
Chase away the winter grays.
All around me lie the wonders
Of the glorious sweet spring days.
Boughs of blossom wake at morning.
Raise their heads behold the sun.
Looking down on God's great wonder.
For by Him all this is done.

Lynn Clarke

Thee And Thou

Stranger by far
Is what you are.
Your body and mind,
I'm sure you'll find
Are joined together
Whatever ...

Frank Cooper

Devil's Bones

As I sit here at my desk
The sun streams in at its best
It's 8:15, a Monday morn
I've dropped off our students from Boulogne

What will today, the work for me
Not a lot I fear it be
My job designing here seems grim
The work load now looks very slim

The Company I fear has lost its way
Production down, as profits sway
My interest is fading fast, not enough
To fill my glass

As we trim down I could be next
Redundant, joining the industrial scrap
The sickness that hits us here
Is just the same in every sphere
The Government strategy of Devil may care
Like a cancer strikes industry unaware.

George Clark

Mathematical Nightmare

Buried by falling numbers.
Volcanoes spewing up hot molten units,
Shards of seven, fiery fives, tons of tens
and trembling twos, hanging in the breathless air.
Swathed in a heavy blanket of fluffy fours
threatening threes.
I sink slowly down
into the churning suffocation mass,
trying to make some sense but can't quite grasp
What it all means.
If ...
If only I could join them, link them in such a way
that they could pose no threat.
Then real them in,
diminish and subjugate them. Climb up and over
into a clean,
cool and light
number free existence.

Hazel Clark

The Sweet Sound Of Summer

I see the bird, on the ground.
No longer to hear his sweet sound.
His time has come
Dead he lies, few remember him.

What did you do?
What was your crime?
You have died, before your time,
So many songs still to be sung.

This day has just begun,
But no song did you sing.
No longer do you cry for the sun,
You didn't wait to see the joy it might bring.

You have taken the knowledge,
You found out the truth,
You found it all too soon.
The price for wisdom — Death.

Your corpse lies
Food for the flies,
Your fire has burnt out
Too brightly you shone.

The sweet sound of summer has left,
My mortality, reflected in your death.

Keith Church

The Brief Romance

Day one, he brought me roses,
Petals from the heart he cried,
Yet he did not know me.

Day two, he brought me chocolates,
I am the sweetness in his life he sighed,
Yet he did not see me.

He walked and talked with me by his side,
His speech directed at himself,
He whispered that I was the apple of his life,
Yet seconds took hours to pass.

His vanity and self-indulgence simmered me out,
I felt not worthy of this man,
The loyalty and faith he felt for himself,
Like only a man really can.

Day three, he spoke of romances dead,
The past, maybe present, buried in his head,
I illuminated briefly for this display of hurt,
But acting is easy when morals turn to dirt.

Day four was the end, I told him farewell,
He said it was a pity as he knew me so well,
I laughed and it struck him that never before
    had he seen me smile
When all was said and done,
    he only knew me a short while.

Jennifer Chorlton

Save Our Afrumasian Race In This Plunitarian Space

Some men of vision visualised a better world
Like Lincoln, Lenin, Gandhiji, Luther King & Hammerskjoeld
Others in this world sang hymns of hate
Opening the gates of hell for everyone's fate.

My plea to all is: Please sit up now and try to realise
What's going to happen to our God's enterprise?
Since fundamentalists are spreading Holy War Religions
As People Of The Book: Jews, Christians and Moslems.

Moses, Christ and Mohammed will be surprised to see
The blood spilt in their name in every county
Each faith perverted or preserved in only name
Dividing human race with hate, without a sense of shame.

This whole humbug brings to light the plight of universe
Shouldn't we learn something now or new before we disperse!
Why not start Caring-Sharing, uniting this creation
Be Hindu, Buddhist, Taoist, Shinto: Go for Re-Creation!

Come, let's now belong to a Plunitarian Space
Let 'Flowers Bloom and Thoughts Contend' our Afrumasian Race:
Red or Pink, Pale or Yellow, Black or Brown masses
Co-exist/Co-mingle/Cross-heart: Evolving Social Classes

Let's hope and pray all goes well by Nineteen Ninety-Nine
In Global Village, pollinate new flowers and plant a healthy vine
Even if past catches on, we can surely have a chance.
To Live, Love, Labor, Learn, Liberate, sing and dance.

Dharmendra P. Chotaniji

The Carton

It lay on the dew-drenched emerald grass
Where Erica Spilt o'er the verdant lea
A symbol of thoughtlessness — of an uncaring soul
Too steeped in bitterness idyllic beauty to see.
The children came, running, cheeks aglowing with sun;
Their pet pounced on the carton, as a prize he had won.
The arsonist watched, trembling, evil eyes afraid.
Lest the dog betray him — his plans thus waylaid.
He had found his father, hideous in death
Hanging in the barn, where life-long he'd toiled.
This sacred place was now used for pleasure
By folks who did not deserve this leisure.
Thoughts torturous and turbid and tinged with pity
For these happy tots from the polluted city,
Soon their respite from care for them be no more
And man's darkest nature they would know for sure.
That night the family returned to the city,
He watched his inferno — feeling no pity,
His friends bought him drinks in the pub that night;
But the carton betrayed him — no more would he fight.

Joan E. Clark

Thoughts

Millions of minds and millions of faces
Millions of thoughts in millions of places,
Some thoughts are good and some are bad,
Sin alone makes this life sad.

If all the thoughts in a million places
Could be good, then all the traces
Of wickedness here and wickedness there
Would change from sadness to sunrise gladness.

If all the thought could hold but love
If they trended their way around and above
What a difference we would find in our own small world
Actions so kind and goodness untold.

Millions of minds and millions of faces
Millions of thoughts in millions of places
Could all the thoughts be but the best
Then the Kingdom could come and ourselves be blest.

Mrs. G. Clarke

Those Were The Days

Black firegrate stands with bricks of red
Hot oven beside to bake your bread
Pole swings out with boiling stew
Those were the days for me and you.

Big oak door, see the brass handle knock
The silent swing of the grandfather clock
Outside the seasons come and go
Never too fast, never too slow.

Big dray drawn by an old white mare
There's time to stop, there's time to share
Old man sits on an old worn log
Reaching out to his faithful dog.

Tin bath steams, tea in the pot
Children bath by a fire so hot
A bite of chess, a crust of bread
They say their prayers then off to bed.

Roving hills in a land so green
Never thinking of the future or the times there have been
Young lovers stare at the stars above
Those were the days that were filled with love.

Peter Clarke

Marooned

"I've got a pain, Mum in my head."
"Well, you'd better go to bed."
These words said, a vision soared,
Shut in a room, totally bored.
No books to read, no games to play
Stuck in an empty room all day.
Next morning I get up for school;
I dread getting up, but I know the rule:
The later I get out of bed
The later we can start to head
On our way to dreaded school.
Being late isn't so cool!
All dressed for school and ready to go,
Mum said to me, "Dear, you look so ...
How can I put this ... white as a sheet,
If hit by a feather, you'd fall of your feet"
"Mum, stop worrying, I'm O.K.,
I can go to school today."
So here I am, sitting at home,
Mum's gone out and I'm all alone.
Sitting here with nothing to do —
My vision of hell has now come true!

Aoife Clarke (Age 10)

Yesternight's Dream

Last night in a dream I met you in a new face
set somehow apart from the rest of the men
hidden repeatedly in covers and corners
in the untouched place. And
beside
between
all around them a single woman
acting several similar parts
through robes of red and blue and gold. And
In between —
Man
seated on your mushroom-stool
strumming golden strings
humming your meanings
by dancing golden earrings somehow old. And
aside amongst
this dream the bead-bearded Man
You — Bead-Blue
acting your part in single hue
trained thought of thoughts of mine
reminding me that somehow I am
a single woman too, 'though hidden
in this strangest space.

Fiona Jo Clark

Rural Lament

As hedges and the trees are stripped away,
The farmland sprawls across in dusty leas
Along the verge of that new motorway.

The butterflies might die as farmers spray
Their crops with toxic mists to halt disease,
As hedges and the trees are stripped away.

The flint-stone barns are falling in decay,
While barn owls move their homes like refugees
Along the verge of that new motorway.

The oil-seed rape's bright poison pollen may
Make oily combs entombing baby bees,
As hedges and the trees are stripped away.

The wild wings could survive the cull, to prey
The safe environment, and breed with ease
Along the verge of that new motorway.

But windmills' fettered sails are on 'display'
And prairie landscapes future artists tease,
As hedges and the trees are stripped away
Along the verge of that new motorway.

Pam Clarke

Mountain Grandeur

Solitary, silent I stand and stare into the still dark tarn
while all around mountains range far as the eye can see.
Above me, patiently erected in stone by stone the small rocky cairn
symbol of success to those whose feet erode the scree.

Grey smoky clouds edge nearer the mighty sun-lit peak
whose ancient rugged slopes attract a strange motley crew
come here to commune with nature when life seems most bleak.
Peace flows through tired minds as they watch the matchless view.

Mountaineers have climbed steep rocks developing new skills
shepherds have searched, listening for their lost sheep's plaintive cry,
and for centuries, men have tramped on these same ageless hills.
Poets, pedlars, travellers all walked this way in days gone by.

I climb on and become forever an infinitesimal part of this scene,
its beauty never to be forgotten, wound always into my very being.

Pat Clarke

Happiness Is A Daughter

You brought such happiness into our lives
So small so sweet a beautiful child
From a child to a woman we watched you grow
From the moment we saw you we loved you so
May you always be happy, your skies never grey,
May you be blessed with a daughter some day
For your caring and kindness we thank you so much
May we never be parted but always in touch
There is no greater treasure in all this world
Than you dear daughter, a wonderful girl.

Catherine Chesters

The Blind Man And The Daffodils

My gaze drifted away from the high banks of the
Roadway that boasted realms of golden trumpets,
Serene, methodical,
To a figure, striding furiously high above, across
A bridge, his reined companion prominent, leading.

And I studied the man,
Oblivious to the wealth that lay below him.

And I focused on the flowers, rampant, exuberant,
And somewhere deep inside, I cried.

N. Clarke

Young Love

My love is a quiet stream flowing,
covering endless ground between us both.
As our two hearts rush together, growing,
bubbling and gushing as we swear love's oath.
I dream of pure, endless and unspoiled love,
consisting of faith, trust, happiness, joy.
Flying to new heights like a peaceful dove,
finding pleasure like a new found toy.
As time passes, and days, months, years go by,
love's ardour wavers, streams dry, love does fade.
Love, faith, trust, happiness and hope all a lie,
a sad ending to the dreams I once made.
I'm drowning in the tormented ocean,
dying, poisoned from love's evil potion.

Carrie Clarke (Age 14)

Monochrome

A cold wind reaps the harvest of raindrops
Tossing them, winnowed on the window pane
And sends them patterning on the loom of glass
Then weaves a trickled fabric from the rain.
The air throws a blanket of toneless damp
And washes the sky with a wintry brush,
Picking out charcoal fragments of tree and bush.
A pencil line of trees stands dark
On a neutral hill of softly moulded grey.
Only the terra cotta roofs
Add muted colour to the toneless day.
The driving rain varnishes the trees
And paths reflect glossily each gate and fence.
Beyond the leaden pavilion the ungreen hills
March away in misty ambience.

Merle G. Clay

Church of Computer Mind

On looking through stained window of one big cross house
The visual display became a small brown mouse
Retrieval of past memory framed an image bright
A graphic of humanity that flickered fright.

With practised stealth the watcher deftly picked proud lock
And entered hopeful hallowed space of granite block
Experience of handling drove the keyboard might
Bounced notes upon oak rafters in a tumbled flight.

Then saw THE BOOK page up beneath a passive face
Without a pause hands lifted it head bent in grace
Examining its worded text 'neath silent clock
Read how Lord Jesus fought corrupt amongst his flock.

His disbelief a cursor that eye could not freeze
Relinquishing control of breath began to sneeze
Unable to suspend rogue though intent was known
He held that book page down as though the words had flown.

His brain began to function with the word falsehood
To check clear field he hid behind a screen of wood
Now cancelling intention holy tome reset
Sought quickly for escape before he faced kismet.

Robin Clayton

Ode To The Recession

This story, I tell, is a warning sent
To all out there, take heed!
Young, strong, virile men
These pages you must read.

There's something out there, I know not what
It creeps up in the night
And drains away a precious thing
Each time out goes the light.

At first you think it will never strike
It's aim's in a different direction
One day when the roll is called
Some are missing from inspection.

Gone, lost, without a trace
Those that once stood tall and stark
Covering each and every inch
Wave upon wave of treasure - dark.

All that is left is a tactical retreat
So I go with brush in hand
To carry on the battle
Gathering together a depleted band.

To guard my scalp from the world outside
It's uphill all the way
Hanging tight, to the bitter (split) end
Hold on in there! Come what may.

Allan Clarke

A Summers Day

I will make you a mantle Mother
A mantle of perfect green
With shades of blue and vivid red
And yellow's golden sheen

I will make you a mantle Mother
Of perfect symmetry
Where royal trees bow down their heads
And greet your majesty

Cloudless sky stems gentle sway
Branches hide her nests
Final twigs are laid in place,
Her precious cargo rests

Purple bells ring out their tunes,
Gentle petals fall
Wings beat quickly across still air
And hurry to their call

All silence now as darkness draws
A veil around your face
Shadows hide your beauty
With scars that leave no trace

Your perfect mantle Mother
Lies deep into the night
We loan you for a moment
You own us as you might

Maureen Cleverdon

Shadows

You are not just the brightest star at night,
Or the bird that sings first in the early morn,
You are the whitest wave in the sea,
Rising above all others.
Many trees shed their leaves, but not you,
You stand an evergreen, and always will,
The rays of the sun become you, warming everyone in sight,
Or the lighthouse that shows people the way through troubled times,
You are the path through the green pasture,
Amidst the flowers that sway in the breeze,
Your colour and fragrance are present and ever near.
When looking in the eyes of a hungry child, I see you,
Frightened, but always hoping.
Through the rain and snow I see you,
Somehow, I feel warmth again.
Soldiers march to war, their courage reminds me of you,
Their medals, your bravery.
Owls swoop from the sky to catch their prey,
The wind beneath their wings is your strength,
I feel your presence, you are always with me,
Memories stay ever near,
I search for you in my reflection, only a mirrored image stares back.
I promised myself that if I look hard enough,
I will find you ... one day.

Sandie Clough

Beneath My Feet

Little insect oh so small
Beneath my feet I see you crawl
In a world of your own
Born between earth and stone
Where raging seas and rivers deep
Are mere pools beneath my feet
If only I were not so tall
Little insect oh so small.

Each blade of grass and buttercup
Bending in the breeze
May give you shelter as you sleep
As do the fallen leaves
What wonders lay beneath the tree
That only you so small can see
If only I was half you size
What would I see with my two eyes.

But as I look toward the sky
And feel each raindrop fall
Just like you my little friend
I'm really not that tall
Though I know not of your world
And you know not of mine
Between this earth and distant star
Are many more divine.

W. Clarke

The Volunteer

So eager was the fine young man
Who blithely went to war.
"Keep smiling," was his cheerful cry,
"Til the lights go on once more."

"This fight," his sergeant-major said,
With a wicked kind of grin,
"Is just a kind of game, my lad,
Which we have got to win."

It's doubtful if the soldier knew
What he was fighting for
As he played his patriotic part
Through six long years of war.

From that grim carnage, back he came,
To the peace that he left behind,
With scenes of stark reality
Impressed upon his mind.

"Yes, war is like a game, my lad,"
A wise old man had said.
"A sinful and expensive game,
Get that into your head.
When a thousand towns are blown apart,
And a million heroes fall,
There are no winners, lad, in war,
Just losers - losers all."

Sam Clayton

Beyond Words

To know you, is to love you
to love you is to find.
That perfect love, I always thought,
my soul had left behind.

To see you, is to want you,
to want to hold your hand.
To walk with you forever,
in this or any land.

To kiss you, is to touch you,
to touch you deep within.
For in that place, is where love is,
and where love, should begin.

To talk with you, is to say,
how much you mean to me.
Beyond the place where words can reach
Is where I long to be.

Brian Cleaver

For Daniel

I want him to be clever, yet laugh like a fool,
To be easy-going but nobody's tool.
I want him to love and be not hurt,
To gamble without losing his shirt.
I want him to forge ahead and not become lost,
To stand and listen, not to be bossed.
I want him to have plenty and give some away,
To know the cool of night and heat of the day.
I want people to like him for what he might be and not own
To stand in a crowd without being alone.
I want him to sway to sense as trees in a breeze,
To hold out yet not brought to his knees.
I want him to deal and sometimes be caught,
To sell himself and not be bought.
I want him to be fair, gentle, loving and kind,
Knowing who or what to leave behind.
I want him to think of me as father and friend,
I want him to want me 'till my very end.

A. P. Clements

Lies

I sat all alone on my seat.
A puddle grew around my feet,
The puddle was tears, I was crying.
I was crying because I'd been lying
The lies had been to Mum and Dad
Now I knew I had been bad
Should I tell them it was me
Who chopped down their favourite tree
Should I tell them the real truth
Who set fire to the garage roof
Do you think they'd forgive me
If I told it was my bee
Would they even let me live
If I told them who put glue in the sieve
Or should I say it was the dog
Who poured ice on the Christmas log.
I told them once it was the cat
Who stuck chewing gum on the mat
My Mum went in a deadly faint
When I said walls were covered in paint
I never blame it on myself
I even once blamed it on a shelf
But even if I told the truth
They wouldn't believe me ANYWAY.

Louisa Clarkson

A Halcyon Heritage - Thank You

You were the pirate king
I sailed my cardboard ship Jolly Roger,
Head on the safety of serge waistcoat,
The woodbines, the runner beans, your trilby just so.

Wisdom in your Irish eyes, smiling.
How could such beauty toil in darkness.
You thought Marx was a comic,
But your children still dream of you.

Ageless in the minds eye, trapped.
Memories caught in time that odours often restore,
Shillelagh waving angel whistling Flanagan and Allan.
Run rabbit run, run to heaven.

Sunshine on young shoulders,
Don't worry, I refuse to let quality fade.
The day when dragonfly threatened,
And you showed him Doc Martin.

"Where's Grampy?' I screamed,
There was no answer, no more Gaelic Jigs.
I searched under the bed for you, you know,
But the rabbit had run.

Richard Allan Clatworthy

Burma Railway

He came home at last
His fighting had been done
His mind and body crippled
Slaving years in swamp and sun.
The railway needed building
Regardless of the cost,
Speedo, Speedo, was the command
Watch out for bayonet thrusts.
Where is this God he wondered
As he watched his comrades die
In squalor and in misery
And wished his time was nigh.
But a little spark of something
Remained within his soul,
That's how he made the headlines
Dead soldier returns home.

(Dedicated to Tom)
Marjorie Clough

Buxton

Buxton with its peaks and splendid view,
Lovely colours that blend to a delightful hue,
And sky in the background looking so blue.
Wending its way, the river flowing through,
Each tree that bends down over you,
This picturesque picture, and morning dew.
Your townsfolk hustling by; some old, some new.
Oh! Beautiful Buxton with gorgeous view.

Lynne Charlton

Away

Would you pluck out my eyes and ask me to bleed?
Would you hand me a book then ask me to read?
Never so vicious has anyone been,
So where does it come from, why am I mean?
I did it to you so what do you think
Do you hate like I do, does your heart sink?
The difference here, between you and I
I never asked permission, yet why do I cry?
Your face was never looked upon, so why does it hurt?
Making no sense like swallowing dirt.
Anger well up and flows inside
All this pain just for a ride.
Something so precious caused so simply
I took it away, I cannot reply.

Jenny Collins

A Better World

Within the world of pain and ills
Of medicine and different pills
The mind is foggy and forlorn
I find no rose only the thorn
The mists of pain and misery
Make it very hard to see.

Though at times I cannot cope
What use is there to cry or mope
For when the body starts to heal
Another world itself reveals
Like curtains being drawn aside
At last I see the world outside.

No longer do I have to fight
Once more in roses I delight
I'll smell the rose, forget the thorn,
Life makes me glad that I was born.

Mrs. B. Charles

Ten Floors 'Till Destruction

With ten floors below
It's too late to say no
Death is before me
With nine floors to go,

Memories flash suddenly
With eight floors ahead
No worries, no problems
In seven floors I'll be dead,

Six floors in the future
My pain will be gone
Five floors to go
I'll not see a new dawn,

Approaching four floors
Until I smash off the ground
My tears will be dry
When the third floor comes around,

Two floors from destiny
For forgiveness I prayed
The spirit world awaits me
One floor 'till my blood is sprayed,

No floors left to fall
And I've wasted my life
I let reality beat me
Another victim of strife.

Vance A. Carson

Letters

Write me letters. (You say). Your letters are beautiful. I can show them to anyone.
Of course I don't, you add hastily. I know they are intimate.
But they are letters of which I can be proud. Letters are allowed.

You drift off into an embarrassed silence.

Letters are allowed I say angrily to myself, wondering what else your husband
Allows and disallows.

But I do not stop writing.

I write you letters. Send them urgent. Special delivery. An extra two dollars.
To show importance. Wing emotion. Make my mark.

Fill a void.

Your morning mail comes heavily stamped with my feelings. (Can he tell? Does he read them?)
While you a void, showing yours.

Here there is no one but me to read the male. For by now I am more obsessed with him than you.
Your letters to me have become his letters to me. He, it seems, makes allowances. (Letters are allowed)
What else will he allow? I scratch danger with my pen nib.

Letters are allowed. Letters reach the edge. But they cannot topple your heart into warm pits.
Warm and waiting. Lazily you still send your mail second class.

Letters are allowed. They cannot spill this wet and jerky wanting.
My fingers parting your wetness leave no trace across the typed page.

Strange. Because the keys are still moist ...

Sally Cline

Thoughts In The Night

I'm sitting here in the middle of the night,
And I just don't know what to write,
I was hoping that I would be inspired
But no, oh no. I'm just so tired,
I won't give up though, oh no not me.
I'm determined to write some poetry,
I really want to enter this competition.
So come on brain, turn on the ignition.
I thought of a poem of what is life?
But all that is too much trouble and strife.
And then I thought, what about the seasons?
But then there's no rhyme and no reasons.
Then it came to me what about birth?
But I'm too tired for all that mirth.
What about time on the Grandfather clock?
But no! I'm so tired listening to its tick tock.
It's ever so quiet, and ever so late.
I'm gonna be up all night at this rate.
Everyone's in bed, not a sound is made.
They're fast asleep, in bed they're laid.
Oh no, just listen, the dog is snoring.
He's driving me mad, the sound is soaring.
I think it's time to say goodnight.
And tomorrow I know, a poem I'll write.

Denise Clitheroe

Missing

Whilst in your perspex cage did you despair
When nought save nature sought for your release
And your redundant husk ungrateful, shed it's flaccid cloak
Exposing in a rude relief you calcic core.
Did you, your only move a wish, appeal
When that shroud of gentle green first screened
Your empty eyes from liquid gold
And humid air dissolved your proud won wings.
How often did the wind in gentle drone or rasping roar
Convince you that your broken bird had lifted free.
Had you once raised your gaze from that inert display
You would have seen in burlesque strip, each day
Reveal the skeleton of your bird, till truly nude
Its form, like yours, laid gaunt and bare.

To the world a form of peace returned
And those who lived could sluice their minds
Of hideous record and forget.
For you, forever to explore, the myriad tendrils of thought
Each certain in its trammelled path,
Always the question posed,
Had your demise so far from home
Ransomed a better world.

Ray Cliffe

Two Enchanting Girls

Solipsism and Serendipity,
Blonde and auburn, oh so pretty,
Lazed on the gate of eternity,
Swaying gold and amber limbs casually.

Up and down, to and fro,
Syncopated feet of toes
Dimpled ocean; ripples rose,
Droplets, eddies, heavens' flow.

Carefree thought their faces shone;
They kissed tenderly, their labours done.
To Solip reflected Serendipity,
"Isn't it lucky that you thought of me!"

Ali Cohen

Friendship

Isn't it lovely to have a friend,
To turn to when in despair,
A friend who will always listen,
A friend who is always there.
A friend who knows when to stay silent,
Or to offer you advice
A friend who will always love you,
A friend who's a friend for life.
'Tis the someone to live fore,
Someone to love,
That the purpose of life depends,
And there's nothing to equal the gladness and joy,
Of making and keeping friends.

Hilda Coe

A Secret Recipe

A secret recipe I have found,
It cost no money not even a pound,
A little laughter to brighten the day,
A word of encouragement to help others on their way,
A little prayer for guidance from above,
A little patience, thought and love,
A word of wisdom to share,
A mind for understanding and care,
A heart for forgiving a yearning for peace,
A voice to heal sorrow and help troubles cease,
A helping hand to freely give,
A contented home for all to live.
If I all these ingredients behold,
There would be little worry for body and soul.

Patricia Campbell

The Hereditary Factor

He checks it from different angles
in different shades of light,
it's got to be just accurate
it's got to be just right.

He scrapes it this way ...
pats it down
moistens it a little,
can't be really rough with it
don't you know it's brittle?

He weaves it neatly into place
careful not to leave a gap
he won't consider disguising it
under any form of cap.

But what he doesn't realise is
I love him all the same,
receding hairline
thatched top lid
or carefully woven mane.

Janice Cluney

White Knight

Out of the light you came,
Saving me from the darkness of despair.
Took me to the garden, repaired my broken heart,
Gave me wings to fly again,
All of this and no reward you ask.

You see the flowers and give them to me,
Each one a gentle kiss.
Like a child I hide in the shadows
Afraid of my emotions
Slowly you take my hand
Leading me toward my own reflection

I must take today,
Hold on to the courage it gives me
There are no dark clouds to spoil the view
Only dark thoughts,
Open your heart and let love in,
Don't hold too tight, for love to grow it must be free.

If I should fall from grace,
Would you see me as you do now,
Or would the candle flicker and fade.
It is not time that scares me,
But of lost love and friendships I am afraid ...

Mrs. J. Coe

A Passing Cloud

I whispered to a cloud, as it was passing by,
Where are you going cloud? and this was his reply,
I am going around the world, I tarnish the sun,
I am as old as the sky, I have been here since time began,
What do you think about, as you roam around the skies,
I think about what I see, he said, between his puffs and sighs,
I travel far and wide, I glide across the sea,
I float across the ocean, I like to be free,
I wish I had wisdom to understand what I witness,
The people of the world, some healthy and some in sickness,
But I pass by slowly, like time I drift away,
Dawn turns to night and then again to day,
Thank you for talking to me cloud, I know you have to travel on,
I turned around to see him and in an instant he was gone.

Julie Collett

Exmoor

Tawny tiger
Summertime tame,
Haunchy minder
Of the scrawny lane,
Now in the sun
Sprawling kinder
Than when wintertime came.

All around,
Unfound,
There's a chuckling water sound,
A purr
In the heather prickled fur,
And, crinkled and creased
This powerful beast,
A bustle
Of intimidating muscle,
Blinks an august eye
In a summertime game,
Wary and wry.

G.G. Collinge

Through A Suffolk Window

When opening the window pane
Sweet air drifts in from country lane
Fields of rape in sunny hue
And meadows wet with morning dew
Delight the eye, refresh the mind
Spring has arrived — the Suffolk kind

Lilac scent lies in the air
The chestnuts hold their candles fair
And in the wide expanding sky
The swallow swoops, birds circle high
On summer wind and gentle breeze
Summer has come — with Suffolk ease

Rain laden clouds sail overhead
The sky is heavy, grey as lead
Buttercups and poppies red
Have lost their lustre, lost their head
East winds blow and trees bent low
Wear autumn tints — and Suffolk glows

With windows closed and houses warm
Bare branches upwards stretch their arms
Chimney pots with curling smoke
Nestle among the mighty oaks
And frost embroiders dense hedgerows
Winter arrived — with Suffolk snow

H. Cole

Auchinreoch

Oh Auchinreoch your stones are so old
The ash in the hearth has long felt the cold
From Falkirk black cattle have passed in the spring
Their hooves have wrought havoc with heather and ling
The collies who snapped at their heels on the road
Their offspring now lounge in their urban abode.

The curlews song fluting in spring you have heard
The moor round your borders the peewits have shared
The people who lived in your austere surrounds
Their children now play with computers and sounds.

Gone are the days when a drink at your spring
Of water so clear and so cold it would bring
Relief to the drover his patience worn thin
By long weary miles no respite for him.

Oh Auchinreoch we long for the days
When summers were warm
The moor clothed with haze
The orchids so pink and so regal in spring
The flash of the merlin so fast on the wing.

Yes Auchinreoch your walls are destroyed
Long years have passed since your children enjoyed
The peace of your setting remote it may seem
Although I have savored your picture serene
Alas in the city it is but a dream.

John Coleman

The Silent Shadow

We looked out to the pavements,
    my lover and I,
where the sounds were as
    bleak as darkness,
in our hearts we led out
    wild horses and turned them loose.

It takes a slow solemn silence,
    my shoes are filled with sand,
love trickles, slowly dying in joy,
    your hands, my heart calling.

Our eyes shone and we
    opened mouths in unison,
I was so much in love with you,
    we smiled and your shining
shadow filled the darkened sky,
    the last memory of you.

Your eyes in a picture frame,
    touch like electric lightning,
you call me until I answer,
    a slow moving dance of days.

Louise Cole

The Journey Of A Letter

In I go, down I float,
Awaiting collection soon I hope,
Protected from the rain, but not the cold,
The van pulls up and on I go.

Bundled in a bag with all my mates,
On we move or we'll be late,
More friends join us on the way,
The sorting office, No Delay!

Glad to be free from the damp cold sacks,
Squashing and pushing no time to relax,
On to the conveyor belt down below,
Stamped to tell them I'm free to go.

Hustled and bustled, rushed about,
Put in a machine and sorted out,
Grouped together and fastened up tight,
Before we're sent off into the night.

In the back of the van, I sit and wait,
To be delivered, I hesitate,
I listen carefully what's that sound,
It's the 'postie' ready for his round.

The early morning sun is strong,
As 'postie' carries me along,
Its relaxing rays make me happy once more,
As my journey ends on the carpet floor.

David M. Cole (Age 13)

The Wandle

The infant river, born in ponds
Is free to run. No longer in bonds.

Through flower-strewn banks
It sparkles and leaps.
Through suburban back gardens, it silently creeps.

Birds preen, dive, squabble and scoot
Heron, Kingfisher, Mallard and Coot

Past red-brick Carew, under bridges of stone.
Your banks may be busy, you go on alone.

Past Morden and Merton. Diverted by greed.
The great wheel still turns, shoppers pay it no heed.

Now to the Thames you have nearly run.
The sparkle is dulled, you are too tired for fun.

Swallowed by Wandsworth, drowned by the tide.
The brave little Wandle has finally died.

Valerie Coleman

In Retrospect

Perhaps I've forgotten the sleepless nights, the piles of
Washing, the occasional fights,
Yet I long for my family home again —
There's a void in my life these days.

I teach music at home and make soft toys
A 'treadmill' I seem to be on ...
I write poems and stories and 'follow the stars'
But where has the magic gone?

When I see a new baby there's an ache in my heart
I would gladly stay up all night:
For slumber lost, wouldn't count the cost
With 'God's miracle' I'd be all right.

There are times when I value my freedom
But that doesn't last very long ...
I feel rather wasted and lost at times
Yet I know that I do belong ...

To a wonderful family, multiplied through the years
Each face similar to the last ...
It's then I look around me, both proud and humble —
Thinking, "What a magnificent caste."

Mrs. M.G. Collingwood

Memories

One night in the Fall, in a raging storm
The Heavens opened and an Angel was born,
The joy of our life, she brought us such love
She will always be with us, but looks down from above.
Our love for her love will never grow less
The bond that we shared no one could guess
Heaven only knows how we miss our dear girl.
Our love never falters as the years unfurl.
Her bed, her toys, her pictures we save,
Cherished memories of an Angel we'll take to our grave.

Mrs. J. P. Collins

A Breath of Life

I rarely rise to anger though I would just like to say
How something seemed to stir me as I wandered out today.
Who was that heartless monster to strike a deed so low,
That it defiled the pavement and yes, disturbed me so?
Did he reap gain from one he'd slain. No! Not any.
Such beauty of a tender life had promised much to many.
Why must you be resentful that you rue your share of fate
Why turn to play assassin and give vent to so much hate
It seems we've lost our values now for bitterness is rife
Destroying all the little things we once held dear in life
My God what a felon can such a man be
That breaks the back of a young sapling tree.

Jack W. Cash

Sharing

The time we have on earth
Is measured in many ways.
Laughter, tears, hopes and fears,
Happy and lonely days.
We yearn for this, we long for that
If only we could see
That sharing makes the world go round
On this we should agree.
So try and help each other
Give and take in turn.
Watch out for those who really care
From these we all could learn,
And at the end of life
When we have done our best
God in heaven will welcome us
To a land of joy and rest.

Judy Collings

Tranquility

I floated aimlessly
In a shallow boat
Flat out
Clasping the moon's reflection
That shone the length
Of the sleeping sea
Pure in all its tranquility.

And lighted bodies
Swam without fear
So we were mixed
In a perfect cocktail
Of unshaken silence
And the moon, fish and I
Passed serenely by
And as I slept
The cold water
Was the only substance
That reminded me
Of where I was bound

For the end of my life is nigh
And in heaven my boat I will
ground.

Paul Collins

Untitled

At the beginning was nothing.
Eventually there was one.
One alone is little better than nothing, useless.
What was its purpose in solitude?
What could it do and what could it be used for?
It could not be used for what was there to use it.
And on its own it could but exist.
Then there was another one, a second one.
One and one.
One and two.
Two.
Two individually were not alone.
They could remain individual, or they could combine.
They could change to either mode.
And what matter which was One, or which was Two;
Or which was first, or which was last?
They each were one.
One and One.
Part of Two.
There they were, equal, sharing existence.
Together, between them, there were possibilities.
Then there were more.
And when there were more, possibilities were without end.

Then came everything

William Geoffrey Collins

Contempt

Contempt it is deeply imbedded in the soul
It seeps into one's mind like a dark flowing oil
And lies there dormant and when you least expect it
It comes to light, a deep infested wound
Weeping a pus it consumes you with hate and mistrust
It eats away at your mind
Slowly but surely turning you blind
Your lips start muttering words so unkind
If it's not caught in time, nothing can save you.
You will burn with a fever straight out of hell
There is no amputation or cure for contempt
It is a seed that is planted in everyone's soul
But only brought to the surface
By the one who would feed it
And the mind that is weak
And the soul that is meek.

Elizabeth Condron

Peace

"They gave their lives", we hear them say
When it comes round Remembrance Day,
We've even got it carved in stone
To stand for time, but we can't atone.

"They gave their lives" that we might live;
Without a receipt, what a price to give.
When it's said often enough then it turns quite tame
'Cause the other blasted side are saying just the same.

They gave their lives to build a new world,
Around the globe this message was hurled;
If what we see is what to go by
With such a mess THEY'LL want to know why.

So let's cut out this trite remark
Before the phrase becomes a nark;
In justice to Ypres, Caen and Somme men
They didn't give their lives - it was taken from them!

N.G. Connell

Release My Angel

I stare at a setting sun across a love lit lake,
Knelt in grasses above my height,
I wait for the stars to rise.
Believe in the beyond,
your vision shall appear.

Beautiful glimmering sky laden with promise,
send me hope of an angel,
ease my ache,
let the burden flutter.

I chose my praying mat of earth from a field of others,
the emptiness beside me is space,
room for heaven's legate.

Rays of hope shine upon my path,
heaven clouded over,
moon lights my absent desire.
My lit cigarette is the only warmth I hold.

A distant haze signals the sun,
moon departs, stars pass from sight,
nature wakes to frosty chill.
The peaceful scent of night withdraws.

I stretch to stand,
alone I walk, alone I pray,
alone I talk,
alone I stay.

Peter Conisbee

An Epitaph To Departed School Friends

Named not on any war memorial these
No battle honours brought them close to fame
Forgotten? No, the memories still please
School friends we ever shall remain.

Gone so soon the reason is not clear
For no corner of a foreign field they claim
Quiet thoughts stray back to yesteryear
When all life's problems were but just a game.

How well we fought with sword and gun back then
Each one a hero of the day
Beaten only, and defeated by the pen
The classroom brought us nothing but dismay.

But four o'clock the "magic hour" did come
Released from bondage, out to prove our worth.
But the freedom that is life was short for some
When manhood's cares about us did engirth.

Play on you noble boys, play on
We left shall toil on best we can
Poorer for your absence, now you've gone
Left drifting on the Lord's eternal plan.

Rest in peace, you boys you've earned your pass
Our memories of you will never cease
All shall one day return to class
We left, just wait the four o'clock release.

Denis Constance

Rain

Rain refreshing upon a summer's day
　　When pavements are dry and hot
Dust laid to the drip from a petal drop

When the light spot hits the face as a downy kiss
　　And the face turns to receive
What the shower would not really miss

The fresh and clean smell it leaves as it does go
　　And somehow a greener green
With a pleasing feeling, and a cooler scene
　　As once more we pass into the sun's glow

But rain that comes also in the flood
　　Tipping down the roofs along the path to the stream
Only to fill and swell until their sides burst as a bud

To carry so much before it bough and fence
　　Homes sometimes taking
Can leave so much heartbreaking
　　And costs more than a few pence

Rain sometimes welcome, sometimes not
　　But to be without water our earth would rot
　　　　Rain

Doris B. Cook

Memories of Childhood

Seagulls soaring, screeching in the summer morning sun,
Sweeping, kissing wavelets in the early tidal run,
Old fishermen whistling, singing, voices carrying far,
Oars lazily dipping, pulling towards the bar,
Women's voices chattering, welcoming the day,
Memories of childhood, swift to slip away.

Helping with the harvest, corn a golden cave,
Hiding in the haywain, quiet as the grave,
Hawks loftily soaring, pouring out their song,
Wind softly sighing, as though the day were long,
Men's voices bantering, sparkling as the day,
Memories of childhood, swift to slip away.

Soft silver evenings, strolling in the glade,
Squirrels swiftly scampering, searching out the shade,
Evening tide arriving, tripping o'er the sand,
Bright red sun setting, majestic o'er the strand,
Children's voices murmuring, sad to end the day,
Memories of childhood, swift to slip away.

Young lovers taking, possession of the night,
Clinging to each other, stars silvery bright,
Moon a loving cup, suspended in the sky,
Soft stillness settling, hours rushing by,
Woo'ers voices wooing, glad to end the day,
Memories of childhood, swift to slip away.

Colum H. Convey

Hostage

The sun went down on another day,
The hostage turned on his bed of hay,
Another day, his freedom gone
Another day spent alone.
Thoughts of home to keep him sane
Will he ever be back again?
The next day dawns,
What will it bring?
Is he just a pawn
In some evil ring?

Janice Combe

Life's Passage

As daffodils begin to die,
And swirling clouds frequent the sky.
I sit and ponder Nature's plan,
That watched me grow from boy to man.
Four seasons come and go so fast,
And then another year has passed.
Which was anew I find has grown,
And now I've children of my own.
Now they must wonder, I've no doubt,
Just what this life is all about.

Kathryn Cooper

Who Cares Anyway

Jack Benny created this stupid trend,
That at thirty-nine, man must pretend,
To cease to count, to bend the truth
To pledge himself to eternal youth.
To perpetrate this tiresome sham,
To parade his mutton dressed as lamb.
To me it all seems rather sad
To say that Grandad's just a lad.

It's better, I'd say, than saving face,
To accept one's age with a certain grace.
To carry oneself with style and poise,
Because this is what separates men, from boys.
For at the final count, when the cold wind blows
When the reaper comes and one's number shows.
It's then he'll ask you, just what you've done,
Not, whether you're nineteen or ninety-one.

John Cooke

Railways Puffing Billy

When I was a child I never thought much about railway engines,
To me it was a huge long train which never had an ending,
It travelled down along the track thundering along,
And if you listened carefully it almost sang a song.

I used to watch it rumble by, smoke was billowing to the sky,
Carriages making such a noise banging and clanging like clockwork toys.
I would see the engine driver as he drove along the track,
He would sometimes blow his whistle, or would wave and I'd wave back.

You could see the huge big furnace with flames and sparks aglow,
Then there were the great big wheels, chugging to and fro.
The huge big wheels went round and round, the engine used to hiss,
Once the train had passed one by it felt like perfect bliss.

The carriages were very plush, seats all covered in velvet,
It also had a window blind to be pulled down in the evening time.
The train would pull into the station for the passengers you see,
Some would alight down from the train to seek a cup of tea.

You would sometimes meet the inspector doing his daily round,
He would punch a hole in your ticket and say, "Don't throw it on the ground."
Alas, those days have now all gone, it is quietness once again,
The tracks have mostly disappeared, no more engines, no more trains.

There are poppies that are growing where the engines used to roll,
The countryside is saddened by the ending of it all,
For now it's just a bridal path for anyone to roam,
But the memory will always remain, of the engines which used to groan.

Elsie Cooke

A Small Piece of Heaven

In this moment as I pray
I heard the Holy Spirit say:
This place I chose just for you,
A place of peace to come to.
Just leave behind the strain and stress
For in this place you will be blessed.
The rush, the clocks, no time to spare,
Leave that behind, this moment's rare.
Look around and above,
The sky is full of God's love.
At day just listen to the sounds
Of farmyard animals all around,
And just look at the stars at night!
Surely they're a wondrous sight.
Take a walk along the lane,
Just unwind and refrain
From looking back to all the sorrow,
For there is a new tomorrow.
This little break will do you good,
So come again when you know you could.
And I'm sure you'll find just like me,
A small piece of heaven you will see!

Ann Cooney

A Celebration: The Passing Of The Berlin Wall

Benign the tumour sits,
exposed,
Its languid lips of brick
that speak adrift beyond the brink,
free,
no longer clipped,
yet, still it preens itself,
not yet spent.

Obscene,
we gather its pieces and enjoy its preservation
as the brick now sits,
in many homes,
breathing hope
each piece alone.

Contamination free
a vision zone,
and, now the stone,
witness to pain, division and control,
watches,
unification of the human soul.

Veronica Cooke

On Ancient Soil I Toil

I see again the twilight
Fall on the evening corn
The patchwork fields,
Make a splendid display
A sight to behold
The powerful horns and patient eyes
Of the cattle on the hill,
Will fill my pockets full.
Rough times and smooth, we have weathered.
Companions to the last.
Fair countryside you wake me to life again.
As on ancient soil I toil, happy and free.

Janet Cooney (Age 13)

The Awakening Passion

Glimpses of your face an body
Hands are shaking, pulses racing
Will it be long, before you notice
How my love for you, is chasing

You set my heart a'fire
Yet, you seem not to care
Yearning for kisses and caresses
How soon, before you're aware

Looking deep into your eyes
Feel my heart rate surge again
Now I see; you feel the same
The love we feel, will not wane

Our hearts and bodies entwined
With passion and hunger quenched
Now forever, we will remain
Being both together, firmly entrenched

Sue M. Cook

Memories

In dreams my thoughts return to days of yore
And children playing on a sun-drenched sandy shore,
Of gentle waves that lap around my feet
And walks thro' dappled woods where waters meet,
And in that dream, you turn and smile at me,
My heart is filled with love and ecstasy,
You take my hand and guide me thro' the years
Of love and laughter — joy and sadness — sometimes tears.
In dreams my thoughts return to days of yore,
The children grown and gone now play on other shores,
Their laughter seems to echo thro' the realms of time —
— These are not dreams at all you see
But my most treasured memories.

Freda Clark

Hard Up And Unhappy

A long time ago, I had two maids for me,
I felt very sorry for them to be,
A long way from home, unhappy and sad,
The money they earned made them glad
They had no choice, no money you see
Their monies were sent home for their families
A long time has passed since then
I think of my maids from way back when
Now times have changed for me they see
I work away from home, for my family
How lonely I am.

Toy Chambers

A Magical Dream

As water flowed along the stream
I saw the ripples glint and gleam
Suddenly the sight I saw
Left me breathlessly in awe
Minute horses zebra-striped
Swimming along to my delight
Two scrambled up onto the bank
Shaking water from their flank.
And grew to large enormity
The larger one came up to me
I gently rubbed and stroked its neck
Its coat was damp, all moist and wet
As it responded to my touch
There passed between us love and trust
His soft coat dampened by the stream
A magic fragment of my dream

Stella Cornell

Celtic Rock

Crow-black notes on the telephone wires
With a quaver of seagull white tones;
As waves thunder forming counterpoint
Now drum on the hard grey stones.
Rock; hard rock; Celtic rock.

A curlew pipes a thin high refrain.
Green seas rumble to dash on the shore;
As cloud shadows dance upon brown fields
Rolling across the windswept tor.
Rock; hard rock; Celtic rock.

Fishing smacks bob in a merry jig
To their motor's rowdy beat. The great
D.J. draws soft curtains of rain
And the disco sunbeams dissipate.
Rock; hard rock; Celtic rock.

Charles Cooper

The Exile's Dream of Home

Oh to see my homeland
Out there some place north-west
Oh to live and die
With folks I love the best,
Oh to tramp the hills and dales
Where I could dream and wait
To hear once more the hoot of owl
Calling to his mate.
Oh to see distant crags
Before it is too late
And sleep again beneath the stars
My dream would be complete.
Oh to wander further still
To reach the highest peaks
My long and lonely years
Would barely seem like weeks,
But I'm far away from my homeland
Where birds are free to nest
In one of God's rare corners
It's where my soul would rest.

Daisy Cooper

The Gulf

Far away in a distant place
Comes the sound of war drums
Drums, so prepare, prepare to fight
It's no disgrace.
The old English spirit has awoke in the night.

Some of our lads are out there now.
Practising killing and playing at war
What'll become of them
Will God teach them how
As from boys to men they are suddenly tore.

Blood stained hands preserving the oil
For that's all it's about
In the desert of wrath.
Boys, they're just boys
Playing at men.
God only knows if we'll see them
And when.

J.M. Cook

Dark Morning

I wake, I stretch, I look and stare,
Is that the time I'm seeing there.
It seems so early, dark and still,
My body's tired, my mind has no will.

I must arise, I must awake,
There's tea to brew and sandwiches to make.
There's the dog to feed and washing up,
Before I can drink my steaming cup.

The air is quiet and still and dark,
Even the dog is too tired to bark.
I wash and dress and brush and comb,
I wish today my work was staying at home.

Breakfast is made and still it is dark,
The dog is fed and already making his mark.
It's time to go out to my work.
Come on now this is no time to shirk.

I'm out now in the dusky street,
There's very few people I can meet.
But this is just another day,
And life has to go on, or so they say.

When my pools coupon comes up at last,
These early days will be a thing of the past.
Dark mornings of autumn will just pass me by,
As I in my cosy bed will lie and lie.

Marie Cove

Confessions

Oh, Jessie, how often I think of you,
I'm feeling so guilty, through and through.
Oh, how I wish I could talk to you now,
Perhaps I could try to explain — somehow.

Why I gave you away, that snow-filled day,
Your cheeks so flushed; the sky so grey.
On the bridge the couple smiled with joy,
Prepared to love you, girl or boy.

Such a vulnerable, wrinkled little mite,
Losing you, broke my heart that night.
Just try to imagine the shame and the fears,
That caused me to hide you all these years.

I was blind at eighteen, I was so immature,
How could I tell Jack? He thought me so pure.
By then, he was always away at sea,
So a "still-born" baby", you had to be.

He never questioned the facts before,
But, suddenly now, he wants to know more.
So sixteen years later, I've told Jack the truth,
That I wasn't a nice girl, like his sister Ruth.

I've confessed, and told all, the secret is out,
At last Jack knows, I was sleeping about.
I have wanted so often to just get in touch,
But the couple, I know, they love you too much.

Victoria H. Crawshaw

Conscience Money

For riches and fame
Don't do down Lottery Lane
A pound a flutter
Don't be a nutter
Foolproof system
You'll not beat 'em
Be a millionaire
No chance there
Six from forty-nine
Waste of time
Money to spare
You'll not share
Wann'a try your luck
You'll come unstuck
You won't heed me
I'll let it be
I hope you win the Lottery
Knowing me, you'll only go to pottery.

John Cougle

The Park in Winter

Stilted swings dank,
forlorn and whining in
vain speech.
The unchaste phlegmatic green,
tempts the unruffled zealot
to bowl.
Rotting leaves clad
the snug seats of the impotent
see-saw.
Provocative
frame lures the infant climber to combat,
the inert pole,
grim, silent and lapsed of
warm hands.
And a plateau of cork,
passive and gratuitous lay
in wait.
Ready for the urchin,
longing for the warmth of companions
in play.

Margaret Corness

The Life We Knew

The bulldozers move in and knock them all down
Those little terrace houses in the middle of town

With white scrubbed steps
And little lace nets
The kettle at the ready
On the old black grate
There's always a welcome
If you're Tom, Dick or Kate

They've moved them all out
The Smiths and the Jones
To a shiny new flat
On the outside of town
With hot and cold water
Bathroom and Loo

But, in the Autumn of Life
Who wants a new flat
I'd give the world, if I could go back
To that two up and two down
Away from this flat
For with all its mod cons
It's not quite the same
As the pub and shop on the corner
And that cosy little chat.

Irene G. Corbett

The Scar

Faster, harder, deeper. Progressive,
Intense concentration saturates the mind.
Adrenaline flows and pulses racing,
Exposed, unaware of enclosing danger.

Excitement seeping from every pore,
Hungry eyes lust longingly at one so close.
Eyes lifting, searching, skilfully plotting,
He's there, smirking, gangling, fixed gaze - flop.

Silence

Relaxation penetrates the soul,
A feeling of warmth protects the fragile flesh,
Drifting further, sinking deeper — falling.
In the distance, voices of agitation.

A sudden stir as heavy lids lift,
Confusion, numbness, surrounded by strangers.
Perspiration blends with the leaking fissure,
The streaked polished floor blemished with scarlet splash.

Never to forgive or forget
The stigma remains a mere memory,
Etched upon the flesh and engraved in the mind,
Forever to dislike the game of hockey.

Sarah Corner

Song of the Band

As the band strikes up loud and long,
The villages around come to hear the song.
Terrific noise from the drums and flutes,
Background from the clarinet — toot, toot.
The conductor waves his baton around
As the band strikes up loud and long.

As the band strikes loud and long,
All the animals sit up to hear the tune,
The workers put their hands over their ears,
Bows hit the violin strings, making a screech,
Villagers complain "How loud it is!"
As the band strikes up loud and clear.

As the band strikes up loud and long,
People thinking it's getting too loud.
Babies crying to the beat of the drum
The band gets louder, enjoying the fuss.
They are all very angry, but they don't care
As long as the band plays loud and clear.

Suzanne Coward (Age 8)

Walking On

Torn and tired, walking on,
Path brambled; leaves damp and rich beneath my feet.
Torch shine the way and light away
The fear of still, quiet darkness.

The path ahead should broaden and ease
Around the corner by these trees
And then more securely I will press on
Without a trip or tangle.

Beside me walks my constant faith,
My friend, my mentor and my guide.
Through the bleak, soaked, world of night
He stays and holds my spirit tight.

The nurturing warmth of my home lights
Wherein lies safety, calms my mind.
Stronger steps lengthen out.
It can't be far; the end in sight.

Rosalind Courtney

Reflections

How lovely England is —
The open Suffolk fields drowsing under the summer sun,
Hedgerows alive with flutter and twitter, the hum
Of questing bees whose work is never done,
Capturing the amber honey drops,
Quintessence of the summer fragrance
To sweeten dark days ahead. The beds
Of cottage flowers, blazing bright,
    aflame with jewelled colour,
The deep brown wheat,
Already shaded like a crusty loaf, wholesome and sweet.
The placid cattle dreaming lie, tails aswitch
To warn the unwelcome fly.
No smoke from cottage chimneys flows
To sully clear clean air, the rose
Pours out its unsurpassed perfume
On all this land — in June.
Let none disturb this peace, this quiet relaxation,
Incomparable land, a summer paradise
Where one can say, in the evening of Life's day
I am content.

P.M. Cox

Thoughts At The Old People's Home

The clock that is a lifetime ticks away
Counting up yet another day
It's Saturday morning on Wednesday afternoon
And another face appears to break the gloom
Lyn Anderson sings on a distant radio
But nobody stops to say hello.

The old lady in the corner, a father's daughter yesterday
She was someone's lover, and someone's mother
    all now far away
Devoid of self-respect or just natural
The thought will linger on eternal

Perhaps there is escape after all
I pass through the aquarium to places I recall
Everyone knows your business, or do they
When you visit you are my privacy

We talk of experiences they did not share
We talk of people no longer there
We talk of places up in the air
We talk and watch the clock waiting there.

Barry Cox

Chertsey — Our Town

To those of us who love it, our town will always be
The town that never quite made the twentieth century.
Many splendid buildings have disappeared it's true
But through the change enough remains to keep the past in view.
Our town still has its town hall, which once was made of wood
It overlooks the busy street — where it has always stood.
Nearby, the splendour of our church, where curfew once was rung
Its bells announce day's start and close, when evensong is sung.
The abbey too was close at hand, and traces still are seen
Of walls and kiln and fish preserves, where Chertsey's monks have been.
The beautiful St. Anns Hill rises high above the town
We still can walk the very road the stage coach trundled down.
And where the Thames winds through the Meads, our seven-arched bridge is found
Resisting modern traffic still — though built for hooves to pound!
The Meads are open spaces now, but were wooded once I'm sure
Many people must have dwelt here, and fished and ate wild boar.
Many major happenings took place in our small town,
A book on Chertsey's history is hard to put back down.

Violet R. Croft

Freedom

Freedom isn't just a word,
It's more a frame of mind,
No need for bars or prisons,
Or heavy chains that bind.

Some people have no freedom,
Confined within a room,
Afraid to go outside the door,
Their lives all filled with doom.

Some others' taste of freedom,
Is governed by the use,
Of drugs, or drink or cigarettes,
Their bodies they abuse.

While others have their freedom,
Curtailed by race or creed,
And others are held prisoner,
By money, wealth and greed.

And there are some among us,
Held prisoner by name,
Their freedom is so limited,
By fortune or by fame.

Next time you talk of freedom,
Just choose your words with care,
Be strong with your convictions,
Be honest, but be fair.

Frank Cumbes

The Horse

Oh for the sound of a horse and cart,
The rustle of harness is a world apart,
The noise of the tyres,
The ring of steel,
There's naught in this world
That has more appeal.

The Milkman's float and Brewerman's dray,
Only the last can be heard to this day,
The noise of the brake has a high pitched shrill
As it trundles along, down the long steep hill
The bowler-hatted drayman, and faithful old mate,
Thank God they're around at this very late date
Two thoroughbreds in front.
And the ale up behind,
They can stay on the roads;
We really don't mind.

Few Ragmen are left with their faithful old friends,
The van and the wagon, are the present day trends
The smell of spent fuel
Fills all with remorse
Oh! For the sight
Of our old friend,
"The Horse"

John Cryan

Is This All?

Is this all? The shell of a man once vital and strong,
A husk to be buried in the ground and forgotten?
The face that smiled upon me now is as carved from stone,
Its tracery of years of love and life lost forever.

Can this be all? But yet even the smallest seed buried
Bursts again into life and that more abundantly than before,
Man is worth more than the seed which growing needs water,
Have my tears not yet watered enough to bring you back?

This cannot be all! When I too, on some distant day,
Am gone into the dark where all must end their days,
Will I find you waiting there to hold my hand again,
Kiss me and wipe the tears of sorrow from my face?

This is not all! You are not dead but alive in me,
And our children, your seed, look at me with your eyes,
I wait in patience for my own call in God's good time
When we shall be together in His love for eternity.

God is all and eternity is His.

Jean Crawford

The Darkness Of Your Eyes

Deep in the darkness of your eyes,
From the smile within.
I see the light, the love that shines,
The happiness I bring.

I'll shed no tears, I'll tell no lies
If you'll just let me in.
I'll hold you dearly to my heart,
I'll love you from the very start.

The wonders of the world, I'll bring to you,
The joys of life, we'll share.
We'll spend such times together,
Showing just how much we care.

But this all lies in times not past,
These times are yet to be.
Because in the darkness of your eyes,
All of this, I see.

Lynne Crawford

Matters

Meet me God if you're a real God,
fill my heart with the love they say is yours
pity my spirit and lift it forever,
into the clouds and through heaven's doors.

Help me God if you're a real God,
if you can spin the planet like they say,
if you can change my future in a day,
meet me God.

Hold me Lord, if you care,
if you can bear,
to show your face here one more time,
both of us are guilty of broken promises,
only a fake God like you would punish such a crime.

Have you spoken?
I've strained to hear you,
perhaps you've been shouting at me all of my life,
maybe my thoughts and emotions are your gift,
must my peace and sanity be your price.

Meet me God if you can hear me,
help me God if you can care,
for I would rather dwell in your house forever,
than languish one day more in this pit of despair.

Andrew G. Craig

Bow

A ring on the doorbell,
My heart began to pound.
Here was the Vet,
To look at my old hound.

He listened to his heart
And said, "It's your decision dear,
But I'd hate to go away
And leave him lying here."

I always knew, this day would come,
As he knelt to open his bag,
It was time for my old hound to go,
And it was, oh so very sad.

Somebody dumped him,
I took him in.
A big bag of bones,
And moth-eaten skin.

This sandy coloured greyhound
Was ever so tame.
I bathed him and fed him
And gave him a name.

That old hound would never
Win a race.
But he won my heart
and left an empty space.

Mrs. M.V. Craven

The Breath of Life

I feel the Breath of Life go through me
And flow through all my veins,
I walk in light and splendour
Without man-made chains.

One moment you are in the womb
All safe and snug and warm,
And then you're being subjected
To the pain of being born.

Life is not easy
You learn that very young,
But life is like a ladder
You climb up every rung.

Happiness, hurt and pain
Are there along the way,
But don't forget that first Breath of Life
That sent you on your way.

If there's times you just can't cope
You feel you can't go on,
Just curl up, nice and warm
And in your mind ... go back to where you
started from.

Maria Currey

Oil Spill

Oil floating, thick and black,
Upon a wavey sea.
How long will it take to clear away?
That's what bothers me.

The gulls aren't calling anymore,
You young ones in the nest,
We've got to clear it all away,
Or at least give it our best.

Seals are coated, head to tail,
And piled upon the shore,
The sound of death is deafening,
As we're hearing, more and more.

Pebbles small, black and round,
As far as we can see,
Will it ever wash away?
But not back to the sea.

The smell of rotting fish,
Is sticking in my throat,
As I start to travel home,
To take a nice long soak.

T.J. Coupe

Nightmares Ridden at Night

A chestnut filly that you ride with zest
Across deep crevices of night —
At first with ease — adventure bound
And by your side Cassandra's hound.
This weird night dream, eerie and strange,
Distorts each picture, some black, some white.
Queer images take hold — and soon
Out of control, a tormented spin.
Cold sweat drips freely from heavy brow
Laboured breath and twitching skin ...
Surreal and haunting; time's clock stands still ...
Thick treacle movements restrict mind's will.

Oh — Heaven sent to wake at last
Breathe in reality at dawn.
Such gullible fear breeds with delight ...
Obsess you mind, ego self-right.
The false appear to seem the norm
But normal desires are just not right.
'Tis well to keep these creatures down ...
Tethered safe the whole night through —
Not set them free — and see too late
These wild nightmares have all come true.
This midnight filly to stalk you still
Through everlasting daylight hours.

Valerie M. Cubitt

Untitled

We've made a hole in the sky
why should elephants die
so that men can make profits
    from slaughter

Do the creatures we slay
Have no vote or no say
to put coats on the backs
    of fine ladies

Why are whales who do roam
so forlorn, so alone
shot by spears form the point
    of a barrel

To the seas that we spoil
with pollution and oil
do the men who cut trees
    have no conscience

It's so unfair, it's so sad
that men are so bad
to the creatures that live
    on this planet

It is true what they say
that man will one day
pay the price for his greed
    and his folly

Paul Cross

The New Loo Roll

I don't know why, do you?
Is it so hard to do
But time after time
You'll never find
The new loo roll hanging true

You may find it on the floor
or balancing on the basin
or even high up on the windowsill.
Does it take a degree to replace it
Where it's supposed to be?

Well I must be qualified in our house
As it seems I am the only one
To replace a new loo roll on the holder
Bringing relief to everyone
Good old Mum!

June Crompton

The Thoughtless Class

Living is the only thing we know,
Dying is for other people,
Goodness always conquers all,
And there's no room for evil.
Who the hell are we trying to kid?
We all see suffering and pain,
We see the old, the sick, the hungry,
The uneven wealth, so vain.
Jealousy doesn't come into it,
Distribution is unfair,
How can the wealthy live like they do,
And never seem to care.
Why does all the deprivation,
Only affect the few?
When like their precious possessions,
Wealth scorns the old for new.

Hugh B. Cron

The Countryside In Spring

The song birds sing; for now it's spring,
O what perfect joy they bring!
The little stream swiftly flows
With water from the winter snows;
Through the meadows and down the hill,
It wanders on some pond to fill.

I take a stroll down a leafy lane;
To see the primroses bloom again.
Each little flower so pale and shy
Their heads uplifted to the sky.
They seem to know once more it's spring!
Their beauty is a wondrous thing.

The cows are grazing on the grass
They hardly look as I do pass.
The little lambs so gaily play
Near their mothers all the day.
The happy lark is soaring high
Way up in the clear blue sky.

I wander back along my way,
Passing the lovely gardens gay
With daffodils and wallflowers bright
They really are a lovely sight!
Contentment to my heart they bring
I love the country in the spring.

Mrs. E.W. Cresswell

Through Two Doors

Drifting through the clouds of life
Searching for direction
There you are, the wings of lust
Bursting pure affection

You play and tease, but never touch
You lure me in and I follow
You've walked the tunnels of my mind
My happiness, pain and sorrow

Through two doors and I am there
Leaving the real world behind
Lust is such a dangerous game
And very hard to hide

You chew me up and spit me out
And laugh me to the ground
I was blinded by your spell
That did not make a sound

I now look back at all I had
Before you came along
It's true I wanted what I didn't have
From a place I didn't belong

Lust is from the head
Not from the heart
It's not really good for you
It will tear you apart

Neil Crisp

A Man of Peace

His words they moved a Nation,
After the bomb in Enniskillen,
He prayed and he pleaded,
Please, please stop the killing.

He lost his lovely daughter,
On that fateful awful day,
They held hands in the rubble,
And her life it slipped away.

Now fate has struck him once again,
His son has now been taken,
But Gordon Wilson still stands strong,
And asks men of violence,
Please right the wrong.

His heart so full of loving,
He continues with his quest,
To have a peaceful Ireland,
While his children lie at rest.

Winnie Curran

The Mission

Check the weapons you have to take
Open the throttle, release the brake
Pull back hard, nose to the sky
You have your orders, never ask why
Faster, higher you start to climb
Check co-ordinates check the time

Cruise through the clouds, 600 miles per hour
The adrenaline flows as you feel the power
Glance at the radar, scan the sky
Swallow hard, your mouth is dry
As you think about another day
The radar blips, target 50 miles away

Check the missiles on the rack
Radar lock, no turning back
Steeper, faster you start to dive
Below, the enemy swarms like bees in a hive
With a flick of a switch with your powerful thumb
The enemy's time has surely come

The missiles strike, the destruction is clear
The screams of death you cannot hear
Mission accomplished head for home
A blinding flash you're on your own
Spinning, falling to the ground
A thunderous roar and then ... no sound

Donald J. Coull

Winter

The snow came drifting down,
Enforcing silence o'er the town,
Quietly stealthily covering all,
A silent embrace in a lacy shawl.
The landscape changing overnight,
Everything turned to a feathery white,
How beautiful each tiny flake,
They are a miracle to make.
What a wonder God has made,
In a single snowflake meant to fade.

Mrs. B.G. Cross

Why

The cosmic jest is best explained
When having cups of tea,
For when you stir them round and round,
The galaxies you see.
They spin like particles profound,
In spirals and in flat,
And when you dunk your biscuit in,
That is the end of that.

George Crosby

Someone Special

Sometime in your life,
There's a certain place,
a certain person,
a certain face,
That makes life bearable,
that brightens your day.
The moment passes,
the years fade away,
But, we will remember,
Here in this place,
For you were that person,
Yours was that face.

Mrs. P.A. Cox

Free Spirit

Deep in the night there comes to me,
A dream of immortality
Be I young or old, my spirit's free.
It roams the world I cannot see.
My body grows from young to old
But life within me stays so bold.
My spirit grows from strength to strength,
While my eyes they dim and my body bends,
There is no end to my desire,
My freedom there within my soul.
For eternity will be my goal
And to return my one desire.

Elizabeth Fredricks

A Changing World

The simple man stared at the sun,
His glazed eyes a picture of confusion.
Around him the landscape is changing,
And the sky is but paint on a wall.
Inside him an image is forming,
That of some trees and a lake.
But the simple man's ride has just started,
And soon he'll be lost in the fog.

Leon Crumbie

The Race

The drumming hooves at breakneck pace
As horses and riders lunge forward to win the race
sweating steeds their nostrils flaring
Headlong, outstretched, wide eyes glaring
Jockeys hunched, to ease the weight
Happy to leave the starting gate
The finishing post a mile away
A rider's dream, to win Derby Day
The excited crowds they scream and shout
And bookies profit without any doubt
The front running horse extends his lead
The punters who backed him shout and plead
Bundles of notes dance before their eyes
And losers tear their tickets in a crowd of sighs.
The winner shoots past the finishing post
And the lucky ones — believe me — love
The first horse the most!

Reg Cross

Birthday
"To Melanie"

I could send you a dozen white roses
As pure as the virgin snow
They would tell you nothing about me
I love you already, you know.

So instead I'll send one solitary rose
As red as the blood in my heart
Hoping you will always be my friend
No matter how far we are apart.

James Ferguson Cunningham

The Snowdrop

Yes January is here again
First month in all the year
When lots of things seem dead and dull
The little snowdrop will appear.

Thousands of dainty little blooms
Sheltering from frost and snow
Bow their gentle heads in state
As if perchance to say hello.

Symbol of love and purity
Silently serene you stand
Perfect in your little white cloak
Unmade by human hand.

May the God who made the snowdrop
Sweet and gentle little flower
Ever show us nature's beauty
And guide our lives in every hour.

Mrs. G. Crozier

The Wedding

I shall be attending a wedding one afternoon
For the union of my grandson which is coming quite soon
While in the church, I shall be saying a prayer
That the sanctity of this marriage will always be there
The love in their eyes is a joy to behold
Please Dear Lord, may it never grow cold
As time passes by, let them both be fulfilled
And the pleasure in each other many never be killed
So when they grow old and all passion is spent
They will both thank their maker, for the life that was lent.

Rose Cray

Australia

It's not a country you can fit into the palm of your hand, it's vast
It's got desert and bush and beaches that stretch for miles.
Kangaroos, wallabies, koalas and pelicans roam free.
It's a land that's filled with opals, sapphires and opportunity.
A country built by convicts, poor people, victims of circumstance,
Who left behind them a legacy of beauty and wealth.
It's a continent so huge you couldn't see it all in a lifetime.
Look down on it from the top of a mountain, it takes your breath away
It's a surfer's paradise, a sportsman's dream, and artist's delight
A land that is still growing with ideas and sunshine.
A place to live, work, smile and be happy
That's Australia.

Ann Creighton

A R T

Art is deep — deep as the flowing stream
Which heaven's waters fill and fill again.
The craftsman's patience and the painter's dream
Sharpen our joy, or else assuage our pain
In harmony of sweet gentility;
Or bring to life with rude vitality;
Or starkly shape the face of tragedy,
Great art throughout the ages can present
To each a share in man's inspired sight,
Yet even our own small efforts trace descent
From the source of all creative power and light.

Katherine H.S. Cruikshank

Believe

God is love — He's all around,
When you believe — then you're found.
He's everywhere; mountains, streams,
In the air we breathe and in you dreams.
He loves everyone — He loves all,
When you hate — then you fall.
He loves you whether you're white or black,
When you do too, you're on the right track.
So don't be racist or prejudiced
Don't be unkind.
Live in peace and harmony —
Love all nature and your fellow mankind.

Michelle Craven (Age 14)

September

In late September's grey-green haze
Aggressive autumn fights old summer out.
Grass lies flat, pale, too tired to grow,
Dew marbles cradled in each blade.
Red berry bodies decorate
The barbed wire of dead bryony.
Nettles strike one last spiteful time
At blackberry pickers in the lane,
On hedgerows, spiders hang huge webs.
A cranefly, careless from the cold,
Blunders in, struggles, and is lost,
Bitten, wrapped, stored with vicious speed.
A thousand tiny battles rage
Beyond our sight, beyond our reach.
Uncaring sheep close-crop the dying grass
And autumn, fighting summer out, will win.

Kate Cummings

Untitled

Crouched in huddled amazement
That you've survived another day
Still questions needing answers
Yet people telling you it's o.k.
Seemingly blank, yet moving
Through the eternity
Never being complacent
Still wanting to be free.
Yet others accept the hum-drum
Scared of the unknown
But quietly screaming enlightenment
And willing to follow what is shown.
Like a lamb to the slaughter
Or lemming meeting the cliff
Blinkered-eyed and dormant
Waiting to be cold, dead and stiff.

Simon Cusick

The Life Line Telephone

No need to feel nervous or all alone,
For sitting by your bedside, is your friendly life line phone,
It's red glow, lights up the room, like a star from the heavens above,
And you know you are being protected, and within reach of those you love.

Remember, when up and about, wear your pendant around your neck,
For no one can ever tell,
Just when you might need to use it,
That precious little bell.

The aged, the sick, and the lonely,
Can now live independent lives on their own,
Safe, in the privacy of their own home,
All thanks to that miracle, the lifeline telephone.

When one becomes a burden on the family,
He loses his self respect as well,
So thanks to all those wonderful people,
Who reply to the urgency of the telephone bell.

24 hours a day they are there, 365 days of the year,
Always courteous and concerned, to help you and me,
To sort out our problems,
And whatever our troubles may be.

I wonder if that canny Scot Alexander Graham Bell,
The inventor of the telephone,
Could possibly foretell, the help he would give to millions,
By the push of a little bell.

Mary Daly

Tryst

Come walk with me, his plea was firm,
So proud yet coy she smiled assent.
Through leafy lane to hedgerow tryst,
They made their way enshrined in love.

In covert glade with pounding hearts,
Fingers entwined together drawn.
Heaving impassioned lips met lips,
Devouring love till rising dawn.

The way so clear and life so short,
His arms reach out, her to enfold.
For consummation's tender thrill,
Trembling bodies tightly held.

Some lust, some love, some never know,
Sated senses afterglow.
That great event in life's short span.
The love of woman and a man.

R. Dallimore

Sixty And Five

Sprite of the morning,
Child of the dawning,
Gay little, lithe little grandson of mine,
Gladly I joy with thee,
I'm just a boy with thee,
Exchanging my sixty years for five like thine.

Fond happy memories
Come flooding back to me,
Of childish pleasures, magic, sublime.
Life is such fun again
Just to be young again,
Brimming with happiness, small hands in mine.

Walk through the meadow sweet
To where bright waters meet,
Sail down the rivers of innocent truth.
Age, I make light of it,
Scorn at the sight of it,
Radiant am I with the freshness of youth.

A. Dando

Think Of Me

Think of me inside this cage waiting for my time to die
To die and be free from pain, final shutters close on sightless eye
Think of me, a new born pup, so happy and so free
Suckling at my mother's teat my brothers, sisters and me
Six months and we were taken away from warm straw and air
Locked inside this clinic state checked with utmost care
Three years I've been inside this cage no loving hand, no tender care
No gentle word, it's so unfair

I've been strapped down burning drops put in my eyes
Injections, creams and so much pain any hope within me dies
My brothers and my sisters gone, not even a chance to say good bye
At least they are out of pain, it's my turn to die
I've dreamt of trees, air, grass and love
Soft hands that caress like the wings of a dove
But reality is sightless eyes, clumps of hair which was once my coat
I sit here helplessly in my own mess, my stomach's begun to bloat
So stop and think of me on that evening out with your make up that
looks just right
Remember I died for that look and think of me as I give up the fight

J. D'Arcy

The Promise Of Spring

It's exciting! Let me tell you:
I'm Spring ... and on my way.
I can hardly wait to show you,
Transformation day by day.

Hedge'rows full to brimming,
New leaf on every tree;
Gardens clothed in flowers,
And Snowdrops bursting free.

Drifts of palest Primrose:
The joy of newborn sheep,
Awakening of the countryside,
Are promises I'll keep ...

I can't be there in Winter:
When snow is glistening white,
Or share your darkest days,
When hope seems out of sight ...

But I'll be there each morning:
As sweet Lilacs scent the air,
And every hue of Crocus bloom.
So tell me ... you'll be there!

I promise: when it's Spring-time,
To lift your heart anew,
Surpass your wildest dreams,
And come again for you.

Evelyn Davies

Delivery

Down the street, towards our house,
Red bag hung by his side
I watch with eager expectant eyes,
What would he place inside.

Would it be something of surprise
That unexpected thing.
A letter from some long lost friend,
Or a fortune I can win.

Will this delivery be for me,
The wife or for us both.
Or will it be that 'junk' type mail,
A thing we've come to loathe.

Nearer now, he is no boy,
His face betrays his age.
Lines upon the weathered skin,
With scar from an earlier age.

His eyes they tell another tale,
Too many paths he's trod.
That weary step, the bend in back,
That says "I'm nearer God."

He's passed on by, no mail for me,
Those steps they fade away.
"I'll wait until tomorrow then,
Until another day."

Anthony Davies

On Stag

In the deep dark, where, at first, a solid wall confronts,
Eyes accustom to reveal blurred outlines and strange shapes.
Out there, beyond full eyesight strain, the enemy hunts;
No metal glint nor movement his eagle eye escapes.

Better look round, but quietly now, sling my Tommy Gun,
Uncocked and off the catch, of course, risking no mistake.
That bush out there! It's closer now! A bush? Was there one?
False alarm. And still an hour and a half to daybreak.

On guard, on stag, on sentry, and here it's just the same;
Tunisia's hills and valleys play tricks when dark and bleak.
Eyes and mind find ways and means of joining in the game,
Like, 'Does George Wood's wife yet know that he was killed last week?"

The night comes clear; the shadows, begin to move about.
It's jitters time and nothing, is what it seems to be.
Letters are weeks behind. It's six months since we sailed out.
Today Len got a 'Dear John'. What sort of bitch is she?

Two nights ago we moved here, listened to the grapevine.
Heard the route was dodgy, map reference confusion.
Previous unit ambushed; went through the German line.
So, we aimed to get there, without the same conclusion.

Another move tomorrow, at sundown on the dot.
Make another bivouac! Another school for brag!
Pray we have no losses, but, whatever there is not,
There sure as hell will be — another stag! Another stag! Another stag! ...

John Daniels

Men Of No Dawn

The cinnamon smoke floats red on the night,
Lies deep in the vapours of old men's minds,
Metal spits and timbers mourn their plight.

Out of the jagged flesh of men, young come,
The mountain gully waits as each one winds,
To stand beneath the broken earth and dome.

When man and mountain, weary of the sun,
Toil once begun, must run their binding pain,
Until, like crippled stones their time is done.

In darkness cursed they hack out womb and tomb,
Then in blindness fall in shadowed pool,
Their epitaph? Not sun to light the gloom.

Black lunged they die corrupted on the bough,
While burial hammers clang out in iron tune
Like choirs, tarred organs, subdued now.

Young women weep deep, to shroud blackened end,
A child screams protestation to it's birth,
And raging lies to rot in rust mold penned,
Wind whispers cold, where wild grass does not bend.

Anntoinette Dubrett

Strangers All

Over a cup of tea they meet every morning
She drowsy with sleep and pent-up anger
He, eyes swollen from the party booze,
Staring empty beyond the kitchen window
Onto the pretty crepe-myrtle floating
In the breeze, and the green lawn
Speckled with crab grass and weeds,
How long had it been, she mused,
This silly routine of the morning cup
This pretence of conjugal love,
When all she craved was the break
Away from the walls, and shatter
The slave bonds of two decades.
Could she do it, was it too late?
The doubts wracked her. She must,
Or call it a day on this sham life.
And what about him, did he know or care?
Of the agony that was splitting her
Apart? Perhaps, Perhaps not.
Who could tell, they never talked,
Never shared their mutual world,
They lived apart. All they had together
Was a bed and twenty years of silence.

Rowshan Daneshy

In A Miner Key
(In Tribute to My Much Loved Welsh Mining Village)

Green mountains high, sharp air so pure, swift streams so clear
By mountain's foot and dusty pit's right hand, fresh planted pines,
Friendly, sheltering our bones from wind's full blast,
Our sight from opencast's deep sear.
Week's workdays cover hours full score and four, in shifts by three,
Leaving thus, small time for play bar precious Sunday on which, divine decree
Proclaims no working man, no slave to coal, shall rise 'til half past three,
Repeat then, every Monday's scene, penetrating dust mixing habitual sweat with grime,
Arriving at work's caged doors, discharged from decrepit chariot,
doubtful of vintage, yet, amazingly, on time.
Later, evening's choice of club or pub or choir,
each a question of 'gentleman please' and marching 'time',
Beaten either by plump pump handle maiden
 or slighter, batoned, Handel-conductor's movement prime,
Answering mutual, high in smoke room, mute in school room,
is the Welsh Male Voice in flood of rhyme,
The glory of rich, round mellifluous tenors, squat basses,
dark-voiced as coal itself and, shining between,
The surge of baritones' line, all vibrant, resonant,
soaring to climax of sound serene.

David G. Davies

Growing Old

With inevitable gradualness the process of ageing
Makes clear the evidence the war nature is waging
The many symptoms and signs, most surely define
The body is experiencing metabolism in decline

Hearing a voice that at one time seemed near
Now sounds so distant, as to make it unclear
Assistance is sought of a technical aid
Our thanks to technology and the advances it's made.

Difficult discernment of things near and far
The pictures are blurred, like a fast moving car
Joints that were once so agile and free
Become sticky and stubborn and creak frequently

Hair once so dark whose growth was abundant
Makes brush and comb, almost redundant
It becomes so sparse and slowly turns grey
Confirming one's time is fast ticking away

A strong sense of unease and foreboding prevail
As fast becomes slow, in pursuit of life's trail
With diminishing verve, and having done its best
The feeble fragile body, is finally ready to rest

Allowing time to reflect in quiet reverie
And ponder life's pattern and imposing mystery.

Dilwyn Davies

A Mother's Memories

Trembling fingers in mine entwined,
Small voice whispers, "is it time, is it time."
Thumb in mouth, quivering lips
As in his haste he stumbles and trips.
Tears near the surface, an occasion so grand,
His first real visit to fairyland.

We awaited our call to the magic door,
He just couldn't believe the wonders he saw.
There were gnomes and elves, bright colours and lights,
Make believe sweet trees in sequinned sites.
Then a white bearded figure with a smile and a wave
Beckoned him into the magical cave.

Uncertainty over, he ran to the knee,
He forgot for a moment how he'd clung close to me.
Quickly he asked for the things he desired
And Santa promised to do what was required.
He said it all depended on the boy being good
And small son said he'd try and do as he should.
"Good-bye," he shouted, as he ran back to me
And he said, "Come on home, Mum, is it time for tea?"

Mrs. D. Davis

Christmas Eve

On Christmas Eve, Santa and his elves
Take all the toys and books off the shelves.
They pack them all ready for their journey to go,
Riding across the mid-winters night snow.
When they are ready, away they fly
Travelling through the dark, starry sky.
Until at last there is rooftops in sight
And there they stop in the middle of the night.
Into the sack the presents go,
Along with bits of falling snow.
Then Santa slowly climbs down the chimney
At the bottom he sees a tree.
He leaves some presents here and there
Then he goes, up the stairs.
At the top he sees two beds,
And on the pillows lie two sleeping heads.
He fills up the stockings with all kinds of treats
While the children soundly sleep.
Then off he goes back up the chimney
Into the sleigh and woosh he's away
Gone to the next house.

Rachel Davies (Age 11)

Hard Times

To be unemployed creates worry day and night,
You dream that one day things will go right,
But then, no matter how hard you try,
The good times in life just pass you by.

Rising each day, full of anticipation,
Hoping the letters you wrote will bring occupation,
But alas, in the mail instead of a thrill,
Your friendly postman delivers a bill.

A feeling of gloom hangs over the room,
What is the answer to this terrible doom?
You've thought of a plan, it could be just right,
But you don't do the pools, money's too tight.
So how do we solve this plight we embrace,
Somehow make us feel better, put a smile on your face.

It's the government who control our social state,
The solution is simple, it's never too late,
Let's have more workers through the factory gate,
They should get off their backside, get on the move,
We the workers have nothing to prove,
We've been there, we have done it, we've shown them before,
Just think back to the times of war.

Give us back our sense of pride,
Abolish this myth that we are here just for the ride,
Come on Mr. Major, stop acting like God,
Bring interest rates down,
GIVE US A JOB!

Neville T. Davies

Wrinklies Rap

I've just had a cruise to Spain
To a lovely place called Santander
The shops are closed every afternoon
So in Santander, you have to meander

The police and people were friendly
Although English speakers were few
We had to rely on sign language
Have you tried making signs for the loo?

The service and food were out of this world
The plentiful drinks the same
Only one thing, when it came to the gin
It had a disgusting name

It was a bit of a thrill, when the ship had a drill
And we all made a grab for our bags
Except for one dame, I really can't name
Who only picked up her glad rags

The weather was swell, the company fine
And I'm really impressed with Spain
So roll on next year, we'll send up a cheer
And do it all over again.

June Davies

My Scented Garden

Stepping deftly between the comforting
Sweetness finding solace in my flowers
At dusk and at night
Through the heady perfume I glide.

My scented garden invokes childhood
Memories which are fused with romance
And dreams of a lost youth
Bountiful and full-breasted I succour.

Through mint and thyme and honey-
Suckle through lavender and rose
I yearn for my sweet love
Exotic balsam love maker juicy.

Skipping and dancing rosemary
Quivering nostrils intoxicated with
Smoke from apple logs and hornbeam
Lungs on fire from the joys of pot pourri.

Peppermint tea drinker was my love
Through our scented garden we
Drank our love full and breathless
Aromatic oils glistening in the sun.

Life passed life gone only my memories
And my scented garden to bring peace
In this cornucopia of wafting dreams
Of love spent but truly loved.

David Dawrant

Bosnia

A dangerous weed with a deadly seed,
Is the seed of hate so bitter
Crushing all that's in its path
And leaving carnal litter,
It stifles all of good intent
That love and care may offer
And robs a nation of its wealth
And leaves an empty coffer,
Warring is a costly job
The tide of fortune fickle,
Death wants payment on the nail
With or without its sickle,
Its tragic that man will persist
To kill, and maim and plunder
Dictating terms in voice of war
The voice of Thor and Thunder
We like to think that civil life
Rents us a room with peace
But war and strife and killing
Seem to have the longest lease.

G. Davis

Insularity

In my heart I'm on an island
In my mind I travel far
I do not need a space-ship
To reach that distant star

In my sleep I'm on an island
Dreams take me back in time
I see the house where I was born
And hear children's nursery rhymes

In busy streets I'm on an island
Crowds and noise don't bother me
I only hear the gentle waves
And seagulls far at sea

In my heart I'm on an Island
Pure gold the virgin sand I tread
This is my own island
And will be 'till I'm dead

Margaret Dorothy Davis

The War

Thousands crumble, they fall and die
The planes are lying low and high,
Bomb and shell, dirt and mud,
Surround the bodies amongst the blood,
Thousands upon thousands die each day
The rest fight on, some run away.

The tracks upon the mud are deep,
Where soldiers upon soldiers cry and weep,
As all their pals get shot and die
This is what appears to the naked eye,
The scream and shout, as the bayonet tears,
Into the flesh of that soldier there.

The sky has darkened the clouds are black,
The enemy comes forward and attacks,
The tanks and planes, all do their job,
And the lonely soldiers' hearts do throb.
The day will come when the world is free
And no more soldiers will die for me.

Michael Dawes

Hope

To what we turn when we are low,
When life has dealt a deadly blow,
The knocks and bumps, still so sore,
Hope springs eternal to the door.

When things we seek have gone astray,
Hopelessness abounds in every way,
When you think life's nothing left in store,
Hope springs eternal to the door.

When outlook's black, and colour's blue,
And there's nothing left you can do,
Everyone's hand held out for more,
Hope springs eternal to the door.

The Samaritans, a port of call,
You just can't seem to climb that wall,
When life seems rotten to the core,
Hope springs eternal to the door.

When nothing good can you find,
Worried, bullied life's unkind,
You just can't take it any more,
Hope springs eternal to the door.

D.S. Davison

Shades of Autumn and Winter

Has it been noticed? I think it will,
The trees are turning, the wind has a chill.
There's beauty though if we look around
The glorious colours that nature can paint.
The red robins arrived on the garden gate
Autumn shades, then winter's here
With the beauty of snow and the hungry deer,
All this God gives us to admire.
So think of all this round the cosy fire
Take notice of everything, it changes fast.
Each year goes quicker than the last!

Mary Dawson

The Morning After (The Night Before)

I look in the mirror at my reflection,
Christ that isn't me!
I look every day of sixty-five
But I'm only forty-three.
What a mess, Hell, what a shambles,
Jesus what a sight,
Mouth as dry as a budgies cage,
Must have been some night.
Can't remember much about it,
God what have I said?
How the hell did I get home?
Who put me to bed?
Sod, I think I'll give up the drink,
Causes me too much sorrow.
But then, tonight is Saturday night.
I'll give it up tomorrow.

John David Davies

Time

Our lifetime is made up of many years,
Of many joys and sorrows and some tears;
The days go drifting slowly by —
Unnoticed pass they into weeks and months.
The months become the seasons —

Drowsing summer follows on sweet spring;
And then the dying year — the autumn, "Fall",
Followed by cruel winter, ice-crowned king of all.
And then the years go marching on and on,
Far back from beyond the dawn of time, they come
Into the future, farther than man can tell or see,
Into the mists where time is not — into Eternity ...

Miss D. Day

Evacuees
Dedicated to Mrs. Stella Waite (nee Lindfield)

The siren sounds
In London town
And children in
To fear are thrown.

To families
They said good bye
And on the train
Sat down to cry.

Evacuees;
They came to stay,
And ran from fear
Both night and day.

And in those days
To wales they came
To find that we
Don't talk the same!

Every Christmas
They send their cards,
And in them send
Us their regards.

Beryl Davies

The Winter Seed

Snow flakes falling
softly to the ground,
everywhere is quiet
no one makes a sound.

Up next morning
children everywhere,
snowballs flying
catch me if you dare.

Snowmen in gardens
sledges at top speed
children laughing, playing,
let the fun time breed.

Why is it at winter
everyone is kind?
reaching out to others,
and never really mind.

Let's take the winter spirit
and plant it in our hearts,
so at year beginning
we'll have a kind new start.

Ruth Dawson

Truce

I had a fall, and you are my crutch.
You must support me until the limb mends.

You pushed me down the stairs
But I did not fight you
Or
Run away.
I thought, at the last moment, you would stop
And I would be saved. I trusted you.

Now my limb is cracked in several places and
Though you regret that fatal push,
It must be others who mend my limb.

Now you see me as a weak being. You are wrong.
People who love and trust are strong.
People, who in the words of the song,
"Dust" themselves "down, and start all over again" are strong.
But those who linger outside the door marked CHANGE,
Those who carry the past with them, and cannot love or trust,
They are weak.

In the detritus that is their past,
In the holdall full of old loyalties,
There is a cruelty, a cruelty that scars those who love them
The new ones whose strong unfaltering steps forward are halted
By Your Deceit.

Ruth Helena Davis

Hospital Visit

These corridors should be cold
Marble floors
Cold grey ceilings
And the air so warm, so false.
I feel any second a nurse
Could jump out
From the shadows
and measure my pulse.

These corners should be rounded
Curved and gentle
Not so stark and sudden
Perhaps easy, as if to glide,
And there should be little
Cut out bits
In the walls
Where a man could hide.

Bob Darvell

In The House

Inside the hollow there sits a black, hovering cloud.
It is waiting for an opportunity to engulf it's case.
Anger and pity.
Hopelessness and fear.
Fear in time-turntable.
I thought long and hard until I was no longer afraid.
My hair was a measure of my years.
I could reach down and touch the floor with my hands flat
My searching was now over.
A peering cat on a window trying to attract my attention.
Nearly all is forgiven languid lady of leisure.
Aroma of dust and shadow.
Of cars moving so fast there is no time to think.
I melt.
Isolated hedges/regimented trees/squadron of colours.
But I am free — dom.
And love so precious I would wear it all the time.
Like a comfortable jewel.
Forgotten houses stare as the day moves along.
I have to contain myself.
Level joy into a more palatable dish.
Although just by the look on my face, anyone would know.

I am the cat that got the cream.

Germaine Davies

Inside Job

The only way we'll win
is if we start to begin
to hear what's within.
It's always been there
and with deep thought and prayer,
I'm sure we all share
the willingness to care,
for the lives of each other
like sister and brother,
let's extend love to cover
whatever the colour,
we are all the human race.

Let's rebuild our souls,
don't allow life just to revolve
reach for some resolve,
the rewards will unfold.
Keep true values in sight,
we must now decide
to get our priorities right.
Then attitudes of mind,
might help us all to find
a pride, in being human kind.

Trudy Dobson

Just Think ...

If they had made a mental note
Of hurt that's never seen,
They might have found the antidote
To quell the in-between.

And healed the darkness of resent
(Where rendered heart befell)
And, brought the peace of sheer content —
Where love together dwell.

Edna M. Dobell

Autumn Day

Today wild horses raced on wilder seas
Then scattered playfully whilst in full flight,
And many gulls dipped in the sapphire sky
Looking for all the world like Chinese kites.

Today I saw so many shades of gold
Not only gold but every shade I've known
But, self indulgently, I wanted more
I wished for you upon my journey home.

Too soon this beauty will just blow away
Will vanish from the sight and from the mind.
Age seems to sharpen sense of joy and pain —
A Passaflora with a Briar entwined.

I gladly bear the years inclement weather
Trusting again we share this scene together!

Juliet Dyson

Birth

Gentle waves caressed the golden sand,
A murmur of breeze stroked the trees,
A silver moon laid a glimmering pathway
Across a sea of glass calmness.
The black velvet sky was cut with a thousand diamonds
That were mirrored in their liquid eyes.
Almost silently they slid through the water,
Her close, constant companion, a shadow
At her side, both knowing, by some force
Of nature, that her 'time' was at hand.
They reached the depths and his great bulk
Gracefully, slowly, soothingly, slipped
Alongside hers as she shuddered,
And gave birth to his first offspring.
The three broke for the surface together
Sending a shower of glittering moondrops
Of water cascading downwards
Onto the joyful family of blue whales.

Diane Davis

Our Diana

She thought that love was everything
When she married the man born to be king,
Two sons and some years on,
She knew that everything was gone,
That all he wanted was an heir
With the other woman this he could not share
Facing the world with a sick heart
While her whole world was falling apart
She's a royal princess, there is no doubt
It's the people who love her
That make her smile
Let's hope she's with us
For a long, long while.

Lily Dawes

The Third Coming

The Jester falls
As we recall
Sweet music in the wind.

A single line
In clear sublime
Before the day has sinned.

The haunted dreams
Of nature's schemes
Compse the rite of spring.

Graces ring;
As silent wings
Forgive, to rise again.

Barbara Davies

Life's Tapestry

What is their use now, what should I do
With remnants and odd scraps, varied in hue,
Cast them in waste? No! Gather them all
Winding the threads in a rainbow-striped ball.

Fitting the pieces of cotton and silk,
Shaping the patchwork, making a quilt.
Blending the colours, weaving the yarn,
Making a garment useful and warm.

Life is composed of the great and the small
There is a place and purpose for all.
And in life's tapestry, O foolish man,
God has a place for you too, in His plan.

Eileen M. Darke

The Flood

How deep the waters run, no bridge nor ford;
No passage to the other side where safety lies.
Swollen foaming torrent run amok,
More than a match for any man who would dare such a force
Yet I must cross this boiling swell
Or die here where I stand, shivering and alone.
Pursuing me, alas, an enemy
To whom no match in strength am I,
Why did I choose this day of melting snow,
No thought of rising flood in my retreat.
Why did I cross that path as if with calling card in hand,
Who knows ...
But reminiscent follies are no consolation now
Any lead I may have had diminishes as sure as seconds go.
Howling, growling, fearsome foe,
Urged on by trumpet call and clattering crushing hooves.
Finely clad horsemen and ladies bold,
Whipping on o'er ditch and hedge
A feather in the cap to them, my brush.
Then I must cross this boiling swell or face the wrath of frenzied foe
How deep the waters run, no bridge nor ford.

John Dawson

Childhood

During early whistling holes-in-trousers childhood
We happily enjoyed ourselves with simplistic innocence,
Walked those pre-responsibility days with ease
And kicked happiness in all directions.

We long for those unashamed innocent hours
When we talked to friends about everything we knew
And threw
Stones and sticks into mirrored ponds and pools.

We could not see our future spread out
As rings in the ponds and pools spread out
Nor could we imagine difficulties in our virginity.

The water, however, is still there, unaffected
Naivety was replaced by fundamental humanistic needs
Whistling has changed tune
And friends passed on as our childhood passed on

But where did simplicity
And enjoyment
Eventually disappear to ...?

John Ernest Day

A Tribute

Like some crone in your jet black hood.
Yellow coat that still looks so good.
The ravages of time have passed you by
And now in repose in my garage you lie.

Faithful friend, treasured memories we share.
Your many years with grace you wear.
You have travelled and driven with zest,
Served me well in you life's quest.

Countless secrets you shared and kept
And in silence you remained while I wept.
My elation. My joy. Of times long past -
To all these memories you hold fast.

As with increasing speed the years race
Your parts with more difficulty replace;
But under your bonnet your strength still lies
And I shall always willingly be your eyes.

Proud Welsh Lady of the Clwyd lanes.
Parked in my garage your usefulness wanes.
Now in peace rest your well worn parts,
For with love you are held in our hearts.

Jannice Day

The Mole

The mole is such an ambiguous creature,
He's nearly blind, many things he's not seen,
But he has one unusual feature,
You don't know where he is but you know where he's been.

He excavates earth, loose or firm,
With talons like spades he tunnels a hole.
He's a predatory hunter searching for worm.
For to survive he must eat, it's his ultimate goal.

His fur is unique by the way that it lays.
It's a shiny black lustrous coating
Each hair can rest in different ways.
You can't help but wonder if he's secretly gloating.

So search on heath, woodland, and pasture
Look for a hill, a tunnel, a hole.
And maybe enjoy such wonderful rapture
As you come across the unique, ambiguous mole.

T. M. Dawson

The Lost Child

Oh, my dearest child,
Now I can never show
The greatest love I feel for you,
And I will always wonder who,
Your likeness would have been.

Oh, my dearest child,
To never know a gentle smile,
Not helped you through Life's hardest mile,
How I will always love you.

Oh, my dearest child,
Though many years have passed away
And you could never with me stay.
You'll always be part of me,
And years will never take away
The dreams I held for you,
Oh, my dearest child.

Maureen Davis

Forgotten Future

Through the darkened corridors of an orphanage,
the sister slowly creeps,
while in the rooms on either side,
the abandoned future sleeps.

Boys and girls of every creed,
abandoned by the world,
forgotten dreams of our tomorrows,
into a black abyss are hurled.

They have no knowledge of life of love,
they only know what is,
They've never known a family life,
or the sweetness of a mother's kiss.

And yet they are our future,
on which we all depend,
like these children, and their children's children,
as it shall be until life's end.

Why are they all abandoned,
like relics from the past,
why have their hearts been broken,
their future's now our pasts.

Victor Robert Allen Day

West Of King's College Chapel

A hidden breach admits my trespass
to lawns beyond the keepers' watch.
On this night so mild, will I keep hold
on my handful of green; my inner child?

At the doors of Henry's edifice of faith,
self-doubt cemented my untried desire.
Now fenced about, the way is barred
but that won't keep the spirit out.

Gothic notes descend the scale,
my seat of stone conducts the bass;
with thunderous play, the vision shivers (despite July)
and the stop within gives way.

Glancing through the ebbing brine,
a pinhead, falling, trails towards the Cam.
Bridging the years, a confiding friend
describes shooting stars, transforming fears.

She'd tasted galling self-deceit,
then anodyne nocturnal skies;
tear-filled hope displacing pain,
in awe at the universal scope.

A convenient philosophy, or truth,
which all the world should learn?
The future's unborn; the possible unknown.
Thus, God meets woman contemplating dawn.

Correna Dcaccia

The Legacy

Child of mine, sweetly sleeping, so innocent and new
I'll wrap the world in ribbons and bows and give it all to you
but will you breathe the poisoned air that slowly fills the skies
will the smog that lingers there cloud your pretty eyes?

Hear the gentle pitter patter on the window pane
the sound that lulls my child to sleep is only acid rain.
Please don't cry my little one, I'll do the best I can
to tell you how the world once was before the end began.

Of open fields that used to lie beneath this urban sprawl
derelict concrete jungle where my baby will learn to crawl.
You will not play in fields of green nor hear a bird's sweet song
stagnant seas, a stench filled breeze, where did the world go wrong?

You tiny hands reach out for me — I'll give you what I can
but is my love enough for you, can you end what they began?
What have I done, my little one, what is there left to give?
The gift I gave my child was life, but not the chance to live.

Teresa Detheridge

Jane Platt

I know most children like a letter
So here's a few lines to hope you're better
Cough and cold having gone away
It's back to school again each day

Awaiting next Wednesday when out for tea
With Tracy and other friends not known to me
Great fun and laughter, games to play
I'm not to know this little one sad to say

To swim again just let me know
With Tracy and maybe Pam will go
Weather may not be finest yet
With indoor pool, we will not get wet

Lighter days and more sunshine
To have a 'Dutton Day' would be fine
Tracy, Jane, and of course, Carol new
One more for Hide-n-Seek chain tick too

To write much more would need a day
Away from school for you to stay
Love to Mum and Dad from visitors one and all
A kiss from me to you at Dutton Hall.

Bryan Dearden

Travel Wish

Over the hill and far away
There's places to visit and I would like to stay
The world's so wide and the sky's so tall
It would take me a lifetime to visit them all.

;But how I would abandon home
To travel the skies to visit Rome
Or the Canary Island I would like to see
I'm told the sand perfectly fine and there's nice blue sea.

I would travel the sea and flow with the tide
And visit a ranch and ride some hide
In cowboy land that would be
Maybe John Wayne would invite me to tea.

I could travel by car and cross the ferry
It takes more time, I'm in no hurry.
I could swim the channel and visit France
I could go by tunnel and arrive in advance.

I'm only dreaming, will it come true?
The decision is purely up to you.
No matter what you think of my simple poem,
I'm only trying to earn me a coin.

June Denton

A Test Tube Son

I know I am my mother's son
My birth certificate says so
But what I do not understand
Where is my dad's name also

There is an empty space
Where his name should be
But mother cannot tell me
Just what that name should be

I know my mother's single
And she's never had a man
But explain to me what made me
And I'll try to understand

I'm told I'm from a sperm bank
Whatever that might mean
So I couldn't know my dad's name
Whoever he might have been.

C. O. Desjarlais

Never Will Free Be Free

What good is this,
This awful desperate struggle
To live, to do, to please.
Grasping at things unseen
Clinging to tenuous ties
To bring the hidden depths some ease.

Cut the umbilical cord
And burn it to ashes grey
Scatter it on the sea
For the wild waves to lift
And wash it free.

Never will free be free.
Never the grip relax
That binds the hidden hold.
Not till the whole be ashes
Both ends of the living cord
And the life that flowed between made cold.

Lillian E. Devlin

Pause For Thought

It is a wondrous moment
That I hold in my hand,
For this is my life
And I am in command.

To choose whichever pointer
On the sign-posted way,
As I live in "the now",
Going from day unto day.

I see the colourful beauty,
The painted picture all around,
Which enhances my inner peace,
That at long last I have found.

Come take my hand,
Be in tune with me,
And let us go forward,
To see what we will see.

A whole world of unity,
Care, understanding and peace,
Where "pure love" is the theme,
And all hostilities have ceased.

Our "God" of the universe
Is always in our heart,
So open up to "Him",
It is never too late to start.

Jade Deacon

The Picture

It's hanging on our bedroom wall,
It's not very wide, and it's not very tall,
There's a beautiful lake,
And some lovely trees,
Whose leave I am sure
Would rustle, in the breeze.
There's a little wooden fence,
And a golden path,
That seems to go all around,
Some pretty little cottages
Are waiting there to be found.
I imagine roses,
Climbing over their front doors,
And perhaps a little pussy cat,
Sitting on the wall.
Their gardens are so neat and trim,
Cared for by the people, who live within,
The distant hill I'd love to climb
It looks so peaceful, and sublime.
Overhead, the sky is blue,
There's a big white fluffy cloud
Up there, too.

Mrs. F. E. Dewfall

Fresh Fields

Oh to walk in fresh fields,
And feel the grasses round my legs
Oh to walk in fresh fields and see
The birds fly above my head.
To see the water trough and horses
Grazing in the fields.
To walk along a country road
While moths dance gaily in my face.
To travel on or rest a while
To see God's blessing all around
Or just reflect upon the hour.

Margaret Dewar

For Piano

It was like every old piano
that waits in silence,
special to you for comfort,
the way it cradled your body,
remembered chords, a quiet key
for childhood, long practised
in speaking loneliness.
Old photographs above.
The soft pedal worn
with crying, for the child
who didn't play.

Tony Dobson

The Heavenly Child

No war nor battle's sound was heard in the world around
When the heavenly child was born.
This was the happy day as the three wise kings
followed the star which lead them to Bethlehem.
It was the season to rejoice, to see baby Jesus,
Who was born in a manger.
That glorious news that echoes around the world
that brings sweet peace and love to all.

Viola I. Delgaudio

Our Choice God's Planet

Inside every person is a brain and a heart
Inside our woman does a child's life start
We are the humans that God did make
The nuclear bomb, that's our mistake
We have a choice between right or wrong
Of wars and riots, or peaceful song
From bombs and guns to a household knife
It's a terrible wrong to take a life
Why do we fail in so many different ways
Why does peace come, but seldom stays
I hope one day, Man can all live as one
Enjoying his planet in the way it should be done
Peacefully.

Paul Diamond

Joy of Living

It's the little things that matter,
As your journey on life's way.
The sound of children's patter,
The break or eve of day.
The handshake of a long, lost friend,
A smile from someone dear.
The person who will always lend,
A sympathetic ear.
The kindly thought, the kindly deed,
The one whose slow to chide,
That friendly arm one gives to lead
Across the other side.
That helpful word when trouble's near,
That favourite little song,
The cup that always gives you cheer.
The friendship that's lifelong.

Thomas Denton

As A Child

As I look at the garden
now overgrown with weeds,
where once I lived,
playing hour by hour.
Dressing up in this and that
sitting in the sun, hat awry,
tangled in a skipping rope
or knocking stumps in with a cricket bat.
Picnics with the teddy bears,
when no one came to play.
Making daisy chains to make a crown,
While I become a fairy queen,
or film star of my wildest dreams.
The fantasies of childhood linger with me still
as I look back at the garden I loved so well,
now overgrown with weeds.

Liz Dicken

Encore?

I never was consulted first, no choice was offered me,
I knew not where I'd go or when nor what I was to be.
I had no footpath clear laid out, no standards to maintain,
I was not told to what conform, what site I must attain.
I had to be a human then but which was never told —
A white, a yellow, brown or black — it did not then unfold
Nor when it was I had no say, I just had to take part
What was decided there and then was made before my start.
I could have been a butterfly with beauty to exceed —
But who would love my beauty there? A bird with chicks to feed?
Or animal with claws and teeth to take another's life
With agonising tear and pull in nature's chasing strife?
No, I was cast without decrees as human — or betwixt
I had to take a place within this world, a place not fixed.
I found myself with new made things that told the men I found
That life could be so wonderful for all who stood around,
If only men would make their lives the wonders they could be
And live together with a will in worlds that stand out free.
But what if I should come again and was consulted then?
Would I another creature choose or land again with men?
A creature, say, to scare those there, to show them who is lord
Might be my choice this second time — if I may pick the word?
But no, I don't suppose I'll come by any choice my own.
Once more it will decided be, my future ready sown.

Albert Dobson

Remembrance Sunday

What is it to us now? Young people no longer
want to become soldiers or sailors.
The regime of education is upon us, and
tells us to use our head,
rather than our heart.
The battlefield is deserted. In its place are the
neat, well-disciplined ranks of the classroom.
Our future is already set out before us;
primary, secondary,
then college or university.
How our desires have changed. Honour and glory no
longer come in the form of medals or colours.
Grades are all that matter now.
Red ticks splatter our exam papers like the
scarlet poppies that splatter the battlefields.
Our dreams are of fame and fortune. We
shun violence and protest against genocide.
Only the older generation are left
to ponder over the past and
recall what life used to be.
And what of Sunday's service? For most of us it is just a
mere ritual to be performed religiously.
The poppies lie dead or dying.
Where have all the knights gone?

Sarah Dilley (Age 15)

The Irate Motorist

The Roads of Britain are in a terrible state
Hey, watch out! There's another raised grate
Yellow blinking lights, red and white cones
Two thirds of our roads are forbidden zones

Why is it that all the ruts are in the lefthand lane
Then they are on the other side when you return again
Tarmac is left to set in great hard lumps
And road repairs are left with peculiar humps

The roads are always resurfaced on a rainy day
Tyres pick up the chippings and carry them away
Thousands of tons of chippings go missing every year
Where they end up is not very clear

Driving through a puddle your car stops outright
Not an AA box anywhere in sight
You step out the car, only to be hit by a wave
A juggernaut swishes by driven by a knave

Detours, restrictions, just try and park your car
You drop in a pothole and receive a nasty jar
Finally the hole is filled in, but the very next day
The Gas Board arrive with a road up display

A hole can be left for weeks at a time
While they dig up another in Ashton-under-Lyme
So somewhere out there in the thirty mile limit
There's a dirty great hole with nothing to go in it

J. R. Dickinson

The Tramp

He shuffles along, odd shoes on his feet
Scruffy and dirty, wandering the street
Tied together with string, like a bundle of rags
Searching the gutters, for food or a fag.

Just by looking at this horrible scene
He makes you feel itchy and unclean
But you wonder as he passes along
About his life, and what went wrong.

Has he a wife and child somewhere
Do they still love him, does he still care
Is some mother's heart breaking for her missing son
Or maybe a villain, who's now on the run.

Perhaps an old soldier, returned from a war
Disgusted with the world, that he saw
Well it could be, he just likes being this way
Living in dirt, and not washing each day.

Olive Dell

Reflections

Have them, love them, then leave them be
Is a conclusion that's very true to me,
To lay the foundation for human life
While taking the part of Mother and Wife!

With experience gained, as through life we go
When we were young we could not know,
Temperaments differ from one to the other
A 'philosopher' is the role of a Mother.

As each day dawned on another scene
No time to ponder on what might have been
We did our best at every turn
And our efforts we should never spurn.

Life is such a game of chance
And richer lives we can all enhance
If all we've don, is our very best
We sit in the wings, and are richly blessed.

Joy Dodman

Lion's Teeth

Fitting like a piece in a jigsaw —
grey against grey ... ground against ground
trodden under foot ... raked over ...
the smile curving with the rising sun
the answer surprised no one
colours flowed under the bridge
flowers stood awkward but alike.

I undid the jigsaw — shook the frazzled pieces
unbuttoned their conformity
denied their status and rights.

I broke the banks of the river
pouring ecstasy into the fields.
I unhooked the stars

dangling their lights in the grey garden.
I plucked the obedient flowers
and strewed them over the grey corpse.

I opened the silence and poured in new sounds,
extraordinary, untamed, flowing sounds.

I counted the teeth in the lion's mouth —
I questioned the cement between the bricks —
I disturbed the graves of well-kept secrets —

the flowers shrieked their answer ...
the secrets danced a shocking dance ...
and the dust glistened, refusing to lie down.

Judy Dinnen

The Creator's Dream

As the sun shines on the garden,
A miracle, silently unfolds,
The beauty of the flowers that bloom;
In hues of reds, pinks, and golds.

God made them with love and tenderness,
In turn, we tend them with love,
For their beauty is a wonder
Which is surely sent from above.

The miracle of tiny seeds,
That germinate, root, and grow,
And the pleasure we derive from them,
Our Lord, on us did bestow.

For to love the plants and flowers,
Is to love the Creator's dream
Of a loving, peaceful mankind,
As Eden would have been.

So now look upon each other with love,
As we look upon a garden yonder,
Because we were made with that same love
And this, can make our hearts grow fonder.

So show kindness and thought to your fellow man,
And try to abide by the original plan,
And one day God will show, for all to see,
Just the way He planned it to be.

Mrs. S.L. Discombe

Christmas Eve

Christmas Eve seems endless,
Children's stockings neatly hung
Trying hard to stay awake,
Will Santa ever come?

Mummy peeps into the room,
Kids pretend to be asleep.
Hoping to see Santa
Filling stockings at their feet.

They try so hard to stay awake
But Mr. Sandman's on his way,
To close all children's eyelids,
So they won't see Santa's sleigh.

In the shadows secretly,
Santa's in the room,
Leaving lots of special toys
In the light of a smiling moon.

Children tossing restlessly,
Fighting with their sleep
Dreaming of the magic day,
Santa's date he said he'd keep.

Terry Davis

Having A Good Time

I'm feeling inebriated
Thirst I have sated
Mind's a bit woozy
Of my steps I must be choosy
Head feeling dizzy.
Stomach's getting in a tizzy
Eyes seeing double
With counting I'm having trouble
Tongue keeps getting knotted
Can't remember how many drinks I've blotted
Hands are unsteady
Spilled more than I've drunk already
Lost count of what I've spent
Ah! Bugger the rent
Of company there's no end
Making friend after friend
When I go to order
They rush to greet me
Even the floors now
Coming up to meet me.

Annie Doherty

Poppies

So this is where it happened.
This peaceful field of drowsy poppies.
Where lovers lie and dream their dreams,
Was once a place resembling hell,
Where gunshots roared and young men fell.
A crueller battle n'er was seen,
Than that 'twas fought upon this green.
Where bullets strewn and cannon blast,
And men were solemn in repast,
And though night came, sleep did not follow,
And morning brought them nought but sorrow.
Yet on this land no scars remain,
To tell of million soldiers slain,
No scars to se yet they are there,
Amongst this ground of beauty rare,
so look once more upon the scene.
The warmth and brightness of the green,
For even nature cannot feign,
This land was not a place of pain.
Beneath the ground lie young men's bones,
The gentle souls so far from home.
And in the wind a mourning sigh,
The echo of a battle cry.

Joanne Dillon

Intoxication

Thicker than water, sinking skin deep,
Co-ordination unbalanced, closer than sleep,
Aimlessly wandering down dark flashing streets,
Breathing carelessly, heart quickens it's beat,
Conversation lingers, what is it they speak?
Another unwanted, limbs taught and weak.

Emotions in torment, those of joy, fear and sorrow,
As the mind flickers over yesterday and tomorrow,
Brain warm and twisted, eyes blind with slurred sight,
The colourless odours disperse on with the night.
The fear of disclosure, as another is poured,
Disbelieving suspension, like a ship that is moored.

Night closely over, have soon to greet,
Stumbling skilfully, yet still full on feet.
The point has gone, of no return,
An infrequent venture, but still just won't learn.
Meeting is over, ill feeling is met,
Night closely over, and emotions lay fret.

Why did one choose to get this way in my head!
Partings finally and they slip off to bed.
Morning, awakening, mouth painfully dry,
No thought of the day that ahead does lie.
All this torment, from just one night,
Effortlessly descending from the bed with the light.

Laura Jane Doherty

Life's Shattered Dreams

Dreams in life should be based on truth, from an early age right into youth
You struggle hard the day you're born, it never ceases dusk till dawn.
Life goes on in stages more, the worst I feel is one to four.
Teaching is hard, learning is worse PLEASE give me a hand where do I stand.
Some are fortunate, some are not, nothing is equal, well not a lot
Children starve, parents fight, no one to teach me wrong from right
The world is round I know for sure, then why so many insecure?
WANTING, WANTING even more, greed takes over from way before.
You must have this, you must have that, WHAT'S the price? YOU'LL manage that.
One day you wake and CHILDHOOD'S gone, it's all so frightening but I must be strong,
To face life's dangers there are so many, friends you think come, ten a penny.
Don't be fooled with all they say, for in the end YOU WILL PAY.
Education doesn't come cheap, what you sow is what you reap.
Avoid the dangers, at all cost, for if you don't lives will be lost.
Heart's are broken, sorrows run deep, life has meaning, we must not weep.
Care for others in every way, then GOD'S LOVE will be here to stay.
What you have may not seem much, compared to some you're out of touch.
Riches in life cost not a penny, please don't say you haven't any.
Look out your window, walk out your door,
There all around you,
FROM GENERATIONS BEFORE.

Doreen Douglas

Be Prepared

If a cloud should hide the sun
If rain should down the window run
If good luck should pass you by
Don't just sit down and cry
Be prepared.
Start a bank account in your heart
It doesn't take much you know
A memory of a happy day
Will help to start you on your way
And then just watch it grow
Each week just add a little more
Anything will do.
A smile from someone in the street
A kindly word or two.
To know that you can see and hear
Now that will help it grow
That you are warm and fully fed
A profit that will show
If you can put each precious gift
Into your bank account
You can withdraw one now and then
When dark clouds hang about
So if your world is sometimes drear,
    don't give into despair
Save from today, and soon you'll find
    you are a millionaire.

Jean Donaghue

Spring

The early watery sunshine
Which in Springtime doth appear,
Bathes all the dull and listless earth
In sunlight bright and clear.

The early yellow crocus
Raise up their golden heads,
And then they proudly spread their leaves,
From out of their soily beds.

The snowdrops droop and vanish
Until another year,
Their fragile ivory petals fall
When Springtime doth appear.

Oh lovely dawn of Springtime,
Please linger — do not go,
We love to watch the plants shoot up
The trees and flowers grow.

Alas, the warmer days appear,
Spring vanishes away,
She leaves behind her splendid work,
The trees and flowers gay.

Oh, lovely dawn of one more Spring —
The birth of almost everything.

G. Audrey Doubleday.

The Farmer's Life

The farmer's life's a busy one,
Because his job is never done.
He feeds the pigs and milks the cows
And the fields still need some ploughs.

The farmer's life's a tiring one,
Because his job is never done.
He rides the horse and picks the flowers,
He never has fun for hours and hours.

The farmer's life's a boring one
Because his job is never done.
He picks the corn and sows the seeds,
And he has to get rid of all the weeds.

But now the farmer's day is done.
As you can see it wasn't very much fun.
But now the farmer wants to rest his head
Upon the pillow on his bed.

Jenny Donoghue (Age 7)

Emma's Dream

Shadow after shadow light through the leaves,
My horse and I following after the breeze.
The tree trunks flicker as we gallop by
Trees, leaves, shadows, silhouettes in front of the sun.
The quickness of light can't catch us.
My horse and I are laughter,
My horse and I are fun.

Life to be given to my horse and I
Life, four legs, the Earth and sky.
And all my summers as free as the winds.
We ride, ride, my horse and I,
And my laughter rides with the wind.

Thomas O. Dodge

The Fox Hunt

A horn sounded on the outskirts of the wood,
All the wildlife scattered as fast as they could.
But a sleek, red stranger just trotted along,
For him life was perfect and nothing was wrong.

Without any warning the hunt had his trail,
He ran like the wind fearing death should he fail.
He ran past the badgers safe down in their den,
And had a strong urge to be home just like them.

His heart raced and pounded as if it would burst,
Just over the hill now — he had to be first.
The hounds leapt upon him with a triumphant bay,
With a scream and a howl his life torn away.

Lisa Dilley (Age 12)

With Love From Sweep

I watch you from my silent world
You are my life, my faithful friend,
My needs are few, I just wait for you
To come home to me when your work day ends
I lie close to you to give you warmth,
And comfort, and sing my vibrating words of love
You reward me with your tender touch
And the unspoken understanding way you have
I feel so sad when oft' I see you cry
I watch you helplessly and wonder why
I lift my paw to touch your stricken face
My way of giving you a fond embrace
You understand my every whim and need
I look at you until you pay me heed
I cannot hear you when you call my name
But I will stay beside you just the same

Jo Doree

Storm

Through oceans dark the ship doth rusheth
Toppling and swaying as she goes.
The dark canvas sails flap and snap
     but amazingly stay in place.
The bright green mast creaks and groans,
The wind in triumphant joy blows gleefully
But in quite the wrong way he blew and blew
Until the ship was safe, at anchor in the bay.

Aleksander Domanski (Age 7)

A Little Beauty

I was walking along this grassy ditch
when I saw these flowers so yellow rich
cascading down like splashes of gold.
Their beauty to my eyes began to unfold
while intermingling with violets so deep
and the pleated leaves of the meadowsweet
with its stems of red picked up by the sun
made these flowers glow. Their beauty won.
They all reflected in the rippling stream
as it flowed peacefully along in an endless dream.
As I wandered along this corridor lush
there were roses of white and strawberry crush,
their colours erupting against the sky so blue
\giving the hedgerows of green a pinky hue.
The stream parted company, beside a field it flowed
where more yellow flowers in profusion glowed.
Their beauty along the streams we must never lose,
this beautiful flower, the little primrose.

Daphne Doy

This Side Of The Bathroom Mirror

Blue nondescript eyes scan humble
surroundings through plastic lenses.
Nose lacking length, rounded tip,
gives way to ovate nostrils.

Coarse whiskers of varying auburn,
now grey emerge, hides a top lip —
pierced by the combination of a
brother's right hook and incisor.

Tongue nuzzles another — chipped.
Recalls that of a metal part;
bullet from fake gun; too long
a game of Russian roulette.

I bite this top lip, reveal
tombstones leaning drunkenly
in defiance of a brace.
They are clenched in readiness.

Tony Downing

The Gifts

Afraid of loving?
Afraid of life
I gave to you a golden flower
From which you scented far off winds
And lands and possibilities;
The petals of gold for food you ate
But in your blood there they'll wait;
In times of famine you can draw on
Banks of love and memory
That no money could you ever buy.

Afraid of speaking?
Afraid of being known
You gave to me a piece of glass
That mirrors the 'window of my soul'
And showed me what I am, and how
To say, to be, to you , to me,
To them.

Helen Yvonne Dowle

Black Horses

The night is black, no moon in sight
Thundering hooves, a flash of light
Four great steeds appear in view
Snorting loud observed by few

Flashing by on their rain soaked way
Perform their deed then far away
Harness straining, dripping sweat
Four great beasts all lathered and wet

On and on throughout the land
Complete their journey as they planned
Moon peeps out to light the scene
No tracks are left where they have been

Through cobbled streets their hooves a-clatter
Time stands still, it doesn't matter
Sparks fly up a screeching halt
Wake the dead, that's not their fault

Up the path their master races
Oaken door, no airs no graces
In and out in a flash of time
No sound he makes, all done in mime

Mounting fast away at speed
To leave this place is their great need
Toward the sky, heaven bound
No trace of visit ever found

L.J. Draper

Thoughts Of The Sea

Edging, and rolling and banging I come,
Seeping, tearing, I'll conquer the scum.
Tearing the earth more each day
To overcome all that lies in my way.

Who are they, these beings who
Bathe and swim and dive?
Lucky they feel to be alive,
They do not know their time is short
But I know as I resort
To plan my task toward their end.

Edging and rolling, I am the Sea,
Won't you come thus unto me.
Ply me with the wind, blow high
Reach me to the bright blue sky.

Bright my edge with raging foam
Onward now to roam and roam,
Forwards I race to take in my path
Oh think, what aftermath.

Lie quiet now, my job is done,
Just me, the stars, beneath the sun,
Peace at last, I'm King, The Sea
Rolling in glorious Majesty.

I'm left alone, the only one
On, on, on, Oblivion.

Frances Down

Winter

As I looked out the window, I noticed that the
great metamorphosis had finally occurred.
I could no longer see the sparrows flying freely,
Or the beautiful colours that surrounded me yesterday.
Instead, a smooth white blanket lay draped over the landscape,
And its innocuous presence caused everything to flee.

As I trudged through the snow, I saw trees stripped naked.
I delved deeper into this curious, yet unforgotten world,
And there on a bough stood the faithful old Robin,
As it nurtured its offspring in the Draconian conditions.
I could no longer see the bright array of Autumn leaves,
But I was aware of the silky spider's web,
And the intricate snowflakes which reflected a different beauty,
As they hung beside icicles which pointed like daggers.

The nights got darker, the winds were stronger,
Yet the people's spirits grew warmer.
Winter was now evident, as men of snow stood erect,
Like sentinels on duty protecting their domain.
Suddenly, the white blanket disappeared,
And the sounds of nature could be heard
Echoing in the distance once again.
Spring, had crept in stealthily,
And won the battle, for another year.

Aidan Doyle (Age 16)

Earth-Bound Galaxy

Lights across the lough appear
Like stars at dusk.
The endless cluster of lights grow
Brighter in the gathering gloom.

Those travelling along
The elongated earth-bound galaxy,
May be like space travellers
Insulated from what's outside their craft;
Regarding others as space debris
In the way,
As they journey to and fro; from where
Those in little worlds of their own,
Scurry along on wheel, or on foot,
Sufficiently aware of those about them,
so as not to collide.

The sky above the phrenetic;
Electrically lit ant-hill,
Glows, blotting out the stars.

Denis A. Dolan

Age

When you see an old man what do you see,
A little boy climbing an apple tree.
Fishing for minnows in a brook,
Using a net instead of a hook.
Playing cricket on the village green,
Or hide and seek so you can't be seen.

When you see an old woman what do you see
A little girl standing by mother's knee.
Clutching a dolly to her breast,
Or looking for clothes in the old oak chest.
Dressing like Cinderella going to the ball,
Pretending to be grown up when you're quite small.

When you see an old couple coming down the street
Bent and shuffling on painful feet.
Remember that they once spent happy days,
Like Christmas and Easter and school holidays.

J. Dudley

Gone But Not Forgotten

As twa young bairns we'd travelled far,
Inspired by fit we'd seen,
The rugged hills and fairy glens in a' their shades o' green.
In Summer, forests came alive wi' birds and scented flo'ers,
The red deer stood sae regal amongst the purple cladded moors.

The swirlin' Autumn leaves now fa', sae gentle on the ground,
The birds nae longer sing their songs, a breeze the only sound.
An' as I look up sae sadly tae the tree that stands sae bare,
I realise, life must go on, though life's nae very fair.
For unlike the scented seasons that return year after year,
Ma freen I've lost forever, ma freen sae very dear.

These memories surround me,
Yer spirit lingers on,
Yer kindness ne'r forgotten,
As I wander all alone.

Ma heart is like a river, that's been frozen o'er till Spring,
An emptiness lies deep inside, nae breath o' hope tae bring.
But as time goes by, that river thaws and sheds its crystal tears,
And fit's left are happy memories that we'd shared o'er a' the years.

Aye those were the days ma freen,
Gone but not forgotten.

Audrey Duncan

Pain, Truth And Happiness

She's growing up and I'm so glad,
Yet sometimes I feel a little sad.
She's very much a young lady now,
And this makes me a mother proud.
Her mother's eyes, her father's nose,
From baby to woman I watch her grow.
I feel the heartache, I feel the joy,
I watch her grow up and marry a boy.
I think she won't be coming home,
Now I feel so very alone.
I must not be silly, I mustn't be grim,
I must not think she only cares for him.
For I've been her friend for eighteen years,
God knows why I'm having these fears.
No one can take away these years,
So why, oh why, am I shedding these tears.
I fear she's been taken, I fear that's she's going,
But I'm being stupid, I shouldn't be moaning.
Instead of losing, I've actually gained,
Three for two a family we've made!

Rhian Dukes

Retribution

His Mam sits in the harsh, bare hospital room.
Alone, but not quite.
Her son, David, lies asleep in the bed,
Half-hidden by the tangle of wires, tubes and drips.
He sleeps more than anything, these days.
It's the morphine, really,
Or whatever it is that they give him.
It's a blessing, she thinks.
At least he won't see himself wasting away.
Slowly dying ...
She wishes his Dad was here,
As much for her as anything else.
But he won't come.
He won't even talk about it.
Hasn't said a word about "it" since the letter came.
She was such a nice girl too.
So bright and happy, and well, normal.
Now she sits all alone
And watches her son die
From "divine retribution".

Cath Dudley

Wars

They rest in silence they're not alone
For they were soldiers — most unknown
Headstones by the hundreds all in line
Amidst green grass, well tended — cut so fine

They were so young when they did go
To fight a war they did not know
'Kill the Germans!' or them so do maim
As so did Germans, did they do the same

Take no prisoners! that was the cry
'Kill the Hun for he deserves to die'
But these poor souls they were just like you
Ordered to kill the lads they never knew

And so it is in all such wars
'Tis not they who fight, the wars others cause
But 'tis these poor souls which lay beneath the sod
They gave their lives, now rest with God.

Leslie F. Dukes

Untitled

Aimless,
Fish in the tank
Swim together alone.
Maintaining body room they keep
Apart.
Neither
Lover nor friend
They companionably float
In a world that's bounded by glass,
Untouched.

Restless
Most of their lives,
Still they keep their distance
Suspended in living water,
Thirstless.
We are
Fish in the tank
Maintaining our distance,
Living apart, untouched, thirstless
As fish.

Keith Douglas

Toast of Xmas Cheer

Mistletoe with berries pale and gleaming bright
Lights upon the Xmas tree
What a lovely sight
Carolers with lanterns sing with
Pure, pure joy
Everyone they celebrate
The birthday of that Boy

It's Xmas Eve again once more,
Goodwill to everyone
We celebrate it every year
The birth of sweet little son.
So drink a drink of Xmas cheer
And raise you glasses
In the air
A happy Xmas everyone
Especially to that little son

He made it possible for us to share
Our table and
Our Xmas fare
So raise you glasses in the air
And drink a toast of Xmas cheer
A Happy Xmas everyone
Especially to that little son

Eleanor Dunn

He Called Me Nurse Today

As she looked me in the eye
Her voice trembled, "Will he die?"
I took her hand and squeezed it tight
And said, "Sit down, I'm here tonight."

As tears of love ran down her face,
He was taken injured, at fast pace,
To the theatre team, just waiting there,
Skilled hands to work and to repair.

A busy ward, work to be done,
But her thoughts were only for her son,
Tired hands and tensions high.
We'll do our best that he won't die.

Nights and days of touch and go
The words she cried, "Son I love you so"
Body broken, no voice heard,
Outside the window, a tiny bird.

Bleeping monitors all around
Was the Mother's only sound.
Long days and nights have drifted by,
Now feeling sure he will not die.

She left his room to walk a while,
And on return, she saw me smile.
I turned and said, "He will be O.K."
"Your son, he called me 'nurse' today."

Beryl Drummond

137

The Lottery

A topic of conversation among gambling folk galore,
Is how to work the lottery, how best to choose the score.
Elizabeth the first 'tis said, began this crazy trend
When dukes, lords and their ladies inheritance did spend,
No mention where the draw was made, could have been on the Hoe,
Sir Francis bowling numbered bowls, some fast and then some slow.
As money came in by degree, committees then to call
On how to spend the guineas to help us, one and all,
Some said we need to use the cash to protect us from the foe,
While others openly declared, "Why must we waste it so?
To cross the Thames we need a bridge where sheep and folks can pass,
Why should we wait for ebbing tide or hand out hard earned brass?"
From parliament and ruling lords loud ayes, nayes, shouts and bleets,
Westminster Bridge, storm shelters, piers, a Swiss chap did complete.
I hope this decade's lottery cash is used in such a way
New generations stop to think of this November day.

Beryl Dyson

Duck And Venison Including Dessert

Delightful, delicious
A veritable feast.
Voluptuousness personified
Incredible beast.
Dejeuner, dinner
My hunger
Can't wait.
I need you
Now,
To touch you, taste you
Yearn for you
Relish you
Eat you.

Jack Diamond

What's Life?

Two wars were tough, yet people pulled together,
Glad to be alive, didn't care about the weather.
Then we got "all mod cons" aye maybe too soon,
Work was there though they even sent a man to the moon.

Not just the rich had cars, everyone was better paid,
Pits worked flat out, whisky too was made.
But we all got greedy, we wanted more and more,
Joined the Common Market, now we pay the score.

There's no longer "Britain" who used to be so "Great",
Now we're "Common", we can no longer debate!
We're a country with no pride, governed from afar,
Lost our 'identity' as it won't fit in their jar!

Is it any wonder, we have all this stress and strain?
We can no longer find work, it really is a pain.
We cant' do this, we can't do that, these others won't let us,
Do they know something we don't, why all this darned fuss?

There's hardly any farms left, because of so many rules,
We won the wars you know, why are we the 'fools'?
Isn't it time we fight, a different kind of war,
Get the MP's to stand up, tell us where to buy our tar!

We should be seeing to our own house, stop all these handouts,
Sow crops, feed ourselves, and don't listen to these louts.
See to crime, drugs, etc., let us make our Britain "Great",
Let us wipe these past few years, right off the darned slate!

Doris Dyer

Poppies

Poppies, poppies
Clean and bright
Shining like a light
Memories of war
Come back to those that fought for us
Poppies shining like blood
Blood everywhere
Today the field of red
I am here today
Only for these men
Who saw so much
We only see on pictures, T.V.
And hear of those many years ago
Memories, oh bright red poppies
What you mean to so many.

Victoria Dyer (Age 13)

The Path Of Life

Life is but a journey
From the cradle to the grave
Innocence of childhood
Left behind to brave
Endless boring school days
Pangs of love and pain
Struggling to adulthood
The passion fires to tame

Another step is taken
Settling down we try
To raise a happy family
Before life passes by
Years slip by so quickly
Bodies growing weak
Struggling with ageing
As extra time we seek

But time will not relinquish
No matter how we try
Time will run full circle
And the will to live will die.

Mary Dunne

Town Signs Of Coming Rain

The Town Hall clock chimes tinny on the town;
The distant diesel brays outside you gate
And rattles round your fence.
The ship in dock is hooting in your ear.
The sound of traffic booms and roars, then wanes
On puffing winds that weave a patterned sky.

Leaves clatter up the street, then rise
In a wild, whirling dance; doors creak and bang.
Smoke-banners drape the walls of those few homes
Where Gran still huddles by an open fire,
Pulling her rug against the swirling draughts
And fidgeting to ease her aching joints.

Unpleasant smells rise from the cleanest drains,
Wafting defiant spiders up the pipes
To crouch in baths and basins. Birds fly home
To country fields that stretch into the town
Then vanish in the rolling cloud that hurls
The first grey drops against the misting pane.

Margaret Durham

Autumn

Oh sweet October day, the world it seems
has paused; morning unfolding gently caught
the trees naked, silent as if in thought
they stand, motionless spell of tranquil dreams.
All around is still; so still. The calm redeems
the storms of life. A canvas clement, naught
disturbs until a bird in song has sought
to write in notes of joy, scattering sunbeams.
O that the lattermath of this, my life,
may lead my way in paths equivalent
unharassed by the curse of crazy care.
A backcloth benign, untainted by strife,
so dawns a new day, the touch of content
and peace a fragrance infusing the air.

Sam Dunn

A Sign Of Hope

The child, surrounded with love,
Gazes with innocence into his mother's eyes.
A soft smile parts her lips
As she bestows a loving kiss.

Watching for any sign of progress
From the years of patiently teaching him,
Helping to open the doors of his closed world.
She silently sheds a tear as he responds,
In a small way,
Bringing him closer to a new tomorrow.

Barbara Denton

Sunrise

Daylight breaks in on the unsuspecting flower
For darkness had ruled so long and hard
But slowly with blinking petals and trembling leaves
It peers over the still sleeping bushes around
To see if it was really true

Yes, sure enough
Even through the blurring fog and deep mist
First with furtive glances in tiny sparks
Then with daring rays and probing glare
The Almighty Sun rises in full array of glory
And shines through the universe
Till all is light for the flower
And hope for you

Charles Dzradosi 1991, Accra

National Poetry Day

Thank God for the travelling library
Thank God for the service they give
Thank God for the care and attention they give us
Thank God — they help us to live.
A book is a quiet companion
Especially if you are old —
And your money is limited
Your spending's restricted
With heating and lighting
Jack Frost's a biting
A bed and a book
Is the best thing to have
Thank God for the Travelling Library.

Mrs. M.K. Dales

Winning Dream

Rush to the shops,
Buy a ticket or three,
Then sit back and dream,
Of winning the lottery.
Pick the right number,
Anyone could win,
Then buy a fast car,
And go for a spin.
Or buy a big house,
Have a ball, have a party,
Buy a whole new wardrobe
Look like a real smartie.
Book a cruise on a liner,
Live the life of 'old Riley',
Mingle with the famous
Tina Turner or Kylie.
It's Saturday night,
Turn on the TV,
Sit down and pray,
Please, let it be me!

Mrs. J. Dravnieks

Debts in Time

Battered and alone like a kiosk phone
She is now but a shadow
Lost in the white washed ward.
Her shapeless, skeleton face and kimono dressing gown
look out of place.

She has been waiting too long
tasting the lonely torture
in the cemetery of her mind.
Only red ribbon making volunteers
dare to fill the orange synthetic chairs next to her bed.

Nobody cares any more
the photographers don't ask her to pose.
The critics have forgotten her name.
Occasionally flowers arrive without a card
from her former, guilt-laden lovers
they have nothing to say to her
for she no longer is the gypsy of the stage
with lush, red lips crowned with a flowing golden mane.

The greed of death easily swallowed her whole
in the cracking yolk of morning light.
but she was ready with her bible and cross.
She left on awkward lipstick stained message behind
I owed debts in time.

Nicola Daly

Peace

The starting of peace
But will it last
As it seems to have happened
All very fast
We all wish for happiness
And peace galore
No more frightened to answer your door
We want fun and laughter
And peace all around
No more bombing
Or bullet sounds
It's time for love
A time for joy
A time to help adults
And every girl and boy
A time for understanding
And a time to join together
Hoping the peace will this time last forever
So ban the bomb, throw down your gun
Let's keep the peace for everyone
We've lived in hell, and all shed a tear
Now let's have a Merry Christmas
And a peaceful New Year.

Anne Downing

The Land Of Make Believe

The thoughts and actions of a child will never cease to be
A source of much bewilderment and full of mystery,
For in their minds there is a world far different from ours,
A lonely place where they abide for many, many hours.

And in this world there is a land of beauty and of joy,
They will must surely seek this place, be it girl or boy,
This land is theirs and only they may enter its domain,
To partake of its happiness in play, and fun, and game.

They seek this place in tender years but as the years go by,
They find it much more difficult to enter, though they try.
For as adults their minds become, the land will fade away,
This world will not now be for them, nor land where children play.

This mystic place can only be exclusive to a child,
Where they may find such happiness they almost seem beguiled,
It is a land where all have been but never will retrieve,
For childish thoughts have made this land The Land of Make Believe.

Wolfe

... or not

Coiled,
Immortal;
Sprung like steel
This stainless soul,
Wrought from fire,
I ought to know;
Fraught with fear
And bought with gold,
Torn to shreds
And swallowed whole.
Spoiled
And mortal,
I shuffled off
This coital thrall,
The cloying stench,
This bar-room brawl.
Oh pure!
Oh free!
Oh God, it's me.

Michael J. Damakin

Morning Star

An air of great despondency was felt around the town.
The last boat-building firm we had would soon be closing down.
The lugger which would be the last to leave the stocks was built,
All saws were oiled and stored away, each hammer in its hilt.
And then began the cleaning up, the locals helped out too,
The shipwrights didn't ask for help, they knew they need not do.

At last the big day came along, anticipation high,
Today it was the launching, 'neath a cloudless, azure sky.
The launching of the lugger was arranged to catch high tide,
When water lapped the roadway just across the other side.
Now today's auspicious launching was the duty of the mayor.
And he'd been know to be a little lengthy with his prayer.
Then everybody gathered round as out the boat was hauled.
The men all clapped, the women wept, but tiny tots just bawled.
At last they all were ready, with the mayor in robes and chain,
And in his hand, for all to see, a bottle of champagne.
He took up his position, which was right against the stem,
And called out, "Let the children see, it's history for them!"
Then with a flourish he did smash that champagne in its jar,
And loud and clear his voice rang out, "I name thee "Morning Star!"
May all who sail in you henceforth be safe from any harm!"
The launchers heaved, and in she slid, and floated like a charm.
Old-timers who have fished for years, on boats both big and small,
Will tell you, (if you ask them) that "The best sea-boat by far,
Is that one which the Mayor launched, that handsome "Morning Star!"

James W. Eddy

Ancient Kings of Nature

A twisting tale of
knowledge
A sturdy bark says
wise
All the world pays
homage
As nature's giants light our
eyes
For giving shade and
shelter
Saving memories of
lives
Accepting pain and
Torture
From initials carved by
knives
Pleasant images of
beauty
In a hundred shades of
green
Sent to perform a
duty
Spread your branches tree
be seen.

Kaye Durant

The M:F:I: Wardrobe

Well time's finally caught up and you old Dad is no more,
And I don't want no weepin' and wailing', no fancy wreaths nailed on't front door,
And I don't want no expensive coffin in polished oak so fine and superior,
And I don't want brass plates and handles that shine or quilted velvet interior.
We've not got money to burn if you'll forgive me little pun,
Yes, I know it's a serious matter, I know I shouldn't make fun,
But I am serious when I ask you, no fancy do's, now mind,
Get Trevor to knock up a plywood box and use those old screws up of mine.
In fact, now I thing on, just tell him there's a M:F:I: wardrobe in't shed,
Get him to knock a few extra nails, in't side that's come loose,
And nail in a board for me head.
And if it makes you feel better get the curtains from that box in the pantry,
And then drape them o'er the old wardrobe door till Trevor comes to fetch me.
He can use that big camping trailer, make sure he ties me down tight,
I don't want to end up in't middle of Stone Road, I would look a weary old sight.
And when it's all o'er and done with and Trev's done these wishes of mine
Give him my old Raleigh bicycle to pay for his petrol and time.
And if there's a few sarny's over (I suppose you'll do one or two)
You can wrap them up in bread paper, and let Trev and Bren take a few.
Now don't forget Duck, no weepin' and wailin', no long faces and silly tears.
Put Max Bygraves on the gramophone and get down one or two beers: Cheers.

John Edmundson

Small Lie, Big Trouble

Poor Geoff Giraffe was feeling bored,
he couldn't use his friend's skateboard.
"Oh come on Peter what is wrong,"
"Well it's like this Geoff, you're too long."
"Oh please, please Peter, I'll be fine,
I ride on Stew Shrew's all the time."
Geoff thought, that's just a small white lie,
"Cos Stew has never let him try.
"OK" said Peter, "have a go,"
So Geoff pushed off with much gusto.
Off down the road he really sped,
"Mind that tree, Geoff," Peter said.
A bang a crash, Geoff's on the ground,
With bits of skateboard all around.
Said Geoff, "I'm really sorry Pete,"
And starts to get up to his feet.
Poor Pete's skateboard's beyond repair,
With pieces lying everywhere.
"I thought you'd ridden one before,
I'm not your friend Geoff, anymore."
Poor Geoff he walked off feeling sad,
He knew that he'd been very bad.
He told a lie to his friend Pete,
that's not a very clever treat.

Michael Earle

Pro Patria?

Where each rise of the ground
was once a prize to be killed for
and hollows stank, one slope
has been mollified; a graveyard,
neat as a dormitory with the grass
trimmed evenly beside each bed
and the soil tucked firmly in.

The first two-thirds are French
— artilleur, capitaine, chasseur —
then the pattern changes. The same
rows, same bare rectangles except
now the headstones are turned,
the names mirror-written, rippled,
the way the wind writes on sand.

With a crescent carved above each
regimental badge, the stones slant —
as a field of sunflowers slants
towards some unattainable desert;
as it, dead, the zouaves have turned
from Douaumont, where every ally
wore the bleached skin of an enemy.

Clive Eastwood

A Secret Place

Whene'er the pace of life's too fast, I have a special space
A secret hideaway of mine, a very mystic place
I stroll along a riverbank so tranquil, calm and green
Together with my collie dog to my hidiehole serene

Where weeping willow's teardrops create circles in the stream
With dragonflies and butterflies I set myself to dream
Of days of youth and lovers lost, of family and friends
I watch white clouds scud o'er the sky and rainbows reach their ends

Whilst dreaming dreams and thinking thoughts, my collie by my side
The hours roll past
Tensions unwind
My worries all subside

As morning kisses afternoon and swallows swoop and fly
An occasional moorhen stabs the stillness with a cry
The sun persuades the water lilies their petals to unfold
Their waxen flowers of pink and white a beauty to behold

A frog leaps up with croak and plop to settle on a leaf
And catch invisible insects to end a life so brief
My dog has smelled all smells around and sniffed at every tree
It's time to wend our way back home, relaxed, unwound and free

So often when at place of work I wish that I was there
My secret place, my haven beside the waters calm
To ponder life with all its care
Be at one with Nature's charm

Angela Edwards

Jess

Golden red summer, emerald blue sky
Landscapes of beauty, mountains so high
Whispers of wind hardly making a sound
Sweet smelling flowers serenade on the ground.

Below us we watch a stream flowing with might
Winding through the valley until it's out of sight,
On it's journey forward to find the great big sea
Through the hills and caves round each and every tree.

My faithful friend has fun bounding down the stream,
Heaven only knows how I'll every get her clean,
Splashing and playing, rolling in the grass,
Chasing all the insects, running very fast.

And so my friend and I have walked for many a mile
I think she's very tired, I look at her and smile.
So we sit and watch the sun go down so very far away
And only hope tomorrow is as beautiful as today.

Joanne Edmondson

Faint Music Of The Distant Drum

I loved my love upon a bed of brier
And fed him honeyed kisses scorched with fire
And bowed my womanhood to his desire;
Now ecstasy has drifted by.

I loved my love in deepest woodland where,
Enraptured by the sweetness, flower fair,
For him alone I laid my secrets bare,
Now gossamer illusions fly.

I loved my love with passionate delight
And followed through enchanted realm of night
Alive with magic shining jewel bright;
Now purple shadows blind my eye.

I loved my love with purity and pain
And golden floods of sacrificial rain
In benediction cleansed the soul again;
My love is gone. Wild roses die.

Anna Easton

That's Me

I'm a leaf on a tree
    That's me.
Roots, branches, a tree
    That's me.
I float in the wind and fulfill my life.
    That's me.

I'm a blade of grass in God's carpet of green
    That's me.
I'll cool your toes and share your dream
    That's me.

I'm a star in the sky on a balmy night
    That's me.
I sparkle and shine — God's gift of light
    That's me.

I'm a clown on a stage, clowning around
    That's me.
I'm living at last what I want to be
    That's me.

Mrs. P. Easty

The Ploughman, The Field Mouse and The Hawk

Autumn is with us
He is safe in his nest
Food store around him
His mind is at rest
Through the peace of his slumber
A rumbling grows stronger
His nest is destroyed
He's at rest no longer
A panic, a scramble
Over mountainous boulders
When over his shoulder
A shadow approaches
The hawk is on target
The field mouse is breakfast
The ploughman looks on
Feeling guilty and helpless

Nigel Dallyn

Untitled

Fifty years hence, old comrades and I will stand
At the cenotaph and silently pray.
The bugle sounds, memories come flooding past,
Oh why! Oh why!
The ultimate price this Christian soldier had to pay.
God, in thy rest his death atoned, let his bravery ever shine,
A light among the stormy way.
Son of a minister prepared to die, so others remain.
Survival of the fittest, pittance to the weak,
That was the reality we had to meet.
The banner raised he answered the call
Worshipped by platoon, L. Cpl. and all,
Refrained all onslaught to the front go
Leader of men to the core.
To all nations let it be known, who wants war?
Not this gallant officer, he did not want to go,
Served country deservedly so
Hell let loose the Reichswald Forest was his fate,
Fought like a tiger, did not flee, died in pain.
His ardennes award repaid in full,
Others saved that was his aim.
In life, did not want earthly gains
But honours shared a minister's son to the end.
"Better death than shame".

T.W. Edwards

Don't Look Back

Don't knock at my door, just walk away,
    What can I do? What can I say?
    Just let me be, just walk away,
    I'll hide my tears of yesterday.

Don't look back, just walk away,
    Don't phone me up, no words to say,
    Just let me be, just walk away,
    I'll hide my tears of yesterday.

Don't look back, just walk away,
    It hurts for me to feel this way,
    Just let me be, just walk away,
    I'll hide my tears of yesterday.

Don't look back, just walk away,
    It's not the time to make amends
    Just let me be, just walk away,
    I'll hide my tears of yesterday.

Don't look back, just walk away,
    Until the time my sad heart mends,
    Just let me be, just walk away,
    I'll hide my tears of yesterday.

Regina Edwards

The Dentist

I hate going to the dentist
Most folk do though, I suppose
I find it so embarrassing
When I'm gazing up his nose
And when my mouth's wide open
And I lay back in the chair
Then he starts asking questions
Like 'Did you go away last year?'
I try to splutter out
That I only stayed at home
And he replies 'How lovely,'
'I've never been to Rome,'
He takes a look around my mouth
And finds some teeth to fill
I grip the chair more tightly
Oh how I hate that drill
He says 'This is not a big one
So it shouldn't hurt you much'
But I nearly hit the ceiling
When the nerve he starts to touch
and when the job's all over
He says 'Now spit in the bowl,'
I feel I'd like to aim at him
If the truth were really told

Peg Edwards

The Laughter of Hell

A sound, a noise,
Stop, listen ... listen.
They hurl themselves at you!
Striving for death, destruction, death.
You see them coming,
Their eyes light up the fields.
You see them stop ... drop,
Their blood colours the dirt.
With no thought you dive,
You feel the earth beneath you,
You know, you will soon be a part of it.
Advance, you do.
Further, closer, nearer ...,
But to what?
You know not of what lies in front,
But you are being driven,
Thrusted toward the laughter of Hell.
Your friends have fallen,
Now you remain.
Hell is laughing ...,
You stand no chance.
In desperation you run towards the laughter,
You feel it rip through you,
Then ... nothing.
It was the laughter of Hell,
That sent you to Heaven.

Damian Edwards

A Day Begins

The dawn of day reveals a covering shroud
Slowly rising, creating mist and cloud
Then clearing to unfold a mystical scene
High mountains with tumbling streams, a joy when seen
Small cottages, chimneys issuing smoke
The telling signs of life for country folk
In the distance can be heard a bellowing cow
Searching for the calf that's been taken from her now
Others are waiting to return to the farm
Before giving their milk, they need to be calm
A triumphant cockerel greeting the day
With a crowing sound that only he can say
Dew laden grass being eaten by sheep
On those far off hills, not so very steep
Birds awakening, delight in their song
Silent they have been keeping all night long
Rabbits scampering in grass long and green
In full daylight they are so seldom seen
Alongside the hedge a fox quietly runs
As he tries to hide before the hunt comes
The sound of a cuckoo seeking a nest
His flight weary wings are needing to rest
Overhead the sun from cloud breaks through
As all life on earth begins anew

Gwendoline A. Ellis

Autumn Wonder

I often sit and wonder how
The leaves know when to fall to the ground
Who changes their colour from green to brown?
Who shrivels them up and blows them around.
Who tells the animals the time has come
To make themselves 'comfy' for the winter months,
Who watches over them as they sleep so sound
In their dens and lairs beneath the ground,
Who keeps them warm during their long winter sleep
Beneath sheets of ice and snow so deep.
Who tells the 'birdies' the time has come
To gather their flock and head for the sun,
Nest in the countries where the sun shines bright,
Far away from the frost, the snow and the ice.
There has to be someone, you must agree
Who cares so much for the plants and trees,
Who loves the animals so very much
To tuck each one in for the winter months.
To guide the birds on their journey afar
Through a maze of clouds lit up by the stars.
The answer to all this wonder and awe
Must be the person who created it all
So as I watch the autumn leaves fall
I thank our Creator, who made it all.

Marie Elliott

A Winter's Tale
(or The Room With The View)

I looked through my window one wintery day,
The fields were all white with a sparkling array
Of snow covered grassland, — a dazzling sight,
Inspiring, exciting, a joy and delight;
I marvelled, then came to this realisation,
How finite is Man and how great God's creation!

The River Trent's wending its own winding course,
For centuries flowing from its secret source,
The soft soothing music of water I hear
As the river goes cascading over the weir,
The trees bare and leafless, bedecked with the snow
Like a fine scenic painting an artist will show.

Inspired by the awe of this wonderful view,
Transcending by far all that mere Man can do,
I pause by my window and silently muse,
How good to have vision to see these great views;
But evening approaches and I draw the curtain
And glad I'm in Abbyfield House here in Burton.

Robert J. Eeles

Friendship

What should we do without it?
How could we live each day?
Without this thing called friendship
To help us on our way.
The handshake and the greeting
The warm and friendly smile
That is exchanged in greeting
With friends we've known a while.
The unexpected phone in
The letter through the post,
These things help keep us going
Just when we need them most.
To me, these are life's treasures
Though no wealth or fame I find,
But I thank God for such pleasures
And for friends, the caring kind.

Mrs. L. Elliott

Animal Sanctuary

A haven run by kindly caring souls
Who take in all dog, cat, or orphan foals
Animals here of every breed and sort
This is a home, their last resort

Some, victims of cruelty and sad neglect
Here cared for, and treated with respect
Scampering kittens, puppy dogs with wistful eyes
Here stables, kennels, cages, and pig sty's

With goats and geese, this and that
Peacock, blind dog, and one eyed cat
Tired donkeys graze with elderly horse
When staying here they're none the worse

Open days are a joy to all
With bargains and gifts on every stall
We make a donation to bring and buy
See dogs running in field nearby

People bring pets for a boarding stay
Leave in safe keeping, when going away
others find working dog, or pet
They're all in good health, checked by vet

Must go now, we cannot stay
Will return again on next open day
Could not wait until the end
This lovely old dog is our new friend

Harold Roy Ellis

Gaudeamus Igitur

Teacups chink and drip on saucers,
Saucers drip on tannined lace,
Two old friends in fading sunlight
Brush their cake crumbs into space.

Dated clothes and walnut fingers
Dipped in yellow-golden light,
Wispy topknots nodding sagely,
Eyes alive and darkly bright.

Long ago, in school together,
They had heard the teacher say,
"You'll remember when you're forty —
And forty you will be, one day ..."

She'd uttered words to jolt their senses,
Outraged youth with alien pain.
"Yes, that day will come, you know."
They'd blinked their eyes and, yes, it came.

Years that passed were rich in learning,
Arcady consumed their days.
Gods drew near in fascination,
Muses envied turn of phrase.

Now, behind the dry old parchment,
Flickers still the Vestal flame.
Two old friends in fading twilight
Tread the sacred groves again.

Denise Elkins

Grieve Not

Grieve not for me when I am gone —
A tear or two perhaps.
But smile awhile and remember well, the fun.
I would not have tarried longer —
A further burden. No! —
Life may end but love and memories linger on.

My time here was good
My friends were many
My family loving and caring
I leave behind fond memories of the past
Which, for my sake, please go on sharing.

Should you forget me for a while and then remember
Do not grieve — Life goes on.
And better you should forget and smile
Than remember and be sad all the while.

Connie Ellis

The Eagle

Cautiously with keen eye,
She swoops and soars above,
The land swirling far below,
The air like cool breath upon her wing,
Her life an open space of freedom,
Her heart light, her worries few,
The grandeur of her stature obscured
By the blue-white, in which she flies,
Her prey lies unknowing in the foliage below,
As she glides with open claws to grasp,
Returning once more to thermal flight,
Disappearing to her high hidden resting place,
Where she feasts upon her succulent catch,
Her beauty forgotten once more.

Ms. L.A. Eaves

Mother to Her Cerebral Palsied Child

Little one —
        The possibilities are there ...
Let us —
        Arouse unwoken senses
                Stimulation

        Exercise your passive body
                Action

        Coax clenched hands open
                Exploration

        Dare stiff legs to walk
                Motivation

        Master independent feeding
                Function

        Release power of speech
                Communication

        Share joys of learning
                Interaction

        Explore worlds of music
                Exhilaration

        Learn to laugh at mishaps
                Affection

        Sleep when we grow weary
                Recuperation

        Prove the sceptics wrong
                Satisfaction

Hazel Emery

The Hardships of Relationships

Collecting the dole is normal,
It's a part of everyday life.
The Job Centre is really informal,
It cuts down on the strife.

The wife she's got a day job,
It helps to pay the bills.
The kid's they do some odd jobs,
For their uncle Phil.

Our life is of a standard,
That we don't go out to drink.
We sit at home, we're stranded,
Our life's gone down the sink.

My wife now wants to leave me,
For another man.
She says she wants to leave me,
'Cos I've gone down the pan.

She left me on my birthday,
That woman could be cruel.
She also took the kids that day,
And took me for a fool.

I do not see the kids no more,
Although I've found a job.
I hear the wife has left him for,
She's found he was a slob!

Mark D. Elwood

Early Morning Call

There's a little Bird a singing, this hazy early Summer's morn,
I've listened to his tuneful notes, since just the crack of dawn.
He seems to know I'm trying to sleep, I've pulled the cover's over my head
But his cheery, happy chirping, even follows me down the bed.
For half an hour, I toss and turn, the bedding's on the floor,
I'll walk around with bleary eyes this morning, that's for sure.
I've evil thoughts about the Bird, if I had got a gun,
I'd shoot the feathers off his back and count them one-by-one!
Soon dressing gown and slippers clad, wearily down the stairs I thump,
To make an early cuppa, 'cos I've really got the hump.
How I'd love to choke that dratted Bird, and silence its cheery song.
Oh, to sleep a few hours, in peace and quiet, is it asking too much? Am I wrong?
But tea in my hand, up the stairs I climb, funny, haven't heard a note.
There's not been as much as a chirrup from that noisy little throat.
Did he pick up my awful thoughts, has he really flown away?
Shall I hear again his melody, waking me on a Summer's day?
What a sad and silent world t'would be, to awake without birdsong,
But not be roused at four in the morn, he's surely got his timing wrong.
I truly wouldn't hurt a feather of his tiny little head,
But I do so wish he'd let me sleep, early mornings in my bed.
It's six thirty now, and seagull's cries arouse me from my rest,
On a wall outside, sits my little Bird, complete with brightly feathered breast!
He's singing such a lovely song. I'm awake. Dreams fade away.
He sings, "It's time to rise, and dress, and welcome a brand new day ..."

Dawn England

He's Not My Dog

A beast of noble bearing
Yet incredibly thick
He has spotted back and spotted face
And a spotted dick!

With naive and total loyally
His trust is unconditional
Though his loving demonstrations
Are completely unconventional.

For there's just one thing about him
That is bigger than his heart
Though it chokes me up to say this
It's his monumental fart!

It can clear a room in seconds
With a stench that's quite appalling
But the scientists at Porton Down
Find it's properties enthralling!

Some say that dog and owner
Will grow more alike each day
And from all my observations
They very likely may!

Heather Ellis

Depression

Why can't they understand,
My body is whole,
I have my arms,
My legs.
No sign can be seen of what is happening to me.
Help me please, try to understand.
The pain I feel inside,
I'm in a turmoil — I can't escape,
I'm trapped in this body of mind,
In a feeling of despair and hate,
A morass of depression I can't define.
Help me — tell me what is happening
To this world of mine?
Why do I hate it so — being alone
Yet when I'm in company — I want to go home.
I can't eat — and my sleep is full of thoughts —
And dreams I want to keep,
They bring back memories of things I loved so dear.
I could tell you about them — if only you had time to hear,
Please someone listen, please someone do
I love the world — my life — my home
I want to be more like you.

Pat M. Ellwood

Thoughts

'The Thinker' thought, "How glad I'd be,
to get up off this risen perch, and clamber down
and see the world, to view mankind as it is today,
not yesterday, when I was made."
"My bronze finger aches to stroke my hair, and touch my limbs,
and set them free.
How unkind was my maker to have imprisoned me thus;
Why haven't I the right to walk this city and choke the dust,
and smell the pollution, and breathe the air?
To see the people, are they really there?
Not clustered round in uneven throngs, fixing me with transfixed gaze.
I ponder from where'st they come, and where'st they go,
Do they really care that I can't move,
or roll my tongue in an unclosed mouth?
Do they really care, that my limbs are bare,
and my body, dark and cold?
They like my posture, and my stance,
but don't they realize, that I can't dance?
Or twirl around without emotion?
My thoughts are strong, they are all I have,
to cling to, in a world so drab.
I can't move, or touch, or feel, and so I make this dumb appeal.
But lesser mortals, I have found, are unable to stand their ground,
Whereas I will never leave."

Joan Emmens

Silent Screams

A shadow falls across my bed,
my mind fills with ugly dread.
A sea of pain awaits me
and I cannot swim away.
Warm, wet hands on my shaking body,
poking and pushing where they don't belong,
touching, hurting and so very strong.
Big, rough fingers of daddy's hand
touch me with evil demand.

Deep inside my tortured head,
a world away from my bed.
A room where only I can go,
far away from my daddy foe.
Dark and quiet with bolted doors,
unable to feel the human claws.
Enters my body, but I cannot feel,
making wounds that never heal.

I scream a million, silent screams
and live in waking, nightmare dreams.
A blind world looks into my eyes.
A deaf world listens to my cries.

Who know when a child dies?

Jez Ellison

Autumn; English Weather

Now it is full Autumn;
The sky is looking grey,
But still the sun can shine, sometimes,
To make a pleasant day.
The winds are blowing, now and then,
The rain appears in showers;
But still, there is some greenery,
Along with Autumn flowers.
The weather changes constantly;
The scenery changes too.
Whatever time of year it is,
We get a lovely view.
Each season has it's beauty;
Each day is quite unique.
No words can quite describe the scene;
No tongues of it can speak.
It's too easy to grumble
About our English weather,
But really it's our climate
Which holds us all together.

Jackie Elvy

Early Morning

The empty swing creaks in the impartial light of dawn
There are no foot prints in the wet grass
Coffee is bitter, with no comfort
The restless, artless quarrel of children's voices, is of yesterday's world
Today — maybe a phone call, heavy with guilt and promised visits
From a strange, grown person in an alien world
Perhaps, joy of joys, some grubby, laboured note from a grandchild far away
A supervised, endearing 'thank you', for a birthday toy
But, no small hands bearing gifts of plucked, short stemmed daisies
No hurt knees to heal with cuddles and Smarties, and promised visit to the park
In Summer days, fledgling birds were nurtured in the secret places of the flower border
Where now, spiders display the treacherous beauty of damp bejeweled webs
The ginger cat demands attention with soft, white needled paws
The touch of a switch, and the clamorous world would invade the quietude
But the hum of the milk float heralds the benison of families sounds
It is another day — a different day..

Mary Extall

A Prayer For Ireland

Oh Ireland, land of my grandfather's birth,
Your beauty embraced in that emerald isle.
Deep are the treasures in your heart,
And yet man's devils, tear you apart.
Sad are the sorrows, that divide,
Your people, kind and Godly, on all sides.
Such misfortune that your children's tears,
Wept blood and heartache for so many years.
The soft lilt of your voices, should blend together,
Joining all your people, forever and ever.
Oh Ireland, if only we could lead you to
A destiny, of everlasting peace and tears of joy.
It's hard to forgive and harder still to forget, but,
It's never too late, always remember that.
The future is there within your grasp, embrace it,
Cradle it jealously, within your ample breast.
If only someone could solve your grief, your pain,
That lies cankering in the souls of the dead in vain.
Now there's a glimmer of peace at last,
Free your ghosts and those tired and weary hearts.
May you cheat the cruel fate of bygone years,
And cast out the terror and the dreadful fears.
Let your lovely Island be full of courage and hope,
And unite all your people altogether, forever, with love.

Leah Everitt

Math Problems

$x + y = z$
2 x 3, find the pair
$x = 7, y = 9$
And 7 = a nightmare.

Solve the circumference of a triangle
2 x pie x r
Add 6 caterpillars to 2 ladybirds
Divide by a large glass jar.

Using $E = mc^2$
Find the difference of 2 signs,
Draw a circle of radius five,
Using only straight lines.

Add the number of politicians who lie,
To the weight of a big oak tree,
Add trees cut down in the rainforest,
Subtract the pollution in the sea.

9 x a hole in the ozone,
Add an apple to a pomegranate,
Do this then solve the hardest of all,
Why mankind abuses our planet.

Michelle English

Passing Clouds

The clouds are passing slowly this night
Across the ethereal blackness of space,
Drifting like lonely distant wanderers
From some benign alien race.

Changing re-arranging
Quietly they pass,
Joining then separating
They travel en masse.

They are more than mere water vapour
More than reflected light,
They are feather light vessels
On the oceans of the night.

Drifting towards the horizon
On a black velvet star specked sea,
I long to travel with them
In the dreamy realms of tranquility.

Jack Ellis

Washday Blues

Has your washing machine let you down?
Causing worry and a frown
Just when you think it is working well
It decides to breakdown and give you hell
When you spirits are low and it's pouring with rain
You really will have to think again
If you think your machine will compensate
For the dreadful weather that you hate
Look out for suds creeping out through the door
Very soon a flood on the floor
Your day will be most frustrating
Nothing you do will be compensating
For all the extra work it will make
No time for a pause or a coffee break
With washing around in many hues
Ruining your day with washday blues.

Evelyn A. Evans

Meat and Veg

On Saturday how I did toil,
To till and hoe and rake the soil
Straight away down to the shops
Packets of seed and four lamb chops.

I thinly sowed these in a line
A sausage sandwich would taste fine
The shoots showed through. Oh! it was great
With ham and chips upon my plate

I watered well and thinned them twice
Now curried beef and savoury rice
I chopped the weeds they's grown so high
And settled down to Shepherd's Pie

The butterflies I chased away
An eight ounce steak is mine today
The plants are grown, the harts are tight
A shish kebab I'll eat tonight

They're ready now, each one's a winner
But what kid wants a cabbage dinner?

K. Evans

Christmas

On Christmas Eve there's magic about.
Children excited and shouting out.
Dressed in their night clothes crisp and white,
Looking all happy in the firelight.
Tree's all aglow, tinsel is blowing
Cold winds tonight "will it be snowing".
Stockings hanging at the fireside,
Mother and father trying to hide.
Expressions that seem as if to say
"Tomorrow is a special day.
A day when a child was born long ago
Because the Bible tells us so.
Jesus was born that same night,
In a stable by starlight.
Wisemen came to bear some gifts,
Over the mountains and down the cliffs.
Following a star that shone above
Because God had sent his child to love."

Sheila Everson

The Day Covers

Not wanting to leave a warm bed
The heart must go into its shallow day,
Awakening from dreams of people that are moulded
Into a symbol of a flame,
It is an illuminated guise of the past and present;
Only one person stands for all of them.

In dreams a force is felt
And I am compelled to ask pestering questions,
Eagerly hoping answers that would tell me
Of those I've known which one she was.

The dreams that open up like torch light
To scan my spirit fade,
Only sparks of memory filter through
To poems
As the day covers such things.

C. English

Earth On Borrowed Time

Dew over the hillside
glistens as the sun rises from its dormant night.
The mist clears
and the morning is revived
for serving the beings who depend on it.
A river runs
ripples are highlighted
by rays from that most powerful source.

The earth is like that
but as in all things
time is of the essence.
It dominates our lives.
For the environmental clock is ticking,
it's only a matter of time.
It can't be frozen and stopped.

It's only a matter of time.
It's only a matter of time ...

Ben Ellis (Age 13)

Cold Life In The City

The city streets look dark and grey
and the evening light just fades away.
The sky looks bare, the clouds unfold
leaving city people to face the cold.
The homeless people out on the street
with their bare feet, no food to eat.
A few shabby houses engulfed in light
to outdraw the darkness of this cold, dark night.
People's homes all cozy and warm
with their TV, beds, records and all.
They're glad they're in, and not outside where the
young helpless kids and adults survive.
Coughs and sneezes and a runny nose
and that's the way their poor lives go.
They go through bins, see what they can find,
a leg of lamb's been left behind.
They wander back to their dark, damp beds,
sheets of newspaper covering their heads.
They lie back down with their crampy legs,
their smelly clothes and whiskey breath.
They wake again to the beep, beep, beep,
of the cars that pass where they sleep.
The drivers give a look but they don't care,
and turn away, and still don't care,
about these poor kinds, with no homes, no lives,
just bus stop digs to stay alive.

Claire Evans

Weep For The World

Do you weep for the world and its many lost causes?
Wars that are lost before they're begun.
We march out bravely, with banners flying
But strength prevails and truth is gone,
I weep for the world.

Do you weep for the world and its starving millions?
Working so hard for its empty plate
Toiling, sweating, starving for nothing
Sorrow and hunger being its fate,
I weep for the world.

Do you weep for the world on its headlong journey?
Rushing so madly through time and space.
Striving to ruin its very own doorstep
Water polluted, land laid waste,
I weep for the world.

Do you weep for the world and its vanishing heritage?
Creatures who walked once, walk no more.
Their share of the goodlife gone forever,
Habitats ruined by Man's tooth and claw.
I weep for the world.

Do you weep for the world in its wanton destruction?
Will there never be peace and place to lie?
Pure clear water and land unsullied,
Room for all to live and die.
I weep for the world.

Jan Eve

A Maritime Matter

If they call a ship a "she"
When its name may be a "he"
Surely that cannot be right?
For then 'twould be hermaphrodite.
So gazing out across the sea
I thought "Why call a ship a 'she'?"
As men we always wear a shirt
Whilst hover craft display a skirt
A ship in port shows lots of bustle
As dockers with her cargo tussle
A vessel has both waist and stays
And oft' at sea, capricious ways
If ladies need a lot of paint
To make them look just what they ain't
I think it is the same with boats
Except they need a lot more coats
To stem the ravages of time
Spent in the ocean's salty brine
My musings have revealed to me
That's why men call a ship a "she"!

John Frew

Tears

A world full of lies and deceit
The tangled web we weave
Empty silence fills the room
When you slam the door and leave
And I'll drown in my own tears.

Why do I so easily fall
With my heart, I completely trust
Then its thrown back in my face
All my dreams, hopes, crumble like dust
And I'll drown in my own tears.

Life proves to me more and more
It's safer to withhold and withdraw
A heart on my sleeve, I never wore
Every wish was clutching at straw
And I'll drown in my own tears.

I'm just too weak to be strong
Anger, hate and bitter scorn
Strong I stand, its where I belong
My heart pierced by a loveless thorn
And I'll drown in my own tears.

Jane Fairweather

The Importance Of The Future

Our future lies in standards set
Or ignored, as maybe the case.
It's to little ones we owe a debt
They're our future good/bad race.

So above the bar of the buggy
Watch language, manners, and ash,
For little ones sitting absorb many things
And standards not crowded by cash.

Do you give children opportunities
In the course of daily life
They see you when the elderly you help to cross
The highways and byways of life.

Often stop and speak to the aged
They can teach you many things
That earthly goods are only lent
'Tis in children we see what love brings.

Do they witness you in frequent bad moods
When you dish out raw and bad deals
When the innocent suffer by your hand
Mind they don't comprehend how it feels.

If all these skills come together
And by high standards are we known
Then our little ones need have no fears
Into our future they will have grown.

Joan Faulkner

Tranquility

Over the fields with their morning dew
Larks on the wing, foxes in view
God did what he could to show us the way
it's good to be alive another day

To stroll by the side of the ripening corn
the Foxglove blowing its gentle horn
to heed the buzz of the working Bee
let the sights sink in of all that we see

The little brook meandering down
working its way and on through the town
all heaven is there if you open your eyes
and Rabbits and Hares not such a surprise

The sound of the silence, the noise of the trees
the silent rush of a freshening breeze
don't frighten the Squirrel as he scurries along
he never thinks that he's doing wrong

But if you sit back in your old rocking chair
and at the ceiling you always do stare
just think for a time let your mind wander on
not of things that are dead and already have gone

Go out in the country as I said before
lift your voice to the wind but don't ask for more
for all that you need is there all around
give thanks to the Lord, keep your feet on the ground

P.F.C. Fairhurst

A Christmas Verse

My favourite time of year must be
when garlands adorn the Christmas tree
Cold crisp nights fill the air
that magical feeling everywhere
Children's faces warm with glee
as they sit upon Santa's knee
The singing of carols may be heard loud and clear
as the old and the young unite far and near
Wars are forgotten, peace is around
If only this feeling could always be found.

Mary Fairclough

Lost Love

Before the sun had reached its brightest glow
The sun went down and he will never know
The Autumn joys, the golden hours that bring
The sweetest fruit, the finest flowers
Before his heart had known the rich
Content of dreams fulfilled
The bright day was spent
And I who love him mourn unconsoled
Knowing a grief too bitter to be told
Whilst he travels on beyond the range of sight
Into the sunshine of a greater light.

Elizabeth Fallais

The Learner My Wife

There's my wife in her learner car
My God, I'm so very proud of her
Starts the engine, puts in gear
I know she's feeling rather queer
Off she goes without a shudder
Nice and smooth in her little red motor
Round down High Street sweet as a nut
Throttle, brake, "oh, damn this clutch"
Oops! did we hit or miss the kerb?
"Look out," shouts Grace, and she has to swerve
Drives a bit just to relax
"Oh, will I ever learn this crap"
Then there is reversing corners
And three point turns, I'm getting warmer
Starts and stops, mirrors, signal, manoeuvre
Somebody please suck me up a hoover
One hour is such a long, long time
If you could feel these nerves of mine
I'm tense, I'm tight, I'm hot and sticky
And I paid eleven quid to make myself sicky!

Robert Farley

Autumn

Alone and weeping willow tree ...
Cold dark river racing on to angry sea ...
Lonely boats, your crew gone home ...
Gulls shrill cry, cold winds moan ...
Fallen leaves, damp underfoot ...
Billowy clouds black as soot ...
Autumn — Bleak and lonely solitude ...
Are you marking time ...
'Til Spring's sweet interlude ...

M.A. Fairweather

The Virginia Creeper

The Virginia creeper is creeping still
It seems to have its very own will,
Last year it seized the garden fence
Now no more creosote, a less expense.
I tie the strands and point the way
It doubles nearly every day,
I protect from fly both green and white
There is much joy when out of sight.
When autumn comes those russet leaves
Will blow about in friendly breeze,
And when they fall at last to earth
Indeed I've had my moneys worth.
I then look forward to the spring
I know what this will always bring,
A growth of green besides the heather
My Virginia creeper goes on forever.

Michelle Francis

At Christmas

Tinsel sparkling on the tree,
Tell me children, what do you see?
Lights abound, above the sound
of excitement and activity.
Looking, longing for Christmas Day
Oh! Mum! Will it ever come?
I can hardly wait to see,
my gifts wrapped at the Christmas tree.
Now I wonder if dad forgot
to get me a hoop, or whip and top,
or a fluffy monkey on a string.
Oh! I want just about everything.
But the greatest gift is already mine!
I don't need to look under the tree.
For with me every day of my life
is my wonderful family.

Eleanor Friston

Suicide

You left, and then I found you, and you watched
But you couldn't comfort me through the pain and the misery.
I tried, I tried to help you, and you cried
For you couldn't stop the agony that ripped away inside of me.

You told me you'd never hurt me
You said it was the last thing you would do
But I never took it literally and now you know I'm Hurting
Yes I'm hurting over you.

Our friendship, it was special, and still is
For although you're really gone the good memories, they go on.
No anger, was there in you, not with me
Through the good times that we shared, you proved you truly cared

You told me you'd never hurt me
You said it was the last thing you would do
But I never took it literally and now you know I'm Hurting
Yes I'm hurting over you.

You wanted me to find you, and I did
Your actions, they were vital, they declared your trust was total.
You left it, and I found it on the floor
And in answer to your letter, I will always love you too.

Wendy Faragher

The Car Boot

Follow signs that glow in the dark
arrows point temporary car park.
People surge towards the event
field of stalls and a marquee tent.

Smell onions from Hot Dog stand
taste coffee of unknown brand.
Stout shoes, empty bag, keen eye
value for money bargains buy.

Glass jars and pots on first table
home produce complete with label.
Cardboard boxes full of old books
records and tapes must take a look.

Squash racquet, an exercise bike
weights for lifting, boots for a hike.
Coats, sweaters displayed on a rail
shoes, dresses offered for sale.

Flowers, shrubs, plant in a pot.
What have I bought? Not a lot.
Go home? I haven't the heart.
Try again, back to the start.

Jean Fairclough

Brigantia

Carved from cold rock, and wooing icy mists
The valleys dream.
Their rivers, like their glacial fathers,
Seek out all the faults and weakness
In this land of Iron.

Cold rivers etch and gnaw their way
In search of subterranean caverns, so dark
That even dreams sleep,
Side by side with ancient warriors
Deep in the bosom of the earth.

Claustrophobic skies hang low,
And scrape the stone.
Bruising darkling fells of old Brigantia.

All night long, beneath a bay of stars,
These heavy, brooding hills invade my dreams.
They loom,
Always in the dying west
Stained red with murdered suns.

Rocks are my pillows under the wheeling heavens,
While the glacial river to Time
Gnaws through the caverns of my heart.
Seeking out the faults and weakness,
In the deep places
Where my dreams are stored.

R.A. Freeman

Time

Time is just a moment, just an image thrusting through
As flowers after rainstorms, or a rainbow arced in blue
Time is falling snowflakes, or leaves from autumn storms
The twilight of the evening, or the breaking of the dawns

Time is fleeting moments that stretch way into years
The parting of a love one that etched a face in tears
Time is fulfilling moments, perhaps of sadness or of mirth
Or just another moment thrusting flowers through the earth

Time is indefinable, which can't be trapped or held
Time is using moments to cast, to forge, to weld
A bonding, a union, making things to last
Looking forward to the future or backwards upon the past

Time is unification, like the circles round the moon
Never starting, never ending, yet comes and goes too soon
Time is wind and water that forever ebbs and flows
A universe of circles, like the wind that ever blows

Time is not a fullstop — as life when at its end
It's going for a quiet walk, holding hands, a friend
It's chasing leaves upon the winds of childish youth delights
Sometimes laughing at the good things, or crying in the nights

Time is what we make it, for time is all too soon
Yet we have it in abundance, like the circles round the moon
Never starting, never ending — it just goes round and round
If you find what its beginning is — perhaps its just the end you've found?

Ron Farrant

The Seaside

Seasides are very special places
Where children have smiling faces
They like to play in the sand
and listen to the brass band

Play in the arcade on the games there
Later on will go to the fair
round and round we will go
Maybe will watch a show

Up and down will go on the big dippers
Sometime later I'll put on my flippers
Go for a long swim in the sea
At the end of the day I'll go home for tea

Go for a walk and see some sights
In the evening look at the lights
We had lots of fun and hope you'll agree
The seaside is a very special place to be.

Dennis John Farnham

It

It was huge
It was enormous
It came dripping from the sea
It wobbled down the promenade
It passed quite close to me

It ruined all the flower beds
It upset an ice cream stall
It was like a giant jellyfish
It had no eyes at all

It burst the turnstile on the pier
As it squeezed its green mass through
It left a horrid track behind
It was like a trail of glue

It reached the pier railings
And it forced them 'til they split
It flopped back down into the sea
And it vanished, that was it.

Matthew Farnham (Age 9)

Ireland

Green was the grass where the shamrocks grew,
Though now, yes now there is nothing to show,
Bullets fly, rocks are thrown,
O' I long for the day when I can go home.

Long past are the days when life was sweet,
Now all I have are lonely hours on the streets,
O' woe is me, I wish I was free,
To live the life as it used to be.

D. Faulkner

Bath-Time Blues

I went to the bathroom this morning
To wash, as I usually do,
And there on my virginal, white porcelain
Were your whiskers, stuck like glue.

My impulse at first, is to clean them away
And turn both the taps full on,
But there's something quite nice about seeing them there
As evidence after you've gone.

There's a hair on my toothbrush, still dripping
My toothpaste lies raped of its life,
My throw-away razor has been thrown away,
And you've just gone home to your wife!

Mrs. C. Franklin

Lost Through the Darkness

I ride my bike into the mist.
My lights shine ahead and my engines run.
Silence and nothingness is in the vortex of darkness.
Hell is here and nothing can be seen
except for the flowing stream of loss and loneliness.
I ride into the eye of silence hoping to find something,
a way out or a place where the music plays.
The sixth sense is aroused as unseen shapes dance
across the corners of my pupil.
I ride on seeing nothing but shadows.
I tremble as another vortex engulfs me. The vortex of fear.
The heart and soul is empty, for things shine here.
Sudden screams can be heard piercing the psyche and soul.
The screams are tortured, in agony and forever restless spirits.
Panic comes over me, I begin to lose control of my path ahead.
It become confusing and disoriented.
The mist fades as the path is lóst
and I am engulfed in eternal darkness.

Nicholas Fawcitt

Dream Of Longing

I lay here each evening,
While the house goes to sleep
I listen to the silence,
into my pillow I weep.
My body is weary,
my mind wide awake,
I relive all the sadness
how much more can I take.
I see all your faces
your voices I hear,
but it's only the longing,
the wish for you near.
If once more I could hold you
or tell you good-bye.
Just to know you are happy
then no more would I cry.
But it's only while sleeping
when my dreams I pursue
that once more we're together,
and my wish has come true.

Pauline Fogerty

Seasons

Winter: The winter snow is coming down,
and all the children start to frown.
The sun has gone, the wind is cold,
now the snowman's looking bold.
Santa's coming with a gift,
to give the people's spirits a lift.

Spring: Now winter's gone and spring is here,
and that's all of the winter deer.
Spring means lambs and daffodils,
and all the birds on the windowsills.
The sun will soon be out to shine,
and the weather will be fine.

Summer: People sunbathing at the beach,
turning all a funny peach.
Splashing about in the sea,
Tommy shouts "hey, watch me!"
Barbecues and summer cakes,
a summer romance hearts break.

Autumn: The leaves are falling brown and red,
making up a wintery bed.
The winter's nearly back again,
nothing's going to be the same.
The seasons go round one by one,
once they're here they're nearly gone.

Helen Fawcett

Winter Prospect

The white shroud of winter descends,
Slow, silent flakes of icy tears fall
Casting a frosty, flawless mantle
Over a polluted landscape
Scarred by human greed.

Field and grave lie covered,
Life and death in shared cerement
Of virginal white.

The snow melts
The ravished earth is revealed,
Rested now and replenished
And it its restoration we have the chance
To begin again.

Shirley Fisher

Eternal Love

My love for you will be there till the end of time
I hold you in my arms and caress your brow
You close your eyes and faded away
The sun streams through the window pane
Emotions of relief and tears roll down my cheek
No more suffering of pain

The memories of you remain with me
Of cherished fifty years we've seen
The flame of love shall burn
Till we are together in eternity
Our guardian angel watches over us
As our souls rest in peace.

Julie Farman

Big Trees

Don't cry big trees
When you hear the smallest breeze
Or when the big gales hale.
We are waiting for you leaves to fall,
To reveal to one and all
The splendour of your twisting, gnarling branches.
Winter has us all in trances
With the beauty of your stark
Don't shy away from Autumn's dress-you-down
We are peeping at your sculptured form
And while you shiver,
Know you will recover
When Spring bedecks you with a brand new gown.

June Hipwell

March Weather

In winter, jumping from my bed
I open my curtains, green and red;
I see upon the windowpane
A frosty, icy land again,
As though a secret, magic hand
Has painted there a wonderland
Of frozen trees and castles tall
And sparkling flowers, huge and small.
But when the sun begins to rise
With beams so dazzling it hurts my eyes
The magic pictures quickly pass
And just leave water on the glass

Danielle Fitzsimons

Midges

Midges! Midges! everywhere.
On face and hands, on neck and hair,
They nearly drove me to distraction,
Never left me for a fraction,
By the river, near the Bridge,
They settled on my Anti-Midge.
The pain I had to bear and grin,
As thousands bit my tender skin.
But simply nothing would repel
Those pests whose bites were perfect Hell,
And all that I could do was moan
In utter anguish of my soul,
And to the echoing mountains fling
My cry "Oh death! where is THY sting?"

F.W. Fenton

Christmas Happiness

To Him who gave us Christmas Day,
May old and young together pray,
And turn to Him with faith renewed,
And joy and love and gratitude.

May God's sweet tender blessings fall,
This Christmas Day on one and all,
May every cherished dwelling place,
The spirit of the season grace.

May every care and worry cease,
May hearts be gay and minds at peace,
May the delights of girl and boy,
The grown-ups all day long enjoy.

In all the old familiar ways,
Observe this holiest of days,
With prayer and song and feast and tree,
A happy Christmas may it be, Amen.

A.J. Fellingham

Bosnia Boy

Yugoslavia, once so beautiful, desecrated and defiled.
Ruined houses, ruined churches, sad bewildered little child —
Sits alone among the debris of what once had been his home,
Young eyes full of pain and terror, knowing he is all alone.

Staring vacantly before him, much too young to understand —
Madness, that has gripped a nation, laying waste his native land,
Neighbours, once so warm and friendly bursting through the kitchen door —
Spraying death and screaming curses, bodies prone upon the floor.

Father, Mother, baby sister — lying on a blood-soaked breast,
Scenes of horror, rape and torture — shattering his innocence.
Stops his ears to sounds of gunfire, snipers bullets, mortar blast,
Screaming women, crying children — panic-stricken, fleeing past.

Night falls, eerie silence cloaks the city in a shroud,
Acrid smoke obscures the heavens like a black enveloping cloud.
Once again the night is shattered by the sound of mortar shell —
Finds its target, flames roar fiercely lighting up a scene from hell.

Now he lies among the rubble, cold and hungry, craving sleep,
No soft pillow for his head, no good night kiss upon his cheek.
Sleep comes softly, gently closing eyes that once were filled with joy,
Will tomorrow bring more sorrow for this orphaned Bosnia boy.

Doreen Diamond Feeney

Liverpool December

the gallery is full of Hockneys now, outside
a freighter, Ghana-bound, waits for the tide,
scarfed blue and white or red and white, a throng
streams up the hill to Anfield or to Goodison
and cheeky-statued Lewis's is full
of grotto-seeking families, the dull
red sandstoned old cathedral frowns down
on Rodney Street, Toxteth and Chinatown,
the ferries ply, the Liver Building's gleam
glances at Wallasey and Bromborough, upstream,
and Woolton, Penny Lane and Strawberry Fields
are haunts for camera-wielding Japanese,
two tunnels, subterranean traffic streams,
two universities, two cathedrals, two teams,
Lime street, Central, a Philharmonic hall and pub,
memories of Canning, Gladstone, Huskisson, hubbub
of students strolling up Mount Pleasant's slope
to lecture halls hard by a street called Hope,
the gallery is full of Hockneys now, outside,
a freighter, Ghana-bound, waits for the tide.

Geoff Fenwick

Weeping Willow

Fazing, through, the sunlit window
I can see, the beautiful, weeping-willow
Through it's branches, the warm wind does blow
it's beautiful blossom, is on show.
Its beauty made my tears start to flow
in the sunlight, they stopped somehow.
The willows branches blew in the summer breeze,
they danced in the wind with such ease.
The willows beauty, to my eye did please,
my sorrow, the willow did seem to appease.
Suddenly the wind seemed to stop still
no longer does it blow from the hill.
Strangely, the willow seemed to be weeping
emptiness in my heart is all I am keeping.
One may wonder, why I am never sleeping,
tears from my eyes, forever weeping.
Today, the warm sun may have shone
but, all hope of love now seems gone.
'Lord' know why on earth I carry on
Perhaps to find my love, 'anon'

John Felton

A Wintry Walk With Children

Slipping and sliding over icy patches, the crunch of frost underfoot.
Glaring eyes were spotted, the dangerous lions killed.

Amid loud cries of triumph, tiny feet shattered frozen puddles.
A large shark, basking in the frozen loch, was rendered helpless.

An elongated hillside on the right, was confirmed a slumbering dragon.
A giant dogs paw print perceived, ensured that we slipped pas silently.

White patches of frost on shaded land, noted and questioned.
Jump, jump over frozen ruts, a new game, a cool game.

Raging torrents crossed carefully on felled tree trunks,
crocodiles lying in camouflage for the unwary. Look out!

Rabbit burrows examined and prodded. Remember when? played again,
A song started to keep us going, only one more mountain to climb.

Linda Ferguson

Life

Life is not always so thrilling
Sometimes I feel lonely and sad
But when looking around I see others
And realize my life's not so bad.

Some people are homeless and starving
Others are jobless and broke
Some have life threatening diseases
My problems must seem like a joke.

Problems like mine seem like nothing
But lots of things cause me stress
Overworking, health problems, depression
It makes everything seem such a mess.

Most of the time I'm so happy
But sometimes it's just an act
I don't want to cause other people worry
They have problems of their own - it's a fact.

When feeling sorry for myself, I just think
Of all things in my life that are good,
My family are worth more than words could say
Problems? - they've always understood.

No one knows how long we'll all live
Everyone has to die
But for now I'll count myself lucky
I'm just thankful to be alive.

Marie Fidell

I Am Homeless

I am not important
I am just so worthless.
I am not a real human,
Now that I am homeless.

I am not to be taken seriously,
I can never speak what is right
I am just one of the "somebodies",
That should be hidden out of sight.

I am just a moron,
I am just a dirty mould.
I should not be in "their" town,
Hiding from the cold.

I am not to be liked,
I am just a disgrace
They just freeze me out,
There is no friendly face.

I am not to be happy,
I am not allowed to smile,
I am just to feel miserable,
As I walk another mile.

I am just so stupid,
With no brain in my head.
The only peace I'll ever get,
Is when I'm stone, cold dead.

Joanne Ferris

Think Of Me Then

Remember me — in quiet moments
When the day's demands have all been met
And your thoughts, released, are free to wander
Over memories we won't forget — think of me then.

Remember me — when shadows form at sunrise;
When lightning flashes pierce a darkened sky;
When with softened breath the zephyr lulls you
Or a rainbow's colour spreads its promise wide — think of me then.

Remember me — in the twilight hour
When melancholy takes its toll,
Or when with joy an early sunbeam
Wakes a response within you soul — think of me then.

Remember me — when you hear sweet music,
When a plaintive strum of harp strings sounds
And woodwinds echo lush and calming,
Seducing with soft falling founts — think of me then.

Remember me — as the seasons change,
In the chill of Winter; in the haze of Summer;
On a soft Spring morn when your steps are gladdened;
When with Autumn's song your heart is saddened — think of me then.

Remember me — when life is ending,
When dreams and memories, sharply focused,
Return to mind — then you'll recall
The moment when our pathways crossed — think of me then.

Jennifer Vine

Passing Shadows

Mark me, in the midst of the family here,
Exchange smile and greeting - inadequate cheer;
Uneasy eye-contact, unnatural pause,
A dignified bearing with so little cause.
Although I believe that for us it is not
A time of finality, measured by plot,
I'm aware (while casting my sprinkling of soil)
That narrow enclosuring makes me recoil.
Not loathing or fear of personal fate,
But knowing I've done this too often of late -
Where coffin is lowered; a life at an end,
Each loss underlining the serious trend.
While others are weeping I turn a blind eye
Presenting a stoic-blank face to the sky,
Where lower the dark-grey monotonous cloud
Diminishes light with its blanketing shroud;
Relentless the wind-driven sleet on the skin
Impresses this wintery hour within.

Jim Finch

A Corby Scot

I was born and raised in Corby
We've lived away and now I've come home
From Stoke-on-Trent down to Devon
No more will I roam.

My parents, they came from Glasgow
Glasgow, that dear ole toon
But when there was the cry of work
To Corby they did come doon.

My mother she was not happy
But thought it all for the best
She gave herself a good talking to
And started to feather her nest.

And so we were brought up in Corby
My sister Irene and Bobby my brother
But I was constantly reminded
Of the land of my father and mother.

My parents have sadly both gone now
My mum's words still ring out a lot
"You're English of Scottish parents!"
I am a Corby Scot.

Sheila Ferguson

Twenty Two

The gold no longer shines so bright,
Owls no longer fly at night.
Most animals have ceased to be,
There are no fish now in the sea.

The snow and ice fight hard to stay,
But the rays of the sun are stronger today.
Waterfalls all dried up now,
Milk no more comes from the cow.

The snake no longer tries to hiss,
Our children aren't allowed to kiss.
Criminals are walking free,
The prisoners now, are you and me.

Aeroplanes no longer fly,
The elderly refuse to die.

These prophesies are coming true,
The warning's clear to all of you.

There may still be time to put things right,
But the gold no longer shines so bright.

Gerald Finlay

Caring

As I sit within my chair
I often wonder if people care.
No one is satisfied today
All we hear is give more pay
Miners — Firemen — Electricians too
Everyone wants to join the queue.

For all this pressure to get extra rises
It's only swallowed up by soaring prices
There is more in life than grab and greed
So why not reflect — and let Britain breathe.
Don't cramp her style while trying to climb
Or back we go in ages of time.

We want to be known, as a country that fights
For all that is precious, worthy and right.
Just try to cherish these things that you love
Whilst you live, work and play 'neath the sky above.
So go forth united — hand in hand
To help one another and be proud of your Land.

Irene Firman

Sight-Reading

Her fingers stiff with age
And her eyes not what they were,
My mother sits at the piano
Stumbling over familiar tunes,
Hymns ancient and modern
And musical hits of her youth.

With a peremptory nod of her head
She urges me to turn the page,
And brings me back with a jolt
From scenes of my youth
When her playing awakened
Nameless yearnings within me —

Creating an unspoken bond between us
Which lay dormant for years.
Now, in response to her need,
My silent tears echoing hers,
Our roles reversed, I turn another page —
Nodding in time to the music of her life.

Anne Finnis

War And Peace

O Lord, your world is torn apart,
With war and battle lines of pain,
Again men pierce you to the Cross,
With selfish greed and destructive aims,
And hearts are cold in self-seeking fame.

O Lord, it seems we cannot see,
The only way of peace we seek,
We cannot hear above the noise,
And we will not listen or let you speak.

O Lord, you weep with pity as you see us strive in vain,
We fail to see the snowdrops
Your strong promises of Spring proclaim,
But look instead upon a tank,
As powerful to be seen.

But peace is found in pardon,
And love is bound in peace.

Margaret Ferguson

Shades of Night

Beings from another world draw night,
I hear their voices rustling like a sigh,
That floats with friendly murmur on the air,
I feel their peaceful presence everywhere.

They whisper softly thro' the quiet skies,
When earth is hushed and daytime's hustle dies.
I hear the gentle tone, the muted breath,
Of those who've learned the mystery of death.

So tenderly they come on wings of night,
Breathing of beauty, telling of delight.
I feel their love encompassing my soul,
Soothing my fears, making my spirit whole.

Dear phantom friends! Someday I too shall be,
Part of your throng, your joyous ministry,
And all the wonders of your world I'll know,
And share your bliss! When God ordains it so.

Laura Fisher

Santa Clause

Moon light moon bright
Santa will come in the middle of the night
Over the rooftops covered in snow
Away on his sleigh he will go.

He will visit the children one by one
Until at last all his work is done
He will fill stockings by the score
And give each child a little bit more.

Some want cars, and some want drums
Some think only of their tums
An apple and an orange was all we got
But now they seem to get such a lot.

Nothing is too big, nothing too small
Some things he has to leave in the hall
Then silently he slips away
Leaving things ready for Christmas Day.

Mrs. E.M. Fisher

Daydream

I sit and stare, life makes no sense
Mind is hopping over heaven's fence
Pictures pass, it's oh, so funny
For once the girl doesn't want me for money
I go through my life and recall all that I've done
Remembering the times when there was lots of sun
(We sometimes cried but it was fun)
I recall all my daydreams they weren't so bad
But now I sit and stare, I sometimes look sad
I love the good old days that we once had
My mind starts going crazy, I get such a surprise
As two evil monkeys pass right through my eyes
All the good times start melting, but I drink them all up
While the two evil monkeys are dancing in the cup
Joyful tunes start ringing through my mind
The monkeys turn green and it starts to rain
Then a bright light shoots through my mind
Firemen start climbing up my spine
For the yellow rain is here suddenly my mind opens
My eyes see reality, the echoes have gone, I see light and
I start to scream, for I am now out of my distant daydream
But only until my mind calls me back
And the firemen run up my back to put me out of the trance
When I have a bad dream of the evil monkey's dance.

Billy Fisher

Ward 22

I opened my eyes as I felt the pain,
Then tried to move, but all in vain,
My right arm encased in a pumping black band
That hissed as it tightened and seemed to expand,
I heard distant footsteps — then something go 'swish'
And saw someone holding a syringe and dish,
A few moments later I drifted away
Quite unaware of the grey foggy day.

I stirred some time later, the pumping had gone,
The pain had subsided, the sun shone upon
The high polished floor and the straight line of beds,
Perfectly made with white pillowed heads.
The days sped by and I walked to the showers,
There were so many cards and beautiful flowers,
My bedfellows were as kind as could be
They encouraged my efforts and sat beside me.

The great day arrived when I could go home,
What a lovely thought — I must go and phone.
My daughter came to fetch me that day,
It would be good to be home, but I really must say
At the hospital things had greatly improved,
People care much more now, and I was so moved
By the help I was given by the young and the new
In the very new wing on Ward 22.

Mrs. C. Fenwick

Street Life

The place which I live in
Is a tourist town
But it's a different story
When the sun goes down.

Out come the cardboard boxes
The newspapers and rags
Then you'll see the homeless;
Out there with all their bags.

No where warm to sleep at night
No soft pillows for their heads
We don't give them much thought
When tucked up in our beds.

Out come all the pushers
Making money by the score
Preying on the hopeless
Hurting them even more.

People don't ask to be born
And they deserve much more
Instead of people downing them
And closing every door.

Some say they have themselves to blame
Maybe this is true
But perhaps just some that blame
Should be put on me and you.

J.C. Fletcher

When I'm Retired

Retirement is a state of bliss,
I'm sure that I shall find,
More than enough to keep me fit,
In body, soul and mind.

I'll rise at nine and have a bath,
And get dressed at my leisure.
I'll take the dog out for a walk,
And breathe the air with pleasure.

At noon I'll pop round to a friend,
And have a drink and chatter.
Or perhaps we'll go out to a pub,
And have a seafood platter.

Folk say it's hard to meet the bills,
For 'leccy', gas and heating,
That being retired is not such fun,
When outs and ins aren't meeting.

But not to worry — life's too short,
The knots we will unravel.
With time to spare, and no more work,
I think I'd like to travel.

I'm sure the State will see me right,
And I'll lead a life of plenty.
But perhaps I'm such an optimist,
Because I'm only twenty!

Margaret Fisher

Upstairs - Downstairs

Idle Woman: "Good morning, Roberts,
I'll not mind, if you gently raise the blind.
The sun is not too strong I think,
The coffee's not too hot to drink.
Pity that the egg's so runny
Don't say you forgot the honey.
Nothing in the morning news
Yes, yes, of course the snakeskin shoes
And run my bath without delay
And quickly pass my negligee."
'The woman really is too slow.
I may decide to let her go.'

Lady's Maid: "Good morning, madam,
Here's your tray. It surely is a lovely day.
Cook thought you'd like the jam instead.
Do you wish to rise from bed?
The velvet suit you'd like to wear?
With emerald brooch and hat with fur?"
'Fat old cow, what bulging eyes
You'd think that she would realize
I simply cannot stand her face
I'll try to find another place.'

M.E. Fitness

Time

What is time,
Which rules our every action?
Sombre indeed when time stops,
We squander it, hour by hour.
What right do we have to steal precious time?
Precious little time is left.
Prisoners are oppressed by time,
For them, time brings no freedom,
What chance do they have to use time wisely?
Whereas time is present for us, taunting,
And daring us to grasp that great infinity
Of which we are so minuscule a part.
However, we, who have harnessed the sun,
Conquered space and power, cannot control time
But to capture it in a watch, or a clock,
Ticking mesmerically, measuring our wasted time, in
Seconds, hours, days; meaningless units;
Divisions of the one power yet to be discovered.
It goes on when we depart.
Memories are made of time.
Without time the world collapses.
And one day,
The clock will cease to tick.

Catherine Fletcher

Our Little Town

Landmarks and buildings old and new,
there are plenty, really quite a few.
Also of history we have our share,
of famous and infamous, of these you'll hear.

All the shops with lots in store,
the local market with bargains galore.
They open early and close late,
some have to close down, that is fate.

Our local artist born and bred,
people throughout they have said,
his paintings so life like and true,
in the art gallery he has one or two.

So if you are passing our little town,
just stop by for a while and do look around.
You will enjoy it, you will see,
so relaxing, happy and carefree.

Maurice L. Fletcher

The River

I
am
born
from
water,
high,
bend,
fall,
flowing
turning
widening,
narrow.
Passing
villages
the towns
open fields
slowing up
the estuary,
river mouth,
dropped silt
out to the sea,
disappearing,
evaporating.
The cycle repeats.

A.R. Fisher

The Old Folk's Home

See them all sitting in their own comfy chairs.
Some with a smile, some haven't a care
Look at their faces, with wrinkles of age
Eyes are not sparkling, they are a permanent gaze
All sitting wondering when their time will come
As the months and years, just roll on and on.

Look at their withered and work torn hands
Some of the men fought in far off lands.
The women, down on their knees, would scrub
And polish door knobs for extra grub,
Or wait for their menfolk to come from the mines,
Then stand for an hour in the ration lines.

They reared their families a long time ago
Now some of their families just don't want to know.
Some sit here waiting for someone to come
Few have visitors, some have none.
They have all got a roof and a bed
But all of their memories are locked in their heads.

Some may not have their faculties right
And just sit about, from morning till night
But it's our job, when we are there,
To show them love and give them care,
To help them all and let us pray
That they may see another day.

Margaret Fletcher

Plight Of My Valley

No more black gold
The mines put to sleep
No more black gold
No vigil to keep.

What now my valley
Does the future hold
What now my valley
Must we be bold.

Dark were the days
Dark were the nights
Dark were the days
No longer man's plight.

The tips are now planted
Young trees to be seen
The tips are now planted
Changing black into green.

What new trades if any
Can we call on
What new trades if any
New life to spawn.

Jerome Fortune

Looking Away
(In Retrospect)

We walked in leafy lanes, showed you butterflies and birds in flight
In sunshine, frost and rain, walked common-land where mouldering tumuli
Lay enclosed with berried hedgerows housing crystal webs and celandine
We fetched brown eggs across the fern-clad hill silhouetted on the sky
We fed the cheeky, funny ducks diving bottoms up
When strolling by the glistening moat so frequently
We mused and browsed among the market stalls expectantly
And yet perhaps you had no eyes to see

We painted eggs and made spring-like displays at Eastertide
I read to you before you drifted into nightly sleep
We made the manger scene I always thought you found such fun
I ferried back and forth to bring you friends
In order that you should not play alone as I had done
And always made those special treats that children love for tea
After weekly trips to that old shop with toys we thought you loved to see
And yet perhaps you had no joy of heart to feel this kind of glee

Mistakenly perhaps, I urged you how to be a good kind boy
How not join in with the cut and thrust
Unwise advice you felt, when all seemed for themselves
Already well adjusted to the 'me' society
Where often love and care held little sway
And in harsh days when you were rudely thrust away
In thought and deed as ever, we told you we were near
And yet perhaps you had no ears to hear

Shirley Flower

His Domain

Brave fox was scenting fearful things
That mounted his displeasure,
Now is the time he needed wings
To flee the downs and heather.

So quick to sense the danger
He could not here remain,
With so little time to linger,
He must abandon his domain.

True to his sense of majesty
In tune with living wild,
Speed on he must, alive to stay,
A will so strong - his chances mild.

So many miles that he must speed
Without rest or food, to measure,
Not yet for him some place to breed,
But with as yet, a life to treasure.

Mrs. V. Fletcher

No Point

There is no point, I heard him say,
A waste of time to go today
Without experience, no jobs at all,
Not worth the effort, or price of the call.

It's a sad old world, no hope, no jobs,
I've really tried, we're not all 'yobs'
The queues are long, the jobs are few,
I'm on the scrapheap at just twenty-two.

As I stood there my heart was sore,
For one so dejected, but there's so many more,
All joining the dole queue, and in the same boat,
With no brighter outlook, to keep them afloat.

But, where lies the answer, Oh! What would I give,
To present to each person, incentive to live,
With hope for the future, and work for us all,
But nobody listens, or pays heed to my call.

Katherine A. Ford

Is This Really Where the Dolphins Used To Swim?

Meetings. Plans stirred surreptitiously with the corporate coffee in air-conditioned comfort
against a backdrop of shadows cast by sunlight filtered through tinted windows.
Always filtered. No personal confrontations with nature's offerings to influence decision.

Locals laughed when we marched along the only street in town waving home-made banners
"NO ... To Drilling in Cardigan Bay. Don't Let Them Chase The Dolphins Away."
Nearby a man in a suit muttered,
"Bunch of nutters. Aging hippies trying to save the world."
He threw something into a bin; and missed; and left it there. Testifying.

We gather on the shore to watch the big ships clutter the horizon,
driving a wedge between us and where the sea meets the sky in perfect harmony.
Shingle scrambling after sucking surf and the laughter of children accuse and condemn
without the burden of speech. Our silent symphony needs no further statement.

Steel black fins break the surface of the water, absorbed in communication and curiosity,
trustingly swimming to the steel that shines less brightly than their own polished pod.
The first explosion echoes underwater like an earthquake of hostility.
The second brings a flight for life, sensors screaming in silent agony.
Some of us cry. The man in the suit cries the hardest of all.

We may stand here again one day, resurrecting half-remembered images
and gathering soiled pebbles to throw into murky water,
slipping through slime.
The only black on the horizon will be swirls of shiny signatures in oil
writing a poem on the surface of a sullen sea,
"Is This Really Where The Dolphins Used To Swim?"

Kath Flowers

Reorganized

There is no sight,
There is no sound,
Upon this flat
And frosted ground,
The air is crisp and white,
No miner's fires burn tonight.

The leaves are frosted over
With ice wrapped round so tight,
The sun's behind a mass of clouds
With no light to trace the ice.

It is so cold and lonely
On this Autumn crispy day,
The pits have frosted over
The ponies gone away.
The hacks and picks have been destroyed
The lamps no longer shine.
Our lives have been reorganized
My fathers, my mothers, my brothers and mine.

Claire Foley (Age 12)

Last Thoughts

Oh dear I think his temper's growing,
What makes him rage like that?
It must be almost fifty years since
Last we heard him stir.
Now look, he's foaming at the mouth.

Nostrils inflamed, breathing fire.
The peace we lived under is gone.
Anger flows out from his body.
We run but there's nowhere to go,
As he engulfs us one by one.

The deafening noise comes bubbling out.
White heat swallowing up the bracken.
Trees just seem to disappear.
People screaming, dying, round me.
Will anyone live to tell the tale?

Brenda Fisher

Purple Heather

Sleep on lonely broken child, amidst the purple heather wild;
Lost for all infinity.
Was it by chance, the hand of fate
Which led you to this dark, forbidding, God forsaken place?
Or the cold painted hand of the red lipped woman
And the man who gripped too tight, spoke too close,
Breathed his warm, sour breath upon your marble face of waxen white?

The dark powers of deception deceived you,
The silver tongued words from the serpent's mouth beguiled you,
Now see the storm rise in their cold, callous eyes
For it's only a matter of time before the black box records their sickening crime.

Suddenly the silence is broken, raised voices, laughter, shattered dreams,
Pathetic cries of anguish as they tape your siren screams.
Cheap perfume fills the air, creatures of the undergrowth inch back,
Watch with restless stare, as the talon fingers wrench and tear.
It's over: Now too late from prayer.
She's dead: Satan's fire of passion fed.
She lies slumped in silent, senseless rest, along with all the rest,
Yet another victim of their evil quest.

From horizon to horizon, the purple heather bows low its tufted head
Wavering like the floundering kelp upon the ocean bed.
Sleep on lonely, broken child, for your cries were all in vain,
The red lipped woman was evil;
Her lover was insane.

Gillian Foley

Final Hours

Winter rays, weak from Heaven,
Lit the room,
From which you felt seconds of tedious hours
Travel into minutes across seven towers
Viewed from your pillow.
And there, beyond your sill,
A living world of change and chance
Albeit without time to kill.
Why? Simply put - remorseless circumstance.
You, who had known lusty eagerness - constitution,
Manhood, like a straight sentinel - thriving,
Now, bent and breathing without breath;
Finding the nearness of death - dissolution.
Time now is a tunnelled railway, end to end.
Drugged in quiet accord, you fill your mind
With dark and silent waiting,
Watching images dancing,
Upon these mirrors -
Of life.

Tom Foggo

Abide With Me

Picture a cottage in your head
Picture dried heather around our bed
Are you moved by the feeling?
Do you find it appealing?

The scent of shalamar fills the air
Nature has blessed the land with otters and deer
The grace of a woman is unknown there
Abide with me and forget you fear

Will you walk with me?
Over fields with their shades of green
I will take you to that cottage
Together we will realise our dream

Up to the rolling hills
It's not much more than a mile
You can wear your summer dress
And your ever present smile

The eagle keeps watch over our land
God has blessed this place with the glory of His hand
When the day is over in the evening's glow we will stand
Did you ever see a view so grand

D.M. Flynn

Just A Thought

Though I am but a single man, I do my best Lord as I can
I don't believe a man should boast far better he stand at his post
Be steadfast — loyal and brave and true in living life — to be like you
I thank you Lord for life itself, for each new day and for good health
For you alone know what I'm worth in biding time upon this earth.

My Lord I think of Calvary — the nails, the insults, bravery
Can we imagine here today your broken heart the price to pay
The tree you carried on you back before they nailed you to the rack
Upon that dark and dreary hill the time had come the time to kill
Your cry was heard, forgive them Father, your work all done was any harder.

I sometimes wonder if you came would you be treated just the same
And in the year of '94 are we so different nearer heaven
What have we learned from all your teaching would you be welcomed hands outreaching
Are we less heathen more devout, I tell you Lord I've got my doubts
And if you came some men would sing but most would shout you're too right wing

Forgive me Father, I have sinned, you died that day that I might live
My soul, your dwelling place within, it's grey and tarnished, scarred by sin
I'm sorry Lord for things I've done, for thoughts I've thought, and lives undone
Is this the way to thank you Lord for what you suffered and endured
My pledge is that I'll do my best, be more like you to stand the test.

Harry Foot

Grief

Sorrow, sadness skim the surface
Solace maybe in sharing,
But grief thrusting with white hot intensity
Into the core of being
Brings searing pain that must be borne alone
Until burnt out
It leaves ashes to be discarded
And a new heart
Refined, restored, at rest.

Zoë Fauvel

Home Is ...

Home is cold and lonely,
No one is ever there,
Music no longer blares out from speakers,
No one cares!

The children have left,
The garden is a mess,
The rooms are all empty and the tables covered with dust.

Home is just the mother and the father now!

Victoria Fox (Age 12)

It's Winter Again

The trees are bare and leaves on the ground
It's dark and windy and damp all around.
So wrap up warm and snug
Or you'll get a cold winter flu bug.
I look out the window it's dull and dark
So I won't be going down to the park.
I will have something hot for tea
And then sit down and watch TV
I look at the time, then go to bed
Pull the sheets right over my head
I'd rather be inside warm and bold
I don't like winter, it's too cold.

Leigh Fletcher

Love

Every heart beat is a creation,
Locked and hidden our secret admiration,
Expressions, beautiful, loving on our faces,
Justified feelings, deep down places,
Our blood mixes like a blow from a knife,
Like doves of freedom, spreading our wings in a new life,
Our two depths of emotion makes one whole,
We bonded in mind, body, heart and soul,
Time has shown, past, future and present,
Our closeness, sensations of attachment,
Together we share life and loves devotions,
Confused thoughts, mixed emotions.

Nicola Fowler

The Berlin Wall

Mama and Papa out for the night
When I wake up no one in sight
I go outside to look and get a shock right away
When I see a wall barring my way.

People protest but to no avail
They can't get gid of that big whale
People want passes but "No! No! No!" That's all you hear
Except for one, the rich millionaire
He paid a fortune to get a pass, but alas he never ever got that pass.

Late one night I look out my window and get a fright
People are out in a big fight
One sneaks away and I get a shock
"Bang! Bang!" His body lies on a rock.

I get a letter from a lawyer to inform me I own some land
But because of that wall I can't get it.

I am older now and I have kids of my own
I hope one day they will see the land that they may own.

We're celebrating now! You ask what for!
The wall has been knocked down
Mama and Papa have come back and now we all
"Chat, chat, chat"

Shaun Foley (Age 12)

Children In Need

Look around and you will see,
Places in the sun
Where the children all run free
But for them there is no fun.

But what good is freedom
Without any joy,
Nothing but starvation
For every girl and boy.

Some millionaires sit idly by,
Well fed and never think,
Of all the help that they could give
To countries on the brink.

Please help the children
Give them all a fresh new start.
Put your hands into your pocket
And give with all you heart.

Ms. M. Fiddes

Time

Time is so precious
And yet we waste it.
We don't take the time to stop,
And say hello.
We always think we'll have another day.
Who knows what's waiting,
Around Life's corner,
If only we could be sure.
Let us try to make time,
For the old and young alike.
Time for your partner or friend,
Make time for them.
We have the gift of time
Let us use it.
Let's take the time now, to say and do
The things we should.
Before it slips away
Please don't let us waste it,
Remember
Everyday is a memory.

Sally Anne Forsdike

Eboracum

Through Micklegate Bar the monarchs would ride
Into Eboracum their steeds astride
This great city where the legions once lived
History, culture and name place would give

Stones of the Minister, the craftsmen have set
Have many a tale to tell ... and yet
Containing the prayers and secrets of any
Gives comfort, peace and enlightenment to many

Now school children stand in continuous file
Curiosity stretching for many a mile
Much is the interest the city retains
Her knowledge and glories everyman gains

Today as you walk through the busy thoroughfares
With buskers and tradespeople selling their wares
Her beauty and history ever shall be
A source of contentment to you and to me.

Linda Fearn

Fragments from Orcadia

late night sky
black as
pitch
lit up
and thrown into
sharp
relief
by the Beltane
fire
of Flotta
flarestack

black
hail choked
sky
unleashes
it's fury
on
silent and luminescent
Brodgar

Stephen Fairclough

Saturday the Thirteenth - 1842

Dawn had just broken, no one in sight,
Except for the few who prepared for the fight.
Women and men, who had little to lose,
Apart from the musket, the sword and the noose.

Their pay had been slashed by some twenty percent,
Their pleas and protest were met with contempt.
The mill owners laughed, and just spat in their face,
They knew from the start, that they held the ace.

They marched down Fishergate, their faces all gaunt,
Their target was Lune Street, their rendezvous point.
They clashed with militia, the police and the Mayor,
The odds were against them, they hadn't a prayer.

Then all of a sudden, a man cried in pain,
As he lay on the ground, blood gushed from a vein.
This angered his comrades, who rushed to the fore,
As brave as they were, they then lost three more.

The workers were speechless, not even a sound,
All they achieved, were four men on the ground
As John Mercer laid in his coffin all quiet,
Richard Palmer, the coroner, said; "He died in a riot."

• • •

If I'd been around in Forty-Two,
    I would have joined them, well wouldn't you.
I would have been at the front of the fray —
But then if I had, my poem would have vanished
    On that sad but brave day.

Austin Ford

Second Childhood

I cringe
you are so kind
as you
wipe my face
say, 'never mind'
I was the one
who nurtured you.
the adult.
You the child
I the leader
teacher. friend, parent
strength was mine to give
I gave
Is this the end.
Where did the two lines cross
You now strong
I now lost
Time took away from me
and now
you and I
roles changed.
I understand
the adolescent rage
and liberty.

D. Francis

A Musical Journey

I sit and listen, in a trance, to music from composers fine
Crescendi wild to make me dance, mystique from where the sun doth shine.
A magic carpet transports me to Spain's hot sands where palm trees sway.
A fine 'bolero' I can see; with swirling skirts to dance all day.

A patriotic sound I hear in Russia, where I march alone.
Was '1812' the fateful year when soldiers young were 'turned to stone?'
The canons blast, the Marsellais is sung, as I just stand and hear
The song of songs, their hearts ablaze with glory, those who know no fear.

Breathe then once more that quietness of lullabies, and let me sleep
Within my Cradle; I will bless that music soft whilst shadows creep.
I shall awake to sounds anew; in Hungary's bounds I'll dance again
On fields so green, with skies of blue, and rhythms pounding in my brain.

Amongst fiords and fjelds I stand where water runs and then doth freeze.
True lovers walk there hand in hand and hear the chords upon the keys.
Norway's concerto loud and clear, its melody that thrills the soul
Just lifts the heart in life so drear, incessant, like the sea must roll.

Let us away from pensive mood ... come waltz with me by forest glade.
We'll stroll along Vienna's Wood and sit and talk beneath the shade.
The cuckoo sings her merry song and swallows in the village fly;
We'll polka down the path along — Perpetual Motion is our cry.

I'm home again on England's shores where Pomp and Circumstance prevails
And down to earth, amidst my chores, sweet memories linger of my tales.
The sound of 'Greensleeves' in my head does compensate for lands afar
I'll dream of "Crimond" in my bed and "Crown Imperial" like a star.

Lynda M. Fradkin

The Antiques Fair

I wander round the antiques fair,
Gazing at the treasures there.
What craftsman, living long ago,
Made that silver teapot glow?
Who made that delicate china plate,
The sparkling chandelier ornate?
Who fashioned candlesticks of brass,
And ornaments of coloured glass?
A child's doll! Oh, who can tell
Who owned that lovely girandole?
The walnut table, old washstand,
Created by an expert's hand.
The mantel clock and leather tome
Were once a part of someone's home.
Those painted cats, and curious dogs,
The carved oak box, containing logs
Once graced a cottager's abode.
That gown was quite the latest mode,
And worn, a hundred years ago.
Who made it? We shall never know!

Audrey E. Fry

Three Pounds Of Sugar

Our flowers of life are our children
Born from God's loving seed
They bloom through His wonderful creation,
Fill our lives with all that we need.
They give love, joy and satisfaction,
Yes, we know, sometimes a tear;
But only God knows the feeling within us
When a child felt snuggle is near.
We gain from them pride and admiration
When they achieve the simplest task,
Small gifts become treasures,
Tiny phrases in memories last.
The moment when we kiss it better
From that small tumble or fall,
Cannot be measured in any way,
A moment not known to all.
But the measure that is the greatest
For Grandad or Grandmother
When asked how much they love you
They answer, three pounds of sugar!

Aer Reg

Antarctic Glory

The great expanse of Antarctica
White with crystal ice,
Giant ice platforms slowly shifting
When nature throws the dice.
Survival is in the lap of the gods when freezing winds start to bite,
The agony of existence continues in a long and hazardous fight.
Seals and penguins, whales and fish have adapted to the freeze,
Seeking food in the icy waters that seem to provide for their needs.
Mountainous icebergs loom on the horizon, snow caves designed by nature.
Windblown snowdrifts appear to be moulded as if created by a sculptor.
Cavernous grottos hung with icicles enhance the frozen splendour,
Pure white landscapes stretch for miles in panoramic grandeur.
Skua gulls and Arctic petrel skim the glassy waters,
Diving down when they spot some food with an accuracy that never falters.
This unspoilt continent of gigantic proportions
Most of us will never behold,
So we read all about adventurous explorers
And what their expeditions unfold.

Patricia Frampton

Hobo

What led to this transformation?
Pressures of your occupation?
Inadequacies as wife or mother?
Disillusionment as lover?
As a spider by slender thread
From its homey web hangs, suspended,
Oppressed you exist in immunity,
Clinging to the edge of society.

Considering your wretched form,
Miserable existence outside the 'norm',
I have no wish to criticize,
To judge your world through another's eyes;
Feeling only anger and dismay
At your choosing to waste your life away.
No ambition, just mindless shifting;
No love, or attachments, simply drifting.

Is this all living holds for you,
Cardboard box, clothes wet through?
Pursuing a state of deprivation,
End it all now - why the hesitation?
Do you wish fate would take a hand,
Prevent you from taking a radical stand?
Perhaps a glimmer of hope - a warm memory,
Will entice you back into life's filigree.

Anna Francis

A Lover's Epitaph

Where you have clipped the wings of my soul,
Emotions flutter against the cage of my heart,
And I know I shall soon die.

Where once my hopes flowed freely,
Soaring high in expectation,
I only see you and the prison of my fears.

I am damned by love.

Where once I existed,
I can no longer see who I am.
I am fettered to the being mirrored in your eyes.

I have lost definition.

I am prostitute.

I am you.

There are demons plucking at the flesh of my mind.
Vulture in on my decay.
Soon I will no longer exist.

In wanting you,

I am dead.

Mandy Foster

Our Heritage

The morning air, pleasant and fresh, encouraged me to take a walk,
A leisured stroll upon my own, unhindered by the need to talk.
The gentle rays of warming sun broke through the branches of the trees,
Caressing little sheltered spots where frost had touched with icy breeze.
And as I walked, quite all alone, meandering where e're I chose,
I marvelled at the beech and oak, resplendent in their Autumn clothes.
I listened to the cooing doves, each calling loudly to its mate,
And saw the squirrels jump and leap and watched the rabbits loping gait.
In some far field the lowing herd, the raucous cry of rook and crow,
Adds to the beauty of the scene and fills the heart with warming glow.
This then is ours. Our heritage. Its riches far beyond our dreams.
But then, on looking round once more, all is not quite just as it seems.
The filth and debris strewn about, a plastic bag, discarded tin,
A mattress dumped beneath a bush, an over-flowing litter bin.
The noisy roar of motor-bikes, young sapling broken "just for fun",
Is this the way to treat our land? Merciful God, what have we done?

W. Francis

Untitled

Come into the garden Maud,
For the black, black clouds have gone.
Come into the garden Maud,
And see what the gales have done!

Your daffs lie drowned
On the sodden ground,
And the flowering shrubs are awry.
Still a blackbird sings
As he spreads his wings
In the brightening western sky.

Come into the garden Maud
But watch the puddle round the back.
Come into the garden Maud,
But don't forget to wear your Mac!

Mrs. E.D. Evans

Love

Love wove a world of dreams,
and the willow bowed its boughs
and wept beneath the velvet moon.

Love bent the silver streams,
and kissed the mornings rushing rays
with Midas gold.

Love gathered summer fruits,
and crushed them with its virgin feet
then drank the wine of pity.

Love donned the purple robes of power,
and cast away the winter's darkness;
Then spilled its sacrificial blood
upon the earth.

H.S. Frost

Stormy Weather

Distant thoughts winging towards an angry day
And even while the sky is clear they gather, grey.
Swirling thoughts kicking up a stormy dust,
Gathering along the paths like love and trust;
Disappearing in my mind's dark hidden dune,
Just a glimpse, a sigh, a word, and gone too soon.
Chasing clouds of golden-bright, remembered hours,
Breezes dancing through the trees and bringing showers,
Softly washing all my dusty dreams away,
Bringing out fresh hopes that cannot stay;
And soon, too soon the time for parting's here,
Another hour, another day, another year.

Wendy Frost

The Ebb of Life

On Lough Swillys fair banks as the Sun was extending
His rays o'er the calm billows blue
I sat down to ponder among the wild flowers
And watched the sea birds float from view.

Before me the billows were ebbing
Gently they touched to the land
One last parting farewell from the waters
Ere the waves made procession to the Strand.

I gazed at the waters before me
At the ebb and the flow of the Sea.
And thought how our life ebbs onwards
To the shores of the Great Eternity.

Mary Friel

Fen Sunset

I love the Winter skies above the Fen,
The pastels painted by the Artist's pen.
The delicacy of the blues and greys
With dusky pink reflections in the bays
And lakes of Cloudland.

The pearly evening darkens into night,
The moon gives fitful gleams of gibbous light,
The clouds now grey and silver on a sable sea
Show beacon stars becalmed in the lee
Of the cloudy shores.

All through the night the starships drift becalmed,
Between the continents they thread unharmed
Until the morning light, all pink and grey
Reveals the dawning of one more blue day
In the country of the Clouds.

Anne Fowler Melville

Journey

Life is a journey, destination unknown
The pathway is marked, by the seeds we have sown.
It winds and it twists, it may rise or may fall
It sinks to the depths, then climbs straight and tall
Our thoughts and our actions can alter our course
Our ability to adapt, is an important resource
We come to a crossroad, which way should we choose?
Is it this way I win? Or this way I lose?
Do we steer straight and clear on the pathway ahead
Or turn and retrace the steps we have tread?
Life is a journey, destination unknown
The direction we take, is our choice alone.

Angela Evans

Branwell

Fragile as glass, your promises were broken one by one.
They lay in fragments all the way
    from Luddenden to London.
You were no genius,
Even the famous portrait of your sisters
Was discarded, left unvarnished.

The blame was not entirely yours.
You were too frail a craft to bear
The cargo of those others' expectations.
There was a darkness in your genes
Inherited from what strange and tragic source?

The mote within your father's eye
Concealed from him the beam that lay in yours.

Barbara France

"Child busy
constructing
with green and blue bricks
Mother takes hold
of fragile calm
to reconstruct her mind."

Jane Margaret Facey

Nature's Gifts

Nature's gifts aren't hard to seek
From lush green valley
To mountain peak
Bubbling brook and tumbling stream
A place where one can sit and dream
Cows in the pasture chewing cud
Perfumed flowers in a wood
Busy little harvest mouse
Bright plumed pheasant
Strutting grouse
And on wing in bright blue sky
Go meadowlarks and butterfly
Prickly bushes, berries wild
The laughter of a little child
All these things on earth to grace
Everything in perfect place.

Kathleen Fox

Ode To Spring

Suddenly there's magic in the air
Music everywhere
Spring
Once again the pulse is racing
All around the great awakening
Intoxicates, captivates, rejuvenates
Everything.

Birth may be quiet and uneventful
Loud and resentful
Rising in crescendo
From a whimper to a scream
The flowering soft and gentle
Ornamental almost, tickling the senses
Like a delicately scented bloom.

Or colourful, robust and riotous
Bubbling like champagne
Exciting admiration
An indescribable elation
In fulfillment of a dream
Life, resurgent, defiant,
Nothing can deny it.

Mary Fraser

The White House

They are building modern houses on the orchard where we played
Four little girls in starched white pinafores.
But the old house is still standing with its garden full of flowers
And hollyhocks still nodding by its door.

But do the rushmats on the landing still whisper in the dark,
As the silent ghostly footsteps pass on by?
Does the door swing suddenly open of the bedroom on the right
And a child, face in pillow softly cry?

Does a mother's quiet footsteps tread swiftly up the stair,
And turn the oil lamp down on summer nights?
And does the wind blow round the corner of the landing with a whine
And the flickering candle flame dance out of sight?

And does a father come running up the path home from war?
His sword banging on the gate as he goes by.
And lift the youngest child high above his head,
While the others group around him quiet and shy.

The past becomes the present, wind rustles through the trees,
The old house lies quietly sleeping in the sun.
But in the silence in the darkness, sound the voices of the past,
In the shadows, in the sunlight, lingering on.

Judith E. Gale

Inspiration

I'm trying to write, looking for inspiration
Should I write about birth or the death of a nation
What about church and a small congregation
Or the stock exchange and world of floatation

I could write about girls and the way that they tease
Or the wonder of Nature and the beauty of trees
I could write about writers that write with such ease
Or of actors and egos and exorbitant fees

Should I be serious, should I be light
Should I write about peace or maybe a fight
The life of a family or a poor orphans plight
A warm sunny day or a dark stormy night

Shall I finish a poem that I started before
Describe a picture or an old music show
What about Rome and emperor Nero
Shall I write about Heaven or Hell down below

No, I can't think what to write today
I'd better put my pens away
For some inspiration, I'd gladly pay
But I've written this, well what can I say

John Gallant

A Wealth of Treasure

Do you dream of inheriting a fortune?
    Or yet of winning the pools?
To just sit and dream
    That is the progress of fools.

Yet we all have may treasures:
    How precious to us is our sight.
The earth is full of such wonders
    When we come outside in the light.

Reach out, and touch each contour,
    Feel its softness or its warmth.
Smell the freshness and scent of the rose
    Or taste the luscious fruits of the earth.

Listen and hear the song of the birds
    Or the quiet hum of the bees.
See the sudden fleeting movements
    Of the deer among the trees.

What a blessing to us is our memory!
    And to people who share good health.
What wonderful things are "our senses",
    Surely we have abundant good wealth.

M.E. Gaines

1548

The Norse of Luffness
lie deep in sleep,
And the men at arms
Their watches keep.

The ships stand at
ease in the bay,
No sign of the English
This Michaelmas day.

Victoria Fletcher

Butterflies

Tiny tapestries take to the air
sailing slight breezes
mainsails a-flutter
Utter a sudden sneeze of strong wind
and they are chaos on display
stringless kites which rise and dip
in helpless disarray

Alight again
adorn the waiting flowers
tasting nectar held in sun-kissed bowers
With parchment wings in diverse colours stained
mix with honeysuckled bees
then take to flight again

Mrs. A. Garrett

The Folly of Man

God created the Earth, sea and sky
He endowed it with forests and mountains, towering on high
Creatures wild and roaming free
And birds sang joyful melodies.

For many years there was peace in the land
Then greed and enmity took a hand
In the form of Man, who was also given life
For many a long year, there was nothing but strife.

Nation fought nation throughout the ages
But still they don't learn from history's pages
Man creates his own hell here on Earth
When it could have been so different, the land of their birth

When will it cease, all of this slaying?
Man killing man, with no thought of paying
The ultimate price, as finally they wend
To face their maker, at journey's end.

Mrs. E. Gallagher

Cairn

Palm warmed stones,
gathered as relics
for Pilgrims to find.

Blackening, as we circle
against the sand tied sun.
Carrying to Hampsfell

All that it owned.
Stacking our journeys
Stone upon stone.

Russell Gee

Liberation

Did you ever see me
        climb a tree
Or kick a football
        high in the sky?
I'm a swimmer, a diver,
        and a racing car driver
I'm no little mouse
        'cause I built my own house
It's fun being me
        up in that tree
I'm a woman you see
        yeah, it's great being me.

Caitlin Gallagher

Summer Song

Sky-blue sky —
Cloudless, bright,
Shot through with sun's rays
Bursting forth.

Hazy shimmers quiver,
As grass cutters cut and hum
With bees the notes of
Summer's song.

Long days — warm, fun-filled.
Squeals and shrieks delight
As ice cream melts
And water's cool tones beckon.

Senses tingle,
Embracing full the
Smell, the feel, the transience
Of Summer's golden promise.

Lynn Gallacher

Woman

Who am I
Wife, mother, daughter
Friend, neighbour, lover, who am I
Where have I gone.
I with so many things to see,
To do,
Who am I.
Am I to be forever a foil
For someone else's life.
Or do I say enough!
Look and see me
This is I

Jean Gee

Lost and Lonely

The time was reached when the dead
Not the living
Were thought about constantly.
No longer did swelling buds
And blossom sprays
Catch the staring dimming eyes.
The long and endless minutes
Ticked slowly by
Reliving past memories.
No night resting of the mind
In peaceful sleep,
But long wakeful soul searching.
To an uncertain future
Now projected
Elderly, lost and lonely.

Lily Gardner

Bereavement

Time brushing gently past the moment,
Moving onwards
Like softly swirling mist,
Leaving hazy memories in its wake.
Mist that covers both pain and joy,
Softening,
Smoothing,
Sharp edges blending into timelessness.
Memories like a vapour drifting along with time;
Joy and sadness evaporating together,
Becoming one,
Moving onwards.
Time.
Peace drawing nearer.

Jean Furness

Friend Or Foe

As I lay down to rest
a burning feeling in my chest.
I think of others, who have gone before,
maimed or dead, through this damn war.

I hope that God can hear my cries
for the ones in charge, to get wise.
Stop sending troops out here to die,
for it makes men sit down and cry.

I hope that I shall live to see
my young daughter upon my knee.
Once again reunited,
although my body has been blighted.
Now I am feeling weak,
but must not fall asleep.

Listen! Is that a voice I hear?
Friend or foe, they're very near.
Am I about to meet my end?
No! Thank God, it is a friend.

Ms. L. Gallant

The Journey

I have to go to work each day
It really is a pain
To see the same old faces
As they climb aboard the train.

But oh, what have we here today
A stranger in the camp,
No suit, no tie, no bowler hat
His hair all curled and damp.

Designer stubble on his chin,
An earring in one ear
The best of Nike on his feet
In his hand a can of beer.

I can't look at his features,
No matter which way he leans,
For I cannot take my eyes away
From the bulge inside his jeans.

I can't look out the window
Read a magazine or book
I know that it's embarrassing
But I do know where to look.

I hope he's here tomorrow
To feast my eyes upon,
At last there's something different
To speed my journey on.

Mary Garrett

The Cyclamen Still Grows

No matter if conjecture flows
Life's unseemly highs and lows,
Or what the mind's eye knows;
The sweet cyclamen still grows.

Tossed though we be by every wind
That fickle fortune blows,
Even saints have sometimes sinn'd;
While the cyclamen, it grows.

Anxieties hasten and hope is slow
Spears of green thrust through the snow,
For summer's song dark winter knows;
The sweet cyclamen still grows.

Fair maiden's pretty head hangs low
Drawn by dark doubts below,
Come, raise your tearful eyes aglow;
And see, the cyclamen will grow!

Years come and fleet-footed go
Youth is quick and age is slow,
Joy comes hand-in-hand with woes;
But the cyclamen simply grows.

Brian C. Gamage

Rendezvous

A war of the worlds sky above.
The moon makes a mercury sea.
And you are here with me.

A couple of winter clouds try to pull the mood down.
But the moon's white light on your pale face.
Makes it summer time anyway.

For one hour you scan the view.
For half that time I study you.
Then I kiss the salt glaze from your lips.

I bend my arm around you and rest it where I find you.
Your warm hand pays me.
The thieving wind steals the only words you say.

So how can it be you're not here with me.
For a moment or two I nearly fell in love with you.
But great loves rise and fall.
We run to catch them all.

Now here in cold blood where we once stood.
A rendezvous with a lost love.
A girl in a red scarf.
And the priming of two young hearts.

S.J. Garnett

Shattered Illusions

Through intellect man has reached the stars
Walked in space and on the moon
This speck of dust with beating heart
Discovering wonders beyond imagining
Time capsuled in their blind endeavour
Realization dawning all too soon

In space did man look down
Upon this blue, green glistening sphere
This world in wonderful illusion
Tranquil in the breathless silence
Cloaked in the mystery of distance
Beyond the reach of pain and fear

Return to earth, feet firmly down
Treading the paths of hope and glory
A generation of bold adventurers
Defeated by the worlds reality
Retreating into quiet obscurity
Visions blurred, adrift, alone

Destroyed by horror of inhuman suffering
Searching for peace passing understanding
Drifting through the cosmos of infinity
Towards a destiny proclaimed by time
Our hour-glass sand fast falling down
Before the dawn of true awakening.

Mignon Garrett

Two Homes

To my very special Mother,
Who I think of every day,
You brought me up from a chilld,
And set me on my way.

I was never Mother's helper,
I didn't have a clue,
It came as quite a shock to me,
To start a home away from you.

I felt so very homesick,
It never went away,
I'd walk back over home to you
And feel I'd want to stay.

I'd come back up to my house,
That didn't have the smells
Of home and you and family,
And things I knew so well.

But then I had my children,
And things began to look so good,
I'd learned to do my housework,
The way Mother said I should.

Now as the years go by,
And my children start to roam
I hope they think of this house,
The way I always think of home.

Lesley Ann Ganderton

Life

From the darkness of the mother's womb, to the light of day,
A whimper of life, my first breath.
A loud cry, the life just starting, the warmth of my parents,
Their loving care giving me strength and growth,
To push my way forward to the challenge of life.

My first meeting place into God's church, proud parents and friends
Looking down on me, my baptism,
The holy water is sprinkled on my face
My audience singing the song of life and ringing out my name.

The learning years, growing up; talking, crawling, walking, schooling.
New friends, their young faces looking for the wind of change
To open the gates of life.
Our paths laughing, playing and tears for the ones who didn't make it.

The golden years have gone, the fun days of school
And my youth taken away by nature's time,
Just memories and photographs to remind me of the past.

The power of love brings forth wedding bells, my parents and friends
With the new generation, once young faces turning into men
Our lives built for this joyous day.

The trial of life is over, my turn to start the day
The cycle of life repeats itself.
The partnership of man and wife, the buying of a house,
Raising of a family and a workplace for life.

Nature's racing time calling in the day, lights of heaven and darkness that day.

Garrett John

A Mother's Price

How can you put a price on something we do
With Love in our hearts everyday though,
I can't say I love ironing, or washing the dishes.
A day doing housework is not one of my wishes.
But all that I do is made worthwhile
When one of my sons flashes me a smile.
My sons were once babies in nappys and such,
The work that's involved is so very much,
But to see them now growing to young men, so fine,
I know I've not wasted all of my time
I'm there when I'm needed, perhaps to wipe away a tear
Or just to give a cuddle, it's so nice to have them near.
And at the end of the day, when the boys are in bed.
I must change out of my role, to a lover instead.
Now you may ask what I'm worth for all that I do.
To say that I'm priceless, just doesn't ring true.
Well you can't pay me in cash or gold for my task,
Just to be loved by my family is all that I ask.

Mrs. H.J. George

Caution - Ireland 1994

The guns and the bomb are quiet now
And both sides have earned the golden cow
Life, liberty and equality now resumed.
The words, stop violence and peace
In my head boomed.
It's hard to believe after all this time
That peace has returned, and it's yours and mine.
But I have to ask, can it be true?
Can I believe it, and can you.
Please be cautious, don't go too fast
Remember our inglorious past.
Opinions from all sides must be considered
Before a lasting peace can be delivered.
All peacemakers must stand up and be counted
So that in God's name, a lasting peace can be mounted.

Marie C.B. Gamble

The Mistle Thrush

My cheekiest most ill-mannered friend to my garden returning
On time, The Trespasser; puffed out speckled breast,
His wings coming in like an attacking Spitfire.

In the centre of the garden, the great feast for birds awaits,
Glowing a translucent white; with its leaves flashed with amber,
Gently falling to the ground.

The hupehensis tree, the white-pink flushed berries
Hang heavy and invitingly to the banquet.
Awaiting tits, finches, blackbird, robins —But no!
Trespasser, the Mistle Thrush, says "Tis all mine,
Till I fall drunk from the tree.
I shall eat to the last berry, you shall have none."

Dawn till dusk he dive bombs
At every bird which dares approach the tree.
Why do I love him — and await his November returning?

Pamela Estelle Gibson

Father To Son

It was only a stop gap.
A cog in the wheel of a production line,
but better than emasculation on the dole queue
and infinitely better than working down a hole
as his father had done, and his father before him.

Hard filthy graft.
Never seeing the light of day in winter,
Edge of hunger always there,
Comradeship. There was plenty of that,
and coughing your guts up.
Exhaustion.
Old age at thirty.

Times are different now.
Soon, he would take his young sons away —
away from those memories
so carefully handed down.
Give them wings to inherit the earth

But then he thought of his father's face,
buoyant with hope and new world dreams
and with the passing years — the slow dimming.
A sudden foreboding rose from deep in his marrow.
He remembered his father's words,
"It's only a stop gap."

Kathryn L. Garrod

Louise, The Pig Farmer's Wife

Look at her. Louise,
with her pinney and her dishes
and her ever ready rubber gloves.
The perfect farmer's wife.

You'd never guess Louise
was trained in Law at Leeds,
and had ambitions
beyond Five Acres Farm.

But then she always said
she couldn't stand routine
and needed a Bohemian
to make her life less dull.
A painter, or a writer
was what she had in mind,
but John the farmer came along
with his pink and shiny piglet
and caught her heart and talked her round
and made her what she is today:
a farmer's wife.

I sometimes stop and think about
her deep brown waist length hair
and wonder if she remembers back
before the screaming kids
to when she hated squealing pigs
and could have chosen ... me.

Martin Gaskell

Storm Quoit

Seven five

A circle pierced by a primeval line
   lies wedged between two storms

Dragons stand up
   repeatedly
   in a slow motion Druidic wave

They hover over Charles I's furniture
   hoping to catch some sun

The circle's roar
   fans out south and east
   neutralising the sting
   of Godrevy's warning wail
   and disappears into the maw of the dragon chieftain
   resplendent over Man

The storms meet
   the circle fades

Just over Gwithian
   a creeping ring of apple fungus
   repaints the rained horizon

Steve Gardiner

The Windows Of The Soul

The eyes are the windows of the soul
Clear like water in a crystal bowl
Gaze inside them, plumb them very deep
Into character you will then peep.

Straight look eyes are steadfast like a hand
Which firmly clasps like an iron band
Round truth and integrity lusted
Conveys this person can be trusted.

Eyes that shift about their gaze
Looking here and there like in a daze
Cannot show trust to put it bleakly
Same as infirm hand shaking weakly.

Eyes can be coloured shades of blue
Green or brown or other type of hue
All twinkle with laughter or sadness torn
It matters not with which sort you're born.

The eyes are the windows of the soul
Clear like water in a crystal bowl
Look in them straight and you shall find
If owner loves — is generous or kind.

Harold Gilbert

White Christmas Wonder

I wonder if this year the ground will be white
When we draw back the curtains at first morning light
To see a white blanket so crisp and so clean,
Covering the world for a Christmas Day dream.

Imagine the joy on a little child's face
To see the earth wrapped up in Winter's embrace,
Enchanted and hypnotised as the flakes fall,
Such magic, excitement, God sends for them all.

Never mind breakfast, they've got to be out,
"Where are my gloves and my wellies?" they shout,
The glistening smoothness all gone with one crunch,
When they've finished their snowman, they'll be ready for lunch!

Presents so neatly arranged by the tree
Wait to be opened by children, with glee,
But the call the Christmas Day snow just can't wait,
They must build a snowman before it's too late.

A scarf round his neck and two coals for his eyes,
A Christmas Day snowman is such a surprise,
But why do we long for a Christmas with snow
To celebrate the birth of our Lord long ago?

Snow didn't fall on that first Christmas Day
In that small town of Bethlehem far, far away,
But in our land the words of the song still ring true,
Each year a white Christmas is dreamed of anew!

Margaret D. Ghori

Whatever Life Delivers Us

We never were that lucky
A bonus folk don't know
Children they just come along
We all must love them so!

But do they always come along?
Of course they always do
Unless by God's deciding hand
They never come to you!

So we've made our life together
Our vows were said so true
Whatever life delivers us
My life I'll spend with you!

You're more than just a wife to me
A pal so good and true
Through all my imperfections
You still love me through and through!

You and I are growing older now
But we never must forget
The family and love we've shared
If we never would have met!

I've always loved you through my days
There's always something we could share
And when our days are over
I know our heaven's waiting there.

Brian E. Gilbert

The Akashic Library

Walking past the vast shelves of the Library,
my eyes focused on what I had been looking for, for so long:
The Book of My Reality. I hesitated, not knowing what to do ...
After a short eternity, I instinctively remembered,
being a Gnostic, that to know of one's existence was to die.
I asked myself if I was ready to go home?
"Yes," I cried — the Masters agreed.
I turned to the Librarian, "Can I Go?"
He too said that it was time.
I was overwhelmed. I had waited for so long,
within this period of incarnation, to see Myself again.
"Thank-you," I whispered. My voice resonated
around the infinite shelves of the Universe.
One day, I knew, I would catch up with those words,
but for now they would be the last I ever spoke.
My arms reached for the Book, it was heavy,
and I had to invoke all my Faith to pick it up.
I turned to the last page, saw my image reflected in a mirror,
and was instantly reunited with the memories of all my yesterdays.
The glass broke, dispersing my image throughout
the never ending passages of Time ...
Then I was back in the sphere of "non-existence" — The Bardo —
surrounded by nothing, aware of everything.

"Hello Father, I've missed you!"

Susan Gifford

The Days Before The War

How well I can remember, the days before the war,
With every day a happy day, that seemed without a flaw;
But that was 1939, we had no notion then,
Of the years that were to follow, the sacrifice of men.

The annual August holiday, filled every waking hour,
That visit to the seaside, with sand and sea and tower
Was soon to be a memory, as clouds began to gather,
And troubles so bewildering, as sunshine turned to shower.

It all seemed fun to children, as we trundled off to school,
With gas-masks on our shoulders, for that became the rule;
The shelters in the garden, protection from the hun,
We didn't think we'd need them, but building them was fun.

The air-raid sirens wailing, the bombers way up high,
Anti-aircraft guns and searchlights, lighting up the sky.
The blackout and the wardens, patrolling in the streets,
The rationing, the shortages, especially of sweets!

I lost my favourite uncle, before the second fall,
I sometimes sit and wonder, at the wastage of it all.
And looking back in sadness, at the things I heard and saw,
I still recall the happy times, in the days before the war.

Doreen Gay

My Great Grandmother's Story

Once upon a time,
Maggie Harkess lived in a Sunderland slum,
an existence she strove to overcome,
with childbearing women prematurely old,
one in the oven, six in the cold.
In a twilight of ill health trying to cope
on heavy washdays with soda and soap.
Unwanted pregnancies, anaemia and worse,
little white coffin, little black hearse.
She had the vote but little cared,
her cross with other mothers was shared
not for the red-taped ballot box
but 'Men laid off in factories and docks.'
Her worries were legion, her possessions few,
but Maggie's spirit came shining through,
a reaching out, a need to know
the reason for living and conquering woe.
Slowly, slowly by degrees,
Maggie rose from her callused knees,
her life no longer a sorry story,
Enlightenment was her Final Glory.

Violet Gibson

Late Autumn

'Neath swirling mist and dampening air
The Earthling, loathe to leave his lair,
Peers out and sees the day begun,
But nowhere does he see the sun.

A grudging lightening of the skies
Is all that will reward his eyes
To mark departure of the night,
And little do to aid his sight.

The Summer went some time ago,
And with it went it's golden glow
Now Autumn sheds its multi-coloured dress
As tattered remnants to Earth's surface press.

Biting wind will soon the mist disperse
As Winter ushers in its curse
Of life locked in 'neath frozen sod,
While Spring awaits its cue from God.

R.H. Gunston

The Snails

The mountains promised an escape,
A chance to grasp a glimpse of peace.
One week to reach out for reality
And seek a precarious sanity.

A day of sweet spring rain
Brought out the thirsty snails,
Searching with instinctive drive
For life-supporting water.

Oblivious to danger, they crept from safety,
To be grabbed by greedy boys
Or crushed by careless foot;
Survivors ignorant of their fate.

Too short the time, too strong the need;
The chance has gone, the risk was know.
Our fragile existence, so very vulnerable,
Crushed by a careless word.

Penelope Guy

Starlight Prayer

On such a night as this my lover died.
On such a day his spirit stole away.
Without good-bye, without a kiss, he left.
Now I, bereft
Of warmth and love and kindly talk,
The paths of lonely bliss shall walk;
And, vainly searching for the sun, the fire, the glow,
I'll only know the night;
To dance under the Moon's cold light.

I tried to say good-bye.
He lay too still to answer with a smile, a wave.
So, desolate, from the grave I sent a prayer
(But who would pray for me?)
Heaven-ward it soared, floating on air
To mingle with the stars.
They caught my love
And held it for moments such as this,
When, wanting him, hearing his voice
And dreaming of his kiss,
My lost gaze travels high.
First the despairing dark, the void,
Then, slowly from the sky
Each spark of shining love is showered from above.
Then I know he prays for me.

Marion Gilliland

I Won't Miss

My little baby's left me
as my tears form a pool,
no, she's not left home or got wed,
she's starting Primary School.

But I won't miss the demands
of sweets when we go to the shop,
or the total defiance, when,
by the roadside, she refuses to stop.

I won't miss the sacrifices
when she switches on the T.V.
and she wants to watch videos,
instead of Home and Away, like me.

I won't miss all of the toys
being scattered on the floor
for me to put them away
then her to go and get more.

I won't miss taking her to town
when I'm shopping in the sales
and we go into a clothes shop
and she's hanging off the rails.

But, I will miss the cuddles
and the help to dry the dishes,
but not as much as those cute
but very sloppy kisses.

Kirsty Garwell

A Visit To

Coventry Cathedral, the bombed and the new.
I went to a dinner dance so I could visit you.
As I lived near London it seemed so far to go,
Just for one thing only in a city I did not know.

I saw the famous tapestry — which I found I could not like.
Bathed in the stained glass, I watched the colours strike
An atmosphere of beauty into all that was around.
THEN — I saw the drawings, my heart sank underground.
I remember very little but the drawings on the stands.
They had a haunting beauty, impressions by many hands,
Of man and hope,
       OF CRUELTY,
              OF ENERGY,
                      FUTILITY.

Great masters, unexpected, I hadn't known they would be there,
They filled me with sensations I still find no words to share.
Drawings from the Holocaust before my soul displayed,
In the hushed Cathedral,
       SEARED
              alone
                 I PRAYED.

Marion Green

Our Dad

Our dad is a special one
The one we all respect,
He brought us up the best he could
And that we won't forget.

Our mum died at 73
The best one in the world
Now dad's tiring in old age
His mind's began to twirl.

He talks about the family
The things we used to do
From walking up to Hardwick Hall
Then home to cobble a shoe.

We won't forget things in a hurry
As he told us not to worry
But as he weakens from day to day
All we do is think and pray.

To see him now is very sad
Because you only have one dad
We know he won't be here forever
And his wishes are we stick together.

Dorothy Gelsthorpe

Friendship

A friend is likened, to a song
So full of harmony
Shows kindness, when things go wrong
Care, trust, and loyalty

Sometimes one hits a low note
And needs a helping hand
A pal, showing affection
Sympathetic, warm, and sound

A friend will hit the high notes
Is reliable and true
A comrade, an associate
A mate, of great value

When friends sing in harmony
Of fondness and goodwill
So genuine, and welcoming
The song of life, fulfilled

But the greatest friend
A man could have
Is a wife, he holds so dear
Pleasing, loving, good company
Sweet music, to one's ear.

Joseph Gething

Against The Grain

I fixed the shelves, it made me feel good,
in shining black ash, the work all mine,
"About time!" she said, eyeing the wood,
"But really, they should be pine."

I offered to wash-up, trying to atone,
"I'll do Grannie's tea service!" she spat.
At such distrust I did not moan,
and left for the pub, grabbing my hat.

Over my beer I pondered long,
I'd worked so hard to be a good man,
but every deed was dismissed as wrong,
I thought some more, then hatched my plan.

Defiant in the garage I laboured all the more,
All week I'd taken, to make this thing so fine.
"Ah, a cuppa — come in darling and close the door,
I've made this for you — lined with lead and finished in pine!"

Triumphant, I took the mug — her face blank,
a long swig prepared me for the final act.
But suddenly faint I caught her smile, my head spun, my body sank,
realising, as my curtain fell, her supremacy — now fact.

D. Goddard

In His Shoes

So at long last — I have arrived.
SENILE.
But not yet deprived of
Eating, Sleeping, Pissing or Sex.
Maybe some dark hex?
The minute becomes a day
and the day becomes a minute —
all in one second.
Sure, it's one strange morning,
but decay safeguards me from any warning.
In a flash I am airborne —
right back to the war, in forty-four,
forgetting my score.
Then back with that French tart
to a secluded shore.
"HARRY!"
Breaks me back into harsh reality,
there's some bitch who's never lived,
spooning me porridge
with great authority.
But everything's good now.
Because I've forgotten.
My one consolation —
In a lifetime turned rotten.

Stephen E. Glover

Untitled

The bullets flew
the soldiers fell
in heaps upon the ground.
Soon no more men stood fighting
one strained to hear a sound.

A sweetheart reads a letter,
posted the week before.
Little did she realize
it was from a love she would see
no more.

There really must be a reason
why men do go to war.
But tell it to the soldier
who lies dead upon the floor.

Since time began
men have fought wars
in the belief that they are right.
The solution to the problem
to take up arms
and fight.

Maybe in the future
there will be some other course.
Where people can solve their problems
except by using force.

D.I. Gaster

What For?

So eager is discouragement to wait outside the door
To knock with great persistence, gain entry, ask "What for?"
It seems the gloom of winter days, bids welcome to this guest
We forget wise words and spoken soft "Just try, and do your best".

All life is for the taking when we truly try our best
Hope rises with the sun, and brightness does the rest
Consider then what lights our lives, the likes of me and you
A night sky has its stars and winter snow has brightness too.

A special star at Christmas pointed to a stable door
Discouragement was left outside and LOVE came in, with power
To overcome the fears of men with courage, faith and hope.
To know "what for" - with certainty, to rise. Have faith and cope!

Olwen Godden

Mill By The Stream

The nettles grow rough and wild
Along the path that leads to the old mill,
Where in the fast-falling gloom
The darkened, broken windows inward gaze.
Green and moist the moss clings on,
To battered roof and dented wall. But
Silver-blue the stream still glides,
Spluttering through the reeds and round the banks.
And musty and mute in sleep,
The dark odours rise and swim in dimness,
While the only sound that calls,
The whispering dirge of the running stream.

Marie Ghoreishi

The Misfit

Outside I'm wrong: Don't fit in
With you who do who pour scorn
On my body, my exterior, my skin.
But of course you are perfect; you
who snigger, and stare, and grin.
United by your own insecurity;
You have no imperfections — they
all manifest in me.
Together share out the jibes and
the insults, the communal spite:
When alone, pause, and consider,
That maybe inside I'm right.

Maureen Godfrey

In The Name Of

Father, see the fullness of creation -
How did you conceive the Word and the Light?
Foul Damnation, divine deviation
Openly trades by God-given birthright!
Son, can you hear the desperate lament
Of pure, honest blood red-soaking the grounds?
Death, their portent, will save further torment
Until your rapture rips open their mounds!
Ghost, how many nations will you inspire
Such a Passion for holy crusading!
Oh, they'll never tire of your cleansing fire
Nor ash-laden baptismal parading!
Can This by they Will? Are These then thy goals?
How much misery? How many more souls?

Bernard Glick

Christmas

The pressure's off, we can relax,
No letters, telephone or fax,
No frantic shopping with a list
Of Christmas things we can't resist!
The pudding's made, the cake is iced,
With busy transport we have diced,
We never thought we could achieve
Success like this by Christmas Eve!
So Christmas Day will dawn at last
In grand tradition of the past,
A message now of hope and cheer
To warm your hearts throughout the year,
Good Luck, Good Health and all you need
Summed up in just one word — 'Godspeed'.

Doril MacMunn Gilbert

From Me To You

A kaleidoscope of images
Whirling through my mind:
Leaves of emerald with
Solitaire diamond.
Warm flesh embracing me on awakening or
Steaming rooms where Neptune and Venus play
Sometimes among cherubs in chartreuse chemistry
But smiling; fulfilled as we.
Pearls of joy; of awe, of pain
Overwhelm us both in pagan rite
Whilst Diana shuns our pure yet unchastened love.
Fearful of intransigence.
Commitments form from air,
Warm through smiling selves.
He sped to glaucous oceans
She to monocolour expressions
Of fictitious phantoms
Where angels lie in wait
As she, Minerva rests.
Hope, dreams and memories
Accompany both.

Gillian Gatley

The Best In Life Is Free

There are some things in life, that money can buy,
But others, you cannot.
Don't measure your wealth, by the coins in your hand,
For some things just can't be bought.

A tree swaying gently in the breeze
The face of a child at play,
An eagle soaring, high in the sky,
For that, you don't have to pay.

The stars, the sun, the moon up above
Are there, for eyes to see,
For money can't buy the gift of sight
It is given us for free.

Speech is another precious thing,
Be sure to use it wisely,
Think, before you utter a word,
Try not to speak unkindly.

A cheery smile, a friendly 'Hello'
Is worth more than treasures untold,
And if you have your health, you're richer by far
Than those with their pots of gold.

So just be content, with whatever you have,
Don't envy the folk next door,
For if you have the love of family and friend,
In this life you'll never be poor.

Jean Grieve

Hello World

Outside, the dreary world
Reflects my mood of dismal self-reproach.
The sorrow and bitterness in the sky encroach
Into my very being and curl
Around me.

Inside, I watch the rain.
With emotions of useless wishes and tears
Of regret I become full of fears
As the rivulets stream down the windowpane
As if in agony.

In the declining light
I enter a world of enveloping isolation
Emotions exhausted, my feelings of desolation
Lifted as it became clear that I must fight
To bring back the sunlight.

In the recesses of my heart
I remember, a love so supreme,
All the joys of the past were not a dream.
The storm clouds lifted, I pulled the curtains apart ...
The sunlight flooded in.

Beryl Elaine Gorman

A Day In The Life Of A Woman

Cooking, cleaning, boring chores,
That's what women do,
Straighten beds and mop the floors,
To make it look brand new.

People come to visit,
Have coffee and a chat,
Talk about their loved ones,
Someone's this and someone's that.

It's nearly time for them to go,
His tea I must prepare,
Take the meat out of the fridge,
He doesn't like it rare.

He walks in, "Had a good day?"
This I always ask,
He flops down, oh so tired,
Hands me his dirty flask.

Back into the kitchen,
Looking at the sink,
Oh, I'd love a break,
This is what I think.

Just to sit, be waited on,
For once in my dull life,
To have him sit beside me,
And whisper "Thanks for being my wife."

Sandra Goddard

Imagery and Innocence

I grasp you with my eyes and thoughts untold
Like some mysterious vision you appear as romance past.
Grant me the heart of silk and gold,
On bended knee these tears I shed my last.
It matters not that I by chance,
Hide such despair and wish my heart free.
I watched nature's embrace and tempestuous dance,
How simple love's soul touches me,
To hear you voice for surely now I know
No more will love's hunger or sorrow be so.
So let all pleasures come to sin's mistress,
Lest not the man who lives within,
As you shall find of love's fired song,
Mingled bodies in life's soft light,
As lips tremble for such impending wrong
I thirst for a foolish summers night,
But brightness trample my gloomy task
No more I the humbler to bend and kiss.
Contented hearts savest such pleasures past
As for relief in hand you smile and give,
And grasp life's hardened youthful embrace,
So shine life's passion be it feigned,
But could your beauty repent or miss,
Or forgive such shallow emptiness?

P.B. Greenway

January

We have seen the landscape all in white,
glistening with frost and snow
A very pretty show!
Now as I stand and stare
There's such a bleakness everywhere
The trees hang bare
Shed of all its golden leaves
And hardly a whisper in the air
But coming slowly through those trees
"Shines the light"
Birds hopping from bough to bough
Singing with all their might.

Presently the scene will change
With many signs of spring in sight.
First again lovely little snowdrops peeping,
So very shyly after sleeping
Watching tiny snowflakes twirl.
Everywhere is budding green
Baby robins among the scenes
Many birds that give delight
Sunsets beautifully coloured, and bright,
So be not sad, January is the forerunner
The crowning month of good things to come
Therefore cheer up. Everyone.

Madeline Green

Sky Rider

He sat upon his motorbike like a cowboy sits his horse.
Screaming up the highway like it was a T.T. course.
Blipping on the throttle to make the exhaust roar,
Touching ninety miles an hour and trying for some more.

Banking round the corners. Burning up the gas.
Keeping well in front of all and letting no one pass.
Defying Death to catch him up, he went a bit too fast.
He only made just one mistake, but his first one was his last.

He didn't see the car ahead until it was too late,
He was dead before his foot could operate the brake.
He went crashing to the left, his bike went to the right,
Both ended up in a crumpled mess and not a pretty sight.

He'll never ride his bike again like a cowboy rides his horse
He'll never treat the highway like it was a T.T. course.
He'll never blip his throttle to make the exhaust roar
He'll never do the ton again. He'll never ride no more.

Beryl Giles

The Door

What lies beyond that dark foreboding door,
What dark secrets have passed through it before,
Its thick wooden timbers ornately grooved,
A large dulled bronze knocker remains unmoved,
Red-rusted hinges grasp despairingly the surround,
To swing with a banshee's screeching sound,
A blackened lock plate hides on one long side,
With a keyhole through which no one has spied,
An iron handle well-wrenched and made grey,
Serpentine it seems to faithfully twist away,
If it were ever to open what would we see,
What unknown abhorrence might we set free,
How can we say if it's a friend or foe,
Can we be sure to ever really know,
Who would chance to venture to go beyond,
To what desolate planes has it once belonged,
With what type of key is the lock turned,
Through what contract is the right earned,
Shall you know and ask to enter within,
Can you be certain to pass without sin?

SEG

On The Blink

We have a television set
That's always on the blink,
And when the colour should be red,
It's a lovely shade of pink.

Sometimes the volume's very low,
And then it goes quite loud.
Sometimes the picture's very clear,
Or else it's like a cloud.

We've asked the engineer to call,
To see what he can do;
But every time he comes around
The picture is like new!

He look at it quite puzzled,
Then he'll say with just a smile,
"I think you'll need another set
in just a little while."

Well, when we get the new one,
And we're sitting down to view,
I wouldn't be at all surprised
If it has a fault or two.

But I couldn't phone the TV man —
That is very plain.
For I can hear him saying now,
"Oh no! Not you again!"

Mavis Goosey

The "Parents" Christmas

"Oh my goodness, Oh my gracious
Christmas is here again," the Parent's said,
Realising Christmas was on its way.

"Out, out we'll dash, coats and all,
With dragging children round the mall,
I want this and that and this, they'll shout,
While we're trying to drag them out.

Toys galore we'll be carrying,
While the children will be marrying,
All the toys they see,
Will they ever think of me?

Lisa Gilbert (Age 11)

Light at End of Tunnel

When I am feeling low and a little depressed
I quickly wash and get myself dressed
I live just across to a beautiful park.
You can stay there all day until it gets dark
Oh to smell the sweet flowers as I walk along
And to hear the birds sing their morning song.
I feed the swans, sit and browse through my papers
Enjoy watching little children get up to their capers
Many interesting people, talk, and sit by my side
If I had stayed home, I might easily have cried
But now as I wander refreshed, back indoors,
I feel the blanket has lifted, I can now do my chores.

D. Gilson

This Beautiful World

Hazy sun reflects off robins breast
Golden leaves stir, move over, then rest
The budding trees echo with warbled trill
Jack Frost takes leave of a morning yet still

The hare starts to bask, so do lizard and snake
Bright yellows and whites shake their heads as they wake
And open their petals to let in the sun's warmth
The butterfly skips from flower to thorn

As the mole and the badger and fox turn to sleep
The ant and the grasshopper scamper and leap
The ground awakes, deep in the grass
The spider lies waiting, watching them pass

And Nature's March day dawns slowly on land
That is blessed with beauty, like a dragonfly's span
Is all this to end by the flick of a hand
By Nature's biggest mistake — Man.

John Goose

The Bomb

So the nameless few drew their knives,
And cut us free from the burden of our lives.
Their shattered minds and blinded sight,
Brought us to this, our final night.

At long last the button was depressed,
Releasing to our world this wicked temptress.
And with her violent and frenzied birth,
She let her fires raze this earth.

Yet barely born, she mates with Hell,
And of these horrors, who'll live to tell?
For the only witnesses there to see,
Are the shadows where people used to be.

And so, with her final orgasmic gasp,
She draws the future into the past,
And with her foul radio-active breath,
She embraces us, into our death.

Melanie Goss

Untitled

Ireland bleeding! Ireland reeling as men with bloody hands
Both Protestant and Catholic roam across her land
Killing for the sake of it - no longer thinking WHY?
Corrupted by a blood lust - it matters not who is to die.
If you asked them why they did it, not one of them will know.
To kill, to kill, to kill again is the only thing they know.
The politicians - north and south - embittered to the hilt
Among them so-called Christians who are only fit for hell.
Yet, bear a bloody guilt they must - with the killers that they hide.
Until their generation dies there's no hope for either side
And parents cease to teach their hate and corrupt the newborn child.

Howard Wallace Gibbs

Making a Cornish Pasty

How are you to make a pasty,
When times have changed so much?
I had the ingredients all prepared,
Pastry, potatoes, meat, onions and swede,
When along came the family and into
The kitchen they came,
Each with a different need:
The first one said no onions for me,
The second said no meat, I'm a Veggy now,
The third said, no swede, and I want Puff Pastry.
So how do you make a Cornish Pasty now?
That's all the cook needs to know.

Betty Gowing

Christmas Poem

A long time ago in Bethlehem
There came a story of three wise men
With gifts of riches they travelled from afar
Guided on forward by a special bright star

Away in a manger on Christmas Day
A child was born to lead the way
He was sent from the Lord up above
To teach mankind and spread his love

With head held high he walked so tall
But in the end he had to fall
On the cross he died not in vain
But so each and everyone of us would remember his name

So when Christmas is here let us all pray
For Jesus our Saviour was born on this day.

A. Gold

Old Empty Rooms

Old empty rooms, what have you seen
Of things and people that have been?
Smiling boys and laughing girls,
Aged folks with silvery curls
Lonely hours of grief and pain
Followed by sweets of life again;
Little joys, much idle chatter
Just simple things that make life matter.

What treasures did your walls once hold!
Loved possessions long since sold.
Polished floors still bear the trace
Where chest and chair had once their place.
Old haunted home of bygone years
That brings the heart so near to tears,
So many things you surely know,
Vanished scenes of the long ago.

J. W. Gosling

My Hero

My hero didn't wield a sword, or wear a coat of mail,
Or ride a fine white charge, to seek the Holy Grail,
He wore a khaki uniform, and joined the service corps,
A bob-a-day, that was his pay, as he went off to war:
He drove a rusty lorry, through miles of Flanders hell,
He gave his youth, he gave his strength,
He served his country well:
He didn't get a medal, all he got was gas,
Only once he had some leave, to see his little lass;
So, when you talk of heroes, however brave and bold,
Fighting famous battles, in the days of old,
I think of all my memories, and oh! I am so glad,
That my darling, dashing hero, was just my dear old Dad!

J.G. Greenwood

All Is Well

Born at Bethlehem for us
    Jesus, a child:
Innocent, felicitous,
    Meek and mild.
'God with us' we now can say,
    Emmanuel.
Christ our Lord — for us the way,
    All is well.

When he moved about on earth
    He healed the sick,
Sinners found in him rebirth,
    Devils the stick.
Lame could walk and blind had sight,
    Temple was cleansed.
Dumb found speech and weak had might
    The dead were raised.

Worship, honour, glory, praise
    Shall never cease.
Angels, martyrs and saints raise
    Hymns of peace.
All creation makes heaven ring
    With endless chorus
So lift up your hearts and sing
    'God is now with us.'

Edward W. Goulding

A Helping Hand

I planted a seed in my Garden
    But I could not make it grow;
My poor hands could only put it there
    Then wait for growth to show.
To wait for warmth from sunshine
    The power of life in the rain;
Each wonderful will of nature
    To spring from the soil again.
So useless I felt in my labour,
    A lovely Garden to grow —
So humble or feeble my efforts
    Happiness to sow.
Then the Lord seemed to say in my wonder,
    "You planted my seed for me
You are my hands in the Garden
    I cannot do that you see!"
I can only work through the hands of Man;
    My mighty works to do
So He put Man to work for him —
    His will to carry through.
To think that I in my sowing
    Could help in some small way;
My hand could help the Lord's hand —
    By planting a seed today!

Rosemary Goram

Once A Living Landscape

Once a living landscape with the abodes of men
for this was our colliery then
Before waves of woods and cornfields —
and the occasional bracken — the tip zoomed high
And the imaged tide that lay beyond became the slurry
And oh! the view — there was no getting over it
The hills became the dirt hills of despair —
and made the miners more aware
To quit the valley of the shadow of time.

Of the yield that lay below there was no trace
Only the dreaded dirt hills and empty space
the beginning of a nightmare and a land laid bare
No more toil and sweat for men to share —
For the bowels of the earth had already been exhumed —
The miner's livelihood doomed!

No soul searching for an explanation
Of the coal cart of man's imagination
Down in the desolate valley of the mine!

Rita Grace

Hill Culture

The hills were a wonderful new discovery for me
although, unknown, they'd encircled me for years:
their protection, beauty, safety, warmth
like a mother's loving embrace.
Once, I climbed
and saw a distant loch
and, not know its name, asked my father
— he wasn't sure either.

I've climbed many hills since then,
but always return to my first love.
I now know the name of that loch
and, in a way, all its many stories:
in its soothing, calming movement
it imparts to me its culture.
But, alas, I cannot tell my father of it
for he's taken his last trip
... but his love remains.

Niall Gordon

Loneliness

Loneliness is a terrible thing
Waiting for that bell to ring
Looking out of my window watching people passing by
Linking arms with their mate, I once had a friend called Kate
Darkness falling, curtains drawing
I now must wait for morning
Sitting in my chicken coop I now open my tin of soup
Cat sitting on my knee, I do wish someone would turn the key
Swaying in my rocking chair I think of how I used to care
Family days I cooked and washed, cleaned the house and
Gave kisses and cuddles and also helped them with their muddles.
Where are they now, I just do not know,
They say you reap what you sow.
WHY do they not write or ring
All I have now is a budgie that can sing.
Coronation Street is now on; I wonder what happened to old Don?
Meals-On-Wheels came today but they did not have much to say.
How I long for a good old talk or someone to take me for a walk
Infirm I may be but daft I am not, and I am not going to sit here and rot.
I can remember when I could run, skip and dance
Stop it, stupid woman, you will go into a trance.
Do not look back they say — I do everyday.
Remembering this and remembering that. Oh come here, you stupid cat.
Undressed and now to bed. Oh dear me, I wish I were dead.

Mrs. M. Groome

If Only ...

If only you hadn't gone Bill, life would be the same
I'd still be pushing you, adoringly down the lane
You left an empty feeling in everyone's heart,
Our not being together is tearing me apart.
If only I had my life over, with no change
You wouldn't go off and leave, me for another plain
A greater force than ours, called you from above
He realised how you'd suffered, regardless of my love
I'm all alone now, so what is new
Memories we did together will haunt my whole life through
Thought we would go on forever, how wrong could I be
Only God knew the time had come to release you from me
I didn't want to believe it, must be a lie
Now I know it wasn't, I'll remember until I die
As we talked together at the latter part
Little did you know, you were pulling at my heart
Time was against us, it ticked and quickly flew
Even as I ponder, thoughts are of you
Time's a great healer, I wonder if that's true
I only know, within myself, there'll never be another you.
For all the sick, and disabled, who from this earth depart
Forever you'll live in everyone's heart.

Vera Graham

Midwinter Sunday

Stark black branches against a leaden sky
    An arctic wind puts a tear in the eye
The countryside lies in winter's thrall
    No human sound is heard, no animal call

Diamonds of mist drop from bush and tree
    The air hangs heavy with malevolency
Vague shadows traverse the village street
    Leaving an echo of ghostly feet

The clock on the church has ceased to chime
    The notes of the organ in sombre time
Weave over the rooftops to hasten the late
    Still busily clearing the breakfast plate

It's hard to move on a winter's morn
    When the air is cold and the house is warm
From the dank grey earth comes the lingering scent
    Of a long dead summer and a life that's spent

'Tis the quiet time when the earth stands still
    Everything waiting for spring's first thrill
The hours glide by in a somnolent haze
    To take up their place in the pageant of days.

Jean R. Gritt

Wouldn't It Be Good?

Wouldn't it be good to fly away,
And leave all our bad behind?
Fly to a world with gratitude,
Where every bad person is kind.
Wouldn't it be good to fly to a place,
Where no disasters occur?
And all you really bad memories,
Were distant or just a faint blur.
Wouldn't it be good to fly to a world,
Where poverty does not exist?
Where everyone is equal,
No man or woman is missed.
Wouldn't it be good if we did what we should?
Oh wouldn't it, Oh wouldn't it be good?

David Guinee

Time To Leave

Time I think to leave this place
time to say farewell
time to join the mad rat race
back to the concrete hell.
Au revoir my babbling brook
good-bye those autumn shades
cries now dim the distant rook
it's the roar of motorways.
I'll feel no more the gentle breeze
I'll miss that sweet caress
back to the fumes, the cough, the wheeze
that restless state — distress.
With concrete slabs and urban sprawl
no more those meadows green
in taxi cabs the city crawls, while I
just gaze just dream

Lawrence Graves

Single Parent

Get up early, seven o'clock
Got to hurry, no time to stop
This bundle of energy want to be fed
The one that's jumping on my head.

Fix the breakfast
Toast or meusli
"Make your mind up,
Don't be choosy."

Trek to school
And then round the shops
Try to keep cool
When the queue suddenly stops.

A quick cup of tea
As the telephone rudely rings
Nearly half past three
And still to finish too many things.

Then as darkness creeps up
And you've had your bath
We read your favourite story book
Your chattering voice makes me laugh.

Just watching you grow
Is the best reward of all
It's all worth it you know
With those three little words you call.

Céri Griffiths

Antiphrasis

I wandered lonely in my shroud
that wailed on high, o'er aching hills
when all at once, I cried aloud
a ghost of haunted daffodils.
And in their wake, beneath the trees
shunned and trampled in the breeze
contagious as their souls are blind
now handed down as price to pay.
Once they stretched in sweet sublime
now rancid flotsam in some bay
ten thousand dead saw I at a glance
hanging their heads in bewildered trance.
The knaves beside them laughed
but they denied those knaves their glee
a poet could not be but sad
by such defeated apathy.
I stood amazed but little thought
what death the blow to me had brought.
For oft when in my grave I lie
shaken by this senseless brood
they dash upon that injured eye
which typifies their platitude.
And then my heart with anger fills
when trampled with the daffodils

Janice Graves

Silent Partner

Strength is a silent partner:
Giving no tender touch or
Look of love,
No conversation, gentle caring,
Thoughtful task and trouble sharing.
Strength gives no praise of grateful thanks,
No company on lonely days
Or nights, when stars are sharp
Like needles prickling pain
That starts up fresh all over again.

Strength is a silent partner
Calmly hiding behind your tears,
Rising, glowering, ever growing
To push you through the mist
Of grey, isolating fears.
Strength gives no need of feeble pleading
To anyone or many wanting you
To fail
Or feel betrayed as they have done.
For strength is a silent partner,
Giving more and taking none.

Susan Gregory

Pollution

Rivers of muck flow down to the sea
Of affluent waste and dregs of cold tea,
They flow from the coal tips, standing there stark,
Rivers of slime that leave a black mark.

Rivers that once were shiny and clear
Look like Stygian rivers of fear.
They flow through the valleys, gaunt with despair
That once were tended with love and much care.

They flow through a village abandoned and lost,
Raped and plundered at a terrible cost.
They sluggishly flow, gathering silt
Through new building sites, just being built.

Then down to the sea, the black rivers flow
Where oil slicks appear at high tide and low.
The fish and the plant life, on which we rely,
Gel fouled and polluted and eventually die.

And then with fear and dread in our breast
This terrible pollution we try to arrest.
For the death of pollution, Man must employ,
Or Man, pollution will surely destroy.

H.W. Griffith

Dawn

Intermittent raindrops fall to the ground
Apart from this, not a sound.
The earthy aroma, as the rain fell,
Overflowing water in the well.

The ground looks fresh and moist and new
Flowers reach their 'necks' to say "thank you"
The sky becomes blue, it now has won
And gives out an orange warmth emitted from the sun.

Look high and wide, the colours we know
Magnificent, stupendous, the arc of a rainbow.
The birds and worms have come out to play
A new beginning, 'tis the start of the day.

The puddles on lanes where the sparrows will drink
Just a small piece of nature, gives you reason to think.
The plant life no more is thirsty, withered and worn
And all because God, gave us the Dawn.

Susan Green

Winter Skies

The sky of dull lifeless grey forlorn
Precedes the cold grey, damp, foggy morn
Whence from his bed, man and beast must crawl
To enter a world entombed by an unending wall,
Where one has lost all identity, shape, and form
On this cold grey, damp, foggy morn.

The glowing sky of beauteous crimson fire sublime
Precedes the serene white morn crisp, and fine,
Where each tree and plant in this enchanted world
Is encrusted with winter's crystal jewels unfurled,
No gilded mortals can these looks, they outshine
On this serene white morn, crisp and fine.

Throughout the changing sky and morn
New life from the hard sod, has taken form,
When earth's soft white blanket has been cast away
Fragile fairies dance in the breeze, whilst lambs play,
Dressed in virgin white the snowdrop and the lamb adorn
Winter's passing sky, that precedes Spring's morn.

Sylvia Greening

Orion

Shapes,
Abstract.
Nameless for Ages.
Seen for the first
"A man with a sword -
from stars!"
A sign from the Gods.
Everything will be OK now?

Now —
Skeptical —
I hope hard.
Orion is my cupid
I've fallen
HARD.
I am aware
How tightly your spring
Is coiled around me.
Everything will be OK now.

Claire Groves

Aborted Child

I am in mourning
For my child.
The one
Who came

A hot scarlet thing
In the cold metal dish
Bruised and silenced
By my will.

You fill
My thoughts
My godly power
Extinguished you.

Your accusatory finger
Piercing as an instrument
Dissects my words
Dethrones me.

Have I your forgiveness
Is your voice sweet?

Ms. A.E. Greaves

Untitled

Some nights
'I' awake
With no point of reference
I don't recognise
The room
The objects
The time
The woman
'Myself'

A part of the Soul
Normally hidden
Becomes clear
Separated from the Whole
One night
'I'll' take a long walk
Away from remembering
Who 'I' am
'I'll' return forever
To
No point of reference

Mark Gott

The West Country

Come to the West Country
And what will you see?
Renowned for its "Scrumpy"
A warm welcome there'll be.

Interesting country lanes
That wind their way through,
The bright village names
That beckon to you.

Luscious green fields
With cows black and white,
Church bells that peel
Across villages at night.

Quiet country pubs
That stock some fine ales,
And serve home-made grub
In many a Vale.

Many beautiful sights
To view on your way,
Your trip will be bright
Each and every day.

Bright coloured orchards
With ripening fruit.
With all this you've heard
You can now plan your route!

Anne Griffiths

Friends

It's been some time now
Since we talked,
Face to face
Or shared our time,
A laugh, a joke
But your image is still clear
In the recess of my mind.
If I close my eyes
Your fragrance engulfs me,
Your touch lingers
And I miss you.
You're not lost to me,
Not forever,
Just a mere heartbeat away
But it hurts to know
I won't ever see
Your smiling face again,
Hear your soft voice
Or feel your warmth.
I miss you my friend,
My heart aches for you
And weeps for you,
And the dreams you left behind.

Caren Grindrod

Winter

Signs,
Begin to appear.
Squirrels gather acorns,
robins arrive.

Trees,
Lose their leaves.
Hedgehogs,
Gradually disappear.

Frost, mist and fog move in,
Taking charge of the mornings.
Scarves and gloves,
Take their places.

Heating,
Warms houses.
Ice forms,
Bringing warnings to many.

Shopping sprees,
Cards and gifts.
Christmas comes,
And goes.

Snow arrives,
Bringing joy to children.
Winter melts away,
Spring signs begin.

Antoinette Gregory

The Fairy?

Have you ever seen a fairy dressed in colours bright and gay?
I saw one in our garden 'mongst the flowers the other day.
She danced between the roses and she fluttered here and there
As the perfume from the honeysuckle floated on the air.

She was a pretty sight to watch as swift she flew
From flower to flower to touch each one and drink the morning dew.
High into the sky she rose on wings of gossamer,
Then down into the orchard green, I quickly followed her.

Among the shady apple trees she disappeared from view,
I couldn't find her anywhere, though I searched the orchard through.
Then John arrived with Oliver; to me they shouted "Hi!
Just come and look inside our net, we've caught a butterfly"

Lily M. Gaskill

New York

Bejewelled crown of all man has achieved,
New York city, splendour, fantasy, greed,
every street corner vibrant with life,
every back alley bursting with strife,
the skyline at midnight, reaching to the stars,
microcosm of humanity, in neon lit bars,
saxophone playing, melancholy but proud,
people are hopeful, though some heads are bowed,
dominant, beautiful, moon in its might,
shrouds in gold shadows New York at night,
enchanting, refreshing, tribute to endeavour,
culture, grime, vitality, that will live forever.

M.J. Gregson

Rat

Darkness falls the time is right,
For the rounds of clubs and dens,
Leaving behind an iniquitous trail,
He steals his rich pickings,
Down the alleys of bins and bags,
He stalks the grimy gutters.
His smooth grey coat,
Betrays his verminous dealings,
Many an enemy yet to deter,
Relentlessly growing fat,
Rodent King,
Mr. Rat!

Jennifer Greenway

Spellbound

The pines whisper a spell to me
Late noon shadows lengthen every tree
Rays of winter sunset emblazon the fells
Under foot, dry leaves crackle like roasting chestnut shells
Darkness is nigh, the woodland is still
No bird nor creature astir on the hill

Twilight is creeping, the breeze breathes a sigh
Dark skeletal fingers reach t'ward the sky
Silvered by starlight and glistened by frost
The age old oak trees stand, gnarled and mossed
The moon is rising, beaming soft tranquil light
Dancing on streamlets, transformed to frozen white

Music is drifting high above trees
The pipes of Pan are calling, calling on the breeze
Enchantment prevails in the sights all around
Breathtaking, magical, to leave me spellbound.

Elaine Goodman

I Can't Make Up My Mind

I'm the sort of person that changes her mind
I'm a woman you see, you know the kind
Shall I wear this, shall I wear that?
Will I look better if I wear a hat?
Blue or red, dress or skirt,
Maybe the black, it won't show the dirt.

What are you wearing? I can't make up my mind
You're wearing trousers; mine I can't find.
Shorts maybe, they will do just as good
Or are they too casual, do you think I should?

Well I have made up my mind
The blue dress I will wear
Shall I wear a hat? Do you think I dare?
Or shall I not bother, I can't make up my mind —
I'm a woman you see, you know the kind.

Margaret Greenall

Feeling Better

Out of sorrow and despair
I did not want to live.
Now that time has healed the hurt
I find that I can give
Help to others, and I find
This keeps the sorrow from my mind.

If I do get low and sad
I look around and see
That there are others
Who are sad, and far worse off than me.

So I hold out a friendly hand
To help them on their way
And feel a warmth
When I can say
I've made a friend today.

John Gill

The Joy Of Spring In Sussex

Can one ever forget Springtime in Sussex
Its winding Country Lanes
From village to village meander,
Coming to life in the magic of Spring.

Abundantly strewn with flowers of every hue
Amidst the shades of endless greens,
The cottage gardens lovingly tended
Coming to life anew.

The Seashore, Marshes and the Downs,
All with their own magic and mystery adorn,
The variety of birds each their own habitat find
Singing in praise it seems for the return of Spring.

How blest are we if we have eyes to see, and ears to hear
The wonder of it all, a parable indeed,
To find our heavenly Father's love
In all creation here.

Mrs. Greenhalf

After The Storm

The branches on the trees are still now.
It's so quiet with only the sound
Of the rain trickling through the leaves,
And splashing onto the ground.

It's hard to believe that only
Just a few nights before,
Those same branches were bending
So they nearly touched the floor.

Who would have known that night
When we were tucked up in bed
That the wind was causing such a menace?
The weathermen had never said.

The noise was so incredible
But now there's not even a breeze,
It's only that continual rain
Trickling through the remaining few trees.

I can still feel the windows straining
And see the lights flicker off and on,
I can still hear the roof tiles cracking
I wondered if ours had all gone.

I can still hear the rushing of the wind
And keep ducking my head in fear
Of whatever could be blown my way,
It was the worst storm for many a year.

Joy Griggs

Folk Dance Queen

The gypsy gave me silver heather,
The band played jigs and reels forever,
You were my dancing queen
Of the folk dance scene.

The coloured lights exploded to neon;
I gave you my shoulder for you to lean on
As the couples last dance polka'd round
To the heartbeat sound.

Then we lay under the star-spangled night,
In the gutter but looking up at the light
Of the blue-rinsed moon
Who sand a salty dog tune.

> With gypsy heather to bring us luck,
> Nothing at all will hold us back;
> Boots of Spanish leather will forge our trail:
> So strong together we cannot fail.

Entwined 'neath blood-orange street light,
We kissed and fused molten white;
You became me;
The two of us were we.

So dance with me till the end of time
Folk dance queen forever be mine;
Glamorous nymph with arrow and bow
Don't ever leave me, don't ever go!

William Greig

Snow

White on white; filling up the sky
And I am smuggled here
In a cradle, in a cloud.

White on white; these heavens and this little earth
Fusing in a silence
To make a blank place.

Lost place nothing place
Where shadows feed themselves
And the sun and the suffusion and the feeling
Of the soil.

The breathing and the tresses
Of a spillage killing nondescript
Take the hand of seasons in this temple,
In this land.

White on white; with the smoothing of a petticoat
Drowning all and seeing all
And being all inside.

White on white; not long before the veil is gone,
Stripping bare the purity
And the muddied bride.

Giles Griffith

Gravity

Where would we be
Without gravity?
Off the ground?
Floating around?
Flotsam and jetsam
Of the air.

Gravity keeps us
On the ground
Trees are fixed
Birds fly high
We are mixed —
Betwixt'.

Gravity of the mind
We find
Amid frivolities —
Helps realities
We all face
In life's mad race.

Sybil Glucksmann

Voices On The Hill

Over the hill I keep walking on
All at once I hear them talking
Voices talking loud and clear
But its only the wind that howls up there.

Where there is naught but wind and black-faced sheep
I sometimes count them in my sleep
And the voices are not always clear
It's only the wind that howls up there.

That lonely hill where breezes blow,
That help to keep away the snow,
So once more over the brow its still,
And the voices stop just for a while.

Then suddenly they seem to come
The sound of the voices in my ear
voices that come from the moorland hill,
But I know that it's only the blowing gale.

The voices are there on the hill all day
It's only when I pass that way
I seem to hear them calling near,
But it's only the wind howling up there.

Edwin J. Greig

Love At Watwick Bay

Tread the grass softly.
The downward slope, slippery,
Dew-wet still, steeply down
To the yellow-sanded garden
Between the high rock — musselled mountains,
Its life-drawing blood surging,
Singing its age-old song.
Come with me love.
Stay with me in this haven
This sun-blessed day
At Watwick Bay.

Search the shore for secrets,
Shout our love to the skies,
Tell the world we want
To live and love together
Under the same sun that
Warms the sand and the sea.
To these gnarled rocks,
Ancient and sharp and proud,
Proclaim our true love aloud,
This love-filled day
At Watwick Bay.

Peter Gwenlan

Awakening

The background noise,
T.V. or radio,
encroaches on consciousness.
Barely there,
but ever more insistent.
Scents carry to the senses.
Not oil or smoke,
clean and sharp, not pleasant.
Now comes the pain.
Wave on wave.
Blank it out with sleep.
Impossible.
That noise again, over and over.
Switch it off.
Will no one help?
Again and again, no relief.
Must switch it off.
Eyes open.
Tears from the watcher.
Joy and relief.
Ten days sleep
now recovery begins.

Neil Groat

Rendezvous

On this afternoon of rain
in rivulets we speak
of want and pain.
The scene we shun, so bleak.
For love of this
our soft oasis.

Eager to speak, we are silent,
denying all we could say.
Ready to love we are haunted
by all that we cant' love away.

There is no touching anymore,
of heart or hand.
A word can never leave the shore,
nor make us understand.

With every aching vein
I wish it were not so.
But sensing truth above the pain
I know. I know.

Gerald Grimsey

Tony The Trucker

Tony the trucker was tough as old boots
He wore a black stetson and chewed on cheroots
He spat with precision from up in his cab
At anyone driving a Volvo or Saab
"I hate foreign motorcars" Tony would mutter
"If you like driving those things you must be a nutter."

Tony the trucker was tough as they come
He drank from a hip-flask containing dark rum
He spat with precision from up in his cab
At adverts for curry and doner kebabs
"I hate foreign take-aways" Tony would mutter
"If you like eating that stuff you must be a nutter."

When Tony the trucker eventually died
His soul was removed by a spiritual guide
And taken to wait in a heavenly court
Where sinners where given their final report
"I hate foreign Judges" was all Tony muttered
"I don't expect justice — my chances are scuppered."

God sat resplendent in all of his glory
And listened to Tony's excuse of a story
Then He spat with precision from up on his throne
And drenched the poor trucker right through to the bone
"To Hell with you Tony" He said loud and clear
"Truculent truckers aren't welcome up here"

Ken Grimason

The Prince Of Peace

Born in a stable, laid on hay,
A royal son came on earth to stay,
Ox and ass attend thy birth.
And just for me you came to earth,
If I were you and you were me
Would I have done the same for thee.

No savage blow came from thine hand,
Not by a tyrant's sway, you gripped the land,
A road of peace lay where you trod,
But still we scorned you, son of God,
If I were you and you were me,
Would I have done the same for thee.

Betrayed by a kiss from a faithless friend,
A cruel cross awaits thine end.
A crown of thorns thy brow adorns,
While a crowd looks on to mock and scorn.
Could I have done the same for thee?
Not me, oh Lord, not me.

So when I feel I need thee Lord,
I pray to thee in faltering word,
I know my plea is not in vain.
And as my life goes quickly past,
I know I'll see your glorious face at last,
And glory in all you did for me.

P. Grinsted

Fond Memories

The summers seemed always long and hot.
In the winter the snow fell quite a lot.
We made sledges and slippery slides.
That came up like glass, on which we'd glide.
There was tin baths in front of a blazing fire.
Only one bath a week, but to go in you had no desire.
There was Sunday School, and Sunday best clothes.
Are we better for it, no one knows?
Sunday School outings on a Dray-Cart drawn by a horse.
We'd go to a farm, had sandwiches and jelly, or course.
On Mondays, always wash-day,
We had Dolly-Tub and Posher in the yard.
In those days time were really hard.
There was the Grate to Black, Red floor tiles to scrub.
Whitewashed walls, and all clothes by hand to rub.
We played marbles skipping, had stilts making us walk tall.
Hula Hoops, Snobs and bounced balls up a wall.
Christmas time the excitement, the build-up I recall.
Home made decorations, the luxury of chicken and all.
On Christmas morning I still remember how it felt.
As we peered in our pillowcases our hearts would melt.
Perhaps one gift, an apple, orange, pennies, a chocolate bar.
But we were Happy, and everyone was on par.
My childhood was Special, I remember it all well.
We had nothing yet everything.
Leaving me fond memories on which to dwell.

Julie Guerin

A Masterpiece

(To All My Children)

They flourish with increased splendour, those that are mine,
    mannerisms each different, a concept so divine.
Masterfully arranged, perfect in every way,
    individually progressing along a separate pathway.
One so headstrong, helpful, and wise,
    another so loving, generous, full of surprise.
One so stubborn, independent, and flighty,
    the identical a temperament, that's so high and mighty.
The last of all, angelically, eyes filled with glow,
    to young to perceive, with time to grow.

As the years pass on, the fruits in full bloom
    perhaps never again to fill a room.
Independently befitting they all become,
    beautifying to others the rearing is done.
Complete and perfected with the will to endure,
    a masterpiece of life completed so pure.

Sheridan Guest

Green Fields

The emerald isle, old Ireland they say,
with such stories as Antrims own Giant's Causeway,
of Leprechauns, their pot of gold,
these stories remembered, always retold.

Its beauty, our wealth,
its tradition, our fame,
those memories of Ireland,
shall always remain.

Though clouded over by trouble and strife,
its war of religion in everyday life.

A difference of opinion,
keeps us apart,
while old Ireland remains,
still close to our hearts.

Kenneth Grafton

Shorescape

Blue with a glitter where the sunlight
scatters the waves with silver coins
shallow waves, breaking gently on to sand
cold sand hard to my feet
as I amble over its slope.

A gull drops like a thrown stone
into the blue, then wings pulling strongly rises
a flash of white in the early morning sun,
a sun hard-edging limestone, coaxing gems
from polished pebble glass.

Alison Hall

Living

One's life is but a very small span,
So it pays to enjoy it while you can,
Don't be a bore, have lots of fun!
But never try to jump the gun.
Laugh and see the funny side,
But never bottle up a silly pride.
Remember, there are folk far worse off than you,
Who still have to mend and make do.
Health, happiness, joy, these are the thing,
Something riches can never bring.
Our world is full of sadness, hate and crime,
So please; try a bit of kindness from time to time.
Do a good deed here and there,
And love costs nothing to share,
Though you have only one heart to give,
Give it — and you will really live.

E. Guest

Images

It seems as I look at the moon on high
I must soon take to wing
And up to her fly
So lovely she looks
In her setting of blue
Like a white ship
With sails of pure silver too
Where would we sail to the moon and I
Perhaps for a while
To watch sleeping towns go by
And then to what! to where!
To an enchanted land
With never a care
To pause! To smile!
To close the door
For my white ship
With sails of pure silver
Has gone once more

Barbara Greenwood

Today

You can have yesterday and tomorrow,
just let me breathe a little today.
Then I will ornament the night sky,
breathe rainbows to brighten the day.
I've lived before, I hope to again,
I've died before, recently everyday.
Let me celebrate today without pain,
juggle the stars, light the milky way,
then tomorrow can be tomorrow again,
with yesterday a repeat of today.
Send the sunlight and make it stay.

John G. W. Hall

Glory

Land of hope and glory
That is what we say.

But do we know what glory is
From all our yesterdays.

Our fathers and our mothers knew
For they have all seen.

What glory does and what glory
Is from all our yesterdays.

But shall we have that glory
In our time as well.

No, all that we have is crime
But only time will tell ...

Patricia Heaton

The Word of God

I am the blush, upon your cheeks,
I am the lustre, in your eyes,
I am the voice, that from you speaks,
I am but wisdom, in disguise.

I am the wind, that fills the sails,
I am the sand, upon the shore.
I am the tide, that never fails,
I am the one, who takes the score.

I am alive, and will not die,
I am the seasons of the year.
I am the maker, of the sky,
I am afraid, but have no fear.

I am the One, there at your side,
I am the One to whom you pray.
I am forevermore, your guide,
I am the "maker" of your day.

G.H. Gray

The War Years

Born and bred a brummie, it was totally different then,
When I recall my childhood, way back when I was ten.
Destruction was all around us, at a time when our land was at war,
I remember the air raid shelters, with a makeshift bed on the floor.

Little back houses we lived in, with a mantle we used for a light,
You could hear every word that was uttered, when we were tucked in at night.
We used the wash-house on Mondays, with soap suds a flying galore,
Us kids used to swing on the mantle, that's what we thought it was for.

Everyone carried a gas mask, not a light was supposed to be shown,
Overhead the air-raid warning, would be sounding all over the town.
Men were called up in the forces, women went to work on the land,
Those in the factories, turned out by the thousands, everyone lending a hand.

Food was scarce, for we were rationed, queuing for hours was our lot,
Down at the wharf, we foraged for coal, but slack was all that we got.
But I want to forget the war years, the blackout, the bombs and the fear,
For the loss of so many who didn't return, is a cross we all have to bear.

We can now look back at things that have past, and remember loved ones who died,
We must think of the present, and live for today, our memories locked deep inside.
For things have changed and now we're at peace, a new generation's took hold,
Yesterday has gone forever, and we of the war years are old.

Lyn Harper

The Path Of Life

The path of life is a long one
To be trod in many ways
Are the memories in the future
Or the past and bygone days.

The path of life has reason
A beginning and an end
To find it we must tread it
And treat it as a friend.

The path of life can be hard
Causing turmoil from within
With harsh and thorny needles
And tethered around with sin.

The path of life can be easy
Gentle loving and kind
If we treat it as our kingdom
Happiness and bliss we'll find.

Don't take the bends too sharply
Or we will find unrest
Take them very gently
To make the path of life the best.

Beryl E. Gwinnett

Go Forth

My sons, before I gave you birth,
    you curled beneath my heart,
close, secure and fiercely loved,
    each one of me a part.

I freed you when the time was ripe,

    to set you on your way,
and with a prayer, I let you go
    to face Life, come what may.

But now the years have rolled away
    you both are wise and strong;
the love that binds us never wanes,
    though I will soon be gone

So this is what I wish, my sons,
    before I leave this earth,
that you will both pass on your love,
    our happiness and mirth.

All friends and family that you meet,
    wherever you may be,
care for, love and cherish all —
    and so, remember me.

Marguerite C. Guile

Memories

When I was little
I fell down the stairs.
I fell down the stairs because my brother
left his bears
at the top of the stairs.
Now I have no cares
about falling down the stairs
because I never got hurt
when I fell down the stairs.

Katie Halcrow (Age 11)

My Mum

You gave me life and watched me grow
Help and advice you gave to me
This I pass on so eagerly
You taught me right, you taught me wrong
To help me grow to someone strong
I pass this on to all my young
In hope that one day they will be strong
Days go fast now and you will soon be sleeping
This will leave me weeping
your pain will go and peace will come
But always remember
I love you Mum

Rita Greed

March Kites In Wollaton Park

Like strangers, indolently isolated
they caress the oncoming air,
slowly, whirling
in their separateness.

Remote, entities apart, they glide
into their cocooned world,
pirouetting, rotating,
in subdued gaiety.

Recognition, curiosity, a nod
a gentle glance,
a cosy tete-a-tete, spiralling skyward
swaying to a fox-trot,
sweeping to a slow tango,
skipping to a Charleston,
simpering together in clownish delight.

Harlequin and Columbine swirl in fun,
into a pas-de-deux and,
in a passionate embrace,
plunge to the earth
as one.

June-Rose Hayes

By Pass

My eyes are open
but do not see
that which is in
front of me.
Is it me or
is it him?
That man who lives
behind my sin.
I pass myself
in a crowd,
pass so quiet,
shout so loud.
The sin of him
who passes by
makes you shout
but never cry.
My eyes are open
I cannot see
he who passes
in front of me.

A. Hamilton

Blind Butterfly

Spread your wings, ascend and depart,
from the putrid nefarious end,
of this inequity.
You may let it sink,
stoop and drift,
without a penalty.

Let the beauty shine,
radiate the unspoilt.
Let the world know the innocence
of freedom in the sky.

Tranquility,
and empty room,
quiet,
a silence of spirit,
of which we slip in your presence.
Watching,
breathing rapidly,
in awe of your devotion to flight.

Good-bye fairy child
the butterfly is blind,
Spread your wings and fly
Good-bye

Miranda Hall-Morley

Tears To Laughter

I always used to wear a mask to hide my loneliness and fears
Only my Mum, now and again, could see my sadness and tears
Family and friends were bemused by my happiness, for how could this be
For I didn't have a husband, lover or child, there was no one for me
Laughing, joking and enjoying myself?
Nobody ever saw that night after night the tears I shed
When I was all alone in my single bed.

I always chose the wrong man, tall, dark and handsome
But they loved me and left me and yet again I was lonesome
Then one day I met a man who said I was everything to him
Until he got me pregnant then he said the child's not his
His advice, have an abortion, termination, get rid
So I got rid ... of my son's father, I was so glad I did
For my son Jaime is a beautiful happy bundle of joy and fun
He's brought back life to me, where before I had none
I saw in the mirror for the first time in years
The sparkle of happiness in my eyes, instead of tears
Now I've thrown away my mask, for now I have no sadness to hide
For five years I've been truly blessed, happy and content, just having Jaime by my side.

Tina E. Hall

Our Hero

Rough terrain and winds so bleak,
Rifle at the ready, pressed to my cheek.
Malvinas or Falklands, I don't give a curse,
As long as they don't carry me off in a hearse.

The big guns roar, machine guns spit,
Over the battle ground the whole sky is lit.
Deathly fear, my eyes full of tears,
No time to run as the enemy nears.

So many dead litter the battle ground,
Enemies and friends scattered around.
A time to live, a time to die,
A time to mourn, a time to cry.

Fields that were green are now bright red,
So many men have laid down and bled.
I did my stint on the hills of Goose Green,
A frightened lad of just nineteen.

We came as boys but left as men,
Our job is done, now it's home again.
I live in hope I won't see another war,
We fight and die, but oh, what for?

The Falklands were saved by very brave men,
For queen and country they would do it again.
I fought that war with the temperature at zero,
Now at last I can rest, for I came back a hero.

Fredrick Meirion Hall

The Things I Love

I love to smell the blossom on the trees
And to feel the warm summer breeze,
I love to smell the grass being mown
And go and collect all the cones,
I love to see lambs in the field
And to smell the corn crop yield,
I love the smell of summer rain
And to walk down country lanes,
I love to walk by the sea
It's nice to sit down for a cup of tea,
I love to have my grandchildren around
And to see the autumn leaves on the ground,
And the fire glowing in the hearth
I love to see the snow on our path,
It's nice to see the rain
Pattering on the window pane,
But most of all I love to be able to see
And to hear everything that is around me,
And to have happiness and good health,
Although I haven't much wealth,
These are the things I love
And that's enough.

Joy Hall

205

Make A Friend

Never be afraid to say
I'm sorry, I was wrong.
Be prepared to give and take,
The road of life is long.
Don't waste your days believing
That you are always right,
None of us are perfect
We each must seek the light.
So go out and offer friendship
With a smile upon your face
For in the heart of someone
You can fill an empty space.

Sheila Hayes

The Presence

Grey time unfolds itself
Voices, soft, fragile run into each other
From the past and beat against my brain.
In the darkness only the breathing of no one there.
A shaft of sunlight confuses the day
And sinks behind watery clouds.
Traces of his image remain and cry out everywhere.
The half torn picture,
A faded flower he gave me.
Rising, I thought I saw a shadow,
But it was no one.
Say good-bye now
As your presence fades.

Tina Ann Harvey

Bee

Monoliths repose and I suppose
I'll do the same. Eventually.
Travelling home from A to B
what will I become, what will I see?

My path unhindered, fulfilled, my life
or a meaningless voyage filled with strife?
And while onboard I'm microsize,
an insect resting in the hive

before the fight to fill and mate,
the queen stands at the garden gate.
A larvae destined to be free,
one day a flutter by will be.

She welcomes me home
pinned straight to breast.
A brooch of me
to adorn her chest.

David Golledge

Behind The Curtain

It was not us crying,
We had our freedom.
We could speak the truth,
Without reprisal.
We did not fear
To condemn or revile
Our political leaders.
From Solzhenitsyn's writings
And Daniel's poems
We were enlightened.
It was Russia crying
From the depths of despair.

Anne Haynes

Hope

My world is rocking around me
Is there nothing to which I may cling
No light to shine through the darkness
Can no one a ray of hope bring
As shadows ever creep closer
And everything shouts of despair
Not yet will hell fires claim me
I think as I whisper a prayer
Not yet am I wholly forgotten
There is one who is ever my friend
Who will lift me up from the darkness
And I shall find joy in the end.

Edith M. Hardman

Untitled

The body is getting older
The bones are getting weak
At last the time is coming
For us to have our sleep.

The Lord will shut the light out
As he lays us down to rest
Some will pray and wonder
But they know it's for the best.

The church doors open wider
As they take you down the isle
There's a weeping in the background
As they rest you for a while.

The Lord sent you here
And now you must go
You have our blessing
Far down below.

F. Green

Trees

What would our landscape be without a tree?
A lofty poplar reaching for the sky,
or graceful weeping willow by the stream,
the shining copper beach may catch your eye,
or mighty oak be seen.

The strong and shady firs in forest glade,
towering over bracken covered ground,
or orchards gay at apple blossom time,
and lovely cherry blossom may be found,
or cool green lime.

Our countryside is rich with woodland scenes,
our byways graced by elm and oak, or ash,
what wonder, just to see chestnut in bloom,
the holly berries, in winter sunlight flash,
or silhouetted by the moon.
What indeed, would our landscape be
without a tree?

Joan Hammond

A Tribute To Sir Winston Churchill

Who was the man who gave us the 'V'
The man who brought us Victory
Whose hand alone did bring us through,
The man to whom the praise is due.

His famous slogan helped us too
To those we owe, so much, the few.
On hill and dale and beach we'll fight
For freedom, and the common right.

"Give us the tools," the great man cried
And on to Victory we will ride.
When this great man assumed command
The country rose to make a stand
Soldier, Statesman, Leader, your fame
History will for long acclaim.

Margaret Hall

Wildest Dreams

A book of verse with tales of love,
Of passion rising like a dove,
Tempestuous amour increasing daily,
As lovers live their lives quite gaily.

Dragons breathing red-hot fire,
Like a blazing funeral pyre,
Knights come charging with their lances,
Dicing with death and taking chances.

Kings, queens, maidens and courtiers shout,
Waiting for the final bout,
All to win the maiden's hand,
To be the hero of the land.

Foam and surf rise up like fronds,
Creating whirlpool-eddy ponds,
The waves splash up to make a spray,
Cooling down this summer's day.

The sky gets brighter than it's been,
All around in country green,
A brook is running through the vales,
Up the craggy hills and dales.

Its ivory voice tinkles on its way,
Resoundingly peaceful in the hazy spring day,
Dragons, tournaments, sea and streams,
These are some of my wildest dreams.

Clare L. Hallas

The Swimmer

I swam in a beautiful sea,
Azure blue and white,
And tiny silver fishes
Flashed in shoals of light.

I swam in a dazzling sea,
Under a blazing sun,
And gentle golden wavelets
Caressed me one by one.

I swam in a murmuring sea,
Washing the white-hot sand,
And green and glassy sea-weed
Made a necklace on the strand.

I swam in a darkening sea,
With coldness all around,
A plaintive sea-bird's cry
The only mournful sound.

I swam in an angry sea,
Under grey and leaden clouds,
Great waves dashed against me,
And the breakers roared and howled.

I swam in a raging sea,
Cruel currents dragged me down,
I fought to stay afloat,
But in the end I drowned.

Pauline Halliwell

Beauty

(To My Daughter Julienne)

Beauty is born with life
It blossoms in your face
Each day that passes
Until the bloom at last
Has reached its best
And shows your beauty
Above the rest.

F.J. Henderson

Brother

I wish you didn't do drugs,
You never turned into a thug
But worse! You caught the bug!
Now that you are not here
I really miss you, so dear
I wish you never took a smoke
For that's where it starts, folks!

Peter Hart

Shock

He grabbed my arm and spoke to me;
When I was out in the street quite innocently
Please give me some money for my next fix
And then the one after that I promise to miss
Please pray for me, for I'm trying so hard
To give up these drugs for I know they are barred
But more prayers are needed, I can't do it alone.
I've sold practically everything from our home,
If I don't give them up before my next but one high
Then I'm afraid that I will turn to crime,
And I fear that I will overdose
For I need more and more.
And then I froze
For he stuttered a bit now, I was mortified
Then he collapsed at my feet
    And there he died.

Margaret E. Hampson

City Strangers

Their brief little faces and little briefcases
Life passing them by when they lose at the races
Their little red faces and their scurrying pace
They're taking the pace but losing the race
They scurry around looking for trains
They don't understand they're looking for planes
Their own little world, in its own little place
That neat little case with so little space
They cram in compartments, sardines in a can
As they follow so neatly their own little plan
They count their numbers in numeric fashion
And dream of a time for their own real passion
They don't understand the life which they live
They stay on the track, with nothing to give
They don't relax they just stand square
These strange city strangers, their souls so bare.

May Hamilton

Feelings

I know not when, I know not why
all my secret dreams, always have to die.
But deep down now, and all alone
my special feelings, are turned to stone.
The untrue love, which I once knew
buried inside me, that long ago grew.
An empty space, which I now feel
someone close to me, will help me heal.
As is a hole, a big black dot
like a war man's grave, an unmarked spot.
Staying happy on the outside
pleasing other people, trying to be kind.
Judging others, is all we do
look in our own hearts, and ask ourselves who.
On the surface, it's flowing free
my hope's that someday, I'll find the real me.

Faye Harris

Close The Coal House Door

Close the coal house door boy,
The coal has all but gone,
The fire is dying, but is trying — to linger on,
Put a log upon the fire to make it burn up bright,
It is cold out in the valleys to tonight,
Tomorrow take a trip to the local college boy,
To learn a brave new trade, and further your employ;
Don't be pessimistic and hope like the politicians say,
In this land of song —
Learn your Welsh and be proud boy,
Your future's round the corner,
And it will come to stay,
Close the coal house door
You're a collier boy,
Close the coal house door boy,
Come what may.

Mrs. V. Harding

The Chain of Circumstance

A child born is not gifted as to whom or where.
One babe will see daylight with the proverbial silver spoon
held for suckling. Whilst another will feel flies adhering
to an already drying mouth, ere death falls.
Thus forms "The chain of circumstance". On a proportion of
infants the chain of circumstance will hover like a gifted halo.
As they grow into adulthood, words uttered become enhanced akin
to the sheen on the links. Sin is the shadow hidden beneath the
glistening chain. Justice serves those fortunate, they need not know
the penalty of being slave to the law.
Alas to some beings the chain of circumstance weighs heavier
than the miller's stone, words spoken become burdened down into
insignificance, misdoings are magnified, and lose their symmetry.
They serve as hapless beings, doomed to serve the covenant of those
who bear the halo, the ring of light, not necessarily earned, and
bearing no relation to God's Christianity. AMEN.

Alex S. Haines

The Seventh Day

Sunday morning.
My bike and I solitary,
a kinship with the lonely skylark
trilling high above in July skies.

Distant hills lined with grey black hills
and green grey trees.
A distant drone of cars.
A light wind disturbs gently the ripe corn
and helps a white fluttering butterfly on her way.

A shy black beetle scurries into the low undergrowth.
Puddles on the dirt track reflect the rain leaden clouds,
and too my wine soaked spirits which, like the clouds
change course helped by some predetermined plan.

Now a pheasant cackles, then a swift, dart-like,
skims over my head.
A distant cockerel crows.
Snails crawl quietly up the dying grasses along the
sides of crop planted fields.

Evocative odours of wild marjoram coupled with Earth's
own pungent smell have me reeling with joy
to join the blood red wine still coursing round my body.

Peace and quietness flooding every corner.
I am one with nature.

Sunday morning.

Janet Hanscomb

Alone

I looked into the mirror
My eyes were filled with tears
Because I had been crying
My widowhood I feared
Please, help me Heavenly Father
To bear this awful pain
I know my husband's happy
He's entered your domain.

We parted oh so quickly,
No time to say "good-bye"
But I know we loved each other
We said so "till I die"
Through the years we oft repeated
"I love you dearest dear" -
"What shall I do without you"
Now, reality is here.

Dear God, I pray for guidance
As forward I must go
Depending on your promise
"I will not let you go"
You said you'd be my husband
In Isaiah fifty-four
Please give me grace to walk with you
Along life's bumpy road.

Val Hamilton

Spring Time

Gardens with flowers, spring time and love
Both go together, like a hand in a glove
Sunshine and showers, leaves on a tree
Buds that are bursting, with colours to see,
Daffodils dancing, on beds of sea green
Blackbirds are singing, their flight is unseen
Blossom is bowing its head in the breeze
Scattering petals which float from the trees
Forests and fields, have carpets of blue
Cobwebs in hedgerows, all shiny with dew
Young boys on the river, with nets on a cane
Looking for minnows, playing at games
Lambs in the meadows, skipping in fun
People are lazing, around in the sun.
Cotton wool clouds drifting high up above
Casting faint shadows on wings of a dove
Mowers are moaning, the grass is too long
Farmers are sowing, now the cuckoo's on song
Spring time is here, thank God up above
For gardens with flowers, and spring time with love.

Gig Hannah

Autumn

Autumn is my favourite season
Perhaps I should supply a reason

I love the dusk as much as dawn
Swirling leaves
And airy breeze

Amber gold and russet tones
Even though night air may chill my bones

Trees stripped of their finery
Stretching up so stark and bare
Lost their tenants to warmer air

All the leaves I sweep up neat
Then like a piper playing sweet
They once again dance around my feet ...
And my heart dances with them
To a more melodic rhythm

Autumn is my favourite season
Can you understand the reason?

B. Harding

In The Shadows

When you see an old woman (that one over there
In the powder blue frock with the snowy white hair)
Do you wonder who loves her, do you wonder who cares?

She sits on a park bench, in the shadow of trees,
And seems to do nothing, but stare at her knees!
— What thoughts are unlocked with her memory keys?

Her sight, her hearing — all fading away.
Though pressed, her frock too, is faded and grey.
What use to buy new when you know you won't stay?

She remembers a time in a house full with life
When she was still a daughter but yet mother and wife.
Those memories, much cherished, still cut like a knife!

Now her life's almost over, her time's nearly done.
Her friends are all dead, her children moved on.
She lives all alone in a flat built for one!

On a park bench, in the shadow of trees,
to the twitter of birds and the rustle of leaves
She sits and she prays to her God — please —

To meet again those loved ones now gone,
Her mother, sister Ethel, her husband, dear Tom.
—So she sits. And she waits. She knows it's not long.

Raine Hänsel-Alexandropoulou

Lament Of A 'Window Shopper'
(Driven To Despair)

Oh! Who invented Window-Gaze!
I see that gown as through a haze.
The passersby, on various ways
Turn round to stare, as though in praise —
Then I recall what ticket says
And, well, I never could wear stays!

The rents, the rates, the 'windows cleaned'
From stocking old, the harvest gleaned
I weigh-up feet. In mirror preened,
Tot-up the price of 'home-machined'
(Now I could swear that model leaned
So from my eyes, price deftly screened!)

Oh! Why should I be such a weight?
My household bills in such a state?
The children grow at such a rate?
And greying hairs be on my pate?
How do some females find a mate
With money in continual spate?

Who e'er invented Window-Gaze
Please, vision from my mind — erase!

Marhala

The Finding

I found Him in the morning star -
    Moving through the dawn
Walking on the gentle wind, towards the early morn.
I found Him standing by the steams
    That rushed towards the sea -
I found Him by the waterfall, which poured in front of me.
I found Him in the meadow fields
    Hem-deep in golden grass -
I found Him by the Rowan trees
    Where my footsteps passed!
I found Him on the hillside - His gown bleached by the sun
I found him in the evening sky
    When the day was nearly done.
I found Him in the blackbird's song
    Floating o'er the earth.
I found Him in my child's tired eyes
    Reflections of the truth!
I found Him in the stinging rain
I found Him "on the air".
I found Him on the rainbows - sleep-deep in coloured prayer.
I found Him in the lily fields where wild roses grow!
I found Him on the pathways leading through the snow!
I found Him by the water pool - standing - still as time
I called to Him, He answered me - saying "You are not alone".

Rosemary D. Harding

My Family

We have a lot of children
and family life is fun
though always short of money
I'm glad I am their mum.

On every Sunday morning
the eldest washed and dressed
is told, now watch the baby
while I deal with the rest.

Now the last is ready
time for Sunday-school
so go on, here's your penny
and sit still on your stool.

Just try to be good
you know you can, you know you should
and don't you dare say that word
when your dad cut his finger,
he swore, and you heard.

Just say your prayers and don't play tag
and don't call your teacher a silly old bag
my eyes are moist as I watch them go
clean little angels for an hour or so.

Patricia Thompson

The Inheritance

Old Grange Hall will Spring returneth
In the shadow of time's flight;
O Rachael gaze, winged dreams entrance thee,
As thee near thy one delight —
Cedar lawn what spirit whispers?
Rachael's dream surround lone heights.

Mellow stone, now time forgotten
Ivy leaf will cling to thee,
Wind blown leaves they sigh around thee
Old Grange Hall, relumed, but free;
Far between tall pine and cedar,
Mullioned windows brightly gleam,
Dark rooks shall fly through the mists of morning,
Flying through dawn's celestial beam.

Old Grange Hall thy spirit charmeth,
Rachael's Spring has just begun,
Season of Spring, when the mind to tower,
Perceives with mystic light, dawn's sun;
O bright the beauty of a higher power
When dark days past are put to flight,
But in life's dreams, finds the immortal hour,
The blazing of the dawn's bright light.

Christine Hare

A Child's Sorrow

One day I saw a little mouse
Laid dead outside an empty house,
It had no roof over its head
And no one cared that it was dead.

But me, I cried and looked and saw,
A cruel wound upon its paw,
I looked again — its eyes were shut,
Because of pain within its foot.

Then I passed on and saw a cat,
Laid cold and still upon a mat,
And I could count its ribs, each one
For it was nought but skin and bone.

"Poor pussy cat" I said and cried —
Why are your eyes so opened wide?
What evil terror laid you there —
Did no one love you ... No one care?

If I had passed this way before
And seen you sit outside the door,
I would have fed you meat and milk —
And you'd have had a coat like silk.

But people pass so quickly by —
They do not even see me cry.

Mrs. F.M. Harrison

Memorial Highway

I cringe at the flurry
Of feathers on the windshield,
But I grin, I confess
At the writing coil after the thump.
Fur, feather, form, might distinguish,
Give clue,
When shell and bone are shattered
It's nothing but a fleeting fossil
Pulp and pelt, pressed flatter and flatter
Onto an asphalt bier.
Little boys, noses mashed flat
On station wagon windows
Relate with relish the goo, the guts
In ghoulish awe (ooh, ah)
The gore of it all.
Given the plethora of puppies
A surplus of squirrels,
They are never disappointed long.
And do the silent wonder,
The bluejay, possum and occasional cow,
A war waged without cause
Or a Darwininan drama, of some moralist's making.
Would scaly cousins grieve
And spotted mothers, mute, mourn?

Rhonda Fleming Hayes

Old Age

Deep stirs the heart that treads black Sorrow's path
in mourning for Innocence long gone,
and sheds string pearls of tears for a cavalcade
of youthful faces, forgotten every one.

Bearing her long-lost children, orphans each,
along the littered road we all must tread upon,
the Soul shuffles, crying out:
"But who will stay the road with me?"

"I will," whispers waif.
"And I," another.
"Me too. For without you how can we shadows be?"

And Old Age, her shrouded eyes dimmed misty with love,
lifts time-worn face to Heaven and smiles at God.

"Face Death alone?" She laughs at Life's great dread.
But as Tomorrow's hour again draws nigh,
Old Age, whose great adventure is to die,
pulls close to hand her children, Memory,
and leads them down the dappled lane into Eternity.

Ron Harper

My Kids

They make a noise from morning till night,
The house is a mess and I look a fright.
I spend hours shouting every singly day,
I never stop cleaning and tidying away.
But when they are asleep in their beds,
No more trying words have to be said.
For as they sleep, their halos glow
Little angels, naughtiness will never show.
I love them all, I love all three,
For they mean more than the world to me.
And when they've grown and flown away
My thoughts will always return to the day,
When they were young and full of trouble,
My life was always lived 'on the double'.
All too soon there will be tiny feet upon my floor,
Padding around and slamming the door.
I'll once more take time to watch kids at play,
"Come on nan tell us a story" They will say.
Once more I'll have noise from morning to night,
The house is a mess, but that's quite alright.

Valerie Harriott

The Fall's Call

High in a depressed summer sky,
A Curlew gave out with plaintive cry,
Telling all of a nest now bare,
How both young and old must take to the air.

The moon may show in her full dress,
Still finds it hard yet to impress,
For her dear sister the day is long,
The heavy air her evening song.

First there is one, then there is another,
Till migrating birds, both sister and brother,
Hold fast upon the salutary air,
Fly south and west to a saltier fare.

High above the full moon sails,
Her sister now grows wan and pail,
For summer now its time has run,
Autumn's turn may now have come.

Walter Hamilton

Winter Feelings

Her hands they were cold,
Her heart it was cold,
Why feel this way?
It's just another day.

The bright lights she saw,
The tinsel like straw,
Cotton wool like fake snow,
Holly, ivy and mistletoe.

The sounds of carols filled the air,
Merry singing everywhere,
Her heart felt lighter,
The street seemed brighter.

Her hands were warm again,
She wondered, now and then,
About this glow that she felt,
Had it made her cold heart melt?

Beth Harris

Winged Horse

I have a horse called Pegasus
He is my favourite friend.
He comes to me each evening,
My boredom he does end.

His wings are pink, he's fleet of foot
His tail is burning fire.
And when I sit upon his back
He takes me flying higher.

Higher than the burning stars
Over the gates of heaven.
Further on in endless flight,
A trip that's never ending.

Then as night draws to a close
Dawn breaks across the land.
He takes me back and leaves me
Lying in the sand.

I awake upon my bed,
It's not a sandy beach,
I'm back at home and in my room,
My dream is out of reach.

He's part of my mind,
Yet he's part of me.
Tattooed on my arm
Forever free.

Jacqueline Harris

Parting

The time draws ever nearer
I know it in my heart
The picture is much clearer
It seems that we must part
Though I will always love you
And try to understand
Another love I always knew
Has led you by the hand.
But I won't weep, or sigh, or plead
Or beg you, please don't go
Nor even judge of any deed,
Or say, I told you so.
The erring heart no one can own
Or persuade from it's intent
Better by far to let it roam,
Love that was never meant.
No band of gold however strong
Is strong enough, you see,
To hold a heart, that ever longs
And pines to be set free.
So there will be no pleading tears
A smile, maybe, instead.
Yet I will mourn our parting years
As a mourner mourns the dead.

Pamela Harris

The Volume Of Imagination

I fell for you between the covers,
Your appeal heightening through the sheets.
You lie open, literally my lover
On demand, you re-enact my fantasies.
I devour every word, image and exclamation
Mark, my words, which are silence to you,
As are my fears that I, like you,
Will be left on the shelf.

You are destined to be,
As unfaithful to me, as I am to you
Our days are numbered together,
And as I caress the leather
That binds our relationship
I read between the lines,
There were no signs, warning me
That you could be, more than just a novelty.

Heidi A. Hammond

The Holocaust

The holocaust is coming, who will count the dead,
No place to rest their weary bones, no place for a last bed.
A desolate earth, all barren and bare,
Who will be left to notice or to care.
Survival of the fittest, this rule does not apply,
Even riches will not buy you a place up in the sky.

This threat is real, it affects us all,
From the highest in the land to the child as yet unborn.
No grass will grow in a world that's still,
No beasts will roam the earth at will.
The winds will blow over all the land,
Carrying death in an unseen hand.

Why has mankind come down to this,
We've had wars and famine and other hardships.
Why should we now have to live in fear,
Of complete annihilation, who is left to shed a tear.
The people in power think that they know best,
Their chance of survival is as slim as the rest.

Of survivors there will probably be a few,
What will they inherit, what will they do.
One lesson they surely will have to discover,
Is to live side-by-side, with each man a brother.
I keep having this nightmare, it's tearing me apart,
A silent plea for world peace comes straight from my heart.

Doreen Harrison

Buy Me a Rainbow

The sun shines bright above me,
 and rekindles my spirit.
The rain falls all around me,
 yet it refreshed my soul
The world is all about me,
 you are my world — I am whole ...

The sharp wind blows right through me,
 and carries me on it's wing.
The freezing snow falls on me,
 yet it heightens my feeling.
The world is all about me,
 you are my world — my healing ...

The day, overcast and dull,
 backdrops colour in your love.
The night-time, settled and still,
 and together we'll stay.
The world is all about me
 you lie in my arms and say ...

Buy me a rainbow, set it in my sky,
 And promise never, ever, say good-bye.

David Hardman

Giro Postman

Social blues and benefit claims,
Filling forms, spelling names,
Where's the money coming in,
Postie's letter makes me sing.
Pay the rent, stay to lodge,
Landlord blues got to dodge,
Pasta and chips, sweetcorn burgers,
Fat and oil, policing surges,
Need to wait another week,
Giro spent before you speak,
Clothes all smelling of sweat and stench,
Up in arms magistrates bench,
Need my giro to survive,
Money in pubs flat alive,
Music blowing in holocaust,
Stoned immaculate totally lost,
Lazy days and morning clocks,
Washing jeans and black socks,
No roll for the toilet just the news,
Where's me giro money blues.
Warmth and gas blue bottled flies,
Matches with fags, docker sighs,
Hold on closely to what you've got,
Giro postman gone to pot.

Paul Harrison

Epitaph

"Do not cry for me" it says up on my grave
"Do not shed a tear for that will not me save.
Though I have gone away - don't mourn for me, my friend
I lived my life to the full, until the very end.
My body is lying dormant, my heart is sleeping sound
My soul is on the wander to wherever love is found.
So keep your heart wide open, for I will soon come home
Give me one last resting place, so I'll no longer roam.
I may see you in the morrow - the morrow of the dawn
So I beg you not to cry for me - just keep my memory warm."

Julie Hourd

Names

Once a driving force, now an aching memory
Down the years the echo of a name still comes to me
Once beloved, and capable of rousing deep emotion
Oft repeated lovingly with tender, deep devotion.
Still your name is with me, like a silken thread
Tugging at my heart strings, and running through my head
It conjures up a vision of sun, and new mown hay
Horses, chickens, sheepdogs and watching children play
The name evokes for me, a word, a smile, a place
In which I was secure, I see a well loved face
In the mystic borderland of now and yesteryear
It makes me catch my breath, lest it should disappear
Is it imagination, which makes me see the name
Written in the greying ash, and in the leaping flame
As it flickers on the ceiling, in the darkened house
When the shadowed room is empty and silent as a mouse.

Irene Hurstwail

My Gift

God gave me a gift one day long ago,
A gift which He knew would bend me down low,
To question God 'why?' never came to my mind
For I know, God is love, God is truth, God is kind.

My gift of a child so lovely and sweet
Soon turned all my life into tears and defeat,
But all the hard journey I knew I could find
My God, who is love, who is truth, who is kind.

Through years of hardship, and sorrow, and tears
Through years of happiness, joy and loud cheers,
Through years of doubt, dark clouds and black mind,
I did not forget, God is love, God is truth, God is kind.

The years have gone by, and I've faced many tasks,
A look of peace, a look of worry, resembles my masks.
No one to know that goes on in my mind —
What a blessing — God is love, God is truth, God is kind.

Rachael Hunter

The Dream

I dreamt I was a winner
And instant millionaire
The number I had chosen
Came out on the night air.

My hand gripped the old arm chair
Heat beating a rapid beat,
I could not find the power
To get up from my seat.

I saw so many faces,
Many desperate in dire need,
I wondered how a million pounds,
Would the poor and hungry feed.

Then my problem ended
I awoke to yet another day
The dream of a million pounds,
That I would just have given away.

Mrs. M. Hanshaw

Pantolines

Wide-eyed children,
Doting grandparents,
Mums, Dads — and Uncle Abanazar,
"Aladdin."

Orchestra tuning up,
An opening of programmes,
A shuffling of feet — and 'eggspectation,'
"Humpty Dumpty."

Cheers for good fairy,
Boos for demon king,
Brokers men — and golden egg,
"Mother Goose."

Kirby's flying ballet,
Buttons, fairy godmother,
Glass slipper — and ugly sisters,
"Cinderella."

Oh! Those childhood memories,
Out in the frosty cold,
Cheeks aglow with joy — and a kiss,
"Sleeping Beauty."

Oh! Yes it is,
Oh! No it isn't,
He's behind you — and tears of laughter,
Pantomime.

K. Harrison

Soldier Boy

I've travelled over the world,
To places far and near,
I've done my service for my country,
And had my share of fear.

They sent me out to places
Where no one ever knew,
I was in the British Army,
One of the chosen few.

I spent twelve years of my life,
Learning various skills,
They taught me how to clean my boots,
And do their marching drills.

They taught me all the things I know,
To make my life secure,
The twelve years in army life,
Were the best for sure.

My final day had to come,
For me to get demobed,
And back into civvy street,
To find myself a job.

Robert Heslop

Our Feathered Friends

It's nice to look out of the window,
To see all the birds chirp and chatter,
They have nut-cake and peanuts to eat,
So it really doesn't matter,
They are happy, they haven't got a care
Providing plenty of food is there,
The birds this year have been Black-caps, Green finches,
Chaffinches, Robins, and the little Jenny Wren,
Great Spotted Woodpecker and family, Starlings,
Sparrows, Blue Tits, Great Tits, and here we go again,
Thrushes, Hedge Sparrows, Lesser Whitethroat,
And House Martins too,
Wagtails, Pigeons, Bull Finches, Doves, Crows,
Blackbird, Kestrel, all in full view,
Now the winter is almost near, the one thing I will fear,
Is enough people will be found to put out some food for
the birds,
If they haven't got a bird table, just put it on the ground.
Just remember birds need to be fed,
We do not want to see *any* dead.

Mrs. P. J. Head

Desert

Whispering slopes of shifting sand
Swirling, blowing reforming
Upon the sighing Saharan simoom
In the heat of desert morning.

How sultry in their arid majesty
These golden pyramids lie,
Locked in a timeless wilderness
Cascading from a blazing sky.

Blistering sand storms spin and surge
Whistling emptily through barren dune,
Rattling the dead, cracked landscape
Forsaken, like the flaky panorama of the moon.

At dark Arctic ice creeps in
Riding a spangled, cold Arabian night
And under the jewelled firmament
Black pyramids dazzle in the moonlight.

At noon, the blazing fire-sun returns
Mercilessly scorching the red earth.
The heat of the Cancerian tropics
Engineering a dusty desiccation of death.

Whispering slopes of shifting sand
Swirling, reforming, blowing
Beneath sun and stars, into eternity
Under the aegis of another knowing.

Katie Hart

Mad Pets

My mad pets
My mad pets
All of them laying
Racing bets.

One mad hawk
That can talk.
One mad pig
Who wears a wig.

One mad parrot
With a beak like a carrot
One mad chincilla
Who is a definite killer.

One mad gerbil
Who is absolutely purple.
One mad cat
Who wears a top hat.

One mad fox
Who lives in a box.
One mad hen
Who lives in a den.

But the maddest of them all
As you see,
With no competition, no opposition,
It just has to be ME.

Iain Heaton (Age 11)

Cubs Jumble Sale

The sale is always a hectic event,
"Little green jumpers" their time well spent,
Knocking on doors, with eyes open wide,
Touting for jumble they'll sell with pride.
At Saturday's sale, the excitement will mount,
"Little green jumpers" are told not to shout!
The buyers arrive, armed with their carrier bags,
Then stuff them full with other folks rags!
Now it's all over, add up the kitty,
Just short of £200.00, what a pity.
"Little green jumpers" go home to bed,
Happy, content "well done" Arkela said!

Marjorie Haywood

The Leaden Skies

The greyness greets the waking day
The shafts of light are far away
Hopeless cries from a solitary bird
Make a deafening sound that cannot be heard
The Leaden Skies are not deterred.

The trees will listen, they will bend an ear
To a dark and dismal atmosphere,
While the wind lets out a sigh of relief
As it blows away a solitary leaf
But the Leaden Skies are full of grief.

The sky has cried a million tears
Over all the many hapless years,
And though they stain the scented air,
Still we are painfully unaware
The Leaden Skies are waiting there.

Colin Harwood

Looking For Work

Filling in forms explaining my life
What have you achieved? Have you still got a wife?
Your religious beliefs, what do you believe?
Any brushes with the Law, or attempts to deceive?
What is you colour? Where were you born?
What are your interests, are you happy or forlorn?
What is your age? An important fact,
You don't get around that one, the files are intact.
Your last three jobs, why did you leave?
Did you leave on your own, were you given the heave?
Forms, facts, dates, what a pain.
If I don't get a job soon, I might go insane.
Ah well, I'll soon get a Giro and there's still the next post.
Thank you sir, we will let you know, till then
I'll keep signing and hope for the most.

Les Heaney

Dawn

The vista of shadow waits as the
Pregnant sky delivers its fruit to the world.
The probing fingers dispel the darkness
Of the womb, sending the beams to dry
The tears on each blade of grass,
Cascading consoling colour on a grey country
To heal the soul.

Unquestioned in a perpetual cycle it grows
To learn, to give its warmth and hope,
Ripening in the radiance of wisdom.
But the essence always dies
And looks for the shadows embrace
For the path to its dark destiny.

Catherine Heenan

There Was A New Baby Born Christmas Day

There was a new baby born Christmas Day,
His name was Jesus Christ,
His mother was Mary, his father Joseph
He was born in the middle of night.

In a stable lay the manger,
All the animals gathered round.
People came from all over
Just to see this wonderful sight.

Three wise men came bearing gifts,
Shepherds with their flocks to graze.
In the sky the brightest star,
Tells the world that Christ is born.

Tracy Heaume

My Mother

My Mother is so kind,
A nicer person is hard to find,
Always in a rush,
Except when she's got her paint brush,

Making pastry is her delight,
I hope it rises and comes out right,
Put Mother to the test,
With her dolls he excels the best,

Her Christmas cakes are crinoline dolls,
Much better than looking at chocolate rolls,
There certainly could not be any other,
To take the place of my dear MOTHER,

I can go to her with any problem,
She will help and guide me all the way,
I will *never find* another like the one I have today.

C.F. Head

Carnousie Howe

Summer sun has long since gone
Autumn sun shines now
Casting, golden shadows over fair Carnousie Howe,
The fisherman is absent seeking pleasures new
The trees have cast their leaves of green
For a richer golden hue
The weeds beside the waters edge
Have slowly bowed their heads
The little squirrels have gathered nuts and lie snug in winter beds
The fields that grew the golden grain to fill the farmer's loft
Lie waiting for the plough share by the lonely little croft,
The pheasant feeds on what remains of summer's mantle green
The River Deveron dark and still completes the autumn scene;
But winter days will quickly pass over river field and bough
Then all will be bright and green again, by fair Carnousie Howe.

Margaret Harrold

Tree

Mighty tree you are so old,
You look down upon me, so wise
you seem, so small am I.
Centuries you have lived
compared to my three decades.
Your weathered skin speaks of harsh and hard times,
the lines of age upon you, of life's experiences.

As I look up amongst you timeless branches
so graceful, yet strong enough
to bare the heavy burdens you must withstand,
I wonder who else has stood here and
gazed admiringly up at you, and
who in another century might do the same?

We humans are like leaves upon your arms,
Some falling whilst still young;
others leaving in a blaze of colour and glory;
another ripped untimely from your nurturing arms;
others withering, to lie upon the ground unnoticed.
Yet you will continue, for longer than I,
to send your seed out upon the breeze
to travel where it will.
Perhaps to fall and grow to carry on
Your magnificence.

Deborah Hearn

A Rose

A rose is a beautiful flower.
It looks up to the heavens above
It symbolizes an emotion
And that emotion is LOVE.
It opens its intricate petals
Like the blinking of an eye.
With colours as soft as the rainbow
After a cloud burst sky.
Roses are like people
They need tender, loving care
And break just like porcelain
Their meagre lives to share.
So stand in a garden of roses
And smell the fragrant air
Knowing they were sent from above
With LOVE, for all to share.

Barbara Helliwell

Pipinella

There will never be another cat
Quite the same as you,
Your little face,
Your dark brown eyes
And tabby twitching tail.

I may get another Kit one day
But never shall I forget,
Your smudged nose and loud purr
Your playful paws and so thick fur.

The sweetest Kit that ever lived
And now you are but gone.
Although I have no pictures,
My memory will never fail.
And always at the front of it
Will be your playful bound,
The way your pounced upon the leaves
As they flew along the ground.

The neatest little catcher
That ever will be born.
Those white sharp teeth,
The lapping tongue.
Although they may be gone,
Always in my mind they'll stay
And never will be wrong.

Hazel Heaton (Age 12)

TV Time

The TV vomits forth black images
To seduce and ensnare the mind,
Grotesque puppets serve as mouthpieces,
Cloying, patronizing, they ensnare the soul.

The whole world in one tiny box,
Riot, death, suicide lead the dance.
We follow the leader, bow to his call
Kneel to pray, let our heads run wild.

Moving picture show, who defaced the star?
Plucked from heaven, cast down to hell,
The disguise dropped, flesh and bone,
Overdosed in the back of a limousine.

No one care, they saw the film,
Only happy endings are served to the addicts
But he was like them, he bled, he breathed, he sucked
Immortal in glorious technicolour ...

Paul Healey

Mary's Sorrow

My hands felt nought though they blistered and bled,
I laid blanket of soil over each angel head,
Then stood as stone while ice winds blew,
To beat my breast where they sucked and grew.

In life bright smiling eyes did shine,
In dying boned red pools met mine,
The stinging sores stole spirit light,
No cries, no coughs to ease this night.

I make no sound, though my soul it screams,
To deafen me, or so it seems.
Left naught, just vast such emptiness,
No skin to kiss, no curl to caress.

Six times the pains of life I stood,
Six times rejoiced my motherhood,
Till savage plague knocked on my door,
To leave me none, of the six I bore.

Miss L. A. Hatfield

Moontime

The evening has vanished in a violet dusk
And as I watch, it darkens to a grey.
The cloudless sky is freedom,
Gone is day.

Wait
   Here,
      Moontime visitor,
      Hear the breezy whispers of the wind.
Come,
   Go,
      In sweet blackness,
      Feel the cool night stillness of your mind.

Calming whispers floating here are soothing
And the spirit has awakened in the night —
But the hush is broken
Suddenly, by something bright.

Darkness now is conquered by a harsh light
And the eyes that loved the peace are made to strain,
They are resentful of the shattered night
And calm gives way to gloom.

Quiet thoughts are gone now, with the false day,
The wind feels like a dull swipe through the brain,
And an artificial sullen light
Leaves shadows on the moon.

Julia Hemings

Loaves And Fishes

Put down your guns you fighting men
and women too who join the fray
Enjoy the world we live in and
rid your minds of evil that is there.
Put down those guns — feel free
and not embittered.
Just smell the sweet earth and the air.

And God, please listen if You are there.

To all those men who plot for greed
by selling guns, promoting carnage.
Do you not see those haunted eyes in
Third World countries — their quick demise.
Rwanda's rape, Sarajevo's shame
Those killing fields to Irish slaughter
Huge lakes of blood fed not a soul.

And God, please listen if You are there.

Put down those guns and stop the tears
It's time for peace the whole world over
No more beachheads full of bodies
of young men who never lived and laughed again.
Remembered by old medalled men with sadness
and widows who never loved again.
Yes, fight for those whose need is great.

And God, please listen if You are there.

Mrs. P. Hearnden

D.J. on the Radio

A tumble of words that bubble from his mouth,
Like lava from a volcano. The tuneless hum
Emitted from the hulk of the receiver.
His ambiguous riddles that are not funny,
But he laughs anyway. Reaching the standard
Of boredom that people turn to, to keep their minds occupied.
Without apparent thought or motive,
He dramatically murders another song.

With the microphone clamped to his lips
Like some grotesque deformity of Mother Nature,
The bland smile interrupted by a swig of barely warm coffee.
The eyebrows raised constantly in an expression of hope,
Only to be dashed by the screech of another syllable.

Half drunk with the words he has spouted,
We sit here and accept what he has said,
Like mindless robots following our leader.
Our ears glued to the speakers, just in case
We miss one word of the drivel that he speaks.
No thought at the meaning of the words,
Only wonder at the sheer audacity at the
Station that broadcasts this.

Screens and pages are not match for this,
This horror of sound. Without which we would be whole again,
Instead of trashing our brains against a wall of sound.

Leanne Heeley

Golfing Fun

Wanting a way to get fit
My boys decided golf was it
So off to the golf club we did go
Was it hard, dear me no

The ball was placed upon the tee
Ready, steady, one, two, three
With the swing they took great care
But after swinging, the ball's still there

Not deterred, again they try
And through the air the ball did fly
To the right and in the ditch
There was only one small hitch

After much searching, it's not found
Oh well! There goes another pound
Nine holes played all much the same
A gallant try for their first game

I thought they gave it a good try
I laughed so much it made me cry
I'm looking forward to next time
And then I'll write another rhyme

Evelyn Heck

I Will Be Lost

When the evening falls and daylight is fading,
I will be lost in the oceans of the night.
For a moment I stray, then it holds me completely.
There in the shadow, no one to follow me.
Forever searching in those deep memories.
Strange how my heart will deliver me
On your expansive shores.
How the waves of memories wash over me,
Even though they break my heart.
As I drift away in my dreams,
This is where I find my peace.
Soft blue horizons reach for me
And I am taken within my stolen memories
To be awakened on your shore
And you are holding me close to you.
Before the days slip quietly through
To take me home
To chase away my fears
Until I am ready to sail back to you.
For unto the night I am lost in this day.
My memories locked within
Until I am again lost
In the oceans of the night.

Pam Helm

Ghosts — 1942-1946 — Hereford

I passed by cornfields golden in the morning sun,
Orchards with apples ripe upon the trees,
later I viewed the river form the old stone bridge,
And ghosts of wartime friends stood with me in the evening breeze.

I climbed the slope to Redhill Railway Bridge,
Strolled gently down through Grafton Lane,
I glimpsed the distant trees of Dinedor Hill,
And ghosts walked with me in the summer rain.

I walked in morning sunshine on the castle green,
Crossed the old suspension bridge above the Wye,
To the lawns and meadows, through the avenue of limes,
And the ghosts were there, accompanying my sigh.

St. Martin's Church with yew trees seemed the same,
The once familiar chapel was hidden from view,
I walked within the cathedrals hallowed walls,
At morning service, ghosts still shared my pew.

I met old friends who still remembered me
Looking for wild flowers on my way,
I shed a tear for all those wartime friends,
For they were young, but I am old and grey.

Dorothy Hodkinson

The Flotta Flare

The Flotta Flare is a wonderful sight.
It lights up the sky on a cold dark night
If it wasn't for Dr. Hammer's pipe line dream
The Flotta Flare in Orkney may never have been seen.

It illuminates the heavens with an orange glow
A big safety beacon at the end of the flow
Tankers arriving are shown where to berth
Planes bound for Kirkwall see its mirth.

The Flotta Flare does not suffer from vertigo
In a Force 10 gale it dances like a hero
It took a disaster at Piper Alpha rig,
To stop the dazzling Flotta Flare's jig.

The Flotta Flare was put up for sale
Oxy rebuilt their rig, Piper Bravo won't fail
Elf bought the lot, held an inauguration ˙
The Flame danced again to a French connection.

The Flotta Flare a symbol of O.I.C. gold?
Helped to build Einar, Erland and Harald, I'm told.
The Flare has watched them escort to and fro
While the oil will comes in through rain, wind and snow.

The Flotta Flare is truly a wonderful sight
From my kitchen window I see its orange glow bright
That incandescent light has helped my own my own home
And to the Flotta Flare I dedicate this poem.

Harrold Herdman

The Clock Of Time

Whilst rolling through the realms of life
One sees love, laughter, trouble and strife
But through all life's problems we always find
The love in our lives is always kind.
The clock ticks on through good and bad
It sounds through all of happy and sad.
No matter what in the past has gone
The clock of life ticks on and on.

Suppose for once there was no time
All stood still, the clock didn't chime
There was no present, no past, just now
No one could promise or preach a vow
A cat couldn't prowl to catch a mouse
You couldn't end up a wife or spouse
Because then there'd be no picture of life
We just wouldn't be here ...

Now think again before you cry
Think about the reason why?
Life's too short to worry about then,
How, what, why or when
So before you pace upon that line
Just think about the clock of time.

Ms. J. Henry

Torment

This torment that I feel inside
is just too much for me to hide
My tears they come like falling rain
Why can't I ease this awful pain
This pain I feel is very real
What can I do to make it heal
The hurt inside is very deep
and that is why I cannot sleep
Sometimes I think I hear a phone
When I am here so all alone
But no one's calling me to say
I love you more each passing day

Noeleen Hendley

The Buttercup

In a field or in a lane
I've seen her once and once again
Her shining head is looking up
To form a little golden cup
Her smile is sweet, her friends are many
They call her little Golden Berry
She says hello and cheers you up
That's Little Golden Buttercup.

Eleanor Herkes (Age 10)

Modern Living

What kind of world do we live in
When there are battles, hunger and pain?
Oh! I would have loved to be able to live
When things were simple and plain;
No planes, no nuclear weapons
No cars or washing machines;
Just to eat the fresh fruit straight from the trees
And wash clothes in the sparkling blue streams.
But! Man decided it was progress
And to me it is quite clear;
I'd swap everything I have right now
To have peace and love and no fear.

Olive M. Hunter

To Mother

Mother's love steadfast and strong
Always there when things go wrong
With each smile we cannot wilt
You share our secrets, joys and guilt
Unselfish to the end
All our needs you tend
We miss you Mother dear
Many a day doesn't pass without a tear
Today we think of you above
With heartfelt gratitude and love
Memories we hold tight
You are still our guiding light
A bunch of flowers we place in the garden of rest
We know in our hearts God only takes the best.

Janet Hobbs

The Red-backed Shrike

Gaily, you adorned those summer skies,
So long ago unto our eyes,
When days were long and your song
Swept through valleys fair and strong.
You came, with flamed, burning, wings
From lands afar, this green your home
As like a star, should never fade.
Winging your way through sunlight and shade
Resting in some unknown glade,
Unaware of man's mortal fate,
You lived and life without a trace
Was bountiful in your waking.
To those who know and those who seek
This one small bird who in retreat,
Sings out its song for one to greet,
And though in vain it cannot meet,
That, which is eternally ours.

Nubia Liana Farquharson

Memory Lane

When eventide and shadows fall
My heart grows lonely, for you it calls,
I take a stroll down Memory Lane
And trace my footsteps back again.

Through the trees there comes a breeze
That whispers your sweet name.
The road is dark and sometimes long,
God gives us light and strength to carry on.

I think of all the lovely times together we had spent
How it all seems a lovely dream;
Together that we were only lent
Each and everyone of us to be handed back
Happy memories forever linger.
Life goes on just the same
Until one day then we shall meet again.

Mrs. D.V. Howard

Man & Co.

Modern times with modern people, men and women on the go
In the city, busy working, where's it leading, do we know?
Modern Miss with modern notions, equal pay and equal rights
Can she build a bridge with concrete, can she man the till on nights?

Will she leave to have a baby, then come back and carry on?
Children need to know their mothers, not just be a fight they won.
While they grow they need affection, not just piles and piles of cash,
Someone there to give direction, not just soothe their nappy rash.

Modern man who thinks he's magic, mobile phone and flashy tie,
PC whizz kid, buying, selling and he drives a GTI.
Loadsa' money, too much ego, burning out before too long
What comes after City limits? Institutions right or wrong.

So much hurry, so much bustle, passing people on the floor
Maybe they've dropped out on purpose, maybe pushed out through the door.
Try imagining the feeling, nothing left, nowhere to go,
Numbness, bleakness, hopeless reeling, trampled on by Man & Co.

Essex Girl or Chelsea Flower, Hooray Henry, Ranger Sloan
Yuppies, Dinkies, Groupies, Wrinklies, move along no-waiting zone.
All the jargon, all the buzz-words, training courses by the score
Cut-backs, lay-offs, automation, thing we will see, more and more.

Where's it leading, who knows best and will it last another year?
Wall Street crashes, black Octobers, bulls we like, but bears we fear.
With the point of saturation, sales curves peak and profits stall
Will we wonder in the future, was it worth it after all??

Jane Hewitt

Christmas In The Town

The noisy lorries raging by,
Jumbo jets dart through the sky.
In the toy shop there's a queue,
People wondering what to do,
Whether to wait or whether to go,
What to do they don't know.
Christmas trees above shop doors,
Chemist shops with creams for sores.
Busy people rushing past,
Trains go by very fast.
Markets crowded with people buying,
Babies in their prams are crying.
The dirty slums are rough and dreary,
The people who live there are always weary.
Their clothes are raggy, they never smile,
They buy second-hand once in a while.
They've no mistletoe, they've no holly,
Not even a present to make them jolly.
Poor and weary, cold and dreary,
They've no Christmas to make them merry.

Patricia Allenby

Someone

Little boy climbs on his garden gate,
Dad's working away,
Mum's job makes her late;
Arm round his dog for comfort and warmth —
If only someone would ask him to play.

The washer has jammed, clothes piling high,
Sink full of dishes,
Toys scattered around,
Toddler demanding; young mother sighs —
If only Someone would lend her a hand.

Rain's pouring down, wind blowing rough,
Too old to go out,
Shops so far away,
Now what can be found to keep hunger at bay —
If only Someone would call round today.

Someone near you is struggling alone,
Can you not see?
Can you not hear?
It takes but a moment to bring back a smile —
If only, if only that Someone were YOU!

Rose E.M. Hilham

Be At Peace

I stood still by the water's edge, serene with peace of mind
The sea lapped round the little rocks, the boats lay far behind
The seagulls swooping down to rest, upon the sandy shore
This wondrous world looked so good, how could I ask for more
And yet inside me was unrest, I could not say just why
What did I want from this small world, a sign to show he was by
A whisper'd word, a shining star, he'd given me life to share
How can I show our dear Lord, how much I really care

I try but it seems not enough, if I knew what to do I would
What are we supposed to do with our lives, make good or just do good
I turn away at the end of the day, darkness is drawing near
I glance once more at the rolling waves, and a face I see so clear
He's smiling and nodding his head at me, then across the miles of sea
A hand reaches out and touches my face, and a voice says "Be at Peace
For when the time comes, you'll know what to do, I'll guide you on your way"
A sign at last, my heart was full, I fell to my knees to pray

Doreen Hodgson

Passage

I have wept to see the glory of our coming and going.
In the warm night of the time of the apple blossom
I have watched the eye flicker and heard the breath fail;
in the cool winds of the leaf-fall I have heard the sigh.

In the soft winds I have waited
to hear the cry and feel the quivering hand of never
reaching blind into the black wilful world,
blind fingers of the will of what is and is not.

In the winter of youth I have seen eternal anguish
wrestle for the peace of the spring of old age,
beat with bloodied fist on the hard earth
which soon must give what cannot be wrought.

In the faces of old men I have seen the heap of things,
of times and happiness and doings and thoughts and hurts;
in the hands of old women I have seen the works
of meals and sons and daughters and the touch of love.

In the blind seed I have seen the eyes;
in the dead wrist I have felt the pulse of forever
pounding and throbbing in the fevered surge
of the endlessly turbulent calm.

And the pink petals fall in a winter of spring snow,
yielding to the new fruit.
In the warm night in the time of the apple blossom
I have wept to see the glory of our coming and going.

Jim Powell Hill

Take A Walk Down Our Street

I'll tell you who's who as we walk down our street
At the cul-de-sac end we've fixed a wood seat
There's a huge old stone house behind its tall trees
Belongs to a man call DeVere if you please

He's built turrets and towers, gables, the lot
Thinks he's lord of the manor, but he's a clot
Talks of Home Farm, the Hunt, his horses and moat
Though he has a stream and a dirty old boat

Professor Vanbrugh has long hair and green socks
His wife will not speak if she's wearing her fox
Then Mrs. McAffer with her tartan coat
You hardly see him but they've got a white goat

Miss Trelawn's posh job needs a very large car
Her washline's out front to show off briefs and bra
Little Miss Bridie in her two room old shack
Has five cats, four geese and a monkey called Mac

We all know it's wash day when Bridie comes out
Monkey on shoulder, hands on hips she will shout
"I'll share your washline Miss Trelawn-ie my dear
I've only long bloomers, I'll hang them right here"

There's Madeleine's mum and Geraint with his Flo
The old lady that spins and her parrot Joe
We're very genteel and we swear with restraint
Take a walk down our street, you'll find it so quaint

Olive Hollingworth

Selina

Selina was a naught cat, she killed her master's chickens,
    But when the old boy got to know, he played the very Dickens.
"That cat" said he "has killed my chicks, for that she shall pay dearly;
    I'll drown her in the garden well, for she deserves it, clearly.

He caught the cat and sad to say, prepared her for the slaughter.
    He tied a brick around her neck, then threw her in the water.
"There now" said he "That's done with her." But he was wrong to think so.
    That cat had such a raging thirst, you'd ne'er think she could drink so.

When he looked o'er that garden well, a shock for him lay waiting,
    For what he saw as he looked o'er was truly worth relating.
The cat was sitting on the brick, a picture she presented,
    Just licking dry her glossy coat, and seemly QUITE CONTENTED.

Horace Hinds

The Trouble With Biscuits

This cellophane has got me licked
I've scratched and pulled and picked and picked.
Still these biscuits won't come out
It doesn't help to scream and shout.
Cursing all those biscuit packers,
I really think I'm going 'crackers'
Oh! for instructions on the pack
Or is it me, should know the knack?
One more tug then call it a day,
Ah! This is it, this is the way
Wrong again, the wrapper tore,
Now all my biscuits are on the floor.

Edward H. Hibbard

Finding God

Man looks up to God
In the Northern Hemisphere;
You'd think they'd look down
In the Antipodes!
When they look out,
He's there in vibrant life;
They look within,
A spark becomes a flame
That lights a new horizon
With the power of Spirit.
The realm of Love is His abode
Simply everywhere!

Mona Hamlet

Lottery Fever

In November '94
Many people thought they'd score.
There was a mood of great elation
And of high expectation.
The National Lottery had begun,
Promising prizes for everyone,
Charities, the Sports and also Art
Would all benefit in part.

Surely it would be no sin
If a fortune I should win.
I thought of all the good I'd do;
I would make some dreams come true —
Some for me and some for you.

But when I saw the winning line,
Alack-a-day
It was not mine.

Mary Henderson

A Christmas Blessing

May the peace of Heaven descend
Upon this house tonight
May the blessing of the season
Upon your heart alight
May the spirit of man's fellowship
With God, be sure and true,
May he touch the souls of absent friends
With love from me and you
May all the joys of life be set
Against this Winter's might
Let magic reign for children
And angels in their height
Will sanctify your dreams and say,
(With God's authority)
"May Christmas be with you, and yours
For all eternity".

Anthony Hilton

Buy Now - Pay Later

Better buy that brand new kitchen
For we know you've long been itching
For that one with real mahogany veneer.
Quickly - go and place your order
'Cause the forest's getting smaller
After all, the price they're asking's not too dear.

And there's another way of caring
Though that's not a fur you're wearing
And your vegetables come from a New Age farm.
Smiling smugly to yourself
Wrapped in western ways of wealth
Can we really be the cause of so much harm?

Love the earth and creatures, yes,
But don't love mankind any less
Though it seems to you supplies are surely vast.
Best respect your fellow man,
Show compassion when you can
And extend the hand of friendship - while stocks last.

Ann Hobbs

Gold and Silver

The sun, now disappearing slowly from the view,
    seems loathe to leave the darkening sky,
and with fingers dipped in crimson blood,
    clings closely yet. Then with reluctant sigh
loosens its tentative hold, and quietly
    slips from out our sight. There is no light -
all is in darkness - frighteningly so,
    with the soft, black velvet that is night.
Suddenly, the moon peeps shyly round
    the edge of the dark mass of cloud.
Then - emboldened - ventures forth, to sail
    serenely on her way. She is so proud,
so noble, nothing dare question her.
    The stars twinkle and dip in salute
as she passes. The night creatures pause,
    to stare up at her, silent, mute.
She is their lamp, without her their world
    would be a dark, impossible place -
no shadows to mix with her pale light
    to form intricate patterns, like homespun lace.
When we are gone, and naught but dust
    how comforting it is to know that sun
and moon will ever travel on their way -
    their journey, unlike ours, is never done.

J. Hockley

The Artist

Ageless hours of waiting, for sleep and dreams to fall
Upon my tired head, as does dusk behind the wall,
That tranquil coat of darkness covering all around
Washing o'er the wall and me, she rests on common ground.
Softly creeping on us, so soft we do not see,
Till suddenly we notice, the darkness, wall and me,
Outlines becoming softer, and fading far from view,
Silence getting louder, sunbeams becoming few.
The lengthening of shadows so graceful and so still
Silently she leaves her gown upon the windless hill.
The wall and I, we know her, her step we never hear
And because she treads so softly her cloak we do not fear
The flowers lose their colours as night invades all things
As quietly, by light of day, she her blackness brings
Her soft and subtle sleeping pill, she bids us all to take
As she blankets last the mountain and the ever moving lake.

Watch her then the artist her brush so deft and swift,
Within moments of her starting, all her canvas is adrift,
Allowed to float forever on a sea of liquid jade
And always stop to wonder, why God this painter made.

Eleanor Hill

Save The World For The Children

What hope do we give to our children?
In a world full of hatred and pain.
What hopes do they have for the future?
Whilst drugs and abuse still remain.

The world doesn't get any better,
We're destroying this beautiful place,
With wars, and death and destruction,
I think we're a poor human race.

The youth of today are the future,
They'll inherit the problems we make.
So isn't it time to take care of this earth?
For ourselves, as well as their sake.

What lessons do we teach to our children?
To do better than we've done before,
To learn from mistakes that we've made in the past
If not — who knows what's in store.

There's still lots of beauty around us,
It's a wonderful world, yes indeed.
But as long as we just keep destroying God's earth,
There will always be Children In Need!

Janet Hill

A Mother's Thoughts

You were loved within my womb,
Throughout your childhood too.
An adult you've now become —
You life's now up to you.

I remember, at your age,
My high hopes and dreams.
Then I couldn't envisage
What growing older means.

You are in your youthful prime,
Striving for success.
I've found, with passage of time,
That my needs are less.

I don't want the rat race —
I'll leave that to you,
Happier with my slower pace,
New interests to pursue.

Though we may think differently,
What matters in the end,
Is that I will always be,
You mother and your friend.

Janet Hewitt

Abuse

GREY.
Chiselled through innocent armour.
Quarried from vulnerable strata.
Chipped on rounded shoulders
scarred from Cosmic boulders
of ancient wisdoms steeped.

Seismic ruptured caverns;'
schizoid chasms.

Strangled compliance;
shrouded compromise.

Secrets suffocate —
consign to vaulted consciousness
—
silent screaming abyss.

Subsidence.

EARTH
quakes —
craters burn.

RETURN —
to that fossilized place
to that sanctified womb
of embracing grace.

Val Hickman

Bournemouth on Canvas

'Old Harry' saw us true and blue,
And we as a mirror saw
Him standing sentinel, in melancholy hue;
A thousand shades and more.

With fickle blended pastel streaks,
Of sienna and ochre placed
'cross Heavens azure, a Lunar path
'twixt maritime mists did trace.

O'er us do watch
Those astral guardians bright,
The Moon, Earth's nearest, ellipses true,
Crescent waxing thro' the night.

Come Autumnal dawn,
The Moon doth horizon chase,
A foraging vixen to den returned,
As the Kestrel hunts with grace.

A gently riven sea,
Of crest and trough doth glide,
The scavenging gull for morsel roams,
Whilst the Swallow on land abides.

Mark Hill

Dignity?

Pale moonlight that falls so pure
Upon the heads of men so poor
Looks down with disbelieving eye
On images forgotten, from years gone by,

And paints a picture so unreal
As to deny the pain they feel,
Now left behind in life's great race,
A hopelessness that's deemed disgrace.

Materialism and self, now are 'in'
To help others a Christian sin,
Pretence of care as words cascade,
To hide a grasping masquerade.

As all around greed and power,
Souls flee and love's paid by the hour,
And ebbs away eternal hope,
Strangled by the rich man's rope.

Still, lying deep, cocooned inside
Burning passion, irrepressible pride
One day rise, again to find
Dignity belongs to *all* mankind.

David Hindle

Untitled

I breathe in your breath,
so close you are to me -
Our bodies, like wax
Melted in the heat of our loving,
Merge into one.

I am pressed in your arms,
Moulded into you -
So inextricably part of each other,
That even when we part
I carry with me the image of your body
Imprinted
On my skin.

Lucy V. Hunt

January

'Tis the time of year when fires burn low
And the time to dream as the embers glow
And 'Spirits of Past' dance, flicker and flame
And a rising spark lights the way to fame.

O the way to fame, is the road to go,
In a glimmer — a speck — say Yes! not No;
Then up with the Stars — so brief — so bright,
But beware of the Dawn — as a 'Child of Night'

For a 'Child of Night' is a soul at rage
And fortune and fame — the bars of its cage
And it hangs in the shadows: (a flutter of wings,
And a feather falls — as the captive sings).

Ernest W. Hughes

To Have

Comfort, and happiness, joy, and pleasure
Nothing to crave for, nothing to want.
A life of love, and that be my pleasure,
A world of happy people, for me to want.
The things I desire, give me that pleasure
Young children, having not to want.
Heaven giveth, and they get pleasure
Helping poor, they should not want,
Winning over enemies, and give pleasure.
Try not to make people, envy of want
Give where you're needed, your own pleasure.
If you're pleased with life, you'll never want,
Having a wife, who gives love, that's pleasure.
Let nothing you see of neighbours, make you want,
For to envy other people, spoils your pleasure.
Waking up in the morning, and not to want,
That's what's a pleasure, to have, and to hold.

J. Hinds

My Friend

My friend, our friendship grew.
A tranquil peace I never knew
Before you came my way.
How could I know a fleeting glance
Could steel a heart away.
"My love", one friendship dies
Confused, disturbed, it lies
How long can dreams fulfill two hearts
When friendship ends and heartache starts.

Betty Marise Heath

Hope

'Tis only just and right that we
Who've touched the heights
The depths should see -

But oh! It was so good on high -
The smiling sun was standing by
With rays so near - yet far apart -
But close enough to warm my heart

Then - suddenly - I looked around
And saw the hard earth on the ground -
My heart - once light - now heavy lay
It pulled me down - I must obey

So down to earth I sadly came
And sank into a pit of rain -
But still I feel a ray is nigh -
IS my warm sunshine standing by?

Marie Hirst

Blue Silk For Sunday

I remember your beloved toilworn hands
yellowed with the stain of pungent onions,
sweating the pace of the seven-course meal,
yet gentle, victim of circumstance, proud.
Served snipe trussed up like little babies
sitting in their gravy on silver salvers.
You, monarch of the stockpot added such
succulent offerings to enhance the 'brew'
and stifled the screams of scarlet lobsters
under the weighty lid of the steaming saucepan.
Whose thumbs grew sore from plucking the duck
but sent it through the hatch brown and crisp.
You laboured long — custodian of the larder,
titillating the bellies of the gentry; yet
on Sundays looked chichi in your blue silk dress
you were Mother Earth, genteel, elite.

Jeanne Hoare-Matthews

The Beauty Of My Mother

Her eyes were of a colour stolen from a dying sunset in Autumn
Amber expression with the clarity of pure honey rich in shades of golden honesty
Eyes that would dance around your whole existence
And draw you toward her like the pleasant warm glow of a fire on a cold dark day.
Her hair was charcoal black that possessed the clean sheen of a raven's proud feathers
Soft waves floating down to white satin shoulders
Like the sea in a subtle alluring mood quietly caressing its spell on the rocks.
Harmonic grace and movement in every natural move
A trained ballet dancer having worked at expression for years
Would, in an instant, lose all the earned attention
By one eloquent glance in your direction
Finding your entire being enveloped in her atmosphere
Intoxicating like the cool silent mist charms the coast.
She's gone — a bright dancing flame of a candle
Blown away in the long moment of seconds
And me — the smouldering wick left behind — with my smoking heart reaching up to the skies
In the glimmering hope that I would feel a star with a unique aura
And then know that she is calmly waiting to take my longing away.

Sarah Hilder

Untitled

They stood side by side at the bus stop
Nobody else in the street.
He was a young punk rocker
She was a Gran with club feet.
His hair was bright yellow, orange and green,
Her mac, was an old faded blue.
He couldn't have given a "monkey's"
She wished others would join the queue.
He noticed she looked rather worried,
She tightened the grip on her purse.
He moved nearer to make her feel better
She backed off thinking things would get worse.
"Alright ma", he said, grinning broadly.
"Alright what!" she said, filled with fear.
"Don't say you've forgotten me already,
I worked with your Albert last year!"
"Our Albert?" she paused, "Are you Tommy?
You stayed over a few nights with us."
"Yea, that's me ma." They grinned at each other.
And along came the Number Two bus.

Vera Hilton

Changes

The world I see so different
Than I did some months ago
I have learned so many things
Things I am pleased to know
I have always said, from all bad
Comes quite a lot of good
This is so true, where I am concerned
Of which I felt sure it would
Quite often we see a fallen tree
It does look so forlorn
As time passes by new shoots appear
And the tree is again reborn
This happens to people
Frail as they may be
They are blessed with strength
Form somewhere
We ask from where could it be
Maybe it is from heaven
Let us all just wait and see

B. Hill

Christmas

Images of crisp white snow
Pine scented air
Baubles that glitter and glow.
Excitement, happiness in the air
A time in our calendar
To give receive and share.
Young children who cannot sleep
Alert and listening
Happy joyous tears soon they will weep.
Families gathered round tables of food
Christmas crackers tugged and puled
Games and jokes to suit the time and mood.
Burning candles and prickly holly
Mistletoe and some bubbly
A time to be merry and yuletide jolly.
Brightly papered ribboned gifts
Smiling faces
It is the heart to receive the thankful lifts.
A time in our lives that we've all had
To come together, reunited be happy and lovingly glad
A moment in our steps in life, to recall the past
Energies needed, peace longed for
To make our Christmas memories linger and last.

Kaz Holman

The Gentle Intruders

Two little black cats have invaded our home,
When my old pusscat died I was lost and alone.
My Sheba was seventeen when she died
And I loved her so much that I just cried and cried.
No more pets for me I firmly said
But sadly, now our friend is dead.
A lasting reminder of her though we see
In two little black cats asleep on my knee.
They were so unhappy when we brought them to us,
So forlorn, lost and hungry and longing for fuss.
They couldn't have known when we fetched them that day
That things were going to work their way,
So nervous and jumpy - they hadn't a clue
Exactly just where they were going to.
But now, full of mischief they're the love of my life,
Though I do wish they wouldn't keep bringing in mice!
Lady and Suzi, two little black cats
I know I will never bring Sheba back
Suzi's inquisitive and so greedy too!
If the doorbell rings there's hullabaloo!
Lady's so different, I don't know she's there
My little black pusscats now haven't a care.
They're fed, loved and happy - no more will they roam
To seek a new owner - they've invaded our home.

Dot Holloway

Winter Time

As I look up at the clock
The summer months I have forgot
Yes winter nights are here again
The long dark nights of snow and rain.

Every hour ticks slowly by
They seem to move with the dark, dark sky
Everything seems so dim
All the houses are lit within.

The snow lies thick upon the ground
No one seems to be around,
The leaves are swirling in the air
The children stand without a care.

Down in the park I go for a walk
I meet a friend, we stop for a talk,
Roll on summer, she says to me
On that I say, I must agree.

Now back at home in my cosy little house
Nothing is stirring, not even a mouse
Sitting down in my chair I go to sleep
The thoughts of summer in my head I keep.

Moira Hitchcox

Lady

It is time you used your strength
For yourself,
Your own path.

It is time to cut all ties,
You are ready,
Do it the little voice says.

It is time to forget Female psyche,
Change gender,
Mentally.

It is time you will be amazed,
How with practice,
It is easy.

It is time to put yourself first,
You have the intelligence,
The intellect.

It is time to use your intuition,
To be ruthless,
Be greedy.

You will be enhanced,
By the speed,
Of Advances.

As one once said,
"the whole world does not revolve around you",
But the Man said ... my world does.

Angela Hodgson

There's Only One Genuine Article

I own a Special Treasure, I got it all for free,
I am one honoured person, pleased it belongs to me.
I gave lovingly for hours on end, its beauty can't be beat.
Every bit of it is perfect and finished off a treat.

It is so tall and slender, stands nearly five feet tall,
Sits within my sitting room, won't stand against the wall.
I give it a wash every day to keep it nice and clean,
Won't let anyone near it, I know it's very mean.

There's nothing in all the world that's more important to me,
I wish it could be on display for everyone to see.
The legs are past their best now and the colour faded a bit
It won't suddenly spring to life with a polish and some spit.

It is so very delicate, could be damaged if knocked to the ground
There's not much chance of that especially when I'm around.
Every inch so priceless with pure diamond sparkling beauty
I guard with love and devotion, not because of duty.
This limited edition so rare and special to view
I don't share it with anyone, but I might make an exception for you.
It will not last forever, that's sadly very true
When I finally lose it, I'll be exceptionally blue.

*(Dedicated to my beautiful but severely handicapped Daughter Paula,
aged 19, who suffers from Tay Sacks)*

S. Hobson

To Have A Woman

How wonderful it would be
To have you lying next to me.
To share my love and ease my pain
And warm me through the winter rain.
To love me for who I am
And not just be a one night stand.
To understand my funny moods
And make me smile, when I feel blue.

To have you close, so I could hold
Hug me as the nights grow cold.
And walk through Dorset countryside
See Hardy's Wessex, through Hardy's eyes.

Share my wealth and share my life
Play the role of a doting wife
And have my kids so they'll take on
My life
And succeed, where I went wrong.

Carl Hodkin

Dreams

To dream
Is to swim in a sea of fantasy,
Floating on a tide of memories,
Unknown faces sweetly kiss awaiting lips.
Mingling with familiar surroundings
Misty yet clear.
Muted yet bright.
Thoughts become reality
Yet are only actors performing a play.
A play in your mind.
Unreal — yet real.
Days and years are only seconds and minutes
Love on one side of the book
Fear on the other.
As memory and imagination turn the pages
Love for a tender caress, a soft murmuring word.
Fear from the crowded shadows.
The turmoil of pain
And the unknowing of the unknown.
To dream
Is but to sink deep into your brain
And awaken slumbering senses.

Miss A. Horn

Just ...

Just when I thought
It was safe to smile ...
I found it went wrong.
Set back a mile,
So glad that I'm strong.

Just when I thought
It was safe to laugh ...
I uncover another disaster.
Nothing happens by half,
I'm sinking, faster and faster.

Just when I thought
I was going under ...
The sun shines bright.
No more frightening thunder,
Life made right.

Just ...
Thank you, Graham.

Elizabeth Lyn Haworth

Waiting To Be Fed

The human cost of civil war
Is flashed up on the screen
In poverty a little child cries
The wanton disregard for life
Is nothing but obscene
As another hapless peasant person dies

This stupid war where no one's right
But no one says they're wrong
Destroys the heritage from former times
With nothing left, the ragged people
Just keep moving on
Skin and bone in desperate human lines

There is nothing left for planting
And there's nowhere safe to sow
A problem brewing up for months ahead
But these folks need assistance
And they want the world to know
In hope, they are all waiting to be fed.

Andrew Hodson

A Housewife's Reward

"And what has been your occupation?"
"Just a housewife," our Margaret said,
And feeling somewhat ashamed
Her face flushed up slightly red.

"Do you have any children, Margaret?"
"Yes, two" she replied with a smile.
"And did you enjoy being a mother?"
"Well, yes, but not all the while."

"There were times when I felt up against it
And I've cried a few tears of despair."
"Was your home clean and tidy then, Margaret?
Did you budget your money with care?"

"Yes, I had to, with no other choice,
When only one wage kept us all."
"And was it a big wage, my dear?"
"Oh no! It was really quite small."

"Then why do you feel such a failure?
You seem to have led a good life.
You've worked hard as a caring mother
And your husband has had a fine wife.
I have no hesitation in opening
These pearly gates for you."

Then Saint Peter, at the entrance to heaven,
Stood aside and let me through.

Margaret Holmes

Quite a Day

WORDS - so much to do with them,
    Writing or waiting
    OR
    Reading when raining
    Doing and
    Seeing.

Whatever you want them to be they will be —
    Wonderful
    Ordinary
    Rare or Redeeming
    Daring and
    Sharing.

We can go where we choose with them,
    Worthing or Wigan
    Osset or Oldham
    Reading (again) and
    Dudley to wow 'em, then down to the
    Sea in Sussex.

After all the traversing, back to the versing,
    Winking
    Ogling
    Rollicking and Rolling
    Doodling and Dawdling
    Snoring and Snoozing - Good night.

Vera Homer

This Game Called Golf

Golf is the most frustrating game that I have ever played
The Pro's, the Hackers, the Handicapped, all speak of shots they've made.
Some days the ball goes flying cleanly through the air
I think I've found the answer and offer up a prayer
The ball will miss the bunkers and roll towards the pin,
All I have to do is putt the little white ball in.
Then comes the rude awakening when next time I do play,
Can't get the ball going, it's all rough and sand today.
What's happened to my swing? What's happened to my play?
Can't someone move that bunker or chop down that tree
How can I hit the Green if the Green I cannot see.
And so I reach the 18th Tee and hit a super drive
Suddenly the sun comes out — it's good to be alive.

Betty Holder

It's Hard To Say You Love Someone

If you went back in time what
Would you see?
Would you change your life?
Say things you hadn't?
Kiss the ones you didn't?
Hold them ...
Caress them ...
Love them ...
Or is it because you just miss them
And wish you hadn't held back.
Life is hard, isn't it.

Gavin Hodson

Angel Of Night

Softly, Softly sweeps the skies,
Curtains of colour, shade and hue,
Drawing a veil before the eyes of Night
begin to glimmer with their starry light
And senses slumber
with dreams of wonder
beyond our imagining:
Ecstasy She brings
on velvet wings,
When dreams come true — how brief their stay!
We beg you to linger Angel of Night,
Let us not awake awhile
until the kiss of Morning's smile
Begins our dreams anew.

Elizabeth Page Hope

Emigration

In a valley in Sussex, where flows the Rother,
three pairs of wild geese honk through the sky,
out through the sunset and on through the evening
away from the valley, as we say good-bye.

Soon we are leaving to follow the wild geese,
but flying much farther and higher than they,
and we are the third pair, leaving the valley
and leaving the old geese, for lands far away.

The old geese are coming, coming to join us
out through the sunset o'er woodland and hill
away from the valley they've known all their lifetime
and out to the young geese, and younger geese still.

In a valley in England, where flows the Rother
four pairs of wild gees will ne'er again roam,
but younger geese one day, adventurous, curious
may visit the valley and the ancestral home.

Mike Hodgetts

The Silent Battlefield

Grim caretaker of bygone hours of pain,
Of quietness where once brave deeds were wrought,
Where dread and human misery were naught,
Where men with disenchanted minds were slain;
Impassive watcher of a thing so vain,
A wilderness enfolding sufferings bought
By mortals with but one demanding thought -
This fearsome hell must never be again;
Where hardened warriors came at length to die,
With weary hearts and memories afar,
Imploring nations never more to vie
In bloody feuds that hope and truth debar:
But still humanity must weep and sigh,
For still the Martian gate remains ajar.

W.H. Hodkinson

An Old Man's Memories

The old memory's not what it used to be,
The old eyesight's fading, but I can still see,
I remember years back as clear as a bell,
And many a good tale I'd be able to tell.

I remember the old house where I used to live,
My mother trying to make ends meet, her last penny she would give,
If someone came who had nothing, they wouldn't be turned away,
She'd sit them down beside us saying, "Pay me another day."

I remember sharing four to a bed, after a tin bath by the fire,
The old black-lead fireplace wasn't much to be desired,
But these are stored in memories that will not fade away,
They were of all the happy years, I remember to this day.

I remember the old pals that went through the war,
I remember the trenches, and the things that we saw,
The air raids, the bombs the sheer destruction,
The fires burning rapidly, as if by some strong suction.

And now as I stand here proudly, with my medals on my chest,
I think of all the pals I lost, but God only takes the best,
There is a special day for them, the poppy tells it all,
They may be gone, but they're not forgotten, as we see the petals fall.

Barbara Holme

What Man Has Done

Haunted by the children's eyes
Looking fearful to the skies
What has man created here
That babies have so much to fear
Man has made the acid rain
That falls on every leafy lane
Each dewdrop now is not a jewel
It's now a weapon far more cruel
It doesn't quench each thirsty flower
It eats them slowly, hour by hour
Now burned and blackened there they stand
A monument on our proud land
Birds of prey, now prayed for birds
Farmers pine for long gone herds
Flocks of sheep no more are seen
Black the land that once was green
Fish float lifeless, seabirds drown
Golden sand now oily brown
Read these words, digest each one
Now you can see what man has done

Gwendoline E. Holloway

Transient Glory

I feast my eyes
On autumn skies.
Copper, red, amber, burning gold
The trees unfold.
But winter traces interlacing
Black among the glorious show
Oh, stay! I cry in vain.
Nature's unfolding is racing
And winds will blow
In showers the helpless leaves away,
Around,
Down to the ground
Where the pitiless rain will slay
To damp and muddy, leafy, mould
The flames of red, copper and gold.
Older I grow,
And want to hold
The autumn glow
To warm me in the winter's cold.

Irina Holman

234

A Child Of Charnwood

I stand in the lee of Iveshead hill and gaze across the land
I see the house where I was born and early life was planned
My mind goes back o'er three score years to when I was a child
When first I learned of nature and the secrets of the wild.
My tutor was a gypsy, a wild unruly man,
Who came to visit us each year with painted caravan.
Although he shunned most people, he seemed to take to me,
Many thing he taught me as I stood against his knee.
How to make and bait a trap, how to set a snare,
Chase rabbits to their bolt holes and find them waiting there.
To walk through woods without a sound, to stand quite still
And watch the silent barn owl stoop down to make his kill.
We'd walk for miles o'er fields and stiles, me learning all the time,
And get back home quite weary, covered in sweat and grim.
I loved the land where I was born, and true, I love it still
But things are very different now as I stand against this hill.
The air which once was fresh and pure is filled with toxic waste
And streams where once I slaked my thirst are now not fit to taste.
Acid rain falls from the sky and strips the leaves from trees,
Flowers with their nectar — a danger to the bees.
Some men with greed for wealth and power are ravishing the land
Pray God someone will stop them and make this pillage banned.

W.A. Berridge

The Infant Playground

On the pavement I stand and stare
Over fence at those who are there
Darting, turning, movements quick
No time wasted as seconds tick.

Jumps of joy, squeals of delight
To me there is no better sight
Sweetness, innocence, beauty so fair
No wonder I must stand and stare.

Memories of yesteryear my thoughts bring
Of bygone days when I, too, was a little thing
Deprive us not this wonderful sight
Old eyes see, value, and take delight.

But those who love want to give our love
To those who grow — so better shall they live
A fence, and years, divides our worlds
The old from infant boys and girls.

Clifford E. Hooper

October Leaves

This is October's sun
When the leaves are almost done
Roasted in the blazing light
Thro' long summer days, till the bite
Of autumn, softens their greens
To mellow yellows and reddish sheens
Wafting madly in the breeze
They thrash their hues this twilight eve
Rotating colours gaily twirl
Amidst the branches to unfurl
A shimmering mosaic of bright tonality
Blended in movement, slowing to finality
Reflecting each, the colours dim
Softly linger and seem to swim
Thrown against the fading light
Before the moon beams milk white
Flicker on, their shades recede
Blanched ghosts, light thin, bleed
Against night's cool blue veil
Evening sighs them to stillness and repose
As dusk subdues, Diurnal Rose.

D. Homer

Tables Meant for Four

Each takes one seat at the tables meant for four,
caught behind barriers others build
and render with their own unease.

Searching eyes stare over the bank of weed,
fix on some point far beyond the waves,
know the reflected solitude.

The wistful girl,
turns to scan the faces of those she doesn't know,
waiting the caress, the promised dream
she saw in the smile of the boy she met
at last night's dance.

An older man tethers his pet to a white, plastic chair,
shrinking the emptiness that crams his days,
while anyplace cod and chips flavours his quest
for footprint shadows, remnant of strolls on tide naked sands
with the wife he buried last year.

And me - stealing an hour at midday,
watching leisure languish,
watching space of trespass hold the lonely in,
watching the ocean amble in her summer dress
hemmed with ripples washing away time;
watching -

and taking just one seat
at a table meant for four.

Anne M. Hughes

Old England

I want to see old England,
Where her streams flow on and on.
Where the heath lays quiet and still
Before it is all gone.

I want to walk her country lanes,
To ret awhile, to smell the heather,
To walk the Cotswolds and the downs,
Before it disappears forever.

To feel the sun's rays warming me,
To see her trees so tall.
I want to see her fields of green
Before there's nothing left at all.

To walk through villages and town's
To take in all and every scene.
Intoxicated by her atmosphere,
To go where I've never been.

I want to ramble through the woods
With sturdy shoes upon my feet,
To lose myself among the trees,
It feels such a safe retreat.

I want to stand upon a hill
To see the beauty of this land
But will she stay always the same?
This place called old England.

L. Hopkinson

Dream On

The palm trees gently wave aloft in a tranquil, graceful way
The cloudless sky of deep azure frames every bright sunray
The rhythmic lapping of the sea sounds like a lullaby
Gazing restfully down the beach I watch the world go by
My cooling drink is close at hand, a novel awaits my eye
My thoughts are wandering as I drift into and out of "shuteye"
The heat of the sun is penetrating into my very bones
Warming without burning it soothes and gently tones
A native guide stands sentinel to attend to all my needs
He gently wafts me with a fan made out of local reeds
He serves a lunch of tropical fruits, the grapes he peels with care
Then he'll cool my brow with some cologne and gently brush my hair
My suite of rooms is furnished in a most exquisite way
I sleep on pure white satin sheets, changed each and every day
I bathe in warming scented foam to ease away the stress
Gentle massage follows with strokes which feel like a caress
My sleep is undisturbed with mind and body so relaxed
No worrying subconsciously about problems raised or taxed
Then I hear a distant bell — I turn and press the "off" switch
Time to wake up to reality — Oh how I wish that I was rich!

Margaret Holyoake

The Secret

This castle has a secret,
I feel it in my bones,
The walls have a noisy silence,
I no longer feel alone.

The dance hall plays its tune to me,
But I do not understand,
As I listen to the music,
Of this ghostly medieval band.

I cannot find the secret,
Of this castle tall,
If only these four walls could speak,
Then I'd know it all.

It could be in the walls,
Or maybe in the band,
Will I ever know the secret
Of the castle on the sand.

Kathryn Hooper

Feelings

A kiss
Like the touch of rose petals,
Lingers in the mind.
No thought of urgency,
Yet,
A desire
Unknown, unfulfilled,
Never to be recaptured.

A tear,
Like a raindrop on a window pane.
Foretells the grief,
Within,
Undisclosed, eternal,
Never to be shared.

A smile,
Tender, like the touch of angels,
Caresses the mind.
Lingering, gentle,
A gift for all time.

Norman Hanley

Malice in Wonderland

It was a pleasure, to see them again
With their usual grace and form,
The King and Queen of the ice rink,
They certainly gave their all.

The physical demands were incredible,
And they should have won the gold,
If the audience were the judges,
The Russians would be out in the cold!

The British judge was not popular,
And has hauled over the coals,
If the contest had been judged by an applause meter,
Then they would have won the gold!

They did everything possible,
And we wish them every success,
It was magic to watch their performance,
They deserve a well earned rest!

N.D. Humphreys

Plea To The Inland Revenue

Tell me something witty,
A little rhyme or ditty.
'Cos I have got the blues,
Since I've heard the news
That in this massive city
There sits a large committee,
And they will not refuse
From amassing all the dues,
So now they're sitting pretty,
Round a pretty little kitty.

Now the nitty-gritty bitty,
Of this silly little ditty,
Is to give you all my views
On your Inland Revenues
So that you may have some pity
On my itsy bitsy kitty,
And maybe I won't lose,
If you leave the fags and booze,
But I'm not a Walter Mitty
So please — tell me something witty!

Donald Hopkins

Lament For The Whale

You have covered the foam,
With our blood.
You pursue us
Wherever we roam.
And yet we've never
Posed you a threat;
And the sea,
Has always been our home.

Our future
Was put in your trust.
Isn't anything
Sacred in your hands?
Even the air that we breath;
Is poisoned by your dust.

Like the giants of old,
We'll be gone.
And they who would stop you,
Will weep.
And your children,
With innocent eyes,
Will ask;
Oh, what have you done
To our beautiful
Friends of the deep.

Windsor Hopkins

A Sailor's Collar

Said Tommy to a smart coquette,
"How much does it cost to cross the ferry?"
For you, young man, just twenty pence;
But why are you in such a hurry?

"Because", said Tommy eagerly,
"A sailor-man has magic power.
I must not miss the ferry-boat,
My mother has been waiting hours."

How can a sailor help to salve
Your problems lad, and you a stranger?
"Because my dad's been gone so long,
And mother fears he is in danger.

So when the sailor takes my fare,
I'll creep behind and touch his collar,
Good luck will follow dad around,
And I'll go home and tell my mother."

Sarah Hunter

Why Death?

What have you done, that you must die?
Gossamer winged, this tiny fly.
Disease and ill to some you spread,
So for this crime you must be dead.

Oh little moth, whose fate is doom.
I cannot have you in my room,
Into my clothes a hole you'll make,
And for this deed your life I'll take.

So hard you work — wee marvelous ant.
From my ill deed, I should recant.
But powder in your nest I'll pour,
Lest you come marching 'neath my door.

What of the grub, the 'wig, the 'pede,
Who spoil my plants and eat my seed?
Beauty you have, but must not live,
Another death! Forgive, forgive!

Greta Hopper

Out Door In The Country

The grass is green along the path,
The tree's fallen in the wind aftermath
The sounds are clearly heard in the air
We walk through the trees without a care.

Do ducks on the lakes,
Realize the freedom they make
For us of the town streets
In the morning, in the country we meet.

The water is blue with calm emotion
It's almost a feeling of poetry devotion
The insects are free to fly around
The birds are with wings of great sound.

The ground under our feet is soft
Alive with warmth and growing moss
The tracks of animals and men insight
Of all the visitors of the night.

Belonging to a beautiful scene
Seems awful rude to leave, if not mean
To live within the city scream
Never to enter the country dream.

Time has no meaning there at all
And the dew of dawn begins to fall
The lake becomes alive with all it contains
If people treasured such places they would remain.

Angela Howe

Why ...

The dirt settles like snowflakes upon barren
ground.
The carpet shouts "dirt."
The vacuum sucks passionately.
The wheels squeak in pain ...
"Oh no, not this bloody carpet again."

The dust rises ... has it aspirations?
Alas to go no further that the tomb of the vacuum
Enshrined, closeted, an underground movement,
Encouraging 'revolt'.

Why is it then, that some escape such fate?
Lie immortal upon rough tufts of twist-pile?
So I'm reduced to grovel, to pick at the carpet's face,
Until I'm satisfied no trace remains ...
To deface my work, my pride ...

Behind closed doors within, confined,
It hides, resides, belittles my achievements ...

Why someone has entered ... spoilt my work,
Trod upon my clean carpet,
Left proof of their presence,
Their foot impaled upon my pride.
From within the closet the vacuum sighs,
And the dust cries "revolution".

AnneMarie C. Howe

Unnatural Selection

A submarine — surfaces at sea, a metal ship full of power
A dying whale sinks in the waves, crying out — unseen,
Jets thunder across the skies, leaving vaporous trails
Oil covered birds die on our shores with fright filled eyes;
Vehicles speed along tarmac roads, to mapped out destinations
As herds of deer, roam through nature reservations.

And man lives on as nature dies, a growing population against extinction.

Crops grow in abundance, soaking up the sun's radiation
Mammals die from farmers spraying — deadly fertilization;
Reservoirs filled by acid rain, falling form polluted skies
We eat the fish that live and swim in poisoned waters — and sometimes die;
We feed upon the honey of the land, polluted by man made poisons
Insecticides, killing all our friends of nature, no bees to gather from her blossoms.

Kelvin Harrison

Seashore Peace

I like peace
And peace is by the sea
Clear cool water: rocks around
An overhanging tree.

I like peace
And peace is by the sea.

The hills beyond are beautiful
The air is fresh and free
I hear the sound of rushing waves
Talking just for me.

I like peace
And peace is by the sea.

Ann Hogarth

Untitled

Now, she is bejeweled with his love,
Gilded with his trust.
Whilst, I am thrown upon the scrap heap
Left to rot — Unjust.

Now, she is put upon his pedestal,
Be-queened upon his throne.
Whilst, I am sat upon my orange-box
Broken hearted — Alone.

But she is welcome to his riches,
His title and his crown.
For all ill fit and tarnish,
Second time around.

Sue Howard

Man's Best Friend

A man's best friend is not his dog,
As many pundits claim,
In fact it is inanimate,
And doesn't have a name.
If you think it is his car,
That gleaming pride and joy,
Then think again, here is a clue,
He treats it as a toy.
Exclusively for his use,
It's always in **his** hand,
And if you wish to borrow it,
There's no chance, you are banned.
When he has mislaid it,
He's impossible to console,
Woe betide, if he should lose
His TV remote control.

Charles Hunter

Edward's Lament

Edward is a little bear,
He has much time to sit and stare
For Edward's home is in a zoo —
Where there's not very much to do.
The keeper brings him food at nine,
Such a silly time to dine.
And after that he walks around
Up and down the stony ground.
He'd like to take a good long stroll,
Or even dig a large round hole
But, all around, the fence is strong
He can't get out, to move along.
So sits and dreams of happier days
And tries to think of means and ways
To end this life of misery,
Forever in captivity.

Barbara H. Holland

The Way Of War

Driven by the power of the man at the helm,
The air turns heavy as they fight for the realm.
The dying embers of a burning land,
The death of a million from a single command.
The poisoned blade of a murderous knife,
That dances and sings as it takes a life.
And the luckless souls that lived to remain,
Screamed in agony as they died in their pain.
Oh such a shock they got,
As their lungs began to rot.
Looking for a cure to all known ills,
The doctor prescribes the demon pills.
The stories they tell are sick and gory,
And all for the quest for love and glory.
Lucifer's kiss and the love of the devil,
In this glory the murderers revel.
The fate of a thousand men goes past,
The murdered souls who sleep at last.
Hear the torturous laughter of the anti-Christ,
At the crazy bastards who took their lives.

Elizabeth-Ruth Hosking

Employment For Young Girls In 1832

Three o'clock in the morning,
When most people are still asleep,
Young girls were lifted from their beds,
And carried down the street,
To the factory they were transported,
To start a long day's graft,
Not knowing what food or drink was,
Until the bell tolled at six or half past,
Quarter of an hour they were given,
To eat and drink their meagre fair,
Then back to the grindstone they were driven,
Not daring to complain or to swear,
For fear of the overbearing overseer,
Who watched them with dismay,
He hurried from one machine to another,
Giving orders as he went on his way,
It wasn't so unusual,
To hear the sound of the lash,
Falling on the back of some young lassie,
Who unfortunately happened to pass,
Three shillings a week was all they were paid,
For all the toil and the goods that they made.

R. Hughes

A Job So Mighty

Across the meadow down the road,
Who would have thought of all the load,
Of trouble and strife to make one big hole,
Men with helmets yellow and blue.
Laying a track to connect us with you,
Who would have thought under the sea,
A job so mighty it would be
Carving earth out with such speed,
Men's sweat and muscle bravery too.
It's no mean task in the dark for you,
A muttered curse and a whispered thank you.

I wonder if the waves above protest
At the intrusion into their nest,
A mermaid seashell too her ear
Hears not the singing of the sea
But hammer's blows,
From down below,
Then far away a voice is singing
Comes down the tunnel a-winging
One day more all will be well
The tunnel will be swell
Two hands across a span of rock
One English, one French
Will link the lot

Edna Hornsby

For A Friend

To value the love and kindness
That friendship so often can bring
The smiles that add so much in gladness
The heart with a song it can sing
'Tis a pleasure to find understanding
A voice that is pleasant and mild
But if I be judged by my virtues
Then let me be as a friend.

To talk to precious companions
With so many thoughts of their own
With regards I know you are special
Than all the folks I have known
Somehow you may find me worthwhile
So willing to be a companion
So happy to lend me a smile.

Give me your trust cause I'm worthy
And not for things I possess
For the joy we really value
Are worth so much more than the rest
A pleasant and heart warming smile
I'll know I am more of a person
Because I care as a friend
If we grow a garden full of truth
There's no need for wealth, fame, or youth.

Edna Houlder

Shadow-Words

Shadow-words, these ...
Inflections of go-between worlds in ghostly communion,
half-sounds distance themselves, will host
no future rubrics.

For future they are not — but serve
yesterday's latest bequest:
a progression of mirrors
whose silvering misses/snatches
on waves of atoning light
chants from earlier solemnities.

Luminous incantations
invoke as gods my responses
purloined until now
by other lives' griefs.
Awash, they spill over,
persist in their vigilance,
mercifully foreclose on the heart's
failure to deliver.

Picturing
completeness, I embrace
ah yes this: the full
moon in eclipse —
the path of totality.

Felicia Houssein

Untitled

The birds, the bees, flowers and trees
Are gone, the young one said
And I, the elder couldn't speak
My tongue was made of lead
    The moonscaped earth and withered land.
Bequeathed through human gaff
Bids welcome to a heritage
That makes the devil laugh
    We hadn't cared in our hide below
Safe through choice of straw
What the fate of others was
Self preservation was our law
    Now in stark reality
The blessings turned to bile
Our days on earth are numbered now
They're only for a while
    Please help us, Lord is our plea
The prayers for everyone
A redeeming light, our voice is heard
And the nightmares gone
    Of flimsy texture dreams are made
Quite quickly they recede
But spectre in the form of doom
If warnings we do not heed.

William Hothersall

The Crippling Companion

A crippling companion to hold so dear
And love and cherish, as you would a friend.
Expensive and demanding, though you keep yourself blind.
The morning, in its freshness,
Holds the hazy recollections of another day passed,
Yet you will not see what has gone before.

Maturity finds you indulging in the same misery
You closely witnessed in your youth.
Intent on being a clone of your parentage
Suffocating and sacrificing the spirit that's your own.
Withholding your sad secrets, to be added to your self-pity
Should ever a happy moment come flirtatiously your way.

This companion you seek, soaks you in its stench
Though you hide it until the daylight hours have died.
Stained and stale, yellowed and pale, sickly and scared
Your life holds no value, until you're at the bottom
Of your bottle, where you new friend waits; so patiently
So patiently; without judgement or intolerance.

Miss M.L. Hull

The Sign

For it was not alike to ought that I knew,
for there shed be such a barren space.
And there no clamour no any din,
and there was nought to view about that place.
And with its all enveloping mist, that layeth,
there ashen grey,
and there portraying its thoughts of the end,
upon that awesome day.
And with the length of all its silent creeping,
and yet through its show that there did'st unfold,
came forth a Sign there revealing, of which I
then took a firm hold.
For above and there all descending,
a light there revealed gain without loss.
For there the all covering then remaining,
showed forth its Sign as The Cross.

Patricia Weir Huntington

Cobwebs and Dust

You are full of cobwebs and dust.
In your eyes I see no trust.
Will the wind blow the cobwebs away.
Will the dust forever go astray.
The past is gone it does not matter,
And high above the storm clouds gather.
So let the wind come rushing by,
Then we together can watch the sky.

Paula Howarth

Where Goes The Time?

Where goes the time that passes by,
absorbed by land and sea and sky.
Where goes the time that is no more,
lost to the night that was before.
Where goes the joy, the pain, the tears,
meshed with 'agos' and yesteryears'.
Where goes the childhood we once held,
lost to nostalgia and memories quelled.
Where goes the time that passes by,
time that elapses the time that flies.
Where goes the day and night that part,
lost to tomorrow, but locked in our hearts.

Julie Howard

Worthwhile

To have a lie-in, it must be heaven,
But alas I have to start work at seven,
To get people up, washed and dressed I know
For it is off to Day Centre some must go.
For it is all the people like me,
I am a Home Care Assistant you see.
We help them to stay in their own home.
Sometimes it is the only one they have known.
Having lived so long as husband and wife,
And worked together all of their life.
Now that one of them has gone,
The other one must soldier on.
They feel in great despair,
It is just as though there is no one to care.
To leave their home is more that they had planned,
It is as though no one will understand.
Many times I have heard it said,
That they wish that they were dead.
And when we make them happy and smile,
I know that my work is worthwhile.

June Hopkins

Silent Song

Clingy-soft and warm inside,
Membrane quivery, moist and mild,
Use your hands on me,
Knead me, thrust them deep inside,
Deep down where my emotions hide.

Reach behind my barricade,
Pull me tremulous from the shade.

Ian Hopkinson

An Era

Dimming moon and rising mist.
Waves lapping against the distant shore.
The wilderness stirs as thunder rolls
And lightening breaks.
Dark cloudlets release their long-held captive
Sparkling drops of water.
The land is moistened.
The rivers and streams replenished.
Rain ceases.
Thunder quietens.
Calm reigns in magisterial silence until
Dawn, when the sun rises from sleep

Rifat Hussain

Leverington Church

There she stands with towering spire
Solid, steadfast, looking eastwards
The camel of God in a desert of sin
Awaiting the sunrise of the eternal morning
O come to her table of love and forgiveness
Guardian of mercy, giver of life
And receive the white horse in your garments of violet
Lest the leopard should be loosened amongst you
Hear the bells sound and feel the heart longing
To enter the hallowed walls of the aged eagle
Where glorious glass speaks colours of truth
Of a greatness beyond Prometheus and Deucalion
Where the shepherd of souls paints pictures of hope
More potent than the brush of Michaelangelo
And by the pit, recalls the ninetieth birthday
The viaticum, the stations, the logos

Gloria In Excelsis

Credo

Judith Howes

If Looks Could Kill

As you day dream in a small cafe
Somewhere in St. Tropez
Drooling over your new plaything
The cat with all the cream
But I stand where I first came in
Going under with nothing
I was wailing on air, nearly there
I really tried and nearly died
For your love and I would still

If looks could kill — if looks could kill
Now I hear you're in Tenerife
More food for the feast
Soon sailing again on his yacht
My, my — you've got a lot
But I have lived in your heart
My sun and moon, my little star
Now I feel like a worn out tyre
On skid row, in the mire
Yet feeling no ill will
I miss you and the thrill

If looks could kill — if looks could kill

Frank Howarth-Hynes

The Life

When at first you take a breath
you live and grow to take the test.
Each friend you make throughout your days
can change your fate and change your ways.
Time it does not wait in fear
it takes the hurt and carries tears
and even grabs and steals the joy
of endless love and your first toy.
A destiny is never planned.
The truth you never understand
and when love hits where pain has gone
you find you cannot be undone.
When you first pass your last exam
or child in arms your biggest fan.
The hopes you have, the dreams you make
can all just be a big mistake.
If when you grow you do a wrong
and you tread bad if you can't bond,
if loneliness is closing in
then hold me close and turn to win.

June Howcroft

The Mistletoe

O' parasite so beautiful
with berries round and white,
evokes the mood of Yuletide
to every child's delight.

Symbolic of fertility
with leafage verdant lush,
when proffered by the suitor
begets the maiden's blush.

When winter's grip has hardened
and frozen is the ground,
the source of song bird's winter food
the Mistletoe is found.

And yet the mind doth wander
through ancient legends told,
revered by Sorceress sinister,
and pagan Gods of old.

H. Howard

The Old & The New

My grandad often said to me
"I'll tell you how life used to be",
I listened with intent and pride
As through the years we took a ride.

Christmas brought him tears of joy
How he treasured every toy,
Once, he got a chocolate train
And a wooden soldier game.

Now and then, the brass band played,
In the park or on parade
Every year, the fair would come -
Bringing side shows, rides and fun.

Then he went to Morecambe Bay,
On a trip, just for the day
He didn't go by train or tram
But travelled in a charabanc.

In his daily working role,
He toiled hard in search of coal
Down the pit he went, quite willing
For to earn his weekly shilling.

I sometimes wonder what he'd say,
If he could see the world today
I think that he would be dismayed -
With all the progress we have made.

Catherine A. Howard

Impressions

In Flander's poppy blood fields scarecrow figures,
flesh decomposed, lay sepulchral grinning.
Imagination sculptures in a face on the sun-bleached bones,
following the contours - improves on nature.
Bible-black within a photograph, name Jack. Manipulated pawn,
though with a cause, died for King and country, scaling ochre
mud trenches, flesh torn gaping, spitting poppy blood to fertilize
a foreign ground.
For him no mournful funeral dirges sang, peaked sad faces,
tears or strong sermons placating grief. A happier place to lie,
among poppy beds beneath a vaulted sky. Kissed by the sun.
Birds heralding his demise with happy song.
Immortalized by name on marble: Jack Jones - a village lad.
Lying in poppies, remembered on stone, and annual revered
silence.
Sharing his name with faceless comrades, who dying for peace
found it in a Flander's poppy field.

Edward L.G. Holmes

Domestic Engineers

I'm a domestic engineer
it's a very demanding career.
It ruins a life, and causes much strife
People say just mother or wife?

A domestic engineer's not a job
a vocation, a lifetime does rob.
From the moment of birth, this job has some worth,
Most important of jobs on this earth.

Domestic engineer's get put down
people often say with a frown,
"Oh! What do you do? Oh! Nothing, that's true,
Some people just haven't a clue!

Domestic engineer's have no life
Just a mother, a paramour, his wife.
As a woman who's kept there's no respect left.
No wonder we're often bereft.

Domestic engineer's get no credit
their hours of toil don't rate merit.
But she does give a damn, she does what she can
She's not an appendage of man!

But domestic engineer's will surmount
their blessings they're willing to count,
I say with a plea, if some could just see,
I'm not just a housewife, I'm ME!

Lee Hoyles

The Darkness

I sit here alone, in the dark,
You couldn't even hear a dog bark.
The dark is like the coal mine,
Not even a shaft of light did shine.

The darkness is within me,
Weighs heavy on my soul.
Taking all the strength away,
As life takes its toll.

The eeriness of night,
Can give you such a fright.
When you are all alone,
And maybe far from home.

Who will light the candle?
As I sit here by myself.
Just to make me realize,
I'm not left on the shelf.

The darkness it gets brighter,
When you have faith in the Lord.
The little light within,
Will strike a final chord.

To receive a candle from a friend,
The light will never come to an end.
To pass a light from one to another,
Then we shall become sister and brother.

Mrs. E.A. Hugh

The Homeless

I walk when silent night sleeps
The windows dark all around
Hurrying footsteps quiet
A world without sound

But what muffled cry awakes
The silence of the night
Carrion vermin jaunting
No other soul in sight

Then shuffling past to nowhere
The lost ones of this life
Despair and anguish in them
Have given up[the strife

A host of stars take over
Far up in the sky
The moon queen now shines brightly
Beckons as they pass by

Oh that they had wings to fly
To dance among the stars
And drift along the moonbeams
Severing earthly bars.

Mary Hudson

Carnival Celebrations

Everything has started
They are all in full swing;
There's so much excitement
Some don't know how to begin.

On to the lorries they will climb
With laughter all around,
To see their smiling faces,
You cannot hear a sound.

The band will strike a note,
Colourful floats will start
And the carnival is marching
Capturing everyone's heart.

The colours are outstanding,
They are all dressed for show
Wanting to show their costumes
That's why they are so slow.

Each have their own entry
Whether old or young,
We will join the celebrations
As we all like some fun.

We don't enter to win or lose,
That's what it's all about;
We are here to celebrate —
To be happy and shout!

Mrs. E. M. Hughes

Our World

This is the world that God created
With Man and Woman who when mated
Produced the children who procreated
And thus began Mankind.

This is the world we can enjoy
As Man and Woman, as girl and boy
Where happy hearts and minds employ
The future of Mankind.

This is the world in which men strive
To cling to love and faith and drive
Out hate and war and keep alive
The hope of all Mankind.

This is the world in which men fraught
With anger and despair then fought
For a better life, but all war brought
Was sorrow to Mankind.

This is the world where hope is lost
Where no one stopped to count the cost
Of war and nuclear bombs, and tossed
Away all of Mankind.

June Hughes

Ladies Football

Looking so proud standing there
Pouring with rain but you didn't care
You scored the goal that won the game
So happy when the crowd called your name

Fist in the air, that scream of joy
Your father said you should have been a boy
That look to the stands to catch my eye
That's my wife I heard myself cry

All your hard work has at last paid off
I remember all those times I used to scoff
Football's a mans game, not for you
All the time your determination grew

The winning trophy is in your hand
No happier lady in all the land
No fights or hooligans just screams of delight
Even covered in mud you're a beautiful sight

The chorus of encouragement from all around
But we are used to a different sound
The sounds of love with arms entwined
So gentle so loving and oh so kind.

Taff Humphreys

She Says, He Says

She tells me go tidy your room, it's a pigsty as usual.
He says you did not wash the car, like I told you to.
He says I just don't care.
I say please listen to me and hear what I say.

She says my sister's not bad like me,
She says that I am stupid,
He says he does not disagree,
I want to tell them I'm just me.

She says that I'm a rebel, He says I'm a pest,
But I'm what's called a teenage, hormones all a mess.
I have a lot of pressures, like exams, homework and job
And just because I don't conform, I'm not bound for prison yet.

I love you all very much, and I talked to grandad yesterday,
He is a wise old man, he told me dad, that you were just the same,
When you were the age I am.

And mum, granny tells me your room was always a mess,
And you stayed out late, and smoked and drank.
You would not listen either,
So please can we compromise, with leeway each side.
And think that I will be through this phase in a few years time.

Karen Hullah

The Epiphyte

Old man near Hemmingway's sea, perched on a quay
Burnt lips, starched face, leather hands
Sun proud as a poem, sucking pipas for salt today
Eyeing yellow mushrooms on the sands

C'mon man, I'm a paragon, a parasite
But in sight no sweet bellied trout play
So he torches, takes a light
To one more Ducados, rubs his stone palms to pray

How come my biosphere's dry
I was promised a reserve
Ain't no carnivore, don't eat hamburgers
So why in all I serve
Slip me out of my niche, my flytackle industry, look
Don't we share no science, co-exist

In the Oldbook
It was just like this
You, me, the rod, a smoke, pipas and sea

I recruited you like a wife, a gilded azure
And I don't call you, you call me
I need to make a living or er ...

I got dry hands
A southern sunset, Spain behind me

Silence

And only so many creatures left, belov'd.

I. M. Humphries

A Mother Recalls

Do I remember?
The big round eyes gazing up at me,
Pearly white smile, captivating charm,
My pride and pleasure as the days rolled by.

Do I remember?
Those crazy hours with an impish tribe.
The hustle, the bustle and tireless drive,
Enjoying being in the thick of things,
And the days rolled by.

Do I remember?
The rainy day games,
Jigsaws, paints, dressing up and shops,
"You be Grandma, and I'll be Dad."
And the days rolled by.

Do I remember?
The sticky fingers of a knee-high horde,
The muddy boots, the battered shins,
Plasters, splinter, cuts and bruises,
And the days rolled by.

Yes I remember.
The hopeful dreams and enthusiastic schemes,
The happiness I recall with affection,
And cherish my memories in peace and quiet,
As the time rolls by.

Vanessa Hughes

Ethiopia

In Ethiopia, where the sun never shines,
On the people who always need to dine.
Small shrivelled faces
Eyes wide and staring.
Rice is their only hope
If the convoys ever come.

Flies spread diseases,
No doctors, nurses, clinics.
War goes on around them,
We say, 'No, can't help'.

We see it in the papers,
We see it on the news.
So be thankful for your food and clothes and shoes,
And remember to spare a thought for the people in the
        FAMINE.
            HELP!

Emma Horton (Aged 9)

Chorus Of Spring

Come join the chorus of spring,
By this fair lady led in;
Wake you from sleep,
Small flowers peep,
Sweet strains of music begin.

Come, join the chorus of spring,
Birds in their nests are akin;
In the tall trees,
Trilling their glees,
They join the chorus of spring.

Come, join this chorus and sing,
You'll soon forget everything,
Heats willed with song,
Never feel wrong,
Dance with the lady called spring.

C. M. Hopkins

Staining The Radiance

Life, like a Dome ...
... The Poet* mused:
But how could he have known
About the shards of blue and red
Which punctuate *my* many-coloured tome?

Eternity is well and truly stained,
Its radiant whiteness spattered
By the sparkling fragments of my life,
Which Life itself has playfully scattered

Onto the blankness of the Page
It spills my colours bright:
My loves, my sins, my dreams, — my fears,
Until cool Death shuts out the Light.

Then blotless White will smirk afresh once more,
Its radiance relieved of every twinkling stain.
The shattered Dome will purge itself —
— But *my* Page of Life will look far from plain!

I have no doubt that the Poet was right:
Eternity holds no unbroken Dome.
But stained bright on the hearts of living friends
My Life-quill has penned an indelible Tome.

* Percy Bysshe Shelley: *ADONAIS* (an elegy on the death of John Keats)

Margaret Hulyer

Ode To A New Knee Joint

This old arthritis eats away
At all our joints we use each day.
It slows us down, it gives us pain,
We sometimes think we'll go insane.
We pop some pills, that sometimes helps,
But then it's back, the pain, the yelps,
We think of all our childhood days
The painless hours we skipped and played.
As time goes by the pain gets worse,
It now has made us fume and curse,
There's hope at last, the surgeon claims
A new knee joint, I can arrange.
His work is perfect, to a 'T'
He knows just how to make a knee.
He wields a hammer, drill and brace,
And quickly puts the bones in place.
The 'op' is done, you're back in bed,
The pain has gone, your legs are dead.
But don't despair, they'll soon awake,
And round the ward a dance you'll take.
You're heading for the open door,
And very soon you're home once more
Completely cured and re-conditioned,
About to start an expedition.

Elizabeth Hughes

The Moth

Oh whispering, flickering, tiny thing,
With death wish 'round the lamplight sing.
'Til daylight brings your homeward charge,
Against a wall in camouflage.

Oft I wonder what you eat
If you dream when you're asleep.
What satisfaction can you gain
By beating on a window pane.
Spreading panic in your confusion
When through a gap you gain intrusion,
Could this be the end you choose?
Crushed to death by yesterday's news.

John Hagyard

Disenchantment

How well behind that ready smile,
Ingenuous and kind, those friendly ways,
You hid your full duplicity!

How well behind those candid eyes,
Whose light would daily shine to dazzle me,
You hid your real mendacity!

And even now, although my own are clear,
And all the sparkle of the sun has left my day,
My painful need is yet to know you as you were,
And not remember you in any other way.

Roxane Houston

All In The Dark

The little kids who roam the streets
Well after it is dark,
Do they look for Martin
Or is it just a lark?
Whatever their intention
It is rather plain to see,
They should all be back at home
With family having tea.
To me it is so very sad
The way things have turned out,
When these children grow up
Will they know what they're about?
It would be so much nicer
If someone thought a while,
And let these kids have futures
That sometimes bring a smile.

Audrey Hoysted

Castles In The Air

When we were young, we built our dreams
Like castles in the air
Rosy plans for a future
In which we two can share

Some dreams are fulfilled as the years pass by
We rejoice that luck came our way
Together with our hopes and plans
We've lived to see this day

Sometimes our dreams are shattered
Our plans all go awry
But while we still have each other
There seems less need to cry

Then one of us is left alone
It's time for a single plan
For a very uncertain future
Lived out any way we can

Half of what was a couple
Building dreams alone, harder to do
But we must try making a life for ourself
In an empty world without you.

Peggy Hunter

Life and Times of Jimmy Caterpillar

Little Jimmy caterpillar lifted his head
I do like these green leaves, he said.
There's plenty to eat
Oh my! What a treat.

He ate so much his skin felt tight
And very soon he got a fright
When his skin split open very wide
A new little Jimmy appeared inside.

As a new day dawned he gave a big grin
When he found that he'd grown a whole new skin
With beautiful colours that warned off his foes
And stretched all the way down to his toes.

He continued to eat and got quite full
But life for Jimmy just couldn't be dull.
The wonderful colours that appeared in his skin
Were much better than being plain and thin.

When his skin shrivelled off he got quite cold
And said I must be getting old.
As a pupa now he could not talk
Hanging on to a piece of stalk.

During winter's sleep, reconstruction anew
Made his form split in two
Though Jimmy's old life was spent
As a butterfly he emerged, heaven sent.

Sheila Hutchinson

The Sheep and the Goats

Whom in the end, O holy terrible One,
Will You claim as Yours? He,
The rich, fat, white man, quoting John-three-sixteen from his
      leather-bound scriptures
And followed all the days of his life by goodness and mercy?

Or starving, beaten and broken by a burning sun
The child, in whose short life never sounded Your name,
Who knew not gospel, nor heaven, nor any thing
But what it is to suffer?
Whom have You chosen to leave, whom to bring?
For whom life was hell must death be the same?

The Power, the Glory, the Right to Choose, for Thine is the Kingdom.
Who are the Sheep and the Goats?

Sarah Houston

City Of Chester

This ancient city, so grand and old,
Holds a million stories, still untold.
Winds that whisper round sandstone walls,
Still carry the cries, the battle calls.
The rolling Dee holds her secrets deep,
She croons them softly, whilst fishermen sleep.
The sighing Rows will tell all they know,
Of loves and heartaches of long ago.
So, listen hard, for all she tells is true.
Let her spin her ghostly tales to you.

Patricia Ingram

Epitaph

Heavy is the burden of my death,
So cold the earth, my sullied bones wet from the worms.
I am dead four and twenty year.
Left in the blossom of my youth,
I never believed a man could die of a broken heart
I am witness and victim both.

Loam my blanket, a rock my comforting pillow.
Insects devour my idle bones.
Supine I rest, till the world above dissolves.
Past is the rancid stench of my fetid flesh,
I am nobody but bone,
Once a kingdom where spiders languished
In the windows of my soul.

The marbled tablet stands six feet above my head,
It reads my epitaph to the visitors of my grave,
Who never come.
All this for a love so deep,
Should I not have loved.
For sin, I am condemned to eternal sleep.

Mark Jordan

Adolescence

Reach for your star of devotion
    whenever there's a starry view.
For when you've a star of devotion
    all your fondest dreams come true.
Stars have a way of revealing, a
    heart that will remain sincere.
In a wonderful way reappearing
    once your true love is near.
Choose the bright blue shining star
    flirtation it foretells.
While with the gold and silv'ry star,
    comes love then wedding bells.
So reach for your star of devotion.
    Remember as they shine above.
May you find a star that will lead you
    to the one you truly love.

J.C. Arthur Ince

For Lorraine

She wore it like a warm cloak,
It clung to the soft pink folds of her dress,
And sparkled
In eyes so bright and shining.
Pervading the hazy air,
It glimmered over children on the lawns,
And danced
In a smile so rich and carefree.
She wore it all around her,
Intangible
And yet so real,
The happiness that was my sister's,
On her Wedding Day.

Juliette Ireland

Maudie

Maudie was four, she lived with Grandma
Who was kind, but often got tired.
Coping with Maudie's long, tangled hair was tiring
While Maudie wriggled and protested as she combed.
Grandma found the solution by cutting it short.

Maudie didn't mind her new short haircut,
She was pleased to be free from the painful combings.
One day, workmen arrived to mend the roof of Grandma's cottage.
Maudie liked to watch them as they worked, but they teased her.

"You're not a little girl" they said, "You're a boy."
"I'm not a boy," Maudie protested, "I'm a little girl."
"No you're not", they teased, "little girls have long hair."

Maudie was cross, stamped her foot,
"I'm not a boy," she said crossly, "I'm a little GIRL,"
At the same time lifting her calf-length dress, exposing her little pink bloomers.
"SEE," she cried.

The laughter of the workmen brought Grandma to the door,
Who promptly marched Maudie indoors and sent her to bed
Without any tea.
Maudie sobbed in her room, not understanding why Grandma was so cross.

Maudie is a Grandma now, and often recalls this tale.
She can laugh now,
As Grandma probably did, in retrospect.

Mrs. M.E. Ireland

What Is It?

This 'commodity' can be lost or found,
It's silent, doesn't make a sound.
Like the wind you can't see or touch,
Sometimes you have a lot, sometimes not much.
It was made when the earth began
And through all the centuries it has ran.
It can be fast or slow or just a bore,
Often we wish we could have some more.
You can have it on your side or hands
Especially musicians in a band.
It is a great healer in times of sorrow
You can take heart and look to tomorrow.
It can be borrowed if you are past seventy
And often proves to be quite plenty.
It's never found to be standing still
Just goes on and on at its will.
Have you discovered the topic of this rhyme
Something we can't do without, it's TIME.

Mrs. M. Jackson

The Silent Welcome

They stood out among the rest
Beside the brassware and china best
And suddenly caught my roving eye
Those smiling clowns perched way up high
With bended knees and dangling toes
Arms outstretched in welcome pose.
Such a warmly invitation
To our east coast destination
Where my friend did loan to me
His caravan so near the sea.
And on that day I vowed that I
Would myself go out to buy
My own clown of similar mode
To welcome all to my abode.
So now when guests upon me call
There to greet them on the wall
Perched high among the bric-a-brac
My cheery clown sits looking back
With bended knees and arms held wide
Inviting all to come inside,
A silent welcome so sincere
From my precious souvenir.

Kevin G. Ibbitson

Love Likened To A Spider's Web

Love's likened oft to a butterfly,
A gentle, fair, fluttering thing,
But shall I compare love to a spider's web
And the soft silks spun therein.

Silken threads set with jewels
'Pon a dewy morn,
Purer than child's tender tear.
Fragile threads kissed with frost
'Pon a winter's dawn,
Like a crystal chandelier.

Oh, how fragile, how harmless, this gentle lace
Softly veiled upon nature's sweet form,
But be wise and consider its other face
Whither 'pon careless souls are worn.

For where danger seems least, hides the greatest threat,
Snares await behind beauty's facade.
Like the web, love's a cleverly woven net
Leaving votaries oftentimes scarred!

Timothy C. Jefferies

A Country Hop

Take your partners two by two
yes, a square dance now to do.
Honour your girl, if you please
have a bow and bend your knees.
Listen to the caller now
for the steps and the know how.
Country music for the ear
laughter, joy and lots of cheer.
Grand chain, star and do-si-do,
basket, cast-off, heel and toe,
promenade around the room,
polka - send away all gloom.
Circle left then to the right
oh what fun and such delight.
To the middle yet again
sing along with the refrain.
Strip the willow time to try
flying Scotsman passes by
People simply in a trance
fun for all at a barn dance.

Margaret Jackson

Fog

The anxious car goes slow in miles
Of gloom; towards us on the road
The glow-worms crawl in pairs.
A smoky creature creeps, inquisitive
To touch the windows, floats disdainfully away
To far lost fields and the obscured horizons
Where should be trees, but Asgard giants tower
And skeletons of pylons march tall from the dead.

Relief should come when Midlands lifted
Mists; yet how I curiously resented
The glaring affront that blinded
And made the journey normal, seeing monotony.
Why did I feel so naked, so discovered
Like some wrong-doer caught out by the switch?
I was a mole forced into daylight
Deprived of my dark deep underground.

Wheels ate quickly at the Northern Road.
Then — veils of vapour made another shroud
To wrap the Sun, and gave me back
To dark imagining; hunchback barns prepared
For treason; cathedral cooling-towers loomed
And threatened. Shawls of grey geese drifted,
Settled damp around the pig-mud farms and fell
On the Crow figure, receding into night.

Patricia Ives

Nostalgia

When you dream of passing years,
Of all the happenings, mixed with tears,
The Precious moments of these days,
You cling to memories in so many ways,
Was it a sister, brother, mum or dad,
Reminding you of presents, that once you had,
In a drawer there is a toy,
Reminding you of yesterday's joy,
And folded carefully in a book,
When no one's there, you take a look,
You see a photo of a lad,
Who wrote the first love letter that you had.
It could be a tree with initials on,
Or a five-bar gate you had sat upon,
A farm, a cottage on the downs,
You recall the moments and the sounds,
The winding lane on its way to the sea,
Those games and fun, happy as can be,
You planned your life with special care,
With love and romance, with someone to share,
The years are passing and you are older,
Those dreams and schemes, a little less bolder,
Don't think of the future, doubts will cease,
Nostalgia brings you dreams and peace.

W.G. Jackman

Flow Gently Sweet Reason

Flow gently sweet reason
Carry my ship of fortune along
Under sun the baked viaducts of time
Toward the salmon leap of uncertainty
Onward ever onward
   'tween the twin whirlpools of mendacity and greed
And into the translucent calm of hope.

Flow gently sweet reason
Through still shadowed green lagoons
Cocooned in isolated aloofness
Onward ever onward
   toward the wide bar mouth of hope
So windswept and fierce
Yet so watchful of bewildered mariners
Where spume capped waves vie for importance
   with seaweed oases.

Flow gently sweet reason
Follow the warmth of the generous sun
Into the ocean wide where kittiwakes and the stormy
petrel hover for food
And basking whales scoff at the midnight stars.

Flow gently sweet reason
Toward the landscape of love
Carry my ship of fortune along
Running the gauntlet of sargasso rocks
Into a sun-filled delight
A kaleidoscope of heavenly vibes
To home.

Paul Harvey Jackson

Got A Conscience?

The key is in my hand
ready to disappear into the lock
the time is now here
and I am ready for it.

All summer long I have wondered
wondered what she could possibly have
hidden secretly away from my eyes
and all the world's eyes in this box.

What could it possibly be?
In this small rectangular box
stolen away, smothered in blankets
deep in the chest at the foot of her bed.

With secrecy it has been kept
secretly and distrustfully
to never see the light of day
that is — until now.

So here I stand
ready to push in the key
no remorse is burdening my conscience
and I am smiling inwardly to myself.

The key fits inside the lock snugly
just a little twist of the wrist
and the wooden lid clicks open
as I take a look inside.

Tony Jackson

The Old Woman

She sits by her window each endless day
Watching the world as it goes on its way
Wandering back to times of the past
The same stage but a different cast.

She lingers in childhood and sees once more
Her beloved parents, a red front door
Now a girl with long brown hair
And a young man handsome, tall and fair.

Tears wet her cheeks as with rapturous pride
She walks yet again her husband's bride
In this little house they made their life
A dutiful father, a mother and wife.

Now all her loved ones have gone before
And wait for her on another shore
Till then she'll spend each endless day
Wandering the path of memory's way.

Maureen T. Isaacs

Entropy Rose

There is an entropy rose of burning light
A rose of burning flames and dark clouds
And soft rain falling like a thousand waves of darkness,
Black rain like tears from the sorrowing god of death.
There is a rose that is
The ultimate gift of a warrior race,
Mankind's shout of glory to the distant stars
Mankind's dying whisper to the universe
It is a rose that fills the sky
Fills every waking moment and the darkest dreams,
It is the most beautiful demon that every breathed fire
The most resplendent dragon to fly the heavens
 The single rose that proves the emptiness of heaven
The darkness of the clouds and the coldness of the air,
The sun that we will never see again.
Too much of our glory in the entropy rose
Too much of our darkness colours the petals of this rose,
This darkest joy of ours that waits, and waits, to fall.

Daniel Jupp

We Are

We are but floating fragments
akin to fractions of the whole.
Belonging to a larger realm
of Cosmic Grace
that couples with each soul.
And proffers no flight,
no escape for Time or even Space
to slip its Godly clasp
and its eternal celestial embrace.
How sweet is this honeyed ceaseless thought
that concedes our Immortality.

Graham Jenkins

The Dark

I curl up in bed and I switch out my light,
It's d-d-dark in my room in the middle of the night,
I close my eyes, I shut them tight,
Because every small noise gives me a fright.
I curl up in a ball as small as I can,
"Oh no what about the boogy man?"
My heart starts beating faster,
My skin starts to leak,
From under my covers I just take a peek,
HE'S HERE, HERE
My door starts to creak,
My legs are like jelly, I feel so weak.
Oh, it's only my dog who starts to bark.
With him at my side
"WHO'S AFRAID OF THE DARK?"

Rachel Jarvis

To Joe

Poor old Joe had had his day,
He used to pull the milkman's dray.
His oldest pal, one of the best,
The milkman now was laid to rest.

The streets in rain he'd walk no more,
To stop and start from door to door.
Sad faced and lonely by the gate
He just seems to stand and wait.

The grass blows unheeded at his feet,
Joe puts down his head, but not to eat.
One day I'm sure he hopes to find
The old man who'd been so kind.
Now to join his friend who's past
Peace to Joe has come at last.

Vera F. Harding

Life and Death, Good and Evil

Live,
Die,
Laugh,
Cry.

Give,
Take,
Make,
Break.

Help,
Ignore,
Love,
Abhor.

Heal,
Scar,
Aid,
Mar.

Please,
Annoy,
Create,
Destroy.

God,
Devil,
Good,
Evil.

S.L. Jackson

The Tragedy Of A Young Miner

A young man lay dying, beneath a great rock,
He was crushed by the weight up against a big chock,
Many a year he had worked down the pit,
But he knew now this time that for him this was it.

Down in the darkness no lights could he see,
Where were his workmates to help set him free,
The pain that he bore was intensely so great,
That he cursed the whole pit with all bitterness and hate,

As he lay there in pain and breathless with fear,
A thought passed his mind of the ones he loved dear,
His young wife called May and the children they had,
He could picture their faces, and shouting "Where's Dad,"

Hour after hour dragged slowly away,
Bleeding and shaken he started to pray,
Then suddenly the darkness became very bright.
And a voice that he knew shouted "Are you all right."

A few years have passed since he last worked down there,
But I'm told that he lives with his family somewhere,
They say he's much better but his nerve he has lost,
Yet I'm sure he's still happy, if your counting the cost.

E.K. Jepson

The Hand

One hand reaching out, ready to help or close to a touch,
Or is it a hand wanting or could it be taking too much?
Does it want to be clasped in a handshake firm and tight,
Is it feeling along life for someone without the gift of sight?
Could it be waving good-bye or offering a greeting,
To one in a crowd or at a chance meeting?
Is it aiding to soothe a child's cut finger or hurt pride?
Is it making a choice — having to decide?
Does it want to clench up and hit out in anger,
Or conducting the sounds of a sweet singing choir?
Is it ready to take when eyes are looking the other way?
Is it ready to halt someone going astray?
Does it want to click fingers to a modern beat,
Or waft cool air on to a brow, red with heat?
Is it calming down in trouble and strife?
It could be all of things in the span of its life!

Shauna Innes

Aspiration

Rare are those moments when my soaring thoughts
Go singing, winging to the higher peaks
Of consciousness, and all my soul is laved
With golden waves of joy; when, poised and free,
Deathless and fearless in that sea of light,
I know the truth of life's infinity ...
And then the glory fades, and though a trace
Of that pure radiance lingers for a while,
Illumining the dark, drear ways of earth,
'Tis but a poor reflection from the source -
That inner, solar light, which soon is dimmed
By doubts and fears and all my worldly cares,
Leaving me yearning on the moon-cold shore.

Marjorie T. Johnson

Bereavement

The sudden stabbing shock of fear and anguish
Brings realization of the fatal blow —
Then weeping uncontrollably is natural,
Like rain in torrents, pouring out such woe.

But when the heart and mind cannot believe it
So unprepared, without a last farewell —
Our desolation numb like anaesthetic,
The valley of the shadow is our hell.

Yet time drags on, and brings a new perspective;
As winter turns to spring, then summer blooms;
The memories heal, not time, with new horizons
Then death is seen as rest, and not as doom.

Margaret Jones

Reflections

While waiting for sweet sleep to steal upon my mind
I feel the tender half-remembered years of youth
When time was kind,
When self was all, yet innocence abounded.
How astounded we would have been
To have foreseen the tide of progress
Surging through the marching years with unrelenting ease,
Littering the seas with human flotsam left behind.

And yet for those with stamina to ride the waves of life,
To philosophise when torn with strife
And take each eddy to renew their strength,
At length will find the peace and joy each girl and boy
Was hoping for.
The memories flutter through my drowsy fading brain,
Calming the strain, till oblivion fills this weary wife.

Jill James

The Proud Dragon

Blue dragon in your cave so bright
Your fiery breath provides the light
You've woken from your daytime sleep
To venture into the forest deep
You look up to the starry sky
Your wings outstretched you start to fly
As high as the tallest of the trees
The beat of your wings disturbs their leaves
You're going towards the mountain side
Through the cool refreshing air you glide
With your head held high you look so proud
You go past the moon with its array of cloud
You begin to disappear out of sight
You fly away into the night.

Joanne Jowitt

Bliss

The softness of a downy pillow.
The sensual touch of a weeping willow.
The sweet caress of a gentle finger.
The summer scents on a breeze, that linger.
Dreams in the peace of a country dawn,
Held in the arms of a golden morn.
Such simple things make a life of bliss.
Who needs more than this, than this?

Paddy Jupp

A Vision

Fearing hope had deserted the poet
Before weary eyes a vision appears
Just like a dream, though this is reality.

Strolling along dim lit road, a cold wind blows
Darkish sky opens,
Colourful light beams down, covering the poet.
Tumbling over into mud filled gutter.

Struggling to break free of broken leaves
Transforms a creator with spiritual needs
Into a butterfly of wisdom, purpose complete.

Alan Jones

Injustice

"Mr. Granville Jones
You stand before this court accused
Of trying to do the right thing.
To this charge, you have pleaded 'not guilty',
Claiming you have led the model life,
Combining alcohol with ignorance
Just like the Government leaflet suggests.
But I put it to you, Mr. Jones, that this is a lie;
We have witnesses, even your own son,
Who have heard you condemn this life;
Neighbours have told of your outbursts,
Our doctors, Mr. Jones, have medically proved
The presence of a conscience.
And finally, massive quantities of guilt have been found
At your house.

It is my job to pass judgement.
Society doesn't need troublemakers like you, Mr. Jones,
I therefore sentence you to life imprisonment."

Next Case.

Geraint Jones

Christmas

We hear them carol Christmas,
It is a winter day.
The world is very troubled
And skies above are grey.

We hear them carol Christmas
And tell of One who came,
To be to all a Saviour
And now comes just the same.

To heal the broken hearted
And take our sins away
And give new life forever.
Listen to what they say.

The berries are red on the holly
And light through darkness has shone,
Thanks be to God forever and ever,
Jesus our Saviour is born.

Hope and strength and comfort
Cheer the future way,
As we hear the joyous carols,
Upon this winter day.

Gwendoline James

Mendacity

To you I might seem to be made of clay
but I'm really made of rock.
So you can hold and squeeze me
I won't break.
What you see when you look at me
is solid and stoic
somewhat deceptive though ... I believe
since I'm really made of rock ... not clay.

You may think I'm made of ... glass
fragile and dainty to the touch,
I won't break though,
as I am firm and solid I know that much ...
I won't break
should you wish ... to put me to the test.

You can try to handle me
a little bit rougher than rough
place your arms around me
and squeeze me tight ... I won't break,
you'll see that I'm right
if you should ... but squeeze me with all you might.

Handle me tough ... but hold me gentle,
yet rough,
I won't be scared to tell you
when ... I've had enough.

Semba Jallow-Rutherford

Wind

Breeze describes its self
Swirled in flexible grass
Bushes belly wobble
Giggling greens
Flight assisting
Constantly searching
Swiftly unseen

Trees show their respect
Corrugated waters
Distortedly reflect

Unselfishly reveal your power
Strength we foolishly judged
In mere m.p.h.

Greg Jones

Gentle Loving ...

Gentle loving
Caring smile
Warm laughter
Selfless consciousness
Breathing
Enjoying
Indescribable content
Graspless tingling
Anticipation
Waiting, longing
Holding forever
Yet never owning
Language inadequate
Words unnecessary
Loving, totally.

Colette Jones

Aberfan

Their breath comes through the faithful flowers,
    To them the freshening years shall cling,
Their precious lives still hold the golden hours,
    And mountain winds to them shall sing.

God has not stilled their sparkling play
    By stream or hill, around each tumbling field,
Have you not heard their voices say
    "Tis your silent grief that bids our joy to yield?"

No timeless ghosts have they become,
    But children of the great white light
Blessed by the moon, warmed by the sun,
    And kissed by the stars through the veil of the night.

Emlyn C. Jones

Lonely Tree in My Garden in Winter

What is it you see oh lonely tree,
Patiently you stand in your frozen land.
Do you feel the wind through your naked arms,
In the mid of the night.
Do you shiver in fright, or do you dream on
of the summer that has gone.
A lovely green tree you again will be, meanwhile
your thoughts are your own.
So who am I to wish them to be known.

Mrs. Q. Jarvis

Death Of The Day

Feel the last drawn breath of day,
Her screams are hushed, death is on the way.
Dressed for the funeral the world turns black,
Evening was her friend now he stabs her in the back.
His knife was sharp, blood on the clouds ran red,
Raped of her pleasure the day is silent, forever dead.
Knowing how she died, understanding her pain,
Scorning the night, pouring out tears, came the rain.
The wind to her aid too late came flying,
Angry at himself now howling and crying.
For her sun-filled smile his heart did please,
She softened his stormy tempest to a slight warm breeze.
Yet submit to me had coaxed the reaper of the night,
Pleasures of the dark are sweeter than those of the light.

Christine Johnson

The Season Of Good Cheer

The cards are up, the tree's ablaze with light
And very soon now, every little mite,
Must climb upstairs, then all those sleepy heads,
Will be tucked up so snuggly in their beds.

Once more, it is the season of good cheer,
When Christmas Day is drawing very near.
We think of loved ones, here and far away
While opening our presents, bright and gay.

But, we should think of someone in a manger,
Who, for all men, heeded no danger.
'Tis the Saviour, whom the shepherds sped to see,
Even Kings fell down, upon their bended knee.

Shirley A. James

A Line Of Dancers

A line of dancers
Shoulders touching, stand impassive
Before an empty stage.
The darkened space beckons them,
And once they enter
A whirlwind of movement
Delights the viewer,
As they transpose their bodies
From one position to the next,
Veering to avoid one another,
Then, in time, interlocking,
Creating emotional shapes,
Caressing each other
In clenched positions on the floor,
Rising to a hypnotic crescendo
Then, finally, rapturous consummation.
When the ritual commenced
The dancers were at the mercy of the audience,
Now it is the audience
Who are at their mercy,
Enticed by their movements,
Possessed by their passion,
Captured in their own seduction.

Kevin G. Jones

The Battle

I thought of the blood that was wasted
Flowing deep from each man's core
Draining into the ageless soil
As Longsword clashed with Claymore

I thought of the hatred that each man had
Both tribe's thinking the other was wrong
How instead of being willing to share the land
Both claimed it as their own

I thought of how each man was a mother's son
And a family would have cried
When it's men folk did not return home
From the border countryside

I thought of shouts and curses
Filling the air in days gone by
How life seemed so expendable
And it was acceptable to die

But now the air is silent
And we stand here feeling the chill
As we remember the carnage
In the Battle for Halodon Hill

Stuart Jeffrey

Someone To Listen

Wouldn't it be nice if things weren't as they seem
I'd wake to find it was all a bad dream
But as I lay here alone on a cold winter's night
Nobody cares if I am all right.
If only Mum had listened, if only she'd tried,
I wouldn't have had to live with his lies.
All I want is a cuddle, someone to care
What's wrong with everybody, life just isn't fair.
Things were great with just me and Mum
But then she had to marry that bum.
He sat me on his knee and touched my young skin
He'd tell me it's normal, I just couldn't win.
He made me promise not to say a word
Children should be seen and never heard,
But then one day I couldn't take anymore
So I told my Mum, but she showed me the door.
She didn't believe me, she said "it's not true"
She loved him you see, what could I do.
So I left that day, it's six months or more
Since I've seen my Mum, since she showed me the door
So I lay her alone only fourteen years old
Wrapped up in newspaper to keep out the cold.

Karen Jarvis

Love Token

I open the drawer of my bedside
Cabinet roughly, and it tumbles into reach.
A white heart-shaped pebble from the beach.

Something that the Emma found, and at that
One love-musing moment, thought of me.
Capturing that shaken second in eternity.

A cherished memento of that day.
Like an old photograph but three dimensional.
More enduring. Less conventional.

For over twelve years our children numbered two,
Until you bounced in, you little mavourneen.
A joyful day and what a joy you've been!

You must have begun like this, a small
Soft pebble in your mother's womb.
Now you've left our seashore. Climbed the combe.

Turning your stone pledge over in my hand,
I read your message, cast upon the beach by Triton.
Love Daddy. 1980. Brighton.

Dick Jarrett

Dancing Class

When we go to the dancing class
we learn to point our toe.
We hold our hands above our heads
while we stand in a nearly straight row.
There's a lady who plays the piano
she wears a hat with a pink cardigan
and smiles at us ever so nicely,
we smile back to her, when we can.
Sometimes we have a concert
when we really dance our best,
Teacher lets us wear our new tu-tu's
and we do not wear our vests.
I think when I am grown up
a ballerina I will be, but,
when I mentioned this to Mummy,
She smiled, and said "let's wait and see."

Maureen B. Johnson

Torment

I miss you when I wake up in the morning,
I miss you when I settle down at night,
I need you when I stop to have a breather,
And when I down my tools to have a bite.

I miss you when I call in at my local,
And yearn to feel the comfort you can give,
But I'm determined not to let you coax me,
For I've decided now, I want to live.

So you can stuff yourself back in your packet
And I'll imagine that we never met
For no matter how I feel I'll not be tempted
I'll never smoke another cigarette.

Jessie Jackson

Uninvited Guests

The pungent smell of sweet tobacco
Lingering in the air.
Crumpled cover, indented cushion,
Tells me you've been there.

I catch a glimpse as you go past,
When I walk into a room.
I hear your footsteps on the stair
In the deepening evening gloom.

You cause a draft as you go past,
Papers flutter to the floor.
Then the rattle of a handle,
As you go out the door.

I think you have a lady with you,
I hear the rustle of her dress.
The heady perfume that she wears
Smells of flowers, sweet and fresh.

Her tread is light upon the floor,
As from room to room she goes.
The nursery chair her favourite place,
As the rocking motion shows.

Some would say the house was haunted,
With people from the past.
To me you are not ghosts at all,
But my uninvited guests.

Joan Jemson

Teenage Rebellion

I listened to a recording today
Of my mother and I.
My mother was thirty two,
I was six months.
She spoke to me with affection,
Her love beamed with every word.
She was my life line,
And I was hers.

But what now?
The days of caring words have past.
My aggression
Makes her tone bitter and distant.
I am now but an object,
A barrier to her happiness.
I torment her every breath,
A denial I feel compulsory
To my teenage existence.

My compassion is now erased.
I appreciate nothing,
And want everything.
But a mother can only do so much,
A child can only push so far.

I pushed too far,
Now she is gone.

Anna Jefferson

Now It's November

Now it's November, trees shed their leaves,
Whispering softly, for each heart that grieves,
For those who no longer await a new dawn,
Who left in their wake, a memory to mourn.

Now summer has yielded to deep autumn gold,
Their legends of valour, return to unfold,
As bright as the poppies we proudly display,
That grace Flanders Field, in a scarlet array.

Now it's November, hearts fill with pride,
Lingering always, for brave men who died,
For us who would one day inherit this land,
Their blood stained forever, the pale golden sand.

Now shifting in silence by oceans that weep,
Where under whose covers, lie comrades asleep.
While we who are grateful still journey on,
Etched in our memories, those who have gone.

Bill Jamieson

Who Am I?

If I were to tell you who I am,
You wouldn't hate me so.
You wouldn't want to take my land,
Or spoil the crops I grow.
Your guns would cease to point my way,
Your anger would soon die.
If ever you did find the truth,
And learn just who am I.

No barriers would bar our way,
No country, creed or race,
If we just looked beyond all that,
Our fears we could erase.
I'll tell you now, so you will know.
Then peace will be our plan.
I'm not your enemy, it's true.
I am your fellow man.

P.A. Ibell

Gentle John

Gentle John desperately stirred the blood in the bucket
As it gushed from the pig's throat,
A torrent of red hot life;
Carefully laid the snares
At the secret entrances to earth's womb,
That held the soft pulsating furry bodies;
Softly shooed the fine-faced lambs
Up the ramp into the dark box,
Which would open to the butcher's knife;
Turned away in shame from the laughing monstrous men
Who indolently admitted the dangling submissive birds,
Undead, into the plucking machine;

Pushed through hostile hedges,
And grovelled in the damp earth
To unjaw the sparrow from the cat's maw;
Picked up the frog
Which pushed fearfully into his hand,
Sending his heart leaping to his mouth,
As he bore it bravely to the safety of the ferns.

I've heard him tell those tales before,
Picking at that childhood sore.
A thousand rescues and a million actions kind
Will not erase, oh, gentle John,
Those murders from your mind.

Audrey Jones

Billy

He walks down the pathway un-aided
Though slowly and forceful each step,
His future — a little more rosy, but
A long way to go even yet.

His life is a permanent struggle
Such obstacles to overcome,
Tears and frustration are part of his life
And for Billy — that's just begun.

Such effort is needed right now as he strives
And a teardrop is visible too,
He continues to walk now against all the odds
And finds inner strength to renew —

His faltering footsteps, are much slower now
But determined he's giving his all,
Please let him make it, the tension is great
He stumbles but he doesn't fall.

So we're willing you Billy come on, love, don't stop
Your goal is a few yards away,
We know you can do it you're nearly there now.
Oh God, let him make it we pray.

We are proud of you Billy, we hug you and cry
For your courage — you bring us such joy,
And you will give hope and incentive to
Some other proud mother's boy.

Mrs. M. Johnston

The Long Sleep

Weary am I, and weak of limb
My once bright eyes are growing dim
I gladly rest my weary head
Down upon the welcome bed

The doctor came, my pulse he took
Then wrote in his black book
The doctor mumbled to my wife
I'm sorry, my dear, but that is life

I know now what is wrong with I
Very soon I am to die
He gave an injection in my vein
To comfort me, and ease the pain

My loving wife beside me on the bed
Gently caressed my weary head
God bless and you to keep
My beloved in your long sleep

The time will come by and by
We shall meet again, you and I
My love for you my dear I keep
Until I too reach the long sleep

We shall meet in God's heavenly land
For ever wander hand in hand
This joyous place with no tomorrow
Most of all ... no pain ... no sorrow

David Johnston

Reflections

The colours of the rainbow
The dew upon the rose,
Reflecting in the babbling brook,
Laughing softly as it flows.
So alike our life, the silver stream
Its ripples shade our mood,
As its bubbles burst then settle
In a quiet interlude.

Crimson sun at early morning
Fires our spirits with its beams,
Lovely pastel shades of evening
Mirror quiet thoughts and dreams.
Nature's glory, every blending
To our whims of patterned ream
Tells a story never ending
Like the ripples of a stream.

Crystal river, stony patches,
Life's endurance can't explain,
Twisting, turning as it snatches
Coloured pebbles — washed in rain.
Just a pick a mix of colour
Which will change from day to day,
But a rainbow always follows
When the sky is tinged with grey.

Beatrice Johnson

Mind Of The Mad

I'm a bat, a bird, a butterfly,
I'm anything I want to be in my visionary mind,
No one can see, so no one can deny,
I'm safe and secure behind my imaginary door,
No one can open it, for there is no key,
Lock me away they can, but happy I will be,
I don't want help, just privacy.

I can fly, I can run, I can see, I can hear
The echoing laughter of mixed up minds behind
Locked away doors.
The tranquility of loneliness, rewards madness in its Self.

I don't want to be free from these four walls,
They're giving me peacefulness to the full,
No interruptions, no answers to give, no questions to have.

Have mercy on a stowaway mind, and let me stay
Till the end of my time,
Until I've emerged ready to fly, from my haven
Of four white walls.

Miss G. Johnston

The Bird Cage

Tall dark shadows creep across the room
As the summer sun streaks in.
At first glance the woman seems at peace
As she lays upon her bed
With her long blonde hair and alabaster skin.

But take another look for nothing's as it seems.
Her hair is unreal and her eyes are glazed
Imprisoned in a body beyond repair.

The bars on her bed cast shadows on the wall
Creating an illusion of a giant bird cage.
But this prison holds no fear
To the woman on the bed
For it will vanish when the sun goes down.

Disease is her cage of no escape
Gnawing at her body — this enemy within.
Doctors and drugs have fought and lost
Leaving her to linger on.
All she can do is silently pray
To be released from this prison of pain
By the welcoming kiss of eternity.

Moira Johnson

That Close Saturday

That close Saturday,
Sun shimmering on the rivered valley,
Dazzling snow-capped mountains
Supreme against slate-grey February skies,
Our love rose to new
Heavenly heights.

White gulls floated upwards
Brightening the leaden sky.
Fur-coated trees firm and erect
On the brow of our valley.
From our mirrored window we watched
Our natural world.

That day we were so close.
Our love covered us
As snow blanketing the valley.
We didn't need to talk,
The icy still silence
Warmth on our heated breath.

We were together then,
As close as ever two could be.
We must stay true
To each other, in harmony
With nature, with seasons
With ourselves.

C. Jones

My Village

Rokelunda was its name,
Now Rockland St. Mary — Both the same,
A village in the fair county
Of Royal Norfolk near the sea.

A shop, a church, a pub, a broad
Where would-be sailors step aboard
Their holiday boats — just moored beside
The pond where many ducks do hide.

And over the road a school is there,
It has been for many a year.
With indoor toilets now a treat —
Saves urgent dash for little feet!

The Gardening Club, the WI,
The Good Companions by and by.
All for the older villagers,
Their own small niche — both his and hers.

Du different is our motto here.
Our words are strange to many an ear.
What's dwile or mawther, do you see?
Or bishy-bishy barny-bee?

And now it's time to take our leave
Of this fair county — don't you grieve,
Come visit when you're down this way
And see the truth of what we say.

Anne E. Jones

Life Before My Eyes

I look at the world through rose-coloured glasses,
I peek at life as it slowly passes,
I test the water of human kindness,
I come face-to-face with human blindness.

I drown in the pool of unrest,
I take the road that looks best,
I smell the rot of all human grief,
I look into hell where there is no relief.

I sit on the fence and take no side
I watch the poor swallow their pride
I see the starving pitifully thin,
I notice the greedy with their lecherous grin.

I watch and watch like a man possessed,
I am so tired I need to rest,
I turn to see my soul rise from the bed,
I am filled with peace for I am dead.

Mrs. H.J. Johnson

Vedere

I can smell you sweet love, but you're not there,
I can taste your warm scent, but you're not there,
I hear your comforting words, I feel your protecting arms,
I sense your great pity, but you're not there.
For all of these things I cannot see, and yet, I have life.

In my mind I can see your warm tender face
In my mind I am running in the games that we played
I remember the sun, the sky and the trees,
I remember the grey days, the snow and the rain.
But as I get older, these memories will fade, will I forget?
And yet I have life.

I will learn how to listen for the birds in the sky,
I will learn how to play again, though I'll always be bluff.
I will sense the wind changing, your mood swings sway.
I will taste the joys and woes, and the sweet smell of
success.
I will feel like I'm whole again, without any sight,
But yes ... I have life.

Graeme Johnson

A New Tomorrow

I would like to see a new tomorrow
One like it used to be.
With no locks on doors, and cheery smiles,
And children running safe and free.

When summer then, was really warm,
And Winter was cold and chill.
Do you remember those walks through snow so crisp,
And sledging down that steep hill.

Swimming in the sea,
When it was clean and blue.
Sunbathing, donkey rides, and walks on piers.
And making sandcastles for two.

Why did we lose such joy of life,
And let it all pass by.
To be left with only memories,
And for those things lost, all we do is sigh.

The world has lost its humour.
It is weighed down with doubts and fears.
And has taken many roads along the way,
Some of which have led to tears.

It is not too late to change the world.
Let us not sit around and mope.
But who am I to dare to dream.
Do you not know me yet — my name is HOPE.

Joan Parry Jones

Old Age

Last night I had an awful dream
I dreamed that I was young
And instead of being past the post
the race had just begun
The thoughts of all those future years
Made my blood run cold
I was so relieved to wake
And find that I was old.

Mrs. B. Jones

A Loving Kiss

Oh what bliss, to share the sensure of a loved one's kiss,
The thrill of the moment of your lover's mouth,
Settling gently in the blending touch,
Lips which urgently drink their fill,
Yet find a space to drink more still,
Greedily clinging in a rapturous thrill,
Which wraps the body in a passionate chill,
The pulsing blood, the surging brains,
The tangled nerves that call for pain,
Sweet pain that cools the aching limbs,
To cool the blood, and burn the brain,
The pressing bows a mite apart,
Seeks to relieve the demands of the heart,
The rosy lips that hypnotize,
The creamy skin, the sparkling eyes,
The eager expression and the panting breath,
All this is the bliss of a loved one's kiss.

S.J. Jones

Little Fifty Four

I studied my tables over and over
Backwards and forwards too
But I couldn't remember six times nine
And I didn't know what to do
'Til my sister told me to play with my doll
And not to bother my head
If you call her fifty four for a while
You'll learn it by heart she said
So I called her my little fifty four
Though I though what a dreadful shame
To call such a cuddly little doll
Such a really horrid name
Next day at school Mary Wrigglesworth
Who always acts so proud
Said six times nine was fifty two
And I almost laughed out loud
But I wished I hadn't when teacher said
Now Dorothy tell if you can
Then I though of my doll, and oh dear, oh dear
I answered - Mary Ann.

June Jones

My Old Washing Machine

He sits in the corner, the love of my life,
Sat square to the wall through our trouble and strife.

Over the years now we've worked and we've toiled,
Sharing good times and bad times, cold water and boiled

Ten years of washing, three times a day,
He's managed to keep stains and odours at bay.

With a purr from the drum and a swish as he goes,
He quickly eliminates dirt from our clothes.

But he's tired and run down now, and can't take the load,
His programs outrun and can't follow the code.

So he'll be going to that great kitchen in the sky,
And I'll always remember him by and by.

When I look in the corner at my new washing machine,
I'll remember the days when he kept our clothes clean.

Sarah Jonas

Talking Hands

Your hands speak words, I do not hear,
Your eyes tell me to have no fear;
You speak to me without a sound,
A language that is so profound,

You came to me when I was young,
You understood my plight,
All alone in a silent world
You taught me how to write.

I watched your lips mouth every word,
Your hands taught me to spell;
I thank you from my very soul
With love, no words can tell.

If all the world could understand,
The language of the talking hand,
Then those who live in silent fear,
Could raise their hands and give a cheer.

Sandy Johnson

Tiger

The slow dance of genes has produced a killer
Lithe in stride and sleek in fur
The fire of the sun and the prison of the jungle
Have all made their mark on this beast
But the greatest force has been man
The hunter, destroyer of which even tiger cannot match
We label it wild untamed and savage
Unaware of the irony, because
We cage what we cannot comprehend,
We cage what we fear
We cage what we see in ourselves

The zoo is a place of control
Our own regulated jungle where we impose order
Then tiger is a symptom, a symbol, neutered in mind
And lax in body, more human than wild
A product of our modern age
A semblance of its former self, more image than reality
Even the myth has died, blame it on the advertisers
And the cars.

Richard Jordan

"She"

As "she" walks by
My whole body gives a sigh
I am afraid to ask in case she says nigh
To my request to feel her thigh

Inwardly I groan as my body demands that I try style
And ask at least for a smile
Or to caress her hair with my hand
For my feelings are getting out of hand

I feel I want to tear her clothes
Till her body is like nature first proposed
Naked and bare just waiting to share

But however we would have to take care
That the world does not see us when we dare
Make love without a care

For if the world should see
A scandal there would be
As it would be obvious to anyone's stare
Upon seeing us laying naked there

Giggling and laughing with glee
That "she" in fact was a "he"
Who was laying next to me.

David Jones

Not Quite The Full Measure

Drifting summer days so hazy, afternoons are lazy
Lying on the grass amidst the daisy chains.
Congratulate me for my pains.
It's such a shame that days like this should end.
Around the bend.
I'm no one's friend.
That's what they said, or what I read
On paper with a crest upon the head.
Put her away, the people say,
She's not sane enough to share our days.
I dream,
Floating on grass of emerald green,
Of places I have never seen.
As time goes by I wish that I could fly
Away from white-washed walls and watchful eyes.
Asylum.
Not my idea of fun, but decisions in my favour
Do not run.
Summer days my only joy, like a baby clutching to a toy.
Please don't destroy my only pleasure
And remember
I'm a treasure
Because I'm not quite the full measure.

Rachel M. Jones

Untitled

Time for bed
Time for sleep
Not another squeak
Perhaps another 'peep
To see if all are asleep
Creep, creep, creep,
Peep, peep, peep
What's that? 'Another kiss'
Now, feet up
What bliss

Joyce E. Joseph

Sadness

Sadness is something you can't see
I feel it like a bee buzzing inside me
I don't know
How I can't show
How it hurts me so

People call me horrid names
But I know they're not games
That is why I'm so sad
I even call for my Dad

I need someone to talk to
Someone to cheer me up
Don't leave me please, I need you
So come and hurry up

Kerry Jones (Age 10)

What Have I Done Since I Last Signed On?

What have I done since I last signed on?
I haven't stopped.
Haven't been able to.
I've got five voluntary jobs, three college courses,
Letters to write, application forms to fill in,
Interviews to attend.
I'm a member of the local Writer's Group
As well as involved with two charities.
What have you done since I last signed on?

Philip Johnson

The Chase

Running water babbling brook
Little fishes off the hook
Rabbits running here and there
Lots of birds up in the air

Horses hooves upon the ground
Then the howling of the hound
All the riders dressed in red
Chasing foxes from their bed

With no thought of country code
Over fields and paths they rode
Only one thing is their aim
That's the fox, is it a game?

I wonder just how they would feel
With twenty hounds around their heel
Would it be a different matter
If THEIR life was about to shatter

Susan Jewell

Pictures on My TV

I saw the child of Africa
Looking out at me once more
I saw the face of want and need
Which I have often seen before
I saw the wizened features
Of an old face on a child
I saw their thin weak bodies
These scenes just drive me wild
I saw a baby suckle
It's mother's milkless breast
I saw a father dig a grave
And lay his child to rest
I saw a young boy guiding
An elder who was blind
I saw the skeleton carcasses
That hunger had left behind
I saw all of this human suffering
With bones just covered by skin
I saw this awful hurtful sight
For our world, a terrible sin
I saw the child of Africa
And it gave me hurt and pain
But the saddest part for me I feel is
I will see it all again.

Frederick Jolly

Interfering

We like to meet her boyfriends so she brings them home for tea.
Her latest seems more suitable than all the rest, to me.
This young man has a haircut and a collar with a tie,
White shining teeth, great big brown eyes and a heartrending sigh.
I know how it annoys her when I want to have my say.
It's my duty as her Mother, so I do it anyway.
To me he seems just like the man her broken heart to mend,
I won't believe her when she says that he is "just a friend".
Quite rightly, she'll be cross with me next time she visits us
But this one seems worth keeping, so I'll try, without a fuss.
He's charming and he offers help as I clear up the meal,
His captivating manners in a man seem quite unreal.
He leaves, and I invite him back — he needn't tell me when.
She whispers "Donald's gay, Mum." I've been sorted out, again.

Judith A. Jenkinson

Break Up

Where did the warmth and passion go?
Our love was true and strong.
The trust we had between us,
Why did it all go wrong?

You crushed my strength, you broke my heart,
My confidence was shattered.
You trod my ego underfoot,
Destroying all that mattered.

My life, my love was torn in shreds,
My being slowly died.
You broke me down completely.
The bruises all inside.

Jacqueline Johnson

Save

Save the world the nations cry
Save the earth and sea.
Save the whale and mountains high
But save a bit for me.

Save the water and the streams
Save the forest tree.
Save the otter and the fox
But save a bit for me.

Save the starving and the weak
Set the hostage free.
Save the lonely and the lost
And then dear God, save me!

Patricia E. Johnson

By the Sea

Cool breezes stroke my face
And above me the birds fly free
While the sands create new images
Sculptured by the sea
I watch the distant waves approach
So secretly they form
From the depths of Mother Nature
Another wave is born
Crested with white horses
That suddenly appear
On their journey to the shoreline
Where they seem to disappear
I can smell the sea's aroma
Carried on breezes in the sky
And in harmony with nature
I can hear the seagulls cry

Tania Jordan

Reunion

The sun was hot when hand in hand
we walked together on the sand;
you whispered words of love to me
and kissed me oh, so tenderly.

The sea was calm, and oh, so blue
when first I gave myself to you;
I love you then, and always will
and though you're gone, I love you still,
and as I walk along the shore,
I feel your presence ever near
and hear you whisper, "love, I'm here."

I walk into the cool calm sea,
my lover's arms embracing me,
and see the shadow of a Dove,
once more united with my love.

Susan L. Jones

A Visit To The Blacksmith's

It was early one July morning,
at breakfast Father did say.
Bonny to the blacksmith's must go,
before we take her to Hawsker show.

I went up the horse pasture,
over several more fields and the stell.
Before I came to the blacksmith's shop,
where Mr. Agar lived, who I knew quite well.

I took Bonny into the stable,
Mr. Agar came in as soon as he was able.
He just seemed to take one look,
and he knew the size of Bonny's hoof.

Mr. Agar then went and stoked up the fire,
and a length of iron he did take.
And within half an hour on his anvil,
a set of four shoes he did make.

The blacksmith then did begin,
to dress the horse's hooves.
After each foot had been dressed,
he burnt on each of the new shoes.

After he had nailed each shoe on,
the hoof around it was tromed.
When all four feet has been done,
it was time to take Bonny home.

Wilfred Jones

Does Anyone Care

How do I feel, does anyone care?
    It's like as if, I'm not there
Just there to see to everyone
    Maybe! They'll miss me when I'm gone!

I'm like a robot, always on the go
    If I didn't stop, they would never know,
Just keep going see to me
    Never mind her, it's me, me, me!

If only somebody would see me
    I have a life as well to be,
I thought I'd found what I was looking for,
    Now I'm really not so sure.

My better half thinks money
    is everything
I wonder how I managed
    before he gave me anything!

It's time he realized about
    life's treasures, they can't
be bought, not by any measures.

A hug, a love, a little thought,
    NO, they can't be bought,
It's something that comes from within,
    How I wish they would from him.

Maureen B. Jones

Single Handed

The hand that rocked the cradle
was warm, loving and able
its skin was fair
nails trimmed with care
the wedding ring new
eternity too
bruising as well
that hurt like Hell
a palm that wiped tears
and covered ears
in moments of sorrow
will rock the cradle tomorrow
in the same unselfish way
as it did yesterday
though it was aching
it was never forsaking
even scared and afraid
the cradle was swayed.

Stuart P. Jarvis

Spring

Oh for the spring
When birds so sing,
The trees in a mantle
of green.

The lovely spring flowers,
And fresh April showers,
I long for that
wonderful scene.

Now autumn is here,
How sad to see
The leaves falling
from the trees.

The swallows have gone
To a land far away,
We know they will
be back one day.

So I will wait for
That wonderful time,
When spring is here
so do not pine.

D. Highman

Nobody Notices

I am heart broken
I'm hurt real bad
But nobody notices
That I am sad.

I'll play solitaire
'cos it's the only game
That you don't need to remember
Anyone's name.

The rest of my life
I'll be alone
But nobody notices
When I get home.

I'm always smiling
To hide the tears
But nobody notices
Nobody hears.

Tamara Jane

Elves of the Morning

Elvan folk of flower and tree
Paint your silver filigree
On every lush green blade of grass
'Til the surface shines like brass
And wake the sun from night-time rest
And put to bed the silver crest
Tell all the birds it's time to sing
The song that endless joy does bring
Your job to wake up life itself
With magic from the land of elf
Until you have prepared the day
In your magic, merry way.

Sarah Kent (Age 11)

Time

Our life is a book of chapters three
The past, the present, the yet to be.
The past is gone, it's locked away,
The present we live with every day.
The future, it's not for us to see —
'Tis locked away, and God holds the key.

Eve King

Jessica's Castle

To celebrate our holiday,
Up the mountain we climbed today.
Past gaping potholes ever so deep,
Some like basins filled with peat.
The impending danger of these holes,
Makes us wary as we stroll.
Like fortified castles very old,
Rocky formations stand so bold.
To Jessica's rock, our way we ply,
Now on this rock she stands so high.
Reaching like "Oread", to the sky,
Or an eagle poised ready to fly.
To the summit we climb, with breathless glee,
Panoramic views with wonder do see.
The wind now cold, it chills the eye,
As the sun dips low in the winter sky.
We hasten down the mountainside,
Where dark of night will soon abide.
With tired feet and aching back,
We finally reach the homeward track.
The cottage we find, without a care,
With door closed tight to the cold night air.
As we sit by the fireside bright,
Recalling to her mother, the rest of the night.
Surrendering to the deepest sleep,
Morpheus now, till dawn will keep.

John de John - *Cumbria*

My Dentist

She bent my head back
She looked up my nose
She opened wide my mouth
To see how my teeth grows

With a burr and a whizz
With a drill that made my teeth fizz
With this object she made a killing
Quickly she gave me a filling

"That's it", she said as she tapped my arm
"I told you you would come to no harm"
My mouth felt it was stretched a mile
At least now I can smile

Slowly I walked out the door
"See you in 6 months to do some more"
The thought of it made me ill
I felt worse next day — I got the bill.

Terry Knight

A Special Union

Our lives are touched by many things,
Especially when shared by a wedding ring.
The deepest of feelings emotions and thoughts,
Our hearts are full, some with sadness are wrought.
However with time, wisdom too,
Life itself can carry us through.
Blessings are many to reflect on and count
Lifting our hearts, helping problems surmount.
Love for each other, with friendship and trust,
To reach out to touch, to comfort a must.
For years of learning of each other's ways
Growing together in hard work and colourful days.
Pulling together side by side,
Meeting each challenge, all problems to override.
To awake each morning to a brand new day,
The feeling of togetherness with love to stay.
Not crossing bridges before they appear,
One day at a time with things we hold dear.
To count our blessings is a must
To know in whose hands we can really trust.
Our Creator has given us so many things
Our thanks and constant praises of Him
The earth should truly ring.

Mrs. W. Kuczaj

Down Memory Lane

I walk along familiar roads and gaze upon the scene,
Thinking of the days gone by and how things once had been.
Rows of terraced houses, not palaces it's true,
But to those who lived there, as each day dawned anew,
This was their earthly paradise, they wanted little more,
Than the comradeship of neighbours, the ever open door.

But now the wind of change has blown and to each passer-by,
The few remaining houses stand, open to the sky.
The old familiar faces are now spread far and wide
Their houses nought but rubble, but memories still abide.

I trace my steps and find myself in my old domain,
Childhood memories fill my thoughts as I look once again,
Upon a house once occupied, now empty and forlorn,
This was my home, this was my past — the house where I was born.
Soon it will fall, but from it's dust will rise,
The memory of those 50 years, my life, my paradise.

Norah Kaye-Lawton

Say Goodbye

Say goodbye to the dolphin
trapped by nets, by spears on skin.
Kind, benevolent and playful like a child,
their only fate is to be beguiled.
In the shadow of an empty world,
they writhe, their tender flesh unfurled.
For easy profits pocketed by scum,
we say goodbye to baby and to Mum.
As Father Dolphin swims away in tears
to the roar of human cries and jeers,
we dread the empty fateful day
when all the dolphins have gone away.

Paul Kennedy

Torness

Blue sky, white lighthouse, green fields of grain.
These are the colours as seen from the train.

Then a monstrous concrete block
A nuclear reactor, what a shock
Imprinting itself on my brain.

Do we need electricity at such a great price?
Will our children in future wish we had thought twice?
The Bible does tell us, we reap what we sow,
But when this harvest's gathered
We'll have died long ago.

S. Kennedy

The Pigeon

You live off the waste and decay of mankind
Ugly little grey thing that begs so earnestly.
No home, no warmth, diseased and despised
You patrol your station, strut so proudly
An old graceful gentleman.
That disregarded ham sandwich, an ancient crisp
May be your first meal in weeks, may be your last.
No concept of time, you only watch the evercoming trains,
Show off your skills, walking on roofs, braving the track.
It get cold, so cold,
Then you entertain,
Fouling on the innocent commuter
You're such a filthy creature, yet
It would be strange not to see you.

Sarah Kent

Mercy

The most beautiful word in the world to me is mercy.
Mercy — when you don't care
Mercy — when you've done it again
Mercy — for every time you go wrong
Mercy — when you know you're wrong
Especially then, because you know
Your guilt will punish you enough
Don't need anymore, especially from the one's you love.
Mercy — to you whoever you are
Mercy — know that somebody cares
You're not alone in what you think
Mercy, not sacrifice, is the way I think.

Jane Kay

Exit Bleeding

The grasp of time slips through my fingers
It stains them purple,
Sat behind a wheel, rushing to death, nothing is certain.
The sky is bright, cascading green and lime light,
A face with so much anguish, like I have never seen before.
Flesh is grey, the lake is red with yellow water,
Red is cold and uninviting, solitude embraced me
Nothing is certain.
One chance, desperate, ebbing away, void and empty
River of blue tail lights flowing and weaving,
Exit bleeding, on coming rush of light arrives
On leaving, faster to death, exit bleeding.
Justice is never done, riots flaring, burning, crying
Girl left dying, radio friendly company.
Escalation, speeding, people sleeping, visibility leaving, deceiving
Another tragedy, souls leaving, nothing is certain
Lifeless, colourful blocks, both sides teaming with life
The river has risen, urban sprawl below.
Blue is warmth, hate is love, orange is purple, confusion,
Exit bleeding, leaving, rain just falling
Slowing, stopping, sigh on arrival
Stepping out and into this kaleidoscope
I'm still not sure, nothing is certain!

John Christopher Kearney

Body

It leaves my body
A train of thought
It leaves my body
But no fight is fought

I'm awake and asleep
Two lives merge and seep
Good and bad in liquid dense
I wonder if this will ever make sense

It leaves my body
The madness mannequin
It leaves my body
Like a saint discards a sin

I'm rich and I'm poor
From the ceiling to the floor
From the eagle to the fish
From fulfilment to the wish

It leaves our bodies
And we are happy again
Every person and being that breathes on this planet
Is equal and equal again.

Tony Keggin

Que Sera Sera

The days pass by so quickly,
    Past life held within your memory.
Looking forward to a brighter future,
    Installed with lots of adventure.

You come across the problems of life,
    Working your way through trouble and strife.
Teaching and learning every single day,
    Trying to understand peoples' thoughts and their ways.

Listen to the power of speech,
    But do not believe it will always teach.
Strange happenings will occur,
    You will never know why for sure.

You will have good times and bad,
    Tears will fall in happy moments and sad.
We all live our lives in hopefulness,
    Creating the fulfilment of success.

Life has to be taken a step at a time,
    Trying not to commit any crime.
You will entangle with love and hate,
    And these will usually be left to fate.

Lemanie Kelly

Mirrored Memories

On Westminster Bridge, the old man stands,
Or perhaps in times gone by?
Beside the stile, breathing in waves of gold,
A young boy of many dreams.
A sailing boat across floating seas,
Glasses of frosted lemonade to cool beaded brows.

The fog, a confused swirl before misted eyes,
Glass tears shattering upon damaged ground.
The man of Westminster remembers through darkened memories
Visions destroyed by fear,
Documented by ebony,
Outlined in scarlet,
Unknown sounds.
Giants of undiscovered lands?
Fire from feared terrain?

"Mother, please pray tell, where is father?
Is he well?"
Briefly, after time has removed the years,
The Westminster fog breaks, perhaps revealing a glimmer of hope,
The man of Westminster moves on
Always knowing her answer.

Michelle Marie Kisby

Friend

The day will change its name, I know,
and in its summer gown will glow
and wrap its winter cloak round tight

Its shape and sound, wisdom and wit
and every colour bright in it
will once more vanish with the night

With sun and wind to touch its face
it has no care for time and place,
it knows no kind of constancy

Only on change can it depend,
but there is you, you are my friend.
Always have been, always will be.

Amanda Kostrzebski

The Island

Waves devouring the rocky outcrops
As the energy released charges the air
With so much hunger and passion
That encapsulates your every care.

Down covered rocks of white
Reveal ganet colonies, huddled so tightly
To shield each other from the bitterness
That prevails so mightily.

Where else does man give way
To enable the humble puffin to burrow and breed
In anonymity for three months of the year
So that continuity will succeed.

The fishermen's guide winks so brightly
The white beam releasing such awesome power
Highlighting the hidden dangers of death
So much faith is placed in the tall white tower.

The wind-torn bleakness of the land
Is relentlessly guarded by granite forts
Whose eyes pierce the horizon with no exception
Protection only for the life they support.

The mutilated landscape stretches ahead
Formed from tainted soil that absorbed so many tears
It can't even support the colour of wild flowers
As so much pain flooded those troubled years.

Mandy Kemp

October 1987

It came in the dead of night
From whence I do not know,
But I was really frightened
Such anger did it show.

The sea, I heard it boiling
Like a cauldron in the night,
And thought of those who long ago
Called their Master in their plight.

I recalled the Bible story,
How, on the sea of Galilee,
Those disciples, the chosen of Jesus,
In a tempest, were fearful, like me.

I thought, He is the only one
Who can calm this troubled scene,
When all around is tumult,
He only, reigns supreme.

The double-glazed windows
Did little difference make,
I heard the roof tiles tumbling
The T.V. aerial shake.

The dawn was more than welcome,
After such a stormy night,
And, how relieved was I to find,
Our damage was so slight!

Anne Keeler

Unemployed

Am oot o' work and peddlin the street, sick "o" heart wi' swollen feet,
Round a' the factories I trail, alas my friends tae nae avail.
No early nise — the back o' eight, slink oot the hoose by the back door gate
Avoid the neebors prying eyes, alas wi' looks o' mean dispise?
"That mans no goat a job ye ken, he's like a' they ither lazy men."
The himiliation o' it wad mak ye greet,
Ye' join the ranks o' this fair Nation and don the cloak o' sheer frustration.

I cast my vote for the working classes, and end up joining the idle masses.
If Scotlands Bard were alive today, Oh! man I wonder whit he would say.
This idle body o' humanity, wad fell gie fodder tae breed insanity.
Am oot o' work still peddlin the street, enjoyin the life and people I meet.
Alas am pittin on too much "beef", and sure enough that'll come tae grief,
But, if everything comes true, and destiny brings tae me whits due —
I'll live on the money pie I oot tae me by the hand o' Social S-E-C-U-R-I-T-E-E-.
Whaur it comes frae I dinna ken, I just collect when I sign wi' a pen.

John Kennedy

The Pine Branch

Sharp and poignant the needles,
Nothing to dull the senses
Or stem the heavy outpour
Of heady essence pulsing
Through the filtering trac'ry
Of dark, brooding mosaics
Etched against the winter's sky.

Yet, removed from eerie light,
Lying beneath questing hand
On familiar table,
Myst'ry yields to memory -
Autumn pine woods, sunsets aflame!
The Christmas tree revelry
Safe-wrapped in love's permanence.

Joan Kelly

Just a Thought

I wonder if he'll know me,
If there should be a here-after,
He, now dead some years,
And me, now past my prime?

Will his glance slide by me
With no sign of recognition,
No memory of the wife I was
Many years ago?

If there should be a here-after
I hope he's there to greet me
With a crisp, "Ah, there you are —
Still no idea of time!"

Iris Kesterton

For Whom The M.P.'s Toil?

They are all there, by us they have been sent,
That's right, our Members of Parliament,
Their conduct at times doubtful — some for the Dunce's Cap.
If that was in school they would get the strap,
Yes that's right for us a near disaster,
Worse still to THAT room to see the headmaster,
In the M.P.'s case, a word from the Prime Minister
No strap, but a caution he would administer
But in Parliament no M.P. gets a fright
But for some unknown reason everyone is right,
Most of the public seem to take it with a wink,
After all they are all right — I think.

P. Keddie

Give Till It Hurts

On comic relief day turn out in force
Starving Ethiopians — feed them of course
Rumanian orphans, donkeys from Spain
Ill-treated dogs — take on their pain

Famines in Bangla Desh, floods in Sudan
Keep giving, keep giving as fast as you can
March to end Apartheid, black music is cool
British born Pakis in your own children's school ...

Hold it right there! That's over the top
It's going too far, it has to stop
Keep Britain white! When push comes to shove
Show your true colours, be a hawk not a dove

Pauline Kazi

Gills and Fins

Wizardry wise, yet not despised, flirting with danger.
Fins always not what they appear, the cordon bleu Cassandra
in a swirling deep, dark concealed place.
Stark, mute, motionless, before it, fools gold.
How did it survive to be this old.

Blood and thunder it's staying under, a swish and swipe
of posture, turbulent, hungry, deliverative assembly.
Focusing wide angled lens, teasing temptation on the barbed hook,
a darting barbed glance, reflection, refraction, reaction.

Everything is moving, seen it all before, a prognostic
just waiting the tug, rocking and reeling, the line chime sings.
Flashing silver twirling, inviting inquisitors, look who's biting.
Perhaps they will get away with the risk, no harm to try,
just a fat fly.

The cold side beckons, a missile lightning strike,
projectile force alined to its purpose.
Waters edge blur, flipping manic panic.
Hook line and sinker, a real skinker,
that old icon was a thinker.

A young fool left to drool, tethered, panting gills,
grasping for life. An excited cry, is it Cassandra?
Oh, it's just Midas comes the reply, an appreciative
radiant wry smile, caught every week, never unique.

Anthony Keyes

The Corn is Red

The sight and sound of breath
Unknowing and still-born
Have left this death
To kiss this summer's morn;
Wading through cornfields
Gazing on the nests of the dead
Made by falling warrior shields
Worn to each bloody bed;
Raced before me the eye and brain of desolation
Squeezed the last wine-drops of hope
Made me drunk with inward fermentation
As I staggered up the slope;
Now the moated hilltop waited
To show me the panoramic view
Like a preacher sombre-coated
Showing strangers to their pew;
But soldiers came and carried me down
Burying me in the grasses tight
By the scene of the battle outside the town
But my grave is empty day and night;
Now like a lonely widowed bird I sit upon this hilltop
Under which all the field's hay must pass
Forever covered with that freckled outcrop
Of bodies jutting from the yellow mass.

Brian King

May It Last Forever

Is it not so exquisite, so very, very nice,
Extremely exhilarating, even tiring,
Can mere words
Describe the elegance and poetry of it,
I think not
But again I must try, must say something,
Pleasing enjoyable most definitely,
Ravishing, ah, ah, mearly there,
Then what about ecstasy,
If any one word can describe it
Then this must surely come close,
To even think about it
Makes the legs tremble,
Brings flashes of delight
To the wee grey cells,
And a firm rigidity, to other famous parts,
Makes you want to shout, tell the world
Just how good it really is,
Oh the joy of it all
Satisfaction and the rest,
May it last forever, from here to eternity,
What, I hear you ask, can it be,
It, my friends, is making love,
Making love, to my wife.

B.P. Kershaw

Truth Amongst Friends

I visited friends who were bragging that their offspring were doing SO WELL.
One was a Captain at Golf Club. One Anything could He sell.
Their daughter was in South America and having a Wonderful time.
While they were about to retire and everything was turning out fine.
Alas, my story was different, so I told them fibs galore
how one son had bought a Hotel, the other a departmental store.
That my daughter was dancing in Las Vegas, and her husband, a millionaire
wanted me to be with them so in their good fortune I'd share.
We spent the evening relaxing with drinks flowing all the while
and soon we were laughing and chatting and all wearing a silly smile.
Then later my friend got tiddley and truth tumbled out of her mouth
how her 'Captain son' was quite lazy and also a boring lout.
And as for her 'Salesman Lad' well he, she could cheerfully clout!
Her daughter had 'just-up-and-left' her so, she was an ungrateful cur
then words became mixed up and muddled, sentences spoken with slur
so, I admitted the hotel was rubbish. A derelict plot of old ground
as for the Store that I'd mentioned, He'd be lucky if rent could be found!
My 'millionaire' son-in-law busked, while my daughter danced to his whims.
And, by the way, have you a bed for me NOW?
After all you said we were friends!

Irene Knott

Indecision!

The thought of a £5,000 prize, brings a gleam to my eyes.
    Shall I enter the competition, though a beginner.
I must conceive an idea, brilliant and clear.
    That will be without doubt a winner.

Should I concentrate on Sport, a reasonable thought.
    No, it has problems, the who, the why and when.
I do not know enough, I would have to resort to bluff.
    Ah! well, empty my mind, start again.

My goodness what can I do, I certainly need a clue,
    for the subject that I am going to pick.
I am not so good at History, it was always rather a mystery.
    There must surely be something to do the trick.

On Geography I was never keen, it was not quite my scene,
    to know where a place was or who it belonged to.
English was severe, I could not grasp Shakespeare.
    Science a complex maze to travel through.

Astronomy is all stars, planets, Venus and Mars.
    Leave the Astronauts to navigational tangles.
Maths and the Hypotenuse just tend to confuse.
    I can live my life without angles.

Unless I find a theme, very soon I shall scream.
    The whole project will drive me mad, if I let it.
So I have decided in the end, I am not going to send,
    my poem in, I am going to forget it ...

James Kerr

Snow Scene

Everywhere is covered with a blanket of white,
Made by the snow that fell in the night.
Sparkling and glistening like jewels so rare,
Bringing a crisp, cold feel to the air.
Children are laughing and playing around,
Throwing snowballs that fall without making a sound.

Rachael Kerby

My Memory

Near and dear, I see your face, in my memory
Like a mental colour slide that saves it all for me
Your face I cannot hold or touch
Your lips I cannot feel
But in my memory's wandering eye
It all still seems so real.
Just like it was when you were here
So it shall always be
Deep in the dark recesses of my memory
The hands I used to hold so tight
No longer wave hello
But in my deepest memories, I still can't let you go
The love and laughter we once shared
They're still all hidden there
Deep inside my memory where no one else can share
So absent you may be, but not inside my memory

Hazel Kendall

Seeing-Eyes

She *heard* his words inside her head
"I love you, love you, love you" he said,
Entranced she watched his eyes intense
Convey in dumb-show, yet make sense,
Expressive eyes, thought transferring
"I love you, love you, love you," staring
Across the table, held her gazing
Fascinating and amazing.
She glanced in shyness, quick to see
If others there had seen what he
Across the table silently
Had beamed with such intensity.
But no, and so her eyes looked in
The depths of his eyes once again
And those dark pools, inside her head
"I love you, love you, I love you" said.
But circumstance decreed that they
Each then must go some other way,
And so it came when she, alone,
Bade him farewell upon the 'phone —
"I love you" truly then she heard
Into her ear, this time by word.

Sylvia King

Lost Heritage

Dark murky streams where dead fish float
Killed by discharge from passing boat,
Whilst factory chimneys black and high
Belch forth their filth towards the sky.
On windswept downs, our land of 'Free'
Covered by sores of old debris.
Our once clean shores becoming fewer
Smell foul from cess and open sewer.
Near beaches black with tar and oil
Are stricken trees, eroded soil.
No longer will you hear the song
From birds who winged their way along,
Your listening will be in vain,
The birds will die from poisoned grain.
What do you want? What sort of life?
A land of wilderness and strife?
I beg of you please count the cost
Or Heritage and you are lost
Each one must help with resolution
To cleanse our land from this pollution.

Peter R. King

Love is All

Christmas came, and love came too,
in the form of a tiny child.
What did we do to deserve such love
In a world sometimes cruel and wild?
'Love begets love', it began at the crib,
That night so holy and blessed.
Jesus our King, beasts surrounding Him,
As in Mary's arms he did rest.

What have we done with that love He gave?
Do we share it where we can?
It appears that greed, ill will and sick deeds
Have controlled the lives of man.
To love someone else who is lonely and scared
Is the message the manger portrays.
Not money, not wealth, could ere be compared
To the comfort that shared love displays.

Bewildered is youth as they seek after truth
We read all about it each day.
And as we grow old, and this world becomes cold
Of faith in 'Our Lord' is our stay.
So let's each make sure that we show
More of the 'love' He would have us all share.
The when we're alone, without friends in our home.
God's love will always be there.

Eileen King

Lunar Bow

On a summer's night of long ago
When the moon was round and hanging low.
There came a hush as tho' to warn
It was the mystic hour before the dawn.

The countryside before me lay
With meadows sweet with tomorrow's hay.
I felt a breeze, a shower of rain
Followed in the zephyr's train.

And then the moon her bow revealed
It spanned the meadows, hedgerows and field
And from the ground it rose up and high
To form an arch in the pearly sky.

A wonderful bow with a silvery sheen
With hints of blue, red, orange and green:
It framed the farmhouse beneath the hill
The lonely spire in the distant still.

It framed the dairy herd, a flock of sheep
The cottages in their slumbers deep:
It was a picture of sheer delight
In the mystic hour of that summer night.

Since then she's waxed and waned many times
Her face has smiled on many climes
But O, that night of long ago —
The night I saw her wondrous bow.

John Keyse

Ode To Bosnia

What has the world got to give
Is this a place for us to live?
Do we live just to die?
To make people suffer
To make them cry.
Bombs crashing, bullets flying
People dashing, babies crying.
No matter what the doctors say,
People dying everyday.
What has the world got to give?
Is this a place for us to live?

Brian King

Reflections

Sitting along and feeling forlorn,
Thinking back, to when you were born.
Precious, pretty and so very small,
Then, before long, you had learned how to crawl.
Uncertain steps, and then you could walk,
Silence is broken, you learned to talk.
Holding you close when you had a fall,
My silent tears on your first day of school.
Together we'd shop and I'd let you choose
Dresses, ribbons and black shiny shoes.
You were my little girl, your secrets we'd share,
When you cried in the night I would always be there,
Feeling so proud when you're in the school play.
Sadness at time that's just slipped away,
A teenager now and you've grown so tall,
But, oh! how I wish that you were still small.
Childhood is waning, but I will never weep!
Because memories are precious, and they're mine to keep.

Kathy King

Brothers of the Underground

Brothers of the underground sleep the life-long sleep
Crawl along the gutters like larvae in the dark
Wriggling towards the light.

Commuters throw a dime and it tinkles on the tiles
And glints like an inspirational flash
Under the drab fluorescence.

Each day they maul the plastic bin liners for their haute cuisine
Or gulp the moonshine from their desperate plastic cups
Thrown down by travellers.

And each eye that passes looks but does not see
Because each life is filled with triviality
And the brothers of the underground watch you and me —
Desensitised ...

Barbara King

To Michael

Tiny little baby on your mother's knee
If only you could realize
How much you mean to me.
Chubby little two-year-old
Playing with your toys
You're always into mischief
But then boys will be boys.
Grown up little five year old
Trotting off to school
Be careful of the traffic
And don't forget the rule.
Smart good looking teenager
Going on your first date
No time to stop and eat your tea
In case you should be late.
The years have passed so quickly
And now you're twenty-one
A handsome man with raven hair,
I'm so proud of you, my son.

Christine King

A Wonderful World

First came the change and the hormone
treatment,
Which played havoc with my vocals,
And the gleam in my eye that you see shining
bright,
Is the sun shining off my bi-focals.

As time goes by, my love life,
Appears to be growing dimmer,
Instead of men surrounding me,
I'm surrounded by a zimmer.

I remember the day's when "chat-up lines",
Were spoken to entice us,
But recently all men seem to say,
Is "Hello, how's your arthritis".

When we were young we would raise our glass
To life and it's many adventures,
We still raise our glass but not as we'd like,
It's only to put in our dentures.

I sit here and ponder on days that have passed,
When I'd happily go to and fro,
But try as I might and with all of my strength,
I can't make my rocking chair go.

On reflection they say that the youth have it all,
But as my life has unfurled,
With the memories I have I can honestly say,
Ah yes ... What a wonderful world.

Frances E. King

Reach Out

When you are feeling life is cruel, reach out and touch a star
there are thousands in the universe, but you needn't stretch so far.
For everywhere about you gleams with beauty and delights,
if only you will take the time to marvel at such sights.
The shimmer on a quiet pool reflecting moonlight beams,
the flashing blue of dragonflies which skim o'er sunlit streams.
And dew glistening on spiders webs like tiny diamonds shine,
while raindrops form upon the leaves, like pearl-drops, clear and fine.
Appreciate all Nature's joys as through a young child's eyes,
and watch exquisite snowflakes fall from out of leaden skies.
Gaze joyfully at frosty scenes sparkling in crystal drape,
and enter Nature's wonderland and for a while escape.

Beryl Kearns

The Flyer

When I got into work today, I met up with the boss,
Who said, "Now John, be on your way, and make for Gerrard's Cross
With thirty-one deliveries, and ten for Wycombe too,
Plus eighteen drops for Rickmansworth, as you'll be passing through"

"You should get that lot finished by twenty-five to one,
Then there's half a dozen Oxfam shops to clear before you're done!"
I said to him, "Now Guv'nor, I can see that you're all heart,
But there's one thing that I must do before I make a start."

"I'll have to go a'searching, a phone box for to find,
To don my costume, red and blue with cape that flows behind.
The reason for this quick-change stunt, is plain for all to see,
You must think that I'm SUPERMAN, the things you ask of me!"

John Keogh

Snowdrops

Oh, delicate white petals from a Crimean home,
Whose bulbous body lies in a rich dark loam,
Heartfelt attraction of when the British soldier was there,
To pick, letter press, and send it home with love and care.
Milky flower, why do you bow your head so low?
Are you studying the frozen jewels in the bed of snow?
Sprightly grassy green stem that hosts white purity,
Chastely objects which retain innocence while developing maturity.
Random carpet, no warp nor weft, but patches and clumps,
Bunches and tufts and gatherings at tree stumps.
A solitary figure on one knee,
Pinches stems to see snowdrops fall, one, two, three.
Days pass by and life's cycle must unfurl,
Aging little petals crack and curl.
What contents do faded love letters have in bottom drawer?
Pages open to reveal poetic verse and the purity of l'amour!

Michael Kendrick

The War

The fire started
The wind blew
The fireworks banged
The fire grew
The fire leapt up
To catch the breeze
The wind breathed in
And then did sneeze
The fire was startled
It jumped back
The fire got angry
And began to attack
The fire licked up
Twigs and leaves
The wind rustled
Through the sheaves
Round and round
The wind went
And into ashes
The fire was sent

Ben Kelly

Talents

What a lovely thing
It is to be able to sing
To sing our thoughts out loud
I cannot make one sound.

But we all have gifts
Given to us to use
Mine comes in starts and fits
Composing poems and tunes.

I love to sit and write
Around a scene I know
Perhaps of children bright
Under a sky of blue.

My friend she does the cooking
I always let her do
Because whatever she's making
Is bound to be good for you.

So keep on doing
All the things we can
Because talents are given
To one and every man.

M.T. Kendrew

Rudolph Valentino
"The Gypsy"

The strong dark gypsy in me
Reflected in my soul
My perfect, sculpted face
Of pores, shaped brows and sensuous lips.
Do they like my aquiline nose
These ladies who talk of Romance?
My dark hair hidden by the bandeau
My coat of sheep's wool
And my uncared for shirt?

If they mother me, smother me
Will I be a star or lose my talent
And be a thing of the past?
Will "it" be lost in early movies,
Or will "I" be "nostalgia" before my time?

The love of my art surpasses love of them.
The script drives me on —
"Blood and Sand" the spur —
Piercing my soul —
Building my character
And then will I be forgotten
Or will I be immortal?

Margaret M. Kirkham

Tempestuous Reminiscences

Rain is falling hard and fast,
Storms are brewing will they last?
Nobody is strolling through the park,
So cold it is enveloped in dark.

Day is past, night is here,
My thoughts reflect the closing year.
Tears of happiness, tears of joy,
This park, alas, was my decoy.

Now it's over I am gone,
I feel so lonely, depressed, forlorn.
Time to move on, forgive and forget,
Especially of times I now come to regret.

The light of day will soon dawn again,
And children will run from down the lane.
I wish that I too could be there,
For happy times I used to share.

With friends and family I belong,
In solitude I've been too long.
Distraught, bereft, perturbed I am,
Inner strife I need to calm.

Jacqui Kirkaldy

Well So You Said

I followed you as a friend,
I had no need to fear.
No ties, no wants — just friendship.
Well, so you said.
We were good together and kept close.
No fear, no fear, no fear.
But suddenly a door locked and darkness fell.
It's alright — well so you said.
I was grabbed by the throat
As I felt your grasps and thumps.
I couldn't breathe, couldn't scream.
Don't worry — well so you said.
Let me shout out,
Your hands cold against my flesh,
Your roughness and fast breaths.
It's normal — well so you said.
Leave my dirty, violated body,
It is not yours.
You leave me and I start to cry.
It's a reaction — well so you said.
My crumpled frame slouched under pain.
It was my fault.
I struggled for days.
I asked for it — well so you said.

Julie Kenny

The Jumble Sale

It's Saturday lunchtime, five to one,
I should be first in the queue, if I run.
Here we are, made it, no one here yet,
I stand in anticipation of what I might get.
Two fifteen, here they all are,
People from near, people from far.
Here comes Philip, he's on the drag,
We're blocking the entrance, the helpers will nag.
I make it two. Yes, they're unlocking the door,
We all make a dash, like a herd of wild boar.
Stalls all around, where's the brik-brack?
Everything from junk to a pretty nick-knack.
I grab a dish, this looks like "Wade"
Only 50p, that's a few pound I'll have made.
That's a nice teapot, oh dear, no lid,
Put that into auction, it won't make a bid.
Philip's bought a radio, that's made his day,
I do hope this time, he gets it to play.
I'll call it a day now, can't carry no more,
Pushing and shoving, just to get out the door.
Goodbye all you children, ladies and men,
See you next week, to do it again.

Pam Knock

September, 1994

Myriads of patterns flowed amongst the leaves,
Sun and wind combined to send them dancing ...
Saplings strained upward as if to reach the heavens:
Conifer and fir sang, while elm and oak moaned.

The wind whipped corn fields in bright array,
White unto harvest; a warm, soft sound.
Rooks gathered amongst nests high in the oaks,
Every hedgerow teemed with starlings, thrush , sparrow.

Sunshine teemed from a bright blue sky:
Summer heat shimmered on the roads.
Cyclists in black shorts, green and yellow singlets
Beat their thighs and machines against the tarmac.

Cars pulled caravans which swayed
In excess of fifty miles per hour.
Lorries thundered in competition with coaches
On motorways: many headed for holidays.

The marathon of the rail strike neared its close,
Business had diverted on the roads,
Towns and cities clogged with traffic;
Autumn brought thunderstorms and a bounty of fruit

Patrick Knight

Life As It Is?

A continuous masquerade,
Of love and giving, and of kindness and courage.
What hypocrites we are.

You say we should love,
Is it love that watches the sick,
And turns away in hate and disgust?

You boast about giving to the needy,
Is it the giving who ignore
The cries of the hungry?

And kindness,
Is it the kind, who
Greet the weak, with oppressive sneers?

And how brave you must be, to
Look on the afraid, and shudder.
We live our lives, and build our dreams.

But on what?
In our lives, is there time for the helpless?
In our dreams, is there space for the forgotten?

Jacqueline Kweka

Christmas

The insurance man called on Boxing Day,
To see the damage done by Santa's sleigh.
He got a ladder and climbed up high,
Onto the roof and gave a cry!

Santa's sled was here and there,
In fact his sled was everywhere!
"Good job this was my last call."
Said a voice from the bedroom wall.

Santa, looking pale and shaken,
Came onto the roof, his big boots quaking.
"I think I took the bend too tight,
It's hard to see in the night."

"I really need specs to get around,
And Rudolph flies too near the ground,
We hit the chimney first, I fear,
I really thought the end was near."

The moon was full, but behind a cloud,
I had my 'walkman' on too loud.
I never heard poor Rudolph cry",
"Santa! We've run out of sky!"

"He's downstairs now, all shaking bones,
I'll never be able to get him home"
"Your insurance won't cover this," he said,
"Next year you'll have to POST instead!"

Adam T.H. Kitcatt

Christmas

I woke up in the middle of the night,
A munching sound gave me a fright!
I opened the window and looked out,
A munching sound without a doubt,
Came down to me from off the roof,
Could I see part of a hoof?

I had to see what I could spy,
So from my window I climbed up high.
Sitting there as clear as day,
A reindeer, munching hay!
Never stopping with his dinner,
He produced a smile, a certain winner!

"He'd better not catch you up here,
Or he will make you disappear!"
"Is he really in my house?"
I asked in a whisper, like a mouse.
"Of course he is, you silly boy,
He leaves all the children a little toy."

"Except the little boy next door,
Who won't be getting any more.
All year the complaints have been coming in,
Enough for ten boys, not just him.
So, he's off the list, it's sad but true,
Behave or the same could happen to you!"

David E.H. Kitcatt

Mother Earth is Crying Now

So much wrong in the world today, injustice everywhere,
Some nations eat while millions starve, pleading, in despair.
Polluted seas and poisoned air, ravaged earth and forests bare,
But Mother Earth is crying now, does no one really care.

I wonder if it really hurt, or if she felt the pain,
When men drilled and dug the earth, to find that vital vein.
They drilled and dug and scarred the earth, out poured the liquid gold,
No time to stop and wonder what the future just might hold.

She bore the pain, as mothers do, if it's for their children's good,
But Mother Earth is crying now, for she's never understood,
That the price of greed and selfishness is paid in a nations blood.

J. Knott

Something On The Hill

Amidst wild flowers on the hill, beneath the belt where air meets sky,
Tiny beings pinch my flesh to drive me from their chosen plot,
Yet here I'll lay until I'm found, with tangled hair and clothes awry.
I hold a message for my loves: a withering forget-me-not.

Through a crystal bead — a limpid tear — a bluey haze pervades my eye,
Kaleidoscoped with transient gold: twinkling glitter from the sun.
I spread my hand to stroke the breeze that passes gently with a sigh
To sweep my soul into the air, and with it, all my breath has gone ...

Patricia H. Kirkbride

Autumn Season

Autumn is crimson, yellow and red,
    from the trees the leaves all spread,
The weather's getting colder,
    for the winter to come,
And it's another two seasons
    until we see the sun.
We'll get our gloves and hats on,
    for playing in the snow,
The winter season's coming,
    and that we all know.
Crimson leaves are scattered,
    upon the grass and ground,
Pretty leaves and ugly leaves
    the children may have found.
We'll put our feet up at the fire,
    and by the end of day,
We'll be very, very tired.

Robyn Kirstein

Anger

I'm angry,
I'm red,
Furious,
Wrathful.
Frustration builds up inside me,
I try to hold my temper,
I'm about to explode
With streams of unpleasant words
Pouring out of my mouth,
Like lava shooting out of a volcano.
It's too late,
I start screaming,
Raging and hating,
Smashing,
Destroying.
Why?
Because of my brother!

Meera Khosla

Tribute To The Queen
on the Occasion of Her Jubilee

Likened to a bride, beautiful, serene,
Crowned head held high, oh youthful Queen
Wed to the nation, to give comfort in need
To rule with wisdom above her years
Dedicated a great nation to lead
Her accepted role without qualm or fears
May the memory of her grace and dignity remain
Implanted in our hearts, through her years of reign

Mary Legg

My Jewels

Pearls, silver and gold
Are precious so we are told
But although they give great pleasure
They are nothing compared to my treasure.

As time went by
Seven lovely grandchildren have I
Dawne, Lauren, and Natalie
Beautiful children for me.

Grandsons now number four,
I wonder if there will be more
Happiness and contentment for me
Such jewels they will always be

Liza Leece

The Rainbow

The rainbow is so pretty,
It's a pity it doesn't stay for long
I try to catch it but it is so high
When it is out of sight I give a sigh!

On rainy days I long to go out,
And as I watch the rain,
The sun slowly peeps out,
Then I see a rainbow very high above me.

I imagined a rainbow in my bedroom,
It has a beautiful band of colours
As bright and colourful as my paintings
Just the same as the one I saw before.

I would love a ribbon,
That looks just the rainbow,
With red, orange, yellow, green, blue, indigo and violet,
I would wear it when the ground is covered in snow.

Hoi Yee Lam (Age 10)

Spring

From latticed window ere I gazed
To grassy meadows dewy glazed
To wooded copse and sun tipped hills
Clothed in golden daffodils.

R.S. Leyman

Condemn Them Not

O ye members of my generation
Consider the youth, of this supposed great nation
And wonder ye not at their unrest
Or why they rise in strong protest

Think ye of decades, of our day
Twas better days then I must say
Late forties, fifties, aye sixties too
Work was aplenty, for me and you

No doubt their manners, not all are right
but we must sympathize their plight
For some their bed and board can't pay
And are cast out to make their way

So condemn them not in their great plight
But lend support, to win their fight
And remember, we had not to thole
The degradation of a lifetime on dole

Andrew Lamb

If Only

If only, when she was small
I'd taken time to mend her doll,
or read the book "with the bunnies in it".
It would only have taken but a minute.

Her birthday party when she was three,
I wasn't there - work you see.
Her presents unopened on the chair,
a tear stained face on the pillow there.

If only I had paused a while,
to watch my teenage daughter smile.
The years have flown - dear God above!
My babe's a woman - and in love.

Money cannot purchase time,
but if all the treasures that are mine -
I'd give them gladly one and all
if I could only mend that doll.

Moira Laing

Untitled

I sometimes feel the stress and strain
as days roll quickly by,
I think about the world's events
my heart just wants to cry.
oh why should all these things take place
upon God's lovely Earth? And I stop
and think of all the good folk everywhere
Some folk will stop and think and pray
but others do not even try
oh if men would stop and think
and pray, there would be no
war on earth today, the stain and
stress is mountains high, because
no one has time to pray, this Earth
is God's and all that's in, why
then should anyone want to
destroy it? Why?

Charlotte Laddychuk

Pawns on a Chessboard

The countryside that once was bare,
Of houses, roads, and thoroughfare,
Where there were meadows lush with grass,
And leisurely the time would pass,
When access was by gate or stile,
And woodland walks stretched many a mile,
Here one would find a shady glade,
Untouched by man with fork or spade,
And trees with different shades of green,
We passed many an hour by a tinkling stream,
On going to school we would travel far,
By foot, and not by bus or car,
When teaching was blackboard and chalk,
With a reprimand if out of turn you talk,
Parents and teachers word was law,
A policeman was looked up to in awe,
Our Sunday was a day of rest,
Not just another day for a shopping quest,
Now children look at you with jaundiced eye,
If you try to tell them, how, where, or why,
Like pawns on a chessboard we are moved through life,
Experiencing happiness, sadness, and strife,
No one can tell how long the game will last,
Or do they know how the die is cast.

Harold Lamb

Autumnal Angst

Earth has reached her menopause,
And in a desperate yen for life
Has decked herself in red and gold.
The pale green shoots of Spring
Are near forgot.
What concentrates the mind now —
The geriatric ward of Winter
Lies ahead.

Laurie Lloyd

The Paperboy

The paper boy is lean and mean,
He's faster than a runner bean.
Up our path, over the walls,
He's gone before the paper falls.
Wet or fine, hail or snow,
He's always fast; never slow.

He does our street in one minute flat,
He even has time to stroke our cat!
There's no other paper boys in town,
As he's so fast to get around.
I really, really, hope and pray,
That one day the paper boy will blow away!

Jeannie Kitcatt

Flowers

Flowers that are scented, flowers that are sweet
Flowers that are red, and the crimson that's so deep
How many petals — two, three or four.
Doesn't really matter, they are flowers I adore
A nice looking yellow, a nice looking pink
a nice looking blue, it's adorable, don't you think
Tall or small, they'll be sure to grow
A small little seed, waiting for me to sow
Put it in my garden, in my favourite spot
And just stand back, I can tell I like it a lot
Nice green leaves, all along the stem
A pretty little flower, I now shall call my gem
Nice scented flowers, they come alive at night
I think they're romantic, call me stupid if you like
My Livingstone daisies, they open with the sun.
These are all my flowers, I've put them in a run.
I always make sure, they are watered every night
So I can walk down the garden, it's a pretty sight.
So let's never forget, all the flowers that we keep
The sweet and the scented, and the crimson that's so deep.

Robin Landen

Loneliness

She sits alone in her humble home
Throughout the night and day
And ponders over things she's done
How the years have passed away.

She thinks about her childhood
The street games that she played
Her school years and her teenage years
And the many friends she made.

She became a wife then mother
Of the many children that she reared
Through the hardship and the struggle
And the poverty she feared.

Then one by one they left her
For lands far far away
Now all she has are memories
To last her through the day.

So now she sits in her humble home
Alone without regret
With memories of the life she's had
And the love she can't forget.

She will sleep tonight and wake at dawn
And silently she'll pray
Please God, for me don't let this be
Another lonely day.

Paddy Lambe

Retirement

This is the time we hope will never come
the Autumn of our life has now arrived.
A measure of self pity may be displayed by some
but I am simply thankful that my memory revives
countless sunny days in peaceful bliss
on England's shores, upon her scented moors
or walking her flower'd fields I could not miss
these moments born of gladness such as ours.

While looking back upon those days gone by
my heart is happy having known such things.
Fishing England's streams by float or fly
or riding her winding roads on equine wings.
Or beating up the Sound on straining sail
rambling her country lanes, climbing her peaks
such scenes etched on my mind I could not fail
to note these things my spirit ever seeks.

The beauty that is England has filled our joyful years
passing all too swiftly since my humble genesis.
I shall forget to tremble and the essence of my tears
will be distilled with laughter when I meet my Nemesis.

K. B. Lambert

"36" "22" "36"

How I wish I'd looked after my figure
When I look at it now it's much bigger
I've lost my neat waist
Eating too much cream paste
How I wish I'd looked after my figure.

How I wish I'd the same measurements
Like a sylph with all the right dents
Curvaceous and slim
So beautifully trim
Attractive to all of the gents.

I wish I'd stop stuffing my face
Then the fat would be in the right place
And not round my middle
Hanging over my griddle
And three double chins on my face.

So take heed all you slender young maids
To avoid all those vile slimming aids
You can have a good feed
Without too much greed
And you'll find overweight you evades.

Sheila M. Lamb

An Early Morning Walk

A new day dawns — pale, shadowy light
Struggling weakly into sight.
Beyond the trees thick mist hangs low
And mingles with the stream's swift flow.

Fine dew lies on leaves and grass —
Footprints where someone has passed.
Cobwebs stretched from branch and stalk
Clutch my face as I walk.

Then suddenly the sun breaks through —
To glint and glisten on the dew —
Making lacy patterns on the ground,
And warms up everything around.

I see a mouse and then a mole —
Slugs and snails, a shrew, a vole.
A small grey squirrel watches me,
Then scampers up the nearest tree.

The merry singing of a bird
Across the lush green meadow heard.
The sun spreads out its warming ray —
Brings promise of a lovely day.

Mrs. J.C. Lane

Beach Friends

The Boy and the Girl
They sat on the beach
The Girl on a rock
The Boy just out of reach

They cooed and they aahed
Like Boy and Girl do
But refused to touch
They hadn't a clue

'Tis just as well
That they could not fathom
How to do the deed
Cause the Boy is four and Adam
And Girl is three and Eve.

Susan Kirk

Life

Happiness and fears — joys and tears
All combine to fill in the years —
Music, and poetry, children so great,
And to humans it's handed on a gold plate.
Then swiftly, and sharply as a bird that flies,
The scenario moves — no wheres or whys.
Much tribulation — so many sighs!!
We have to seek strength —
We have to seek power
Or life would become an ice cold shower!!

Julia Lever

Super Sonic Splat!

Spider man zoomed through the air.
Waiting for Batman who was
Putting on his underwear.
Superman forgot
How to fly.
So he caught the 'bus
As it went by.
Batman was very soon ready,
Superman remembered and he started
Flying steady.
Then the Spiderman lost his grip,
Fell off the building and he did slip.
He fell and fell and then he landed,
On top of Superman and they were stranded!
They fell and fell and fall they did,
They landed on Batman and they were SPLAT! dead.

James Lascelles (Age 10)

Illusion

It seems just only yesterday you called my name,
I was too absorbed in self to hear your cries of pain,
I did not realise your flesh was solid to my hand,
Nor did I note the hours sift away like sand.

I did not listen to what you had to say,
Nor did I give importance to the minutes of your day,
Never tried to get to know you really well,
You were like a story I had no time to tell.

My eyes were blind to the pleading on your face,
I glanced away your hurt without a saving grace,
Never cared about the depth of your distress,
Or tried to comfort you with the warmth of a caress.

I did not see you as you really were,
Building in my foolishness a future cross to bear,
Too ignorant to know we cannot choose to stay,
So, unthinking, I threw the story of your life away.

All our life time hopes forever lost,
Dead reckoning to be the final cost,
For suddenly, like a book not completely read,
I turned a page of life and you were dead.

Dorothy Laycock

Countryside Awakening

A warm haze floats gently o'er the ground
In it's wake laid a carpet of glistening dew
Tranquility of morning broken only by the sound
Of the lark's merry shrill as skyward she flew

The sun rises as if to set the horizon alight
Shadows scurry away apparently in mortal fear
The wise owl rests exhausted from its searching night
Into shelter nocturnal visitors hastily disappear

Stirring rodents awaken from nighttime dreams
Birds abandon nesting comfort in search of food
Insects busily dance o'er rippling streams
Wildlife sounds now interrupt the once silent mood

Fragile petals of wild flowers bathe in gentle heat
Thus exposed, their fragrances invite insects to feed
Trees burst with green splendour, majestically complete
Safe havens for many creatures, predators to impede

Wild thoughts or imaginings are needed not
To realise the wealth and beauty of these things
Awe inspiring splendour in wonderment caught
Agape at what natures' countryside awakening brings

David S. Laing

Trees

Trees have always been, to me, a source of pure delight,
Whether small young saplings, or of great towering height.

While slumbering through winter's chill, with naked, frosted bough,
To soften bleakened landscape, they, a stately charm endow.

Then springtime kisses urge the sap to rise, like mercury,
So soon, the boughs once starkly bare, will raise a canopy.

Extending arms to welcome back returning birds that sing,
While hoarding hidden treasure their nest building will bring.

Displaying leaves and blossoms of every scent and hue,
Wonderful varieties to beautify a view.

Abundant foliage above will cast a shade for me,
While I, in admiration gaze, as far as eye can see.

Playing host to numerous small creatures in their time,
To those that burrow under roots, or those that swing and climb.

Autumn's palette never fails to paint a masterpiece,
To compliment the passing year — then to the harvest feast
Of fruit and nuts and berries, ripened by summer's sun,
A final lavish gesture, before the year is done.

Oh Lord, how dull this life would be
Without the beauty of a tree.

P. Launt

Essentials

Look God I want that racing car set, you know
The one I wanted last year but didn't get.
Also I need a robot that fires missiles, plastic of course,
And, oh yeah, two pairs of trainers, the best ones of course.

Holiest Father, take pity on my family and friends,
We need food to eat, water to drink, I implore you to send.
Manna from heaven, a miracle maybe, a passing cloud or
Slight breeze, anything to show us that you're around.

Thanks a lot God, guess what? No racing car set,
The wrong robot in this parcelled box as well I bet.
One pair of trainers, can anything else go wrong?
Only for you, you've just heard your last prayer and song.

Holiest Father, I sit here and watch the crying,
Everyday, I know more will soon be dying.
Do my prayers go unanswered, what have I done wrong?
No will not question you Lord, my faith remains strong.

Michael Lambshead

A Young Girl's Dream

I saw a bright, new shining star
Way up in the sky
I tried so hard to reach it
But it glistened far too high
I held my hand toward it
As further up it cruised
As it moved away from me
I felt so sad, and bruised
I thought I saw it smile at me
But then, I'm not so sure?
It moved away so suddenly
And that hurt even more.
I've tried hard to be happy
Be strong, and bright, and bold
I'd just love that little star
To call mine, and to hold.
I would not have to own it
Just loan it, now and then
Borrow it a little while
Then, put it back again.
I guess I'll never have my star
Or that's the way it seems,
So I'll make a wish upon it
To be always in my dreams!

Donna Lawrence

No Need of Shamrock
(A Remembrance)

I knew not any one of them
No — not even by sight,
But they became my bothers
That wild St. Patrick's night.

They left to do their duty
As they'd done so oft before:
How could they even guess that
They'd see Brims no more?

Caught 'twixt pride and sorrow
We, who, remain, recall
The stunning shock we suffered
When the sea became their pall.

We have no need of shamrock
To remind us of that day;
The tears we shed have lessened —
The grief is here to stay.

But, when the March north-easters
Display their awesome might
We remember — yes, we remember
That black St. Patrick's night.

For the Longhope Lifeboat
lost with all hands 17/3/1969

Ruby Leslie

The Snugs
(from a child's dream)

When I went down beneath the sea,
I met the Snugs and had some tea,
and they were busy as can be,
rolling out their panels.

The Father Snug thus welcomed me,
bowing low with pleasure.
Mermaids, crabs, and octopus,
on panels took their leisure.

When after tea, they guided me,
through green and swirling bubbles,
up to the surface once again,
I thanked them for their trouble.

One little mermaid, pink and fresh,
swam up and kissed my cheek,
then blushed sea-green and swam away,
as all her sisters, who had peeked
from out their panelled shells.
Laughed with delight, and clapped and sang,
their lapping, swishing, gurgling song,
and waved me out of sight.

When I went down beneath the sea,
I met the Snugs and had some tea,
then, left them all contentedly,
rolling out their panels.

Frederic Lamont Law

The Letter

A letter arrives, it's what you dread
"I'm not coming home as I said,
I want to go further afield
Experiences I can yield."

"I'm very sorry Mum and Dad
I know this will make you sad,
Extra fares I'll have to pay
If I come home for Christmas Day."

The party will have to be put on hold
Cancel the friends that we have told,
"You'll all be invited again next year
When the date is made more clear."

"I'll write back saying "It's okay
We understand" What else can we say!
"Have a great time and take care
Yes love, we're a funny pair."

We want you home, then tell you to stay,
To show our love, it's the only way.
You'll come home when you're ready to
Just remember, "We love you."

Mrs. P.A. Leach

Solitude

In solitude I like to be, where a mind can wander free,
free to search the corners of one's mind.
Hidden away from long ago are parts of life that you've let go,
the wonders you thought you had forgot,
or the heartbreaks that you have not.
Bit by bit you will recall the tiniest memories
when you were small,
Sometimes they pain, we think, "I won't recall that again"
But if you do the hurt goes less and helps to
find you happiness - and happiness you will find.
It is locked away within your mind.
So find the key, and turn it slow,
and let your thoughts and memories flow,
let them be released
in solitude
and peace.

Betty Lancashire-Frain

To Be A Child Again

Did I once play as you do on this shore
Letting the soft sand run between my toes?
Was I ever a child like you my son
Sorting shells and putting the pebbles in rows?

Yes — then I was carefree
With no worries that age can bring.
Then I was happy
Free as a bird on the wing.

If I could only leave my burdens here
Watch as the tide washes them away
Then run and jump and
Like the children play

In and out of the sparkling sea,
With net in hand
The fish and shrimps to catch
Or tiny crabs before they hide in sand.

But — can I recapture
That special thrill
That awe and wonder and
Excitement still?

Mrs. J.A. Larner

Of All The Things In Life You Want To Be ...

I want to be a radical, but I'm in the C of E,
the most non-conformist thing I do, is drink fairly traded tea.
I want to fight for honour and glory,
in battles fought hard and won,
but I stand, sit and kneel when I'm told to
and turn my page to sing hymn thirty-one.

Churches lay cold and empty, the homeless have nowhere to stay,
so we wait til Sunday to open, but people have all stayed away.
They've gone to Marks and Spencers,
where even the parking's free,
their gospels marked won 50p this week
with a money back guarantee.

I want to shout out the good news, but people don't want to listen
and besides, it's comfy to sit here in these pews.
But I believe in God the Father,
so say we all with one accord,
and I've got my lottery ticket,
if I win, it's 10% to the Lord.

I want the church to be different, like we were called to be
not dress up nice with best hats on for songs of praise on T.V.
Where is the voice from the wilderness,
to cry aloud again,
make way prepare the way of the Lord,
so we wait, and when, when?

Ian Lightfoot

Isca

I recall the day of the Caerleon trip, the thick, grey, lowering cloud.
The drip-damp mist clung all around, the trees shrunk, shrouded, bowed.
We made our way in silence through a bleak and sombre park,
In an atmosphere repellent, it felt evil, heavy, dark.
A short-shiver walk and we huddled close, on sodden, beaten grass.
Our ankles deep in mounded mist that squirmed, but did not pass.

We stood on that same boggy ground, where once the Romans stood.
Those alien soldiers far from home, in a savage land that would,
To them have seemed a place accursed, with its chill and hostile clime.
They'd surely dreamed of home and friends, unregimented time,
In which to live in happy peace, to laugh with girls and men.
And not be stood where we were now, chilled and wet, as then.

I felt their presence in that sad, old place, a place, and not their home.
Isca, now exposed for all to see, a fortress built for Rome.
Like sly intruders we slunk away from that dank and eerie place.
And I shuddered sharp and uncontrolled, as cold mists brushed my face,
Like fingers of grey-cloud ghosts, who still and silent stood.
Holding fast to conquered land as all good soldiers would.

And I was glad to leave that place, to those who'd never leave.
Unloved and far from spirit kin, they weep eternal, grieve.

Graham Lewis

You Are My Friend

Far away across the miles
each day I think of you,
when I'm feeling up or down
happy, sad or blue.

It doesn't matter what my mood
at any day or time,
we always seem to have a chat —
completely in the mind.

It's either in the kitchen
or lunching in the town,
drinking coffee all day long —
oblivious to what's around.

The best of gifts that I have
which you have given me —
is to have a friend like you;
it means so much to me.

You really are the best of friends
that anyone could wish,
I thank you on this Mother's Day
—
you are a special gift.

Julie Lloyd

Liar

I told them I was best,
I told them all I was great,
I told them
and I told them,
so much that I told me.

I told them I could do anything,
I told them what I could be,
I told them
and I told them,
so much that I told me.

I told them one day I could dance,
I told them I could sing,
I told them
and I told them,
so much that I told me.

I told them that I'd travelled,
I told them that I'd flown,
I told them
and I told them,
so much that I told me.

And then one day I realised,
and then one day I knew,
that I'd told them
and I told them,
so much that I'd only lied to me.

Miss Z. M. Leech

No Visitors

People never call, to see the wife or me.
So we have a little cat to keep us company.
A pretty little thing she is, jet black and pure white.
She likes to sleep the day away sometimes half the night.
She has her funny little ways
and shows it in the way she plays
She flicks a ball along the hall
Then waits for our applause
And she likes to think she's clever
When she sharpens up her claws.
She'll sit and listen to what we say.
Then she'll turn her head away.
I can't be bothered with all that
For I'm only a poor little pussy cat
Because no other food will do,
Felix is her main menu.
We have to be thankful that she's living here
and willing to let us stay too
So because she's so dandy,
We're calling her Pandy,
We think she's lucky,
Don't you?

T. Leach

The Sorrowing World

The world stands upon a brooding precipice
Her eyes with sorrow filled
Her hands pluck at the strings of peace
Her arms hold countless killed.

Her fingers caress the sodden mounds
Graves too innumerable to count
And even as she ponders
The cost in humans mounts.

Her ears throb from the pounding guns
Evil hovers where once lived joy
Her feet wade in rivers of blood
Tentacles reach out to destroy.

Her habitations desolate
Her seas suck foulest air
Protestations silenced by command
Leave her heart in spasms of despair.

Oh world, I weep at your destruction
Man sees your loss as gain
But I see a day of retribution
A night of endless pain.

Anthea Elizabeth Leah

Autumnal Forest

Still, the scrunching sounds
Of elated swishing feet
Through golden brown, sun seared carpet
A russet counterpane of life
That once was lofty forest canopy
A mere two seasons past.

Stay, exuberant romp
To imbibe this magical wooded sanctuary
Where sight, sound and fragrance
Interweave to a capricious tapestry,
A volatile pageantry
That intoxicates our being.

Hark, amid proud sentinels of Birch and Oak
The overhead, raucous conversations of irascible Rooks
Punctuated by dissonant disconnected note
And fleeting glimpse of brilliant plume
Revealing furtive presence of marauding Jay,
In tantalizing undergrowth.

Attend, hasty retreat of wary Blackbird
To wreathed thicket refuge,
Scuttling across parched carpet
Accompanied by rustling of industrious squirrel
Foraging forest's brown fallen mantle
Now tinted gold by late autumn sun.

Stan Lee

Butterfly Ten Thousand

Once there were ten thousand butterflies
To every single one that lives today,
Fast flakes of ever moving life
Sipping sunlit syrup of nectar
Cracking, splitting fissures through chrysalis shells,
Children of the dizzy heights
Brimming into adulthood,
Perpetuating infinitesimal dreams,
Battling against sultry breezes and rising gales,
Dying in puddles like upturned yachts,
Cat caught, pawed into a delicacy,
Hibernating in a mesh of life-suspended leaves
Hugging the old barns rafters,
Bunched in one harmonious breath
Gentle as tomorrows sigh, weaving fantasies
In and out of eight legged gossamer,
Copulating in the updraught of vernal pleasure,
Feeling with wire bent antennae their way
To further fields, flower filled meadows,
Laughing, if they could, at existence,
Winging down vibrant ways like messages
Caught in the cornstalks of ten thousand harvests,
Daring the night in black crevices,
Feeling the nearness of the distant stars.

Gail Mary Leadley

The Sea

Wild is the sea,
Deep, thundering, roaring,
It's almost as if the sea is crawling
On to the rocky shore,
The sea crawls up more,
Very soon it covers up,
All the sand, it's gone, gobbled up.
Right out in the middle,
Someone's in trouble
The Wild, roaring cold, cold sea
It's far, far too dangerous for me,
But forget that for now, about that boat
Will it be able to keep afloat?
The lifeguard's coming, is it too late?
Oh my! Oh no, no, no never too late,
But it is. Oh you horrible sea
Who will forgive you?
Certainly not me.

Kirsty Langley (Age 9)

He Didn't Choose To Go

I really am excited
This day has come at last.
But will he be delighted
Our parting's in the past,
Will he rush towards me,
Or treat me with disdain,
Or does my absence, he now see
As thoughtless given pain?

I know it was essential
To stay away so long,
But hurt is influential,
Such pain it can prolong,
Oh yes, I'm apprehensive,
And will until I'm there
Feel guiltily defensive
About his 'kennel care'.

Grace Leeder-Jackson

Life Is ...

What makes a day worth living?
What makes life seem worthwhile?
Why do we sometimes feel the urge
To greet all with a smile?

Surely it's not the great unrest
Of worldly situations,
Certainly not the weather
Which defies our expectations.

No, it's the simple things in life
Which cost us not a penny,
And if we stop to look around
We'll find that there are many.

The first flowers after winter snows.
The hedgerows slowly stirring
From winter brown to leaves of green —
A kitten gently purring.

A kind word when we're feeling low,
A helping hand when needed,
A sunny morn, a dewy rose —
These ne'er can go unheeded.

A fire bright, a candlelight,
The warmth of family chatter,
Friendship, good neighbours, kindly deeds —
These are the things that matter.

Molly Leplar

Joe

When Joe was but a little lad
He said he'd grow up like his Dad.
No great ambition bothered he,
A trusty weaver Joe would be.

But Fate, who deals out joy and strife
Appoints to us a place in life.
With all the skill that he could muster
Joe grew up to be a "duster".

Every morn with scathing looks
I watch him disarrange my books.
Every time I put them straight
He dusts, with fiendish delight.

When 'ere, with concentrated frown
I stand them up, — Joe dusts them down.
He follows me without a sound
Wreaking havoc all around.

I pointed out for many days
The monstrous error of his ways.
I tried and tried to make him see
Those book were all in all to me.

But slowly I gave up the right,
Resigned myself to life's grim fight
To suffer as we mortals must,
Take up thy duster, Joe, — and dust!

Jean Lees

Look Around

What has happened to this world of ours
That should be filled with love and flowers
That should be more often happy and gay
You must have heard the grumblers say.

Well, it is great if we find time to look
There are sunshine and flowers and a babbling brook
There's joy round the corner in very good measure
If we only recognise the things we should treasure

The goodness of people as they help one another
Be it a neighbour, a friend, or a brother.
The smile on a face before they join the rat race
Thank goodness they stopped flying off into space

The trusting face of a child so innocent and pure
They care only for us and want to make sure
We are there by their side the world is so wide
Hugs and cuddles aplenty helps to breach the divide

The gardens created are a beauty to see
God didn't rush the growth from sapling to tree.
The flowers that he gave us with colours so bold
Can compete with anything we care to behold.

And so as we see the treasures so rare
And look around at the people who care
WE must always remember the joys that abound
If we only take time to look clearly around.

Jean Lees

The Aftermath of a Storm

Life is sometimes like a savage storm,
Its passions rise and swell,
The peace we get from tranquil life
Replaced by raging hell.

When first we met, I felt the stir
Like waking from a trance,
Excitement filled the air about
My heart began its dance.

The two of us were so in tune
As song and lyric, blend,
We cared not for the world around
Or how our song would end.

Each day we filled with memories, dear,
The precious wine did savour,
The sunlit days in which we moved
The spice of love, for flavour.

You did not choose to go away
But knew you had to leave,
How I hope you'll never know
How my poor heart did grieve.

But now the pain no longer aches
And no more do I weep,
The void that I once called a heart
Returns, once more, to sleep.

Monica Leman

Silence

Do you hear the silence of people all around?
Footsteps vibrating echoes, soundless on the ground,
Lips enunciating conversation, words you cannot hear,
Need shadows cast upon the wall to know someone is near.

Do you listen to the silence, see birds in feathered flight,
Movement tells you they are there, for you rely on sight,
You cannot hear the music of their trilling beauteous calls,
You do not know that they are close when darkness on them falls.

Do you listen to the silence of the passing City bus,
It looms upon you unawares, you start, but do not cause a fuss,
The hustle and the bustle of those busy teeming streets,
You do not know the hum of rain as it bounces down in sheets.

YOU may drink the cup of silence and enjoy the sweetest sip,
And thrill upon the whispered sounds of waves upon a ship.
But to live your life without the strains of melodious refrain,
And to always hear the silence, is a source of unrelenting pain.

Glenda Lawrence

Four Seasons in a Week

Monday's chucking it down,
All the fields are muddy and brown.

Tuesday's warm with sun,
Children playing in the park having fun.

Wednesday's heavy rain,
Hitting the window pane.

Thursday is a gentle breeze,
Flowing through all the trees.

Friday is thunder and lightening,
We sometimes find it frightening.

Saturday's snow and ice,
To go skating would be nice.

Sunday is warm and hazy,
Just the day to be lazy.

Rhea Lewis

Depression

I ran and ran, my heart was beating fast.
    Had I escaped this thing at last.
I went on and on, until I could go no more.
    Had I escaped, this thing before.
I came upon a clearing, within my mind.
    Had I left this thing behind.
I was numb and tired, and did not care.
    People passing, just look and stare.
I felt down, and dejected, with despair.
    It caught me, when I was unaware.
What is wrong with me, people never ask.
    They could help me, with the task.
My voice shouts out, aloud inside.
    This is an illness, you cannot hide.
My voice within, just screamed and screamed.
    Is it only, just a dream.
These chains that damage, you cannot see.
    Will someone please, help me.

R. Lee

Time

When in her hour of darkness,
All 'lone and in pain,
Fear crept up behind her
When she thought that no one cared.
She took the tablets that lay there
And said "Now my time will come."

Then in her desperation she realised
What she had done,
She called a friend and said,
"Now my time has come."
Help was quickly on its way,
For her time had not yet come.

After more pain and suffering
The Lord reached out his hands,
He wrapped her in his robes of love,
And took her in His care.

The Lord took her across the water
To the other shore,
He took her to his garden
And gently sat her down.
With loved ones all rejoicing,
So happy to have her there.

June Linn

What will be left?

What will be left when I am gone
To that far place where you may
no longer see or hear me?
What will remain when my body has been
thrust into the cold unwelcoming earth
Or consumed by flames?

What will be left when my voice is still
and my touch is gone forever?
Will I live for a while in the hearts
of those that love me?

But if I have no issue,
where then a smile or likeness to hand to posterity
And I have done no deeds of daring.

For my name is not perpetuated
and no record has been noted in the Book of Life
Yet I lived, loved and cared
for those about me,
I was aware of Mankind,
though they were unaware of me.
So, what will be left to show
that once, I passed this way?

Mary J.T. Lewis

Sweetheart

Once again you have to go
to make you better than you were before
I pray to God, both day and night,
He will help to put you right.

As I lay each night and rest,
I ponder and think, AND,
My thoughts of you are of the very best.

Our travels, joys and pleasures,
That have now all past,
Oh, that they could forever last.

Our time is now getting shorter each day,
But the Lord has treated us both O.K.

I love you Mother, I think you are swell,
More than any tongue can tell.
I see your face in every flower,
I'm thinking of you hour by hour.

So, goodnight, Sweetheart.
When it comes time to part,
You'll see Gladys TATTOOED all over my heart.
GOD BLESS YOU (LIGHT OF MY EYES)

Glyn

Perky

Perky the hamster is sleepy today.
She won't come out when we want to play.
But rattle the box with the hamster food in it,
She'll come out in half a minute.
Nostrils quivering, whiskers shivering,
Ready to take all we have to give.

Perky the hamster is lively just now.
She doesn't mind if we make a row.
Whirling and turning around in her wheel,
Sitting up begging with such appeal,
Coat so smooth, eyes so bright,
What a pity! It's nearly night and
I have to go to bed.

Phyllis M. Lewis

Winds of Time

Once again our paths may cross
ships drifting gently in the winds of time
remembering the love which is now lost
the mist of morning dripping from the vine.

Now and then we may yet see the dawn
the sun rising against the burning cloud
and the proud silhouette of golden fawn
as it stands still on the shore crying loud.

I was in this silent place when you drifted
on the waters of the loch slowly into view
the thoughts in my mind softly sifted
through my dream saw the coming you.

Now we have parted and heavy is my loss
torn apart now as the ships of the line
all that is left of you my love is the cross
in memories and dreams that once were mine

Gordon Longmead

Second Best

Discarding second best in a whim of vanity
Sods Law threatened to inherit his sanity.
The answer to it all as he ended up with third
was to show a mild indifference and that was his last word -
on the topic of success which eluded him pretty well.
He stumbled, tripped and blundered in an effort to to quell
What he really was in life.
There is a price to be paid when you cannot face what's real.
A price to be paid when always hiding what you feel.
A price to be paid when insisting black is white.
Such a tragedy life is wasted
When you cannot see the light.

Irene Leech

This Feeling, Now

A cow upon a cattle grate knows how I feel:

For though the freedom lies but yards
From where she stands, stuck fast and hard
Those cast iron devils serve to prove
She hasn't got the power to move.
Stare she may and wish she will
And strain her neck ahead, but still
However much her thoughts are worth
Her holds will bring her back to earth.

I see her now, she waits in vain
For someone to relieve her pain.
To set her loose, to lead, to guide
To take her to the other side.

On cue, the farmer in his truck
Laboriously wades the muck;
But though the beast has her release
She's even further from her peace.

She knows not how to bridge the gap
Which keeps her in this open trap.
So lives, so sleeps, so dies this cow.
This is the feeling I have now.

Nicola Elizabeth Lister

My Dad

My Dad had a truly wonderful spirit.
When asked how he was, the reply was 'fine'.
Though gasping for breath from pneumoconiosis,
A legacy from the mine.

Badly shell shocked in the first world war,
Returning only a frame of his former self,
The pits alone were open to men, for
That or the dole, there was nothing else.

Travelling to Aberpergym every day,
Costing six shillings out of his pay,
Coming home very dirty and worn,
His moleskin trousers could stand on their own.

Soaked through to his waist very often
To bath before the fire in the kitchen.
No privacy was there at all to be had,
He was not allowed to be modest, my Dad.

Two pounds ten minimum was the outlay.
What would miners say to that today?
Not that he would begrudge them, no indeed.
"Good luck", he would say. "Well deserved."

Dad was only sixty when he passed away.
I loved him so much and was very sad.
But that same spirit he kept to his dying day.
I shall always be proud that he was my Dad.

Elizabeth Lewis

Now Sleep My Love

When you, my love with smiling eyes, invite me to your open arms
Cascading hair on radiant cheeks aglow with all you grace and charms,
And kisses fresh as summer breeze blow warm caresses, oh I feel,
That all the world is fantasy and only you and I are real.

Afloat upon a sea of dreams, we drift together lost in bliss
Tender thoughts, and words sweet lover whispered gently as we kiss,
Thus enchanted I sink down in velvet softness of your thighs
Melting together in sweet fulfillment then all is silence save for sighs.

Passion past we nestle close, locked in each others arms, at rest
With eyes now closed in peace my love, you hold my head against you breast
We have dear love in precious time submerged to spend these wondrous hours
And as sleep comes in soothing calm tranquility once more is ours.

Edward Littlewood

Leaning Over The Gate

Leaning over the gate — watching the whispering grass
Waving in the easterly breeze in a solemn mass,
Seeing the bumblebee floating from clover to clover,
Pollinating each flower, doing its daily task.

The cattle in the meadow, chewing as they lie,
The lash of tail is frequent to disturb the hungry fly,
The trees display their foliage — bisecting the rays of sun,
The stream its waters shallow, a little slower runs.

The whin and hawthorn green garnished with their bloom,
Gives sweet fragrance to the air,
A deeper breath — a silent thought,
A little thankful prayer.

Leaning over the gate — I see the sheep upon the hill,
Their winter coats discarded a duty they fulfil,
The swallows twisting, bending in energetic flight,
Ever seeming tireless feeding in the light.

The wood birds singing merrily, each in their distinctive tone,
The lark high up in the sky singing on its own,
The passing plane unknown gives applause that all do hear,
An orchestra of music to the inclining ear.

Oft' times I pause and ponder over God's creative wonder,
All cares and worries I forsake,
When the mind is free, a million things I see,
Leaning over the gate.

Robert Lynn

Springtime

The countryside is green at last,
Rare beauty all around.
Now the harsh sad Winter's past,
Spring flowers can be found.

You almost see them bursting through,
On Parklands Woods and Hills.
Much beauty can the eye behold,
And Nature's dream fulfils.

Tiny snowdrops — bow their heads,
To welcome in the Spring.
Chattering birds are building nests,
Of matchsticks twigs and string.

The elegance of the towering trees,
Swaying gently to and fro.
A breath of just the mildest breeze,
That makes the windmills go.

A rippling stream — down by the bridge,
Has come to life once more.
Tadpoles, newts and croaking toads,
Are signs — it's Spring for sure.

Sprightly lambs they romp and play,
For Springtime is their pleasure.
The more we see through Nature's eye,
Much more we have to treasure.

Mary P. Linney

Poems

Writing poems isn't easy
Sometimes you just can't think,
As words seem hard to come by
And you totter on the brink,
Rhymes just seem to fail you
And you wonder why you bother
Then in your mind you have it,
First one line, than another.
If you enjoy the writing
The reader will enjoy the verse,
For poems do give pleasure
There are things far, far worse.
So all you budding poets
Draw near and to take heed
Keep up the good work, do your best
write when you feel the need,
It gives great satisfaction
And boredom it will relieve,
You'll be surprised at what you do,
And what you can achieve.

Margaret Logan

Wandering

Wandering around the summer blooms
Inhaling the sweet scent
Memories of long ago
Fresh bread and jam
Clean washing on the line
Ground coffee, not from a jar
Mince and dumplings in a pan
Bring back memories
Of long ago
Silent rocking of a cradle
The crying of a baby
Warm milk and soothing breast
Comfort a hungry child
Memories from long ago
Skating up and down the hall
Snow fights in the garden
Paddling in the stream
Burned hot in summer
Oh those memories from long ago

Carole Lofthouse

Survivors of War

The war may be over, but we forget the real misery.
The fractured lives, tormented with hate,
Distraught and left behind.
Homeless, fighting for peace,
Courageous but mournful.
An empty world, derelict and abandoned,
Collapsed and destroyed,
Only shattered lives remain.
Tortured souls with no life, children with no future
In need, desolate and solitary,
Born into a constant danger.
The possessors of cruelty and suffering,
Living reminders, bearing hope and contentment.
They are the symbols of victory,
Yet through this their lives are ruined,
Ruined by those who now live,
Live in comfort and in care,
Celebrating their victorious defeat,
Bearing no concern for those who now suffer,
Those who are hungry and afraid.
The fighting may have ended, but the war is not over,
The ominous survivors remain.

Amy Lithgow

Day Dreaming

I had a dream the other day,
of a whitewashed cottage far away.
On a windswept island across the sound,
with clear blue waters all around.

A neat little garden overflowed with flowers,
a haven where one could spend idle hours.
A small green boat was moored to a pier,
filled with creels and fishing gear.

Peace and tranquility reigned supreme,
broken by the murmur of a mountain stream.
A seal bobbed up from the mirror like sea,
and gazed across the water at me.

I wended my way to the end of the isle,
and looked across the placid kyle.
I stood on the waterline all alone,
listening to ocean caressing stone.

I retraced my steps through stooks of hay,
and returned to the cottage far away.
If I have another dream the same,
I'd love to return to that island again.

Frederick Pryce Lloyd

My Dad

My dearest loving Dad means everything to me
I've always had just what I want but not spoilt or free,
Memories are the best joy, so full of warmth and love
Of all things I used to do, flown away like a dove.
I loved the place where I was born, but it makes me sad to remember,
The happy days I spent there, now it's just like a cold December.
My Dad was sad when we left there, losing what he loved the most,
The farm sale was so degrading, he wasn't a man — just the 'host'.
It didn't seem fair to have worked so hard, then to have it all taken away.
He made that farm into what it was, it wasn't done just in one day.
But life goes on as we all know, with bitter things to recall.
But he stood firm and proud, still wondering what else could befall.
Of all the things that have happened to my Dad in his full life
He didn't moan or grumble, yet a lot of it has been strife.
Now he's had a heart attack, I don't know what to do.
I prayed to God he'd live and get back healthy and new.
Now Jesus has you Dad, in His tender loving care,
Giving you all his kindness, that we one day will share.
I know that you cannot return, or be with us anymore,
Yet how I'd love to see your face, just coming through my door.

Pauline Lobb

Oscillate Wildly

As the night falls and my emotions rise
Morning hides behind my eyes
That's chased by a future of wanton regret
And held down by the loss of 'great minds' that forget

While bitterness unites my life of such lonely
With passionate nights of one so despairing
A prosperous book filled with literary lying
That wakes up the dead to torment the dying

I live for this genius, this poet and saint;
To picture his beautiful Dorian Gray
And thank God for my books and my eyes and my God
For without them there would be just an 'immoral sod'

And without them there would be no insatiable soul
No reasons to be earnest or important at all
And now that I know him I can waken my sorrows
But delay once again all my lonely tomorrows.

Here comes the rain.

Louise Llewellyn-Jones

Beyond This

I dream of a world in contrast to this,
Above clouds and rain and prevailing mist,
There I will meet a man full of glee,
As he turns around I see that man is me.
I bow to me gently, myself I bow back,
"Falsehood or real," I inquire without tact.
"Oh real," he says, pausing, "indeed very real."
I look at him quizzically, he knows how I feel.
"I did not steal you and leave you to die,
I have always been you and you always I."

Dream, am I dreaming, I pinch my arm to see
Ahhh! Maybe not, he therefore is me.
I take time to think, to collect my mind again.
I stand in a black room and black are the men.
My likeness does beckon, "come hither to me."
I walk to him hesitant, for what he wants me to see.
Stare into this screen and watch from above
As you true loved ones shower you with love
A love that lies dormant upon an empty shell.
He changes and bids me good welcome to hell.

Gary Lightbody

294

Acrostic Eulogy
A Cotswold Village

Endless delights in EASTLEACH dwell
As if Elysian fields and glades
Still sleep along the river's edge.
Turville, Beerfurlong, Sheepridge spell
Life in past ages. Cote Farm shades
Ecclesiastic linger; sedge
And cresses, daffodils, warm stone prevail;
Churches, not one, but two! Sweet peace pervades
Hillside and valley, our dear privilege.

Jane Lofts

That Word!

Old Bill was a farming man of skill in high degree,
Few others could produce near half as well as he.
The local folks oft questioned him, what made the crops so sure,
Old Bill's reply would always be, "Manure, manure, manure!"

Bill's daughter was a pleasant lass who sought her Pa to cure
To bring the old man up to date, and drop that word manure.
She called her mother in, to see if she'd advise her
On any way to get her Pa to call it fertilizer.

"You leave him be," said she, "His ways you must endure.
It took me twenty years, and more, before he used that word Manure!"

C.J. Lockett

No More: — A Widow's Lament

No more walking hand in hand discussing all our dreams and plans
No more secret messages only you and I alone knew
No more "Little Angel" or "My Little Love" from you
No more laughing at your jokes, or at your ready wit
No more cries of "Grandpa fix it" when the toys appeared in bits
No more golden silences with no need for spoken word
No, no more tears, is that your voice I heard?

No more the joy of Christmas which we always held so dear
No more holidays for two, not once but twice a year
No more searching for antiques looking for bargains and anything unique
No more "The Girl That I Marry" our song you sang to me
No more the special meals you cooked for anniversaries
No more goodnight kisses, caresses or tender word
No, no more tears, is that your voice I heard?

Mrs. E. Loman-Brown

A Life's Tale

My life has changed a lot this year,
no longer filled with lonely tears.
At last I've found my perfect mate,
so there's no need to fear my fate.

It has been one lonely haul,
after every step there came a fall.
I never knew love so good
and never thought I ever would.

So now my tale has been told,
Life I can face so strong and bold.

No longer will I lie awake,
each day I'll grasp and hold and take.

For every dawn that shines on me,
says how good life can be.

Angela Linskill

Kiss of Life

He started with a kiss
A dot in the dark
So easy to miss
Leaving no mark

He grew and he grew
In his cosy nest
From a cell to a few
Our new little guest

He began to move
This way and that
His presence to prove
Soothed with a pat

She talked and she sang
He jumped and he danced
New life with joy rang
Our days now enhanced

He sleeps and he sleeps
Some day to awake
The whole world weeps
For his poor parents' sake

Our dreams are no more
Our hearts ache and ache
HE our souls will restore
And our future remake

Ceri Lusk

Down and Out

In the big cities with the bright flashing lights.
In the rural town with the bobby on the beat.
You can see them on every corner,
With the sign of life hanging wearily round their necks.
Shabby shirts sitting scruffily on their backs.
Their homes are detached boxes borrowed from anywhere.
The light in their eyes is all but extinguished,
Their souls are ready to pack up the fight.
They find themselves in a situation that is not their fault,
And there is nothing they can do to escape.
The system seems to be unable to cope with them,
They are trapped in a circle, going round and round and round.
How can you ignore their pitiful faces
As they hold out their bowls in front of you.
Yet I can scarcely believe what I am seeing,
People living on the streets.
Maybe, in some poor, third world country.
But this is the civilized world,
A developed country.
Millions are spent developing new technology,
For the pleasure of the rich.
What have we done wrong?

David Lord

Softly Glow

This night shall a candle be lit for you my love.
As if in one last gesture of hope within my means.
To ease troubled minds painfully trying to rise above.
Only to despair in awakening to frightening dreams.
Shall this flickering light be a pathway to hell?
Or yet soft steps to a heaven, whoever can tell?
When you lost your way, then your smile wore sorrow,
You had misty sad eyes, no sparkle, so hollow.
Then nothing made sense, no future then to view,
Such surging deep anger, confusion; poor lost you.
Forgotten the knowledge of this life's fatal blow,
That the world goes on round, but we reap as we sow.
Not admitting most downfalls are rules we then bend,
And then portrayed as misfortune to a loved friend.
Contentment and balance such heartaches to find,
It's all there, but we stumble in darkness, so blind!
So pass not by this tiny yet such powerful light,
For you it burns gently, through each day and night.
Follow this pathway, release your troubled despair,
Hold tightly to loved ones, for you they are there.
In the glow which surrounds, as each day you unfold
To gain such strength and direction, a mind so bold.
Until then shall this candlelight softly glow.
How precious you are, so wonderful to know.

Jo Long

November Roses

Pale sisters of summer's flush,
Beauty still in bud, slow to open;
Gently bent on lanky stem,
Parchment clad in leafy gold,
Ink stained.
Rotund yellowed hips
With claret spines compete,
Vibrant in the watery light,
Ripe for the pruner's secateurs.

Denise Lynch

To Share

Days of sadness I have shared
With none but myself,
Hours alone to think and brood
Over past happenings —
That chilled me
And put me in melancholy mood.

Strange this should be so!
But oh when joy
Fill the room, and fills your heart,
To measures over-whelming
And delight
You need to share it so! Lest it past!

Jenny Linehan

Don't Go

Say you'll always love me
Say you'll always care
I will always love you
And I'll always be there

Take me into your heart
And keep me for all time
Just say you'll always love me
And you'll always be mine.

Your love is so special
I hope that mine is too
All I ever want to be
Is right here next to you

So baby don't you leave me
Please don't go away
I want to spend my life with you
Each and every day

Gary Long

Spring

White blanket cast aside, once more
Mother Nature tingles with delight
As the harmony of feathered song
Accompanies the symphony of bursting life.

As sun smiles down its ochre warmth
She opens her arms in wondrous joy.
Embroiders rainbow dreams upon green velvet
Expertly stitched as she alone knows

The fluttering wings of gossamer days
Fragile, fleeting ever moving, our
Untiring, infinite cycle of life revolves,
Turned by the breezes of timeless wonder.

Sylvia Lycett

'My Son, My Son ...'

The boy sits upright on the shaggy pony,
No saddle, thin legs dangle in the warm fur.
The big dog stands head level with his master's heel.
Dog died, long gone his bones, black pony to some
knacker's yard —
And you, my son, and what of you?

Each brushmark conjures up what should have been
Such happy childhood years;
But also does preserve the watching of it all.
Photos bring back memories, but nothing like
The searing pain which heats the tears
Falling on the unfinished canvas.

Rachel Luce

Life At The Moment

Sitting it out in a darkened room,
Occasionally moving into beams of light
Thrown by moments of interest.
The rest - just monotony.

Once I was optimistic, despite all.
Now pessimism becomes a way of life,
Without it I'd feel bereft.
Happiness - a threat I couldn't get used to.

To have joy causes fear - fear of its loss.
Why should it last, why should it happen to me?
If caught out in enjoyment I'm bound to be punished.
No, joy isn't for me.

And yet "at the moment" holds hope.
Maybe there will be more than beams
In the darkened room sometime.
Maybe not soon - but sometime.

Angela Lowle

The Autumn Poplar

Away on a bank a small poplar tree
Growing barely four feet high
With its autumn leaves a-trembling
Fluttering as a butterfly
Quivering, quivering here and there
Then dancing from right to left
Expressing so much happiness
Giving forth very Heavens best
Only to find little tree crying, bereft,
As those leaves fall earthward exhausted.

Phyllis Ludgate

Until ...

I will love you today forever,
Until the stars flee from the sky,
Until the moon no longer wakes each night,
And birds no longer love to fly.

I will always be your best friend,
Until the sun falls far from grace,
Until the sea at last is standing still,
And your dreams begin to know your face.

Until every song has ended,
Until every word has gone,
Until time has no more meaning
And our hearts now beat as one ...

Mrs. J. Lowrey

Negative Equity

The house, the car, the lovely yacht
And all the things his wealth had got
Could not delay the awful day
For what his doctor had to say.

The house, the car, the lovely yacht
And all the flings his wife had got
Could not erase one lonely night
That married life could not make right.

The house, the car, the lovely yacht
And all the things they never got
Amount to just a hill of beans
Now they've passed on in spite of means.

The house, the car, the lovely yacht
And all the things they now have not
Are falling into disrepair.
No one to know. No one to care.

David R. Lucas

When Opportunity Knocks

If -
    I should trespass upon your door,
        With a rap, to gasp your startled vagaries
    Deeply acute; into their innermost chamber,
        Wherein all dreams acquire secrecy; to secrete what implore

Invites -
    To befit all such ragged wanton,
        Within, that embodiment of creation,
    Enquiring beyond, life's daily, mundane, tailored contour.

Will -
    You hasten admission, with a turmoil akin
        To the excitement within an eager without caution
    Upon that threshold beyond all elation past breath,
        Before its spiral, creates, an apex through spin

Or -
    But inwardly compose through a peephole compute,
        An outline; with the whim in its fantasy
    Assuming, such a presence should admit; an opportunity within.

P.J. Lyons

Don't Cry For Me

Don't cry for me as I am asleep
I am at peace so please don't weep
Don't grieve too long I ask of you
Please be happy and don't be blue

Don't let your tears fall too long
Try to smile and please be strong
Be strong for me and know I care
Although in life we no longer share

Think of me as I'm free of pain
Until the time we will meet again
I am happy so don't feel sad
Start again and don't think bad

I still surround you with my love
Even though I am now with Him above
Although for now we are apart
Smile again, don't break your heart

Don't cry for me as I am at rest
Live the life you have and just be blessed
Don't think of me as gone away
We'll be together again someday

Lannette Lusk

Untitled

Each night I greet your smiling face,
The love it shows makes my heart race!
You hold my hand so very tight,
As together, the world we fight.
We have our moments when we don't get on,
But for each other, we'll always be strong.
No matter what blows this land has to give,
For years to come, together we'll live,
For the love we share is simple and pure,
It's a kind you can't lose, there is not a cure.
Though the time will come when you leave my side,
But my true feelings I shall deeply hide,
When a new girl walks into your life,
And you decide to make her your wife.
I will be happy that she is here,
Though secretly I shall shed a tear,
Because I'll know you have found the one
That makes you happier than I can, SON.
So please remember the times we shared,
And also that I have always cared,
As though your Dad and i might be apart,
The two of us love you with all our heart.

Karen Lyon

One Mind's View Of The Universe

I am going back to basics in my purposes of mind,
I am setting out to tell you VERY TRULY what I find,
For I guess all human beings are much the same as me,
So ONE TRULY UNDERSTANDING MIND can represent the whole menagerie.

I remembered William Shakespeare from my days in English School,
"TO BE OR NOT TO BE" was cited as the BASIC RULE.
For everyone, at every stage, from babe to wise old age,
I will tell you now I set my mind to try to be a sage!

I was young and very healthy so I CHOSE the way of LIFE.
I had found a mate with courage who had said she'd be my wife.
I was not very wealthy but I had thought what I could do,
To REFORM the world's BASICS as I still aim to do.

One FLASH of UNDERSTANDING had brought home to my mind.
THE BASE of having ONE GREAT TRUTH: ere I TRUE TRUTH could find,
ONE MIND I had, ONE TRUTH for me, was very plain to see,
That HENCEFORTH I would be content to let SEARCHING motivate me.

One UNIVERSAL MYSTERY is our environmental stage,
One World, One Folk, One Cash, One Tongue should be our equipage,
One Race, One Faith, One Law will work to PACIFY the World,
Collective HUMAN UNITY WILL WIN: with ONE WORLD FLAG unfurled!

GLORY! GLORY! HALLELUJAH!
GLORY! GLORY! HALLELUJAH!
GLORY! GLORY! HALLELUJAH!
LET MANKIND'S SEARCH GO ON!

Edward Graham Macfarlane

Executive Stress

The time is now, my love,
The time is now.
While your lifeblood runs young and your spirit still soars.
While your love is still urgent and your loving still warm.

The time is now, my love,
The time is now.
While your body complains that you're running too fast.
While you're chasing the things that you know will soon pass ...

The time is now, my love,
The time is now.
Time to give to yourself what you're giving to all
Your time,
        Your time,
                Your time.

Helena Landers

The Shore

What a horrible beach we have
For nobody cares
It's greasy and stony now
For nobody cares
Children like playing, making sandcastles too,
But not now,
For nobody cares.

Everyone's complaining now
For nobody cares
Complaining about their children,
Being muddy when they play
All because of the dirty beach
For nobody cares.

Kelly MacLeod

Interrupted Dream

The space around my body is occupied by a scented cushion of water,
It ebbs and flows over my form like gentle summer waves.
Thoughts drift on clouds of steam, fighting with sleep,
Closing heavy eyelids, I open my mind for developing dreams.

Bounding my circumference, lemon shaped soap, a striped purple flannel,
frayed in one corner, trying to cope with a dried up split peach stone,
(remains of my supper)
All balanced precariously on the bath's rim.
Falling together, creating an avalanche
Into the deep subterranean cave
Mysterious, murky and dim.

Sudden intrusion of unwanted objects brings startled awakening.
Bursting the bubble of blissful contentment.
I pull the plug.
Down the drain a peaceful mood is lost.
The stresses of life's problems will resume again.

Elma Lumbard

Bereavement and Grief

Do not feel alone when your loved one has passed on,
The loved one's Soul still lingers. Only flesh and bone is gone.
The tears you shed in sorrow will help to ease your pain,
Then look towards tomorrow when Souls shall meet again.

'Tis true one feels the ache of sorrow
Deep within one's receptive Soul.
The pangs of anguish slowly follow,
Despair sets in and takes its toll:
Its grip — likened to tightened rope.
The gut responds and strives to cope
With the agonising sensation
That sorrow provokes from its creation.

One then resigns oneself to keep
The grieving sorrow sunken deep
Within the wounded Soul. There's no release
Till one expires, then — longed-for peace
Instills itself to penetrate
The sorrow it will obliterate.

Animals, birds and marine life, too,
Experience grief like me and you.
They're not immune from shedding tears
When the ugly head of doom appears.

Tina MacInnes

The Killer Sandwich

In the dark, dark depths of my lunchbox,
There is a bag which is government protected.
For in there is a sandwich as sly as a fox,
And it is mentally defected!

It lives on fingers which try to touch it,
And it sits on a carpet of mould.
Once an elephant it bit,
Then pretended to be as good as gold!

It is made of brown bread with crusts,
And lettuce and strawberry jam.
After some freedom it lusts,
It eats meat like chicken and lamb.

I'll soon have to take it to the zoo,
To have it locked up forever.
The manufactures of it I'll sue,
It has just eaten all my leather.

So beware of foreign pasties
And of sausage rolls and pork pies,
They could be killers or nasties,
Or maybe just made of lies.

Sarah Macdonald (Age 13)

Sunset On Hoy

The evening stilled and clouds appeared to lie
Asleep on brooding hills of speckled brown
While shafts of orange streaked the upper sky
Changing to burning crimson lower down
To meet the sea horizon in a blaze
Of rippled redness where a glowing ball
Was half submerged beneath the gentle waves.
And soon a colour mix spread over all
The hemisphere like shattered rainbows cast
Aloft by random hand — a scattered light
Whose sheen seemed pining for the day now past.
This sad cathedral calm was such that night
took longer to approach — still loathe just yet
To fade the glory where the sun had set.

R.A. MacBeth

When Hope Has Gone

Love is a stranger
I have never met
Fear and pain
my constant companions
Death is what I pray for
with every breath
Hope is what I remember
in my distant past
Oh God, if you're out there,
release me please from this hell
Let me embrace death —
my one and only true friend

Jean McMann

Untitled

I sit through the hours of many a night
In pain and hell with all its might
And the thing that helps me se it through
Is the love and joy I share with you.
I don't always share the feelings of my heart
But without you I'd fall apart.
Just knowing that you are there
With your love and tender care
So instead of feeling blue
I thank God that I have you
These aren't the rantings of a silly old man
But to let you know my feelings if I can.
And hope to God these words will do
Just to let you know a little of the way I feel for you.

You probably think I am quite mad
You're right — *and you need another writing pad.*

W.A. MacDonald

Me

Alone am I, within myself,
Among the crowd, alone I am,
With family near around my side,
A vast array of empty space,
Like single, one, and on my own,
To me I speak, and I do hear,
I'm glad to have myself to listen,
'Cause nobody knows just how I feel,
Image in front, hidden insides,
No one to know, what cries within,
To be like them, I cry for change,
Not to be shy, or anxious,
Moods that change like passing clouds,
Thinking happy, but feeling down
Momentary acts set mind ablaze,
Control, control, control the rage,
Joyful scenes behind the mask,
Embarrassment, hoping time will pass,
Alone am I, to be carefree,
It's me who only can escape,
To fight myself, but which side wins?
The strongest power is felt within.

Graham MacDougall

Bus Station

Beyond us a city of strangers
Joined the evening discotheque.
Among them the great diesel rangers
With dozens swaying on deck,
Glad to be snug as winter bears
While eternity suspended our trek.
The bench held a self-conscious cast
Sombre lives, mutely examining the past.

The sound of a purse overflowing
Caused one youth to sink to his knees.
The noise was like a Gatling,
Soon he was crushed by the squeeze.
Discipline kept us from cheering
Another tragedy by Euripides.
This long-haired, cane-battered hero
Felt the terrible pain of subzero.

A sceptical mood embraced us all.
It's not difficult to understand why
Fear sparks the inevitable brawl.
Gale-lashed, static, lost above the cry
And a glass fridge for landfall.
Such trials would warp a samurai.
Years of little defeats can splatter on
Then suddenly the armour has gone.

Maureen Macnaughtan

Soul Searching

Happiness is found at the Spirit within
Spread your wings,
Shine on through.
Have faith in all things good.
Believe.
Have faith and thou shalt receive.
Have faith and thou shalt go forth.
Have love and thou shalt be loved.
Respect they wishes and go hence with love and compassion.
Love thy neighbour.
Love thy friend.
Love thine enemy.
Only then will come peace and harmony,
Within.

Mrs. G. McGeechan

The Answer

When you feel sad and lonely and no one seems to care
Then just kneel down in silence and speak to God in prayer:
For He will ease your burden, He'll bear your heavy load
And He will walk beside you, along life's unknown road.

Your sins they may be many, but God waits to forgive,
New life He'll freely give you so trust in Him and live;
Your life will have new meaning, new tasks for each new day,
If you will only take time to humbly kneel and pray.

You'll find your each tomorrow has joy none else could fill.
As day by day you serve Him and know you're in His will;
Then count your many blessings for all that Christ has won,
Until you stand in glory and hear the great 'Well Done!'

Iris MacKinnon

My Hopes in You

You look up at me smiling your toothless grin
How much I love you to tell you I don't know where to begin
Your arms outstretched that look in your eye
It's enough to almost make me cry
Your tiny little body made perfect in every way
Getting bigger stronger and wiser with every passing day
So small so trusting and dependent on everyone here
You have to take the chance that for you we will care
I look down on you now I hope that I will do you right
To protect you from your fears by day and by night
And hopefully as you grow older you'll learn by your mistakes
I hope that you will get the chances get the lucky breaks
For our generation our chance is gone our time is overrun
But for you my little child your time has just begun
Don't waste it don't throw it carelessly away
Plan for your tomorrows not for our today
Our people our planet our hopes all look so blue
That's why my child I place our hopes my hopes in you

Karl McAreavey

The Pipe Band

I hear them in the distance
And as they're drawing near
I feel like jumping up and down
And letting loose a cheer
The sound just makes me shiver
My very toes, they curl
I love a Scottish Pipe Band
The drum beat and the skirl
Marching out at their head
Is the leader with the mace
He throws it up into the air
My heart does madly race
What if he didn't catch it
As it comes falling down
He'd feel a proper Charlie
A failure and a clown
But oh — aren't they real bonnie
In Clan tartan oh so braw
You can have your Pop or Classics
The pipe band beats them a'

Jean MacLeod

Spring!

The rainbow
    shines through the trees
    like a brand new day in June.
    I'm dancing like frost through leaves,
    In my own cocoon.

The clouds
    keep cunningly changing
    just in the blink of an eye.
    Dancing uncensored around the sun,
    carefree around the sky.

The rain
    drip-drops, refreshing
    upon my electric pulse.
    All in a passing shower.
    Dancing, hitting, all the leaves,
    writhing in overwhelming power.

The sun
    twinkles through the trees,
    the leaves make way.
    Oh how I do so love early Spring!
    Dancing like a lamb.
    This sunrise
    Keeps my heart bobbing on a string.

Laura E. Macpherson

behind glass

i love you in your 'uncertain' look which shoes you've seen my eyes
        and i love you as you kiss me into oblivion and daze me with your touch
and when our bodies merge
        and when your warmth is mine

i love you with our hands deep in our pockets — just in case we forget
        and i love you in the silence
i love you in the open with salt spray and laughter
        and i love you in the morning with giggles and clatter
                and six o'clock nonsense
                        and peering through windows
                                and saying hallo fondly as we step over milk

                        and leaning round corners
                                dodging men with binoculars
                        and smiling in mirrors
                                and turning away

i love you
        and you smile
                and i take your smile with me into the rest of my life

Cara Mackinnon

Life

At age sixty, we all look back
At life, to see what we've achieved.
We remember all the heady stuff
The goals, the points, the scores,
The tears, the laughs and glory
Years of fun and woes.

Things might have been better
We should have tried to make
The most of opportunities
That life placed on our plate
The points could maybe have been goals
Hills perhaps were not that steep.

Would that life be like a cine film
To view and view again
Fast forw'd that silly time we had
It's not worth a second look.
Pause here and let us see once more
The magic of that special day
'Twas happy, but why did I look so sad?

Who's the operator here, I want it to be me
To rewind the film of my life again
To look, to pause and to rewind.
Unfortunately it just can't be.
I only had one starring role, mistakes or not — that's me.

Patricia McCarry

Farewell To My Canine Friend

I put my face down close to yours
        To tell you that I loved you.
I tweaked your ears, I stroked your head
        And said how much I'd miss you.

I reminded you of happier days
        When you were young and strong.
How you romped with the children in the snow
        And loved to chase a ball.

You were always faithful, always brave
        In defence of your smaller brother.
The beach and sea were your delight —
        Or to walk in a leaf-strewn forest.

You always were a friendly chap
        With a happy, long-tongued grin.
And even in pain you never moaned ...
        You knew we'd do our best.

"There's a place in my heart that no other can fill"
        So says the Irish Ballad.
But you'll never know just how true that rings —
        There'll certainly be no other.

So you lay on your bed whilst I sit by your side;
        We're both helpless to alter our fate.
You cannot be cured — and the decision is made —
        For you to fall gently to sleep.

Doris McCartney

No Deliverance

As snowdrops droop I remember
How you slithered into the world.
A miracle of folded pink perfection
A foil for your robust brother.
The final piece in the jigsaw of our lives
You flawed creators gawped in awe,
At downy hair, rosebud mouth and amaranthine eyes.
For eight drowsy weeks
we rarely touched the ground,
Until that April morning when I found you.
In your bassinet of duck-egg blue
Limp and purpled.
At anniversaries we feign forgetfulness
Immersing ourselves in spurious tasks.
In fervid avoidance of each other's stare.
Lest we should find there
A mirror image of our own despair.
Siblings in your slipstream,
Found me too fearful
Though I tried to conceal my scar tissue.
Years later the strangest things stir up my pain
There is no deliquescence for so viscous a sediment.

Maureen McAteer

A Dog's Life

If some dogs could speak,
Then this they would say:
"I am tired of sleeping,
Doing nothing all day.

Of chewing on bones,
Eating scraps from your meal,
Wearing collars to walk
And always made to heel.

Eating food that you've chosen,
Told off when I mess,
Now I know why they say:
'It's a dog's life', I guess.

You don't think as you watch,
For I cannot speak;
I've feelings and strength,
But sometimes I'm weak.

If I packed up my bone
And walked out the door,
There'd be no one as faithful
Living here anymore."

Kim McDonald-Payne

Tae Laureate wi' Frustration

Fightin' for genius but I just canna spell it
Typin' the words cause I canna recall.
Searchin' for endin's better than this,
Wishin' for clarity, tae Hell wi' it all.

Readin' ne'r writin', spellin's tae poor,
But when I see, hear or smell it my heart does fly.
Pretendin' the pretence but I just canna halt,
I'll say what I feel before I lie.

My English is broken, my Scots worse still
Form is a stranger and rhyme a bitter pill.
Vernacular my comment, foreign my tongue,
But when it comes tae frustration, my personality reigns.

They told me to read more but I feared o' readin' tae much.
Work takes it oot oh me and the old scone's scunnered.
You just sit there in exaltation, producin' your prose with ease.
Mysel' ... it takes me a lifetime tae jot doon my list.
Must avoid that pretence and I *will* find that thought!

Scott D. McArthur

Games We Played

As I sit by the fireside
I think back on the days
Fin I wiz a youngster
An the games that we played

There wiz chasing an rounders
And skip we a rope
Bools in a kipie
And beddies we hopt

In the lang winter nichts
Fin we didna get oot
We wid sit roon the fire
And wid a reed a book

Maybe wid play
A gamie o cards
Snakes an ladders an ludo
Draughts wiz nae bad

I mine noo on dotties
An X an Os
Hang the man
An dominoes

I we were contented
We little te dee
The kids noo dee nithing
Bit watch the TV

Iris L. McRae

Metre

Should a poem rhyme? Or do we just keep the metre;
should it be sublime? Or do we keep walking down
 the line, and keep the metre ticking long, or short, but fine.

It seems to matter not what we say, but how we deign
to say it, if reason be the food of love, let's not
pick up the pen, and when reason begins to falter, we
can surely start again.

If line after line the rhyme stays, and the sound is
easy to taste; and a story is told be it mellow be it
bold even be it in haste, then think not of the rhyme
or the reason, just keep the metre pace.

If love the story should enter, be sure not to be too
refined, be curt and remote, don't let words clog
your throat, chew them up, spit them out, rule the mind.

When ending your saga, be it long, be it short, be
sure the story is told, for you hold in your pen, the
world at its best or worst or neither, for the story
is all, for the lilt and fall of the metre.

Newol

A View Of Christmas

I love this brumal landscape
The night-time of the year,
When dawn is dressed in silvery frost
And the air is crisp and clear.

When the wooded ways of England
Stand bare for all to know
By morning they'll be clothed again
In a mantle of pure white snow.

The way the frosted grasses stand
Decked out in Winter's jewels,
While bulrush stand bedraggled,
Trapped in ice bound pools.

Like ice topped cakes the hedgerows stand
Capped white, rich browns below,
While here and there a rose hip shines
In pale December's glow.

Yes, I love this winter season
Its colours and tannic smells,
With its grizzled fields of corduroy
As the year bids its farewells.

Colin McCombe

Quite Disjointed!

Soft banana splodges — deep in pockets of the car.
I stab pickled onions through the bottom of a jar.
Look how slanting moonlight silvers a dusty frieze!
What about my briefcase? Why are you on your knees?
Tired Hansel and Gretel, prancing Unicorn.
(It's zigzag cortex *slumber* — not straight logic of the morn!)

On grey Glenfinnan's shoreline, our touring children play.
How come Flora McDonald lives just across the way?
Marks and Spencer's doorway, the cat sits on the mat.
These will never fit me! Where did you get that hat?
Along the hillsides, warlike Redmen muster.
Our confidence is waning — we're standing here with Custer!

Please take some three times daily, while coughing on the train.
That hellish sump called Sellafield, milk goes down the drain.
Who will give me credit for smart remarks at tea?
Why does our men's choir sing — "Three Little Maids Are We"?
From purple potholed pit, float strange fading yells.
I'm roused from mental subways, by German alarm clock bells.

Stagger back from the bathroom. Snuggle down in my dream.
Purloin a plate of biscuits — then single out the cream!
Childhood talents flourish *now*, long-dead parents smile —
Till, with such approbation, *youth* comes back a while.
Drat tickling duvet! My deep-down world is gone!
I'm awake! Still quite *disjointed*! — In the dull and dismal dawn!

S.A. McElroy

The Cat

Her coat is black and silky
Her eyes luminescent bright
She glides along with dignity
Is a hunter day and night.

She is always independent
No alliance will she honour
But she tolerates the human race
Who fuss and fawn upon her.

Her ancestors roamed the hill sides
The forests and the moors
She will accept your hospitality
But she never will be yours.

There she sits cold and aloof
Watching and listening as though in reproof
Judging the world through eyes that can speak
One of the strong despising the weak.

Her heritage is a proud one
From forest, valley and dale
You can see it in those glowing eyes
In the haughty swish of her tail.

Then off she goes back on the prowl
In the dark dark world of the bat and the owl
Tail erect and eyes gleaming bright
One of the mysteries of the night.

Bernard McDonough

For 'M'

Out of the press and throng of a hostile world you came
Like a long-forgotten song, like a dear-remembered name.
You came when my need was great and the flame in my soul burned low,
When the clock of the world chime 'late' and the clock in my breast beat slow.

You came and my day grew bright with the warm white light of love,
And all that was wrong came right, and all that was rough turned smooth.
So beloved, take my hand: no! Not my hand, my heart!
For you will understand that it dies alone, apart

Like a shed leaf, or a rose from its parent plant detached,
Or buds when a bleak wind blows, or artlessness when watched.
You have restored my faith and hope has returned to me
That all that was lost is safe in Time and Eternity!

So come, leave the world and rest in arms that have waited long
To shelter you, dear heart, from the press and the hostile throng.

John McClennan

Pirates In The Sky

She huddles by her window as battle commences
With that first ominous rumble heard from afar
The world with baited breath waits wondering, yet
No one yearns for it more than she.

Needle bright light splits the
Sullen sky, splintering through the clouds
A gasp is torn from her spirit
She is captured by the storm.

Crackling, rolling round the dome of sky
Thunder follows lightning as night
Must follow day. Blue-white forks
Plunder the sky in jagged sharp bolts.

Pirates in the sky, they raid the earth
Nature's warriors, riding to battle
To be victors or vanquished, who can say?
Mere mortals cannot comprehend

Except, perhaps, the girl who watches
Eyes wide, fear bright, thrilling to the splendour
The storm touches her with its savage beauty
Deep in her soul, she hears its cry.

Rachel McClusky

Real Lonely Freedom

The best things in the world are free,
Constant chorus of the birds carefree,
Warm mild May rain,
That brings growth and renewal again.

Smell the greasy, horsey air,
As cattle lose their ould matty hair,
The long winter they have survived,
Now with lush grass they'll thrive.

I am relieved that this time is here,
Life at its best.
Like times before, perhaps! I'll remember,
'Now' in a different distant year.

Colour schemes and joyful things,
Nothing as bad as ever it seems.
Life takes with it splendid springs,
A time of change and new dreams.

Wish you were here,
To enjoy yourself,
Yet even I don't understand,
The beauty within this sphere.

Mr. McCaughey

'Paws' For Thought

Last year, Christmas was such fun, with toys and gifts for everyone,
A special present (that was me), lay underneath the Christmas tree,
The sweetest tiny ball of fluff, the family couldn't love enough,
One ear stood up, the other down, I was the cutest pup in town,
We played, we walked I'd fetch my ball — so clever for a dog so small,
I didn't have a pedigree, but what the heck, they still love me,
The novelty did not last long and soon my rights had changed to wrong,
As weeks passed by my size increased, the walks and games by now had ceased.
All day locked in a tiny room, I cost so much to feed and groom.
I didn't mean to scratch the door, or leave the puddles on the floor,
Or chew the cushions on the chair, bark so loud or cast my hair,
The family found they could not cope, and led me on a length of rope,
Into the woods, tied to a tree; some lads passed by and set me free.
I knew survival would be hard and leave me hungry, cold and scarred.
Roaming the streets and scrounging bins, for scraps of food or opened tins
Became a way of life for me — a far cry from that Christmas tree.
So spare a thought for me today, I don't deserve to live this way.
Please heed the theory of this rhyme and don't give pets at Christmas time.

June MacLeod

Untitled

Don't believe you've gone
The real rose
No more smiling eyes
Gone to a better place

The world didn't deserve you
But you deserved the world
A heart so full of sadness
Can anyone understand

A big gaping hole
In the world today
So many tears
For a rose that withered and died

So alone in this simple world
Just couldn't live any more
A body too tired to go on
But a spirit that can fly

So fly, spirit, fly
While the memory keeps you alive
Travel high on the wind
Till your home again

We're all just drifting
Existence is but a dream
I hear you whisper in the trees
While the wind gently blows.

Sonya Matheson

A Lonely Man's Thought

A band of soldiers
Dance to a tune
Their shadows cast before them
Reflected by the moon

The violin plays
As if by itself
For below the toadstools
Dance the fairies and the elves

A ring of seven
Went the men round the fire
Brought down like angels
By the evil man sire

True black and chanting
Eyes red with hot blood
He walks through the fire
Throughout the winds and the floods

Oh, desolate hero
Show me your heart
Pick me a beginning
From which I did start

Tangled in reeds
Below rough ridden seas
Could the waves have drowned me
The way they did thee.

D. McKay

Starstruck

The wine-washed heavens cloud my mind
Though clear in their purity
Rocking my innate sanity,
Reflecting an inner expanse as vast
Yet compounded into its usual mass
Of futile hellish reason.

A cerebral mind warp of adverse electricity?
Or universal collected thought pervading each being?
For who can shut out every spark of such intense feeling?
And who can stop the questions making life seem harsh?
And if we knew the answers wouldn't we be parched
With thirst for any mystery to take away the sting of knowing?

And yet to know is too enticing,
Out of reach and tantalising.

Dare I let go and learn to live
Or suffer on preoccupied,
Gnawing away this self inside?
These doubtful questions create more doubt
So any faith is all but cast out.

Donna McGarel

Childhood Friend

Standing alone in the playground
She watched her friend draw near
He was old and grey and crumpled
But to her was very dear
He told her funny stories
Above the playground noise
And sometimes gave out sweeties
To special girls and boys
Billy's job ensured
He was never far away
She laughed when he called her Goldilocks
And cuddled her each day
He was her one and only friend
She trusted him completely
And when she sat upon his knee
He spoke to her so sweetly
He said she was a good girl
But she must never tell
Of how when Billy touched her
It made his trousers swell.

Jacqueline McGregor

Discovery

Nobody told me that I would become
Invisible.
I expected the wrinkling face and thickening waist;
I accepted the diminished hearing and hair.
But I was quite unprepared for
Invisibility.

Nobody noticed me in streets, pubs or shops:
I was completely overlooked at bus stops.
And at home my slowly focussing eyes
Watched the chocolate box passing quickly across
The shabby barrier arms of my chair
While my hand, poised to select, silently retracted
Like the miniature crane, without its prize,
In the glass box on the pier of my childhood.

But today I discovered a way
To make myself undeniably and gloriously visible.
I simply made myself extremely
Audible.

In the street they walked around me very carefully.
In the shop and the pub I was served immediately,
And I was helped most solicitously
Onto the bus, which they had stopped for me.
Oh yes! I have learnt the lesson of my second childhood:
Old people have to be heard to be seen.

Margaret McMichael

The Queen Of Sheba

Stroking tresses so sleek and sensuous
this harem lady deserves attention
princess and seeker of diversion
coils round legs so lascivious,
loving, sweet, obsequious,
life companion, faithful friend,
soul-mate, sleeping.

But under the mask lies tempered steel
sharp rapier claws in velvet paws
and razor teeth in deadly jaws,
keeping guard with eyes half-closed,
sleeping, yet not asleep.
A sentinel on duty, one ear cocked,
quiescent, watching.

When hunter's moon shines ghostly white
she mounts her solitary night patrol,
disturbing dustbins, near the coal shed,
pads under bushes, by the flower-bed.
Faint scratches and a tiny rustle,
betrays a tiny creature's bustle.
A lightning bolt,
with sapphire eyes.
Assassin.

R.W. McDonald

A Tribute To A Border Collie

I had a dog, a special dog, I affectionately called him Sheppie Pie,
One thing I knew for certain, I was the apple of his eye.
He used to get me up for work and I was never late.
When I trudged wearily home, he was waiting at the gate.
He was always pleased to see me of that I had no doubt.
Oh how I loved him, he was always bossing me about.
He was great with my grandchildren when they stayed for the night
He'd pad from bed to bed making sure they were all right.
Yes, he was a worker, a friend loyal and true
That's why I'm sitting here crying, 'cause I really miss you.
He had that one quality that very few possess
That very special something that equals happiness.
I love my Pie, my Sheppie Pie, I'll love him till the day I die.
There is few like him I will confess, He did not want to cause me unhappiness.
A noble lad was he who met his death with dignity.
If there is a life hereafter and that journey I have to take
I hope my pal comes for me to see me to Heaven's Gate.

Sarah McGowan

When Night Time Falls

When night time falls, on the edge of sleep I wait,
The thoughts of the day that were suppressed
Come floating in the mind.
Like a turbulent tide crashing on the shingle beach,
The torment arrives and spreads along
And into each nerve and fibre of my brain.
Cold and stark my brain reacts to shut away
These unwanted thoughts.
Go away disappear, my heart cries out.
I hold my breath the memories ripple along
And invade my being.
Slowly I release my breath and count to ten
Relax my body from toes to head.
Gradually my thoughts subside my heart beats
Get steady, my body gets warm.
My bed feels soft like a lamb's skin cover.
I drift and sigh into a dream,
Will I remember when I awake or am I awake
Who knows.
My thoughts flash past on a turning tide who cares
What they are as once again they are locked inside.
Come the sunrise and the day and once again
They will subside.

Pamela Madlen

The Critical Path

And it came to pass
That out of soft bone meeting oyster flesh;
Myself. From womb through mangle muscle
Stumped by antiseptic wicket-keepers; out.
Into the pavilion of thought, padded perception,
Purpose, unexplained bodily functions,
Smiles, smells and screams. Pneumatic milk,
Sleep and dreams of that warm jacuzzi;
Immersed in the sweet fruit of incubation,
Stagnation. A holiday of a lifetime.
Then the gravel palms and nettle knees of reality;
The curriculum search barefoot among the white coals,
The goals of the critical path.
Where to look? How to look or be seen to look?
The black toes, blistered souls, molten cramp,
and quicksand bends of journeys end;
Where both heart and mind are spent
Of social integration, the gritty salt of interaction,
High hopes, expectation.
Discomfort — the bee among wasps,
The jelly fish acquaintances brushing past an open sore,
Makes one ask: Is judgement the mirror
Or that which lies beyond the door?

Keith Manning

New Year

Now a new year begins
We hope for lots of things
A safer world for you and me
For all friends and family

We hope the new year brings
Lots of friendships near and far
Good health and happiness to all
Peace on earth forever more.

Mrs. L. Mansfield

The Waiting

The ghosts of my ancestors,
Wait at Dundalk station,
Suitcases in hand,
Caps and scarves,
Upon their heads,
The final immigration,
The journey of the dead.

Michael James McShane

The Windows of Wonder

The face in the mirror is not the same,
The face in the mirror is only a frame.
The eyes ask questions direct from the brain,
The eyes are the mirror reflecting the same.

Different windows various size,
All in the search of the hidden prize.
Ever changing seeking truth,
Then looking back at their fading youth.

For the eyes that wonder
The mirror will always reflect
The light through the windows,
The language of effect!

Christine McDaid

Lights

Scattered crystals, sparkling fairy ice
From ages past, beyond recall,
A sea of friendly eyes are looking down,
Vast, awesome distances made small.

Wrapped in evening's velvet cloak, I stand;
A valley of stars below me spills.
Across the rift, an ordered snake of lights
Winds around the purpled hills.

Twinkling reflections of the past and present,
Above my head, beneath my feet,
Matching beauty in a darkened quiet,
Natural and man-made magic meet.

Joan McClung

This Other Man's Hell

There's darkness on the edge of noon;
All life eclipsed, as arms exalt the phoenix
Risen from the ashes of its own destruction.
He walks; a sordid beggar with opium
Covered eyes, towards a serene death.
Around the sky shroud falls, and beside him
Death's ambush treads: it steps lightly,
With a slow tapestry of movement.
In his mind's shadows the comrades watch: all dead,
A high school photograph of standing corpses,
With only him to take his place.
Death moves closer ... its open womb-like arms
Reach out to him — in this place only death has honesty —
He stops ... waiting for the call to free him
From this other man's Hell ...
And it comes ... clear as day.

Eamonn McGinty

On My Way Home

Last night I saw God, (on my way home),
His hair was untidy, so I lent him my comb.
"Well", said He, "you're doing all right,
Keep eating carrots and fight the good fight."

Last night I saw a dog, (on my way home),
Reciting Shakespeare whilst gnawing a bone.
"Well" said he, (just before Othello),
"I was talking to God, what a nice fellow.
This is for you", and he gave me my comb;
God had apparently taken it home.
"He asked you to visit, said you'd be a welcome guest,
Oh, and by the way, the comb has been blessed."

Last night I smiled to myself, (on my way home),
Gently clasping the hallowed comb
Secure in the knowledge my soul had been saved
And hoping my hair would be permanently waved!

Fiona E. McGrouther

What Idleness Of Thought Brings You To Such Thinking As This

What idleness of thought brings you to such thinking as this?
What lack of understanding makes you believe in your ... understanding?

When he left, you played your favourite record twice,
the melancholic one,
with the bleach-blonde singer quietly singing between fretless bass hums
and synthesizer chords ringing indulgence in your ears.

When he wrote,
the walk upon the beach that did not seem long enough
and you hear your heart miss beats when you picked up his letter,
yet
your happiness soon dwindled as each word reread lost its power.

And in few words and slight pause, in passing mention of this,
you become momentarily dulled,
quickly skipping over it,
like an issue which lovers want to skirt around when knowing
(but ne'er admitting) that it's finished.

What loss of love do you push into yourself?
What distance of length (time and miles) tortures you like this?
What lack of understanding makes you believe in your understanding?
What 'love' that you speak of brings you to melancholy as this?
What idleness of thought brings you to such thinking as this?

A. McIlveen

Love Song

Shall we walk together, I and you?
   Among the sandworms on the sweating shore,
Where the small curls of sea-lace edge the blue
   Breakers that ebb and flow for evermore.

And as we walk, the wool-wisp clouds are trailing
   Across the vivid canopy of the skies,
Wreathing around us, feather-light, and veiling
   The love-light that I hope is in your eyes.

And will you tell me of the things you dream?
   Or leave them in your secret heart still dwelling?
Things you have never told before, that seem
   Too precious, almost, to survive the telling.

Ah, but I would not carelessly receive them!
   Your dreams are mine, beloved, your heart my treasure,
I would not toss them on the wind nor disbelieve them,
   No, for I share your dreams in fullest measure.

Then let us walk together by the sea,
   Tracing our way across the shell-strewn sand,
The warmth of love enfolding you and me,
   Our hearts entwined as one, and hand in hand.

Betty McIlroy

Wee Babes

Over the moon so far away,
Angels dance and children play,
Gone from this world, the one we call Earth,
Happy in Heaven and full of mirth.

Wee babes with shining wings,
Playing while the Angel sings,
Lullabies straight from the heart,
Plucking gently on a harp.

In our world too ill to live,
Given all there was to give,
But not enough to keep them well,
So Jesus saved them from this hell.

He sprinkled stardust in their hair,
Said some to Heaven, I'll be there,
He reached down and took their hand,
Said come with me, I understand.

Over the moon so far away,
Angels dance and children play,
Cherished and nurtured and free from pain,
Never to be hurt again.

Allison Magee

The Sea

The arrogant waves tossed the fishing boat, on a sea that was swollen, black, edged white.
Backwards and forwards, unrelenting as the Tempest reached it's height.

The Skipper, fighting with the wheel, cast a practised eye at the charts,
and prayed to reach safe haven and wished with all his heart
that he were at home.
Boots off, pipe full, fire blazing in the hearth.
Hot supper on the table, much cosier than his berth.
Or, perhaps sitting in the Local, mellow, supping with the boys,
laughing, joking, comparing catches, lost in the smoke and the noise.
Then taking pleasure in lingering, anticipating warm bed and wife.
Snuggling down together, soft and welcoming, this is the life!

When the violent sea is raging, doubts may come to mind.
But then, the storm has passed again and he gazes round to find
it has become his mistress. Soft and welcoming, and calm.
Waiting to be wooed and won, not wishing any harm.

Waiting to be harnessed, holding him in her embrace.
Asking who would come in first if this were a race
between the Land and Sea.

He knows it is hard choice.
And he waits, as though listening to the Sea's seductive voice,
It seems to him that it would say, "You know deep in your heart,
I am the one, that you truly love, we will never be apart,
and, for all of the tenderness, and your wife's loving ways, She knows, and I know,
It's with me you will stay".

Lynette Shaw McKone

A Woman's Place

A woman's place is in he home,
    While man the beast goes off to roam,
And woman never should complain,
    Cause it only gives her man a pain.

Look after his kids and never bore,
    Her great big Ape by asking for more,
Money to feed and clothe the kids,
    He'll make excuses and they'll all be fibs.

A woman has to be subservient,
    Do her duty and be quite fervent,
Be his lover in the bedroom, his slave in the kitchen,
    And never dare dream of a day that she'll ditch him,

She should be satisfied with her lot,
    And never criticize the man she got,
Close her eyes when he goes out the door,
    Broken promises she must ignore,
Smile though defeated and carry on
    Was it to satisfy man that woman was born?

Rosaleen Mallett

The Gray Headed Kestrel

Up above the motorway
The gray headed kestrel flies,
Searching, slowly searching
For an early morning prize.
In the air he gently hangs
As he scans the ground below,
Looking for a mouse perhaps
As it scurries to and fro.
Cars and trucks they thunder by
All throughout the day,
And crows and rooks and rabbits too
Just get in the way.
Then kestrel spots a movement
As he hovers way up high,
And tail and wings are folded
As he drops from out the sky.
For down there by the roadside
In amongst the hay,
A harvest mouse sits terrified
For it is the kestrels prey.

John McLaughlin

Us

In the beginning it was hurried meals,
long smooching over candlelight would wait.

Only the years seem to have flown.

Vast distances exist between the plan and
execution; there's never a convenient date.

You set the table now for few, then fewer.

Our children going gives us time to plan.
Untroubled; set for two, for candlelight, for calm.

Trevor McMahon

Your Future Rock

Life is like climbing a mountain,
You don't know what's going to happen,
On your way to what you want at the top,
Trying to reach for your dream from destiny,
Destiny from your climb on your future rock,
It's a hard rough track you will have to see,
When things don't go the way you want them to be,
From a sudden fall or a bad knock,
As time goes past so fast on your life clock,
You have to pick yourself up though,
Even if you're hurt, weak or filled with crying,
You have to get up again and keep on trying,
Because out of everything bad there always comes good,
That's what you have to see on your way to the top,
So keep on going for you must not stop,
For what you want from your future rock.

Ivan McConnachie

Running Scared

What will I do? Where will I go?
I'm so confused I really don't know.
Who will I run to? Where will I hide?
What are these feelings I'm having inside?
Where will it end? What lies in store?
I wish I could see behind these closed doors.

I wish I could turn back the clock again
And get rid of this turmoil, anger and pain.
It is all this pretending and living a lie
It feels like I have given up and lay down and died.

How can I make things better once more?
To go back to the way we were once before.
The questions are plenty, the answers are few,
So dear God up in heaven, please show me what to do.

Gillian McKenzie

Untitled

I'm sinking, I'm sliding,
I'm drowning but fighting.
In a tunnel, no light, no sound,
Trying to scream, going around and around.
Darkness closing in, smothering.
The dank blackness always covering
Pleasant thoughts that spring to mind,
Locking them away, unable to find.
Voices scream, chant and call,
Invisible hands that try to maul
My sanity away from me.
Now I'm crying, crawling towards the light
That's always just within my sight,
Slipping back into reality,
After glimpsing the hells of insanity;
God, am I going mad?

Elizabeth McMullan

Our Garden Heritage

Round, rosy robin, freckled thrush,
Noble blackbird, tiny wren.
Each decorates the lifeless brush,
A living garden ornament.

With yellow flash emergency
A finch, regardless of the rain,
Makes the sorry cherry tree
An interesting place again.

Whilst underneath the hawthorn hedge,
Unseen, except for heaving leaves,
Small birds of clever camouflage,
Seek warmth among their relatives.

And up above, on every roof,
The starlings in a state of schism,
Make light of order, peace and love,
In favour of materialism.

Yet every winged variety
Knows well its place and keeps its pride
And does not threaten harmony,
Creation's laws to override.

The garden is our heritage,
The city was not meant to be,
Destroying life is sacrilege,
Our birds have wisdom, what have we?

Margaret Mann

The Cotswolds

Some several thousand years ago, in Neolithic times,
As the glaciers slowly melted in those dread and icy climes,
Was left, by Nature's accident, a more gently contoured scene
Which some many centuries later grew forested and green.

Then — man settled in the borough combes and dwelt within the folds
To graze his sheep and cattle upon the grassy upland wolds -
Deforested by now.
And he used oolithic limestone, left by some ancient sea,
To build himself a cottage home and leave the legacy
Of Castle combe and Bibury,
Wyke Rissington and Asthall Leigh.

And —
Somewhere within Jurassic rock
Springs source of Thames near Lechlade Lock
From which a tributary flows through Bourton on the Water
And down the timeless quietude of High Street, Lower Slaughter.
And always those surrounding hills, with view of seven counties
Beyond a clump of native woodland beech and birch and oak trees.

So, as we walk the Cotswold Way
And delight in all we find today,
Remember, though by accident, man also had a hand
In moulding such a landscape in this green and pleasant land.

Marion McNaught

The Peaceful World

A peaceful world I would like to live in,
Wake up in the morning and hear the birds singing.
Walk down the path and smell the fresh flowers
As they blossom in Spring.
To meet people with a big smile saying, good morning,
Isn't it a peaceful, bright, lovely day.

A world where there's no hatred, fear
Discrimination, war and famine, drugs and diseases.
But where there is peace and harmony, caring and sharing,
Love and comfort, helping and showing the right way in life.

A world where Man doesn't destroy nature and wildlife,
But they can live together as one.
A world where people don't say the wrong things to each other —
Offending and upsetting this can be.

A world of no sin and shame but of purity and righteousness
For all mankind to live in.
A world where people don't live by the gun or bomb,
But start living for Jesus.
There can only be peace through knowing the one who gives it.

Brian McKay

Still waters

I am weaving a basket
with reeds gathered
near the still waters
despite the mosquitoes.

My wife is pounding grain
to flour — hour after hour
beside the still waters -
despite the mosquitoes.

Our kraal is sad, is silent now,
no longer do the children splash
and play in the still waters —
how I hate those mosquitoes.

Thomas McGonigle

Birdy

Crazy girl
scally-wag child,
in black donkey jacket and scarf
that dangles.
Hopping
in and out
of the gutter
on sparrow thin legs.
Scattering
the leaves
in your second hand shoes
and flapping
jumble sale dress.

Ayelet McKenzie

Untitled

Bone-white mist coils slowly
Pervades the stubble field.
Rent earth, dyke and thorn-brake
Shrouded, lie concealed.

Washed out landscape grey
Steady, steady fall.
Reeling, flapping, flailing
Raw-voiced ravens call.

Withered wind hisses
Skittering, scattering gust.
Dusk descends softly
Moth wing dust.

Then-veined branches scrape
The belly of the sky.
Sickle moon slices
Night shade creatures fly.

F.E. Mackie

Circumstantial Departure

Light's frame flung gently on the floor,
Silent departure beckons at the door.
You tread softly by, breathing words to catch my ear —
Circumstance interferes.
She steals the moment into her trance,
Illusion lies in her fluid-filled glance.
Slowly you breathe her mysterious sighs,
Alone with sweet promise I bid good-bye.

Siobhan McMahon

To Lincolnshire

This hallowed ground which now I tread.
What life it gave to me,
To be at one with earth and sky.
In its own bosom 'til I die.
With pleasures still to be.

How often do we find a niche,
That dreamers long to see.
But look 'tis there for all, I know
And faithful hearts will find it so
With waiting arms for thee.

But time outruns our dancing feet,
To seek the heavenly choir.
We take our leave,
And part of thee
O, Lincolnshire, O Lincolnshire.

Celia Maddison

Lonely Boy

He stands alone watching, never smiling
He wants to go and join the fun
"Come on" they call "you can play"
He runs and climbs, he's one of them
Suddenly he stops, he doesn't see nor hear
His mind just suddenly rids itself of thought
Falling to the ground his body jerks
And then at peace he sleeps.

He stands alone watching, never smiling
He wants to go and join the fun,
"No!" they call "you're different, you can't play"
He just walks away, his head hung low
The tears of so much unhappiness just fall,
His head is so full of vivid thoughts
Falling to the ground his body jerks
And then at peace he sleeps.

Helen Machin

Alpha - Omega

I am the youngest fawn of spring
I am the oldest tree of the forest
I am the rushing torrent of the mountain stream
I am the still and deepest dark lake
I am the drifting wind-blown desert sand
I am the immovable granite slab
I am the deepest valley and the highest peak
The soothing breeze and the furious wind
The strongest bough and the weakest twig
All these things are me,
For I am Heaven and I am Hell.

Christopher A. Madeley

The Weak and Strong

How can a man who is strong and tall,
Hurt a child who is weak and small,
How can a man take a child and slay,
When all he has done is go out to play,
How can a man rape a girl or boy,
Then throw them aside like a broken toy,
How can a man who seems gentle and kind,
Look at a child with murder in mind,
Too many children alas have died,
Too many mothers and fathers have cried,
How can a man who is strong and tall,
Hurt a child who is weak and small.

F.M. McKendrick

Death Of A Planet

What have we all done
To poor old Mother Earth,
mankind is slowly killing her
since day one of our birth.

A big hole in the ozone layer
Letting through ultra-violet rays,
Now is the time for drastic action
We have got to change our ways.

The polar ice now slowly melts
Causing oceans and seas to rise,
Land and towns will disappear
Washed away, buried, before our eyes.

Next time you pass a factory
Watch how the filthy fumes rise,
Just one more unwanted help
Towards your, and my demise.

Patrick McCann

Hostage

Your work was dedicated to our Lord
In a foreign land, language unknown
Captors held you hostage
Crime was spreading God's word
Kept you hidden in a small dark room
Revealing little light
Chained you to a wall, not knowing day from night
Days, weeks, months drag into years were many
Holding you against your will, from your family
They kept you from humanity
Only yourself to talk to, smile or cry
They hadn't feelings how you felt, or looked but
You know what is written in the Holy Book
Not anyone in authority could separate you from God's love
He surrounds you with his angels and a peaceful loving dove
Continued prayers on bended knee it is written
Nothing is impossible with thee
After five long years, through many a tear
Your captors set you free
This time were tears of joy, celebrates the world
You're home my friend
On television a brave and smiling face
I watched with happiness
The joyful events that took place.

Violet J. Maidment

The Oxfam Shop

In many a High Street shopping scene
An Oxfam Trading shop is seen
With familiar lettering - yellow on blue
Linking the third world with me and you.

    Volunteers arrive in rain or shine
    To open the shop soon after nine;
    Bags left on doorstep are manoeuvered,
    Shelves are dusted, carpet hoovered,
    Cash float checked, so come what may,
    Ready now to start the day.
    (Theirs is not to reason why
    Some will browse and some will buy!)

Enter a couple looking for bedding,
A lady requiring a hat for a wedding,
A collector examines a silver spoon,
A reader heads for 'Mills and Boon'!
See baskets made in a far off country
Where water is scarce and children are hungry;
Cushions from India, snazzy socks from Peru,
Fair trade helps in getting aid through.

    The sale of these items as Oxfam makes known
    Enables wells to be dug and seed to be sown;
    So dual the shop's purpose, the third world to feed
    Whilst endeavouring to satisfy customer need!

Mary Marshman

Love

I'm dying to hurt you
Cut open your skin
Draw out blood
Drain you thin

Suck on your dirty flesh
Till it stings red raw
Bite into your bones
And chew them sore

Scratch your smooth eyes
To a painful shade of blue
Inflict agonizing torture
Like you never knew

Sharpen each nail
To dig holes in your skin
Push hard as I can
Force my way in

I'll gnaw to shreds
Your repulsive lips
Drag on your tongue
Until it rips

Scrape away your vulgar face
Strip your body, leave no trace
No ugly reminders of what you did
And then of you I'll almost be rid.

Sonia Mallett

Dust In The Wind ...
Always And Forever I'm Still Missing Your Love

I miss you more than anyone knows
As each day passes by the emptiness grows
I laugh, I cry, I play my part
But beneath it all lies my broken heart
No length of time can take away
My memories of you from day to day
Loving thoughts a silent tear
Always wishing you would return home here
The face that I loved is missing
The voice that I loved is still
A place is vacant in my heart
That only you could ever fill
I'll always remember you as someone so precious and dear
Never a day passes me by
When I sit and think and wonder why
Someone so special, loving, caring and true
You choose to leave me for someone *new* ...!
The heartaches in this world
We have shared so many
But losing you was worse than any
They say the memories are golden
And maybe that is true
But I never wanted memories
I only ever wanted you.

Colin Marshall Esq.

A Friend

Someone to give advice when needed
Not to say, ah you should have heeded,
Hopes and dreams scattered like sand
Someone there to hold your hand,
To give a kind word
When life seems absurd,
Not to say, that you're a fool
Nor to scorn or ridicule,
A shoulder to cry on
When you need one,
Someone to crack a joke
Though you could choke,
When you're in a state
You need a mate,
A friend in your darkest hour
When all around is sour,
That friendly smile
Will take you a mile
Sharing your heavy load
Along the winding road,
There at the end
Your FRIEND.

Dennis Manton

The Seasons

White, crisp and glistening; it lays upon the ground,
Grasping all and everything from anywhere around.
It creeps upon us in the night when stars and sky are clear,
The magic dust that's cold and sharp: to show the frosts are here.

White and crunching underfoot, the softly falling flakes,
The sky is grey, the ground is bright, the children are awake,
Playing, shouting, throwing, whizzing on a sledge,
Building Sam the Snowman from drifts beside the hedge.

Dripping from the branches pouring from the sky,
The melting of the Winter that makes the rivers high:
Rushing, tearing, flooding, it rapes the banks and towns,
Killing all that's in its path, Spring has come around.

Repairing all the damage, it warms and shines upon us,
Encouraging the flowers and birds to sing their chorus.
Everyone goes to the beach, to bathe and have some fun:
A sudden change of temperament, discovered by the sun.

Hidden in the branches, gold appears from green,
The colours of the Autumn, completely change the scene.
Falling softly to the ground, again the leaves are lost,
Patiently awaiting the coming of the frost.

Rachel Mallion

Why Do We Do It?

Most of us who are so inclined,
    Take up our pens and write
Of things which, uninvited come to mind
    To be recorded ere they've taken flight.

We receive a fleeting inspiration
    And our senses tell us we must give
In words born of our imagination
    A picture which may make the image live.

Even as an artist with his paints,
    Lays down on canvas that which pleases
Other eyes than his, without restraints,
    And many others ... teases.

So, the words we write may make some frown
    And wonder how they give us pleasure
And why we need to put them down
    In rhyming form and in poetic measure.

Perhaps we wonder this ourselves ...
    Is it that we have an inflated ego?
Should we put our verses on the shelves
    And as others not inspired go, we go?

I put it to you, are we overrated?
    Or are our minds with rhythm saturated?

Eileen Martin

A Winter Morning

On a silent winter morning,
When the world is a glistening white.
In the undisturbed churchyard
There are many magnificent sights.
An owl glides, then swoops to the ground
A timid field mouse he has espied.
But when the creature, small has seen him,
Too late, alas, he is eaten, and has died.

On the shimmering pond, by the graves,
A rabbit signals to his friend
To come and glide across the ice.
Then springs the fox,
But the rabbit's life is not at an end.
The swallows they have all flown south,
A robin is softly singing.
The enchanting melody fills the air,
Love, this tune is bringing.

Fatemah Mafi

The Black Cat

Late on a damp, dull August night:
With shabby coat that matched the night,
A tom cat crept along a path,
His gaunt frame full of feline craft.
His target was an open door:
His object food. His chance he saw
When someone came in sight. He took
His chance - and chance draws to it, luck.

September came, October fell,
November's here - that cat as well.

He's handsome now, and knows he is;
And knows what love is: chicken. His
Ship's in. Now Sooty squints with pride:
A king beside his fireside.
It's said that luck and black cats go
Hand in hand. Well, I now do know
It's true. And I know something else -
This cat kept his luck for himself.

Diane E. Maltby

The Opera House

How sad I felt on Thursday night
When I saw her standing there.
A gateway hole for all to see
Her insides laid bare!

This place I'd often gone to
And laughed the night away.
Is now an open wound.
She's been blown away.

Her walls have rocked with laughter
Her rafters rang with song.
All classes there together
United in one throng.

Faceless men have done this
What's the reason why?
What did she ever do to them
That says she must die.

Like to Phoenix she'll rise up,
Of this I have no doubt.
Proud and grand, restored once more
To bring the people out.

May McFarlane

The Radish

Looking upwards all the Time,
Hoping for a little light,
In the ground it's dark and cold,
Looking at filthy mould

Winter has gone, now summer comes,
Growing upwards in the sun,
It's so great
It's such fun,
Growing upwards in the sun.

Being picked now is the worst,
Being pulled from the earth,
In the Basket here I lie,
In the Basket it's so high.

In the kitchen here I wait,
Time is passing it's so late,
Sitting on the cutting board,
It's not fair that I'm so bored.

I'm for tea,
Not just me,
Here I go in the mouth,
Now I'm going downwards South.

Martin Makinen

And On The Seventh Day

Walk with me, take my hand,
Follow me, yes you can for you were there!
Lead me on, show me all
Comfort me, I need to know where I went wrong.
Be my eyes, guide my path
Save me, I have to live for who are left.

Stay with me, tell me why,
Speak the truth; no more must die through words unsaid!
Towers of strength, perfumed colours,
Roaming life; so pure I rested proud and satisfied.

Shield me, reproach me
Forgive me, I slept through the death of a dream.

Moira Main

Reflections On Our Times

We pamper the prisoners, featherbed the felons,
Mollycoddle the murderers, release the rapists,
Vanquish the victims, penalise the pensioners,
Ignore the innocent, indulge the immigrant,
Obliterate the ozone and slaughter the seals.

We poison the crops with pesticide,
Uproot the hedges — birds cannot hide,
The forests of the Amazon are bare,
The wildlife gone — but where?

What is man doing to planet Earth
That he should destroy his land of birth?
Where are the values we held so dear
As now we live in endless fear?

Satellites invade the sky
Beaming their messages from on high
To planet Earth, to sate man's eternal greed
For wealth, while poorer nations cannot feed.

Successive governments make ponderous statement,
And plunge us headlong, without abatement
Into a life of untold frustration,
Without supporting the population.

They pursue their aims with determination,
Having no thought for the plight of the nation.
When will all this stupidity cease,
And man be left to live in peace?

Margory Martin

A Poem For Richard *(who is autistic)*

In your own private world,
You go through the day.
Eat, sleep, no play
Content just to be,
No kisses for me.
Order and structure
Friends not inviting.
Do you know I love you?
Do you feel for me?
Sometimes I think you do,
And sometimes I think you go
Away to a place I cannot follow.
If you would take my hand
We could go together.
I will show you my world,
And you can show me yours.

Cheryl Mann

Old Woman

The mirror and the calendar
Compete in cruelty and in theft,
The blushing rose has disappeared,
The disagreeable thorn is left.

Self-pity rules this dismal hag,
Cosmetics caricature old charms,
No pleasing prospects cheer her heart,
No lover clasps her withered arms.

Soon death will end her discontent,
For buried dust lies quiet and still,
While avaricious relatives
Fight fiercely over her last Will.

Margaret Clare Maison

Drop of Rain

On the window pane,
In one small drop of rain,
I see a young girl picking flowers;
They are orange flowers.

Her dark green dress
Mingles with the grass
As she kneels there.

Her apron is of the purest white;
Pure, like the tear in her eye
As she bends her head to cry.

And the tear turns into a drop of rain
That trickles down the window pane.

Dot McKown

My Place

The rocks below seem to invite
The waves that lap and excite
The sea a bed of tranquility
The wind caressing every part of me
The flowers peep out to see the view
Yet here I sit once more with you
You close your eyes and rest a while
At least this place can make you smile
A chill comes sudden and makes me shiver
And then my body starts to quiver
Anticipation of an ending could be the reason
As if our love was meant for just one season.

June Woodward Martin

The Message

Give me love, give me joy, give me hope and prestige,
Give me health and the friends that I crave.
Take me out of this pit of sorrow and strife,
Let me ride on the crest of the wave.

When all look beyond their own wants and needs
And care for their fellow man;
The troubles that threaten to engulf all mankind
Will instead be transformed into sun.

It's by giving not seeking that life turns around.
When misery drenches you most;
Stop asking for love and the joy you desire —
Take up the banner — play host

Sheila Manners

Winter

And then, suddenly, the first winterday.
With cold north-westerly winds,
with rain and hailstones.
The thoughts of leaving the warm place at the fire
makes you shiver.
The closes and lanes empty and bleak,
the dim light of the sparse streetlamps
mirrored in the wet flagstone pavement.
Not even the croaky calls of the gulls.
The houses nestle together,
their wet roofs shroud themselves
in the smoke of their chimneys.
The gentle days of peedie summer
fade into memories
when the tiny boats heading for their anchorage.

Con Mara

Another Day

When the children are in bed,
and all the things have been said,
I breathe a sigh of relief
and grumble quietly through my teeth.

With all the bath things put away,
another ending of the day
I love this time on my own,
a lovely quiet happy home.

Now's the time for washing-up,
a knife, a fork, a spoon, a cup.
When all the things are put away,
it's time to start another day.

Jackie Manning

Gratitude

There's a bunch of men in Kenya
In the sweltering Middle East,
Though miles away from England
Are thought of, far from least.

They wear a yellow Hackel
On a nice smart blue beret,
And they go on fighting Mau Mau
In the aberdares each day.

Time from them is lonely,
But we can smile now through our tears.
Because in time we'll sing an anthem
To the Lancashire Fusiliers.

Dora Margieson

Man's Will

For the dying of creation
Thanks be to Man!
For the famine in the nation
Thanks be to Man!
For the eroding, dumping, spilling
Silent growth while we are sleeping
All our future is dissolving.
Thanks be to Man!

All for self we do our labours
Man's will is done!
Selfishly ignore our neighbours
Man's will is done!
In the sufferings that confront us
War and killing all around us
And the lies which still surround us.
Man's will is done!

Lynsey Marks (Age 13)

Unnatural Dreams

It happened in the dark of night
A city torn with fire and light
And what of the people it killed!
Enemy not bothered, just thrilled
As they ran ranting and raving
About the bloodlust they were craving.
The opposition practiced and drilled.

The birds with iron wings soared the sky
Hoping to oppress yet another lie.
The demons they carry bursting with power
Leading nearer to the doomsday hour
And all around, everywhere it be,
Dust and sand of a long lost sea.

In the distance a sound, a baby's cry.
There it was, a sudden piercing scream
Makes the world think what does existence mean.
Sudden explosion, power unleashed,
World torn apart folded and creased.
No more resistance
End of existence
All is now left to our unnatural dreams.

Dominic Marshall

The Wind

Hark now the wind it blows by night
while gently rustling leaves
still hidden is its power and might
its soft caressings on my slumbering ears
faint murmurings soothe away my doubts and fears
and as I lie so close to sleep
its whispering voice my soul and heart will keep
then suddenly as if replying to some tortured soul
what was once a whisper is now a muffled howl
stronger and stronger now it blows
crashing dustbin lids and making bottles roll
all at once the air is filled with noise and rain
lashing gusting blowing all before it in what seems a hurricane
a flash of lightning lights the distant gloom
as ghostly shadows dance around my darkened room
great rolls of thunder jar the wind-swept night
the voice of God within them showing us his power and might
at last the raging force is spent
slowly I close my eyes and fall asleep, content.

D.A. Martin

Memories

Memory is a fickle friend
When you're three score years and ten
You know you should go somewhere
But you can't remember when.
You mean to ring up Mary
Then find you've dialled Mabel
You make yourself a shopping list
And leave it on the table.
When in bed you try to sleep
Doubts creep into your mind
Did I switch the fire off?
It really is a bind.
If someone asks about the past
Your memory serves you well
You recall in minute detail
And many a tale can tell.
It really is quite comforting
Remembering the past
Even when our memory fails
Memories always last.

Lily Marsh

Prince Vagrant
(full of tears)

He hides in a whiskey jar,
A jar full of tears.
He died long ago,
Long before his fears.
He's everywhere and nowhere too,
In his world full of pain.
It's been so long unused,
He's misplaced his own name.
His turpentine tears flow,
From the sea of despair.
Staining the face carved
By those who don't care.
He sleeps now anywhere,
But dreams no more.
You've all seen that man,
Outside your door.
His clothes are tattered and torn,
And breaking at the seams.
Mirrored by his life,
And the loss of his dreams.
As the leaves of time
Fall gently to the ground.
So his dignity drains away,
Never to be found ...

Delwyn Marsh

Untitled

It grieves me so to see you worried and sad,
I love to see you carefree and glad,
A nasty word or thought of you won't be had
Please my love believe what I say to you,
I shall not toy with your love and affections.
I will love you as one loves life,
Nothing I shall do, be contrived,
But are my heart's true reflections.
I shall prove my love, should you desire
This I can do and grant your wishes,
Showing I am no liar.
I have loved before in the days gone by, now I am wiser
You for the rest of my life I desire.
I would give everything for thee should you wish it,
The truth is, I would give my life for you,
For you already have my heart and soul,
Please do not doubt it.
My love for you shall be forever
Tears of sadness in your eyes, I shall see never.
So my true love, be happy and full of joy
As you for always be my girl, and me, your lover boy.

N. Maniar

Happy Days

She made our dresses, smocked with care,
tied scarlet ribbons in our hair.
She taught us how to knit and sew
sat round a blazing fire aglow,
with toffee apples, bags of chips
Easter eggs and lucky dips.

We'd walk along the country roads,
picking blackberries by the loads.
Blackberry jam and pies galore,
some to eat and some to store.

To Emma's chalet we would ride,
and gather cockles in the tide
Laughs and games and lots of fun
and singing till the day was done.
Always happy, never blue
because we always were with you.

Such happy days are past and gone
But memories still live on and on,
The years that passed cannot erase
My memories of those happy days
And the one that made them all worthwhile
A look of love, my mother's smile.

Christine Molloy

Don't Turn Away

He is still yet three
This child of ours.
Don't turn your back
Don't walk away.
When he reaches four
He will need you more.
Gaze upon that small face.
What do you see?
Love is there. And trust.
Hero worship for you, not me.
Show him you love him.
Show him you care.
Not just today, but evermore.
Tell him for you he's special.
Never ever close that door,
Don't shut him out this child of ours.
Our gift from heaven above.
Proof of our undying love.

C.A. Moggach

The Vision

Last night I lay in silent thought
In my dark and lonely room,
When, my reveries they brought
A vision, to me, from the gloom ...

Scarcely did I dare to breathe,
My heart was pounding in my breast
Yet, in my fear I did perceive
The vision was with beauty blessed ...

Gold and white the robe all flowing,
Proud and beautiful, the head
With translucent aura glowing,
Lighting up my lonely bed ...

And so, courage I was finding
To address the vision, "Lo!
"Who art thou, with light so blinding?
What power makes your form to glow?"

The vision smiled and came yet near,
I gazed upon the lovely face
In the eyes, so bright and clear,
Every movement fashioned grace ...

"Behold, your heart will know the story
I've been chosen to convey"
I listened, ... then in mists of glory
The vision faded fast away ...
Now I'm telling you to listen, but to never ask for proof
That I saw thro' eyes that glisten, one dark night,
The form of 'Love'.

Kathleen Millington

Love

We stood together mother and child
Mere warmth of her touch filled me with pride
I was so young but still I could see
The unfathonable love in her eyes
That shone only for me
Hear the fear in her voice at my slightest pain
Feel the kiss on my cheek like a shaft of sunshine
That appears after rain
In life many friends more love there will be
Maybe many and more
But never again the gentle inexpressible love
That non but a mother alone can bestow.

Mary V. Ciarella Murray

Reflections

A long time ago, in a faraway place,
Dwelt a mighty king, of an ancient race.
And this mighty king, of a long time ago
Ruled with the sword and feared no foe.
He sacked and pillaged, raved and swore.
He bathed in blood, and revelled in gore.
Thunder and lightning he proclaimed,
The land was blighted while he reigned.
The a wise old man of the king's domain
Sought, with reason, the king to tame.
He faced the king in private chambers.
His logical words were sharp as sabres.
But the mighty king of the ancient race
And the wise old man of the faraway place
Rued each other and from each other ran.
For they looked in a mirror and saw the same man.

Thomas Morris

To Diet or Not To Diet?

I am going in for this "slimming lark" I think.
Yes, I intend to try this famous "drink",
The one where you eat only one meal a day
That will be easy on my purse anyway.
Then after two weeks, (so they say)
I can then buy a dress that will fit, anyway,
Perhaps a size 16, now that would be a treat
For the size I am getting, soon "shan't see my feet".
I struggle and pull at a size 22, then find it is 26!
Now this can't be right, so with all my might
I am giving up sugar and sweets
Biscuits and cake, the kind mother makes.
Now what does that leave to eat?
No bread and no fat, just salads and that.
I don't even think I can do it.
My will is so weak, I do like to eat.
No, I am certain, I really can't do it.

Amy Martin

Rights and Wrongs

What right has he ...
　　　　to threaten me
　　　　to attack my family
　　　　to steal my property?

What rights have I ...
　　　　to defend myself
　　　　to protect my family
　　　　to save my property?

　　　　What's right?
　　　　What are my rights?
　　　　The Law says NONE!

Theresa Munson

Kingfisher On The Brun

A flash of electric blue passed by
Quicker than the winking eye
Skimming liquid light
Perhaps looking for a bite

Not rod or line this fisher needs
He is good at hiding in the reeds
Nesting in the hollow bank
Along the river brun

Colours of every hue
Rare beauty in the night
The old Kingfisher is in flight
Oh can't be missed, this rare sight

Alert, sitting on his bough
Keen eye searching, spotting now
Moving under water, tasty dish
Sparkling spotted silver fish

A.E. Marshall

Friendly Time

When representing time we use a figure
Who carries in his hand a sharpened scythe,
An hourglass to represent the rigour
Of passing moments innocent and blithe.
A figure used in representing fear
Of chances that have long since fallen by,
In hindsight opportunities so clear
Of aspirations scattered to the sky.
And yet why fear time, for times a friend
The rule is that everything must grow,
And having grown must fade and make an end
It matters not how quickly or how slow,
For death is hope of better things, a friend
Perhaps of life that will not have an end.

David Stephen Marshall

Ode To An Angler

One summer's morn, it wur four-thirty sharp
Owd Sam rose early, like proverbial lark.
Wi' basket, rod and line he went.
Water's edge wur his intent.

Poor Sam sat theer, near aw' that day
And not one fish had come his way
He watched his float, till near boss-eyed
Then sad at heart, just sat and sighed.

As he sighed his float went under
Cried Sam, "I've got a bite, by thunder!"
He grabbed his rod, reeled in aw't slack.
And promptly fell upon his back.

It must a' bin a whopper, for it pulled him in
And poor owd Sam, he couldn't swim
Alas, alack, he never come up
Reet fast, on't bottom, in't mud, he stuck.

Neaw if thet passing by this spot
And see's water, sorta bubblin' up
It won't be a fish, that you can bet,
It'll be poor owd Sam, he's strugglin' yet!

T. Mason

Nature, Life and Love

We're here as beings, thro nature and love
Born with wings like the dove
Earth's glory full of life
Ready to face any strife
Tiny, small, big or large
All as one on this great barge
Floating slowly, wending our way
Waking up to each new day
To see what treasures are in store
The gift of love and something more
Tolerance for those we know
Who've somehow fallen very low
Into the depth of deep despair
Let us tell them that we care
It doesn't take long to say
We are here for you each day
For who knows too what may happen
Us could follow a self same pattern
So let's think, and remember
We're part of one burning ember.

Rose Mason

Untitled

In a village, a cottage small
Brings sweet memories which I recall
Black lead grate, the fire glow, steel fender,
Lamplight, the love so tender.

Coconut matting, pegged rugs
Mingle with the loving hugs.
Children playing amongst the coal,
Washing hands in an enamel bowl.

Cosy parlour, decorations,
Meeting all of our relations.
Mince pies, Christmas pudding,
Scuttle by the fire to keep the wood in.

Christmas carols and the laughter
Will stay with me forever after.
Times change in many ways,
Yet these memories will always stay.

Helping us to value the things we now have,
Understanding that simple things make us glad.
Memories of this village and cottage remain
Help me to carry on through sunshine and rain
I treasure the peace and love which was there.
Where Christmas was a time to share.

Mrs. P.R. Martindale

Immortal

Clasp my hand then you will be
Forever special and defended by me
Walk with me throughout your life
And united we'll stand when trouble is rife
I'll always be there when you need me
Ready to face any foe
When danger raises it's ugly head
I'll be there to shield and console
If you should feel lost and all alone
Feel the world has turned to stone
I shall warm you with my immortal fire
And lift you up from out of the mire
I shall whisper you name on the wind when it blows
I shall be your crystal on the pure white snow
Wipe away your tears if they should fall
I am everything you need, and you will be my all
Seek no further for peace of mind
Though all men have said that I am blind
My eyes see only beauty wherever I go
For this I reap, for it is beauty I sow
I am here for all eternity
And have been since time began
I am wherever you seek me, below and up above
I am your comforter, your saviour, I am love.

Alma Mason

Allamistakeo

This was in the past;
A good time, back then.
And it wasn't Far, out of Town —
Tiny new Houses were Cutting through the trees.
But she was clearly in the clearing unHappy:
She turned the Light up till I could hear it
Freckle her dress ...
I sat Down in the Shadows and mud.
Total fool.

I explained,
But She explained,
— I Knew what she meant —
So, Yeah, we kept up the Jokes ...
No idea what to do.

The sweet breeze had been cut away to
Cold and Damp by then. I felt DISEASED:
But do YOU think she Remembers ...?
She only remembers a Joke.

Could've died of claustrophobia.
Left Alone as lone as Sever in the Dirt.
Without a thought, I sat there.
Sunset.

Ross May

O My Century

This century is a psychiatrist
who hears whispering in the attic
and is afraid

It is the Holocaust

It is the poor who starve across the world
from hate, oppression
or the dearth of crops

It is the dead of two world wars
which altered many cases

It is the sheathed and languid
woman of society
watching the Jarrow marchers through the open window
or the corner tobacconist,
ex-serviceman,
living the decent life with a small profit

It is the smoking gun
and the flaccid sermon

It is the lie triumphant

It cannot find another world than ours:
its fervid huge beginnings
make it a time of ending

H. Massy

Untitled

Whenever swirling mists confuse your eyes,
And life ahead has lost all direction,
Beyond the grey and stifling cloud, there lies
The mystic beauty of love's perfection.

If ever hope is crushed by black despair,
And faith succumbs, a cold fatality,
Then stir your aching wings and fly to where
You find the gold of love's reality.

When paths are tortuous, wild and overgrown,
The hands of caring friends will lend you through,
There's no real darkness though you feel alone,
For very near, your sky's a sunspoilt blue.

Submit yourself to love of heard and mind,
And wonder at the timeless joy you find.

Rita Martin

The Evil Tongue

A plague on you, you utter shrew,
For lashing with your vicious tongue,
Great hate and venom you construe,
With all the praises left unsung.

You slander'd every local lad,
Attacking them, their loving mothers,
Without remorse, they all were bad,
All them, their kin, and many others.

You criticized the Blacks and Whites,
And neighbours' each and every fault,
Your poisoned tongue works days and nights,
Without a stop, without a halt.

To err is ugly in your sight,
Mistakes and faults and slips alike,
Your wicked tongue is full of spite,
That overflows and floods the dyke.

There's no one left in your small life.
No honest, decent, simple man
No sister, brother, husband, wife,
Worth saving in God's master plan.

In time the world will come a'right.
And good beat evil in the test,
But not until some faithful knight,
Has laid you and your tongue to rest!

Stan Mason

My Lodger - The Hedgehog

I think he must live in our garden
Somewhere. Hidden among leaves and mosses
A little home he's found.
It's difficult to discover exactly where.
But I suspect it's behind the brambles
Where twigs and tussocks lie in tangled mound.

On Autumn nights I watched, breathless,
When he came to feed under my window,
His bristles silhouetted in the artificial light.
I heard him crunching
And I smiled as his shiny, black nose
Upturned each morsel prior to every bite.
Then silently and secretly, slipped back
Into the night.

Several times from the opposite corner of the garden
A young one came.
And rummaged through the brittle leaves
Close to the window pane.
But it was very timid and seldom stayed for long.
Then on soft, black feet and scraggly little legs,
Away he'd run.

Pauline May

The River

Black is the grass, so red is the sky
Who pressed the button and why oh why
Are there no green trees left, not even a flower
Years of evolution destroyed in an hour.

It was only a river, a conveyor of water
But ultimately it led to the slaughter
Of millions of people of all race and creed
One government's ego, one government's greed

A boundary dispute, it's only a line
Drawn on a map with a pen so fine
But that line so fine always drawn red
Means thousands are wounded and hundreds are dead.

So who has succeeded and what have they gained?
Was it worth all the thousands that they have left maimed.

The river is dead, the land has no life
Man may take a woman, but never a wife
For the radioactive fall-out has rendered them sterile
There can be no future, to go on is futile.

And as the cloud spreads a mushroom of death,
lay down, make your peace, then draw your last breath.

Clive Maxwell

Anne

So near and yet so far
Apart and yet so close
Does she think of me I
wonder
In these sombre Autumn days.

How well I remember her
Dark, shining hair
and soft tanned skin
Swimming like a fish
without a care.

But time will heal
Spring will return
She'll become a young woman
With thoughts of her own
And love in her heart.

Who is she? you ask,
Oh, didn't I say
She's Anne, my granddaughter
— I miss her.

Carole Mehigan

Untitled

Nana's little sweethearts
Lovely girls and boys —
Darling dainty little girls,
Lovely handsome boys.
As I hold you closely,
Love flows from my heart,
Time flies all too quickly,
As your growing starts —
When I stand and watch you,
I think of days gone by —
When your Mummies and Daddies,
Were the apple of our eyes.
I'm now getting older,
And darlings so are you,
I hope one day that you'll be blessed —
And be a Nana too.
Nana's little sweethearts —
Nana's little pests,
Always into mischief —
Always full of zest.
Time to go to bed now —
Put away those toys —
Nana's darling little girls,
And cuddly little boys.

Valerie Mawford

Off the First Tee

It looked so easy and good
So I set out with a wood
To hit the ball - no trouble at all
Stood on first tee with trembling knee
Placed ball on tee- hope no one can see
With a tremendous swing - ball should take wing
But alas and alack - missed the thing
A blush to my cheeks did it bring
Once again with shrug of shoulder
Felt myself becoming bolder
Must get off this tee ere much older
Tis getting late - feels much colder
Could not believe that I missed again
Would hate to score first hole "ten'
T'would cause a laugh among the men
Can hear them say try knitting hen
Third time was lucky - felt plucky
Till spied the ball in rough quite mucky
A spectator cried you can do it, ducky
Took my sand wedge - hit ball into hedge
Felt like jumping off a ledge
Instead took a pledge to give up the golf game
'Cause I am just a dame, not looking for fame
The golf game I cannot tame.

Beth Meek

Mersey Lights

When I was just a boy of four,
I used to walk the Mersey shore,
Taking my Grandad by the hand,
We would run along the sand,
Being born a "Billy Boy,"
They say I was his pride and joy,
And at night returning home,
Along the water's edge we'd roam.
There often appeared in the sky,
Trails of light just passing by.
"What are they," I used to ask,
Sitting down he took a flask,
"A cup of tea for you my son,"
Then the wonder tales began.
"God is in his Heaven above,
Those shooting stars a sign of love,
In giving us his only son,
He prayed that peace on earth would come —
And so a bright star is his ploy,
Telling of a newborn boy,
Somewhere on earth this night,
A new male child has seen the light."
Though many years have passed by,
Memories like this will never die.

R.G. Menarry

Lingering Aromas In Time

I still recall the wonder of those moments
Of long forgotten lingering aromas in the air
Of ginger spice, and all things nice
That corner shop, where we would stand and stare

Hams hanging up in rows, the smells of bacon
Teas and coffee, adding to the aromatic feast
Tasty fresh oven bread, and long crusty rolls
A thousand and one exotic spices from the east

How they stir up the memories within me
Strings of sausages and hot meaty smelling pies
Cheeses that add their flavour to this wonder
The Bisto kids, who the smell of gravy mesmerized

Where are all those familiar nostril tempting odours
Vanished into so many containers stored on racks
Rubber tasting foods with long E numbers
Tinned, frozen or sealed, in vacuum plastic packs

How can we enjoy those many shopping flavours
Alas but by colour, size or advertised delight
No longer can we savour tempting aromas emitted
Redundant nose, now gives way to sign and sight.

Carl R. Menkin

A Mother's Reward

"What do I owe to my Mother?"
Is a question any youngster may ask.
To answer it, so that a child can understand,
Is quite a formidable task.
This task usually falls to the father
To answer on behalf of his wife;
One obviously reply for the father would be
"To begin with, your mum gave you life.
As her baby, she fed and she clothed you
And loved you as no other could
She nursed you through illness and always tried
To train you in all that was good.
At times she would buy you a present
And she would, perhaps, do without.
Unselfishly mothers will do this
Saying, 'That's what motherhood is about'."
So if you ask your mum what you owe her
She'll say "You owe me nothing my dear
My reward is your good health and happiness
I thank God for every day you've been here."

W.S. Maxwell

My Sam

Oh how I miss you my faithful Sam
No more to bury your wet nose in my hand
I loved you more than anyone knew
Now you're gone forever leaving me blue

In your eyes I saw your pain
Your telling me was not in vain
Because I loved you and you trusted me always
I stayed with you till the light went out on your days

Never will I forget how you guarded the house
Barking at the postman, milkman, even a mouse
Never would you harm unless provoked
What you loved most was being stroked

At the age of thirteen you departed from this life
The pain I felt still stabs me like a knife
I'll always remember my faithful Sam
One day we'll walk again paw in hand

Mrs. J.L. Merchant

I, The Poet

It's three forty-five, in my bed I lie awake
Contemplating thoughts, the next move to make
Darkness falls, so slow and so deep
Daytime's over it's time to sleep.
The night so peaceful, space to think
Into the void of dreamland I'll sink.
The colours so bright, the sounds so clear
If I could stay, so be it here.
My world is quite empty, the mind is so full,
Without my dreams, the world very dull.
The words arrive, at my brain they are knocking
Sometimes sweet, sometimes shocking.
I've been given a gift, to this world I must speak,
Protecting the innocent whilst saving the meek.
I am the voice of the generation Youth
I'll tell no lies, I speak only the truth
The poet I am this society I'll save
Before the system sends us all to the grave.
I write for the people, their voice to be heard
Anti-establishment, yes, but never purged.

David Melvin

Where Can Our Children Play

There is a lovely wood and meadow nearby
Where hedgehogs snuffle around
Where foxes and squirrels play hide and seek
And the moles tunnel underground.

Go down to the river and stand on the bridge
See the swans swim majestically past
In the shallow water it's safe to play
And children fishing lines can cast.

In the meadow a ball you can kick really hard
Or let a kite soar away up high
You can even climb trees — if you take good care
Trees that nearly reach up to the sky.

When we were children we could play all day
In the meadows and woods on our own
Yesteryear it was safe — now it's only a dream
It's not safe now for a child alone.

How sad that our children can't share that dream
To be free and roam woods all day
What makes a person so twisted inside
Our children aren't allowed out to play.

Mary Millar

My Perfect Day

A beautiful day with a bright blue sky,
Small fluffy clouds pass slowly by,
Down to the beach with its clean golden sand,
My beachmat and towel clutched in my hand,
I swim in the water so cool and clear,
While small shoals of fish come quite near,
As I swim towards them suddenly go,
Quickly darting to and fro,
A yacht sails by so majestic it seems,
As its chrome in the sun shimmers and gleams,
Its sails fully blown like a huge ball gown,
Till suddenly they sag as the wind dies down,
I float on my back in the sun kissed sea,
And let the waves wash over me,
The gulls overhead they screech and scream,
Awaking me from my floating dream,
Refreshed by my swim I head back to shore,
And feel the sand under my feet once more,
The sky suddenly turns to an ominous grey,
An abrupt end to a perfect day,
The wind starts to blow and whips up the sea,
I pick up my things and head home for tea.

Joan Mayer

A Tree

How beautiful a tree is, standing proud and silent there
How beautiful the blossom, that sways in centre air
Soon the wind will scatter the blossoms to the ground
A carpet of soft petals will cover all around
Once more in all her spendour her fruits she will display
Showing off her wares to those who pass her way
As weeks go by she sheds the fruit, she has borne this year
Her leaves she'll shed for winter, they'll scatter everywhere
But spring is round the corner, she'll bloom again you'll see
She'll burst with buds and show once more the splendour of a tree.

Mrs. J. Meyrick

First Light

Dawn was breaking and falling to the floor,
    The cottage that hid behind the rose bush lay still.
The cabin's lights were slightly dim,
    As the lamp was extinguished from the draught of still air.
Only the fidget of the pair of Tawny owls awoke the solemn landscape.
    Their cry of 'Kerwic-to-whoo', echoes round the forests cove.
The moon's tender beams shined through the orifice's,
    Formed by the abrasion of speckled rocks.
The passing hour, spread its thoughts still fully,
    As the glowing pimple rose.
Down on the shore, the fragile wavelets broke to create white horses,
    Dancing on the first sun's rays listening on the sea.
Energy of light was sweeping through the morning clouds,
    That hung in the sky, suspended on heaven's chains.
The alarm clock rang vigorously, brought this picture,
    Of tranquillity to a halt.

Harry James Mitchell

How I Felt When I Lost You

A tiny star shines up above, it seems so far away
Just like the love that we once had, no longer here today
A sunny glow that filled my world when you were here with me
And now a cloud that will not lift, for you I cannot see

A tear that falls upon my cheek, I cry these tears for you
If only you could be my love, my skies would turn to blue
In my heart I hold a torch, for the one I love so dear
I'll care about you always, whether you are far or near.

A broken heart that will not mend, a pain that will not die
A love that cannot be forgotten as each day passes by
Memories that will always stay, locked inside my heart
Of all the happy days we had, before we had to part

So someday when you are old, and feeling sad and blue
Remember how you broke my heart, how I felt when I lost you.

Goog

Sun Alone

I am a sun alone
In this dark universe anon.
No planets upon which to shine
No centre 'round which I've spun.

No days or seasons
Orion constellations
Existence without reasons
Challenges, consolations.

Michael Gerald Meade

Childish Wonder

The mighty oak has stood there
Since before my dad was born
A solid lofty living thing
In the middle of the lawn
Now here's the thing that puzzles me
As I look out each dawn
The oak tree it still stands there
But my father he has gone.

W. Mehaffy

Rape Of The Land

Meadows once full of buttercups
Show now a placid blue.
The vivid yellow rape fields
Are yet another hue.

The motorways spread wider
Into the country lane,
Changing for our children
Forever the terrain.

We travel on the motorway
And reach a roadworks scheme,
The land is torn and terrorised,
A devastating scene.

The greenbelts torn asunder,
Suffering pillage and rape,
The white chalk downs now sliced
Resembling a moonscape.

The ribbon road snakes on,
There is a return to green,
It does no good to dwell on
The land that we've just seen.

Meadow sweet and Foxgloves
Are banked beside the way
Perhaps in spite of all this rape
They'll bloom another day.

Joan Mitchell

Scenes From Jamaica

I was waiting my turn in the travel agent's shop.
As I waited I listened, and I watched.
There was one elderly lady with tears in her eyes.
As she begged for her ticket for the aeroplane ride.
She was told, one more payment that's what it takes.
Perhaps by next week she would raise the stake.
As she turned, her thin and gnarled hand brushed a tear away.
To be replaced by someone else eager to pay.

I'd seen the London Buses in Kingston last week.
Advertising milk and honey, in the streets.
The mother country needs you, it had said
Here were the loyal people ready to be led,
And willing to save their every shilling.
To go to London at the mother country's bidding.

I'd seen laughing people leaving last week.
From the Palisaidus airport, it looked like a treat
In their Sunday best clothes of yellow sateen.
And light coloured sandals of orange and green.
No one had told them, it would be cold, and might snow.
They were so excited they just wanted to go.
It filled me with a dreadful despair, to listen their chatter and hope.
If only they knew, living and working in London is no joke.

Mrs. J.D. Miller

The World's Children

Look into your childhood, what do you see?
Loneliness, sadness, or days filled with glee.
Where you guided with meaning, feeling loved and secure.
Or were you condemned into an unknown future?

'You are what you eat' dieticians exclaim
How we are brought up, is exactly the same,
People and incidents are like a play and its cast —
The way we are now, can be found in our past.

To a child, bad experiences, physical or emotional
In some form or another, eventually take their toll,
Sometimes guilt or resentment, but certainly grief —
Which often takes a long time to find relief.

Our "little people" are the world's only hope
And patience with understanding will help them cope,
They'll gain insight, with awareness for the Earth —
Feeling there is reason and purpose to their birth.

What more can we from our children expect
Than returned love; treasured memories, and respect,
Be fair to them now, and in return —
Life's lessons, they will be ready to learn.

We all have regrets in things said and done
But at least trying is where we hope to have won,
Climbing into their heads and hearts is the key —
That child is *you*, that child is *me*.

(Dedicated to Rowanna and Aila)

Lynda Miller

Dancing on the Sunlit Air

Drowsily I opened my eyes
    To see two butter flies
Dancing on the sunlit air,
    Happy to be without care.

It was such a beautiful day,
    The world was mine and as I lay
I drank in all that loveliness
    And felt a wondrous happiness.

The day was drenched in perfume,
    It filled my nostrils and my room
From all the many flowers,
    So highlighting the sunshine hours.

Will that stillness captured in time
    'Ere again return to be mine?
It was a day I'll remember
    Through many a chill December.

J. Millington

Ghost

From the nightwood, o'er the wet grass,
Past the waters of the lake,
Drifting, moving, ever onwards
Seeking, searching for her mate.

Owls are hooting, clouds are scudding,
O'er the new moon's shining face,
Dark ahead the ruin lies waiting
To enfold her ghostly grace.

Once this place was filled with laughter,
In those golden days of yore,
Hand in hand with her young lover,
Here they walked in love so pure.

Now she screams and yearns to find him,
Through those portals dark with space,
Every new moon she's returning
Seeking, searching for his face.

Down the darkened silent hallways,
Bats aflutter overhead,
Moonlight glitters through the windows,
As she vapours, arms outstretched.

Though two hundred years are passing
Still she haunts, and still returns,
'Til she finds him and then can rest,
Arms entwined, to sleep at last.

Mrs. J. Mizrahi

1994

I used to be shocked and used to cry,
Over all the human misery and tragedy,
But over the years my tears have run dry,
As it happens every day with no remedy.

Mornings, I waken and turn on the TV,
Ethiopia to Rwanda, headlines the same,
Listen to news and violence is all I see,
The horrors of war are always to blame.

Today it's happening all over the world,
Starved children with mutilated parents.
Food from other countries is long-hauled,
Yet no guarantee of providing nutrients.

They fight for their next breath of air,
Besides something to fill swollen bellies.
Aid workers plead for money, for the care
Of the beleaguered millions of refugees.

We are in 1994, with no sight to an end
To all the bloodbaths and wanton carnage.
Deprived of freedom, most without a friend
And all we can give is goodwill ...
...and helpless patronage.

Robert Milnes

The End of the Road

I looked across the room, and saw the empty chair,
My dearest love had died, and was no longer there,
For sixty years, we had shared our life together,
And battled on, through very stormy weather,
We made our vows in nineteen thirty-three,
Promised to love and cherish, no matter what may be.
Two world wars we've seen, and still survived,
Was thrilled to bits, when our only son arrived.
Money was short, but who cared about cash,
We paid our bills, we were never rash.
What we couldn't afford, we just had to bar,
In fact we were sixty, when we had our first car.
We enjoyed the things, which were always free,
Such as pure air, the flowers, and movements of sea,
And the many good friends, we have made on the way,
I include everyone, when I kneel down to pray.
Some of our young ones, have gone raving mad.
Battering old folk, it's all so sad.
I'm glad I'm not a youngster, growing up today,
With so many temptations standing in my way,
I no longer plan for things ahead,
No interest now my husband is dead.
My tears still flow, time heals they say,
We'll meet again, on the final day.

Mary Milverton

Who Needed Fred!

The robin hopped down the unswept path.
His tail drooped, his eye was sad.
Where was the man, stooped and grey,
the friendly gardener,
whose name was Fred?

The robin scratched in the barren earth,
but the wily worms were deep far down.
No gnarled old man was here today,
to dig the soil,
unearth the grubs.

The robin twittered in the rose-hip tree
swinging low by the potting shed.
Sometimes Fred scattered crumbs
on the flags of stone ...
but, not today.

The robin flew to the garden wall.
His bright eye twitched at what he saw.
The square below had dark rich earth ...
freshly turned ... a feast of worms.
Who needed Fred!

Felicity Minifie

Santa's Lost Boot

Father Christmas has lost his boot,
While travelling in his sleigh.
All the children hope he finds it,
Before it's Christmas day.

The reindeer are very sad,
The elves and fairies too.
Because they help Father Christmas
To bring your toys to you.

Don't worry, Santa, the children cried,
As they frolicked in the snow.
We will help to find your boot
Before it is time to go.

They searched among the sacks of toys
He had upon his sleigh
And lying at the bottom
His big black boot lay.

On went his boot and through the snow
He strode without delay
So he could deliver all the toys
In time for Christmas Day.

Mrs. E. Moneypenny

Autumn

Suddenly — the brilliance of summer days is over
Almost without our realising,
The trees, recently clothed in bright-coloured leaves
Now look in sorry state
Where the last of their autumn dress
Has been rudely stripped
By unrepentant gales.

Their naked branches give a grotesque look
As if stretching up to ask for divine grace,
Like the arms of someone drowning,
Reaching upwards with last minute appeal
For resuscitation.

But, they waste their time;
For God in His wisdom grants them His sleep
Until the great awakening of Spring,
When He, with loving care, when the time is right,
Will cause the sap to rise and give new birth
To all those stark and lifeless forms, when they
Will live again.

Joan M. Minnitt

I'm Fine

"How are you?" they say. "Fine," I reply.
Oh why can't they see that I'm telling a lie?
I'm not fine at all. It's all a facade.
Outside I'm smiling. Inside I'm afraid.
Outside I'm happy, talking to folk.
Having a drink and sharing their jokes.
Inside it's different; inside I'm crying;
Inside I'm drowning; inside I'm dying.
"How are you?" they say. "You look a bit peeky."
"I'm fine" I reply. "Just the kids being cheeky."
I'm not fine at all. All is not as it seems.
Can't they see me crying? Hear my silent screams?
They ask me for gossip, for scandal, for news.
Not, "How are your feeling? Are you scared and confused?"
And I'm good at pretending that all is OK
So polite conversation. "Nice weather today."
They don't seem to notice an old friend in pain,
Who can't possibly cope under all of this strain.
Oh please, open your ears and listen to me!
Open your eyes. Tell me, what do you see?
I'm not fine at all. I'm not doing well.
I'm not a bit happy. I'm lonely as hell!
But I'll keep on smiling. I'll hold back the tears.
Until they all leave me, alone with my fears.

Karen Mitchell

The Story of Santa

Santa is coming soon,
He comes way after noon.
Come on and join the ride,
With Santa at your side.
Rudolph will be your light,
As you travel in the night,
But then day arrives,
So go back to the girls and guys.

Kieren Marston (Age 8)

Autumn Thanksgiving

The family sat down
All eyes stared at the turkey
"Cluck, Cluck," The infant imitated.
The knife was lowered
A leg fell off
"Owwww" screamed the infant holding its leg.
The meat was served
The grace was said
"Yummy" said the infant.
Everybody started eating
Chewing filled the room
"Yuckky" the infant said, spitting out the food.
The mother got up
And took the infant to bed.
"Shucks" the infant whispered.

Scott Metcalf

Passing By

She cannot speak as she lays there still
I want so much to give her some of my will
I take her hand let her know I'm there
Please God, let her know I love her and care
Her eyes open slightly so tired and dreary
Her body is frail so weak and weary
What has her life been like in the past
So many question I'd like to ask
Her lips form a smile as she clenches my hand
She looks far away as though in another land
I whisper comfort close to her ear
Oh God, I pray, please let her hear
Wanting anything? I manage to say
She points to her rosary, she wants to pray
As I place the beads across her chest
Her eyes slowly close, she has gone to rest
I wonder who this lady was, I sigh,
I didn't know her, I was just passing by.
Words of comfort doesn't need pay
'Cos love isn't love till you can give it away.

Theresa M. Mitchell

The Burial of an Unknown Woman in Highgate Cemetery

There is the smell of freshly turned earth
and damp laves,
Of wormy cells and tree roots freshly stripped
And bleeding,
The air is heavy with mist, clinging and cold,
There is mud on shiny shoes
And vapour on frozen breath,
Few words are spoken
Only the clatter of falling stones
Breaks the silence, and condemns her loneliness
To the grave.

M.J. Michalak

A Brief Moment In Wandlebury

Ah! How the sun shone for us today!
As we probed and teased out our lives to each other.
Our music was the birds.
Our contentment was our company.
We planned your future, knowing mine has been.
The sun danced in your eyes as you laughed.
I saw it.
You were happy.
I counted the gold in my treasure chest.
Then let the pieces of eight slip through my fingers.
Wandelbury took us to her bosom.
And held us tight!

Phillip Mason-Wright

Love Is Such A Lonely Thing

Love is such a lonely thing
when evening falls
like waves of helpless soldiers
on the beachhead of Dieppe,
hours of youthful promise
now forever unfulfilled —
building blocks of history
draped in black.

In the hours of deepest darkness,
when the weary world
has finally found its rest
inside its silence
the spirits of the dead
will rise uneasy from the beaches
and cry out through their agony
to lonely hearts
that love has rendered sleepless in despair ...
and beckon with the promise
of remembrance everlasting.

Douglas Meale

The Flats

A flat on the landing with only one tap
A welcome to everyone on the old mat.
A blackleaded grate with a roaring big fire
No new three piece suite or TV on hire.
We worked hard for a living just a few bob
Keys in the letter box nothing to rob.
Girls played on lampposts, boys with a ball,
Old folks looked after by one and all.
They called the flats slums
And pulled them all down
In Kew Street they were
In old Liverpool town.

Mrs. A. Murray

Black Gold

The moon is silent on the edge of life
As though to be forever in our sight.
The sea that's known a fury made in hell
And crashed its power upon the shore, now sleeps,
Decked in sequins sparkling in the beams,
The sea bird's cry still echoes on the breeze,
A scene for dreams.

Afar I see the glistening of the gold
As black as any night without a moon,
And in the light of day will sea birds fly
Or drift amidst the ebony to die.
So on the morrow with the changing scene
And no sad echo on the evening breeze,
We'll know she wept.

Luciane Murfitt

Identified?

I might make myself available,
I might be in the right place.
I might spend all my money
To provide the right resources.
I might sacrifice my time
With those who need me
In order to be with those
I could help.
I might get myself beaten up,
I might be taken for a ride;
I might be taking myself
For a ride
If the only reason I do all this
Is so the undeserving poor
Can hear the Good News.
I may be identifying with
them —
But do they identify me with
Him?

Ian Marron

Britain's Chapter Of Seasons

The seasons are like four chapters we read about at night,
Starting with winter in its silent shroud of white
Looking like a fairyland in a beam of light,
Life around seems so peaceful on such a winter's night.
Spring is chapter two which is wake up time for me and you
Beauty all around unfurls itself making the earth a picture of wealth,
The flowers are so colourful the music from the birds
Make spring create a paradise helping the summer to look so nice.

Spring brings us chapter three what fun is had on holiday.
Children playing in the sand, splashing in the sea,
Squealing, shouting and giggling with tremendous glee!
Some adults prefer a walking spree, for them that's the perfect holiday.
Such picturesque and pleasant places brings a smile to all their faces.
What a sight on a clear summer evening watching the sun slowly disappearing.
Spreading out peace as it sets in the west giving us time for some much needed rest.
Autumn has now brought us chapter four the scent in the air is nearly pure.

The leaves on the trees are an artist's delight
A painting on a canvas brought majestically to life.
Britain has the mountains in beautiful pleasant Wales,
The splendour of the Sussex Downs through Harting and around
Spreading out to surround us on our journey now northward bound —
To Scotland with its mountains, lochs and glens and purple coloured heather
Growing on the roadside around each bend.
Thank you chapters, one, two, three and four, bringing us the seasons to admire forever more!

Eileen Joyce Molland

NATO Fleet on Exercise: Nineteen Fifties

Anchoring quite close inshore
First one, then indistinctly many more,
Those towering shadows coming through the fog,
Flashing signals,
Sheathed might.

Amplified orders heard throughout the night,
A bugle call at dawn;
The great ships, pale grey
In pale grey mist, dissolve away,
Silently, stealthily.

An unforgettable sight of resolution,
Quietly magnificent, awe inspiring.
A memory kept all these years, distinct,
When service did not suggest reward;
A time extinct.

Jean Mitchell

The Great Divide

You don't have to build a wall to see
The division that's creating in our country
It isn't just the North and the South
It's here all around us, a callous tongue in the mouth
It doesn't have to be bricks and cement
Sometimes it's just over your garden fence
Take John Smith with his UB40
He's not lost his job for being naughty
Unemployment — that dirty word
Went and reared its ugly head
Friendships we've known, now are dead
Families we've loved from the start
What are they now — torn apart
But don't despair, keep your pride
Only clouds, the sun does hide
After dark, there's always light
Britain one day — will unite

Mandy Mitchinson

Sailing on a Metaphysical Sea

I sit in your boat and watch my dreams float,
　　as I drift across your lake of time.
I hear your sweet words as they ease my stretched nerves,
　　like pure honey laced with wine.
And I know we're naked from the soul up we have tasted,
　　more riches than in a gold mine.

　　we're sailing on a metaphysical sea
　　just hold my hand and set me free

We have touched the stars with our passion for hours,
　　your body has melted into mine.
You dazzle me in sounds of colour I have found,
　　myself resting in your shine.
And there is no god above who can show me more love,
　　my religion is with you, divine.
We break through words barriers
　　nothing could carry us higher than our bodies mime.

This valley is so deep my mind cannot sleep,
　　I touch you through the fabric of time.
Nothing could break us apart nothing could take us,
　　we have grown together, entwined.
I cast my troubles to the breeze my blues into the seas,
　　I smile at myself knowing you're mine.

P. C. Moody

"Blossoms-In-The-Dust"

Pretty are the flowers that bloom this wooded lane
Silence here is golden, never more to wane
Evergreens of "spruce and pine" stand erect in line
Casting shadows through a glade now a communal shrine
Pilgrims tread this sacred ground weeping years of sadness
Remembering atrocities carried out in an act of madness

Ugly are the visions that cause a sleepless night
cries of disillusionment herald a ghastly sight
Degraded tottering skeletons, unaware of the smell
Are herded towards oven doors — gateways to scorching hell
Sadists and perverts wade through a sea of groans
Wielding barb wire whips, shearing flesh from broken bones

Black smoke swirls from chimney stacks to hover overhead
Furnaces blazing hot, devour the crackling dead
Overloaded pushcarts carrying corpses' ashen-grey
Are dumped into an endless pit of squalor and decay
Grotesque and barbaric scenes no country will surpass
A legacy from "The-Weinmarcht and Himmlers Black-Mass"

Time is the healer of every "genocide"
No epitaphs or crosses on a mound of earth abide
Garlands of "eidle-weis" perfume this reverent place
In memory of Jews annihilated - Germany's disgrace
The winds of change have swept away debauchery and lust
For souls at rest, forever blessed, now "blossoms in the dust"

James Montgomery

The Fox's Den

I am a fox
I live in a den
Sometimes for dinner
I eat a fat hen.
People hate me,
But how can this be?
You eat the chickens
Why can't you spare one for me.
Now this is the end of my sad diary.

Nathan B. Moffatt

Untitled

I look for my father's ivory paper knife
to open my post.

　　My father opened his letters neatly
　　and kept his papers in order.
　　I open my letters neatly.

My father daydreamed for an hour or two
and came up with his master plan.
I daydream for an hour or two.

　　Every few years my father moved house
　　and the change was for the better.
　　Every few years I move house.

My father died and for sure he went to heaven.
I haven't died yet ...!

Jane Molnar

From A Manx Garden

A clear blue sky, a gentle bracing wind —
But more than this, worth so much more —
　　A stillness and a calm.
The sounds of silence, barely-broken quiet,
Save only for the gentle, murmuring hum
　　Of bees - a heaven-sent psalm.

A seagull's sudden scream, ear-shattering,
But briefly shocks the sleepy Island's peace;
　　The balm of quiet remains.
And over all the unseen humming song
From all around, continuous, content,
　　Sweet soothing heart-felt pains.

The toot of passing tram is heard below
In valley depths, before the passive sea
　　Sweeps all beneath its feet.
And still the music of the bees sings on,
A thousand drowsy purrings, Nature's balm,
　　Soul-restful, honey-sweet.

Maureen Mitchell

A Friend Is To Another

A friend is to another, as is a bosom to a lonely lover,
as the stars are to the skies which hold them,
as nectar is to the humble bee,
these are but small comparisons to all that you are to me.

To see the sun rise in your perfect piercing eyes,
is to see the moon glow above the emerald isles,
is to watch a sibling bird fly as it never has before,
is to witness a baby enter the world through its mother's door,
as this is in feeling only a speck of the delight you bring to me,
I am not blind if I see nothing else but thee.

If you teach me a million things hence, one per day,
it is my secret garden where my thoughts can play,
it is my life's blood within my very veins,
it is a lark's song veiled by the morning rain,
and if I learn slowly, as lessons should be taught,
let me die happy for I have found in you more than I have sought.

In short ... you make my heart sing,
you bring more volumptuous words to my lips than from a jester's to a king,
for if I am weary you wipe my furrowed sweated brow,
I know you love me, but I still wonder how?!

S.D. Moore

Heralds of Winter

Jabber-jangle, frenzied honkings
Great flappings, long necked seasonal travellers —
Brazen in pillage of carrot tops
They feast.
Such Journeying deserves regard.

Back down my years
In spaces where instinct lives
Where self exists
I'm wired,
Inner ear receives first goose cry.

I hoard this gift, this V-shape.
Calculated flight across my skies
Personal heralds, polar scouts,
Bird-voice sings off key
No symphony this!
Third eye beholds the image of a grief.
True leader, compass bearer-spear
Receive this silent mourning for
She who died.

Listen! You can keep it safe within your flap-beat —
I will catch the echo of it next year.

Susan Anne Moore

Goodbye Cruel World

I've been down here for hours and hours
Someone covered me up with earth and flowers
I had a pain in my chest and back
It must have been a heart attack
Now I'll never be ill, nor ever well
Is this what it's like, down in hell?
        I think, I must be dead.

It's dark and cold and quiet here
Nothing to see and nothing to hear
Nothing to do but just lie here
No more worries, nothing to fear
I've always wanted a place of my own
Now I'm down here, all alone.
        I must be dead.

Now I've gone to meet my maker
Meeting family and friends of long ago
No more will I see the earth or sky
No more will I hear my grandson cry
I leave behind a cruel world.
        I'm not sorry, I'm dead.

Sheila Myers

Flowers

Flowers are gathered in the rain,
Sheltering each other from the pain.
Liquid droplets forming on petals, delicately beaded.
The young want, hope and plead to be needed.
One smiling and tall,
One shy and pretty.
They don't mind the rain,
They can share all their pain.
The petals of the flowers curl slowly around them.
Secret from us, form their own sparkling gem.

Kirsty Moore

Homeless

The homeless lay there on the ground.
No one to care only the sound
Of footsteps passing all around.

People hurry on their way
To start another busy day.
No money or food to eat
As they lay huddled on that cold wet street.

The police pass by and move them along.
You can't stay here among this busy throng.
Weary and tired they move along.

If only someone would stop and say,
There's a room for you, a place to stay
Where you will be loved and fed.

No more to roam round and round,
Hoping someone will give you a pound.

Jessie Moody

Bitterness

Silt lying at peace on the river's bed,
Is gently stirred by the rumbling rocks that roll,
And bounce their way through currents, flows, and ebbs,
As they journey towards their unknown goal.
The river calms, and the residues fall,
Sedated once more among the dark depths,
Where they lie in wait, waiting to be called
Into action. Sometimes, in violence,
These residues are whisked into an all-
Blinding blizzard of frenzied action by
Eddies of anger, and into a squally
Sense-retarding blur that clouds the eye.
Pain may settle like sediment, yet,
Although we forgive, we never forget.

Chris Moores

flowerssunsetmoonsnow

anonymous yellow mix
unconsciously creating
their own fluid dynamics

pink over concrete high rise
clashing with a faltering
neon Tetley sign

thumbnail clipping coy
amidst an Early Learning
blue painted sky

unique white auditory quality
subtly damping
the vibrations of the city

Catherine Moore

Homeland

Steam trains still run in Yorkshire,
The moors still hold their peace.
Men still toil with earth and beast
To bring forth food and fleece.
The deep mines are mostly gone now,
The cotton mills long dead,
The rivers creep by sluggishly,
Too long by poison fed.
The Pennines keep majestic sway,
And their people proud and strong,
Bound to this sleeping giant
Who perhaps has slept too long.

Mark J. Morris

Signs Of Winter

The Autumn mist was fading,
And the sky became clear
The moisture on the rose petal,
Looked like a tear.

The dew was sparkling
On the spider's web,
The sun made it look,
Like a gossamer thread.

A red-breasted robin
Was hopping around,
Ever hopeful, to find
A few crumbs on the ground.

The berries on the shrubs
Were turning red
All were signs
Of the winter ahead.

Enid Morris

Eduardo Et Morte

I'm writing to you daughter dear, with news you will not want to hear,
Mother cried 'til her face was red, I've got to tell you, Teddy's dead.
He was perched on top of the wardrobe, he slipped and fell on his side
We feared the worst, his stitching had burst, the stuffing oozed out and he died.

He was a faithful companion, he'd listen and not answer back,
His mother was one of the 'Paddington' bears, his father a Russian called Jack.
Yes, his father must have been Russian, for when you stop to think,
That must have been the reason, his fur was coloured pink.
We'll never forget poor Teddy, the lopsided grin on his mouth,
We'll remember with tears, his large pointed ears, pointing opposite ways — North and South.

You confided to him all your secrets, while you and he did play,
And he never told another soul until his dying day,
But now you're grown, I'll tell you why, the reason he never snitched.
Poor old Teddy couldn't talk, because his mouth was stitched.

We cremated poor Teddy at midnight, your Mother and I alone,
We had to wait 'til the streets were bare, we live in a smokeless zone
He disappeared in a puff of smoke, no Sympathy Cards or Masses.
When the postman next knocks, he'll deliver a box, with Teddy's glass eyes and his ashes.

A.W. Morrison

Red Point Croft

The wind howled round the croft house night and day.
It lashed white horses up onto the rocks in spray.
The pregnant sky hung heavy with the mounding cloud
And seagulls shrieked their warnings far and loud.

And yet the rain withheld and would not fall
Except in sudden grey-sheet-shrouding squall
Which then departed quickly to another place —
The howling wind the chaser in the race.

The shags stood silent on the spume-soaked rocks.
The otters hid, though gannets swooped in flocks.
Across the Point ʼupon the Salmon Bay
The new-dead carcass of a grey seal lay.

A sudden lull — the wind becomes more gentle
Then screams again with forces elemental.
Here I face this nature as I stand alone
Upon this land Man vainly seeks to own.

I seek an understanding of Man's past,
Yet here an ancient presence seems to last
Forever. All Man's greatness seems to me
Just like a speck of flotsam on the swelling sea.

M. Louise Moran

A Trip To The Valleys

The future here looks grimmer,
Don't live in the past, but look to the future.
A past washes away, like coal dust from a face,
Blue scars left behind is a symbolic trace,
Of our miner's last days.

By tightening one's belt and making do,
Is a system and knowledge, we each have gained.
There is a closeness here like no other place
Look the world over, there is only one Wales.

Hills and vales go hand in hand.
This truly is the place to stand,
And look at beautiful views,
Should you just listen quiet enough,
You will hear the mountains, call you back.

With an urgency, it will cut like a knife,
Slicing deep, like the devil in the wind.
To leave, is to return, if only in your mind.

Be proud to be Welsh, and never forget, be loyal,
Always think of your kind.

Maria Morgan

Soliloquy

Where is the love so lately tended
In place is harshness, iron will unbended
Is this then cold reality — no warmth, no sun-filled days?
Or merely life's rough pattern, always testing, low in praise.
No fondness or indulgence at the foolish spirit's cravings
Once more to tread the lonely ways with sorrowing heart
O'er pavings sharp, rutted choked with thorns
Does each soul struggle onward even though it mourns?
Still onward yet, as always striving for life's treasure,
Must this be sought alone — no sharing gift of pleasure.
... But hope wells up eternal or life is not worth living
E'en tho' the content lacking without the joy of giving.

June Martin

Homesick

The cloudy nights, the glistening stars,
The things that I can't see.
Why couldn't it go to some other place?
I don't know where I belong,
Where I used to be.
My mind tells me that someday,
I'll find a place where I belong,
Where I was meant to be.
A lot of things which are around me,
Remind me of my home,
When other things just don't,
And I feel all alone.
And someday I will find a world where I belong.

Samantha Morgan (Age 9)

Summer

Summer is the season of love,
Its warmth pacifying the cruelest heart.
Birds fly in their freedom in the blue sky above
While a horse pulls a hay-laden cart.

Butterflies flutter and bees buzz around
Among the flowers of pink, blue and red.
The fields are yellow from wheat on the ground
Like a huge blanket upon a warm bed.

If summer were human it would be a woman
Who sings carefree among the sweet corn.
She's happy and laughing and knows that she can
Bring pleasure to all the new born.

The bright sun shines like the crown of a king
Casting shadows as sharp as a knife.
The heart dances with joy and the feeling it brings
Is a feeling of love for this life.

Nigel Morgan

A Lloyd's Name

She walked erect, proudly striding out,
The pavement like a catwalk.
A queen at centre court,
Glancing neither left nor right
She made her stately passage.

The coat, dark navy, tailored classic,
Had worn well, suited her
Classical stance, coiled hair.
Shoes, high heeled courts,
Not suited to that rough weather.

The umbrella spoke gave her away.
Silently it poked awry
Allowing a rain drop to cry
Down that haughty face.
Ignoring it, on she travelled.

Once there had been a Jaguar
Chauffeur driven, highly polished,
To take her shopping at Harrods
But now she patronized the local Spar.
It was a lifetime's short journey.

Liz Morris

Breathe Little Child

My baby's born blue,
What can I do?
Quick, run for the doctor, the minister too.
Oh God hear my plea,
I need you with me.
Breathe little child, my baby ...
The doctor came quick,
(The child was so sick)
To restore life he tried,
A priest,
At his side,
Took action
Right there.
On his knees
With a prayer,
Named the child in God's eyes
Laid it down, fraught with sighs
O God, hear our plea,
We need you here, don't you see?
Breathe little child, tiny baby ...

A splutter, a cry escaped me,
God heard their plea.
I breathed ...
I was that child, that baby.

Dorothy Morrison

Winter's Sky

As I stroll home on a winter's night,
I look at the sky, what a wondrous sight.
Out of the black, a million stars shone
Their twinkling light so many years born.

There's Cassiopeia and the Great Bear,
Leo the Lion is still in his lair.
The Seven Sisters are unusually bright,
But Taurus the Bull seems to have been in a fight.

Aries the Ram is bedraggled and torn
It looks to me he's minus a horn.
The Gemini Twins are dancing with glee
Could they know where the horn might be?

Orion the Hunter his belt is lost,
An angry cloud his path has crossed.
More stars begin to disappear,
The predicted storm is drawing near.

A distant rumble fills the air
A gust of wind blows through my hair
Must hurry home to my feather bed
Before the storm comes overhead.

Marie Mort

Season's Colours

The colour of Spring is crystal bright
Daffodils gold in the yellow Spring light
New leaves on the trees are the brightest of green
Meadows are carpeted with Buttercup sheen
The woods are awash with the brightest of blue
As the Bluebells explode with their wonderful hue
The colour of Spring is crystal bright.

The colour of Summer is kaleidoscope bright
The flowers are all bathed in the gold Summer light
A rainbow of colours neath the blue of the sky
Ponds sparkle like diamonds for the green dragonfly
The butterflies dance like jewels in a crown
As nature is clothed in her rich Summer gown
The colour of Summer is kaleidoscope bright.

The colour of Autumn is orange bright
Trees shimmer topaz in the soft Autumn light
Dressed in the splendour of russet and brown
A carpet of amber as the leaves tumble down
The berries are growing bright yellow and red
Food for the birds in the Winter ahead
The colour of Autumn is orange bright.

The colour of Winter is dismal grey.
There's no more to say.

Janet Morton

Elephants

With flapping ears and ponderous feet,
These animals are quite unique.
For many years they've tramped the earth,
The bulls looked on, the cows gave birth.
These gentle giants, they feared no one,
Till greedy man let lose his gun.
Poaching is a ghastly game,
Their lives will never be the same.
They wander around, they do not know,
Is that man friend or foe?
Has he come to slay them all?
How could humans be so cruel!
What price to pay for ivory,
Too high a price, 'tis plain to see.
One day, with luck, this death will cease,
And elephants will live in peace.
Freedom to live their lives once more,
Guns laid down, and heard no more.

Mrs. M. Moss

Hiraeth

(Nostalgia)

We have a little home in Wales
Close to the Sea it's called "White Sails".
To reach our cot the path is steep,
But Oh the peace, how deep our sleep.

"A jewel set in a Silver Sea"
was how Tom Parry described to me
Beguiling, beauteous Borth-y-Gest
Where Sea and Country folk are blessed

The mountains oft-times mauve with heather
Are ever-changing with the weather;
Now sparkling white with winter snow
Their rushing streams all silvery flow

To join the Glaslyn, Dwyryd, Dwyfor
Where Salmon leap in turgid river
And hurry into lovely bay
Where Fishermen and children play

On golden sands on summer's day
or scramble rocks if clouds are grey;
And little boats set sail and glide
Out to the bar on wind and tide.

When summer's end brings Harvest Gold
The fruits of autumn fill the Fold
Still Sea-Birds scream and whirl and dive,
And Oh it's good to be alive.

Joyce E. Morrison

Singing Songs

Singing songs for all the people
Singing songs for all the land
Singing songs that make us happy
Makes life feel just really grand

Just putting smiles onto faces
And chasing clouds of grey
Making everyone feel happy
As they go from day to day

We sing songs of love and laughter
We sing songs to charm the birds
But the songs that give us pleasure
Are those with simple words

So let's all sing together
And some happiness let's gain
Let your voices join together
With this simple short refrain

Singing songs for the people
Singing songs for all the land
Singing songs that make us happy
Makes life feel just really grand

Roy G. Muckart

Legacy

I have seen that image once before
A long, long time ago
That expression on a familiar face
That used to thrill me so.
The way those eyes in deep intent
Read the book, held your hand
Strange to see that face again
So hard to understand.
You in the future, your life ahead
Yet he was from the past.
Your heritage so plain to see
That life itself had cast.
About to take familiar paths
A calling to the sea
How strange to be reminded
Of a similar memory.
This great profession, your own choice
May it be the perfect one.
To bring success, achieved with pride
For you, my dear grandson.

Mrs. O. Muir

Homecoming

Open the door with firm, unflinching hands,
Hands that fear not the other, inner side.
O traveller returned from distant land
Open the door then, set it standing wide.

Stillness within, then faintly, from above
Into the waiting quietness "Who is there?"
"It cannot be! But oh, it is, 'tis he."
Then rushing footsteps crowd upon the stair
The voice in breathless laughter hurries near
And arms are wide as when true lovers meet
After the lonely unrelenting years.
Be silent time! Eternity is sweet.

Look round you now, and see how clean, how bright.
Yes, this new, but that we've had always.
How long it's been, and yet the years invite
Delightful memories, bridging days
Of separation, as a river's length
Is cut across. How changed we are,
And yet the same. Perhaps a little strength
Is added to your face, and frown lines mar
My own. But dearest, it is really thus
I love you best,

Now let us close the door.
The gentle quietness shall hold for us
The beat of life — and who may ask for more

Vivienne Morris

Suggestion

I looked around and saw an ox
I looked again and saw a fox.
I stood and waited for them both
Who came along but Mr. Sloth.

Now Mr. Sloth is quite a guy, very droll, very dry.
With just three toes on long forearms.
A nice fur coat to keep him warm.
He takes his time and travels slow,
But always gets where he wants to go.

I looked around and saw a bear
I looked again and saw a hare.
I stood and waited for a chat,
Who came along but Mr. Cat.

Now Mr. Cat is quite a guy, sure of feet, sharp of eye.
He likes to prowl both night and day
Hunting for his favourite prey.
With lots of caution he does roam
And usually brings something home.

Now these two chaps have a message for you
To keep in mind in all you do.
To act in haste and full of wrath
Hinders you along life's path
So take things slow but very sure
And that hard road you will endure.

Damian Mort (Age 14)

Teashop Countesses

Every Sunday afternoon,
We rise from floral comfy chairs,
And humming Vicar's favourite psalm,
Will flock to olde-world tearooms.
We thousand genteel women
Decked out, dressed up in our best hats,
Shall sit here sipping endless cups
Of tea, through redsmeared lips,
While whisking crumbs of current buns,
From new plaid skirts and leaf motifs,
On crisp white linen cloths.

These old tea rooms,
Have stayed the same since 1935,
When we as girls, upon the Green,
Met village boys, long passed away.
But now, we concentrate on pleasant things,
The sun that shows a dusty haze of stars
Through leaded panes into our corner,
And rooted to its wooden perch,
An ancient cage bird sings,
For these are precious moments spent,
Where we remain, while time stands still,
Contented 'mid the sweet calmness,
That seeps from fruitcake and eclairs.

Rosie Murdie

Kyleakin

This is a cherished scene
I know it well, this lonely shore
I know the water's sheen
Though I have not been here before
How can this be?
Have I seen it through a glass?
Or am I haunted by a spectre of the past?

Deep in my memory
Another time, another place
She is a part of me
Her reflection wears my face
Where is she now?
Have I left that girl behind?
Or is she watching from the shadows of my mind?

A silent mystery
She won't forget, she can't forgive
She is my history
And my past was hers to live
But even now
She is tearing me apart
Her voice is calling from the reaches of my heart

I hear her cry
Through these crumbling walls of stone
And deep inside me know, I know I have come home.

Fiona MacKenzie

Winning Through

You look around and others see
And ask, "Does grief touch them as me?"
The answer you many never know,
Nor what they've had to undergo.
A man may suffer deep, deep down,
Yet often smile and seldom frown.
His struggle to accept his fate,
Unknown to us, may have been great.

He may have felt such pain and woe
As you or I may never know.
Just stop and think. What you can do
That, in the end, you may win through?
If happiness you cannot find,
Then just to know some peace of mind
Is something you may yet acquire,
Like metal tempered in a fire.

Performing tasks for others' sake,
Giving more than what you take,
Winning the fight that seems in vain,
In some such ways peace you may gain.
Such true contentment in your soul
Could make you, once again, feel whole.
Then someone may say, at the end,
"I loved that man. He was my friend."

Isma Munro

Tears of Caledonia

Though you live far from home your
Heart and soul still belongs to Caledonia

And even though you may travel wide and
Far, your mind travels back to Caledonia

And when you have reached your
Destination and you're flicking through a
Magazine and your eyes fall upon a scene

Of running burn, soaring mountains
And deep loch.

Your eyes fall upon wild deer running
Free down the glen.

With tears welling up in your eyes
And a lump in your throat.

Your mind takes you back across all those miles.

Across the big wall at the border to where you
Belong, back home in your beloved Caledonia

And as you return home with your bride on
Your arm, and under the watchful gaze of
MacGregor Rob Roy and your home
Caledonia.

Thomas Morton

This Place

Again I am drawn to this place
Enchanted, untamed, ageless
Conceding only to changing seasons
And Nature's rebirth
I feel it touch my eyes and my mind
I hear the sound of childrens' laughter of long ago,
Lost in the wind
I see the reflection of a lover's kiss
Captured in the still water
Childhood footsteps retraced by new youth, now grown
And I, now in my autumn time
Once more intrude upon this place
To absorb its beauty, comforting sameness, to remember,
A whispered promise of returning carried on the breeze
I tread softly as I leave

Gail Morgan

Although I Am Tired

Although I am tired,
the wind will not cease

from hurling the white
words hard at the window.

The hollow eyed face
of the woman refusing

my offers of shelter.
Yet still she forbids me

the peace of the unsmoored
peat fire of dreams.

Tim Morrison

Consumed

We're all so scared, running with fear,
Like rabbits being chased by foxes,
We must keep paying and so we pay,
Working all day, day after day,
For our semi- or detached little boxes.
I wonder if we experienced death
Before we experienced life,
Would we want to waste anything then.
Even a second on strife?
We've mortgaged our souls for a box.
The rabbit's consumed by the fox.
Now we're so consumed by our greed
That when we see money we grab it,
But only one going to heaven is
                    ... THE RABBIT!

J.F. Munson

The Day I Loved A Whale

One day in the month of May
I wasn't the same I'd forgotten my name.
We went to the pool with the school
We were talking about whales with big long tails
Ever since that time, felt fine
But I loved whales so bad, that I went mad
People kill them with harpoon
And I sit crying in my room
Oh why, why do they kill them so
They don't even give them time to grow.

Jill Murphy (Age 9)

The Waiting Game

Suddenly life is different
More meaning with an added inner glow
Strange flutterings become an obsession
Strange rumblings become a compulsion
Eating, sleeping, dreaming alters course
Conversation falls into a single track
Taking care of oneself becomes main preoccupation
Being spoilt by all around second nature
Accepting it and accepting vulnerability is the norm
Slowing down to a snail's pace but thinking in overdrive
Preparing, washing, cleaning everything in sight
Will this new little person ever appreciate
Mum's waiting game?

Jane Munt

Beachy Head

Cliffs so high and chalky white,
Fields of green, so many shades
Trees of all shapes shiver in the wind
The sea roars over the rocks below,
Above a lone seagull emits an eerie cry,
This is the place I choose to die.

Peace, peace, beautiful solitude
So near to where I uttered my first painful cry,
Forced from my mothers womb
Into this ever changing world,
Sometimes happy, sometimes sad.

With outstretched arms I leap into space
To fall beneath the cliffs with grace,
Too late now to turn back now its done,
The ache and pain will soon be gone.

Barbara Morris

It's A Charity

O Morgan from Glamorgan you're as godly as they come.
You walked the roads of Ireland to raise a generous sum.
To make a bend and move the trend from jumbo jet etc.
And clasp the handles of the humble wheel barrow set.
Your unselfish thought and deed has bought the true reward.
The beauty of your country, from the weary roads you trod.
Rwanda reaps the harvest from the land of saints and you,
Who left your home and comforts to surely think of thee.

Mary Aigneis Murphy

I Say! ...

Cherish the highs and lows, not mediocrity,
The saturated solution of all that you now see.
Chance would be a fine thing, if it could only be,
Shoving amorphous lives into the rolling sea;
Man overboard from HMS Security.

With the dreams you absorb from media and friends,
Tomorrow's plans pre-lived, the where and whens.
Arrogant self-confidence, home is his castle men,
Flagging dead ideas, relative values to pompous ends;
You hide from life and survey it, indignantly through a lens.

I talk to you, trusting, my words bounce off you reeling,
As with weary composure, you begin the standard routine.
Name and career details, conveyed to a count of fifteen,
Your duty ended by an offish smile, leaving me to glean
Such Rubbish as may be all there
         is behind your ancestral screen.

Tom Murphy

Your World

War, oil, birds, fish,
What have these in common — people
Nature is cruel but we are crueller
For instance
Tigers are killed for their bones and your rugs
Whales are killed for the oil in your lamps
Bears not so much dancing as dying
Foxes and hares hunted for miles
Elephants killed for your ornaments
Rhinos slaughtered for your health
Meadows destroyed for your luxury homes
Landscapes demolished for the quarries for the rock on your roads
Rainforests wiped out for your fancy furniture
The ozone layer breaking down as you use your smelly aerosols
Why not stop now and think about your world
It's everyone's problem
So do your bit to help before it's too late.

Rebecca Murray (Age 13)

Dad

We asked you what you wanted
To celebrate 80 years of life
You said you had everything
Including a perfect wife.
We said "What about a cardi,
A scarf, a tie or hat?"
You said, "No, not really
I don't need owt like that."
Then you had a brainwave
You were thinking well ahead,
You said you needed something
To put upon your bed.
We asked "What? A pillow, a sheet,
A quilt filled with feathers from a duck?"
"No", you said, "It's for my bed of roses,
What I really want is 'oss muck."
Impressed as we all were
With such an original present
We couldn't bring it here today
Cause it smells rather unpleasant.
So here's a little sample
Of what will come your way.
When you let us know
That it's muck spreading day.

Janet Mustill

A Bit Of String

Balloons floating high and low
Tied with a bit of string
Sledges bouncing over snow
Pulled on a bit of string

Boys and girls winning shouts fly
Conkers tied on a bit of string
Wooden tops spinning by
Tied on a bit of string

Corn cut, guided by binder sails
Sheaves tied with a bit of string
Progress bringing round or square bales
Tied with a bit of string

Brown paper parcels large or small
Tied with a bit of string
Destinations labelled on card tall
Tied with a bit of string

Sheeps fleece in long hessian bag
Tied with a bit of string
Wheat and potato sacks sag
Tied up with a piece of string

The farmyard gate secured
Tied with a piece of string
A few of life's problems solved
With *a bit of string*

Mary Mycock

Compulsion

Once I was asked "What makes you write?"
As I scribble notes by day and night,
An interesting question, food for thought,
Could it be Anger, Therapy, Compulsion or pressure of another sort?

It is rather difficult to decide but is probably compulsion,
An irresistible force, stronger than a horse, or other means of propulsion,
For one who has this hidden urge, output has been rather light,
But age takes its toll, of course, as much as we try to fight.

However and article well done at leisure,
Plus a few letters for good measure,
Is an ideal way to spend a day,
Creating a good deal of pleasure.

There are many things to write about,
An endless supply year in year out,
From Cabbages and Kings, Ceiling Wax and things,
Plus the weather which is always with us, no doubt.

On checking all ideas for the magic turn on,
There is one that shines like a beacon when all others have gone,
Its beam is an inspiration, by day and also night,
So Compulsion can't be wrong, if it makes one always write.

Robert Murphy

Queen Elizabeth In Russia '94

She smiled with dignity so borne
Elizabeth our Queen made history once more.
Russia's Tsar and family so long gone,
But in their memory she opened a new door.
On her head the sapphires, diamonds, shone —
A head held serene and elegant.
Above, chandeliers glittered, with gold adorned,
A tiara on a Queen's head so reliant.
From the famous to humble she took their hand.
She was a new light in a Russian Realm,
The great hall, winter palace, was so grand,
Great riches of art, treasure,
When Tsar Nicholas was at the helm.
Red square, St. Petersburg, Leningrad she paid homage.
Philip was always close by
Our proud Queen in the frontage
Saying to an old world, good-bye.

Janet L. Murray

By the Window

By the window in my hospital bed
I watch the birds fly overhead.
Each day they gather, each day there's more
Getting ready for flight to a far off shore.

I look at the trees so strong and bold,
Leaves changing colour to yellow, orange and gold.
Then in the breeze falling gently to the ground
There's a colourful carpet spread around.

I watch the clouds as they drift by
Seeing faces and shapes as I look at the sky
And as the sun goes down to rest
This is the time that I love best,
For in the distance the sun is so low
Casting a wonderful colour a wonderful glow.

All this I see as I lie in my bed,
Things taken for granted and I shake my head.
Tomorrow when I wake up and open my eyes
I'll look all around me and thank God I'm alive.

Mrs. S. Musgrave

On Seeing Ikeuye - Seki's Comet
(Southern Hemisphere 1965)

Sparkling trail of diamonds, low on the horizon
Reflecting the unusual in the pre-dawn sky,
Daily getting fainter, then alas — it's gone
Leaves a feeling of some sadness
Like the autumn loss of swallows,
But the splendour stays a memory,
A truly awesome sight,
One of such rarity, remembered with delight.
One knows that the splendour will not be seen again,
That the knowledge of its visit will remain a mystery,
And just like Halley's comet, become a part of history.

Mrs. M.R. Nelson

The White Rabbit On The Motorway

A white rabbit crossed the motorway
I am so glad it got away
The bus lights flashed as it dashed past
I did not want to see it bashed.
The little thing it sped across
It was in a frightful rush
No wonder the little thing rushed out
It must have had an awful fright.
I hope it's safe across the field
A safe return is its need.
To find a place, to find a home
So that it won't need to roam
Across a busy motorway

Lena Newton

Poetry Day

On Poetry Day
This is what I'd like to say.
Paint a picture in the mind,
People nature and all such kind.
Close your eyes and have a think,
On 6th October that is the link.
Words are what it's all about.
Make it known and even shout,
The praises of our Poetry Day.
In other words, hip-hip-hooray!

Robert J. Murray

Autumn

Leaves drift gently in the autumn sun
and carpeting still earth,
whose warmth ebbs
in reminiscence of the fading breath on dying lips.

Such intransigence from this season's mellow statesman,
herald to an annual ceremony
of re-occurring richness
embroidered on a changing landscape.

Pulchritude surrounds
more lovely for the perfect haute couture
from Nature's St. Laurent.

A seasonal collection of converging colour
presented to a captive audience
limited by time.

Glenn K. Murphy

Winter Once More

The chilling wind of a cold November's day
Begins to lay the foundations
For a winter, once more on its way
The wildlife of the forests
Curl up and go to sleep
To avoid this season so bitter to them
While the snows start to fall
And the land's rivers freeze hard
As the boughs of the trees sigh
Knowing that their blossoms
Have long since died
And still the sun shines.

John James Murray

Wind

Have you thought of the wind as a spirit, a spirit like Jekyll and Hyde,
Or like a giant colossus which all through the world will stride.
This uncontrollable force, which smites or caresses mankind
Can be either a curse or a blessing, but never with chains can one bind.
In the height of a tropical summer, a slight breeze is a god in disguise,
But whither it will pay you a visit, is merely a guess or surmise.

Deep in the Arctic Circle where howling winds can blow,
And the face becomes a pincushion for needles of driven snow.
If you are caught out there in the open you pay with death the price,
For anything out in the open in a few minutes turns to ice.

In the days of sail it was wind that drove ships through the sea,
And when they were marooned in the Doldrums it was wind that set them free.
Typhoons are malevolent winds filling sailors hearts with fear,
Dominating the Eastern seas at certain times of the year.
Hurricanes scything o're land, destructive as an atomic bomb,
Is second cousin thrice removed from a gentle breeze waving the corn.

Strong gales cause structural damage, and uproot large trees in their way,
While the weekend yachtmen in oilskins for a force five wind will pray.
A gentle wind turning the mill sails lets the miller grind the corn.
And chases the clouds away as a hopeful new day is born.

Alex Noble

Holiday Extracts

Abandoned porn mags and bikini tops await our entrance
The cockroach lays, squashed, crushed to death on the kitchen floor
Stolen sand dunes lay pressed against the balcony door
Mountains of Coca Cola cans pile against the wall.

Moby and other freaks flounder helpless to the incoming wave
Crashing pounding waves dragging me into cartwheels of terror
Pointless, juvenile games I evolved from years before
Radioactive cat leg with a lettuce for a friend.

Synth bass booming drumming pound techno sound
In raving early morning heaven till dawn
Irish centres, drunk and food 1%'s, fake gold and hashish sellers
Trying to entice everyone in total abstract failure.

On starlit mornings copulating couples screwing in deserted stairways
On backseat coaches tongues wrapped in unison
Spent ravers on lonely benches throwing everything up in your face
As you emerge from the maze to find the way home.

Transvestite lady-men await on the corner
Trying to convince everyone they're fully laden whores,
With nothing hidden away
But no one can ever be that gone, can they?

In grey clouded drizzle mornings you touch down home
With the arsehole drivers on the Orbital go around
Work Problems, Money Problems, Girlfriend Problems
Everyone's problems just seem to drag your happiness down.

Stephen Newton

Despair

I am the shell
Washed up on the shore,
Pounded by waves
For evermore,
Moved by the tides
From near and far,
Tugged by the moon
And watched by the stars;
Drifting and swirling,
Stormy and calm,
Lashed by the rain,
Then the sun's warm balm;
Pushing and grinding,
Never at rest,
Pulled north and south,
East and west,
Centuries passing
'Til time is no more -
Still I remain
On the desolate shore.

Dorothy Neil

Red-Shift

Don't be embarrassed
By the red-shift
Or the Hubble constant

If the universe expands
It may belong to someone else
Or no one

A contracting cosmos
Belongs to you, not me;
Own up to this.

A question can't be asked
If there's no answer,
So consider:

If the power of gravitation
Is a force to be reckoned with,
Why do we miscalculate

The gravity of power,
Of mine over yours,
Of hierarchy

As we move together
With incohesion
Don't mistake

Or be embarrassed by
The power of need,
The inchoate.

Steve Murray

The Old Dear (1897 - 1987)

That room's available,
The old dear died last week.
Blessed relief we all thought,
Seemed to do nothing but whine, you see.
If she'd been left to me
I'd have had her put away.
Always on about the War,
Told us her sweetheart joined up and died.

Odd the way she used to hide.
Called us her enemies
And she was in the trenches
Just like her darling Ronnie had been —
Wounded 1916,
Returned to the trenches
To be killed properly
Near a village called 'Passion ... something'.
Last week she went missing,
Wandered through the gardens.
She seemed to be reaching out
And tangled herself in rusting wire.

Alan Newbold

Untitled

These thoughts I know, will have been written before,
But through my life I realise more
That all we feel and see and do
Is very precious, this is true.

In our younger years, time had no end
But then it changed, do you agree my friend?
Christmas was always forever away
Yet each one now, seems like yesterday.

The time passes quickly, ticking away
Year by year, not just day by day,
So let's all be happy, enjoy each event
Rejoice in knowing our time's been well spent.

Our offspring are grown now and out through the door,
No longer tiny, not children anymore.
Now we can stop and take stock of our lives,
We've all been so busy, like bees round the hives.

This is the time to relax and unwind
Live life to the full, leave worries behind.
Savour each new moment, be it happy or sad
For with each experience, there's knowledge to be had.

We're guests on this earth for a very short time
So let's play it for real, not act and not mime.
Let's be full of hope, with each bright new day
And forget the clock, ticking silently away!

Jean Newell

Most Precious of Gems

Peace, a gem so very rare
Possessed, it seems, by few,
Not many can say they have no care
Quite the reverse is true.
A gem which we all need to hold
In a world so torn by strife,
More precious by far than silver and gold
So hard to attain in this life.
Slow down, life isn't just a race,
This wearisome strife must cease,
We need to stop, to ease the pace
To know this gem called Peace.

Lilian New

Michael

"You shouldn't have done that!
You shouldn't have done that -"
A Derry woman's voice screams
In anger,
Then wails in hopeless grief
Cutting through the grey Saturday air.
She cradles his hurt head in her lap
And whispers,
"Hush now, love, you'll be all right,"
As his life's blood flows down a wet
Shipquay Street
Under the feet of stunned shoppers.
He is now paying the ultimate price
For wearing the dark green uniform.
How could his blinkered assassin know,
Michael was a Catholic.

Patricia Newman

Faith

A Christian's wife dies giving birth,
He spends twelve days in pain and grief,
Yet, laying his eyes upon the cot,
He thanks his God for all he's got.

In a far away land, hit hard by war,
A mother mourns her youngest born,
Scorning laughter, forgetting fun,
At sweet sixteen, he took up gun.

Despite her terror-stricken days,
At night she bows her head in praise
— to Buddha, for life in better times —
And asks forgiveness for her crimes.

Why do we fight for recognition,
And let men die for their religion?
If we all have faith; accept our lot,
Does it really matter: faith in what?

Anne Neininger

A Day By The Sea

The white rippling waves roll along the golden beach,
Strewing shells and seaweed out of its reach.
The sun sits high in a clear blue sky,
Who could wish for more? Certainly not I.
The warm, soft sand between your toes,
the endless ocean, I wonder where it goes?
Gulls soaring on a gentle breeze,
I wish I could capture this day in a frieze.
If people would only look around them and see
that the best things in life are always free.
The sea, and the sand — the sun in the sky,
these wonderful days, money just cannot buy.
So thank you my Lord, for all that you give
we should all enjoy it as long as we live.

Anne Naylor

Ancora

Your love enwraps me like heaven's mist,
And your touch soothes my being numb, I am in love.
When you hold me close and when I am kissed,
My heart ignites and takes flight as the dove

Of John: So baptize me. Force me under,
Hold me down, with hands slipping, hear me gasp;
Hot, close, see the lightening, hear the thunder.
Push, panic, punch me, feel me grasp.

Just don't let go. I don't want to lose you.
Let me breathe and let me love you. I hear
Your voice, and I grown calm; I listen to
Your words, and I know I have nothing to fear.

You are my anchor in this love; this sea,
For you hold me still, and you cradle me.

Chris Newman

Winter Wonders

The sky is pink and peach and red
The little birds have gone to bed,
This wondrous scene on a winter's day
Foretells that frost is on the way.

This glowing sunset looks like fire
Fingers of colours spreading higher,
With silhouettes against this glow
The dark, black trees put on a show.

But rising east, so clear and bright
The lunar lantern of the night
Spreading a bright white light around
Transformation without a sound.

The moon is sailing higher and higher,
And gone completely all trace of fire,
Just quietness and light through the frosty night,
Soon dawn will break all crystal and white.

Anne Nice

Gale Force Winds And Blustery Showers

Air in more or less natural motion
Shouldn't cause any frightful commotion,
But it does.
Round the house hear it moaning and screaming,
Leaving the puddles foaming and creaming,
Down from the gutters the water is streaming,
Washing we humans away from our dreaming.

Robbing dustbins with unholy clamour,
Using an eldritch unseen hammer,
Frightening us.
Taking lids with ill-fitting flanging
Way down the alley, crashing and clanging,
Freeing cans to their echoing banging,
Newspapers writhing, blowing, then hanging.

Now there's fear for the slates as they tremble,
Gutters all fill and blown leaves assemble
To block them.
No one thinks that these traits are endearing,
Only feels glad when the storm clouds are clearing,
Glad to rest quietly, not lie there hearing
Banshee delight at the damage we're fearing.

Joyce M. Nicholson

The Visitor

A spaceman travelled to Earth one day,
from a planet left of the Milky Way,
For he'd heard mankind was a civilised race,
and his dream was to meet with them face to face.

So he travelled the world, and his wonder was great,
at the beauty and culture, mankind could create.
He gazed at castles, great pillars of stone,
the wonder of Egypt, the beauty of Rome.

He gazed at the cars, computers and planes,
the wonders achieved through man's versatile brain.
Yet his heart became heavy, his spirits were low,
for mankind was lost, they had nowhere to go.

There were people surrounded by opulent wealth,
while millions of others were starving to death.
Parasites squandering money for kicks,
or selling their souls for a snort or a fix.

He saw animals slaughtered, by man at his worst,
so women could walk about dressed in their furs.
He saw sadness and badness, where greatness could be,
people enslaved, who would never break free.

Old people lying, like rubbish in streets,
children who never get kindness or treats.
His heart, filled with grief, as he said his goodbye,
but his thought as he looked back at Earth was WHY?

Kathleen Nicholson

Planet Earth

Planet Earth, are you only
A tranquil sphere, doomed to be lonely;
A minute speck in outer space;
A beautiful haven, going to waste;
A beacon of life in a sea of dark;
A rock where Man has left his mark;
A mass of blue, and yellow, and green;
A hole in space, polluted, unclean;
A strange creation, evolved by chance;
Orbiting the Sun in a weird dance;
A part of the Universe dirty and obscene;
Dominated by men corrupt and mean;
By the year 3000 you will be no more;
For Homo sapiens knows nuclear war.

Scott Nixon (Age 13)

Goodbye

I remember when I was a little girl,
how you would sit me on your knee
and tell me stories of long ago,
the way life used to be,
you would take me walking
and I would hide in fields of heather,
laughter always filled the air
when we were together.

But time soon passed us by,
you grew old and I grew tall
and in those fields of heather,
you had a painful fall.
Oh Grandad, how I miss you
for I didn't think you'd die,
I never told you that I love you,
and I never even said goodbye.

Lynn Noblett

Magic Moments

I've never seen a lovelier sight
Than herring sea-gulls in full flight.
Their wings outspread they sail and swoop
And sometimes seem to loop the loop!
Then as they twist and turn about
grey feathers shine like silver trout.
And rose-pink legs are well tucked under,
I stand and stare in silent wonder.
Then as they follow wake of plough
The noise they make — you'd think they row!
And in a crowd they land on earth
To feast on worms beneath the turf.
Then up, up, up, against the blue
They head for home till out of view.
'Tis strangely quiet now they've flown
But magic moments I have known ...

Gwen Mould

Deception

Stitched into a shroud
by Bitterness
I longed to break free.
I forgave, then I forgot.
Suddenly I was free!

But last night
Memory came, and
used a stronger thread.

Dorrie Morrison

Not Enough Love For Three

If you really want to go, go quickly
Please baby, don't hang on
Don't look at the child who's crying
And don't come for one last kiss from me
It would only make it harder
If not for you — then for me
I always thought it would come to this
I only wish it hadn't
Because how do I explain to the little one
When he grows
That even though you loved me
There just wasn't enough love
For three.

Angela Nicholas

To An Apple

Your perfect shape
and glossy skin
Offers a promise that all's well within

Yet should I dare
to put to test
That upon which my eyes now rest

Maybe I'll tarry
for just a while
And let your beauty me beguile

On canvas framed
you would endure
Still I would never know for sure

It's better to
have loved and lost
So I'll take your pledge at cost

Your fate's decided
I'll take a bite
You've kept your promise to my delight.

Mrs. D.J. Nodwell

Hobo

I am but a man who dwells by the sea
Everyone seems to be rich but me
For what have I but the sea and sky
No time of day does pass me by
A mind on the breeze that sings in the trees
All of these things are my every day needs
So why am I not the richest of these
I am I am said my head on the breeze
Not every one has a mind that is free
A mind that walks and talks to the trees
Alas, I am but must not conceive it
Or shall cease to be free.

Richard Northwood

Dolly

Like a single star, in a sea of night,
Glistens one eye, a contrast to fur of white
A beautiful eye of amber and green,
A more startling cat just can't be seen!
With feet and nose of palest rose pink —
Your tongue's the same colour, when you have a drink!
Your magnificent coat, which trails the ground
As you noiselessly trap birds without a sound.
Then crashing about with your ping-pong ball
And sliding through cat biscuits out in the hall
A truly outstanding Persian Cat,
Safe in the knowledge — no one can dispute that.

Lucille Norton

The Genetic Imperative

Spilled from the womb of time,
Unknowing or when or where,
My destiny planned, no choice of mine,
Blind, chance chose any cross I bear.

The paths I follow are laid for me,
The result of my inheritance.
My code of genes will my master be
Will chart my life in any circumstance.

Constituted by my heritage.
A unique mix from the lives of others,
I cannot change my ways or colour,
Or oppose the directive of my lineage.

Whether good or evil be my lot,
As I blindly follow my creators plot,
I cannot choose the broad or narrow way,
For I had no choice in the cards I play.

Christians should consider, think, again,
Examine any doubts or fears,
For the evil all men do, refutes the claim
"God is Love", then why, why? This vale of tears.

John Newell

Untitled

Being deep inside this mire
I have but one big desire
well before it's time to expire
for my heart to be set on fire

Not by some sweet talking liar
with whose promises I would tire
I've no need for goods and chattels
they only lead to financial battles

Of my hero, I do ask
one enormous, precious task
that's to be strong and very brave
and my company he should crave

My mind, my body and my soul
he should want me as a whole
and when a problem rears its ugly head
he should go where angels dread

With a soft and compassionate tread
weaving a strong and binding thread
and as through life together we will walk
we must never forget to talk

Oh, my Lord, please hear my plea
and send him now, right here to me

Helen Nicolaou-Allan

Dreams

'Tis the place where dreams are made
when per chance we fall asleep;
The people of another world
our secrets of the night they keep.

Who are these people of the night
not all familiar faces;
Are they travellers of the past
or transported figments of our imagination?

Projections of past and future merge together
muddled voices yet some so crystal clear;
Loved ones no longer with us
but telling us, nothing from them should we fear.

Kaleidoscopes of colour fill our unconscious mind
pictures, places, people unravel daytime thoughts
so in our waking hours tranquility we find.

As from our slumbers we awake
our conscious mind now overtakes,
'Tis welcome to the real world
but ponder on this, as who's to say
which one, the night of dreams or day?

Patricia Nurton

351

You're Too Small To Ride

"You're too small," I said to my friends, "much too small to ride"
"I'm going on the waltzer, you're half an inch too small,"
"There are one hundred white knuckle rides,
I'm going on them all."
I felt them watch me spin and twirl and have my photo on the coaster,
And splash on the flume and scream as I zoom on the carriage of doom.
Their faces were full of jealousy,
As they sat on the carousel with the melody,
"I'm glad they're too small" I thought,
"I'm glad they're too small to ride."

I loved the rides each one of them,
My little face was full of glee,
As Daddy held on tight to me,
I felt so bold, so big and strong,
It was so excellent,
And nothing went wrong,
But they were too small to enjoy all the fun,
"I am the heroine," I thought as I spun,
"I'm glad they're too small,"
"I'm glad."

Holly Owen-Frawley

God's Covenant

A magnificent sight,
We rarely see,
A vision of glory,
For you and for me,
Raise our eye,
Look above — at the sky,
Wonderful colours
We cannot deny,
Forming an aura,
Half circle, so bright,
A gateway to heaven,
Leading to light,
The sun and the rain,
Create an infinite glow,
Praise to the Lord,
A beautiful rainbow!

M. Owen

Words Of Mr. Taciturn

O one year too many,
With delicacies for the chatterbox.
Though I be laden with words filling a trolley,
I shan't salivate for our Grob, Royal or Tory.

Not of the 'Mellor-dious' Adam
Severally seen sinning in Eve's arm;
Cast away from the Garden of 'Heritage'
And now, from a discordant matrimony of an age.

Where 'Mellor-diously' he sang "Music for the divorcee."
His lyrics; of man's frailty to aphrodisiac.
No nothing about him shall I gossip;
Better of granting my tongue some sleep.

Not of our Di,
Thought to have turned a Dinosaur
But suddenly emerged from the blue;
Now palling with The Great, Meek and Dangerous.

Nor of His Majesty
With a life's romance un-majestically unmasked,
And a Grob
Smeared in a leap to Grab.

Never of an arm-in-hand Major
With threats to mess my 'mail'
Now pacifying my Quaking heart with this story:
"You can make quids from the lottery."

Ifeatu C.A. O'Koye

Death Dream

With tree seeds
Plant me
When I die
Sow me in your
Garden
The naked sky
And body earth
Shall grow me
In your gaze
From Mother's arms
I'll spring to life
Each bud exploding
Feeling
In seasons' robes
Reveal to you
The centre of my being
The night shall share
Its past with me
The sun shall kiss
My bough
Yet silently I'll wait
For you
My core, my soul
My reason.

Marie O'Brien

The Stolen Grandad

He sits in his chair, looking frail and uneasy
Staring at walls but sees nothing
What's he thinking about? What are his thoughts?
Does he have any?
He smiles and laughs but does not know what at
He recognizes no one but greets everyone
Why has it done this?
Taken him away,
Why has it robbed me of a Grandad and friend?
Why have I not been allowed to know him?
Have I done something wrong? Am I to blame?
His body lives on but his mind dies slowly.
His premature death is so unfair.
Where is the grandad to take me fishing
And to show me his medals?
Where is the Grandad who would have been so proud
At the achievements of his grandchildren?
Where has he gone, we shall never know
But something out there does
It laughs at it's victims, too many to name
And looks on as we suffer with no one to blame.
This thing is Alzheimers, the illness which kills the mind
... And the family's hearts.

Victoria Odwell

The Future

Listen here and I will say what I saw yesterday.
I saw a world of famine and fear
Of those who had lost loved ones near and dear.
Children were crying there, mothers were dying.
Fathers were praying and they were saying
There is one life, there is one life
There is one world, that's what you heard
Covered in fog, covered in smog
Where are the plants? Covered in mud
Where are the birds? Where are the bees?
Where on earth are the trees?
We are the children of the future
Listen to us, we're the future
We can tell you what to do
Plant back the trees, oh please do
Then in the future we will say
You should have seen yesterday
There were no birds, there were no bees
There wasn't even a morning breeze.

Kelly Oakley (Age 12)

Indifference

Rarely content, and never satisfied,
Wanting he knows not what,
Though eagerly to get he may have tried
Despising the things got,
What is this longing which man has inside,
Blowing now cold now hot?

What but the longing that filled Adam's heart,
To realise with pain
No more in Eden he could have a part,
Nor walk with God again;
Instead of prime integrity, the smart,
Sour knowledge of sin's stain?

And yet, the fact that longing still was there
In the old Adam then
Was known by God, whose pity could prepare
A covenant for men
And vow that in time's fullness one would bear
A Saviour ... Ah, but when?

At last He came, the Ransomer, and lo'
Was laid in stable stall,
How many did in longing to Him go,
Still rather stay in thrall
To sin? God, for the indifference we show
Have mercy on us all!

H.O. Brian O'Neil

The Silence Within

Heavy silence brings no joy. It delivers frustration.
The mind is unoccupied, waiting, expecting, anticipating.
Anxious but never comprehending
No sound is heard, no rhythm felt
Just a room full of nothingness
Where is the noise I long for?
The one that keeps me sane
I wish to hear it again.

But my little box is still, like the air that is dead.
It contains such mystery. Like this feeling inside of me.
It no longer speaks or whispers
Of words of wisdom or content
It sets aside in the dark corner
Watching my presence of nowhere
Observing my blank stare.

Will it ever rise again, to exchange joy of my pain.
Will it ever come alive, to welcome me as I walk by,
With that sweet familiar tone, to tell me I'm not alone.
Or will it simply drift away
Like the soft melody it used to play
Will it fade away and go
Like a friend I used to know
Will this mystery ever unfold
Of me, and my silent world ...

Nina Ovanessian

Sweet Contentment

I sit in peace
And tranquil silence
Thoughts flow softly through my mind
Calm and warming they surround me
Easing burdens all the time.

Stillness is a heavy moment
Darkness is a soulful place
I rest my weary tortured body
In the waters sweet embrace.

Refreshing cleansing and surrounding
It washed through my troubled mind
And for just a moment
Sweet contentment
That I hope one day to find.

Cathy O'Reilly

The Traveller Emmanuel

Snowflakes danced beneath the winter moon
As the traveller walked the cobbled streets.
Icicles, straight and proud, shimmered under the starlit sky
As a chill wind swirled around the lamplight's glow.
And still the traveller walked — never pausing,
His footsteps breaking the virgin snow
As he was engulfed within the stillness of the night.
Suddenly the silence was broken by the chimes of the
                church clock striking midnight.
As their final echoes faded away,
The traveller disappeared into the regained peacefulness
                of the night,
His image reflected in us all,
As we rose to celebrate the Christmas dawn.

Patricia O'Gorman

Motherhood

Bleary-eyed, stumbling from a warm comfortable bed,
Her steps follow the hungry wail of wanting to be fed.
Arms reach out to tenderly grasp an infant in full cry;
Soothing words and gentle hums bring forth a contended sigh.
The infant snuggled and warm, being fed,
The mother gently lays back her weary head.
To think of days not so long ago
When sleep and dreams were allowed to flow.
A gurgle wakes the mother from her repose,
The infant smiles and wiggles his tiny toes.
All thoughts of yesterdays vanish with a smile,
The tenderness of the two makes all worthwhile.
Mother and infant bonded by a cherish hold.
A treasure, a gift, which is greater than gold.

L.V. Osborne

Growing Up

Once there was a little lad
Who thought he had a wicked Dad,
He would shout, kick and cry,
His Mum would bake him an apple pie.
He hated her as much as Dad,
All this makes you feel so sad,
If only he would be a good little lad.
Perhaps one day when he grows old
He will read this poem I have told,
When we were young we did the same
I put myself in his shoes,
Gave my Mum a lot of blues!

Mrs. B. Newsome

Apple Time

An autumn day on a lonely path
That runs along a rill
Air frosty-fresh and redolent
Of disemboweled drill
Orchard trees fruit laden
Leaves approaching sere
The music of conversing birds
Ever pleasing to the ear
Savouring the forbidden fruit
As I stroll a peaceful pace
I become somehow, somewhy alive
To another time and place
No dreaming, no imagination plies
No effort to sustain
Yet for one eternal second am
Not a man but a boy again.

Sean O'Kane

Until Winter Has Passed By

Favour not the child
Who sips from a silver spoon,
Rather, avert your eyes
Listen, the pitiful cries
Of a child, the victim of hunger.

Favour not the athlete
Who runs for Olympic gold,
Rather, raise your hand
Salute he, unable to stand
A man, the victim of defect.

Favour not the orator
Unless he speaks the truth,
"We cannot have summer
Until winter has passed by
We cannot experience joy
Unless pain once clouded the sky."

Pauline B. Ogilvie

Peaceful Interlude

It's waters dark and cold, the river flows,
Reflecting buildings on the old quayside;
By alders bare, and willows, on it goes,
Its sombre hues relieved by mallard, pied.

With plumage pure, and regal head held high,
A silent swan glides on with graceful ease:
I turn from city traffic rushing by,
And pause here for this interlude of peace.

Margaret Grace Ong

January

"Oh, when will it snow?" the children cry,
"When will the world be white?"
Morn after morn, a despondent sigh -
(They'd *prayed* it would snow in the night.)

Sullen, the grey skies threaten and glower,
Pavements, all rain-washed, shine.
Suddenly, sunshine for an hour,
Then the cruel wind's shrill whine.

Born now is God's own baby Son -
Some of us thought of that.
Funny, how when December's done,
Everything seems so flat.

Round and about the grown-ups walk;
Gone is their Christmas glow.
Of sales now, and cheap Summer hols. their talk.

But the children wait for the snow ...

A.M. Olive

Cancer

Monday to Friday I stay out of sight
Flowers grow wild and shine so bright
Inside my fortress I shiver with gloom
Silence surrounds me inside this colossal cocoon
I clutter around like a condition of cedar
I'm engulfed in this fever it's an epidemic inside
But still my flowers grow beautiful and wild.
Wistfully I wonder will I withstand this plight
Will I keep going, will I make it tonight
Could someone please tell me how long I have left
Before this thing inside me starts eating my flesh.
I dance thunderbound up the mound
And I ponder on past pleasures I found
Wearily I weep as I remember those days
Out in the wilderness where happiness stays.
It now seems so distant as I fade slowly away
This thing inside won't shed me another day
But it has shed many tears day and night
Still my wisteria hangs so beautiful and bright.

Ryan O'Toole

My Mum

Shortish,
Loathes computer games
Unlike Dad and I!
Excellent cook,
Choc-a holic,
Extremely witty,
Always cracks jokes,
Complains of cold ears
When watching me play
Rugby.
Does keep fit —
More like get fit!
Hates glasses but unfortunately
Can't see without them,
Likes shopping for clothes
But hates food shopping,
Would like to win the Premium Bonds
And/or Pools.
My Mum.

Adrian John Ordish

The Road Making Machine

Tear it down, gobble it up,
Destruction is my game,
I have power to destroy,
Vandalism by any other name.

Who can have such power as I,
Nothing stands in my way,
Man can talk as much as he wants,
But I always have the final say.

There is a beautiful wood,
That needs to be destroyed,
Just call me on the telephone,
And I shall be overjoyed.

So much destruction to undertake,
In the wonderful name of progress,
Who can flaunt my reasoning,
Or doubt my ultimate success.

I hear some doubts and murmurings,
They must be quickly squashed,
I am the mighty road machine,
A cause that must never be lost.

Tear it down, gobble it up,
Destruction is my game,
I have power to destroy,
Vandalism by any other name.

Jean Oldbury

Untitled

Reality throws me onto bloodstained canvas,
As in the ring you swing another painful blow.
I crawl in retreat to my cold blue corner
As warm red blood begins to flow.
They're not the words I want to hear
It's feeling I need you to show.

Fouled at the halfway line,
So for you it's the yellow card
And still I spill my soul out,
While you're so Goddamn hard.
In the ring you'll throw another punch
As I let down my guard.

We can't go on denying this,
Are you scared to give some more?
The whistle sounds, the flag is up,
But what's the final score?
It's nothing each, we're just the same
As we've always been before.

Saying contact sport's your preference,
Means this distance run's not smart.
So at speed I'm looking round for you
Spikes tearing through my heart,
But we're nowhere near the finish line
Did you ever leave the start?

Honor Owen

I Spat Out My Sex

Devalued by 'beauty', trampled by 'grace',
Submitted to shout from corners unheard,
I lift my face from a history of dirt
And cry for my part in the pitiful horde.

My race, my roots, my sex - my shame,
Letting themselves be used,
Clawing for lusty worshippers,
Giggling to be abused.

In the flaking, burning pit of my soul,
Stained scarlet anger gnaws and corrupts,
I force calm, it smiles, "deep breath" deep death,
A surge of injustice flows from my guts.

Shaking, I glare as you walk into view
Hating that which draws me to you
I am tripping Judas, failing my will
Failing and falling, but clenching you still.

The pictures of dumb blondes pandering to brutes,
I kick 'round my head with my no-nonsense boots,
And alone with you and your mountain green eyes,
I try to forget those whom I despise.

Wendy L. O'Shea

Black Wednesday?

Some called it Black Wednesday,
for in their view the pound
was blacked out
on that day.
Others called it White Wednesday,
for in their view the pound
was bailed out
on that day.
So whether the pound
was blacked out or bailed out
on that Wednesday,
was for the experts to sort out.
But one thing wasn't in doubt:
on that Wednesday,
the money dealers used their clout
to bloat out their bank accounts.

Charles K.N. Owusu

Carers

Carers are worth their weight in gold!
Their kindness to old folk is manifold.
What ever the weather; rain, sleet or snow,
Cheerfully on their rounds they go.
They know old folk are not all alike
Some like to get up early,
Others like to stay up at night.
They listen to their cares of who,
Have them smiling
Before it's time to go.
God bless you, carers,
For the work you do
Helping old folk
Keep in their homes
As they wish to do.

Eva Osborne

My Labouring Mother

I gaze into her eyes and see tears swelling
I view her gnarled hands and picture tree-felling
I listen to her heavy breathing and wheezing
I hold her limp body polluted and freezing.

Through her eyes I see the seduction
Through her hands I feel the destruction
Through her breath I sense asphyxiation
Through her body I construe mortification.

This is my mother that bares all before me
This is my love that permits me to see
This is our planet wantonly destroyed and crying
This is our dear mother earth carelessly dying.

John M. O'Sullivan

You Are

You are the sunbeams in my trees
And the dancing shadows in the leaves
You are the gold in the morning sun
And the moonshine when day is done
You are the colours in a perfect rainbow
And the love that makes my heart glow
You are the beauty in all the flowers
And the freshness of the April showers
You are the breath that's in my chest
And the dreams when I lay down to rest.

L.C. Paget

'Spring Ah! Spring'

Wander with care through morning mist I do.
Ripples the stream by glade of green and dew.
The darting squirrel! Skylark or cuckoo!
To see and hear
Wind blowing wild and free.
Here and there a daffodil, tulip, buttercup or bluebell.
A hue of colour rare hard to compare.
Light and dark across the sky
Clouds they glide.
The sun bright and clear.
As rain begins the downward fall.
Now to the wonder, a rainbow appears!
As if from nowhere.
'Spring Ah! Spring'
Slowly, slowly fadeth all, for low and behold
Summer is here.

Percy T. Padley

To A Road Hog

The midnight knock — the rusty bolt drawn back —
The door ajar, as far as chain allowed —
A woman's querying face — a policeman shorn
Of cold authority and pomp — all cowed.
Forgive him! He was young — he'd never faced
The task of breaking news of someone's end.
He's older now — he's often had to say
"Your husband's dead — it happened on the bend"
It's commonplace — they do it everyday
Some twelve or fifteen times — it's brutal fact —
Some policeman, somewhere, has to break such news
With sympathy, sincerity and tact.
So Road Hog, in your thoughtless race today —
Without regard for other lives or laws —
For God's sake ponder on that baby cop.
He'll knock a door tonight. It could be yours.

Paddy

Along The Golden Sand

Let's go to the seaside,
Let's walk hand in hand,
Beside the gentle flowing tide,
Along the golden sand.

We'll leave foot prints in the sand,
While the gulls go gliding by,
As we walk hand in hand,
Under the summer sky.

We'll watch the children paddle in the sea,
And build castles in the sand,
We hear them laughing merrily,
As we walk hand in hand.

We hear the Punch and Judy Show,
The jingle of the donkeys bells,
As hand in hand we go,
Among the coloured shells.

Ever nearer comes the flowing tide,
As we walk hand in hand,
We can no longer bide,
Along the golden sand.

Barbara Patterson

Cotswold Queen

Cotswold oolite garden river down to sea
Frith of flowers stupendous sight to see.

Rocking rolling riding
Bobbing in the breeze
Like a mighty army
Beauty their supreme.

I viewed in amazement
Others shared the scene
Eyes lit up faces red
Smiles of ivory sheen.

Suddenly someone said
I know where we have been
She has taken us to her heart
This Cotswold Oolite Queen.

Reflections from the splendour said
You must paint this scene
More colours than a rainbow
And polished to a dream.

Completion of the portrait
The sun shone down to be
With his favourite flower
Dressed in rural green.

We walked on together along her oolite way
The wonder of these Cotswolds make this a special day.

David Pollard

Autumn

The leaves from the trees come tumbling
down
With colours of red, orange, yellow and
brown.
Days may be dull, but the beautiful hue
Of many trees rustling beside lakes of blue.
Rivers of silver, rippling in the sun,
The sound of the robin has just begun,
His territorial message to warn other birds
That they may stay clear, in so many words.
Chestnuts are falling, to walk is rough.
Paths through brambles, really tough,
With scattered leaves and the like.
People out walking, or riding a bike,
Children laughing, gathering nuts as they fall,
Dogs barking, running to their owner's call.
Squirrels are active, they need to store
Food for the winter, all as before.
The sunsets in Autumn are really the best
Giving a glow to nature when it's time to rest.
We thank our God for the beauty we see,
Then realise that the best things are free.

Dorothy Parish

Cats

Cats like to sit on a table,
A cushion or a chair,
Cats need comfort,
And great loving care.

Cats like to gobble food,
And lashings of milk,
Cats like to sleep all day,
On sheets of silk.

Cats like to keep fit,
Hunt and run around,
They can easily jump on birds
And not make a sound.

Cats are excellent runners,
Could beat anyone in a race
Cheetahs who are in the same family
Can speed up to a tremendous pace.

But mostly, after a long hard day,
After catching birds and prey
Can you guess what secrets they keep?
All they do more than anything else is
Sleep, sleep, sleep.

Victoria Elizabeth Parker (Age 9)

Don't Take Life For Granted

They say God only takes out the best,
The rest of us left put to the test.
Accidents happening each and everyday
Always to others, never us we say.
One day life's all rosy or so it seems.
The next a tragedy shatters all your dreams.
A fatal accident in town, victim my brother.
Oh hell no, are you sure it's not another.
Thank God he never knew and he never suffered pain.
We'll all suffer that, those of us that here remain.
He wouldn't want us to be sad, of that I'm sure.
I tell myself that everyday, but it doesn't cure
This feeling of despair I often feel inside.
To the outside world I do quite well to hide.
If I could turn back time I'd have visited him more
Than I ever did do I know that now for sure.
Many accidents in the news happening still,
I notice them more now and think I always will.
I know one day we'll be together again.
A comforting thought slightly easing my pain.
Steven if you're looking down from heaven above
You'll know how we all miss you and send you all our love.
Life carries on at this end as we all know it must
So until we meet again, we leave you in God's trust.

Debbie Palmer

Untitled

Sweet melodies of string float gently
Through twilight's blue haze
Recapturing touch of bygone days.
Melancholy rhythm plucked gingerly
With fingers soft and warm and yet
So free, in his mystical musical reverie.

Please listen to me with your hearts
Is all that's asked.
Let worries of this world depart
And language of another kind
Soothe your lost and tired minds.

My friends, my music is not new, of that I know
But truth and justice forever grow
Within the hearts of able men.
Please listen is all I ask of you.

Fingers lightly strum and fade
His last sweet sounds tiredly played
One by one the shadows lengthen
Darkness beckons, it's peace at last.

And so his soul is once more
Taken high free to soar
Amongst realms of heavenly bliss
Perhaps one day we too will know
Happiness such as this.

Marie Parker

The Unthawing

Stilled in white frost silence I breathe
Black bogs scree; with silver burnishings.
Frost sprite, knuckled white and cold
Crisping twig and brittle leaf.
Blighted within dark December's brooding,
Virgin snows drift from passive hills
Never to feel the thawings.
Twilight, on this dead December night, moon masked hard in glassy reflection.
The snow strays between white whiskered avenues
Hiding gruff wall, house and hot hornet chimney.
No breath of smoke, or saffron light - man's wolds;
Alien in their silence, stopping the thaw in man's dimension
Stopping the thaw in me.

Savage snow and ice soon disperse,
Dispirited in sudden change and quick vanishing.
Earth shallow in It's tending will reap again
Barely waiting to release It's progeny to Spring.
Why place a shroud so *white* to cover you?
To prick it black with tears.
In dead Decembers I remain; chill in shadow, unbleached by light, dead within
Excepting thoughts of you.
Never warm, within ghosts of suns, within pale seas
My vigil, my unthawing, my love of you.

Jane Park

Cancer

The bedclothes laid across your body
As you slept
They heaved and sighed in time
With your irregular breathing.

Without me beside you
You would be peaceful I thought
I wanted to wake you and tell you
That God was no longer on our side
Death had set his sights
And was intent on taking your life.

I would sit here forever I thought,
And fend him off.
For a second I closed my eyes, tired of life,
I silently begged him to make a mistake.
And take me instead.

When I looked again,
The bedclothes were still,
Your pulse was also sleeping,
Death wore armour plating
And I had no weapons at all.
I will curse myself forever
For closing my eyes
The very second that death chose
To walk through the door

Clare Page

My Life So Far

I can't remember much
    Of the very early years,
But what I do remember
    Is of love and not of fears.

I have been very lucky
    In the choice of Mum and Dad,
As mine are filled with goodness,
    Yet some are filled with bad.

The holidays we have had
    Filled with fun and mystery.
Even those that did go wrong,
    They all seemed great to me.

The best years of your life
    Are at school, as people say.
They're filled with friends and memories,
    And, you'll realise this one-day.

The decisions in my life
    Have always been right up to yet
I honestly can't remember
    One decision I regret.

I know I ask a lot
    But I hope our kids will be
As happy with their life,
    As mine has been to me.

Mandy Parker

The Video Machine

Grown all his days with the unearthly power
Of the time control switch
Lord of all life, he sat in his armchair
Resurrecting the dead
With the lifting of his hand
Wrapped round the remote control button
Granting instant gratification
To those who squealed for particular pleasures
Suspending the moment in the trembling present
For as long as it took to sate the palate
Then moving on, rushing past dull moments
Withe the second's press on the fast forward button.

Surveying his kingdom with that sublime confidence
Granted only to mortal souls
He fast-forwarded past Sybil
And Faust and Dorian
And only on that day when the control button jammed
Did he, fleetingly, terrifyingly,
Get the picture.

Marcia Parish

At Grass 2

Tucked away in a corner, forgotten,
The gallopers stand, under the trees,
Beside the railway track. Heads
All facing the same direction, as if
Sheltering from wind or rain.
Their paint brown and rusting, their names a blur,
Their roundabout long since replaced
By a larger, brighter, newer model.

You can hardly imagine children astride them,
Shrieking with glee on forgotten holidays,
Captured on Box Brownie shot in
A long closed album.

The train passes, back to the station,
And the present, "Shall we have lunch
Before we see the craft workshops?"
Leaving the gallopers to dream.

Rosemary Parry

Christmas Day

This festive season, it is Christmas time;
The holly may be clad with frost or rime,
The bells will chime for all on Christmas morn,
Given to the world our Saviour was born.

To remember the world is God's big home,
With scrumptious meal you may select a pome;
Heedful care, listen to the carols sung,
Life given to us from the cross he hung.

Turkeys, chickens, mince pies and drinks galore
With cheers and merriment more, more and more,
Forget not the reason for Christmas lore,
God's only way to open heaven's door.

Have a silent thought in your banquet hall;
He paid the ransom for one and for all;
Born in a manger in the old inn stall,
The brightest light to shine in every thrall.

The light of Jesus shines for you and me
In the eyes of children round Christmas tree;
If courage fails, you wish Christmas away,
Remember Jesus, Christmas every day.

The wise men's gifts and shepherds showed the way.

Dennis Parkes

Untitled

Three heads turn, green eyes bright
As six white ears hear a solitary bark
And three noble felines of regal descent
Prepare for their time to prowl in the dark
Of nooks and crannies surrounding the cottage
Worn with age and the harshness of weather
But for a moment they pause - all three
In the open doorway, waiting together
As immobile and silent as statues of ivory
Coast gleaming, each as silky as another
Perfected by hours of careful cleaning
And the industry of two washing the other
Now the leader edges forward, sniffing warily
Inspecting the air outside the door
The kink in his tail shows the Siamese trademark
Which is also the reason he raises his paw
And with cautious movement he pads at the ground
Ensuring no enemies are awaiting, beyond
The security of the cozy, warm kitchen
And the family's company of which they've grown fond
No dangers lay waiting and so softly, yet swiftly
From the house and quickly out of sight
Race three white scamps, highly strung and jittery
Ready again to conquer the night

Suzanne Parkin

The Rowan Tree

For weeks it stood, bearing the weight of brilliant berried bunches.
Glorious with colour beneath the sun and rain
Spreading its branches to shelter the wild wooded creatures.
Repeating its annual bounty again.

Then came the day for the harvest of songsters - how did they know?
The tree was a flutter of hundreds of wings.
They gathered together to guzzle and gobble and chatter.
Enjoying the savour the bright berry brings.

In the evening the branches were light for their berries were gone.
Leaving the leaves for their dance in the autumn
Changing their colours from green into pink, bronze and copper.
Blown by the breezes, bare in the sun.
It's harvest was done.

Valerie Partridge

Despair

Alone.
Charging through this endless corridor
    of confusion.
The sunken ground filled with objects
    of torment, hallucination and sadness.
Sorrow and tears are what linger in this sombre air
    of pain
With an eerie emptiness of certainty, but an abundance
    of insecurity.
Amity and philanthropy do not,
    exist here,
For this is the place for the living, but, not the place
    for me.

Donna Payne

Apocalypse

Four minutes, two hundred and forty seconds,
Three hundred and sixtieth of a day.
The only warning the butchers can display.
The button with its fiery shade awaits the movement to be made.
The gliding hand, the final press, just one man's choice
through strain and stress to end it all.
Soot like sky, sun like heat,
A racing pulse with a thundering beat.
Then nothing, nothing but bleak white mist.
And shadows of what used to be,
A man with sight, a man with dreams,
A man with threatening death machines.
A man with science, that special skill,
Is a man with a new age choice to KILL!

Dean Perks (Age 14)

The Hungry Peasant

His back was hunched the plough was heavy
But he kept on going steady
All were weary and ready to drop
But determined to never stop

The wind lashed across the cheek
Making them very weak
And as they trudged on in the bitter cold
Their features withered and became old

David Pearce

Four Seasons

The trees stand brave against the wind,
The leaves have long since gone.
Snow is deep upon the ground,
The winter seems so long.

The snow starts thawing in the sun,
Spring is on the way.
April soon, followed by May,
Oh! What lovely days.

Then comes summer, nice and warm,
And trips down to the coast.
These golden days, are special days,
Of which, please make the most.

Autumn comes, leaves will start to fall,
They flutter to the ground.
Soon the snow will also fall,
It will fall, without a sound.

Jean Palmer

Untitled

A rich man and a poor man both sat beneath a tree,
The poor man looking all around at the wonders he could see.
The rich man sat so deep in thought, so troubled and so sad,
Which man do you think you would rather be, if ever the chance you had.

A small child walked over to them both and asked,"What is your name?"
The poor man answered straight away, the rich man did not say.
It was not because he did not hear, it was because it had been a while,
Since he had know the comfort in the wonders of a smile.

He cleared his throat and spoke his name, the boy seemed satisfied,
Then both men rose to leave the park, they walked together side by side.
As they came to where their roads must part, each took a backward glance,
The poor man with a heart so rich, wondered, had they met by chance?

Kelly E. Paterson

The Gift

"Get up, you'll be late for work" said a voice.
I rise with a feeling I should rejoice.
Go downstairs (washed and dressed) — now fed.
The sun aslant on the garden shed
The coffee's hot, the rolls are fresh
Strawberries agleam with their leaves enmesh.
Rat-a-tat, there's a knock at the door,
Someone crosses the polished floor,
Then comes back, "There's someone for you."
I open and gaze, can it be true?
A dozen roses of crimson hue
And just the message — "I love you"

D.J. Parry

Freedom

I was bored looking out of my window;
For I needed something to do.
I was tired and feeling a bit low,
So I ran off to Timbuktu.

Yet I would rather have gone to Kabul
But something stopped me from going;
For common sense had made me so careful,
With all this to-ing and fro-ing.

My holiday in Spain was just nothing
When compared with great Alpine climbs.
Oh, but how could I ever do this thing;
Idle and waste my precious time!

I enjoyed my trip to the Orient
And oh, for those long Prairie nights!
My travels are usually spent.
I just wish I could see such sights!

Barbara Pearce

Ode For A Job

The grip of morning greets me
Holding hopes anew.
Will anybody out there
Help me find something to do.
Something useful, something worth while.
Maybe a job that will bring a smile
As folks hurry by on their way
To me its just another day.

Irene Pearce

Thoughts of Vincent

His hand worked wonders with his heart
And expressed in colour, his isolated
Self.
Misunderstood, mad or beautiful,
His style was a class
Apart.

Love he craved and love he sought,
In violent, erratic endeavours,
Burnt hand or slashed ear,
He offered all he had.

Rebuffed by lovers or their families
Consolation for life was sparse,
And farmyard suicide called
Like crows in cypress trees ...

Dying redhead with pipe in hand,
Your last wish was "to die now",
May immortality of your art bring justice,
And life in heaven, an abundance of yellow.

Kate Park

Monte Cassino

I watched an English mother and her son kneeling on the ground heads bowed in prayer,
their sadness touched my soul and tore my heart in two as I stood waiting there
in that so silent place with every stone as white as purest driven snow.
Loving families all around from near and far had vowed to ever keep them so.
They made our sons their own, became their mothers in our place and tended them with love.
Red rosebuds at every head, green grass as smooth as velvet — with not one blade above
another — spread all over that vast reach of silent holy earthly space.
God's peace was over all. Enriched in heart and mind and soul, I saw His face.
Angels caught in shafts of heaven's light, kissed the names on every stone —
of those brave young men who gave their lives — gossamer wings sparkling in the sun.
When I left that peaceful, moving, yet stirring place, forever etched upon my memory
was the suffering represented there for those young lives that never were to be.
Let all unite in one great fervent prayer, "Please God may wars in other lands forever cease"
and evil be transmuted into good, that all men everywhere may live in peace ...

Madge H. Paul

Silhouettes

Wave after wave of silhouettes
As I stare into the evening sky
Young soldiers dancing pirouettes
As they spin in agony and die.

My world is a vista of sun and star
Days and nights I've lain in slime
Silhouettes float over this man-made scar
Like a Mephistopheles pantomime.

Shadows passing, a tear, I weep.
Bayonets fixed as they leap the trench
Dead and wounded in a heap
Whilst I lie here amongst the stench.

Again I see the silhouettes
Against a mustard coloured sky.
Disjointed dangling marionettes,
Chlorine, Phosgene, Alkali.

The horrors, the torment, the mustard gas
The blinded eyes as the deadly cloud stings.
Another wave of silhouettes pass
I hear the beat of angels' wings.

Young soldiers under Flanders' sun
You were a silhouette, I saw you leap
Across the trench towards the Hun
A final pirouette and sleep.

James Andrew Patience

Without You

What would I do without you,
Each day how would it be,
As the sun slowly lifts the dawn's shadows,
Bathing in light each beautiful tree.

As I gazed at your empty pillow,
There'd be no voice to greet me and say,
'Good morning my dear did you sleep well'.
Or even, 'I think it'll be a nice day'.

The kitchen would be strangely silent,
No kettle 'singing' for tea,
No clatter of cups and saucers,
Being prepared by you for me.

Sadly I'd discard the bedclothes,
Then slowly prepare for the day,
The emptiness stretching before me,
No word of love, helping me on my way.

Time would drag on and on before me,
I'd see your face in all that I'd do,
At homecoming there would be silence,
No word of love to greet me, from you.

What would I do without you,
As time passes how would it be,
I know; life would seem not worth living,
Without your love, to comfort me.

R.C. Peach

A Moment Stolen

Empty of players the play-park is grey and
park pathways and footbridge glint metal in the rain and
grey water flows from the socket of the bridge and
a man enters the park by leaping the puddles and
he turns up the collar of his wet raincoat and
wipes moisture from his face and
moves to the flooded stand of trees and
there under her dripping umbrella
he embraces his arrived sweetheart.
Soft sweet sad embrace.
Embracing
tenderly achingly moistly.
And there under her dripping umbrella
she embraces her arrived sweetheart
and departs the flooded stand of trees
and wipes moisture from her face
and she turns down the collar of her raincoat
and the woman leaves the park by ignoring the puddles
and grey water flows from the eye of the bridge
and park pathways and footbridge glint metal in the rain
and empty of players the play-park is grey.

John Pearce

The Artist

God went out with a paintbrush today
With rain and shine and dabbled away
He created a rainbow

A golden orb he tinged with red
Then sunk it slowly into bed
He created a sunset

Vibrant colours of gold, red and brown
He changed green leaves and tossed them down
He created autumn

Mountains and rivers, people too
He painted with love, me and you
He created Earth

Off to the Heavens his favourite place
There is so much to do out there in space
He is painting creation

Mrs. A. Pendrous

'Will We Remember'

Hustle, bustle, toil and queue,
It's a busy time, I agree, don't you?
There are lists to make and presents to buy,
A cake to bake and, of course, some pies.

There are friends to contact, to see if they'll come,
Valerie, Barry, Susan and John.
Mum, Ann and Ken, if he's able,
What a happy gathering to be round the table.

There will be clatter and chatter, oh, what a din.
Plenty of food to eat, carols to sing.
Lots of fun to be had by all,
But! Will we remember Jesus at all?

Will we remember those who live alone,
Who have no one to share their food or their home.
Will we, like Jesus, go and see,
In someway bring comfort and make them happy.

Let us remember this time of year,
The old and the lonely living near.
And as we share our joy and our care,
Let them feel Jesus, who was also there.

Sheerah Ruth Peachey

The Visit

We paid a little visit,
To a famous Susex town,
To see its ancient battlements,
And have a look around.

A mixture of the old and new,
I know which I liked best,
Its narrow cobbled streets,
With time have stood the test.

There's a thirteenth century inn,
And antique shops galore,
A typical English beach,
With shingle on the shore.

They fought a famous
battle here,
The year 1066,
The name of course is,
Hastings,
The visit all too quick.

Barbara Petty

364

The Queen Of All Flowers

That I may walk
in the praise of England
and know life's sweet desire,
reach out and touch the gloaming
see crimson sunsets on fire.

Just to walk in green acres
paradise is found in quiet hours,
where it behoves the men of England
to behold the Queen of all flowers.

And measure that feeling
his heart only knows,
for England does, and England will
forever, wear the rose.

Joan Parsonage

Autumn Glory

I look up into the sky
And see the white clouds hurrying by.
The wind is whispering through the trees.
Golden leaves twirl in the breeze.

On the boughs the squirrels chatter
As they gather winter matter:
Hazel, beech and acorns sweet.
Awaken all for winter's treat.

Twirling, whirling, falling, curling,
Sycamore, lime and elm are swirling,
Riding on the dying flow,
Hither and thither the sweet fruits go.

By the path a rabbit scurries,
On the scent an old fox hurries.
The hedgehog peeps through matted boughs
Whilst in the fields graze tranquil cows.

On the pond a splash and ripple,
Fishes swim and turn and tipple.
The old frog croaks with deep disdain.
There's a sound of a distant train.

Quietly soughs the evening breeze,
Into their homes the animals squeeze,
Ears alert for any danger,
Watchful for the hungry stranger.

George Edward Pearson

Troubadour

He threw a rose,
        Then tuned his lute;
So sprightly, by her bower.
        A token-pledge,
From love-lorn youth;
        She was his fairest flower.

He struck a note,
        It vibrates still;
Against her shuttered tower.
        Then turns away,
His song unsung;
        Love's memory gone sour.

Johnny Pottinger

The Mug Mass

Mealy-mouthed mistresses,
Standing, waiting for the crowds,
Controlling the counters.

Campbells coaches coming,
Slowing, heading for the mills
Offering the passengers.

Big-bully bosses,
Rushing, changing cards around
Swindling the customers.

Lucky locals
Looking, screwing their faces
Walk out.

Angela Pearcey

Lament for the Oaks

They call it progress, I know not why.
Oak trees fallen, gnarled broken,
Chopped and twisted, by a bulldozer guy.

He hacked their base, tore their limbs
Bashed and bashed with certain aim,
While the lovely oaks cried out in pain.

Now being placed on a funeral pyre,
When evening comes the man will fire.
Black smoke will pall the evening sky
And I cry inwardly, and ask myself
"WHY OH WHY".

Dear Oak Trees, you have not lived in vain
I will plant acorns and make it right again.

Hazel Phillips

Forgotten (?) Youth

You remember that night — the night we sat
beneath the stars, and kissed under moonbeams
in absolute bliss? I remember ...
In all my life, I shall never forget
the memories of your youth ... when the sun was warm,
and the sunbeams danced upon the autumn leaves.
Birds flew over our heads, and we laughed
till our cares flew away with the wind.

Do you remember that stormy, winter night?
The gales howled through the trees, and we sat
huddled before the fire, toasting our toes ...

Our love was strong then but it has
mellowed with the years. Can we do nothing
to rekindle what we had? Life is so short —
so short — but yet, so long.
Our youth was spent in sharing
ideas and fears and hopes. But times have changed —
you read ... I sit and mope.
Do not despair — the end is not here yet.
The best days may have gone
but at least
we won't
forget ...

Caroline Pettit

The Little Things

God give me grace
To heed the little things.

The dainty butterfly
With silvered wings.
The furry bee
Whose droning sound
Brings tranquility
To all around.

All little birds
Alert and shy,
The timid mouse,
The tiny snail
Who marks its way
With a silver trail.

The little flowers
That hide away —
Such beauty lost
If none can see
Perfection in
Fragility

God give me grace
To see the little things.

Margaret Parry

Out Of The Mist

Was it so long ago? That cherished, vanished spring,
when the swan of the dawn brought life and light,
mystery, to us, and happiness, brief happiness,
gliding to our radiant world upon immaculate wing
out of the cloudy past, out of a cleft in the night.

Oh, to wander again in olive groves under the sun
where still lascivious satyrs loll in the shade
and the shadows of long-dead centaurs prance
in the perfumed breeze, their dance that never is done!
Oh, that time were young again and my world new-made,
the face of the morning bright and promise of summer fair!

I remember the flash of the light on the living stream
and — so well — the plash of the waterfall,
the blossom entwined in your hair!
Was it only a dream, that myths are true,
the song the cicadas sing —
that we were there?

In the pool of time,
if you must,
look deep:
On its surface I saw, and I trust,
the image of you.

Stephen Lewis Ingham Pettit

A Tree

Though poor am I,
yet poorer still is he,
who looks, yet sees,
no beauty in a tree.

How ill does Man
compare,
with yonder monarch
standing there
majestic and aloof,
deep rooted as a rock,
untouched by tempests
which have tried to mock.

By each gnarled root,
each fairy leaf is fed,
to form a verdant green
about his mighty head.

With arms uplifted
to the evening sky,
each passing breeze
becomes a fervent sigh.

Does he implore
the heavens to impart
A love of Nature
to the human heart?

Reg. H. Penfold

The Girl Next Door

I am the girl who lives next door
I live with my Mum who I adore,
I'm the biggest girl you ever saw
But I do the fussing, and lay down the law.
I'm a beautiful white chested Tabby,
But I'm afraid I'm no laddy,
I have two little sisters, who I've never seen
But my Mum takes care of we three.
I talk to my Mum, and we both understand
What each other has to say.
I won't be picked up, but I like a fuss
My Mummy thinks I'm a lovely Puss,
When I go to rest I lay on her chest.
Then my Mum thinks I'm a real pest
When the bell rings, I answer the door.
I will look after my Mum for evermore
To my friends, I give my weight, but they ignore
But my beautiful face they all adore.
Here is my story, I haven't told a fibby
Love from Tibby, the girl next door.

Elsie Pickthall

Love

A mother's love is instinct,
Borne from deep within
A lover's love is passion,
An exciting kind of thing,
A sportsman's love is perhaps a game
Or a new kind of machine,
While to the very young
It's some romantic dream
But love to me is a footstep,
When someone's been away,
That feeling of belonging
When you're kneeling down to pray
Love is a hand resting close in mine
When I'm feeling rather sad,
Or the warm glow you feel,
When you think of you mum and dad.
Love is a walk in a garden
Filled with singing birds.
Love is when two people
Have no need for words.

Marjorie Percival

The Lady of Cardboard City

Shards of stress took her laughter away,
Her beautiful looks she has lost,
The husband she loved was inclined to stray,
Now sadly she's counting the cost.

It started with just a glass of sherry,
To warm and give her a glow,
Later it progressed to being rather merry,
With speech that was slurred and slow.

Then came events she couldn't recall,
She drifted along in a daze,
Losing her children was saddest of all,
While lost in that tragic maze.

Gone are her family and home, what a pity,
But the poor lady isn't to blame,
Her lonely nights spent in cardboard city,
Pricks her conscience with guilt and shame.

For what do we know of her anguish,
Her heartache hopelessness and pain,
Her wistful dreams and burning wish,
Never to be fulfilled again.

Olive Pentoni

Food

Food we take for granted
We eat well every day,
But life in the third world
Will never see that day.

They grovel in the dirt each day
To find a single crumb,
While we grow fat and podgy
And sit upon our bums.

They lay there dying in the sand
With sadness on their face,
And little children sit and cry
With all the hopelessness they sigh.

They long for food which never comes
They watch their families die,
And all for the sake of wholesome food
Which we stock up in piles.

You'd think that in this day and age
The problem would be solved,
But there is no solution
When there's politics involved.

J.E. Phillips

The Evacuee

I don't really understand what this all about
They say it's to protect me
I've to be good or get a clout!
They say it will be safer
Safer for who?
That's what I want to know
They can stay at home
It's me that's got to go.
I'm sitting on me suitcase
With the few things that I own
Inside there's some striped pyjamas
But they are just on loan,
I'm all packed up with me Micky Mouse gas mask
Trying to be brave,
That's the hardest task
'Cause me Mam's eyes are red
She's trying not to cry
Me Dad's stood at the railing
Waving me good-bye.
I hope that family's nice
I hope I make some friends
I don't really understand all this
I hope this war soon ends.

Margaret Phelps

All Gone

Gone are the wheels that used to turn
With ropes that let the cages down
The inky blackness of the pit
Where man and boy worked underground

Gone is the clang of pit-top dram
And gritty feel of coal-dust grime
Shimmering as it fell upon
Those houses of another time.

Gone is the coal that once was king
That fired both the grate and heart
and left a legacy of hate
Which often ripped the soul apart

Gone is the miner and his lamp
With blackened face and thin blue scar
Reminders of those years of toil
And searching for a place too far.

Haydon Phillips

November Delphiniums

A single leaf twists through hollow air,
rain picks at my face,
black ribs of hawthorn
score grey skin of sky —
then, whisper of sun
slides through staleness of morning,
flakes metaphore of memory
in the mind's turning,
and I see them;
late delphiniums,
two columns of colour
set out of time, echoes of a coda lost
somewhere in dark-leaved summer;
one white as indifference,
other blue as love,
now distilled, blended into vapour of sleep
against slow freeze of night.

The colours do not fade,
air swells and warms,
brackish water sweetens.
What's left in the soul to suffer
will blaze to its apotheosis
in gentle plume of flower.

David Perry

Cornea in October

No other sounds
Only the crashing water
Against the rugged cliffs
Like rumbling thunder.
The low swish of the waves
Pounding in steady rhythm
The pebbles on the shore incessantly,
Devouring with greedy tongues
Evermore of the beach.
White spume, riding like horses
On the sea, grey, restless,
Like a heaving monster brought to bay.

What great primeval force
Is there at work?
What unknown power has designed
And then created, out of a void,
The ordered pattern of our world?
Man in his arrogance
Is just a puny speck,
A fleeting moment
In this immensity,
To his small mind so inconceivable
Of the entire universe
And of eternity.

Ruth Peel

A Treasured Place

My garden is a treasured place, full of wealth untold,
It fills my heart and senses with the wonders that it holds.
But most of all it teaches me life's lessons day by day
And gives a set of values that guide me on my way.

I watch the tiny seedling as it struggles hard to grow,
The spider's graceful symmetry as it dances to and fro.
And when that seedling starts to blossom and the mist bejewels the web,
I see that patience truly is rewarded just as the proverb said.

And if I'm vainly boasting of the garden I have made,
The winds and rain berate me and the sun affords no shade.
But as I stoop to tend the damage and I'm down upon my knees,
I'm taught the lesson of humility and my pride begins to ease.

Sometimes when I am tired from the efforts of the day,
I sit and watch the wildlife at their work and at their play.
The bees, the birds, the butterflies, the shy vole as it darts,
And I'm shown that life's a fellowship in which we all must play our part.

Every season of the year has a beauty that's sublime,
But I also know their changing marks the turning wheels of time.
And though the folds of time for me are nigh unfurled,
The seasons promise constancy in an ever-changing world.

And when at last I come to meet my Maker face-to-face,
I shall tell Him of my garden, of that very treasured place.
And I'll thank Him for the beauty and the wonder that it brought,
But most of all I'll thank Him for the lessons that it taught.

Heather Philpott

Family At War

We enter this world, to live our life
But all around is pain and strife
There's always fighting, killing and war
We all want peace, and love not more.

Our life is run from higher ranks.
We struggle on with not much thanks
Some of us hope our jobs are for life
To provide for the children, and also the wife.

But all too soon, it comes to an end
Then join the queue on the downward trend
With money scarce, we just scrape by
No wonder people give up and die.

Pat Potter

Concord

Memories, when you're not near,
Interject all that I do.
Insistent images appear
Of winsome form, charm, my dear.
Oh Chloris; how I long for you!

But harmony as we two greet.
Thoughts forging unbroken chain;
Link follows link, each one complete:
Our latest parting, bitter, sweet,
Forgotten till we part again.

Now I hold your eyes in mine
And listen to your music while
Clutching this moment so divine
Fingers eager, touch, entwine;
Patience rewarded by your smile.

Edmond Philpott

Who Gives A Damn?

Aging, aging, I'm going insane,
another white hair and a varicose vein.
Just twenty-two with a future ahead,
surely this stomach's not middle age spread.
Shopping's more of a chore than a fun expedition,
to realise loosing a stone is my main ambition.
I try a size ten, just fooling myself,
then discreetly return with a sixteen from the shelf.
I try to look happy, though my smile starts to wilt,
as friends assure I'm not fat, but just well built.
A burly body-builder conjures up in my head,
then I know for certain I've a few pounds to shed.
But how can I diet when everyone else,
is sitting around me stuffing themselves.
They order a pizza, but I've already eaten,
when the aroma arrives I try hard, still I'm beaten.
I grab a slice wondering will I get fatter,
my good friends assure me that one piece won't matter.
A topping of cheese, peppers, sausage and ham,
do I want to be slim? No I don't give a damn!

Kerry Phillips

The Elusive Reason

When the sea engulfed the land,
there was no apparent point,
although the reason,
was hidden in the sand,
it drowned,
before it could be caught.

As the reason choked,
in the saline mass,
and the sand slipped away,
leaving truth naked
upon the beach, when,
the ocean retreated,
leaving it marooned,
out of reach.

A cool, transcendental breeze,
cast its breath along the coast,
now the reason,
anointed with calm,
perplexities of the past,
and dissatisfactions,
just memories, just a ghost.

Paul Phipps

The Workers' Song

Come all of you workers who toil night and day
By hand and by brain to earn your pay
Who for centuries long past for no more than your bread
Have bled for your country and counted your dead.

In the factories and mills, in the shipyards and mines
You've often been told keep up with the times
For your skills are not needed they've streamlines the job
With slide rule and stopwatch your pride they have robbed.

But when the sky darkens and the prospect is war
Who's given a gun and then pushed to the fore?
And expected to die for the land of his birth
When he's never owned one handful of earth.

The first one to starve and and the first one to die
The first one in line for that "pie in the sky"
And always the last when the cream is shared out
For the worker is working when the fat cat's about

All of these things the worker has done
From tilling the fields to carrying a gun
Yoked to the plough since time first began
And always expected to cary the "can".

Ed Pickford

York

This beautiful city of God,
With Churches old and new
This city of many tears —
Its secrets known to few
Narrow cobbled streets —
Beautiful city walls
Tiny latticed windows —
In churches, mansion and hall
One looks towards the splendour
Of the ancient minster there
Fine old architecture
Which speaks of toil and care.
One enters through the doorway
And sees the vast expanse —
Beautiful stained glass windows —
They call for more than a glance
A stranger sees the beauty —
But rarely the ancient days
Which tell of toil and bloodshed
And men with primitive ways!!
Today I sit and ponder —
How the city stood the test
But if I look in its inmost soul —
I would see "By God it is Blest".

Neil Pinkney

To Autumn

It's wonderful to take a walk in Autumn
To see the changing colours of the trees.
From green to yellow, through to red and auburn
Bright coloured piles and drifts of fallen leaves.
To shuffle through the heaps of changing colour
Like little children, kicking them in glee.
Oh it's so beautiful this world of ours to live in
If only we have time and eyes to see.
The fiery berries on the prickly holly,
The hawthorn shining brightly in the rain
Providing food in plenty for the birds who stay all winter
To cheer our hearts till Spring is here again.

A. Phipps

The Way It Was

How my memory wanders back to precious childhood times
When streets were cobbled and bakers shops had little "Hovis" signs
When bread and jam and Wensleydale were all there was for tea
And rows of smoky chimneys were all that one could see
When rag and bone men gave balloons and donkey stone in blocks
In exchange for Dad's old torn clothes and worn out woolen socks
When playtime meant a skipping rope and bubbles in a jar
And spinning tops and hide and seek and hopscotch in the yard
When kids could take the tram alone, spend hours in the park
And people left their front doors open even after dark
How I wish the old times were with us once again
And children could enjoy the innocence of life that we knew then.

Joy Pickering

Untitled

A funny thing happened to me walking down the road
Ahead of me I could see a yellow spotted toad.
As I approached to take a look, it brought me to my knees
For as I got near I heard it say "Hello" in Japanese
Well, knock me down with a feather, then pick me up again
For when I asked what he was doing "In on my way to Spain"
How come you can talk and why the funny colour
"Do you know" said the toad "I've starting going duller
When I set out on my travels I was a pale pink
But as you see and must believe, I'm yellow now I think
How I came to talk is very much more bizarre
For waking up from a dream I was in Zanzibar
Next to me in my room was a frail and lonely man
He gave me three wishes and then the tale began
My first wish was to travel, see as much as I could
My second wish I whispered and was barely understood
The third wish to say the least is very extreme
For when I slept for the night I was in the same dream."

Keith Perry

Pollution, "94"

As I watched the river black and grim,
Choked with filth up to the brim;
Silent, sullen, bearing down
The refuse from the busy town,
I asked myself if it could be,
God made a thing so foul to see;
Then thought how higher up the stream
Shone with a clear, translucent gleam.
And then I knew, and knew for sure,
God made the stream and made it pure.

I mused upon the stream of Life
The cheating, hating and the strife.
And said, "God surely must be blind
To make such things as human kind".
Then looked and saw a baby's eyes,
Blue and clear as summer skies,
And knew whatever may be the man,
God made him clean when he began.

Hubert Proctor

Me And My Skin

I wear an expensive suit,
it keeps the rain out
and me in.
Though what has been has marked it.

Over time it sheds itself,
but I stay inside, holding it together.
Forever.
I see it as a blackboard for those
I've yet to meet.

They will look at me and say;
He has laugh lines,
he must have laughed,
or;
He must have worried,
see his furrowed brow.

And here's how
will they ever know?
because happy lines don't show
and I can't tell them.

What you see and what is within
is me and my skin,

can you guess me?

Jason Potts

"The Lifeboat Men"

As a tribute to the men who man the lifeboat,
We stand and sing their praises in a song,
We give our thanks to those who man the lifeboat,
And go to sea when things are going wrong,
Without a thought of fear for their own safety,
They head for where they know someone's in need,
For courage and for bravery you never will their equal see,
Lifeboat men are special men indeed.

If red flares light the sky at night in summer,
Maroons will boom out like a quarry blast,
From near and far the lifeboat men come running,
Each call for help is always answered fast,
We hold our breath until they start the engine,
Then as a man we wish them all God speed,
Wives and sweethearts left behind pray tonight the sea be kind
Lifeboat men are special men indeed.

In December when the winter winds are blowing,
And we are by the fire snug and warm,
It's off to sea again these men are going,
To rescue fellow travellers from the storm,
Close to rocks and reefs where there is danger,
The lifeboat men will go and pay no heed,
In cottage windows candles burn as we pray for their safe return,
Lifeboat men are special men indeed.

J. Pugh

Motherhood

When all the push and stain is done and labour's now complete,
They put into your trembling arms small hands, small face, small feet
And misty eyes gaze into yours
While gently soft you smile.

And you are there when first he smiles, and you are there to coo
At wobbling steps and lisping words and that first potty poo.
And trusting eyes look into yours
While gently soft you smile.

And you are there when e're he falls to kiss and make things right,
To teach him nursery rhymes and songs and read to him at night
And happy eyes laugh into yours
While gently soft you smile.

Then comes the day, that fateful day, when your angel has to leave
And bravely he walks into school, and even though you grieve,
His nervous eyes look into yours
And sweetly soft you smile.

But you are there when he comes home and says "Hey Mum, piss off!"
And asks you "What does fart mean?" (finds poos and bums a laugh),
And knowing eyes stare into yours
And, greatly strained, you smile.

Catherine Pope

Class Working; Or Working Class

Head down
Worried frown
Shoulders stooped
Factory cooped
Bonus, bonus
Onus, onus
Job to keep
Worrying losing sleep
Morning boss!
Running at a loss
So work faster
Please the master
Or it's a big black
hole
Called the dole.

June Plaskett

Point of View

Life is just a ritual
A well established thing
The process is predictable
As Daffodils in Spring
Seasons in their sequence
Summer's youthful song
Autumn age and changes
Winter old and long

Saplings in their element
Adapt when Tempest blown
Adjust without a murmur
Only old trees moan
Lithe, carefree, the younger
Swing with youth's wild fling
The older, knurled and leaning
To their status cling

Through its many stages
Life has one set trend
Regular in its phases
Routine to the end
All is so foreseeable
The Tree of Life unfolds
Fantasies — realities
Then the whole thing folds.

Jack Pritchard

Footsteps

We were young, madly in love, happy and carefree.
His call-up came, our world fell apart quite completely.
Good-bye at the station, broken hearted but crookedly smiling,
He had gone, I was left quietly crying.

The postman's step. Would he pass the door?
The quiet certainty he'd stop, and then no more.
Embarkation leave was a warning of how it would be,
But the waiting, the listening, was torture to me.

At last, at last! The postman's stopped.

As I flew down the stairs, I knew there would be
Dozens of letters, and each one for me.
No hint where he is, and the joy the joy,
He's alive and well and still my boy.

Not now daily letters, only now and again
The months stretched to years, and then —
He's coming home! I can't believe it! When oh when?
Next month, he says we'll get married then.

That loud step never, the one I had known,
Quietly he walked, weary and alone.
I looked at his dear face, no longer young,
I looked at a man for whom life had begun.

Arms around each other, very little to say,
Five lonely years simply melted away.
Tomorrow we would become man and wife,
Step forward together, forever through life.

Lillian Jane Price

A Cook's Tour

What shall we have for dinner tonight? I fancy something nice.
Something out of the ordinary, with a little bit of spice.
Get my foreign cook books out, seeking inspiration,
Browsing through the recipes on a journey of temptation.

"Lapin aux pruneaux" we ate with friends in Northern France.
"Bouillabaisse with rouille" we had down in Provence.
At Aubusson the most delicious "Bouchees de la Reine"
And after that was ice cream, over which they poured champagne!
In Paris "Steak au Poivre", on an island in the Seine.
Then Paella in a village in the hills of Southern Spain.
Moussaka was the favourite on our holiday in Crete.
And in Greece our first Baklava, a memorable treat.
In Cyprus with a kebab, pitta bread and brandy sour
We'd sit and watch the world go by for hour after hour.

Oh look, how time has flown while on my gastronomic tour.
The clock is striking six and when I started it was four.
When looking through my cookery books, it always is the same —
I don't have to cook much, so it's bangers and mash again!

Betty Pople

The Humble Bumble

There's a busy bee in the foxglove,
I can hear a noisy hum,
But all I can see of the busy bee,
Is its little humble bum.

Violet Puxty

Shadows

I hear you calling, softly calling,
As you called me long years ago.
Mists of memory, stirring faintly,
Bring back faces I used to know.
Joys and sorrows,
Tears and laughter —
All I find in memory's store,
Echoing voices,
Tender moments —
Shades of those I'll see no more.

Jack Prince Gardner

Winter Wonders

Winter is with us once again
Bringing frost, snow, ice and rain
All the trees are brown and bare
Not a leaf shows anywhere

Many birds have flown away
To far distant lands so gay
Where the sun is warm and bright
These birds sing freely with delight

But some in England here do stay
To brighten up each dreary day
They sing so sweetly with their song
As if to say Spring won't be long

The robins are our faithful friends
They stay with us 'til winter ends
Among the cold, the ice and snow
Although the blustery winds do blow

The blackbird and the thrush so gay
You also see them every day
The starling and the sparrow sit
Beside the tiny sweet blue tit

The squirrel is a pretty sight
But now he's disappeared from sight
He hibernates 'til Winter's past
Then out he comes again at last

R.G. Potter

Nomadi

A burning light, throwing incandescent flames across the horizon of thought.
An old woman kneeling beside a bench which bears the memorial
Plaque commemorative utterances of her deceased hubby.
She stoops and crumples up her weak legs like a master contortionist.
The wooden one helps her back up with great difficulty as the
Structure groans with the supporting of such dead weight.
In the gloomy light which once glowed with neon explosions,
Rays of sunbeam choking its way through Cumulo Nimbus hoards
Of water vapour: The old, frail and helpless lady walks off.
Her face lost in the crowds of desolation.
The shop fronts stare out onto a cold, oblivious street.
The waste gathers in a stranded corner against the mortar
Of a crumbling, decaying church, which once celebrated
The birth, marriage and death of God's children.
Now only the carved stones put up for ornamentation and
Remembrance prove that life was once present and past.
Now ... there is no future.
Everything has stopped.
Man has invaded his own territory, one machine, one scientist.
One giant mushroom cloud.
Now an empty shell.
Now, no life,
Nothing.

Barnaby Pout

Lady Of The Road

You see her in the town
Bundles at her feet
She sits there with her thoughts
Her home is the street.
Why is she here?
Who made her this way?
Trudging round the town
No place to stay.
Did she have a sweetheart
Who left her, or who died?
Could she not hold her life
No matter how she tried?
Were the disappointments just too much to bear?
The sadness within her, just too much to share?
She'll carry on living
Existing day to day
On handouts from people
Going busily on their way.
No matter how we wonder what made her live this way.
Her secrets are hers alone,
And in her heart they'll stay.

Elizabeth Powell

Reflexion

See the old man struggles to be free
His silver cord and golden bowl
Weakened by capricious years of greed
Past glories give no solace to his failing ears and eyes
And he; he thinks what might have been.

David's son and king by royal decree
Wealth and works, wine and wives
Devoured his pantheon days
"Everything my eyes desired I took"
Said he; now he thinks what might have been.

Once Sheba breathless at his pomp and majesty
Once Heaven's glory crowned his best design
Wisdom's rubies mined from fathomless store
Poured justice into troubled lives
But he; he thinks what might have been.

See the old man struggling with his destiny
Head as white as Kenya's mount
Dispensing life and joy to nature's youth
"Remember thy creator, enjoy Him while you may,
Pity me; I know what might have been."

Maurice Powell

374

Storm

The moon flies high in a raging sky,
A shining ship on the ocean,
It tosses and reels, way over it keels -
Then sturdily keeps in motion.

Magnificent seas are the clouds that fly,
So dark and threatening tonight,
But the moon that rides in those sullen skies
Is a full - a glorious light.

Rough elements toss, but cannot destroy
That beautiful ship in the sky,
It silently glides between cumulous waves -
While travelling seagulls cry.

Cold rain has drenched, the wind has dropped,
It is calmer, the cloud-waves have gone;
The moon, in full sail, so majestic now,
Glides silently, silently on.

And man has trod its shining deck
As it sailed in a blue-black sea,
Just 'one small step' in space and time,
But 'forever' - in history.

Sylvia A. Price

The Hill

I stood on the hill in the evening,
As the sun dipped below yonder trees.
And gazed out across the old airfield,
All I heard was the whispering breeze.

Spread out before me in the gathering dusk,
Though I thought it could never be so.
Were the huts the workshops and hangers,
Of the station I knew long ago.

I heard the sound of aircraft,
Of gunners testing their guns.
And the roar of Hercules engines,
As a Halifax started its run.

There are voices all around me,
Unseen airmen both young and old.
Coming back to the camp from the village,
Back to huts that were always so cold.

I was back on that hill in the morning,
Impatient for dawn to arrive.
As I waited a Halifax landed,
Just the one of them all to survive.

The sun came up and cleared the mist,
My old station was down there no more.
Gone were the hangers, workshops and huts,
'Twas the sixth day of June '94.

Clifford S. Poole

Legend

Land of hills and mountains high
Appears to reach the leaded sky.
Merlins mystery still is here
To cast his spell on all who near.
Castle walls still echo song,
And knights of old still pass along,
And eerie bird calls in the night
Send all who listen into flight.
Legends abound, on moor and hill,
For this is Wales, it's Magic still.

Gwyneth Pritchard

Thundering And Lightening

Three forks at once,
from the brown bruise
of beaten clouds,
and we cannot do what we wish to do.
As if the land was always there
to be some drum set dancing,
a boom and a crash
and a vibrant metal.
We ran indoors
to count seconds
between sight and sound;
to watch the droplets jumping
upon the varnished ground.
Its heart was miles away
yet still we were trapped.

John Pownall

Old Scythe in a Thorn

I saw you hanging in a thorn
With rusted blade and handle worn
Not needed now, your day is gone
Old scythe your day is past

No longer the day of shining blade
Of well made bow and sturdy snead
Machines are used today instead
Old scythe your day is past

Where is the man in sunny morn
Who swung you singing through the corn
With crop and stone your blade got worn
Old scythe your day is past

But remember scythe this world runs fast
The oil and tractors may not last
When modern ways aside are cast
Old scythe is your day past

Eddie Polland

Joys Of Nature

I wandered on the windswept cliff,
Seeing life through a haze of pain,
When suddenly, above my head, I seemed to hear the sound again.
A tiny bird from way above, sang to me a song of love.
And further up and further out, towards the sea,
A flighty flock of seagulls danced for me.
They danced and floated through the clouds,
With windblown wings and voices loud.
While down below on the dark grey sea,
Strong white waves tossed joyously,
Like wild white horses raging high, to rage and race across the sky.
Suddenly, clear-eyed, I looked around
And by my feet, there on the ground,
A tiny snowdrop raised its head, awakened from its wintery bed.
And there, close by, beneath the hedge,
Daffodil leaves seemed to give a pledge,
Of spring to come, and sunny days,
And contentment that comes in many ways.
Then home I walked and though in pain, I closed my eyes and saw again.
The tiny bird upon its way, the seagulls and the waves so gay.
The snowdrops and the leaves so green,
And all that happy, hopeful scene.
Then contentment filled my mind for I was blessed, like all mankind,
With heart to love and eyes to see, the joys of nature wild and free.

Mrs. J. Proctor

Speckled Light

When you see the sunlight dancing.
Through the leafy mantle shining
Shimmering there on breeze a prancing.
Like a fish's scales aglow.
See a moving diamond blanket, or as many sequins shining
On the dewy earth below.
Golden sun in all its glory broken in to patterns rare.
Beauty in a space of seconds.
Changing, brightening here and there.
Such embroidery, Nature's wonder, cannot be the same again.
Cause: Leaves are growing, world is moving.
Different shadows on the lane.
In the dells and wooded hollows, bathe in dapples that are bright.
All that sparkling, glittering silver.
Like a shower of heaven's water.
Drench yourself in speckled light.
Then the energy reflected, will your human spirit raise.
By speckled light that spread and changes,
In so many wondrous ways.

Ronald Powell

Bursting Cupboards

For lack of words
We say too many,
This I know is true.
For if we took the time to think,
Our nonsense would be few.

Why do people, not say what they feel?
Is the truth too hard to take?
Perhaps grown-ups
Should take a tip
From the children, to relate.

So years go by, hiding truths in cupboards,
Just waiting to burst out.
Most people choose finding faults in others,
To have something
To complain about.

Carolee Price

Untitled

Desert Wasteland,
Arid dunes of drifted time
Are these hollow days of dust, of wearing masks.
The irksome tasks ...
Sandfly biting
And my heavy, leaden feet
That drag; interminably they drag and scuff
The shifting sands
Grain against grain
Until they whisper your name.
Left, right, on, on, day, night, on, on, on and on;
The dreary chill
Of endless night
And each fevered, lonely day
Merging into grey oneness, shadowed, overcast;
But, here and there,
Exquisite amid dry rock
Blooms for one hour a desert flower; fragrant,
Fragile, transient
Hope that we may
Yet bear high the leaves of palm
We gathered from each oasis home we passed,
Fulfilled at last.

Irene F. Priestley

Nostalgia

Life's clock just goes forward; we can't turn it back;
Yet lost in nostalgia, we dream.
Remembering the good times with family and friends,
Those loved ones — our favourite theme.

But would we have changed what has happened before?
Decisions we made in the past?
It then seemed alright, and our pathway seemed clear.
But some things were never to last.

Life's full of surprises and changes occurred,
Knocked back; but then rallied again.
The future seems bright, great contentment in store,
But joy can be mingled with pain.

We just never know from one day to the next —
Which cards in this life we'll be dealt;
But we'll be on our guard, and we'll watch for the signs
And pray no more heartache be felt.

Jan Portlock-Barker

This World

Oh, this world that we live in
With famine and wars everywhere
Is this what we're leaving our children
The thought of it makes me despair.
Oh, this world that we live in
With new roads, and so many cars
I wonder, would it be safer
If we all went to live up on Mars?

Why can't we all live together
In harmony, peace, and love.
Or is it that we have forgotten
Our Father in Heaven above.
Will the next generation
Discover the things we all missed
Or is it going to continue
Till our world no longer — exists.

Susie Pratt

Gravestones

In the churchyard, tilted
In drunken stance, gravestones stand
shoulder to shoulder for support,
On sentry duty till eternity.

Potted biographies planted
deep in the earth in once neat rows
until time and subsidence destroyed
their regimented perfection.

For centuries they stood,
lurching to the left or right,
guardians of the family plot,
examples of the mason's art.

Sacred tablets to the departed
But now, this sanctity abused
they lean against churchyard walls
so the land can be re-used.

I gaze at them and wonder whether,
if they could the dead would return
to haunt the perpetrators of
this modern day sacrilege?

Janis Priestley

The North Wind

Oh winter wind, who with piercing force,
doth travel from the icy north.
Whose claw-like fingers burn the face
of children, who in hurry, braced
against thy touch, in hat and coat,
with thickest scarf around the throat,
go homeward bound, to thaw the chill,
and sit round roaring fire till
their sleepy eyes can see no more,
and into fluffy pillows snore.

Oh cruel north wind, who's moaning cry,
at night doth make us restless lie.
Thee lifts the slates from barn and shelter,
and sends them rolling helter-skelter.
Take back with thee thy bite of ice.
Thy strong embrace like gripping vice.
I shan't be sad when thy demise,
sends warmer climes across the skies.
Take with thee all thy misery.
Oh no north wind, I shan't miss thee.

Jan Pugh

Black Widow

The courtroom was hushed. Proceedings began.
The judge settled into his chair.
My defender rose — that dour Mr. Leith
(Still vigorously checking for food in his teeth!)

"Your Honour" he said — in his best nasal tone
"I fear prejudice by the press.
Due to misfortune, my client's been named
'SPIDERWOMAN' — such a great shame."

A titter ran — nay, raced — through the room
As he offered more reading that claimed:
"An 'Arachnaphobic' is this ex-deb —
Who's name is also Mrs. Webb!!!"

"But she's an innocent victim of her own fear,
A condition that' s dogged her for years.
Accused of MURDER!?? — I'm appalled!!
She only shot a spider that crawled!!"

"ONLY shot a spider that crawled?!?!"
Prosecution was now on its' feet.
"This widow's third husband has now had his lot.
Like the others, he stood near a spider she shot!"

Oh, the traps I've set, the tales I've spun —
But no three times lucky for me.
Now trapped by my craft, I'll accept defeat
And stop spinning those silky-like webs of deceit!!

Marian Profit

The Lost Child

You came and stayed awhile
with lovely face
and happy smile.
You brought us joy
and love galore
but left before we knew you so.

The sunshine went
The darkness came
Years of misery to remain
but as time has rolled away
Peace and tranquility are here to stay.

Memories of you are all we have
As life's journey carries on
Not lost and gone forever
Just a pause until we meet again.

Margaret Pritchard

No Exit

Cold and isolated
Lost in tears of rain,
Helplessly calling you
Trying once again.
This time a different refuge
All attempts in vain
I walk over cracked dream stones
Through puddles filled with pain
And then my hopes, suddenly
Trickle down the drain,
For I have broken down in a
Dead end called Memory Lane.

Vivien Phillips

Michael

He sat upon the chair,
his favourite blanket wrapped around him,
More for comfort than for warmth
— and that is where I found him.
In the dining room, alone, just staring into space.
It broke my heart to see the sadness in his face.
He's seven years old and knows his friends
Don't have to move house every year.
To leave their homes, their school, their toys,
To run away in fear from 'new dads'
Who have a fondness for the beer.
I knelt beside him, held his hand,
Not knowing what to say or do
And he, wishing his childhood years away said,
"When I am older Grandma,
I am going to come and live with you."

Moreen Place

Arousing the Poet Within

An inconspicuous column of newsprint on the twenty-ninth page,
Some poetry competition open to anyone, any age.
And though reluctance had defeated me countless times before,
For some reason this was an invitation difficult to ignore.

Almost instinctively a voice inside urged "write!"
Temptation was present, the mood felt right.
But then Old Doubt tapped my shoulder, whispered in my ear:
"Why bother? You've no chance, just forget the idea."

After all, the poet's an illusionist, his magic comes from inspiration
And a huge, black, padlocked chest crammed tight with imagination.
God knows how he conjures up all kinds of romance,
Come on! Did I really stand any kind of chance?

Besides, what should I write about? I hadn't a clue,
Apparently the poem should be original, maybe something new.
Whatever the subject that I eventually chose
Surely far greater craftsmen existed in verse, in prose.

Cautiously therefore, I started scribbling down raw ideas.
Without realizing, I was already losing inhibitions, losing fears.
This curled up, overslept imagination was slowly stretching, slowly yawning,
Perhaps the very purpose of it all was also finally dawning!

It's not about first prize or claiming a runner's-up award,
It's the pleasure, the satisfaction of writing, that's the real reward.
It makes no difference whether some of us lose, some of us win,
The important thing's arousing the poet that each of us conceals within.

Michael Prosser

The Mouse That Lives In My House

There is a big mouse that lives in our house,
He is black and white,
But dare pick him up he will probably bite,
He's been there for years now,
But I don't know how,
I'd have thought he'd have moved out by now.
Every night he scurries across our floor boards,
Carrying nuts back and forth,
Mom puts mouse traps round the house,
Trying to catch that elusive big mouse,
No wonder the mouse traps won't succeed,
I take out all the cheese!
Don't tell Mom what I do,
I'd be in deep trouble too.

Joanne Prosser (Age 11)

Hidden Extras?

Dear, adulterous, deceitful liar,
Your spouse and children torn
On every fearful briar
Of the bramble path you tread.
Abandoned;
Bleeding self-worth, respect and trust,
They are caught
Like so much litter in the thorns
As you choose to sacrifice them
On the altar of your utter
Selfishness.
Will you ever perceive the pain you cause,
Each time your vanity thrills
In illicit intercourse?

Christine Pryor

Images of Childhood

Images of Childhood are as books upon a Shelf,
Hidden in the attic of our inner Self.
Some of these books we love to read, and often bring to mind
However, some we hate to read or even try to find.
Some of the happier moments we just love to share and nurture,
There are others that remain untouched lest they influence our future.
To have some happy memories then is envied by so many.
There are a lot of people who really haven't any.
It's thought these lovely images just may have been invented
By people who don't have any, they may often be resented.
Whatever images you hold they are just part of you
They may be hopeful wanderings or very starkly true.
Hang on to happy cheerful things that stand out bright and bold
But don't forget the hurtful ones which may need to be told
Use incidents from near and far to help create just who you are.
Bring forth those memories, sometimes I put them right away.
But treasure any pleasant ones, don't let them go astray.
Use any of your images to give you instant pleasure.
Like those books upon the shelf,
They are your personal treasure.

Jacqueline Pudsey

The Garden

There's a gentle peace in a garden
When the end of a day's work is done
And long before ill thoughts can harden
The intent to forgive has begun.

There's a fertile peace in a garden
With the seedlings all striving to grow
That some will succumb is no bar then
In expecting to reap what you sow.

There's an endless peace in a garden
Every season brings concord to mind
Serenity will ease the burden,
And the answer to problems you'll find.

There's a joyous peace in a garden
With squeals of delight to uplift you
In knowing that happy young children
Are enjoying their childhood anew.

There's a tranquil peace in a garden
When the evening sun has dipped low
And the distant clouds are all golden
And we marvel how quickly days go.

William Austin Pugh

Snow

Silently snow falls during the night,
Changing the world from black to white,
Bringing your face clear to me again
Bringing memories of a day with two alone.

Walking in blizzards holding hands,
Walking on moors, then stopping to stand,
Staring and wondering at a world below us,
Changing from green to white all around us.

Moments that might not return to us both,
Lost in thoughts of only each other
Wonder at nature and her power
Thinking of love growing by the hour.

Where do we go from here was one thought
As we kissed and held each other tight.
Snow blowing, snow falling, snow landing,
The air was cold but warm was our loving.

Standing on the crest of a hill, parting slowly,
Speaking to one another lovingly, quietly.
This picture before me during the night
As I watch the world turning from black to white.

Jan Purdy

Aunt May, Mum and Me

We go to tea on Sunday to Aunt May's, Mum and Me,
She gives us strawberry jam with home made cakes and cups of tea,
She's small and round and rosy and her hands are red and rough,
And she smells of lavender and herbs and all that kind of stuff,
Aunt May was never married but on the fire place is a picture,
Of a soldier with a lovely smiling face,
And when I ask her who it is Aunt May just turns away,
He's just a lad I used to know is all she'll ever say,
She lives alone that is except for Sam her big black cat,
Who seems to spend his lifetime asleep on Aunt May's lap,
He sits there almost smiling curled up upon her knee,
And I have to say move over Sam, come on make room for me,
We sit there by the fire while the flames they dance and leap,
And Aunt May tells me stories till I almost fall asleep,
And when Mum says come on it's time that we were on our way,
I always feel unhappy and I always want to stay,
Aunt May hugs me and I hug her and as we go I say,
Good bye, God bless, I love you, see you next week Auntie May,
She went away last Wednesday although I don't know why,
Cos it's not like Auntie May to go and not even say good bye,
Mum says she's very happy in a special kind of place,
And she's sure she's with her here soldier with the lovely smiling face,
But I know she'll come back to us then just you wait and see,
Will we have fun together, Auntie May and Mum and me.

Margaret Puffett

Rwanda

The millions they trek in the heat of the sun,
While we fly to enjoy our holiday fun.
They scavenge in dirt for food they can eat,
While we dine with friends and people we meet.
Their home is wherever they can lay their head,
Tragically beside loved ones who are dead.

Who will care for these children who cry?
We are too busy, so we'll have to deny.
And enjoy our life with homes full of fun,
While they wander and wonder what they have done,
To deserve such a fate, where nobody cares.
So give them your all and share, just share.
You may save a life and show them you care.
Open your hearts, they'll know someone is there.
If we all give together, the difference will be
The millions of people may be like you and me.

Mrs. M.E. Powell

All Change

My motorbike's broken down Mum,
So I'm going with my mates in the car.
I won't be very late, and we won't be going far.
But that was the last I saw of my tall strong son.
Because the car was crashed by half past one.
And after he lay, so quiet and still,
Many months in his hospital bed
Never to be my son again,
A stranger quite different instead.
He looks the same
He answers his name
But brain damaged the rest of his life,
He never will be my son again
And it tears at my heart like a knife.
His motorbike stands in the pouring rain
And only a mother can know such pain.

Molly Prince

The World

I stand and stare with wondrous eye
At stars like diamonds in the sky
A thousand eyes all twinkling bright
Among the inky black of night
I drift along in timeless space
Staring at the world's mysterious face
And wondering just how small is man
Compared with life's gigantic span.

Audrey Quinn

The Sea of Ice

Unexplored, like a new found country
Still and quiet, like a rabbit being hunted.
Smooth as icing on a cake,
and yet as white as a snowflake.

With white scenery all around,
And yet not a single sound,
A crashing wave crushed cruisers,
Deviously destroying anything it chooses.

Barren, like a deserted town.
Lifeless, not one sign of living around.
Cold, like standing in a freezer.
Only one season called Winter.

Naureen Qureshi

Confines of Freedom

The boy is wandering dazed and confused,
Unsure of his surroundings,
Yet following a map burnt deep in his memory.

Once he played, happy and free
From the rules of the adult world.
Now those constraints lie shattered like the buildings.

He does not cry, the fighting has shocked him
Into a silent world, no music, no laughter.
He does not yet mourn those dead.

He survives on instinct alone,
Hides when the soldiers arrive,
Watches as they rob the bodies.

The boy cannot comprehend the nature of war,
Has no feelings for the country's fears,
No sympathy for his countrymen.
He does not share in the fight for survival
But in time, in time he will.

Lee James Quaggin

Diana Mabel (Drowned 1934)

The smell of the dung filled brook
hung dank and acrid
in the air
when they laid her on the table
beside the baking tins.
Her swollen fists
still clutched
the melted chocolate bar
we had given her
in the morning
when her baby hair
was brushed
so bright and fair.

Doris Palgrave

USA

Sorry, you've caught me in a bit of a state
Though my money system makes sense
People trying to be civil are starting a war
Crafty ingenuitive agents all over
Only representative is Mickey Mouse
Drowning in the Atlantic as the Pacific pushes
With eyes staring from the river
Lost angels gloat over the west
Pets from a reservoir out on video
Uncomfortable stones lurk around eating places
And a log with Christmas leaves on hosts the stars

Sarah Quilliam

Waves

Racing towards the mountainous dunes,
Closing like fuming racing steeds,
They pay credit to the name 'white horses',
Crashing early, they leave their seething foam,
To creep and crawl up the shortening spit of sand,
They suck back taking their share of before unwetted land.

Curling and roaring as they topple forward,
They bend their new head back as though braking hard,
But then in contradiction, the foam lunges forward,
Spreading until its momentum is lost,
It slides back to be met by the next onslaught,
In and out, in and out, in and out come the waves.

Day in, day out, tide in, tide out, never a wave the same,
Far into the distance the horses rear and buck,
Some days they are placid,
Lying low beneath the surface it seems,
The next they are mad, hurling spray to the air,
But always, they come back.

Cameron Queen

Friends

Appreciation of friends not realised,
Their worth only realised in their absence,
Lonely days and nights,
Longing for a return to the past but realising the future to be the only escape,
The realisation of thoughts being the essence of satisfaction in life,
Their return commands celebration in mind and soul,
Their presence now appreciated,
A loss of contact brings friends closer,
The tedium of Life requires the off-loading of heavy burdens,
Their absence weighs heavily on the back of a weak soul,
Protect them in their needs, as they like me, require more than Life can give,
Thank you for their safe return, and guard all those to whom my friendship is given,
Un-deserving, I have been given friends who exceed the bounds of appreciation,
As I weaken may they gain strength,
The long night over, the dawn again returns.

Tim Quick

Dick Turpin

In 18th century England, far away and long ago.
There was a young butcher, whose life would end in woe.
From a humble butcher to a legend he became.
The famous highwayman, Dick Turpin was his name.
He had a pretty horse, its name it was Black Bess.
And everytime he rode her, the people liked him less.
He got in with old Gregory's gang,then with old Bob King.
A hanging at The Mount in York is what his life did bring.

Juliet Pyke

Morning Splendour
(To Jane)

Beautiful red and white roses
Bejewelled with morning dew.
Caught in a ray of sunshine,
Casting a silver hue.

Droplets of dew shed tears
Nature's cultured pearls
These things remind me of your beauty
As this Valentine morn unfurls.

Elusive as the Pimpernel
As beautiful as the Rose.

T.B. Ratcliffe

Reynard From Pusto Wood

This fox was fast, very good at running,
He could run for hours and still be cunning.
But the cry from the hounds was nearer still
They were going to hunt him and then to kill.
They were going to chase him until his blood clogged
On his heart as his brush with mud,
Until his back arched up and his tongue hung flagging
His belly and brush would be filthy from dragging,
He would meet with me, have none for a friend.
He did not want this untimely end.
So he crouched stone still dead, beat and dirty
With nothing but teeth against the thirty.
Then he upped his brush, ran with a will
Straight across Drywoods to Mattersey Hill
Did a u-turn, his mission to fill, sped up the track
To Blaco Hill, hid in the bushes to cool his blood
And away back home to Pusto Wood.

T.W. Redford

My Peter

He kicks your bin
He pulls your flowers
He makes a row for hours and hours
He knocks on your door
He swears in the street
In fact he's a nuisance to all that he meets

You don't like his hair
You don't like his face
And look at his clothes
They're such a disgrace

But please get your facts right
Don't repeat what you hear
It isn't my Peter
'Cos Peter's not here!

Judi Ruddy

Mind Over Matter

The mind is a very complex thing
It can make you cry, or make you sing
Many memories are stored in there,
Plus a wealth of information which we can share.

We can make time stand still whilst searching through the mud
Reliving times and folks who were kind,
Or banish all misery if that be our will
Yes, truly the mind is a complex remarkable thing.

Mrs. M. Radford

Wanting You

Watching you and wanting you
But you never ever look my way.
What can I do to make you care
To make you glance my way and stare
I might as well be invisible, as you just don't see
So I touched you on the shoulder, and you turned, and looked at me.
At last, I understood why you never looked my way.
Your dark, dark eyes told me your world is black night and day
I didn't have to speak, for you know my feelings for you.
And when you touched my hand, I could tell, how you felt too.

Linda Roberts

Untitled

Mother Oh Mother what have we done
The breed of destruction the destroying one
Gone are the trees that once filled this fair land
Now piled brick and mortar in their place does stand
More tarmac, more mortar, more concrete, more glass
Destroying nature so man can have class
Run from your arms mother that's what they do
They'd rather collect things than give love to you
They're not told of you they don't realise
When brainwashed forever to close up their eyes
I pray for them mother, I pray they find light
To tune to you rhythm and dance to it right
To spread health around you, to mend damage done
To walk in your love true oh life giving one
Your soul everlasting touches me from within
Opening pathways where wisdom begins
Oh lady so great to walk your sweet earth
To be free from hate on the wheel of rebirth
I'll strive to teach of your love in rhyme
To help begin a brand new time
When you'll be loved by all so sure
Earth mother you'll rule as queen forever more.

Anton Reddy

The Sanctuary

In the hills and coombes of Devon
The donkey finds its peace,
From hunger, toil and loneliness
And from cruelty release.

"The tattered outlaw of the earth"
Is groomed with brush and comb,
And finds its health and dignity,
But most of all a home.

So face to face with humans
It now gets love and care;
Its sweet and placid nature
Restored for us to share.

The donkey is a blessed beast,
His cross it bears with pride;
A sign for all of us to know
Of him who once did ride.

Philip G. Rawlings-Smith

The Best Is Yet To Be

It's never too late
To do your own thing,
Get out of your rut
And make your life zing.
Don't let your fears
And doubts worry you,
It could be surprising
Just what you can do.
Avoid all the people
Who push you around,
Be firm, resolute
And stand your own ground.
Age is no barrier
I know this true,
Hear wise advice offered
Have confidence in you.
Remember our creator
He loves each one too,
So never feel lonely
He's always with you.
Here's to your new life
I hope you agree,
Each day is for living
THE BEST IS YET TO BE!

Sylvia Reedie

The Dragonfly

A strip of turquoise, shimmering green,
Flits past my window, as yet unseen.
Full of art, full of grace,
You fly past in your endless race.
Veined wings like gauze so fine,
This dragonfly - this creature of utmost design,
Has unfurled itself to my sight,
This helicopter, this King of Flight.

Shagufta Rafique

Remembrance Sunday

When the silence ends and the last post sounds
A lonely soul stirs in his grave,
As he remembers the battles on foreign ground
The screams and the shouts of the brave.
The blood flowed red from the wounded and dead
And endless peace reigned when they died,
Their lives they laid down for country and crown
And the widows at home sat and cried.

Margaret Robertson

The Loneliness of the Old

Loneliness is a distant cry unheard,
That flutters in a singular room,
And speaks but not with spoken word,
And listens, hearing naught but gloom.

Loneliness is a longed for friend,
A glimpse of hope amidst the night,
But like the spark the fire did send,
A tinge of temporary light.

Loneliness is a moment often pondered,
In nostalgic scenes and seasons past,
When others were the ones who wondered,
And you thought that your youth would last!

David Reavely

True Love

When first you flashed those eyes of blue
That's when I fell in love with you
Your eyes looked so big and bright
That I fell in love at first sight
You smiled at me for the first time
And I heard bells begin to chime
Your smile is like the rising sun
Your eyes reflect your feeling of fun
Your nose turns up at the end
Any broken heart it can mend
It is so cute and just suits you
No wonder my love is so true
Your hair is the golden colour of corn
Swaying in the breeze of the early morn
Like spun gold at the end of the day
When the hues of the setting sun do play
I really am a hopeless case
I just have to look at your face
With the first look the die was cast
This was true love at last
It will endure for the rest of my life
Though I could never be your wife
I am your granny, my boy bold
And you are not yet one year old

Margaret C. Rae

Words In Poems

Words in poems, rocks in pools,
brick walls round gardens, yards, green
places where children play, all
these uphold the substance and

the vigour of fish swimming jamjar
style, won at a fair by a boy who's
skiving from school; milk bottles
whistled to your step, letters, earth

scraped flat for a workshop floor, each
carries the strength of fruit preserved
in pots and the echo of a voice in a cave
hollowed first by a prehistoric sea ...

a lamp turned on in an attic where
pictures hang with webs and the silver
is wrapped in silk, a clenched fist
ready to open up a secret, a dab

of scent on the wrist, illustrate
the spot in the glade of a forest
untouched by man, where pines
chill shade and the springs rise

quickly for the taps of a house
that the valley harbours safe
as a boat on the homeland shore ...
Words in poems, rocks in pools.

Annabelle Rankin

Horsey Pals

Murphy, mi pal ye'r gettin aul, a bittie like masel,
Aat's the geese fleein ower, anither winter, seen be feedin fae the pail,
I ken yer legs is whiles sair, an ye'r nae sae prone tae gallop,
Bit, Na! ye ken dampt fine, ye'l niver get a wallop,
Seen be a score o years that we'v gaed aboot thgaither,
Yokett in the bonny gig, prancin in fine sunny weather,
An you showin aff, wi ye'r dancin doon the street,
An masel, sittin sae prood in the drivin seat,
Bit, come the neist fine day, an it's nae like tae be some rain,
We'l maybe get aa yokett, an dae it aa over again,

Ae, ye ken jist fine, errs a sweetie in mi pooch,
God-al-michty, Murphy, ye'r still a bloody mooch,
I ken ye like yer sweeties, aboot aat I winna yell,
Ye'v fairly gotten a sweet tooth, a bittie like masel,
Noo, awa inside o yer hoosie, an keep oot o the caul,
Cos you an me thgaither, are baith ower bloody aul.!

Mary Rayne

Fingers And Thumbs

I'm man's best friend and intelligent too
But there's so many things I find I can't do
I can't hammer a nail or turn a screw
Oh, I wish I had fingers and thumbs like you

When I practice hygiene on my parts down south
I have to use the tongue in my mouth
You find this disgusting, for you that's quite true
But I haven't got fingers and thumbs like you

I can't bend down and pick up a pin
I can't eat my food until you open the tin
And everyday you invent something that's new
Oh, I wish I had fingers and thumbs like you

But I'm having doubts and wonder of late
Does the way you are going make inventing so great
And would I follow the same path too
If I had fingers and thumbs like you?

When you invented arrows and guns and knives
You invented orphans and made widows of wives
And that unknown soldier who someone once knew
Didn't he have fingers and thumbs like you?

But I'm still you friend and always will be
Although I don't understand what binds you to me
But I thank my God and I wish you knew
That I'm glad I've no fingers and thumbs like you

W.G. Ralph

The River

Flowing river, timeless river,
Take my thoughts down to the sea;
Wash them in the endless ocean,
Then return them fresh to me.
Cleanse my mind of wars and hatred,
Violence and suffering;
Let them vanish, leave no traces,
Let the doves of peace take wing.
As I stand and watch the river,
Pleasuring in it's constancy,
The world is fighting, starving, dying,
Always chained, and never free.
As the river flows, it carries
Waste from forest, field and plain;
Take as well men's thoughts of evil,
Make them pause, and think again.
Let all trouble flow within you,
Rid the world of endless pain;
Then we'd be each other's brother,
Thus to be re-born again.
Then we'll throw away our weapons,
All our means of waging war;
Mankind shall stand beside the river,
Hand in hand, for evermore.

Anne Redshaw

The Family

The memories shared of happy days,
The sadness and the tears.
The laughter, love and special thoughts,
Which join us through the years.

The older generations,
Who sadly have to go.
The new, such tiny babies,
How we welcome and love them so.

The Christmases, the birthdays,
Christenings, weddings too,
The holidays, shared jokes and fun,
Happy days which simply flew.

The special bonds which bind us all,
The affection which goes so deep.
Children who suddenly grow so tall,
And the sentimental weep.

The family's always changing,
But somehow stays the same,
Grandparents, parents, siblings,
Loved by whatever name.

Remember now to tell them,
Please don't make them wait.
How very much you care for them,
Before it is too late.

Heather Rayner

Nature's Beauty

To stroll across a Wiltshire down,
Far from the grime and dust of town,
A dewdrop on an wild rose see,
Here nature's beauty I perceive.

To hear the ripple of ripening corn,
When on a gentle breeze is born,
Golden ears like waved conceive,
Here nature's beauty I perceive.

The skylark high sings his merry song,
Then dives to feed his hungry throng,
A squirrel through the trees does weave,
Here nature's beauty I perceive.

As newborn lambs gambol in play,
The rabbits watch, then run away,
Then mothers come, their lambs retrieve,
Here nature's beauty I perceive.

Nature's sounds and nature's peace,
From the cares of the world release,
Then with the falling shadows I must leave,
Nature's beauty that I perceive.

Levire

Mischief

Peace reigns at last for a short while
Eyes wait anxiously for that big smile
Tiny limbs rest so comfy and snug
Before the onslaught of the toys on the rug

Eyelids fluttering from the land of dreams
Body recharged with more energy to scheme
It defies all logic that someone so small
Can sustain such vitality to out-run us all

Inquisitive fingers explore all within reach
Best hide the trinkets and the sink bleach
No malice is ever intended, and yet
The outcome of some escapades makes one fret

Plants in the garden cringe and dig deep
Hoping their roots will hold them this week
Watch for the spade to launch them afar
And beware of the impact from the toy car

The impish laugh that keeps the world right
The soft purring sound of an infant at night
The smell of a new-born babe on one's arm
Just how can anyone wish a child harm?

Maureen Rawlings

Halloween

George was going home very drunk,
Worried what his wife would say,
God! She wasn't a pleasant woman, even on a sober day,
She grat and niggled from morning till night,
It's not much wonder his head felt not right,
To save a bittie of time, and try to keep her quiet,
He cut straight through the graveyard
Ghosts? No, he just didn't buy it!
Stories of bloody hands clutching daggers
And demons rising out of the ground,
It all went through George's brain
Fun was not to be found,
And then there rose, in sight of him
A creation in hot breath, horns an' smoke,
A bloody business like wicked dreams
Witchcraft, an' murder of good folk,
His red eyes gleamed and blazed,
From his mouth he spewed out fire,
An' snarled to George, "I am Satan,
Of eating folk I never tire!"
George, he blinked his owlet eyes,
With face beginning to blister,
An' said, "Man, I'm pleased to meet you,
I'm married to your Sister!"

Sandy Rayne

When I Was Very Young

When I think back to my childhood days,
When I was very young,
We used to go down to the beach
And enjoy the sand and the sun.

We used to wait til the tide went out,
And climbed out over the rocks.
We caught a lobster with our cleek
and cooked it in one of mum's pots.

It tasted really lovely,
And we thought it was so grand.
Sometimes I wish I was young again,
To build castles in the sand.

We used to climb Macduff Castle,
And rummage round about.
But in half an hour os so,
Mum and dad would shout.

Come down from there, you silly kids,
Before you have a fall.
So down we came to mum and dad,
And clambered over the wall.

I used to fall asleep at night,
And dream of all we had done.
And I want to let everyone know,
We really had a lot of fun.

Janet Rennie

Fulfillment

Flowers for the living and flowers for the dead,
A situation I must have misread.
Why did she have to die, the best friend I ever had?
Our times were so happy, but life can be sad.
There must be a reason, some reason to live,
I'm seeking fulfillment and try to relive.
I have to be happy, and must not despair.
The one thing I believe in, I always will care.

Dean Edward Ragis

Running Free

Down in the city streets the old lady walks alone,
Leaning heavily on her stick, hurrying to get home,
Up fifteen floors lies a beaten wife,
Her husband, drunk again, she has no life.

A young girl sleeps uneasy without the security of home,
Dreaming of street devils, she dare not answer the phone,
Out in the back streets beneath the little red light
A fourteen year old scruffy kid canvasses throughout the night.

But I am different, I left school
To ride with my new brothers, to keep a different rule.
In gully ways and stations, that is where I'll be,
Running through the city streets, running wild, running free.

Mrs. G. Richards

It Kills

Hey, I bet you've heard about it,
It's the latest craze.
It hurts you and everyone around you
it makes you mad and then it'll makeyou cry,
and sooner or later it'll make you die.
You're climing a hole that's way too steep,
and when you cry for help you'll be in too deep.
It ain't too late you gotta stop now,
or later on you'll wonder how!
Your life is going to be turned upsidedown.
You are using up your time.
                    IT KILLS!
Later on, when you're at death's door
you'll wonder what it was all for.
Please be listening, my words have reasoning.
Taking drugs ain't fun. So many have died because of it.
Think about your family.
Taking drugs ain't the easy way out.
                    CALL HELP

Beth Revell (Age 11)

The Family

Father, this I know for sure
We are all one family,
Doesn't matter if we're black
Doesn't matter if we're white.

For I know that you are true.
Every day in all our lives.
In this one earth that we live
We do know that we are one.

When we play or when we work
We do know that this is true.
Me and you are one family
For our God is good to us.

Diane Elizabeth Ruston (Age 11)

High Summer

He mounted the farm gate
The summer smelling blood and gold
And stared across the worked fields
Staked out between the hedgerows.
He stretched along the furrows
Feet to the distance
Listening to the old, old land.
Watched a magpie, coming for his soul.

J.G. Reynolds

Questions of Longing

What will I do when you're not here
How will I feel when we're apart
Where can I find that special love
To fill the emptiness in my heart.

To whom will I owe my allegiance
And where can I spend lonesome hours
With who's heart may I share all my secrets
To whom can I send special flowers.

Who's name will I speak on awakening
Who's body will I long to be near
Who's face will I see full of laughter
In the morning ... when you're not here.

My God ... how I'll miss you my dearest,
It is you that I do idolize
When you're gone ... I'll only have memories
And maybe some tears in my eyes.

James A. Ryan

My Dream

My name is Garry Reynolds, I'm just a wee boy yet,
But I had a dream the other night,
I never will forget.
I had signed for Manchester United and I was their newest find
Just flown in from Northern Ireland , fresh on everybody's mind.

Old Trafford was just wonderful, so big and green and vast
As I ran on that football field says I, "I'm here at last"
I heard the cheers ring in my ears for the newest Irish Rover
Achieving my ambition, now my wandering days are over.

On that pitch for the first time I was in it heart and soul
And just when my team needed it, sure I went and scored a goal
They chaired me off that football pitch
Among the cheers and laughs
And I was dizzy afterwards just signing autographs.

Well, as I said at the beginning, I'm just a wee boy still,
But I have that dream, that lovely dream and I think I always will
\And stranger things have happened, who knows what is to be
Perhaps I'll get to Wembley yet, I'll just wait here and see.

Garry Reynolds

The Haunted Cathedral

The ancient walls now stand alone
With glassless windows framed in stone,
And roofless arches rising high
In silhouette against the sky.

But what is this? The moonlight fades,
The grass-floored aisle is filled with shades.
A white-robed choir begins to sing
A chant in praise of Christ the King.

Am I awake? Or do I sleep?
And why do all these people weep?
Is that a coffin carried in
To be sent forth, absolved from sin?

The service draws near to its close,
A soul is seeking for repose.
The priest intones "Go forth in peace,
From all you sins you've gained release."

The music fades, the scene grows dim,
A cloud unveils the full moon's rim
Which starts to light the empty space ...
For the mourners there's no trace.

Lionel Reid

The New Lifeboat

A scowling Landlord stared at me
As I approached the bar
"Yes," he said with solemn face,
"Have you come from afar?"

Ah, an ex-naval man thought I
He's bound to help a little
After all he understands the sea
And how it can be so fickle

I stood there with sponsor form
Held tightly in my hand
"In aid of the New Lifeboat" I said,
"Would you care to lend a hand?"

But alas my words were all in vain
As they fell on stony ears
He had only one thought in mind
To fill his shelf with beers.

So take heed you would be supporters
And choose your sponsors with care
Men like these are hard to find
Thank God they are very rare.

Mrs. J.E. Roberts

Boredom

A restless mind flits and flies from thought to thought,
And from thought to action, then back to thought again,
It seizes opportunity of quenching its unceasing thirst for fulfillment,
Then casts it off as the longing changes its course.

The aching hands fidget with boredom,
And freely show their feelings through the tap-tapping on the table top,
They slink and glide across the surface,
Trying to suppress each rising emotion.

The heart beats loudly, consistently, insistently,
A hot sweat breaks out on the tightly drawn face,
Each nerve trembles from head to toe,
Fighting the fatigue which plagues the brain.

Empty vessels, once of blood, explode into the gloom of nothingness,
Nothing can crush the rising volcanic surge of frustration
Which melts all forms of possibility and drowns the soul,
Diluting hope, inspiration and lust for achievement.
Boredom is all:
Gripping, biting, chewing.

Heather Render

Photo Shoot

A woman stripped bare
who cares?
Men come and position her
for the benefit of the camera
From forced grin to spread thighs
the camera never lies
Crude objects strategically placed
amidst the leather whips and lace
Her image used solely for pleasure
for them to pour over at their leisure
If the photographer's hands wander too much
has she the right to refuse his touch?
After all, she belongs to him his object
he can do whatever he wants with his subject
If it takes her degradation to leave him pleased
she is forced down like a dog, to her knees
Why in the pursuit of this unattainable fame
do they have to partake in this sickening game?
There's a queue round the block willing to pay
enough meat to last for many more days
Another woman stripped bare
who cares?

Michelle Jessie Raeburn

Tribute to Padstow Lifeboatmen

The winds they howl,
The winds they roar,
As the waves remorselessly
Pound the shore.
Away out there
Across the sky,
A rocket's flare, shines on high.
A foghorn moans, as if in despair
To try and warn those out there.
The lighthouses' flash for all to see,
Not by man's hand, it's electricity.
Through the gloom and spume
A light appears,
Bringing help to those in fear.
As the lifeboat rushes from the land
At its helm is a man named "England"
He and his crew, oh! so brave
Risk their lives for others to be saved.
The peril is over,
All are safe on dry land,
Thanks to the crew, and their coxswain, "England".

Mrs. D. Richards

In The Beginning

Are we carved from the Tree of Life?
Are individuals branches and roots?
Did the touch of the Master Carver make us wake?
Can we compare sap to blood?
Are our hearts flesh or wood?
The wind whispers and leaves listen,
The grain is the pattern - the way we should take.

Are we merely tossed on the ocean?
Soul, mind, body and pure emotion?
Did the Trident of Neptune stir us in the Primal Sea?
The colour, depth, waves and the force
Our souls ride free on a white horse.
Silent surface - shimmer of moonshine,
Lunar motion - tidal response: one more link for you and me.

Are we part of the continuum of space,
Where souls shall blend from the Human Race?
Did the One intend that we should die alone?
Life is waiting in starry, black hollow,
The Universe beckons - souls will follow.
Realm of beauty beyond belief.
The quest is over - peace in reunion - we are Home!

Sue Roberts

Tolerance

Children playing together
All white but one,
A little black boy
Accepted as he is:
The innocence of children.

The same boy,
Older now,
Tormented by those who know no better,
Ridiculed because he's black:
The ignorance of youth.

He's left school now
Looking for work,
"Sorry, we don't employ blacks"
Always the same reply:
The narrow-mindedness of men.

In later life
(He's married and settled)
He has friends — though few,
The rest are indifferent:
Tolerance?

Jill Riley

A Chance To Die

Searching for survival, reaching for a hand
The victims are afeared as armies storm their land.
Men and women cluster, diseased of moral pride
They're searching for their freedom, yet know they cannot hide.

Violent, evil soldiers, from these killers they have fled
Desperate search for honor, morale's already dead.
Prisoners don't get taken, their bodies crucified
Storming for their safety, thousands tried and died.

These men they have no reason, they're doing it for lust
They cannot stay afar from the abyss of truth and trust.
They're killing for their country, their honour, pride and hate.
Failure's not an option as the victims face their fate.

You're running through the darkness, footsteps all around
Screaming fills the moonlight, bodies fill the ground.
Trudging over corpses you hear a bitter cry
The soldiers, they surround you, you're given a chance to die.

Dying for religion, dying for belief,
Shooting, burning, crying, kick back in the teeth.
The men they fire their shots, the evil deed is done,
The bodies drop so quickly - there's nowhere else to run.

The screams they filled the air, a-crying and a-dying.
The sadist soldiers fled, their lying and defying.
The tranquil air is silent - the night-time strangely cold
Families mourn their loved ones - the dead, so brave and bold.

Colin J. Richardson

Rare Visitor

The other sunday afternoon
To old Wainfleet we went
To see a lovely snowy owl
Was our main intent.

Down the lane, just past a house
Along the dyke we stole,
Keeping quiet as a mouse
That rests within its hole.

Then nearing other watchers, who
Had been there quite a while
We spotted him upon a bank
As he sat there in style.

Someone said, "Look through my scope"
It was a lovely sight
To see him close, too much to hope
With plumage snowy white.

This beauteous bird has come from afar
To grace our Lincolnshire land,
T'was privilege great to see him there
In majestic beauty grand.

He seemed to lap up all the fuss,
And sat so still and calm,
I think he waited just for us
May no one do him harm.

Rhoda Roberts

Dying World

There's beauty for us everywhere if we will only look.
In flowers and trees and sandy shores
Sunlight dancing on a rippling brook.
The miracles of nature all around us
Are there for those of us with eyes to see,
But so many rush around and never notice
The loveliness of new buds on a tree.
Can we really be so very busy
We have not time to simply stand and stare?
To appreciate the wonders that surround us,
Or is our load so heavy we don't care?
It saddens me, the acid rain, pollution and the rest,
The desecration of our planet is a sin.
It has to stop so all of us must do our best
To make our world a good place to live in.
Let our children inherit it with pleasure and with pride
Regard its keeping a sacred duty,
So its rivers and its forests and every mountainside
May be protected and preserved in all their beauty.
Make time to see and hear, enjoy every lovely thing.
Discover for yourself the serenity they bring.

Edna Ridge

Emily Jane

Emily Jane, a little dot and your Life began
The love of your parents you were part of a plan
Each day you grew a little bigger
Alongside your Mother's figure.
Sick and tired, feeling weary
But always thinking very clearly.
Hoping and praying everyday
You would be normal in every way
Your Mum and Dad anxious and fearful
Sometimes beyond them making them tearful.
The day arrived for you to join them
Your Mum was asleep, you were a Caesarian
Although your Mum slept, her heart was full of love
Waiting to hold her miracle sent from God above
No one knew what you were to be
A game of waiting and longing to see
Your Grandmas and Grandads, Uncles and Aunts
Great-Grandparents, Great-Aunts waiting to glance
Nine minutes to three 'Welcome *our* little Baby Emily'
Welcome to the world and all your family
A beautiful girl, nine whole months we waited for you
Perfect in every way, again to God we say 'Thank-you!'
Emily Jane my precious Great-niece
I wish you always health, happiness and peace.

Elaine A. Brocklesby

Untitled

Only knowing when to die, could ease my living
And only then if it came early.
If I knew that there were no tomorrow,
Then surely I'd enjoy today.
I doubt it, for even happiness brings me sorrow.

Stephen G. Rymell

Promise Of Spring

The daffodils in glory stood
Around the border of the wood
Heads held high
To the morning sky
Clothed in green
Their heads so clean
Rose proudly from their regal dress
Sunshine kissed and dewy fresh
Rusty brown the buds dried husk
Beauty bore, before the dusk
Living, laughing, loving light,
Golden trumpets open bright
Glorious daffodils' short-lived youth
Telling the world their message of truth
Promise of Spring
And Summer to bring
Glory to us and everything

Gwen Robbins

Dreaming

Last night as I lay sleeping,
tucked up in my bed.
I began a dreaming, strange
thought's filled my head.
The snow was falling softly
and covering the ground.
Coming from the distance
I heard the sweetest sound.
The sound was children singing
around the Christmas tree.
While stars above were twinkling
a wondrous sight to see.
Then along came Santa, his gift's
were a delight.
For he bought love and peace to
earth, on that Christmas night.
But that was only dreaming, I wish it
could come true.
My Christmas present to the world,
with love from me to you.

Muriel Richards

The Ride To Dent

The question was, where shall we go?
Said the driver member of our family trio.
Being asked, and given the choice,
I thought of a road I knew — agreed — that's just what we'll do.

Remembrance being rather hazy, our number one member had a map.
Our number 2 member said "It's crazy" — nursing instructions on her lap
Very soon, number 3 member began to have a doubt,
Murmuring, quietly at first, "I can't see the tower used for looking out".

The narrow road started to climb —
We three saw the gate, thinking — it takes a little time —

Meeting a cyclist, we had to wait.
Bikers ahead, in twos and threes
Tackling this steep ascent, each side, instead of trees
The earth in half was rent.

Emerging round the curve of road, a sign warned —
One-in-four — anxiety, and prayers bestowed.

Descending — eyes closed as before — sensation of flying at this point
As down and down we sped; fear and cramp in ever joint —

However full confidence in our number one with nerves of polished steel.
The road only inches wider - another bend reveals a sign
Which said "Dent" ahead, with hillside farms each side.

We three in the game decided there and then —
No repeat performance;
Concluding "Never again"

Iris Robertson

Through The Window

Little spiky hedgehog, running on the lawn
Seeking food and titbits, in the early dawn
Lapping at the morning dew as you hunt for bugs
Scurrying tiny insects, slow and slimy slugs.

Dark and bright eyed blackbird
And the splendid spotted thrush
A sly and sneaky tabby cat
Hiding behind the bush.

Starlings fighting sparrows
Over the stale and mouldy bread
A beautiful little robin
With his chest so red.

A fat and ugly spider working on his web
Midges playing hopscotch on the tiny ponds ebb
Busy queen bumblebee, buzzing to a fro
Step into the garden and watch them up and go!

K. Riley

Summer's Wake

When sunrise turns back night's black cloth in folds
the day wakes up in pastel shades of blue
The crests of smoky hills are burnished gold
and birds silenced by night from treetops flew
The burning azure skies are edged with peach
as summer's blazing eye surveys our earth
And then those joyous birds' crescendoes reach
in celebration of this season's birth
The musky scent of grass and fragrant flowers
that nod themselves to sleep by dappled lanes
pervades the breeze that loosens blossom showers
from cherry trees still lush with springtime rains
And droning bees like music notes do bound
between the wavering staves of tall bluebells
The sinking sun brings dusk and keener sounds
as silence breathes a sigh on moon-kissed fells
And although wakened summer slumbers now
new dawn will soon be on horizon's brow.

Scott Richardson

They Keep Mything

There is this wild haggis, he's Hamish by name
By nature he's reclusive and not very tame.
He lives on the hillside and feeds with the sheep;
Likes munching the heather, and needs little sleep.

In winter the hunter comes out with his gun
But Hamish is cunning and man can he run.
His right leg is longer than the other and so,
Swiftly round mountains anti-clockwise can go.

He's just a round blur as he speeds round the hill
And the hunter keeps missing for he never stands still.
He looks very smart in his plaid and his kilt
And his voice though not Gaelic has broad highland lilt.

However, should you meet him at a social event
You'll find on survival he's very intent;
But his eyes become steely and you'll get seriously attacked
If you say that he's fiction instead of a fact.

David Robb

... The Voice of Nature Cries

Mrs. Rabbit in her burrow prepares her bunnies tea,
Complains the taste of lettuce is not as it used to be.
Blames pesticides, atomic dust, falling acid rain,
She can't change their staple diet, though health is on the wane.

Mr. Rat and Mr. Vole survey the river bank,
Once a pleasant spot to live, now odorous and dank.
Industrial foam, tin cans, dead fish, all go floating by,
To swim is now a hazard — they wish that they could fly!

"Not so," declares a bird family, slowly flying past,
"We're looking for a nesting site, but hedgerows vanish fast.
We thought we'd move near to the sea, until alas, we saw
Oil coated seabird cousins dying needlessly on the shore."

Once, out in the farmyard, hens could peck and freely range,
Now battery concentration camps, for most a sorry change.
Immobile, caged, condemned to lay, but when the eggs are few,
Another fate awaits — poor tiny, fluffy chicks — they grew!

We love Nature's smaller creatures and we bemoan their lot,
But even large and powerful ones are likely to get shot.
The lumbering elephant only slain for tusks of ivory,
Its size can't help the mighty whale when harpooned in the sea.

I've written for the animals, their woes they cannot tell,
Whilst in our Third World countries the suffering poor must dwell.
We must use our strength and purpose; we'll have ourselves to blame,
If we leave an awesome legacy — to our everlasting shame.

Doreen E. Roberts

Phantom Thoughts

Beware the phantom
thoughts of night,
So clear so bold
so true so bright,
But torn to shreds by
cruel light of day,
Pure thought but etched
in dreams that gently
fade away, away, away.

And bereft of dreams
the thought no longer
endures the mind,
Therefore cast out to
fade, or flourish if only
fate would be so kind,
So beware the phantom
thoughts of night,
So clear, so bold
so true, so bright.

J.R. Richardson

A Lady in Distress

You have paid me a visit
And depressed my flush
Now please don't depart
In such a rush.

Spare one more minute
And listen until
You're sure you can hear
My tank refill.

More often than not
It doesn't and so
The next time I'm used
My flush won't flow.

My ballcock gets stuck
And so I'm afraid
My tank remains empty
And I need first aid.

The treatment is simple
Though not very thrilling
Just wiggle my handle
'Til you hear my tank filling.

Don't deny me this help
I'm depending on you
And I'll always be grateful
Yours sincerely — The Loo

Sandra E. Ronson

Old Pwllygarth

Oh how I dream of bygone days, of the street where I was born.
Elderly people sat by their doors, in old Pwllygarth and watched the children at play.
Children would roam the fields, and play safe by night and day.
We skipped and played games galore, as children did years before.
Safe in our world without fear.
People had time to stop and chat, and sometimes joined in our games.
Front doors where always open in old Pwllygarth
Old and young welcome in every domain.
Street parties were held, we had such fun.
Jellies and cakes made by everyone.
My childhood dreams of bygone days,
Of old Pwllygarth, nicknamed the bay.
Money was short, work was hard, men worked long hours for their pay
No carpets on floors, women scrubbed and toiled, but home,
Was our haven, come what may.
Now! No open doors in old Pwllygarth, no elderly people sit by their doors.
Children no longer roam the fields, to pick wild flowers as we did in our teens.
So thank you Lord for my childhood dreams.

Sylvia Roberts

English Language

Whatever became of our spoken word
When Americanisms were seldom heard
Instead of "Hello, how are you?", it's "Hi"
And everyone speaks of a man as a 'guy'.
It's becoming the norm for someone to say
"So long" and "Hey, have a nice day"
And now to the pictures a 'movie' we see
With popcorn and gum, no more ice cream
'Sneakers' not plimsoles or pumps on our feet
A 'walkway' for pavement on avenue or street
Hamburgers, fries, what happened to chips?
Pieces of celery put into dips
It's muffins in teashops, not just a cake
And candy and cookies, for goodness sake.
Where's all our own vocabulary gone?
Our nice way of speaking, a way of our own
Why do we have to copy the Yanks?
No way! We are British, just say "No Thanks!"

Jan Roberts

The Daily Memory

We laugh at you when you talk to yourself
And make fun of your ill health
Yet you stumble on wheeling your old bike
Taking as much time as you like
We talk about you behind your back
While you deliver papers from that old news rack
You live alone and you'll die alone
Probably in that dirty place you call you home
Yet you savour each moment as you walk by
As if to each letterbox you say good-bye
You fumble with each paper to fold it neatly
And then push it through the letterbox weakly
Maybe each paper is a dream or a thought
Of times that were happy of things that where bought
For the wife that you loved, a rose bush or two
Primroses, a lilac, and forget-me-nots blue
Time took her away and you're waiting alone
With your papers each memory gets a new home
Until you're together.

Natasha Ritchie

Echoes From The Past

Ancient forests; mist curling many fingered through the trees;
Dark leaves, moisture pearled, hang flaccid in the lifeless dawn.
Strange whispers, the scent of danger, dry leaves rustling in a sudden breeze.
Sharp eyes piercing opaque veils drifting silent over steamy marsh.
Senses probing; dark and secret hollows trailing tendrils of unease.
Silence broods, no bird is singing, no joyful call to rend the air
Just the dank smell of rotting vegetation, and moisture dripping from the trees.

Is racial memory, then, so strong that on an autumn stroll today
I feel the ghosts of ancient fears that linger still, relics of our past?
And what for me is self-indulgence, mere imaginative play,
Was felt in deadly earnest by our ancestors who walked this way.

Sheila Rolls

The Call

Waiting for your call.
Coffee cups, plates and my face
need a wash,
and the cat's peed in the hall.
Beds to make,
Cakes to bake,
Blank faced, I just stare at the wall.
Brain and limbs refuse to function at all.
And soon (I'm sure) the phone will ring
And I'll spring to my feet
And greet you, with the first
smile of my day.
And feel you smile at me
from your world,
Where now you can be, and do, and see
'Cause you've spoken to me.

Janet Roberts

Time

Time is precious, do not waste it,
Use it wisely every day.
Make each moment count for something,
As you go along Life's way.

Time is precious, gentle traveller,
Let it take you by the hand.
Help to take you on your journey,
Through this green and pleasant land.

Time is precious, so be happy,
Make each day a pleasant one.
Leave behind your love and laughter,
When your time on Earth is done.

Helen Roberts

Earthache

I am a mountain where streams rippled in Spring.
    Rebuild my ruins.
I am a forest where birds used to sing.
    Heal my wounds.
I am a river and I once flowed with pride.
    Tend to my sores.
I am an ocean across a mighty divide.
    Cleanse my shores.
I am a landscape where flowers bloomed so proud.
    Erase my scars.
I am a desert now shrouded in cloud.
    Let me see the stars.
I am the past and the future of Earth.
    Nature created me.
I am a Planet. What is my worth?
    What is my destiny?

Theresa Rafferty

Moonbathing

When the sky is like crushed velvet,
The colour of deep blue sea.
Then the moon has power over the earth,
And night time has unlocked its key.

I spy two earthly beings,
Laying among the grass.
Taking in the wonder of darkness,
The varying blue mass.

A time to gather thoughts,
Think deeply about life,
Because there's no stress in moonbathing,
Unlike living on the edge of society's knife.

Perfect peace and tranquility,
At harmony with fellow man.
Moonbathing; the perfect hobby.
I do it as often as I can.

Elizabeth Rice

Monday Blues

Oh what's that noise, oh can it be, my mother's voice a-calling me?
"Come on get up, you sleepy head, it's a quarter past seven, get out of bed."
"Oh mammy, let me stay awhile, I can't get up, I want to lie";
But does she falter? Not one bit, "Come on miss, get out of it".
She never tires, and will not quit, until within the car I sit;
Then off to school, where I will be free from all my misery,
where Monday blues will fade away, for I love school, on any day.

Helen Reynolds

One Day

One day you will wake up to find
that all the stars have fallen
from the skies and lay on your pillow.
Wipe your eyes and find
that your tears have been stolen
and placed in the velvety skies above.
Your smiles shall replace the sun;
your sorrows replace the moon;
the whispering winds your only breath;
the flickering flame you soul;
the smoke on the hills your memories;
the caressing sea your blood beating heart;
the baby's cry your dying song.
Then on this day, hold high your death
so that life might not
creep up and steal it.

Gillian Robson

A Mother's Blues

I'm full of love, and very proud
as every mom should be
but sometimes as if to spoil it all
darkness folds around me.
Perhaps if I could just explain
what it feels like to be
deep down inside this hopeless void
unable to get free.
I love my babies very much
and all of me I'll give
that they can grow wise and strong
as they learn to live.
I hope and pray that as they grow
and adults they become
I'll be the woman I once was
not just the children's mom.

Mrs. Sandra Robinson

Release

Here I sit in my lonely room,
Awaiting my impending doom
Surprisingly, I know not fear
Having lost all that I hold dear.
Soon I will take my final breath,
To find the peace there is in death.

Once I thought I had it all,
For you to come I need only call.
But sadly you have passed away,
Was it really only yesterday?
Together again with my final breath
We'll find the peace there is in death.

We laughed and cried through good and bad,
But no regrets — I am not sad,
The next world waits — I'm on my way,
Tomorrow is not another day.
As now I take my final breath,
To find the peace there is in death.

J. Rickard

The Rowan Tree

Standing lonely looking upward
Thinking of the sunny spring
When next year I'll stand much stronger
Glory forward — harvest dream.

Birds don't give me time to cherish
All the berries of my life
In the town I grow and flourish
Seed of birds so — dropped in strife.

Honour loved my life in country
Cherished much by sun alone.
Wind and rain help me grow stronger
Rowan green with beauty sewn.

Drop the berries small wee brown bird
Drop it were it will be seen
By God's clever way of making
Tall and lovely Rowan's green.

Anne Robson

Untitled

Denzil Morrison loves this land, pays his way and makes a stand.
He wants for nought his nest egg gone, booze cigs and drugs too, giro heaven,
So much for the few. Spirals of vapour in our forties sky mock on high
And frame the lie. Roll on through, heroine, crack, cocaine grow your own and smoke a few.
Peerless war, heroes homes, forgotten and gone, a bad joke.
Denzil drones his thin lament from the stage of flat cement,
Caught in the trap below the line, cardboard box for you next time.
Beg for Britain, re-locate get on your bike, circumnavigate.
Divide and conquer, pay and play, lose your will anyway.
D.H.S.S. turns water into wine, a miracle sign, water into cash, a financial splash.
Dam the system, damn the man, another term is the plan.
The horseman's wait is nearly done, his horizon hides the nuclear sun.
Streets are scourged and clean Denzil's gone and so has Jane.
We happy band we five percent will own the place, as it was meant.

Peter Rothwell-Frear

The Old Tin Bath (1930's & '40's)

The old tin bath hung on the outside wall,
in a corner, right out of the way,
Its presence no one really noticed,
'Til it was required, every Friday.

Then it was carefully brought indoors,
with lots of newspapers under to protect the floor,
It was then wiped clean 'til it gleamed like silver,
with the firelight flickering on it like golden slivers.

Lots of hot water would then be brought,
to fill up the tin bath, from the copper,
and a huge bucket of water stood at the side,
in case the bather needed it hotter.

Around the bath was put the wooden clothes horse,
with the towels draped to afford some privacy,
and one could bathe in comfort by the fire,
without intrusion on one's intimacy.

After the ablutions the old tin bath,
had to be emptied and cleaned,
then hung up again in its corner plot,
where it shone like a shilling and gleamed.

Friday night was a bath night,
a regular ritual at that,
but although it was always a horrible chore,
we miss, the fun in the old tin bath.

Joy Robinson-Judd

Mothers

I wander alone, awash in sorrow
    Below, God's flowers breathe in sleep,
Today, will become tomorrow
    People will still laugh and weep.

Their world is blessed and tranquil,
    No tears to shed for living,
No fearful cries to pierce the will,
    Of a mother's desirous loving.

In every man, a mother cries,
    In every seed, a thirst for growing
The infant souls, devoid of lies,
    Baptised in the Elysian sowing.

Ages pass, the mind profound
    Dead winds caress the graves,
On Earth — but mendacious evil sounds,
    Victory will sleep, in us the brave.

Today, on the streets of Aberfan,
    In every face I see,
The deluged morning, of moving land
    Forever forged — in eyes to weep.

The shimmering stars of timeless light,
    Who kiss the white sentinel stones,
Their kith and kin in life entwined
    Look down, on flowers immune to blight.

Robert Rowland

The Ghosts of Summer

Acolytes' passage repass the midsummer shadows of hallways, through which the
Spirits of Sunshine have Trodden, bearing
Tokens of Tea to blazing green lawns;
the cup of happiness and the cakes of fruition.
The Ghosts of cooler bowers, Supine within
dreaming alcoves, where Sentinels of mechanistic and celestial Time maintain their
crystalline Rhythm for the heart of our
Tomorrows.
Gyrating wells of Solar gold kiss the Oak of
both parquet and panel, mayflies cavort
within and without these gilded pillars of
stellar glory, adorning lily and vase,
the gossamer wings of microcosmic messengers stir upon the cyclamen blessed
currents of quiescent atmosphere,
The delicate lace of white curtains floats upon the Dancing Air.
The warm metallic voice of college and cloister bells beckons the floating thoughts
of summer Dreamers to the schoolrooms of
Youth, where their fancies ran free in the
meadows of Sun,
and cooling fountains decanted pristine
jewels of water upon the delicate windows
of Time.

Mark Rogers

My Teddybear

Today I found my teddybear
    lying battered by my bed,
I picked him up and hugged him
    and dropped a kiss onto his head.
He stared at me with two glass eyes
    and his little button nose,
I only know I love him
    from his ears right to his toes.
I straightened up his faded bow
    that's tied around his neck,
I thought I ought to make him
    a waistcoat in blackcheck.
I dusted off his rich brown fur
    but he looked a sorry sight,
So I popped him in the washer
    and hung him from a height.
He swung upon the washing line
    pegged up by his ears,
I found him out a ribbon
    my eyes were filled with tears.
I really didn't care at all
    I'd found my once best friend,
My very battered teddybear
    that Mother used to mend.

Stephanie Robinson

Defeated

We couldn't be together,
I thought I'd lost the fight.
I couldn't take the pressure,
And now it's growing light.

Don't want to be the meek one,
Defeated lying form.
Abandoned to the high winds
That raged in last night's storm.

I want to rise above it.
I need to feel I'm free.
Good-bye to all the torture,
Destroy the treachery.

I need to form an army,
I've got to gather strength.
I'll try a new approach, can't stand
This struggling on at length.

The battlefield is long dead.
I can but take my leave.
Attacked by fierce sun and scent,
While caffeine and I grieve.

I pray tonight is different,
My sanity to keep.
I'll crest those waves so wakeful,
And dive deep into sleep.

Alison Roe

A Kindred Spirit

I know what it's like to be homeless like you,
Oh, my heart goes out to you, for I've been there too.
There's no need to speak about hunger or thirst,
For believe me my dearest one, I was there first.

When dear friends desert you, I know how you feel,
Your heart feels as if it's been pierced with cold steel.
Have you ever been punished by someone's false claim?
Place you hand in mine dear one, I've suffered the same.

You'll never shed teardrops, or sweat that's blood red,
Lying prostrate in prayer, on Gethsemane's bed.
Surrendered to those whom your death they would seek,
Betrayed by a friend, with a kiss on your cheek.

But this was God's love gift, his Son's life to give,
I suffered the pain, so that others might live.
To die on the Cross, bearing everyone's sin,
Put your faith in me dear one, let God's love come in.

Robert Ross

What's Happening

Oh town so dark, so drab, so bare
With just the odd tree here and there
Full of pollution noise and smoke
Pavements littered with cans of Coke.

Men sitting around with bottles of wine
This is how they pass their time
Fag ends and packets litter the streets
Paper and plastic wrap round our feet.

When night-time comes the yobs come out
Windows are smashed and things thrown about
Cars are stolen and taken for rides
When petrol runs out they are set alight.

Muggings and drugs are everyday things
Sniffing solvents from pressurised tins
What is happening in the world today
Perhaps one day we shall all have to pay.

Betty Rose

The North

The grime and the smoke that used to belch
From the factories and the mills
That covered the towns in dust and soot
And obscured the fields and hills.
It now is gone and the place is clean
No more chimneys or mills to be seen.
The hills can bask in the warmth of the sun
The trees and the fields are once again green.
When Lowry painted the matchstick men
They were true to life for conditions then.
Everyone seemed to be drab and grey
In the caps and the clogs of yesterday.
They worked long hours they wouldn't work now
With the strength of their arms and the sweat of their brow.
Those men and those maids of the old working North
Were true grit and pure and the salt of the Earth.
The mills have all gone and the old cobbled street
Echoes no more to thousands of feet.
Idle the factories and closure of mine
A North that is facing a time of decline.
The people are there in the heart of the North
Wholesome and true and knowing their worth.
They will rise from the ashes of chimneys and mills
They will tremble the mountain and shiver the hills.

M.E. Royle

Tempus Fugit

Time like silent tears slips past,
And man, a youth, the years does cast.
Old age with wrinkled days draws nigh,
And life goes on and passes by.

Time is life, when life is o'er,
Man desireth clocks no more,
His need for time is left behind,
A present for the child to find.

But why should life by time be ruled?
Why should man by time be fooled?
He wastes it, spends it, makes and gains
From time, what pleasure for his pains?

His life by time is then measured,
His hours, days and years are treasured.
But life is not a span of time to live,
It is a gift we all are given.

A regal crown for man to wear until
The Gods decide the role he can no longer fill.
And then the crown, worn thin with care.
Renewed, is given to the newborn child to wear.

Jenni A. Rose

Message To The Conscience

Oh God, if you had known him, you wouldn't point that gun,
Nor dared to pull the trigger, as the crather tried to run,
He was such a perfect gentleman, no malice in his heart,
His only love was music, his singing and his art.

He chanced to pass you way that night, you had nothing else to do,
You were sent to kill and innocent, regardless of his view,
You lay in wait, he came that road, travelling from afar,
Not fearing any enemy, the poor fella stopped his car ...

He'd think your van had broken down, maybe you needed aid
That was the type of guy he was, he'd never be afraid
To come to the assistance of a neighbour or a mate
Such kindness and compassion, sadly was his fate.

The story that you put about, "he's a rebel psychopath"
You knew well then, and still know now, he took no active part
In any deed to hurt a man, a woman or child
You just were trigger happy, your hatred running wild.

All I ask of you today is, when you're on your own.
You've friends of plenty now, I know, but one day they'll have flown
Remember that you took his life and changed that of another
To you he was a target, but to me, a special brother.

Repent to God and tell him of the guilt that's on your mind,
Ask him to forgive you, tell him of the kind
Of lies you told to make your deed, seem somehow justified,
And think of us heartbroken, and the many tears we cried.

Eithne Ryan

Muddled Mother Nature

Thank goodness the winter is over,
I think, with a sigh of relief.
Now that April is here, the tulips appear,
The trees are producing new leaf.

I'm in bed, and think of spring cleaning,
Oh! There's such a lot to do.
I'll clean all the windows, and polish the brass,
Till everything looks like new.

There's the bedroom, kitchen, bathroom and lounge,
Which room shall I start on first?
But wait — the birds — they're not singing,
So I jump out of bed, with a burst.

I open the curtains, say, "Well I'll be blowed"
And back into bed I creep,
For there overnight, my world had turned white
It's snowed, so I'm off — back to sleep!

Joan Romain

Christmas

Excitement grows as Christmas draws near
Santa Claus will soon be here
Little faces glow with joy
Waiting for that special toy

The nativity plays are in full swing
The angels looking sweet all sing
Mary and Joseph together stand
Each holding the other's hand

The presents are all wrapped and bright
Waiting for that special night
Excitement grows and children say
Here comes Santa with his sleigh

The Christmas tree is sparkling bright
The night is dark, the ground is white
What joy there is on Christmas Day
As with their gifts the children play

J. Rolph

The Wars

Children's faces gaunt and sad
Nothing but bloodshed
Gunfire through their land
Scared and frightened at what they see
Women crying, screaming on bended knees
Men and boys dying everywhere

Where women and girls were raped and taken
When the soldiers came, like bad cruel demons
Bloody scenes through their lands
Nothing can be done
To stop these evil doings
To help the old
To help the poor ones

No peace
No silence
Just the terrible remains
After the soldiers had come
Blood running down the streets
Like a flowing river passing by their feet.

Isabel Ross

When The Milklight Breaks On The Moon's Dead Eye

When the milklight breaks on the moon's dead eye
And the slate night hewed from quarried cloud,
Fainter are the stars than the homebound fishing fleet
Ploughing the deep dark soil of Irish sea,
To the gull's whetted shriek — a razor of hunger.
In the crabapple wind on the fish-smelling quay
The boy-man stares in his turn at the helm,
While the dream is his and the boy was I.

When the mistmilk churns on the sun's warm breath
And the men mending nets and smelling of tar,
And rotting boats with their bowlegged bones
Sticking out of the mud and riddled with gribble
Beneath weed slippery slime, a ghost fleet
Is swashbuckling under my crab-shared command.
The man-boy stares at his returning tide
With a shell to his mind and brine in his eye.

When the gleamgreen sea of war-tangled night,
Its wild grey mares, its stallions white
Stampede 'twixt ship, the devil and iron shark
Flinging its one-minute foaming fin
Burying its nose in thundering rust!
Darkness cries in human gulls,
Our dying whale dives and stays below,
And the man-man shakes — the man was I.

Jonathan Russell

Untitled

I watch as you sit staring
From the corner of the room
I speak but still you sit there
Staring at the gloom

I see your eyelids blink
When I get up to close the door
I wonder what I did wrong
That you don't love me anymore

I go and close the curtain
As it's getting very late
I sit down and put my feet up
As I really need a break

When nearly I was sleeping
I felt you kiss my nose
You look at me so sweetly
I know you love me so

As you turn away
I give you bum a tap
I wonder what I'd do
Without my temperamental cat!

Barbara Rodgers

Untitled

It's hard to write a poem
Harder than it seems
Even though most of them
Come from people's dreams

Poems could tell a story
Of a persons life,
Some are written of love
From a Husband to his Wife

Some will tell of lovers
Walking hand in hand
Some are written in order
To say you understand

They also tell of heartbreak
Of when two people part
Then the words that are written
Are always from the heart

There are many types of poems,
Of love, of hate and joy
Poems of newborn children
Of a little girl or boy

There are poems of sadness
Like when love has all run out
And I'm sure that there's a poem
That tells what love is all about

Andrew Ross

Peace

If everybody loved and shared
If the people of the world helped and cared,
then the world would be a better place,
A happy smile and a friendly face.

If the wars were over and never came back,
If we could fill a person's empty sack,
If the rain would fall and the sun would shine
If the world could love then we'd all be fine.

If the moon would glow in the dark night sky,
Then the world would be better for you and I

Amanda Roy

The Diet

Years ago, when I was eight,
No one worried about their weight.
But today it is a different tale,
We must diet, without fail.

We mustn't eat this, we mustn't eat that,
Not too much sugar, not too much fat.
We have to eat vegetables, and plenty of fruit,
If we want to get into that slim-line suit.

If we have a cream cake, we feel really bad,
But I love cakes, and it makes me feel sad.
So I'll have a carrot, and maybe a bean,
And then a crispbread with margerine!

Mrs. I. Roshier

Backtracking

Biafra.
I had forgotten about you and your hungry tears.
Until tucked away on a video tape
You stared back across the years.

A black matchstick child
With empty saucer eyes
Still starved in front of mine.
A doctor kissed a dying boy
As the world looked on.
Struck blind.

Still blind
The world looks on
At the starving and the damned.
Forever the matchstick child
Holds out its starving hand.

Dave Rogers

Untitled

From the news
I answered an ad
Requesting poems
Good or bad.
Words of Wisdom
Truth
of reality
My eyes see
and my heart feels
So
I can't ignore
The hurt and shame
The glut of gore
Who's found fame
There is good too
becomes lost,
vague,
Hard to see
Through the driving rain
of obscurity.

Robert Ross

Why?

Fear and insecurity haunt my days.
Knowing, but not knowing
The reason why.
Lies all lies.
Our marriage is a sham,
A charade.
I'm alone.
Doubt clouds my mind.
The sun has gone down.
The light is dark.
The spark is dying.
The fire is out.
True love no longer comes my way.
False love,
Just words,
Hidden behind deceit
Are thrown at me.
Why?
Pain stabs my heart
My body
And pain lingers on
Growing with every hour
And the burning question
Why?

Karen Rooks

A Game of Chance

Life was given us for free
To do with as we choose
To us it is a game of chance
We either win or lose

We all make a mistake or two
We learn as we go along
When we have a weakness
We try to make it strong

Some of you have made it
In life you're at the top
But don't look down on others
Whose lives have been a flop

We'll never get a second chance
So at least we ought to try
To do whatever we want to
Not let our days pass by

So when a chance for you arrives
Don't pause to pick and choose
Take the chance while it is there
Be it win or lose.

Sheila Rowley

Savings?

20% off, the sign proclaims,
Save fifteen pounds today,
But can you tell me what I 'save'
When I've still the asking price to pay.

The shops are full of all these signs,
All claiming that we're saving,
Reduced by this, reduced by that,
I find it so amazing.

I toddle off down Nottingham,
To find something to tempt me,
I 'save' on everything I buy,
But still my purse is empty.

Can someone kindly please explain,
Why this should be so,
I've thought and thought and racked my brain,
But still I do not know.

Perhaps the best thing I can do,
I know it may sound funny,
But if I do not buy at all,
I'll then save all my money.

Maureen Rowe

Autumn

The leaves will soon be falling
And berries appear on the tree
The beautiful colours of Autumn
Are there for all eyes to see.
As we wonder what tomorrow brings
Nothing can dim the memories
Of walking through Autumn leaves.
As the evenings grow darker
The flowers begin to fade
God hope's the world remembers
Golden moments of Autumn Days.

Joan Ruddick

Friend

When you're lonely, take my hand,
Talk to me, I'll understand,
You need never feel alone,
Think of my house as your home.
I will not be far away,
Call on me both night or day.
Do not think you will intrude,
I'm always in receptive mood.
I will always give my time.
I will make your troubles mine.
If you need a quiet while,
If you need to share a smile,
If you're troubled with a tear,
Come to me, that's why I'm here.

Maggie Robinson

Umbrella

Large, bat-like harbour
Erupted from such a placid object.
Once modest and compact,
Now strong and exposed
Offering comfort from earth's
displeasures
Snow! Wind! Rain!
Be gone!
You cannot win —
This body resists your malicious force.
It is man's protector,
The ultimate bodyguard!
Ever reliable, ever amenable
Defensive, dogged dome.

Tracy Revell

Mendip Season

September, and a sea sound
Shivers through the grassy reeds
That edge the causeway path
To Priddy mineries.

As the tide of summer ebbs
It leaves a surfy strand
White with sandwort, eyebright,
And bubbles of sea campion.

Ripe seed of willow herb
Flies from each foamy wand
And floats downwind to rest
On tussocky gruffy ground.

Across the bay tall barques
Ride at anchor; green masts stand,
Their shrouds tread air and heave
Dark in the Stockhill roads.

The watch I keep is brief
Old Mendip ticks and sighs
Summer's hour glass runs
And another seasons dies.

John Rumming

Autumn Walk

I had no need to turn the stone
For it was not a stone turning day.
Why take autumn's leafy walk
With view to winter's way.

Why tread the winding river path
Upon which the stone was worn
When all along the tossing turn
It winds since we were born.

Should darker side of under rock
And deeps of fast river flow
Determine my depths of mind ahead
When it is backward I wish to go.

Bending as the ochre leaf
Upon a barked bough unsure
Who with a slight sigh flutters
For the green that's gone before.

I am holding for just a moment
Sweet spring and summer sand
Before shuffling on along my path
And letting go their hand.

Norman Royal

Oak-To-Be

Although your heart
Is not yet beating

Your bud
But new-budded thought,

The centuries overhead
Are creaking, acquiring

Tortuous membranes,
That flesh-out your future

Unbidden.

Spencer Redfield

Magic Moments

When the love in my heart and body is expressed,
I wonder if my heart is ever at rest,
My love for you is forever growing,
I am always thinking and forever knowing,
That you'll be the one on my mind,
You're sweet, loving, yes, my kind,
I wish you felt like that about me
Because I'm in love with you ... you see.

Emma Rogers

Tender To Percussion

Tender to percussion,
the gentle lapping wave,
the pounding of the ocean,
the echo of a cave.

Sand that's locked in motion
while I'm moving standing still;
the sound of bubbling water
running through a beetling mill.

Tender to percussion,
the billowing of sails,
the sound of roaring laughter,
the resonance of whales.

Tender to percussion,
the rolling of the deep,
the tender tread of angels
falling quietly to sleep.

Pauline Rushe

Mean Season

Coffee coloured sky.
Cream cheese on my chin.
Brick Lane, a strange tongue. A stranger.
Underground travel. Hot pigeon shit.
Yellow leaves in gutters stink.
A mean season coming.
Black swans, screeching, rock pools and reeds.
Ducks glide past, making a wake in shallow
reflections of low light.
A mean season coming.
The pain I feel is real. It is constant.
The drugs I take, the booze I drink, the sad
and lonely life I lead, remind me of the
poets I once knew.
Hallucinations rack my brain, and California is far away.
Winter is almost here. A mean season coming.
Milky sun. Low clouds. Dark days.
A welcome fire, bare branches, and barefoot children
still play — on bleached sidewalks in a different
time zone.
Glorious days will be, the poem writes itself.
Chocolate on my lips.
Not before. A mean season coming.

Daniel S. Scott

In The Interest of Science?

Get the harpoon ready; explosives in the nose:
Hearken to the lookout's cry, "Ahoy there; thar she blows!"
Cruising through the waters, majestic in its going,
Spouting like a fountain, blowing ... blowing ... blowing.

Let the harpoon go boys, let it burst inside;
Not enough to blow it up, but bring it alongside:
Knives and saws all ready, busy as a hive:
Start the cutting right away .. so what if it's alive?

It's just an animal you know, I'll tell you once again:
They're not like us, they do not feel the slightest bit of pain;
We're doing this for science, to help save human lives,
'Though no doubt the odd whale or so will fall to forks and knives.

It's just like when your angling, and put fish in a pail;
We're doing just the very same, but on a larger scale:
So give the wind your scruples; let the red blood flow:
The world has too many whales, as you and I both know.

Carve the monster up at once, let the scuppers run:
Just think of when you get your pay, ashore, and having fun:
It's not as if we're killing men, like soldiers have to do;
Besides, we all are partial to some whale meat in our stew.

Alexander K. Sampson

lost in heaven

I dream that
heaven is blue
that the sun
shines all day through
that there is
much love
much more than
I thought
the air is so clean
as I look around
I see the flowers blooming
everywhere
but I know
when I wake up
all I will see is so
much heartache
as I know I am back in
the land of the living
until it is time for me
to go back to heaven

Tracy Salt

Look Ahead Together

Gone are the pits,
Gone are the black hills,
Gone is the black dust
That came from the coal.

Mourn for the miners,
Mourn for their passing,
Mourn for the men
Who are now on the dole.

But then, look to the future,
Welcome green valleys,
Welcome the clean air
That will fill our valley homes.

Smile, for the children,
No more breathing coal dust.
Smile for the young men,
Saved from that black hole.

Keep all your memories
Of our brave miners.
Let history books be written
Of their heroic fight for coal.

Let's all walk together,
As we go into the future,
Hand in hand together
In our proud valley home.

Joan Samuel

What Is Love? My Thoughts

Love it seems is many a splendoured thing, To some a wedding and a diamond ring.
I see love in a very different angle, let my thoughts to you untangle.

Exhilaration, ecstasy and excitement, with my partner, there is such enjoyment.
But is love just a physical attraction? For two human beings a feeling of compassion.
Let me go further and explain, of the difficulties, the sorrow and the strain
I am talking about the complexity of my job, who do I turn to when I wish to sob?

My partner and family, they do not understand, that my mind is constantly on over-demand
Difficulties arise when I wish to address my partner
So where do I find mental security but with a friend, another
Being emotionally in tune, this is a trend
To reach out their mind, the soul and lend.

A relationship without any sexual activity, you might think, what such negativity!
A feeling of being appreciated for what I am
Without the misunderstanding, out goes the sham.
Is there such a think as combined happiness?
Without the pain, the tears and the nastiness.

Faint heartbeats and soulful glances, temporary insanity and emotional trances.
A relationship where two minds think alike, this is the beauty,
To share, to confide, to laugh, to cry — is there such poetry?
I believe there is, please forgive me if otherwise, my thoughts I have shared, these I prize ...

Think back and read again the above, this to me is ... Love.

Mohammed Sayeed

The Dancing Maid

Oh Maiden dancing on the village green,
With fleeting bare feet, and tambourine,
Those fiery red lips, and jet black hair,
Has me spell bound, while standing here.

Your Romany features, those flashing eyes,
Are like twinkling stars, in darkened skies,
Those nimble moving limbs, in erotic dance,
Holds me captive, to your hypnotic trance.

Since I was a lad, so many years ago,
I have seen you come, and quickly go,
Watched you dance, listened to your song,
And wondered why, you remain so young.

What strange magic power do you hold,
To keep your beauty, and not grow old,
While I can only, stand and leer,
And grow older with each passing year.

Could it be perhaps, you exist only in my mind
A vision of torment, so alluring, vivacious, unkind
Why must it be when I reach for you, or wander near
You fade from me into darkness, and disappear.

Arthur Saunders

Bring Me Your Dreams

"Bring me your dreams" said the haunted man
As the child stood before him in play.
"What will you do when you are a man?"
"I will fly to the stars on that day,
To see other worlds and the wonders up there,
And travel the universe far
To see living things on the planets in space
And look for a bright shiny star."

Said the man who was haunted, "I too had a dream
To travel the universe wide;
I flew to the moon and looked at the stars
And saw that the planets had died.
There is no life now in the universe,
The moon and stars lost their light.
I stood on the moon and looked back to earth
And saw a most terrible sight;
The earth, it was dying, my soul shrivelled too,
And that's why I am as you see."
The boy looked in horror upon the dead man
And cried "Give back my dreams to me."

Muriel Sandham

Rose Tattoos

Outside, the wind is roaring
Round the rose tattoo
The serpent forgotten in sleep
A melancholy in the air
Which can't quite come forward
    Enough to weep

She knows the gangsters in government
They are drunk, not her concern,
Like an advertising agency crowd,
Like someone else's letter
    Blowing down the street.

Big men can't reach her,
No clue how to treat her
Causing the dogs to crawl, the saxophones to weep
Angel witch the touch of the child
Naturally chic.
Colours untouched by the rain are there to enjoy,
So we'll play her game.

Gerry Scales

Advice to a Friend

Stay with him forever,
Don't cut his heart in two,
No one will ever love
The way that he loves you.
Don't you love another
And you mustn't be untrue,
Don't think "it won't matter",
You'll cry when you are through.

Solicitors and courts —
That's the path you'll follow.
Why find another man
Whose heart may be hollow?
So do your thinking now,
Whilst you're able to compare,
Because a broken marriage
Isn't easy to repair.

And this much I know for certain —
Divorce is the final curtain!

Amanda Jane Scarborough

Just A Working Dog

She lays there so peacefully,
Her working days are done.
And through her mind go thoughts of sheep
And all the miles she's run.

Her coat a little shaggy now
And nose a little dry,
Her young days have long gone past,
But she will always try.

She moves a little slower now,
Her eyes grow dim with time.
I sometimes sit and wonder how much
Longer she'll be mine.

In all the days I walked the fields
She followed every step.
And now her working days are done,
I keep her as my pet.

I know she longs to be out there when I tend the sheep
I'm sure she dreams she is with me, even in her sleep.
A faithful friend, a working dog, no better could I find.
I know that when her days are done, she'll never leave my mind.

If dogs do go to heaven,
I know that she will be,
Waiting at the gate,
Hoping I'll arrive, to always be with me.

R.J. Sandom

Loneliness

Loneliness is a ticking clock
Inside an empty room
That echoes round inside your head
And you feel just like a tomb
It's a cacophony of silence
As you stare across the street
And desperately want to hear
The sound of passing feet
To watch and see the happiness
Of others passing by
Whilst you are sitting quietly
Watching clouds go by
You know the room so intimately
Everything in its place
At times you feel it's choking you
And smothering your face
Deep down there inside of you
There's just an empty space
Of broken dreams and memories
Why can't they take place?
And so you drift off to your bed
To try and get some sleep
Days and nights can seem like years
Tomorrow, maybe peace.

P.V. Sanders

Iridescent Awe

Skies of golden satin embedded in them there trees,
Desperately reluctant to devour a new horizon,
Amber strands intertwine, colliding, and riding with the breeze,
With this their last fleeting chance to lighten,
Turn not suddenly, look not hard, for this timid sky does wander
to dare to scatter afar,
Dusk contemplating the shrouding of a nation,
Ready to adorn the beacon blue in a midnight celebration.
Be still not to miss its brilliant departure sink beneath our land,
We'll meet again at the same time, same place, as planned,
Once the day emblazoned with its disquiet abdicates for retire,
And then and only then can the golden one return to once more reign its realm
and many a heart inspire.

Stephen Sayers

Living with Redundancy, Part 1

My husband was made redundant first,
I said "Don't worry, things could be worse!"
"Oh!" no sooner said than done,
The next to get it, was my son.

Things got very hard indeed!
Couldn't buy all the things we'd need.
My nerves were getting very tight,
Tensions would snap, then we'd fight.

My cupboards became almost bare,
It was awful, seeing nothing there.
It was meal times that I hated the most,
We seemed to live on baked beans on toast.

A friend would say, "Please don't despair!
God gives us the burden he knows we can bear."
Inside of me I wanted to shout and shriek!
"Well, my dear, that must make you very weak!"

Who was she to give out advice?
Her life was comfy, safe, all nice.
Paranoid was what I became,
Things would never be quite the same.

I felt she was being, an insensitive bitch!
For compared to me, she was downright rich.
But although her words made me boil inside,
I held onto my dignity, I kept my pride.

Denise Sanders

First Visit

My nightmare journey has begun
As the gates securely lock behind me.
Innocent until proven guilty
Are words the media love to shun.

Can anyone else feel the pain and grief?
Pain so bad it grips the very soul.
I fear not, it is a personal thing
From this torment there is no relief.

I climb the stairs, name and number given
Past other mother's sons so forlorn and young
Beloved and precious just like mine,
Awaiting their turn to be forgiven.

Snatches of time so eagerly sought
Give messages from home of love and hope,
Longing to feel my arms enfold you
And win this battle that must be fought.

Fear and distress etched on your face
What lies ahead we can't foretell,
No promises dare to be made
In this cold, unfeeling place.

My son stand tall, stay strong and pray
For those who love you just like me
Know truth will conquer in the end,
As the judge pronounces not guilty on the day.

Pauline Scobie

Satellite TV Dish

Working steady all through that day
'Rentokil' men, masked, safe in protective clothing
Disinfect and preserve with brush and spray.
Thorough, over all woodwork in that small flat
Attack each room from front to back.
Quickly, efficiently eradicate all dry rot.
But is now replaced by electronic fungi above the hall,
Sprouting from, distorting, the outside wall.
No longer danger of spreading dry rot -
Instead, ceaseless beaming, insidiously spreading
Deadly, mindless brain rot!

Robert O. Scott

Fishing

Fishing is a cruel sport I hear people say
I'd love to go fishing everyday.
Sitting on a river bank with rod and line
Relaxed and excited both at the same time.

The float it goes under, excitement it grows
What have we caught, until it's landed who knows.
Take off the hook gently, see what you get
Then place it carefully in your keep-net.
Bait up your hook again, cast in the lure
Best pastime ever fishing is for sure.

Pouring rain or sun high in the sky
The fish that you catch never ask why.
At the end of the day you weigh up your batch
Then put the fish back in the river for others to catch.

John Scripps

Memories — Ballyfinigan — Barefoot Days

A memory — what power you wield
A boy, a dog, a horse and sheep
Cattle cows all in one field
The boy supreme is in command
A whistle, shout not yet a man.
He walks sedate, then runs with joy
His feet caressed by Nature's jewels
Moistened grass and small wild flowers
Green and gold a touch of pink
Between young toes with love they cling
Memories, memories, back and forth
You conjure joy and sadness both
A balance on the wings of time
Reach out, reach out, be bold be kind.
And neither age or fleeting time
Will conquer joy in a young boy's mind.

Thomas Seale

Mid Life Crisis

Mid life crisis, a confused mind
All the answers you're trying to find
Searching for a new direction
Which route will you take at the intersection?

Old wounds you thought had healed
Cause you pain
Living your life all over again
Searching for something you may never find
Is contentment within the mind?

David Scott

Sonnet On An Eightieth Birthday

Slowly, saliva dribbles down his chin
To fall unheeded on his birthday shirt.
He lifts his face and gives a vacant grin,
And through his empty eyes, I see his hurt.
Encased in birthday slippers, warm and red,
His restless feet are rustling paper round —
Perhaps to drown the voices in his head;
Or then again, maybe he hears no sound.
Stiffly, he rises from his sodden chair,
And shuffles off towards the bolted door,
Forgetting, on the way, just why or where
His weary legs intended him to go.
     Oh Dad, my Dad, so lost, so sad, so old!
     But dignity returns with death, I'm told.

Maureen Settle

Enigma

She in the radiant springtime of her life,
He in the golden autumn of his days;
May and September fusing into one,
Sunshine and shadow merging into light.

All summer long they daily strolled the park,
Arms fondly linked, supportive in caress;
Pausing, from time to time, to turn and speak,
Eyes meeting eyes, contentment in their gaze.

But, from the day the leaves began to fall
They came no more; and never have returned.
Yet often in the loneliness of night,
I see them still, and wonder who they are.

What bond cemented such apparent love?
A love that heeded not the span of years
Between the radiant springtime of her life
And the golden autumn days of his.

Jean Scott

When Eight Meets Eighty

I cried when I saw him sitting there,
Old and alone with time to spare.
Lonely at home, he'd come to the park
To watch children play and hear the dogs bark.

He found as he sat, in the distance to stare,
As lonely here as he had been there.
The sun fierce and strident covered his face,
His mind wandered backward, life's dreams to chase.

A smile lit his wrinkles, he felt her so near,
Her hand fast in his, down his cheek ran a tear.
Then a shout broke his slumber, a ball hard on his back
Left his love back in neverland, the sweet mirror cracked.

He turned fast in anger, a choice word to throw,
His gaze travelled downward to an angel below,
He'd freckles a plenty, and curly red hair,
"Sorry mister, I di'n't mean i'", his voice full of care.

In that moment, old was just a word,
The child asked "Can yer teach us to 'ead?"
Oh, the feeling of joy bought by that little boy
In the few simple words he had said.

The next time I saw him, I had to smile
The tears were far away,
For daily they'd come and knock on his door,
"Can yer come out ter play?"

Mandy Shora

Offshore

Dawn is breaking once again, fishermen walking down the lane
Harbour wall is just in sight as rising sun replaces night
The tide is rising, buoys are bobbing, fishing boats' old Diesels throbbing
Crew's aboard, they leave the shore out to search the shoals once more
There's work to do as they travel on, nets to mend and maintenance done
Wind is rising, swelling the tide, bigger troughs and crests to ride
Radio begins to clatter, fishing grounds are near
Louder now the skippers' chatter as other boats show clear
Nets are running fast and free, spewing into the foaming sea
Speed is down now as they start to trawl
The crew are stood at ease
Waiting to retrieve their nets
Ever hoping their catch will please
The order's given, the winches turn
Trawl's coming in now over the stern
The tension is rising, the nets take the stain
As a voluminous catch lands in the holds again
Now it's "stow away the gear lads, hose down the decks"
Everything's safe as the Skipper checks
Forward the throttle, hear the old Diesels' roar
All eyes to the coastline and home once more.

Dennis Shrubshall

Frightened

You cannot
You cannot
Shake off this
sometimes shoe
That you call
Frightened me.

Louise Simpson

Yukon's Moon

Silhouette their tall
Wintry shapes,
Tinted in silver
Draped in firs
Majestic ...
Deserts of snow,
Eternally the crystals
Dance and glow
By lunar light
Where famished green-eyed
Lupine lurks and rakes
In Yukon's wilderness.

Terrence St. John

Love

Love is kind
Love is your neighbour
Love is eternal
The sun in the sky.
Share love
Find his glory
For love's a heavy burden.

No greater our love
Through that of actions
Love is bonding
Never to part.
Love is friendship
Love is trust
Love is being together.

Love is God.
Love is being loved.

Owen Shields

My Dream After All

I once had a dream to show the world what I could do
And for a while it seemed that dream just might come true.
For one fleeting moment I caught sight of the real me
I had a glimpse of life the way I always wanted it to be.
There seemed no reason it would stop, no chance that I would fall
For I had made it happen, it was my dream after all
So why did it go wrong, what made it fade away?
What made me lose my grasp on what was there just yesterday?
Was it circumstances that did it, life having the last laugh
Showing me a happiness that I could never have
Or did I just grow up, become part of the real world
Finally become a woman, leaving behind the girl?
Maybe a grown-up is not supposed to dream
And not supposed to understand what happiness can mean.
Maybe life's meant to be full of stresses and of strains
Worrying about the same problems time and time again.
Living hand to mouth, never getting anywhere,
Hoping that someday you will find someone who will care
And yet surely we can rise above it, reach for that highest star
Live life to the full, believe in who we are
For I once had a dream and I once let it fall,
But this time I'm keeping hold of it, it is my dream after all!

C.M. Seddon

Fly Away To The Sun

Computer weary eyes scan now the white
And curling continent below and minds
Attuned to balance sheets relax to piped
Refrains and cocktails from the friendly hostess.
This great bird has gathered us to her bosom
And will take us to the kingdom of the sun.

"Shelter us!" we cry out to the sun,
"Wrap us in your comforting blanket.
We play for you on white and gold beaches;
We make pilgrimage to stone bright ancient cities;
From Orient to Occident we search for you;
Dazzle us awhile to our cold reflections."

Wrapped in warmth we come back to life
Like mid-day lizards, then dart away
To build sandcastles or carve our initials
Where they will be seen. How hard we work,
How cleverly we direct our lives to reach
For pinnacles that crumble as we climb.

So quickly — too quickly the time passes.
Return snatches us away from dreams
And romance. Can I be the only one
To feel regret? What have I to take back
With me? Did the shrine yield up it's secret?
Or must I return again and again?

J.N. Sell

Life's Seasons

I have sat and thought of reasons
For life having nature's seasons.
For birth is spring as a new life will unfold
Crisp and fresh and brave and bold.
Like nature's world, full of wonderful things
A new life finds its roots and spreads its wings.

Summer comes and brings forth the sun
Only time for now and not what's to come.
We blossom and burst and spread our seed
We adventure and brave any daring new deed.

But autumn comes and brings forth a chill
Which creeps in and removes some of the thrill.
Into our life may come our very first storm
But summer has not long gone and still we feel warm.

Autumn gives way to winter's cold
We are not so brave and not quite so bold.
Our petals drop and our heads hang low
Our roots become brittle and no longer grow.
We shrivel and die in what seems a day
And back to the earth we are taken to lay.
But for the loss of that flower we should not mourn
As come the spring it will be re-born.

D.J. Seneschall-Morgan

Journey To A Pine Forest

The journey seemed long, he'd travelled far,
It was bitterly cold and the snow lay deep.
Majestic pines stood guard in the forest
Like sentries at the door of a keep.
Row upon row of sturdy branches
Decreased in size as they reached their peak.
The woody aroma enveloped his being,
Spurring him on, new heights to seek.
Branches creaked and groaned under foot,
Sporadic needles dropped to the ground.
Icy water trickled down his neck
As snow quietly melted all around.
The wind howled round his face as higher he climbed,
Groups of needles fanned to and fro,
Sun rays flickered and darted about
Routing out cones that were starting to grow.
His hand grasped the trunk and the pine tree shuddered,
Supporting his weight with its outstretched arms.
The saw was raised high for the finishing blow,
The tree gave in, submitting its charms.

He'd cut down many a tree by profession
But this was to be his own possession.
And he thought, as the trunk he began to sever,
This was to be the best Christmas ever.

Ruth Shepherd

Little Birds

Little birds
Say tiny words
As they rush
Through the trees
As they fly
The say goodbye
To the strong
And windy breeze

Andrew Shora

Thoughts of Him

Food? Not for me.
Ill? No.
Yes, my hands shake
- But I'm all right.
What was that?
I'm touchy? - Sorry.
My breathing?
Yes, but I'm fine. Really.
What? You haven't guessed?
My trembling
And that warm wet glow?
Don't know?
It's thoughts of him.

Cathy Saunders

Whispers From The Gutter

Your gaze is ice, you judge me scum
Your ignorance asks where did I come from
Had a life like you, warm and safe from harm
Not always lying on the street with needles in my arm
Naive move to the city, foolish young and bold
Dreams are dead these streets are paved with shit and not with gold

Too late to go home
Cannot face the shame
These heartless streets I roam
My only friend is pain

You eyes say junkie, but where do I run?
My family tome a myth, from nowhere have I come
You have no pity 'cos I put this death into my veins
But what else is there left for me, serendipiters disdain
Sell my arse to perverts, battle to survive
Rotten food from dustbins to keep myself alive

Too late to go home
Cannot face the shame
These heartless streets I roam
My only friend is pain

Ian Sen

Fear At The Crossroads

A rock in his hand
by the lych gate,
A rock where his heart
should have been.

Alone and in fear
new ghosts will appear
Along country lanes at this
time of the year.

He is standing there threatening
death to all comers.
The fear in his eyes
amid dangerous skies
and terrible, violent greens.

He has taken his fear
to the crossroads.
But what is it, pray
he has seen?

Derek Sculthorpe

Wherever

Darkness marched across the land,
And in the wave of a bloody hand.
All that was good and kind before,
Was swept away in a path of gore.

It takes very little for the demented
To kindle old hatreds and ferment them
So that each tribe and clan rise up,
To destroy each other and cannot stop.

In time the country is demolished,
And the living are abolished,
To distant borders as they flee
And settle in camps as refugees.

Then the world watches on T.V.
The plight of these people and their agony
As they die of hunger and disease,
Like Typhus, Cholera and Dysentery.

But whatever is done, it's always too late
For after all, this could be any country's fate
Where the darkness can erupt,
And all we can hope for, is it to stop!

S. Seed

No Choice

Like many that have gone before us,
That time must modify,
We follow in their steps, not much wiser,
And a better world passes us by.
The violence of life we experience
Is sire and dam to our art,
And the fear that is always present,
Is the fuel that keeps us apart.
We are the prisoners of evolution,
Whose account we all have to pay,
And it's reality that stirs and whispers
"You are mortal, this bill you must pay."
So any faith that you may have,
Is yours by right to hold,
For the soul by faith is ripened,
And it's all you have that's gold.
You may feed on thoughts of joy and love,
Those sacred fruits eternal,
But don't get too fond of this earthly pond,
It's ruled by powers infernal.

W.E. Sherratt

Trouble With 'Id'

"Just be yourself," said my mother,
As we waited for the door to open;
And, knowing that the trap was baited,
I wanly smiled my acquiescence,
Resigned to all the noisy malice
Of other children at the party.

Even now, that same injunction
Tantalizes like Browning's heaven —
A promised chalice, always just
Out of reach. For who am I?
Or what is self? What makes
'Every' distinct from 'Each'?

Is self perceived through
The looking-glass of others; every image
A different truth? Or am T
Unique: A P.I.N. in genetic code
Undeceived by mirrors, though deluded
By a mirage in a different mode?

I can't remember what happened at the party —
No doubt relief that it all had ended —
No doubt relief that uncertainty would be transcended,
And yet, as I hear my mother's voice again,
The exhortation would still confuse.
And mean as little now as then.

William G. Shaw

Autumn

Summer has gone, without even a whimper
And the long, hot days have no place.
For regal Autumn has burst upon us
And captured us with its grace.

Autumn means fields of waving corn,
And the Harvest Moon shining bright.
A golden ball in a glittering sky -
A star-studded canopy of light.

Out in the forest, the short Autumn day
Is a myriad of colour, all aglow.
Bronzes and browns, mellow yellows and fawns.
With the wind a freshening blow.

The woodland scene is a pageant of blaze.
The pines are of six different greens.
There's a touch of ice on the sparkling pools
And the resident woodpecker preens.

Autumn nights bring the grey swirling mists
That sometimes render us lost.
But inside the house there's a cosy fire;
Outside - unheeded - the glistening frost.

So wrap yourself round me, majestic Autumn.
Let my days with your magic be blest.
For you wear the crown - you are supreme.
Of all the seasons, you are the best.

S. Shaw

The Dreaming Of A Painted Horse

When painted horses dream
Do they ride the merry-go-round
Or gallop in the rye;
Are they coupled in the hunt,
Or bareback,
Riderless in the desert.

When painted horses dream
Do they dream of summer scented figs
At the shores of an oasis,
Or are they limited;
To the roundabout of their wooden life,
Being moved in circles, at the machine's command,
With oil for their wounds
And a stake through their heart.

When painted horses dream
Can *you* tell me what they see?

Dayv Sherriff

Untitled

Through Winter's chill the withered leaves and bracken lay
As if to guard Earth's treasures from the light of day
But when the first warm gleam of sun appears
Crocus and snowdrop lift their pale green spears
Raised up by Nature's beckoning
To bravely greet an early Spring.

So if dark days have come to us
And we are suffering pain or loss
Take time to rest with Nature's healing
Until with faith in God revealing
New hope to help us stand upright
Renewed in strength to face new light.

Barbara L. Shaw

The Gardener

He was very busy working, pulling out weeds
The next time that I saw him he was busy planting seeds
I passed a few months later, my how the seeds had grown
Hedges neat and tidy, lawn all freshly mown

Hours of work and loving care, flowers blooming everywhere
Not just for him alone, but beauty all could share
Alas not all took pleasure in the work that he had done
Someone came and wrecked it, I suppose they thought it fun

I never saw the man again, perhaps he just lost heart
To spread a little beauty, at least he'd done his part
No flowers bloom there now, no lawn all freshly mown
Where a patch of beauty lay, now lies a square of stone.

Mary Shepherd

Free To Be Me

Azure horizons
fading
misty outlines
I hold your shapes, colours, textures
just for that moment
when I know you are mine
alone.
The crystal sharpness
is frosted there inside me
after all that striving, yearning,
churning
to capture the sense of me
through the senses of others
when what I see is mine ...
... and it is wonderful.
The moment is gone
mountains crowd in and fade away
always beyond a single vision
never meaning to be captured
and yet,
I still hold the beauty
glinting inside
as cold rock touched by sunlight.
I love my truth.

M. Sedgley

A Bathroom Ode

So you like your bathroom
Every time you have a bath
Or is it so old fashioned
It makes you want to laugh?

You think of all the years
You have put up with the thing,
Shall we? Shan't we? Have it changed
Now it's coming spring.

Dare you let in visitors?
When they ask to use the "loo",
What will they think when they go home
That you're old fashioned too?

Never, never you will say
Let's go to the arcade
I'm sure they'll help us out
Now the decision is made.

The bathroom is now fantastic
You really can't believe it,
The only trouble now of course,
NO ONE WANTS TO LEAVE IT.

Clare Shetliffe Smith

Childishness Happiness Loneliness

Are ye comin oot tae play the day, We'll go up the farm and mess the hay
Or else we'll play chapdoor run, anything for a bit o' fun
We can get empty cans and make oor stilts as long as them lads don't look up oor kilts
Play at statues or hide'n'seek. Shout after the teacher wi' the big red beak.

Play at beds wi oor polish tin peever, skip in and oot ropes like a weaver.
Shops open come and buy. That wis wan familiar cry.
As time went past and we got older, then oor games became much bolder,
Hospitals, nurses, whose the doctor, truth, dare, double-dare, torture.

Catch me if you can, kiss and tell, next, the sound of a wedding bell.
A hurried up weddin' wis a common sight, aye they say, she's 'up the kite',
Ten years later on in time, up to your elbows in hoosework an'grime.
Whit did a dae tae deserve a' this, it's all the result of that chaseme kiss.

Five wee wains roon ma feet, a man in the pub, a lia an' a cheat.
He's never oot that bloody place, he'll come in late and belt ma face.
It'll be moan an' groan, git the wains to bed, when is a man gonna git fed,
If I don't git a move on, he'll go back oot, spend ma paye, an I'll be left withoot.

Tae git some money I'll hav tae pawn ma weddin' ring, it's all I own.
But the dinner's got tae come from somewhere, ye canny eat, if the cupboard's bare.
They're all away noo, all grown up, I sit at ma windae sippin' oot ma cup,
I watch the wains playin' at chases, ropes an peever, shops an' races.

Dae they know where they'll all end up
Sittin' at a windae suppin' oot a cup.

Elizabeth Young Simpson

Step Father

No, not a Rembrandt!
The label lifted
the price tag fell

The label lifted
and to some
as with horses or cattle
breeding was all

You think Eden could grow in this desert
if 'scaped by Ezra and not by Eliot?

Though shadows fall
the eyes defy
and the helmet
will not be dimmed

And so my father
stepping to his title role
fathered
though he had not sired

For even if Bacon as Shakespeare did pose
that wouldn't sour the smell of a rose.

Philip Shepheard

Time As A Freeze Frame

crossing the black eagle's nest
                                    room
the candle burns blinding
the Visions vision alight
Freeze Frame universe

a blinding infinite
                    shadow soiled
                    ashen oil curling
                                    Fume
                                    wicked

like the wicked child's
                    Night aye

we come from an aquabasen
to disperse an inferno
and start an aerial red
                                    again

          Times a smart appearance
          and you can see, it's only naturally

Lel Shirra

Who's Scared Of The Dark?

I'm not scared of the dark and the reason is pretty plain,
I'm not scared of the dark, just thought I'd say it again.
Mum can turn my light off, I'm not scared, in fact I'm fine,
But then why shouldn't I be, after all I'm nearly nine.

I was scared when I was younger, and often woke with fright
I used to say to Mummy, please don't turn off the light
But Mummy says the nighttime, is the daytime's friend, a guest,
Who comes round every evening, to give us all a rest.

Mum said, when the good Lord made the night, he new the benefits we would reap
He knew that little girls like me would need to go to sleep,
He knows that we have schoolwork, He knows we play at break,
He knows if it was light all day, we could never stay awake.

Mum says He made the nighttime dark, so our dreams would be a treasure,
So when I go to sleep at night, well for me, it's just a pleasure,
Mum says her explanation is true, she's very sure,
Because her Mummy told her, when she was only four.

I'm not scared of the dark, and the reason is pretty plain,
I'm not scared of the dark, just thought I'd say it again.

John Shine

Somebody Loves Me

Could one honestly call me a sexy young sight
As I slip 'twixt the sheets on a dark frosty night?
In thick woolly bed-socks, unsightly yet warm
And an ancient grey tracksuit distorting my form,
I doubt I'll be enlisted for x-rated porn,
SUCH is my sad lonely plight ...

Could one seriously question my unsullied soul
When I slurp low-fat soup from a small china bowl?
Watching with bemusement the sex-ridden soaps,
Doubting the reality of the muscle-clad blokes?
Wondering if I dare a more blatant approach,
SUCH is my self-doubting role.

Could anyone care for my bunyons and flab,
And a backside which looks like a large London cab?
Tolerate my need to write thousands of cheques,
Withstand the charm of my heavy-duty specs,
Endure the vacillations of a nature so complex?
For SUCH are the charms of a hag!

But do I really need a partner to make me a wife
To bolster my pride and support me through strife?
Though mother won't kiss me in *that* special way
And she'll never buy me roses on *that* loathsome day ...
Still she'll love me impartially whatever I say ...
Ah! SUCH is the wonder of life.

Karen Simpson-Harris

Something Fishy

Goldfish, coldfish, swimming in your tank,
For your food you have me to thank.
In that safe world you have no troubles,
Flitting in and out of the filter bubbles.
To watch you gives me pleasure,
Your gold and silver shining like treasure.

As you dart about going through your paces,
I wonder what you think of the strange staring faces?
Is it fear that makes your stare look blank?
Or are you oblivious to the world outside your tank?
You look more surprised than you do cowed,
As you go around open mouthed.

Tell me little fish, with your bright red tail,
How do you get on with the water snail?
I know he's not bright and moves very slow,
But he cleans your tank as he moves to and fro.
Are you happy when you see him approach?
Or would you sooner be friends with the weather loach?

With the water plants ever so green,
You and your friends make an eye pleasing scene.
As you swim around in your own private space,
You bring a look of cheer on this old face.
And so to you we raise our hats,
As we watch you make fools of the household cats.

Anthony Simmons

417

The Donkey And The Tramp

A donkey lived in a meadow, a tramp in the nearby lane.
The continuous bray of the donkey nearly drove him quite insane.
At the same time, the smell of the tramp made the poor donkey feel very ill.
So each day they glared at each other, oh dear, if those looks could kill.
Then at last they settled their problem, down by the clear meadow stream.
The tramp agreed to bathe daily so he and his clothes would be clean.
The donkey said he would bray quietly so that way he would not offend.
The donkey and tramp I am happy to say, now called each other "Friend".
So remember all those who are thoughtless, when habits and ways can upset.
It is nice to have friends but not enemies, that is something we must not forget.
Just remember the tramp and the donkey and how they both mended their ways.
If only we humans could compromise, how carefree would be all our days.
Please think of these words, "Do to others as they would do unto you."
Believe me your days would be worthwhile, so try it your whole life through.

Janet Short-Windsor

A Poem For Easter Sunday

I saw a field of rubble and my heart sank to the floor,
What used to be so beautiful wasn't like that anymore,
I remember daisies growing
And grass so green and lush,
What has happened to our country
What has happened to us?
Man has become so envious
And to satisfy his lust
He set the bombers over
And reduced our land to dust.
I wandered on still further
Then something caught my eye
A tiny little flower
Head pointing to the sky.
God had heard my silent prayer
He had sent to me a sign,
For it was Easter Sunday
The day life was born anew,
On that day so many years ago
Christ arose to give hope to me and you.
So give thanks this Easter Sunday
Think of that little flower
God will surely help to restore
Joy and peace to this land of ours.

D.G. Siddall

The Lady Of The Night

The seducing vibes she sends out,
Can be felt by males all over the city.
A chill enters the air,
Her chill invites the unsuspecting males.
These males are being let to their doom,
Like lambs to the slaughter.

They are strangely attracted, pulled, captured,
These are her powers.
She traps their hearts and souls.
She needs them to survive
Living of their flesh and blood
To maintain eternal life.

She seeks out her prey.
Males are the vampire's prey
From which one shall live
She sinks her teeth into the punctured skin
And drains them of mortality,
Taking them to a world that vanishes.

It vanishes from the human eye,
And their lives are non-existent.
They too, in turn, provide her with life.
They are her source, her life, her power.
Discarding un-needed flesh and tonight's feed,
She sleeps, preparing for another night.

Caroline Shouksmith

"Rollup Rollup"

The fairground lad, riddled and bad,
With a winning smile, and style he had,
a confident aura, that appeased the girls
As he strut his stuff amid the spins and swirls,
The glint in his eyes, stories told, beleaguered lies,
Living on one-night love, beer and pies.
This nomadic life only suits some —
The lost, the outcast and those on the run.
Calloused you have to be, to fit in,
Not shy of a brawl, or occasional sin
That brings in more trouble, of which you've no need
Thrills paid for loose, greasy, gypsy, breed.
From the big dipper to the coconut shy
I've been watching you, and I gotta ask "Why
Do you live like this?" Hey don't take the piss."
"Cos I don't like ironed, shirts, and regular stuff like this."
"For that comfortably starched, news at ten lifestyles, not me,
When I peg a new field, and lubricate imagination,
On what it's like to be free."

P.J. Sharpe

The Moonlight and Me

The moon shone brightly onto the sea
Laying a path of moonlight in front of me.
The pier was lit up, its lights shining bright,
Silhouetted against the blackness of night.
Smells floated by on the cool evening breeze;
Of the salty sea and the nearby pine trees.
And couples walked by, so much in love,
Surrounded by stars that twinkled above.
But I stood and waited until everyone was gone,
Until everything was still, and I was alone.

I imagined myself walking across the sea.
The moonlight path was calling to me;
"I know your secrets, I know your dreams,
And I hold the answers in my moonbeams.
Just walk up my path, walk into my light,
Look into my world where everything is right."
For a while I was tempted, I wanted to find
The answers to the questions in the back of my mind.
But did I really hear what the moonlight said,
Or did I imagine the voice in my head?
One thing is for certain, as I stood by the sea,
The only ones there were the moonlight and me.

Rachel Sidebottom

Animals

Dolphins swim, dolphins hide,
Dolphins play in the tide,
They play tricks in the water
Over rope that couldn't be tauter.

A dog swims with a furry coat,
In the water chasing a boat,
It swims ashore and shakes it's body,
And water flies on everybody.

A cat appears in a hedge,
So quickly see the sparrows fledge,
The sparrows settle in their nest,
Time for their long days peaceful rest.

A cat chases a tiny mouse,
And leaves it's footprints through the house,
It escapes through a very tight gap,
Where it has its long night's nap.

Two little foxes chase each other,
Until they hear the call of their mother,
They hide behind the long tail grass,
Until the cruel poachers pass.

Peter Shora

November 11th - Remembrance Day

Every November I wear with pride,
A poppy in memory of the men who died.
In two world wars they gave their all,
In answer to their countries call.
The supreme sacrifice they all made,
And now in foreign fields are laid.
May they sleep in peace for evermore,
The innocent victims of two dreadful wars.

Mrs. K. Schofield

I Have Never Regretted

I want you to know, of that year in the past
I have never regretted, meeting you
And the happy times, we have spent together
I have never regretted, marrying you
And the many times, that were cruel and hard
I have never regretted, caring for you
And with all our tears, of joy and sadness
I have never regretted, loving you
The times you would need, a shoulder to cry on
I have never regretted, holding you
And when you brought our children, into this world
I have never regretted, helping you
And throughout the years, of your love and care
I have never regretted, knowing you
And I want you to know, through the passage of time
I will never regret, being with you.

Robert Sibbald

A Love Song In Springtime

Down in the green dales, the young lambs are leaping,
On heather-clad hills, the roe deer roam free;
High in the blue sky, a skylark is singing,
And my thoughts are winging, home towards thee.

On open pasture, the green grass is growing,
The soft rain is falling, so pleasant to me;
O'er woodland and lea, the cuckoo is calling,
And I am fast falling in love, dear, with thee.

On every tree, fresh foliage is forming,
Bluebells are blooming, so lovely to see;
All birds are nesting, ring-dove and starling,
My own love! My darling! I'm in love with thee.

Over the hills, a rainbow is shining,
The sun is declining, out over the sea;
This spring day is fading, the lambs they are lying,
My darling, I'm dying, for love of thee.

S.J. Short

Old Man

As time went by
His will had grown weak
While gazing at the sky
His manner turned meek
The courageous heart
The pillar of might
Had been the start
Of his vainglorious fight
First came the temptation
Then the addiction
The endless frustrations
Of the perpetual affliction

James Salt

The Food Of Love

The table is diversely laid;
That for one course alone
Is ushered by a single beat,
As if desire might vanish with a chord.
Should feeling stay so bare?
Yet it may daub with brighter hues
Lives mouldering in a drab world.
But deeper in the spirit lies
A hunger for the full repast,
With harmony conjoined,
Digesting sweet and bitter fruit
With joy and sorrow, each
The provender for tears.

Dr. W.I.D. Scott

Follow Me

Close your eyes and follow me,
Through the darkness to eternity.
There to find what you aspire,
To dream the dream of your desire.

Trace the heavens in the sky,
Climb those mountains way up high.
Explore the wonders out in space,
Leave the earth, the human race.

Alight upon an unknown land
Blow the stardust from your hand.
Pluck a moonbeam from a tree,
Shut your eyes and come with me.

Together we will build a dream,
Side by side we'll be supreme.
Sleep, to let us make a start,
Close your eyes, let us depart.

B.E. Simmons

Rwandan Boy

The wee boy sits in the burning dust,
His eyes lack lustre, his stomach out-thrust,
Bewildered and starving as fool doesn't come
He scrapes the parched earth in the hope of a crumb
The innocent victim of war and of strife
No one to help with a long, cool drink,
No one to care, or even to think
Of the wee boy
Out there in the dust.

In the lights of the city the banquet goes on,
Given in honour of some favoured son,
Piles of rich food and endless champagne,
Most of it wasted with lofty disdain
Money uncounted on jewels and dress,
Laughter and boredom, no sign of distress,
They're dancing for charity,
"My Dear, yes we must,"
And the wee boy rolls over,
And dies in the dust.

Clara M. Sims

The Myth Of The Poet

Shouldn't a poet's life be hard?
Don't good poets suffer for their art?
No one there to lend a hand,
No one there to give them a start.

Doesn't a good poet dream of hell?
With recurring nightmares again and again.
Isn't his mind consumed with lingering doubts?
His body racked with pain.

Isn't his home a crumbling old garret?
Or one solitary room in a tower.
Doesn't he have trouble exercising his mind?
While over him, others exercise power.

Isn't he commanded to write this or write that?
To a deadline impossible to meet.
Doesn't he go home to his hovel each night,
Dreaming of shoes for his feet?

Isn't he a person gaunt and thin?
Driven on by lack of food.
Doesn't the hunger in the pit of his stomach
Create his poem's mood?

Perhaps poets like that really existed,
But only in art or in books.
Because in spite of all their deprivations,
They're depicted with stunning good looks!

Stephen Sippitt

The Man And The Beast

It was time to feast,
So out set the man and the beast.
Both hunters, both hunted,
Both cunning, both running.
Both in time to meet,
But which was to be the other one's meat?
Neither it seems, as they kill each other,
And the Vulture swoops down to eat.

Carson Scott

She Said ...

I want to lie and muse with you
By the fire and watch the patterns flow.
I want to drink of life anew
And feel the pulse within you grow.
But as flame borne pictures change and move
Our lives together slip and fold
To drift apart by distance torn
Caught in life's throw that others mould.

Cool now the embers of our simple tryst
Black now the colour of my heart's torment
But deep in love's ashes the heat remains
To rekindle the fires when we next meet
In some part of this unfamiliar orb
Where our lives resume their rightful being
Two tortured souls to join again.

Richard Sharpe

The Return

I gallop through the mist enshrouded trees
And where my feet have trod, flowers grow
I sniff the scent floating in the breeze
Of magical spells of long ago

I toss my head and rainbows fill the skies
The skylark's love song breaks the silence
My tears, reflected in the curlew's cries
Are for this sad world of endless violence

With pointed horn, I draw a circle on the ground
And mystical music lingers in the hollows
The sunset spreads its cloak of gold around
My bed of moss and ferns among the shadows

The purple brooding night ends,
And with the dawn,
I dream that peace returns with me —
The Unicorn

Grace Sim

Salisbury Plain

Long ago born a pleasant scene
In an open land of green
Around the chalky gorse bank hills
A ghostly peaceful atmosphere stills
There beyond under a circle of trees
Gusting gently a fresh hill breeze
Surrounded by tired limbs creaking
Rests a lamb mildly bleating
Here on the roving grassy dales
Stood sheep dips, dew ponds and mossy bricked wells
Where wide old shepherds once told wise tales
Flocks of sheep and sweet tinkling bells
Busy sheep dogs crossed flowering downs
Passing neglected burial mounds
Woods and glades untouched, so wild
The wonder of every nature's child
Here twittering larks still proudly fly
Soaring high in deep blue skies
A timeless place to be alive
It could be 1885
Dream of this again and again
Beloved beautiful Salisbury Plain.

Edward Phillip Smith

I Thought The War Would Never End

I thought the war would never end
Perhaps it never did
I was just a young boy then
God, I was just a kid!
Now I'm just an empty shell
A man without a mind
One too many bombshells
Exploding out of time

Out there on the battlefield
There was glory to be won
Out there on the battlefield
My daring deeds were left undone

Now I'm trapped by what I've seen
My mind is trapped in limbo
These walls are scrubbed so very clean
And there are bars up at the window
We were all just young boys then
Yes, we were all just kids
We thought the war would never end
For some it never did.

Richard Sims

A Husband's Tomorrow

I'll fix that gate tomorrow if I can find the time,
paint the garage doors again, repair the washing line.
Attention to the garden, really is a must,
but I cannot use the mower till I've removed the rust!

Once the mower's working, I'll quickly cut the lawn,
then I'll mend the lounger, I see the corner's torn.
Tomorrow if it doesn't rain, I'll give the car a clean,
that should please the 'better half',
    she said she thinks it's green!

Perhaps I'll dig the borders and plant some flower seeds,
but then, of course, I can't do that
    till I've removed the weeds.
When I've finished planting I'll connect the garden hose
but I first must mend those little slits,
    from where the water flows.

Tomorrow if it doesn't rain, I'm going to be so busy,
the thought of all the jobs to do, makes me feel quite dizzy.
Perhaps I shouldn't do too much, there's always other days,
Rome wasn't built in only one — so everybody says.

So tomorrow on reflection, whether rain or sun,
I'll have another day to think about what's to be done.

Mrs. E. Smith

My Family

I have got seven lovely daughters
Also I have got four boys
When they were all much younger
They had loads and loads of toys

There were dolls and prams and footballs
All strewn around the floor
Whips and tops and marbles
One could hardly get through the door

Well they are all more or less grown up now
With children of their own
Somewhat my family has dwindled
There's just one son and me left at home

I'm a widow and thought I'd be lonely
I miss him and always will too
But now there's the grandchildren, all twenty-eight
So I've no time at all to feel blue

The love that surrounds us is wondrous to see
What more could you really expect
After all I'm a Mum and a Nanna
And this then, is my family

J.M. Skitrall

Healthy Reading

Have you ever sat down to look,
Through an A-Z household medical book?
Giving details of illnesses and infections.
Not to mention the various injections,
Listing the symptoms, prognosis and cure,
You know the kind of thing, I'm sure!

Well, I started to read one last night,
And to be honest, I'm now filled with fright!
After reading, my whole body shook,
Since, I recognised every symptom in the book.
My chances of survival are slim, no doubt,
Because, I've had every disease they have written about!

I only managed to read up to the letter 'G',
Which reminds me, I must go to see my GP.
I have to get treatment for my back pain,
And really, should check out this weight gain!
Perhaps, I should discuss getting my appendix out,
And while I'm there, I could always mention my gout!

Before I go, I should get on with my reading,
In case there's any other information he'll be needing.
So on with the letter 'H' I'll go,
Oh! This one looks very interesting you know!
In self-diagnosing — I've definitely got the knack,
And one thing I'm sure — I'm not a Hypochondriac!!

Elizabeth Sirrell

'Tis Not 'Good-bye!'

Sleep, sleep, my dear
My very dear, my Love!
For Mother Earth extends her arms.
She longs to hold you gently,
Soothe away the years,
The ears grown deaf, the eyesight dimmed.
Sleep! Sleep, my dear,
My very dear, my Love!
And do not strive to wake again
To age and its infirmities.

And I shall stroke the living grass
That wraps you,
Watched by bright pansies' eyes
That see you,
Whispering to the talking leaves
That hear you,
You will be always there, my dear!
My very dear! My Love!

Miss M. Salter

In Search Of Minerva

It will be all right they said
when seals on shiny beach lay dead.
When whales meet a bloody fate
in lonely search to find a mate.
Dark seas from darker rivers fed,
it will be all right they said.

When the young in corners sleep
in hopeless, homeless, timeless deep
and jobless men in mounting tide
search aimless weeks and stolen pride.
When women fear the devils leap,
left bloody bundle, loved ones weep.

Behind this dark stage curtain seen,
in desperate search when times are lean
Minerva is so hard to find,
whose gentle magic closely bind.
Once looked back in secret dream
and still the forest since has been.

J.P. Simons

Nature

We cannot believe that autumn is here
There's quite a breeze and chill in the air
The summer was long and hot and dry
With never a cloud in a perfect blue sky.
The beautiful flowers are beginning to fade
While the leaves on the trees turn to all different shades.
The swallows have long gone to lands far away
To follow the sun but return they may
When winter is over and spring comes again
Gone is the snow, frost and rain.
And nature will have completed its circle
With the wonder of life we call a miracle
That things can die and yet remain
From year to year exactly the same.
The colour, the scent, to see and smell
No matter how long your thoughts may dwell
The mystery of Nature is from heaven above
Where everything lives in perfect love
So that is why the beauty of flowers and trees
Are given to remind us of all these.

Ann Smith

Christmas With God

Christmas with God, Oh what Joy,
The beautiful face of a Baby Boy,
God in his childhood, just like Thee,
Smiling and happy and full of glee.
Christmas, Christmas.

Christmas with God, all Glory on High,
Tells of the good news reaching the Sky,
Hour after Hour of enchanting delight,
The wondrous stars showing their light.
Christmas, Christmas.

Christmas with God is Prayer and Peace,
Family Love is widely increased,
Young and Old, together at last,
Sharing their future, reliving their past.
Christmas, Christmas

Christmas with God on Christmas Day,
Long may it last, forever we pray.

Margaret Silcock

Facts of a Modern Life

Watch out it's out there
Too many people don't seem to care
The fools believe you can only catch it is you're gay
The fact is more heterosexuals are catching it every day.

We live in a permissive society
The age of sexual variety
Safe sex is not a problem
This is the time of the condom.

HIV is a virus without a conscience
Does not suffer from prejudice
It will not matter what colour you are
Turning a blind eye will not get you very far.

Aids is a problem that will not go away
Unfortunately it's here to stay
In time this illness will be beaten
But what a high price mankind will pay.

Being permissive without protection
Only increases the risk of infection
If you're not careful you risk being another statistic
So use a condom let's be realistic.

Mark Slade

A Visit to Santa

We set off to the shopping mall
With my daughter dressed to kill.
I knew that seeing Santa
Would give her such a thrill.

So we put her onto Santa's knee
She giggled and she laughed.
"Oh yes", I thought "It's going to be
A perfect photograph."

But then to my embarrassment
She grabbed old Santa's beard
Off it came in pieces
And everybody cheered.

And as if that wasn't bad enough
Poor Santa came to me
And showed me that he had
A little damp patch on his knee!

The excitement had been all too much
My daughter made it clear
That we'd have to just content ourselves
And try again next year.

Janette Sloan

Our Favourite Garden Seat

I dreamed I saw the future as in my usual retreat.
I sat among my flowers on my favourite garden seat.

I saw a young man garden with what was tender loving care.
He told me of the flowers that his grandad had planted there.

The flowers painted pictures which came up brighter year by year.
And the young man proudly said that his grandad had put them there.

I enjoyed our daily chat although I had not known him long.
I was the grandad mentioned and I had died when he was young.

Then appeared by his side a gentle lady grey of hair.
And although she could not see me she knew full well that I was there.

She spoke to the handsome lad "Is grandad here again today?"
"Yes grandma" he said I was so she decided she would stay.

Then she shuffled to the shade to escape from the summer's heat.
She came and sat beside me on our favourite garden seat.

John Smark

Memories

As I look back through the years,
All of the memories reduce me to tears,
I think of the times when we used to play,
And in my heart you'll always stay.
In the winter we sat by the fire,
And in the spring we walked by the briar,
When summer came we bathed and shared our ice cream,
Oh, these memories, how long ago they seem.
Autumn and we'd walk through the leaves,
Your lead in my hand,
We'd stand,
And watch them fall from the trees.
Enjoy your sleep my little one,
Snoopy "Old Son".
One day, you'll wake,
And I will take,
You into my arms.
We will sit in a heavenly land,
With beaches and palms.
Until then, enjoy your rest,
Don't forget you are the best.
Because my little Snoopy, I'll always love you true,
You're my Snoopy - That's who!

Laura Smith (Age 13)

The Magic Flageolet

On the coastal path from Lyme Regis,
Under Ware Cliffs, near where the Landslip
Cataclysm occurred one Christmas Day
(In eighteen thirty nine, "actually"!)
We found a penny-whistle - possibly left
By some sprite of the ample woodland there?
Welcomed as a magic omen
That not one of us knew how to play,
We took it to Sidmouth, then back to Lyme
And, down from Broad Street, sat, resting,
Looking out beyond Lyme's broad Bay.
Two backpack-youths were seated nearby.
"Pardon me," one of them politely said,
"But did you, maybe, find that penny-whistle
Beyond the Cobb?" Treasuring an omen,
I respectfully replied: "If it's yours -
Then play it - to make it yours again!"
The youth did: made Lyme's air dance a jig!
So ... up Broad Street to a tavern, where
Two generations harmonized
With themselves - and lost property found -
In the form of a magical penny-whistle!

Herbert Smith

425

Depression

Bemused am I today, what sad and ill-gotten thoughts lie within my heart
I feel an ache inside which should be shed, like a seed to the wind,
Blown far away never to take root again.
This world takes the blame for today, it is upside down, and throwing me around,
I am on my head, and can't think straight,
Go away my poor heart bleats, it's time you took your heavy load,
And trundled off to where all burdens go.
Leave peace and quiet, not torment tugging at my strings,
Why was it only yesterday I heard a blackbird sing.
But not today ill-fated though I feel, doomed like a tiger in a cage,
Yes I do feel this is not the way my poor heart should suffer,
So I say pain and misery, ache and woe, please won't you just go.
Fly like a bird if you so wish, leave my heart and me in tranquility,
Becalmed with peace of mind, for tomorrow when I awake I will be myself I do so wish.

Dorothy Smith

Childhood Lost

High above the webbed skies I can see no lies,
Way below in dark warm earth I can hear no cries.
A dream I have of children set free with no worries or cares;
Parents no longer afraid of their dares.
Why is it nowadays little children are not safe on our streets
Years ago it was not like this is it real I weep.
One day will they once be free, or will this society now so
Changed allow their invisible bonds to remain.
Every child in all the world should be able to play without
The worry of their day.

C.I. Smith

A Fruit and Nut Case

I can't get away from the thought of food
This diet is driving me mad
I still feel I look like a pudding
('Tho a syrup one wouldn't be bad!)

I can't get away from the thought of food
It's a weakness of mine - I know
So I'm taking two weeks away from it all
In a Black Forest Château!

Bev Scott-Fagg

Requiem

All the young men have gone,
Abe, Hiram, Bud and Ike, Billy and Cyrus,
Who chewed, cursed, gambled, feared, and dreamt
Of Pennsylvania, Iowa and Kansas.
Their dreams are dead, their longings spent,
Nothing is left but half-forgotten tales,
Crumbling concrete where the flight path went,
Stubble and marshalled lines of barley bales.

All the young men have gone,
No longer shall we bid them sele o' the day,
Only the night breeze scythes their orison,
The Suffolk girls they kissed have long turned grey,
The swing-time songs they sang have floated far away
Beyond the steadfast everlasting fields.

Norman Sinclair

Mother

Mother, why are you sad?
I hate to see you cry,
Is it something that I've done, mam?
Please tell me and I will try
To make your life more pleasant, mam
Because I hate to see you cry.

I know you have always struggled mam
When we were all at home
You never ever left us mam
Never left us on our own.

Now you are growing old and wrinkled
With silver in your hair
But we will always love you mam
And we will always care.

David Smith

Within Four Walls

In the east the rising sun,
Proclaims "a new day has begun",
A chance to put the world to rights,
Or just to watch the grown men fight.
Within four walls they can't be heard,
Their arguments go undeterred.

A mother lays her child to rest,
No longer will he need her breast,
Her tears of sorrow, anguish, pain,
Help console a heartfelt drain.
Within four walls it can't be seen,
Where his cradle would have been.

Grown men journey through the rain,
To their place of work again,
To be told they're unemployed,
Is something that they can't avoid.
Within four walls it can't be felt,
Humility, embarrassment.

In the west the setting sun,
Tells me that this day is done,
Different people everywhere,
Different stories of despair.
Within four walls I'm locked away,
Keep me safe, O Lord I pray.

Derek J. Starkey

Where There's Life

Ah, yes, come in, she's over there
We dress and sit her in that chair
She never speaks, but like her food
So keeps quite well we can conclude

Hello — it's me again
Your skirt — that looks a nasty stain
Don't stare through me at the wall
Aren't you pleased I've come to call?
Now stop that sobbing — we must believe
That you feel nothing and cannot grieve

We can't know — you don not tell
Is life for you a barren hell?
Eternal night as cold as stone
A battle you must fight alone
Or is there light behind that gaze?
Perhaps you dwell in bygone days
When he world was your oyster and you its pearl
Each hour an adventure for an eager young girl

Who knows? Not us — we just surmise
A total void beyond blank eyes
Oh, please — no more empty tears
For surely they're not joy or fears
Emotions you don't show or share
But deep inside, are they still there?

Gary Smith

Alone

She sits staring.
Smiling, like she is happy.
She pretends to listen, but doesn't.
She thinks, she dreams.
She wishes to be elsewhere.
But she isn't. She will be stuck there,
Forever.
In the dark, lonely corner of life.
Alone.

Greig Smith

Autumn Leaves

With light and gentle action
They make their way to earth,
In dress of bronze and copper
That changed their green of birth;
In helpless, sad surrender
The lovely leaves of Autumn
They drift upon the breeze
Now severed from their trees.

The soft rain falls upon them
And footprints press them down,
Till dark and cold and quiet
They pass into the ground:
But from the rotted leaf mould
New glory shall appear,
And other leaves find nurture
To meet their glad new year.

Ann L. Smith

The Solemn Vows

The solemn vows were spoken
One year ago today
To cherish, love and honour
Is what we heard you say
A candle was ignited
As in the days of old
And placed upon your finger
A simple band of gold.
Love was all around you
And on your shining faces,
A little tear had trickled down,
And left its tiny traces.
God bless you both my children
And in the years ahead
May love be ever present
Wherever you may tread.

Betty Shanks

Autumn Leaves

The leaves are falling from the trees,
Brown, red, yellow and gold.
Carpeting the fields and lanes.
A precious sight there to behold.
Crisp and crunchy underfoot,
And dancing in the breeze,
Happy that their job is done,
And they have left the trees.
The trees are stretching out their limbs,
Their message is quite clear,
Good-bye, dear friends, it's time to sleep,
Now autumn time is near.
Your precious gift of life is passed,
The joys you gave unswerving,
For when you dwelt upon the trees,
In glory you were serving.
And now the time has come to rest,
And we shall slumber on,
Till Spring comes round again once more,
Our duty we have done.

Edith M. Smith

Grandma

I know that grandmas are full of moans,
"My poor old feet, my aching bones."
When they visit you purse your lips,
Don't guzzle your drinks, take little sips,
Because they're watching for a chance to say
"We didn't do that in OUR day.
We were well behaved, had manners too,
We crooked little fingers dipping bread in stew.
We stood up whilst old folks sat,
Always wiped our feet on the door mat.
I don't know what it's coming to
If we're to depend on the likes of you!"
But I wouldn't mind if mine said that,
Or if she visited me for a little chat,
Because mine sits and groans upon my bed,
I'd rather visit her instead.
All I want to do is hide
Because its ten whole years since she died!

Karen Smith

Untitled

To stand and stare at a withering tree
A tree that's older than you or me
To wonder when the seed was sown
Back in the distant days of old
To think of eternal everlasting space
To think that there may be another race
To know that man's life span is short
Against the eternity of it all
Then surely we must pause and think
Of the bickering ways of the human race
We cry aloud that they are black
And they in turn in anger answer back
We go to war and kill the foe
And find that after all he was only John Doe
He was the same as you, the same as I
But caught in this mad race, he had to die
We spend and build for another war
Whilst little children starve next door
We work and sweat and make a name
But when we've gone it's just a shame
Then why not look into outer space
Or at a tree that lives out the human race
Then someday we may learn to know
That we are but grains of sand in a world that's grand.

J.W. Smith

The Skint Granny

I read your notice in our daily paper,
And thought I'd try this poetry caper.
I'm a Granny with six grandkids,
And Christmas presents need many quids,
But paying the bills is a bit of a curse,
And always leaves me with an empty purse.
So gifts get smaller, and the kids they huff,
'Cos I can't afford this computer stuff.
We go down to the shops to have a look,
But they'll probably get the usual book.
I'd love to buy what they'd really like,
A couple of games, or a mountain bike.
This would be possible with some spare cash,
That's why I decided to have a bash.
So now I'll trust to Lady Luck
To see if I've earned an extra buck,
But if I haven't I'll try next year,
And wipe away a little tear.
I've got some tissues nice and handy
But if I don't need them, that's just dandy,
'Cos if I'm lucky, and I win your prize,
I'll see delight in the children's eyes.
Then all the judges I'd like to thank,
And the remainder I'd put in the local bank.

Jay Mil

Rose Of Peace

Like a tear drop on a cheek
On a rose petal raindrops sleep
The morning breeze like a sigh
Moves the petals who seem to cry

Oh Rose of Peace so aptly named
Of creamy face and pink tint framed
Your beauty's there for all to see
In a garden of glory forever free.

Phyllis Smith

The Ballet Of The Trees

As I look thru the window on a windy day,
I see the trees all dancing across the way,
Tall poplars sway to and fro,
As if they hear the music come and go.

Bowing and waving with such delight,
It surely is a wonderful sight.
A ballet in all its beautiful splendour,
Is being performed for our blessed maker,
Thanking Him for their leaves so green
They truly make a wonderful scene.

But when the wind has ceased, and the trees are at rest,
That's when you can see them at their very best,
So tall and stately, full of majesty
Just as God made them to be.

Irene May Smith

Fear Of The Unknown

Death is darkness, the unending night,
The fear of the unknown, gives each the strength to fight.
Another battle, another day.
To strive to keep the inevitable away.

Pain, oh how it tortures our bodies
It saps our will, robs us of our hobbies,
The daily tasks that were such a chore,
No longer seem to be a bore.

Pills and potions, gels and creams,
Popping them, dropping them, I want to scream.
Why me, why me, and every day
My life is ebbing away, fast.

Turn back the clock, turn back the time,
Give me the body that once was mine,
End the agony, end the pain,
Bury me in the sunshine, not the rain.

P. Skipworth

Untitled

Beauty is to the beholder
that is true to say
but we all see things of beauty
in an individual way

Some see it in a young child
full of smiles and grace
some in an old woman
as she deftly weaves fine lace

Others see it in the dawning
with dew on grass and flowers
some in the deepest heavens
which they study long night hours

Some see it in the oceans depth
with coral growing on its bed
some in the colours of a diamond
or in a ruby's deepest red

All our world is full of beauty
sky, sea, land and tree
but my own things of beauty
are as individual as me.

A.G. Spall

To A Snowdrop

O you tiny little thing
    Are you the Herald of the Spring?
From the ground, where you stay,
    Looking for the light of day.

O you pretty little thing
    Are you the Harbinger of Spring?
On stilted legs, you tiny face,
    Ever dancing, full of grace.

O you lovely little thing
    Crowned in glory, like a king,
Nodding here, and nodding there
    Looking around you everywhere.

O you dainty little thing
    Beautiful as a butterfly wing,
With tiny petals, white and clean,
    Ever waiting to be seen.

You arrive out of the blue
    When no one is expecting you,
You surprise us every year,
    When we see your form appear.

You are not with us very long
    But we miss you when you've gone,
Back to the Earth, to sleep and rest,
    And to return, looking your best.

Joan Smith

Pigs That Fly

Last night what should I see soar through the sky,
But those rarest of birds — pigs that fly;
And as they glid on silken wings,
That flock of hogs did gently sing.

Like a heavenly host they grunted their tune,
Heard by the listening Earth, stars and Moon,
An all of those stood close below,
Who by Fortune's chance did witness the show.

Through the night air the words shimmered down.
Soft on the lucky ones, there on the ground.
A message for all the faint, down-hearted.
A message that shall now be imparted.

"We are the pigs who fly through the sky,
The ones who even gravity defy.
We shall never be tethered, butchered or sold,
We are the pigs who will never grow old.

"We are the pigs who shall ever be free,
The ones who eat acorns straight from the tree.
We are the ones who are truly real,
The pigs who exist for those who believe.

Mark B. Smith

A Perfect Stranger

One day — while walking by the river
    I met a man more fair than most
He bore the shoulders of a warrior
    Yet wore the pallor of a Ghost.
He said "I'm listening to the river
    As it rushes to the sea
It's saying that a perfect stranger
    Will pass this way and comfort me."
I gave him water from my flagon
    And broke in half my humble bread
His sapphire eyes grew wide with wonder
    And in a voice of silver thread
He said "I've come from o'er the water
    I've walked a thousand lonely years
My feet are black and sorely broken
    Their only salve has been my tears."
He said in all his weary travels
    That I alone had bade him dine
My humble bread became a banquet
    My flagon overflowed with wine.

Margaret Morley Smith

Memories

You've a smiling face and I know you care
As you smooth out the knots from my tangled hair.
But I know sometimes you think I'm not there
When you look at my eyes and see a vacant stare.

It's not that at all, I'm just far away in the
Lovely world of yesterday.
Where the summer days were gloriously long,
And I remember the words of a well loved song.

I am growing old, near my three score and ten
But I see it all so plain again.

I can't always remember from day to day,
But can bring back memories from far away.
Some of them joyful, some of them sad,
But now even those don't seem so bad.

The friends I had, I have some still,
Who have been to my bedside while'st I've been ill,
With the good Lord's grace I'll be up again
Leaving behind this bed of pain,
With my memory refreshed and my body healed.
It is marvellous what power love and prayer can yield.

So to my good friends and nurses so kind,
There is just one thought left in my mind,
How can I thank them, what can I say
But only remember them when I pray.

Mrs. M.H. Smith

My Borders

Three mighty sentinels proudly stand
Watching over their borderland
A land of beauty, a place so fair,
Where run freely the fox and the hare.

Winding rivers, a gurgling stream
Waterfalls raging — a photographer's dream
Heather clad hills, moors coarse and wild,
Steep-sided gullies, gentle valleys so mild.

Beneath craggy peak or rolling hill
Lies a loch — its waters so still
Swans and waterfowl gently swim by
As the peewit utters its plaintiff cry.

The Ettrick shepherd sits watching the shore
A land of history — and folklore
Gravestones so old nestle on the slope
Where blanket preaching gave covenanters hope.

Thomas the Rhymer and his fairy glen
Wallace's statue in its leafy den
The Abbey where lies The Bruce's heart
Brings us back to our journey's start.

Three Eildon hills stand in line
The guardians of this land of mine.

Marilyn Smith

Impressions

If a travelling spaceman landed on earth,
How would he assess her inhabitants worth.
The lasting impression this stranger would get,
Would largely depend on the people he met.
Would they show him the beauty of a tree, of a flower,
or explain the logic of nuclear power.
Would they show him our creatures, how birds swoop and soar,
or strategic positions in our first or last war.
Would they treat this man kindly, with truth, trust and love,
or show him the hatred we're capable of.
Would they tell him how grateful we are for our sun,
or lead him away at the point of a gun.
Would they dismiss all he said 'out of hand'
and crucify him 'cause they don't understand.
What would he take with him of that he has seen,
Has this man yet to come, has he already been?

Elizabeth E. Smullen

The Game of Chance

In every walk of life - there are so many kinds
Some seem so content - whilst others have troubled minds
There are so many lonely folk - their plight is so heartfelt
And they must play as best they can - the hand that they were dealt

Some will seek their fortune - will search from near and far
Others get so much pleasure - from a simple shooting star
For some its just the high-life - always on the "Scene"
Try sitting in a valley - by a flowing silver stream

Some overflow with happiness - they make the most of time
Happy smiling faces - eyes like sparkling wine
For some there is love gone wrong - best that they should part
How can you measure time - to heal a broken heart

Those who have their riches - can always pay their way
For many other people - another hungry day
Life is just a gamble - but you should not lose face
If you ever get your chance - then you must play your "Ace"

In this world there's so much hurt - and if we knew the truth
Most would love to live again - the seasons of their youth
Those whose world has fallen apart - I'm really sure that they
Would trade in their tomorrows - for just one yesterday

Life if just a game of chance - it sometimes seems a curse
But if you look around you - there's always someone worse
Don't give up, play your hand - see how things unfold
Just keep on chasing rainbows - and find your crock of gold

Alice Sobczak

Jealousy

I envy looks and personality.
Talent, wealth and originality.
I hate people who wield great power,
And grow more famous by the hour.
I despise energy and youth,
Whilst I grow longer in the tooth.
In spite of this, I have a prize:
A glaring pair of big green eyes!

Mrs. S. M. Solden

Home the Prison, Valium the Keeper

She can show you courage,
at the opening of a door,
and a long, lonely walk
down an overgrown path
towards freedom.

She can show you fear,
at the wild beating of a heart,
and a trembling hand
that searches out safety
from a tiny bottle.

Julia A. Smith

Hope

In passion and pain,
Jesus Christ dies again.
Let's hope not in vain,
To our eternal shame.

Every murdered child,
Will open his side.
Each innocent lost,
Nails him on that cross.

ALL hatred and scorn,
Crowns him with thorns.
All things grotesque,
A lance at his chest.

It's never too late,
Save him from this fate.
Be Christian and true,
Let God's light shine through.

You could say a prayer,
Should never despair.
He'll always be there,
He'll never leave you.

Mark Sims

The Road

The road is long and winding
And when we think we're finding
What we're looking for
We often reach another unexpected door.

It can leave you scared if you feel unsure
So reach out for God's gracious hand
And he will make you more secure.
He will lead you, if you let him
Through that mysterious door
And guide you on the winding road
The way you weren't looking for.

But it's difficult to see the road
When you are down and feeling blind
Self enemies, like ugly toads;
Crouching, leaping close behind.

Don't let impatience falter your foundations
Or bitter self-pity blind you with temptations
It's hard to die to self-will when pride gets in the way
So just follow Jesus gladly and he'll brighten your darkest day.

Each time we stumble, each time we fall
Just remember to give our Lord Jesus a call,
He will come running with staff and rod in hand
He will lead us along the winding road on to the promised land.
Alleluia!

Ioana Soord

in a strange land

     the Norman cow country looked very like Berkshire
the woods of Burgundy could pass for the Chilterns
but we have come at last to an alien land
to southern Dauphiné where it borders Provence
     a long-settled country where enterprising Greeks
came from Marseille to trade and brought vine and olive
Hannibal's elephants lumbered their way across
     slim pointed churchyard trees authentic cypresses
stand very straight and black against a flawless sky
blue like Our Lady's robe quite unspotted by clouds
     the wide-arched balcony faces more or less south
the sun is quite early lost behind the high hills
we can sit on unchilled to watch the moon rising
     an evening of peace but a night of thunder
with pouring rain to swell the Aygues by the morning
from yesterday's trickle to a rushing torrent
     days oppressively hot from high humidity
come only now and then and the mistral clears them
a chill blast from the north but it brings back the sun
for sun-starved Northerners this is the place to be
     come here from late August until mid-October
and again in the spring but never cheat yourself
never think that for you this is a place to live
this dry land of the south too strange to be a home

Muriel Smith

Heathcliffe's Ode to Cathy

I cannot die without my soul,
I cannot live without my life,
I cannot love without my heart,
Fore 'ere I walk, I walk alone.

For shadow's dark and deep,
Into my very soul they creep.
'Ere I have loved someone so fine.
Until death doth strike,
May she be mine.

Where heather 'White' grows 'abound,
May they find me on the ground.
And to the castle, 'bove 'Pennistone Crag',
Where skies are blue, and birds do sing ...

Promise me, one final thing,
That you'll bury me where my heart lies.
And pray for me, with all your heart,
That one day as it was meant to be,
Hand in hand, and hearts entwined,
That she and I will walk away,
Into that 'Sunset', faraway ...

Suzanne Swift

Total Rejection

Just because you couldn't hear me,
It doesn't mean I wasn't there.
Just because you couldn't touch me
It doesn't mean I didn't love you.
I might have been a footballer,
a rock star or a top chef.
But I wasn't given the chance to live.

Didn't you want to hold me,
touch my hands and watch me smile?
Was total rejection the only way
you could cope with me and while
I waited to be murdered
you went about your daily life.
You didn't count your blessings
and I waited for the knife.

Next time you see a baby
Out for a walk, inside his pram
All dressed up to thrill his parents
Think of me. I was ... I am ...
The twinkle in my father's eye,
the cuddle in my mother's arms
I'm outside looking in. I can't
enter, just stare with hollow eyes
and a piercing scream.

Total rejection. Help me ...

Stella Smith

Overheard In A Bus

Bacon and eggs for breakfast
With coffee, black and strong.
A bus to catch,
The clock to punch,
A job to do,
And then to lunch.

Silly chatter,
Nitter, natter,
"Top of the Pops"
The Beatles, the cops,
Nylons and curtains, birds and men,
The state of the world without end, Amen.

Back to work, another half shift
Bus back home, or cadge a lift,
The wife, the kids sat down to tea
Going out? or watch T.V.?
The horses, the dogs, the Mirror, the Pools
The pub for a pint, Bingo where fools
Can fill their time and waste the hours
Till bed or death calls, or age devours.

Till then,
Bacon and eggs for breakfast
Ad infinitum, Amen

T.O. Smith

Questions?

Death, destruction, confusion, noise,
Life who chooses girls or boys.
Silence amid the chaos around us
Arrivals, departures, our platform of life.
Strangers become friends and lovers
Fluttering in and out of our lives.
Changes, endings, beginnings emerging form
Ourselves like butterflies.
Searching, seeking, always questions?
Will our knowledge harmonize.
Can we reach this body deep within
Free it from all guilt or sin?
Plan our pathways by meditation
Dictated by our contemplation.
Are the facts of life so simple
That we have choice of every dimple.
Love and hate, good or bad, heaven and hell
Are within us in every cell.
Can we rise above our low vibrations
Uniting colours, creeds and varied nations.
Is that our task, why we were born
Questions to answer not to scorn.
Can we fill our lives with love
Answers please, dear God above.

T. Stock

The School Teacher' End Of Term - July

It will not always be like this,
The school, pupil-less, a few last leavers
Adding their decoration
To the desks and wall, braiding their cuffs
With felt tip graffiti. The young girl preening
In the toilet mirror. Having looked up
From the daily chores, pause a minute,
Let the mind take its photograph
Of the school's scene. Something to wear warm
Against your heart, until the cold September!

R. Peter Smith

My Canine Friend, Bran

I know a young dog whose name is Bran
he doesn't do much but he does what he can.
He loves to walk and wag his tale
and I guess if he drank, he'd probably drink ale!
A braver dog I've never known
he barks at cats, even the telephone,
He lives a life envied by most
and lays awake at night guarding his post.
His hair is long and legs are short
but that doesn't stop him from being a good sport.
So here's to Bran whose talents are many
may he live long with his owners Penny.

Gary Snowball

Barn Owl

He was perched on the wall of a ruin,
I thought he was asleep,
So quite and still did he sit there,
But his eyes must have been open a peep,
I wanted to see a bit clearer,
So I took a step or two to the side.
And the wily old owl who had foxed me,
Took to flight with wings open wide.
As he soared to the sky above me,
With hardly a whisper of sound,
The barn owl kept a vigilant eye
For any movement on the ground.
I stood there in the fast falling dusk,
Watching his graceful flight,
And felt a little saddened,
As he disappeared from my sight.

Evelyn Smith

433

Untitled

I stood upon a fair green hill and
    viewed the country o'er,
I travelled back to childhood days
    and was a boy once more.
I lived again those happy days amongst
    trees and fields and flowers,
So long ago, so far away those happy
    carefree hours.

I saw again the laughing brook that
    wandered through the glen,
The stepping stones, the little bridge
    long built by hands of men
Long hours I spent (though all alone) I
    was not lonely there,
In all the world I have not seen a place
    that could compare.

Now that I'm old the scene has changed
    The glen forgotten dreams,
The brook for me is not the same, the
    laughing's stopped, it seems.
For time so quickly seems to pass as on
    through life we go,
And I shall never live again those days
    of long ago.

Gordon Smyth

The Green Field And The Brook

Not so very long ago,
When toddler's steps we took,
How wonderful in knowing
The green field and the brook

A magic world of daisy chains
And leap-frog in the grass —
Of paddling in the water
As summer days would pass ...

Simple little pastimes
To fill the childhood heart,
'Til waiting in the shadows
Were grown-up days to start

Too soon they came and with them brought
No time for joys we knew
To keep up with the Jones's
Is what we learned to do ...

Life goes by — we wonder why
Contentment's never met —
There's always something extra
We never seem to get ...

And now we buy our pleasures —
But if we cared to look,
No joy on Earth has e'er surpassed
That green field and the brook!

Doug Southall

Instantaneous Combustion

Shirts shout orders to be obeyed.
And I lie them uniform, upon the
Shirt chair — which they like
More than my back.

The chair cradles starch.
And I wince at the thought
Of creases — which I make so crisp,
And sweat to straighten.

Wincing comes direct from white:
Which must never be sullied!
It's always there —
There, upon the Christ Almighty chair.

In the middle of the dark, cold night,
Or miles from home where out of sight:
I lie awake — arise flash fast —
To straighten. As if my last!

Yet in your life, there are no chairs,
Or Regimental Sergeant Major Starch:
I trash those Christ Almighty shirts,
And lie crumpled in a heap with you.
Resurrected.

Tim Southwell

On My Father's Death

If with slow, sad footsteps I had thought
'Twas you we followed to the grave,
Then with tears fast flowing I had brought
Hurt to the brave.

That dear form, so icy-cold, so still,
Is but the instrument outworn
Not the musician's self, he will
Forbid us mourn.

Now anew on finer instrument
Tuned to his theme he weaves his song
With a divine accompaniment,
Joyous and strong.

Freed from the trammels of mortal strife,
Anxieties still increasing,
Suffering destined to last with life,
Pain unceasing,

The music rises to purer height,
The melody deepens and flows
And love yet burning, though veiled from sight,
Diviner glows.

This our firm belief and, even though
'Twere proved mistaken, sorrow's end
By death has been achieved; former foe
Now kindest friend.

Marguerite South

Good-bye
(Dedicated to my Dad)

As I stood next to your coffin to pray,
Hoping you'd give me strength for the next day,

Upon your face I could see a smile,
I talked to you for a little while.

I know you heard what I had to say,
I'm sorry that you had to go away,

A little tear drop rolled down my cheek,
When I realized you could not speak,

I wished I had the time to cry,
But instead kissed your forehead and said Good-bye.

Jacquie Smith

Ode To A Violin

Sweet violin play, music, play,
Hypnotise me with that melody I so love,
Mesmerise me with your gentle sway,
The music is rich as it blows, like blood.

Every beat of my heart in time with your tune,
You make my spirit sing and my soul swoon,
As I dance the night away under the waning moon,
Pity the dawn must arrive too soon.

The lonesome player stands, somewhere outside,
Making his bow strike those fragile strings,
My dance is a long journey, no end to this ride,
The night is serenaded by the music it brings.

Hayley Abigail Smith

Raindrops

Hundreds of tiny raindrops fall from the sky,
Splashing, splattering on the window pane,
Small globules of water from clouds up high
Hitting cold clear glass again and again.
Chalk pictures on pavements all meet their doom,
Damp clothes and hair, everything soaking wet
Coloured umbrellas burst into full bloom,
Dripping rooftops and shining streets of jet.
Damp fresh air, cold, clammy and foggy,
Sloshing through wet muddy puddles and pools,
Crispy leaves that once crunched go soggy.
And spider webs ornate with raindrop jewels.
People hide from rain like inky splashes,
Whilst outside the roaring thunder crashes.

Sally Spenceley

No One Knows Why!

No one knows how or even knows why
It can make you feel sad,
And it can make you cry!
The gift of feeling, caring and sharing,
Is a most precious gift,
But it can let your heart down,
Or it can give it a lift!
It does not warn when it will strike,
But when it does, it makes your heart shine,
Like a star in the night.
When you feel the pain of a Cupid's dart,
It can bring you joy,
Or tear you apart!
That is the power of a Cupid's dart!

Sandra Spinks

Sounds

What sounds do I love?
Church bells ringing on a Sunday morn,
Calling to worship our God up above.
The bird's chorus at dawn,
It's so wondrous to me how,
So simple a thrush can make such melody.
Music from the opera, Puccini,
And Andrew Lloyd Webber,
When I'm quiet and alone,
I could listen forever.
My children's laughs,
A rippling brook,
The purr of a kitten,
Turning the first page of a new book.
What a cruel place
The world would be,
If the sounds that I love
Were lost to me ...

Mrs. V. Soronow

Mother's Day

You really are a sweetie to think of poor ol' me
Who's never been a mother, but wished that she could be.
To receive a gift on Mother's Day, I was quite overcome,
A lump came into my throat — I became "Mum"

Thanks for the card you appropriately chose
And the pretty hanky adorned by a pink rose.
I shall always keep that lovely rose
And I'll think of you when I blow me nose.

While having had this little say
In a somewhat jocular way
Deep down these words are meant to convey
What it means to be remembered on Mother's Day.

Audrey V. Sutcliffe

Twilight - An In-Between Time

A slow, steady drift of light is leaving our world.
There is a sense of constriction: rigid anticipation.
Everything is suddenly prominent and taut.

A gust of wind on trees is met with adversity,
Their branches appear brittle and motionless;
Precise and waiting.

Tiny flying creatures dance around in their frenzied whirling groups.
It is darker, and the clouds are beginning to drift;
Our grey sheet slants slowly sideways, revealing a lighter clearness.

Is this growing coldness awakening something?
The gnats circle and swerve; down up, down up,
The grey sheet shifts into the distance, leaving the lighter clearness and its tendency to dim.

A sharp chirp above me,
Three birds silhouette across the clearness,
Wings flapping fast on a return flight.

Dark grey ridges stretch humungous long fingers across the sky,
Reaching for the slanting grey sheet.
Trees twitch at a slight breeze, their leaves give a shake; then still.

The clouds meet I feel what has been waited for has just arrived.
Whatever it is, is icy, likes stillness, and is dark.
Darker, and darker; then dark.

It has a smell of cold, misty freshness, smothering itself over the land.
This is night time:
Slipping through the trembling, opening door of twilight.

Jakqui Spedding

Back To Basics

Housing, buildings, mansions
    Construction or destruction,
These do not create a town.
    It is the quality and the customs
People handed down,
    This creates a living town.

To create a friendly, humanitarian atmosphere
    Free from hate or fear
That is deep within the memories
    Of those who dwelt therein,
A place which they held so dear.

These are the basic needs
    To sow the seeds
Which create an environment
    To live in freedom
From desolation or despair,
    A heritage of hope and trust
Handed down
    In a real home town.

S.V. Smy

Hypocrisy

I brought the wise men to my eyes
And read their worth that I may see
Through faith and fear and outright lies
And God retained His mystery

In life's long din I held my say
For fear I missed the savant's call
To glean his mind and find the way
To see the truth that answers all

I looked and longed that I may find
The lighted path that sets one free
But checked these chains for love so blind
Could shed no balming light on me

Deliverance was not my gain
If indeed there's such a thing
But pious paragons I disdain
Who love His way but hold their sting

And as I rest, my days but gone
Still wondering what life's all about
I marvel at these jewels that shone
And spoke so fine through devilled doubt

A.L. Spence

Flight

Cool grass beneath my feet, sun warms my face.
Toes softly caressed by dew, I'm free.
I leap into a frenzied dance, my hear does race.
Hair flows about my face, laughter fills the air.
Boundless energy born of loneliness reaches for the sky.
A butterfly joins my dance, a grand partner.
We twist and turn, his wings, my feet fly.
Songbirds our music no sweeter can be found.
The sun is slowly setting silently creeps in the dusk.
I see her, an old lady, grey hair bent of back.
She beckons, I do not want to go, but I must.
With heavy heart slow of step, I walk back into myself.

Sybil G. Smithson

The Empty House

On moonlight nights the empty house is dark.
It stand alone, forbidding, grim and stark.
A ghostly echo whispers through the eaves,
No breeze, but rustlings come from nearby leave.

From old, cracked windows gleams an eerie light
But four stone walls are still as black as night.
A distant clock chimes twelve, the midnight hour
When bats still circle round the lonely tower.

The musty rooms are dreary, damp and cold.
In darkest corners lurk huge spiders bold
Waiting and watching, black and still as doom
Among the cobwebs in that murky gloom.

The house is talked about for miles around.
Some say that ghosts and evil things abound
And other tell of many things to fear,
But no one *knows*, for no one dares go near!

Pat Smith

Currency Crisis

Floating currencies have become an international nightmare
Resulting in frequent bouts of monetary warfare
Between different currencies all over the world,
As speculators manipulate, the exchange rates are whirled.
There are regular fluctuations, as they play their finance game
Purely for their benefit as they continue to gain.
They compile their vast profit over and over
Whilst nations are left to take action to cover.
Countries need to spend reserves to counter a run,
No sooner has one ended before another has begun.
This results in pressure on countries and individuals too,
Bringing deprivation, anguish and ruin for the benefit of a few.

Ron Simmons

Untitled

Sitting by the window
Watching the rain
Listening as the droplets
Hit the window pane

The sun has disappeared
Behind the blackest cloud
What a dismal day
I want to shout out loud

I think about the weather
And the changes it brings forth
No two days the same
Just like South and North

I still sit by the window
Waiting for the sun
The clouds have gone
The sky is bright
You and me are one

Delia Spalding

Thinking Of You

Cornered by hands
In the wafer-thin light,
She shakes off antiseptic dreams
For a rash of speckled sand
And fingers of sunlight
Stroking her skin.

Feet baptised in barnacle pools,
Tokens exchanged in bingo halls:
She shuffles her thoughts
Of Blackpool days. Pearls of memory
Nestled in a time warp
Ticking like a bomb.

Water slowly trickles
Over cracked elbow ridges,
But her mind is racing
With the retreating tide
Shell-shocked with pleasure
As the big wheel turns.

The tired heart slips
Into starched white sheets,
Caught in a circus
Of neon. A clown's face
Twists into a shadowy pout.
All out.

Alan Spencer

Thoughts of Toya (Not Just an Ordinary Dog)

I am a thoroughly decent girl and Toya is my name
And here I hate to mention class, some say we're all the same.
My hair is short and very smooth, the colour it is gold,
And need I say that's quite high class, or so I have been told.
My mistress goes off to the garage, she's gone to get the car.
I hate to mention it of course it is a Jaguar.
She puts my rug upon the seat, it's here I settle down,
Then in she gets and off we go to our other house in town.
We roar off up our private drive, just leaving clouds of dust,
Instructions left for all the staff, this really is a must.
When I'm in town and on my rounds, I pass the time of day
By talking of my country seat, with rooms for work or play.
Now all at once the weekend's here and off we rush once more,
Off to our country residence with roses round the door.
We purr along our private drive, of gravel and small stone,
A reassuring feeling when you know that it's your own.
There's Doug the outside working staff, an ordinary sort of fellow,
Sometimes I let him pat my back when I am feeling mellow.
Vanessa is the indoor staff, she cleans up all around,
And checks, of course, to make quite sure my basket's been put down.
My master is due home quite soon and feeling full of stress
But he must keep up the pressure, if we're to have the best.

Douglas Spencer

Sombre November

No sign of sun, nor hint of rain,
But canopy of grey o'er head
As mist that shrouds topmost mountain,
Not here, tho' where the path has led.
Eerie stillness presses down
Wrapping itself round coloured bark.
Russet carpet covers ground,
No bird song breaks the silence. Lark,
Thrush, robin, blackbird — none are found
As I walk through this woodland park.
Distant throb of engines sound
And fade, then, As I tread, the sharp
Crack of twig, now leafy gowned,
Wakens senses, warns the hart.
The sleepy wind gives gentle sigh.
As poppy petals on Remembrance Day,
Crisp Autumn leaves drift from the sky —
Remind us of loves passed away.
A drop of dew no touches eye.
Distant memories cloud our way.
Deadness tells us Winter's nigh
As nature's shawl 'neath feet doth lie.

Violet Sprigings

The Miners Lament

Men have mined since coal was found
Many miles deep underground.
For them there was no sun or air
The comfort of an easy chair.
With pick and shovel, lamp and boots,
Digging coal out, was their roots.
Backs a-breaking, arms that's aching
Death and dust, bolts that rust
In their God they put their trust.
Many died, widows cried,
Children ran away to hide.
Now the pits, like tombs, lie so still,
No longer hear a canary's trill.
Ponies too, are gone to grass
But what of men, Welsh miners sang
When in the valleys, pick axes rang.
Never to hear again that sound,
Another hole, left in the ground.
Slag heaps all, cast aside,
Swept away on an outgoing tide.
To drift forever
On tears they cried.

S.M. Stacey

No. 11 2:45 am 6th October, 1993

In heaven we will see the ones we love
if on Earth we come to the above,
if only we'll listen to what He has to say
for He has all the answers for
each night and each day.
So please I entreat you let Him meet you,
talk with Him, walk with Him,
He's your best friend, He's my best friend,
there's not one who can love like the one above.

Barbara Ann Spicer

Cardboard City

Lost in the City, frightened and alone,
A damp cardboard box is my only home.
Abused at home, so to the City I fled,
To find a job, put a roof over my head.
No jobs to be found, so to my utter shame,
I beg on the streets, I won't go on the game.
I've kept off drugs, and from the bottle I'm free,
No one's going to make a bag lady of me!
A strip wash in the toilets, I've got my pride,
But I've got no real friends, in whom I can confide.
I'm in utter despair, I don't want to be here,
But I can't go back home, to live again in fear.
Please God give me hope that one day I'll find,
Someone who is loving and caring and kind.
Who'll see the real me, not the shell I have shown,
And we'll be happy together, in a real family home.

Marjorie Spooner

My Daughter Wendy

I had a daughter, years ago
A beautiful baby she was you know
But babies grow up very fast
And suddenly babyhood is past
From toddlers to teens, the years fly by
You give your all, the best you try
One day she says she wants to leave home
To face the big bad world alone
She thinks it's great, always in a hurry
While I can do nothing but sit and worry
To stray off the right path is easy to do
But Mum's always here, if this happens to you
Mistakes you will make, pitfalls you will find
And sometimes love will make you blind
But as you get older, about life you'll learn
And sometimes just for home you'll yearn
But you'll marry someday and then I'll say
Finding happiness was all that took you away

Elaine Spalding

Christmas Thoughts

At Christmas time,
We think of friends dear,
Especially those away,
As well as those near,
Some are very fortunate,
And have all things just right,
While others of less means,
Seems to be in a plight,
Some children make do,
With plastic toys and paper games,
While others, an electric car,
Can be had for their pains,
Whatever the reason,
Old friends are not forgotten,
Even though the weekly budget,
Lies at rock-bottom,
It's Christmas time again,
So let's fill each other with joy,
It really doesn't matter,
Whether you're a girl or a boy.

D. Suckley

Christmas Feasts

A table laden with richest fare,
the hall ablaze with light,
the guests in decorative costumes,
a vivid and colourful sight.

Nearby, at the Church's altar rail
a woman knelt in prayer.
Her clothes were poor and the figure thin,
as she bent in reverence there;

looked up at Nativity pictures,
their colours rich and rare.
She bowed to the Cross in devotion
and offered up her prayer.

But now she must leave this sanctuary,
go back to her solitary lair,
no Christmas feast awaited her
whose cupboard was almost bare.

Her way led past the mansion
whose riches blazed in the light,
but she did not envy its bounty
or feel pity for her plight,

for *she* had dined with her Saviour,
had tasted His Bread and Wine,
and she thought, as a believer,
that *her* feast was just as fine.

Geraldine Squires

Captivity

This sea of sand, my eyes, mouth and ears has clogged.
My mind's becalmed. My senses by inertia dogged,
What genie's twisted mind has this fate conceived?
Five days before I'm 21, of jewelled liberty relieved.

To thoughts of death or wounds my mind has sometimes turned,
But with youth's impulse to survive, they were quickly spurned.
To be captured by the foe, and held behind barbed wire stark,
Not for one moment did my mind on this strange theme embark,

Time no longer marches on. The clock fingers now seem filled with lead.
Life's contours now are changed, they're flat, variety's dead.
If we in captivity for long slow years must be detained,
How can we ensure that alive and sane we shall remain?

This dreary state of mind cries out to be reversed.
And soon bright rays of enterprise our camp traversed.
Choirs, worship, bingo sport emerge: Talks, crafts and exercise abound,
The captives forward move. The way to survive they have found.

Today the gates stand open, our liberty's restored.
Some shout and sing: some quietly sit, just overawed.
Soon now through those gates in droves we'll pour,
On the journey of a lifetime. Each to his own front door.

Warwick Steels

Untitled

It shivers and sways, as light as air
Move to one side you can see it there
Have I imagined it, must put it out of my mind
But when the lights go on it's there to tantalize and blind.

It's growing, thinks it's at home,
With shining thoughts as it just dances along.
Mockingly knowing it's out of reach
As you try and flick it away,
But it's up high and safe in it's own niche.

I ask very nicely
"Can you move it away?"
But am told "Why worry about it:
So there it stays.

Now I look upon it as a friend
Whose out-stayed it's welcome
But I'll win in the end.

I won't let my spirits drop to a low ebb
All because of a family of cobwebs.

Frances Stagg

Majesty

Towering cliffs, breathtaking views,
Rolling breakers, white crested flume.
Granite rocks by crystal pools,
Ruined tin mines and chimney stacks.

Valley of the rocks, St. Necterns Glen,
Rushing waters, tumbling streams.
Leafy valley, bluebell woods,
Technicolour caves with hanging fronds.

Arthur's Castle, wrecks of ships,
Deepest harbours, tiny creeks.
St. Michael's Mount, Bishop's Rock,
Truro Cathedral's soaring spires.

Goonhilly's might dishes,
Brunel's viaducts and bridges.
Man made mountains, china clay.

Huge stone tors on Bodmin Moor,
The Lizard's pearly beaches.
Lands End's mighty roar,
Dosemary Pool,
Excaliber ...

Lydia E. Stanton

Next Time

Don't look back or dwell too long on what might have been.
It's over now and we should go our separate ways.
For one breathtaking moment our lives touched and we held each other spellbound,
In some strange unreality.

Treasure that moment, just as it was, for it will never come again.
We knew each other and that intimate knowledge enriched us both.
We each gave each other something very precious of ourselves ...
We gave life, yet in the same instance took life away.

Don't be bitter, for bitterness cripples and destroys.
Just be glad that we were privileged to meet.
Resolve to use what we learned from each other and in that way,
Prevent the hurt of a next time.

Jenny Stacey

'A Little Child Shall Lead Them'

Although I am so very small,
Not big and strong —
Nor very tall —
I know that Jesus died
Heaven's gate to open wide.

And I know, although I'm small,
Jesus loves us, loves us all.
He has washed away our sin,
Bids us all to enter in.

Olive M. Spurgeon

Life

As the snow melts and turns to water,
It travels down the hills of strife.
Passing over,
Going under,
Moving round,
Until it finds the lake of life.

There it stays, sustaining love.
Admired and feared,
Silent and still.
Reflecting light,
Reflecting you.

Paul Spencer

Fathoms Of The Deep

Foaming, frothing, rushing waves,
Crashing over jagged rocks, forcing into caves.
Cold and biting, icy waters, bitter, roaring angrily
Vast expanse of the deep under world,
Deep dark fathoms of the sea.

I stand way back out of reach,
Howling waves crash the beach.
The wind is stopping, waves are dropping,
Waters calming once again,
The sea flattens, dripping echoes, ripples in the water
From falling rain.
The sky brightens and dark clouds go,
The sea is sleeping now and calm and peaceful
Waters flow.

Diane Stanley Sr.

Sleep

Sleep, sleep she washes over me
As gentle as a lover's touch
A sweet caress, a welcome friend
A perfect partner at day's end
Takes away the pain of the day
And restores the shadow of hope
She lies with me, warm and loving
And like a child, forgiving

Icy fingers of dawn wake me
Drag me into another day
Faces I didn't want to see
Caught in the open of morning
I fall, a victim of my fear
Trapped with no hope of returning

D.L. Sutton

Hive of Industry and Dreams

Beeswaxed cord made the spinning wheel soronously hum
Soporific, the food on the treadle beats like a carder drum
Honey coloured spindles shimmer in the sun's spun rays
Round, rich rolags like cumulus clouds in a basket, laze
The eye draws flabellated, fleece fibres into the flyer
Endlessly the silver beech wheel turns, churns, doesn't tire
Whirling, whorling wool, winds around the busy, bobbin spool
Spin, spun, span. Maiden uprights keep serried wool to rule
Hands drafting easily, spinster in reverie, dreams of Arachne
A mortal, besting goddess Athena, condemned to spin for eternity
Of wind blown sails, woven of handspun, for Ulysses voyages
Gandhi on his charkha, spinning a sacrament, making his raiment
Furrowed brows and restless roving souls in the traveller wheel assuages
A plethora of plied yarns and dreams spun, spawned. Spinner spent.

Rae Staples

The Nightmare

The nightmare starts when signs appear,
'ROADWORKS STARTING — NEXT WEEK — HERE'

Despair descends like thick black fog
no detour to my daily slog.
That fateful day I stand in line,
have I allowed sufficient time

To pick my way through unknown tract?
If late again I could get sacked.
Approaching foes gain unjust bites
of time allowed by spiteful lights.

I'm spared from being left behind
to lead the next lot through and find
the secret path through leering cones
safeguarding deserted zones.

I smugly wait the following day
confident I know the way.
My turn to lead a valiant band,
but in the night a ghostly hand

Maliciously and without warning
has switched the cones around for morning.
With vision blurred by panic's haze
I guide my party through the maze.

Next day I wake with aching head,
I'll ring in sick and stay in bed.

Winifred V. Stubbs

The Cruel Countryside

The greens of trees and meadows,
The yellow of the corn,
Hawks aloft on outspread wings,
On zephyr breezes bourne.

In silence in the skies they glyde,
And spy their prey below,
Suddenly they plummet down,
Like arrow from the bow.

True to the mark they speed their way,
Their talons outstretched reaching,
Then in the marshes down below,
Their quarry ceases screeching.

G.E. Seeley

Living

There are so many reasons for living,
For laughing and loving you know,
So why don't we put into practice
This gift which is easy to show.

Take time to say a Good Morning
To smile at a very sad face
It may just help someone to know
That the world is not a bad place

Your day may not start very happy
Bad weather or just a bad dream
Don't take this bad mood out on someone
Just sing and your face'll become a sunbeam!

So smile and be happy for someone
Never mind the bad dreams or upsets
There's always a better tomorrow,
Get ready, don't hurry, don't fret!

Dympna Slattery

Watching

I watched a frog
Springing on the dainty water lilies
Resting on the still water
Diving into the clear pond.

I watched a fish
Glistening in the sunlight
Diving into the quiet water
Swimming through the Forget-me-nots.

I watched a nymph
Killing its prey with its claws
Pouncing on the tadpole,
Shedding its old skin.

I watched a dragonfly
Swooping down to lay its eggs
Mating in the warmth of the sun
Dying in the dark.

I watched a tadpole
Zig-zagging on the pond
Growing legs and getting bigger
Changing into a frog

Alison Sowden

Happy Thoughts

Oh gentle breeze you touched a furrowed brow
And wiped away the turmoil of the day.
Oh gentle sun you warmed the very breath
That I and many others learn to live upon.
Oh moonlit nights that light the darkest hours
You spread your vision far beyond the sky
Oh gentle rain that sinks below the ground
And stirs the spring time flowers to abound.
What magic in our world can still be found.

Daisy E. Shire

Life

Life is like a garden,
Ruled by season's climes,
Seedlings are like babies,
Needing nourishment to thrive.

We aim for healthy perennials,
As years begin to mount,
We lavish all our love on them,
Trying not to throw them out.

But as one cycle ends its span,
And new growth comes along,
Spring opens up its arms once more,
Life's garden blooms again.

Doris E. Strickland

Apotheosis

'Entia non sunt multiplicanda praeter necessitatem'

Apotheosis is a way of seeing
all things as they appear to God. Can we
avoid, within a universe of being,

hiving energy in comprehending
the infinite — not stifle pansophy?
Apotheosis is a way of seeing

energy — without creating or destroying,
without mundane perceptions — as, purely,
a void. Within a universe of being

all life must be repudiated; cleansing
our eyes of images reveals what the
apotheosis is: a way of *seeing*:

to perform all parts of a drama, culminating
in the role of audience, and finally
the void within. A universe of being

holds a silence where reflection, propagating,
is allusive with synaptic energy;
apotheosis is a way of seeing
the void within that universe of being.

Martin Steward

Eday - Red

Red the rugged sandstone,
rising from the sea
Clear red the legs of Redshanks
piping just for me.

Rouge red the poppy dancing,
amongst the gold of corn
Blood red the drunken July sun
bouncing dawn to dawn.

Dark red the hips of roses,
after flowers fair
Rusty red the shoreline
rusty red with ware.

Dusty red the sorrel,
in fields not cut for hay
Crimson red the wattles of
the cock who greets the day.

Pat Sullivan

Honour And Glory

Brave men march towards their fate
Dreams of honour and glory await
Distant guns pound the earth
Silencing the deafening cries
As flares light up the midnight skies.

Stumbling, fumbling through the misty night
Blind men still hunger for the fight
Knee deep in mud and Man's own slime
We march along this never ending line
We curse with every step we take
Nearer and nearer to our untimely fate.

In the shadows we can see
Our brothers in arms fall helplessly
Creeping like a thief at night the dawn, she slowly awakes
We gaze at Man's destruction and weep
For here where an Eden once stood
Daybreak reveals a river of a generation's blood
Their brave limp bodies embrace the mud.

Please forgive me I pray
On this I fear to be my judgement day
As for the honour and glory
We all so much crave
We shall take to our unknown grave.

Veronica Stott

Final Journey

Through blurred vision watching,
That bright beacon of flickering light,
Reaching, grasping, unerringly ever closer.

> Distraught yet despairingly decided,
> He stands,
> All alone.

Twin lines of smooth steel,
Stretch,
Gleaming coldly and efficiently.

> As a rabbit mesmerized, regards a hawk,
> So the flickering light is regarded,
> As it swoops ever onward,
> Larger and larger, still it rushed,
> Till loudly squealing, sparks fly,
> Flickering light shrieks its protest.

Released from paralysis, slightly shaking,
With flickering light screaming on,
Confident now, he swiftly steps,
Looking onward, not back,
To stand between those lines of steel.

Calum Stewart

Omega

A House is a House is a House — But is it?
Upon the structure of this place my life is built,
Not bricks alone, but all my strength and blood is spilt
In raising up these walls that shelter me,
Secure and safe, whose arms enfold,
A fortress from the outside world so cold.
Yet comes the final closing of the gate,
And, on the other side, I now must seek my fate.
My steps will echo on the empty floor,
I know not how to shut and bar the door.

A House is a House is a House — But not this one.
By every blade of grass and leafy tree I'm known,
My hands are recognised by polished wood and stone.
The air is filled with voices heard no more,
Children at play — a little dog that listens by the door.
This one unchanging thing throughout the years
Stands solid, through the laughter and the tears.
Memorial to a generation now gone by,
But in whose hearts this plot will never die.
My spirit in this sphere will ever roam,
That knows not anywhere but here, as Home.

Mrs. E.H. Stilley

Hypothetical Suicide

If I were to attempt suicide
I'd embrace the secrets of the sea;
Where it's mighty undulating form
Would invite me to an Atlantis type utopia;
Overwhelm me, and take the decision
Irrevocably from my grasp.

The resolution now made,
There's no retreat:
I flounder; strength and will diminishing
In collusion with the ebbing of the tide,
Upon which my now inanimate form
Will coincide with distant continents;
A free sea passage to the places of my dreams.

Eventually, after decay
We would become one; the sea and I,
Slowly eroding the great land masses
Until we were jointly, all powerful.

In life, I had nothing;
But you see,
In death;
I will have inherited the earth

Jamie Karen Stewart

The Ballad of Johnny Martin
1850 - 1868

When Johnny was a young boy One-Eyed Jake rode into town
A silver handle on his six gun he was the fastest man around
He'd come looking for trouble as he drew on Johnny's Pa
Young Johnny vowed that he'd get even as his daddy hit the floor

It was in the months that followed a young boy turned into a man
When he came down from the mountains with his father's favourite gun
He went out to search for One-Eye to arrest him as the law
'Cos the town had made him sheriff and he wore the old tin star

But now the town it was deserted there was no one in the street
One-Eye was in the bar room drinking whisky tall and neat
Johnny stood outside awaiting the sun standing high at noon
And he knew for him or One-Eye life would be over very soon

One-Eye ambled down the sidewalk his pistol hanging low
The silver handle taunted Johnny as it glistened in the sun
For a while his eyes were blinded then One Eye he drew first
Johnny felt the bullet get him as he dropped and bit the dust

A sudden shot rang out of nowhere One-Eye turned to make a run
A bullet caught him neatly and darkness replaced the sun
His arms were waving as he stumbled his frightened face looking around
There was nothing he could see 'cos his other eye'd been closed

When the noise and dust had settled a shadowed figure stood its ground
'Twas a little grey haired lady a smoking gun was at her side
For a moment no one realised who took the outlaw's other eye
And as she walked into the sunlight they could all see Johnny's Ma

Sing the ballad of Johnny Martin who took on One-Eye Jake who's fast
But on his eighteenth birthday Johnny Martin drew and lost

Geoff Stone

Daybreak

Come let's roam through fields of green,
the dawn is here and there's lots to be seen.

The cock is the first to disturb the peace,
he wakes up the dog who strains on his leash.

The sun peeps o'er the mountain top bare,
the fox after hunting sleeks back to his lair.

Dew laden grass sparkles bright in the sun,
but will soon disappear its purpose been done.

The country's alive, birds still heralding dawn,
as if thanking the sun for its beams gentle warmth.

So let's praise God with joy and mirth,
a day is born, the Earth's given birth.

H.J. Stapleton

Vierte Reich

They're making bricks and hard cement
in readiness to build again
a wall between the minds of men
in Germany.
The slogans on street corners warn
of 'purity' and 'hope reborn'
where young men march in uniform
and harmony.

In stirring tunes and rousing rhymes
those ancient themes come down through time
to stimulate again the minds
of angry men
whose fathers thought to clear, at last,
the ghettos of the 'lower' castes.
Among the ashes of the past
they sin again.

Lawrence Stewart

No Flowers

Seven days have passed without a word.
Were we really that careful that none have
heard of me?
Do I deserve their acrimony?

I am to be spared the place at the bedside
The place at the graveside, my handful of dirt.
Maybe to them, I am less that.
The dirt under his nails.
I am to be scrubbed away.

I guess my nameless, claimless one is gone.
Although in my childish hope I wait for his ring.
Waiting, waiting, endless hesitation
Voiceless Mary knows her station.

No black dress peace for me,
No last dignity, no peace,
No right even to grieve,
No flowers, they say, and none I receive.

You had him first,
And you had him last.
I was his Mary-home-by-ten,
You were his light and his Amen.

Kirsty Stonell

A Candle for Katy

She came soft as thistledown,
Like a snowflake,
A winter baby,
A Christmas baby,
A gift.

We had made her
But we had not fashioned her.
Some other hand furnished her gifts,
Her seraphic smile,
Her rich contentment,
Her eyes ...
Round, so blue, burning bright,
They seemed to contain the universe.

A beautiful child,
All the secrets of the cosmos were hers.
But she was not ours —
Just briefly lent for an allotted spell.

On the anniversary of her birth
We will light a candle,
And warm ourselves by its glow,
And watch it burn out
And melt away
Like Katy.

Clarice Stevens

Remembering

The thud of a letter through my door this morning
Can bring happiness, laughter and tears,
For remembrance of friends, though they live far away
Is a heart warming gesture, so dear.

Time taken to write is not time that is wasted
Indeed it's a gift, now quite rare,
But it brings its reward in a number of ways
As we give love and have plenty to spare.

There are cards now for birthdays, for every known happening
And they are quite nice to receive,
But if sad, can a letter not say it much better?
If happy, write screeds 'fore you leave.

Paper and notelets, all colours and texture
Give writers the choice of the year.
Use yellow for sunshine, blue for the clear skies
And green for a soothing note, dear.

It's amazing how touching, a small scrap of paper
Can show to a friend that you care
And they can re-read it, and fold it and keep it
When your memory has gone yesteryear.

Now put pen to paper this very next instant
Add caring and light to this world,
For a letter can help put a smile on a face
And reach even the heart of a child.

Elizabeth M. Sudder

Patience

Patience is what the angler needs
As he sits by the loch beneath the trees,
As dragonflies dance amongst the reeds
That gently sway against the breeze,
Patience is what the angler needs
As he sits by the loch beneath the trees.

Patiently he sits and waits
Hoping fish will take his baits
When suddenly his line goes tight
And struggling fish begins to fight
It pulls and leaps into the air
A bar of silver, gold and green
The biggest pike he's ever seen
When suddenly his line goes slack
The fish is off and swimming back.

As mist and time roll slowly by,
A distant buzzard is heard to cry
Soaring high above the trees
All these things are sent to please,
But now its dusk and time to go
There's always next time, and he should know
Patience is what the angler needs
As he sits by the loch beneath the trees.

Brian Stott

Elephant's Foot Curio

Mighty one with care-worn eyes
how we bring your wisdom down
how we cut you down to size
tawdry harness, tinsel crown.

Tasteless antics for the crowd
swaying cargoes on your back
logbound labour in the sun
on some twisting forest track.

Dignified in gait and mien
till that mighty spirit crack
we, by rights, should weep to see
your foot, amid the bric-a-brac.

Isabel G. Stewart

The Walking Stick

I have travelled many a Mile,
    Always managing to raise a Smile.
Up the hills and down the Dales,
    I have never been known to fail.
Through a Lock and on a Train,
    The help I give is very plain.
Visited Edinburgh and Gretna Green,
    Also, the famous Loch Ness I have seen.
On holiday in glorious Devon,
    Across the moors is Heaven.
Then I climbed the Blackpool Tower,
    That took a lot of my willpower.
This stick tells the Tale,
    For a Crocked-up Old Male.

Mrs. R. Smith

Course True

You are that world we knew in yesteryears
When wings were surfacing the overcast:
A world of gently moving stars and spheres
Acknowledged then as beauty unsurpassed.
For in your face is all its purity
And all its breadth and depth is but your mind;
Its light you eyes reflect with surety,
Your heart and hopes are with its heights enshrined.
To shrink the splendid spaces of your realm
That I may fill the mean extend that's left,
To let possessiveness so overwhelm
That of all previous joys you stand bereft —
    In not such way do I my love construe
    Else love is not that which I have for you.

Rob Stratton

The Devil

He's there when you lie
or when you're mean and sly
The little man with horns
as spikey as thorns
He fights for the evil and rules against good
And if you listen to him
he does as he would
that's tell you the wrong
and sing an evil song
Then he's off in a puff
like a bit of grey fluff!

Sarah R. Statman (Age 10)

Unmarried Mother

Dampness descends upon the room
clouding every surface.
The soggy washing, limp and sad,
steams before the fire.
The cabbage boils
and adds to the greasy paper
its own disgusting, stinking vapour.
A chill November fog
Steals through the cracks.
The child cries and she smacks
her; barely more than a child herself.
Listless she prods at the cabbage pot,
nor heeds the bawling infant in the cot.
Last week, next week, any week.
She lifts her crumpled apron to her
cheek.

Greta H. Stratford

A Mother's Son

He played his part
That lad so brave,
And for his King
His life he gave,
And now once more
We think of him,
That brave young lad
Whose name was Jim,
Who fought until his very last gasp,
And in his hand that lad did clasp,
A locket that was made of gold,
And in it a photo that was old,
And on it was written there
To my own dear son "Take care",
Oh, what could that mother's thoughts have been
When she heard her son was dead
And never anymore would she see,
Her son's fair curly head.

P.W. Stevens

Kids

I sat and tried to write a poem,
But found it hard with a child on the roam.
"Mum, can I have, Mum what's this?"
Oh! peace and quiet would be such bliss.

Just as the words start to form, seem to flow,
"Mum, I want a wee wee, can't reach, have to go".
Up I go with my three year old son,
"Come on, hurry up, are you sure that you're done?"

All tucked in, and back down I sit,
"Mum I can't find my Action Man Kit".
Oh! give me patience, Oh! for solitude,
"Mum, if you say bum bum, is it naughty, why's it rude?"

"Please, please be quiet, Mummy has to think",
"Mum, look at me, I can climb in the sink".
OK! OK!, I've finally given up,
Let's go and search for the elusive 'Garfield cup'.

"Mum, have you finished? I though you were writing a letter",
A poem, but never mind, time for playschool (then things will get better).
Ah! peace at last, now I can start my poem,
I can't think of anything to write, I wish my son was home.

Mrs. A.J. Sutcliffe

Locked From My Freedom

I'm thrown in a cage, locked from my freedom,
But I already know the torture's just begun.
I see all the animals wasting away,
I know I'll be like that soon one day.
I see a man approaching my cell,
Whatever he does it's sure to be hell.
He picks me up — he's got a strong grip,
I've got to escape, I scratch and I nip,
He doesn't let go, he keeps hold of me,
I know I'm in trouble, I just want to flee.
He holds me down and gets out a needle,
I can't escape, he's strong and I'm feeble.
The next thing I know I'm back in my cell,
I don't know what he's done but I don't feel well.
I try to get help but no one knows,
That the pain I'm suffering just grows and grows.
A day has passed, it seems like a year,
I know my end will soon be here.
The man approaches ready to kill,
There's nothing I can do, I know he will.
He takes me away, out of the room,
Into his lab where I will meet my doom.

David T. Sutton (Age 14)

Four Seasons

Through fading mellow autumn light,
The towering forest Monarchs soar,
Misty crowns about their heads,
Bespeak their majesty and power.

Sad silence echoes in the bowers,
That yesterday were filled with song,
When feathered suitors plighted troth
And earth with burgeoning life was thronged.

Yet joyous wave the leafy flags,
Of fiery red and yellow gold,
Like trumpets blast their beauty breaks
The silence and its eerie thrall.

If winter creeps in autumn's wake,
White mantled silence to bestow,
'Tis only God's snow eiderdown
To cradle infant life below.

Assuredly unfailing spring
Shall rise again to bloom and bless
And summer join the seasons choir,
In "Lord great is thy faithfulness".

William Sutherland

The Miners Past

With a little gladness and sorrow,
I shall be leaving the old pit tomorrow,
Looking back on many a year,
Brings back a smile or a tear,
Through a life of sweat and grime,
In darkness most of the time.
Tired body and weary heart,
Many is the time from the pit I would like to part,
But with a family to upbring,
The only work to do was mining.
If I had my time to come again,
I'd be on that cage and paddy train,
With my mates I've played my part,
With all the strength at heart.
We've laid a good foundation,
For this organization,
The moral to the story I have told,
It's that I am now sixty-five years old.

Lancelot George Sutton

Mother Earth, The Big If

Oh Mother Earth, how bountiful you have been
To all animals, creatures great and small
Feeding us by the green you grow
Your Sister Sun to give us warmth
Without you both we would all die
Providing us with the trees and stone
To make our shelters for comfort
And the food we grow and fish to catch
Now Mankind has developed so fast
To destroy our Mother Earth
So the question, how long will it last?
In one hundred years the damage has been done
Question how long to repair the damage
Man has done or must we continue on
The path of self-destruction
Or can man reconstruct the Big If?

Sam Smith

Untitled

If the path you walk is stony
And your feet are worse for wear
If the hill you pick is the steepest
Then you must not despair

If you cannot find an open gate
But have to climb a wall
Remember you are not the only one
It happens to us all

We never make life easy
And often live a dream
We always want the other side
Where the grass is ever green

The simple things in life we miss
By looking far too hard
All the things we really need
Are in our own backyard

Life is what we make it
The pain we self-inflict
By being far too greedy
And wanting things too quick

So make the best of what you've got
And treasure what you find
Enjoy your life and what it holds
Then you will have peace of mind

V. Sykes

Splitting Logs

Small straight grained logs
Offer no resistance to the sharp
Long handled wedge shaped axe.
One deft blow down the middle
And they are quickly parted.

But larger closely grained logs
Are attacked from the edges,
Go for the middle and the axe
Just bounces off, quite painful!
Better still use a metal wedge
Or two, driven in with force
The splits appear and soon
More logs go onto the pile.

The hardest of all logs are
The knotty ones, those that
Branched out to bear the
Leaves, flowers and fruits
Yearly to perpetuate themselves.
These logs are so intergrained,
Interwoven and reluctant to part,
That they become trimmed to size
And only the fire parts them.

Relationships are like logs.

Vic Sutton

You Never, Never Know

Over the past few weeks everyone's been going mad.
My friends, colleagues and even my dad.
The National Lottery has reached fever pitch,
Everyone's convinced they're going to be rich.
What on earth would I do if I won all that cash?
Well, for a start I'd throw a big family bash.
Then I would set out to have some real fun,
The first thing I'd do is take a break in the sun.
I'd think about buying a large stately home,
With a red porsche complete with mobile phone.
No longer would I go to work,
Even the ironing I'd be able to shirk.
All I have to do is get the numbers right,
Predict the balls that'll come out on the night.
The task doesn't seem all that difficult to me.
My birthday's in March so I'll have number 3.
Only another 5 numbers I have to choose,
I don't really see how I can possibly lose.
By this time next week I could be a millionaire,
Very, very rich with not a single care.
Up until now I've scored a complete duck,
But it must be my turn to have some luck.
So this week I'm going to have an extra go,
Well, I really feel lucky and you never, never know.

Lynda Smoult

The Party Is Over

Rock of evil sprung like mushroom across the countryside,
Its chimney stuck up like a sore thumb,
Among the scenery in the twenties,
The called it euphemistically, 'mental institution'.

Rock of evil where lives wasted and ruined,
Where vagrancy was a mental illness,
Where maid's pregnancy was a crime,
Where wives were locked up for rebellion,
Where doctors were tools of the ruling classes.

Rock of evil where 'rules of law' was an alien,
Where staff ruled by fear and force,
Against those who could not afford,
To hear, to see, to speak up or to think,
Where managers turned blind eyes to their members' crimes,
In the rock of evil, where patients retired at five in the afternoon,
To make room for the party's chosen few,
Where on Friday at five, they sang and danced,
Until Sunday at ten, they slept and snored like pigs.

Then at last, Thatcher's flag ship in the mid eighties,
The rock of evil was marked for closure,
Staff and managers crying like spoilt children
The fat lady has sung, my friend;
Time to go home, the party is over.

S.A. Suffee

Stretching The Bond

Closed back,
Speechless chair.
Turned to talk;
you weren't there.
Friendship past
Years gone by,
Lessons learnt;
lonely tears cry.
Crowded room.
Wicker face.
Promise dissolved
and left no trace.
Excuses given:
'Dear John ...'
But, no longer there,
I have moved on.

Jessica Sumner

Evening Walk

Every day
For a run he goes
I love the way
His muscles show

Following him
He must tell
That his every limb
I know so well

He looks behind
And sees me there
Brown eyes so kind
Glossy blond hair

I think he knows
As past I walk
My love may show
Though we never talk

I turn around
to retrace my trail
Up to me he bounds
Wagging his tail

Mary Rosamund Stewart

Who's That Man

A gentleman comes to our house each year.
Now what's his name? — It isn't clear
He doesn't come in June or May
He only comes on Christmas Day.
With beard of white and cloak of red,
He only comes when you're in bed.
You must be sure to be asleep
You dare not look or dare not peep.
Down the chimney he will come,
With books and toys for everyone.
On his sleigh he will ride
A sack of toys at his side.
Rudolph with his nose aglow
Pulls him safely through the snow.
You've guessed his name
Now let's applause.
A big Hooray for Santa Claus.

Yvonne Taviner

Heron Death

Today I count the goldfish in the pool:
Under the ice in sluggish winter glide
They move to safer depths when from the side
My shadow's menace falls upon the school.
They cannot know how I protect them from
The hungry heron and marauding cat!
They graze the weed and, growing golden fat,
See not the net which holds back Nog and Tom!
Are we as blind, swimming our dappled pond,
To plunge with terror from each threatening shade
Which may be our defence from threats beyond?
And do we, by our stupid greed betrayed,
Gobble unseeing, each next morsel seek,
And slide towards a vast, immobile beak?

Eric Swainson

My Homeland

I wish that I might go to far off lands,
Might make an Argosy of sounds, smells, things,
Might jostle with the natives in Bazaars,
And echo through the Palaces of long lost kings.

I'd go to where martyrs bled, where Homer sang,
Where beauteous Helen launched a thousand ships,
I'd savour smells where many races met,
And hear the sounds of Babylon from their noisy lips.

I'd tread the ageless sands where Pharaohs trod,
See mighty monuments which were their pride,
Jumbled by time, and feel my littleness,
I'd ponder immortality where Jesus died,

Know the Ganges where the Hindus dead,
Raise fiery vespers, awesome Gods to please,
There would I marvel at the gilded shrines,
And pity the untouchables their filth and fleas.

A wealth of wide-eyed wonder I would cull,
From Orient Southern sea, and all the grand
Americas their present conquers east,
And having garnished come again to my own land.

Oh England, England, thou would still remain,
My heritage, my jewel set in sea,
And all earth's treasures, all her gems,
Would add but to my pride, my joy, my love of thee.

Blanche Taylor

Retirement

Some folk, I know, complain they're too old
To do this, or do that, or whatever;
Past eighty they plead, their tale is told
And to act as if young, seldom clever.

I'm long in the tooth, yet I disagree
And believe life holds much still in store;
I'm still compos mentis at age eighty-three,
Looking forward to many years more.

Retirement for all is a wonderful chance
To do anything he or she wishes;
Join a choir, read the classics, learn how to dance,
Play bowls or play bingo, cook foreign dishes.

I have to admit I do draw the line
At rugby or cricket or long distance running,
But gentler pursuits I can tackle just fine
Those calling for skill or low cunning.

I enjoy competitions that need concentration,
Questions to answer, slick slogans to devise;
Crosswords and puzzles that improve my education
And usually offering a very fine prize.

Most often I lose, occasionally I win
But one thing is clear from the start;
As long as I live, through thick or through thin,
I intend to remain young at heart.

Alan Tate

Dreams Of Vincent

Concerning the facts of his existence
I know less, perhaps, than the most
perfunctory dilettante;
yet I can see him
out walking with canvases, thin, haggard,
copper beard and once white smock.
A slow recovery on the rutted track
from all the meaningless, persecuting
interrogative world;
puddles flashing in the swelling sun
cornfields glowing hot with burnished bronze.
Stopping to touch a wildflower
let the dew soak his palm,
senses so alive in a universe of coloured gifts.

In his little yellow house
a wave of madness came and engulfed him.
He bequeaths us pain and beauty
which was his life,
is life more than facts,
this misunderstood and hurting man.

David Taylor

After The Cross

After the cross they were empty
After the cross they were sad
After the cross it was finished
For Jesus was all they had

Now He had gone and left them
Now they were full of despair
Now they had gone to the tomb
And found there was nobody there

Now they could see what He'd taught them
Now they understood what He'd said
Now their Lord had risen
Jesus was no longer dead

Now He had gone to the Father
Just as he told them He would
We may also join Him
Just as he said we could

Now we must come in repentance
And seek to be pardoned from sin
Now we must open our hearts
And let the Lord Jesus come in

Annabell Taylor

Look And See

When I look out at the sky so wide
Twinkling stars and clouds they glide
Passed by once, they've been before
Is there life out there? Of this I am sure

The clouds, the shapes they enter my mind
Changing in form in every kind
With sky and mind, ever so vast
Surely a suspicion, 'Aliens' can be cast

The twinkle of light-one, then more
Seem to be knocking on heaven's door
A mirror message maybe, to you and I,
"Come join us up here in the sky"

With heavens so wide, great, with no end
So many people, earth can send
In many a vessel to the stars advance
Where our MOTHER can twinkle at a glance

We can learn from others, make a better earth
Time for our world, for a new rebirth
A way in which we can share time, and space together
Where it can be like this, forever and ever.

John Taviner

The Playground of War

The children do not hear.
They do not hear the sound of a playground.
The sounds of bombs, guns, artillery
Are their companions.
The children do not see.
They do not see the sights of happiness,
Just misery and pain surround them,
The derelict buildings are
Their playground.
The children do not know,.
They know only soldiers
Not fathers, uncles, brothers.
Mothers, sister, aunties all
Suffer in their pitiful lives.
The children have no hope.
Brothers missing, fathers fighting,
When will their peace return.
The children have heard,
The children have seen,
The children really know,
The children have hope.
We must hear, see, know, hope,
Like the children in the playground of war.

Debbie Tatton

Resurrection

The fated Mary Rose is risen from the solent's silted blanketed
      murky bed.
Four centuries of undisturbed muted rest with only fish to admire
      her timbered hulk.
Gleaming skulls, scattered tragic bones lurking in leather shoes,
      Tudor caps give evidence of Tudor heads long dead.
Once King Henry's favourite warship, it sailed the Solent, flags
      flying and golden Tudor roses painted on her hulk.
Splendid bronze guns arrayed in a double row with strong armed
      anchors ready to face a large numbered French foe.
A brown towering warship with romance in her sails, but sadly
      overloaded, doomed, before her last aggressive show.
The ships motley crew, sailors, soldiers, gunners in their appointed
      positions, handicapped by armour as she sank beneath the waves.
The Mary Rose disappeared with indecent haste to rest, with only
      seaweed instead of flowers around her lonely grave.
Sound waves of the drowning men could be heard rotating round the
      stricken ship for many a year,
Until time itself stilled all cries and kindly left the hulk for
      posterity to share.
And now at last in this progressive era of nineteen hundred and
      eighty two,
The flagship's crew of many bones are resurrected, perhaps to find
      solace in their belated discovery true.

Evelyn Tatlow

Tears

Tired — yes, so very much
Unsure of what I'm doing, slowly losing touch
Of all my surroundings and dreams coming true
Now it seems reality has jumped out of the blue

Trying hard to find what it takes to be strong
Hoping to survive in a world that seems all wrong
Where people are insensitive or just don't understand
That we sometimes do have feelings, we're not completely bland

Someone laughed aloud, another had a look
At some unfortunate person who hadn't got what it took
To be like all the others who prance and pose around
As long as you're with the in-crowd, you're definitely sound

But it's the people who are laughing that I feel sorry for
Their hearts are like the apple skin, they haven't got a core
They haven't time for anyone who ponders for a while
You're just another misery, who never has a smile

But they'll never really know you or even try to find
What lies behind the serious face
Is there something on her mind?
For if they did I'm sure they would learn the reason why
This person isn't smiling - Look!
She's just begun to cry

Deirdre Henderson-Tabb

Love Is Blind

"I don't love you and never have"
Did I hear it right
Was he going mad?
My joy was having him around.
My love for him just knew no bounds.
I could not agree
That his love for me
Had really been
Pretence

He went away.
Why was I blind
To the fact that he
Had never loved me?

The divorce absolute meant I was free.
But the love still
Lingered inside of me
The ache has gone,
The future for me
Is to give to friends
And my family
The love that is still
Inside of me.
And let God
Judge his adultery.

Ella Taylor

St Elizabeth's Hospice (5th Anniversary)

Paint a portrait of St Elizabeth's, and of her personnel
Create a vivid picture, and choose your colours well.
Arrange every helper, each moulded to their trade
Sketch as matchstickpeople, selfsame as Lowry made.

Norman, the domestic girls, the flower ladies too
Set them by the riverside, down where the rushed grow.
Workers behind closed doors, the office and canteen
Present them in wide pastures, so they are clearly seen.

Blending harvest tinges, yellows, golds and tans
Depict the welfare, and the Daycare artisans.
The many volunteers who give so freely of their hours
Draw them in a garden bright, amidst exotic flowers.

Angela presiding over each and every one
Portray her on green and purpled hills, 'neath the morning sun.
The nurses ever vigilant, with tenderness serene
Place them on your canvas, in a tranquil scene.

Matron, doctors, management, Chaplain John, God Bless his heart
Give them a place of eminence, in your work of art.
For the patients and their loved ones, emulate the pale blue skies
With white clouds gently soaring, beyond to paradise.

For each bright star departed, for every soul asleep
Show in abundance butterflies, near where the willows weep.
To commemorate the Anniversary, exquisitely display
Five birds of Divine Beauty in varied tones of grey.

AND

When your work's completed, place in a gilded frame
Entitle "St Elizabeth's" then pray "LONG MAY SHE REIGN".

Caleta Thomas

The Rival

The lady walks among delphiniums,
Above her head their blue spires shame sky's blue
But not her eyes their echoes — at her feet
Cornflower, larkspur, lupins in colonnades
Stretch out their scents to touch her passing through.

Oh, lady with the larkspur-coloured eyes,
How was my Springtime scarred with envy of you!
Where are you now, I wonder, are the skies
Above you still delphinium-aping blue?

Now in the heart of golden Summer's height
I in a rose-enamelled garden stand.
Orange and scarlet, crimson and cream and white,
My Love's love gave me this enchanted land.

I have forgotten how it feels to cry,
Coloured and perfumed is my paradise,
And yet I never see delphiniums
Without recalling cornflower-coloured eyes.

M.E. Tribe

Just a Dandelion

I'm just a common dandelion,
Some speak of me with scorn,
Yet I've a bright and bonny face
And countless places I adorn.

Little children seem to love me,
They gather me and smile,
And when I see their happiness
I know that I'm worthwhile.

And when my golden bloom has gone
I've a globe of feathery down,
And my seeds fly away on wispy wings
Over countryside and town.

And you know, I've got a special name
That makes me feel a King,
For old countryfolk still call me
'The sunflower of the Spring'.

Alma Taylor

Dawn Of A New Day

Dark grey leaving
Misty pink arrives
Dawn is fast approaching
Ghostly fingers in the sky
Soft droplets falling
Caressing tranquility
Spring-time flowers
Quench their thirst
May-time gentle showers
In the morning
Perfumes the garden
When day is dawning
Sun arises
Brightly shining
And a new day then appears
Warmth of day
Persuades the blossoms
Unfolding petals everyone
Exquisite beauty
Splashed with rain drops
Diamond glitter in the sun.

Eunice Hughes Thomas

The Headland

The mowers primed, and horses hitched
And off they go to be bucked and pitched
On mountain field, with rocks all strewn
From local quarry, sometimes hewn.
The headland first, a nightmare cut
Of blades that jam, in deepest rut
Rotting sacks, household rubble.
Gypsy cast-offs, last year's stubble
A grassy knoll, concealing stones
And farther on, a dead sheep's bones
A dozen stops, to clear the cutters
The farmer swears, and growls, mutters.
Amid chattering blades, the unheard squeals
Of field-mice nests, beneath the wheels
The shires twitch, with rolling eyes
tormented by the wobble flies
Old swathe board breaks, tied back with string
This first cut is a dreadful thing.

(Mowing 50 years ago)
M. Thomas

Genesis

I watched and cried, dear mourning world
Did strain to hear your laughter,
And as in darkness buds uncurled,
I walked through your disaster.
And as the four dark horses,
Rode across our barren land,
A milk white steed appeared to me
I fed it from my hand.
My food did reek of moral sin
Of which the horse had eaten,
And as it rose and cried for more,
I knew they could be beaten.
The horse did bleed and look away
As from the air came thunder,
And from the sea a giant wave
That called your people under.
In fear I climbed upon the horse
And joined it in its plight,
We trampled who, through lust and greed
Were hidden from the light.
For seven days the storm did rage
We rode the angry tide
And when at last it fell away
We buried those who'd died.
I watched and cried dear mourning world,
Did lie on soft good earth
And as in darkness, buds uncurled
I revelled in your birth.

Linda Taylor

The Sea

The sea washes the coastline all the way round,
And embraces the people who come from the town,
On holiday they speed to its wide open arms
And they splash and they swim without any qualms.
Yet safe it is not, due to our senseless misuse
So stop and think, there's really no excuse.
The rivers bring pollution from the factories in town,
Killing people and wildlife on their journey's down.
There's sewage too, all washed down and away,
What right have we to treat it this way?
It accepts all our waste and we don't seem to care,
Then it spews it all back, leaving the coastline bare.
No plants or animals can live it its wake,
It's had all the pollution it can possibly take,
Birds smothered in oil cry for our help
As they struggle in beds of poisonous kelp.
The sea we are killing by day and by night,
The pity is there's no way it can fight.
For into the sea it's all being pumped
Any old thing, it's all being dumped.
One day we shall find there's no life at all,
We are rushing ahead with our own downfall.
It's our duty to protect the land and sea
We must stop this slaughter — you and me.
The end — or is it?

Roy Taylor

The Four Seasons

Spring
    In the light meadow children will play,
    While adults spring clean before it's May.
    Daffodils and tulips both start to grow,
    And the men have the grass to mow.

Summer
    The beaches are drowned with the rich scent of skin cream,
    Ice cream stands are packed while others lie and dream.
    The waves, dance on the sea, a donkey gives a girl a ride,
    At half past five the beach is still and rushing in comes the tide.

Autumn
    Crinkle, crunch, snap go the leaves on the ground,
    The crisp, dry leaves make a scuttly sound,
    As they flutter and scatter around the tree trunk,
    And gather up piles of copper colour junk.

Winter
    Everyone is sat indoors
    Chitter chatter goes the children's jaws.
    When it's Christmas turkey's eaten,
    And outside the grass is beaten.

James Taylor (Age 11)

Grandad

He just fell asleep and he didn't wake up,
    his tea by his side has gone cold in the cup.
The smile he'd have given when I entered the room
    has now gone forever and adds to the gloom.
He's looking so peaceful his cares gone at last,
    gone and forgotten remain in the past.
Now who shall I ring? His brother down south
    Oh I know he's a pain and he's got a big mouth.
He did have a sister but I think she's passed on,
    let's look in the 'phone book, now where has that gone?
His doctor should call by right I should think
    if he's not informed there'll be such a stink.
There's certificates to sign to make it all right,
    if they're not in order I'll not get a mite.
Insurances, now then, there's a thought,
    of these he had many, they'll have to be sought,
Let's look in his pockets to find such a clue
    to seek out a policy to see what I'm due.
His arm it moved slowly, his eyes start to blink,
    Ee I'm glad you've come back love, please make me a drink!

Vernon E. Taylor

Den My Gentle Bricky

Den my gentleman Bricky
He is so bold and true
He pops his head around the wall
And asks Liz what shift are you.

And when he's busy working
And the rain begins to fall
He's worried about my washing
As he leaps across the wall.

We went to Barry on a day trip
I was lying on the sand
I looked up and saw you standing there,
You're trowel was in your hand.

I know of no one like you
You are so true and bold
You're always doing for others
'Cos your heart is full of gold.

Liz Thomas

Johnny Never

Johnny never was one of the crowd,
Maybe his face didn't fit,
Maybe his shirt was too loud.

Johnny was a traveller,
He walked a lonely road,
Sometimes people crossed his path,
Or else he stayed alone.

Johnny was a drifter,
People didn't know his name,
He didn't have a wife,
Now isn't that a shame.

But Johnny was still searching,
He hoped for better times,
He was an honest man,
Who never had a dime.

But Johnny was a dreamer,
Who waited for the breaks,
He would keep on hoping,
No matter how long it takes.

It was on a winter night,
That poor old Johnny died,
No one shed a tear,
O even cried.

John never was one of the crowd.

Simon Taylor

Inner Feelings

These are the feelings we can find it hard to express,
These are the feeling we sometimes curse, not bless.
These are the feelings which lie deep inside one's gut,
These are the feelings over which we often tut.
These are the feelings which divide the good from bad,
These are the feelings you can have for Mum and Dad.
These are the feelings that separate 'like' from 'love,
These are the feelings that are warm just like a glove.
These are the feelings which some fight hard to hide,
These are the feelings that ebb and flow like a tide.
These are the feelings which often cause most pain,
These are the feelings, that help to keep you sane.
These are the feelings that can give you butterflies,
These are the feelings that are always true, not lies.
These are the feelings which occur in times of stress,
These are the feelings which hard upon you press.
These are the feelings that leap, and fly, and sail,
Without these feelings, common sense would not prevail.
These inner feelings, without them life would be drear,
Because these inner feelings help us to see more clear.

Elizabeth M. Thom

The Thaw

My words meant nothing to you then,
So why then should they now!
The grey lag has landed in the fen,
The swallow left us once again,
And frankly I do not see how

New words might undo what is done;
So why the raised eyebrow!
When the green flights of April are on
The hawthorn and the snows are gone,
All being well we may see how

A natural thawing might have been
Something to disavow
In so partisan a scene.
And as for words, what can they mean
Except the image we endow.

Ray Thursfield

Love on the Dole

When things are not right
And money is very tight
When the electric man is going to cut off the power
Would you have the strength of a tower
When the money is very short
Would you still love me with all your heart
When I have a splitting head
And butter but no bread
When we've had rice pudding three days on the trot
Would you give me all the love you have got
When we have only a one bar heater
And no money for the gas meter
When we are fumbling around in the dark
Would we be able to talk
When the giro didn't come on time
And all we've got to listen to is the clock's chime
Would you tell me I'm pretty then
Or would you call me a crackling old hen
Life is not easy I know
It doesn't take a lot for a cheery hello
Bear a thought to the people in the street
And give a pleasant smile to the people you meet
They may have no soap and covered in muck.
They may through circumstance's be down on their luck

C. Thomas

United Kingdom?

The battered edges of this isle so green
For so many only here to be seen
And left with memories so clear
Gently fading until next year

The bitter truth is left behind
Simmering with those who are left to find
A way to survive a winter with needs
A far cry from those who decide your destinies

We are so far from that most "Exclusive Club"
Like splintered spokes on a revolving hub
Never mind our constant yearning
We *must* follow the wheel that's turning

The forgotten lands that rarely shine
West of Severn, North of Tyne
Though not when listening to politician's patter
But the truth of too few voters to matter

They'll create new jobs, "to prevent a slump"
And fob us off with a chemical dump
Or a nuclear plant with radiation strong
And tell us that there's nothing wrong.

We are still waiting for the special treat
For we feel we're constantly under their feet
But whether in vale or glen or on hillside
They'll never suppress our Celtic pride.

E.G. Thomas

Untitled

This is the tale of a shipwrecked man whose life of loneliness began
When he sailed away on a little raft which was not a very suitable craft
There was not much room, for the craft was small, but of course it was better than nothing at all
At least it was much better for him for without it he would have had to swim
But he couldn't settle himself complete for he had nowhere really to put his feet.
As being so tall he was ill at ease, his chin always resting on his knees
So he dangled his legs down in the water, a thing he didn't really oughter
For a passing shark whipped them off to the knee' stead of six feet tall he was the five feet three
On the raft he used to stump around for now he was nearer to the ground
But looking up in the air one day a seagull took one eye away
With two legs, one eye now gone you see he wondered what the next thing would be,
When an octopus rose from out the foam and whipped him off on its way home.
As he struggled hard and tried to block it, is other eye flew from its socket
And landed on the raft as he disappeared beneath the sea.
The eyeball went rolling to and fro wondering where next it had to go,
When of a sudden there was a heavy swell and overboard the eyeball fell
As there was nothing else that could befall, that's the end of the story, good-bye all.

Colin Thomas

Untitled

From Alpha to Omega,
Words without end;
Enjoying those enduring Gems-of-Wisdom,
Just as a reliable friend.
So, perhaps, when we have time to criticize,
We may also have time to help.
Who knows? Then we could suddenly realize,
We would be forgetting our selfish-self.

R. Tutte

Raindrops

Raindrops fall 'neath cotton cloud
Flower and leaf, endure unbowed
Ray of sun on mist adorn
Coloured arc, a rainbow born.

Raindrops but to stem in vain
Tumbling down the window pane
Rivulet trails to journeys end
Await return to cloud ascend.

Harold Taylor

For Honour and For Him

Somewhere a man is toiling,
Fighting with might and mane,
Thinking always of one dear face,
And whispering oft, your name.

Somewhere a man-husband-sweetheart, friend,
Is fighting. A fight, the fight that soon shall end,
That those he loves may live in peace once more
And forget the horrors of this dreadful war.

To you he looks with honour, reverence too,
As he toils always, his mighty task to do.
Thinking of the day, when you, and he, united,
Shall live in peace, nor day, nor night be blighted.
Will you, who mean so much to him,
Do ought, his faith in you to dim,
No, honour him, and keep unsoiled your own,
Then, what joy for both, when he comes marching home.

W.H. Twigger

The Bridge

Flowing through the lush green valley,
Its destiny the sea so far.
Keeping life in reed and rushes,
Its way so clear none can bar.
To cross this river man has ventured,
He has built a bridge of stone,
There it straddles all this beauty,
Without life, it's all alone.
Every secret of the river
All has passed the bridge untold,
Friend of man, yet friend of water
It respects the river old.
If it was not for this river
It would never have been built,
For once man has conquered water,
With stones so strong it will not wilt.

E. Morgan Thomas

The Pools

"Mr. Littlewood", here's my coupon, that I've sent to you,
I've tried to write a winning line for weeks and weeks it's true,
But every Saturday night, I just can't get them right
If I could do my 1 x 2, I'd be a winner of the "Football Pools".
Oh "Lady Luck", please see me through,
If I could do my treble chance, I'd go to "Monty", "Biarritz" and "Cannes".
Oh "Lady Luck", I'll bank on you,
I've tried the easy four, and the easy six as well,
I've tried the eight selections, but the same old tale they tell.
If I could do my 1 x 2, I'd be a winner of the "Football Pools".
Oh "Lady Luck", I'll bank on you.

Mrs. S. Taylor

Time Is Relative

In the time it takes one person to break one heart
One person can jump off one bridge
In the time it takes one year to pass
One second might seem like one year
In the time it takes one to see the light
The light has changed to darkness
In the time between birth and death
Life is only present in the present tense
In the time it takes for life to end
There is no time at all

Martin Thirkettle

From Out of the Blue

Clouds drift across the blue,
forming and reforming as they often do.
Sometimes there's buffalo on the plain,
wild horses, a wagon train.
Dragons in hasty dance,
knights of old with shield and lance.
Snappy alligators, lions and mice.
Towering cities made out of ice.
Charging elephants, polar bears, snow.
Clouds drifting and changing,
always on the go.

V. Taylor

Our Jane

A winding lane, a country lane,
No poor, thought simple as our Jane,
And yet her eyes, most quizzical eyes,
No stone unturned, no tit, no old magpie
Escaped her notion or her mind.

Oh How I'm bored, her clump like frame!
"I'm tired of looking at you, Jane."
Yet on she went, half stooped,"
Half bent and fully lame
With everlasting gruesome pain.

But oh, her eyes, blue flashing eyes
Reflects sweet violets and the sky,
Her wisdom, ever wisdom wise
Her mind immortal, shattered mine.

We turned the corner,
Oh the pain
The coming on of sleet and rain
And looking up,
Her smile was blossom in that country lane.

C.R. Thornton

The Killing

Hazy rays zigzag in the watery depths.
An orange orb above the transparent skin.
From the waterside a barking beast
erupts into the stillness
to retrieve its toy.

A lone sleek figure stands poised
to catch its prey.
Among the willow he stays perfectly still,
bill angled to strike.

Teardrops explode on the wrinkled surface.
Ripples echo to the shore.
Ducks dabble among the choking weed.
Silver darts through the murky torrent.

In an orgy of panic a tail hangs
obtrusively from the razor sharp chasm,
and all is hushed once again,
but for the ripple of the gentle rain.

Miss C. Thomas

Passing Thoughts

Day has dawned, and with it too, flowers refreshed with morning dew.
Raised from ashes of perpetual change,
Endlessly searching to improve their range.
And as in Nature's curious way, rarely fails to have its way.
Wind with wild imagination, randomly sows new expectation.
As I ponder o'er thought and deed, would it be different, would I take heed?
If only I could the past erase, another time, another place?
On life's experience I could feed, and probably sow a better seed.
Before you realise what you've done, your bones will bleach beneath the sun.
Beware! Make haste, let it not be, do it now, wait not for me.
The urgency that lies within, suggests that time is wearing thin.
Basic feelings on a theme, self-awareness, or a dream?
Hidden memories, vague but real, stir up thoughts, reel after reel.
Fleeting glimpses, events long past, dance through the mind, but do not last.
How do time and imagination blend; the subtle changes of fashionable trend.
With lots of things I have been showered, I've flourished, yes!
But never flowered?

Selwyn L. Thomas

Felixstowe

A dozen miles east of Ipswich, hard by the Suffolk coast,
Where the Orwell and the Deben meet the sea
And Martello towers watch for Napoleon's ghost,
There have I chosen my place to be.

Where Felixstowe stands on harbour-guard
And the North Sea pounds the beach
And the winds from Jutland blow strong and hard
As the doors of the Haven defy any breach.

From Landguard Point up to Levington,
Past the marshes and Trimley's Saints,
Along the riverbank to Nacton
Where the artist stands and paints.

From Waldringfield and the Maybush Inn,
And Woodbridge down to Bawdsey,
Or sail across to the Ramsholt Inn
While the river winds on to the North Sea.

To hear the clack clack clack of a hundred sheets
As they slap against upright masts,
When the wind blows strong and the heart fast beats,
With the deafening air-horn blasts.

By Felixstowe Ferry and the Ferryboat Inn
And the meandering Kings Fleet river:
Here may a man his journey begin,
Or end it with his soul all a-quiver.

Laroche

Silent Love

Under the dark green cypress tree,
Beneath the Italian sun,
Sits a lady fair,
With earth and sky as one.

She dreams of her love so far away,
Fighting on distant shore,
And longs for the day to come,
\When he will claim her hand once more.

She wistfully gazes across the land,
Where the sun burns bright at noon,
And thinks of her love so sadly there,
Under an August moon.

A soldier he must do his duty,
She at home must stay,
But all the while she longs for him,
And for his safe return doth pray.

She sits upon that rise each day,
And eagerly scans the view,
Seeking the return of her soldier love,
Under a sky so blue.

The day will come she knows it so,
When he will return to she,
But for now she must be still,
And her thoughts her comfort be.

Patricia A. Thomas

Clique Clique

What's all that noise?
(clique, clique, clique)
Can it be the poets,
(clique, clique)
verbal knitting?
(clique, clique, clique)
Creating a self-importance,
(clique, clique)
saving the world!
(clique, clique, clique)
"Poetical knot tying",
(clique, clique)
why use one word when ninety-seven will do!
(clique, clique, clique)
Are we making ourselves clear?
(clique, clique)
No?
(clique)
No???

Andy Thompson

Tranquillity

The moon reflects on a water fall
The whole world is still
A farmhouse light, glowing bright
On a far-off hill.

A lonely cry from a newborn lamb
Its mother has wandered far
And disturbing all this stillness
Is the sound of a motorcar.

The mountain tops capped with snow
Cast ethereal shadows far below.
A pebble falls, disturbed by a sheep,
Rouses a farm dog — fast asleep.

The motorcar comes to a halt.
The lamb has found its mother,
The rolling pebble rests by a rock
And the farm dog runs for cover.

The rain pours down relentlessly
But the stillness will remain
Until the first light of day
And it's daytime once again.

Gail Thompson

The Heavens

Sun is eighty billion years old,
and goes on five billion years to dissolve,
Mercury, nearest to the sun,
And its ground dry as a crumb.
Venus, a little further away,
Can be seen on some days.
Earth is the ground we live on,
Some years it is dry as a scone.
Mars is the other side of us,
We cannot get there by bus.
Jupiter is the biggest of ten,
It's made up of gases in its glen.
Saturn has large rings,
But still not large enough to be king.
Uranus sits on its side,
Its rings go up and down abide,
Neptune is number nine,
And is a little smaller to wind.
Pluto is not like the others,
It travels out into space and back to its brothers.
Planet eleven, opposite the earth and behind the sun,
UFOs come from there by passing the sun when they come.
The stars live ten million years,
Then explode and disappear.
All the above is universe,
That's the end of this verse.

E.M. Thompson

And We Go On Pretending

The arteries of corridors,
the cubbyhole of space,
where you've been shelved,
rescinds my hope,

And we go on pretending.

I fiddle with the curtain,
uncertain what to say,
Mythical tales of the
future seem apt,

And we go on pretending.

They come to change your drip,
the nurse repeats prosaic
quips — she knows her lines,
the play, the scene,

And we go on pretending.

Vast estuaries of time
run out, I kiss your effigy.
Tomorrow may be just
a promissory note,

But we go on pretending.

Jacqui Thomas

The Field Mouse

Redolent rodent resting in yon rustic wall,
What wayward thoughts do you this time recall?
Do feral cats impinge upon your brain
With images of suffering or pain?

Or are you happily at ease
Doing what you will where'er you please?
Feckless in a field of nodding maize
Blissful in these long, hot summer days.

Or do you fret about you naked brood,
Asleep and blind in straw-lined nest so crude?
The season's warmth too soon will pass you by
And fallen leaves will wither up and die.

Then winter cruel and callous will arrive
To taunt your every instinct to survive
Until at last the healing, vibrant force of spring
Disturbs your slumbers with a rude awakening.

Some troubles passed, more troubles still remain,
The energies of reckless youth now wane;
Curse not the passing of the fleeting years
But soldier on and wipe away your tears.

David Thompson

Untitled

Let your Christmas spirit
shine on me
Let it shine throughout the world
for all to see

Everyone join together
spirits in harmony
make the world a better place
for you and for me

No more wars, guns or drugs
no more mindless thieves or thugs
no more famine in an ideal world
There's not much time
to change your ways
before the judgement day

So let your Christmas spirit
shine on me
Let it shine throughout the world
for all to see

Susan Thomas

The Silent Telephone

The telephone torments me. Its silent sulkiness
Angers and frustrates me, and yet I must suppress
The love and longing deep inside, the misery and pain
Of willing it to ring, that I may hear your voice again.

Each time that I have rung you, your voice gives me a thrill.
I treasure each inflection, the sound is with me still.
But conversations oh so rare and meetings all too brief
I had to stop, I had no choice, but I am filled with grief.

If only you could see a way to contact me instead,
You know my number, where I live. Oh, why can't you be led
By my silent thought waves calling out your name?
Lift the hand-set, press the buttons. Make me whole again.

The phone can be so noisy calling for attention.
At times so intrusive, Mr. Bell's invention
Is sure to ring both loud and long when we need some quiet.
It insists on being answered. We cannot deny it.

But for that one special call it stays mute and dumb.
I wait and listen and I pray. Will that call ever come?
My love, sharpen your senses, listen with your heart.
Call me now, please call me. We've been too long apart.

Where e'er you are, my thoughts reach out, every single day
Hoping you'll receive them, that love may find a way.
Thoughts of love and tenderness meant for you alone.
Listen, darling listen, to my silent telephone.

Susannah Thompson

Still Flying

I am the smallest of the ducks
Still flying up the stair.
What I have seen and I have heard,
Repeat, I would not dare.

We've been here now for forty years,
Washed regularly in spring.
But should we be hung yet again?
Well now! There's the thing.

The young folks tried to ban me
And the others flying here,
But the older generation,
In hearts, held us most dear.

Our colour's slightly faded now.
We still fly up the stair,
But we can hear a change of tone
In the young who visit here.

Each wants to be the chosen one
Who will inherit us.
Those people who, some years ago,
Consigned us to the dust.

It seems that as the years have passed,
Our value it has risen;
And now we are collectibles
We'll one day fly to Heaven.

Alison R. Thomson

Comino

Please may I have a moment of your very busy day
Just close your eyes and I'll take you to a land not far away.
It's peaceful and it's quiet and it's just the place for you.
It's set in crystal waters under skies of china blue.

The sea around the coastline holds colours you've never seen,
Of amethyst and turquoise and a million shades of green.
The majestic cliffs soar upwards then slope down to rocky coves
And in the evening when the sun goes down, they burn oranges and mauves.

The land is not a fertile place, full of forests of tall trees,
But barren, open, rugged with wild herbs to scent the breeze.
It has a beauty of its own which takes your breath away,
And if I'm very lucky I might see you there one day.

So raise your glass and drink with me and together we will toast,
To "The Island of Comino" just off the Maltese coast.

Val Thompson

Victorious

As the gigantic whale cuts through the sea,
Undulating waves, wash over it's back.
It slips through the water with strength and ease,
The power is nuclear, and there are men in it's heart.

There, on the fin, men stand watching.
Observing the ocean and the cloudless sky,
No monster this, but a man-made machine,
To keep the peace, they do not ask why?

The men disappear quickly as the hatch it closes.
Then comes the signal, dive, dive, dive.
The great mass submerges beneath the waves,
Not a sign is left, only the ripples survive.

Silently it sinks below the surface,
Down towards the bottom where Neptune sleeps.
Will it come home to port, when it resurfaces?
Or will it forever be lost in the deep?

The men on board have an aim and a goal.
Living proof they are heroes of our time.
Working and playing, a self-sacrificing role,
Deep down, underneath the brine.

Dedicated to life, beneath the waves,
Their lives for their country, courageously they give,
Bravely valiant, with no thought of fear.
Peace for mankind, on to victory they steer.

Shirley Thompson

My Mind's Eye

Where is the land that once my father's knew?
Whose image, rugged strong and grey
I kept within my proud mind's eye
When I was oh! so far away.

No land this for holding petticoats
Of Mamma's busy scrubbing coal black vests
Away to cook and sew for grander folk
From morn 'til night, they put you to the test.

But through it all, in my mind's eye
I saw my Dad come singing from the mine
I saw the winder wheels so tall and
I was home again with folks so fine

The streets with laughter rang whene'er
They gathered for a wedding or a birth
no locks upon their doors they kept
For what was theirs, was yours to share it's worth

I see them now, in my mind's eye
I taste small beer with Sunday dinners
The chapels and the workmen's clubs
Both had their share of saints and sinners

There are no more the winder wheels
The miners song is just a sigh
But they will always be with me
Brought to life, in my mind's eye

Gwyneth Tilley

What's Happening To Me?

I know I'm old, or so they say,
That's what they told me yesterday.
They tell me "Dear, go here and there"
When I'm quite happy, in this *my* chair.
You see, I know this chair is mine
Because I sit here all the time.
Now they want me to try and rise,
They just don't know, with these old eyes
How hard it is to go some place. Oh! how demeaning — a zimmer race!
There's plenty of time, I'd rather wait,
It doesn't matter if for dinner I'm late.
Here they come, "The toilet Dear?"
I wish they'd leave me sitting here
It's my legs you see, they're not so good.
After all I'm eighty, and I would if I could
Here we go, "I'll give you an arm", don't they know they're doing me harm.
To make it worse, I can't hear too well,
Everything's muffled. It really is hell.
You know, it's strange, I don't seem to know
Or remember much of the past day or so.
Yet I can see before me spread, my youth, my loves, the life I've led.
Slow, bit by bit, I go through it all and smile to myself as I sit in this hall.
The girls are nice, and good, you see
I just wish I knew, "What's happening to me?"

Jane Thomson

"I Don't Have Green Fingers!"

The lawn is off-centre, the paths aren't straight,
The colours are fearsomely blended,
The hedge, (give it time) means to swallow the gate,
There's lettuce where none was intended!

The packet says 'DWARF' and the blooms climb the wall,
The 'GIANT'S' knee-high to a daisy —
Anemones planted to brighten the Fall,
At Christmas are blooming like crazy!

The dainty Lobelia grows anywhere but
It's prim little line in the border,
The ranks of the Lupins close in on the hut,
Advancing in strict battle order.

I follow instructions when planting my seeds —
Comes a gale and all Nature is seething,
(I once saw some asters of mine among weeds,
In a field very near Inverkeithing!)

I don't have green fingers — an obvious fact,
My friends find my efforts confusing'
"How colourful, quaint: they remark with great tact,
"And isn't the lay-out, well, amusing!"

Patricia Thorburn

Crows and Geese

The crows are wheeling
Round the copper-clad spire of the cathedral
Vying for a place on the weather-cock
They are canny birds
And like to know
Which way the wind will blow
I like to keep a weather-eye
On the golden cock too
But I can feel the wind wintering
And need no proof of direction

Another sign
A skein of wild geese flying south
Straight and true
In their V formation
They too had felt the north wind
And were running before it

I marked their position in the sky
As I travelled east
But when I looked for them again
They had gone

Michael Thorpe

464

The Bright Spark

A long time ago, they worked as a team
Bathed in fire's glow and droplets of steam
Over sleepers and stones their engine worked hard
With wheezes and groans and goods from the yard
Steam was no trouble as they charged up the hill
The fireman with shovel and the driver with skill
With heads quite askance and eyes that were keen
At signals they glanced, red, yellow, or green?
"She's steaming well mate" so the driver notched up
Unaware of his fate as he drank from his cup
A spark from the fire all glowing and red
Climbed higher and higher as it shot up his leg
It caused him to roar when it lodged at his knee
The pain was quite sore, the bad language free
As the fireman looked over, stifling his mirth,
Flames danced all o'er the driver's large girth
With bucket in hand and hose at the ready
He obeyed the command "Put me out Eddie!"

Jim Towle   .

All's Well in Poppyland

Early morning crab boats, chugging up the coast,
And the roar of North Sea breakers conjure up the ghost
Of Henry Blogg the lifeboatman, Samaritan supreme,
Whose statue on the clifftops marks the townspeople's esteem.
While his stone eyes scan the seascape, the pier and the sand,
Then the gentle folk of Cromer know all's well in Poppyland.

Meandering along the seafront or lounging on the pier,
Day trippers watch the anglers, before sampling the beer
In Bert and Barbara's "Bath House", the cosiest pub in town,
While on the promenade outside, the lads walk up and down.
Along the pier stroll pensioners, and lovers hand-in-hand.
The friendly folk of Cromer know all's well in Poppyland.

Eastwards on the cliff path, the lighthouse in our sights,
Upwards to the golf course, the greensward on the heights
Beyond the Happy Valley and the Country Club above;
Down below, the dogs yap on the beach they know and love,
Sniffing every boulder on the route to Overstrand.
Even Cromer's canines know all's well in Poppyland.

My window overlooks a copse of oak, ash, fir and birch,
And, further west, red rooftops, clustered round the church.
Now I see the grassland and the gorse in Happy Valley,
With its pathside benches where the clifftop hikers dally.
With such beauty all around me, I think I understand
Why the gentle folk of Cromer know all's well in Poppyland.

Alan Titley

Stranger Danger

Children stay away from DANGER
NEVER talk to any stranger
taking sweets may be nice
but oh dear children
do think twice

if in doubt just run and shout
let them know what it's all about
tell mummy, daddy, teacher too
or a policeman
they'll help you

Mark Tann

To A Spider

Run away, little spider, run away.
I know that it's a fine, sunny day,
But can't you weave your web
When I'm asleep in bed?
Go away, little spider, go away.

Run away, little spider, run away.
I know that you really want to stay,
But I've got things to do.
I'm sure that you have too.
Go away, little spider, go away.

Mrs. P. Thomas

Secrets

Secrets are special gifts
Bestowed on us, by others
Never to be told, or shared
Especially those from mothers

Keep them locked inside your heart
Under lock and key
Maybe after death
We dare to set them free

It's so hard to keep a secret
And we sometimes long to tell
But if we should unleash it
We may be doomed to hell

So listen to my story
Take heed of what's been told
Keep secrets safe forever
And smile as you grow old

Elizabeth Thorpe

Raspberries

Some fruits the gods made for themselves:
Strawberries, complexioned peaches,
The moulded pear,
The red jewelled ear-rings of the cherry tree.

And some the gods made for mortals:
Bitter-sweet berries, for the most part
Guarded if nominally by barbs
Pointing the moral of take if you dare
Sample and be sorry.
And none of them suits so well the tainted delight
Of our compromise with heaven
As the raspberry.

Lack-lustre, it pleases the eye that shuns brightness:
Not one but is blemished in some little part —
Rotten at core, ephemerally firm
Or damp to the touch.
Raspberries are parodies of people
Sharing their dull and sinful natures
Mocking their marks of weakness.

The gods have a delicate irony all of their own.

W.H.H. Tucker

Patience

Smothered, mis-spoken anger, killing true feeling,
Finally disperses with the helping hand of God,
Making way for grief at another's pain.
Disbelief spoken too loud, too soon,
Causes the cut to go deeper where healing should have been,
And again God comes with gentle chastisement —
Then peace.

Fear, disguised as anger, or even laughter,
Subtly takes over, enveloping all emotion
And taking it prisoner.
Tears then have their way, dissolving the chains
That fear has wrought in its pride
And they lie crushed and defeated —
Then freedom.

Longing, crying out for a depth of God
Only glimpsed in divine moments, all too brief,
Yet capable of bringing peace at their memory.
Searching for a knowledge beyond human understanding,
Searching 'til the earthly curtain falls

And the heavenly curtain rises on all the answers —
Then life.

Penelope Tilzey

Ode To My Sincerity, For Alex

I wondered lonely as a cloud
Well, Wordsworth did but I'm not proud
His poems are so much better than mine
I'm sure he wouldn't mind if I pinched a line.

Anyway as I was trying to say
In an unpoetical kind of way
I have no money and future is bleak
But I've plenty of love, it that's what you seek.

Ian Thompson (BA Hons.)

The Spirit Is Wailing
But The Flesh It Creeps

Words are a
Waste of talent
That stems from
Nervous energy
That serve
No other purpose
Than serving
As a therapy
So if no one
Pays the piper
Will he still
Scream out a tune
And will it go on endlessly
(Manic-obsession — lost — last impression)
Wailing ghost locked in an attic room

Paul Tilley

"No Known Grave"

There's a little bit of England,
    in the Flanders coastal plain,
Where the poppies in their thousands bloom,
    and fade, and bloom again.

Through the changing seasons,
    and the slowly passing years,
Hallowed by the mem'ries,
    nurtured by the tears.

There's no stone to note his being,
    nor verse to laud his fame,
Just the poppies in their thousands
    in the Flanders coastal plain.

Rest well, you son of England,
    'neath your quilt of Belgic sod,
Though gone, you're not forgotten,
    for your name is known to God!

Roy Tyler

Pernicious Zone

Loitering is not a consideration on the South Downs late at night,
Internecine feuds of good and evil continue to battle, wrong and right.
A large black moth of death around light does flitter
With disciplines from hell, twisted, tarnished, bitter.
Envoys from Satan beneath the full moon and the chalked Long Man,
Stirring up horror, mayhem and terror as considerable as they can.
From times gone by candles flicker medieval in mist and haze,
Under the watchful nocturnal Barn Owls steadfast stealthy gaze.
Then out of nowhere into the hushed pagan air, a vision of darkness,
Stalking with vindictive malice and venom so black with acidness.
Sorcery and magic work in harmony in the martyrdom of this night
Silver electrical bite leaved fingers with excessive force and might.
Across the open fields at high speed and with utmost clarity,
Far away into the distance, brash vulgar and with such barbarity,
Endless power of this master, a being epicene — to further confuse
And in the morning, when all is good and new, my mind is washed unable to accuse.

Georgina Allison Ticehurst

Years Ago

A lang time ago at a mertimas term
I accepted a bob tae work on a ferm
It wis oot o' the wye quite unknown tae me
Bit wi promises made, wis determined tae see

I fixed ma auld bike an a pedalled for miles
Hummin an singin the road tae the isles
Fin there on a brae this auld ruin appeared
Wid this be the pace, it looked affa weird

I knocked on the door an the fermer cam oot
He asked if I winted a look roond aboot
I thocht tae masel there's nae muckle tae see
Jist a run doon craft an a auld oak tree

The stable door needed a wee bit a force
A'fore I got in for a look at the horse
They braw beats haed shrunk as far as I'd seen
There wisna much left, bit some skin an been

The bothy wis next, so I opened the door
An mice gaed scamperin ower the steen floor
A chaff-bed wis riddled like a fisherman's net
It felt raither cosy, the tykin wis het

I'd wasted ma power comin ower for a look
At the meagre existence an time that it took
Handin back the arles, I'd made it quite plain
That I widna be joinin his grand race a'men.

O. Turner

Jodi

"Dad!" a shout, a cheeky grin
She wants to raid the biscuit tin
"What do you say?" I said in tease
Head on shoulder, puppy-eyed, "Please".

"Ask your Mum you cheeky pest"
She runs off with the same request
"It's nearly dinner" Mummy said
"Go and play with Dad instead".

In the air and up and down
She laughs so much when thrown around
Jumping, falling, she's so bold
God! She's only two years old.

Dinner's eaten, it's bath and bed
To look for stories I haven't read
She's now asleep without a care
I sit beside her and just stare.

Her long brown hair and perfect skin
Button nose and little chin
On her front, and bum in air
I sometimes want to shed a tear.

Two a.m., woke up, she's screaming
I'll kill the bogey man she's dreaming
Dummy in, all is fine
It's Mummy's turn in two hours time.

Leslie James Turpin

Scarlet Poppy

Demanding my attention, this red flower of the field
Stopped all my careless thoughts and made me yield,
I gazed in utter pleasure, such delicate beauty fair!
Waving gently above the grasses with a defiant air,
Then breaking through my transfixed mind,
For a moment, down this country path were lined —
Ten thousand soldiers, marching for their king.
It seems in dreams, ah! the memories you bring!
Each one so weak, so human, and so frail,
But marching together could defy the gale,
And so now you stand my friendly flower
In all you weakness, showing us such power.
A sad, brave beauty passing swiftly by,
Like the tanks and soldiers, out of place, 'neath summer sky,
Soldiers have gone and fields are planted out once more,
Yet still your redness shouts for victory as before,
As this new season you declare in no uncertain terms
                    "LIFE GOES ON"
Leaping from the earth and all its gentle shades
You come, and speak, in triumph, before the summer fades.

Vera Torbet

The Handbag

It's not so much a handbag, well more a cabin trunk!
And most that lives within it is nothing more than junk.
Let's open it and delve around, let's take a peek inside
It's mysteries I will reveal, from me they cannot hide.
A paperclip, a safety pin, some loo roll (just in case)
A tube of hide and heal — you know, for spots upon my face
A biro that is topless and one that just won't write
My tube of indigestion pills for when I'm ill at night
A polo mint that once was white but now it's soft and brown
My mum's disabled sticker for when we park in town.
A nail file and some scissors, some perfume to enhance,
And look there's even tickets from last year's Christmas dance.
A coupon here with 10p off, the money I shall save,
The contents of my handbag are like Aladdin's Cave.
Some glasses for the sunshine and so's I can read.
Yes everything lives in here everything I need.
A bunch of keys are jangling, a spare one for the car,
A screwed up silver wrapper from a sneaky chocolate bar,
Yet, once a week I sort it out it has a Sunday treat,
I organise it carefully and get it clean and neat,
But then I think I'll have it exorcised, I think I'll call a priest.
'Cos somewhere in the lining must live an impish beast.
For next time that I open it there stands a glorious mess,
Excuse me whilst I search inside ... now where's those pills for stress!!

Barbara Trippier

Sorrows of Spring

The flowers are fast opening
Another day starts anew
I look around the room I'm in
But all I think of is you
Outside the world is happy
A spring day full of hope
But inside this room my heart is heavy
I feel I cannot cope

Ann-Marie Tolley

Dawn In The Kitchen

The tap drips in the corner
Steady as a heart beating at its cage
Of curved long bones.
Somewhere a cold electric hum
Runs with the precision of planets.
The striped cotton shanks around
Strung arms and legs still
Stiff with the stress
Of sleeplessness. I brood
Down the empty roads of night,
Dumb with thoughts of grim days
Bolted and barred against a past
Lit by long memories of sunshine.
Numb with a lack of expectation
I perch until frost-light
Bars the window-blind
And then I douse the kitchen lamp.

Bryn Treadway

Robin

The robin flitted in the snow,
His little beak began to glow
Against the dark earth,
Which was becoming to be seen
And a tiny amount of the grass so green
Began to gleam,
He began to look for food
A worm, some bread, a berry,
But alas he could find none
So he waited all alone.
He was not having any fun
His feathers ruffled
To keep him warm
Would he get some food?
Or would he be forlorn?
An old lady went down her path
And answered his mirth.

Rachel E. Todd

468

A December Night

Flakes of pure, innocent white,
Against the evil black of night,
Confused, like a plague of flies,
But floating gracefully from the skies.
A never-ending film of white,
Is seen with the help of the moon and its light,
My eyelids, weighed down with sleep,
The outlook is no longer bleak
For now in my dreams the outlook is bright
Away from the dark, depressing night.

Angela Triffitt

The Fox

His padded feet make no noise
Against the thickly covered forest floor,
Making his way towards the nearest tree
The fox hears a rustle in the undergrowth.
Warily
He moves forward
Seeing a rabbit dart among the ferns
Crouching
He is ready to spring.
The fox leaps
And pins the rabbit to the ground.
Content at last the fox slinks back to his hole
As the first rays of sunlight
Appear from the east.

Sarah Thornley

Early Spring

Shafts of sunlight filter
Through an archway of leaves
New born to early spring.

Coltsfoot and daisy dance
To the tune of a gentle breeze
Enchored by early spring.

Birds in their finest plumage
Preen to court a mate
Conceived in early spring.

Daylight lengthens every passing day
When nature comes alive
In the warmth of early spring.

Jenny Treacher

Time For Thought

The simple joys in life are free,
Like sunshine after showers.
We take so much for granted
In this wonderful world of ours.
Daffodils dancing in the breeze,
Blossom on the apple trees,
Poppies in a field of corn,
Birdsong heralding the dawn.
A rainbow after sun and rain,
All is right with the world again.
Winter brings the frost and snow,
Carols round the Christmas tree,
Children's faces all aglow,
Living in a land that's free.
The changing seasons come and go,
Summer, Autumn, Winter, Spring.
Through the clouds the sun will show,
Thank you Lord for everything.

Evelyn M. Tuckwell

Shades Of Summertime

I can't wait for the summer, when the sun always shines,
To see sweet flowers bloom in the warm summertime,
I love their beautiful shapes and their fragrance divine,
Their nice pastel shades looking oh so sublime,
I can't wait for the sun to come out and shine.

It's nice to see squirrels scurrying around on the ground,
Gathering acorns and looking furtively around,
You have to be quiet and not make a sound,
As they're quick as a flash and then they are tree bound,
I can't wait for the sun to come out and shine.

We can ride on a tandem and sing lovely tunes,
Take a picnic basket out on the dunes,
We can go for a paddle and play the fool,
Or go for an ice cream, to keep us cool,
I cant' wait for the sun to come out and shine.

We can harvest the corn and the fruits of the earth,
Grow grapes on the vine in the lovely sunshine,
As the fruits of the earth, make beautiful wine,
We can drink it outside in the warm summertime,
I can't wait for the sun to come out and shine.

P. Thompson

Time

When you are small you run and play
You don't think of the seconds ticking away,
Then you're a teenager you think you know it all
Still the seconds are ticking
But you're having a ball,
Into your 20's you're planning your life
Still the seconds are ticking
But now you've a wife,
Into your 30's you have children too
Still the seconds are ticking
But you think not for you,
Your 40's and 50's pass by in no time
Still the seconds are ticking
But you feel fine,
You 60th year has crept upon you
Still the seconds are ticking
But what can you do,
Now into your 70's
You treasure each second
Because you suddenly realize
With time you can't reckon.

Janis Tyson

Friend Oak

Oak, strong, silent,
master of the woodland,
sanctuary for a thousand creatures.

Witness to a thousand seasons,
watching the changes,
feeling the sun,
bending in the wind,
drinking up the rain,
holding the frost and snow.

What have you seen?
What do you know?

Let me shelter near you.
Let me lean on you.
Let me hide in you.

Your whispering leaves
hold a thousand secrets.
Let me tell you mine.
Friend.
Oak.

Lesley Tyler

Looking Back From the Future

City of fallen grace
Once a proud place,
Its towers were tall and mighty
Libraries, halls, galleries sightly,
The men were tall and strong
But through arrogance it all went wrong,
They sought for power and wealth
Thinking only of themselves —
Down came the towers and halls,
To unhearing gods went their calls,
The kingdom was laid to waste,
No more bustle, no more haste,
There I rest my solemn case —
Is there no hope for the human race?
but
After every night there is a dawn
And from every sleep there is an awakening:
After every war there is peace
And from every plague there is recovery,
Always there is light at the end of every tunnel
And always a dove amongst the lions.

James Tunstill

Nature

I like the brilliant sunshine
        And the softness of the rain
The untold mysteries of nature
        We find so hard to explain

I like the many colours
        We see among the trees
The beauty of the scenery
        And the gentle summer breeze

I like the mixture of flowers
        Some wild and from the past
With scent like expensive perfume
        A fragrance meant to last

I like beaches of sand and gravel
        Around the coast of this isle
With its varied rock formations
        Showing an individual style

I like all things close to nature
        The animals, birds and bees
Humans have a lot to learn
        From the nature of the trees.

James G. Turner

Released

My emotions were in a state of calmness, free from plight
As I lay on the cool fragrant grass,
The moon illuminating the vast sky at night
Stars looked like teeth in a huge gaping mouth.

The sound of a busting city, heard in the background
The taste of freedom lingering around my mouth.
Thinking of all the lives, enduring hardship and strife
All the lonely housewives, living life by the knife.

The cool crisp air was gently caressing my lungs
As I lay free, in a tiny part of a disgraced world of madness
But still in my mind, all I could hear
Were bells chiming songs of peace.

Paul Scott Taylor

A Poem On Childhood

I know it's in my cupboard, though my mother says it's not,
But Daddy says it might be, if I bother him a lot.
I hear it when the lights are off, shuffling around,
The slobbering and sliding, the 'let me eat' you sound.
At night my Mummy tucks me in and opens up the door
But it hides itself, I know not where, perhaps beneath the floor.
I'd really like the light on, but Mum says I must be brave
And Dad he always says that there are power bills to save.
So in the dark I tremble when its thoughts invade my head
When it asks me, "open up the door and let me in your bed".
So just what can I do, to stop this awful, frightening sound,
Well I snuggle 'neath my duvet and I wrap it round and round.
And I think about some nice things and I think about my Mum
For I know when Mummy's in my head the monster will not come.

P.B. Thornton

Untitled

Last night I had a funny dream, it left me feeling blue
They say pride goes before a fall and now I now its true.
I courted a musician and I heard his pals all say
He really was quite famous though I'd never heard him play
I bragged to all my girlfriends about this handsome gallant
And wasn't I the lucky one to catch this lad with talent
I knew they would be envious so I planned for them a treat
The night he had his concert I booked them all a seat
Would he play the violin with encores asked non-stop
Or would it be piano, classical or pop
I knew that from this moment my whole life would be changed
Never time to all my own, autographs to be arranged.
The curtain rose majestically, my pride burst like balloons
For there was my beloved playing Mozart on the spoons.

Margaret Toplis

Elegy

Quiet
Are the fields
Once again.
Muddy hoofprints
Blurring
In the rain.
By the gate
The trough stands
Full.
Dispersing now,
Some windstrewn
Shreds of hay.
The cattle went
To market
Yesterday.

M.E. Tengwall

Spider in the House

The spider's web is worked
like lace and traced
in needlepoint
finding patterns
in the blank space of the wall.
Heavy bellied
Shadow lover
Puppet stringed and
tightrope walker
God of unspun airways
uncharted courses
naked bodied
Spider in the house.

C. Taylor

Inter City

They sit, unspeaking.
A quartet, travelling.
He reads, unknowing.
She writes, unthinking.
He looks, unseeing.
She sits, unsleeping.

They watch, fearing
Someone speaking
And so disturbing
Their non-communicating.
Eight eyes avoiding
Each other facing
But slyly looking
And perhaps wanting
A little coming
Together before departing
And forever separating.

Les Thornley

The Speech

Ladies and gentlemen,
Lords and tramps,
Giant gorillas and Killer Ants,
Enormous beetles and pussy cats,
Birds and dogs and don't forget bats,
Tiny elephants and massive bees,
Huge mice and square fleas,
Baby tigers and cute snow deer,
Raise a glass of beer,
To Mr. and Mrs. Leech as they prepare to
Make a speech.

Kevin Thorpe

The Storm

With racing foam that once did crash.
In pithy spite the storm winds lash.
On steely sheets of sombre shades.
Of curling knives with slashing blades.
Of promise made by restless steel.
Now falls away to peace reveal.
The tranquil peace when turmoil rests.
From bucking waves and roaring crests.
Where tossing seas in calm new found.
When silence comes with ne'er a sound.
In stillness calm of sunny seas.
With salty tongue of salty breeze.
From ripping grey to glassy blue.
Then see the fair reflection view.
That raging seas and tempest's groan
Will never conquer peace's throne.

John Taylor

My Small Boat

Rippling waters, take me afloat,
Carry me and my small boat,
Take me to another land,
Where the sun will glisten on the sand,
Where peace and happiness can be found,
Where apart from birds you hear not a sound,
Where kindness is spoken from people unknown,
Where in the blackness of night you can still roam,
Where children can play without any tears,
Where people can live without any fears,
Where money is nothing and love comes first,
Where people aren't living in hunger and thirst,
Where animals are free and live as they please,
Where you can walk in the forest, admire the trees,
Where blood shed and fighting will be no more,
Where you can sleep at night with an unlocked door,
But these things I know will never be,
For my small boat is a fantasy.

Samantha Treadgold

Untitled

Let me show you fields
Of coloured glass
To fill with flowers
And paper worlds.
Let me show a lane
Of rainbow forests
So that you can sit in the earth
And paint the sky onto your eyes.

Louise Tiplady

God's Only Son

Faces come and memories go
Life moves fast yet the earth moves slow
Stars shine but only at night
Birds sing for the hours of daylight.

Lessons in Life are learned each day
Thoughts remain and never go away
Dreams are shattered and replaced with pain
If you could live life again would you live again.

Everybody learns by their own mistakes
A chance in life is a chance to take
The odds are high on who will survive
It's the fitness of Man that keeps us alive

But still we kill for the status to be
God's only son for us all to see.

Paul Trotter

The Stars Look Down

Stars high up and far away,
blazing across the heavens.
Suspended there for all eternity.
Placed by hands unseen but
not unknown.
Old, old as the dawn of Creation.
Silent witnesses
to all the foolishness of Man.
Do they weep for a fallen and
divided world?
Where that which was conceived
and wrought in Love is turned
to dust?
Must beauty die, poisoned by greed?
The dew that settles on this earth each day,
can this perhaps be your tears
O stars?

D.H. Taylor

Seasons Of Life

Green buds, new shoots
New life, just like a baby
Bright clothes, strong roots
A long full life? Well maybe.

Dark days, cold war
Battered leaves and wind-blown
Thin children beg for more
Huddled, tired and still moan.

Brittle twigs, crisp leaves
Old ones too ill to care
Spring, Summer, now Autumn grieves
Winter too soon laid bare.

White snow, silver hair
Ravaged by the years
Seasons fast we all must share
Happiness, pain and tears.

Bare trees, cold and strife
Waiting for the sun
Embryos just starting life
The seasons almost done.

Browyn Terry

The Old Tin Bath

The wife rushes in with steaming water
more cold lass, chuck it in.
The zinc bath almost full t'brim
the linoleum will be saturated,
when the old fella he steps in.

'Ere catch it pet, mucky shirt t'boil tomorrow
pass us coaltar and the brush o'er there.
The muscles covered in grey and grimy sweat
cry out for want of sudsy massage,
Mother come on give us hand.

Those lads out in the yard are shrieking
they'll soon be down the pit themselves.
Two more years at school 'as Harry
Stevie's dead set he won't go.
Frightened of the filthy water, gouged with grey grime
of long ago.

Viki Twist

Untitled

Strong march winds and summer sun
October fogs and we were young
Flying kites and having fun
Catching frogs and wasps that stung

Chasing girls on old town green
Catch them kiss them not be seen
Come home late where have you been
Not so young but just eighteen

Called away to serve the king
Fond good-byes and tears that sting
Foreign shores sad songs we sing
Sailing home a wedding ring

Married now no longer free
To chase the girls or cross the sea
Three young sons for all to see
Invite the in-laws home for tea

Three young men now fully grown
From the nest will soon have flown
Another spring the seeds are sown
The harvest now we are alone

Bill Underwood

Friendship

Times there were I could have penned
Of your being a special friend,
Close at hand and goodly neighbour
Responding readily to a favour.

Such happy times did we share,
Laughing along without a care,
Shopping trips ... housewives together,
Off we went ... whatever the weather.

And before coming home an added perk
Of coffee break before housework.
Oh yes, joyful days and memories galore,
But alas, alack all these are o'er.

Who could foresee or justly portend
Their sudden, abrupt and startling end?
A misunderstanding which sadly led
To harsh and untruthful words being said.

Now silence reigns as a black cloud
Golden friendship within a shroud
Disillusionment, mistrust ... such a surprise
The only sparkle ... tears in my eyes.

Mrs. S.M. Unsworth

Love Remembered

George, do you remember when we first met?
You said, "I'll be your Romeo if you'll be my Juliet>"
George, do you remember when you were full of lust?
So romantic, keeping me out from dawn 'til dusk.
Then you went down on one knee
And said, "Gladys, marry me."
George, we tied the knot on the fifth of November,
That night there were fireworks in the bedroom, that's for sure,
Somehow we don't have them anymore,
Is it because I used to run my fingers through your hair?
Sadly now it's no longer there!
As for that athletic body I used to cuddle a lot,
After much Guiness, has now gone to pot.
George, it's our wedding anniversary today.
I'm sorry, Gladys, I seem to have forgot.
Yes, George, forgetting things is what you do best.
Go lie down for your rest.
As for me I'll remember our youth so wild and free,
When you were so madly in love with me.
I know deep down we love each other still,
But what really kills romance at night
Is when you take your teeth out before you switch off the light.
Whatever you say, Gladys, you're always right
Goodnight, George, goodnight!

Sally Vale

Cornwall

Cornwall is the place I long to be,
With its rugged coast and raging sea.
Where the pace of life is slowed right down,
But work still gets done in the village and town.
The leafy lanes with their abundance of flowers,
To wander along them, forgetting the hours.
Down there you're in another space of time,
away from the bustle, and the dust and grime.
To visit the harbours so pretty and quaint,
With their tiny cottages coloured with paint.
The sound of the seagulls flying high above,
All of these things are what I really love.

And when in Essex, all I do is dream,
Of that lovely county of clotted cream.
Until I go there again on my summer vacation,
To make the most of its scenic location.
For every year Cornwall seems to beckon to me,
To the place of golden sands and crystal blue sea.
I expect its because my father was Cornish,
I've got it in my vein,
To return to my second home, time and time again.

Rosalind Venus

Dead Days

Down through the years we've been apart
Dead days return to haunt the heart.
Empty now the sweet sad place
Where once we lay in close embrace,
Soft shadowed by the sunlit leaves,
A world in which the young heart weaves
Dreams of a future flushed with gold,
An unfolding tale of love, its ending never told.
There summer passed us swiftly by
As we caressed neath a sun-bright sky
Blue windowed by the curtains of the clouds,
Cradled in love, far from unwanted crowds.
Too short our joy, too brief its stay,
A love, not lost, but thrown away
Unwanted by a heedless heart
That made rejected love depart.
Too late I saw what grief it cost.
Too late I knew what I had lost.
Now dead days fill my thoughts again,
Awakening near forgotten pain.
Through the aching years we've been apart
Dead days return to break the heart.

Fred Vaughan

Memories

Memories of a policeman walking the beat,
A boy on a bicycle delivering the meat,
The milkman came round with the milk in a churn,
And our Friday penny we had to earn,
With carbolic soap we were given a scrub,
In front of the fire in a large tin tub,
Toilet rolls were not the in-thing,
It was newspaper squares hung on a string,
Our diet included dripping on toast,
But jam roly-poly was what we liked most,
When we were at school we were not always good,
We didn't behave, like we knew that we should,
For bad behaviour we were given the cane,
We knew then for sure we'd not do it again,
But we were most of us happy, in those days gone by
When I look at life now, I just heave a sigh.

Mrs. D. Vine

A Name

What's in a name
Yes! What is a name?
We are all different
Yet some bear the same.
We shall be known by it,
Esteemed by it.

What's in a name
We can be called a failure
By that same.
A name can be
Your stepping stone to fame.
When someone calls
How can he without name?
Once thing we know,
Some use it just for show,
Far, far better that we should
Carry through our lives
A name that's good.

Kathleen Mary Vaughan

A Widow's Quilt

It is the sole assertion of a life
Of her own. It is spirited from black magic.
Like a trick of the light, it parallels her life.
The horizontals are woven through with
Blood, sweat, tears, all of which she is
No longer able to offer, so keeps to comfort herself,
Thought turned to lonely evenings
Now darkness draws her in.

It won't be more than a winter's wear.
She is used to cutting corners,
The scissors to her wedding dress,
Scarlet for the lining, that she cannot find.
When she thinks about it so much is missing
She hardly dare dream of the end.
So she pieces snippets of their old duvet together,
Rough, coarse, awkward-edged,; yes, she is used to making do.

Unlike the young girls of today,
She has known no other. She remembers the tension,
Unpicks frustratedly, wished she could start again.
She continues, though her pace ever slower, such is old age.
She pricks her finger, feels sleepy. The clock stops,
She winds and rewinds. Is it really so very late?
Finishing, she bites the thread, feels her life come apart.
She rests a moment, pulls the quilt about her and is gone.

Ms. V. Vaughan

Winter Chills

The autumn leaves turn red and brown
Soon winter winds will blow
Their ice cold blasts will chill the air
Bringing clouds and snow.
Snowflakes will drift quietly down
To cover houses, trees and all around.
The sunrise in the mornings
Will light up this wintery scene
Of long hanging icicles
And snow topped evergreens.
Children playing in the park
Some sliding on the ice
Old people carefully pick their way
For them it's not so nice.
Soon church bells will send a message
On a star-lit night
People will go to church to pray
And sing with all their might.
Once again it's Christmas
A time for love and cheer
Softly falling snowflakes
Quietly close another year.

Alec G. Vale

A Winter's Tale

I'm aware of all the seasons
and the weather all year round,
as I rose from bed this morning
I saw snow upon the ground,
I gave thought to all my feathered friends
the blackbird and the thrush
the robin and the sparrow huddled in the brush.
I gaze upon the laden trees to me they look quite sad,
with every falling snowflake their branches start to sag,
I see children with their sledges racing up and down,
watching for the snowballs whizzing all around.
As the day progresses the snow begins to freeze,
with every crunching foot-step
I can feel a chilly breeze.
There are twinkling stars above me
and I see this awesome sight,
the snow that I am standing on
makes day-light out of night.
I'm not as young as I used to be
but I don't feel very old,
I'm wrapped up snug and warm but my nose and ears feel cold.
Now when the snow has melted and the birds begin to sing,
the yellow of the daffodil
then I'll know tis turned to spring.

Ron Veitch

The Car Park

Ramble, bramble uphill scramble.
Team up, clean up, pulling green up.
Old place — needs space — set sights - set pace.
Improve — mess move — shift, shovel, make smooth.

Plan well — tree fell — rotten wood — bad smell.
Be strong, work long hours till time's gone.
Grass out — glass out — large things pass out.
Slime out — grime out — can't take time out.

Scraping, raking, hard back breaking.
Chopping, cropping, feel like dropping.
Hacking, cracking, heap high stacking.
Gripping, ripping, rubbish tipping.

Swinging, clinging, foliage thinning.
Clearing, shearing, no end nearing.
Clipping, tripping, with sweat dripping.
Shaking, taking rest from aching.

Spade down — laid down — with work weighed down.
Can now, wipe brow — job done somehow.
Weedless, seedless, leaves in breeze — less.
Flower — less, powerless — tall growth tower — less.

Stare ground - bare ground — wear and tear ground.
Play land — grey land — have no say land.
Dead land — bled land — tears all shed land.
Dry land — cry land — had to die land.

William Varnam

Stone Steeped in Rydal

Stone steps
take you down
Stone meets
Nature's transparent garment
Fluid
rock sprayed
sun dipped
deepened in parts
folded and formed
inviting immersion
with rippled suggestion
Stone bridge
takes you over
Ivy warmed
Green formed
Spanned
with stone hut
windowed
with rustic view
tree-scaped idyll
Stone steeped
in Rydall

Carol Tyson

Summer

Screaming gulls, smelly bins,
ice cream, tanned skin.
Traffic jams, can't park,
can't swim, what shark.
Summer tops, flashing boobs,
cool drinks ice cubes.
Hot sun, gentle breeze,
more rubbish, bloody fleas.
Heat wave, radio noise,
sexy girls, sexy boys.
Sun tan, Summer haze,
sun cream, lazy days.
Coconut oil, nice smell,
skin cancer, bloody hell.
Holidays, long breaks,
sea side, fishing lakes.
Half board, full board,
more Emmets, aw gawd.
Smile please, camera's clicking,
SHUT UP ..., couples ticking.
Blue Lagoon, sea shells,
blushing bride, wedding bells.

F. Vosper

Grain

A fulsome grain of wheat am I in the cold dark earth
A slim green sheath will pierce the soil when I give a birth
For the sweet spring rain will kiss me and tempt me from my sleep
Warmth from the sun will flatter me and my growth complete.
I'll thrive and my harvest will be good before the sharp scythes reap
And my plump seeds fall in the bustling wind
To the cold dark earth and sleep.

Life is as short as the corn is green
As breath of an April spring.
Life is as long as the old gray years
When birds no longer sing.
A season of blithe young ardour.
A season of rich sweet cream.
A season of fruit in the larder.
A season to only dream.

God giveth a babe to a maiden.
God giveth love to a youth.
God giveth wisdom in autumn.
In winter — He giveth truth.

Fran Vincent

Untitled

No movement,
Sky hanging, lifeless.
No blue, just grey.
Trees dripping, branches bare.
Skyline sharp, empty of life.
Stillness everywhere, no shadows.
Ground, brittle and dry.
Animals burrowed for warmth in hidden places.
Mist lies over the dying leaves.
Silence echoes against the day.
No feeling in the air.
Everything waiting for a brighter time.
Winter.

Sue M. Townsend

Another Day

The alarm clock rings to start the day
No one knows what will happen today
A thought goes racing through your head
And you lift yourself out of your nice warm bed

Down the stairs still half asleep
To wake up with a nice cup of tea
You sit there staring into space
Thinking of all those bills to pay

Back to the bathroom for a shower
It feels like you've been awake for hours
Out you jump and then get dressed
Now you don't feel quite so depressed

Back to the bedroom to make sure you look right
You kiss the wife and say good-bye
Down the stairs once again
And don't forget to phone today

Yes my love I will let you know
Where I'm going to be all day
Through the door and off you go
In the car and down the road.

Barry Vincent

Open Your Eyes

People do not feel the wind;
They let each wisp and gust go by ...
And waste so much.
They rarely see the setting sun
And accept its rise without a thought —
Yet each day is a miracle in itself.

When did you last see a bird?
Or notice that there wasn't one around,
And if you say "today" —
Did you really see it?
Or was it that it happened to be there.

When last did you truly breathe the air,
And thank the trees for making it so fresh.
Does your conscience ever prick you
That the river isn't clean?
Or do you just say 'shame', and then forget.

Do you admire the countryside
From the window of a car?
And ignore the tarmac scar
That lies beneath!
How more pleasant it would be
If the roadway wasn't there;
Then I don't suppose you'd be there either
Would you?

M.J. Volp

Ages of Transport

First the sledge, then the wheel, and from reed to timber boats,
Man's endeavour in transport on land and water promotes,
He harnessed the horse, the wind and running stream,
Then took coal from the earth, and made the power of steam.

Horse and cart, cab and stage, gave way to car, and steam on rail,
While iron tramp steamer took passenger and cargo, from tall white sail,
Then networks of motorways takes preference, from lane, road and byway,
And now steam must give way to diesel, then electric railway.

Determined pioneers of flight, triumphantly took to the sky,
And later opened the Heaven's airways, and Man at last can fly,
Then Man's first flight to the moon, far out in space,
Where he walked and talked, to the whole human race.

Space and under sea travel, is Man's ultimate and possible dream,
And all of this the Channel tunnel, is the first stages to be seen,
Next intercontinental travel in comfort, at the speed of sound,
Through stainless steel tube under Ocean, both under and above ground.

G.T. Vincent

Memories of Scapa Flow

Here come the divers to dive in Scapa Flow,
Clothed all in rubber cheeks all aglow,
Air bottles full, weight-belts galore,
All aboard the dive boat cast off the shore.

Out to the grave site, out in the deep,
Where rusting hulls of battleships twist in their sleep.
In and out of the hatches, octopus and wrasse,
Conger eels and lobsters, seals, monster crabs.

Lush sea anemones along with deadmen's fingers,
Sponges and tangles, history still lingers.
Wreckers find their treasures, in the sunken mass,
Portholes, propellers, brick-a-brack and brass.

Photographers' bulbs flashing, scoop their winning shots,
Posing divers, mounted canon, broken pots.

Suddenly it's over, air is running low,
Back aboard the dive boat with memories of scapa flow.

Margareth Van-Den-Heuvel

Only a Handshake

It's hard to have to give a parting handshake
When one you love is bidding you farewell,
Though king and country needs me,
Do not let this parting grieve thee,
Good bye, God keep you safe and well.

It's joy, my dear, to give a hearty handshake
When one you love is welcoming you home,
Though sea and land divide us,
Our love will always guide us,
Sweetheart, one day we'll all come home,
Let me remember the joys of the past,
Here in a handshake so warm and steadfast.

Only a handshake that means au revoir,
Only a handshake till we meet once more,
The wars have meant partings for old and young,
Yet in our hearts we are still as one,
Let me remember a sweet smiling face,
Put it right here in this parting handshake.

Margaret Vinall-Burnett

Travel

Today we hop aboard a plane and fly across the ocean
To visit lands so far away, wherever we've a notion.
We board a plane, a boat, a train as easy as can be,
And yet not so very long ago, people never even saw the sea.

We go to places on the map we've read about in books,
It's all so very easily arranged by Thomas Cook's.
We take a cruise upon the Nile, or go to Hyderabad,
We can look upon Mount Everest or dream in old Baghdad.

The mysteries of the Far East are mysteries no more,
Wherever we would like to go someone's been before.
America no longer is a wild and untamed land,
The red Indian says welcome, just have cash in your hand.

Australia is now a trip to visit our relations.
We don't even need a visa to visit many nations.
We can go as we please and no one thinks it funny,
But there is just one condition, you've got to have the money.

Mrs. F. Walkington

Heaven?

My tide is ebbing to its flow,
The sunsets fiery, golden glow,
Is nearing for me here below
So have no pity when I go.

Disregard the shepherd's warning,
New scenes for me are dawning,
I'll be on my way ere morning,
Now the gateway ahead is yawning.

Beckoning to pastures new
Could you but see the lovely view,
Maybe, one day, you'll see it too,
The drifting, restful, rosey hue.

My ponies waiting in the clover,
Now their working days are over
Dogs are bounding from their cover,
As though to greet a long, lost lover.

Alex waiting cap in hand
For me to join the happy band,
I see now in the promised land,
I have but to wave my wand.

B.E. Waddell

Two's Company

I'm so looking forward to Christmas
'Cause for once, I won't spent it alone
Last June I drew out all me savings
And then, went and ordered a clone.

I remember that day at the clinic
When I looked at myself and looked back
I shook hands with myself, said how do you do
And handed a cheque to the quack.

When we got home, we played tennis
But the end of each set was the same
So we called it a day, put our racquets away
And agreed that we didn't like the game.

We decided to play the piano
Every crochet and minim tune
My clone loved Debussy, and of course, so did I
So we played a duet — Claire de Lune.

We went shopping today, bought our presents
And we've hidden them under the bed
Eh ... I've just had a thought ... while I'm sipping me port
Nobody will know when I'm dead.

I'll just phone the quack, ask the question
'Hello ... you must see me at once
You say you're not there? — this is certainly queer
He's gone out with himself — for his lunch.

Joan Wallace

The Prodigal Son

I sat in silence by an open fire,
My memory sought your face,
I dreamt that you and I my love,
Were in some other place.

I dreamt we dwelt in marbled halls,
Just as the poem says,
I dreamt of open fields, my love,
Of all our yesterdays.

I dreamt of days when we were young,
Of happy days, and sad,
Of golden days beneath the sun,
Of all the fun we had.

I sat in silence by the fire,
The embers slowly died,
And as I thought of you my love,
My tears I had to hide.

Not tears of sadness those my love,
Just simple tears of joy,
They told me you were coming home,
To me my son, my boy.

E.A. Wade

The Soul Of Nature

In the rain, in the rain, in the dense feeling of life,
My brain flutters the world. I see in my mind's eye, countries
afar, deserts, aquaseas and safari lands.

I imagine the muscular bodies of barbarian athletes, roaming the
earth in harmony, black hearted. My thoughts flow like a stream,
into theirs, their movements become mine, their feelings enter me
without warning. My relationship with nature, becomes so great and
overcoming, I enhance the strength of a great lion.

The warmth of the sun hits my heart like a rock, I feel so happy
I could dance and sing in the sun for hours and hours. For me that's
where the dreaming finishes, when there is nothing left to dream,
when there is nothing left to want.

In the rain, in the rain, in the dense feeling of life. Fantasies of
happiness just seep away, my soul drips slowly back into the tiresome
and depressed existence I am trying to lead, these dreams are all I
seem to have.

Lucy Dawn Walker (Age 14)

And You Scream Why

For years on knees we hoped and prayed for her
Cartoon figures filler her room
Her cot, her new womb, warmly waiting
But she never came home

A twisted red screwed-up face
Little eyes closed fearing life
We were there, always would be
She should fear nothing we would tell her
When she opened her eyes
But she didn't

Her little white coffin rested gently
In her daddy's hands
As snowdrops dotted the graveyard
And the sun smiled with embarrassment

Her name, it's Claire
We still talk to her
It's like being touched by an invading light
Filling every nook and cranny of our very souls
Then snapping off
Leaving a cold grey ache

Our hearts, they still stubbornly beat
But please, oh please
Hide us away somewhere, anywhere
Until they stop

Shane White

Harbingers of Spring

O 'tis such a glorious sight,
To see a yellow aconite,
And know that Spring is on the way,
Dispelling Winter's clouds of grey.

The dainty snowdrop shows its flower,
E'en while the fearsome snowstorms glower,
Heralding signs of coming Spring,
Enticing birds to chirp and sing.

The varied coloured crocus blooms,
That open wide when sunshine looms,
Filling the ground with petals bright,
Uplifting spirits with delight.

Majestic, golden daffodil,
With gratitude our senses fill,
What grace! What glow! these flowers employ,
To cause our hearts to leap with joy.

Then there's multi-coloured heather,
Clustering their blooms together,
Making carpets flushed with beauty,
To gladden eyes of you and me.

It would be nice if we could bring,
Our praise and thanks to God our King,
For all the flowers that we enjoy,
Each man and woman, girl and boy.

L.E. Whitfield

Love From Afar

I see you walk with her, talk with her —
I say nothing
I see kiss her, you say you miss her —
But I say nothing
You say you love her, no one's above her —
And I say nothing.
But what do you feel for me?
No, don't tell me!
I know the answer —
Nothing ...

Sally Wilford

Lament For The Chosen

She lies in a ring of fire
High, high, higher
The chaste maiden robed in white
Alone on her sacrificial throne.

Awake from your sleep my dream webbed sweetheart
Come of age fair child
The tree is laden with rich fruits
Forged golden and gilded
Take sustenance and rise
Sun Queen
Rain god
Dogmatic plea to your existence.

Lament for the virgin
Rejoice for the crimson river.

Rhys Warren

Home Of Mine

Ageing buildings and wondrous dales
Green-clad hills and rambling vales
With wheatfields that nod
And rivers that flow
Where cattle are grazing
In pastures below
With towns and gardens, cliffs and rocks
Ministers and churches with very old clocks
The charming woodland in all its greenery
The Wolds stretch for miles
In all the scenery
The moorland solitude is something rare
With heather almost everywhere
People surrounded by ecstasy
With all this wonder all must be
The end of any anthology.

Barbara Ward

Why

You said goodbye, just walked away,
You made me cry, no words could I say.
The dreams that we had, just didn't come true.
Why did you go, did you find someone new?
Why was it so, we drifted apart?
Why must I live with my broken heart?
If you're filled with regret, but too proud to admit,
May my love guide you back to me here as I sit.
Then happy I'd be, no more would I cry.
No more to doubt or ever ask why.

Raymond White

True Happiness

It's folk who are friendly
And folk who are kind
That makes life worth living
And bring peace of mind.
It's hands that are helpful
And ready to bless
That makes all the difference
To joy and happiness.

Doris Welford

Get Off My Land

Denied of having a party
now freedom is banned
when you travel to the country
the police say "get off my land".

When you drop out of society
to travel, life free
M.P.'s are quick to say
that the land doesn't belong to me.

Funny how the times have changed
once we had free speech
inflation hitting down on choice
is what the Governments preach.

Now we can't even protest
about what they're trying to do
because they've installed a system
to curb our point of view.

A justice bill for criminals
is what it's going to be
when innocent folk are sentenced
whilst M.P.'s and rapists still walk free.

Beverley Warner

D Day 1944 - 1994

It is hard to perceive what the Allies achieved all those years ago
landing on War-Strewn beaches many miles from home; I was not born
when flags were torn and Soldiers killed in Normandy that very Morn.

Sacrifices were made because Europe was enslaved by Nazi Tyranny.
If I find it hard to perceive; will younger generations find it hard
to believe as World War Two veterans fade away.

World War Two was still fresh in our parent's minds; they told us
stories of deeds done; how Uncle Bill chased out the Hun; Arromanches
Bayeux; Caen; Villers; Bocage; and Falaise; the road to freedom led to Paris.

Tank battles were fierce with many dead on both sides; Artillery
barrages killed many Civilians as shell splinters didn't choose sides.

The sounds of combat recede; the wind blows them away; surviving
combatants march away; tears shed; Prayers been said for their dead.
The fallen now rest in peace: where once shells rent; blackbirds lament;
a man of fifty-two visits his father who died in battle aged twenty-two.

So our heads of state pay their respects today: This is the fiftieth
anniversary of D Day: Old Comrades shake hands and march away; the last
Post having been played the last notes fade.

Was their sacrifice necessary for freedom's sake? Let there never be another
World War for our sakes.

R.J. Wallach
6 June 1994

Yesterday Was Sunny

Yesterday was sunny, yesterday was fine,
Yesterday we picked roses, yesterday we drank wine.
Yesterday together in the park, yesterday hand in hand on the beach,
Yesterday was autumn leaves, yesterday so far from reach.
Yesterday we walked in the snow, yesterday we laughed in the rain,
Yesterday is just a memory, yesterday won't come again.

Today I can but dream, today I'm on my own,
Today I'm far away, today I am not known.
Today I sleep alone, today I don't know what to do,
Today I wonder where you are, today I ache for you.
Today I lay awake, today I gaze at the moon,
Today there are no answers, today can't end too soon.

Tomorrow I'll say I love you, tomorrow I'll say I care,
Tomorrow I'll tell you I need you, tomorrow I'll be there.
Tomorrow I'll take you in my arms, tomorrow there'll be no others.
Tomorrow we'll be together, tomorrow we'll be lovers.
Tomorrow I'll be yours, tomorrow we'll be alone,
Tomorrow you'll be mine, tomorrow I'll be home.

Michael Whight

A Thankful Heart

If I were to be born again
And parents I could choose
My first thoughts for my mother
Would be eyes as deep as pools

Where from the first beginning
I could see myself reflect
All her patience joy and love
My inner self infect

Knowing close beside her
Was an honest upright man
Always there to comfort
And to listen and to plan

What more could be desired
For those tender wondrous years
From childhood to maturity
Foundations firmly laid

These are the things that matter
Born of selfless sacrifice
They are God's best gift to children
He alone can know the price

Audrey Ward

Getting On

It's nice to be "getting on" you know
With do be careful! Mind how you go
Let us carry your shopping and mop your floor
And should you need more help we are only next door.

I never thought old age brought such style
When they take one for car rides mile after mile
Call in at a cafe and say with a smile
Would you like tea and cakes and rest for a while?

They say come to dinner each Sunday at one!
Offer second helpings before it's gone
Do stay to tea for some jelly and pears
And sorry the "loo" is up all those stairs.

How nice to have friends who treat me so well
After years of hard work how can anyone tell
Just what it means to one "getting on"
To enjoy such kindness before we are all gone.

Marjory Watson

Evening Storm at Brookenby

So still, so quiet in the darkening day,
No breath disturbs the rye.
Along the hedge the white scuts play
Beneath the glowering sky.

The stalking cat ghosts through the gloom,
No prey to pounce seeks he.
But a lover's tryst on the darkened green
Before the rain breaks free.

The stuttering storm ignites the dark
Toward the silent sea.
The wold tops stand out black and stark,
The world belongs to me.

Raindrops spit on the thirsty earth,
I take the homeward track.
From flickering sky to flickering set,
Reluctantly turn back.

Peter James Wallis

A Drought Too Long

The scouts float by like balls of linen; innocuous,
While the infantry congregate in the distance
And begin to march forward consuming the light.
The wind sounds their onslaught as the first
  Mortar tastes its target.

Above the legions swarm, growing awesome and angry.

An orchestra of infinite splashes is playing now
With intense authority from heaven,
While the trees humbly bow in the breeze
As if to say grace for the ineligible offering
  From above.

With a thought the composer commands
  And the orchestra calms
The legions disperse for they have done their job.

Like fields of corn they stand and gather,
Blown in by winds of promise of rains of
  Refreshments.
They stand tall and stretch and gasp but they wither,
The grim reaper has havested death with his Scythe.
Where the clouds have deserted to feed other environments.

Throughout this world there is a drought,
  Of starving souls I have no doubt;
If like the clouds we come together
We can fee these lands and brave the weather.

James Walsh

A Walk In The Country

I was up with the lark
at the break of dawn
so in the country I went
for a walk that morn

I kept on walking for about a mile
to my pleasant surprise I saw a stile
So I thought I would sit
and rest awhile

I hear a pleasant sound
so I took a look
Not far away
was a babbling brook

So after my country walk
to roam
I retraced my step
and headed for home

I thanked the lark
for the country to see
the things that I saw
are for you and me

So get up with the lark
and come with me
for the beauty of Nature
for you to see

Mrs. E. Warren

Cruel Paradise

This is the ballad, of someone not you.
Who was compelled to drugs, and all sorts o' glue
The true friends he had, shook heads in frustration.
He's dead now, so I'll warn the nation.

Acid, hash, hot knives and speed, a fair amount o' ecstasy,
That was the trip, that brought him here.
See his cold body next to me
He was a selfish man, although not really cold,
It's all very difficult, but the kids must be told.

He searched for something special,
It truly eluded him well,
It hinted signs o' paradise,
Instead it gave him Hell.

One long final search, a plastic bag placed o'er his head,
A last wearied inhalation,
Now he lies stone dead.
His short ballad's almost over, a tiny detail I must add.
Will his kids need a fix, to go and find their Dad.

Alan Watt

Council Centenary Year

Come all you village people,
Old minutes books to spy,
Unfold your minds from slumber,
Note all the years gone by.
Count all your many blessings
In photos and in rhyme,
Looking to the future.
Count all things back in time.
Encompass all your feelings,
No thoughts should go astray
Try and see more clearly, in
Every passing day.
Not all is ere forgotten,
After one hundred years.
Remember past achievements,
Yet have no lasting fears.
Your future is before you,
Even though it's not too sure
Although it's not so brilliant
Reflect on days of yore.

L. Gordon Ward

Live With Spirit

Is life on earth but a futile waste
    Whatever one's breed or caste?
Vain futile chase for love, for joy
    'Til death claims each girl, each boy.

Escape this knowledge — drink, smoke, drugs — what?
    Search for copybooks to blot.
Then what? Survive the stress of it all
    Yet still will come death's bleak call.

Create wondrous works of art profound —
    Why for? Death doth yet abound.
Breed profusely as animals do
    Then worn out, last days be few.

So what to do with talent and brain?
    What's the secret of eternal life?
Is the universe a school to train
    The soul by suffering irksome strife?

If this the purpose for our being
    Our ego clouds the way of seeing.
But why not when young this way be know
    And guidance given — we to be shown.

If purpose be high, our souls to learn
    Both candle ends we may not then burn.
Why then material being — why, why?
    Let all be spirit in vacant sky.

R.G. Warrior

Down and Out

I see the beggar on the street,
He doesn't have enough to eat,
He sits there rocking to and fro
He's there in sunshine, rain and snow.

I look at him and I could cry.
There but for the grace of God go I.
He's cold and lonely, living rough
My fiver doesn't seem enough.

The coat wrapped round his body's torn
His shoes are well and truly worn,
People pass him every day
'Get a job', I hear them say.

This poor man hangs his head in shame
Once he was proud, he had a name,
No one wants to know him now
He'd help himself if he knew how.

He's old, he should be somewhere warm
Where he would come to no more harm.
Clothes to wear and food to eat
And slippers on his weary feet.

He won't live long without some love,
Soon God will take him up above.
This man is just like you and me,
A branch from someone's family tree.

L. Wall

I Watch

When the world is late, and dark,
And every creature's well asleep,
Then I go about my tasks —
Then I creep and peep.

I watch drunks stagger homeward,
Dragging their feet and swearing;
As they enter one door the wives' lovers are out the other:
Urine-stained Y-fronts or boxer shorts and socks are all they're wearing.

I watch dogs chase cats and cats chase rats,
I watch foxes scrabble through old tin bins;
I watch vicars at their altars in the "wee small hours"
Secretly confessing their non-existent sins.

I watch ghosts rise thinly in the graveyards,
Disfigured wrecks of both distant centuries and more recent years
Raging silently at injustice, screaming mute agonies of pain,
Uttering soundless curses, crying wetless tears.

I see accidents and terrors, ignorance and death,
I watch owls take squealing mice;
I see souls burning in Earthbound hells,
I watch fevers break on ice.

Late in the night, with headphones blasting, I record these images:
I do not cry for innocence, I never judge the deed;
What guilt could there ever be in such a world —
What hurt could ever register, as I feel the Earth's hear bleed?

D.A. Warne

An Original Thought?

The cynics argue that it's all been said
That there is nothing new beneath the sun
Each step I take in someone else's tread
No matter what I do — it has been done

Can there be grains of truth in what they say
These thoughts of mine have marked some yellow page
My life is lived in someone else's way
A permutation from some bygone age

Those famed ones of the past in well-earned sleep
Disturb them not in question of their fame
Or is the tomb a passing tryst they keep
To masquerade in someone else's name

Will Hitler live again — perchance old Nero
Was fiddled while some other city burned
Would I be knave or might I play the hero
Where would my role be cast if I returned

My ego tells me this cannot be so
Something I've said or done must be unique
But then I wonder if — long years ago
In Athens — some fool thought the same — in Greek!!

Murdoch Ward

Carole

Against every full consequence
She feigns a dull indifference
To a torture so tender it
Can make its victims defend it
Beaten by the cartoon blizzard
Of a Christmas far too busy
To weep at the naivete
Of this simple nativity

From dreams like summertime picnics
She can only truly pick which
Fence to fall at rudely — but
Could she faultlessly refuse it
Swelling with barely hidden hurt
Splattering sinks with just deserts
She turns thick gag to laughing stock
From punchbag to sandbag and back

Revealed by a lack of coat, she
Looks hot but feels cold, deep
In the heart of an uncivil war where
Even the poor live in ivory towers
If beggars can be choosers she may
Not get dressed at all today.

Bill Watt

The Last Christmas Of Childhood

Is one to remember
It's magical thrill will be with you forever.
Flushed with excitement you get ready for bed,
Colourful thoughts fill your head.
Rudolf with his bright red nose bringing
Santa in his toy laden sleigh.
As you settle to sleep, a smile on your face,
Your stocking hangs by the fireplace,
Two mince pies on a plate nearby.
You close your eyes hoping Santa enjoys them
As the stocking he fills.
Morning comes early,
Mum and Dad open the door.
Are you ready to come downstairs to see
What's under the Christmas tree?

Next year it's different, at school being told,
Your Mum and Dad buy your toys at a store.
That morning it all looks the same
Just feels so different without the magical thrill.

E. Watkins

Winter Memory

The grey-day sky had darkened
to inky black of night.
The deep smooth snow
had silenced all sounds.
There shone no light of moon
or stars above
to guide my stumbling feet
as on, on,
homeward bound
I yearned for rest and heat.

Chill morning dawned in splendour
of sun on jewelled snow
and icicles
like pendants of crystal in a row
hanging from the eaves.
On looking upward
I could only gaze bewitched
for there, against the sky —
a back cloth, brilliant blue —the silver birch tree stood;
white hoar-clad twigs and boughs
like lace
A poem in wood.

Maimie Waugh

Lord Jesus Christ

Lord Jesus Christ bearer of our sin,
Redeeming love comforter in our pain,
Glorious, victorious over evils reign,
Son of the Father, make us born again.

Creator of the universe, foretold and yet unknown,
Through our blessed Mary, a manger for a throne.
At Christmas time we celebrate
The Messiah's Holy birth,
Peace and Goodwill to all men here on transient earth.

Taking away our blindness, showing us the way.
Miracles abounding, teaching how to pray.
The scriptures show, how you love us so
With Divine inspiration.
Our Hope with you is that we can truly
Resist all temptation.

How can our Lord, so full of Grace
Have to drink the cup alone
And still by the ultimate sacrifice
Become the cornerstone
At Easter time the world is still
In memory of your passion
Fill our hearts with fire Lord
To love and inspire in immeasurable ration.

P. Warren

The Writing On The Wall

Buses burnt, no wages earned.
Wandering aimlessly among the rubble
Children bolting out and through
No one knowing what to do!

'No Go' areas, 'Troops Out!'
Flags of Creggan blowing about.
Men without faces ordering crimes
Women peeping through their venetian blinds.

Suddenly it erupted in '69, bin-lids clash
To the intrusion, chanting question,
Converse, confusion,
Guilty? Innocent? Who's to know!
Both will anguish, both will mourn
Over there or here at home.

'Motor Man' at 4 o'clock
Raiding houses in the dusk, who's the victim them or us?
Asking "What's the reason?"
"We don't know, just following orders, come on let's go."

'Free Derry Wall' standing at the Bog,
Each week a different lament,
A delusion of wanting dreams
In the chaos of event
Pictures of collected thoughts painted on cement.

C. Weir

Terra Santa

Hosanna Jerusalem, land of religious greed, fulcrum of three creeds
each true to same God, yet false to each other.
Wake up, Jerusalem, cast aside dark shadows of past
to ONE Father abide and in ONE fraternity find
how to be the salvation not the curse of mankind.
Mirror yourself Jerusalem, can you rejoice when your arid soil
avidly saps the flesh of those who are slain
when salty tears seep through salter terrain
and the dried grass grows greener with the red fluid of life
of the ones born in blood to die in blood?
Toil, pain and strife touch you Jerusalem, touch and rebound on your
wailing wall, and for the all who weep the sound echoes deep
with songs and throngs and crosses of Crusaders.
That cross is still with, Jerusalem, for you to bear
until you learn to tear the veils of time and cross the rimes.
Recall the beginning, Jerusalem? Where is the manna now to appease
hunger and anger and bring peace? Not to bring forth spines
and thorns did the shrub light up divine for Moses, nor was the prophet
of AL-MADINAH bellicose, he taught love and brotherhood, as did the
child in Bethlehem born. Who for war stood? Who invented the 'infidel'?
Ah, tear the veil, tear the veil, Jerusalem.
Age upon age you fathomed and fanned a bloody human tragedy on your stage.
Don't let the curtain fall.
Not in TERRA SANTA.

Jo Wassell

The Lonely Year

Gone blooms and blossoms of the spring,
With all the dreams that they should bring,
Past summer days of humid heat,
Those sleepless nights in lone retreat,
Now shades of autumn, fill the scene,
Where once new hope of life had been.
Lightening with thunder, rend the air,
Releasing ions everywhere,
Soon, misty days with early frost,
Will herald winter, with its cost,
For extra light, and fuel to heat,
Those frozen fingers, and cold feet.
How quick will come the 'Christmas Tide',
Along with presents, you will hide,
Followed by New Year's hopes and schemes,
Once more to spring time, with its dreams,
More lonely hearts will seek their fate,
Another year to find a mate,
'Companion adverts' in the press,
Perhaps a year to answer, 'Yes'!

Aquilla

Winter Sleep

When the snows of the year began to fall
We walked down the lane, looked over the wall
There he was

All curled up, the frosts all around
Shouldn't be here, should be close to the ground
But he's not.

We had to do something, had to be bold
Couldn't just leave him to suffer the cold
So we helped.

We scraped out the hedgerows, did our best
Gathered the things that would make him a nest
And cradled him up.

He opened one eye and gave a good snort
We settled him in, his awakening was short
We were glad.

This was one little creature whose life we had saved
He had tried very hard, the elements he braved
The little hedgehog.

Judy Watson

Bruno's Story

For twelve long months I sat there waiting for you to arrive,
I greeted every visitor, and for affection I did strive.
You found me in a corner of a small and dirty shed,
I fought for food with others and had papers for my bed.

I knew when I first saw you, that you would bring me cheer,
A happy home to live in and a family to be near.
It took me one whole hour to realise sofas were just fine,
And fires were warm to sit by and a dish put down was mine.

For twelve long months I waited for someone to call my own,
Now I have love and laughter where once I felt alone.
I don't know where I came from, I was too young to know,
But I am so glad you chose me and I'll always love you so.

You say I make you happy, keep you fit and on your mark,
I tell you when the postman comes — cos then I always bark.
I frank the mail a second time, just to check it's not alive,
And always take the paper in if I hear the boy arrive.

For twelve long months I lay there in that cold and dirty shed,
But now I have thick blankets and a special comfy bed.
I dream sometimes of those dark days and always hope and pray
That each and every dog in there finds happiness one day.

Wendy J. Wearing

Retirement

Retirement is approaching, days dreamed of for so long
The time when routine changes — now can that be so wrong?
No more rushing for the bus or standing in a queue
Say good-bye to colleagues then onto places new

Maybe take a holiday and try on a sarong
Stay in a Hotel where dinner is called with a gong
Struggle to climb a mountain just to admire the view
Delight in all the flora, even a tall Yew

Back home, lots of visiting to those dear and belong
Maybe take up Politics to air ideas so strong
Attend to a zillion things instead of a few
Hobbies, now in fashion, will need to be reviewed

Leisurely walks, stroll in the park, listen to bird song
Pause to watch the flowers grow, hear a clock chime Ding Dong
See children run to feed the ducks, racing through the dew
Play games on swings and slides acting Captain and Crew

There must be something else to do before Evensong —
Could help the gardener toiling (whose fork has lost a prong)
Neighbourly assistance with chores and some shopping too
Entertain and baby-sit for friends who are true

Premeditate the future, measured, as a furlong
Then watch for life's surprises, twists and turns, as when young
A diary full of happy times and skies always blue!
Thankful to the Lord for this, the prayer from the pew

Ellen Wayland

Utopia

I dream about the mountains,
I dream about the sun,
I dream about the open fields,
Out where the rabbits run.

I dream about the valleys,
I dream about the seas,
A world so far from traffic jams,
A world of quiet and peace.

A world where life is tranquil,
No crime and violence there,
Where people help each other,
And have the time to care.

No crowded city pavements,
No endless city blocks,
A dream like that is precious
But dreams are all we've got.

P.M. Walsh

Untitled

To be or not to be
That is the question
Could be he, or she
Who cares at conception?

To live or not to live
For weeks, months, years?
Wait, worry, then to give
Decision, joy or tears.

To save or not to save
This tiny, unborn life
Which, if it could would crave,
To be a man, or wife

To love or not to love
There is no answer
When quested from above
And now a prancer

To meet or not to meet us
No longer a question
Poor, poor foetus
Terminate, for attention!

(With apologies to Wm. Shakespear)

Len Wade

The Corner Shop

I still remember that little shop on the corner of our road
Where neighbours met and had a chat, their worries to unload.
My Johnny he's got measles, and Bert he's got the flu,
Ah yes, I want a loaf of bread and half of butter too.
Now have you heard about our Mary, she's expecting once again
And Tom's fell out with Alice, and now going out with Jane.

Many things had to be weighed, the sugar, fats and tea
Sweets and biscuits, dried fruit too; quite a task you must agree.
Pots and pans, and paraffin, pegs and other goods
Could all be purchased in that shop, along with kindling woods.

They were such a friendly couple, whether spending pounds or pennies
For a bag of spuds, a tin of peas, or just a packet of Rennies.
In there you'd always get to know, someone who'd lend a hand
To do a bit of papering, or perhaps to till your land.
A phone call to your doctor, a bet on Derby day
Was part and parcel of their service, for that was just their way.

Now all those things have been and gone, the shop's no longer there
So we have to use the Supermart, not quite the same I fear,
For one is just a number to swell the coffers of the rich
But we have no alternative, as more and more like that they ditch.
But they can't wipe out our memories, of those carefree shopping days
For they'll remain with us forever, until our dying days.

Mabel Weavers

The Honeymoon

Hear the thunder, the pouring rain
Beat against my window pain
Table setting candles glow
We start to dance, the music's low
I feel your body, close to mine
Our lips meet, arms entwine
Tonight my darling you'll be mine

Hear the music, feel you sway
Rub against me in a special way
My fingers gently probe, caress
Awkward button on your dress
Feel you quiver, shake, implore
You've never been this far before
Please don't rush, take our time
Tonight my darling you'll be mine

Do not disturb is on the door
Dress is lying on the floor
The sun is up, hear the rooster crow
Feel our love start to grow
Once more our bodies do entwine
My darling wife, I've made you mine.

R.G. Walker

Schooldays

They say that schooldays are your best,
writing essays, taking tests.
The squeaking of the blackboard chalk,
teacher shouting "work, don't talk".
Cookery was my favourite class,
while maths I knew I'd never pass.
In science I was never good,
I'd skip most lessons if I could.
P.E. swimming, games, and sport,
the playgrounds where we played and fought.
Now thinking back they weren't that bad,
there were some happy times I had.
I do look back with sadness now,
and often think what, when and how?
are the friends I made back then,
of whom I'd love to see again.
The school chums that we made for life
are now a husband or a wife.
Yes I miss those happy days,
now friends have gone their separate ways.
Though there were times we'd rather skive,
they were the best days of our lives.

Belinda Whyatt

A Lovely Land

Once upon a fairy tale my mother said to me
And told me of a long lost land that nobody could see.
You see that hill with plants and trees
And dickey birds and bumble bees.
Well at the top and down a bit
There is a place where you can sit.
Or on the sand where birds eat from you hands
And wild horses you can stroke and ride,
This is a land where no creature has to hide.
All the animals live in harmony
And this is the way the World should be.
But if you just turn left and round that bend
There is a wicked place called Earth the end!

Sarah Way

Summer Memories

It's nice to go out on a warm summer day
and walk down a lane with a sweet smell of hay,
listen to a skylark high in the sky
watch bees and butterflies fluttering by,
hear the hum of a tractor in yonder field
cutting the corn, its harvest to yield,
see the sun setting such a beautiful sight,
hear church bells ringing on this clear peaceful night,
gaze upon a blackbird as he sings his nightly tune,
see again the rising of a new crescent moon.
Suddenly a field mouse goes scurrying by,
hiding away from the owl's watchful eye.
The countryside then sleeps until another dawn —
when a chorus of birds will awaken the morn.

Mrs. K. Webb

Generations

The poignant pellets are preaching pain
As my body slumps into a water-filled crater.
My senses are extinguished en-route to my brain
But I remember the words of my dear old Pater:
"It's every man's duty to fight in the war,
Like those Boers and those Zulus — we gave 'em what for!"
I remember the pride in the things that he said.
Well thanks a lot Pa, now I am dead.

Long after I've been buried in my matchwood casket,
My children will have a question,
But I'll never hear them ask it.
I'll never see the face of my youngest lad,
When he says,
"What did *you* do in the Great War, Dad?"

Ian Webber

The Glorious Years

One Hundred and fifty years ago
On the South Cliff, Scarborough
The elegant Crown Hotel was built
With views down to the harbour.

People came from miles around
Some to stand and stare.
They came by coach, or hansom cab
But mostly carriage and pair.

Ladies in all their finery
Young men sporting cravats
Debutantes with parasols
Gentlemen in top hats.

The service at the Crown Hotel
Was far beyond compare
With friendly staff all waiting
To serve the sumptuous fare.

Today it's been updated
But these traditions can still be found
And you'll always find a welcome
When visiting the Crown.

Marie Whiteley

Wishful Thinking

"Do you think they'll choose me?!"
Said the fir tree to the oak,
"No, I certainly don't think so,"
Giving him a poke.
"You're small and frail and ugly,
Not the kind they're looking for,
Someone tall and graceful like myself,
I'm sure would suit them more."

The little fir hung his head
Quite sure the oak was right.
But who should come with stealthy steps,
In the middle of the night,
The father of a family
Too poor to buy a tree.
"This one's fine," he muttered
As he quickly pulled him free.

On Christmas morn all decked in gold,
He thought about his past.
His branches spread, his head held high,
He gave a happy, breathless sigh,
"I'm a Christmas Tree at last!"

Sandra Watson

Dudley Castle

High on the hill above the town,
Stands a castle old and grey
With memories of great men renowned
Who aboded there one day.
Great forests once around it grew
Where deer there could be found
And caverns deep with mystery too
That echo every sound.
Nobles, earls and royalty, have stayed
There through the night.
And men have fought with loyalty
To defend the castle's right.
Long bows were drawn, and swords were flashed,
To defend the castle's keep
And above it all the cannons crashed
Where now the lions sleep.
But peaceful times, it's also seen
When all were merry each day.
Of dancing on the village green
When celebrating May.

Albert Wheeler

Almost A Cherub

Tumbling and twisting in muddy water
deep
Friends stood watching in disbelief
From the pond side I did fall
Wished I never had climbed that wall

Over and over I seemed to turn
Choking, struggling, my lungs did burn
Suddenly between fish and weed
Calm came upon me, no fight, no need

I felt I was back inside the womb
Not knowing the closeness of my tomb
A small child with his father so tall
Said "...please Daddy fetch me that ball."

What he saw was in fact my head
Seconds later is would have been dead
His father realised my need
He jumped in clad amongst the weed

My lungs he cleared of murky water
He had saved my mothers' daughter
The first I remember, I was in bed
A saviour had saved me, I was not dead

It made the headlines the very next day
Seconds from drowning or so they say
Thank you for saving my life on earth
A second chance, a second birth.

Rosalinda Whalley

Untitled

Her cheeks are pink
her clothes just right.
Who is this just hove in sight?
Is it a model with skin so clear?
She's far too nice to be working here.
Is it a mirage, I think not.
This isn't the desert, it's not that hot.
Is it a fairy from some place hence?
She's far too big to sit on a fence.
Is it an angel, have I just died?
Are you sleeping?" My wife cried.

Gary Westwood

All My Love Mummy

The way I feel deep down inside
holds a special kind of pride.
The joy that comes from a child
just one look that loving smile.
As each day I watch them grow
how much do they really know.
For even though I'm in a muddle
there's always time for a kiss 'n cuddle.
So I just hope they understand
when I shout or give commands,
that my life I would lay down
just to keep them safe and sound.

Kathleen Walker

Emotions Call and Struggle

Like a restless herd before the stampede
Nudging one to the other, the air is still,
The pond lies still, draped in mist
As the mind is.

Emotions rustle as leaves in the Fall,
Each one eager to be off, to find a salvation.
The mind shakes and as the branch, will twist
As the wind blows.

An emotion will call, struggle to be heard
Above others which are but muttering yet,
Later to clamour for attention, insist
In their turn.

J.M. Whiteway

Untitled

Inside of me burns an eternal flame
To you my love it will always remain
For you are my life, my reason to be,
The thoughts that I think, the air that I breathe
When harsh words are spoke in times that are hard
The tears and the pain won't tear us apart
The flame will burn stronger and deeper in me
For you are my love, 'till the last breath I breathe.

Melinda Wagstaff

The Letter

I must write a letter
To my friend Etta
There's no one better than Etta.
She sent me some flowers
I beg your pardon
T'was half the garden.
So now in my moments of quiet repose
I dream of those flowers, including a rose
And I think of the wonders of nature's store
And the blessing she showers on rich and on poor.
So thanks for your kindness enriching my days
With friendship and goodness and beauty and praise.

F.M. Welch

Down from Oxford

What a brilliant spirit.

Naturally we keep her room
Just as it was. Not a thing's been
Moved from her little domain,
Not that quaint LP with *Begin the Beguine*,

Nor the tortoiseshell hairclip
Or broken-toothed comb
I bought her very much on the cheap
From some word-coining gnome

At a stall on Blackpool beach.
In those early days, any affluence
However modest, was out of reach.
You saved the shillings, counted the pence!

Of course she reached the top of the school,
One of the brightest of our nation.
Where brains are concerned, *I* am the fool,
With my overreaching expectation.

Here at the back is a second stair,
(Mute token of my increasing wealth!)
And, standing there, the little chair
Beside the rail where she hanged herself.

Allan Wells

Three Years Ago Today

Three years ago today.
Cold. At the back door step, he lay.
Repossessed. No notifying call to say
It would happen. Three years ago today.

Blue. With a trickle of red.
And a little pebble-dash graze to the fore-head
I wished his name was Lazarus instead
Of Jim. Three years ago today.

Ms. Watt

Not Like Bosnia

"They're animals", the man said coldly,
"They're not like us."

SOHO FIREBOMB — 10 DIE
BABY BATTERED TO DEATH
YOUTH STABBED IN RACIST ATTACK.

In the field the cow lazily chews the cud.
The pig ruts comfortably in the mud.
The horse nuzzles its foal.

Jennifer Webb

Thoughts of Home

I thought last night of my home town
And all that it means to me.
Of loved ones, far away, yonder,
With thoughts that are dear to me.

I thought of the River Leven
Where chestnuts great overhang,
The path that leads to the garden,
Where my heart so often sang.

I thought of lanes that I'd travelled
Dear country, — second to none!
The hills standing guard around it,
The becks flowing gently on.

Loved Cleveland! There's no place the same!
Dear home — we're fighting for you.
When this strife is ended and over
Sweet home, I'll come back to you.

We fight — for Peace everlasting
Safe surety — come to our shore!
Freedom, that really is freedom,
We treasure; come, stay evermore!

Sgt. J.S. West
Stokesley (6.6.44)

Well It's My Body ... Isn't It?

My silent screams echo down the year.
My unloved, unloveliness washed in many tears.
I lived inside my skin longing to be dead,
As each night a monster crept into my bed.

Now I have my body back again at last,
The over-weight-abusing-unclean-misusing, is of the past.
No! The penetrated-violated, dead body of another time,
Belonged to someone-hated, isolated, it was never mine.

My body I can now enjoy
Run with it till my heart pounds.
My ears hear music. My eyes see beauty.
I have found a joy that knows no bounds.

My nose smells the scent of many flowers.
Gone is self-hate for things beyond my powers.
No more feeling unclean, full of insalubrity.
I have been cleansed with greatest purity.

I met a man whilst deep in deep despair,
I asked him what he was doing there,
He said I died to make you whole and clean.
Now never, never more yourself demean.
I will all you hurt avenge,
Forgiveness is the best revenge.

Gene Weston

Lest We Forget

His shoes are brightly polished, his suit is clean and pressed
His military bearing belies his mode of dress
He marches with his colleagues,
Shoulders straight and head held high.
He wears his medals proudly and his Regimental tie.
The band's continued playing — the drum's persistent beat
The music ever louder drowns the sounds of marching feet.
He remembers his dear comrades,
How they all fought side by side
So few were there this morning to honour those who'd died.
Those boys he had commanded, he knew them everyone
Their courage never wavered when they were called upon
To take up arms for Freedom, Oh God, they were so young
They never had a chance to live
In the peace that they had won.
He mourns the years of carnage —
The wars that caused such strife
The suffering and grievous pain and every wasted life.
He stares ahead unsmiling, his face serene and calm
But then responds so readily to the pressure on his arm,
He turns his head a fraction, and with unseeing eyes
Looks left, for there's the Cenotaph
Pointing proudly to the skies,
'They grow not old' the Poet said,
'Ah, yes' he knows that's true
Their faces were the last he saw — thus he remembers you.

Mrs. E.C. Westbrook

Open Cast

No skylark sings it's happy song
Then spirals from the sky,
Only Man's machine that scars the earth
And won't let beauty lie.

No hiding place for fox or cub
To settle in their lair,
The metal rapist rages on
Till all the land's laid bare.

No meadow sweet! No buttercup!
No grass to lie and dream,
That oily trickle in the mud
Was once my rippling stream.

My country walk, now piled up high
The hedgerows are no more,
How could they change this beauty
Into an open sore.

If I could only backwards turn
Life's clock and change the past
I would erase this evil
The Devil's open-cast.

G.F. Westgarth

Winter

The skies are grey, the trees are bare,
There's a frosty feeling in the air.
The fog comes down it's winter time,
Trees and hedges are white with rime.

It's bitter cold, but what a sight
Like fairyland in bright sunlight,
Other days bring wind and rain,
To beat against the window pane.

The days are short, but pass so slow,
Now silently fall flakes of snow,
Children sledge on slippery slopes,
The frozen lake raises skaters' hopes.

The wind is howling through the storm,
And soon the drifts begin to form,
'Older folks will dream and say,
'Twas different in some far off day.

The snow plough driven by automation,
Moves bulk beyond imagination
The road is clear, the cars rush on,
But winter snow has not yet gone.

There's work to do, and stock to feed,
Perhaps some families in need,
The thaw will come, perhaps some rain,
Then soon it will be spring again.

L.G. White

Maud

She hurried along the high street,
As always dressed in her best.
Her brown handbag and shoes, a perfect match.
Maud in her twenties would have been quite a catch.

The ring of the bell above the shop door,
Now what is it that she went in there for?
Next stop the Post Office it was always the same,
Three o'clock Wednesdays was the time that she came.

You could set your watch by her.

The second-hand book shop was next on her list,
A bargain she sure wouldn't miss.
She smiled to herself as she closed the shop door,
So pleased with her purchase, she couldn't be more.

A cheery 'hello' from old Ben on the corner,
He'd been to The Drovers for a pint and a chat,
He didn't get drunk, he knew better than that.
Her shopping done, her time was now free,
Maud treated herself to afternoon tea.

Maureen Angela Wheatcroft

The Miner's Son

My dad's been down the pit again,
There's coal dust in his eyes,
And big blue marks all o'er his hands,
For the victor what a prize.
His daily fights against grim death,
When lumps of coal go flying,
While on the pit-top mother frets,
Inside she's slowly dying,
She knows the danger deep within
The bowels of the land,
And when my dad comes home again,
I see her take his hand,
She fills the tub, by fireside,
With ladle from the rack,
While in her mind, she thinks one day,
Perhaps he won't come back.
I ask my dad why he works there,
Way down that big black hole,
"Well someone's got to do it son,
We need the Bloody Coal ..."

Roy Weaver

A Person Of Special Significance

At any proper wedding which is guided by the Book
The most important figure hardly gets a second look
And yet in every family relationship that's good
The Father-figure proudly stands where every Father should.

He's far from a nonentity, this person of renown
And minuscule perplexities don't ever get him down
Unruffled by emergencies but overwhelmed with pride
No one is more essential than the Father of the Bride.

Without participating in paternity way back
In lawful loving wedlock he'd have had a grievous lack
Of daughters, but predictably, he took it in his stride
And made long term arrangements to be Father of the Bride.

Then, having nurtured nubile girls of comeliness and charm
He realised a Share Account would cushion fiscal harm
And as the girls matured his endowment multiplied
Until he could afford to be the Father of the Bride!

The Mother of Bride ensures that everything gets done
And suits herself, and gets a hat, and treats it all as fun
But who provides the counselling? It cannot be denied
The master mediator is — the Father of the Bride.

The poor Bride isn't Number One on her great day of days
Although composed and radiant, and relishing the praise
For on arrival at the church, the escort at her side
Is not her novice husband, it's the Father of the Bride!

Kenneth W. White

Where Angels Weep

On top of a pit in the valley
An angel stood alone
Where once the sound of footsteps
Echoed on the stone

No more the sound of singing
As miners made their way home
After a day in darkness
The pit was left alone

The valley now a ghost town
as people moved for work
Pit ponies, left to wander
When once they could not shirk.

On that pit in the valley
The angel faced the town
Empty and deserted
A tear upon his frown.

No more a sound of singing
Or laughing on the line
No more the church bells ringing
This was the end of the mine.

James G. Walkingshaw

Lord Gideon F. Fitzwilliam

Lord Gideon F. Fitzwilliam was not his complete name,
But it is not for his long title that Fitzwilliam has his fame.
Nor is it for his collection of medals from the war,
It was the fact that Old Fitzy was an incredibly boring bore!

His tales of heroics were regularly told,
He'd talk all through supper while his meal was getting cold.
Of how he was once shot down by a German fighter plane,
And other such stories until his guests were far from sane!

I don't know which was more boring; his tales of war or cricket,
For he also spoke in depth upon the invention of the wicket.
Also about the test match and who was playing who;
One soon ran out of excuses to leave like, "I rather need the loo!"

Discipline and punctuality were very much his scene,
And if you didn't turn up for tea at four, you'd soon look rather lean!
You must admit he doesn't sound the most entertaining man,
Although I may be biased as I'm not his biggest fan.

He'd march around his house all day, in his old uniform from the army,
Yet he wasn't exactly pompous, just incredibly barmy.
It's amusing to watch him with his bullet-wounded hip;
His thick and bushy moustache and his stiff upper lip!

Samuel J. Wigley (Age 14)

The Little Place

There's a little place that's nestled in some trees in Cambridgeshire
With winding roads and thatches and a river running near.
With here a lane and there a lane that lead to church and mill,
And just to make it charming here and there a little hill.

Now this little place that's nestled in some trees in Cambridgeshire
Has lost so very many of the things that we hold dear.
Gone the tinkling on the anvil in the forge we knew so well
Gone the call to lessons dreary from the noisy old school bell.
No longer does the muffin man or hurdy-gurdy call,
Gone the children from the village green with skipping rope and ball.

When Guildhall corner gathered all the children there to play,
The season would dictate the game to dominate the day.
The traffic was no problem in those quiet old days of yore
And while we played white aproned wives would wait each at their door.
When horse and carriage graced the roads and cows went to and fro
Our little world was quite complete, to town we'd seldom go.
We roamed the vast arena that Whitser could contain,
As kids we even ventured to the top of old Bar Lane.

But they buried all the milestones and the name of old Bar Lane,
And when the war was over didn't dig them up again.
They cut down trees and badly scarred a mellow ancient wall
They could have left intact and still provided homes for all.

So we must all wake up in time our efforts to employ
To save the beauty of the Place for others to enjoy.

Edna Wight

Existence ...

A man that was
but is no more
returns to earth
his goodness stored,
among the leaves
his whispers tease
neither was nor is
forever he lives.

We are all one —
merely parts of the sum.

James Wade

In Summer

Who is that screaming?
Oh, terrible, like a cry
of pain!

Yet summer gleams
on the garden,
the river glides smoothly by.

There, — it scythes again,
like one in agony!
Oh, who screams so?

It is the peacocks
under the cedar tree,
crying primevally.
Nothing is here for tears!

Jo Westren

The Woman

The woman in my life
be placid of nature,
though when roused be
quick to anger,
she be beautiful
though very humble.
God who is mightiest
I am a lucky man.
She does her best,
her man is too quick
to anger,
but remember these lines ...
that man who learnt to
trust in her love and
laughter,
loves this woman with
all of his matter.

Timothy William Webster

Untitled

Memory will cease to be, should she fall into disuse;
Or, she is indulgent luxury of beguiling winsome ways
That spins her host on whirlwind tour,
Down alleys dark and wide.
And in these chasms enter friends — Creativity and Pride;
Each may wear a mantle that is kinsman to Disguise.
The choice is ours to linger,
Yet, beware where Memory lies.

Linda Wilbur

A Victorian Garden — Daylight's Brothel

Flowers are little flirts!
Look how they display without a hint of shame
Bright glowing colours intent to catch the eye
Opening up their petals in that disgraceful way
Revealing all! Absolutely nothing left to the imagination.
Tarted up in hues of violet, bright pink, yellow and orange
What is one to think? Absolutely shocking.
Luring all kinds of creatures into their lair
How the poor bees and butterflies are deceived
They are pleasing only at nightfall
When they close up their petals
And repent of their outrageous behaviour.

Miss A. Whytock

The Word

After scrutinising the X-ray he indicated a small
eruption of cells, tapping the spot with his papermate.

Resting his other hand upon hers, he delivered the word
CANCER.

Blood evacuated her brain and sent her spinning into
oblivion, but there was no solace there in the blackness.

Standing on the sidelines, she watched herself
experiencing the procedure on automatic pilot. Blood
test, examination, needle biopsy, counselling.

One by one the innocent victims entered the dock for
sentencing. Six months, five years, life,
some lucky ones even got parole.

Death appeared more imminent as malignant, mastectomy,
metastasis bounced off the scrubbed white walls.
She was angry, frightened, humiliated, sad,
EXTRAORDINARY.

Her sexuality was in jeopardy, nice legs —
shame about the boob.

She remembered her mother's ethereal caress
and that the sun was shining.

P.A. Wicks

A Three Year Old's Impression Of Santa

He seems to be all over,
In shops and on T.V.,
His voice is always different,
Just listen and you'll see.
So is there a production line,
Up north in the snow?
And which one brings my presents here?
Well ... I'd like to know.
Everybody says he's nice,
But if you ask me,
I think perhaps there's something wrong,
With sitting on his knee.
What's behind that beard?
Is it good or bad?
I wouldn't like to face it,
Without my Mum or Dad.
When I grow up and get a job,
Santa's what I'll be,
And frighten people all day long
Just like he does to me.

Adam Whitbourn

Through The Seasons

When the bluebells spread their carpet
Along the leafy lane
And the trees are thick with blossom
And the cuckoo calls again
When the air is filled with fragrance
From the lilacs after rain —
          will he still love me?
When Summer sun brings roses
And there's shade beneath the trees
When the air is filled with birdsong
And the humming of the bees
When the earth gives off her incense
Upon the evening breeze —
          will he still love me?
When Autumn comes and tints the trees
With russet brown and gold
And the last of summer roses
Try to beat the frost and cold
When the evening sun is slow to fade
And the year is growing old —
          will he still love me?
When Winter comes, and winds are cold
And snowflakes start to fall
When petals of the winter rose
Unfurl, delight us all
And looking back, through seasons past
Sweet memories I recall
          I know he'll love me!

V.M. Whitehead

Memories

Old age is a time of looking back to where you've been,
For remembering special moments and reliving them again.
To think of all the pleasure life has passed on to you,
Recalling years gone by and time spent with friends, old and new.
Smiling as the faces of your children come to mind.
The laughter and the tears,
And wondering how you had the time
To cook and wash and to keep the house clean.
It seems now as if this time has never been,
But most of all old age is a time set apart
To look within and cherish all the memories in your heart.

M. Whitley

Friends

Today I lost another dear friend of mine,
All I can seem to remember are the good times.
Always a cheery word and a happy smile,
When we would stop and chat a while.
Caring for her family, pets and birds of the wild,
A loving kind word for any small child.
She loved to garden and see things grow,
As she watched with excitement at the small seeds she would sow.
Her house she kept as clean as a new pin,
When you called you would always get a welcome, "Come In."
This is two very good friends I have lost in a short time,
And I am very proud to say that they were friends of mine.
God bless you both neighbours in heaven from now on you will be.
Linda and Janice who were good friends to me.

C.A. Waldron

Diving!

My dreams of skimming nymph-like at forty metres deep
Are about to happen as off the boat I leap!
Graceful, moving swiftly, I belong beneath the sea,
I say to all the fish, "My dears, what do you think of me?"

I feel just like a mermaid, sensual and all aglow,
As I toss my curls and play sea games with all my friends below.

But wait a minute — what's that thing hanging on the wall?
It's my wet suit, and wearily in to it I crawl!
It's like a horror movie, the monster from the deep,
I hear a bloodless curdle as my hubbie takes a peep.

Encased in armoured neoprene, I'm not a pretty sight,
At least I'm sure of one thing though, the sharks won't take a bite!
No mermaid I — more Moby Dick, as I slurp towards the foam,
I've scared so many people, how I wish I'd stayed at home!

Marlene White

Summer Showers

A thousand sparkling diamonds
Run down the window pane
Outside the wind is blowing
The squalls of summer rain

Soon the sun will dry the showers
And the wind will cease to blow
Then once again the children
Outside to play can go.

Splashing in the puddles
Reflecting rainbows hue
Their faces fill with pleasure
As only children's do.

Mary Wigan

Said Rosemary

Write me something, said Rosemary
Squaring off her books
But what shall I write, Rosemary
She saw my troubled looks.

Write me a poem, said Rosemary
Making for the door
Find rhythm in your verse, my dear
You'll beat a rhyme, I'm sure.

But what shall I do, Rosemary
With rhythm, beat and rhyme?
Word music for the deaf, my dear
Write paintings for the blind.

K. Waterhouse

Freedom

One cold December morning
When snow lay crisp and white
A robin hopped on a windowsill
And saw to his delight
A cosy room with flaming fire
And children gathered to admire
A little feathered friend

At first he envied that sweet bird
And thought how nice 'twould be
If he were in that cosy room
With love and sympathy,
But on reflection he said "Nay"
He spread his wings and flew away
He could, yes, he was free.

Kitty Webster

Children In Need

Take care of the children
Give them your love and care
Guard and protect them through
Life's evil ways.

Take care of the children
Teach them right from wrong
Good from evil
To be obedient.

Take care of the children
Remember they're not yours, but a loan from God
Don't think of tomorrow it never comes
So take care of the children and God will take care of you.

Margaret Wilson

Anniversary

From deep inside my heart, to the foundations of my soul
I acknowledge that, if not for you, my life would not be whole.
You are the spark within my life, which I search for, oh, so long
You've given me an inner peace, you're the words within my song.
Because I believe that Someone in Heaven high above
Decreed that it was meant to be, for us to share our love.
A love we both look up to, which will never go away
A love which means so much to me, and has done since that day
When you and I before our God, were joined as man and wife
To share our love together, for the remainder of our lives.
So upon this day, I thank you for your love and friendship too
And God knows that you deserve those thanks for simply being you.

Peter Wilson

Silly Suffolk Sam

In an olde worlde ale house, not too far from here
Sat old Silly Suffolk Sam, a quietly sipping beer.
Now he grabbed a busty handful as the barmaid did pass by.
She turned and swore some nice words and she didn't half smack his eye.

Then calling for the landlord she said "Throw this old sod out"
The landlord looked him up and down then grabbed him by the snout,
He led him to the pub door, and kicked him up his seat
And poor old Silly Suffolk Sam fell headlong in the street.

He picked himself up saying "If there's one thing I detest"
"It's making all this bloody fuss because I grabbed her breast."
It ain't she weren't expecting it, she's not that daft I'm sure
I've done the same thing everyday since nineteen sixty-four.

I always thought she liked it, now I'm not so sure
I s'pose I really out to think of not doing it anymore.
I don't know what to make of it, it's been a funny life
You'd expect it from a stranger, but not you darling wife.

Steve Williams

Animated Spirit
(Dedicated to Martin Auckland)

The spirit dances
Up around
Its joy, elation
Knows no bounds.

There is today
a great divide
But tomorrow's
dawn shall nothing
Hide.

When night and day
shall be no more
Then on Horizon's
golden shore
We shall meet
to dance once more
With nimble feet.

Sing and dance
till kingdom come
Then ...
Dance on, dance on and on.

Teresa White

Queen Moon

Shepherd herds his sheep away
From her white light
Which stretches over fields,
Seas, roads, nowhere can escape
The night-light touch of
Queen moon,
When she decides,
It's time to call the shot,
Before the drunks
That sleep in graveyards, start
Believing they are safe,
She pull the earth
From under them,
Sends them visions against
The stone, they feel
The fingers on their
Throats, she casts a shadow
Over those who once, used
The dark of night to sell,
Their dope, she lights
Them up, exposed,
They seek to run and hide,
Cannot escape Queen Moon,
It is she who rules the night.

Eileen Winnington

The Blue Bird

A circle of feathers upon the green grass
Blue and grey.
Standing guard with hostile stare
the bird of prey.
Inside the circle, lifeless, still,
the small blue bird.
With lowered head, the cruel beak pecked away
till all was gone.
Then, satiated, he flew away.
A circle of feathers upon the green grass
just a memory of a small blue bird.

Gladys Walker

Not As A Stranger

Do not treat me as a stranger
when eventually again we meet.
Distance hurting when once so close,
from caring warmth in distance froze.
Goes time slowly passing
longer then we sleep.
Once more with open heart
your arms
Soon lovingly to greet.

Audrey P. S. Williams

Nightmare

You may enter my nightmare if you so wish,
It begins with an opening door.
And I'm just a child hiding under the bed,
Trying hard to be part of the floor.
But I cannot succeed, for they know where I am,
So they drag me out throw me up on the bed,
Then they tear me apart, I scream in my mind,
For I know I'd be better off dead.
I should never have watched all those horrible films,
That mam said were only pretend,
'Cause I know when they creeep from their holes in the wall
They have dastardly plans for my end.
So where can I hide? How can I sleep?
Whilst these ghouls round my bedroom are roving,
Would you like to live here in this haunted old house?
'Cause I'm seriously thinking of moving.

Allan George Weston

The Happiness Cake

So many ingredients;
easily made by experienced hands,
lovingly exhibited through
the plate glass window of life
with all its sorrows and joys.

How would the happiness seem
when the space no longer exhibited the cake?
Would people remember
the goodness of the creator, the human effort
and, perhaps, the human failure?

C. Smith & T.H. Widdowson

Owed To Sir John

Alas, Sir John, I knew you not
But life with such things is fraught.
You'd say that poetry cannot be taught,
Original thought (unlike sin) cannot be bought.
A cornucopia of concepts, emotions flowed,
Dripping jewels, crystalized thoughts on parchment you showed,
Masterly skill, interwoven with art,
Needling, nurtured feelings set free on a raft,
To voyage the seas of eternal mind,
Without stumbling, or stuttering, but binding with kind.
No dryness of desert, no barren drought,
To jeopardise the jungle of juices you brought.
In secret drawers and forgotten places,
Touched and opened by imaginary faces.
Who can light future time and space?
Shouldering your mantle with fitting grace.

Sally Weston

Walking The Pennines

I've trod the 'thrufts' on Pennine hills
through pastures sweet for grazing
and rested, back to dry stone wall
whilst in the sunshine lazing.

I've felt the wild wind pluck at me
the arctic rain come stinging
as lightning rips across the sky
and the Devil's anvil ringing.

I have trudged the drovers' paths
where flocks were seen to gather
then driven on the market towns
to feed the hungry worker.

The lonely 'thruft', the crumbling walls
that stride across the heather
lure me back a thousand times
no matter what the weather!

Brian Wickins

Our Companion Departs

Can't forget his face that last afternoon,
A face we love.
Watching his every motion for the last time.
Tears we try to hide.
Just close your eyes and thoughts remember,
Thoughts of yesterday.
What's the use of going on,
Prolonging the agony felt by him inside,
And by us in our hearts.
He always appears to smile,
As if to thank us for everything,
But in his eyes,
His sorrow and pain shows.
Out to the vet he goes,
An outing from which he'll never return.
No more impatient barking as mother serves dinner.
No more contented murmurs behind the sofa.
No more drying of paws on a wet spring day.
Thinking of him as he slips away.
Clock ticking.
Wonder where his soul is tonight.
Good-bye brother Kim.

Peter Williams

Monday Morning, 6 AM

I awoke on Monday morning
and you were by my side,
brown PJ's and black hair rumpled
sleepy dust in your eyes.
Your face was crinkled
your fists clenched tight
as if to fight off daybreak,
I watched in silence and stroked your face
not wanting you to wake.
I put my arms around you,
you sighed and pushed your nose to my chin,
And as your head lay heavy
on my beating chest,
I drank your beauty in.
You were so warm, you felt so soft,
I held onto you so tight.
I thanked my luck stars as I lay there
and waited for daylight.
As I cradled you in my arms,
I promised to never let you go,
And when you snuggled closer to me
I whispered in your ear as you slept
that I love you so.

Paul Wigmore

The Future — 3010

In the year three thousand and ten
There are no diseases or wars
People believe they've found Paradise
As nobody dies any more!

To cope with the population explosion
Something had to be done
So open spaces were replaced with buildings
Now concrete jungles - everyone!

Plastic trees and flowers
Are now used everywhere for show
Because there is no space anymore
For the real ones to grow!

Crops are no longer required
With synthetic foods being eaten instead
Coloured powder dissolved in water
Replaces meat, fruit and two veg!

Animals no longer roam the Earth
Birds no longer fly in the sky
It's heartbreaking — as looking through old books
Our children ask us —Why?

With no more room left to build on Earth
Houses are setup in Space
Think for a moment all I've said —
Is this the future of the Human Race?

Joanne G. Wilding

Rocks And Stones

I'm not daft and I'm not a fool
I don't go in for fantasy as a rule
But I believe and I know I'm right
That rocks and stones move about by night

I walk the field around my home
Up the mountainside I roam
And I'm convinced by sound and sight
That solid stones become mobile by night

How do they move I ask myself
Is it the fairies, an imp or maybe an elf
Why they move is a puzzle too
I have no answer but I know they do.

I wonder if some seek the shade
In some cool and restful glade
Or some may think it would be fun
To move in the open to catch the sun

Do some go seeking a rocky mate
Or go to a stream their thirst to slate
Do they go hunting tasty pebbles to find
And leave stony partners waiting behind

One day when the white coats come for me
I will tell them straight faced and seriously
That I believe and I know I'm right
That rocks and stones move about by night.

Alan T. Williams

Autumn's Approaching Shadow

Autumn's approaching shadow, with its serenity slowly begins to fall,
All those colours in a rainbow, painting leaves on trees so tall,
Perching along cables and power lines, swallow, martins with swifts line up and wait,
Patiently for their fellows, across our coastal waters they will all migrate.

Brent geese and many wildfowl, are mirrored in a red Autumn sky,
Circling over mudflats, soaring in thermals they climb and fly,
A seasonal time of movement, many will leave our isles,
While others are heading towards us, traversing untold miles.

Wooded corners of rolling countryside, that stirs our inner being,
Enhanced by the odour of damp earth, a ritual assurance we are seeing,
Rustic hues on crisp leaves, vestiges of summer they still cling,
Arousing dormant melodies from a fieldfare, as across wildwoods his song does ring.

Evergreens of a pine forest, spreads a carpet of needles upon green floor,
Red berries on blooming holly, while moss and lichen spread once more,
Roe and red deer wander, through your clearings and your glades,
Misty shadows linger, as Autumn's pale light fades.

Wintergreens with lesser twayblade, add beauty to your ground,
Red squirrels with pine marten, quietly forage around,
High above perch buzzard, sparrow hawk and long-eared owl,
Silently among white birches, a fox is on the prowl.

Autumn's final splash of delicate magic, upon a sombre forest floor,
Erica's tinting colour, paints fresh pictures across an open moor,
As those last leaves of Autumn, gently make their fall,
They echo the majesty of this season, a heritage for one and all.

Jim Wilson

Now You're 60
'The Golden Autumn of Your Life'...
is a brand new page

No clock to watch, your tide of life
Is turning now, to one without strife.
Stroll down the days, the golden honey
Is not your pocket lined with money.

When once you had that coveted dime,
You did not always have the time ...
Now the hours are yours, what a wholesome pleasure,
To consume one's life with total leisure!

The freedom is yours, and cannot be bought,
Like other plans you may have sought.
Forget the cash, time is precious,
But, we don't want to sound officious.

We are quite envious, you're taking the halter,
Come gird up your loins, and do not falter.
Throw out the clock, damn the wage,
The Autumn of your life, is a brand new page.

Jennifer Wright

Sensations Of Love

I hear a whisper, I hear you breathe,
I hear the motion of the leaf,
I hear the sound from beneath,
The sound of love, full and complete.

I long to touch you, to feel you move,
To feel the warmth from within you,
I hear your heart beating so clear,
I feel moist breath upon my ear.

I hear the sounds of birds in song,
I feel this place where I belong,
I know this love cannot be wrong,
A love fulfilled, a love so strong.

Call to me, call my name,
Touch my face, send me insane,
Touch my skin, feel it's heat,
Feel my fire from head to feet.

Quench my thirst, feed my soul,
Leave me wasted,
Leave me whole.

Tracey Worley

Famine

I look over my shoulder,
To see him standing there,
His baby black face showing nothing but despair,
He so wants to cry but the tears just won't come
His big swollen belly, enclosed in fragile skin,
Then I see his parents laying side by side
Life taken from their bodies to save their son,
They'd tried:
"Why" he whispered, "will my parents not come?"
"Please help me," he begs, but the damage is done.

Rebecca Louise Winter (Age 12)

Memphis Man

Memphis Man they call the King
Cause everybody liked to hear him sing.
Born in Tupelo, Tennessee,
His name was Elvis Presley.

"Love Me Tender", "All Shook Up"
They filmed him from the waist up,
The people cried the night he died,
For they knew there would never be another Elvis Presley.

The Memphis Man will never die
So people please don't cry
For they say the King is still alive today,
His music anyway,
God Save The King

Ian Wilson

Untitled

Imprisonment is a way of penalty for misconforming
to a well established code — a behavourial mode of life
for society who purport to be — civilized ...

To live within a community amicably and comfortably
there has to be an honourable way to establish fair play
All have to subscribe to a varying degree
for a healthy and wholesome environment
for growth and prosperity and ultimately harmony -
and content ...

But is there a way for the offender to pay
that will eventually lead to remorse for the deed?

To do unto others what you would have them do unto you
Should provide a valuable clue ...

Dorothy Williams

Illegitimate Love Child

She loved him like a lioness
loves her cub
She longed for his presence
by her side always
Her eyes bled tears of aching
while he was away

She saw him perfect like a sun set
she begged for his love
when he tormented it from her
Her heart shrieked with pain
when he left

He found her pleasing to the eye
He wanted the sweat from her
naked flesh all over him
His every wish was her pleasure

He began to suffocate in her cage
He wanted back his freedom
His use for her was complete

He was free
She would never be

Michelle Whitham

Absent Friend

It's disbelief - that's what it is
That awful news they brought
It doesn't happen - not to us
At least - that's what I thought

I feel the panic in my chest
Which courses through my veins
My heart keeps telling me 'it's true'
But it doesn't reach my brains

I think of other people
Who have lost a wife or son
But it doesn't matter what I think
The tears still carry on

Why can I not be as strong
As others seem to be
Because it hasn't happened
Not to you and me

But this was just beyond me
And I think you really knew
The only time in 16 years
That I couldn't pull you through

But death came sooner than I thought
I wasn't well prepared
I didn't help you to the end
The only thing not shared.

S. Wild

Acid Rain

Where are our delicate ragwort,
And our champion white and pink,
The bluebell so pretty, a paler shade of ink.
Acid Rain.
Where are our dandelions and buttercups so bold,
Our wild crocus and snowdrops, which gently unfold.
Where are the tall, elegant, grasses, so fine and discreet,
And the bracken so vivid, knee length and green,
These carpeted our woods where we strolled through and dreamed.
Rustling the leaves loudly, between our two feet.
Acid Rain.
The sting of the nettle and thistle so keen,
The elder and cowslip rarely now seen.
Ponds full of creatures we loved to observe,
A reflection of joy as we peered over and stared.
Acid Rain.
Acorns, conkers, holly and chestnuts,
Pussy willow, catkins and brambles that cut.
Dragonfly, butterfly and daddy long legs,
Caterpillars and Horsefly, where have they all fled.
Acid Rain.

Loraine Woodward

The Artist

A jumble of colours
in pots
spills over the table top,
indistinguishable from left-over
egg and beans
on a plate.
A brush, like a chimney sweep's
cast-off,
descends into the butter-tub
pond,
then splurges
from colour to paper to colour
to paper again,
leaving a trail
of blobs on the in between pine.
The once plain,
virginal paper
brightens, begins to live,
speaks and shouts
loudly
at the bidding of
my daughter's imagination.

S.J. Wilkinson

Remembrance

Remembrance Day is with us again,
Heads bowed in silence, to the chimes of Big Ben.
Black-coated figures, with poppies so red,
standing together, to honour the dead.
The laying of wreaths, in solemn procession,
each one remembered, from every profession.
Sadness on faces, of people together,
huddled against the inclement weather.
The sound of the bugles, playing the last post,
above and around us, the invisible host.
All thought of, with joy and pain, never to see their like again.
They gave for their country, with no thought of self,
some are still caught, in the throes of ill health.
Limbless, in chairs, with eyes that can't see,
all to make sure that we would be free.
The march past begins, medals shine in the sun,
we are proud of you all, each and everyone.
Remember them all, not just on this day,
wars are still raging, although far away.
What a wonderful world this could really be,
if arms were laid down, across the sea.
If men could learn to respect one and other,
no creed, no religion, just brother to brother.
The last stroke of the chime, comes from Big Ben,
Remembrance Day is with us again.

Mairearad Wilson

The Pearl
(From Ridiculous To Sublime)

The one exalted smooth and pure
Grandiose as haute-couture
Adoration of its wealth
Plucked from out the sea itself.

Molluscs lurk in fathoms deep
Know not of the gift they keep
Growing precious over time
From sand ridiculous to pearl sublime.

Elevated from the brine
Majestic child of living time
To adorn with beauty true
The necks of just a wealthy few.

Simple sand and molluscs hard
Played this metaphoric card
Ungratefully the shell torn wide
To justify the prize inside.

The pearl will die if not kept warm
The lustre bright will be forlorn
So respect it's beauty deep
And it's metamorphic sleep.

Maria Wiles

A Highland Tour

Among the hills and bens at early dawn
A mist hangs over, then is gone
A beautiful picture comes into view
Those hills and bens have changed to blue

The dark blue lochs and silvery streams
Are awakened by the sunlight beams
The winding road where shadows fall
Of trees, so stately and so tall

The tourists amble on their way
With scenery changing every day
And as the sun sinks in the west
The weary traveller goes to rest

No hurry or bustle, tomorrow will do
Like a boat in the water without any crew
This is the life of the people up there
In the heart of the highlands, no place can compare

The holidays over and making back home
With beautiful memories I won't feel alone
I'll picture those scenes and remember always
The highlands and islands with colour ablaze

Jessie Williamson

Call To Prayers

Dawn; and I hear the call to prayers.
From a wooden minaret, a crow,
A black robed muezzin cries;
Solitary in silence, a shadow on the sky:
God is Great; God is Great

In morning; a sink to drain the font of night.
When washed of sin to sin anew,
The perfumed body of which I take part
Moves clamorous ahead without its heart:
God is risen; God is risen

For day; in bowing to the wall that
Bounds my life, I sing its praises.
This construction of sense which
Keeps me sane; this limit of time
Upon which I claim: God is one

Into night; when sight fails the hour
of sudden gloom: the dark intoxication.
The blinding of reason within my room,
Where sole abed, lies witness to my grave,
Such sleep: for god is dead; god is ...

Glyn Williams

This Wonderful World

This wonderful world that God has made,
Through my eyes it will never fade,
Mountains so high and topped with snow,
Beautiful trees where rivers flow,
Sunshine that gives us a wonderful sight,
And then the darkness in the pale moonlight,
Flowers with colours of every shade,
An incredible sight so perfectly made.
A carpet of grass, so green and lush,
The swell of the sea, comes with a roar and rush,
The wind blows so freely, to sweep the world's face,
And gently tears of dew with everlasting grace,
The sunrise in the morning that lights up all the sky,
The shadows in the sunset seems to lay down and die.
A gently fall of the first snowflake,
The biting wind adds ice to the lake,
The fish all beautiful with colours so rare,
The animals of our kingdom, with faces of care,
Up there above us gentle birds in flight,
With delicate feathers so perfect and bright,
From the dull rainy days to the warm sun above,
I stand here in wonder, and thank God for his love.

Horace Williams

A Perfect Night

As we stroll hand in hand together,
Treading softly through the heather,
There's a stillness in the air tonight.
Wild geese wing their way in flight,
Vixen, gives her mating call
Somewhere 'neath the pine trees tall.
As we wander through the gloom,
Soon will rise the harvest moon.

Woodsmoke scents the autumn air
Something makes us stop and stare.
A rustling in the leaves close by,
A hedgehog moves and owls cry.
Now the moon is out in full,
Church bells ring to bellman's pull.

When we reach our favourite place
We'll rest awhile, there is no haste.
As we gaze out through the night
Those twinkling lights, oh what a sight.
From cottage, farm and every place
The air is so pure we almost taste.
Glow worms shed their share of light
And we enjoy this perfect night.

C. Williams

Walney Island

The air is clear and the day is bright
The sea is green and still
And over on the horizon lies a cloud
That covers Snaefell Hill.
A swirl of birds like a curtain pass;
And the sand is hot underfoot,
A lark with a song in its throat
Rises up from the marram grass.
While a curlew's cry like a long lost soul,
Echoes its lonesome flight,
As if glad for the day and passing of the night.

Mrs. I. Wignall

Two Little Angels

Most have one or maybe two,
Do yours make a mess? I know my girls do,
Backwards and forwards collecting from school,
In the summer they shout "mum, fill up the pool".
Sticky hand prints around my front room,
One's spilt the Daz, get out the broom,
"Get out of my cupboard, don't touch, sit down",
I glare at them both with a meaningful frown,
"Neighbours" is on, it's time for a bath,
The bathroom is flooded and they just sit and laugh,
All clean and tired, their story is read,
It's nearly 8 o'clock, it's time for bed,
Playing me up they really push their luck,
Wait 'til they're asleep,
I'M GOING TO WAKE THEM UP.

Clare Williams

Pilgrimage To Walsingham

The sweet sound of bells on the evening air,
As we stroll in the garden, free from care.
We've come here, five pilgrims, to pray at the Shrine,
Wherein there's a silence, something divine.
There's no explanation, as we kneel and pray,
The feeling of peace that surrounds us each day.
Hundreds of pilgrims pass to and fro,
Many thousands before us have knelt here of yore.
Wherever you are in this beautiful place,
There's time for a greeting from each smiling face.
An oasis of peace in a world full of strife,
Where pilgrims have gathered from all walks of life.
We've laughed, and we've cried, now once more we pray
To come back to Walsingham before many a day.
We leave with reluctance, and many a sigh,
But we vow to return, Liz, Nell, Beth and I.
For I know at the Shrine, I will surely find
God's gifts of tranquility, hearts ease, peace of mind.

N. Williams

Remembrance

They were young and in their prime
In our nation's darkest time
When we were forced into a war
To keep the enemy from our shore
They were sent, far and wide,
To stand, together, side by side

They fought and killed and shed their blood
As on foreign shores they stood
They faced the perils of the deep,
Many, to find, eternal sleep,
Or, fought our battles in the skies
Never, again, to see a sunrise

They did not choose, to fight and die
Nor did they ask the reason why?
They fought for us, to keep us free,
As we were really meant to be,
Remember them, they played their part,
Keep them, forever, in your heart

J.R. Wilcox

Winter Sport

The season came — you played your hand
Game suitor with a magic wand
Delivered proudly to my door
A trophy that I must devour.

Abracadabra! You waved your gun —
Swift the killing trick was done.
Glorious mallard had become
Flesh and feathers left to hang ...

Until I plucked up the nerve,
Wore your colours in my hair
While white feathers flew everywhere
Softly floating down.

I took the knife — off with his head!
I chopped right through bright orange feet,
Working 'til he looked like meat
All dressed up ready for the table.

My slippery fingers probed inside —
Drawing out the slimy mess
Hey Presto! Bloody bits and pieces.
No fanfare now. No secrets.

But what a feast the wild-duck made —
So dark and rich and strong!
I thought of you, feeding my guilt,
Not satisfied for long.

Bewick Wilson

Death or Life?

I see her frail hands, her wasted face,
Her crumbling frame, her silver hair,
Her strained breath.
I see her despondent eyes, her resigned posture,
Her loneliness, her hopelessness,
As she looks out the window.
I imagine she sees herself —
The blossoming child, the blushing bride,
The proud mother in days of happiness
But more importantly Life.
I see her pain as she watches all these decay,
And fade into memories.
I see her despair as she looks at her friends grow
Old and wan and die.
I see her realise her own fate.
But I do not see her long for freedom, for peace.
I do not see her young, vibrant spirit of the
Blossoming child, blushing bride and proud mother,
Beating on the hollow walls of its collapsing age.

Victoria Willson

Nocturne In Blue

Blue shades the velvet soft, of Eve,
velvet dark too! the sounds;
hurried steps, purr o' motors, hooting owls,
tones of sleep descend:
the great gate of Night, opens.

Orange-gold the orb, rises high,
magical, the aura begins;
the aura of nocturne, blue:
when trees look! like black umbrellas,
stars decorate the Heavens above;
the scene! is a picture in silhouette.

Dawn breaks in a blush o' silk,
birds sing a grand chorales;
flowers of every hue, open their eyes,
fresh! from dew-washed tears;
life begins with a smile,
and it's good Morning to you.

Bernard Williams

The Fragile Border

The day the local butcher started selling fish
I felt my mind tremble.
Pale pink salmon slices wrapped in plastic
Nestled cosily beside the fillet steak.
"Times are hard," he said when I protested
"We must diversify."

And how could I explain
That for some of us
That fragile border dividing mad from sane
Is a wispy silken thread which stays in place
Only so long as bakers sell bread
And candlemakers candles.

When butchers sell fish — why anything might happen.
At church on Sunday the vicar might preach atheism,
While outside, a green sky overhangs the purple grass.
Cows might bark as I walk home through fields of wool,
Past the woods where silver birches rehearse the Stabat Mater
To the sound of the Palestrina in the wind.

I stumbled from the shop.
Was the pavement still the pavement —
Or had that white line in the middle of the road
Been painted for me to walk on?
Reality blurred at the edges
And in the distance I saw the asylum beckon.

Caroline Windsor

The Beauty Of Scotland

The rugged shores of Scotland
The splendour of the sea
The lochs and glens with all their charms
Are wondrous things to see.

The deer they are majestic
The eagles they do fly
Whilst salmon leap into the air
From rivers running high.

The pipers they are piping
They ring out loud and clear
Tunes to suit the young and old
Sweet music to the ear.

Ben Nevis is a treasure
Its glory plain to see
It lures one in its clutches
How thrilling that can be.

Loch Ness may have a monster
One that is never seen
It may one day decide to peep
Perhaps next Hallowe'en.

When the sun sets over Oban
Or Barra, Coll and Tiree
It makes one glad to be alive
So Scotland is for me.

Mrs. W. Winner

People's Plight

So they've got you trained
Holding your gun,
A child with a toy.
A man! ... you're barely a boy.
Shoot and play
Can you kill, will you maim?
Live for today, tomorrow will come.
Play with your toy, a slaughter is done.

Suzanne K. Willox

My Friend Ben

I have an imaginary friend
His name is Ben
He comes to me in the day
But then he floats clean away
He teaches me about the birds in the trees,
About the lush green grass and the honey bees.
The buttercups and the poppies red,
Bright fiery daffodils growing in a
Damp, dark flower bed.
He teaches me of the windmills
And the cornmills in motion.
The fish and the seaweed
And the deep blue secret ocean.
He teaches me about the colours
About the trees and about the flowers.
He helps me paint pictures in my mind,
Ones I'll never see because I am blind.

Talia R. Williams

The Bird

The bird is such a graceful thing,
When it flies the skies and expands its wings;
There is never a need to hurry or race
As it slowly glides its way through space.

When dawn arrives the birds awake,
I know this is so by the noise they make;
The morning chorus sounds so fine,
As they are perched along the washing line.

The young wait anxiously in their nest,
While the adults go searching for food that is best;
They finally arrive back with a worm or some bread,
As the little ones fight to be the first one fed.

The time has come round to now say good-bye,
I'm sure if I was their mother I would be tempted to cry;
The world is so endless for them to now roam,
After being brought up and leaving their home.

Dianne Wilson

Nature's Cathedral

I heard a lovely choir of birds
So beautiful to hear.
I seemed to understand their words
They told that God was near.
This church was built of stately trees,
The roof a cloudless sky,
Old Nature gave to me the keys
I could not ask her why.
The alter was a bank of flowers,
Old Nature's font was there
The windows were of leafy bowers
The atmosphere a prayer.
The congregation was the flowers,
The birds and rabbits too.
This lovely scene watched for hours
In Nature's cooling dew.
The organ was a gentle stream
Its notes so sweet and clear,
To me t'was but a lovely dream,
To tell that God was near.

Moyra Wilding Rome

Swan Lake

The maestro has lowered his baton,
Bringing the overture to its close;
Now the retinue of dancers
Take up their graceful pose.

Right on clue, the prima ballerina,
Exquisite in her swan-like dress,
Pirouettes, as light as thistledown ...
A vision of loveliness.

If only I could dance like that,
I would be famous overnight;
But I can't dance ... I can only dream.
Of things that might have been.

If only I'd bee trained like that when young,
My chances of stardom might have come.

So I will make myself a coffee,
Strong and sweet, with lots of cream,
And sit before the TV screen;
But I can only watch and imagine
That the sylph-like ballerina's me ...

Sit and watch and dream of things
That now, alas, can never be.

Patricia Suzanne Winder

November

On this cold November day,
I look around me everywhere,
And see the trees are looking bare,
Leaves are scattered here and there,
I sweep them all, and think that's tidy.
Alas next day they are back, oh Blimey,
The birds there are just a few,
Big crow, blackbirds, and seagulls too,
My favourite bird is little Robin Red-Breast,
He tries for crumbs, without much success,
Come back Robin, when the big birds have gone,
More will be put out for Robin,
As he sings his song.
Autumn flowers still in the gardens
Jack Frost's been about through the night,
Nipping some, I'm sorry to say.
Soon the gardens will look all bare,
Christmas time will soon be here.
Snow and holly everywhere,
Then once more a New Year too,
Spring and summer to look forward to.

Jean Wilson

Ode To The Fields

Contemptuous May!
You thought your iron hold would clutch forever,
To stifle Spring, ransom Summer;
But the hour has come.
Beneath your dreary skies,
The tiny shoots have fledged and fattened.
With gentle persuasion slowly rising,
Each unseen but together a mighty army,
Who wreath in supple splendour,
On May's rusty girder.
The sunshine may yet be captive,
But green meadows stand exultant;
Littered with yellow, violet, mauve,
And rustic ochre on the crests of the field.

Beauty until my heart bursts!
How I long to smother my discord,
With your narcotic calm.
Lick the wet leaves, drink the soft raindrops,
Bury my hair in the folds of green.
I wish that time would not rush on;
For Summer will surely scorch
The exuberant petals and vital stems
Just top sink to the drenched roots of oblivion,
And cease to want for all that I will never find.

Hannah Wingrave

Meg

Swirling mist and rain like needles
Across the bridge, approach the brow
The hill is steep, the man exhausted
His thoughts thump back "Where is she now?"
She loathed the dark, afraid of storms
What made his beauty brave this night
Did my shouting rage surprise her
Before she scuttled off in fright?
A street light casts a pool of welcome
Is that a shape — or just a trick?
He stops, caresses damp, furred body
Receives with joy ecstatic lick.

Shona White

The Important Day

Over the channel we sailed away
For we did know it was a gruesome day.
France lay ahead, we came to the shore,
We ran up the beach in '44.
The Germans stood, before our eyes
There were many deaths, and many cries,
We stormed the forts, and cleared the land
But British blood, lay among the sand.
A winner and loser had to come
We'd soon find out with the rise of the sun
Triumph was ours on this important day
Britain was back, we are here to stay.

Andrea Wilkinson

The Fox

I was stalking a rabbit on the hill one day
When I heard the sound of bugles over the way.
I stopped and I listened, then I started to run,
In the hope that I'd get away and not be the one,
The one that they chose to chase and to kill,
The one whose blood would please and thrill
The men on horseback, the men with guns
And lords who thought that killing was fun.
As I rushed, I stumbled and fell
Up ahead I could see the Dell.
The Dell was a hill where I used to live
And with all the strength I had to give
I made a dash to see if there
Was somewhere for me to hide up there.
The hounds were getting nearer and nearer
The sound of the bugles was getting clearer.
I got up on the hill and then
I dived into a deserted den.
The hounds and horses raced on by.
And I knew I wasn't going to die.

Cara Williams (Age 13)

At The Gate

Until my hair turns white
And my lips turn blue,
I will wait for you.
Until the sky cracks open
And the sea's black and swollen,
I will wait for you.
For when the angel of death
Comes to steal my last breath,
I will be thinking of you.

Aaron Whitehead

Children

What greater gift can you give to Man
Than a child! a soul! that you have planted on Earth
You bless their parents with riches
From the day of their birth.

And we are their gardeners
We have to dig and prune
And fashion their natures
So they will grow and mature
Your love and grace Lord
Is our lives' manure.

And at the springtide of life
Our garden will be full of colour
For it's only your love Lord,
That's kept us from being a wilderness
And at the time of the harvest
You'll gather us all to your breast.

Mrs. M. Wood

The Tropical Sea

Your warm embrace and comforting calm,
From enigma, adventure, to quick alarm,
Awaken my soul and capture my heart
You are beautiful, you are art.

Nature's love has been kind,
A wealth of treasures to love and to find;
Variety divine and spontaneous life
Eruptions of colour as sharp as a knife.

To every island and every beach,
There is no limit to your reach;
Crystal clear, to golden sand
Created first by God's great hand.

Though I live in a dismal place,
With solemn skies to grey my face;
I live and dream about the sea
So my soul and mind can wander free.

Damien Wilkinson

Age

Age now has clamped your limbs
and numbed your mind.
The isolation grows.

You have no joy but this,
Death stands waiting
beside the final void.

He cradles in his arms
the child you were
and beckons with a grin.

P.G. Williams

It's Lonely

Four grey walls, an empty chair
Picture someone sitting there,
Tell a joke, speak in rhyme
Anything to pass the time
        It's lonely
At the window looking out
People pass, I start to shout,
It's in my head but not aloud
Even with this passing crowd
        It's lonely
Perhaps it's just a state of mind
And if I try someday I'll find
Someone, somewhere just like me,
A friend who will help me see
        It's not so lonely

Hazel Wilson

Shattering Silence

Silence stood
As clear as water
When seen through mist
By a clouded moon.
Each move
Expressed by thought
It's strength
Magnified
As their eyes turn
To avoid the changing mood.
Their pain
Intensified
By the numbness
Of each sip of wine.
How silence stood
Laughing in it's glory
Watching the lighting
Shatter the words between them.

Sonja Wilson

The Passing Years

Far hiv 'a the years gane
Just memories left o 'a that's been
School days fin worries cam fae books
An learnin' 'a oor 'p's and 'q's.
That days auld age seemed far awa'
We never thocht we'd age at a'

Syne cam the carefree days o' youth
We learned tae cope wi a' oor growth.
The warmth o' freens tae help us thro'
Fin' mist an clouds shut oot the sun
There's much in life we'el leave undeen
Fin age begins tae 'dim the sheen.

Bit lookin' back thro' 'a the years
Life comes tae us wi hopes an fears.
Tho' memories we aye can share
An a ain has their ane.
"The brae noo needs a second look
Let's tak a rest an close the book".

Sophia D. Winchester

The School Gala

Hush! Hush! Now go in there gently,
Can you see what I can see?
Yes! You can, it's Grandmama,
Snoozing away in the old rocker
Peter and Penny, are really out to shock her!
To shock her!

Well! Well! Well! Grandmama is listening
To all their fun and games,
Cos she has heard it all before
Oh, so many, many times,
A fleeting smile, flickers, around
Dear old Granny's face.

A School Gala! Well! that's very modern.

"Oh! I'm so excited, Peter, me too, Oh! Penny
What a lovely time, we're going to have —
On that merry-go-round, that goes round and round."

Grandmama is feeling tired, oh so very tired,
As her dearest, great, great grandchildren
Do high jinks and handstands, all over the room.
Even balancing on top of the chairs,
Grandmama, suddenly so fed up with all this!
Razzle, dazzle, quietly, oh so quietly —
Falls back to sleep again.

Ruth Wolstenholme

Untitled

The autumn winter has just begun,
No longer we feel, the warmth of the sun,
The lovely green grass, is turning brown,
The leaves off the trees come tumbling down,
and soon we shall have the snow,
Making our feet and fingers glow,
It's then we turn to our cosy home,
No longer our parks to roam.

E. Wilford

War

Shells and bullets pass me by
missiles and bombs fill the sky.
Houses destroyed,
there's nowhere to sleep;
innocent people,
flocked together like sheep.
Soldiers on the left and on the right
armed to the teeth ready to fight.
People lie wounded, dying and dead
a child in the gutter, shot in the head.
Will these wars ever end
please, let us have peace
in the message we send

Michael Patrick Williams

Earth's Treasure

Gentle rhythms pulsating beat,
Cool ice hardness, liquid fire heat,
Enrolled in a crystal beyond craftsman's cut.
Lines pure straight edges, gleam to a tip,
So perfect, earth's teardrop chip.
Light and shadows dwell within,
A doorway you will find,
To give retreat, the echoes of the mind.
Rainbows swirl with ice diamond blaze,
Breathless beauty, basking in man's gaze.
Created from nature, nurtured by earth,
Crystals of every shape, size and girth,
Evidence of the planet's spiritual birth.
Blossoming in sunlight, they sparkle and gleam,
Haunting creation, an alchemist's dream.
Energies flare and spark a bite,
The most tender, pure, spiritual light.
They heal, they soothe, they give out love,
A gift so unique it came from above.

Patricia Wilson

Ploddy Plodderings

'Ploddy' is a little sugar,
And he likes playing 'rugger',
He scored two tries for England once,
Then, the ball hit him on the 'bonce'.
That was more than 'Plod' could take,
So, the England Team he did forsake.
Off he went to New Zealand to live,
And to the 'All Blacks' his services her did give.
They loved him,
SO HE'S NOT COMING BACK!!!

J. Wilson

Carnival

A labyrinth of circles whirling around,
Painted mask face looming up on a clown,
Helta-skeltas, firecrackers, roaring of sound,
Smithereens of stardust smothering the ground.

A Harlequin sways on high stilted tread,
Polka-dot pantaloons gleam mauve and red,
Black velvet bolero, green turban on head
He juggles the balls like a tumble of thread.

Roundabouts rotating, faces giddy, white,
Whirly-gig music bursting into the night
Shattering sleep, I awake, slowly aware
Of marshmallow pillows and noiseless night air.

Annabel Teviot

Searching

Closely look through the chasm of time,
Looking for that, which you seek to find,
Danger torment, endless trials await,
Seeking the place they all congregate,
Look to the future, what do you see,
You don't see nothin', 'cause there's nothin' to see,
If you can't believe, you don't belong,
Time is the master, so sing to his song,
He whistles a tune, which has no rhyme,
Overcome logic and seek what you find,
You don't know what it is,
That you desperately seek,
Then your future decays and looks, oh so bleak,
For to come to the end,
There must be a start,
Find your purpose, and you'll be allowed to depart.

Stephen Wilkinson

The Romany Boy

I love to roam, my dogs and I,
And sleep beneath the starry sky,
Or course my dogs o'er field and plough
And play beneath the wooded bough.

I never learned to read or write
But sit beside our fire at night,
With ash wood green across my legs,
Sit with my father, making pegs.

My mother always used to say
She'd seen the fairies out at play,
Mother comes form County Clare
She's seen the fairies dancing there.

We crossed the sea to Liverpool
A big white van, a mare and foal,
We wandered down to Epsom fair
And met a lot of cousins there.

We may return perhaps in the fall,
To the rolling hills of Donegal,
Perhaps I'll be back when I' a man
And drive my own white caravan.

Eric Woods

The Window Pane

Weary eyes survey again
The sobbing, throbbing window pane,
Where water runs or hangs like tears
Of all Mankind across the years.
Spread across the meadow lies
A lake, reflecting leaden skies.
Muddy water's leaving slurries
O'er the roads where traffic scurries.
Those who need to venture out
Go splashing, squelching all about
Battered, blown by wind and rain
And deluged by the cars again!
Their sodden garments, wet and cold
Hang from shoulders, young and old.
Senseless hands clasp rainsoaked shopping
Icy feet trudge home; not stopping.
But fearless children find much fun
In endless days of absent sun.
Clad in boots and mackintosh
In every puddle love to splosh,
While their elders' sole desire
Is comfort by a cheerful fire,
Content to watch the wind and rain
From INSIDE the window pane.

Patricia Woodley

Your Mam

Last night, I dreamt I saw your mam.
She looked well and had just moved house.
I took our daughter to see her,
to show her our girl.

Our girl who looks so like you.
She said that had she met her
she would have known her to be one of her line.
Looking her over she smiled
with a pride that a grandparent has.
Another grandchild, child of her youngest,
not seen before. The first of our love.

She was sad to have missed her first days.
All ther grandchildren had sat on her knee
but this one is special, to watch from afar
and to meet only in dreams.

We didn't talk of meeting again
and I don't remember saying goodbye.
I woke suddenly with tears in my eyes,
feeling warm and cold and happy and sad,
with a hope I would visit this dream again.

Julie Wood

Scary Encounter

A crooked nosed gnome near magicked me,
as I picked mushrooms for my tea.
I knocked a toadstool with my hand,
and out popped he in a temper grand.
He puffed a chest like a hatpin head
"Curse you, human child" he said —
    "May the star-witch snatch you on her tail,
    to far-off Pluto's ice and hail,
    then; frozen, hurl you into space
    to Sirius with the white-hot face.
    May meteor goblins prey on you
    and twelve-eyed moon-bats clutch at you.
    May the blackness of a dead world be
    your prison, and should you break free
    let goblins, witches, toads and bats
    pursue you to the utmost flats
    of coldest outer universe,
    to do their part within this curse."
I fell to my knees in trembling fear,
I closed my eyes, and blocked each ear,
but nothing happened, no one came,
the sky and earth remained the same.
I peeped — and gone was the angry gnome,
then so was I, running hard for home.

Frederick W. Wood

From The Train

Land of the bed-sits row upon row
Some with a bathroom on landing below
Some with a window commanding a view
Some disturbingly next to the loo
Some with a kettle plugged in with the lamp
Some shared with spiders and rising damp
Some with the washing thrown over the chairs
Some with a trip hole on landing or stairs
Some with a one minute light by the door
Some with a futon thrown down on the floor
Some with old curtains, tattered and thin
Some where the main meal comes from a tin
Some with a gas ring and some with a Belling
Some where the kitchen forever is smelling
    of dishcloths and cabbage or curry or stew
Some full of pots where the cheese plants grew
Some where the flowers are plastic or feathers
Some where the rooms remain cold in all weathers
Some where the book shelves are covered in dust
Some where the window frames buckle with rust
Some where the telly stays on all the day
One where a lonely head bows down to pray
Some where the tenants mysteriously go —
Land of the bed-sits — row-upon-row.

Rita Woodall

Young Love

We sat and talked!
Romance was ours ...
That lovely Summer's night!
Face to face,
I kissed away your fears.
We felt the bug of 'youth's love'
Take its bite,
And threw our reasons for past cares!

We said our vows
(Ignoring each written stone)
Friends shook our hands,
While we mimed the Virgin's 'Blush'.

Too soon, the mating urge became outgrown,
Leaving past years to write their passing
In our flesh!
Now you have gone!
... So too you babes have gone
I kneel ... my fingers touch the mounded earth

So much to me, this message on the stone,
That I had shaped, to mark your simple grave!

Thomas A. Woodley

Christmastide

What does Christmas mean to you?
In a world so torn with strife.
Where sickness and poverty is rife.

Is it Bethlehem with its stable bare?
The ox, the ass, the sheep.
Or is it Jesus lying fast asleep?

Shepherds with their flocks of sheep
A blinding light they saw,
And angels proclaiming Peace for evermore.

Wise men with their precious gifts.
Bowed down on bended knee.
God's gift, so all men shall be free.

Or do you look at the tinseled tree?
The lights aglowing there,
But never at the people in despair.

Think of that first Christmastide,
The stories which are told,
Then its wonders you'll behold.

Mrs. D. Wustrack

Never You

I heard a voice in the evening calling,
Softly whispering my name,
And I hurried along, hoping, searching,
To find from whence it came;
But it was only the wind in the treetops sighing,
Sighing for the passing of day,
And in my mind the remembered voice
As I turned and walked away.

I saw a face in the distance, smiling,
With a smile like the morning Sun,
I wanted to reach and touch your cheek,
And my feet began to run;
But it wasn't you with the smiling face
That I'd hurried along to find,
It was just the smile of a passing stranger,
And you were in my mind.

I felt two lips, so sweet and gentle
Softly kiss my face —
I raised my arms to hold you close
But l met with empty space;
A butterfly's wing had touched my lips
And my eyes, with tears, were blind,
For I knew your tender loving kiss
Was only in my mind.

Leslie Woods

The Prisoner

Weary of your empty chatter
Concerning only you not I,
I long to flee, from words be free,
To turn my face to the sky;
And in my untamed imaginings
Feel the wind on my cheek,
And listen long to the birds at song,
Yes, this is the freedom I seek.
But, unheeding in your self-esteem,
You little know or care,
Though my mind roams free
Still my body must be —
Nailed by your voice to a chair!

Irene Wood

The Secret

Mother, I didn't tell you
About the old rocking chair,
I rocked it so hard
We both tumbled through the air,
I found myself hurling backwards
And the chair followed behind
To say I looked undignified
Would put it very mild,
My first thought, was your sideboard
Had I scratched the wood at all?
I scrambled back into the chair
When I heard you in the hall,
You don't have to be a child
To get into a fix,
I was the mother of two
And my age was twenty six.

Margery Wilson

The Eve Of All Hallows

On a haunting eve like Hallowe'en
when the lightening makes the thunder scream
and the trees are lifted from the ground
and the rain can wash away a town
how useless is the technology race
when Nature puts us in our place
and while we waste our resources
and pollute the earth
and have no respect for its worth
one day Nature will become so angry,
with an anger so supreme
that on a haunting eve like Hallowe'en
the whole damned earth will scream.

Patricia Withnall

Evacuees

T'was on a bright September day that lots of children went away
With canvas knapsacks on their back and everything that they could pack
They went to places far and wide to seek a place that they could hide.
Away from all the sounds of war, t'was same for rich as well as poor.
They went to stay with families that were strangers to them all.
And try they did to make new friends when they started their new school.
They waited eagerly for news of bombs that fell around,
And hoped that they would hear soon their folks were safe and sound.
T'was hard to be away from home, from family and friends
How long they wondered would it be before this damn war ends?
And end it did after six long years to everyone's delight.
And there were lots of joyful tears 'cause we had won the fight.
And back they came to homes they knew, no longer did they fear
To be united once again with those they held so dear.

Sybil A. Woods

What The Willow Tree Says

I am not as sad as you think
As I lower my head into the water.
When the wind blows, my thin rods
Will sting and whip you with anger.

But afterwards kneel by my trunk
In the cool of a summer shade
And hear my soft words,
Feel my beauty and my grace
As you run your fingers through my green hair.

I give you my tenderness and my resilience
Which neither heat of sun nor fury of storm
Will ever destroy.
My tears will pass for I am in touch
With the flowing river and the ocean beyond.

Christopher Woodland

Bird Brain

What joyful larks
those birdies are.
What happy little wrens.
With tuneful thrush' and starling chatter
the envy never ends.
Don't you just wish
that you could fly and
swoop and sail
about the sky;
and sing
so happy — just the same.
What wondrous mites
those birdies are —
'tis pity about
their brain!?!

Sheila Woodmansey

My Camera Is My Memory

Like a squirrel, in my Autumn years
    I'll store the food of memories
In pictures, for the Winter which I dread
    When I am old and ill
And cannot walk on hilltops with my dog
    Nor run at speed on grassy river banks
I'll recall, when I need to,
    The images I've taken with my camera's eye
Of joyous youth and health in days long gone
    To look at and be glad; I'll taste again
The fruits of Salad Days; drink longer draughts
    Of memory's wine I only sipped at first
Recall the scenes of childhood in my mind
    Of happy times, of people I have known
From pictures which I took long, long ago.

Alan Wilding

Stone Flags

Grey stone flags, old stone flags,
    Set in Earth side by side.
Time goes slow to old stone flags.
Cold, wet, sometimes hot as seasons pass
Young feet, old feet, walked, ran, scuttered
    Over old stone flags
    Leaving yesterdays scars.
Picks, prod and lever and old flags
    Shudder then yield.
Old, broken flags, cast aside
Now concrete ones lie snugly in their place
Broken old flags cast aside to lie on a council tip.
Strong hands lift and carry away
To set criss-crossed in rural paths
    Proud old flags
    Sleeping on again.

R.A. Wilson

Christmas

Christmas time will soon be here
Bringing with it lots of cheer
Xmas trees and lights all glowing
Look out the window, now it's snowing

Soon it will be Xmas morn
When sweet little Jesus was born
Mummy makes dinner and Christmas pud
Oh it's lovely it does taste good

After dinner we watch T.V.
When I sit on Daddy's knee
I've opened my presents some are toys
One is a keyboard it makes a noise.

When night time comes I go to bed
There I rest my little head
I've enjoyed myself in my own little way
And tomorrow morn will be Boxing Day.

Michelle Anneka Whittle

My Solitude

On a cold night quiet and lonely
Sits a lady, longing, waiting.
For the bell which does not ring
Or even telephone to sing.
Clocks ticked out of synchronization,
Sounds of footfalls in the street.
Reading finished and poetry written,
Thoughts of you pass slowly round.
Uncanny are life's saddest moments
Loneliness has a dreadful sound.
Dreams like smoke, drift to the ceiling,
Trying to reach you through the air.
Can't you feel my love lies waiting.
In the stillness of the night.
You are all in life to me.
You are my pure and sweet symmetry.

Eileen Woodhead

Rejection

She was a woman, much as any other,
Undistinguished in a crowd,
Taking a pride in her work and her home,
Yet she was not proud ...

She had been born into a on overwhelming family,
Loved and cherished, and although rather plain
She grew up expecting love to follow
And so was unprepared
For the subsequent rejection — and pain ...

But she married, and became like the others,
Chatted to neighbours,
And was sufficiently sincere to deceive everyone
Except her closest friends,
— And those she had cause to fear —

She could be quite amusing at parties,
People wondered, when she smiled,
What she was thinking — how could they know
That deep in her long-tormented soul, she was wild, wild ...

Once she found, unexpectedly, a great love
As perfect and impassioned as her own ...
A god who stepped down briefly from Olympian heights,
— For an amusing interlude between goddesses,
And left her forever unsatisfied ...
But how could she have known?

Catherine Lucy Woodward

Spring Is Here

Free from the winter's icy grip
The gentle rippling stream doth flow
The silvery leaf of the willow tree,
Sparkles in the sun's warm glow.

O'er the deep and dreaming pond,
Iridescent in her flight,
Skims the lovely dragonfly,
Dancing till the fading light.

And lambkins gambol in the spring,
And catkins tremble on the bough,
The happy bird is on the wind,
Spring is in the country now.

The bright green moss beneath the trees,
In the woodland starts to spread,
Soon, we'll hear the busy bees,
Hovering round the floweret's head.

The golden cowslip in the field,
Gently sways before the breeze,
The cuckoo pint behind her shield
Peeps, through her dark green glossy leaves.

Behind the hedge's lacy screen,
The little bird begins to nest,
And, covered by the soft sweet green
Sleeps, when the sun sinks in the west.

Violet Jessie Wright

The Village Craftsman

Reed upon reed, in perfect symmetry,
The patient thatcher plies his ancient trade;
From sturdy ladder rung, conscious of village unity,
He sees a creed of self-sufficiency displayed.

Well seasoned elm and oak; wheels for a wagon or mofrey,
The wheelwright's hands design with chisel, stock and bit;
Created by the carpenter, a Windsor chair or hive for honey bee,
Reflected in the candle gleam, the skillful tailor sits.

To deftly sew a seam, a bridal gown, a faulty hem to alter;
The saddler's window, flush with purses, belts and tack;
Alluring smells of fresh made bread pervade the bakery,
The dry stone wall surrounds the crops; corn dollies for the final stack.

Treen from the turner; the basket maker weaves the willow,
Hedges are plashed and laid; the besum maker brushes clean;
Willed to him by his father's hand; the anvil, forge and bellows,
Outlined by flame, the blacksmith strong completes the scene.

Mrs. D. Woollas

The Ever Changing Sea

Grey, majestic, constantly thrashing
Wild horses onto seashore, crashing
Giant waves and spray sent flying high
Reflect a tortured, angry sky.

But wait! the sun has struck the grey and angry chords
And in an instant rays of gold as from a mighty sword
Reach down to change the waves to shimmering silver hordes,
And its wondrous beauty takes another form.

Maureen Stella Wright

My Love

Pictures inspire and excite me
Canvasses outstretched wall after wall,
Paintings and drawings of objects and people,
But no palette or brush can portray love;
A feeling, a mystery.
Something that brings happiness and joy,
And you.
My inspiration, my art form, my love.

Fiona Wilkes

My Great Loss

I commit myself to paper as I write upon this page
Trying to come to terms with internal emotional rage
A rage that makes me feel that my whole body is in pain
When I conjure up your picture, mentally, again and again.

I watched you getting better from the illness that you had
And everyone was pleased for you and really very glad
But fate can play some dirty tricks and really turn the knife
Especially when it really meant the taking of a life.

We gathered around your bedside and helplessly we stood
We tried to show our love and care and hoped you'd understood
But little did I know that day that you had felt so ill
Ill enough to give up on the hold of your life's will

Now when I open up my arms I find this empty space
A space that is not for refill and never to replace
For it's hard to lose your mother whether young or very old
Having only empty heartache and memories to hold.

Wendy Winslet

Memories

A pile of bricks? Nay, not so,
For these were homes not long ago.
Homes where people once resided,
Lived and loved, and softly chided
Children, who throughout the years,
Grew up amidst their toil and tears,
And in their turn, lived in these houses
With their chosen ones for spouses.
What memories lie buried here,
What joys and sadness, frights and fear,
Of births and deaths, and love and care,
Of cries and laughter, songs and prayer
All gone, as if they'd never been
A vital part of this street scene.
But when the bricks are cleared away
New homes are built, and children play,
But they'll not think about the past,
But toys and things that never last.

Jack E. Wheeler

Snorkel And Mask

With this new aide,
I began to wade,
As I slowly put them on,
The world above has nearly gone.
My body and head beneath the sea,
A new world is born to me.
I swim along and look beneath,
Follow the shape of a gorgeous reef.
Now I've opened this vast new door,
My eyes are hungry to see even more.
The colours hit me in the face,
My heart now beats a quicker pace.
Of the colours I couldn't describe,
It's more a feeling deep inside.
This experience I'd like to share,
With all the people for whom I care.
I quickly wake up from this dream,
The sea may be cruel and also mean.
I swallow water and begin to choke,
Kicking water and trying to float.
Fighting for breath to stay above,
The world I've found and now I love.

Les Worthington

Time Passes

When young, our time seems never ours
Our minds are full of ivory towers
We dream about what we can play
What shall we do to fill the day?

In later years time brings us love
No time to ponder or to prove
Our thoughts are logical or correct
Such was my love, I recollect.

There's never time, or so it seems
To satisfy our many dreams
Life seems so full and yet we ought
To spend more of our life in thought.

For time will last until the end
No matter how our lives we spend
Then let us think of others too
For life's but perfect for the few.

When time is good and life is full
Sometimes alright, sometimes it's cruel
Then take that time, forget the stress
And time will help your life to bless.

J. Thomas Wright

Untitled

The last few weeks I have done nothing at all,
Just sitting there looking at the wall.
Nice and warm by the fireside,
Listening to the wind and rain outside.

For quite a while the rain and cold,
Will sure be felt by young and old.
So anyone calling to see me,
Will find me by the fireside, drinking tea.

What better way to pass the day,
Till the days grow warmer at the end of May.
It would be nice for anyone to call,
Just top have a chat about anything at all.

We all have something we would like to say,
To someone we have not seen for many a day.
Someone who is worse off than yourself,
Will make you feel better, if you've been able to help.

For it's nice to know, if you live by yourself,
There is always someone willing to help.
So if it's possible at all,
Do one good deed a day, however small.

James Woods

Cake

Cakes invited to birthdays, weddings and wakes
Christenings, reunions, anniversary dates
Travels to Madiera, Battenburg, Dundee
By royal appointment to Her Majesty

Cakes historically famous: Alfred burnt his as you know
A king told the peasants to eat some and go
Ever heard of Kipling, Cadbury, Lyon, McVitie
Green, Walker, Waitrose or Sainsbury?
Cakes are round, oblong, square and often in tiers
Because they're repeatedly beaten, sliced with knives
Hidden in cupboards, imprisoned in tins
Squashed, burnt, prodded and thrust into bins

Cakes wears a rich coat of icing decorated with fruit
Grated lemon bow-tie and fresh cream suit
Marzipan waistcoat trimmed with almond and cherry
A burnt sugar cane; and coffee shoes laced with brandy

Cake rises to the occasion, and makes a proverbial speech:
"You can't have me and eat me you know
Yet the more you have, the more you seem to want
Yes, too many cooks did spoil me
That helping hand saved little time as I recall
If I'd known you were coming to bake me
Then I wouldn't be here at all!"

Davina Worton

Burning?

That first kiss, yes 'that' first kiss
What could have possessed me
To want a second and more?
Where was my head then?

Even though I knew
You would never be mine,
Maybe I had something of yours
For a short time.
The gaping hole,
My sense of loss,
Maybe you can tell me
If this is called 'bearing your cross'.

So what of the future?
Run away, try to forget?
Where is my head now?
In bits, with memory banks
Locked away for all eternity?

No, I live in the real world
And you will become someone I never met.
At least until the next time
I am possessed by you.

Cathy Yoxall

My Mate Scooby Do

She came to us at two months old
And would not do as she was told,
Full of black and spikey fur
She often sought my tea to stir.

In often landing from the sofa seat
Her nose would skite upon my meat,
In finding plate with piece of cake
You always found it in her bake.

In bed at night she always snored
And woke me up when she was bored,
Along the balcony she would run
To meet her Jo and have some fun.

When Flo came home to meet with barking
She always knew t'was only larking,
With dainty paws and white tip tail
When young I thought she was a gale.

But then the years they did advance
We had to walk a slower stance,
Then came the day when doggy doctor
Must sadly say "I cannot help her".

At the bottom of my garden there stands a tree
And from there I know each other we see,
With her name and roses red she hears the cuckoo
In the good old summertime, my mate Scooby Do.

Joyce Young

The Grim Reaper

How go you about your business? Old Man Death.
How is it that you choose who shall win, who shall lose
In the gamble to decide on life's last breath?
You and Destiny, brothers in the sands of time,
Running out life's mean allotted spell,
To cancel when you alone think well.
The mortal dwelling lowly in despair
You pass him by so close, yet leave him there.
While bouyant youth loving life with me
You lightly touch, then celebrate with Destiny.
Some day I'll be meeting thee, Death and fellow Destiny
And maybe linger for a spell that I might celebrate as well.

Ron Wood

Prelude

The air is still,
Grey skies look down
On quiet fields
And grimy town
And mist lies waiting
On the hill.
Soon the rain,
Sweet and swift
Will tumble down,
To wash each
Grimy window pane,
To swell the book
And green the grass,
And thirsty earth
Will smile again.

G. Whitehouse

Autobiographical Viper

"Writing in Snake is easy ...
long, complex formulae
and simple words of wisdom
lie in my coiling wake —
and poison-pen letters ...
Prey, walk my way,
passionate embraces
are my consuming interest ...

While the calculating adder
counts his swallowed mice —
legless, in the long grass,
in a satin dream
without a seam,
I shed my scaly skin ...
and the story of my life,
written in Snake,
truthfully, lies."

Eunice Wyles

We Call This Love?

To want to be near someone,
We call this love.
To feel warm inside,
We call this love.
To feel our heart beating fast,
We call this love.
To remember songs and places with longing,
We call this love.
To smile for no reason,
We call this love.
To feel jealous of your past,
We call this love.
To lie awake watching you,
We call this love.
I love you ...

Lynne Wyles

Come Home

How do we measure time?
A span of days spreads into weeks.
Nothing alters.
Not the way I want it to.

Time passes, my heart beat slows, my breath is even.
Yet still my teeth are clenched, my jaw set.
Still I think of you daily.
On awakening, retiring and frequently in between.

My soul is lost, wandering aimlessly without you.
I need you.
And time just goes on.
Another day, another night.
My life, your life.

I love you totally.

All I do is nothing if you are not there to share it.
All I am is empty without your being in my life.
All I feel is numbness if I cannot taste your kisses.
All I want is death if you're never to be mine.

I believe one day, one day we shall be together.
A battle will be fought and not an easy one.
Many tears and mixed emotions and you will be the victor.
I know I cannot win but just to be involved will feed my need for you.

Come home, come home, come home.

Elizabeth Young

Emmanuel

The down curve of the year
Falls through drear November
And strikes primeval chords of fear,
For year's end in December.
Decreasing light declares
No hope of life renewing,
And pagan man despairs
At winter's stark ensuing.
December's breath blows cold with death,
Blows cold with death.

What! Now behold a blazing star
With shepherds blinded by its glare
And kings who travel from afar,

So all mankind may now remember
That hope was born in man's December.

Mary York

Untitled

In broad daylight a candle burns
As Adam reads, and my soul churns.
He squats beside an eerie flame
Adding weight to all our pain.

If one did stop to ask of me
The fragrance of insanity
Then candle wax I'd have to tell
Is madness with a waxy smell.

Linda Zulaica

Dark Nights

Dark Nights,
Are spooky and whooey,
Make my knees go all gooey,

Owls are flying, bats are flapping
Round and Round
What a sound!!!

Their beady eyes look on the ground,
I wish I could see what they've found.
Bats call 'eek'
Owls call 'oooo'
All what's found they leave around
Just look what they've found.
Bats call 'eek'
Owls call 'oooo'
Home's where I'm going to.

Hayley Jane Wright (Age 8)

BIOGRAPHIES OF POETS

ABBAS, WAHEEDA: [b] 6/1/68 Burnley; [p] Abdul & Remmat Remman; [ch] Arsalan & Intanaan; [ed] Nelson & Coine College, Burnley College; [occ] interpreter; [awards] N.N.E.B.; [activ] volunteer ethnic minority groups; "I have written many poems, I am very pleased seeing the first one published, it has given me more encouragement."

ADAM, ROBERT: [b] 4/11/31 Tarland; [p] George & Helen; [ch] June & Charles; [ed] Tarland Jr. Sec.; [occ] rtr'd; [pub writ] two poems - Buchan Heritage magazine, four poems - Aberdeen Press & Journal; "I started writing as an outlet for my thoughts as, despite my headmaster's urgings at school, I declined to further my education because of a bad stammer. I recently had my stammer cured in Kirkaldy"

ADAMS, MARC RICHARD: [b] 24/9/72 Brackley Bucks; "I believe no matter what someone has to say to you, you should listen, no matter who they are. They might say something that will change the way you perceive something or even your whole outlook on life."

ADAMSON, MARY: [b] 24/10/20 Kirkcaldy; [ed] Viewforth Sec., Kirkcaldy College of Technology; [awards] exam passes resulted in being named Print Room Technician at Kirkcaldy College; [activ] volunteer - 'shelter'; [pub writ] poetry in Ntn'l Anthologies, church magazines, local newspapers, verse for greeting cards; "Retirement at 65 presented me with ample time to indulge in my favourite hobby, writing poetry. I would say my senior years have been my most rewarding."

ADDISON, HAZEL L.R.: [b] 8/4/36 Logie Coldstone; [p] Robert & Helen Porter; [ch] George Ian; [ed] Gordon Schools, Huntly.

AITKEN, ROBERT M.: [b] 31/1/12 Glasgow, Scotland; [p] John & Isobel; [ch] John & Peter; [ed] Stockton Sec., Sheffield Univ.; [occ] school master (rtr'd.); [awards] BSc '33, 1st Class Honors Geography, diploma - Education; [pub writ] poems/letters in local newspapers; "A rather cloistered career in teaching, broadened by five years active service in the Army and participation in the politics of a teachers' union."

AITON, RUSSELL: [b] 22/4/64 Lincoln; [p] Judy & Al; [ed] Yarborough High School, Lincoln Tech. College; [activ] fund-raising for local charities/groups; [pub writ] book - "An Open Heart: Verse of Discovery", Minerva Press '95; "My business "An Open Heart" is to date my greatest achievement. My poems are a culmination of my life to date, and reflect the love and wisdom given to me when I needed them most. My greatest joy is being able to share them."

A'LEN, CONSTANCE: [b] 13/4/30 Watford; [p] Beatrice & Sidney Gilbert; [ch] Paul Edward; [ed] Secondary Ed. Cert. - Watford; [occ] social care; [awards] diploma - hairdressing, certificates - care of elderly/disabled; [activ] church member, animal welfare, pottery, drawing; [pub writ] poems and short stories in church magazine; "The greatest pleasure in life is God's creation. Such beauty for us all to enjoy, we really do have a lot to be thankful for."

ALEXANDER, LORNA: [b] 13/2/30 Wartle, Aberdeens; [m] John; [p] John & Annie Connon; [ch] John & Valerie; [ed] Aberdeen College of Education, Invervrie Academy, Daviot Primary; [occ] head teacher (rtr'd); [awards] diploma - Education; [activ] volunteer secretary/treasurer local village hall; [pub writ] poems - Leopard Magazine, local publications and Anchor Books; "Since retiring from being a primary head teacher, I have taken up writing short stories and poems, as well as joining a Ladies' Barbershop chorus."

ALLAN, HELEN N.: [b] 7/3/27 London; [p] Onisiforos & Angeliki; [chl] Tyrone; [ed] St. Angela's Girls School, Palmers Green; [occ] training officer; [awards] Institute of Training & Development Certificate; [activ] parent/governor - Manor Hill Greek School, Barnet; "Being judgemental/selective on visual beauty we tend to miss the most valuable beauty that comes from within."

ALLAN, MARGERY H.: [b] 5/4/20 Essex; [p] Tom & Mable

Harington; [ch] Penelope Jane, Duncan Ferguson; "I have always written for my own pleasure."

ALLEN, CAROLYN.: [b] 18/11/47 Cornwall; [p] Jack & Ruby Lee; [ch] Mark, Matthew & Rachel; [ed] County Primary School; [occ] housewife/homemaker; "I am a housewife and mother. I get much pleasure from running the home and taking care of my family. If expressing my thoughts, in words and verse brings pleasure to others, then that is one of life's bonuses for me."

ALLEN, CATHERINE A.: [b] 30/1/61 Plumstead; [m] David; [p] Dr. and Mrs. Head; [ed] St. Joseph's Convent, Abbeywood; [occ] secretary/personal assistant; [awards] RSA Secretarial Qualifications. Advanced Qualifications - piano/ballet, BFBS; [pub writ] poetry in book "Christian Poets From Southeast England", church magazine; "Appreciate good health and simple pleasures and when something proves an effort, steal yourself — you will always be surprised at what you can do! Thanks to my mother, father and husband for their wisdom, understanding and humour — you always have and always will, inspire me."

ALLEN, MARY: [b] 23/3/30 Worcester; [ch] Kim & Nicola; [pub writ] poems in several anthologies; "I first began to write poems a few years ago for my Grandchildren. This one was written before the arrival of the sixth to try to explain how I could love them all equally."

ALLEN, MURIEL: [b] 18/5/18 Liverpool; [p] Ethel & James Phillips; [ch] Brian James; [ed] Stand Grammar School [occ] rtrd; [mem] Bury Parkinson Disease Soc., church choir member; [pub writ] poem in book "Sparrow's Worth", church magazine; "My poems are my thoughts I have to really experience the situations I write about. They are a true therapy when I am feeling low; they lift my spirit as I write the words. I looked after my husband for 15 yrs. during his long illness when he suffered strokes and Parkinsons Disease. The poems were my true therapy, certainly a gift from God."

ALLEN, REBECCA L.: [b] 8/2/83 Manchester; [p] Keith & Larraine; [ed] Sale Grammar School, Cheshire; [occ] student; [awards] acclaim for historical project - Stretford over the past 50 yrs.; "I have, for as long as I can remember, been interested in writing, poetry and short stories. I enjoy illustrating my work and hope, one day in the future, to be a famous author and illustrator."

ALLISON, DAWN P.: [b] 1/9/74 Kirkcaldy; [ed] Viewforth High, University of Stirling, Telford College; [occ] student; [awards] Sound Control Trophy - drum kit '91, sr. prefect, yr. rep. at university; [mem] Ntn'l Youth Ensembe of Scotland; [activ] played percussion - Stirling Orchestra & Kirkcaldy Orchestral Soc., sunday school teacher, youth ldr.; [pub writ] work in anthologies, magazines, newspapers, exhibitions; "There's a great communication in writing. In a short poem or essay a lot of emotions and sentiments can be expressed. Saying little can mean so much. I see my writing as a means to reach out and educate others on various issues."

ALLISON, GEORGINA: [b] Colchester; [p] Terence & Audrey Coleman; [occ] poet/writer/lifeguard/childminder; "Writing makes everyday a celebration of the heart so give your effervescence a pen and make a start. Let the words flow in torrents onto immaculate paper, if you avoid it now you will have forgotten it later. Extempore your expression true pleasure to impart, writing makes everyday a celebration of the heart."

ALLSOP, VALERIE: [b] 22/2/32 Hounslow; [p] Mary & Percy Court; [ch] Joy & Frances; [occ] nurse tutor (rtrd); [awards] nurse, clinical teacher, community tutor; [mem] church and Royal College of Nursing; [pub writ] poem in book "Outcasts" - 'Thoughts on Bosnia' publ. in US; "I find writing a medium for expressing my views on many issues in society today."

ALLSWORTH, PHILIP: [b] 19/10/61 Trowbridge; [m] Debra; [p] Jack & Eileen; [ch] Jenna & Connie; [ed] Wyvern School; [occ] truck tyre specialist; [activ] fund-raiser CLIC & LEPRA; "I would just like to thank my wife and two children for making me send the poem in and for believing in me."

AMBLER, DAVID J.: [b] 8/10/39 Wallasey; [m] Christiane; [p] Harold & Blanche; [ch] John, Louise, Rachel, Anthony & James; [ed] Wallasey Grammar School; [occ] sales executive; [awards] prizes for creative art in company and local authority exhibitions; [activ] Old Wallaseyans Club, Wallasey/Merseyside; "I have always been interested in creative art, poetry, psychology, and humourous writing. Family responsibilities and participation in sporting activities, mainly football, have to date restricted my creative productions but I hope in the short term to branch out more along these lines, eventually, hopefully moving to Paris to write and paint as my wife is a French lady and we have family ties there."

AMBLER, ELIZABETH A.: [b] 29/12/46 Leeds; [m] Stuart; [p] Nellie & William Pearson; [ch] Paul & Andrew; [edl] Woodhouse Sec. Modern School; [occ] dental surgery assistant; [activ] Leeds Parish Church, District Church Council; "I have always tried to see the good in others. Being slow to anger, gives one time to reflect and not offend. Writing poetry gives me great pleasure and tranquility of mind."

AMENDOLA, KERRY L.: [b] 21/1/65 Worksop; [m] Carlo; [p] John & Susan Dunk; [ch] Daniel & Scott; [ed] Ordsall Hall Comprehensive - Retfore, Notts; [occ] housewife; "I have always enjoyed writing poems and verse, my husband and children have been a great influence to me, but until now they have never been published. I am very pleased."

ANDERSON, MAXWELL: [b] 30/4/63 Dunfermline; [m] Kirsty; [p] John & Beth; [ch] Adam; [ed] Inverkeithing High School; "Understanding and figuring people out can be difficult but seems far easier expressing it with pen and paper, and with inspiration always at hand from my wife Kirsty and son Adam."

ANDERSON, PAULINE: [b] 1922 Cambridge; [p] Hilda & William Saddington; [ch] John, Paul & David; [ed] Central Higher Grade School for Girls; [mem] U3A in Cambridge (University of the Third Age); [activ] volunteer - local hospital; [occ] rtrd.; [pub writ] poems/articles in church magazines; "You only get out of life what you put into it — also try to see the funny side of life, expecially when you're feeling low."

ANDREWS, PAUL: [b] 17/12/64 Birmingham; [p] Valerie & Colin; [ed] Wath Comprehensive School, Sheffield Polytechnic, Sheffield University; [occ] teacher/maths; [awards] BTEC - mechanical engineering, Maths Degree, PGCE; [activ] church choir, assisted with Sheffield Marathon, Abbeyday JuJitsu Club, fund-raising for charities and schools; "Financial gain, however nice, could never compensate for the love and support of family and friends. It is nice to have this opportunity to thank them in black and white."

ANSTY, JOHN R.: [b] 17/4/55 Guildford; [m] Carol [p] Peggy & Terrance; [ch] Katherine & Gareth; [ed] Sheerwater C.S.S., - Surrey, Peoples College - Nottingham; [occ] electrical engineer; [activ] served in Blues & Royals, Household Cavalry Regiment Brigade of Guards, fund-raising local charities; [pub writ] several short stories and poems; "A poem will never show its age. It will pass through the years blissfully unaware of the restrictions of time, and will be as fresh as new always. Poetry captures time for us all."

ANTCLIFF, CHRISTOPHER J.: [b] 1/10/61 Nottingham; [p] John & Joan; [ed] Open University; [occ] student; [awards] BA Hon. (Arts) '86-'94; [activ] Committee of League of Friends of Cedar Medical Rehab. Unit; [pub writ] poems in poetry digest, 'Poetry Now', 'Poetry Nottingham', Keyworth Baptist magazine; "I am severly disabled which caused the need to write initially, a therapy, then it grew in scope and understanding, a sense of fulfillment."

ANTHONY, KAREN: [b] 4/2/64 Sunderland; [p] Florence & Andre; [ed] Laygate Infants & Jrs., Mortimer Comp.; [occ] student; [awards] Certs. - painting/ decorating, City & Guilds - CAD-CAM, Robotics,

C.N.C.; [activ] body building, camping, cycling, rock climbing, drawing, reading, writing poetry; [pub writ] 3 poems pub. various books - Arrival Press; "I am a pretty easy going person, and get on well with people. I have just started to dabble in writing children' stories, but I love writing peoty and all my poems, apart from the funny ones, come from the heart. I hope my poetry, if a success, reaches other people's hearts too."

ARMSTRONG, NANCY: [b] Belfast; [m] Bob; [p] Tom & Elizabeth Crawford; [ch] Alistair; [ed] Skegoniel & Saintfield Academy, Trinity College of Music; [occ] home executive; [awards] certificate - Trinity College; [activ] hospice care support; "I dedicate this poem to my two grandchildren, Neil and Colin."

ASHFORD, JEAN: [b] 13/8/39 Leeds, York; [p] Jane & Ernest Pearson; [ch] Susan, Matthew & Emma; [ed] County Primary Comprehensive; [awards] S.E.N. Nurse, Loudon Academy Music and Dramitic Art; "There is a story in every person, and a poem not far behind. Life treats us all in different ways; it is our experiences that make us individuals and interesting."

ASHWELL, JOANNA: [b] 20/4/72 Barnard Castle; [mem] Poetry Book Society; [pub writ] (Arrival Press) '94 Anthology N.E., Book of Caring, Emotional Ties (Poetry Now Anth.), Write Around Poetry Anth., "Breathless" Poetry Now Regional Anthologies for North East '92, '93 & '95, British Poetry Review '95 Anth.; "Poetry is a window to my inner-most thoughts and feelings. I use it to express knowledge, messages and to share the mystery and discoveries of life."

ASHWORTH, MARGARET E.: [b] 22/1/51 Bebington; [m] Ronald [p] Veronica & Alfred; [ch] Gary & Angela; [ed] St. John R.C. School; [occ] housewife; [activ] Cancer Research, Age Concearn; "I like to put my observations of life down on paper and also try to see life through the eyes of others, also I enjoy writing childrens' stories and poems."

ATHERTON, JEAN: [b] 10/9/43 Sheffield; [p] Frances & John Hayes; [ch] Stephen Michael; [ed] Secondary Modern, Colley Sec. Modern School; [occ] credit controller; [awards] K.F.A. Certificate - Keep Fit; [activ] teacher 'keep fit' classes; "I enjoy writing my poetry and find it easier to put my feeling on paper rather than speak them. I am known at work for my little verses and am called upon to write one whenever a special occasion arises."

ATHERTON, ROSEMARY: [b] 6/1/47 Lydney, Glos.; [p] George & Audry Thomas [ch] Angela; [ed] Chepstow Larkfield Grammar School; [occ] children's nursery supervisor; [awards] diploma - children's writing; [activ] counsel bereaved/abused children; [pub writ] poems in anthologies and local newspaper; "Writing poetry is a welcome respite from my hectic lifestyle. I enjoy penning childrens verses and use them as a gentle introduction to the world of poetry and as a foundation for their future enjoyment of literature."

ATKIN, POLLY: [b] 30/7/80 Nottingham; [p] Richard & Irene; [ed] Grosvenor School, Nottingham High School for Girls; [occ] student; [awards] 1st prize essay competition - school; [activ] drama group; [pub writ] stories and poems in school magazine, report in local theatre club magazine; "I love writing, music, drama and art. I don't think poety is about stringing words together just to sound pretty, it's about expressing an emotion, or a point of view. It's about life, and dealing with it, and also a certian amount of escapism. Expressing myself through creativity helps me through life until a time when I no longer need the help."

ATKINSON, ALASTAIR B.: [b] 11/11/81 Haslingden; [p] Patricia & Alan; [ch] Cameron Alan; [ed] Queen Elizabeth's Grammar School - Blackburn; [occ] student; [awards] '94 - First Year Form Prize, Commendations for English/History '94; [mem] Mensa [activ] Methodist Church; "My attitude to life at the moment is to experience as much as possible. At shool I am a member of the choir, swimming team, rugby team (captain), school community action team, house quize team, basketball, football & athletics teams. Hobbies include Scouts and playing the organ."

AYRES, CAROL: [b] 23/1/41 Swansea, S.Wales; [p] Flossie & William Thomas; [ch] Josephine Rebecca; [ed] Greggs Commercial

Private College, Swansea; [occ] artist/poet; [awards] 3 'O' levels - English, Maths, Geography, RSA English, L.C.C. English, diploma - typewriting medical secretary; [mem] Church of England; [activ] volunteer; [pub writ] 'Night and Day', 'Long Remembered Day', 'An Easter Poem', 'Echoes from an Inkwell', 'The Avenue Dry Cleaner'; "I write what I feel — it releases me — the written word. I especially like to write how I love Jesus and share these poems with others."

BAILEY, ADAM S.: [b] 19/6/72 London; [ed] Bexley-Erith Technical High School for Boys; [occ] student; "Experience is life's greatest teacher so I enjoy writing about things my heart and mind have learned."

BAILEY, CASSARNDA: [b] 12/4/44 Kniveton, Derbyshire; [p] Charles & Mary Wood; [ch] Joy & James; [ed] Ashby Girls School, North Lindsey College; [occ] nursery manager; [mem] Methodist Church - class leader and pastoral visitor; "Being a farmer's daughter I have always worked close to nature. As the seasons change, so the beauty of the earth changes. When I write I feel so full of love for my Creator and His creation."

BAILEY, EDNA: [b] 2/10/13 Doncaster; [p] Edward & Florence Tyler; [ch] Alan & Roger; [ed] Doncaster High School, City of Leeds College; [occ] teacher (rtrd.); [awards] Teaching cert., French diploma, Art qual., poetry/prose awards, Cert. of Honour (Professional Assc.); [activ] Guiding, Red Cross, National Exec. (Primary education), Art Socs., Yorks Countrywomen's Assoc., church; [pub writ] poetry in "Yorks Countrywoman", church magazines, book - "Poems For Friends"; "A happy childhood and marriage, with an involvement with music and painting have served my writing well. A long life has furnished countless memories to write about!"

BAILEY, MARGUERITA: [b] 11/5/36 Charsfield, Suffolk; [ed] Nottingham University; [occ] teacher (rtrd.); [awards] Certificate of Education, 8 G.C.S.E.'s, 1 A level Art/Design; [activ] choir, art and music; "The poem 'Realisation' is my first attempt. As a mature 'A' level art student in 1993 I used it as a basis for various aspects of course work. Music, art and literature are my interests."

BAILEY, WALLACE: [b] 1/10/38 Kent; [m] June [p] Reginald & Dorothy; [ch] Nigel, Amanda & Belinda; [ed] Morehall County Sec. School, Folkestone Technical College; [occ] builder; [pub writ] poetry in church magazine; "I enjoy my work, my wife and I do enjoy sequence dancing and theatre."

BAINE, MARK: [b] 31/3/68 Belfast; [p] Samuel & Marie; [ed] Queen's University - Belfast, Heriot-Watt University - Edinburgh/ Orkney; [occ] marine scientist; [awards] Degree - Zoology, MSc - Marine Resource Development & Protection Degree, MSE Profession Diver; [activ] charities; [pub writ] poetry in school magazines, modern anthologies, and scientific literature; "Poetry is a wonderful way to release one's emotions. It is the next best thing to a 'heart-to-heart' with my girlfriend, Penny, family or friends. There is such pleasure in the delivery of a good poem, such a joy to be creative."

BAKER, EDWARD J.: [b] 11/7/31 Eastbourne; [p] Bessie & Tom; [ch] Sharon; [ed] St. Mary's Boys, Stasden Mixed; [occ] warehouseman; [mem] P.O. Union; "I am retired, I like gardening and keeping busy. I also enjoy words and writing."

BAKER, KAY: [b] 9/11/61 Near Bath; [pub writ] several poems in anthologies, England and USA.

BARBER, VICTORIA J.: [b] 2/8/79 Radcliffe; [p] Susan Barber & Keith Mills; [ed] Radcliffe County Primary & Junior School, Radcliffe High School; [occ] student; [awards] flute - graded 3+; [activ] volunteer local youth group, deputy head girl (school); "I enjoy writing my poems and find it is a good way to express my feelings. I hope to continue with my writing throughout college and university."

BARKER, MYRTLE: [b] 2/4/33 Takeley, Essex; [m] Brian; [p] Sidney & Daisy Mary Carr; [ch] Linda, Angela & Diana; [ed] Mole Hill Green C of E, Thaxted C of E.

BARLOW, ELAINE: [b] 8/1/51 Oldham; [p] Leslie & Florence Hopwood; [ch] Dale Anne; [ed] South Chadderton Sec. Modern; [occ] home help; [activ] animal welfare, charity work; "I have always liked poetry and wrote several poems, though I have never sent any to a contest before. Going on a sensory course inspired me to write this poem."

BARNARD, J.F.: [b] 18/4/42 Scotland; [p] Alexander & Margaret; [ch] Lee, Karen & Jenny; [ed] Christchurch Secondary Modern School; [occ] housewife; "No matter which type of background you come from, if you really want to achieve something you can do it, all you need is faith in yourself."

BARNES, PAULINE: [b] 20/13/48 Prittlewell, Essex; [ch] Kriston & Jaron; [ed] Eastwood High School for Girls; [activ] volunteer - ambulance service, church activities; "I love the countryside and its natural beauty and simplicity. Greedy, selfish people are unhappy, miserable people and don't understand why they are not liked or loved. My thoughts are manifested through my poems: To be at peace with oneself is to be at peace with the world."

BARRETT, WILMA: [b] 5/10/44 Peebles; [p] Rober & Jessie Brown; [occ] homehelp; [activ] volunteer, fund-raiser, talking tapes for the blind, community work; [pub writ] "Poets" '92, "Scottish Poets" '94 & '95, letters in magazines and local newspapers; "I get great joy from helping children and old people. I like peace and harmony in my life and I love a challenge. Writing poetry I believe, for me, is a God given gift."

BARROW, SUSAN: [b] 13/8/48 Bath; [m] Mike; [p] Bill & Barbara Jones; [ch] Matthew & Amanda; [ed] City of Bath Girls Grammar School; "I have always enjoyed writing poetry to express my feelings. This is the first poem I have ever entered for a competition/publishing probably because it's very special to me."

BARTER, ELAINE C.: [b] 15/3/48 Scarborough; [p] Mr. & Mrs. J.W. Coulthard; [ch] Peter James & Paul Andrew; [occ] hairdresser; [awards] 'O' level - Eng. & Art, Hairdressing General Certificate Lds/ Gents, C+ Guilds, Advanced Hairdressing; [activ] YMCA - Judo/Yoga; "I am writing a book which will be entitled 'World of Poems', as I write I feel about the world and its environment."

BARTON, JEAN: [b] Eastbourne; [m] John; [p] Jane & Walter Harris; [ch] Alison & Malcolm; [ed] Eastbourne High School, Eastbourne Art College; [activ] art group co-ordinator, piano, watercolourist; [pub writ] magazines/local paper; "By expressing our true feelings in the written word, we can communicate and understand one another when looking for the harmony of life."

BARWOOD, CLIFF: [b] 29/9/34 Kent; [m] Barbara [p] William & Madeline; [ch] Nicholas, Mark & Paul; [ed] Rye Sec. Modern; [activ] R.S.P.B., Sussex Ornithological Soc., Rye Haroubr Nature Reserve; [pub writ] articles in Sussex Ornithological magazine and report; "Life long interest in natural history, ornithology, conservation, my poetry reflects all aspects of nature on and around Romney Marsh."

BATCHELOR, MARGARET: [b] 14/4/47 Folkstone; [p] Alex & Maude Rose; [ch] Kim; [awards] cert. child care; [activ] community work - young offenders, children; [pub writ] poems in newspapers; "I spent most of my life as a young person in Fegans Children's Homes, which was a great upbringing. They taught me everything and I am grateful to them. My hobbies include writing poetry, reading and walking the dogs. I love every day and take one day at a time."

BAYNARD, LILIAN: [b] 29/7/21 London; [p] Edith & Solomon; [ed] St. Georges in East Central School; [occ] manufacturer/retailer (rtrd.); [mem] education committee; [pub writ] poems & short stories in local newspapers; "I was guest artist on BBC 1 Walter Love "Day By Day". Reading my own poems, also American papers. Spoke to school in Michigan."

BEARD, RICHARD: [b] 18/9/41 UK; [p] Bernard & Lilian Beard; [ch] Andrea & Martin; [ed] Alleynes Grammar School, Uitoxeter Staffs, Bucks College of Higher Education, High Wycombe; [occ] sawmiller; [awards] BSc. Timber Technology; [mem] Muscians Union; [pub writ]

'Fude For Thought' - book of music & song; "I took the degree at the age of 39 which changed my attitude. It taught me to teach myself, I learned to read music and play the piano at the age of 48, and have published music myself. My book contains short, catchy, easy to learn songs about family and caring for others — things that matter to everybody."

BEATTIE, FRANK: [b] 11/7/52 Kilmarnock; [p] Frank & Margaret; [ch] Fraser & Grant; [ed] James Hamilton High, Kilmarnock Academy; [occ] jounalist; [activ] volunteer - Ayrshire Railway Preservation Group; [pub writ] Yang & Grogg, local history publications; "Look at the world with your own eyes. Listen with you own ears. Think things through for yourself."

BECK, EDWARD: [b] 19/11/35 Liverpool; [m] Jeanette, [p] William John & Jane Elizabeth; [ch] Jane Elizabeth & Rachel Alison; [occ] rtrd.; [mem] Royal British Legion; "I have never written poetry before and who knows if I will again. But having retired prematurely due to anxiety, I needed to reflect on the previous 12 months. What better way than verse? The result 'Hindsight'."

BEEKE, LANCE: [b] Maidstone; [ch] Tiphanie & Jemma; [ed] Orphanage Kent, Maidstone College of Art; [occ] fine artist; [awards] exhibition of paintings locally and abroad.

BELL, JENNIFER: [b] 5/6/46 Purley, Surrey; [m] Stuart; [p] Alfred & Doris Lock; [ch] Ian & Clive; [ed] Roke County Sec.; [occ] photo assistant; "I hope I bring pleasure to people through my poems, and even more so with the songs I write as well; my son has used a couple with his band."

BELL, JOSEPH: [b] 19/6/10 Maryport; [p] Robert & Martha Ann; [ch] Elsie Lillian & Irene Ann; [ed] Workington Sec.; [occ] civil service (rtrd.); [awards] two piano contest wins - Carlisle & Workington, Cumbria; [mem] life member Sight Savers; [activ] National Trust, Lifeboat (Governor), Friends of the Lake District, church.

BELL, SHEILA M.: [b] Southampton; [p] Jack & Kathleen Locke; [ch] Micheal O'Keefe; [ed] Convent boarding schools Southampton, Bath, Nova Scotia, art college Philadelphia; [occ] writer/illustrator; [mem] chess club, family history societies; [pub writ] letters/articles for magazines; "My interests lie in child and animal welfare, 'green' issues, art, cycling, chess, education and family history."

BENNET, NELL: [b] 4/5/13 London; [p] Jessie & Henry Hall; [ch] Jean & Brian; [occ] typist (rtrd.); [awards] gold medal - ballroom dance; [activ] Keep Fit, Mother's Union, Civil Service, choir, reading, [mem] Church of England; [pub writ] poem in Civil Service magazine "Ode to a Civil Servant"; "Since moving to Suffolk from London, I have made friends and enjoy a very nice social life trying to help others and keep well. I also belong to Heart Beat."

BENNETT, NORAH M.: [b] 30/12/29 Cirencester; [p] Helen & Walter Gealer; [ch] Timothy, Michael & Michelle; [ed] Watermoor C of E School; [occ] housewife/hairdresser; [mem] Pres. Cirencester Operatic Soc., [activ] church; [pub writ] poems published - 'To The Forces In The Gulf', 'A Mother', & 'The Beauty Treatment'; "I love writing poetry and seeing the final result. I find it very fulfilling and relaxing knowing the written word will last long after me."

BENTON, KATHLEEN: [pen] Toni Francis; [b] 19/5/36 Trimdon; [p] Sep & Mary Hannant; [ch] Carol, Susan, Bernadette & Toni; [ed] St. Williams - Trimdon, C.F.E. - Stafford; [occ] Marie Curie nurse; [awards] Marie Curie nursing award, diploma - typing; [activl] nursing, volunteer - cancer aid; [pub writ] poems in local magazines, 'Now' publications; "Working with poorly or terminally ill patients helps me to appreciate life. I find it easier to put my feelings and ideas down on paper."

BERWICK, THOMAS W.: [b] 30/6/18 Lochhead Farm; [p] Melville & Marjorie; [ch] Peter; [ed] Coaltown-of-Wemyss, St. Monans - Balcurvie; [occ] rtrd.; [pub writ] poems in local newspapers; "I wish to be at peace with the rest of the world, and be allowed to continue my close love and friendship with the countryside into which I was born, and to which I am grateful."

BEST, DENNIS: [b] 16/3/46 Tadcaster; [p] Dennis & Dorothy; [ch] Karen Denise & Colleen Michelle; [ed] Parlington Sec., Modern school - Aberford; [occ] scaffolder; [awards] Editor's Choice Award - National Library of Poetry (USA) for 'Bad Weather'; [activ] writing poetry for Micklefield Historical Soc., and Micklefield Against Development; [pub writ] 14 poems published, one book out (A Bit About Life); "I have just finished my first play which will be performed next year and have written 14 songs to accompany the play. I have also just writren my first short story adapted from one of my poems."

BICKERSTAFFE, ELIZABETH: [b] 28/11/60 Lytham St. Annes; [m] Kim; [p] Carles & Nita Sturrock; [ch] James; [ed] Queen Mary School - Lytham, Bristol University; [occ] housewife; [awards] B.A. Honours in Modern Languages, Diploma - Bilingual Secretaries, CAM Cert. in Communication Studies, Best Marketing Student - '88, ROYDS McCann Advertising Award '88, Nat'l Magazine Company Award - marketing '88; [mem] Soroptimist Int'l Club, P.I.P. (Preschool Integration Prgm.) - disabled children; [pub writ] publicity material; "I would love to indulge in writing poetry again! For now my creative energy is channelled into caring for my delightful disabled son."

BIDWELL, JOAN A.: [b] 28/3/09 Devon; [p] Rev. F.W. & Zoë; [ed] Christopher's Private School, Art School - Lowestoft; [occ] display artist (rtrd.); [awards] prizes for window displays; [activ] RSPB, Whitstable Improvement Society; [pub writ] 'Supper Being Ended' in "100 Contemporary Christian Poets", poetry in church publications; "By its very nature my professional work of window dressing was transient: it is nice to know my poetry my last a little longer."

BIRD, GEORGE A.: [b] 18/9/30 Edinburgh; [p] George & Mary; [ch] Pamela & Margaret; [ed] Boroughmuir High School; [occ] civil servant (rtrd.) [awards] Scottish Higher Learning Cert.; [pub writ] poem in "Poetry Review"; "I've written countless poem and short stories, mostly at 2 a.m. I write the entire poem in my head before committing to paper. Afflicted by the melancholy and sentimentality of the Scot, I try to infuse a certain mysticism into my poetry or prose; that, combined with a simplicity and directness of style."

BIRD, RACHEL: [b]19/9/80 Bury St. Edwards; [p] Jon & Helen; [ed] County Upper School, Bury St. Edwards; [occ] student; "I'm a committed Christian, so God is the centre of my life and through writing my poetry I want to bring glory to Him."

BISHOP, EVELYN: [b] 8/5/44 Wigan; [m] Edward; [p] Lily & William Aspinall; [ch] Brian Edward; [ed] Giplow Sec. School, Springfield NR Wigan; [occ] housewife; [pub writ] poems published - "Love Is", "Home Sweet Home"; "I write poems for friends, for various occasions; humourous, births, sad poems. I find writing poetry very restful to my inner self."

BISHOP, HELEN M.: [b] 11/2/39 Blackheath; [p] Arthur Henry & Jennie Helena; [ed] Roan Grammar School for Girls - Greenwich; [activ] writing poetry for pleasure, day classes.

BISHOP, SHARON J.: [b] 16/8/72 Belfast; [p] Mervyn & Winifred; [ed] Wellington College - Belfast, University of Ulster - Jordanstown; [occ] student; [activ] volunteer - Project Phoenix Trust (overseas study tours for the disabled); "Writing is the main channel through which my honest emotions flow in their true intensity. My poetry is the key to understanding me — a personal diary."

BLACK, JOHN S.: [b] 28/10/50 Kelso; [p] William & Anne; [ch] Sarah-Jane & Lee-Anne; [ed] Kelso High; [occ] concrete technician; [awards] 'B' class degree - sales, City & Guilds Electrical; [activ] sports especially rugby; "I find that writing poems for friends etc., enjoyable and rewarding. I have never before tried to have any published although I have written for many years."

BLADES, M.J.: [b] 26/10/60 Surrey; [p] Mr. & Mrs. Watson; [ed] Guildford County School; [occ] housewife; [awards] 10 'O' levels, 3 'A' levels, Duke of Edinburgh Bronze level award; [mem] church choir - Birkenhead; [pub writ] school magazine, editor for "The Oasis" - magazine for people with mental health problems; "I am but a happy cog in the great wheel of life — if I have influenced just one person to happiness, then my heart is complete."

BLOMFIELD, MARGARET: [b] 22/1/36 Ipswich; [p] Phyllis; [ch] David & Steven; [ed] Copleston Sec. Modern for Girls; [occ] cleaner; [awards] winner talent competition; [mem] Woman's Institute, Royal British Legion; Hadleigh Amateur Dramatics; "When I was a child and through my teenage years I was a very shy girl, and dearly wanted to do something important, and as the years rolled by my shyness gradually disappeared. I only discovered my talent nine months ago and decided to do something about it."

BLOOR, CLAIRE L.: [b] 21/11/81 B.M.H. Rinteln, W. Germany; [p] Allyson & Gordon; [ed] Southlands High School - Chorley; [occ] student; [awards] school - Achiever of the Term (Summer '94), Gr. 1 Music Theory, St. Johns 1 Cross Award; [mem] R.S.P.C.A., hockey and netball teams; "I would like to become a veteranarian but to achieve this I will have to keep working hard at school which I intend to do."

BOARD, BARBARA A.: [b] 22/8/42 Taunton; [m] Ray; [p] Fred & Ann; [ch] Mark & Glenn; [ed] Banwell Primary, Churchill Sec. Modern; [awards] Pitman's Diploma - shorthand/typing, Silver Rose Bowl Award - lyrics; [mem] church and local social club; [pub writ] 3 poems in various anthologies; "Born into a farming family on the Blackdown Hills I learned to love nature. I enjoy walking, the theatre and dancing but the biggest thrill has been to see my poems in print."

BOAST, JOYCE O.: [b] 8/10/19 London; [p] Norah & Arthur Walters; [ch] Graham & Horward; [ed] Lynton House School - Maidenhead; [occ] rtrd.; [mem] local music society; [activ] piano, gardening, crosswords, visiting hospital patients; "By becoming aware of other people's troubles, I have learned to thank God for my blessings."

BOCKING, JOHN: [b] Essex; [m] Lyn; [p] Rober & Selena; [ch] Julie, Tony, Sean, Lee, David, Scott & Laura; [occ] factory mgr.; [awards] Quality certificate, Fire Marshall Certificate, vrts. sport trophies; [activ] show producing, song writing, poetry, sports team mngmnt; [pub writ] magazine reports - sports coverage, company portfolio; "I have always been interested in poetry but have never entered before. I would like to write in celebration cards, I feel very despondent at many cards on sale regarding the quality of the verses. I excell in specific topic poetry and feelings/expression."

BOLAN, MICHAEL J.: [b] 13/1/34 Birmingham; [p] George & Evelyn; [ch] Stephen; [ed] monastic - The White Fathers; [occ] painter/ writer; [activ] resident painter - Lichfield Festival; [pub writ] "The Book Of Jonah" '94; "Sir John Betjeman wrote that he "much enjoyed" my poems. Simplicity makes the best poetry."

BOND, JOAN: [b] 19/5/49 Grantham; [p] Fred & Doris; [ch] Glen & Haley; [ed] St. Hugh's Sec. Modern, N.I.H. - Swansea, Clarendon College North; [occ] cook; [awards] N.I.H. diploma, City & Guilds Cookery; [pub writ] poem in - As Seen On T.V.; "I believe in not having any front — what you see is what you get — and always have a good sense of humour."

BOONE, CAROLE A.: [b] 26/6/55 Plymouth; [m] Howard; [p] John & Edna; [ch] Marie Anne; [ed] Haverhill Sec. Modern School; [occ] housewife; [awards] City & Guilds - hairdressing; [activ] painting/ sketching; "I have found writing poetry expresses my feelings and thoughts, also it is very therapeutic for an introvert such as myself."

BOULTON, SYDNEY "HUGO JOHN": [b] 24/9/38 Hebburn; [m] Mauree Joyce; [p] Robert & Mary; [ch] Mandy, Robert & Sandra Jayne; [ed] Comprehensive - Senghenydd, Caerphilly Mid Glam; [occ] miner (rtrd.); [awards] trophies for sports activities (rugby); "I like racing pigeons and writing poetry, I also like solitude, peace and quiet and compiling crosswords."

BOURNE, ROGER: [b] 21/6/45 Bath; [m] Mary; [p] Syndey & Mary; [ch] Maureen; [ed] Bath Technical College; [occ] music publisher/ interior design; [pub writl] poems, short stories, in Poetry Now, Mast Publications, local newspapers; "Poetry is the gateway to self-knowledge.

Self-knowledge is the key to spiritual awakening and enlightenment ultimately leading to peace, harmony and understanding."

BOWYER-SMITH, NANCY: [b] 7/3/18 Egham, [p] Rosa & Raymond; [ch] Jill & Diane; [ed] Kingston Day Commercial College; [occ] housewife; [awards] Blaikley Salver, C.F.W.I.; [mem] W. Institute, Old Cornwall Soc.; [pub writ] various poems in anthologies and magazines, Poetry Now, People, Natures Power, selfl-published for charities - 'Poems & Potato Peelings', 'Mixed Musings', 'Star Stuff' 'Giggly Rhymes for Giggly Kids' & 'Animal Facts & Fancies'; "I began writing comic and serious verse when my children left for college life. I have been much encouraged by Dr. Charles Causley of local and national fame."

BRADLEY, GLADYS: [b] 10/1/17 Haworth; [p] John & Margaret Alice; [ed] Haworth Council School; [occ] rtrd.; [mem] Haworth - O.A.P. Welfare, Methodist Church, Parish Church Luncheon Club, community/church work; [pub writ] poem in "Poetic Sixty's" and church magazines; "Not very talkative but I enjoy writing long letters. I have written many poems, both serious and funny, which I read at our church meetings and sometimes other churches but I've never tried to publish them until now."

BRADSHAW, DIANE: [b] 3/7/41 Thurlby; [p] John & Vera Sandall; [ch] Sarah & Richard, Ian & Stephanie; [ed] Bourne Grammar School; [occ] housewife; [activ] ex-pres. W.S.P.C.L local group; [pub writ] poem in "Poetry in Motion" '94; "I was widowed at the age of 40 and remarried 5 years ago. I'm new to writing verse with some success last year in 1994. I'm very motivated to write more poems and short stories."

BRADSHAW, RAYMOND A.: [b] 2/7/48 Leicester; [p] Raymond & Laura; [ch] Laura-Jane; [ed] Rushey Mead Sec. Modern, Charles Keene College; [awards] 'O' levels, various City & Guilds Engineering certs.; [mem] assoc. member Royal British Legion; "I've written songs - one actually made it to a recording on Decca. I've been runner-up in local poetry competions and had some movement with television scripts and school plays. I write from the heart and the whole piece 'comes in one go'. I have to get it written before it fades."

BRAHMS, SONYA: [b] 4/2/28 London; [p] Leon & Carlotta; [ed] Bromley Theatre School, Park School, Portsch's Sec. College; [occ] rtrd.; [awards] Matric. RSA Sec. Diploma, 1st stage Ballet and Pianoforte, 3 gifts of my verse/floral arrangements accepted by Royal Family; [pub writ] 5 poems in various anthologies, articles in local newspapers; "Most of my work transpires from a sudden inspiration and is accompanied by a storyline and sketch or floral arrangement. My ambition is to have a book of my poems published and write my family history. Though my writings are not prolific I have varied interests and am a keen observer."

BRAMLEY, EDWARD: [b] 28/9/23 Ashington, Northumberland; [p] Edward & Georgina; [ch] Martin & Alan; [occ] reg. staff nurse (rtrd.); "The main occupations of my working life have been coalmining and as a staff nurse in psychiatric nursing. I've experienced most things in life except death — I'm leaving that till the last! A born wanderer, my poem "A Walk At Dawn" was inspired by an actual experience of my own."

BRAMMA, BETTY: [b] 21/3/30 Worcester; [m] Donald; [p] JOhn & Louisa Banks; [ch] Susan; [ed] Worcester Grammar School for Girls; [occ] housewife; [awards] Cambridge School Certificate; [activ] Gold Award blood donor; [pub writ] local newspapers, "British Poetry Review" 1993; "I enjoy gardening, creating a haven for birds, butterflies frogs, etc. I get inspiration from nature's beauty and wonder and hate the devastation that man has caused."

BRANSON, ROSEMARY: [b]14/9/29; [p] Anelia Richelieu & John Affleck; [ed] Richard Hind School for Girls - Stockton-on-Tees; [occ] rtrd.; [pub writ] various poetry magazines, collections and competitions; "Why do we do it? Become a poet, write words so apt and wise, reveal our thoughts and all our dreams, to other people's eyes. Disclose the inner most angles of the mind, and the arrogant folly of Mankind, and live with life as it should be, in balance with Nature's harmony. But who out there would understand the writings of a poet's hand, except of course for you and me, the odd one here and there maybe, and as for me, the unknown poet, what will be left of me to show it. Scraps of paper, reams of rhyme? Ashes and memories on the winds of time!"

BRAY, ROSEMARY: [b] 8/9/38 Cornwall, [p] Beatrice & Ben Madron; [ch] Anthony, Sharon, Elizabeth & Catherine; [occ] housewife; [awards] diplomas/medals for ballet; [pub writ] poems in various anthologies; "I enjoy my life and love writing poetry. My ambition is to have more of my work published in the future."

BREEN, MICHAEL J.: [b] 26/8/49 Down Patrick; [m] Irene; [p] Michael & Elizabeth; [ch] Deirdra, Conor & Michael; [ed] St. Patricks High, University College, Dublin; [awards] Batchelor of Arts.

BRENNAN, MARY: [b] 11/7/50 Ipswich; [m] T.G. Brennan; [p] Grace & Derek Hunt; [ch] Jessica, Jennifer, Michael & Catherine; [ed] Sacred Heart - Swaffham, Norfolk; [occ] housewife; [awards] S.R.N. - 1971; [mem] Parish Council 1980-83; "Writing for me has been therapeutic, but has also given me a great sense of fulfillment. I hope it will also give to my children just a little insight and understanding of life."

BRIDGEMAN, JOHN H.: [b] 16/7/15 Bourne Fen; [p] William & Rose; [ch] Noel & Shirley; [ed] Bourne Fen Elem., Bourne Lincolnshire; [occ] farm foreman (rtrd.); [awards] herdsman awards, gardening awards; [activ] Mayor of Bourne 1952-53, served as councillor 9 yrs.,local preaching; [mem] Age Concern Gardening Club; [pub writ] poems in local newspaper; "I left school at the age of 14 yrs. I have always been interested in poety, but did not start writing until my wife died. It is one of God's gifts which was hidden in me."

BRIERLEY, MARGARET A.: [b] 3/2/09 Preston; [p] Luke & Cathering Robinson; [ch] Christopher & John; [ed] Gottam R.C. School - Nr Preston, Lancs.; [occ] housewife; [activ] nursing - general and private; [pub writ] 'One Mysterious Night' in Poems Of The Northwest.

BRIERLEY, MARILYN: [b] 15/7/45 Nelson; [m] Fred; [p] Jane & Albert Williams; [ch] Amanda-Jane; [ed] Littleborough High School; [activ] Int'l Fellowship of Healing; [pub writ] one poem in anthology plus poems in local newspapers; "I feel I have inherited my ability for writing poety from my mother who had a book published. I find beauty and inspiration in the world around us and in it's people, also the love of my family."

BRIERLEY, RORY: [occ] Lawyer/antiquarian/bookseller/writer; [pub writ] "The Kingdom Beyond The Eyes", "Raw Food Compendium", (pen - Mark Everley), 2 books in prep. - "Writing Poetry For Oneself" & "Walking As The Basis Of All Endurance"; "I encountered poetry early in life through my father and Shakespeare and classic poets. After translating Book VII of Virgil's 'Aenid' from the Latin and later on becoming a reluctant lawyer, I learned to appreciate words. I wrote much verse but not necessarily good poems, I learned to know the difference. I learned much from The Rationale of Verse" by Edgar Allan Poe, a most illuminating essay. I could readily compose mere verses but a poem would come out of the blue and I would write it down like a scribe. A satisfying, but rare happening."

BRIERS, KATHLEEN I.: [b] 26/1/24 Kegworth, Leics.; [m] John; [p] Thomas & Mildred Grimley; [ch] Rachel Anne; [ed] Loughborough High School for Girls; [occ] housewife; [awards] Oxford Cert. - Loughborough, 2 prizes for verse; [activ] treasurer Church of England Oaks-In-Charnwood (Leics.), Mother's Union Brand (C of E), church choir; [pub writ] poems in church magazine; "I have a strong Christian faith and if my attempt at poetry gives pleasure to anyone then I'm happy. I like to express my love of nature, my sense of humour, anger, happiness, thoughts and feelings through my poems. I am inconsistent with my writing and tend to write as the mood takes me."

BROCKETT, MICHEAL M.: [b] 5/10/46 Blackwood; [m] Janice; [ch] Andrew & Joannah; [ed] The Lewis School - Pengam, The Cardiff College of Education; [occ] teacher; [awards] BSc. Math; [mem] Islwyn Art Group; [activ] semi-professional artist (would like time to develop further); "With age one realizes that the best things in life are the simple

things — good health, good friends, a happy family. I thank God for giving me all these and the ability to express myself creatively."

BROCKETT, ROBERT: [b] 23/10/20 Lancashire; [m] Betty King; [p] Hilda & Robert; [ch] Jeanette & Jennifer; [ed] Kilmarnock Academy (Scotland), School of Mines (South Wales); [pub writ] short stories and poems in nat'l magazines and local newspapers; "I am a locally known artist, a painter of minings scenes — particularly underground scenes. Painting and poetry express emotions and feelings."

BROOKES, BRENDA: [b] 8/4/43 Wigan; [m] John [p] John & Annie Dawber; [ch] Shelley Anne & Simon Thomas; [ed] Wigan Girls' High School; [occ] district nursing sister; [awards] reg. general nurse, District Nursing Cert., Community Practice Teacher Cert.; "Good communication is vital in all areas of my life. By my poems I feel that I can more clearly express my deepest beliefs and feelings about life."

BROOKS, DOREEN: [b] 16/6/39 Letham, Fife; [p] Alexander & Catherine Lumsden; [ch] David & Rosalind; [ed] Bell Baxter High School - Cupar, Fife; "This is the first time that I have ever had the 'courage' to submit my work for possible publication. I am absolutely thrilled to have got this far."

BROWN, CAREN TANIA: [b] 14/9/67 Douglas, Isle of Man; [p] Joyce & Dave; [ch] Cara & Leana; [ed] Dhoon Primary, Iom and Ramsey Grammar School; [awards]6 'O' levels & 2 'A' levels; [activ] enjoy the company of my children, travelling all over the island with them. My hobbies include walking, reading & writing; [pub writ] 3 poems published; "Having been born Manx has been by inspiration for writing. I live a fairly quiet life here and am very thrilled that someone somewhere may appreciate my work. Thank-you."

BROWN, D.W.: [b]29/6/29 Plymouth; [p] William & Doris; [ed] Plymouth Art College; [occ] company director (rtrd.); [awards] engineering and some success in painting competitions; "I am a keen painter, though amateur. I am interested in the relationship between portrayal in painting with that in poetic wording."

BROWN, DOREEN M.: [b] 12/11/31 Scarborough; [p] Alice & Sydney; [ed] Falsgrave Girls School; [occ] rtrd.; [pub writ] poem - "Love" - British Poetry Review; "Late in life the inspiration came to me to express my feelings, thoughts, imagination and awareness of life in poetry and short stories, giving me pleasure and delight and the same I hope to those who read it."

BROWN, ELIZABETH: [b] 15/3/27 Acton; [ed] Acton Primary School, Sudbury High School for Girls; [occ] medical receptionist (rtrd.); [awards] 2nd prize for adult poetry '83; [mem] Acton Church choir, Acton's Women's Institute; [activ] press correspondent for over 55 club and W.I.; [pub writ] poems in village/church magazinesm, poetry magazines, also poem in "Wish You Were Here"; "As I am severely disabled with C.M.T. (a form of muscular dystrophy) writing in any form helps! Poems are my children."

BROWN, IVY C.: [b] 5/2/17 Hackney; [p] Madeline & Charles Wicks; [ch] Eric Douglas; [ed] Ongar Residential School (Council Orphanage); [occ] housewife (rtrd.); [awards] Scholarship - Domestic Science/Housewifery; "During 1940-44 I was part of the London Meal Service Team in Forest Hill, in later years I had a variety of jobs. They were challenging but I always found a humourous side to various situations and took pleasure in putting it to rhyme."

BROWN, JAMES S.: [b] 10/5/39 Kirkcaldy; [p] John & Isabella; [ch] James & Stephen; [ed] Kirkcaldy High School Sec.; [awards] Cert. of Merit - electronics course '75; [mem] photography and snooker clubs; [pub writ] several poems in local newspaper; "I find that writing poetry helps to keep me sane and also provides some amusement for my friends and relatives."

BROWN, KATHARINE C.: [b] 31/7/62 Kent; [m] Lawrence; [p] John & Joyce Webb; [ed] Hope High School - Manchester; [occ] optical advisor; "I find that being a keen observer of nature has taught me much about life, expecially that there must be a Creator. The best teacher though is the Bible, as it tells the future of Mankind."

BROWN, ROY F.: [b] 3/3/31 Wokingham, Berks.; [p] Reginald & Lillian; [ch] Clifford; [awards] Editor's Choice for 1975 Regency Press; [pub writ] poems in "I'm Rich" - Poet's Corner Anchor Books, 'Songs of Praise', 'What Is A Man', 'Ours Is A Nice House' Treasurey of Modern Poets 1974. 'A Call To Arms', Spitfire Charioteer', 'St. Crispin's Day'; "Writing, but not poetry, was the only subject which I was any good at and which I enjoyed at school. I was hopeless at anything else."

BROWINING, SUE: [b] 22/10/62 Wolverhampton; [p] Patricia & Ernest Randles; [ch] Nathan & Charlotte Porter; [ed] Aberdare College of Further Education, Cardiff Insitute of Higher Education; [occ] student; [awards] B'Tec Ntn'l Diploma; [activ] volunteer - social work; "I find writing poetry very satisfying. I enjoy expressing myself with rhyme and ryhthm. Most of my poetry is very personal and subjective."

BRUNTON, NEIL E.: [b] 21/10/65 Nottingham; [m] Tracy [p] Martin & Gillian; [ch] Nicholas & Clare; [ed] Christ The King Comprehensive School, Arnold, Nottingham; [occ] police officer; [awards] Certificate of Administrative Management; [mem] Inst. of Admin. Management and Facilities Mngmnt; "I believe that the key to success is having a positive approach to life. By adopting this approach potential achievers will undoubtedly achieve, regardless of class, attainments or influence. I enjoy putting my own feelings and experiences into writing, and a llittle humour is never too far away."

BUCKLEY, ELLA: [b] 5/4/21 Shaw; [p] Elbert & Edith Pears; [ch] Doreen & Jacqueline; [occ] housewife; [activ] R.N.L.A., R.B.L., R.A.F.A. - St. James Church, Holy Trinity Church; "My task now is taking care of my dear husband, a victim of osteoarthritis and stroke. We hope to rejoin our friends again someday."

BUNGARD, ROSALIE: [b] 23/6/33 London; [p] Mabel & Cyril; [ed] Tollington High for Girls, Rolle College; [occ] teacher (rtrd.); [awards] Cert. of Education, Advanced Diploma Linguistics & R.A.; [mem] Elder of U.R.C., N.T., R.N.L.I., & R.S.P.B.; [activ] volunteer - G.D.B.A., Pestalozzi, Traidcraft; [pub writ] church magazine; "Retirement proved to be a new, challenging and exciting experience. Becoming involved with voluntary oganisations keeps me busy enabling me to meet many interesting people. Living in such beautiful surroundings has inspired me to express my thoughst and emotions in verse."

BURGESS, GLADYS A.: [b] 13/5/35 Kingsbury; [p] Clara & Frederick Dixey; [ch] Sylvetee, Coral & Susannah; [ed] Brodesbury & Kilburn High School, Northwood Bible College; [occ] artist; [pub writ] Editor's Choice, Spring Poets, Our National Heritage (Regency Press), "It's Lilac Time" (Regency Press), Poetry Now, Talking Volumes, Life Through Poetry; "Our school was evacuated during war years, when the pupils returned they had compiled their little books of favourite poems. Although the clocks all registered 12:40 when the bomb dropped, we managed to continue our interest in poetry."

BURGESS, MARGARET: [b] 30/12/43 Woodford Green, Essex; [p] Marjorie & John Borkett; [ch] Stephen & David; [ed] McEntee Technical School; [occ] housewife/receptionist (part-time); [mem] local Women's Institute; [pub writ] poems in various anthologies and local newspaper; "I love life and want to live it to the fullest extent of my abilities. Any talent that we have is a bonus and should be enjoyed as such. Poetry is to me a way of sharing my thoughts and feelings with others."

BURKITT, EVELYN: [b] 22/9/41 Epworth; [p] Fred & Freda Farr; [ch] Caroline, Sonia, Beverley & Andrea; [ed] Church of England Epworth, Ashby Girls School; [occ] caretaker (rtrd.) [awards] R.S.A. - bookkeeping, G.S.E. - accounts; [activ] Befrienders Disabled Group; [pub writ] "Child's Eyes", "My Mum", & "Yesterdays"; "I like writing, also helping people. I believe you should not do ill to others as it could return to you. I also love my garden and cats, and I have lots of good friends which everyone needs."

BURLEY, MICHAEL: [b] 13/10/67 [p] Norma Frances; [occ] photographer; "I write poetry in memory of all the things I've forgotten and all those things that I choose to forget."

BURNSIDE, MARK: [b] 23/7/77 Chelmsford; [p] Michael & Gloria; [ed] Moulsham High School, Harlow College; [occ] student; "Poetry is a good way of expressing my feelings, I am inspired by Jim Morrison of "The Doors", who once said, 'Poetry is so eternal'."

BURTON, NORA: [b] 12/11/38 Chorley [m] William Melvin; [p] Arthur & Ann Nicholson; [ch] Ivan & Marie; [ed] Sacred Heart School, Chorley; [awards] 3rd prize - Norwich Carnival '78; [pub writ] two recipes - Bolton Eve. News Christmas Competition; "my Happiness is my home, grandchildren and husband. In my Daddy's words, 'You can only try to do your best, and your best is always good', you only get out of life what you put in so I always try to keep happy."

BUSHBY, JOYCE: [b] 12/3/34 Beckenham, Kent; [m] Victor; [p] Eric & Gladys Squirrell; [ed] Balgowan Sec. Modern, Bromley County Technical School; [occ] rtrd.; [activ] Romney, Hythe & Dymchurch Light Railway Assoc., & R.N.L.I.; [pub writ] poetry in ntn'l magazine plus various anthologies; "Living facing the sea on the edge of Romney Marsh, I draw great inspiration from this area for my poetry."

BUTLER, BRENDA: [b] 11/10/44 Hanworth; [p] George & Elizabeth Herrieven; [ch] Gary & Angela; [ed] Leiston Middle School; [occ] supervisor; [awards] qualified healer; [activ] meditation, volunteer - community work with elderly; [pub writ] poetry (2), book (1); "I have worked with elderly people (mentally handicapped) for 33 years in homes and private. I am an investigator into the paranormal of all types. I get a lot of satisfaction through writing."

BUTLER, RENEE: [b] 2/6/22 Preston; [p] Harold & Florence Wilkinson; [ch] Nancy & Patricia; [ed] Preston Liverpool, I.O.W. & Bournemouth; [occ] housewife; [activ] sunday school teacher - G.F.S., ballroom dance teacher; [pub writ] "Reflections" - church magazine; "My poem reflects my life — I was guilty of taking — not giving."

BUTTLE, MARY: [b] 3/9/38 Birmingham; [ch] Terrence, Susan & Deborah; [ed] Beardall St. Hucknall, Edale Rd. Secondary, Nottingham, Clarendon College; [occ] student; [awards] B'Tec 1st Diploma - performing arts Clarendon College; "I only realised I could write poetry at the age of 55 after working 20 years on school meals. Being made redundant I went full time to Clarendon College."

CAFFREY, ROSALEEN: [b] 11/4/20 Irish Republic; [p] Mr. & Mrs. Carter; [ch] Stephanie, Olive, Val, Robert, Margo, Maurice (dcd.) & Eddie; [ed] St. Patrick's School - Drogheda Co. Louth, I.R.; [awards] 2nd place - Ntn'l Handwriting Competition 1933; [pub writ] several poems - "The Keepsake", "The Gardener", "The Leprechaun"; "My daughters Stephanie and Olive are established writers and Eddie is a radio presenter on LMFM Radio in Drogheda. Writing is in the family."

CALVERT, ALAN J.: [b] 1/5/48 Leeds; [p] Joseph & Doris [ch] Helen, Elizabeth, Laura, & Daniel; [ed] Foxwood High School, Kitson College; [occ] foreman fitter (rtrd.); [awards] G.C.E. 'O' level engineering science; City & Guild - mechanics part 1,2 & 3, I.M.I. & I.R.T.E.; "After 30 career years which a stroke cut short, I can now enjoy family friends and life through new eyes."

CAMPBELL-LYONS, PATRICIA: [b] 11/2/18 Pangbourne, Beaks; [ed] Convent Boarding School, Limegrove Art School; [occ] performing arts instr.; [mem] Royal Soc. of Literature, Soc. of Authors, Scientific/ Technical Group; [activ] singer, dancer, drama teacher, pianist; [pub writ] 12 pantomimes, four pieces in 'The Lady' Magazine, also published in 'Woman's Own', 'She', 'Evergreen', the 'Sunday Times' & 'The London Anthology'; "Have written a three act play (drama) and am just completing my first novel, an Edwardian fantasy about children 'The Brighton Train'. I have a large portfolio of poetry should any publisher be interested."

CAREY, LORRAINE: [b] 11/5/73 Coventry; [p] John & Roisin; [ed] C.C.S. Carndonagh & N.W. Institute of Further & Higher Education; [occ] childminder; [awards] B Tec, Ntn'l Diploma in Travel & Tourism, 'Tourist Guide' cert.; [activ] Greenpeace supporter; "Poetry is a wonderful outlet for my thoughts and expressions. Poetry is beauty personified, each one of us has unique qualities, developing these enriches our own lives and the lives of those around us."

CARLIN, ANTHONY V.: [b] 11/2/39 Coatbridge; [p] John & May; [ed] St. Augustine's RC, Smyllum Park School, St. Ninnians House of Falkland Fife; [occ] window cleaner; "I love wildlife and the countryside where I visit as often as possible and have written many poems about what I see and hear, and hope to get published someday."

CAROE, TIM: [b] 14/3/74 Aylesbury; [p] John & Linda; [ed] Eastbourne College, Pembroke College; [occ] medical student; [awards] MA - Medical Sciences; [activ] Capt. Cambridge University Rugby Fives Club, member comedy review team; [pub writ] poem in East Sussex Anthology - Arrival Press; "I enjoy being creative, writing poetry, music, short stories and drama, while juggling and unicycling help to provide balance. I also spend a lot of time performing — both on and off the stage."

CARPENTER, JANE: [b] 15/12/66 Caerphilly; [p] Joan; [ed] Heolddu Comprehensive; [active] volunteer work; "I have been writing poetry since I was nine years old. I write about my feelings and personal tragedies."

CARROLL, ANNE: [b] Wigan; [m] Gerald; [ch] Treena; [ed] Alfred Turner, Manchester; [occ] housewife; [awards] Computer Diploma, S.S.V. medals from Whitbreads; [activ] volunteer - Wigan Hospice (reception); [pub writ] "The Wedding" - Northern Voices, "Haigm Snow" - Talking Volumes, "Heaven" - Christian Poets from the North West; "Most of my work is life experiences, but not all. I don't sit down and write, it just happens, amazing."

CARSON, VANCE A.: [b] 20/12/70 Glasgow; [ch] Kane; [ed] Marr College, Advanced Technology College, Cardonald College; [occ] student; [pub writ] various poems in ntn'l magazines & anthologies; "I know that I exist in a thought, but here's a point that can't be missed: Whether or not that thought is my own, if only in thought, 'I exist'."

CARTER, SARA J.: [b] 8/1/71 Leeds; [p] Michael & Barbara; [ed] Cliff High School, Threlkfeld Primary, Keswick Sec. School, University of Dundee Med. School; [occ] med. student; [awards] Duke of Edinburgh Awards, school prizes; "My interest in poetry was founded by my Grandmother (who also has a poem published in this book.)"

CAXTON, JOAN E.: [b] 19/7/28 London; [p] George & Leah Wilson; [ch] Martin; [ed] Lillie Road School, Fulham Central School; "I am married to a Pole and spent holidays in Poland. In 1993 my husband was recalled out of retirement and sent to Poland. We spent 13 months there and we visited Warsaw often."

CHADWICK, MAGDALENE: [b] Yorkshire; [p] Mr. & Mrs. Whitley; [ch] Christine; [ed] Teacher's Training College, Goldhall School of Speed & Drama; [occ] head teacher/owner private school; [mem] Society of Teachers of Speech & Drama; [activ] leader - Rainbow Guides; "I love music, playing the piano, flute and violin. I teach different instruments for my student, I like Classical Ballet which I also teach."

CHAKRAVARTY, ANITA: [b] 27/12/72 India; [p] Manas Chakravarty; Juthika & Arun Chatterjee; [ed] St. Xavier's, Bokaro, Lady Shree Ram College, India; [occ] student/playground leader; [awards] B.A. (Honours), L.O.C.N. - Caring For Under 8's; [activ] volunteer - social services (UK), National Service Scheme (India); [pub writ] poems in 'The Statesman' - newspaper (India); "Yesterday is a bygone memory, tomorrow an uncertain vision, today is life — the time to love, help, give and smile. Have faith in your mind and body temple and remember every torch is lit to light other candles."

CHANNON, TONY: [b] 11/9/25 Malton, Yorkshire; [m] Elizabeth; [p] Guy & Kathleen; [ch] Jonathon & Gillian; [ed] Oundle School, 1939-45 Aberdeen University, 1948-52 Birmingham University; [occ] plant pathologist (rtrd.); [awards] BSc (Aberdeen) - Pure Science, PhD (Birmingham) - plant pathology; [activ] Barrow & District Soc. for the Blind - newstape reader; [pub writ] book - "Random Reflections" Eliton Books; "Was in the R.A.F. from 1944 - 1947. My interests include

hillwalking, bagpiping, woodturning and carving, and writing poetry."

CHARLTON, LYNNE: [b] 2/6/50 Ilkeston; [m] David; [ed] Michael House School, Derbyshire; [occ] housewife; [awards] certificate for an Eistedford; [mem] Assemblies of God Chapel, and two fan clubs; [activ] volunteer; [pub writ] 1 poem in magazine and 5 in books; "[I write poetry] because when I'm dead it will be a part of me left behind and maybe help others one day. I have learnt that just to smile brings happiness and makes life worthwhile."

CHESTERS, CATHERINE: [b] 22/8/31 Birkenhead; [p] Mary & John Wray; [ch] Ann, Elaine & Julie; [ed] Conway St. Secondary School, Birkenhead; [occ] cleaner (rtrd.); [activ] animal welfare; "I started writing poetry as a hobby for the amusement of my family and friends. My inspiration came from a Doberman named 'Zak' and I would write ideas on beer mats while cleaning at a social club."

CHOTANI-JI, DHARMENDRA P.: [b] 25/10/28 Br. India; [p] Prabhu Datt & Daropdi Chotani; [ed] BA (Hons.) Hindi, Polictical Sci., & Eng. (India), Dip.Ed. (Santi-Niketan) Vishwa-Bharti (India), Dip.Ed. (Queens Univ.) UK, [occ] Intn'l Eng. teacher; [awards] known as 'Indian Douglas Bader' since 1964 (UK), won awards in disabled sports 1960 (India), U.N. Year of the Disabled 1981, Educational Inst. of Scotland; [activ] editor: Bimonthly Manuv Sundesh (Humanist Herald), inititiator: 'Inglishinto' - based upon phonetic English to promote a world link-language in place of 'Esperanto'; [pub writ] 'National Overhauling' (Eng.), National & International Problems & Solutions, A Blue Print for New United Nations and Design 1999; "I call myself an Afrümasian teacher and philospher. Born in British India; became a victim of partition holocaust 1947 when shifted to Simla in Himalayas to experiment with my (Gandhian) Global-Village schools. Lost both legs in a tractor accident in 1954, travelled and taught (despite artificial legs) in sub-continent & overseas during 1946-82. Still keep on working for One-World Vedantic views inspired by Hindu-Humanism."

CHRYSTAL, C. A.: [b] 5/10/32 Huntly; [p] Ernest & Mary; [ch] Thomas, William & Joshua; [ed] Gordon Secondary; [occ] housewife; [mem] church; "I love writing and have done ever since I was a child. My ambition is to get some of my work published. My three sons are an inspiration in this."

CHURCH, KEITH: [b] 12/9/76 Dumbarton; [p] Lennie & Joy; [ed] Hermitage Academy, Helensburgh.

CLAGUE, JAMES R.: [b] 26/11/41 Douglas; [p] Clague-Callow; [ch] Joanne, Judith, Jeanette, Jillian & Jonathan; [ed] Laxey Primary, St. Ninians; [occ] general/local authority; [mem] Local Authority, R.N.L.I. (chairman), Mens Fellowship (chairman); [activ] young farmers clubs, music, writing; [pub writ] local newspapers; "Over a number of years I have written poems for weddings, speeches, concerts etc., often humorous. I often say to my audience to put a smile on somebody's face is worth a fortune but costs nothing."

CLARK, GEORGE: [b] 16/4/45 Cowley, Middlesex; [m] Rae Stevens; [p] William & Elizabeth; [ch] Victoria; [ed] Manor County Rolslip Open University; [occ] packaging designer; [awards] over 15 British Design Awards, World Star 1985; [activ] football referee; "I enjoy helping others, in writing poems and short stories a recent change of direction for me, I've found a new buzz to life."

CLARK, JOAN E.: [b] 21/8/24 Liverpool; [p] Frank & Olive Leeson; [ch] David, Paul, Lucinda & Joanne; [ed] convent school; [occ] State Registered nurse/midwife/health visitor (rtrd.); [pub writ] a novel - "The Brooch" - Minerva Press; "It is never too late to start writing. After a very busy life, I hope I can reflect some of my experience in my work."

CLARK, JUNE: [b] 3/6/36 Middleton; [m] Jack; [p] Herbert & Grace Kenny; [ch] Valerie, Karen, Lynn, Robert, Anthony & Caroline; [occ] housewife; [pub writ] poem in church magazine; "I have spent most of my adult life caring for my husband and children. I find this reflects in my poems quite a lot."

CLARKE, ALLAN S.: [b] 17/3/62 Helensburgh; [m] Sheila; [p] Joe

& Helen; [ch] Scott; [ed] Cardross Primary, Hermitage Academy, Dumbarton Academy; [occ] shop manager; [awards] Cardross Tennis Club - Doubles Champion '88, '90 & '92; [pub writ] magazines; "I enjoy getting my thoughs down on paper. When they leave an impression with others, that is a bonus indeed."

CLARKE, KATHLEEN: [b] 25/9/68 Belfast; [p] Kathleen & Thomas; [ch] Matthew, Aisling, Aaron & Ross; [ed] St. Mary's - Kircubbin, St. Columba's, Portaferry, Kircubbin F.E. College; [occ] civil servant; [awards] diploma - secretarial studies; [mem] N.I.C.S.S.A., Peninsula Writers Group; [pub writ] 'Finality' - Norther Ireland Poets, Arrival Press; "If you are a writer and you are not writing, then you will never gain personal happiness."

CLARKE, PAM: [b] October 1932 London; [m] Roy; [p] Kay & Jimmy Mason; [ch] Belinda & Virginia; [ed] various schools, St.James College, London; [occ] freelance tutor/examiner/adjudicator; [awards] Oxford Matriculation, Teaching Licentiateships - London Academy Music/Dramatic Art (Hons.), Guldhall School of Music, London; [mem] council mem. Intn'l Soc. of Teacher of Speech/Drama; [pub writ] "To Toto" - L.A.M.D.A. Examinations Anthology Vol. 11; "Recitations by my father and grandmother during childhood travels were exciting and inspirational. Today the challenge of writing combats stress — but I have to wait for the Muse to hit me. Then it's 2 days on black coffee in the Garden Room — a wonderful way to slim!"

CLARKE, PETER J.: [b] 18/6/50 Halesowen; [p] Sydney & Irene; [ch] Timothy, Matthew, Simon & Daniel; "I am disabled with Spina Bifeda. I am a watercolour artist, musician and write extensive poetry on varying subjects and topics."

CLARKE, WILFRED: [b] 2/9/40 South Wales; [p] Mabel & Wilfred; [ch] Maria & John; [ed] Bedwas Comprehensive, S. Wales; [occ] computer operator; [activ] music, reading & playing snooker; "My personal motto is 'Forgive me for the things I do wrong — love me for the things I do right.' Happiness is a contented mind, brought about in the knowledge that there is always someone worse off than yourself."

CLARK-SMITH, KATE A.: [b] 28/11/79 Tittensor, Stafford; [p] Stephen & Susan; [ch] Jamie; [ed] Kingsmead High, Staffordshire; [occ] student; [awards] distinction awards - Elecution for Spoken English; [pub writ] poetry published; "I enjoy poetry, reading and Karate. I usually write poetry about the things in life that I feel strongly towards, whether it be caring for someone, or homelessness. I feel writing poetry releases my inner feelings and thoughts which helps give me a good outlook toward life."

CLATWORTHY, RICHARD A.: [b] 27/11/63 Merthyr Tydfil; [p] Allan & Margaret; [occ] teacher; [awards] BA Honours Eng. Lit., Cert. in Education, Cambridge Cert. - English as a Foreign Language; [pub writ] poems published in University of Glamorgan magazine 'Head'; "I have a strong belief in the power of the English language to break down barriers."

CLAY, MERLE G.: [b] 26/3/38 Purley, [p] Margaret & Len Holmwood; [ed] Dorking Gr. School, Wimbeldon School of Art, U of London, Goldsmiths; [occ] art teacher (rtrd.); [awards] Intermediate Diploma in Design, Natn'l Diploma of Design, Art Teacher's Diploma; [pub writ] school magazines, B.T.F. magazines, poetry anthologies; "My father taught me the love of the written word, this and painting help me to colour my writing."

CLAYTON, ROBIN: [b] 1/6/52 Leeds; [m] Alexandra; [p] Stafford & Jean; [ch] Jonathon & Matthew; [ed] Cow Close School, Matthew Murray School, Park Lane College, Leeds; [occ] civil servant; [mem] National Trust; [activ] volunteer, hospital broadcasting - radio; [pub writ] selected poetry, self-published anthology; "I wish to encourage the triumph of individual will over the dark forces of evil through the power of the pen."

CLINE, SALLY: [b] 5/1/38 London; [p] A.T. Cline & A. Harns; [ch] Marmoset Carelyn; [ed] Durham University, Lancaster University; [occ] writer/lecturer; [awards] BA Honours Eng./Philosophy, M

Lit.Social Sciences, BBC prize - short story '93, Eastern Art Fiction Bursary '94, shortlisted Eastern Arts Fiction Bursary 1989 & 1993; [pub writ] Through Andre Deutsch Pub. - "Reflecting Men At Twice Their Natural Size" ('87), "Just Desserts: Women and Food" ('90), "Women Celibacy & Passion" ('93).

COE, JENNY: [b] 11/6/56 Hereford; [p] Mary & Charles Bundy; [ch] Stacey, Christopher & Sarah; [ed] John Kyrie High School, Ross-On-Wye; [occ] confectionary asst.; [mem] DAG - Dean Archaeological Group; "I consider myself an active, observant person who is inspired by life's twisted ways and surprises. My philosphy is to 'captivate' all life's energies however trivial they may seem. As a true romantic, I consider myself a student of life."

COLE, DAVID M.: [b] 28/12/80 Hull; [p] Sue & Mike; [ed] Trumacar County Primary, Heysham, Lancaster Royal Grammar School; [occ] student; [awards] winner poetry writing - Morecambe Musical Festival '89, three 2nd places for poetry reciting, North West finalist in school's challenge quiz; [mem] school athletic club & quiz team; [pub writ] poem in "Write & Shine" regional anthology '95; "I am the eldest of four children and enjoy a wide range of physical, mental and literature associated activities. I find I respond well when set challenges."

COLE, LOUISE: [b] 18/7/72 Oldham; [p] Leslie & Elizabeth; [ed] Breeze Hill School, Manchester Metropolitan University; [occ] library asst.; [awards] Library Studies Degree - BA Honours; [pub writ] four poems in anthologies '90-'94; "I started writing during 'A' levels and it has become a big part of my life. I rarely edit anything and have written several hundred poems since 1988."

COLEMAN, JOHN: [b] 29/7/51 Dumbarton; [m] Georgina; [p] John & Sarah; [ch] John, Claire & Linsey; [ed] St. Patrick's High, Dumbarton; [occ] manager; [awards] diploma - industrial management; "I am very keen to preserve the heritage of Dumbarton in verse."

COLLETT, JULIE A.: [b] 21/8/59 West Midlands; [p] Don & Brenda Pritchard; [ch] Charlotte & Adam; [ed] Albright High School, Oldbury; [occ] housewife; [mem] local drama group; [pub writ] 3 poems - "Living Poets" '77, 1 poem - Autumn Anthology '78; "I have written poetry from the age of nine. As the years roll by, my thoughts reflect in my poetry and give me tranquil peace from today's stressful world."

COLLINGE, G.G.: [b] 29/6/28 Birmingham; [p] George & Lena; [ch] Martin, Simon & Justin; [ed] R.H.S. Edinburgh, Chippenham Grammar School, Bristol University; [occ] schoolmaster (rtrd.); [awards] BSc - mathematics, Certificate A - education; [pub writ] local literary society magazine; "My wife Joan and I travel widely and we both play a lot of golf. I came to the writing I do as an antidote to mathematics and as a record of our travels."

COLLINGS, JUDITH: [b] 31/12/40 Norwich; [m] Brian; [p] May & Louis; [ch] Giovanna, Niall & Lisa; [ed] Blyth Grammar School, Norwich, Ipswich College, Norwell College; [occ] health service mngr; [awards] City & Guilds NEBBSS; [activ] volunteer - Age Concern; "The most important role that I believe in is helping others where possible and keeping the family unit together."

COLLINGWOOD, M.G.: [b] 15/4/25 Bury, Lancashire; [p] Alis & George Bestall; [ch] Rosan (dcd.), Jim, Sylvia, & Barry; [occ] housewife; [awards] secretarial certification; [activ] Friend of the R.A.F. Assc. - volunteer entertainer; [pub writ] poem in church magazine; "I count my blessings daily, thank God for the many gifts he has bestowed upon me. Love my neighbour as myself. Try to stimulate my brain as much as possible. Thankfully, I am a born optimist!"

COLLINS, PAUL: [b] 7/2/66 Epsom, Surrey; [p] Jack & Jenny; [ed] St. Andrew's RC School - Surrey, Southbank University - London; [occ] building surveryor; [awards] 4th Year PT. BSc (Honours), Building Surveying; [mem] Wildlife Aid; [activ] mountain biking; "I have written 200 poems to date; people and the planet are my inspiration. I can't paint or play an instrument so I write poetry, it keeps me sane and hopefully stirs thought in others. In a lifetime so much can be left unsaid and precious feelings are so often lost forever — my words may live on."

COLLINS, WILLIAM: [b] 13/8/24 St. Marylebone; [ch] Geoffrey, Philip & Stephen; [occ] rtrd.; "I have written essays on various subjects including creation and parthenogenesis. These are unpublished. I have attempted to draft poetry but could not decide whether it is literate or simply absolute nonsense."

CONISBEE, PETER: [b] 5/4/69 London; [p] Audrey & Tony; [occ] police officer; [awards] 1 commendation for Bravery & Dedication to Duty; [mem] Q.P.R. Supporters Club; "Six years ago, with the death of my grandfather, I found difficulty in verbalising my emotions. I began to write my feelings, and now whenever in a stressful or emotional situation, I find poetry becomes an ease."

CONNELL, NORMAN G.: [b] 24/12/19 Glasgow; [p] John & Kate; [ch] David; [ed] Huntly Gordon Schools; [occ] chemist (rtrd.); [awards] Diploma M.P.S., M.R.H.S., F.S.A. (Scotland), L.C.S.M., F.R.G.S., M.B. Ch. A.; [activ] town councillor, v.p. Ex-Serviceman's Club, v.p. and pres. Huntly Cricket Club, Parents School Representative, Chairman Alexander Scott's Eventide Home; [pub writ] snippets in local paper "Bogies (N) iders"; "Father was poetic; wrote short songs; own education at school set in beautiful surroundings (very effective). Huntly itself is full of many others equally gifted."

CONSTANCE, DENIS: [b] 26/5/32 Padstow; [m] Mavis; [p] Sheraard & Vera; [ch] Kevin, Karen, Karl, Wayne, Sean, Kathy, Seamus; [ed] Padstow Boys School; [occ] construction site agent; [awards] apprenticed carpenter/joiner.

CONVEY, COLUM: [b] 21/1/36 Co Down. N.I.; [ch] John, Stephen, Lorraine, Katrina, Michael, Colleen; [occ] rtrd.; [activ] golf, art, reading, walking; "My poetry comes from my heart. I have written other pieces unpublished."

COOK, SUE M.: [b] 2/4/49 Berkshire; [p] Ivy & Earnest Wakefield; [ch] Deanne & Andrew; [ed] Carters School - Berkshire; [occ] insurance clerk; [pub writ] school magazine; "I try to give out good thoughts and feelings to people, as life has taught me what you give out you get back. Poetry helps me to express those thoughts and feelings into words."

COOKE, ELSIE V.: [b] 17/7/29 East Ruston; [p] Ethel & Charles Pratt; [ch] Sally; [ed] East Ruston Primary, Stalham High; [occ] housewife; "I started to write poetry whilst recovering from a fall fifteen years ago. I have a knowledge of bygone days. I like to write topics from the aged to the young, also about the countryside."

COOKE, JOHN: [b] 14/2/26 Bolton, Lanc.; [p] Margaret & Edward [ch] Gary, Lynn & Sara; [occ] sales director; [pub writ] British Parachute Assoc. magazine - 'Sport Parachutist'; "I took up Sport Parachuting at the age of 40 and was later founder member of Parachutists Over Phorty. I received a request for membership from the wife of one of the sport's leading personalities (a surprise for his 40th birthday). On receipt of this he apparently went quite 'potty' - hence the poem. I have written over 100 items of verse, mainly humorous and mostly to do with the antics of people. I have had several read on local radio and many more published in Sport Parachutist."

COOKE, VERONICA: [b] 17/7/64 London; [m] Peter; [p] Doug & Freda Sims; [ch] Madelaine; [occ] housing manager; [awards] Social Administration & History Degree.

COONEY, ANN: [b] 13/4/45 Charshalton SY; [p] Violet & Stanley; [ch] Nicholas, Maria, Matthew, Stelphen, Sharon, Shaun, Aron; [ed] Elmwood Sec. Modern School; [occ] school helper; [mem] New Life Christian Centre; [activ] swimming; "I have always yearned for a country life, but have spent my life bringing up a large family (7 children) and haven't had much time for anything else. I love to take my youngest child and my three labradors to my little caravan on a farm in deepest Sussex where I get the inspiration for my poems and ponder awhile."

COONEY, JANET: [b] 9/6/81 Newcastle; [p] George & Donna; [ed] St. Malachy's High School, Castwellan Co. Down; [occ] student; [pub writ] verse in ntn'l and local books/magazines; "It (writing) has taught me how to communicate with people, how to become more self-confident. I get a great feeling from seeing my work in print."

COOPER, CHARLES: [b] 8/12/25 Twickenham; [p] Arthur & Elfrieda; [ed] Beckenham Art College; [occ] artist writer; [awards] National Diploma - Design; [activ] Hampstead Filmmakers - chairman; [pub writ] stories, poetry & illustrated articles for magazines, newspapers in England, Ireland & Spain; "Although I have written for and performed in films, radio and T.V., I find that poetry encapsulates the world in a microcosm. Like the Chinese poets, I like to paint in addition to writing."

COOPER, DAISY: [b] Dent; [m] Roy; [p] George & Elizabeth Moffat; [ch] Irene, George, Bryan & Alan; [ed] Sedbergh Primary; [occ] housewife; [pub writ] 'Tale of the Pig'; "My first published poem was 'Tale of the Pig', since then I've had four more published. I am now an eighty-two year old widow with arthritis, and my spare time is writing poetry which keeps my mind active and is something I enjoy."

COOPER, FRANK: [b] 23/9/32 Derbyshire; [p] George & Minnie; [ch] Gail & Brett; [ed] Derby College of Arts & Crafts, Derbyshire College; [occ] shop manager (rtrd.) [activ] computers/electronics; [pub writ] local newspapers; "To me life without poetry, books, and good music would be no life. Poetry is emotion on paper, books are the windows of the world, and music calms the inner man."

CORBETT, IRENE G.: [b] 14/1/32 Birmingham; [m] Les; [p] Irene & William Haywood; [ch] Paul, Anthony, Amanda & Leslie; [ed] Sec. Modern, Day Continuation, Bakery School; [occ] confectioner (rtrd.); [awards] silver medal - bakery, R.S.A. - English; [activ] village church P.C.C., secretary - village W.I., Children's Soc.; [pub writ] poetry in W.I. reports, church magazine; "Poetry and verse is a way of expression, of life, nature, and the way one looks at happenings, of the world, today and yesterday."

CORNER, SARA M.: [b] 28/3/76 Preston; [p] Roger & Denise; [ed] Preston College, De Montfort University, Bedford; [occ] student; [awards] A.S.A. Teacher's Prelim, Award of Merit, Advanced Resuscitation Award, C.S.L.A., Netball Teachers Award; [activl] C.S.L.A. - teaching netball, lifeguard; [pub writ] Poem-Alone in an anthology & local newspaper work; "I have been writing poetry for two years and enjoy expressing my thoughts and feelings in this form. I hope to continue and improve my worrk and hopefully continue to publish my poetry."

CORNESS, MARGARET: [b] 6/10/32 Leeds; [p] Rena & Richard Garrutt; [ch] David & Richard; [ed] Secondary Modern, Morley Victoria Road School; [occ] nursing officer (rtrd.); [awards] S.R.N., Q.I.D.N.S. (now under N.H.S.) F.E. Teachers Cert., 1st/2nd Line Management; [mem] radio communication Heydays - Leeds Playhouse Theatre, debating group; [activ] creative writing, volunteer - samaritan; "Lifelong involvement in decision making for other people — now enjoy myself in early retirement making decisions for leisure."

COUGLE, JOHN: [b] 17/5/34 Arbroath; [p] James & Emma; [ch] Ian & Lynn; [occ] miner (rtrd.); "As a former soldier and miner my roots are working class and I feel a great affinity to what is termed the 'blue collar' worker. So whatever Life throws at me I take it with a pinch of salt and a good laugh."

COUPE, TONI, J.: [b] 23/10/66 Crayford, Kent; [m] Simon; [p] Anne & Ivan Northfield; [ch] Jessica & James; [ed] Dartford West Girls School; [occ] housewife; [activ] creative writing, volunteer - brownie pack; [pub writ] poem - 'Refugee'; "I just started writing and find it exciting not knowing where it could lead. I find writing poetry relaxing and wish I had started years ago. To write poetry you just need to write what you feel."

COURTNEY, ROSALIND: [b] 11/10/52 Cirencester; [ch] Charles & Ralph; [ed] Cirencester Grammar School, Avery Hill College; [awards] Teaching Certificate - Eng. & Art, diploma - community management; [activ] projects development officer for Citizens Advocacy; "Writing is a joy to me, a way to express life and so understand it better and most importantly to share it with other souls on the journey."

COVE, MARIE: [b] 15/4/36 Nuneaton; [m] David; [p] Ernest & Lucy Fletcher; [ch] Ian, Jane & Robert; [ed] Atherstone Grammar, Secretarial College; [occ] secretary; [awards] 'O' levels, certificates - shorthand/typing; [activ] sunday school teacher, M.V. leader; [pub writ] book - 'Lucy's Story', poems for church; "My greatest joy is in being a wife, mother and grandma. Writing in any form; stories, poetry, etc., is part of my life and has been since childhood days."

COX, BARRY: [b] 2/2/47 Everdon; [m] Diane; [ch] Mark & Chris; [ed] Everdon Primary School, The Daventry School; [awards] Blue Peter Badge; [mem] chairman Crombie Memorial Club, Institute of Advance Motorists, Institute of Vehicle Recovery; "I have found that money will buy you a dog ... only love will make it wag its tail."

COX, POLLY: [b] 1/4/40 Scunthorpe; [p] Alfred & Elizabeth Hutton; [ch] Susan & Angela; [ed] Schunthorpe Grammar School; [occ] sales assistant/housewife; [pub writ] several poems in various anthologies; "Writing poetry, although self-taught, stimulatees my power of thought."

CRAIG, ANDREW G.: [b] 13/3/72 Writtle; [p] Margaret & Michael; [ed] Rainsford High, Anglia University; [awards] Business Adminstration Degree; [activ] Save The World, MENCAP; "Life's a laugh and death's a joke."

CRAVEN, MICHELLE M.: [b] 11/2/80 Caerphilly; [p] Catherine & Philip; [ed] Ysgol Gyfun Cwm Rhymni; [occ] student; [mem] Cwmpas Theatre Group; "Set yourself goals in life and as long as you have love and determination in your heart you can accomplish anything."

CRAY, ROSE E.: [b] 14/4/13 Trebanog, S.Wales; [p] Morgan & Lilian Rees; [ch] Philip Henry (dcd.) & Heather Lilian; [ed] C.E. School; [awards] Cert. of Merit - knitting; [pub writ] 'Wales - A Christmas Story', 'The Wedding', 'The Midas Touch', 'Hands'; "Eldest of eight, never was able to skip (with babies to look after), just turned the rope."

CREIGHTON, ANN: [b] 1/3/45 Bacup; [p] Fred & Mary Horrocks; [ch] Annette, Carl, Stephen & Lynsey; [ed] St. Mary's RC School; [occ] machinist; "I am quite an easy going person most of the time, but I will make a stand for something if I thnk it is right."

CRON, HUGH B.: [b] 9/6/67 Irvine; [ed] Mainholm Academy, AYR; [occ] self-employed baker; [pub writ] National Library of Poetry - 'Scotland', 'Silence of Loneliness' & 'Afterdark'; "It is a pity how so much 'undiscovered' talent stays that way because of one person's opinion. The vicious circle of the unpublished, no interest scenario disheartens us all. These compilations and anthologies are the hope of all unpublished writers."

CROSS, BARBARA: [b] 7/3/29 Coventry; [p] Edith & Redvers Cobb; [ch] Nigel, Lynne & Rod; [ed] Coventry Art School, Handsworth School of Art & Dress Design; [occ] rtrd.; "My husband is incurably ill in a nursing home and I seem to write poetry when thinking about life in depth and the meaning of it all.

CROSS, REG: [b] 13/12/23 Liverpool; [m] Helen; [p] Bert & Ellen; [ch] Helen, Janet, Doreen & Carol; [ed] Council School Butler St. - Liverpool; [occ] rtrd.; [awards] Wartime - Royal Artillery, wounded Monte Cassino, Italy; [activ] factory shop steward, sunday football secretary; [pub writ] letters to press, short stories - army convalescent camp newspaper; "A happy family is the most important thing in life!"

CRUMBIE, LEON K.: [b] 12/11/72 Eastbourne; [p] Alice & Clive; [ed] Ratton Secondary, Eastbourne College of Arts & Technology; [awards] City & Guilds Electrical Engineering; "I believe that writing is the most fulfilling and powerful tool available to us. It enables its users to project their thoughts into the minds of others."

CUBITT, VALERIE M.: [b] 10/1/43 Eastwood, Essex; [m] Robert; [p] Thomas & Cicely Speight; [ch] Stephen, Martin, Jacqueline & Paul; [occ] special needs assistant; [mem] Philatic Member (Essex), R.S.P.B., W.W.L.F.; [pub writ] short stories for children and poetry; "I have many interests; animal welfare, stamp collecting, writing and jigsaw puzzles.

I enjoy walking holidays with my husband. I also enjoy cricket and football."

CULLEN, MAUREEN J.: [pen] Elizabeth Fredricks; [b] 6/4/35 Preston; [p] Leslie & Vi Walker; [ch] Maria, Catherine, Peter & Michael; [ed] Trinity Secondary, Preston; [occ] care officer HFE; [awards] 'O' level English, Management Certificates; [activ] working with seniors; [pub writ] letters to local newspapers; "I have been writing many years and was encouraged by my in-laws, hence the pseudonym Elizabeth Fredricks, in memory of two wonderful and much loved people."

CUMBES, FRANK: [b] 22/2/36 Hereford; [m] Maureen; [p] Reg & Alice; [ed] Hereford High School for Boys [occ] factory hand; [awards] school certificates - English Language/Literature; "I have alway enjoyed words and how they are formed. I have always been able to get along with people and find that being honest and open in everything always pays."

CUNNINGHAM, JAMES F.: [b] 17/4/13 London; [p] Emma & James [ch] Carole; [ed] West Sivertown School; [occ] aircraft engineer (rtrd.); [mem] British Airways Retired Assoc.; "As I've grown older I've come to appreciate and value more and more the wonderful world we live in. The beauty of nature that tends to pass unnoticed during one's working life, and the special relationships that can arise between people of different generations. These are the main subjects of my poems although I am sometimes moved to write about the injustices in society. Writing keeps me young."

CUSICK, SIMON T.: [b] 12/7/65 Bury; [p] Thomas & Josephine; [ch] Zachary; [ed] St. Gabriels High School; [awards] City & Guilds - Bricklaying; "Our duty is to develop ourselves, to expand ourselves wholly in all our potential. It is to succeed in becoming fully what we feel ourselves to be."

DALES, MARY K.: [b] 12/10/27 Knottingley; [p] Joe & Annie Shaw; [ch] Robert & Charles; [ed] Ferrybridge J.M.S.I., Selby Art & Technical; [occ] housewife; [awards] R.S.A. shorthand/typing; "Can make a poem about anything that pleases or annoys me."

DALLIMORE, RON: [b] 6/4/21 Rhondda Valley; [p] Gwladys & John; [ch] Jennifer; [ed] Tony Pandy Sec., R.A.F. Apprenticeship - College of Further Education, Merseyside; [mem] chairman Wallingford Art Club, [activ] volunteer - hospital; [pub writ] 'Welsh Connections' - Clamorgan Archive Service, poems/short stories - town magazine; "I started writing as a means of alleviating my grief on the death of my wife in 1991 and have found it most helpful."

DALY, MARY: [b] 27/2/27; [m] Peter (dcd.); [p] Peter & Bridgid Devlin; [ch] Peter, John, Helen, Annie & Bernadette; [ed] Adavoyle Primary, Sacred Heart; [occ] clerk (rtrd.); [awards] 13 secretarial awards, road safety slogan, 1st. prize local competition; [mem] I.C.A.; [activ] Jonesboro Luncheon Club; [pub writ] pomes in local papers/magazines & N. Ireland Anthology; "I enjoy writing poems, rug making and gardening. I enjoy social functions and outings."

DAUNCEY, JUNE A: [pen] Jade Deacon; [b] 15/8/41 Devon; [m] Michael; [p] Joan & Dennis; [ch] Joanna; [ed] Lynton House Public School for Girls, Berkshire; [occ] housewife/wholistic therapist; [awards] R.S.A. Certificate - counselling; [activ] C.O.G.; [pub writ] poem published - 'Pause For Thought'; "Over the last few years I have developed a personal philosophy with an wholistic approach. I think we have to find the "me" beneath the conditioned "I" and feed our four quadrants (mind, emotion, body and spirit) in the way that creates balance and fulfillment for our inner self. Everything based on love."

DAVIES, ANTHONY: [b] 19/3/46 Ystrad Mynach; [p] Dorothy & James; [ed] Graddfa Secondary Modern, Mid. Glamorgan; [occ] charge nurse/paramedic; [awards] State Reg. Nurse 1979, N.H.S.T.D. Cert. Paramedic; "Life is a wondrous thing, seeing people as human beings is an added bonus, helping them at times of need is, I feel, a duty."

DAVIES, BERYL: [b] 4/7/46 Carmarthen; [m] Jos; [p] Thomas & Rachel Davies; [ch] Heddwyn, Heuly, & Eurfyl; [ed] Lampeter Sec.,

Cardiff College of Music/Drama; [occ] housewife/mother; [awards] svrl prizes - 'Eisteddfodau' - hymn writing incl. £100 prize; [activ] organist since '73 - Soar Y Mynydd, Nr. Tregaron, Dyfed; [pub writ] many hymns in song books.

DAVIES, DILWYN: [b] Bargoed; [ch] Barbara; [ed] Bargoed Grammar School; [occ] fire officer (rtrd.); [awards] C.U.I Diploma, C.M.D.; "it's said that ageing dulls and impoverishes the mind but where there's will and determination succes is still attainable. As tutor (self-taught) to my daughter's musical success, this fact is vividly illustrated."

DAVIES, EVELYN: [b] 24/3/30 New Brighton Wirral, Cheshire; [p] John & Henrietta Courtman; [ch] Derek John & Janet Christina; [ed] St. Pauls C of E, Kirkdale, Manchester University; [occ] housewife/retail grocer; [activ] environmental issues; [pub writ] poetry published in anthologies and Southport paper; "Lived in Liverpool Fire Station as a child and was evacuated in war time. I felt free to seek my natural mother when adoptive parents died. I've enjoyed writing from an early age and found that humour 'lightens the load'. My favourite Greek proverb: 'To love is nothing. To be loved is something. To love and be loved is everything'."

DAVIES, FLORENCE A.: [b] 4/10/38 Nanty-Glo-Gwent, Wales; [p] Annie & Redvers Jeffreys; [ch] Mark & Carole-Anne; [ed] Nanty-Glo Grammar School, North Gwent College, Crosskeys College; [occ] writer/singer/artist; [awards] 'O' level Art, Eng. Lang./Lit., French (with oral proficiency); [activ] Blaenau Gwent Chorale, soloist, Gwent Singers, Brynmawr Choral Soc., soloist with Beaufort, Ebbw Vale, & Newport Male Voice choirs, Toured abroad singing in Germany, also Gloucester Cathedral; [pub writ] 6 books, 1 short story, 5 poems: "Voices from the Valleys", "A Taste of Wales", "Desperately Seeking Someone", "Snap", "Too Many Cooks"; "I love singing, writing and painting (Chapter 5 of a novel already underway). I love meeting people, giving pleasure through all three aspects of my work. I began writing 6 years ago."

DAVIES, JOHN D.: [b] 2/2/48 Cardiff; [p] Trevor & Gwendolyn; [ch] Tracy, Renata, Alun & Geraint; [ed] New Tredgar Technical College; [occ] driving instructor; [awards] City & Guilds Engineering, M.O.T. A.D.I.; [mem] pres. local labour party; [activ] community councillor, local school governor; [pub writ] poems in local papers & National Coal Board magazine; "Apart from my poetry I play guitar and harmonica in a local band and write lyrics for my own songs mostly from personal experiences."

DAVIES, JUNE: [b] 17/2/27 Enfield, Middx.; [p] George & Mabel Woodards; [ch] Laura, Stephen, Richard, Mary & Irene; [ed] Enfield Church Shools, Edmonton Technical College; [occ] housewife; [awards] fully trained dressmaker/milliner; [activ] over 50's club - Healthy, Wealthy & Wise, ELY Explorers Club, ELY Eisteddfod; [pub writ] poems in 'South Wales Echo', 'Poetry Now' and 'Wish You Were Here' "I love watching people and the written word, so to combine the two is a fascinating hobby."

DAVIES, NEVILLE T.: [b] 18/4/39 Bebington; [m] Beryl; [p] Stan & Ethel; [ch] Gary, Jacqueline, Denise & Michelle; [ed] Bebington High for Boys; [occ] works manager (rtrd.); [awards] City & Guilds Tyre Distribution; [activ] Lord Napier C.G.B.; "Patience and understanding helps me put pen to paper. Life is a magical thing most precious when shared with others."

DAVIES, RACHEL: [b] 30/4/83 Trethomas; [p] Jane & Kelvyn; [ed] Tyn-Y-Wern Juniors, Bedwas Comprehensive; [occ] student; "This is the first time I have ever had any of my work published and I feel privileged to see it in print."

DAVIS, DIANE: [b] 3/2/57 Mansfield; [m] John; [p] Arthur & Ivy Porter; [ch] Jessica Louise; [ed] Blackdown Comp, Leamington Spa, Headland Comp, Bridlington, East Yorkshire College of Further Education; [awards] R.S.A. 1 typing/word processing, City & Guilds - office procedures; A.T. (Adult Training); [mem] Neurofibromatosis Assoc.; [activ] Bridlington Writers Group; [pub writ] short story - New Fiction, 3 poems - Arrival Press, 1 poem National Magazine; "Inspiration for my writing comes from local scenery, family and friends. I place

great stead in these and hope to extend my writing career."

DAVIS, MARGARET D.: [b] 24/9/40 Beckenham; [m] David; [p] Kathleen & Thomas Hopkins; [ch] David & Matthew Lee; [ed] Secondary Modern Marian Vian, Beckenham, Kent; [occ] poet; [activ] volunteer - St. Mary's Church, Willington Amateur Dramatics; [pub writ] four poems published since 1994; "I have only written poetry during the last five years and get the most satisfaction in writing to family and friends. It is a bonus to see my work in print and I'd like to write a book."

DAVIS, MAUREEN: [b] 19/5/41 Wadebridge; [m] Keith; [p] Walter & Violet Dalley; [ch] Teresa Kay Blake; [ed] Bodmin Grammar School; [occ] housewife; [activ] M.S. Society, hospital car co-ordinator, John Betjemen Ctr.; "Since becoming housebound owing to M.S. I have swapped musical activities for personal writings thus proving for me not all change is bad."

DAVIS, RUTH H.: [b] 28/2/45 Manchester; [p] Beatrice & Richard; [ch] Heide Benyair; "I do research for plays, or dance drama on information required about pagan folk-lore or old customs. I'm currently writing a book on a child's eccentric childhood in the 1950's and a play called 'Giving Up Guilt'."

DAVIS, TERRY: [b] 16/8/38 Rochford; [p] lila & John; [ch] Carl & Rachel; [occ] courier; [awards] composition awards, First Aid, Advanced Driver's Cert. (ambulance); "I have written many children's stories and poems but never tried for publication. I enjoy writing them. I also enjoy music and play piano and organ (self-taught)."

DAWSON, JOHN: [b] 5/1/43 Bannockburn; [m] Doreen; [p] John & Margaret; [ch] John & Janette; [ed] Bannockburn Jr. Sec.; [occ] joiner; "Humour in verse both in English and local dialect is my favourite way of describing life, but controversial subjects are given to much deeper thought."

DAWSON, RUTH: [b] 9/7/64 Harrogate; [m] David; [p] Eva & John Hemsley (dcd.); [ed] St. Aidans C.O.F.E. High School; [occ] homemaker/ assist. supervisor playgroup; [awards] Cert. of Christian Service - Faith Mission Bible College; [mem] Baptist Church; [pub writ] church magazine; "I feel that peotry is an expression of what you feel within. Through the school of life there are many lessons to learn and poetry is created to help people with those lessons."

DAY, VICTOR R.: [b] 22/4/50 Chelmsford; [p] Jack & Mable; [ch] Lorraine Caroline; [ed] Sandon Secondary Modern School; [occ] insp. Cat Protection League; [awards] City & Guilds - Continental/Oriental cooking; [activ] Chelmsford Male Voice Choir; [pub writ] The Sound of Poetry, National Poetry Library (USA) - book/cassette form; "Poetry to me is the rose among the thorns of verbal communication, and after letters from the Royal Family and Vatican, is my whole world."

DCACCIA, CORRENA: [b] 6/7/63 Birmingham; [ed] Thomas Becket Upper School, Northampton, Christ's College, Campbridge; [occ] teacher; [awards] Theology Degree (MA), Post-graduate Cert. - Education; [mem] Catholic Theological Assoc. of G.B., Catholic Women's Network, Amnesty Int'l; [pub writ] articles in national religious journals - 'The Sower', 'Priests & People', 'Forum'."

DENTON, BARBARA M.: [b] 23/12/39 Salisbury; [p] George & Susannah Cavanagh; [ch] Hayley, Caryl, Cheryl & Stephen; [ed] Convent High School, Colwin Bay; [occ] music teacher; [awards] music wards, Pitmans Shorthand/Typing certs., R.A.D.A. awards, certs. - clerical computing; "My three daily 'exercises': 1) Live each day is if it was you last. 2) Never say 'I can't' — 'I will' gives you the determination to succeed. 3) The Qulity of life depends on the quality of your thoughts."

DESJARLAIS, CHARLES O.: [b] 20/5/17 Solihull; [p] Joseph & Edith; [ch] Tony, Michael & Amanda; [ed] Friarage School, Scarborough Yorks; [occ] rtrd.; [awards] gold watch - retirement 25 yrs. construction; [activ] former member I.I.SO., voluntary work Wigan Leisure, play groups; [pub writ] Northern Lights, Clogs & Reeboks, Poetry Now, Between The Lines, Christian Poets From The North; "I find that at my age, writing poetry keeps my mind active, and gives me an aim in life. My wife also writes stories and we often confer together. It is nice to know that someone else reads your work."

DEWAR, MARGARET: [b] 9/4/29 Stirling; [p] Jane & Jimy; [ch] Pamela, Rosalynd, Gilbert & Charles; [occ] housewife/book binder (rtrd.); [activ] church [pub writ] 2 poems - 'October In The Wee Country', 'Ode To A Wheely Bin'; "I find I am always moving on in this life."

DIAMOND, PAUL: [b] Dumbarton; [p] Elizabeth & John; [ed] St. Peters R.C. Primary, St. Patrick's R.C. High; [activ] radical multicultural socialist; "This poem is my opinion of Man's unwillingness to make radical change for the better and is dedicated to peace in Ireland and Sacco and Vanzetti."

DIAMOND, JACK: [b] 12/12/74 Tandragee; [p] Anthony & Noreen; [ed] Banbridge Academy, Queen's University, Belfast; [occ] dilettante; [activ] local historical soc., Ulster Architectural Heritage Soc.; [pub writ] "The Linen Houses of Banbridge", various articles on aristocracy; "In this life nothing has a meaning, which I find fascinating. I also find the aristocracy fascinating ... I'm easily fascinated."

DINNEN, JUDY: [b] 24/12/48 Colchester, Essex; [m] John; [ch] Tom, Jo & Toby; [ed] Colchester High, Coldsmith's London Open University; [occ] special needs teacher; [pub writ] poems in anthologies/magazines; "I began writing years ago, inspired by a creative writing course at Iona Abbey. Since then I have followed Chrysalis (poetry course) and done a course with O.C.A. (Open College of the Arts). I am writing a novel about child abduction, exploring issues of right and wrong, and the place of change in our lives. I am interested in writing not only as a medium for exploring issues but also as a form of self-expression."

DISCOMBE, SANDRA J.: [b] 28/4/53 Greenwich; [p] Charles & Alice Barber; [ch] Anthony & Christopher; [ed] Catford County Girls, Sec. Modern, Comprehensive; [occ] housewife/mother; "After suffering heart problems and subsequent operation last year, I have found myself with time on my hands. Subsequently my love of reading and writing poetry, from way back as a teenager, has been rekindled. I am slowly putting together a collection of my own favourite works. So far only family and friends have ever read them, if other people enjoy reading them then it will give me the confidence and also a great pleasure to carry on writing poetry."

DOBELL, EDNA M.: [b] 31/1/32 Eastbourne; [p] Bert & Elsie Weaver; [ch] Corinne & Craig; [occ] dispatch clerk (rtrd.); [activ] volunteer - literacy tutor, correspondence course (short stories), tennis; [pub writ] poems in magazine/anthology; "Make every day count. Make it an achievement. Make it what you will — but make it. My inspiration in my daily routine and my writing."

DOBSON, ALBERT: [b] 20/3/14 Macclesfield; [p] Samuel & Florence; [ch] Pat, Alan, & Helen; [awards] various related to amateur theatre, Manchester; [pub writ] various mainly plays; "I've had various plays broadcast on the radio, four from Manchester. Also commentaries of plays in the magazine 'Amateur Stage'."

DOBSON, TRUDY: [b] 14/11/58 Mansfield; [p] Bernard & Irene Parkhouse; [occ] housewife; "Some advantages come from what we think is a disadvantage, it just depends on how we look at it. I look on the serious side of a problem then try to find an amusing side. Then when I look back on the serious side I find it's not so bad and I find I can smile."

DODMAN, JOY: [b] 18/2/28 London; [p] Ada & George Simmons; [ch] Sue Joyce & Kevin Leonard; [ed] Dominican Convent High School, Suffolk College of Further Education; [occ] dressmaker (rtrd.); [awards] City & Guilds 1&2 - fashion dressmaking/design; [activ] volunteer recept./secretary, pres. Ladies Club - St. John's Methodist Church; "In 1945 we lost our home to a V.2. Rocket. All six of us lived to tell the story. It made me realize that people come before material things."

DOHERTY, ANNIE: [b] 29/10/46 Letter Clonmany; [m] Patrick; [p]

Bernard & kathleen McLaughlin; [ch] Brian, Martin, Anthony, Patrick, Annette & Michael; [occ] housewife; [pub writ] 'Penned Into Submission' - self-published plus various poems in magazines; "When I sit down to write it's like starting out on a thrilling adventure, I never know what's going to happen or how it will end. I feel so lucky to have the priviledge of taking part."

DOHERTY, LAURA J.: [b] 23/5/75 Scunthorpe; [p] Deborah & Neil; [ed] St. Bede's R.C. Comprehensive, John Leggott College; [occ] student; [awards] 'A' levels Eng. Lit/ Psychology; "From a young age it has been an ambition of mine to write and be published. I have now begun to fulfill that dream. I have learned to believe in my ambitions in order to achieve them."

DONAGHUE, JEAN: [b] 10/5/30 New Mills, Derbys; [m] John; [ch] David & Stephen; [ed] New Mills Board School; [activ] past chief ranger - New Mills Court, Ancient Order Foresters; [pub writ] By Arrival Press Poets, Winter Gold '91/ Midland Words '92/ local newspapers; "I began to write poetry on retiring in 1990. I write on any topic I hear or see during each day. A delightful pastime."

DOREE, JOSEPHINE: [b] Sunbury-On-Thames; [m] Arthur (dcd.); [p] James & Gladys Halsall; [ch] Stephen & Susan; [ed] St. Ignatius R.C. School, Sunbury On Thames, Middlesex; [occ] legal secretary.

DOUBLEDAY, AUDREY: [p] Mr. & Mrs. T.C. Davies; [ed] Waterloo Park School for Girls; [occ] housewife; [awards] WRNS '41 - Squadron Staff Officer - Fleet Air Arm; [activ] Merseyside Conservative Luncheon Club - chairman '80-'82 [pub writ] 'Spring' - Spring Anthology - Oxford University Press 1937, song in newspaper; "I am now a grannie to my five grandchildren. I am writing my life story but keep finding excuses not to finish it!"

DOUGLAS, DOREEN: [b] 7/6/44 Invergordon; [p] Angusina & Norman (dcd.); [ch] Selma & Hayley; [ed] Invergordon Primary, Secondary; [occ] shop assistant; [awards] British Red Cross - cert. of Commendation/Meritorious service '92; Voluntary Medical Service medal '93; [mem] Tain Parish Church; [activ] volunteer co-ordinator Christian Intn'l Aid - 'Blythswood'; "'Life's Shattered Dreams' is dedicated to the children of today and adults of tomorrow. Always have faith and you will never be alone or afraid. A very special thank-you to my late Mam and Dad for their love and wonderful upbringing, through good times and bad."

DOUGLAS, KEITH: [b] 26/6/43 Liverpool; [m] Dorothy; [p] Clarence & Gertrude; [ch] Jeanette & Gavin; [ed] Liverpool Institue H.S., Liverpool University; [occ] teacher (rtrd.); [awards] MA - Eng.; [pub writ] several poems in Forward Press anthologies.

DOUSE, ANGELA M.: [b] 9/10/30 Halstead; [p] Irby & Dora Chapman; [ed] Primary school Church of England, Grammar school, Halstead; [occ] housewife; [activ] floral art club; [pub writ] poems published in: Rhyme Arrival (mag.) '94, Poetry Now Eastern '92, Eastern Promise '94; "There is much encouragement for poets/writers of all ages these days. It is good to see this upsurge in the appreciation of the written word."

DOWN, FRANCES: [b] 22/7/46 Penzance; [p] William & Kathleen Horn; [ch] Phillipa & Angela; [ed] St. Ives Jnr., St. Ives. Comp., Cornwall College; [occ] housewife; [awards] Pitmans/RSA Shorthand, 'O' level Eng. - Civil Law; [activ] assisted husband to reform Constantine Silver Band '77, secretary of Amy Rice Appeal Fund; "I have an accute sensitivity to people's thoughts and my love of life and interest in mankind gives me the desire to put thoughts into poetry form. Most of my poems are event related as well as mood aspects of experiences of my journey through life."

DOWNING, ANNE: [b] 16/9/54 Belfast; [p] Robert George & Annabel; [ch] Leanne & Nicola; [ed] Blackmountain Primary School, Cairnmartin Sec.; "I've always enjoyed making words rhyme to make a poem and it's been a great achievement for me to get this far. Thanks to my family and friends telling me to 'go for it'."

DOYLE, AIDAN: [b] 20/4/78 Banbridge; [p] Sean & Margaret; [ed] St. Patrick's High, St. Michael's Sr. High; [occ] student; [activ] youth ldr. - Discover Programme for Young Adults; "I ejnoy writing poetry as I feel that it is a true reflection of the world around us. Words can paint a thousand pictures and the imagination can allow us to perceive a poem from many dimensions. I feel that poetry is the most creative art form and I get tremendous satisfaction in interpreting my thoughts into words."

DRAPER, L.J.: [b] 21/3/42 Loughborough; [p] Owen & Joan; [ch] Karen, Wayne, Dean & Claire; [ed] Humphrey Perkins Sec., Modern; [awards] City & Guild - engineering, BA Hons. - Open University; [mem] O.U.S.A - region rep., O.M.E.G.A.; [pub writ] poems in Arrival Press '93, '94, and Local Echo Press; "The idea of putting thoughts to words came to me after going through 8 years of O/U essays. I enjoy writing and have started writing a novel. I would like to break into writing full-time."

DRUMMOND, BERYL N.: [b] 18/12/43 Scotland; [p] John & Helen Wilson; [ch] Stuart & Rachel; [ed] Church of England School; [occ] state reg. nurse; [awards] Cert. Counselling Skills, S.R.N. - welfare officer; [activ] folk singing, study of human psychology/behaviour, song writing; [pub writ] two books, a story, poems in local magazines; "'So many emotions we cannot express, and yet, we speak volumes in the silence of the spoken word', I believe in speaking for those who cannot speak for themselves, that is, those who are mentally ill/handicapped."

DUDLEY, CATH: [b] 16/3/65 Isle of Man; [p] George & Sheila Jones; [ed] Douglas High School; [mem] Greenpeace, Anti-Nazi League; [pub writ] poems 'Disposable Assets' 'Mother' - Greenpeace Anthology, 'Sleeper' - A Dry Eye Anthology; "I write to try to explain how I feel about what I see and feel."

DUDLEY, CHRISTOPHER: [b] 16/12/81 Birmingham; [p] Irene; [ed] Leasowes High School; [occ] student; [awards] up to and incl. Gr. 4 - Ballet; "My great passion is dancing. I trained for two years with the Birmingham Royal Ballet and appeared in Peter Wright's production of the Nutcracker Suite. I ave also danced in Los Noces at the Symphony Hall, Birmingham. I am learning to play the piano."

DUDLEY, JAMES: [b] 22/6/20 Clay Cross; [m] Lorna; [p] George & Gertrude; [ch] Peter, Janet & Richard; [ed] Clay Cross Sr. Boys School of Commerce, Norwich Technical College; [awards] Assoc. Company Accoutants; [mem] Gideons Intn'l; [activ] marathon running; [pub writ] poetry - books, local magazines; "I have lived a varied active life in various occupations as well as serving in WW II - 1939-45. I like swimming and travel which provides inspirations for writing poems and short stories."

DUKES, LELSIE F.: [b] 19/4/13 Retford; [p] Fred & Elsie; [ch] Jason, Maurice & Rosalie; [occ] bricklayer/builder (rtrd.); [pub writ] poetry in svrl anthologies of verse, local papers; "A good listener before making my opinion. I would like to publish most of my own work, so far, too expensive!"

DUNCAN, AUDREY: [b] 4/3/53 Aberdeen; [m] Peter; [p] Walter & Hilda Boyne; [ch] Steven, Paul & Neil; [ed] The Gordon Schools; [occ] admin. clerk; "Writing peotry in my local dialect, interior designing and music are a few of my favourite hobbies all of which give me great satisfaction and are a wonderful form of relaxation. Contentment is my answer to personal happiness."

DUNN, ELEANOR: [b] Birkenhead; [p] Charles & May Brandes; [ch] David, Jaymie & Paul; [ed] Prenton Sec., School, Painting School of Art, Laird St.; [occ] antique doll restorer/housewife; [awards] prizes - poetry/short stories, fine arts recommendations; [activ] charity work various organizations, Spina Bifida Assoc.; [pub writ] work in magazines/ local papers; "I have a mind that speaks poetry to me most of the time. I write lots of funny poems and children's poems. I really enjoy my writing and it gives me great satisfatction."

DUNN, SAMUEL: [b] 13/12/53 Ballyclare; [ed] Carrickfergus Secondary, Ballyclare High School; [occ] bank official; [awards] Banking Cert. - Institute of Bankers in Ireland; [activ] East Antrim Harriers - athletic club; "I think that poetry is about truth; going directly and unashamedly to the heart of things, sifting out what really matters, capturing the essence."

DUNNE, MARY: [b] 11/1/26 Liverpool; [m] John; [p] Robert & Bridret Davies; [ch] Paul, Angela & Brian; [pub writ] "The Tree", "I Feel Fine" & "The Widow"; "I started writing poetry after I retired, to pass the time away and I find it very relaxing."

DURHAM, MARGARET K.: [b] 17/11/14 Preston Langs; [m] Douglas (dcd.); [p] Walter & Maggie; [ch] Jean (step-daughter); [ed] Secondary School, Ipswich; [occ] postal officer (rtrd.); [awards] Corontation Medal '53 - postal service; [activ] volunteer - St. John Ambulance, serving Sister, Order of St. John '64; "My main interest lies with art; drawing, painting and needlework."

DYER, DORIS J.: [b] 3/8/41 Aberlour; [p] Bill & Jean Fraser, [ch] Kevin, Lorna, Siobhan, Craig & Fraser — Billy, Francis, Jim & Ann Marie (step-children); [ed] Abelour Primary/High School; [occ] caravan park warden; [mem] Red Cross, Aberlour Bowling Club; [pub writ] newspapers/magazines; "I was a nanny with the forces, then later bacame a cook, I have travelled to the Far East and all over Scotland, Ireland & England. I work with the public in my job, and it is very rewarding, I'm a happy go lucky kind of person who loves animals and writing when I find time to do it."

DYSON, BERYL R.: [b] 14/9/30 Gt. Livermere; [p] Mary & Bertie Cutter; [ed] Livermere Magna, West Suffolk County School; [occ] florist (rtrd.) [awards] recognition - floral exhibits; [activ] volunteer helper; "I enjoy meeting people, helping and giving pleasure through my efforts. I am helped and encouraged by my husband."

DYSON, JULIET: [b] 27/4/37 Westminster; [m] Ian; [ch] Jayne, Anne, Benjamin & George; [pub writ] county publication, local magazine, two natn'l publications; "An evacuee from a broken home in blitzed London inspired to raise family in country. I have a devoted interest in family, community, Nature, music, photography, watercolours, and writing."

DZRADOSI, CHARLES: [b] 11/1/63 Kumasi; [p] Fritz & Mary; [ed] Tamale Sec., University of Ghana, University of Liverpool; [occ] development planner; [awards] degree - Geography & Regional Science; [activ] community church leader; "All over the world, people are searching for true meaning to life. To me, Jesus is the way, the truth and the life. Through my lifestyle and poems I try to let people know Him too."

EADES, WILLIAM: [b] 15/10/02 Tipton, Staffs; [p] Enoch & Gertrude; [ch] Alan & Michael; [occ] clerk (rtrd.); [activ] secretary Westley & General Agents Soc. 1931-39; [pub writ] book - 'Poems By Wolfe'; "I have written 130 poems on all subjects of life including: politics, children, royalty and Nature. My inspiration comes suddenly from a feeling I have; then I sit down and write a poem in a short space of time. The poem 'In The Land Of Make Believe" was written in as little as 25 minutes."

EAVES, LYNETTE A.: [b] 8/12/51 Liverpool; [p] Frank & May; [ch] Zara, Jed, Daniel, Hannah, Joe & Ida; [ed] Liverpool Girls College; [occ] housewife; [activ] volunteer - bereavement counselling, visit elderly, local toddler group, relief supervisor play group; [pub writ] svrl. poems; "My life is simple and I enjoy the outdoors and wildlife. Inspiration plays a great part in my poems. My large family keeps me busy and I write in my spare time. I am a fun-loving person and this helps make life easier with the family."

EDMONDSON, JOANNE M.: [b] 21/1/73 Cleethorpes; [p] Bud & June; [ed] Kibworth Jr./High School, Frickers Academy; [occ] shop assistant; [awards] jr. county golf champ. '92, most improved player '92; [mem] Torksey G.C., Carholm G.C., Owmby G.C.; [activ] Lincs County Golf Team; [pub writ] 'Man At War' - Arrival Press Poets, Eastern Chorus; "I enjoy writing poetry and short stories and have recently completed my first full length children's book. I would love to travel, play golf and write."

EDWARDS, DAMIEN P.: [b] 10/5/78 Ballarat, Aus.; [p] Gary & Kym; [ed] Mr. Clear Secondary; [occ] student; [awards] academic award '93, ballroom dancing awards; [activ] basketball, ballroom dancing; [pub writ] computer software report - local newsletter; "I would like to thank my grandparents, Patrick and Yvonne Edwards, for entering my work on my behalf. I feel poetry is a way in which I can express any thought or idea for others to experience. It is a wonderfully unique form of expression."

EDWARDS, JACQUELINE: [b] 15/7/60 London; [m] Terry; [p] Frank & Iris Traveller; [ch] Jonathan & Daniel; [ed] Chalvedon Comprehensive, Southend Technical College; [occ] cook; [awards] City & Guilds - catering, Advanced Cooks course; [activ] volunteer - special needs children's club; "I try to treat people how I would like to be treated. I get a great deal of satisfaciton from my family who give me the inspiration for most of my poetry."

EDWARDS, THOMAS W.: [b] 21/4/16 Aberdare; [p] Martha & Watkin; [ch] Susan Dawn; [occ] butchery manager (rtrd.); [awards] military medal (Battle of Ardennes 1945); [awards] written composition - winner S. Wales area; [mem] Old Comrades - Aberdare; [activ] board of directors - Aberdare & Dist. Co-op Soc., ex-chairman USDAW, Royal British Legion, avid reader (biographies); [pub writ] 'Racing Post'; "Counter Psychology is education itself. Keep smiling under adverse conditions. I like to help people less fortunate than myself, gain people's respect by being a good listener. The most important, health is the ingredient to happiness."

EELES, ROBERT J.: [b] 26/12/10 Reading; [p] Howard & Lillian; [ch] John Martin; [occ] minister (rtrd.); [pub writ] words/music - 'Festival of Male Voice Praise', various church magazines; "From childhood I have always been fascinated by rhyme and metre, combined with music composition. My work is chiefly church music. Many of my pieces are sung by Male Voice Choirs in the U.K. and Australia."

ELLIOTT, MARIE: [b] 23/11/50 Letterkenny, Co. Donegal; [m] Eamond; [p] Jim & May Ferry; [ch] Linda, Damien, & Brandon; [ed] Loreto Convent, Letterkenny; "Through poetry I can express my thoughts and feelings about the simple but priceless things in life which we so often take for granted. Writing about my thoughts makes me more aware of their existance, beauty and value."

ELLWOOD, IVY: [b] 12/12/22 Bristol; [p] Florence & Richard Thorn; [ch] Jane Margaret & John Anthony; [ed] South St. Girls School, Merchant Venterurs Tech College; [occ] housewife; [activ] bowls club, various women's groups; [pub writ] Relationships - An Anthology, Bristol Reflections, Entitled Elders, British Poetry Review 1993, A Dry Eye 1994, West Country 1994, local paper; "I had a stroke two years ago, but I find pleasure in writing poetry."

ELWOOD, MARK: [b] 21/2/80 Leeds; [p] David & Christine; [occ] student; "Through my poems, I am able to express my thoughts and reflect on things that I hear and see happening."

EMMONS, JOAN: [b] 12/5/52 Woodridge; [m] Chris; [p] Margaret & John King; [ed] Farlingaye High, Suffolk College, Trent Polytechnic; [occ] V.D.U. operator; [awards] various C.S.E., R.S.A., G.C.S.E., 'O' level & 'A' level art passes; [activ] Breastcare Assoc.; [pub writ] short stories/poems - school magazine; "I am very enthusiastic about creative photography and have made many new friends through this medium. I als try to be creative in my writing."

ENGLISH, CHRISTOPHER: [b] 10/12/50 Harrogate, N. Yorks; [p] Jean & Freddy (dcd.); [ed] St. Mary's School, Chilton Cantello House, Harrogate Art College, Loughborough College of Arts; [occ] painter/ fine art; [awards] BA Hons. Fine Art Painting; [pub writ] poems - York Poetry Workshop - 1984-85, poems & paintings - Yorkshire & Shumberside Arts 1988, poems - Harrogate Arcade Gallery Publications 1984; "Writing poetry and painting pictures is what I like to do. Over the years I have used the imagery of my poems in my paintings, either directly or indirectly. The relation between poetry and painting is interesting to me."

EVANS, ANGELA: [b] 23/5/56 Sunderland; [ch] Sammy & Kerenza; [occ] reflexologist; [mem] Institute of Patentees and Inventors; [activ] Reiki practitioner, qualified hypnotherapist; [pub writ] poetry; "My poem says it all!"

EVANS, EVELYN: [b] 21/7/25 Crowborough; [occ] housewife; [pub writ] book - 'Home Truths' plus poetry in 17 anthologies; "I have written poetry, including poetry for the Royal Family, for the past twelve years. I also paint animal portraits in oils. I have the need to express my innermost feelings in verse."

EVANS, KEITH: [b] 30/3/38 Maesteg; [p] Tom & Evelyn; [ch] Ceri, Martyn & David; [occ] fitter; "I saw the competion advertised in the S.W. Echo and even though I'd written no poetry before I decided to enter. When I received your request to publish it I was absolutely amazed."

EVERSON, SHEILA: [b] 21/2/44 Cwncarn; [p] Joseph & Nora West; [ch] Julie Christine; [ed] Cwmcarn Comprehensive; [occ] housewife; [mem] I.F.A.W. & Labour Party [activ] Neighbourhood Watch co-ordinator; "This is one of many poems I have written and would one day like to have them all published. I enjoy writing them and I am still writing many more and have written many about my family."

FAIRCLOUGH, JEAN: [b] 6/8/45; [m] Edward; [ch] Gillian, Andrew & Debra; [occ] secretary part-time; [mem] Ormskirk Writers and Literary Club [activ] committee member/competition co-ordinator; [pub writ] short story - natn'l magazine, svrl poems in small press pubications; "I have never regretted joing a writers circle. Apart from the friends I have made I have gained knowledge of the literary world and continue to learn from other member's experience. The group's support has given me confidence to continue and a desire to succeed."

FAIRHURST, P.F.C.: [b] 8/7/36 Wigan; [p] Elizabeth & Francis Cyril, [ch] Darrel, Gary, Carl, Kristian & Stuart; [ed] St. Josephs R.C. School; [awards] Safe Driving diploma; [activ] helping other people, caravaning, fishing & wild countryside; [pub writ] Preserve/ Poems of the North West, Tranquility/Island Moods and Reflections; "I like to write for pleasure, and about all kinds of subjects. I have also met many famous people, and I love the countryside and nature."

FAIRWEATHER, M.A.: [b] 26/9/43 England; [m] Alan; [p] Violet & Fred Hubbard; [ch] Jamie, Michelle & Tracy; [ed] Costessey High School; [occ] cashier; [pub writ] poetry in various anthologies: 'Out of the Kitchen', 'Skin Deep', 'Love Lines'; "I started writing stories for my children about 20 years ago, it's only recently tha I have turned once again to writing as a excellent form of stress relief."

FARLEY, ROBERT: [b] 9/7/49 Hertforshire; [m] Linda; [p] Ernest & Kathleen; [ch] Mark & Sarah; [ed] Peckham Grammar; [occ] gov't. officer; [activ] creative music & bookkeeping, volunteer - community works; "Family is first priority for happiness. I get the most satisfaction through my music and poetry and take nothing too seriously."

FARMAN, JULIE: [b] 13/5/62 Stockton; [p] Terry & Edith; [ed] Ian Ramsey, Stockton, Cleveland; [occ] laundress/EPH; [awards] Sign Language, Photography; [activ] music clubs; "Julie died suddenly 11/ 25/94. She loved music, photography and her cat. She was a beautiful daughter, caring and good. She would have been proud."

FARRANT, RONALD: [b] 9/8/32 London; [p] Alfred & Catherine; [ch] Susan Irene, Stephen Leslie, & Lawrence Raymond; [ed] Hermit Road High School, London; [occ] supervisor Ntn'l Health Trust Hospitals; [awards] arts/crafts; [activ] Bury Knowle Art Group, Marston Chess Club & Windmill Road, Headington Cons. Social, snooker club; [pub writ] ntn'l magazines, calligraphy in local newspapers; "The purpose of life is to create for yourself and thereby for others all that you require in life. Often these are basic, simple things, for nature will convey your thoughts."

FAWCITT, NICHOLAS: [b] 27/4/79 Farnbrough; [p] Shirley & Peter; [ed] Priory School, Orpington; [occ] student; [awards] various Judo awards; "I believe tht every new day you learn something new. You must learn from your mistakes before you gain anythng from them. I enjoy writing poems and I think I'll always enjoy it until the day I die."

FELTON, JOHN: [b] 4/10/41 Birmingham; [p] John & Ethel; [ch] Elizabeth & Simon; [ed] St. Chad's R.C. Sec. Modern; [pub writ] "Tears of Regret", "A Beautiful Dream", "The Midland's Man ; "Discovered writing by accident and wish to bring my work to a wider audience."

FEWICK, CYNTHIA: [b] 29/9/29 Scunthorpe; [m] Dennis (dcd.); [p] George & Maud Camplin; [ch] Peter John & Joy Elaine; [pub writ] 'The Gardener' - Anchor Books '94; "I am very happy to be able to share my thoughts and feelings in verse with the many poetry lovers of today — and tomorrow, I hope."

FERGUSON, LINDA: [b] 4/11/39 Castle Douglas; [p] Margaret & Thomas; [ch] Mandy, Steven, Maureen, Jane & Grant; [ed] Castle Douglas High School; [occ] bookkeeper; [pub writ] poem 'Lost Love' - British Poetry Review '95; "I am at my happiest with my children and nine grandchildren around me. Most of my peotry is inspired by my children and everyday living and dying."

FERRIS, JOANNE M.: [b] 25/10/81 Newry; [p] Mary & Colin; [ed] St. Josephs Convent School, Our Lady's Grammar School; [occ] student; [awards] Life Saving Qualification; [activ] Newry Swim Club; "I write poetry for my own pleasure. I am greatly influenced by media coverage and like to think I am contributing to public awareness of certain issues."

FIDDES, MAUREEN: [b] 20/2/36 Byker, N/C; [p] Bill & Nancy; [ch] Malcom, Julie, Kevin, Alison, Clark, Shaun, Beverley & Lee; [ed] Secondary Modern, Bolam St., Byker; [pub writ] poem in local paper 'Daytrip Ferryboat'; "Never be afraid to let your family know how much you love them and you're always there when needed, even if it's just for a cuddle. Also treat all human beings as one, no matter the colour nor the creed, and always be there for people in need. Give a shoulder to cry on."

FINCH, JIM: [b] 24/1/33 Bircotes; [m] Sheila; [p] Linda & John; [ed] St. Josephs College, Blackpool De La Salle Trianing College, Manchester; [occ] head teacher (rtrd.) [mem] Charter 88, Amnesty Intn'l, National Trust; [pub writ] poems in Poetry Now magazine and anthologies - Arrival Press & Poetry Now '92-'94; "Literature, including poetry, has always been imporant in my life. As a teacher I attempted to communicate this love, and I am still passionate about story-telling and poetry readings. When my own muse awakes it is persistant."

FINLAY, GERALD: [b] 8/7/36 Leeds; [m] Shirley; [p] Harriet & Arthur (dcd.); [ch] Samantha, Nigel & Susan; [ed] Royal Air Force Technical; [occ] engineer; [awards] Sr. engineer, 2nd place - poetry competition, awards karate, swimming, running and triathlon; [activ] fund-raising for charities; [pub writ] poems published locally; "Poems and music are inspired by countryside. I dislike lack of responsibility in people, a lack of morals and the break-up of family life, I am a Christian."

FIRMAN, IRENE F.: [b] 29/12/18 Birmingham; [p] Minnie & William John; [ed] Secondary/Technical College; [occ] civil servant (rtrd.) [awards] Nursing certificate; [activ] P/D Society, church member; 'I love people and try to do all I can for them whenever my disability allows me. I try to be a good friend if I am needed."

FISHER, A.R.: [b] 9/11/74 Worlingham, Suffolk; [p] David & Miriam; [occ] freeland writer; [awards] 8 GCSE 'A' grades incl. English/English Lit.; [mem] Ntn'l & Intn'l computer clubs; [pub writ] regular columns/ articles in computer press; "'The River' is a very descriptive piece, twinning a shape-poem (like Lewis Carroll's Mouse's Tail in Alice in Wonderland) and narrative. I hope to publish a short story anthology in the near future. In addition, I share the same birthday as Roger McGough, which inpires me to write more..."

FISHER, BILLY: [b] 27/1/71 Preston; [p] Patricia & Fredrick; [ed] R.H.H.S. Ribbleton Hall High School, Preston College; [occ] hairdresser; [awards] City & Guilds - hairdressing dip., 1st place - gents. hairdressing; [mem] priesthood - Church of Jesus Christ Latter Day Saints; [activ] writing poetry, martial arts, football; "Everything is beautiful. What if

there was nothing? God is great, the Earth is small, one day we'll come together and our poetic minds will meet."

FISHER, BRENDA: [b] 19/5/35 Harrow; [p] John; [ch] Mark, Kevin & Deona; [ed] Sec. Modern, Belmount; [occ] housewife; [activ] church - ministry of healing; [pub writ] short story in local newspaper, poetry in Christian book and magazine; "My awareness of Christ in my life is first and foremost. I enjoy writing short stories and poems, my husband is a great encourager."

FISHER, SHIRLEY: [b] 8/11/51 Burton-on Trent; [p] Betty & Leonard; [ed] Salisbury Memorial School, Burton John Taylor High, Barton-under Needwood Open University; [occ] student; [awards] certificate in Local History (University of Keele); [mem] RSPB; [activ] animal welfare; [pub writ] poetry in anthologies: Poetry Now, Arrival and Mast; "Through studying the past, painting and poetry I have deepened my appreciation of the complexity, beauty and fragility of nature and of life. If I can meet the challenges I set myself and still find time to help other I will be content."

FITNESS, M.E.: [b] 1/11/23 Blackpool; [p] Constance & Alfred Locke; [pub writ] poem in 'Northern Lights'; "More than anything I love words."

FLETCHER, CATHERINE: [b] 30/7/80 Bath; [p] John & Wendy; [ed] Bath High School; [occ] student; [awards] Sr. School Scholarship, runner-up BBC Wildlife Poetry Contest '94; [pub writ] poems in BBC Wildlife magazine, and school magazine; "I enjoy many outdoor activities and so find the natural world fascinating. Family life is also important to me. I enjoy reading and playing the clarinet and piano. I find writing a useful and enjoyable means to express myself."

FLETCHER, VICKY: [b] 8/2/42 Edinburgh; [p] Col. David Fletcher & Lady Daphne Stewart; [ed] Convent of the Holy Sepulchre, Chelmsford Essex, Diens High School, Berwickshire, Telford College; [occ] physiotherapist (rtrd.); [awards] Chartered Physiotherapist - '64, Dame of the Order of St. Lazarus of Jerusalem; [mem] East Lothian Antiquarian, Hay & Stewart Socs., [pub writ] poetry in Poetry Now (Scottish Anthol. '93), East Lothian Life Mag.; "I am currently writing a book called "The Children of Yester" about my childhood in my Grandfather's house (the 11th Marquis of Tweeddale)."

FOGERTY, PAULINE M.: [b] 13/3/57 Morecambe; [m] Scott; [p] Edward & Alice Bird; [ch] Sarah & Claire; [ed] Ripley St. Thomas School, Morecambe & Lancaster College of Further Education; [occ] elder care; [awards] City & Guilds - cosmetics, college diploma; [pub writ] "Richness of Love" - Anchor Books '93, "Eddie" - British Poetry Review MAST Pub., '94; "I try to take each day as it comes and cope with what it has to offer. My poetry is a form of release when I have a lot on my mind."

FOGGO, TOM: [b] 17/10/27 Lochgelly; [m] Helen; [p] Thomas & Helen; [ch] Steven; [ed] St. Andrews Madras College of Commerce, College of Education, Dundee; [occ] teacher; [awards] diploma - Primary Teaching; [activ] St. Andrews Operatic Soc., New Golf Club; [pub writ] short story - New Fiction, various poems - Arrival Press; "To leave behind a fraction of one's inner feelings, built into the wall of history, must surely be greater than the wealth of the world and its universe."

FOLEY, SHAUN: [b] 4/11/82 Lanark; [ed] Greyfriars Primary, St. Andrews, St. Mary's Primary, Lanark, St. Aidans High School, Wishaw; [occ] student; "I enjoy writing poems and short horror stories as I have quite a vivid imagination which works overtime when I am writing stories. I also like to write poems which are based on facts of the past as these are constant reminders of things which actually happened."

FORD, AUSTIN: [b] 7/12/26 Preston; [m] Jean; [p] John & Mary Ann; [ch] Angela & Trevor; [ed] St. Joseph's R.C. Elem., St. Richard's R.C. Sec.; [activ] A.P.C.A.P.T. - campaign against the Poll Tax - Preston; [pub writ] poems in 'Poets Chorus' and "Here, There and Everywhere'; "I am at present writing quite a few poems and short stories, both sad and humourous, as well as a book "Thatcher's Legacy" which is now complete, but I'm having difficulty getting it published — 90% relates to the adverse effects of the Poll Tax."

FORD, KATHERINE: [b] 15/1/33 Inverness; [m] David; [p] Sandy & Violet Thomson; [ch] Susanne & David; [ed] Secondary School - Pitlochry; [occ] aux. nurse; [pub writ] 10 previous poems in 10 different books; "I'd love to have book of my own poems published, It's a great feeling seeing your own poems in print."

FORSDIKE, SALLY A.: [b] 27/10/54 Ipswich; [p] Robert & Rhoda Forsdike; [ch] Jennie; [occ] retail; [activ] reading, history, cookery & swimming; "I am the second youngest child and have six sisters and one brother. I've lived in Felixstowe since 1994 with my partner, Paul and my daughter, Jennie."

FOSTER, MANDY: [b] 3/9/62 Haverford West; [p] Howard & Beryl Jeffries; [ch] Sean; [ed] University/College Cardiff, Open University; [occ] education manager; [awards] BA (Hons.) English Lit., MSc - Adv. Social/Educational Research Methodology; [mem] Regional Women's Committee UNISON (branch secrt.) "I always attribute all of my achievements to my mother, who is one of the strongest women I know, and who has alway encouraged me and has faith in everthing I do."

FOWLER, NICOLA: [b] 16/8/68 Bath; [p] William & Christine; [ed] Corsham Comprehensive; "I try to keep an open mind and to be tolerant of others. This I find gives me a positive attitude. I enjoy poetry as a way to express myself and give enjoyment to myself and hopefully to others!"

FOX, KATHLEEN: [b] 11/3/28 Harden, Bingley; [p] Thomas & Ada Chamberlain; [ch] Barry & Tony; [ed] Bingley Modern & Technical; [occ] housewife; [activ] volunteer - Cancer Research, OXFAM; [pub writ] 2 poems on local subjects, 1 poem - Harvard University; "Smile, be happy with your lot and brighten someone's day. Be ready to help others and receive it back three-fold when needed. This and the countryside gives me joy."

FOX, VICTORIA: [b] 5/1/22 Doncaster; [p] Richard & Sandra; [ed] Orchard School, S. Leverton, Notts; [occ] student.

FRAMPTON, PATRICIA: [b] 22/6/40 Dulwich; [p] Joan & Jim Hallett; [ch] Carole, Neil & Graham; [ed] Wandsworth Grammar School; [occ] florist; [awards] Scholarship to Guildhall School of Music/Drama; [mem] Isle of Wight Poetry Soc.; [pub writ] poetry book - "Pictures From the Mind's Eye", 11 poems in various anthologies; "To me poetry can express feelings on all subjects, making all issues readable and easily understood. I would like one day to have some of my poems used in education."

FRANCIS, ANNA: [b] 7/6/47 Chipping, Sodbury; [m] Brian; [p] Frank & Kathleen Turner; [ch] Joanna & Jonathan; [ed] The Ridings School, Winterbourne, Soundwell Tech. College, Bristol; [occ] sr. secretary; [pub writ] articles/poems in local magazines and newspapers; "Basically I'm a romantic with a deep admiration of works by Hardy, Dickens, Du Maurier and contemporary writers such as Catherine Cookson. If I can express a fraction of such genius I will have achieved my goal."

FRANCIS, DOREEN A.: [b] 13/4/44 Saunderton, Buckinghamshire; [m] Kenneth; [p] Martha & John Woods; [ch] Maria & Clare; [ed] Princess Risborough County School; [occ] company director; [activ] Conservation British Heritage; [pub writ] Poetry Now anthologies contained within six books, poetry in local newspapers; 'I find writing poetry and also reading poetry gives me an insight into humanity."

FREEMAN, ROBERT A.: [b] 8/12/50 Leamington Spa; [p] Thomas & Eva; [ed] Plymouth University; [occ] engineering design consultant; "With one grandparent English, one Canadian, one Hungarian, and one German, it has taken two World Wars just to get here!"

FREW, JOHN M.: [b] 1/7/21 London; [p] Thomas & Jessie (dcd.); [ch] Stuart & John; [ed] Southfields, London, County Farm Institute, Winchester; [occ] civil servant (rtrd.); [activ] committed Christian, church member and bible student; [pub writ] Shell African Farmer; "I

began writing humourous verse more than 40 years ago about life's situations, and more recently, poems with a spiritual message for church magazines. Being blessed with a strong sense of humour, imagination and observant eye help tremendously in my work."

FROST, WENDY P.: [b] 15/10/48 Walthamstow, London; [p] Jim & Joan Frost; [ch] Ruth, Steven & Sylvia; [ed] Gt. Yarmouth High School, Open University; [occ] childminder; [awards] 'O' level, BA (Hons.); [activ] Childminder's Assoc., specialized childminding for social services; [pub writ] poems in anthologies, ie. Poetry Now (N. Ireland) and MAST Publication Anthology/Review; "Writing poetry helped me in bad times when I found no one to confide in. I just wrote my thoughts down and they became my poems. This is thanks to my mother who advised me to write my thoughts if I couldn't talk many years go."

FULLELOVE, REGINALD: [b] 25/6/30 Brownhills; [m] Brenda; [p] Ellen & David; [ch] Lynda & Karen; [ed] Brownhills Elem.; [awards] British Empire Medal '84; [mem] Methodist Church; [pub writ] three booklets - 'Two Sides of Mer Reg', 'The Best of Mer Reg' & 'Treasured Thoughts'(self-published); "My writing is a gift given to share with others, my inspiration and suport is my wife, Brenda."

FURNESS, JEAN: [b] 2/6/34 Norwich; [p] Herbert & Edith Flowerdew; [ch] Stephanie, Vanesa, Ian & Craig; [occ] housewife/writer; [activ] care worker to prostitutes "Magdelene Group", church activities; [pub writ] small book "Love is His Meaning", poems published by poetry clubs, plus theological articles; "Experiencing life's joys and sorrows and discovering new insights into life through these experiences enables me to 'write from the heart'."

GALE, JUDITH E.: [b] 7/3/37 Yoxall Staffs; [ch] Julieanne, Antony, Katherine Christina Nicholas & John; [occ] housewife/mother; [pub writ] articles in local history publication - Keele University; "I began writing when my children were small. It provided me with an alternative occupation — something of my own. I enjoy describing the countrside where I live."

GALLACHER, LYNN: [b] 12/6/61 Bedford; [p] Ena & Bernard Hutchings; [ch] Sam & Hannah; [ed] Bedford High School, Oxford Brookes University; [occ] physiological measurement technician; [awards] BA (Hons.) - German.

GALLAGHER, CAITLIN: [b] 7/11/51 Canada; [ch] Tara; [occ] counsellor/aromatherapist; [awards] Cert. Social Work, Massage, Reflexology, Aromatherapy; [pub writ] short stories in local magazine, poem in Canadian feminist magazine; "I have written some songs which I like to sing, and poetry as a way to heal myself from past hurts. Writing and singing are liberating mediums for me to express myself creatively and politically, especially in relation to women's issues."

GALLANT, LYNN: [b] 26/4/48 Hornchurch; [p] Fredrick & Dorothy Roberts; [ch] Lee, Zak, Ula and Jed; [ed] Suffolk College; [occ] family support worker; [awards] Access, Sociology, English, Maths; [activ] psychology/law A levels, volunteer; "I re-entered education at the age of 45, 'it is never too late to learn'. A whole new world becomes attainable, through which it is possible to help others."

GAMAGE, BRIAN C.: [b] 4/7/40 Canterbury; [p] Charles & Joan (dcd.); [ch] Bradley, Julia & Grant; [ed] Tunbridge Wells Tech. School; [occ] gov't officer (rtrd.) [awards] 'O' level Eng. language/literature, 'A' level Law (homestudy), Higher National Certificate - public admin.; [mem] parish church choir, Fed. of Kent Writers, formed writers group 'Tonbridge Scribblers'; [activ] active Christian; [pub writ] various poems in regional anthologies; "I was one of top 22 winners in a nation wide B.T. short story writing competition recently. I enjoy creative writing and sound syntax. I have written a two act play based on John Bunyan's 'Pilgrim's Progress' which was perfomed in 1994 at a local theartre. I enjoy writing both Christian and secular work."

GAMBLE, MARIE C.: [b] 10/2/46 Hebburn, Co. Durham; [p] Mary & Hugh Driver Mitchell; [ch] Suzanne, Yoland, Daren Sally & April Dawn; [ed] Maysfield Sec., grammar school Sarrow, St. Vincent de Pauls Convent, London; [occ] housewife; [awards] degree - social sciences, BA - Open University; [mem] Disabled Access Group; [activ] volunteer - teacher's helper, playschool organiser; [pub writ] poems 'Old Age - Anthology North East '90, 'Loneliness' & 'In a Walk Down Memory Lane' - Anchor Books, various poems in local papers; "This poem, 'The Guns and Bombs Are Quiet Now' is about Northern Ireland, as is most of my work. I lived there and most of my family were born there. I was disabled by a bomb. The people and place are fantastic. I find it best to think of people for what they are, not for what they do, I try to understand."

GANDERTON, LESLIE A.: [b] 15/12/57 Caerphilly; [m] Keith; [p] Tom & Sylvia; [ch] Russel & Lisa; [ed] Lewis School for Girls, Ystrad, Mynach; [occ] housewife; [awards] 5 'O' levels; [mem] Lupus U.K.; [activ] fund-raising Lupus; "I would like to dedicate this poem to my mother and all the memories I have of years gone by."

GARDNER, LILY: [b] 1922 Clapton Park, London; [m] Frederick; [p] Albert & Rebecca Millins; [ed] North Hackney Central School for Girls; [pub writ] 'The Dance of Progress' booklet of 20 poems - Outposts Publications, magazines and local newspapers.

GARRETT, ANGELA: [b] 12/7/57 Newport IOW; [m] Ged; [p] George & Susan Stubbington; [mem] Greenpeace; [activ] volunteer - Warwickshire Wildlife Trust, spear-headed successful campaign to save Ensor's Pool, Nuneaton; [pub writ] 4 poems - Poetry Now & Arrival Press; newsletter articles, letters local newspapers; "I love nature and poetry; bringing them together is, for me, the ultimate therapy. The ongoing encouragement of my primary school teacher, Noel Watkin, plus family and friends' support are invaluable to my writing and my life."

GARRETT, MALCOLM: [b] 28/8/41 Cardiff; [p] William & Winnifred; [ch] Raymond, Susan, Michele, Ceri & Jason; [ed] Sec. Modern - Severn Road, Kitchener Road - Cardiff; [activ] help old people, son's football; [pub writ] 'My Wales' - Poetry Now; "Hard word for companies doesn't pay, they'll still get rid of you. Always have a smile and be ready to help, don't be taken advantage of."

GARRETT, MIGNON: [b] 1/3/31 London; [p] Henry & Frances Morgan; [ch] Jane Victoria; [ed] Sutton High School, Benhilton College - Surrey; [pub writ] 'The Sound Of Feelings', 'My Cornwall', 'The Wonder of Youth'; "I have lived in Cornwall since 1952. I worked in Newquay Library for fourteen years and belong to the Pendragon Literary Workshop."

GASTER, DAVID I.: [b] 7/2/51 London; [m] Penna; [p] Jack & Phyllis; [ch] Francine & Christophe; [ed] Shoreditch College (Brunel University); [occ] teacher; [awards] long service award - ILEA; "I discovered my interest in writing poetry whilst courting my wife."

GATTLEY, GILLIAN: [b] 23/1/60 Croydon, [m] Trevor; [p] Joy & Geoff Wiggins; [ed] King Edmund Comp., SEEVIC, Hull University, Manchester Polytechnic; [occ] teacher; [awards] BA (Hons.) (French/Spanish) PGCE; [activ] member Anglican church; "As an Arts Graduate I enjoy reading and created this poem in 1983 in recognition of literature and also as a celebration of love."

GAY, DOREEN: [b] 8th, October; Huddersfield; [p] Ellen & Albert Ellam; [ch] Rosemary & Mark; [ed] Huddersfield Polytechnic, London Art College; [awards] diploma (honours) - London Art College; [activ] music/voice production, operatic socs., NODA, church; [pub writ] poems - Anthology of Yorkshire poets, church magazines, newspapers; "To try to be pleasant and friendly at all times is my aim. To be a good companion to my family above all, and to put my thoughts into words as in my latest poem 'The Written Word'."

GEE, JEAN: [b] 23/7/42 Bacup; [m] Michael; [p] John & Elizabeth Goggins; [ch] Sharron & Deborah; [ed] St. Mary's R.C., Bacup; [occ] officer-in-charge home for the elderly; [activ] theatre, reading & socializing; "I enjoy people for whomever, or whatever they are. It's what a person says, not how they say it that really matters. No matter what material possesions we possess, in the end it's the people in our lives that count."

GEE, RUSSEL D.: [b] 21/3/66 Cumbria; [m] Cheryl; [p] David & Margaret; [ed] Cartmel Priory School - Cumbria, Open University; [occ] museum curator; [awards] BA (Hons.), Degree - History; [pub writ] 'Views From the Shelter House' - Mountside Press, Kendal, contrib. 'Valleys Of Thought' - anthology; "Writing poetry helps me to ask questions about the world. These questions lead not to answers, but raise yet more questions. In so doing, I explore what I find around me."

GEORGE, HAZEL: [b] 3/1/59 London; [m] Kim; [p] Irene & Donald Cash; [ch] Christopher, Martin & Tony; [occ] housewife; "I have enjoyed writing short stories and poems since my early days at school. This is the first poem I have ever submitted and it is such a thrill to know it will be published."

GETHING, JOSEPH: [b] 1/6/40 Stoke-On-Trent; [p] Joseph & Florence; [ch] John, Carol, Jill & Peter; [ed] Queensbury Road Normacot, Stoke-On-Trent; "After a serious illness and with time to spare, poetry has become an avid interest. I am writing my life story in simple verse - 'Serene'."

GHORI, MARGARET D.: [b] 30/5/51 Worthing; [p] Hilda & Fred Jackson (dcd.); [ch] Sarah Yasmin & Humerah Shaheen; [ed] Worthing High School for Girls, Worthing College of Further Education; [occ] practice manager; [awards] diploma - Assoc. of Medical Secretaries (with distinction) 1994; "I find that poetry is my own way of expressing my personal feelings on any subject important to me at a particular time. I feel greatly satisfied upon completion of a poem which has expressed my thoughts and views adequately."

GIBBS, HOWARD W.: [b] 27/3/38 Maidenhead; [p] Harry & Betrice [ch] Anthony Howard; [ed] Slough College of Further Education; [awards] Inst. of Office Managers, Inst. of Work Study Practitioners, Inst. of Works Managers;[pub writ] local magazines, Age Concern magazine, poetry 'Simple Pleasures' - Anchor Books; "I am a member of USA Marlborough Creative Writing Group and was active in amateur stage work until four years ago when ill health forced me to give up most of my hobbies, including retirement from work, also owned village shop and post office for 20 years. I am a long time amateur archeologist."

GIBSON, DAISY: [b] 28/12/22 Walthamstow; [ch] William, Glyn, Alison & Norma; [ed] Secondary - Staples Road, Loughton Essex; [occ] housewife.

GILBERT, DORIL M.: [b]Wolverhampton; [p] J. & N. Kislingbury; [awards] music (piano), tennis; [activ] amateur dramatics, languages, gardening, design/paint greeting cards; [pub writ] magazines/newspapers; "Grandmother, P.J. Kislingsbury, awarded Bronze Medal for poetry. My first poem was composed when I was eight, in the bath, my mother ran for paper and pencil. I have written severl hundred on countryside, religion, flying wartime, topical subjects."

GODDARD, LEAH A.: [b] 16/7/08 Cwmcarn; [p] Leah & William Watson; [ch] Patricia, Brian & Leslie; [ed] Fairview, Blackwood, Gwent, South Wales; "I am almost 87 years of age, live in a council house with my cat called 'Toot' and if I was fortunate enought to win the £500 first prize I would take a holiday with my son who has been forced to retire because of ill health."

GODDARD, SANDRA: [b] 22/2/51 Manchester; [m] Colin; [p] Benjamin & Ivy Lane; [ch] Joanne; [ed] Flixton Secondary School for Girls; [occ] housewife; "Thank-you to my husband, Colin, for giving me the time to write my poetry. I love you."

GOLLEDGE, DAVID: [b] 1/2/67 Sunderland; [p] Ernie & Vera; [ed] school in Sunderland, UNL & Birkbeck, London; [occ] production/design officer; [awards] degree - geography; [mem] Royal Geographic Society, Greenpeace; [pub writ] 'Wideyes' - Poetry Now/War On Want Anthology, 'God Machines' - North East 1994.

GOODMAN, ELAINE: [b] 24/10/48 Oldham; [p] Kenneth & Doris Clarke; [ch] Martin, Alison & Robin; [ed] Fitton Hill Sec. Modern School; [occ] student; [awards] College of Preceptors certificate - English Lang./Lit., ULCI cert. - office skills/typewriting, Duke of

Edinburgh's award; [pub writ] Poetry Now Anthology, Poetry In Motion (North) Anthology - Arrival Press, A Taste of Summer Anthology - Anchor Books; "I inherited the gift of writing from my great-grandfather who was also a poet. The wild beauty of the north of England countryside inspired me to write poetry. I have also written four novels."

GOOSE, JOHN: [b] 17/2/42 Epsom; [m] Carole Ann; [p] Tom & Lillian; [ch] Terry, Jo (Joanne) & Karen; [occ] manager; [awards] certificates - tyre sales, managerial recognition; "I have an easy going nature which helps me to tolerate the stress of others and appreciate those of a like nature to myself."

GOSS, MELANIE: [b] 4/5/67 Leicester; [p] Tony & Barbara Conway [ed] Burleigh Community College, Loughborough & Reading University; [occ] insurance clerk; [awards] BA (Hons.) History; "As we go through life, we wander the bricks and mortar of our personalities, eventually settling at our favourite window in order to view the world about us. The wonder of poetry is in finding a new, as yet undiscovered, window."

GOULDING, EDWARD W.: [b] 31/12/23 Liverpool; [m] Margaret; [p] Edgar & Mary; [ch] Paul & Janet; [ed] Liverpool Institute High School, College of Estate Mngment, St. Aidan's Theological College; [occ] vicar/prison chaplain (rtrd.); [awards] school cert., A.A.L.P.A. (now A.S.V.A.), general ordination exam; [activ] fund-raising various causes; "I am a disabled ex-serviceman (1943-7 army). A number of friends were less fortunate and were killed. I have never forgotten a sermon from St. Martin-In-The-Fields heard on a radio in an army canteen about 1944. This phrase I pass on to others — it was repeated many times by the preacher: 'When milions of men have been killed, what are you doing alive?'"

GOWING, BETTY: [b] 14/6/25 Slough, Bucks; [p] Annie & Edward Daines; [ch] Lorna, Barry, Cath, Jim, Wendy, Ted & Nigel; [ed] Church of English; [occ] housewife; [awards] Electrical & Mechanical Engineer on Hawker Hurricanes WWII; "I was delighted, as I have other poems and I have never entered any of them before."

GRACE, RITA: [b] 23/6/34 Annesley, Woodhouse; [p] William Henry; [ch] Valerie, Stephen, Russel & Roger; [ed] Kirkby Woodhous Jr. & Infants, Vernon Road Sec. Modern, Clarendon College, Nottingham; [occ] housewife; [awards] Booth Edison Trust Award, E.M.E.U. & R.S.A. - Shorthand/Typwriting, English, Maths & Composition, winner 1st Peter Davis Award Phab Magazine; [mem] P.H.A.B., Newstead Abbey Byron Soc.; [pub writ] articles for Ashfield (CHAD), 'The Belles of Byron' - 1995; "Writing and poetry hve become my passion. I get inspiration from my thoughts, from my surroundings and from historic occurrences."

GRAHAM, VERA: [b] 19/1/30 Billingham; [p] Bertram & Eva Smith; [ch] Linda, Michael, Lorraine, Vivien, Billy & Richard; [ed] Bousefield Lane Girls School; [occ] housewife; [mem] I.C.I. club; [activ] writing, Good Samaritan of the Skies, Care for Carers; [pub writ] 'Birth of I.C.I.', short story - 'Butterfly Silk'. "I have had letters published in The Evening Gazzette regarding the disabled; let's bring sunshine into disabled lives."

GREAVES, AUDREY: [ed] Winchester School of Art, Open University; [occ] R.G.N.; [awards] scholarship - Winchester School of Art, [activ] drawing/painting, writing poetry, illustrating and producing children's books. "I am a visual artist and lyrical poet. In my paintings form takes marginal precedence over colour. The poems are personal without being confessional. The theme of my work is the interdependence of all living things encompassing birth, love, motherhood, nature and death."

GREEN, SUSAN: [b] 22/2/64 Sutton-in-Ashfield; [p] Pearl & Peter; [ch] Jamie Robert & Carly-Jo; [ed] Shirebrook Comprehensive, Clowne in Derbyshire College; [awards] recognition for charity work, fund-raising medals - Multiple Sclerosis; [activ] writers club, volunteer fund-raising; [pub writ] poem - 'A Soapy Saga' - Anchor Books; "I feel that everyone needs a dream to live up to and by my joining the Writers Club my hobby has kept me happy in the knowledge that I now have two separate pieces of work published."

GREENWAY, JENNIFER: [b] 1/7/43 Ashford, Mox; [occ] advertising rep.; [activ] Runnymede Arts Assoc., scrtry Runnymede Writers; [pub writ] short story - New Fiction Shorts from Surrey, poem in regional anthology; "I enjoy writing, and find it helps me see a lighter side of life."

GREGORY, ANTOINETTE: [b] 11/2/81 Bury St. Edmunds; [p] Nigel & Julie; [ed] County Upper School; [occ] student.

GREIG, WILLIAM: [b] 25/5/56 Winchester; [p] Philip & Susan; [occ] lecturer; [awards] MA - Social Anthropology; [mem] Friday Folk, Beg. Eng. Dance Club, St. Albans, HERTS; "The poem 'Folk Dance Queen' was written as a song. If any singer or musicians are interested in singing it please get in touch through PIBI."

GRIEVE, JANE: [b] 5/11/41 Fraserburgh; [m] James; [p] John & Beatrice Noble; [ch] Gary & Gail; [ed] Fraserburge Academy; [occ] production worker; [activ] Scottish Motor, Neurone Disease Assoc.; [pub writ] poem - Poetry Now '95; "I lead a quiet life with my husband and three cats. I love gardening, crosswords, listening to music and writing poetry. I am a deeply caring and compassionate person and try to put these feeling into my poems."

GRIFFITH, GILES A.: [b] 8/11/75 Wiltshire; [p] Angela & Duncan; [ed] King Jame's School, Greenhead College; [awards] school awards - English; [pub writ] poem - Poetry Now Yorkshire Reg. Anthology.

GRIFFITHS, CERI: [b] 25/6/66 Birkenhead; [p] Ron & Lilian; [ch] Fay Devon; [ed] Park High Sec. School, Birkenhead; [occ] mother/student; [awards] diploma - creative writing; [activ[volunteer - teaching English to overseas students; [pub writ] poem 'The Fish Tank' - Winter Anthology '91, short verse for greeting cards; "I wish to be a successful writer/poet. I find a lot of inspiration for my work comes from watching my daughter grow. The best of my work has been written while listening to relaxation tapes ('Moods')."

GRIGGS, JOY: [b] 19/12/55 Perth, Scotland; [m] Stephen; [p] William & Joy Mullenger; [ch] Ricky & Laura; [ed] Featherstowe Road School; [occ] housewife; "I have written a few poems and children's books for my family on special occasions. At the moment I am researching my family tree."

GRINDROD, CAREN: [b] 11/11/59 Altringham; [m] George; [p] Bill & Eileen Grindrod; [ed] Brookway High School, Fielden Park College of F.E.; [occ] secretary; [awards] AMS Cert. - medical secretarial, Manchester Tec Bus. Enterprise Programme cert.; [pub writ] poem - 'Lift The Veil' - anthology Writers Bureau '94; "I married George Christophorou, February 2nd, 1995, whose love, support and encouragement has given me the energy to pursue my ambition."

GROAT, NEIL L.: [b] 9/7/53 Kirkwall; [m] Karen; [p] Tommy & Bessie; [ch] Kane & Alison; [occ] airline agent; "Music and the written word feeds the soul of mankind."

GROOME, MARLENE: [b] 28/8/37 Romford Essex; [ch] Geoffrey, Michelle & Michael; [occ] housewife/carer; [pub writ] poem - Anchor Books; "Thrilled to bits. I have written twenty-five poems which have not been seen — hope to publish a small book of them."

GUEST, SHERIDAN D.: [b] 17/3/59 Scotland; [p] Rita & George Russell; [ch] David, Christopher, Jamie, Nicky & Lauren; [ed] Kings School B.F PO 47, West Suffolk College; [awards] 5 'O' levels - child psychology; [mem] Local Council Tenants Forum, Brittle Bone Soc.; [activ] song writing/poetry; "Ideally I would love to have my songs recorded and sung by a good artist and would like to write more poetry and songs."

GUINEE, DAVID: [b] 2/11/78 Cardiff; [p] Pat & Laurence; [ed] Lianrumney High School; [occ] student; "Writing poems is a way in which I can express my thoughts and feelings clearly without irritating people. I also gain a sensation from writing lyrics."

GUY, PENELOPE: [b] 19/4/47 W. Sussex; [p] Peter & Kate Greenyer; [ch] Tabitha, Victoria & Hannah; [ed] Worthing High School for Girls,

Whitelands College; [occ] teacher; [awards] teaching cert., T.E.F.L. cert.; [mem] life member - National Trust; "I am going to live in Crete next year and hope to find a lot more time for writing."

GWENLAN, PETER: [b] 16/6/40 Tredegar; [p] David & Ann; [ed] Lewis' School, Pengam; Caerleon Training College; [occ] headmaster (rtrd.); [activ] Milford Haven Town Band, Celtic Saints Jazz Band, Milford Haven Squash Club, St. Ishmaels Church Recorder Group; "It's never too late to take on fresh challenges. If you have a dream, pursue it."

HAGYARD, JOHN: [b] 29/9/50 Wakefield; [p] Kenneth & Olive; [ch] Victoria, Neil & Aimee; [occ] community carer; [activ] Gr. 1 football ref., (local leagues); [pub writ] poems - British Poetry Review '94, Winter Celebration; "By writing poetry I can capture my thoughts for all to see and discuss. As an artist would put on canvas what he/she thinks and sees, a poet paints a similar picture using the written word."

HAINES, ALEX: [b] 3/6/29 Weston-Super-Mare; [m] Barbara; [p] Sydney & Edith (dcd.); [ch] Pauline, James, Caroline, Connie & Alexander; [ed] Waliscote Road School for Boys; [activ] founder/sole member WIMP - Weston's Individual Madman Party; [pub writ] newspapers, Arrival Press, Anchor Books; "I feel I have messages to give to this world — more so after a few pints ... don't we all?"

HALL, JOY: [b] 20/5/30 Somersham; [p] Millicent & Percival Barlow; [ch] Enid, Gibbs, Vivienne, Benton & Colin; [ed] Slepe Hall Private School for Girls; [activ] British Legion, Agricultural Assoc., Friendship Club; [pub writ] local newspapers; "I enjoy being with people and joining in their social activities. Writing my poems makes me feel good and relaxes me."

HALL, MARGARET I.: [b] 13/3/38 Norton, Malton; [m] Edmund; [p] Herbert & Beatrice Rowsby; [ch] Gary & Martyn; [ed] Norton Primary School, York College for Girls; [occ] bank clerk (rtrd.); [activ] volunteer - OXFAM, Cancer Research, Arthritis Assoc.; "I enjoy life, play bowls and whist. I belong to the Mothers Union and local church. This is my first attempt at poems."

HALL-MORLEY, MIRANDA: [b] 10/12/66 Nottingham; [ch] Jacob Reece; [ed] Col. Frank Seely School, Arnold & Carlton College; [occ] advertising consultant; [awards] award - creative writing, diploma - advertising (Guam USA); [activ] Roundabout Theatre Co., Co-operative Arts Theatre; "To achieve goals you have to have dreams, take those dreams and make it happen. Anything is obtainable if you want it enought."

HAMMOND, HEIDI: [b] 1/10/75 London; [p] Alf & Linda; [ed] Chislehurst & Sidcup Grammar School; [occ] editorial assistant; [awards] school prizes - art 'A' level, J.H. Walsh English prize - 'A' level, Venture Scout Award; [activ] Venture Scout, local health authority, peer ed. rep. HIV-AIDS, Greenwich Young People's Theatre; [pub writ] poem 'A Twisted Compliment' - school magazine, brochure copy - Thomson's; "If I wanted to be pretentious I'd say 'Poetic inspiration is like a child, conceived half by accident during the expression of emotions, with fears and doubts but no guarantees. When born, the reward is that whatever happens there is living proof that for one moment at least, you were blessed with the chance to make a part of yourself immortal.' But to be honest, I believe life's about doing the things you enjoy, and if others can enjoy them too, it's a bonus."

HANSCOMB, JANET: [b] 29/9/38 Crayford, Kent; [p] Hilda & Cyril Fulker; [ch] Gregory & Stuart; [ed] Dinorben private school; [occ] care assistant; [awards] Wadebridge Music Festival - 1st prize for original poem - 1992-94; [mem] Wadebridge Choral Soc., Writing Group, Camelford Inner Wheel; [pub writ] 'No Way Out' - Poetry Now South West 1995; "I enjoy singing, writing and painting, gardening and reading. Much of my writing has developed in my mind whilst excercising my two dogs."

HANSHAW, MURIEL: [b] 30/12/22 Leeds; [p] Lillian & Clement Ashton; [ch] John & William; [ed] C. of E.; [pub writ] local newspaper; "Since major heart surgery I write purely for pleasure to motivate myself. My ambition is to write a TV script."

HARDING, ROSEMARY D.: [b] 8/4/44 Cheshire; [p] Philip & Patricia Handley; [ch] Simon, Katherine & Sharon; [ed] R.C. Boarding School, Ladies College; [occ] housewife/artist/poet; [mem] International Dolphin Watch, I.F.A.W.; [pub writ] 'Counterpane of Cats', Little Manx Cats', 'My Late Father', magazines; "All of my best poems have been on Manx radio, in newspapers and magazines. I have discovered lately that the majority of people love to share another's deepest thoughts — no better way than poetry to bring comfort and communication."

HARDMAN, DAVID: [b] 4/3/66 Poynton; [m] Helen; [p] George & Jean; [ch] Imogen & Gareth; [ed] University of Hull, University of Manchester; [occ] Methodist minister; [awards] BA (Econ/Pol. Soc.) BD - (Theo.); [activ] guitar in rock band, sport; [pub writ] poems in various anthol.; "Putting pen to paper helps me to express myself. Often poems become songs for the band. Other's musical ability combined with my words gives energy and passion to my feelings."

HARE, CHRISTINE: [b] 9/5/47 London; [p] Harry & May Baker; [ch] Oliver; [occ] housewife; [awards] class prize - Harrow; [activ] collector for Help the Aged; "Observation has a transforming effect on many minds when infused with inspiration. And certainly, the mind reflects, and thought creates thought. Yet, there is no doubt that the poet's vision is often inspired by the transitional and haunting beauty inherent in nature."

HARPER, LYN: [b] 20/12/30 Birmingham; [p] John & Violet Hurley; [ch] Jean, Pru, Denise & Christopher; [ed] Lea Village High School; [activ] volunteer - Age Concern, avid reader of non-fiction, elder care; [pub writ] poem - Age Concern magazine; "I get immense satisfaction knowing that most of my poems bring pleasure to others, and having at last found the courage, to enter one in a competition."

HARPER, RON: [b] 28/5/53 Walsall; [m] Carole; [p] Arthur & Vin; [ed] Willenhall Central Sec. Modern, Walsall Technical College; [occ] journalist; [awards] NCTJ - proficiency cert.; [pub writ] various technical pamphlets, books, video scripts; "Poetry is my way of saying things that I cannot put into words!"

HARRIOTT, VAL: [b] 10/2/52 Wimbledon; [m] Roy; [p] Jean & Les Moss; [ch] Sharon, Dawn & Roy; [ed] Sandhurst Rd. Infant School, Franciscan Rd. Junior, Tooting Sec.; [occ] childminder; [activ] church, National Childminding Assoc.; [pub writ] 2 poems - Triumph House (Christian publication); "I am excited to know that a hobby of mine that was, up until now, my own thoughts and feelings, my ups and downs, could bring pleasure to others. I feel honoured and humble."

HARRIS, BETH: [b] 20/5/49 Edinburgh; [p] Elizabeth & Edward Hurley; [ch] Mikyla, Adam & Vicky; [ed] Boroughmuir Sec., Firhill Sec.; [occ] housewife; [awards] Creative Writing, guitar; [pub writ] short stories/poetry local newspapers; "I was very surprised and delighted to hear from you. I love writing, but I didn't thnk it would ever be published in a book."

HARRIS, FAYE: [b] 11/4/77 Scunthorpe; [p] David & Denise; [ed] Vale of Ancholme School, Brigg & Brigg 6th Form; [occ] student.

HARRIS JACQUELINE: [b] 12/3/59 Edinburgh, Scotland; [m] George, [p] James & Grace Cooper; [ch[Emma & Allan; [ed] South Queensferry High School, Kirkland High School, Glenrothes College; [occ] shop supervisor; [awards] Eaton Special Merit Award, various Scotvec modules incl. creative writing level 1; [activ] Red Cross volunteer.

HARRIS, PAMELA D.: [b] 18/7/35 Walsall; [p] Henry & Dorothy Wells; [ch] Pamela & Kathleen; [ed] North Walsall School; [occ] Environmental Health Assist.; [activ] church member, gardening, animal lover; [pub writ] poetry in two books; "My husband died 15 years ago in tragic circumstances and I became something of a recluse. I began to read poetry for consolation, and putting my own thoughts into verse. This helped me to realize my world had not ended. I am now looking forward to retirement and devoting more time to my poetry."

HARRISON, DOREEN: [b] 30/12/46 Tipton, W. Midlands; [p] Charles & Evelyn Munday; [ch] Helen & Marie; [ed] Willingsworth Comp. Tipton; [occ] receptionist; [awards] R.S.A. - shorthand/typing; [activ] scrtry - Morecambe Raiders - country/western club, fund-raising; [pub writ] verse in c/w magazines, short articles; "I get a lot of personal satisfaction from helping to organise the many charity events held at my local club. My writing gives me pleasure and a sense of achievement."

HARRISON, FRANCES M.: [b] 2/5/1899 Hemingborough; [p] George & Helen Parkinson; [ch] Herbert, Veronica May & Francis; [ed] Hemingborough Comp., South Duffield Comp. Otley Road (Bradford) Comp.; [occ] housewife; "I obtain personal satisfaction from writing poetry, and even at my age (coming up to 96) I leave my bed at night to jot verses down. I have written many poems thoughout a long life."

HARRISON, KEITH: [b] 2/5/33 Leeds; [m] Shirley; [p] James & Hilda; [ch] Lynn, Julie, Andrew & Paul; [occ] cellar man/porter; "Taking English G.C.S.E. at evening class has inspired some writing and a desire to continue to 'A' level English or a Creative Writing course. 'Pantolines', my second attempt at poetry, is based on childhood memories."

HART, PETER: [b] 27/5/61 Edinburgh; [p] Muriel & Thomas; [ed] Broughton High, Telford College; [occ] painter/decorator; [awards] City & Guilds - paint/decorating, 'O' levels - Eng., History; [mem] cycling club, British Legion; [activ] roadman for pro-fighter; "Feeling strongly about a subject is like having a colourful window in your mind; write it down before the curtains close."

HARVEY, TINA A.: [b] Birmingham; [p] David & Jess Penn-Francis; [ch] Francesca Elaine Birch; [occ] writer - music/poetry; [pub writ] 6 poems - 'Poems For The Open Mind' Anthology, 'Poetry Now' Southwest 1992, "Passages" Westam Poets Anthology; "I love to write, writing is my live. The intangible needs in all of us need poetry as an escape from everyday life, through the mind's many hopes, dreams and fantasies, I love you all."

HARWOOD, COLIN: [b] 18/9/59 Nottingham; [p] Margaret & Dennis; [ed] Farhurn Comp.; [occ] civil servant; "I've always written poems from as far back as I can remember. I am also a songwriter and, as such, try to incorporate my poetic ability through the lyrics I compose. I occasionally write amusing anecdotes based on modern living!"

HATFIELD, LORRAINE A.: [b] 29/12/65 Bridlington; [p] Kenneth & Sheila; [ch] Luke & Jodie; [ed] Headlands Upper School; [occ] housewife; [awards] Art GCE, 'A' level Eng. Language GCE; [mem] National Asthama Campaign & Eczema Soc.; "Being a busy mum, spare time is a luxury when I indulge myself in poetry and painting. I plan to write/illustrate my own children's books on subjects inspired by my own children and my childhood."

HAYES, JUNE-ROSE: [b] 12/6/27 London; [m] Geoffrey; [p] John & Mary Earl; [ch] Graham, Keith & Neil; [ed] Highgate Grammar School, Derby College Higher Ed.; [occ] WEA tutor; [awards] poetry adjudicator (Nott'm Writers Club), diploma - adult education, R.S.A. secretary, joint winner Derbyshire Festival Short Story Competition; [mem] Nottingham Writers Club; [activ] volunteer speaker - Methodist Church Guild/Fellowship, WEA rep.; [pub writ] poetry in local magazines, Welsh anthology, 'Poets of Midlands'; "We are all uniqe. However great or small, our talent is God given and we must use it wisely and well. I believe that we should share our success and happiness for the good of others. Writing has hopend up new doors for me and changed my life for the better. The first step to helping people appreciate others is to help them to appreciate themselves."

HAYES, RHONDA F.: [b] 3/7/56 California; [m] Thomas; [p] Glen & Loree Fleming; [ch] Hannah & Will; [ed] Calif. State University, Fullerton; [occ] mother/writer; [awards] BA Foreign Languages; [pub writ] poetry in regional journals (Southern US), several essays for metro newspaper columns; "After living in England for the past year, I know the true meaning of "Anglophile", for I have become one. It's good to know that some of my writing will remain here after I have left."

HAYES, SHEILA: [b] 11/6/38 Wallasey; [p] Mr. & Mrs. Auchinleck; [ch] Donna, Kerri & Matthew; [occ] housewife; "I started writing poetry at age 12 but never thought about publication. Started writing stories for my chldren and grandchildren."

HAYNES, DAPHNE, A.: [b] 28/11/48 Brighton; [m] Duncan; [p] Daphne & Eric Vale; [ch] Timothy, Daniel & Martin; [ed] Blue Coat School, Royal Walstead Herts; [pub writ] poems in local magazine.

HEAD, CHARLES F.: [b] 22/2/52 Swindon, Wilts.; [p] Charles & Pamela; [ed] Fradon Forest School; [occ] car valet; "I get great satisfaction from putting my thoughts onto paper. To be courteous, understanding, helpful, considerate, plus having a good sense of humour equal happiness."

HEANEY, LES: [b] 9/12/40 Liverpool; [p] Leslie & Cathrine; [ch] Mark, Darren & Dawn; [ed] Liverpool Sec. Modern; [occ] artist; [awards] M.M. and (C.D.F. - France) - ex-foreign legion paratrooper/ British Special Forces); [activ] pres. Re-Beat Club - cardiac patients support group, hospital fund-raising; [pub writ] poem - Poetry Now '95; "I wish only in life to be healthy and happy and pass a small helping hand to my fellow man every day I am allowed to inhabit this wonderful earth."

HEARNDEN, PAULINE: [b] Chester; [m] George; [p] Joseph & Frances Williams; [ch] Beverley & Andrew; [ed] Christ Church School, Dee House Ursuline Convent; [activ] C.A.B., chair local Townswomen's Guild, local community groups; [pub writ] 'Chester' - 1994; "I believe you only get out of life what you are prepared to put in. That welcoming smile goes a long way to breaking down barriers — and, of course, we all need to feel valued."

HEATH, BETTY M.: [b] 12/8/27 Trethomas; [p] Iris & Charles Mortimer; [ch] Shirley & Alan; [occ] housewife; [activ] collector Wales Cancer Research; [pub writ] one poem; "I just find that poetry releases my emotions."

HEATON, PATRICIA: [b] 13/12/46 Middlewich; [p] Harry & Dorreen Gallimore, [ch] Matthew, Aiden, James & Reanne; [activ] volunteer - church committee, Christian Viewpoint lunches, Chadwick Court; "I like to help others and I love everyone. I get a great deal of satisfaction from the poems and songs that I write."

HEAUME, TRACY M.: [b] 7/10/74 Derby; [p] Iris & Derrick Tallett; [ed] Paget High School, Burton Technical College; [occ] nursery nurse; [awards] Bus. Admin NVQ1, NNER diploma, Duke of Edinburgh Bronze, Silver (Gold in progress), First Aid; [activ] volunteer - Cub Scout, first aid; Duke of Edinburgh Award Scheme; "I am 20 years of age and enjoy writing poetry. I write for my own amusement. I attend Paget High School and entered poems for my Englis exams. I put my feelings and thoughts/emotions into peotry as it comes naturaly to me most of the time."

HECK, EVELYN: [b] 14/5/45 Essex; [p] Mary & Eric Warne; [ch] Donna, Allison, Graham & Shane; [occ] domestic engineer; [pub writ] 'You' - poetry anthology; "I'm 49, have four children and two grandchildren. I enjoy all literary pursuits, gardening, quizzes and I'm looking forward to my 50th birthday party."

HEELEY, LEANNE: [b] 6/10/73 Ashington; [p] Eileen & Dave Parker; [ch] Samuel & David; [awards] BA Hons. Degree Student; "Although I have many other commitments I enjoy writing poetry, and hope that my success with this will lead to much more succes in other areas of my writing."

HEENAN, CATHERINE: [b] 21/9/76 Caerphilly; [p] Eileen & Patrick; [ed] Heolddu Comp. School; [occ] student; [mem] R.S.P.C.A., school editorial board; [awards] taking up my place at Cardiff University to read English in the Autumn of 1995; [pub writ] "Bargoed Bygones" - local history book; "My study of literature has profoundly influenced my outlook on life and it is my ambition to articulate that view in what I hope is my own unique voice."

HELLEWELL, BARBARA: [b] 6/3/40 Huddersfield; [ch] Mark & Anne; [ed] Scisset Sec. Modern & Huddersfield Tech. College; [occ] housewife; [awards] student Writers College; [mem] The Examiner Travel Circle (Huddersfield); [pub writ] 5 poems published in 6 books & local newspaper (1st yr. of writing); "I am very honoured that my poem "A Rose" has been chosen by the Poetry Institute and hope it give lots of pleasure to the reader. Thank-you."

HERDMAN, HARROLD: [b] 10/10/51 Orkney; [p] Bill & Betty; [ch] Damien & Eve; [ed] Hope School, Kirkwall Grammar School; [occ] marine operative; [activ] fund-raiser.

HERGLI, NUBIA LIANA: [b] Pendle, Lancashire; [ed] Whitfield School, Burnley College of Arts & Technology; [awards] English Lang. & Creative/Soc. Studies Awards; [activ] Mid-Pennine Arts, Writers Group, R.S.P.B.; [pub writ] book poetry/prose, illustrated - 'Changing Seasons' - Janus 1995; "Inspired by the natural beauty of the countryside, my thoughts and feelings are expressed through the medium of poetry and prose. From an early age, writing has been an influential and creative activity that I have pursued. It gives me immense pleasure and satisfaction when it is shared with others."

HERKES, ELEANOR J.: [b] 9/1/84 Eastbourne; [p] Richard & Jenny; [ed] Willingdon C.P. School; [occ] student; [activ] Church Pathfinder, piano, clarinet & ballet; [pub writ] poetry in church/school magazines; "I find great pleasure in writing short stories and poems. I started when I was five years old. My love of music helps me with my poetry. I have started to write songs too."

HESLOP, ROBERT: [b] 30/1/45 Stirling; [m] Catherine [mem] Freemasons; [pub writ] MAST Publications 'Christmas Cracker' '94, British Books Poetry 1993-95 - Poetry Now '94, 'Power of Words '94 - Triumph House; "My poetry started off as a joke two years ago and has gone from strength to strength from then as I have had lots of success and support from my wife Catherine and friends and my mother-in-law."

HEWITT, JANET N.: [b] 1/11/47 Doncaster; [p] Audrey & George Harris; [ch] Jayne & Colin; [ed] Percy Jackson Grammar School; [occ] midwife (rtrd.); [awards] nursing/midwifery certs.; [mem] St. Peter's Church; [pub writ] poems in several anthologies; "Having a wide experience of life' I have found it is better to reflect on yesterday, live today to the full and look forward to tomorrow. I enjoy writing and exprssing my feelings in verse."

HEWITT, PATRICIA: [b] 19/462 Brigg; [ch] Brian; [ed] Baysgarth Comprehensive; [mem] N.A.H.C.; [awards] Gr. 2 English CSE; [pub writ] poem in school magazine; "Writing poems gives me a great sense of expression and achievement. Believe in yourself and you can do anything, all you have to do is want it enough. Never give up on yourelf — and people will never give up on you."

HICKMAN, VAL: [b] 30/7/52 Birmingham; [mem] active member of local Wildlife Trusts; [pub writ] poems 'Awakening', 'Hunger', 'Armageddon', 'Homage to Keats', 'The Ripening', 'Homage', 'Josef'; "Personal trauma and turmoil as enriched me with a 'been there — done that — wore the T-shirt' type education. I am pasionate about Nature. The forces have combined within me. through a therapeutic partnership with my pen, they have given me a voice. A voice which I hope would aspire to fulfill (I believe) a poet's aim — to touch — to reach receptive/ unreceptive souls."

HILDER, SARAH: [b] 8/6/62 Keston, Kent; [p] Joan F. Goodchild; [occ] adminstrator; [activ] photography; "Life is full of beautiful things — if only we stop to see them."

HILL, ELEANOR: [b] 1955 Kirkcaldy; [p] Elizabeth & David; [ch] Louise & Stuart; [occ] housewife; [awards] L.A.M.D.A. Gold Medal, Poetry Society Gold; [pub writ] poems local press.

HILL, JIM P.: [b] Scotland; [m] Daphne; [p] Thomas & Ada; [ch] Thomas James; [ed] University: Glasgow & London; [occ] translator/ lecturer/speech writer; [awards] Degrees - Hispanic & Russian Studies; [mem] Amnesty International; [pub writ] speech manual, one novel,

verse in university and national publications; "I believe strongly in freedom of expression, in access to information, in proportional representation and more direct public participation in government. I also believe that writers and users of other media can effectively promote the implementation of these principles."

HILL, MARK: [b] 9/2/64 Eastbourne; [m] Jane; [ch] Charlotte & Victoria; [mem] Deanery Synod [activ] church council.

HILTON, VERA: [b] 29/3/44 Denton, Manchester; [m] Jim; [p] Walter & Sarah Harwood; [ch] Steve & Darren; [ed] Egerton Park Sec. Modern; [occ] department manager; "If this poem makes you smile then I've achieved a lot."

HIPWELL, JUNE: [pen] [b] 2/8/47 Halifax; [p] Hilda & Alan (dcd.); [ed] Crossley & Porter Grammer School for Girls; [occ] housewife; [pub writ] 'Clwyd' - Welsh Poets Anthology; "'Big Trees' is the first poem I ever wrote inspired by Whitty Lane, Warley, Halifax. I have written over 60 since. More to be published later this year I hope."

HITCHCOX, MOIRA: [b] 10/5/53 Bradford; [m] David; [ch] Kirk; [ed] Fisher Moore High School; [occ] perfume top processor; 'I enjoy writing poems, I write them quite often for people for special occasions and I find it relaxing."

HOBSON, SYLVIA: [b] 7/12/43 Washington; [p] Bill & Grace Lonsdale; [ch] Paula Michell & Ian Edward; [ed] Usworth Sec. Modern School; [occ] housewife; [pub writ] 3 poems in local magazines; "I get a lot of enjoyment in putting my thoughts about everyday true experiences into poetry."

HOCKLEY, JOYCE M.: [b] 26/7/22 London; [p] Albert & Elizabeth-Maude Killman; [ch] Michael & Sally Anne; [ed] St. Cuthbert's College; [awards] 3rd place - short play competition, 1st & two 3rd place in songs contests for lyrics; [pub writ] poetry in 4 anthologies; 17 children's short stories, weekly articles local press; "Writing is my hobby — poetry, short plays, comedies, short stories — for children and adults. Just give me a pen and paper and I'm in my element!"

HODGETTS, MICHAEL: [b] 12/12/36 Watford; [p] A. W. Hodgetts; [ed] Merchant Taylors School, London University; [occ] chartered surveyor; [mem] fellow - Royal Inst. Of Chartered Surveyors; [activ] past president Rotary Club of Perth W.A.; [pub writ] Building Ezontrust of Australia, editorial writer 4yrs.

HODGSON, ANGELA: [b] 15/12/56 St. Albans; [p] Wally & May Woods; [ch] Oriana Rose; [ed] Oaklands Convent Hants; Portsmouth College of Art & Design; [activ] equestrian, dogs, reading, painting, architecture & interior design; "I started writing poetry after a 'near death' experience while convalescing after the birth of my daughter. I hope to pursue this interest utilising my artistic ability to conjure up images and thoughts with words in a fashion pleasing to myself and others."

HODGSON, DOREEN: [b] 19/9/42 Horncastle; [p] St. John & Kathleen Withers; [ch] David & Caron; [ed] Gartree Comprehensive; [occ] catering manager; [activ] local art group, Sugar Craft Guild; [pub writ] poetry in local magazine; "Taking up painting in watercolours two years ago as a hobby has opened my eyes to the beauty that is all around us. I now notice the colours of an autumn sunset, and how bare winter trees stand stark against a dark threatening sky. As I get older I put love, friendship and family above all material things."

HOGARTH, ANN: [b] 21/6/48 Dunfermline; [m] Hamish; [p] Annie & James Muir; [ed] Lochgelly Jr. Sec.; [occ] p/t care assistant; [activ] caring for pets/dog training/obedience/shows, walking, swimming and music, writer's workshop, knit for charity; "I have learned that one finds happiness from doing things for other people and making others happy rather than seeking for oneself. I like working with elderly and disabled people and doing things for charity. I also love animals and detest cruelty."

HOLLOWAY, DOROTHY: [b] 4/5/48 Oxford; [m] David; [p]

Eleanor & Jack Anns; [ed] Icknield Sec. School, Oxford College of F. E.; [occ] housewife; [activ] committee member Minster & District Social Club, founder Faringdow Singles Club, church member; dance club; [pub writ] reg. contrib. church magazine, poem 'God's Paint Box' - A Pocketful of Verse - Anchor Books, self-published 'Verse and Decidely Worse'; "My hobbies are making soft toys, bellringing, sequence dancing, nature study, singing, Scrabble and writing. I am a Christian, love children and animals, the countryside and swimming. I use my poems as a testimony to God and to explore my sense of humour in life."

HOLLOWAY, GWENDOLINE E.: [b] 16/7/36 London; [p] George & Daisy Self; [ch] Laura & Emma; [ed] Eastham Grammar School for Girls; [occ] secretarial/pa; [pub writ] some poems have been published; "I am a vegetarian with strong views towards protecting our environment and totally against cruely to animals. I love cats especially and I am writing my autobiography."

HOLMAN, KAZ: [b] 14/6/64 Weybourne, Norfolk; [p] Stephaine & Jack Clarke; [ed] Sheringham High School; [occ] housewife/tarot consultant; [mem] Psychic & Clairvoyant Society, Swords of Pendragon Re-Enactment Society; [pub writ] poetry - 'Mother Earth Is Dying' - Anchor Books '94, 'If Life' - Anchor Books '94' "I feel in my years of writing poetry I have gained so much inner reward. It is my belief that what we put out, so will be returned, and 'we are what we think, having become what we thought'. If we think happy, we can become happy. My poems have shown me if we 'cause' so we will 'effect' so a good 'cause' does bring a good 'effect'.

HOLMES, EDWARD L.: [b] 30/9/22 Birmingham; [m] Norma; [p] Laura & Leonard; [ch] Robert & Madeline; [ed] Halesowen College; [awards] sport/athletics trophies, 3 wins Hundred Mile Handicap Veterans Race, 10 Mile win - Midland Counties; [pub writ] 5 poems in various anthologies - Anchor Books, one poem in magazine; "I wish to dedicate this poem to my wife, Norma Holmes and my best friend Teresa Rudge who have always supported and encouraged me with my poetry."

HOLMES, E. MARGARET: [b] 1/1/35 New Silksworth, Co. Durham; [m] Bob; [p] Dora & William Snowball; [ch] Nigel & Alison; [ed] Seaham Harbour Girls Grammar School, Ilkley College of Housecraft (Teacher Training) [occ] teacher/medical clerk-typist; [awards] 7 'O' level GCE, Teaching Cert., Elem. Typing Distinctions, Early Grade Piano Certs.; [pub writ] 60 children's short stories - Sunderland Echo, poem - Horton Writers Group '86, poem - Poetry Now Northeast '92; "I was brought up a Methodist and sang in church choirs. My God-given talents are a musical ear and a sensitivity to words as a means of communication. After suffering and recovering from a very bad spell of agoraphobia I have acquired a greater understanding, awareness of empathy for my fellow human beings. My life has been richer, though not easier, for the experience."

HOMEWOOD, MAVIS: [pen] Leslie Woods; [b] 12/6/21 Ashton-On-Mersey; [p] Lilly & Ernest Mawson; [ch] Roger, Keith & Ian; [ed] Sale Central School; [awards] A.V.C.M., L.V.C.M., & F.V.C.M.; [mem] Ramsbottom Heritage Society; [activ] film-making, sec. Bury North Homewatch Committee; [pub writ] 8 poems various anthologies, 6 poems published '72; "I have written since I was eight years old. Many things inspire me and I write stories in verse as well as short ones. I also write stories for children."

HOOPER, CLIFFORD E.: [b] 5/4/27 Cheslyn Hay; [p] Percy & Lilian (dcd.); [ed] Cheslyn Hay Sr. & Further Education; [activ] chairman local Historical Society, friend of local schools; "Children are my great love and main inspiration. My ambition is to have a book of illustrated educational poems published, worthy of aiding and pleasing children now and long after I have gone. I include humour in some and keep children's abilities in mind as I write."

HOPE, ELIZABETH: [b] Seaham, Co. Durham; [p] Robert & Elizabeth Hope; [ch] Mervyn, Gaynor & Glenda; [occ] artist; [awards] teaching diploma - Leeds, commissioned Xmas cards - Leeds Lord Mayor, art exhibitions - civic hall/'conserved' church bldg.; [activ] volunteer - visit the sick - Eucharistic minister, Leeds painting & sketch club; "I achieve self-fulfillment in the seeking of beauty through creation,

and in communicating my innermost thoughts with words and paintings."

HOPKINS, JUNE M.: [b] 19/6/34 March; [m] Michael; [p] Tom & Annie Henson; [ch] Teresa, Paul & John; [ed] Hereward School; [occ] homecare assistant; [pub writ] 'On The Wings Of A Dove' - Dec. '94; "I only started to write poems the night before my father's funeral in 1984. I still cannot believe they are worth publishing."

HOPKINSON, LEONORA: [b] 13/3/43 Sheffield; [p] Norah & Leonard; [ed] Hurlfield Sec. Mod. School for Girls; [activ] volunteer - Imperial Cancer Research/Rotherham; [pub writ] 2 poems - anthology '75; "I am a born again believer in Christ. I believe I am patient and a good listener. I love to write poems and paint landscapes."

HORTON, EMMA: [b] 2/1/85 Leeds; [p] Diane; [ed] Aspin Park C.P. School; [occ] student; [activ] ballet, tap dancing, flute & recorder; "I like writing stories and poems. I save them on my Grandpa's computer. I get lots of ideas from the books I read and all my friends and family."

HOUSTON, SARAH A.: [b] 2/1/74 Belfast; [p] Barrie & Anne; [ed] Belfast Royal Academy, Trinity College; [occ] student; [activ] amateur dramatics, choral work, community work; [pub writ] poetry in student magazines; "Poetry is the ultimate expression of one's feelings. As a painting does for an artist, it encapsulates the poet's innermost thoughts in a way in which the reader may unparcel and experience them for himself. This is what I aim to achieve."

HOWARD, CATHERINE A.: [b] 5/2/53 Elland; [m] Leslie; [p] Edward & Audry Poe; [ed] Elland Grammar School, School of Commerce; [occ] gov't officer (rtrd.) [activ] foreign travel, vehicle restoration; [pub writ] 'Elland In Old Picture Postcards', poetry in various books, magazines; "In 1989 I took early retirement due to contracting meningo-encephalitis. I have limited mobility and concentration, but having always had a flair for poetry I decided to compose. The results have brightened my life somewhat."

HOWARD, DORIS V.: [b] 16/5/16 Sunbury; [m] George (dcd.)[p] William & Alice Derbridge; [ch] Nigel; [ed] C. of E. School, St. Saviour's Staines Road West; [pub writ] 'Untitled', 'How Much Shall I Remember: When I Am Tired And Old' - Anchor Books '94; "Widow of the late George John Howard, car hire proprietor Sunbury-On-Thames, son of Devonshire family (late) Henry & Sarah Howard. I have on son Nigel, married to Susan (nee Brown), daughter of Joan & Peter (dcd.), two granddaughters Joanne & Katy. I love writing poetry on life and what it is all about."

HOWARD, HARRY: [b] 24/6/32 Rochdale; [p] William & Annie; [ch] Noel & Angela; [ed] St. Edwards, Castleton; Castlemere Central, Rochdale; [occ] engineer; "I am, I suppose, what could be described as an erratic poet. Dependent on mood, I sometimes create a work within minutes whilst at other times, it can be months before I apply pen to paper."

HOWARD, JULIE: [b] 31/3/62 Rochford; [m] Steven; [p] Sylvia & Norman Cribb; [ch] Steven & Vikki; [ed] King John School; [occ] housewife; [pub writ] 'Simply The Best' - Soap Wars - Arrival Press; "Writing poetry has always been a passion of mine. It can dramatically change everyday events when described in verse. It releases tensions & emotions and gives me great satisfaction."

HOWARD, SUSAN: [b] 14/3/53 Exeter; [p] Victor & Elizabeth Balkwill; [ch] Lewis, Shari, Leonie, Stacy & Steven; [ed] St. James School, Shelly School Crediton; [occ] housewife; [pub writ] poem in Poetry Now - South West '92, 2 poems in local magazine; "Since a small child poetry has been a major part of my life and my poems reflect the events of my life, the ups and downs."

HOYSTED, AUDREY: [b] 15/2/24 Shorncliff, Kent; [p] William & Alice; [ch] Sarah & Karen; "I've loved writing letters and poems in local newspapers for over 30 years. I did voluntary work in the past and have a keen interest in politics."

HUDSON, MARY: [b] 19/4/18 Glasgow; [p] Margaret & William

Penman; [ed] Mumlochy Public School; [awards] Editor's Choice Award - Outstanding achievement in Poetry - National Library of Poetry (North America), hymns sung in church, book of 46 religious poems; [activ] entertainer OXFAM, cancer research; "Thank God daily, walk humbly. Raise a laugh, help to uplift everyone you meet."

HUGHES, ANNE M.: [b] 5/5/52 Llandudno; [p] Veronica & Samuel Aston; [ch] Pamela; [ed] John Bright Grammar School, Llandrillo College; [activ] sec. Sword & Acorn Writers; [pub writ] poetry in various anthologies & ntn'l poetry magazines; "Poetry, one of the earliest forms of communication, is still a powerful medium and my hope for the future is that poetry becomes an intrinsic part of everyone."

HUGHES, EDITH M.: [b] 26/6/18 Hengoed; [p] William & Margaret Brown; [ch] Alwyn & Judith; [occ] housewife (rtrd.); "I have been retird for the past ten years, and enjoy writing poems. This particular poem I wrote when our village was preparing for the Carnival; I enjoyed watching my grandchildren taking part and getting excited on Carnival Day."

HUGHES, JUNE: [b] 29/6/36 Worksop, Notts; [p] Gladys & Bob Willcocks; [ch] Janette, & John; [ed] Technical College, Worksop; [occ] housewife; "As a wife, mother and grandmother I have written over the years, mostly poetry and children's stories. This is the first time I have submitted anything."

HULL, MARIE-LOUISE: [b] 11/11/70 Cornwall; [p] Fiona & Ronald; [ed] Hayle Comp. School, High Lanes, Hayle; [occ] holiday co-ordinator; [awards] BTEC Bus. Studies Cert., Cert. Personnel Practice, Cert. Private Secretary; "Still trying to work life out."

HULLAH, KAREN: [b] 19/9/56 Harrogate; [p] Elizabeth & Ernest Sykes, [ch] Debbie & Jamie; [ed] Duncan Bowen Sec. School; [occ] care officer; [awards] training awards, Youth & Community Diploma, City & Guilds - Hairdressing; [activ] school governer, judo (black belt); [pub writ] poetry in 12 anthologies, freelance for local paper, short stories in magazines, local activities booklet for young people; "I enjoy writing and get a great deal out of it in terms of seeing my work in print and feeling a sense of achievement."

HULYER, MAGGIE: [b] 7/6/52 Wisbech; [m] Derek; [p] Noel & Maisie Cawthorne; [ed] Wisbech High School, Nottingham University, Ealing Tech; [occ] librarian; [awards] Theology Degree, Diploma - Librarianship; [activ] solo/choir singer: Anglo-Catholic Cantrix; [pub writ] poem regional anthology, poem accepted - National Anthology; "In my social, working and musical life, effective communication is a high priority. My poetic self-expression therefore aims to be comprehensible, but also knows that the spiritual intellect needs enigmatic stimuli."

HUMPHRIES, IAN M.: [b] 8/10/60 Newark; [p] Kenneth & Brenda; [ch] Ezra; [occ] playwright/actor; [awards] joint winner - South Bank University Poetry Award '92; [activ] ex-boxer, member A.B.A. (Amateur Boxing Assoc.), gardening (roses); [pub writ] 'Broken Resolutions' - Poetry Now, 'Strangers In Conversation' '84 - pub. Public Arena, various plays; "I am currently writing a children's book (Myths In Poems) and am attempting a collection (Poems Unselected) and various short stories based in London, Spain & America."

HUMPHREYS, NORMAN D.: [b] 12/5/20 Abercynon; [p] Annie & Arthur; [ch] Linda, Patricia, Helen, Michael & Norman; [pub writ] poem - factory magazine; "Although I am 74, I did not retire until a fortnight ago."

HUMPHREYS, TAFF: [b] 19/3/51 South Wales; [awards] military medals; "Always take cash before a cheque and Wales for the Grand Slam!!"

HUNT, LUCY V.: [b] 24/5/68 North Yorkshire; [p] Mary & Peter; [ed] Ripon Grammar School, Harrogate College of Arts & Technology; [awards] Cert. Teacher of English as Foreign Lang.; [mem] Greenpeace; [pub writ] poems in Poetry North anthology '92 - '93; "I am forturnate to have been brought up in a family who encouraged me to express myself through art, music and writing, (my mother, in particular, encouraged me). I believe that the arts provide a tangible bridge between the imagination and reality, providing valuable insight into the very best (and worst) of the human condition."

HUNTER, CHARLES: [b] 7/12/52 Anglesey; [m] Hazel; [p] Charles & Violet; [occ] engineer; [pub writ] poems in various anthologies; "Through my poetry I have found a long sought release valve to get things out of my system."

HUNTER, OLIVE M.: [b] 12/1/34 Aberdeen; [m] Norman; [p] Mary Ann & Charles Bruce; [ch] Kimberley & Paul; [occ] housewife; [mem] Sweet Adelines Intn'l - choral singing; [activ] indoor bowling; "I have travelled extensively during my life, I have lived in New Zealand for seven and a half years, also Portugal. My singing and writing have given me great confidence. I have led an exciting and active life."

HUNTER, PEGGY: [b] 15/4/26 Morley; [p] Ethel & John Snow; [occ] hire/sale controller; [pub writ] poems in various magazines & anthologies; "Since retiring, writing poems has given me much pleasure and satisfaction. I also enjoy reading my poetry aloud to various groups, as and when the occasion arises."

HUNTER, RACHEL: [b] 10/10/46 Sale, Manchester; [m] Ian; [p] Charles & Kathleen Estcourt; [ch] Paul & Alexandra; [ed] Jr. School, Sale, St. Winifred's Girls School, N. W.; [occ] housewife/carer; [awards] Gr. 1-8 - singing, City & Guilds - catering; [activ] volunteer - disabled, church group; "Caring for my severely disabled daughter has made me feel so humble. I count it a privilege that God thought us fit parents to be blessed with such a lovely, sweet daughter. Poetry seems so right to put my inner most thoughts down."

HUTCHINSON, CONNIE S.: [b] 30/8/24; [p] Harry & Jennie Hardwick; [ch] Nina, Scot & Louise Storry; [ed] Sutton-In-Ashfield Grammar, Trent University, Nottingham; [awards] cert. - Education; [activ] Sherwood Archaeological Soc., Victorian Soc., Nottingham; [pub writ] school/college magazines.

IBBITSON, KEVIN G.: [b] 7/12/50 Leeds, [p] Fred & Violet; [ed] Gott's Park C.S. School, Leeds; [occ] printer's engineer; [awards] Queen's Award - Export Achievement '76, 25 yrs. Continual Service Award '91.

INGRAM, PATRICIA: [b[12/5/50 Chester; [p] Ernest & Elizabeth Jones; [ch] Collette & Lynsey; [ed] West Cheshire College, Chester College; [occ] student; [awards] diploma - animal science, R.S.A., C.L.A.I.T.; [mem] League Against Cruel Sports; "My late return to education has been like the unlocking of a huge, old, creaky door. Now the door is open, I am free to go in whichever direction I choose. I am who I choose to be."

INNES, SHAUNNA: [b] 23/1/61 Dunfermline; [m] Richard; [p] June & James Lumsden; [ch] Jamie & Craig; [ed] Inverkeithing High School; [occ] pt VDU operator; "This particular poem I wrote was a favourite of my late Gran, Isabella Fleming."

IRELAND, MAY E.: [b] 7/5/15 Norfolk; [occ] civil servant (rtrd.); [pub writ] poems pub. in magazines, 'This England' & 'Evergreen', poems in 9 anthologies; "Born in in Norfolk, I am now living in Essex. I joined a Creative Writing class, and Writers Group after retirement. I have one son, two daughters and three grandsons."

JACKSON, PAUL H.: [b] 27/6/34 Belfast N.I.; [p] Mary & Harvey (dcd.); [ed] Rockport Prep. School, Co. Down & Trinity College, Glenalmond, Perthshire, Scotland [occ] information officer; [activ] N.U.J. (Ntn'l Union of Journalist), Inst. of Supervisory Mngmnt; [pub writ] children's book - 'Stephen's Pigeon', poems, travel articles, short stories in various newspapers, magazines and anthologies, story - Royal British Legion Year Book, poems for charitable booklets; : Whilst I always try to give of my best at whatever I do and believe in the philosopy 'Do as you would be done by', I get the most satisfaction from putting my thoughts, feelings and ideas into written words through my short stories and poems"

JACKSON, SIMON L.: [b] 26/9/70 Scunthorpe; [p] Brian & Pam; [ed] High Ridge Comp., North Lindsey College; [occ] acting manager; [awards] B Tec 1st diploma - engineering; "I believe people should express their feelings through words and/or music more often than they do. I try to, and think we all should try to enjoy and make the most of our lives, as we only have one."

JALLOW-RUTHERFORD, SEMBA: [b] 4/12/52 Jamaica; [p] Elijah & Linda Rutherford; [ed] University of B'ham, Leicester University, U.C.E.; [occ] lecturer; [awards] degree - sociology, PGCE, CCYW; [activ] Equal Opportunities Steering Group, African/Caribbean Educators; [pub writ] poems 'Black Heart Black Voices' Vols. 1&2; "My words are not mine, they are the thoughts and ideas of others before me, penned by my own hands. Poetry is used by me as a means of releasing innermost thoughts, feelings and observations."

JAMES, SHIRLEY A.: [b] 16/8/43 Penrhiwceiber; [p] Hester Ann; [ed] Mt. Ash Grammar School, Aberdare College F.E.; [awards] G.C.E. 'O' level - English, Welsh & German, City & Guilds Cert. - community care practise, Achievers Cert. '90; [mem] church choir, M.U., St. Winifred's Branch; [activ] knitting, sewing; "I first began to write the odd poem from 1975 onwards. Just for my own pleasure and for friends. I received letters from the Queen & Queen Mother for one or two 70th & 90th birthday occasions and for the MU Centenary tribute to the MU Founder Mary Sumner."

JARRETT, DICK: [b] 1927; [ed] Marine Technical College; [occ] Marine Chartering Accountant (rtrd.); [activ] treasurer - 'Churches Together' (Esher & Dist.), volunteer - Princess Alice Hospice, golf & swimming; "I am interested in creative writing, my four granchildren and my 'old lady', (not necessarily in that order)."

JARVIS, KAREN: [b] 22/11/58 Chesterfield; [m] Paul; [p] Jack & Hazel Wright; [ch] Rachel, Daniel & Adam; [ed] Hasland Hall School; [occ] housewife; "I feel so strongly about the subject of child abuse which is why I put pen to paper. Nobody really seems to listen anymore, but things could be so different if they did. 'Someone To Listen' is my first attempt at poetry."

JARVIS, STUART P.: [b] 28/4/57 Crail; [p] Eric & Mary; [ch] Abby & Jason; [ed] Waid Academy, Anstruther; [pub writ] 5 poems - 'Poetry Now' Arrival Press; "Throughout my life I have been in stressful situations, I have found if I take my pain and write it down, the created verse serves as 'valium' — tension is released and my mind is cleared. Though, if it weren't for stress, I wouldn't have poetry."

JEFFERIES, TIMOTHY C.: [b] 5/3/70 Loughbrough; [p] Trevor & Barbara; [ed] Manvers Pierrepont Comp. School, Forest Fields College, South Nottingham College; [occ] security officer; [awards] City & Guilds - photography; [mem] Worldwide Fund for Nature (WWF); [pub writ] poems in 3 anthologies: Simple Pleasures - Arrival Press, Life As We Know It - Anchor Books, Earthly Love And Divine Love - Beehive Press; "I am interested in music, art, poetry and philosophy. I believe that these things reflect that which is divine in Man. They represent the universal aspiring of Man towards the plane of higher consciousness, towards the Divine Ground!"

JEMSON, JOAN: [b] 1/10/40 Loftus; [m] Brian; [p] Edward & Caroline Money; [ch] Karl; [occ] housewife; [pub writ] 13 poems in various anthologies; "Relaxation to me is keeping the hands busy with crafts, lacemaking, china painting, embroidery etc., leaving the thoughts free to create the poems I write."

JENKINS, GRAHAM: [b] 25/7/36 Cardiff; [m] Gina; [p] Arthur & Dorothy; [ch] Kerry, Stephen, Alan & Adrian; [occ] engineering rep.; [awards] diploma - stress therapist; "My ambition is to become a successful author. I have recently completed an unpublished book 'The Why Factor', designed to reach the enlightened mind. My poem 'We Are' has been extracted from its beginning. It is hoped that by the publication of this poem a further interest will be created in my writings."

JOHNSON, BEATRICE: [ed] Market Street Girls School; [awards] diploma - Social Work; [activ] choir & other musical activites; [pub

writ] 8 poems in anthologies, Ntn'l Annual, Ntn'l Magazine; "To write is to express. Reserved by nature I find achievement in my poems which does not surface in communication, and find fulfillment in acceptance."

JOHNSON, GRAEME: [b] 16/2/67 Newcastle Upon Tyne; [m] Carol Ann; [p] Robert & Doreen.

JOHNSON, MARJORIE T.: [b] 24/2/11 Nottingham; [p] Ellen & George Johnson; [occ] book research; [awards] 1st prize (2) poems - East Midlands competition - "Platform" & Nott'm Festival '72, book prize & publication - article "Everyman's" Summer Holiday competition '31; [pub writ] poems, articles, short shorties, local & ntn'l papers/ magazines, verses for greeting cards; "I am a vegetarian & anti-vivisectionist, and I believe that humanity will never find peace and healing until it stops its appalling cruelty to animals. Writing keeps my brain alert and relieves my pent-up feelings."

JOHNSON, MAUREEN B.: [b] 24/10/40 Rugeley; [p] Edward & Phyllis Brandrick; [ch] Jamie & Kay; [ed] Bilston College; [occ] nurse; [awards] N.N.E.B.; [activ] Save The Children, World Wildlife, Cancer Research; [pub writ] 5 poems various anthologies; "My writing reflects my interest and love of working with young children."

JOHNSON, PHILIP: [b] 18/7/60 Cheshire; [mem] Ntn'l Assoc. Colitis/Crohn's Disease; [activ] Northwich town councillor; [pub writ] local, regional, ntn'l newspapers, Mid Cheshire Writers Group Promp; "Thanks to English Language Tutors, Jane Dunkerley & Tony Davis for encouraging me to develop my writing of poetry."

JOHNSON, SANDY: [b] 6/6/45 Kinghorn; [m] Kate; [p] Thomas & Agnes; [ch] Lynn, Sandra, Katherine, Sharon & Pennie; [ed] Kinghorn Primary, Burntisland Jr. Sec.; [occ] scaffolder; [pub writ] poem - "Ode to Alexander" - Poetry In Motion Anthol of Scottish Poems - Arrival Press '94; "I have had various poems printed in our local paper. I enjoy reading, writing, fishing and transferring my thoughts on to paper."

JOHNSON, TRICIA: [b] 26/4/42 Stockton, Tees; [m] Allan; [p] Matthew & Nancy Dinsdale; [ed] William Newton School for Girls, Stockton & Billingham Tech College; [occ] countryside info assist.; [activ] Stockton Music/Drama Comm., volunteer warden - countryside park; [pub writ] 1 poem North East anthology; "Never let anyone stop you from writing. If I can do it — you can."

JOHNSTON, DAVID: [b] 7/9/31 Kinglassie; [p] William & Robina; [ch] Stephen & Helen; [ed] Kinlassie Primary School; [occ] miner (rtrd.); [pub writ] poems in local papers; "Be polite to others, if you can't do a good turn, don't do a bad one."

JOHNSTON, GAYNOR: [b] 24/2/66 Buckinghamshire; [p] Leo & Ann; [ch] Alexander Leo; [ed] Meols Cop Miam, Lancashire University, Southport College; [occ] social worker; [awards] diploma - social work; [activ] LACS - Greenpeace; "My son, genuine friendship, animals and my love of nature have all enhanced my life, with not only love but laughter both of which I believe are essential food for the soul. As long as I continue to receive these gifts of life, I will live in happiness."

JOHNSTON, M.: [b] 19/3/36 Derbyshire; [occ] housewife; [activ] WVS, treasurer - self-help group; [pub writ] hospital nwsltr, local newspaper, poem in Easter ed. 1st book "Traveller" series; "Great satisfaction from writing poems, which I moved on to from short stories for children."

JOLLY, FREDERICK: [b] 23/11/27 Bearpark, Co. Durham; [m] Dorothy; [p] Thomas & Ethel; [ch] Barbara; [ed] Bearpark County Council Elem.; [pub writ] self-pub. poetry book "Reflections", poems in anthologies; "I started to record my poems in books in 1985 and have written about 400. I write mostly for family and friends on their special occasions. I enjoy life and people but have great empathy with those less fortunate."

JONAS, SARAH: [b] 2/1/60 Kilmarnock; [m] Kevin; [p] Ian & Sadie Angus; [ch] Andrew & Michael; [ed] Kent School, Germany (R.A.F.); "I love transforming everyday thoughts and situations into poems. It shows that even the most routine tasks can be fun."

JONES, AUDREY: [b] 7/12/35 Manchester; [m] John; [p] James & Clara Berry; [ch] Mark & Simon; [ed] manchester Comp., Worcester Training College for Teachers; [occ] teacher; [awards] BA - Literary Studies M/C University 'Degree by Degrees'; "Writing poetry with my students and sharing our experiences and ways of expressing them has led me to believe that writing poetry is a most accesible means of self-expression and creativity for children of all abilities. Their writing has afforded me the greatest pleasure and insight over the years."

JONES, COLLETTE: [b] 20/10/66 Poringland, Norfolk; [p] Patricia & Tony; [ch] Zoë; [ed] Derbyshire College of H.E.; (Matlock) Durham University; [occ] teacher; [awards] B Comb Studies (Hons.), PGCE; [activ] golf; "Whatever I choose to write here now will only serve as an embarrassment in years to come!"

JONES, DAVID: [b] 5/3/43 Harefield; [ed] University of Lyton; [occ] student; [awards] Merit Prize '92, 1st Prize, 3rd Prize & Merit Prize in Koestler Award, Playwriting for TV/Stage; [pub writ] poem - "Love" - British Poetry Review '94; "I am a poet and writer, I have had vaious poems published in free magazines and newspapers. I am at present a mature student at University of Lyton."

JONES, EMLYN: [b] Bangor, N.Wales; [occ] pastor/pt tutor; [activ] hon. adjudicator Prose/Poetry - Lancashire Authors' Assoc., chairman Preswich Literary Soc., pres. British Council of Churches N.Wales; "I like to get the odd little poem off my chest now and then. My philosphy of life is rather simple; always remember to keep your feet very warm and your head very cool."

JONES, GERAINT: [b] 11/9/73 Merthyr; [p] Granville & Sylvia; [ed] Pen-Y-dre High School, Swansea Inst. of Higher Ed.; [occ] student; "I am currently studying for a degree in Literature & Media at Swansea I. of H.E. Something is wrong when a writer like Dennis Potter is surrounded by misunderstanding and misconceptions. Education must encourage the opening of minds."

JONES, GREG: [b] 31/7/71; [p] Ken & Jan; [ed] Aberdare Comp.; [occ] factory worker; [activ] guitar, exercising, collecting rare records; "Thank-you Kathryn, for the much needed encouragement and inspiration. Words are read by most, but digested by few."

JONES, KEVIN: [b] 29/3/51 Battersea, London; [p] Rosina & George; [ch] Ryan, Matthew, Jennifer & Steven; [ed] Bennetts End Sec. Modern, Filton College, Weston College of Art; [occ] artist; [awards] Commonwealth Essay diploma/ M.I.T.A.; [mem] Pinnacle Group Assoc. of Exhibiting Artists; "I find writing poetry a natural reaction to living. It is a passionate response to feelings, observations and personal experience. As with my art, it is by my very nature that I define a line."

JONES, MARGARET: [b] 29/6/37 Hornbury; [m] Ken (dcd.);[p] John & Nora Naylor (dcd.); [ch] David & Philip; [ed] Horbury St. Peter's Girl School; Wakefield College of Art, Leeds Metropolitan University; [occ] student/housewife; [awards] 2 'A' levels - Eng. Lang./Lit., 'O' level Art, BA degree - Literature/Psychology '94; [mem] Brontë Soc. Haworth, Methodist Church; "My poem is written from the heart, my husband Ken died suddenly three years ago — a month after my mother had died. I live alone, and am 'owned' by my cross/lab dog 'Diamond'.

JONES, MAUREEN B.: [b] 22/4/45 Manchester; [p] John & Alice Haughey; [ch] James & Rachel; [ed] Our Lady's Sec. Modern, Prenton, Wirral, Merseyside; [occ] carer - soc. serv.; [activ] photography; "I am so pleased that I can express my thoughts and feelings in words and other people can enjoy and relate to what I have written."

JONES, RACHEL M.: [b] 21/1/71 Bath; [p] Alan & Mary; [occ] secretary; [activ] WWF; Whale & Dolphins Conserv. Soc., British Fantasy Soc., [pub writ] poetry/short stories various anthologies incl. 'The Science Of Sadness' - Barrington Books; "Whether or not they enjoy my writing, I would like people to be affected by it and for it to leave an impression long after they have finished reading."

JONES, SUSAN L.: [b] 14/2/47 Hillingdon, Middlesex; [p] Emily & Henry Pembrooke; [ch] Martin & Sharon; [ed] Swakeleys College, Middlesex; [occ] secretary/PA; "The inspiration for my poetry comes from observation of people; their actions and mannerisms. My poems are based on life, love and sorrow and I also enjoy writing satirical prose. I gain immense fulfillment from writing and my ambition is to one day have my own anthology of poems published."

JONES, WILFRED: [b] 15/2/26 Marton in Cleveland; [m] Annie; [p] Percy & Hilda; [ch] David, Eric, Kathleen, Susan & Philip; [ed] Hawsker C.E. School; [occ] farm guide p/t.; [activ] branch scty. Ntn'l Union of Agricultural Workers (20yrs.); [mem] Redcar Male Voice Choir, Langbaurgh Singers; "Some of my memories of the 1930's: oxen yoked into the Astoria Suet Cart, Alan Cobhams Flying Circus and The Mallard, majestically puffing its way between Whitby & Hawsker Station, after it had won the blue ribbon as the fastest steam train, from The Flying Scotsman. Also a poem 'A Visit To The Blacksmiths'."

JORDAN, MARK C.: [b] 26/5/69 Halesorwen; [p] Keith & Carol; [ed] Earls High School, Halesowen Tertiary College; [occ] quality engineer; [pub writ] poem - reg. anthology; "I enjoy writing poetry, expressing my feelings & thoughts in verse gives me a great sense of freedom."

JORDAN, RICHARD: [b] 18/1/77 Devizes; [p] Angela & Alan; [ed] Devizes School; [occ] student; [mem] Bath Rugby Club; [activ] Devizes Writers Group; "I wish in the future to be a published novelist and have plays performed as I believe I have the talent for these ambitions."

JUPP, DANIEL: [b] 11/4/74; [p] Colin & Rita; [ed] Essex University; "I am currently in the final year of a BA in History and Literature at Essex University."

JUPP, PADDY: [b] 8/1/35 Levallois-Perret, France; [m] Leonard; [p] Melville & Gwendoline Matthews; [ch] Timothy & Sally; [occ] housewife; [awards] 2 Victor Ludorums - athletics; [mem] Quiling Guild; [activ] W.I. (Cornwall & Essex); [pub writ] poetry in svrl anthologies incl. Women's Institute & local papers, magazines & newspapers; "Enjoy writing poety and participating in several different craft forms, art and photography and reading."

KAYE-LAWTON, NORAH: [b] 17/8/18 Horden, Co. Durham; [m] Matt; [p] Henry & Emma Kaye; [occ] clerk (rtrd.); [pub writ] "Roses In December", Childhood memories of mining village, published in local newspaper; "The daughter of a coal-miner, educated at the local village schools, I was married at the age of 50 years (from the house in which I was born) to Matt G. Lawton, local Park Groundsman. I am fond of music and am a former chorister. I write poems and articles dealing with factual events."

KEARNEY, JOHN C.: [b] 26/12/63 Germany; [m] Val; [p] Bill & Doreen; [ed] Glossop School; [occ] courier driver; "I like to dig a little deeper, then jumble everything around, my life's like that, it helps me to write; darkness is sometimes light."

KEARNS, BERYL A.: [b] 22/7/37 Weston-Super-Mare; [m] Terence; [p] Gladys & Bertie Tripp; [ch] Jillian, Della, David & Steven; [ed] St. Johns School Sec. Modern; [occ] housewife; [activ] volunteer - local hospital; [pub writ] svrl poems in anthologies; "I hope that my poems will give pleasure and perhaps they will help to lighten someone's load as they face problems in their lives."

KEDDIE, PETER: [b] 17/7/21 Galashiels; [p] Harry & Jemima; [ch] Stuart, Gordon & Harry; [ed] Galashiels Academy, Strathclyde University; [activ] church elder, gala rugby com., loc. Brawlad Gathering com., sec. pigeon club; "I like everybody and assume they like me. I like to do good turns to people and like to co-operate and help."

KEGGIN, TONY: [b]20/4/70 Liverpool; [p] James & Shelagh; [occ] civil servant; [awards] 1st prize - "Summer Lyric" competition; "This a great achievement for a working class, Merseyside boy. I've been writing for 5 years and now scratching the surface of success."

KENDRICK, MICHAEL: [b] 17/10/46 Hugglescote, Leicestershire; [m] Beryl; [p] Les & Betty; [ed] Skerry's College, Allerton Grange School, Leicester College of Technology; [occ] sr. technician; [awards] degree - footwear mngemnt; [mem] National Trust, Western Front Assoc.; [pub writ] poems/memoirs in book/ntn'l magazine; "Nostalgia is an important ingredient in my life and hopefully my writings convey the sentiments that are involved."

KENNEDY, JOHN W.: [b] 7/1/26 Edinburgh; [m] Helen; [p] John & Christina; [ch] Alan & Colin; [ed] Boroughmuir High School, Edinburgh & Heriot-Watt College; [occ] engineer (rtrd.); [awards] Mech. Eng. Technician Pt. 1 & 2; [pub writ] bio of childhood memories - Argyllshire Advertiser; "I love writing letters and comical poems about work. Love to travel anywhere except beaches."

KENNY, JULIE: [b] 3/3/77 Co. Fermanagh; [p] Ursula & Tommy; [ed] Collegiate Grammar, Enniskillen; [awards] Public Speaking - N. Ireland Awards; [activ] sec. local youth club; [pub writ] school anthol.; "Poetry is my means of expressing my emotions. It is like the musician's piano and the artist's paint, it is a thoroughly beautiful thing."

KERSHAW, BRIAN P.: [b] 5/8/53 Yorkshire; [m] Linda; [p] Arthur & Hilda; [ch] Hanah, Sarh, Stephen & Brian; [ed] Littleworth Sec. Mod., Barnsley, Hills & Glens of Ross-shire; [mem] Easter Ross Rights of Way Assoc.; [pub writ] 2 poems "To The Islands Gone", "A Walk Down Scotsburn Glen".

KEYES, ANTHONY: [b] 15/4/60 Weston-Super-Mare; [p] Robert & Carmel; [awards] commendation - Weston & Southwoodspring Poetry Contest (3yrs.); [activ] exhibitions - Weston Heritage Ctr. - Weston Civic Soc.; [pub writ] book - author/photographer "Weston-Super-Mare The Sands of Time" pub. May '95, celebrity interviews, 9 poems - various anthologies; "The job of a poet is to be distinctive, to create different moods, challenge many styles and at the end of the day, leave one's own individual stamp on each work."

KHOSLA, MEERA: [b] 4/9/82 Barnet; [p] Anil & Nili; [ed] Dame Alice Owens School; [occ] student; [awards] L.A.M.D.A - speech/drama awards, swimming - silver, gold & honours, Gym 6,5,4,3 BAGA, Music Gr.1 - piano; [mem] speech/drama club, squash club; "I like reading poetry books by T.S. Elliot. I love acting in drama and I enjoy modern music."

KING, BARBARA: [b] 26/3/53 Merthyr Tydfil; [m] David; [p] Audrey & Douglas; [ch] Matthew & Wendy; [ed] Bargod Grammar School, University of Wales College; [awards] BA (Hons.) Eng. Lit., Cert. Ed. (FE); [mem] Blackwood Writers Group; [pub writ] 5 poems in svrl anthologies & S. Wales Echo; "I am interested in Jung's theory "collective unconscious" as the source of imagination and creativity. My writing seeks to revive the intuitive and spiritual side of human experience masked by the burden of everyday modern life."

KING, EILEEN: [b] 23/1/38 London; [ed] Rosecroft Private School, Goldworth County Sec.; [occ] S/Nurse (rtrd.); [awards] svrl. medal/cups/certs. - solo singing, music festivals; [activ] volunteer - 'Crossroads'; [pub writ] 1 poem; "Writing peotry when inspiration invades my heart is my pleasure! Often I sing the words to music with guitar accompaniment, but I never dreamt to be counted good."

KIRKALDY, JACQUI: [b] 12/5/79 Birwick-Upon-Tweed; [p] George & Maureen; [ed] Berwick High School; [occ] student; [awards] Eng. Speaking Union, Public Speaking Cert., winner - Yr. 9 Debating Competition, Cert. of Commendation - creative writing; [activ] youth orchestra & ceilidh band; [pub writ] 'Flight by Night' - Squat Diddley by Sarah Andrew; "I enjoy studying languages. Public speaking and debating gives me a lot of satisfaction. My ambition is to study law. I derive pleasure from travelling abroad."

KIRKBRIDE, PATRICIA H.: [b] 18/2/40 Lancaster; [p] Ronald & Jennie; [ch] Maxine, Billy, Lesley & Robert; [occ] company accountant; "Creativity is our destiny: it is everything we are and everything we do, but most of all, it is God's soothing prescription. I would like to dedicate this poem to my Nanna Carradice."

KIRKHAM, MARGARET: [b] 30/3/34 Goodmayes; [p] Mr./Mrs. Whitley; [ch] Andrew, Theresa, Stephen & Helen; [ed] Convent St. Philip's Priory; [awards] SRN, Youth Leader award, civil service; [activ] YMCA Board of Management, support for bereaved; Eucharistic minister, museum group; [pub writ] poems - "Life is Good" - Anchor Books; "I am able to express feelings through poetry. I feel the need to help others by listening. Being positive is good."

KIRSTEIN, ROBYN L.: [b] 7/8/84 Kirkcaldy; [p] Charles & Evelyn; [ed] Tanshall Primary School; [occ] student; [awards] various ballet, gymnastic & swimming awards; "I get a lot of joy out of writing poetry, it helps me to express how I feel about things and people."

KNIGHT, PATRICK: [b] 17/12/49 Foochow, China; [p] Rev. Frank & Patricia; [ed] Loughborough Grammar; [awards] 5 'O' levels, 3 'A' levels; [pub writ] booklet - "These Fruits Of A Greater Tree" - Chandlers Ford Church Hants '89; "Being a Christian is my main motivation. My experiences, love of life, nature and relationships find fulfillment in writing poetry."

KNOCK, PAM: [b] Suffolk; [p] Phoebe & Alf; [ed] Beccles High, Lowestoft College; [occ] admin. assistant; [awards] Royal Soc. of Arts - Commerce & Word Processing; "This is my first attempt at submitting a poem for publication and I am thrilled at being successful."

KNOTT, GEORGE W.: [b] 6/8/25 Whitworth; [m] Rachel; [p] Violet & Joe (dcd.); [ch] Jacqueline; [ed] Lloyd St. C of E; [awards] City & Guild - textile inst.; [activ] calligraphy; [pub writ] poems in anthologies/magazines; "Personal satisfaction in seeing my poems in print for other people to enjoy. I believe that poems and calligraphy enhance eath other."

KOSTRZEBKI, AMANDA: [b] 15/12/63 Nottingham; [p] Alan & Sheila Dury; [ch] Anthony & Samuel; [ed] The Frank Wheldon Comp. School; "The writing of short stories and poetry is, for me, a way of looking at life through new and different perspectives, each day is another interesting place to sit down and write about."

KWEKA, JACQUELINE: [b] 31/3/79 Tanzania; [p] Edward & Josephine; [ed] Our Lady's School; [occ] student; "Most of what I write is greatly influenced by my experiences. I find it hard to talk about what I feel and so I put it in writing. It's very satisfying to see a finished piece of work and know that I did it."

LAMB, ANDREW: [b] 19/6/44 Glencraig; [m] Mary; [p] Martha; [ch] Margaret, Ricky, Alex & Andrew; [ed] Ballingry Sec. School; [occ] security contractor; "Writing poetry has kept my feet firmly on the ground, helped me to tolerate life more easily and see people and surroundings in a different light, and has made me a much happier person."

LAMB, HAROLD: [b] 27/11/30 Cardenden; [p] William & Mary; [ch] Kenneth; [ed] Denend School, Auchterderran Jr. High; [occ] train driver (rtrd.); [mem] Rugby Club, Field & Equipment organiser; [activ] branch sec. A.S.L.E.F.; [pub writ] humorous poem in local press; "Realised the social life I missed out on with shift working on railway. Inclined to write humorous verses about working life situations."

LAMB, SHEILA M.: [b] 11/8/33 Montreal; [m] Bill; [p] Mary & Duncan Carmichael; [ch] Lesliey, Bill, Susan & Stephen; [ed] Alloa Academy; [occ] wage clerk; [awards] Lower Music - singing; [mem] Lledo "Days Gone" collectors club (vintage models); "One of my hobbies is writing verse for special occasions for my friends. I also compose melodies but have never submitted any for publication."

LANCASHIRE-FRAIN, BETTY: [b] 12/1/32 Chadderton, Oldham; [p] John & Hilda; [ch] Anne, Christine & Peter; [ed] Mills Hill Sec. School; [occ] civil servant (rtrd.); [activ] volunteer care for disabled; [pub writ] svrl. poems; "Happiness for me is caring for people, especially my family. My instpiration for my poetry is simply through love and life."

LANDEN, ROBIN: [b] 16/8/58 Deeping St. Nicholas; [m] Karen; [p]

Iris & Fritz; [ch] Debbie Anne & Gavin Lewis; St. Guthlac's Sec. School; [occ] vehicle technician; [awards] accredited technician; "I love writing verses, 'Flowers' is special to me. As my work started out as poems of criticism until 'Flowers' came along. I also enjoy songwriting."

LANDERS, HELENA: [b] 21/9/56 Swansea; [p] Joan & Roy Greenway; [ch] Robert, David, Matthew & Bethan; [ed] Llwyn-Y-Bryn School, Polytecnic of Wales; [activ] church, volunteer - children' charities, first aid; "I have been writing poetry since my early teens. It is often my way of expressing very strong emotions. I wrote this poem for my husband a few months before his cancer was diagnosed."

LANGLEY, KIRSTY M.: [b] 15/11/54 Blackpool, [p] Phil & Cherie; [ed] St. Bernadette R.C. School; [occ] student; "I live with my family and cat Josh in Bispham which is by the sea. I have always enjoyed writing short stories and poems and have been encouraged by my family and teachers."

LAW, FREDERIC L.: [b] 28/3/32 Glasgow; [p] Wiliam & Jean; [ch] Virginia, Richard, Adrian & Geraldine; [ed] Whitehil Sr. Sec. School; [awards] F.E. Teaching, C&G Cert.; [activ] boating, charity collecting 'People In Need'; [pub writ] short story - "The Tricksters" - London Eve. News '69; "I enjoy the satisfaction of creative writing. Keeping the spark alive within my family."

LEACH, PATRICIA A.: [b] 15/4/41 Bury St. Edmonds; [p] Carl & Samantha; [occ] housewife; [activ] Womens Section Royal British Legion; [pub writ] "Bowlers" - Shifting Sands - Anchor Books; "I enjoy writing poems about my feelings, it's just a pleasant hobby."

LEAH, ANTHEA E.: [b] 6/7/35 Taunton; [p] Isabel & William O'Connor; [ch] Mark & Tania; [ed] North Town Sec. School; [occ] housewife; [awards] 3 Editor's Choice Awards - Ntn'l Library of America, 5 Best Poets of '95 In America; [mem] Intn'l Soc. of Poets; [pub writ] "Poems To Reflect On" - Adelpi Press; "I believe we need to take a real look at the suffering, pollution, and treatment of others outside our own ambitions and the materialistic world we live in, for I believe we have lost our way."

LEE, STANLEY G.: [b] 23/8/27 East Ham.; [m] Maureen; [p] George & Jean; [ch] Julie & Mark; [ed] Becontree School, S.E. Essex Tech. College; [occ] chief industrial designer (rtrd.); [awards] Chief Designer of Ferguson Radio Cpn., Thorn-EMI, M.S.I.A.D.; [activ] volunteer - Dr. Barnardos, Christian Aid; [pub writ] poetry in local newspaper; "Since retiring from designing, my sporting interests (competitive bowls and golf) have been supplemented by two creative activities: painting in oils and writing. My poetry attempts to chronicle rustic experiences of my youth. Contentment and tolerance, more easily achieved, one finds, in a rural environment are two aims for which I strive with only partial success."

LEES, JEAN: [b] 13/2/28; [p] Violet & Charles Tanner; [ch] Nicholas, Gillian Suzanne & Jonathan; [ed] Chipping Sodbury Grammar, Manchester Poly.; [occ] librarian; [activ] Country Friends (walks), Keep Fit class, ice skating; [pub writ] poem in local paper; "I write poems for fun, I love words and take delight in rhyming defficult words. I don't like poems that don't flow or scan."

LEES, JEAN: [b] 22/8/28 Birstall; [m] Frank (dcd.); [p] Will & Annie Ackroyd; [ch] Alan, Russell, Mark, Clinton & Ruth; [occ] housewife; [activ] Brownhill Church P.C.C., Mother's Union wrkr.; [pub writ] poem - Mother's Union Journal; "My family and my Christian faith are the two most important things in my life. I enjoy writing letters and poems and meeting people."

LEGG, MARY: [b] 1/12/15 Middlesbrough; [p] James & Matilda Cassidy; [ch] Tony, Jane, Anne, David, Raymond, Denise & Ernest; [occ] housewife/writer; [pub writ] story - Common Thread Anthology (writings of working class women); "I am now retired from writing but proud of this final inclusion."

LEWIS, ARTHUR G.: [b] 5/5/09 Glygorrwg; [p] Martha & Arthur; [ch] Joan, Joyce, George & Pauline; [ed] Port Talbot County Grammer

School; "Had Parkinson's Disease for fifty-five years and write as a hobby. I can also write backwards!"

LEWIS, ELIZABETH: [b] 28/7/18 Merthyr Tydfil; [p] Kate & Lewis; [ch] Anne & Alun; [ed] Georgetown Girls School County Grammar; [occ] housewife; [activ] Merthyr Writers Circle; [pub writ] children's stories - Brimax, Cambridge, stories/poems in 7 books - Writers Circle; "Writing, reading and puzzles, helping to care for my family. My best asset being a sense of humour."

LEWIS, GRAHAM: [b] 16/12/15 Penarth; [p] Clifford & Flora; [ch] Anthony; [ed] Penarth County Grammar; [occ] diagnostic radiographer (rtrd.); [awards] Qual. radiographer '51, M.S.R.R. S.R.R.; [activ] pres. Normandy Veterans Assoc. S. Wales; [pub writ] short story - "All On An Autumn Day", poems, "Who Will Remember", "Hepzibah", "Last Parade", & "Falaise"; "Remembrance of the horror and humour of war, and the mental and physical scars endured by those at the 'sharp end'."

LEWIS, PHYLLIS: [b] Blaina; [p] George & Lilian Price; [ch] Roger & Reece; [occ] teacher (rtrd.); [awards] Co. Supt. St. John Ambulance, S. MON. - care of school animals - USK Agr. College; [activ] bowls club, Art Soc., sewing; "My poem was composed from observations made by the children of Bedwas Infant's School, Reception Class - ages 4½ to 5 yrs."

LIGHTBODY, GARY: [b] 15/6/76 Newtownards; [p] Jack & Lynne [ed] Rathmore Primary; Rockport Prep., Campbell College, Dundee University; [occ] student; [pub writ] 4 poems in various anthologies - "October", "Strawberry", "Beyond This"; "Poetry is an opportunity to be the one person no one else sees — yourself."

LIGHTFOOT, IAN: [b] 4/7/58 Liverpool; [m] Shirley; [p] Alan & Edna; [ch] Lee & Christopher; [ed] Ormonde Drive Sec., Modern; [occ] print manager; [awards] B/Tec Ntn'l Diploma - Printing; [pub writ] poems in various anthologies; "Written words have a beauty all of their own, they communicate not only to the brain but affect our emotions. God revealed His glory in the word made flesh. When words affect our will they become powerful."

LINEHAN, JENNY: [b] 21/4/49 Hornchurch, Essex; [p] George & Maud Lufkin; [ch] Charlotte & Ashley; [ed] Westborough High School for Girls; [occ] window dresser/nanny; [activ] youth leader - local church; [pub writ] poem - Anthology London '94 - Arrival Press "A Memory of Time"; "I am thankful for my life, my gifts, my friends and especially my God who makes it all possible."

LINNEY, MARY P.: [b] 18/3/30 Woodlands, Doncaster; [m] Roy; [p] Edward & Mary Franey; [ch] Sharon, Patricia, Rita, Michael, Dawn & Paul; [ed] Woodlands R.C. School; [awards] 'A' grade - Eng., 'C' grade - Lit.; [mem] Doncaster Network of Writers; [pub writ] 6 poems in Doncaster N.O.W. Anthol., 10 poems by various publishers, local papers/magazines; "I have always loved writing but never had the time, bringing up a large family. Retirement gave me the opportunity to achieve my ambition; to express my thought into words and see them published, also passing GCSE in Eng. Lit."

LINSKILL, ANGELA: [b] 8/7/71 Leeds; [p] Rodney & Janice; [ch] Ryan Dean; [ed] World Wide Education Services Tutor/ W. Africa; [occ] teacher; [awards] NVQ levels 1&2, 730 Teachers Award, Word Processing, RSA 1&2, C.L.A.I.T. 6 'O' levels, 4 'A' level; "I express my feelings and emotions through my writing which gives me a good release when I read my work back, it gives me a clearer perspective of the situation at hand."

LITHGOW, AMY: [b] 6/3/79 Whitehaven; [p] Val & Dave; [ed] Woodgord Lodge High School; [occ] student; "I enjoy reading and writing poetry in my spare time and I am very happy that my poem is being published."

LITTLEWOOD, EDWARD: [b] Nov./33 Leeds; [p] Charles & Helen; [ch] Anthony, Graham, Stephen & Susan; [ed] State School Sec. Modern; [occ] engineering; "Sometimes a moment of happiness or sorrow, or even an item of news in the media will inspire me to put pen to paper. Although not to everyone's liking I try to write the truth — despite the consequences."

LLEWELLYN-JONES, LOUISE: [b] 11/4/74 Shrewsbury; [p] Heather & Rhoss; [ed] Llanuiltud Fawr School, Coleg Glan Hafren College; [occ] secretary; [awards] GCSE's A-levels, Blue Peter Badge; "I am currently writing a futuristic novel 'A Perceptual Lie' and short children's stories - 'Touched by the hand of Moz!!'."

LLOYD, FREDERICK P.: [b] 22/4/33, Southport; [p] Gladys & Fred; [ch] Darren; [ed] Birkdale High School, Leigh Tech. College; [occ] joiner (rtrd.); [awards] accom. artist, fndr. Leigh Art Soc., 'Studio 77'; [activ] writing on politics; [pub writ] poems various church mags/ local newspapers/club mags. and anthologies; "I find that playing with and studying words brings a lot of satisfaciton. Poetry, art and music are open to everyone so I can only encourage others to have a try!"

LLOYD, LAURIE: [b] 4/5/22 Coventry; [p] Reginald & Agnes; [ch] Gill, Philip & Jonathan; [ed] Bablake School; [occ] schoolmaster (rtrd.); [activ] parish councillor, volunteer - Hospice of the Good Shepherd; "I write for pleasure, if then others enjoy reading what I have written, that is a bonus."

LOBB, PAULINE F.: [b] 19/7/45 Cornwall; [m] Ian; [p] Francis & Marjorie Beare; [ch] Robert, Sharon, Glynn & Helen; [ed] Wadebridge Sec.; [occ] housewife; [activ] support First Air Ambulance, British Heart Fndtn.; [pub writ] poem - St. Minver Link Mag. '85; "I think I am a happy person most of the time, but words come easier when I'm in a melancholy or sad mood."

LOMAN-BROWN, EILEEN: [b] 11/3/29 London; [p] John & Eileen Bragg; [ch] Linda & Ian; [ed] Kingston Day Commercial College; [awards] college scholarship; "I think it is important to make time for people, I am told I am a very good listener; I also put my thought into words whenever I feel strongly about a subject, be it serious or lighthearted."

LONG, GARY: [b] 2/4/66 Isleworth; [m] Anita; [p] Ronald & Joyce; [ch] Daniel; [ed] Longford School; [occ] warehouseman; [awards] City & Guilds - carpentry/joinery; "I would like to dedicate this poem to my wife, Anita."

LORD, DAVID: [b] 8/8/72; [p] Harry & Elizabeth; [ed] Colne Park High, Burnley College, University of Central Lancashire; [occ] geotechnical technician; [awards] O.N.C. & H.N.C. - Bldg. Studies; [activ] lay preacher, sunday school tchr, youth group ldr., bass guitar, juggler; "I have found that poetry is an excellent way of puting across my views on the destruction of the environment; pollution of the land, air and seas, the plight of the homeless and other serious and not so serious subjects. I have found that the key to a happy life for me has been to exercise mentally and physically, to find time to relax, and also have a strong Christian faith."

LOWE, NORMAN: [b] 15/4/29; [ed] Basic (some lost through war) only reaching 4th grade. Sat City & Guilds Installation course, 2 & 3, at the age of 36 years; [awards] British Rail (foot plate), National Service 1947-50, Post Office engineering (28 yrs.) becoming Leading Technical Officer, Licensed Public House (3 yrs.), Caretaker Hanson Corner (mental health ctr.) until April 15, 1994; "I have written bits of rhyme and prose for many years, but was too busy making a liveing for it to become an important part of my life. But now, with retirement, I find it a most satisfying pastime, which certainly destroys any sort of boredom. So I now pass a lot of my time doing just that."

LOWREY, JO: [b] 15/1/71 Barton-On-Sea; [m] Andy; [p] Soo & Graham Glashier; [ed] Priory High School, Exeter College, Open University; [occ] health care wrkr; "I wish to dedicate this poem to my husband, Andy, and to send my love to my parents."

LUCE, RACHEL: [b] 19/4/35 Storrington, Sx.; [p] Phyllis & Cyril Binet; [ed] Our Lady Of Sion, prvt. tutor; [occ] sheep frmr/philosopher/ artist; [awards] Degree - philosophy; [pub writ] poems - 3 anthologies, articles in farming press; "Man is at the fusion of two worlds, it is

important to be in contact with both; to feel with nature - animals, plants; to have friends and everyday to endeavour to find something for the body, somethng for the mind and spirit; to be able to create and communicate and trust in the goodness of God."

LUDGATE, PHYLLIS: [b] 18/9/13 Kent; [p] Olivia & William Joiner; [ch] Carolyn & Ross; [ed] C. of E. School; [occ] housewife; [awards] GCSE's in Eng., Eng. Lit., Red Cross Adv. Certs.; [activ] church, flower guild, W.I.; [pub writ] poems - church mag./local press/ W.I. News; "Having an optimistic outlook and trying to see the best side of people and situations tends to enrich my own life. I feel that poems are born of the emotions; from beauty, sadness, comedy, etc."

LUMBARD, ELMA: [b] Kingston-On-Thames; [p] Ernest & Sarah Wagner; [ch] William & Sarah; [ed] Tiffin Girls Grammar School; [occ[research scientist (rtrd.); [awards] diploma - sociolgy, scientific qualif.; [mem] Molesey Photographic Soc., Molesy Art Soc., [pub writ] scientific papers/articles in mags. and newspapers; "I find that now I've retired, I have time to let my creative ideas flow. I am able to indulge in photography, writing and painting."

LUSK, CERI E.: [b] 13/5/54 Newport, Gwent; [m] Kevin; [p] Harry & Anita Bishop; [ch] Thomas (dcd.); [ed] Newbridge Grammar, Leeds University; [awards] BA (Hons.) - French, PGCE; [mem] SANDS (Stillborn & Neonatal Death Soc.), Life & Milnrow Evangelical church; [pub writ] church magazine, local newspaper, Grace Magazine, Confident Life, SANDS Nsltr, Compassionate Friends Nsltr.; "All my recent poetry and prose has been written as a result of the tragic stillbirth of our firstborn son, Thomas. My aim has been to put down my innermost thoughts in writing as good therapy for myself, as a memorial to Thomas, as a help to others in a similar positon and in order that our friends may share in our pain with a better understanding."

LUSK, LANNETTE: [b] 19/7/59 Laindon; [m] David; [ch] Ellis; [ed] Laindon School; [occ] systems administrator; "To be happy and to see my newborn son grow up content and happy. I use my poems to reflect my feelings, moods and situations around my life."

LYCETT, SYLVIA: [b] 15/9/45 Cannock; [occ] nursery nurse/ aromatherapist; [activ] animal welfare, school govenor; "I believe that life is a great leveller and we get from life only as much as we put in. I try to treat others as I would wish to be treated myself."

LYNCH, DENISE: [b] 15/9/42 Letter Kenny; [m] Tim; [p] Jim & Caroline Deasy; [ch] Aoife & David; [ed] Convent of Mercy, University College, Cork; [occ] general practitioner; [activ] scouting, Amnesty Intn'l.

LYONS, PATRICK J.: [b] 14/5/44 Waterford Eire; [p] James & Anne; [ch] Diane, Steven, Karen & Adam; [ed] Wykeham Sec. Modern, Kilburn Polytechnic; [occ] bldg. manager; [awards] City & Guilds - plumbing, HNC - building; [activ] mem. various local committees, fund-raising for local organisations; "I have been writing for a number of years as a hobby. During this period I have completed a selection of short stories, a couple of novels and a large selection of poems. I am currently working on a couple of plays."

MACBETH, RONALD A.: [b] 10/9/19 Inverness, Shire; [m] Mairi; [ch] Rhona, Iain & Mairead; [ed] Inverness Royal Academy, Aberdeen University; [occ] headmaster (rtrd.); [awards] degree - science; [pub writ] poems in 3 anthologies; "I love the countryside, sea and mountains. I am perplexed with some of Einstein's theories."

MACDONALD, SARAH: [b] 21/1/81 Cardiff; [p] Pam & Ian; [ed] Lewis Girls Comp. School; [occ] student; [activ] clarinet, keyboard playing, drama, reading & badminton; "I enjoy writing poems and this is my first one to be published."

MACFARLANE, EDWARD G.: [b] 12/3/11 Auchtermuchty; [m] Geo Laing; [p] George & Fanny; [ch] Grant, Roy, Linda & Margie; [ed] Bell-Baxter, Cupar Fife, Dundee Teachers Training College, Preston Tech. College; [occ] teacher; [awards] Dayschool cert. in Cupar, diploma, H.N.C. (Distinction), Preston (Mech. Eng.); [activ] started the

World Parliament Party in 1947, contested by-election to Westminster 1952 Dundee-East Constituency; [pub writ] poems, articles, letters to press, 2 books "Truth" '81, "Cosmopolis" '84; "I aspire to create a single world unionised state based on persons and not on nations or competing churches etc. I oppose all competing sovereign nations and terrorist movements."

MACKINNON, CARA: [b]22/8/55 Glasgow; [p] Donald & Pat; [ch] Erik, Kristyn & Kane; [ed] Hillhead High School; [mem] Palace Players Drama Club; [activ] children's drama group 'Surprised Halibut'; "I enjoy music, dance, writing, theatre, art and photography in fact all forms of creative expression and communication and use of mixed media."

MACLEOD, JEAN: [b] 18/7/30 Doncaster; [p] Alexander & Doris Wood; [ch] Alexander, Fiona, Donald, Norman & Amanda; [ed] Portknockie Sec.; [occ] housewife; [awards] home-study Eng. 'A'; [activ] swimming tchrs. cert. prelim., WRVS member, volunteer; "I get a lot of satisfaction from writing short poems and reciting at senior and disabled local social events."

MACLEOD, JUNE: [b] 31/1/50 Dundee; [p] David & Elizabeth; [ch] David & Lorraine; [ed] Beath High; [occ] stores assistant; [pub writ] limericks & poems; "Always imitate the behaviour of the winner when you lose."

MACLEOD, KELLY: [b] 21/8/81 Inverness; [p] Angus & Vivienne; [ed] Park Primary, Invergordon Academy; [occ] student.

MCAREAVEY, KARL: [b] 27/1/66 Bury; [m] Wendy; [p] Rev. William & Jean; [ch] Emma, Paul & Zoë; [ed] Hindland Sec., Anniesland College; [occ] driver/delivery person; [awards] Ntn'l Diploma - Computer Studies; [mem] Poetry Soc.; [pub writ] 3 poems - 3 anthologies; "I find it hard expressing my feelings and find the best person to talk to is myself. Putting pen to paper helps me in my own way to communicate with the world. It pleases me knowing that my thoughts help others to relate to something personal in their lives."

MCCANN, PATRICK: [b] 30/3/59 Kelso; [p] Patrick & Bridget; [ch] Lea, Zoë, & Kadi Lynn; [ed] Kelso High; [activ] darts, pool; "Althought I've suffered from epilepsy since I was 14 I try not to be held back by it. I can still eat and drink when I want, millions world-wide can't."

MCCARRY, PATRICIA: [b] 15/3/36 Ireland; [p] Hugh & Mary Coyle; [ch] Brenda, Hugh & Peter; [occ] secretary; [awards] various certs. in secretarial courses & Royal Soc. of Arts; [activ] various local committees; [pub writ] articles in local newspaper; "At school I loved writing essays and since then I have always loved writing little pieces. A great part of my work entails helping people and I enjoy helping my family."

MCCAUGHEY, HUGH: [b]31/8/66 Clogher, Co. Tyrone; [p] Michael & Mary; [ed] Christian Brothers Grammar, agricultural college, Foundation Studies; [occ] student/farmer; [awards] 'O' levels; [mem] Fermanagh Writer Circle; [pub writ] "The Painter" - British Poetry Review '94, "Solidarity" - N. Ireland Poets '95; "I am fascinated by life and its mysteries and find poetry an enjoyable way of capturing life experiences by attempting to paint with words a living scene."

MCCLUSKY, RACHEL: [b] 1/9/78 Ashton; [p] Joyce & Allen; [ed] Glossopdale Community College; [occ] student; [awards] Gr. 5 RNCM piano with merit, Gr. 4 RNCM - flute; [activ] Mensa; [pub writ] poem - Roald Dahl Poetry Competition '94, poem in 'Poetry Now' - "Single Minds"; "I would like to make a career in writing and journalism. My great love is literature and I enjoy all aspects of life, especially foreign travel and new experiences."

MCCOMBE, COLIN F.: [b] 5/9/53 Moreton; [m] Suzanne; [p] Keith & Harriet; [ch] Maxine, Lee & Colin; [ed] Wallasey Grammar School; [occ] boilerman; [pub writ] poems in 'Poppy Fields' & 'World At War', local mags. and papers; "Seeing the world through the eyes of a poet enables me to appreciate the simple things and to cherish what I have and what I am."

MCDONALD PAYNE, KIM: [b] 24/6/61 Aberdeen, Scot.; [p] William & Irene; [ed] West Ridge High, South Aerica, College of Tech., Basingstoke; [occ] customer serv. agent; "I enjoy the simple observations and experiences in life with the ability to put my imagination and ideas into words in a way which others may appreciate and understand."

MCDONALD, RONALD W.: [b] 31/5/35 Aberdeenshire; [p] Ronald & Annie; [ed] Aberdeen Grammar School, Aberdeen University; [occ] principal/teacher; [awards] MA, M.Ed.; [pub writ] plays/short stories pub. in various anthologies & periodicals; "I was only recently encouraged to try poetry as a new medium of self-expression."

MCFARLANE, MAY L.: [b] 22/12/40 [m] James; [p] Elizabeth & William; [ch] Marcus, James & Michaela; [occ] housewife; [pub writ] poems - local press; "I feel things very deeply, especially the 'troubles' and the environment. I like to put my thoughts down in poetry."

MCGAREL, DONNA: [b]22/12/64 Larne; [p] John & Iris; [ch[Kerry & Jordan; [ed] Larne Grammar School; College Bus. Studies, Belfast, East Antrim Inst. of F.E.; [awards] 8 'O' levels, 2'A' levels; [mem] WWF; "I feel that we must all at least try to rise above our own selfish drives, foibles and even emotional traumas to become more objective and work towards a greater good for others and for ourselves."

MCGEECHAN, GWEN: [b] 26/1/60 Doncaster; [p] Gwen & Tom Cliffe; [ch] Lisa, Wayne, Christopher & Benjamin; [ed] Wheatley High School for Girls; "I have had a rough time over past years and am now more involved with the spiritual side of life. Things have improved tremendously and writing is my way of expressing my feelings."

MCGINTY, EAMONN: [b] 22/2/70 Derry; [p] Kathleen & Edward; [ed] St. Josephs Sec. School; [occ] clerical assist.

MCGONIGLE, THOMAS: [b] 31/7/30 Paisley; [p] Thomas & Ioland; [ch] Marina, Fiona, Lisa-Maria & Thoma-Paul; [ed] St. James' Sec. School; [occ] welder; [awards] art exhibitions - Hexagon House & Manchester Round Library; [activ] church, committee member, church magazine; [pub writ] short stories/poems in local press and anthologies; "I think peotry for me is the best way I can express myself, if I make sound and sense. And give someone else pleasure in the reading."

MCGOWAN, CYNTHIA B.: [pen] Patricia; [b] 9/7/22 Birmingham; [p] Harry & Beatrice Newberry (dcd.); [ch] Dudley, Elizabeth, Jane, Virginia, Catherine, Peter, Paul, Robert & Mark; [ed] St. Mary's Girls School; [occ] secretary (rtrd.); [awards] cert. shorthand theory, scholarship Mosely Art College; [activ] reading, music, choir, chess, bridge, letter-writing; [pub writ] poem "Cinemas" in 'The Picture Palaces' by Chris & Rosemary Clegg, book of poetry "A Selection of Poems" self-published; "Apart from rearing a large family I have always enjoyed painting and writing. I have had two painting exhibitions ('86 & '89) in Sutton Coldfield Library. Currently I am writing my autobiography which covers many years, even before my birth."

MCGREGOR, JACQUELINE: [b] 15/3/66 Belfast; [p] Christina & John; [awards] Poetry Soc. Awards, Eng. Speaking Board Award, diploma - short story writing; [pub writ] verse for greeting cards, article - Newstatesman & Society Mag., poems in 7 anthologies, appeared in "We Are The People" book; "I find poetry a great release, a kind of therapy, emotions leak from pen to page, cleansing the mind but sometimes leaving the soul bared."

MCGROUTHER, FIONA E.: [b] 27/1/53 London; [p] Margaret & Neil Murray; [ch] Robert; [ed] Kilmarnock Academy, Stirling University; [occ] housing officer; [awards] degree - Sociology, post grad. diploma - housing [mem] Chartered Inst. of Housing, Royal Zoological Soc. of Scotland; [activ] sec. Murieston Community Council; "I see poetry as a natural extension of my being, allowing me to express my feelings, emotions and in a medium which brings pleasure to others and satisfaction to me."

MCKONE, LYNETTE S.: [b] 4/7/54 Rotherham; [p] George & Audrey; [ch] Sarah, Dave & Adam; [ed] Bolling Girls Grammar; [occ] clerk/driver; [mem] Maltings Art Ctr. Adult Performance Group; [activ]

sec. Berwick Writers' Workshop; [pub writ] 2 poems - "Nets, Unfurled", "My Hero", various articles/short stories; "Writing comes from the heart, not from the pen, the more you feel, the better you will write. You shouldn't just create words, you should create images."

MCKENDRICK, FLORENCE: [b] 26/8/47 Northumberland; [m] George; [p] Thomas & Esther; [ch] Sharon, Emma & Tammy; [ed] Seaton Burn Sec. School; [occ] kitchen porter; [activ] parents committee; "I am rather a quiet person who finds it easier to write my thoughts down that to speak about them. Sadness in the world moves me deeply."

MCKENZIE, AYELET: [b] 4/1/57 Israel; [p] Stanley & Sandra Taylor; [ed] Primrose Hill School, Park Lane College, Crewe & Alsager Collage; [occ] housewife; [pub writ] poem - anthol - Aural Images; "I have a history of mental illness, and find writing to be very important to me."

MCKOWN, DOROTHY: [b] 12/8/48 Oldham; [ed] Breezehill School, Manchester Music College; [occ] teacher (rtrd.); [awards] degree - music, diploma - teaching; "In addition to poetry, I have also written a few songs. Simple pleasures such as reading, knitting, cryptic crosswords, T.V. and radio. I collect bookmarks and like Leonard Cohen songs."

MCLAUGHLIN, JOHN: [b] 4/4/59 Paisley, Scot.; [p] Joseph & Margaret; [ch] Lorna-Jane; [ed] Sacred Heart High School, James Watt College; [awards] City & Guilds - shipbuilding/engineering, Craft Studies parts 1&2 credit; [activ] volunteer, environmental issues; "I have always been interested in nature, and most of my poems are about this subject. To sit out in the countryside helps me to concentrate and put my thoughts down on paper."

MCMAHON, SIOBHAN: [b] 28/3/71 Limerick, Eire; [p] Joan & Michael; [ed] University College, Galway; [occ] teacher; [awards] degree - Eng. & Philosphy; "Words merely express an inner vision, which is further diluted and transformed by interpretation and critical evaluation."

MCMAHON, TREVOR: [b] 7/1/51 Belfast; [m] Margaret; [p] Margaret & James; [ch] Lara, Ashley, Ruth (dcd.) & Christian; [ed] Royal Belfast Academical Inst., Queen's University of Belfast; [occ] schoolmaster; [awards] BA (Hons.), PGCE; [pub writ] various anthologies, magazines, pamphlet (Mandeville Press) Trio (Blackstaff Press); "Look to detail. It may interest readers that this poem is an acrostic - Amor Vincit Omnia."

MCNABB, HOPE: [b] 26/3/33 Renown, Sks., Canada; [m] Gordon; [p] F.G. & Annie Patrick; [ch] Cynthia Ann, Rocky Gordon, & Todd Dalton; [pub writ] Mid-Island Co-op Nsltr., 2 self-published '92, '93, local newspaper, 2 Ntn'l Library of Poetry; "My words I pen may awaken some readers to taste the wonder of connection."

MCSHANE, MICHAEL J.: [b] 18/2/67 Crossmaglen; [occ] technician; "Each thought, dream and event is poetry, you just need to get it down on paper; this is the art of poetry. Thanks to my friends for listening to my rantings, K. & R., and all. Slán."

MADELEY, CHRISTOPHER: [b] 1946 Liverpool; [ch] Christopher & Catherine; [ed] St. Francis Xaviers College; [occ] photographer; [awards] Cert. Visual Arts, Cert. F. E.; [activ] church and arts; [pub writ] poems/writings various anthologies/books; "I have been writing poems/thoughts/prayers, for 20 years and although many copies have been requested by individuals during this time, it is only quite recently that I have offered them to be published. I believe all talents blossom when shared."

MADLEN, PAMELA: [b] 27/6/41 Huntington; [p] Alice & Cyril Dodd; [ch] Stephanie & Nina; [ed] Huntington Sec. Modern; [occ] f/t carer; "My life evolves around many people of different nationalitites. I care deeply for other people's pain, to ease my thoughts I walk in my local forest all year around and lock each different day in my mind."

MAFI, FATEMAH M.: [b] 20/9/84 Bury, Lancashire; [p] Mozzaffar & Helena; [ed] Bury Catholic Prep.; [occ] student; [awards] Gold Merit

Award '94 - Academic Achievement & Contribution to School; [mem] Ramsbottom Rascals Swimming Club; [activ] church, pianoforte, singing, dance, play descant and treble recorder; "I learnt that one of the best ways to express your feelings is to write a poem about your feelings. I take pleasure in writing poems because poems create a whole new world where the imagination knows no bounds."

MAIDMENT, VIOLET J.: [b] 15/7/31 Pawlett; [p] Alfred & Matilda Hurford; [ch] Brian, Joh, Clive Westney & Mark; [ed] Jr. Pawlett, Sr. School Huntspill; [occ] cheese packer (rtrd.); [awards] bronze & silver medals - ballroom dancing; [pub writ] 6 poems in various anthologies, 2 poems - church magazine; "I wrote the Prime Minister a poem on 'back to basics' which I was delighted to get a thank-you for. Life and people are my subjects, prayer has always been my back bone in life."

MAKINEN, MARTIN: [b] 13/4/80 Tokyo, Japan; [p] Seija Makinen & Bob Savage; [ed] Penryn Community School; [occ] student; [mem] Pony Club, Creftow Art Gallery; [activ] Penryn Army Cadets; [pub writ] S.West Voices - Anchor Books - Jan. '95; "I hope that I will become successful as Oliver Goldsmith."

MALLION, RACHEL: [b] 15/9/67 Pembury, Kent; [p] Mr./Mrs. I.A. Corke; [ed] Weald of Kent Grammar School for Girls; [occ] assitant accountant; [mem] Assoc. of Accounting Technicians (MAAT); "As I came from the town, much of my poetry was inspired by the countryside. Friends requested that I write poems for certain occasions which I did, realised that I had a certain gift when my poetry made people cry. My friends and family encouragd me and I would like to thank them for this "The Seasons" is one of my collection of approximately 100 poems."

MANIAR, NARENDRA: [b] 12/8/51 Blantyre, Malawi; [ch] Puja & Anand; [occ] sub-postmaster; [awards] diploma - engineering, B.Tech (Hons.) - Mech. Engineering, diploma - industrial management, prizes - insurance sales, high achievement; [activ] "If you have faith in what you do, have hope for yourself and fellow man and practice charity, then it will be a beautiful world to live in."

MANN, CHERYL ANNE: [b] 23/9/55 London; [p] Patricia & Rober Burford; [ch] Laura, Sarah & Richard; [ed] Porters Grange Primary, Dowsett High School for Girls; [occ] housewife; [m] Ntn'l Autistic Soc.;[activ] sec. P.T.A.; [pub writ] "Heavy Dreams" - Poetry Now '94, Talking Volumes; "I enjoy writing poetry, being a mum and I also make salt dough plaques which I sell in the village shop. My hobbies are reading and writing letters."

MANN, MARGARET, R.: [b] 21/2/43 Skegness; [p] Colin & Ruth Storey; [ch] Timothy & Christopher; [ed] Skegness Grammar School; [occ] housewife; [activ] volunteer, Bible education; "'As apples of gold in silver carvings is a word spoken at the right time for it.' - Proberbs 25 v. 11."

MANSFIELD, LILY: [b] 16/4/31 Huddersfield; [p] Jane & Joah Kaye; [ch] Audrey & Robert; [ed] Spark Hall School, Crow Lane School; [occ] textile operative (rtrd.) "Since retiring I have had more time to reflect on past life experiences which has inspired me to begin writing poetry. I find it therapeutic and relaxing."

MARGIESON, DORA: [b] Dec./30 Everton, Liverpool; [p] Dora & Robert Kennett; [ch] Peter & Sheila (dcd.); [ed] Rupert Rd. Sec., Wavertree Day Trade; [occ] tailoress (rtrd.); [awards] tailoring cert.; [mem] Horticultural Soc.; [activ] St. John Ambulance Aux.; "I like helping people, I am very patient and tolerant. I have written my poems when I get inspiration from everyday events and thoughts."

MARTIN, RITA A.: [b]24/3/40 Bury; [p] George & Olive Heys; [ch] Colin & Gillian; [ed] St. Chads Primary, Church Central; [occ] mobile hairdresser; [activ] volunteer - Bury Hospice; "My poems were all written at times of deep personal events. I wish to dedicate them to the memory of Mr. Raymond Frederick Petts."

MARSH, DELWYN: [b] 28/12/71 Caerphilly; [p] David & Meriel; [ed] Heolddu Comp. School; "I find writing, especially poetry, to be a great source of enjoyment. Getting my work in print is a great thrill and

I hope people enjoy reading it as much as I enjoyed writing it. And maybe it will make people think of the problems in today's society."

MARSHALL, ANNE: [b] 22/4/36 Colne, Lancashire; [p] Ivy & Jack Ormerod; [ch] Melanie, Howard, Vanessa, Mathew & Karen; [ed] convent education; [awards] Technology Applications [activ] volunteer wrkr - Age Concern, social group for elderly; [pub writ] currently taking writing course, 1 poem - "New Born Day"; "As a child I was sick and missed much schooling. After convent I decided to improve myself, between bringing up five children, I think I have managed this."

MARSHALL, COLIN: [b] 5/12/60 Barking, Essex; [p] Helen Coenen; [ed] Comp. School Robert Clack; "This poem is dedicated to the beloved ones I've lost. In memory of my loving brother Trevor who died April 24, 1991 aged just 34 years. This poem was written on recycled paper, please help our earth to survive."

MARSHALL, DAVID S.: [b] 8/6/52 Oldham; [p] Mary & Alfred; [ed] Our Lady's R.C., Salford college of Technology; [occ] music teacher; [awards] BA - Band Musicianship; [pub writ] poems in Weekend Chronicle & Anthologies North West '94 and Dolly Mixture; "I have a deep interest in music, literature, drama and the arts in general."

MARTIN, JUNE W.: [b] 1/6/43 Wolverhampton; [p] Ethel & Harry Payne; [ch] Roger & Gail; [ed] Bineley Sec. School Mod.; [occ] housekeeper - Abbeyfield; [activ] care for elderly residents; [pub writ] 2 poems "Time" & "The May"; "I began writing poetry when I moved to Cornwall and was under going a crisis. It is my own personal therapy."

MARTINDALE, PATRICIA R.: [b] 7/2/27 Gillingham; [m] William; [p] Rose & Harold Bulmer; [ch] Brian, Alan & Keith; [activ] volunteer; [pub writ] 5 poems - Poetry Now, 1 poem - Arrival Press, 3 poems - Anchor Books; "I started writing poetry when I was about 50 years old. Many inner feelings came out in my writing. I have read my poems at a couple of meetings giving pleasure and help to others."

MASON, ROSE: [b] 13/9/37 Surrey; [m] Alan; [p] Ronald & Lillyan Hardy; [ch] Paul, David, & Philip; [ed] Doncaster Sec. School, Scunthorpe School; [occ] Marie Curie Nurse; [awards] Palliative Care cert.; [activ] Cancer Assoc., Marie Curie; [pub writ] verses in anthology collections; "I like tending people, caring for them and giving my support to their families. When I write, it is my thoughts and feeling for other people."

MASON, STAN: [b] 19/6/34 London; [m] Angela; [p] Doris & Joe; [ed] Davenant Grammar School; [occ] writer; [awards] FRSA, FCIB, FIMgt., ACIS, DipM. M. Inst.,M, M. Inst. A.M., MIRC; [mem] PIC - Playwrights In Cornwall, Redruth Amateur Operatic Soc.; [pub writ] numerous books, plays for radio & TV, films, poetry, short stories; "Writing is the most thrilling activity in life. A writer creates characters, plots and stories and can manipulate them at will. Excitement in writing has no end. It is infinite!"

MASON-WRIGHT, PHILLIP: [b] 11/7/29 Aldershot; [p] John & Eve; [ch] Anthony & Timothy; [occ] cancer research; [mem] Fellow of the Inst. Of Animal Technicians; [pub writ] short stories, poems, articles (fiction & technical) 2 books; "I have always felt that poetry is a form of short story; each telling a tale. 'Poets are born not made' (J. Clare). I am priviledged that I have contributed in a small way to Clare's belief in the form of my writing and local broadcasts."

MAWFORD, VALERIE: [b] 28/3/20 London; [m] Jack; [p] James & Louisa Spencer; [ch] Jack, Maureen, David, Linda, Michael & Brian; [ed] Eastbrooke Rd. School; [occ] housewife; [activ] charity work; "I get my feelings to write when things happen to people. I feel a great love for my family and Mankind, a lot of feelings for people."

MAY, PAULINE: [b] 18/8/39 Birmingham; [m] Michael; [ed] St. Agnes' Convent (Dominican); Birmingham College of Art & Design; [occ] teacher (rtrd.); [awards] N.D.D. & A.T.T.; "I have always enjoyed writing poetry and short stories and plays. My particular interest is in Natural History. I enjoy the writings/poems of the Northamptonshire poet, John Clare, and greatly admire his detail to flora and fauna."

MAYER, JOAN P.: [b] 17/3/36 Cheadle, Cheshire; [m] Gordon; [ch] David & Sandra, Anthony, Rachael & Joanne; [pub writ] poem - 'Chow Chat' magazine; "I enjoy seeing the family. My pastimes are exhibiting my Chow Chow dogs, caravaning with my husband Gordon and the dogs, knitting and sewing and meeting people."

MEADE, MICHAEL G.: [b] 21/2/70; [ed] University College, Cork; [occ] computers; [awards] Bach. of Civil Law; [mem] The Wooden Key Theatre Co., Amnesty Intn'l. "See poem 'Sun Alone'."

MEEK, BETH: [b] Coatbridge; [p] Eva & Frank Sinclair; [mem] Yoga Assoc., Art Ctr.; [activ] Gen. Art, French conversation; [pub writ] poems "Busier Than Ever" Musings - book, "The Blue Mediterranean", "Ripples In Time", "Karmic Cuts" - Yoga Magazine; "I have many enjoyable interests but find that a good book is a favourite thing. It can enable me to do or be anything I wish. I would love to write one."

MEHIGAN, CAROLE A.: [b] 12/4/41 Kent; [p] John & Anne-Marie Clinch; [ch] Susan, Daniel, Priscilla, Michael & Richard; [ed] St. Joseph's Convent Grammar School; [occ] dental secretary; "I love writing letters to my younger partners, friends and family and keep every personal letter I receive. I have a collection of poastcards going back to my childhood."

MELVILLE, ANNE F.: [b] 16/11/32 Brentwood, Ex.; [m] Colin (dcd.); [p] Keith & Nell Fowler; [ch] Elizabeth & Diana; [ed] Brentwood High School for Girls; [occ] writer; [awards] typing cert., General Teaching Cert. Eng., BA (Hons.); [mem] March & Doddington Writers Circle; [activ] group activities, short story competitions, readings for elderly, produce magazine "The Quill"; [pub writ] poetry in Lincs. & Cambs. Co. magazines, short stories in local mags., letters to newspapers; "Currently doing Access Course at Peterborough F.E. College as remaining active is vital at an older age. I hope to publish a novel eventually. I also go to an art class, enjoy oil painting, play piano and am very keen on film video."

MENARRY, ROD G.: [b] 12/7/42 Liverpool; [m] Ena; [p] George & Elsie; [ch] Paul & Andy; [ed] Liverpool College of Technology; [occ] design engineer; [awards] HMC - engineering; [mem] Inst. of Engineering Designers; [activ] committee member "Alzheimers Disease Soc."; "To my grandchildren: Robert (6), Joe (4), Thomas (2) and Lucy (Born 24/1/95) with love."

MENKIN, CARL R.: [b] 19/2/27 Liverpool; [ch] Allan, Peter, Clive & Joy; [ed] Sec. Modern School, Flintshire, Merchant Navy Training at 15 yrs. of age; [occ] Nuclear Sales Manager BNFL (rtrd.); [awards] Galley Boy to M.N. to Sr. Exec. Grade, various courses in technical school & management; [activ] guest speaker, volunteer walker to aged, poetry readings, ex Chairman of Council, volunteer walker MS Group; [pub writ] MIND publications, local newspapers, Maritime Museum Archives, newsletters, book; "I compose some poetry, other poetry just flows from inspiration. I have no delusions of grandeur. The only person you would delude is yourself. I have an open mind, observe all things possible. Be cheerful with all people."

METCALF, SCOTT C.: [b] 13/7/83 San Francisco US; [p] Michael & Sharon; [ed] Aus. & US schools, The American School - Switzerland, Tasis - England; [occ] student; [awards] honour student, swimming awards; [activ] boy scouts, woking, swimming club; [pub writ] poems in local newspapers (California, US); "I like writing poetry and short stories. I daydream on the school bus and then write down my thoughts. I also love swimming, backstroke is my favourite stroke."

MEYER, MARGI: [pen] Goog; [b] 5/1/58 Melton; [p] Roy & Kitty Spink; [ed] Maidstone Rd. Infants, Felixstowe Middle, Felixstowe High; [occ] aux. nurse for elderly; [awards] hairdressing, dancing - old time/ballroom; I try to keep happy and to help other people the best I can and I like to put my feelings into poetry."

MILLER, JEAN: [b] 29/3/30 London; [m] Gerald; [p] Leonard & Alice; [ch] Deborah, Linda & Lance; [ed] The Willows Girls School; [occ] health visitor (rtrd.); [awards] S.R.N., SCM, H.V.F.W.T. - nursing in Eng. & Jamaica; [activ] Bourne Art Soc., church; "My poems and short stories are based on some of the most interesting poignant and emotional aspects of my life, and the search for the right words to express my privileged experiences is a constant challenge."

MILLER, LYNDA: [b] 3/8/66 Belfast; [m] Richard; [p] Frances Sullivan; [ch] Rowanna & Aila; [ed] Princess Garden School, St. Ninians High School (I.O.H.), Douglas College of F.E. (I.O.H.); [occ] psychiatric nurse; [awards] 6 CSE's, 8 'O' levels, 2 'A' levels, Reg. Mental Nurse (R.M.N.), City & Guilds N.V.Q Trainer/Assesor; [pub writ] 6 poems published; "I believe we are all on this earth for a purpose; and helping one another along the path as we go is our key to happiness and peace."

MILLINGTON, J.: [pub writ] "The Cat" - American Poetry Anthology '88 and The Cream of Short Stories and Poetry by Cheshire Writers, book of 100 poems, poems and stories in magazines, anthologies, newspapers etc, and three children's books.

MILNES, ROBERT: [b] 11/6/54 Withington, Manchester; [p] Marie & Joshua; [ed] Two Trees Sec. Modern; [awards] F.E. awards - Machine Engineering; [activ] reading, listening to music and writing poems; "I have a very laid back attitude towards life in general and enjoy the company of others. By observing friends and others I'm able to write both critical verse and love poetry. Any poems that do get published is due to my very close friend for her resounding frienship and gentle persuasion to submit my stuff to competitions, I'm always indebted to her for the encouragement."

MITCHELL, JEAN G.: [b] 25/11/20 Wimbledon; [p] George & Helen Gibb; [ed] Sherbourne School for Girls; [mem] Ntn'l Autistic Soc., Ntn'l Trust & Scottish N.T.; [activ] observer for regional councils 'Fife Nature'; [pub writ] National anthologies & spec. interest journals; "I find writing poetry highly therapeutic!"

MITCHELL, JOAN: [b] 2/5/28 Portsmouth; [ch] Sharon & Michael; [ed] Central School, Southlands Teacher Training College; [occ] teacher (rtrd.); [mem] W.I.; [activ] OXFAM volunteer; [pub writ] 1 story in Short Stories from Kent, 10 poems in Bluebell Railway News; "I taught infants for twenty years, (I always wanted to teach since the age of 11) and worked for my qualifications at evening classes and correspondence courses. Since I was 8 years old I have enjoyed expressing myself in poetry form. I also enjoy short story writing and have always read avidly."

MITCHELL, HARRY J.: [b] 4/2/80 Gt. Yarmouth; [p] John & Sally; [ed] The Royal Albert Memorial College (Framlingham College); [occ] student; [awards] bronze - Duke of Edinburgh Award; [activ] sailing and music; "I enjoy poetry, music and reading. I enjoy playing the piano, saxophone, and doublebass, and base lots of my poetry as topics to the music I compose."

MITCHELL, KAREN: [b] 21/2/64 Rochdale; [p] Eamonn & Arline Ronan; [ch] Laura & Jack; [ed] Bishop Henshaw Memorial R.C. Upper School; [occ] secretary.

MITCHELL, MAUREEN: [b] 28/5/41 Guildford; [p] Leslie & Miriam Quirk; [ch] Alexis; [ed] Guildford High School, Guildford Co. Grammar School; [occ] housewife; [awards] diploma - secretarial; [activ] church musician, treasurer - Ragdoll Cat Club; [pub writ] letters - local/ntn'l newspapers, poem in anthology - 'North West Chorus'; "I returned to my Manx 'roots' after the death of my Cornish husband. I so appreciate the beauty and diversity of the Isle of Man, I try to convey its charms in my poetry."

MITCHELL, THERESA M.: [b] 14/11/42 Scotland; [p] Catherine & Peter Hughes; [ch] Lorraine, Allan, Jason, Samantha & Emma; [ed] St. Patricks R.C. School; [occ] housewife; [pub writ] poem - 'Poetry Now' Anthol. '91; "Writing my poetry has been a therapy for me as most of the ones I've written are facts that have happened to me in my life."

MOLLAND, EILEEN J.: [b] 25/10/46 Shoreham-By-Sea; [m] Anthony; [p] Walter & Kathleen Goodman; [ch] Jeffrey, Roger & Julia; [ed] St. Margarets Convent School; [occ] knitwear manufacturer; [awards] 1st prize knitwear - local show Wales, 1 prizes - flowers; [activ]

amateur country/western singer; [pub writ] poems accepted; "We must all keep up our morale in these recessional days which is why I chose to write poetry. It releases tension and builds up self-esteem, as we must all have a goal to aim for in life."

MOLLOY, CHRISTINE M.: [b] 16/7/47 England; [p] Jean & Keneth Fones; [ch] Lisa Ann; [ed] Walney Co. Sec. School; [occ] housewife; [activ] painting/drawing (Howard St. Furness College); [mem] Barrow Artist Soc.; [pub writ] poetry - 'Stepping Stone to A Better Life' by Patricia Perry (Austr.); "I like to spend my leisure time writing poetry and painting. I would like to dedicate this poem to my mother and to thank her for my happy childhood."

MOODY, JESSIE: [b] 6/2/32 Old Farnley; [p] Alice & Alf Fleming; [ch] Patricia & John; [activ] enjoys giving little messages from the Spiritworld at the Spiritualist Church; [pub writ] poems - 'Book of Winning Poems In Scotland' - C. John Taylor, poems - Poetry Now, local radio in Leeds, 'Evening Post', church magazines; "I like writing poems of the Royal Family, I have received letters from some of them thanking me."

MOORE, KIRSTY: [b] 16/6/78 Cambridge; [p] Malcolm & Janet; [ed] Bottisham Village College, Hills Rd. Sixth Form College; [occ] student; [awards] Duke of Edinburgh Award - Silver; "I am looking forward to what life can offer me and what I can offer life."

MOORES, CHRIS: [b] 12/1/58 Rawtenstall; [p] Alex & Dorothy; [ed] Bury Grammar School, University of Central Lancashire; [occ] student; [awards] City & Guilds - hairdressing, 7307 cert. - Teaching Further & Adult Education; [activ] volunteer path warden - Rossendale Borough Council; "Seeking happiness was a futile occupation: only when I opened my eyes wide enough did I find inspiration, pleasure and contentment everywhere around me."

MORGAN, MARIA D.: [b] 6/1/63 Risca; [m] Mark; [p] Reg & Maureen Mann; [ed] Pontymister Sec. Modern; [occ] housewife; "People's abilities differ. What is easily grasped by one can be difficult for others. Learn not to rush, instead lavish time upon yourself and wait for your moment of confidence, I did, and it helped me to express myself."

MORGAN, NIGEL: [b] 4/8/67 Portsmouth; [p] Frederick & Marion; [ed] Lewis Boys Comp.; [occ] voluntary wrkr; [activ] volunteer - R.V.D.C.; "I am interested in drawing and writing. I also enjoy outdoor activities. I am the 6th out of 7 children and I live in a shared house."

MORLEY-SMITH, MARGARET: [b] 3/4/32 Heworth, Gateshead; [p] Elizabeth & Earnst; [ch] Anthony, Phillip & Neil; [ed] Scarborough, Birmingham, Newcastle; [pub writ] poem "Just Looking" - Arrival Press Anthology 'Words Work'; "Most of my poems are of childhood memories which I hope one day my children and theirs will appreciate."

MORRIS, FLORENCE V.: [b] 7/12/16 Largs; [m] Hugh (dcd.); [p] Alexander & Florence Simpson; [ed] Ardrossan Academy, studied Music/Piano, Organ, Singing - A.M. Polly Henderson, Glasgow; [occ] music teacher (rtrd.); [awards] ATCL, LTCL (piano teaching), ARCM (singing/teaching), LACW Radar Mech.; [mem] St. John's Cos. Largs. Toch, RAFA, Historical Soc., SWT (Largs branches) [pub writ] poems - 'Let Me Walk With You', (priv. pub.) J & R Simpson for charity, '42; "I strongly believe in continuing zest for life to the limit of one's strength, both physical and mental. Writing is therapeutic and often influential. It's fun as well!"

MORRIS, LIZ: [b] 19/5/53 Cardiff; [m] Ray [ch] Jenny & Karen' [ed] Whitchurch High School, Open University; [occ] housewife; [awards] 2 'A' levels, B.A. '85; [activ] clerk to governors of daughter's school; [pub writ] poem - Poetry Now South '95; "I have only recently started writing poetry seriously but find it an effective means of expression for my feelings."

MORRIS, THOMAS: [b] 24/9/30 Cardiff; [p] Jeremia & Gwen; [ch] Christopher, Dawn, & Tracey; [ed] 'O' level equivelents during Service (R.N.); [occ] bricklayer (rtrd.); [awards] City & Guilds - bricklaying;

[activ] swimming, reading, oil painting, writing.

MORRISON, DOROTHY: [b] 15/8/36 Scarborough; [p] George & Christina Bond; [ch] Michelle & Shona; [ed] Gladstone Rd. C.P. School, Convent of the Ladies of Mary Grammar School; [occ] teacher (rtrd.); [awards] Cert. of Ed. (Teaching), Cert. of Literature, Cert. Environmental Ed., City & Guilds - computer studies; [activ] local historian, some work on archeological digs, school swim club, school activities; [pub writ] local history in evening newspapers, res. history Scarborough Police Force 1850-1947 for archives, poems in creative writing book, also 'Family History' magazine; "Although a science teacher I have always enjoyed a wide range of activities and in quiet times greatly enjoy reading and writing poetry. It is a window to the soul!"

MORTER, MARY: [b] 8/5/50 Essex; [p] Annie & George Horton; [ch] Clair & James; [ed] White Bridge Primary, Brook Sec. Modern, Loughton College F.E.; [occ] housewife; [awards] 'O' & 'A' levels - art & Eng., G.C.S.E. - needlework; [pub writ] poem - "The Visit" in Ntn'l Library of Poetry Anthology '95 'Echoes of Yesterday'; "I believe that poetry should enlighten and inspire the reader. Through my work I hope to share my personal philosophy and life experiences with all who read it."

MORTON, JANET: [b] London; [p] Harry & Violet Sheridan; [ch] Sheridan John & Rebecca Jane; [ed] Sec. Grammar School; [occ] admin. clerk; [pub writ] 3 poems in last 2 years; "I tend to write in verse all my thoughts and feelings about life and family, and hope one day to publish all my poems in one book."

MORTON, THOMAS: [b] 3/10/60 Glasgow; [m] Mary; [p] Thomas & Wilma; [ed] Eastbank Academy, Glasgow; [occ] papermill wrkr; [pub writ] articles pub. 'Pints of View', S.E. Scotland Nsltr for CAMRA; "I wrote the poem for Steve & Lynne who were to be married at Balquidder, Rob Roy McGregor's resting place. The poem was my contribution to their big day."

MOSS, MARION: [b] 8/3/54 London; [m] John; [ed] Rainsford Sec. Modern, College of Technology, Lincoln; [occ] civil servant; [awards] 9 'O' levels; [pub writ] poem local works magazine; "I enjoy reading, completing crosswords, playing scrabble and writing poetry."

MUCKART, ROY: [b] 4/5/37 Dundee; [m] Barbara [p] Dodo & Sandy; [ch] Angu & Fiona; [ed] Haris Academy, Dundee; [occ] holiday park accom. mngr.; [activ] local/ntn'l philanthropic organizations; [pub writ] articles/verse in RAF mags. and quarterly journal of R.A.D.B.; "Writing verse and songs and playing guitar are my way of relaxing from a stressful occupation."

MUIR, OLIVE: [b] 11/7/20 Ipswich; [p] Alfred & Ann Hayward; [ch] Wendy, Barie & Lynne; [ed] Nacton Rd. Girls School; [pub writ] 2 poems - "A Prayer" and "Memories Of Childhood"; "I've been writing poems since I was a teenager and express my feelings and thoughts in poetry which still gives me great pleasure."

MUNT, JANE: [b] 13/10/52 Newport, Isle of Wight; [ch] Roushka & Hoffi; [ed] Carisbrooke Grammar School, Westminster College, Oxford; [occ] student; [awards] C & G - literacy & numeracy; [activ] studying for B.Ed (Eng. Lit.), volunteer tutor Basic Ed.; "I have enjoyed reading and writing poetry since I was a child and hope, in the future, to be able to share that enjoyment with others."

MUNRO, ISMA: [b] 24/5/21 Braemar; [p] Bert & Ella McAndrew; [ch] Deirdre (dcd.); [ed] Banchory Academy, Aberdeen University, Aberdeen Training College; [occ] school mistress (rtrd.); [awards] MA degree, Teacher's Cert., Proxime Access It, prize at school; 1st class certs. - moral philosophy & botany; [activ] S.W.R.I committee; Scots Language Soc., Tain Civic Trust Committee; Clan Munro Assoc. Council; volunteer - Tain museum; [pub writ] poems in mags. & anthologies, 1 poem/1 short story broadcast; "I write only when I am in the mood and have an idea. I have never joined any writer's group as I wish writing to remain a pleasure and not become a chore. My lifetime motto 'If you cannot have what you would like, try to like what you have.'"

MURPHY, ROBERT: [b] 8/11/17 Cheshire; [p] Robert & Edith; [ed] Council School; [awards] R.N. Engine Room Charge cert., Dale Carnegie Award - salesmanship; [activ] volunteer collector many societies, volunteer with disabled; [pub writ] short stories; "We pass this way but once to help one another."

MURRAY, ANNE: [b] 14/3/43 Ireland; [p] Patrick & Kathleen Dunne; [ch] Tony, Anne, Kevin, Andrew & Patrick; [ed] St. Anthony's R.C. School; [occ] housewife; [activ] lady's darts, bingo; "I am just a wife, a mother and a grandmother but I love being all three, and I like putting my thoughts on paper."

MURRAY, JANET: [b] 19/1/20 Morningside; [p] Margaret Mollins; [ch] Ronald; [ed] Morningside Village School, Newmains Public School; [activ] art classes resulting in exhibits; [pub writ] svrl. poems pub. "Peebles-shire News", poems in 'Cracked Mirror' & 'The Way of Life'; "I have realized since my husband died, I must live again and I do through writing poetry; now I try short stories. I have had a colourful life. Love is all to me."

MURRAY, JOHN J.: [b] 17/9/54 Leeds; [p] Peter & Elizabeth; [ed] St. Michael's College; Park Lane College, Swarthmore F.E. Ctr.; [mem] MIND - mental health organisation; [pub writ] poem "Happiness" in 'Simply Read' (Swarthmore's 1st magazine); "I write for my own personal enjoyment, hoping to share this with others when they have read my work."

MURRAY, MARY V.: [b] 7/11/28 Sunderland; [p] Peter & Margaret Ciarella; [ch] Shiela, Peter, Susan David & Anthony; [ed] St. Joseph's School; [pub writ] 1 short story "Second Hand Rose" in 'I Remember the North East' Recollections of Yesteryear, many articles/poems in local newspapers; "I find one is never too old to learn, each day brings new beginnings and life is one unending path of discovery no matter what age. You only have one chance at life, so use is wisely. My life has been more precious than most, my husband Peter and five children have been my awards in life, but not least, the gift of life itself. God Bless."

MURRAY, ROBERT J.: [b] 29/1/39 Magheraflet; [p] Robert & Mary; [ed] Primary School currently reading art at Open University; [occ] painter/decorator; [mem] local SPRED group; [pub writ] local correspondent for prov. nsltr., 1 poem "Orange And Green" in poetry anthology; "My motto is: With malice towards none and charity toward all."

MURRAY, STEVE: [b] 22/4/57 Rochdale; [m] Sheila; [ch] Iain & Nicola; [ed] Bishop Henshaw Sr. High, Middlesex Polytechnic; [occ] healthcare analyst; [awards] Reg. Gen. Nurse; [pub writ] poem in 'Poetry Now Connecting' - Forward Press '95; "Nothing I could say in such a short space would be adequate. Isn't this what poetry tries to do?"

MUSTILL, JANET: [b] 15/2/57 Wakefield; [ch] Stephen; [occ] deputy payroll mngr.; [activ] badminton; [pub writ] poem in parish magazine; "Total surprise to be entered but this has given me courage to look at submitting other poems. I don't expect too much from life so I am seldom disappointed. Generally I'm a happy person."

NAYLOR, ANNE: [b] 23/6/50 Cambridge; [p] John & Annie Cameron; [ch] Sarah, Jamie & Anna; [ed] Secondary, Secretarial College; [occ] housewife; [activ] volunteer - bereavement, visitor - hospice; "My poety is generaly quite personal and I hope to give as much satisfaction to others who may read it, as I derive in writing it."

NEIL, DOROTHY: [b] Cardiff; [p] Thomas Dorothy; [ed] Lady Margaret High School; [occ] shipping clerk (rtrd.); [activ] arts group, studying French, theatre, music, cats; [pub writ] poems various anthologies and local newspaper; "I have found that being tenacious and persevering when faced with adversity, has paid dividends; my best poems have been written when under emotional stress. My motto is: Unto thine own self be true."

NETHERWOOD, ERNEST: [b] 30/3/04 Castleford, W. Yorks; [ed] Elementary followed by eve. class studies Wakefield College; [awards] 1st class Colliers Mngrs. Cert.; [pub writ] poems and short stories; "I spent 49 years in the mining industry. I commenced writing after my wife died nine years ago. I shall be 91 years old in March."

NEWELL, JOHN: [b] 7/8/10 Leeholme; [p] John & Ethel; [ch] Molly & Jacky; [ed] Alderman Wraith Grammar School, Spennymoor, Co. Durham; [occ] coal mine official (rtrd.); [activ] Derbyshire C. Council, parish councillor; [pub writ] letters to papers; "A man's actions cannot be fairly judged, his intentions are the genuine criteria on which to form a judgement. Forming an opinion is mere speculation and inevitably in serious error."

NEWMAN, PATRICIA: [b] 3/3/45 Armagh; [ch] Clare, David & John; [ed] Convent of the Sacred Heart Grammar School; Teacher Training College, Fenham; [occ] teacher; "I don't have a gun, I'm not a politician. I don't have a voice. Putting words down on paper is my safety valve."

NEWTON, LENA: [b] 2/12/23 Barrow-In-Furness; [p] Beatrice & William; [ch] Leonard, Paul & Derek; [ed] Victoria Girls School; [occ] aux. nurse (rtrd.); [pub writ] 1 poem "The Prayer" (about the oil disaster); "We were the choir, on our way home from Lancaster after singing at the College one night. I was on the front seat of the bus and out popped this lovely white rabbit, darting across the motorway. I started writing after I retired mostly."

NICHOLSON, JOYCE M.: [b] 5/2/15 Bolton; [p] Nellie & Frederick; [ed] Bolton High School; [awards] Teaching Cert.; [activ] volunteer garden work for disabled; "After a busy working life surrounded by people I now live alone and find a satisfying outlet for my thoughts by writing verse. I rail at the follies of the 'powers that be', weep at the sufferings of today's unfortunates, revel in the joys of the countryside and laugh at life's sorrows."

NOBEL, W.A.: [b] 12/5/18 Symington; [p] W.R. & A.G. Noble; [ch] Alexander; [ed] Kilmarnock Academy, Glasgow University (Vet School); [occ] vet. surgeon (rtrd.); [awards] Hall Memorial Award - pig diseases, M.R.C.V.S.; [activ] volunteer; [pub writ] svrl. papers on pig diseases, poems - "Drunken Chiropodist", "The Sky", "Christians", "Cabbridgeshire Fens", etc.

NOBLETT, LYNN C.: [b] 17/2/71 Preston, Lancs.; [p] Frank & Jean Noblett; [ch] Katey & Karl; [ed] Holy Cross High School, Chorley Public, Largo High School (Fla., US); [awards] Editior's Choice Award - Ntn'l Library of Poetry; [pub writ] poem - "After The Storm" - Ntn'l Library of Poetry (US), "Dream Don't Dream" - Aural Images, local newspapers; "I live for every moment and I cherish every day, and every memory I keep is another verse of my poetry ... let the light of love shine on."

NORWOOD, JOHN T.: [b] 22/1/34 Old Hill, West Midlands; [m] Jean; [p] Samuel & Gladys; [ch] Rachel; [ed] Halesowen Boys School, Martineau Teacher Training College, Birmingham Polytechnic; [occ] Training Ctr. Mngr (rtrd.); [awards] diplomas in teaching, management & preaching; [activ] church secretary and lay preacher; [pub writ] poems in Midland Verse '93, Poetry Now '94, words for choral/orchestra pres. Prom. Praise W. Australia '90, hymns & children's songs locally; "A passion for poetry has always been part of my life. My own verse includes devotional poems and hymns, narrative & humourous poems and verses for my grandchildren. Verse affords me a vehicle by which to convey those thoughts and emotions which enrich daily living."

NURTON, PATRICIA: [b] 4/3/40 Iselworth; [m] Michael; [p] Hilda & Paul O'Daly; [ch] Julie, Lilly, Jane & Wilson; [ed] St. Edmund's Infants School, Kneller School Girls Jr. (Lordsfield Boarding School), Open University; [awards] sociology - pass certificate, fully trained florist, book prize - literature; [activ] fund-raising for MS Soc. through my Clouds & Silver Lining Poetry books, member of pen pal group; [pub writ] articles, poems in local newspapers, poems in books (4); "My gifts of poetry and writing have enabled me to share inner thoughts and feelings with others. My greatest challenge now is to write my autobiography to leave behind for my grandchildren. Seeing my first poem in print was magic."

OAKLEY, KELLY L.: [b] 5/10/82 Stourbridge; [p] Gerald & Marie; [ed] Gigmill Rimary, Ridgewood High School; [occ] student; [awards] piano grds. 1 & 2; [mem] Kinver Operatic Soc.; [pub writ] poem "Sarajevo Christmas 1994" - Poetry Now '95; "I like writing poetry and try to project a point of view to people. As I am a child I think that it is harder to make people listen to my point of view, so I write poems and hope more people will become aware of the suffering in the world."

O'BRIEN, MARIE: [b] 14/10/55 Derry, N.I.; [m] James; [p] Gerald & Lavina O'Doherty; [ch] Roisin, Deirdre & Cora; [ed] Waterside Girls School; [occ] civil servant; [activ] creative writing class; [pub writ] local books/mags.; "Poetry to me is the breath of the heart and mind in words. Whether people, nature or the universe. I cannot envisage life without writing poetry."

O'DOHERTY, LEON: [b] 16/7/74 London; [p] Geraldine & Raymond; [ch] Lee & Rebecca; [ed] NorthWest Inst. of Higher and Further Ed.; [occ] student; [awards] B-Tec Ntn'l Diploma Leisure & Tourism (Leisure/Recreation with distinction); [activ] semi-pro cyclist; [pub writ] Weymouth Publications, Arrival Press, local newspapers; "From a first hand and personal experience I use my poetry as a medium to 'explain' my reflections of life in N. Ireland. (Knowledge is power.)"

ODWELL, VICTORIA: [b] 11/12/78 Westcliff-On-Sea; [p] Dennis & Gillian; [ed] Westcliff High School for Girls; [occ] student; "This poem expressed my personal feelings and I hope by having it published it will give an insight to this condition. I therefore dedicate this poem to my grandfather, George Odwell."

OGILVIE, PAULINE: [b]19/6/56 Derry; [m] Thomas; [p] John & Eileen McCauley; [ch] Tony, Caroline & Heather; [ed] Open University (studying for a BSc - Maths); [pub writ] 3 poems - "Mirrors Of Time" ('92), "Just Before Dawn" ('93), "The Birth Of Road From Mountain Track" ('94); "When my six years of study with the Open University are completed, I intend to devote more time to writing poetry and short stories."

O'KANE, SEAN: [b] 9/5/40 Maghera Co. Derry, N.I.; [m] Joan; [p] Barney & Tillie; [ch] Felicity, Shiona, Deirdre & Kirsteen; [ed] Seminary - Congregation of the Cross & Passion, Probation Officers Training; [occ] social wrkr.; [awards] Cert. of Qualification - Probation Officers (Scottish Office); [pub writ] one forgettable letter to The Scotsman!; "Everyone has something to say or tell worth listening to, and the discipline of poetry helps us say or tell it succinctly; all we need else is the courage to risk ridicule."

O'KOYE, IFEATU C.: [b]26/4/68 Portharcourt, Nigeria; [p] Sir Christian & Lady Beatrice; [ed] University of Nigeria Nsukka, Loughborough University of Technology; [occ] engineering/post grad. student; [awards] B of Engineering, Master of Science (Computer Integrated Manufacture); [activ] Anglican Soc., choir, general community services, organist; "Powers that be must listen to subjects that are, per providence, to their orders bound, discerning when to turn their ways around. Mankind must her creation's mystery retrace; for though technology's face smiles for his large paces he's helplessly frowned to discover his limits. As a SUPREME FORCE unrolls challenges unlimited."

OLDBURY, JEAN: [b] Warrington; [p] Leonard & Violet Daintith; [ed] Warrington High School; [occ] nurse; [awards] nursing - R.G.N. & S.C.M., B Tech - creative therapy; [mem] Mother's Union; [activ] Christian, member Church of Eng., bellringer; "I find it difficult to express my thoughts and feelings verbally, but much easier with a pen in my hand."

O'NEILL, HILARY O.: [b]26/2/13 Liverpool; [p] Thomas & Caroline (dcd.); [ch] Patrica, Ruth & John Justin; [ed] Liverpool Institute, Sefton Park Teachers Training College; [occ] school master (rtrd.); [awards] Teacher's Cert.; [activ] sacristan at S. Mary's Wellingborough; [pub writ] 3 books of poems printed for charities, poems in anthologies, words to hymns; "My writings are mainly religious - 'Ad Maiorem Dei Glorium'."

O'REILLY, SANDRA J.: [b] 26/4/71 Lewisham; [p] Franklyn & Patricia Adshead; [ch] Danielle & Jayson; [ed] Crown Woods School; "It gives me great pleasure to write about children and spend endless time writing poems."

OSBORNE, EVA K.: [b] 28/4/11 Elmsett; [p] Walter & Ann Pryke; [ed] Village Church of England school, Elmsett, Suffolk; [occ] pensioner; [pub writ] 2 poems in local Evening Star; "I enjoy reading poems, biographys, 'who dunnits', T.V., cards, darts, carpet bowling. I had a very happy childhood working in the fields. My parents were wonderful and worked hard to give us children a happy childhood."

O'SHEA, WENDY L.: [b] 11/6/75 Melton Mowbray; [p] Brian & Valerie; [ed] Penglais Comp. Aberystwyth, Exeter University; [occ] student; [activ] ed. univ. newspaper; chair student/staff committee, Exeter Poetry Soc., Debating Soc., Exeter Ladies Football Team; [pub writ] university paper - reviews/articles; "Being chosen for this anthology is a wonderful 'pinch' for me as it lets me believe that I'm not just a dreamer with sugary aspirations. My Career Advisor may crumple his brow, but perhaps there is hope for a hyper-sensitive, ecstatic, angry, nineteen year old who wants to be a writer and a poet???"

O'SULLIVAN, JOHN M.: [b] 6/9/43 Castle Donnington; [p] Violet & Jeremiah; [ed] Alleyn's, Dulwich London, Free University, Berlin; [occ] TEFL teacher; [awards] TEFL Cert. '89; [activ] folklorist, travel, languages (fluent in German, good in French/Spanish); [pub writ] poems in 'Yorkshire 1995' and 'The World Turns' (1994); "I have lived at various times in Germany, France Holland, Israel and Cyprus. Only after becoming an English teacher in 1989 have I been able to express these experiences in poetical form or as short stories."

OWEN, HONOR; [b] 2/11/70 Alexandria; [p] Margaret Laidlaw; [ed] Vale of Leven Academy, Dunbartonshire; [activ] volunteer/paid work with children of single parent families, women's aid establishments; "Human interaction has always fascinated me, but none more so thatn the man/woman relationship. Most of my work is on this theme as I'm not only affected by my own personal circumstances, but am sensitive to the emotional conflicts and dissatisfaction that exists in those around me."

OWEN, MURIEL: [b] 6/4/25 Netherfield, Nottingham; [p] Alfred & Caroline Porter; [ch] Vivienne & Julie; [ed] Carlton Girls Sec. School; [occ] sewing machinist (rtrd.); "I enjoy expressing my inner thoughts in verse, hoping to delight and give joy and peace to others."

OWEN-FRAWLEY, HOLLY: [b] 26/12/82 London; [p] Angela & Nick; [ed] Upper III Perse School for Girls; [occ] student; [awards] BAGA - gymnastics, school prizes, (English) dancing; [mem] Huntingdon Gymnastic Club; "My parents are divorced and I live with my mother. I love gymnastics, poetry, rock and roll, guinea pigs and my Mummy and Daddy. I would like to be satisfyingly rich when I grow up!"

PADLEY, PERCY T.: [b] 15/5/30 Bulwell, [ed] Claremont Senior, Carrington Nott.; [occ] machine operator (rtrd.); [awards] Progress Prize 1944 3A, gold watch - 25 yrs. service; [mem] Bestwood Park Church; [activ] Nottingham Music Hall Assoc.; "This is the first poem I have entered. I like racing, music and art. I served in the R.A.F Ntn'l Service L.A. 1948-50. I read poetry sometimes and know most of their names, (the famous ones)."

PADWICK, DENIS: [pen] Paddy; [b] 7/1/14 Romsey, Hants; [m] Lena; [p] Charles & Ellen; [ch] Alan, Patricia & Janet; [ed] Barton Peveril, Eastleigh Hants Sec. School; [occ] police officer (rtrd.); [awards] Long Service Medal; [activ] founding member - Basingstoke & Hart Male Voice Choirs (1964-91); [pub writ] about 70 poems - Police Review (1951-66), letters to newspapers; "Choral singing was my 'life' for 27 years. Shortness of breath, due to angina, puts this pleasure beyond reach now. So I am quietly enjoying my old age — along with my dear wife — my best friend for the past 63 years."

PAGET, LEONARD: [b] 17/5/28 Swindon, Wilts.; [p] Edward & Florence; [ch] John, Paul, Dawn, Mark, Hayley & Ian; [ed] C of E; [occ] farm worker (rtrd.); [awards] Ploughing Award, Garden Show Award - Veg/Flowers; [activ] love gardening and music; [pub writ] poems in local newspaper; "I love to write poems of things seen through my life and put them to music. Always lend a helping hand, you will be repaid three times over."

PALMER, JEAN M.: [b] 15/10/51 Isleworth; [p] Phyllis & Gordon; [ed] Kneller Girls School, Middlesex; [occ] collater; "I try to look at other people's point of view. I enjoy writing short stories and also my poems."

PARK, JANE: [b] 25/3/56 Bradford; [m] Graeme; [p] Geoffrey & Clare Cosway; [ch] Andrew & Emily; [ed] City of Leeds & Carnegie; [occ] sculptor/poet; [pub writ] 2 poems in anthologies; "I began writing poetry at three years of age, but stopped in my teens, confusing verbiage with meaning I suspect. I started to write again in September 1994, eight weeks later I wrote "The Unthawing": I especially like to paint landscapes with my poetry which reflects the mood of the person or subject I am writing about. Poetry by its very nature should be diverse and honest."

PARKER, MANDY: [b] 8/11/67 Nantwich; [m] Simon; [p] Pat & Derek; [ch] Danica & Dalton; [ed] Middlewich County Comp.; [activ] volunteer - Barnardos; "I enjoy writing poems and have written many, mostly relating to family and friends which gives me and all my family lots of happiness."

PARKER, VICTORIA, E.: [b] 17/7/85 Birmingham; [p] Terence & Vivienne; [ed] St. Mawgan In Pydar C.P. School; [occ] student; [pub writ] poems in local newspaper/magazine, also anthology book; "I am nine years old and have been writing poems and stories since I was five years old. I want to be a successful writer one day."

PARKES, DENNIS: [b] 4/3/19 Springfield, Rowley Regis; [p] James & Edith; [ed] Compulsory State School; [occ] factory wrkr/lorry driver; "My identity and family is now at West Bromwich Registrar, transferred from Dudley."

PARKIN, SUZANNE: [b] 18/1/73 Birkenhead, Merseyside; [m] Colin; [ed] Winterton Comp., S. Humberside; [occ] insurance clerk; [awards] 9 G.C.S.E.'s, Cert. of Insurance Practice; "Reading has been my passion since I can remember — and so has given me the inspiration to create my own ideas for writing of all kinds."

PARRY, ROSEMARY: [b] 1947 Loughborough; [ed] Loughborough High School, University of Warwick, Loughborough University of Technology; [occ] freelance writer; [pub writ] article in local mags., Sherlock Holmes Magazine.

PARSONAGE, JOAN: [b] 14/11/43 Liverpool; [m] John; [p] Henry & Emily Roberts; [ch] Dawn & Fiona; [ed] Sec. Modern - Liverpool; [occ] arts/crafts; [awards] Youth Leadership Diploma; [activ] youth leader - local arts/crafts; [pub writ] poems in ntn'l magazines and local newspapers; "I write partly about nature, for the wilderness is in our keeping, and creation is more marvellous than yet we know."

PATERSON, KELLY E.: [b] 6/3/61 Kirkcaldy; [p] Alexander & Ann; [ch] Dawn; [ed] Kent School (R.A.E.) Germany, Glenwood High School; [awards] 7 'O' grades, Scotbec Awards, R.S.A. awards; [pub writ] short story - Women's Own Magazine; "The love of my caring daughter, Dawn, and a wonderful family have helped me through the most difficult times in my life. If my writing can in any way touch someone else's life then I will feel a true sense of achievement. A big thank-you to my sister Karen and brother Cameron and a special thank-you to my beautiful daughter, Dawn."

PAYNE, DONNA: [b] 6/3/78 Canvey Isl.; [p] Robert & Lynda; [ed] Cornelius Vermuyden Comp.; [occ] shop/display assist.; [awards] art/design award; [activ] volunteer - animal sanctuary; [pub writ] poetry - local anthology; "To be happy is my only goal in life and words help me achieve this. My poems are my feelings so they may be hard for others to interpret, but I hope people see them as original and enjoy them for that reason."

PEARCE, BARBARA: [b] 14/9/74 Plumstead; [p] Terry & Anne; [ed] University of Luton; [occ] student; [pub writ] poems in various anthologies, letter in local press; "I find that creative writing is relaxing in my hectic schedule. Writing poems is one medium in which to express my ideas and ambitions."

PEARCEY, ANGELA: [b] Scotland; [p] Elma & James; [ed] Dumfries Academy, Lady Mabel College, London University, Open Univeristy; [occ] teacher; [awards] BA, BEd., Dip. Ed., L.C.S.P.; [activ] reading writing, walking, sports clubs; [pub writ] articles/short stories; "I find listening to sounds and playing with words a means of seeking clarification and simplicity in this highly complex world of ours. The varying moods and forms of poems reflect the nature of life."

PENTONI, OLIVE: [b] 21/5/45 Irish Republic; [ed] Togher Ntn'l School; [occ] Vauxhall worker; [pub writ] book ' Don't Look Back', svrl poems; "I find that writing is a wonderful therapy. There is a certain magic in the written word and each piece I write is from real experiences."

PERCIVAL, MARJORIE: [b] 23/9/29 Derby; [p] Richard & Mary Broughton; [ch] Richard Knowles, Mark, David & Nicholas Percival; [ed] Ashby School for Girls; [occ] housewife; [pub writ] poems - "Remembrance", "Life", "Divorce" - Treasury of Modern Poets 1980; "You are never alone when you have an affinity with words, and a good imagination."

PERKS, DEAN: [b] 11/6/80 Hereford; [p] Rosemary & Martin; [ed] G.C.S.E (1st yr.); [occ] student; [awards] LAMBDA & Mime Awards; [activ] public speaking, Hereford Youth Theatre, Hereford Amateur Pantomime, fencing, snooker club, music group "Classified"; [pub writ] "Falling" - regional anthologies, "Fireworks Night" - Invitation to Poetry, "Parents and Teachers" - Through The Hoop; "I enjoy writing poetry for two reasons: one, it is fun and two, it aids me with my drama work which I hope to continue as a career when I leave school."

PETTY, BARBARA: [b]27/4/52 Londonderry; [p] Jean & James Thom; [ch] Graham; [ed] Templemore, Londonderry; [occ] housewife; [activ] volunteer; [pub writ] poems - "Ulster or Not" & "Hillsborough" - Arrival Press '93 & '94; "I find great satisfaction in the fact that my poems are being recognised and put into print."

PHELPS, MARGARET: [b] 27/11/46 Normanton; [ch] Angela & Karen; [occ] p/t shop assistant; [activ] Normanton Amateur Operatic Soc.; [pub writ] book of poems self-published; "After writing my very first poem, a teacher said that I 'certainly had a gift'. Thank God that gift has remained with me. Being able to express myself in verse, has brought me a lot of pleasure, hopefully bringing that same pleasure to a lot of people."

PHILLIPS, HAZEL: [b]24/7/26 [ch] Michael, David, Martin & Hugh; [ed] Secondary; [activ] local art soc.; "I live in a lovely valley in S. Wales. My roots are anchored deeply like my beloved trees: I will strive to preserve that beauty forever."

PHILLIPS, JENNIFER E.: [b] 8/7/50 Llanbradach; [p] Daniel & Ann Seaborne; [ch] Nadina; [ed[Caerphilly Sec. Mod., Rhydfelin College; [occ] pharmacy assistant; [awards] City & Guilds - hairdressing; [pub writ] poem - "Life" Poetry Now 1994 (Wales); "I find writing poetry brings out my innermost thoughts of what I feel is happening in the world today."

PHILPOTT, HEATHER: [b]13/4/42 Kent; [p] Helen & Charles Osborne; [occ] nurseryman; [mem] Herefordshire Community Health, NHS Trust, Leominster Voluntary Action Group; [activ] choral soc. member; "Moved to Herefordshire in 1988 and have since created a garden and nursery from two acres of farmland. The garden is open to the general public under the National Gardens Scheme during the summer and is the source of inspiration for my poems together with the surrounding countryside."

PHIPPS, JEAN: [b] 15/3/28 Watford Herts.; [p] Ernest & Yvonne Gibson; [ch] Michael, Christopher & Robert; [ed] St. Joan of Arc convent; [occ] housewife; [activ] church activites, horitcultual soc., volunteer; [pub writ] poem in Catholic newspaper, local club magazine; "I am the fourth daughter in a family of seven girls and one boy. I usually write when emotionally moved."

PHIPPS, PAUL: [b] 6/30/67 Windlesham; [ed] Horsell County Sec. School; [occ] musician; "Satisfaction for me is self-expression through writing and performing, giving entertainnment and enjoyment to an audience."

PICKERING, JOY: [b] 22/3/42 Liverpool; [m] Dennis; [p] Helen Quinn; [ch] Paula & Ché Edward; [ed] Huyton Hey Sec. Modern, Abraham Guest High, Adult Ed.; [occ] housewife/artist; [awards] 'O' levels - English; [activ] Homewatch co-ordinator, animal supp. liberty; [pub writ] 3 poems; "Secure in my marriage and the knowledge that my children succeeded against the odds. My creativity in art and poetry exudes, and with the backdrop of my beloved adopted town, Wigan, and its people for inspiration I shall always write. It is a bonus that someone should read it."

PLASKETT, JUNE: [b] 8/7/47 Bolton, [m] William; [ch] Brian & Susan; [occ] shop assistant; [pub writ] 7 poems in various anthologies, svrl. in local newspaper; "I enjoy writing and reading poetry and I have completed a drama televion script and have recently submitted it."

POLLAND, EDDIE: [b] 7/12/37 Co. Down, N.I.; [m] Mary; [p] William & Elizabeth; [ch] Jenifer, Barry & Anne; [ed] Primary School Glassdrumman P.S.; [occ] civil servant (rtrd.); [awards] commendations Long Service & Good Conduct medals; "To use hands and mind to the best of individual ability brings satisfaction to life."

PORTLOCK-BARKER, JAN: [b] 14/7/35 Didcot, Oxon.; [p] Robert & Violet Beck; [ch] Colin & Tony; [ed] St. Helen & St. Katharine, Abingdon, Oxon, Oxford & County Secretarial College; [occ] secretary (rtrd.); [awards] R.S.A. - secretarial skills; [pub writ] 6 poems in anthologies, church magazines, local magazines: "I find that poetry is a very expressive form for my personal thoughts. Challenging to write but easy to read and understand."

POTTER, PAT: [b] 7/2/59 Bromyard; [p] Phillip & Frances; [ed] Queen Elizabeth Comp., Bromyard; [occ] supervisor - electronics; [awards] NEBS - management award; "I don't spend too much time wishing, as time is best spent doing. You only have one life, so make sure you live it. There's no going back for a second chance, so everyday I try to live to the full."

POTTER, RONALD G.: [b] 24/10/23 Weston Colville; [p] Frank & Mildred; [ch] Karen, Hazel & Helen; [ed] Weston Colville Village School; "Have been interested in writing poetry since a teenager, just for my own pleasure, I often made up poems for work mates."

POTTINGER, JOHNNY: [b] 6/1/24 Stromness; [ed] Stromness Academy; [occ] seaman/taxidermist/museum attend. (rtrd.); [pub writ] poems/artcles/short stories various newspapers, books, magazines; "Life is wonderful! One can learn much from the past. This is mostly reflected in much of my creative writings."

POTTS, JASON T.: [b] 20/2/65 Scunthorpe; [p] Brian & Margaret; [ed] Thomas Sumpter Comp.; [occ] steelworker; [activ] pro animal rights; [pub writ] various poems in local press and books; "I believe there is no such thing as a bad poem. Any arrangement of words, from this rich language of ours must always count for something."

POWELL, ELIZABETH: [b]24/10/34 Manchester; [m] Charles; [p] Lilian & James; [ch] Beverley, John & Lesley; [ed] Crosslee Sec. Modern School for Girls; [pub writ] poems in anthology, local newspapers, church mag.; "Since a child I've always enjoyed writing but over the years never found the time. Having early retirement forced upon me through ill health I found I had the time and also the inclination. Oh, what a joy I've found."

POWELL, MARGAET E.: [b] 13/4/45 Barrow-in-Furness; [m] Dennis; [p] Patrick & Sabria McAloone; [ch] Simon & Claire; [ed] Our Lady's Crosslands Convent, St. Aloysius Sec. School; [occ] school meal assist.; [activ] church steward, choir, prompt for amateur dramatics, volunteer collector - charities; [pub writ] 2 poems in local evening paper;

"I am happiest when with my family and friends. Patience and understanding are important to get on with people."

POWELL, MAURICE: [b] 17/10/33 Tipton. W. Midlands; [m] Gail; [ch] Janet, Linda & Andrew; [ed] Tipton Central Grammar; [occ] pastor; [activ] church, lay preacher; [pub writ] poem "The Old Castle" - W. Midlands Poetry Now 1995; "Now that I have retired from a career in the N.H.S. and the foundry industry I want to give more time to short stories and poetry, particularly Biblically based."

POWELL, RONALD: [b] 27/12/21 Oldbury, W. Midlands; [ch] Brian & Lynne; [awards] 5 War Medals; [activ] church volunteer - charities/nursing homes; [pub writ] "I'ronny In Verse" - Ripples On The Pool Of Life; "At this end of life to pass on experience if possible and help make this world a better and happier place."

PRICE, LILIAN J.: [b] 21/7/19 Wedbley, Herefordshire; [m] John; [p] Ann & William; [ed] Jr., then Vaynor & Penderyn Grammar School; [awards] G.C.E. (Hons.); [pub writ] poems; "My gift of words was acknowledged at school. I am now studying to write publishable prose, and eventually my autobiography."

PRINCE, MOLLY L.: [b] 10/1/35 Bristol; [p] Tom & Rose Andrews; [ch] Andrew, Philip, & Robert; [ed] Connaught Rd. Sec. School; [occ] housewife; [activ] volunteer; "I like to put my thoughts down on paper, things I wouldn't say. I am not a very confident person but when I write it is as though I expose the hidden me and what I really feel."

PRITCHARD, GWYNETH: [b] 26/1/29 Banwen, S.Wales; [p] Violet & Evan James; [ch] C.A. Roberts; [occ] train announcer (rtrd.)/housewife; [awards] paintings in National Exhibition of Housewive's Paintings, by IPC newspapers, the people; [activ] life member RAFA, sec. 1223 Squadron ATC, Smooth & Wire Fox Terrier Club of S.Wales; v-pres. Caerphilly Art Soc.; [pub writ] poems - Poetry Now (Peterborough), Natures Notions (Wales Anthology '94), Poetry Now 1995; "I enjoy both painting and poetry and find it very rewarding and relaxing, wish I had more time for both, which is rather limited, mixed in with running the house."

PRITCHARD, JACK: [b] 13/4/23 St. Margarets, W. Herefords; [p] John & Mary (dcd); [ch] Derek, Graham & Sheila; [ed] Newton Primary; [occ] land reclamation/transportation (rtrd.); [awards] 1st prize - Ploughing with Horses 1937 (cert.), garden awards; [activ] reading to Women's Institute; [pub writ] chuch mag., 'Mature Tymes', Poetry Now; "Country born, now a city dweller, my aim is to write realistically and portray in lasting terms impressions, reflections, trends and country moods in many 'fields'. To contribute to life."

PROFIT, MARIAN: [b] 24/5/54 Canada; [m] Chris; [ch] Rachel; [ed] Holy Heat High School, Nfld., Canada; [occ] singer; [activ] animal welfare; [pub writ] 2 songs, 1 poem; "The world needs healing. Making someone smile is a step toward that. I find that acting a little insane sometimes helps keep me sane — releasing a smile, hence a step to self-healing. Try it!!"

PUGH, JAN: [b] 12/8/46 Staffs; [p] Charles & Cicely Dyble; [ed] Broadacres Sec. Modern; Staffs College of Further Education; [occ] housewife; [awards] Cert. shorthand/typing, Eng. Lang., Eng. Lit.; [activ] sec. local Allotment Soc.; [pub writ] svr. poems in consumer nwsltr, 1 poem - British Poetry Review 1995; "I get satisfaction in life by trying to help other people; I relax by painting pictures of wild flowers and writing children's stories and poems on any subject. Whenever I see a wild flower, there is usually a poem just waiting to be written about it."

QUAGGIN, LEE J.: [b] 3/8/71 Isle of Man; [p] Paul & Shiela; [occ] student; [activ] about to finish 2 yrs. 'A' level studies, aim to study Celtic History; [pub writ] poems - Northwest Anthologies, "A Dry Eye" & "Affairs Of The Heart"; "Although I have been writing poetry for four years, I feel that it has improved dramatically since my return to education. I would like to produce an anthology of Manx poets at some point in time."

QUILLIAM, SARAH: [b] 30/12/80 Manchester; [p] David & Kate'

[ed] Ballakermeen High School; [occ] student; "I enjoy writing as it's one of the few things in life that's not a passing fad. I also enjoy acting. I wrote my poem when I was 13 and my ambition is to enjoy life and carry on writing."

QUINN, AUDREY: [b] 18/2/35 London; [occ] housewife; "I just love writing poetry nothing more, nothing less."

RADFORD, MARTHA: [b] 17/1/24 Durham; [p] James & Mary Ann Moore; [ch] Christine, Lesley & Paul; [ed] Durham & Essex; [awards] medallions - War work (home nursing), real estate managemen (US); [mem] WRVS; [activ] hospice volunteer, sr. citizens social organiser; [pub writ] poems in church magazines, WRITTLE newspaper, one book of poems 'Dolly's Mixture'; I get great satisfaction from putting my stories into rhyme and have made many new friends from this worthwhile pursuit."

RAFIQUE, SHAGUFTA: [b] 2/6/66 Pakistan; [p] Mohammed & Gulzar; [ed] Paget High School, Burton College, Bradford University; [awards] Eng. prize - school; [activ] OXFAM volunteer; [pub writ] poems/letters local newspaper; "Friendship has played a major role in my life. The friendship of my bothers and sisters, my parents and that between God and myself. The most valuable gift that I possess is my imagination."

RATCLIFFE, TERENCE: [b]10/2/41 Goseley; [p] John & Mary' [ed] Mount Pleasant Sec. Modern School; [awards] medal - Long Service Special Constabulary, Royal Humane Soc., Scroll; [pub writ] 4 poems in books, 1 in magazine, 1 in paper; "I enjoy writing poetry and stories, from the ridiculous to the serious, and I hope to do so for a lot more years."

RAWLINGS-SMITH, PHILIP G.: [b] 5/4/12 Rotherham; [p] Alice Edna; [ch] Susan Rosalind; [ed] Rotherham High School; [mem] Rotherham Metro Dist. Local History Council, Rotherham Soc. of Artists, Wickersley Probus Club; "Believe your beliefs and doubt your doubts but don't fall into the error of believing your doubts and doubting your beliefs."

RAYNER, HEATHER: [b] London; [m] Ray; [p] H.B & D.E. Peake; [ch] Mark & Grant; [occ] co. director (rtrd.); [activ] fund-raiser charities, Conservative party; "I enjoy writing and have had press releases published in connection with the advertising agency I owned jointly with my husband, Ray, when he was Chairman and I was Deputy Chairman."

REDFIELD, SPENCER: [b] 3/1/64 Bishops, Stortford; [m] Elisabeth Hill; [ed] King Alfred's College, University of Sheffield; [occ] press reader' [awards] BA (Hons.) Eng./Drama; [mem] Mervyn Peake Soc.; [activ] 1st yr. study - M Phil., Amnesty Intn'l; [pub writ] contr. British Poetry Review 1995; "For me poetry is the perfect expression of an innermost language, a mode of thought; I particularly admire Kathleen Raine and Geoffrey Hill in this field."

REDSHAW, ANNE: [b] 19/2/45 Bridlington; [m] Kenneth; [p] Mary & Eric Bornwell; [ch[Stephen Mark; [ed] Bridlington Girls High School, N. Riding Teacher Training School, Bridlington & Driffield Hospitals; [occ] state enrolled nurse; [awards] UKCC State Enrolment (nursing); [activ] member Olde Tyme Music Hall, write revues for local hospital, write quizzes for teams; [pub writ] poems in local papers/mags.; "I would class myself as a 'loner' my ideas and inspirations from stories and poems come mainly from keen observation of others, particularily from things they say. Poems arising from deep personal feelings are not written by me, they write me. Once an idea is in my head, I cannot rest until I have expressed it on paper to my statisfaction."

REEDIE, SYLVIA: [b] 1/1/47 Dunfermline; [m] Alan; [p] Rocco & Helen Cascarino; [ed] Waid Academy, Anstruther; [occ] administrative assistant; [activ] C. of S. sunday school/youth church leader/teacher, Gideon Auxiliary (sec., ex-chairlady); "A Christian, I believe love covers a multitude of sins, treat others as you wish to be treated, God sees and knows everything, goodness will prevail ultimately. I enjoy writing."

REEVES, LES: [pen] Levire; [b] 1921 Bromham Wilts; [ch] Michael,

Alison & Patricia; [ed] Bromham Council School; [activ] town councillor, carnival committees, crime prevention; [pub writ] various poems, letter, & articles, folklore book; "Very interested in folklore and folk music. I enjoy walking for inspiration. Abhor pollution caused by mankind. A Wiltshireman by birth and nature I enjoy spending time on the Isle of Man."

RENDER, HEATHER: [b] 4/11/71 Oldham; [p] Harold & Diane; [ed] Failsworth School, University of Central Lancashire; [occ] student; [activ] working twrd degree, Eng. Lang. Studies; [pub writ] poem in local newspaper; "The colour of life holds a great fascination for me and I have always tried to reflect this in both my poetry and pastel portraits. Tolerance of people is an important aspect of life and everyone should work towards this goal."

RICHARDS, DORIS: [b] 3/2/15 St. Minver; [p] Francis & Amelia Tremain; [ch[Donald, David, Richard, & Philip; [occ] housewife; [pub writ] poem "Betjeman" - Arrival Press; "I have written many poems, also a book of life and events, dating from 1915 with illustrations. Two publishers would like to print, but I cannot meet their fees."

RICHARDSON, COLIN: [b] 10/8/78 Ipswich; [p] Tony & Jane; [ed] Woodbridge School, Farlingaye High School; [occ] student; [awards] 10 G.C.S.E.'s, Gr. 6-8 Bronze Medal - "Verse & Prose"; "This piece of verse was originally written as a song for the band in which I play. I am a keen musician and also very much enjoy drama and performing arts."

RICHARDSON, SCOTT: [b] 6/4/67 Oldham; [p] Arnold & Jean; [ed] South Chaderton Comp., College of Technology; [occ] salesman; [pub writ] short stories in ntn'l fiction mag., poems in anthologies; "Creative writing is a gift. It is up to those lucky enough to possess it to harness the skill and commit to paper the literary enjoyment for future generations."

RIDGE, EDNA: [b] 23/1/33 Kidderminster; [p] Molly & Edward Hinton; [ch] Les, Michael & Mark; [ed] Sec. school - Halesowen W. Midlands; [awards] R.S.A. - Eng. Gr. 1; [activ] Rainbow Group, volunteer 'Scope' shop; [pub writ] poems various anthologies/mags.; "I enjoy writing long letters to friends (three from my school days). I write poems about things that happen at work, mostly amusing, I would love to write a book someday but need to get a move on!"

RIDGLEY, SARA: [b] 23/1/57 Bucks; [p] Joyce & Ed Woodwark; [ed] Beaconsfield High School, Bucks College; [occ] writer/entrepreneur; [pub writ] cookbook - 'Simply Pickles', articles in Garden News, contrib. Poetry Now & Chiltern Writers Antholog. & Dates From Hell; "Released by redundancy from a 15 year recruitment career, I am nurturing and exploiting talents I always knew I had. A TV script today, a songbook tomorrow and a novel next week! I put pen to paper and the creative cuircuit connects."

RILEY, KENNETH: [b] 18/3/54 Stockton; [m] Susan; [p] Alfred & Irene; [ch] Clair & Alexandra; [ed] St. Josephs Infants, St. Bedes Sec. Modern, Stockton; [occ] crane driver (rtrd.); [activ] Five Alls, Sea Angling Club, glass engraving, writing poetry; [pub writ] poetry - British Poetry Review '94, Poetry in Motion N/East '94, Paving The Way '94, A Xmas Cracker '94, local paper; "I started writing poetry in '94. I tend to think if you use true feelings, have a vivid imagination and write what you feel when you see a subject, there is great pride in seeing your work published."

ROBBINS, GWEN: [b] 1/7/11 Bath; [p] Clara & Albert Crump; [ch] Christopher, Brian & Angela; [ed] East Twerton Jr., Oldfield Sr., Bath; [awards] Bookbinder Cert. of Award "Royal British Legion" Poppy Appeal; [activ] RBL, M.U.T.G. art group; Bath College - Hard of Hearing; "I am old but that does not bother me, I 'think young' and 'feel young' and the wonder of nature never fails to amaze me."

ROBERTS, JAN: [b] 31/7/42 Hastings; [p] Jim & Vera Riley; [ch] Clive & Jane; [ed] Claverham Community College; [occ] housewife; [pub writ] 5 poems in anthologies; "I believe in saying what I think, incorporating anything I feel strongly about into my poems."

ROBERTS, JOAN E.: [b] 30/4/22 Cromer; [p] Nelly & Cecil Woodhouse; [ch] Anthony & Rosemary; [ed] Aylmerton; [activ] volunteer - Friends of the Hospital.

ROBERTS, SUE: [pen]; [b] 12/3/65 Ormskirk; [m] Pierre Wysocki; [p] Bill & June; [ch] Kimberley; [occ] teacher/translator; [awards] BA (Hons) Fr. & German, PGCE (Sec. Ed. Lang.); "Life follows a predestined path; no matter how you deviate or follow other routes you will always return to Destiny's Plan, therefore try to find happiness in what you've got!"

ROBINSON-JUDD, JOY: [b]15/1/33 Nottingham; [m] Philip; [p] George & Winifred; [ch] Kevin John & Julie Ann; [occ] gov't. officer PA; [awards] secretarial skills, First Aid/Nursing, diploma - Writing For Children; [pub writ] articles - Nottingham Historian; poems/children's stories in local press & Country Life; "Writing poetry and stores is a tremendous form of relaxation for me, and indeed I have been writing since the age of 11, when I won a prize at school for a composition and a poem."

ROBINSON, SANDRA: [b] 1/9/54 Sedgley; [m] Philip; [p] Trevor & Eveline Totney; [ch] Lorraine, Louise & Lloyd; [ed] Siviters Lane Girls Sec. Modern; "After a lot of knocks in my personal life, I have found great satisfaction and relaxation by expressing myself through writing."

ROBSON, ANNE: [b] 1/10/32 Cumbria; [p] James & Georgina Maxwell; [ch] Susan & Yvonne; [ed] Church of England School, Longtown, Royal Academy, Tain, Ross-Shire; [activ] church - St. Andrews Church of Scotland, St. Andrews Club of Berwick-Upon-Tweed; "I find compiling poems is not only a way of relaxation, but also stimulates the mind. Through an extension of my own thoughts I attempt to give the reader a picture or scene I envisage."

ROGERS, DAVID: [b] 23/7/47 Dingwall; [p] Alastair & Helen; [ed] Dingwall Academy; [occ] warehouse wrkr; [activ] Labour Party, Ross County FC.S/C. [pub writ] school magazines; "I have a love of poetry."

ROGERS, EMMA: [b] 12/12/80 Basingstoke, Hampshire; [p] L.E. & P.S. Rogers; [ed] Harriet Costello Sec. School; "To express my feelings on paper by the form of poetry gives me great pleasure. To discover my inner emotions I found with ease when I had the inspiration from someone who I admire in many ways. Thanks to B.W. and thanks for the satisfaction of making such a happiness complete. I've learned to make the most of all situations, turning bad into good, and good into better. Thanks again."

RONSON, SANDRA E.: [b] 2/3/43 Marple - Nr Stockport; [m] Edwin; [p] Stanly & Sylvia Allen; [ch] Donna, Darren & Matthew; [ed] Thornton-Cleveleys High School for Girls; [occ] reg. nurse; [awards] Serving Sister Order of St. John '74, Officer of the Order of St. John '90; [mem] St. John Ambulance (41 yrs.); [pub writ] poems - St. John Mag., books of poetry about St. John Ambulance; "I am usually inspired to write a poem by the need to communicate information. The subject of my poem is situated in the Lytham-St. Annes, St. John Ambulance Hdqtrs."

ROOKS, KAREN J.: [b] 26/8/67 London; [p] Fred & Diane Rooks; [ed] Queen Mary's College, University Combined School of Nursing; [occ] staff nurse; [awards] Reg. General Nursing Cert.; [mem] St. John Ambulance; "I didn't start out to write a poem but with the intention of merely setting down my true feelings and thoughts at a particularly emotional period of my life."

ROSS, ROBERT: [b] 8/11/28 Cardenden, Fife; [p] Robert & Grace; [ch] Margaret & Robert; [ed] Auchterderran High, Fife; [occ] caretaker (rtrd.); [activ] ordained elder - Church of Scotland, hospital visitor - Christian Caring Course - Aberdeen University; [pub writ] poem "No One Is Perfect" - Poetry Now Scotland '92, poems in church mag.; "I am guided by God in my writing as I pray to Him before putting pen to paper each time I write a poem or compose a hymn."

ROWLAND, ROBERT: [b] 14/9/29 Taliesein Wales; [p] Richard & Ann (dcd.); [ed] Llancynfelyn Primary, Ardwyn Grammar School Wales; [occ] stone mason; [activ] recreational trustee of village Angling

Club, O.A.P. activities; [pub writ] "Music On The Wires" & "The Conversation" - White Rose Literary Magazine, short listed - Raconteur Magazine - Annual European Short Story Competition; "It is logical to realise that words are the apparel of one's thoughts. In my work as a building mason, you fuse stones or bricks into one, and you see images, which are in harmony with your mind, thus: you write them. Writing is the complete relaxer, from a manual working day."

ROY, AMANDA: [b] 4/4/83 Greenock; [p] Yvette & Gordon; [ed] St. Mary's Primary; [occ] student; [awards] Piano Exam 1; [activ] Guides, pony club, piano, horseback riding, writing poems; "I wrote the poems because I am against war and other unrest in the world. Most of the poems I write are about what the world would be like if there was peace on earth, others are about the damage done to earth. I feel strongly about the injustice in other countries."

ROYAL, NORMAN: [b]15/8/43 Cardiff; [p] Doreen & Clifford; [ch] Neil Alexis; [ed] Herbert Thompsons School of Cardiff; [occ] artist; [awards] Koestler Awards (6) Art, 18' Mural of Derby Day - Gloucester Prison; [activ] helping the homeless//hungry; [pub writ] poem - "Moments" - (New Haven) US, short stories in various local papers; "I am as driftwood on Life's sea. My youth spent in approved schools, borstals and prisons. My adult life travelling the world the hard way. I have to express myself in words, it is all I have left."

RUMMING, JAS: [b] 12/1/30 Birmingham; [p] Denis & Bertha May; [ed] City of Bath Boys School, Bristol University, P.G.C.E. King Alfred's College, P.G.C.E.; [occ] headmaster (rtrd.); [activ] started own pub. bus. "Summerhouse Press", Bath, ind. candidate for Bath '92, member "New Britain" party '94; [pub writ] 40 educational books (Math/Sci.) pub. U.L.P. (Hodder & Stoughton) James Brodie & Pergamon, 10 poetry books in West Country Series - Summerhouse Press, Bath; "I am a Capricorn, known for hard work and late rewards. My work is informed by the spirit of Thomas Hardy, and the living influence of Laurie Lee who told me at a recent meeting to "carry the torch.""

RYAN, EITHNE: [b]20/3/42 Co. Armagh; [p] Patrick & Mary Murphy; [ed] Cregganduff P.S., Newry Technical College; [occ] school clerk (rtrd.); [awards] shorthand/typing proficiencies; [mem] RSPB & WWF; [activ] volunteer - social serv., reg. carer; [pub writ] poem - Poetry Now Reg. Anthol.; "Very interested in anything cultural - traditional music, set and ceili dancing. Joined an art class and enjoyed that very much. Love putting my thoughts and inspirations onto paper. Took part in 2 plays some years ago."

RYAN, JAMES A.: [b] 1/9/37 Dublin; [p] Kathleen & James; [ch] Hazel & Seamus David; [ed] National School; [occ] fireman; [awards] Cert. Fire Service Engineer; "I have written quite a lot of verse over the years, but did not submit it to anyone until now. I enjoy writing it and although I don't class myself as a poet, I like to think that I have recorded some happy and sad moments of life as it is."

RYMELL, STEPHEN: [b] 22/5/67 Croydon; [p] Frank & Audrey; [ed] Kendal Grammar School; [occ] ins. claims controller; [awards] Associate of the Chartered Insurers Institute; "If I could look up, I might see another day to take the pain from my writing. After five years, there must be change."

SALT, TRACY: [b] 19/3/64 Liverpool; [m] Robert; [p] Roselle & Frank Webster; [ch] Jessica, Lorna, Rosalie, Richard & Dwain; [ed] Meois Cop, Comp., Southport; [pub writ] Poetry Now; "I can now stop looking back and start looking forward to greater things ahead and use my talent as best as I can."

SAMPSON, ALEXANDER K.: [b] 1/11/23 Cowdenbeath; [m] Mary; [p] John & Elizabeth; [ch] John & Elizabeth; [ed] Ballingry Public School; [occ] electrical engineer/civil serv. (rtrd.); [awards] Diplomas - Creative Writing - Dunfermline & Dist. Arts. Council; [activ] Salvation Army musician, office bearer, & Sal. Army Cops. Press Officer - Dunfermline S.A. & District; [pub writ] 8 poems in various anthologies, local newspapers, articles in church magazine; "I enjoy making poetry; especially when family and friends ask for special birthday, weddings.

and other special occasions to be recorded and aired in verse."

SAMUEL, JOAN: [b] 22/7/37 South Wales; [p] Martha & William; [ch] Gaynor, Steven, Lyndon, Helen & Glenda; [ed] Secondary ed., Pre-nursing School ed.; [occ] housewife; [awards] St. John Ambulance/ Home Nursing Cert.; [activ] writing for local charities, about local people/events; St. John Ambulance activities; [pub writ] anthology - "Village Tales" (about village life past/present); "As I have lived in a small welsh village all of my life I believe you have to write from the heart and my heart is in Wales. My grandfather was one of those killed at the Universal Colliery disaster."

SANDERS, DENISE A.: [b] 16/5/38 Corsham, Wiltshire; [p] John & Frances Lucas; [ch] Michael, Helen & Jayne; [occ] carer/housewife; [pub writ] 7 poems in anthologies; "Now that my family's grown up I can spend more time writing poetry about all the things I have seen or heard during my life, also the rewards of helping others."

SANDOM, RONALD J.: [b] 26/2/38 London; [p] Shirley; [ch] Gary; [ed] Garth High Modern, Surrey; [awards] R.A.F. fire service; police qualified ambulance person; [activ] prison serv. review committee, War Pension Committee; "I would like to write more poems. I often write when the thoughts come into my mind, I could write many."

SAUNDERS, ARTHUR: [b] 31/3/23 Birmingham; [p] Arthur & Ruth; [ch] Patricia, Richad & Teresa; [ed] Grammar School, Bilston; [occ] engineer (rtrd.); [activ] Variety Artists Club - Birmingham/W. Midlands, tenor singer; [pub writ] poetry/short stories (topics of local interest); "I found from my very early youth, I had the gift for writing. I take great pleasure in putting my feelings and thoughts into both verse and prose. This year I received a medal from the minister in Caen, Normandy, during the 50th Anniversary of D-Day (I was among the first to land in Normandy)."

SAYEED, MOHAMMED: [b] 30/9/62 Nottingham; [m] Saeeda Begum; [p] Mohammed Ismael & Iqbal Begum; [ch] Safara, Aneesa, M. Obaid, & Asmaa; [ed] De-Monfort University, Nottingham Tren University; [activ] working toward diploma in Social Work, p/t Masters Degree - equal opportunity, p/t youth worker, casual comm. service supervisor, various community organisations; [pub writ] poems local/ ntn'l newspapers/mags., anthology for Black Writers Course (Anon Foundation); "I started to write poetry because it allowed me to reflect my inner urges and speak from the language of my heart. Those who will read it, will find in it an experience similar to their own hopes and ideals."

SCALES, GERRY: [b] 20/5/46 London; [p] Mina & Henry (dcd); [ch] Sam & Melinda; [occ] singer; [activ] Song Writers Guild; [pub writ] "The Best Forever Yet" - Somewhere In Time Album (Pinto Bennett), various small publishings; "I believe in self-fulfilling prophecy, that you can do anything, but keep track of receipts. A 'hip' lifestyle, good lyrics, any religion that gets you there, and the cowboy way."

SCOBIE, PAULINE: [b] 25/12/45 [m] Derek; [ch] David & Darren; [ed] basic comp.; [occ] housewife; "I would like this poem dedicated to the memory of my son Darren who was my inspiration and would have been proud of my achievement."

SCOTT, DANIEL: [b] 23/1/54 Los Angeles, Ca. (US); [m] Patricia; [p] Charles & Michelle; [ch] Marie Anne; [ed] Palos Verdes High School, Ventura College; [activ] volunter reader - school children, Poetry Society; [pub writ] "Open Secrets" - Sussex Poetry, Poetry Now '94 S.E. Anthology; "I love the written word and enjoy reading and writing verse. I hope to create better poems and in the process find a better world."

SCOTT, DAVID: [b]13/7/59 Kirkcaldy, Fife; [m] Alexandra; [p] Arthur & Annie; [ch] Alexandra (stpdtr); [ed] Viewforth Jr. High; [occ] operations & maintenance tech.; [awards] City & Guilds - mechanical engineering; [activ] Glenrothes Round Table, Kirkcaldy Art Club, folk music (guitar, pipes); [pub writ] poem in Poetry Now Anthol. Scotland '95; "I believe it's never too late to start something new, you may not become the best, but you can achieve a lot. Be kind to people, enjoy life."

SCOTT, ROBERT O.: [b] 5/9/27 Glasgow; [p] Robert & Mary; [ed] Govan Sr. Sec.; [mem] R.S.P.B.; [pub writ] poetry book "Some Assynt Yeas" (about Assynt in NW Scottish Highlands); "I found that writing poems of my memories helped me after my wife's death. I have lived most of my life in the Scottish Highlands and many of my poems deal with its wildlife (animal and human!)"

SCOTT-FAG, BEV: [b] Isleworth; [p] Kathleen & George Naylor; [ch] Gillian, Julie, Susan & Richard; [ed] Gumley House Convent School for Girls; [occ] writer; [pub writ] various poems/letters; "Self-confessed 'steamy' writer, most work penned in the bath. Have just written a tender poem on the back of a pink facial tissue. It was very (re)moving..."

SCRIPPS, JOHN F.: [b] 31/12/33 Norwood; [p] George & Doris; [ch] Julie, Lisa, Tony & Jody; [awards] Certs. Turbine Driver/Boiler Operator - C.E.G.B.; [mem] Diabetic Assoc., R.S.P.B.; "Started scribbling poems in 1989 during night shifts on security duty. Found it helped to relax and stimulate me. Strange feeling, my wife encouraged me to send this work in."

SEALE, T.S.: [b] 6/8/19 Galway, Eire; [p] Catherine & Thomas; [ch] Sheila, Anthony & Patrick; [awards] Military Medalist - Grenadier Guards; [activ] British Legion, Ramsbottom; [pub writ] poem - "How Green Is Your Crown" - South West Voices anthol; "I spent my youth in the wilds of Galway, Eire. Apprentice builder/Soldier (1939-45) - Africa & Italy. Short sojourn as porter in Library & Museum, Bury. Mystic of words, benign old age."

SEDDON, CHRISTINE: [b] 19/11/58 Manchester; [ch] Jennifer, Suzanne & Robert; [ed] Astley Grammar School; [occ] housewife; [activ] fund-raiser - Ukraine, Friends of the Earth, support Achon Aid, WWF; [pub writ] 4 poems and a regular article in local paper; "I try to see the other person's point of view, to be fair and truthful, and above all, to retain a sense of humour!"

SEDGLEY, MARTIN: [b] 9/7/56 Bedford; [p] Fred & Lily; [occ] pers. devel. consultant; [awards] degree - business studies, certs. - counselling/hypnotherapy; "The mountains of my adopted home provided the inspiration for my poem 'Free To Be Me', written at a time when my self-belief was being challenged. The Scottish Highland have been a consistent backdrop to my personal growth during the last decade and I now enjoy fulfillment from running personal development programmes for other people in this beautiful environment."

SEN, IAN: [b] 12/5/73 Bridlington; [p] Jean Sen; [ed] Headland School, East Yorkshire College; [occ] student; [awards] O.N.C. - engineering, 'A' level - Art; [activ] I am currently studying forestry, interested in animal rights/welfare; "I wrote this poem because I thought it would be a challenging and important subject to explore. I believe that all art should be as original and uncompromising as it can be in order to maintain its potency and remain free from banality."

SENESCHALL-MORGAN, DEBORAH: [b] 22/5/56 Grimsby; [p] Shirley & Anthony Sutcliffe; [ed] Technical Grammar, Grimsby; [occ] regional co-ordinator; "Writing has allowed me to place my confusion on certain situations in my life into juxtaposition with my thoughts. Always producing a clear verbal picture of my true feelings and from this I find direction."

SHARPE, PETER J.: [b] 23/3/56 Dover; [p] Jean & Michael, [ch] Kane & Tara; [ed] primary/sec. for boys, appren. Construction, Carpentry & Joinery; [occ] builder; [pub writ] 1 poem - anthology 'To Love And Be Loved' - Heritage Press; "Sometimes it's never really like just writing, more like bleeding all over the paper. I would love a collaberation with a musician to take the words one step further."

SHARPE, RICHARD: [b] 29/4/50 Bristol; [m] Sara; [p] Anthony & Marion; [ch] Christopher & Caroline; [ed] Penarth Grammar School, Barry Tech College S. Glamorgan; [occ] sales/marketing mgr.; [mem] Hon. Life Member - Sully Sailing Club, governor Intn't Society Weighing & Measurment; "I travel the world for a living and I find that writing helps me to keep a base within myself when away from home for long periods. I currently live in Los Angeles."

SHAW, STAN: [b] 2/4/23 Cheadle, Staffs; [m] Mary; [p] Bernard & Eva; [ch] Janet & Christine; [ed] Sec. school - Cheadle; [occ] civil servant (rtrd.); [pub writ] poem "The Church" in Midlands Poetry Now Regl. Anthol. '93; "I have never believed years to be the yardstick of age. In our case, our granddaughters Karen & Joanne keep us youthful in both spirit and outlook. They also bring us much happiness in our lives."

SHEPHERD, RUTH: [b] 5/5/47 Manchester; [p] Robin & Dorothy Thompson; [ch] Dawn & Sarah; [ed] Clarendon School, NW; [pub writ] poetry local mags.; "I have always enjoyed writing short stories and poetry, and found after settling in the U.K., after 21 years in S. Africa, it was very therapeutic expressing my loss through creative writing, especially prose."

SHERRATT, WILLIAM: [b] 11/1/34 S.O.T.; [p] Norman & Frances; [ch] Jacqueline, Jennifer, Joyanna & David; [ed] Hanley St. Johns; Peoples College, Notts.; [awards] diploma - animal husbandry; [activ] Royal British Legion; [pub writ] poetry in local newspaper, 1 poem - anthology; "I believe good poetry should have magic, mystery and music: the first for imagery, the second for imagination and the third for dignity and beauty."

SHERRIFF, DAVID: [pen] Dayv; [b] 2/3/63 Leicester; [p] Colin & Audrie; [ed] Lea County Primary, Mutton Grammar, Preston College; [activ] Goon Show Preservation Soc.; "Poetry, for me, is the discrete interpretation of a point of view. It's a thought process that combines one's humanity (or understanding of it) with careful useage of language to hopefully trigger an emotive response. It's the ideal medium through which to explore two of my main passions; the study of humanity, and correct useage of English. One day I hope to include my other main passion, music. I include amongst my heros: Spike Milligan, Douglas Adams, The crews of the Star Ships Enterprise, and Shakespeare. Make of that what you will."

SHIRRA, LEE: [b] 12/9/74 Bellshill; [p] Margaret; [ed] Glenrothes High, Breiton Arts College; "Poetry is a state of 'becoming', a philosophy of revaluation and necessity, not of aesthetics. A reorganization and 'scripting' of the writer; it should challenge and unsettle, the writer included."

SHORT-WINDSOR, JANET: [b] 9/11/33 Brighton; [p] Kathleen & Sydney; [ch] Stephen; [ed] Wistons Priv. School; [occ] library/tourist officer (rtrd.); [awards] 2nd prize three short stories; [activ] assist. sec. Hailsham Choral Soc., Sussex Singers, Sussex Opera & Ballet Soc., patron - Hastings Opera, Canford Summer School of Music Choir, Eastbourne Sinfonia Choir; [pub writ] 3 short stories; "Ballet dancer (on points), ice skater and singer (several years ago). I still sing and enjoy writing. I wrote words and music to a lullaby for my son when he was small. The Choral Society is going in for choral competition in France this June. I love classical music and poetry."

SHOUKSMITH, CAROLINE: [b] 1/5/76 Newcastle-Upon-Tyne; [p] Peter & Pauline; [ed] Teesside High School for Girls, Harrogate Tutorial College, Teesside University; [occ] student (business); [awards] 'A' levels; "From a very young age I have always been complimented on my creativity and potential in writing. Starting poetry helped me to express what I couldn't talk about. This publication has given me a tremendous sense of achievement and will continue to inspire my work, hopefully improving with every piece."

SIBBALD, ROBERT: [b] 31/7/55 Glasgow; [m] Gillian; [p] Elizabeth; [ch] Jason, Ross & Darren; [ed] Wellshot High, Glasgow; [occ] H.G.V. driver; [awards] I.A.M. award, L.G.V. Driving Instr. diploma, Lord Lieutenant's Cert., sports awards (Karate, pool, football); [activ] territorial army (15 yrs.), collector; [pub writ] "I Found My World In Dreams" - (Between The Lines Paperback) 1993; "I see and hear certain situations, and like to put them to verse, but also imagination can make wonderful poems, and to my wife, Gillian, this is dedicated to you."

SIDEBOTTOM, RACHEL: [b] 4/11/73 Glossop; [p] William &

Hilary; [ed] Bishop Grossetste College; [occ] student; [activ] college choir, church youth leader.

SILCOCK, MARGARET: [b] 1/6/36 Wirral; [occ] school secretary; [ch] Jenny, Carol & Helen; [activ] reading, music, crossworD puzzles; "I enjoy meeting poeple, special interest in children - hence my career choice. I get a lot of satisfaction from challenges and as this is my first attempt at writing poetry I am absolutely delighted with the results so far and hope to go on to further success."

SILVESTER, THOMAS L.: [b] 16/9/24 Liverpool; [m] Jean Marie; [p] Albert Edward & Carmen Silva; [ch] Graham & Sylvia; [ed] Toxteth Tech. Inst., Central Tech College, Tech. College, St. Helens; [occ] surveyor (rtrd.) estate managment; [awards] RICS Pt II (Val), Earl of Derby Prize (Constr. Dwg.) [pub writ] occ. articles for in-house journal and professional journal (on request); "It is never too late to achieve anything, but to make the attempt requires concentration. A Welsh Bard amongst my ancestors has, perhaps, been resuscitated."

SIMMONS, ANTHONY: [b] 26/9/38 Birkenhead; [p] Edward & Annie; [ch] Kevin, David, Karen & Paul; [occ] bricklayer; [awards] City & Guilds - communication skills, cert. for creative writing - City Lands Neighbourhood Colleges; [activ] adult student; "I like watching all sports. I am interested in wildlife and conservation, and I support the Labur Party. I am also an avid reader."

SIMMONS, RONALD: [b] 24/3/39 Loughborough; [m] Marjorie; [p] Lawrence & Elizabeth; [ch] Stephanie, Andrei, Lorraine & Anthony; [ed] Limehurst School, Loughborough College, Nottingham Tech. College; [pub writ] "The Middle Years" - Poetry Now (Midlands) 1991; "I began writing poetry whilst a patient in 'Barts' hospital in 1984. I feel I have gained greatly from life threatening experiences in childhood and as an adult. I believe these traumas have given me increased sensitivity, appreciation of love and life, the importance of family life and the value of a good sense of humour."

SIMONS, JEFF: [b] 30/6/40 Dagenham; [p] Pauline & Philip; [ch] Martin & Louise; [ed] Cooper Company Grammar, Bow London; [occ] engineering draughtsman; "This is my first poem to be published, I hope not my last. Previously I have written poems and short stories for my own amusement."

SIMS, MARK: [b] 19/1/51 Wales; [m] Susan; [p] Stan & Kathleen; [ch] Melanie; [ed] Catholic Boys School, Merthyr College, Royal Air Force; [awards] Royal Observer Corps. - Loyal Service Medal; [activ] fire service (Mid-Glam), Royal Observer Corp. (12 Grp.); [pub writ] 10 poems in various anthologies/competitions, 1 short story; "In my poetry I try to reflect my views and experiences of life, my short stories are pure fantasy."

SIMS, RICHARD: [b] 22/8/64 Hull; [ed] Hough Side High, Leeds; [pub writ] poem - Contemporary Verse 1992.

SINCLAIR, NORMAN: [b] 21/10/10 Nottingham; [p] Mensing/ Sinclair; [ch] John & Jean; [ed] Sec. school, Education College; [occ] teacher (rtrd.); [awards] diploma - art; [mem] Liberal Democratic Party; [pub writ] poems in local papers; "Happily married and retired."

SIPPITT, STEPHEN: [b] 12/2/54 London; [occ] bank officer; "Whatever it is you are writing, enjoy it. Be part of it and enjoy it."

SKITRALL, JEAN M.: [b] 13/7/27; [p] Bertha & Edgar Hughes; [ch] Joy, Carol, Peter, Yvonne, Iris, Dianne, Sandra, Kevin, Garry, Tracie & Paul; [ed] Meliden, N.Wales, Bond Street School, St. Mary's & St. Modwens Schools; [awards] plaque for being a Super Gran 1963; "I write poems for amusement and have several about my family and friends. It was my eldest grandaughter Tracy who got me to enter the competition. I love poetry, if something comes into my mind, night or day, I put it down on paper. Next day I work at it and turn it into a poem."

SLATTERY, DYMPNA: [b] 14/5/28 Eire; [p] Patrick & Marcella O'Reilly; [ch] John, Anthony & Seamus; [ed] Catholic National School, St. Louis Convent; [occ] pub landlady (rtrd.); [mem] Catholic Womens'

League; [activ] volunteer hospice worker, Weston Care, hospital visits; "Poetry is my relaxation, it makes me aware of the good things in life, away from sadness and worries."

SMITH, ANNE L.: [b] 1906 St. Agnes, Cornwall; [p] William & Henrietta; [occ] nanny/clerk receptionist (rtrd.); [awards] Cert. English, medals: War Service and Red Cross, poetry prizes (Women's Inst.) prize for epitaph - church paper; [mem] P.C.E., W.I., Old Cornwall Soc.; [activ] volunteer - Red Cross, church work.

SMITH, CLARE S.: [b] 1/8/07 Newton In Furness, Lancs.; [p] George & Hannah Gibson; [ed] Cross Green Church of England School, British & Dominions School of Drawing; [awards] grammar school scholarship, 2 art diplomas, scholarship cert. school of drawing ('28); [mem] Modern Sequence Dance Club; [activ] dancing, R.S.P.C.A. volunteer; [pub writ] woman's mag., local weekly paper, church mags.; "Being elderly I write articles and verse to keep my brain active. Try to see the best in everyone, have a keen sense of humour, my motto - Don't worry when you can pray."

SMITH, DAVID: [b] 4/4/42 Rotherham; [m] Lorraine; [ch] Paula, Steven, Lisa & Sarah; [ed] Badsley Moor Jrs., Spurley Hey Sec.; [activ] computer course; [pub writ] 4 poems in various books; "I get a lot of pleasure out of writing poetry. To put words on paper, and to enjoy every minute of it. Getting my poems published is just a bonus."

SMITH, EDITH: [b] 24/3/32 Salford; [p] Philip & May Haines; [ed] Council School, Haslingden, Lancs; [activ] church choir, Mothers Union - local choir, sing for disabled etc.; [pub writ] Poets Corner - local newspaper; "I have found that a pleasant attitude toward others gives me a delight which I can share by putting my thoughts and feelings into verse and rhyme."

SMITH, EDWARD, P.: [b] 1/2/60 Devizes; [p] Robert & Beryl; [ed] Market Lavington Comp.; [awards] Gr. 1 - English Lang./Eng. Lit. CSE's; [mem] Wilts Trust for Conservation, Friends of the Earth; "Through my writing it is necessary for me to express my feelings and thoughts in a creative and positive way. I hope that my poems will help others to look to the light within themselves."

SMITH, EVELYN: [b] 27/6/44 Barrow-In-Furness; [m] Colin; [p] James & Evelyn; [ch] Angela, Gillian, Jennifer & Kevin; [occ] factory wrkr; [activ] volunteer M.I.N.D.; [pub writ] poetry in local newspaper; "I write poetry, firstly because it's inside of me and needs to be expressed and secondly if my poetry can bring a smile to someone else I feel my living has not been in vain!"

SMITH, GARY: [b] 9/9/57 Rougham (Nr. Bury St. Edmonds); [p] Colin & Gwendoline; [ed] Rougham Primary School, Beyton Middle, Thurston Upper; [occ] tree surgeon/head teamaker; [mem] Guild of Master Teamakers; [pub writ] various short poems, greeting card verses; "Always seek out the good that is inherent in everyone and respond to it."

SMITH, GREIG: [b] 13/4/76 Kirkcaldy; [p] Derek & Doreen; [ed] Kirkcaldy High School, Glenrothes College; [occ] student; [awards] Primary Six, 1 trophy 2nd prize - essay comp.; [pub writ] poem - "See" - Fife Leader (lcl paper); "No matter what people say, believe in yourself and you'll get there someday. But most of all, live life to the full."

SMITH, IRENE A.: [b] Aberdeen; [p] Elizabeth & William; [occ] nurse (rtrd.); "I have four brothers and one sister, I have three daughters and one son and my husband. I have six grandchildren (3 girls/3 boys) and another expected soon. I'm always writing short poems or stories for my growing family, simply for fun!"

SMITH, IRENE M.: [b] 23/2/28 Walsall; [m] Leslie; [p] John Edward & May Jacom; [ch] Gerald Andrew; [ed] Wolverhampton Road Infant, Jr./Sec. schools; [occ] housewife; [pub writ] poems - The Way It Is - Anchor Books, church mag., Rushall Post; "I started writing in 1989 with encouragement from my husband. I like to write about the simple things and the things around me that I see everyday."

SMITH, JOHN: [b] 28/1/25 Leeds; [p] Leonard & Anne Wallis; [ed] Palatine Ctrl. Girls School, Blackpool; [activ] Brownie guider, P.R. Blackpool S. Div. Rainbows/Brownies & Guides, Blackpool S.W. Dist. Badge Sec. & P.R., church member; "After 20 years as a Brownie Guider and English my worst subject, I joined a Creative Writing & Literature class (night school). I learnt so much and find that I now can put my thoughts in words."

SMITH, JULIA A.: [b] 3/4/55 Huddersfield; [m] Ian; [p] June & Arnold Quarmby; [ch] Lindsey & Deborah; [ed] Newsome Sec, Huddersfield; [occ] care assistant; [awards] Sci./Technology Award, Computer Studies Award, various certs.; [mem] assoc. mem. World Wildlife Fund; [pub writ] svrl. poems in various anthologies; "I receive great satisfaction from my job, but also feel the need to be continuously learning, whatever the subject. I get great enjoyment from my writing. I also read a great deal and could not comprehend not doing either."

SMITH, KAREN: [b] 16/5/54 Uttoxeter; [p] Herbert & Elsie Croft; [ch] Laura & Heidi; [ed] Alleynes Grammar School; [occ] school sr. supervisor; [awards] 5 'O' levels Eng. Lang./Eng Lit.; "A 40 year old human whirlwind, I enjoy noting down the funny things people say and turning it into verse. Although I have written a great variety of poetry, this is my first publication."

SMITH, LAURA: [b] 25/9/81 Burton On Trent; [p] Micheal & Karen; [ed] Oldfields Hall Middle School, Uttoxeter; [occ] student; "I have always loved poetry. I enjoy writing to express my true feelings, I wrote my first rhyming poem at the age of ten and have since compiled an extensive file of poetry on different subjects."

SMITH, MARILYN: [b] 24/12/47 Galashiels; [m] Brian; [p] James & Olive Graham; [ch] Robert & Carolyn; [ed] Galashiels Academy, Moray House College; [occ] SNR cashier; "This is my first attempt at a 'serious' composition. A great personal achievement, I dedicate this poem to my late father who instilled in me a love of the border countryside."

SMITH, MARK: "My career is careering and my occupation is life. I have still to be born and reside in no place. By trapping the world in nets of rhyme, I propose to halt the passage of time."

SMITH, R.: [b] 17/12/27 Tunbridge, Wells; [p] Reginald & Ivy Woodcraft; [ch] Glennis & Lorna; [ed] Speldhurst Primary, West Kent Tech. College, Tonbridge, Kent; [activ] Brown Owl, charity collecting (children in need & R.S.P.C.A.); "It gives me pleasure to write poems about my family and pets. Very relaxing and I love people."

SMITH, REGINALD P.: [b] 30/10/39 York; [p] Reginald & Mary; [ch] Maria Jane; [ed] Manor School, University College, Scarborough; [occ] teacher; [awards] BA - Open University 1982, qual. (A.I.S.T.) ; [activ] chairman Scout/Guides 1st Scalby, swim instructor - swim club; "Poetry is, to me, a reflection of inner feelings of a particular moment, yet can be shared by many."

SMITH, SAMUEL: [b] 24/12/32 Colne, Lancs; [p] Herber & Margaret; [ed] Primet Sec. School, Lancs; [occ] builder/antique dealer (rtrd.); "Due to age/illness and being on my own, I find pleasure living close to nature and writing poems and stories. I write fiction stories under nom de plume 'OReilly Smith'."

SMITH, STELLA: [b] 12/10/51 Luton; [m] Jim; [p] Margaret & Fred Mills; [ch] Robert, Edward & David; [ed] Luton High School for Girls; [occ] school secretary; [activ] sunday school teacher; "My poems are the wallpaper of my mind."

SMITHSON, SYBIL G.: [b] Bury St. Edmunds; [m] Harry; [p] Henry & Agnes Lomax; [ch] Janis, Kim & Glenn; [ed] Guildhall Feoffment, King Edward VI Upper; [occ] florist (rtrd.); [pub writ] poems in various anthologies; "To be sincere when listening to other's joys or sorrows, and sharing my own, heightens my awareness of life. From these genuine feelings comes the poetry I love; a mix of reality and a strong imagination."

SMOULT, LYNDA: [b] 1/3/54 Newcastle Upon-Tyne; [m] Bob; [p] George & Delia Douglass; [ch] Robert & Beverley; [ed] Sacred Heart Grammar, Newcastle Upon Tyne Polytechnic; [occ] Teacher; [awards] B.Ed. (Hons.) 2:1 Specialising Maths/Sci/Tech.; [activ] crosswords, writing poetry, ballroom dancing; "I like to live life to the full. We must make the best of what we have, and see good in all those we know."

SMY, SAMUEL V.: [b] 30/4/19 Scarborough; [ed] Graham Sea Training & Engineering School, Technical College, Scarborough; [occ] nurse (rtrd.); [awards] SRN, SRMN, Cert. BTTA (cert.), MSSCH; [mem] Ntn'l Geographical Soc., British Red Cross; "A short verse of what life has revealed: - As we pass along life's highway, we cannot turn back. But what the world wants are the gifts we have got, it cares nothing for those we lack."

SOORD, IOANA: [b] 30/3/67 Harlow; [p] Maurice & Jean; [ch] Samuel Boon; [ed] Latton Bush School, Harlow Tech. College; [occ] p/t nanny/teach aerobics/mother; [awards] RSA (teaching exercise to music); [activ] keep fit, read, write poetry/letters, drawing; [pub writ] poems in church mag.; "I would like to write a book about how the love of Jesus transformed my life. I sincerely hope that this poem will encourage Christians to run the good race. I thank God for the personal relationship I have with Jesus and for inspiring me to write."

SOUTHWELL, TIMOTHY M.: [b] 11/6/76 Rugby; [p] Michael & Susan; [ed] Colston's school, Goldsmith's College, University of London; [occ] student; [pub writ] poem - Poetry Now (West Country Anthol. '95); "I believe in people, for people hold everything. They hold the future."

SOWDEN, ALISON: [b] 8/11/86 Barnstaple; [p] Kelvin & Jan; [ed] Halwill Primary School; [occ] student; [activ] reading, swimming, walking on Dartmoor."

SPALDING, DELIA: [b] 17/12/49 Ipswich; [m] Philip; [ch] Lee & Samantha; [ed] Westbourne School, Ipswich; [occ] p/t refreshment person; [pub writ] poem in local Evening Star paper; "I enjoy writing poetry and find I can best express myself when I put pen to paper."

SPALDING, ELAINE: [b] 10/8/47 Bridlington; [p] Arthur & Doris Nicholson; [ch] Wendy; [ed] St. George's Sec. Modern; [occ] housewife; [activ] R.S.P.B., Hawk & Owl Trust, British Trust for Ornithology; "I have a great love and concern for nature and like to write poems about the reality of life."

SPALL, ALAN G.: [b] 23/10/30 Barking, Essex; [m] Jean Perry; [p] George & Ann; [ch] Susan Linda & Robert Alan; [occ] vehicle accident damage repairer; [mem] Institute of Motorists 1982; "I consider I am a very fortunate person, having had a great deal of job satisfaction from 45 years of work, and considerable happiness and pleasure over 35 years of marriage."

SPENCE, ALAN L.: [b] 17/7/48 Middlesbrough; [p] Colin & Vida; [ed] Eston Grammar School, Middlesbrough; "Words are jewels of infinite salvation, words are weapons of eternal destruction. Measure well before use, harness their power."

SPENCER, ALAN: [b] 17/12/63 Oldham; [p] Carlton & Sylvia; [ed] Oldham Hulme Grammar School, University of Leeds; [occ] civil servant; [awards] Degree (Hons.) - English/History, post-grad. diploma - Librarianship/Information work; [pub writ] short stories in anthologies & mags., poems in anthologies, local newspapers/mags.; "I have always enjoyed creative writing and hope to reach a wide range of people through my work."

SPENCER, DOUGLAS: [b] 14/9/39 Bridport; [ch] Vanessa & Susanha (stpdtrs); [ed] Beaminster & Netherbury Grammar School; [occ] property renovations; "Having for years written what can be best described as ramblings and nonsense for the amusement of my family. I have been persuaded by them at the late age of 55 to do other than consign them to the bin."

SPENCER, PAUL: [b] 12/9/57 Jersey C.I.; [p] Roy & Kathi; [ch] Aaron; [occ] musician; [pub writ] poems in various anthologies; "I wrote "As The Snow Melts ..." for Amanda, whom I love very much."

SPICER, BARBARA A.: [b] 18/6/39 Dover, Kent; [m] Eric; [p] Thomas & Dorisie Potter; [ch] Christopher & Roberta; [ed] Barton Rd. Sec. School, Dover; [occ] housewife; [mem] Christians Together in Dover; [pub writ] 1 poem pub. Triumph House, Peterborough; "I've written 14 poems after discovering God. Over the last 6 years I copy scenes, large scale, from the children's Bible for my church's Sunday School, St. Peter's & St. Paul's River Dover."

STACEY, JENNY: [b] Manchester; [m] Philip Young; [p] Joe & Nancy Stacey; [ed] Whalley Range High School, Man.; Birmingham University; [occ] clinical nurse specialist; [awards] SRN, RMN, diploma - Adolescent & Family Psychiatry, cert. Marital & Family Therapy, ENB 998 - Teaching & Assessing in Clinical Practice; [activ] friend of the Theatre Royal, Bury St. Edmunds; [pub writ] 3 pt. serial "The Manor Mystery" pub. Manchester Evening News", poem - "The Empty Room" pub Poetry Now '95 (East Anglian Reg. Anthology of Verse); "I have always been fascinated by the written word as a means of self-expression and over the years have written quite a collection of poems. It is only recently with the encouragement of my partner Philip, that I have put them forward for publications. The first few have been successful so I am now keen to do more."

STANTON, LYDIA E.: [b]16/9/36 London; [p] Lydia & Richard; [ch] Donna, Kay & Lynne Elizabeth; [occ] pastry cook; [pub writ] poems in 3 anthologies; "Although born in London, I love Cornwall very much and through my poetry I hope to portray the beauty of this lovely county."

STARKEY, DEREK J.: [b] 4/10/69 Pontypridd, S. Wales; [m] Joanne; [p] Marjorie (dcd.) & David; [ch] Thomas (dcd.); [ed] Bryn Celynnog Comp., S. Wales, Royal Air Force School of Tech Training; [occ] engineer; [awards] OND - engineering, NVQ - plastics moulding; [activ] Christian music writing/composing, church member; [pub writ] cartoonist for local church mag.; "I have found that the most precious things in life cannot be owned or achieved. They must be earned, received, or at best, given."

STEELS, WARWICK: [b] 26/6/21 Midway, Derbyshire; [p] Walter & Charlotte; [ch] Jennifer Ann; [ed] Swadlincote Council School, Stockport College of Further Ed., Liverpool Poly; [occ] local gov't officer (rtrd.); [awards] CQSW, Methodist Local Preachers Examination 1941; [activ] Methodist Local Preacher 54 yrs.; [pub writ] poem - "A Child's Unspoken Plea" in Christian Poets in the North '95; "Left school at 14. Worked on brickyard. Then 5yrs. 2 months army (3 yrs POW). Post War various jobs. 1966 Social Work. Motivation Christian and Socialist convictions and family (49 yrs. married). Interested in social issues and sports."

STEWARD, CALUM: [b] 25/6/71; [p] Graham & Alison; [ed] George Watsons College, Edinburgh; [occ] agriculture; "The best poems reflect strong emotions. I try to contain these feelings and not let them take over. In the future there is always potential for happiness — I never lose sight of that."

STEWART, ISABEL G.: [b] 5/3/26 Alloa; [p] Thomas & Jean; [ed] Alloa Academay, Duncee college of Education; [occ] teacher (rtrd.); [awards] Cert. of Education; [activ] volunteer - Red Cross, church choir, "Friend of Alloa Tower", "Friend of Alloa Museum Committee"; [pub writ] article on local history for newspaper, Scottish poems in BBC publications & mags., poetry in English ('Scotsman' Newspaper); "When writing poetry, I use a variety of "voices" which seem to relate to the content — rhymed, blank, spare or more ornate. Lallans Scots also offers variety in creative work."

STEWART, KAREN J.: [b] 18/11/46 Buton-On-Trent; [p] Jamie Stewart (mother); [ed] Coventry University; [awards] Ntn'l Diploma - Business/Finance; "For me, the magic of poetry is the ability to create a sense of empathy; therefore forging some kind of bridge between the poem's creator and its audience, who can then realise that they are not alone in the midst of sometimes their most painful thoughts and emotions."

STOCK, TOM: [b] 11/7/34 Londong; [p] Daniel & Mary; [ch] Sandra & Daniel; [ed] Hedingham Sec. Modern; [occ] bricklayer; [activ] U.R.C. Church member, currently studying for lay preacher membership; [pub writ] 1 poem "Memories" Unto Us A Son - Triumph House, poems/ articles in church mags.; "Book of philosophy nearing completion, struggling to find publisher. Ambition: to counsel people who are finding life difficult to cope with."

STONE, GEOFF: [b]29/4/44 S. Wales; [p] Iris & Victor; [occ] accountant; "I play and teach the guitar and in 1990, decided to try and write a song. With encouragement at its success among friends, I wrote more. To date I've written approximately 35 songs. However, "The Ballad of Johnny Martin 1850-1868" is my first poem!"

STRATTON, ROB: [b] 29/8/21 Bath; [p] Robert & Ruby Stratton; [occ] civil servant (rtrd.); [activ] city councillor (former); [pub writ] local newspaper sports column and various occ. articles; "Shelley and Wordsworth showed me the glories of our language when disciplined into rhyme and metre. No divine spark has exactly come forth, but appreciating the beauty of words, set one with another, is everything isn't it?"

STRICKLAND, DORIS E.: [b] 23/9/28 Preston; [p] Frank & Evelyn Fish; [ch] Christine, Susan & Edward; [ed] Harris Institute Day Commercial, University of Ctrl. Lancashire, Preston College; [occ] NHS (rtrd.); [awards] Degree - Health with Education (Hons.) 1994; "Writing successfully for my own and other's enjoyment has been a dream. That dream is now becoming a reality. Education has unlocked doors hitherto closed."

SUDDER, ELIZABETH M.: [b] 16/3/37 Edinburgh; [m] Colin; [p] Mary & William Ellacott; [ch] Ruth, Anne, Rosalind & Jennifer; [ed] Mary Erskine School for Girls, Edinburgh; [occ] organist/piano teacher; [awards] Assoc. Board Exams - Gr. VIII piano, Gr. VI organ, Gr. VII flute; [mem] Soc. of Organists, [activ] organist/choir director at church, Red Cross; [pub writ] Drama & Mime for 6's to 9's & 4's to 8's - words/ music, articles in magazines/papers, concert crit. newspaper, 2 poems; "I enjoy writing hymns and poems for specific occasions — weddings, harvest, etc. In the past I have written words and music for 2 children'cantatas which have been performed. Also love letter writing!"

SULLIVAN, PAT: [b] 13/3/42 Yorkshire; [p] Leslie & Mary Wolsey; [ch] Kevan Catherine & Anna; [ed] Elsecar Cofe Junior, Ecclesfield Grammar; [occ] crofter; [awards] S.E.N.; [activ] p/t registrar, Crofting activities, carer; [pub writ] poems in local press plus Scottish Anthologies '93, '94, & '95; "Encouraged to appreciate the written word from childhood. I write for the pleasure of it. My inspiration stems from the unspoilt surroundings I live in."

SUTCLIFFE, ANGIE J.: [b] 5/11/60 Lancashire; [m] Phill; [p] Edith & Reuben Hurst; [occ] market stall holder/party plan mgrs. (self-employed); [awards] Self-Defense Course, First Aid; [activ] spec. constable 2yrs., charity works; [pub writ] poem "Poetic Justice" - Voices, Anchor Books; "I try through my poetry to let people see the real me; my hopes, fears and outlook on life. My greatest achievement would be to stir peoples emotions."

SUTTON, LANCELOT G.: [b] 4/10/34 Leeds; [p] Ivy & George; [ch] Paul, Faith, Dawn, Tracey & Peter; [ed] Primrose Hill Sec. Modern, Yorkshire; [occ] miner (rtrd.); [activ] charity work R.N.L.I.; [pub writ] letter on subjects in newspapers/mags.; "I am writing my autobiography. Open minded as to life and world in general. Easy person to talk to and good listener, but take things at face value."

SWIFT, SUZANNE: [b] 24/12/68 Liverpool; [p] Pauline & Keith; [ed] Abergek High School; [occ] support wrkr - mentally handicapped; [awards] Certs. Care of Elderly, Care of Children, First Aid; [activ] Tour of Duty Fan Club, childminding; "I enjoy writing short stories and poems. I enjoy reading biographies. People from all walks of life fascinate me."

TABB, DEIRDRE: [b] 27/1/62 Derry; [p] Kathleen & Hugo Henderson (dcd); [ch] Lucy & Paul; [ed] NorthWest Institute of Further & Higher Ed.; [awards] 'O' & 'A' levels; [activ] singing, dancing, reading; "Over the years I have been inspired to write poetry by my mother, who was forever quoting Shakespeare at home. To express myself through writing poetry is a joy in itself."

TANN, MARK: [b] 21/12/73 Hastings; [ed] Canterbury College of Technology; [awards] R.S.A. - retail; [pub writ] "The Castle Nursery" in Diapers & Dimples pub. Arrival Press; "I enjoy working with children and find a lot of fulfillment in this work. I am also a committed Christian and get on with people of all ages and enjoy writing poetry."

TAVINER, JOHN M.: [b] 1/8/70 Caerphilly; [p] Michael & Yvonne; [ed] St. Ilans Comp., Istran Mynach College; [occ] shoe shop mgr.; [awards] Management Course, 'O' level Maths/Art/Tech. Drawing/Physics/Computer Stds.; [activ] record clubs; "Personal thoughts are put on paper purely for pleasure. I believe there is more life beyond the stars and we have yet to discover it. I hope one day this will be proved."

TAVINER, YVONNE: [b] 19/6/47 Tredegar; [p] John & Irene Williams; [ch] John; [ed] Gwyndy School for Girls, Ystrad Mynach College of F. E.; [occ] crecit controller; [awards] R.S.A. & W.J.E.C. various subjects, Eng. 'O' level; [activ] environmental activities, geneology, horse owner/rider; "I write poems to put a bit of humour into people's lives. My poems are usually personal for birthday celebrations etc."

TAYLOR, CATHRINE: [b] 24/2/72 Essex; [p] Maureen & Barrie; [ed] Burnt Mill Comp., Harlow College, Loughborough University; [occ] retail; [awards] Degree - drama; [pub writ] poems in anthologies - 'Together Forever?', 'Green Shoots' & 'Talking Volumes'.

TAYLOR, DAVID: [b] 6/11/67; [ed] Greenwich University; "Amateur writer and musician, currently working as a driver but hope to train for librarianship this year. Have travelled extensively in the US and Europe."

TAYLOR, ELLA: [b] 27/7/21 Rochdale; [ch] Joan; [activ] sec. Rochdale Stroke Club, attend workshop Rochdale Infirmary; [pub writ] short story/poems in 'Rochdale Writers', poem in 'Write On 17'; "After suffering a stroke in 1979 (left side), I joined a writers group at Balderstone High School (nightschool). The group has now disbanded."

TAYLOR, ROY: [b] 4/8/38 West Bromwich; [p] Henry & Rose; [ch] Kathryn & Sally; [ed] Albright High School; [mem] Of Foye Bowling Club; [activ] coastal walks, writing verse/poetry for local people; "This a beautiful planet, with its peoples and creatures, we must help each other along the way, we need each other."

TAYLOR, SARA J.: [b] April 12th, Leeds; [ed] Catholic school; [occ] housewife.

TAYLOR, VERONICA: [b] 7/3/43 Chadderton; [p] Albert & Annie Windsor; [ch] Denise, Christine & Julie (stpdtrs.); [ed] St. Mary's R.C. Sec. Modern, Oldham Lancs; [occ] housewife; "I like to keep an open mind and believe that to see things from another person's view is to learn something new."

TENGWALL, MARION; [b] 20/6/38; [ed] Collegiate School for Girls, Leicester; [mem] R.S.P.C.A.; [pub writ] poems in school mag., article church mag.; The poem "Elegy" was written while living with my husband and family in a rural community close to the sea on the island of Anglesey, N. Wales."

THIRKETTLE, MARTIN K.: [b] 20/5/55 Norwich; [p] Norton & Gene (dcd); [ch] Anna Louse; [ed] The Paston School, N. Walsham, University of Salford; [occ] town planner; [awards] Degree - Social Studies, Post-grad. Diploma - Environmental Planning; [activ] safety officer - Anglian Branch Football Supportors Assoc.; [pub writ] short story in reg. anthology, articles in ntn'l/local football mags., ex-co-editor football fanzine; "Life is football! Football is Life!"

THOM, ELIZABETH: [b] Manchester; [ed] Withington Girls School, Edgehill College; [occ] tutor; [awards] Certs. - clarinet; [mem] English Bridge Union; [activ] local theatre member, foster carer; "I have written poems and stories since I was a child and find the written word is an

expression of myself and inner feelings — a great way of reducing tension."

THOMAS, CALETA M.: [b] 18/8/32 Burstall; [p] Hannah & George Hardwicke; [ch] Hazel; [activ] volunteer: hospice & Meals On Wheels; [pub writ] numerous anthologies; "I am a typical Leo, I enjoy fun, laughter, and positive thinking. I like sunshine and Mediterrranean light and atmosphere; a legacy from a very happy marriage. I love everybody."

THOMAS, CAROL A.: [b] 14/12/74 Carshalton; [p] John & Maureen; [ed] Therfield High School, Bath College of Higher Education; [occ] student; [activ] at present doing a diploma in Eng. History and Creative Studies in English; "I have moved around a lot in the past few years and I have begun to see things in a new light. I hope to put some of my experiences on paper, via my favourite genre, poetry."

THOMAS, DENTON: [b] 13/10/11 Blackwood, Gwent; [p] Thomas & Elizabeth; [ch] Anthony & Marilyn; [ed] Gladstone Elem. School, Cardiff Tech. College, day/eve. classes; [awards] cert. - interior decor.; [activ] 16 yrs. scout movement; [pub writ] pub. in church magazines; "I have found even in business, that difficulties are more easily overcome by the use of poetry. Rhythm and rhyme is basic for poetry to reach a certain standard."

THOMAS, SELWYN L.: [b] 30/10/29 Hartlepool; [m] Annie; [p] John & Mary; [ch] Selwyn, Carole, Michael, Patricia, Winifred, Pauline, David & Sharon; [ed] Hartlepool Sec. School, Hartlepool Tech. College; [occ] builder (rtrd.); [activ] member of local council, organist, painter/artist; [pub writ] 5 poems in regional/gnrl anthologies; "I believe that 'Life is what you make it' I have adopted a positive approach and hope to make some contributions with my poems."

THOMPSON, ANDY: [b] 9/9/61 Portsmouth; [ed] Exeter; "I started writing poems as love poems to my then girl friend, now wife. That was four years ago and I find that I'm still writing! I write on a variety of subjects, a number of which I have had accepted for publication. I have had two pieces of work accepted by "Poetry Nottingham", the magazine of the Nottingham poetry society. Two pieces accepted by "Poetry Now" for publication in anthologies. "S.O.D.E.M." have accepted four of my poems. Some of my railway poems published in the Summer newsletter from the Bodmin and Wenford railway preservation group. Recently made contact with The Devon River Poets and am finding the contact very useful."

THOMPSON, IAN: [b] 31/10/70 Rotherham; [p] Keith & Christine; [ed] Wolverhampton University, Rotherham College of Arts/Tech. Wath Comp., Bretton Hall; [occ] student art teacher; [awards] BA (Hons.) - Fine Art Degree, painting, BTec Diploma, Art/Design, PGCE - art specialism 9/95; "The only restriction in life, is life itself. I have found that with positive thinking and with love, I can achieve anything. If I close my eyes I can fly."

THOMPSON, GAIL F.: [b] 3/2/48 Aberystwyth; [p] Tom & Milly Owen (dcd); [ch] Ian; [ed] Dinas Sec. Modern School; [occ] hotel receptionist; "Have been 'scribbling' since a child for my personal pleasure, putting into rhyme and verse those moments that I treasure."

THOMPSON, P.: [b] 9/8/41 Blackpool; [p] Mr. & Mrs. Penny; [ch] William; [ed] Litherland Sec. Modern, Liverpool; [pub writ] 1 poem "Liverpool", 1 book "Here, There & Everywhere"; "I feel very proud I have been chosen for your book, Island Moods & Reflections. It is a great accomplishment to me, it is something my parents & grandparents never did."

THOMPSON, SHIRLEY: [b] 6/10/35 Kelso Roxburghshire; [p] Helen & George Crozier; [ch] Lesley, John, Lindsey & Alexander; [ed] Kelso High School, Balmulloch College, Cumbernauld College; [occ] housewife/poet; [awards] Editor's Choice Award '93, & '94 - National Library of Poetry (Maryland USA); [mem] Peterloo Poets, Intn'l Soc. of Poets, The Poetry Soc. and Verse Poets; [pub writ] poems pub. Poetry Now anthologies, svrl poems pub. National Library of Poetry (USA); "Poetry is a way of expressing myself, searching and drawing on that reserve of knowledge and words, to be able to share with my fellowman, to strive for peace through poetry."

THOMPSON, SUSANNAH: [b] 26/8/36 Hordle; [p] Robert & Phyllis Cooke; [ch] Fiona & Simon; [ed] Watford Girls Grammar, Wallhall College Aldenham, Watford School of Music; [occ] teacher (rtrd.); [awards] Cert. of Teaching, L.R.A.M. - teaching singing; [mem] Woodbridge Choral Soc., Suffolk Poetry Soc., [activ] volunteer - hospice, art classes, flute; [pub writ] 'Poppy Seeds' a small volume of poetry, 1 poem - "Couplings" Poetry Now Anthology; "After retiring because of ill health, life seemed rather bleak. Now however, my voluntary work and love of music and writing are so fulfilling thay have opened up a new world for me."

THOMPSON, VALERIE: [b] 24/2/43 Weston-Super-Mare; [p] Ernest & Catherine; [ed] Winterstoke Sec. Girls School; [occ] shoemaker; [activ] hockey - Somerset, TV appearance "Come Dancing", team mem. "Scofields" formation, theatre, dance, taught tap dance, enjoy sports, travel, fund-raising - cancer; "I have been writing poetry for a long time especially for family celebrations and fun, but always thought I wasn't good enough for bigger things. Now you have told me that I am good, and that feels great! I love challenges and believe that everyone should have a goal in life. We all are good at something."

THORNTON, CHARLES R.: [b] 3/6/25 Richmond, Yorks; [awards] Intermed. Clerk of Works, Buildings; [mem] Darlington Arts Soc., Richmond Writers Group, Civic Soc., Ramblers Assoc.; [pub writ] 1 book (accepted by 4 publishers); 1 poem "In Bishop's Park" - Arrival Press Peterbourough; "My book, "Moles Awakening" which, I hope will be on the shelves this summer, concerns children of all ages grouped with 10 watercolour pictures (one for each chapter). It is self-produced.

THORNTON, PHILIP B.: [b] 24/7/44 Thrybergh; [m] Ann; [p] Henry & Nora; [ch] Stephen, Shaun & Robert; [occ] Plumber; ["It has always been an ambition of mine to write to give others pleasure. Only in the last year, now our sons are grown up, have I had the time."

THORPE, ELIZABETH: [b] 28/3/35 Bury, Lancs; [m] Ron; [p] Margaret & Robert Hayden; [ch] Robert, Nicholas & Samantha; [ed] Our Lady of Grace R.C., C.T.A., creative writing class; [occ] poet; [mem] Labour Party & CND; [activ] volunteer: HM prison Strangeways, 'Barnados'; [pub writ] poetry - 4 anthologies, local poetry mag.; "At the age of 50 I started writing poetry and found my 'niche' in life! I am now 60 and living proof that 'it's never over till the fat lady sings'! Many thanks to family, friends and tutors for their support."

THORPE, KEVIN: [b] 12/7/81 Basingstoke; [p] Janet & Walter; [Richard Aldworth Community School; [occ] student; [awards] 2 medals - running; [activ] writing poetry, short stories, football, music, reading; "I am delighted to be chosen to be entered for the main contest and have my poem published."

THURSFIELD, RAY: [b] 12/1/27 Cannock; [p] Ray & Eva; [ch] Andrew & Maxine; [occ] engineer (rtrd.); [awards] National Cert. Engineering; [activ] exhibit own paintings (expressionist); [pub writ] poems in company anthology; "Hispanophile, linguist and one-time seaman, greatly appreciative of the works of Lorca & Neruda. Enjoy expressing my imagination with the written word and in painting. I like jazz."

TILLEY, GWYNETH: [b] 16/2/20 Bargoed, S. Wales; [m] William; [p] Evan & Lilian Bartlett; [ch] Douglas, Derek & David; [ed] Tynywern Sec. School; [awards] Bedwas, Trethomas & Machen Community Council Award - Poetic Achievements '92; [activ] volunteer various charity/fund-raisings, church member/worker; [pub writ] svrl. anthologies, church mag.; "Brought up in a mining village, I experienced my Father's death in the mine. My poems are mostly of real life."

TILLY, PAUL: [b] 15/11/59 Caerphilly; [p] John & Syvia; [ed] St. Martins Comp., Caerphilly School; [occ] bakery operative; [awards] 3rd place - local bodybuilding comp. '92, singer 'Buzz & The B Days' - semi-finals of Sony Rock'n'Pop Challenge; [mem] 'Fitness Connection' - local gym; [pub writ] poem in Poetic Visions '91 - Century Press, vocals on album - 'Mutant Surf Punks Hang 11'; "Once in a while I feel the need

to empty the contents of my head onto paper, shame that most of it seems to be toilet paper... I think, therefore, I write."

TILZEY, PENELOPE: [b] 12/9/62 Bromley; [p] Eileen & Gilbert; [ed] Reigate County School for Girls, Hotel Career Ctr., Bournemouth; [awards] diploma - travel/tourism; [activ] various church activities, assist. soc. activities at college for the blind; [pub writ] poems in Poetry Now '95 & church magazine; "I enjoy music, books, film, and the countryside. Poetry enables me to communicate my deeper feelings, and I hope, help others. I am also known for my humour which provides a healthy balance."

TITLEY, ALAN: [b] 8/10/29 Gravesend, Kent; [p] James & Gladys; [ch] Lorna & Brian; [ed] County Grammar School, Kent; [occ] children's entertainer (rtrd.); [awards] Higher National Cert. Business Studies (with Distinction); [mem] R.N.L.I.; [activ] house mgr. Cromer & North Norfolk Festival of Music, Drama & Dance; [pub writ] poems in local newspapers/church mag., "Like every good Libran, my philosophy in everday matters is to avoid confrontation whenever possible by seeking a compromise. Within the context of verse and prose, however, creative writing encompasses my more deeply held beliefs, and serves as an emotional safety valve."

TODD, RACHEL E.: [b]17/6/68 Melton, Suffolk; [p] Elizabeth & John; [ed] Thomas Mills High School, Suffolk College; [occ] care assistant; [awards] Lifting Cert., Parencraft Cert., English Speaking board, City & Guilds - numeracy/communications; [mem] Wickham Market Flower Arrangement Club; [pub writ] poems in the 'Nafas' - The East of England Ed. no. 90 nwsltr.; "I enjoy writing poetry on a variety of subjects. When it's quiet I am able to contemplate my thoughts, therefore express myself."

TORBET, VERA [b] 12/12/37; [p] James Robertson & Hannah May; [ch] Julie Mary; [ed] West Park Sec. Girls School, Sunderland Tech College (secretarial), College of Further Education; [awards] CGE 5 'O' and 1 'A' level, S.R.N. 1962; [activ] fund-raising - cancer, correspondence (international), Baptist church member; [pub writ] 9 poems in various anthologies as well as self-publications; "I like to convey how I see the world around me, and within, by writing. I hope that by sharing my experiences and thoughts others will be helped to live peaceful lives as they read, and be encouraged to use their creative abilities. I think everyone can leave something beautiful behind them to enrich the world."

TOWLE, JIM: [b] 6/10/43 Dunfermline, Fife; [m] Margaret; [ch] Gail & Claire; [ed] Queen Anne College, Dunfermline, Fife College, College of Fuel Technology; [occ] boilermam; [awards] techical certs., City & Guilds - Boiler Operators Cert.; [mem] Scottish Steam Preservation Soc.; [activ] volunteer fireman; [pub writ] humorous illustrations - "Quite By Accident" pub. Square One Publications; "Experience of life brings inspiration at unexpected moments. Anyone who stops learning is old. Anyone who keeps learning stays young."

TOWNSEND, SUSAN: [b] 5/6/46 Oxford; [p] Ivy & Percy Lester; [ch] Guy; [ed] Carswell Jr. School, Larkmead Sed. School, Abingdon; [occ] learning/support assist.; [awards] R.S.A. English, R.S.A. Cert. of Cont. Ed.; [mem] P.H.A.B.; [activ] swim club member, painting & drawing; "My family are very important to me, and I try to have a positive outlook. I enjoy the company of friends and like caring for, and helping people. I wrote my poem on a cold November day."

TREACHER, JENNY L.: [b] 18/2/35 Chalfont St. Peter, Bucks; [p] Grace & Eustace Knight; [ch] Susan; [ed] Durants Sec. Modern School, Croxley Green; [occ] housewife; [pub writ] 2 poems - Arrival Press, 1 poem - Poetry Now, 1 poem - Anchor Books; "My first poem published was in 1991 after my daughter, Sue, persuaded me to enter a competition. My thanks to her. I receive great satisfaction from writing about places of beauty. My Great Grandmother, E.A. Lemprière Knight, was a poet."

TREADGOLD, SAMANTHA: [b] 5/6/73 Southend; [m] David; [p] Keith & Wendy Brown; [ed] Cecil Jones High School; [occ] housewife; "Writing I find is very relaxing and the result can be very rewarding. It's the best way to express myself and very satisfying."

TREADWAY, BRYNLEY I.: [b] 5/2/27 Epsom, Sy; [m] Jennifer Oliver; [p] Frederick & Edith; [ch] Judith & Katrina; [ed] State school/ eve. classes; [pub writ] poems "Little Balls of Rubbish", "Star Begotten" (collections of poems), poems in various quarterlies, etc.

TRIPPIER, BARBARA: [b] 20/8/43 Wirral; [p] James & Nora Landreth; [ch] Simon & Jamie; [ed] Oldershaw High School; [occ] dental receptionist; [awards] runner-up in 'Poetry Digest' Fun 1993 Comp.; [activ] swimming, dancing, cycling; [pub writ] poem in local papers 1977; "I write purely for pleasure inspired usually by the everyday things in life. I think a sense of humour is probably the most important asset. I like to see the funny side of life and hope people smile along with me."

TURPIN, LES J.: [b] 5/6/67 West Thurrock; [m] Wendy; [p] James & Ann; [ch] Jodi; [ed] Torells Comp. Essex; [occ] production supervisor; [activ] karate, fishing, reading; "Obviously inspired by my beautiful daughter, Jodi. She matured me overnight. Love to you always, Dad."

TUTTE, ROY: [b] 16/12/32 Epsom, Surrey; [p] Thomas & Lillian; [ed] Royal Navy - Electrical Branch, various tech. schools; [occ] informaton researcher; [awards] City & Guilds certs.; [activ] local charities; [pub writ] short items local/ntn'l newspapers, literary competitions; "Approaching the Twenty-First Century, and reminded of the troubled Twentieth Century, it is encouraging to discover that there are many, many good and worthwhile people everywhere. I enjoy observing and meeting such folk, and learning so much from them, thankfully."

TYLER, LESLEY: [b] 21/7/48 Sussex; [p] Joanne & Noel Stevens; [ch] Karen & Paul; [ed] Ipswich High G.P.D.S.T., Hockerill College; [occ] teacher; [awards] Cert. Ed., A.C.E.; [mem] Natn'l Assoc. of Field Study Officers, Natn'l Assoc. of Environmnental Education; [activ] volunteer - conservation; [pub writ] NAFSO Journal '94 & '95, local community news sheet; "I take life as it comes and make the most of opportunities. I write poetry for emotional therapy!"

TYSON, CAROL: [b] 13/4/48 Liverpool, [m] James; [p] Elizabeth & Richard Durkin; [ch] Jamie & Sam; [ed] Loraine St. Girls Sec., Kendal College; [occ] proprietor - guest house/aromatherapist; [awards] diploma - hotel reception/business studies, diploma - aromatherapy/anatomy/ physiology; [activ] Greenpeace, Amnesty Intn'l, Dr. Barnado Committee, M.I.S.P.A.; [pub writ] 2 poems (Emotional Burning Hoops) (Rapt In Barbed Wire) - Foreward Press - Shiver of the Heart (Separate Lives) Anchor Books; "I am most happy when I've done something for the right reasons and not because it is expected or required. I hope always to aim for the light and the open spaces inside and out."

UNDERWOOD, BILL: [b] 17/2/29 Devizes; [p] George & Ethel; [ch] David, Matthew & Simon; [ed] Southbroom Elementary.

UNSWORTH, SHEELAGH: [b] 8/6/30 Bristol; [p] Kathleen & Herbert Hunking; [ch] Simon & Christopher; [ed] Redland High School, Bristol; [occ] typist (rtrd.); [awards] school prize - Latin; [pub writ] short story - Bristol Evening Post 1936; "Verse and stories encouraged a smile during husband's terminal illness and continues."

VALE, SALLY: [b] 31/12/58 Ipswich; [p] Cintra & Douglas Crascall (dcd.); [ch] Kirsty (dcd.), Katie & Jodie; [ed] Claydon Sec. Modern, Suffolk College; [occ] homemaker; [awards] City & Guilds - hairdressing/ wigmaking, R.S.A. - commerce, R.S.A. - typewritng Stg. 1 & 2; [activ] volunteer - school, circuit training, sport, local playscheme; "Always be positive, enjoy life to the full. I write poems for pleasure. Ambition: to write a best-selling novel."

VAN-DEN-HEUVEL, MARGARETH: [b] 23/5/45 Mylor, Cornwall; [p] Joan & Piet; [ch] Robin & Jessica; [ed] Quarry Hill Sec., Falmouth Commerce/Journalism, Royal Cornwall School of Nursing; [occ] nurse/ lecturer/diver; [awards] Scuba Instr. Magiciene, Woman Of Today '92; [activ] spec. in care of elderly & nutrition, northern most Vegetarian Info Ctr. in U.K.; [pub writ] Envoi/Poetry Now, short stories in ntn'l mags., freelance rprting; "I am a happy and relaxed person, I aim to achieve something 'mega' every year and my ambition is to dive under the Antarctic ice. I have dived all the oceans of the world. I am a dedicated conservationist."

VAUGHAN, FRED: [b] Merthyr Tydfil; [m] Violet; [ch] David Huw; [ed] Cyfarthfa Castle Grammar School, University College, Cardiff; [occ] school master (rtrd.); [awards] BA (Wales), frmr head of History - Afon Tâf High School; [pub writ] various articles on local history in various journals.

VERNON, ADA: [b] 4/6/25 Liverpool; [p] William & Ada Lloyd; [ch] Norman, John, Maureen & Alan; [ed] Knaphill Central School, Surrey; [occ] housewife; [pub writ] poems in local paper; "I'm a good listener, I find people like to talk to me. I like to write about many things. Poetry is a stream of thought that fills your mind at difference times."

VINALL-BURNETT, MARGARET M.: [b] 3/10/13 Haslemere; [p] Arthur & Frances Bennyworth; [ch] Nancy, Albert, Caolina, Robert, Rosalind, Dorothy, Jefrey & Kenneth; [ed] Village School, Cross-In-Hand, Sussex; [awards] at 17 worked with Margaret Rawlings; [mem] N.A.L.D. & Action for Disabled, Sussex; [pub writ] 2 poems put to music/pub. Paramount 1939, 4 poems in Disabled Magazine '70's, and in 'Something To Say', Devon & Dorset Poetry Club."

VINCENT, BARRY: [b] 15/3/50 Chesham, Bucks; [m] Patricia; [p] Joan & Ashley; [ch] Emma & Wayne; [ed] Raans County Secondary School, Bucks; [occ] motor engineer; [awards] City & Guilds - engineer 1 & 2; [pub writ] 1 poem '94; "I have just started writing poetry after 32 years from leaving school where I got an internal award for poetry. I have also written some ballad/love songs but I have not yet tried to have them published."

VINCENT, FRAN: [b] 9/7/26 York; [p] Rose & Harold Sparling; [ch] Christopher; [ed] Higher Grade Girls School; [activ] OXFAM, church member, trained singer/choir member; "I have been writing poetry from the War onwards but have only now decided to offer them for publication. Many have appeared in church magazines and also in The Northern Echo. I also have a book of poetry and church recipes coming out hopefully in the Summer."

VINCENT, GILBERT T.: [b] 15/11/20 Middlesbrough; [p] Edward & Mable; [ch] Margaret, Lilian, Vera, Lynda, Gilbert, Edward & Paul; [ed] council schools, Easington Colliery, Redcar & Middlesbrough; [activ] serving brother, order of St. John (rtrd.), Supt. Wingate D.U., Mem. Rats of Tubruk; "I have written about 18 poems since 1940, never tried to have any published. Also three books, not yet edited. I got the most satisfaction from teaching First Aid in schools and factories."

VINE, JENNIFER; [pen]; [b] London; [ed] Enfield County School, Open University; [occ] housewife; [awards] Arts Degree; [mem] National Trust; [activ] volunteer; [pub writ] article in National Magazine, poems in anthologies/local paper; "I am pleased to have time now to write poems and short stories. I also write stories for my grandchildren. I enjoy words and the thinking that is required to use them creatively."

VOSPER, FRANCIS: [b] 24/6/57 Munster, W. Germany; [m] Nicola; [p] Alan & Margaret; [ch] Emma & Kerri; [ed] Bodmin Sec. Modern; [occ] catering mgr.; [awards] City & Guilds 706/1 and 706/2, Community Sports Leader Cert.; [pub writ] "Driftwood Spars" in Poetry Now South West; "I get great pleasure from writing and a buzz of people like what I write. My family encourages me to put pen to paper with my poems and short stories."

WADE, EDWARD A.: [b] 2/9/39 London E7; [p] Edward & Kathleen; [ch] Simon & Nathan; [ed] John Clare School, Northampton; [occ] project supervisor; [awards] Despatches Aden 1964; [activ] officer - Yorkshire Army Radar Force, Assoc. member Royal Soc. of Health; [pub writ] Aden Reflections 1965 "A hopeless romantic, I enjoy good books, fact or fiction, love writing. I have enjoyed poetry since childhood."

WAGSTAFF, MELINDA: [b] 19/2/69 Catterick; [p] David & Geraldine; [ed] Risedale School, Hipswell Catterick, N.Yorks; [occ] cafeteria mngrs.; [awards] GCSE English, Eng. Lit., French,City & Guilds - beauty therapy/electrolysis; "Life should be lived to the full and disappointments and hard times only lead to greater happiness and well-being."

WALKER, KATHLEEN E.: [b] 14/9/66 Berwick; [p] George & Violet Maltman; [ch] Danielle & Michelle; [ed] Eyemouth School; [occ] homemaker; "After having children I don't want as much for myself in life. To enter my poetry in the contest was a major step, I didn't know I had it in me."

WALKER, LUCY D.: [b] 10/9/80 Bury St. Edmunds; [p] Brendon & Pauline; [ed] Hadleigh High School (starting 9/95); [occ] student; [activ] fund-raising for animal welfare, children in need & Comic Relief; [pub writ] some work in school magazines; "I have never looked at poetry as just rhyming words. I have always thought it was a perfect way to show my feelings. Writing has always relaxed me and when I let my mind go, my thoughts become words."

WALKER, ROBERT G.: [b] 10/5/34 Befast; [m] Agnes; [p] Richard & Annie; [ch] George, Heather, Ann and Elizabeth; [ed] Beachfield Primary, Templemore Avenue Intermediate; [activ] darts, writing; [pub writ] "Mixed Thoughts of Winter"; "My wife and myself enjoy long walks and are concerned about the environment."

WALL, LINDA: [b] 13/3/55 N. Ireland; [m] Christopher; [p] Duncan & Margaret Campbell; [ch] Matthew & Jennifer; [ed] Ripley St. Thomas C. of E. School; [occ] stock controller; [awards] diploma - computer studies; [pub writ] poems in 9 anthologies; "Never expect anything from anyone to avoid disappointment. Trust your instincts. Don't take things too seriously."

WALLACH, RICHARD J.: [b] 13/2/52 Windsor, Berks; [p] Jim & Zydia; [ch] James Michael; [ed] St. Ignatious Sec. Modern, East Barkshire College of Technology; [pub writ] poem "Geevor Mine" in Poems of the South West Anthol. pub Arrival Press '93; "Life is a rich tapestry of inspiration for myself as a writer, writing in whatever form is Mankind's legacy for future generations."

WALKINGSHAW, JAMES G.: [b] 20/5/54 Aberystwyth; [p] Mr./ Mrs. J. Walkingshaw; [ed] Dinas Sec. Modern, Aberystwyth; [occ] clerical assistant; [activ] trained First Aid, St. Johns Ambulance; [pub writ] poem - Arrival Press (Spring '94); "Sometimes when I'm down and sad, I think to myself o, how glad, to live with nature and be free, with God's creation all to see."

WALSH, JAMES: [b] 30/8/67 Lisburn; [ed] Lisnagarvey High, Lisburn Technical College; [awards] G.C.S.E.'s (2); [activ] Dromore Angling Club; [pub writ] "The Queen of Hearts" & "Encounter With The Aquatic Pedagogue" - Poetry Now anthologies; "The words that utter from the heart are poems themselves and play their part, to unite the man."

WARD, AUDREY: [b] 22/11/19 Redcar; [p] Harriet & Arther Hannan; [ed] Westdyke School, Redcar; [activ] Justice of Peace, W.R.V.S. - Scalby & Dist. Business & Prof., Scalby Church member; "The first poem written after death of mother. I enjoy art, writing, music and people, holidays and life with my husband. I am the youngest in a family of seven."

WARNER, BEVERLEY: [b] 2/10/67 Harlow; [p] Rod & Val; [ed] East London University, Harlow College, Brays Grove Comp.; [occ] student; [activ] volunteer work with homeless; [pub writ] 4 in various poetry books, some work 'Talking Newspaper' for the blind; "I am a stand-up poet in clubs. To write poetry it helps to have had experienced life in the gutter and in the loony bin to receive a balanced understanding of life."

WARREN, P.: [b] 11/12/51 Clevedon Avon; [p] Stan & Helen; [ch] David & Catherine; [ed] Nailsea Grammar School; [occ] postal officer; [awards] Inst. of Supervisory Management; [pub writ] cassettes of my original songs; "The inspiration for this poetry is to the glory of God."

WARREN, RHYS: [b] 30/9/73 Skegness; [p] John & Maureen; [ed] Skegness Grammar School, De Montfort University, Leicester; [occ]

shop assistant; "'The road of excess leads to the palace of wisdom' - Blake."

WATKINS, ELIZABETH: [b] 20/12/31 Ynysybwl; [p] Sara & Huw Jones; [ch] Elwyn Huw & Jane Merryl; [ed] Ysgd Ganol, Abercynon; [activ] Poetry Society; "Rediscovering a childhood longing to write to satisfy an inner need. Now drawing on a reservoir of memories, rewarding in so many ways, not least of all filling the space in my life emptied by present circumstance. Your acceptance has rekindled the fire within me."

WATSON, JUDY: [b] 6/11/45 Yorkshire; [m] Michael; [p] William & Dilys Harwood (dcd.); [ch] Ross & Lee; [occ] civil servant; [pub writ] poems in anthologies, story in National Magazine; "I often write poems for other people and delight in their pleasure on receiving them. My philosophy for life is to take 'one day at a time'."

WATSON, MARJORY: [b] 10/9/25 Dalton on Tees; [ch] Derek; [awards] Cert. in Music; [mem] Yorkshire Country Women's Assoc.; [activ] church organist; [pub writ] 2 poems '94' "A farmer's daughter who loves the countryside and animals, I'm a keen gardener, and I like antique fairs."

WATSON, SANDRA: [b] 24/4/34 Essex; [ch] Carole, Sharon & Jolyon; [ed] Westcliff High School, Brentwood College of Education; [occ] teacher] [pub writ] half dozen poems, one or two articles; "Most of my poems are concerned with stories about children at school, or experiences of my own grandchildren."

WATT, ALAN: [b] 24/8/54 Aberdeen; [m] Ida; [p] Alexander & Elizabeth; [ch] James, Shaun & Siobhan; [ed] Powis Academy, Aberdeen; [occ] artist/writer; [awards] diploma - Creative Writing; [pub writ] various poems; "A thousand sleepless nights to know it. A thousand reasons why to show it, it's all within you, you can grow it. Call it the curse of the all probing poet."

WATT, JANICE E.: [b] 23/7/61 Belfast; [p] Eliza Jane & James; [ed] Ballyclare Primary and Secondary; [occ] process operator; "I prefer to write than to talk."

WAY, SARAH L.: [p] Anne & Trevor; [ed] Thorpedene Jr. & Shoebury High School; [occ] student; [awards] Basic Reflexology Cert.; [activ] stable work/horseback riding; "I would very much like to have my poetry read by everyone. I am into conservation and would like to see a better world. I have horse riding lessons and work in a stable."

WEARING, WENDY: [b] 18/5/39 Chipping Norton, Oxon; [m] Roly; [p] Cecil & Vera Money; [ch] Steven & Stephanie; [occ] secretary; [mem] NORCAP; [activ] geneology, Christian Spiritualist Church member; [pub writ] poems in various anthologies; "It is better to express emotion and feelings than to keep them pent up inside. Putting these thoughts into words on paper often helps me put things into perspective."

WEBB, JENNIFER: [b] 21/2/53 Reading; [m] Roderick; [p] Geoffrey & Francine Taylor; [ch] Robin & John; [ed] Kendrick Grammar, Geore Watson's Ladies College, University of East Anglia; [occ] p/t/ teacher; [awards] degree - comparative literature, diploma - creative writing & P.G.C.E; [activ] local charities; [pub writ] articles in country mag., "I have taught creative writing to children for many years and am now discovering the pleasure of distilling experience and capturing moments in time for myself."

WEIR, PATRICIA A.: [b] 25/3/43 Lancaster; [p] Joseph & Barbara Barraclough; [ch] Caron, Debra & Tina; [ed] Dallas High, Lancaster; [occ] care assistant; [awards] various poetry commendations; [activ] charity appeals; [pub writ] poems: Moods, Devotions, More Of Moods, Reflections, Sacred Offerings, Impressions, Adorations, plus 9 anthology works, short stories; "I try not to think of self alone when I write, but for others who might derive some pleasure from my collective thoughts when they read the written words."

WELCH, FRANCES M.: [b] 18/2/05 Tywardreath, Cornwall; [m] Dr. Cuthbert Welch (dcd.); [p] Rev. Cecil & Mary Norris; [ch] Eleanor,

Barbara & Daphne; [ed] Truro High School & soprano voice training; [activ] solo singing, Sussex Rural Music School, Eastbourne Music Club, All Saints Church, creating pressed flower pictures, crafts for fund-raising for church, cancer research; "A positive outlook is a key to contented living. Each day life begins anew. I am now 90 years old and embarking on a new venture writing down my poetry to share with others."

WELFORD, DORIS M.: [b] 6/6/28 Norwich; [p] Mr. & Mrs. Griggs (dcd.); [ed] Comprehensive School Norwich (Lakenham), Colman Girls School (Primary), Larkman Sr.; [awards] hospital work, machinist, engineer, Capstan Lath, N.A.A.P.I. 1950; [activ] church work, St. Johns Red Cross (2 certs.); [pub writ] winner of 4 awards, came 2nd on Radio Norfolk; "I want to write a book. My poems come inspired, once it's there I must write straight away or the idea is gone."

WELL, GERALD: [pen] Aquilla; [b]7/4/31 Fexixstowe, Suffolk; [p] Gwendoline & Reginald (dcd.); [ch] Michael & Nigel; [ed] Christ Church C. of E. School, St. Georges School, Army Ed. Corps (Pt. 1,2 & 3); [occ] civil servant (ind.) (rtrd.); [awards] served Royal Scots Greys (5 yrs.); [pub writ] various anthologies; "As an inspirational poet, poetry is my hobby. Now at retirement I am persuaded by my two sons and future daughter-in-law Gillian and have decided to 'go public'."

WESTGART, G.F.: [b] 20/11/24 High Moorsley; [p] Lelie & Florence; [ch] Kenneth & Anne; [ed] Eppleton Council School; [occ] blacksmith (rtrd.); [activ] sec. Hetton & District Art Club, painting, sculpting (mostly mining subjects); [pub writ] poetry in local papers, cartoons; "I love a challenge, doing something different; at present I'm helping people who are recovering from mental problems to paint pictures. I love to see the joy when their first effort is framed and hung."

WESTON, SALLY ANNE NISBET,: [b] 1/2/50 Haddington; [m] Eric; [p] Margaret & William Weston; [ch] Andrew & Amanda; [ed] Knox Academy, Dunfermline College of Physical Education; [occ] loose cannon/housewife; [pub writ] poem Scotland Anthology '92; "Thanks to my husband, Eric, for his continual financial support in the eternal pursuit of philosophical and literary truth, stray cats and the perfect sauce Bigarade."

WESTREN, JO: [b] 1914 Essex; [p] Grace & Robert May; [ed] governess & boarding school; [occ] poet/journalist/artist; [awards] nursing exams Royal London Hosp.; [mem] Poetry Book Society, fnd. member Suffolk Poetry Society; [pub writ]articles & stories in Nat. Publications, 2 War poems "Brief Sanctuary" & "Behind the Screens" pub. "More Poems of 2nd World War" (Dent). Poem broadcast twice in "Not For Glory" 2 on TV, also selected for tape presented to Queen & featured by Thomas Nelson in "Poems of 2nd World War". 4 poems included in "Suffolk poetry 1952-62", 2 feature poems in "Anthology of Hammersmith Festival of Poetry" 1979. Own anthology "Harvests" pub. by Outposts 1978. Poem in "Poet's England" 1994. Also a poem in "Christian Poets of Eastern England: 1994; "Poetry is integral to life if you know where to find it!"

WHALLEY, ROSALINDA: [b] 21/5/47 Sunderland; [p] Kate & Ivan Spithray; [ch] Julie Ann & Norna Louise; [ed] Castle View Sec. Modern, Sunderland; [awards] Instructional Techniques/Communication Skills, Health & Safety Comm., St.,Johns Ambuland, First Aid; [activ] Salvation Army helper, Neighbourhood Watch; [pub writ] short story, children's hymn, Pebble Mill; "Writing my life experiences in poetry, fulfills my soul so strongly the release of all my yesteryears just flow from my heart."

WHEELER, JACK E.: [b] 30/11/16 London; [p] William & Ada; [ch] Ian & Anne; [ed] Elem. & Royal Hospital School, Greenwich; [occ] civil servant (rtrd.); [awards] B.E.M. (Mil), 3 trophies - horticulture; [mem] St. Andrews Art Club, Friends of the Byre Theatre, St. Andrews Horticultural Assoc., [activ] patron St. Andrews Amateur Operatic Society, amateur artist (acrylics) landscapes/harbours; [pub writ] poem "Steam Trains" in This England Autumn 1992; "I am a lover of nature who likes to love and be loved with an awareness of all the good things of life around us. I am grateful to have lived so long to be able to

appreciate them."

WHEELHOUSE, JAMES: [b]13/7/19 Edinburgh; [p] Catherine & Alexander; [ed] Ramsay Tech. College, Royal College of Massage; [awards] Diploma of the Royal College of Massage; [activ] actv.serv. R.A.O.C. (6 yrs.) Port Ordinance Detachment; "My poetry and short stories give me great satisfaction. Though I have not forwarded any for publication so far."

WHIGHT, MICHAEL: [b] 16/2/64 Ipswich; [m] Jean; [p] George & Gina; [ed] Thurleston High School; [occ] local gov't officer; [activ] films, music, coin collecting & foreign travel, football; [pub writ] 1 poem in book, svrl. quizzes in intn'l magazines (football) "Writing is the ultimate freedom of expression, be it poetry, novel writing or keeping a diary. My motto: 'Don't worry about it'."

WHITBOURN, ADAM: [b] 9/9/77 York; [p] Wendy & Tony; [ed] Broughton High School, Runshaw College; [occ] student; [awards] 9 G.C.S.E.'s, 'A' levels; "I find that I have a great interest in my surroundings and this is reflected in my poetry. I am still fairly new to this and I write for my own pleasure rather than gain. The publication of my piece has greatly encouraged me."

WHITE, MARLENE: [b] S. Wales; [ch] Michelle & Andrew; [ed] Weston-Super-Mare Tech. College; [occ] soc. services/carer; [awards] secretarial qual.; [activ] Buye Theatre Club, Camelford Operatic Soc., Intn'l League for the Protection of Horses, novice diver; [pub writ] poems in local paper/mags.; "I am ultimate proof that you don't need to be an egg-head to write poetry! Just pick up a pen and take a deep breath ..."

WHITEHEAD, VIOLET: [b] 19/4/20, Kent; [p] James & Min Cackett; [ch] Vyvian; [ed] Village School C. of E., Hextable; [occ] housewife; [pub writ] verses in parish mag., & Natn'l Mag.; "I have realized that adversity brings strength. Putting my thoughts about everyday life gives me mental satisfaction and pleasure."

WHITEWAY, JUNE M.: [b] 14/1/25 Dorset; [ed] Convent school, London, State school, Kent; "I have found in writing poetry a release of thoughts which often I could not speak of."

WHITTLE, MICHELLE: [b] 5/9/86 Nottingham; [p] Maurice & Ann; [ed] St. Marys School, Edwinstowe Notts; [occ] student; [activ] Brownies Grp.; "I am pleased to have been selected. I do lots of competitions as a hobby."

WHYTOCK ANDREA: [b] 19/11/66 Dulwich, S.E. London; [p] Anthony & Joan; [activ] travel, Tai Chi, contemp. dance; [pub writ] poetry in local newspapers & booklet (fund-raiser for homeless), poetry in alternative press; "Each piece of writing is crafted like a tapestry. I try to make it as perfect as it can be with the creative energy I have at the time."

WIDDOWSON, TOM H.: [b] 4/7/41; [occ] retail; [pub writ] poem in Poetry Now East Midland Anthology '94, Christmas story in CANDIS, and church mags.; "I never set out to write. It used to scare me (still does!). I would also love somebody to write and tell me what they think of my work."

WIGAN, MARY E.: [b] 6/12/45 Wigan; [m] William; [p] Winifred & James Spencer; [ch] Paul; [ed] St. Patrick;s R.C. School, Wigan; [occ] cleaning supervisor; [award] Cert. of Merit - Ntn'l Essay Competition for Schools; [pub writ] 3 poems "Summertime" in North West Voices '92, "Untitled" in Poems of the North West '93, "Christmas Joy" in Faith in Verse '94; "I started to write poetry when I was recovering from an operation, then I wrote one for a friend's retirement. Other people asked me to write them for special occasions, so I decided to send one forward for an anthology and was delighted when I heard they wanted to publish it."

WIGHT, EDNA: [b] 1913, Whittlesford; [p] Harriet & Albert Merry; [ch] William; [ed] Whittlesford Elem. School; [awards] 1st - Elocution; [activ] drama, poetry; "Thanks to my head teacher, Mr. Rudling, who fired me with the love of English Literature, poetry & music."

WIGLEY, SAMUEL J.: [b] 29/6/80 Canterbury; [p] Andrew & Marilyn; [ed] Thurston Upper School, Suffolk; [occ] student; "I have always enjoyed writing poems, short stories and screenplays. My primary interests are art and cinema and my ambition is to be a film reviewer. I shall always indulge in creative writing and treasure this book containing my first publication."

WIGMORE, PAUL: [b] 22/6/67 Reading; [p] Pauline & Barry; [occ] journalist; [awards] BA (Hons.) - History; "This poem is dedicated to Janet."

WILFORD, SALLY: [b] 5/4/77 Sutton-In-Ashfield; [p] John & Josehpine; [ed] Lorne House School, Ranby House School, Worksop College; [occ] student; [awards] won poetry comp. - Woodard School, creative writing prize, G.C.S.E.'s, 4'A's, 2'B's, 2'C's, Gr. 1 (distinction) flute, academic prizes; [activ] choir - soprano, 6th form committee (college); [pub writ] college nwsltr, yearbook; "For as long as I can remember I have written poetry and I know I always will. It is my solace and the only way I can truly express myself; for me it is a way of life."

WILKINSON, DAMIEN K.: [b] 19/12/76 Bahamas; [p] Brian & Chris; [ed] Rmasey Grammar School, Isle of Man; [occ] student; [awards] School Humanities Award, Public Speaking Awards; [activ] volunteer - Age Concern; "The greatest asset in life is imagination. With knowledge and understanding a man can climb high, but without imagination he shall never fly."

WILLIAMS, ALAN: [b]27/2/37 Rhondda Valley; [p] Meredith & Florence; [ch] Alyson & Judith; [ed] Aberdare Grammar School; [occ] riding school prop.; [mem] Rotary International; [activ] charity - "Riding For The Disabled"; [pub writ] poems on local papers, anthologies, & mags.; "I didn't start writing until I was 48 years old, now I can't stop! I get so much pleasure from putting my thoughts on paper. I am now writing short stories."

WILLIAMS, AUDREY P.: [b] 6/12/36 Sidcup, Kent; [p] Albert & Emily Stapley; [ch] Clifford, Maxine & Gregory; [ed] Sec. Modern, Blackfen School, Kent; [occ] writer; [pub writ] "Don't They Know" (theme related to unemployment); "I have had a very varied life and occupations and have enjoyed writing poems, stories also, and a couple of short plays (radio/TV). I have begun to write a novel which I intend to complete."

WILLIAMS, C.: [b] 20/2/68 Ipswich; [p] Maureen & Bill Griggs; [ch] Chelsie & Tayla; [ed] Rosehill Primary, Copleston High School; [awards] 'O' level - art; "I find myself putting everyday situations and circumstances down on paper. Thoughts, problems and troubled minds can sometimes be explained and understood easier on paper. I enjoy adding just a touch of my own sense of humour to my poems."

WILLIAMS, CECIL: [b] 24/10/17 Cicely Ford, Trellech Monmouth; [m] Irene; [p] Cicelia & Albert; [ch] Patricia; [ed] C. of E. Trellech nr. Monmouth; [occ] postman (rtrd.); [pub writ] 4 poems in World of Verse 1975, 1 poem in Arrival Press 1995; "I like studying local history, photography, painting, walking, reading, music and sequence dancing."

WILLIAMS, DOROTHY: [b] Liverpool; [activ] Amnesty International, Greenpeace; "Deeply concerned about moral confusion and social disorder."

WILLIAMS, MICHAEL P.: [b] 25/10/62 Caerphilly S.Wales; [m] Margaret; [p] Alice & Tom (dcd.); [ch] Emily & Mathew; [ed] St. Cenydd Comp., Caerphilly; [occ] signalman; "I like to take life at a steady pace, I find that I'm not over ambitious. Being with my family, to me, is ideal happiness. If you want something in life, you've got to go out and get it, be yourself and believe in yourself."

WILLIAMS, NORMA: [b] 17/8/26 Rhymney; [p] Susan & Edward; [ch] John & Keith Thomas; [ed] Lewis Girls School, Further Ed. College, Merthyr, Tydfil; [occ] clerical officer (rtrd.); [activ] St. Davids Church Guild, Rhymney Amateur Dramatic Soc.

WILLIAMS, P.G.: [b] 15/2/30 Merthyr Tydfil; [m] Jean; [p] Leyshon & Doris; [ch] Richard; [ed] Cyfarthfa Castle Grammar School, University College, Swansea; [occ] university tutor; [awards] BSc. & MSc Mathematics; [pub writ] short stories/poems in national mags./ anthologies; "Poetry should always be comprehensible."

WILLIAMS, PETER: [b] 26/7/65 Mansfield; [p] Ron & Pat; [ed] Dukeries Comprehensive, Open University; [occ] land surveryor; [awards] BSc - Earth Studies (OU), HND - mine surveying; [mem] Woodland Trust; [activ] R.S.P.C.A. member; "Poetry I found so tedious when younger, It's only recently that I've discovered what a great tool it is in getting thoughts and feelings out into the open."

WILLIAMS, TALIA R.: [b] 12/6/80 Caerphilly; [p] Merril & Lyndon; [ed] Heolddu Comprehensive School; [occ] student; "I am pleased I am able to express myself in a way that others can enjoy. I like creative writing and I am hoping to make a career of it. Hope you enjoy the poem!"

WILLOX, SUZANNE K.: [b] 28/2/74; [m] Adrian; [p] Michael & Suan Chapman; [ed] Neale-Wade Community College, March & Isle College, Cambridgeshire; [occ] housewife; [awards] 'A' level - sociology; "Poetry exists deep inside everyone; so live, breathe and feel it. Discover youself as I have discovered myself."

WILLSON, VICTORIA: [b] 2/8/76 Leamington SPA; [p] Peter & Sandra; [ed] Tremough Convent School, St. Hugh's College, Oxford; [occ] student; [awards] Royal College of Music - piano Gr. 6; [activ] Oxford Union Soc.; [pub writ] poems pub. in poetry mags.: "First Time", "Dial 174", "Otter", "Omnific"; "I started writing out of a teenage whim but I hope it never leaves me. I believe writing is the best therapy. My only ambition in life is to be happy."

WILSON, DIANE: [b] 13/12/62 March, Cambridge; [p] Grace & John (dcd.); [ed] Hereward Comp., Isle College, Cambs.; [activ] Ileostomy Assoc. & Internal Pouch Support Group or G.B. & Ireland; [pub writ] 2 poetry books "Highway to Hope" & "Reflections" (proceeds to Ileostomy Assoc./cancer research), poems in local/church mags.; "Having experienced many years of illness in my life, my philosophy now is to live life to the full and make the most of each day, thus hopefully to enable me to help others that are less fortunate than myself."

WILSON, IAN: [b] 28/7/60 Keith; [p] William & Helen; [ch] Robert, Ian Jr., Sarah Anne; [ed] Keith Grammar School; [occ] blacksmith engineer; [awards] Coded Welder, Agricultural Engineer, blood doner; [pub writ] "Memphis Man" - runner-up MAST Publications Poetry Review 1995; "I am truly honoured to see my work in print and it makes me even more ambitious to land a major publishing deal."

WILSON, JOHN E.: [b] 16/7/34 Cumbria; [ch] Andrew & Ian; [occ] security officer; [mem] Union A.P.E.X; [activ] plane spotter - photography, model construction (planes), caring for my beloved cats; [pub writ] letters in local newspaper 'Oxford Mail'; "I get my inspiration for poetry/verse when I am all alone, by myself, on night duty (10 hrs.), and it's too wet to go out on my patrols. So I put pen to paper until it 'fairs-up'."

WILSON, MARGERY: [b] 10/4/30 Lisburn; [p] John & Violet Hull; [ch] Errol & Brian; [ed] William Foote Memorial; [occ] housewife; [activ] intercessor for healing - St. Marks Church, poetry reading to sr. citizens; [pub writ] poems in 12 anthologies, local papers, Hammer Mag., and church mags.; "Since my eldest son's death in 1992, I found a new walk of life down the path of poetry from sad "Mother's Lament" to fun "The Secret"."

WILSON, SONJA: [b] 21/9/69 Horden, Co. Durham; [p] Norma & Fred; [ed] Shotton Hall Comp., University of East London; [occ] student; [activ] pres. taking New Tech. BSc Hnrs. Degree, [mem] Free Writers, Amnesty Intn'l; "I find writing is great fun for me as well as being a reliable silent friend. Recently I have learnt to share this friend which has proved to be just as enjoyable."

WINDER, PATRICIA S.: [b] 3/3/32 Cornwall; [ch] Paul; [activ]

contr. poems to charity magazines; [pub writ] booklet of poems, 'Echos', poems in local paper and Radio Cumbria; "I have gained pleasure from giving to charity and helping those less fortunate than myself. Though I suffer from ill health, I try to help and cheer others."

WINDSOR, CAROLINE: [b] 6/10/48 Kent; [m] David; [p] Rollo & Lorna Lempriere; [ed] Farringtons School, Chelsea School of Chiropody; [occ] chiropodist; [awards] Cert. London School of Journalism; [mem] Soc. of Chiropodists; [pub writ] short stories, articles, poems in various mags./local newspapers; "I enjoy writing prose and poetry; fact and fiction. There is a form of writing to suit every mood."

WINNINGTON, EILEEN: [b] 5/7/76 Enniskillen; [p] Victor (dcd) & Joyce; [ed] Jones Memoria Primary, Eniskillen Collegiate Grammar School for Girls; [occ] student; [awards] Bronze Medallion - Life Saving Award; [activ] swimming, reading (love authors: Stephen King & James Herbert; "I believe that poety is most often what the reader takes from it, not always what the poet gives. I love writing, it's one of the greatest forms of expression, sometimes the hardest emotions to express can flow when the right words come."

WINSLET, WENDY: [b] 30/8/52 Ystrad Mynach; [m] Peter; [p] Eunice & Brinley Roberts; [ch] Cristian & Dawn; [ed] Caerphilly Girls Grammar School; [occ] aux. nurse; [awards] First Aid/Communications Award - St. Johns Ambulance Brigade; [activ] sec. local St. John Ambulance Brigade, geneology; [pub writ] svrl. poems in various anthologies; "Enjoyment about writing is essential."

WOLSTENHOLME, RUTH: [b] 22/1/16 Whiston; [p] George & Ruth Sayles; [ch] Edgar; [ed] Whiston Church School; [awards] Creative Writing Diploma, Study Passport, Programme of Work Women & Health; [pub writ] 9 poems in anthologies, poems in church mags., short story - Lifestyle Mag.; "I have found my interest in literature to be a great blessing. Being a widow, it gets rid of the feeling of loneliness."

WOOD, MOYA T.: [b] 8/12/41 Horden; [p] Thomas & Thora; [ch] Catherine, Robert, Paula, Donna, Anthony & David; [ed] R.C. Jr. Sec. Modern School; [occ] housewife/factory cleaner; [awards] won comp. & cup - diving (13 yrs. old), won swim competitions; [mem] Catholic Womens Guild; [activ] knit, sew, cook, cycling, writing; "My writing is the outpouring of my heart."

WOOD, RON: [b] 22/3/22 London; [m] Dawn; [p] Harding & Ethel; [ed] Borough Polytechnic London, St. Martins School of Art, London; [occ] artist/sculptor; [awards] qual. - engineering, entry in 'Dictionary of British Art Vol. VI 20th Century Painters & Sculptors' pub. Antique Collectors Club, Suffolk; [pub writ] articles on sculture, scholastic publications, WWII RN Navy exp. Sea Classic International & Sea Breeze Mag.; "I like to keep in mind the fact that a rocket travelling at 100,000 mph across the Milky Way from end to end would take 670 million years to make the journey. And here we are living our short lives on a tiny planet within the Universe. A sobering thought, that hopefully might put some of our over-emphasised earthly concerns into perspective."

WOODLEY, THOMAS A.: [b] 16/11/22 Llanbradach; [p] Frank & Edith; [ed] Pontllanfraith Elem. School; [awards] War Service Medals; "I have laboured hard and long all my working life — and sought and enjoyed the tenderness of my fellow man and the beauty of nature."

WOODS, JAMES: [b] 7/3/13 Standish; [ch] M.P. Rourke (dtr.) & J. Eccleston (dtr.); "My father is almost blind and with various other ailments doesn't get out very much other than to an Old People's Day Centre once a week. His first poem was at my daughter's wedding, nearly 6 years ago, which he memorised. People have to write them down for him." - M.P. Rourke.

WORLEY, TRACEY: [b] 26/3/64 Chiswick, W. London; [m] Daivd; [p] Christopher & Patricia Smithers; [ch] Jordan, Kellee-Jade & Karis-Amber; [ed] Abbotsford Comp. School, Mddx.; "I have written a variety of poems in the last few years. I particularly enjoy writing children's poetry. This poem I wrote especially for the P.I.B.I. Competition. It is my first attempt at competition and I am overjoyed that the P.I.B.I. deemed it good enough for publication."

WRIGHT, JENNIFER A.: [b] 3/12/43 Sale, Cheshire; [m] Peter; [p] Renee & Wilfred Renshaw (dcd.); [ch] Mark & Tracy; [ed] Wellington School for Girls, Cheshire; [occ] solicitor's legal cashier; [mem] Leisure Centre, Women's Institute, Institute of Advanced Motorists; [pub writ] 3 poems in Arrival Press & Anchor Books; "Animal lover, gardener, reader, music lover, photographer and outdoor person. I enjoy food and wine and the company of friends. I am impulsive, creative, contemplative, but seek solitude, peace and quiet for personal leisure."

WRIGHT, MAUREEN: [b] 1947 Bedfordshire; [p] Steven & Elsie; [ch] Paul & Steven; [occ] catering mgr.; [awards] City & Guilds - catering; [activ] volunteer - Steam/Diesel Train Footplate Crew; "I find the poems I write are linked to times of spirtual awareness and emotions, heightened I think by my coming to live in north Norfolk, by the sea."

WUSTRACK, DAPHNE: [b] 3/9/42 Scunthorpe; [ed] Sec. Modern, Grimsby; [occ] midwife; [awards] Certs. Gnrl Nursing & Midwifery; [activ] local W.E.A. creative writers group; [pub writ] articles in local newspaper/hospital mag., short story in The Direction, church mag., poetry in Poetry Eastern Now; "I believe that by putting God at the center of my life He has given me the ability to put my thoughts and feelings into a structured form of either poetry or prose. I have gained extensive experience through working for many years in the public sector."

WYLES, EUNICE: [b] 22/5/33 Denny Stirlingshire; [m] Ian; [p] Alexander & Bridget Thomson; [ch] Sandra, Kenneth & Laura; [ed] Denny High School; [occ] school secretary; [awards] Secretarial Certs., Computing/Wrd. Processing, teach qual. - Scottish Yoga Assoc., Dialect Poetry Prize - radio Scotland (BBC); [mem] Stirling Literary Soc., Poetry Digest, Leics.; [activ] F.E. teacher, dressmaking/design, creative crafts; [pub writ] short stories/poems in mags. & Scottish anthologies; "One of the pleasures of writing poetry is to discover, that on occasion, the sentiment expressed and reflected upon, so accurately touches the reader as to provide a uniqe and lasting souvenir; perhaps, even one of a collection."

YORK, MARY: [b] 1912 Northampton; [p] Sidney & Gertrude Carpenter; [ch] Susan, Richard & Patrick; [ed] Northampton School for Girls; [awards] Secretarial Cert. - London Chamber of Commerce; [mem] Suffolk Art Soc.; [activ] church, Local History Soc., W.I. & Bures Art Group; "Watercolour painting is my chief hobby."

YOUNG, ELIZABETH: [b] Warwickshire; [p] Margaret & Tom; [ch] Matthew, Marcos & Samuel; [ed] Hallcroft Sec., North Notts College of F.E., Brackenhurst Agricultural College; [occ] secretary; [mem] Kuy-Shin-Do Karate (college); [pub writ] short story in local newspaper, 2 poems pub. Poetry North; "Being a full-time mum and holding down a full-time job leaves me little time for myself. My safety valve is my poetry."

YOUNG, JOYCE: [b] 5/2/43 Belfast; [p] James & Eileen; [ch] Jo-Ann; [ed] Hillcourt Girls School, Heidlberg University, Queens University; [occ] chairman - charity for the disabled; [awards] degree - languages, degree in Dental Therapy (QU); [activ] community activities, Co. director L.E.D.U.; "Being disabled, I have found the best thing is to be busy and I am rich in family love with my daughter and grandson. They help me through any adversity."

ZULAILA, LINDA: [b] 18/3/53 Preston; [p] Bill & Muriel Balchin; [ch] Mima, Adam, Solly & Babby; [occ] care worker; [pub writ] "Create To Survive" (Full Book of Verse), "Every Mother's Lot" Poetry Now '92; "If only I could earn our crust, from writing — nine 'til five ..., But inspiration ain't enough, to keep us five alive!"

INDEX TO POETS